Graphic Novels

Genreflecting Advisory Series

Diana Tixier Herald, Series Editor

Hooked on Horror: A Guide to Reading Interests in Horror Fiction, 2d Edition
Anthony J. Fonseca and June Michele Pulliam

Make Mine a Mystery: A Reader's Guide to Mystery and Detective Fiction
Gary Warren Niebuhr

Teen Genreflecting: A Guide to Reading Interests, 2d Edition
Diana Tixier Herald

Blood, Bedlam, Bullets, and Badguys: A Reader's Guide to Adventure/
Suspense Fiction
Michael B. Gannon

Rocked by Romance: A Guide to Teen Romance Fiction
Carolyn Carpan

Jewish American Literature: A Guide to Reading Interests
Rosalind Reisner

African American Literature: A Guide to Reading Interests
Edited by Alma Dawson and Connie Van Fleet

Historical Fiction: A Guide to the Genre
Sarah L. Johnson

Canadian Fiction: A Guide to Reading Interests
Sharron Smith and Maureen O'Connor

Genreflecting: A Guide to Popular Reading Interests, 6th Edition
Diana Tixier Herald, Edited by Wayne A. Wiegand

The Real Story: A Guide to Nonfiction Reading Interests
Sarah Statz Cords, Edited by Robert Burgin

Read the High Country: A Guide to Western Books and Films
John Mort

Graphic Novels

A Genre Guide to Comic Books, Manga, and More

Michael Pawuk

Foreword by Brian K. Vaughan

Genreflecting Advisory Series
Diana Tixier Herald, Series Editor

A Member of the Greenwood Publishing Group
Westport, Connecticut • London

Library of Congress Cataloging-in-Publication Data

Pawuk, Michael.
　　Graphic novels : a genre guide to comic books, manga, and more / Michael Pawuk ;
　foreword by Brian K. Vaughn.
　　　p. cm. — (Genreflecting advisory series)
　Includes bibliographical references and indexes.
　ISBN 1-59158-132-X (alk. paper)
　1. Comic books, strips, etc.—Bibliography. 2. Comic books, strips, etc.—Themes,
　motives. I. Title.
　Z5956.C6P38　2007
　[PN6710]
　016.74153—dc22　　2006034156

British Library Cataloguing in Publication Data is available.

Library of Congress Catalog Card Number: 2006034156
ISBN: 1-59158-132-X

First published in 2007

Libraries Unlimited, 88 Post Road West, Westport, CT 06881
A Member of the Greenwood Publishing Group, Inc.
www.lu.com

Printed in the United States of America

The paper used in this book complies with the
Permanent Paper Standard issued by the National
Information Standards Organization (Z39.48–1984).

10　9　8　7　6　5　4　3　2　1

Copyright Acknowledgments

The author and publisher gratefully acknowledge permission for use of the following material:

Cover design by Martha Rago from *Pedro and Me* by Judd Winick. Cover design © 2000 by
Henry Holt and Company. Reprinted by permission of Henry Holt and Company, LLC.

All cover images used from Dark Horse Comics, Inc., reprinted with permission. Dark Horse
Comics® and the Dark Horse Logo are registered trademarks of Dark Horse Comics, Inc.

Cover art of *Clone Wars Adventures: Vol. III* © 2005 Lucasfilm Ltd. & ™ and *Star Wars: Rite of
Passage* © 2004 Lucasfilm Ltd. & ™. All Rights Reserved. Used under authorization. Unauthorized depiction is a violation of applicable law.

Cover from *Bone: Out from Boneville* by Jeff Smith. Published by Graphix, an imprint of Scholastic, Inc. Jacket art copyright © 2005 by Jeff Smith. Reprinted by permission.

In loving memory of my Baba, Motria Swyrydenko, who taught me that all of life's problems could be solved with love, compassion, generosity, and a heaping plate of pierogies; my aunt, Sandra Swyrydenko, who bought me my first Batman comic book (I have been a Batman fan and a lifelong comic book reader ever since.); and my mother-in-law and fellow librarian, Linda Loos, who no doubt would have loved to use my comic book collection to make her own handcrafted cards. You are all missed. May their memories be eternal!

To my son, Nathan, who truly is a gift from God.
I sure hope you like comic books.

Contents

Foreword

Brian K. Vaughan

Growing up in the suburbs of Cleveland, Ohio, I took a weekly bike trip that always involved two stops. First up was Westlake's Porter Public Library, where I would check out as many novels as I could fit into my backpack. My second stop was Baluk's Newsstand, where I would buy what few comic books my allowance would afford.

Back then, I never would have imagined a day when I would be able to find comic books at my local library. Then again, I also wouldn't have imagined a day that I wouldn't be able to find comics at the newsstand.

Graphic novels (for the uninitiated: self-contained, book-length stories told with a combination of words and pictures) have definitely changed the landscape of the industry I'm now fortunate enough to be a small part of, and libraries have been instrumental in this evolution of our medium.

Now that single-issue monthly comics can mostly be found only in comics "specialty stores," these ongoing series are sold primarily (though not always, thankfully) to an ever-shrinking group of lifelong collectors, destination shoppers who know exactly what they want and where to find it. While this "secret society" mentality can be fun for fans, it makes it very hard for new characters and new concepts to reach out and find the wider audience they need to succeed.

Recently Runaways, a new series I co-created for Marvel with artist Adrian Alphona, was very nearly canceled. This subversive kids' book, which deals with a group of teenagers who discover that their parents are actually super-villains, was a critical hit, but it had a difficult time surviving in a marketplace crowded with X-Men and Justice Leagues, and consumers who seemed to want mostly stories about characters they grew up loving.

But when our comic was finally collected into a series of graphic novels, it became an instant hit in bookstores across the country, where young readers were starving for all-new adventures about heroes with whom they could identify. Like a movie that underperformed in theaters but became a cult favorite on DVD, Runaways was blessed with a second life, and it's still being published today (as both a monthly comic and a series of graphic novels).

But even before my work started selling well in bookstores, I was hearing from readers who discovered my writing at their local libraries, where librarians (always a forward-thinking, progressive bunch) had started stocking the shelves with graphic novels years ahead of the current commercial craze.

I'm immensely grateful to these librarians for being among the first to recognize that graphic novels are not a genre (like super-hero adventure, Western, true crime, etc.), but a medium, like painting or literature, a medium where anyone and everyone can find something to love.

If this is your first exposure to the world of graphic novels, I'm jealous, and I hope you have as much fun discovering what words and pictures are truly capable of as I did on a long bike ride a lifetime ago.

BKV

Brian K. Vaughan is the Eisner Award-winning writer and co-creator of Runaways, *the post-apocalyptic social satire* Y: The Last Man, *and the sci-fi political thriller* Ex Machina. *He lives in California with his wife and their several hundred books.*

Acknowledgments

I would like to thank the following for their assistance and support for this book: Di Herald, editor Barbara Ittner, and the staff at Libraries Unlimited for all their input and advice; The Browne Popular Culture Library of Bowling Green State University, the Ohio State University Cartoon Research Library, and the Russel B. Nye Collection of Michigan State University for the many hours I spent researching their collections; the fellow members of the Graphic Novels in Libraries Listserv (GNLIB-L) for their invaluable assistance and support, including, but not limited to, Steve Miller, Dawn Rutherford, Steve Weiner, Francisca Goldsmith, Steve Raiteri, Michael R. Lavin, Kirsten Edwards, Kristen Fletcher-Spear, Meredith Jenson-Benjamin, and many more; my fellow members of YALSA's Graphic Novel Task Force: Kat Kan, Jody Sharp, Michele Gorman, and Robin Brenner; all the graphic novel companies, publishers, and distributors, including Dark Horse Comics, DC Comics, Image Comics, Marvel Comics, IDW Publishing, VIZ Media, TOKYOPOP, Cartoon Books, Lucasfilm LTD, Antarctic Press, Slave Labor Graphics, Top Shelf Productions, Diamond Comics, Baker & Taylor, and countless others who gave me copyright permission for this publication and those that were able to send me review copies of their titles for this publication; John Gavin of York Comics & Cards for supplying me with the graphic novel titles I purchased for "research"; Sean Kollar for his illustrations in the comic book section of this collection; fellow Clevelander and Eisner Award-winning author Brian K. Vaughan for his foreword; my twin brother Paul, who has shared my love for comic books even since we were kids; and most important, this couldn't have been done without the support of my parents Stephen and Ludmilla Pawuk who have been supportive of my love for comic books ever since I was a child, and my wife, Laurie, who has been supportive of this hobby of mine and this project since Day One. I owe you, Laurie, many make-up dates for all the years when I spent Saturday nights typing instead of taking you out on dates. I love you with all my heart.

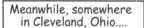

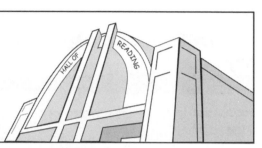

Hi Everyone, My name is Mike Pawuk and I'm a Teen Services Librarian for the Cuyahoga County Public Library system.

And I'm Mike's friend Sean Kollar. I'm a comic book artist and I'll be drawing this adventure into libraryland.

I want to talk to you about something that is near and dear to me: Comic Books and Graphic Novels. I've been a huge fan of comic books ever since I was a kid. My parents got them for me at the local comic book stores, grocery stores and more. I even remember that they used to have them at my local library too.

Oh, back in the late 1970's - early 1980's there weren't that many.

GRAPHIC NOVELS

There were only 4 or 5 graphic novels in the Adult-Non-Fiction area with the good old call number of 741.5973

but every time I went into the library, I'd still go back to that same section and reread books like Marvel's "Bring on the Bad Guys" and "Son of Origins".

SON ORIGI OF MARVEL C

Years later, when I became a Teen Services Librarian, I wanted to give a little back to the community and build up a graphic novel collection for the next generation of teens who came into the library hoping to find comic books and graphic novels.

I've been very fortunate. Adding graphic novels has been one of the most rewarding decisions I've made as a Teen Services Librarian and the positive feedback I've gotten from patrons of all ages has been great, attracting both reluctant readers as well as avid fans.

Plus, it's wonderful seeing teens walking out of the library with a HUGE stack of graphic novels in their arms.

Graphic Novels In The Library???

Well, why should we have Graphic Novels in our libraries? They're nothing but trash!

Well, first impressions are hard to change...

but...

....does your library carry other popular reading materials in your collections?

Do you carry music and movies in your collection?

Internet access?

Then you're already a popular culture center for your community and reaching out for the needs of your patrons. Graphic Novels are another popular culture medium that will fit in well in your community.

But, it's just trash!

Yes, not all of the stories could be considered as award winning...

though there are awards in the comic book industry

such as the Eisner Awards and the Harvey Awards.

You should compare it to your own materials in your other collections.

Not all of the books won awards. Not all of your movies are Academy Award winners. Not all of your music in your collections won Grammys.

Besides, we all like to read a little trash sometimes and teens are no different.

A Very, Very Short History of Graphic Novels

But it's got pictures? Reading's not supposed to have pictures!

The use of art to tell stories has been with us since the dawn of man. From prehistoric cave paintings....

...to icons of the Christian Orthodox Church and more.

Here's some food for thought: Why is it that artwork in children's picture books is so important for a child's development...

...but after a certain age

Aa Bb Cc Dd Ee

READING
WRITING
ARITHMETIC

using pictures to tell a story is no longer acceptable?

It's a strange paradox that artwork isn't acceptable in literature

Yet in a museum, art is a revered and cherished form of expression.

Graphic Novels are that wonderful blend of text and graphics that is a unique visual medium for telling a story.

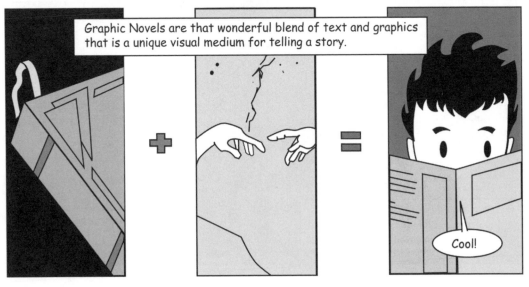

Cool!

Who Reads Graphic Novels?

Why focus on Teens?

Aren't comic books just made for kids?

Actually, you'd be surprised to know that most of the comics to today are written with teens and adults in mind.

In fact, the average age of a comic book reader is about 30 years old.

I had NO idea!

That archaic stereotype of "comics are just for kids" will probably be with us for a long time.

Just like our own of librarians being old ladies with buns in our hair.

In fact, this age gap might be a potential stumbling block with library staff or patrons.

They might be shocked to find some content not suitable for a younger reader.

Even library-favorite creator Jeff Smith admits that his hit series "Bone" is written for an older target age group.

However, it's popular with younger readers as well.

So, who reads graphic novels? Everyone?

One of the most interesting things I've noticed since building my library's collection

Is that it's heavily used by other age groups.

What did you find?

Well, I expected that a lot of children would be checking out the collection due to the appeal of a graphic novel.

What I didn't expect was the large amount of adult readers that I see browsing and checking out the collection as well.

Don't be surprised to find both children and adults looking for the latest graphic novels in the Teen Area.

Unless your library already has a separate area for them.

Comic Books, Trade Paperbacks and Graphic Novels

What's the difference between comic books, trades and graphic novels?

Are they just the same but different?

Oh yeah!

Well most of us are familiar with a comic book.

It's typically a 32-page pamphlet-sized publication. It can be a self contained or part of an ongoing plot.

Here we have an example of the comic book "Ultimate Spider-Man" published by Marvel Comics.

The single issues were collected and reprinted as a trade paperback

A trade paperback is a collection of comic books that were once sold as individual single issues. It can come in paperback or hardcover.

You can usually tell from the table of contents section of a book if it's a trade or not. For example the USM book says the following: "Originally published as USM #1-7, (c) 2002."

A graphic novel is a self-contained publication by the publisher. It was never done in a comic book format and it was only printed just like the way you're seeing it now.

Creatu

by Doug TenNapel

It can feature all-new characters or feature familiar characters such as Batman and Spider-Man.

THE JOKER

Comic veteran Will Eisner coined the term as a way to have his work stand out from the standard super-hero titles of the day.

The term has stuck, for better or for worse, as an all-encompassing term for both trades and graphic novels.

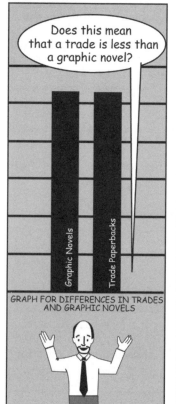

Graphic Novels Are More Than What?

BETTER THIS WAY. QUICK. CLEAN. FINAL.

Jean, No DON'T

SCOTT!

One of the concerns you might have for your readers is that unlike a novel, graphic novels visually show the reader events that are happening.

Is it called a "graphic novel" because it has a lot of pictures of naked people?

Nope.

All it means is is that it's a visual novel.

Here's an example of prose vs. a graphic novel.

It's a small segment from Homer's classic epic poem The Odyssey to show how describing a scene and visually showing it can be portrayed.

Wow- I feel like I'm in High School again! Toga! Toga! Toga!

When my men and I were sure that he was asleep, we took our weapon, which was a very long, and thick stick of wood, put the point into the still burning fire, crept up on the sleeping Cyclops, and then we thrust into the Cyclops' eye. He screamed, and yelled so loudly that all the other Cyclops came running to see what had happened.

Now we wait, AND WAIT, as Sean draws this in page form.

WHEN MY MEN AND I WERE SURE THAT HE WAS ASLEEP,

WE TOOK OUR WEAPON,

WHICH WAS A VERY LONG, AND THICK STICK OF WOOD,

PUT THE POINT INTO THE STILL BURNING FIRE.

CREPT UP ON THE SLEEPING CYCLOPS

AND THEN WE THRUST INTO THE CYCLOPS EYE.

HE SCREAMED AND YELLED SO LOUDLY

THAT ALL THE OTHER CYCLOPS CAME RUNNING TO SEE WHAT HAD HAPPENED.

As you can see although the same words were portrayed in a graphic format, you only saw what Sean wanted you to see. The writer/artist has complete control over the scene, while the prose format lets your imagination run wild with your view of it.

As a rule of thumb, when it comes to selecting graphic novels, I recommend that you should select them with the same precautions that you would consider a novel for your teen section. Remember, there are some titles that are better for older, more mature teens than younger teens.

Where can You Get Graphic Novels and Find Recommendations and Reviews?

When you're trying to add graphic novels into your library,

I highly recommend checking your local comic book shop. Stop in, talk to the store owner, and see what's available and appropriate.

I usually find something for myself, too.

Andr
Dun

Check with your local bookstores too. Many bookstores are catching on due to the huge popularity with teens and Japanese manga. They now carry a wide variety of graphic novels, including many mainstream U.S. titles. Now many book vendors list graphic novels as well including BWI, Ingram and more.

Diamond Comics Previews magazine is a monthly catalog of all comic books, graphic novels and more that are being published three months in advance. Most comic shops order from here.

Many professional review journals now review graphic novels. VOYA's reviews by Kat Kan stand out as some of the best.

Other journals that provide reviews include Booklist, Library Journal, Publishers Weekly and others.

Also, if you're including popular magazines in your teen area that talk about comics

I would recommend Wizard: The Guide to Comics and Comic Buyer's Guide.

Many librarians have written books on graphic novels in libraries.

They range from genre guides to ideas for programming and promoting.

For a complete list, check out the back of the book

The Internet is also a goldmine for graphic novel reviews, help from other librarians, as well as news from the comic book industry.

Also, I highly recommend that you join the Graphic Novels in Libraries listserv. It's designed specifically for librarians. Send an email to GNLIB-L-subscribe@ topica.com to subscribe

Cataloging and Displaying Graphic Novels

One of the biggest dilemmas to having a graphic novel section is cataloging.

Good ole' 741.5973XXXX.

For a public library using the Dewey Decimal system, graphic novels have been shelved in the non-fiction 700's call number.

Of course, they still work out fine, but part of the problem is that the majority of the stories are fictional. They've mainly been cataloged in the 700's due to their illustrations.

I have a question--are all of your children's picture books cataloged as non-fiction?

Of course not!

Fictional stories are cataloged differently from non-fiction titles. Graphic Novels should be no different.

Though there is no correct way to catalog them

I've seen libraries catalog them as fiction.

That works well, as long as you don't integrate them with your fictional titles.

They'll get lost in the fiction collection and will never stand out.

I recommend cataloging them as a separate medium, similar to how you might catalog visual formats such as DVD's and CD's.

That way they are cataloged by the medium of Graphic Novels and then can include fiction and non-fiction titles. Plus it helps to keep the media in their own separate section.

On to displaying and promoting the collection!

Promoting the collection

Why do I have to promote it?

Promoting it is a way to let the teens know that you've got the good stuff.

Well, think of it as a way to highlight your teen section.

Contact your local press.

Feature Creator/ Character Displays.

You've seen the **Movies** now read the **Books**

SIN CITY

Fantastic Four

Spider-Man

X-MEN

Posters and Bookmarks

Can be store bought or your own.

Booklists of recommended titles.

BOOKLIST
1. Batman
2. Crisis
3. Spider-Man
4. GI Joe
5. Transformers
6. Star Wars
7. Fantastic Four
8. X-Men
9. Star Shooters
10. Y: The Last Man

You can make up your own or use ALA/ YALSA selection lists.

Booktalk Graphic Novels at schools.

Comic Book/ Manga Club.

Drawing class with an expert.

"Create a Comic Book" Program.

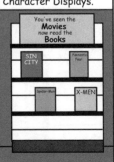

STAR SHOOTERS

Free Comic Book Day tie-in.

Usually in May/June at your local comic shop.

FREE COMIC BOOK DAY

There are many other ways to promote graphic novels. I suggest checking other recommended sources in the Appendix for more books on the subject.

Promoting the collection

Why do I have to promote it?

Well, think of it as a way to highlight your teen section.

Promoting it is a way to let the teens know that you've got the good stuff.

Contact your local press.

Feature Creator/ Character Displays.

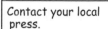

You've seen the **Movies** now read the **Books**

SIN CITY

Fantastic Four

Spider-Man

X-MEN

Posters and Bookmarks

Can be store bought or your own.

Booklists of recommended titles.

BOOKLIST
1. Batman
2. Crisis
3. Spider-Man
4. GI Joe
5. Transformers
6. Star Wars
7. Fantastic Four
8. X-Men
9. Star Shooters
10. Y: The Last Man

You can make up your own or use ALA/ YALSA selection lists.

Booktalk Graphic Novels at schools.

Comic Book/ Manga Club.

Drawing class with an expert.

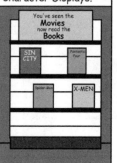

"Create a Comic Book" Program.

STAR SHOOTERS

Free Comic Book Day tie-in.

Usually in May/June at your local comic shop.

FREE COMIC BOOK DAY

There are many other ways to promote graphic novels. I suggest checking other recommended sources in the Appendix for more books on the subject.

HOW TO USE THE BOOK

Each year thousands of graphic novels are published.

In 2005, over 2,700 titles were published in North America.

Wow! That's quite a lot!

I hope that you can find this book useful and that, in here, you find the classics, the hidden gems and more. It's been tough cutting out some titles, so I apologize if your favorite is missing.

It's pretty daunting. There's a lot of great works out there and it's sometimes tough to find a great new title.

The title listings are broken down into overall basic genres

including: Super-Heroes, Fantasy, Science Fiction, Action and Adventure, Contemporary Life and more!

Each genre has it's own symbol on the right panel of the book, for easy searching.

Within each genre, there are sub-genres listed as well. For example:

SUPER-HEROES
SUPER-HERO ICONS
OTHER SUPER-HEROES
SUPER-HERO TEAMS
TEAM-UPS & EPIC EVENTS
VILLAINS
SECRET ORIGINS
ALTERNATE TIMELINES
ELSEWORLDS & WHAT-IF
    WORLDS
ANTHOLOGIES

Some titles do like to blend genres, so it was tough nailing the single genre that a title could be listed in. You might not agree that "Groo" is a Humor genre more than a Fantasy genre, but hey--you write your own book! :)

For each annotation, there is an age-appropriateness guide for the books. Here's a simple rating level for each title:

A= All Ages
Y= Youth Ages 10+
T= Teens 13-15
O= Older Teens 16+
M= Mature Readers 18+

I've also embraced for this book fellow librarian Michael R. Lavin's criteria for including graphic novels in your library:

1. Popularity
2. Suitability
3. Age Level
4. Genre
5. Writing Quality
6. Artistic Quality
7. Artistic Style
8. Format
9. Reputation
10. Awards and recognition recieved.

Also listed after all of the main chapters is a list of publisher addresses and web sites.

I will also recommend other sources, including other graphic novel titles as well as web sites and magazine articles of interest.

Wow. That's all in this book? If they're all in here, then what's behind you?

Uh, behind us are the next 2500+ graphic novels coming out next year. By the time you read this book, there's many more great titles already for you and your library patrons to discover and enjoy.

CRASH

I guess I'd better start my next book.

GROAN

Epilogue

As a librarian who works with the public every day, we're always out there to serve and help find what they're looking for.

We help the public, but we don't always expect to get a "Thank you" for what we do. It's sometimes hard to know if we're doing the right thing—

—adding so many different mediums into our libraries.

One day while working the reference desk, I got an amazing three "thank you's" from:

A pre-teen,

Cool! Thanks!!

A teen,

Thank you!

and an Adult.

Thank you!

—all of them thanking me personally for adding graphic novels into the library. I don't think I've had such a gratifying experience.

I hope that all of you will have that same feeling of happiness and satisfaction adding graphic novels to your library like I have.

I hope you enjoy the rest of the book!

THE 'EVER LOVIN' END

Introduction

Graphic novels have become a growing part of the collections of public libraries, bookstores, schools, and more. Readers of all ages have embraced the format, and today there is an unprecedented variety of titles available for teen and adult readers. This graphic novel explosion can be credited in part to both the diversity of the publishing companies in North America today as well as the influx of titles originally published in Japan, Korea, and China that have been embraced by North American culture. Even in the library world, graphic novels have found a place of respectability, becoming more and more a common medium in libraries for not only young adult departments, but increasingly adult departments as well. Graphic novels now also frequently appear on YALSA selection lists, as program topics for discussion at the American Library Association conferences, as well as at an all-day preconference on graphic novels, held in 2002. In 2006 YALSA created a selection list solely for graphic novels. Called "Great Graphic Novels," the list will highlight the best graphic novel works with teen appeal for the previous year.

According to the Diamond Comics weekly listing of graphic novels released each Wednesday in comic book shops across North America, in 2005 there were more than 2,600 graphic novel titles published. The titles included new graphic novels published in North America, reprints, and titles originally published in Asia and Europe. This is up from 2004, during which approximately 2,000 titles were published. This trend is expected to increase each year as publishers release more graphic novel titles to meet buyer demand.

Purpose and Audience

Although there have been many notable titles written by librarians and fans of the medium on the subject of graphic novels that have helped to guide readers to many great titles (see appendix 1 for a list of recommended titles), there has not been an in-depth genre guide to the medium since the 1995 publication of D. Aviva Rothschild's *Graphic Novels: A Bibliographic Guide to Book Length Comics* (Libraries Unlimited). *Graphic Novels: A Genre Guide to Comic Books, Manga, and More* is intended to help readers and readers' advisors find the graphic novels readers most enjoy for all age groups. Titles that may appeal to children, teens, and adults are listed. This publication organizes and describes more than 2,400 original graphic novel titles and collected graphic novels series by genre and subgenre. Original graphic novels are defined as graphic novel titles that were created solely in a bound format and were never before originally published as a comic book. Collected graphic novels (also referred to as a trade paperback by many comic book publishers) were previously published as a monthly comic book and after a period of time were repackaged in a collected paperback or hardcover format. For brevity's sake, the titles are all referred to as graphic novels.

In addition to the graphic novels annotated, this guide lists a wide variety of publishers of graphic novels, including publishers of mainstream super-hero stories including DC Comics, Marvel Comics, and Image Comics; smaller independent publishers, including Dark Horse Comics, Fantagraphics Books, Top Shelf Productions, NBM Publishing, Oni Press, and Slave Labor Graphics; mainstream book publishers who have also ventured into publishing graphic novels, including Random House's Pantheon Press and Roaring Brook Press' First Second; and a wide variety of Asian publishers, including VIZ Media, TOKYOPOP, ADV Manga, and many more.

This guide is by no means a comprehensive overview of titles by specific writers and illustrators. It is not intended to serve as a guide to what could be considered "safe" or "clean" graphic novels, or even what can be considered "best of" collections. Instead, it is hoped that this guide will help readers' advisors and readers build their graphic novel collections and find graphic novel titles that will appeal to both adult and teen readers. It is also hoped that public librarians, school librarians, educators, booksellers, and others who work with readers of all ages will find this to be a valuable and useful aid.

This book is also not intended as a beginner's introduction to graphic novels. Though only briefly covered in the illustrated "Tales from the Library" comic book section of this book, there are many wonderful works written by fellow librarians and comic book historians that focus on the origin and history of the comic book and graphic novel. Featured titles as well as recommended Web sites are listed in appendix 1.

Like prose fiction, new titles, authors, publishing companies, and subgenre fields appear constantly, and it is impossible for a book such as this one to remain completely up-to-date. Readers of this book looking for further graphic novel titles of interest should supplement this guide with book reviews; visiting your local comic book shop, library, or bookstore that carries graphic novels to browse the latest releases; and asking fans of the medium what titles they recommend.

Scope, Selection Criteria, and Methodology

This publication lists all major genres published by graphic novel publishers and includes publications written for children, teens, and adults. Most of the titles were published within the last fifteen years, but on occasion older titles prior to 1990 are listed. The selections include titles popular with readers, as well as critically acclaimed and award-winning titles, and those that have stood the test of time and have helped to define the medium.

Unlike most prose fiction, whose readers often look for what is new for their respective age group, graphic novels tend to transcend age groupings. Similar to the appeal of other popular culture media such as motion pictures, music, animation, and video games, most graphic novels, regardless of when they were originally published, can still find themselves in the arms of a reader. Note that there are always exceptions to this rule, such as the all-ages appeal of J.K. Rowling's popular Harry Potter series of novels. Many graphic novel titles originally published decades ago can still be relevant today. In fact, this trend can be clearly seen with the hit Japanese manga (manga loosely translates as the Japanese word for "humorous pictures") titles that are current hits with readers, particularly teens. Many of the manga and other Asian titles that are currently popular in North America today were originally published several decades ago and have recently been retranslated for an English-speaking audience.

Many of the authors and illustrators that are featured in this guide are well known to fans of the medium but may not be to the average reader. If you are an avid reader, librarian, or readers' advisor with minimal knowledge of graphic novel creators, then names such as Neil Gaiman, Alan Moore, Jeff Smith, Stan Lee, Art Spiegelman, Jack Kirby, Frank Miller, Will Eisner, Brian Michael Bendis, Rumiko Takahashi, and Brian K. Vaughan may already be familiar to you. Their works are featured in this collection. Also included in this guide are a wide variety of creators who have helped shape graphic novels for decades, including Chuck Dixon, Mark Waid, Kurt Busiek, Walter Simonson, John Ostrander, and Arthur Adams, as well as up-and-coming creators of graphic novels such as Craig Thompson, Bryan Lee O'Malley, Chynna Clugston, Jill Thompson, Bill Presing, Kazu Kibuishi, Andy Runton, Josh Howard, and countless others. Through this guide, I hope you become as intimately familiar with the creators as many other graphic novel readers and I have done.

All titles listed in this guide were reviewed by this author, with the exception of multiple volumes in series collections and anthologies. For series titles and anthologies, a sample title from the collection was read, reviewed, and deemed appropriate for inclusion in this guide. As with other literature, it is advised that educators always read a graphic novel before recommending it to young readers.

In this book I have included

- original graphic novels—stories published exclusively in the graphic novel format, and

- collected graphic novels—book-sized reprints of a comic book.

I have left out

- collections of newspaper, magazine strips, and web comics (aside from those published by comic book publishers; see chapter 8 for a brief list);

- children's picture books;

- non-English-language material;

- sketchbooks and art books;

- fotonovelas; and

- single-issue comic books.

This publication features titles published throughout the world, with a focus mainly on North American and Asian publishers. Although some foreign-language titles from Europe are listed on occasion, they do not stand out well enough to be singled out. There is an extremely large portion of the book featuring Asian titles, mostly due in part to the "manga explosion," which has reinvigorated the graphic novel field with the influx of titles now available for many readers whom North American publishers typically have ignored: girls. I have included a brief content indicator after the age rating (see below for an explanation of the age rating) if a title was originally published in Japan, Korea, China, or a North American publication mimicking the format. The content indicators are as follows:

- **Japanese manga** = Asian graphic novel titles published originally in Japan. Manga is the general name given to comic books published in Japan. Popular publisher examples in North America include TOKYOPOP, ADV Manga, and VIZ Media, LLC.

- **Korean manhwa** = Asian graphic novel titles published originally in Korea. Popular publishers include TOKYOPOP, ADV Manga, and CPM Manga.

- **Chinese manhua** = Asian graphic novel titles published originally in China. DrMaster Publications, Inc., and HK Comics are publishers who print comic book stories originally from China.

- **Neo-manga** = North American graphic novels made to appear almost identical to the Japanese manga format. Popular publishers of these titles include TOKYOPOP, Antarctic Press, and Seven Seas Entertainment. Thanks to manga and anime specialist Gilles Poitras for the title suggestion.

There are many recently published and forthcoming books on the subject of the influx of Asian titles and of their own comic book history in Asia. Recommended titles on the subject are listed in appendix 1.

Like many other popular culture media such as film, television, and music, comic books and graphic novels also have awards and honors recognizing best works in the industry. The following awards and recognitions for graphic novels have been given to books listed in this publication:

- **Will Eisner Comic Industry Award**—Started in 1988, this is one of the highest honors in North America for comic book professionals and is named in honor of the pioneering writer/artist Will Eisner. The awards are given each year at the San Diego Comic Con and are known in the industry as the "Eisners." Due to space limitations, not all Eisner Award winners are listed in this publication. Award categories of note listed throughout the book include Best Single Issue/Single Story, Best Short Story, Best Serialized Story, Best Continuing Series, Best Finite/Limited Series, Best New Series, Best Title for Younger Readers/Best Comics Publication for a Younger Audience, Best Anthology, Best Graphic Album—New, Best Graphic Album: Reprint, Best Writer, Best Artist, Best Writer/Artist, Best Artist/Penciller/Inker or Penciller/Inker Team, and Talent Deserving of Wider Recognition.

- **Harvey Kurtzman Award**—Started in 1988, this award is voted on by comic book professionals and is named after the pioneering artist and editor Harvey Kurtzman. The awards are also known as the "Harveys." Due to space limitations, not all Harvey Award winners are included in this book. Some categories listed in this book are Best Writer, Best Artist, Best Cartoonist (Writer/Artist), Best New Series, Best Continuing or Limited Series, Best Graphic Album of Original Work, Best Graphic Album of Previously Published Work, and Best American Edition of Foreign Material.

- **Ignatz Award**—Started in 1997, this award recognizes outstanding achievement in the industry and is awarded at the Small Press Expo each year. The award is named in honor of the character Ignatz Mouse from George Herriman's classic comic strip Krazy Kat. Due to space limitations, not all Ignatz Award titles are listed in this publication. Titles listed in this publication include Ignatz winners categories such as Outstanding Graphic Novel, Outstanding Series, and Promising New Talent.

Over the years a variety of graphic novels have been selected by the book selection committees of the Young Adult Library Services Association (YALSA), a division of the American Library Association (ALA). The following notable book selection committees have listed graphic novels in their selection lists. The YALSA-recognized works are listed throughout this publication and are listed in the following recognition awards:

- **Best Books for Young Adults**—a selection list created by a committee of the Young Adult Library Services Association, a division of ALA

- **Quick Picks for Reluctant Readers**

- **Popular Paperbacks for Young Adults**

In order to identify graphic novel titles that have won awards or have been recognized, I have included the symbol 🏆 following the content indicator listed after the age rating if a title has received recognition from within the comic book industry or by the American Library Association.

Other icons are also used throughout the book to denote graphic novels that have tie-ins with film, television, gaming, and Japanese anime, as well as core collection titles:

◎ core collection title

🎬 has been made into a film

🖥 has been made into a television program

🎮 has been made into a game

あ is Japanese anime

Organization and Features

As previously mentioned, this guide organizes titles according to genre, subgenre, and theme, and sorts them into similar groups for readers and readers' advisors to find like titles. There may be some debate among readers about whether a specific title belongs in one chapter and not another. My decisions were reached by consulting publishers, asking colleagues, and reading reviews on the ideal genre for specific titles. However, genre labels are always somewhat subjective, and in the end, the final decision was mine.

Books featured in the chapters in the appropriate subgenres are listed alphabetically according to the main title of the graphic novel, a graphic novel series, or in some cases (such as the super-hero chapter) by the name of the featured character. Unlike prose fiction, in graphic novels the focus is not always on the creators (i.e., writers and artists), but on the particular characters featured in the title or series. Many readers may not know creators such as writer Stan Lee and illustrator Steve Ditko, but they are most definitely aware of the hero Spider-Man, whom both men created. For that reason, the titles in this guide are listed not in alphabetical order by the writer's last name, but by the title of the graphic novel, graphic novel series, or featured character. Due to space limitations, no contributors to a graphic novel—inkers, colorists, editors, translators, and more—other than the writer and artist are included in this publication. I fully recognize that comic books and graphic novels are the product of more than just the talents of a writer and artist, and I apologize if I have left out any creators who have also played a role in the creation of a series.

Entries for all graphic novel titles covered by this guide include the title of the book or series, writer and illustrator, publisher, publication year, ISBN, and a brief description. All graphic novel series title listings are sorted by the volume number, and collections featuring specific characters or series titles are sorted according to specific themes that help to distinguish the titles from other books. Featured sections in the chapters focusing on specific characters (such as Batman) or series titles (such as Star Wars) include brief descriptions of the overall subject, followed by short annotations highlighting the specific titles in the sections. Also, titles published in hardcover are noted in the annotations; all others are softcover.

Following the year of publication is an indicator of recommended reading levels. The designations used are

A = all ages
Y = youth ages ten and above
T = teens ages thirteen to fifteen
O = older teens, ages sixteen and seventeen
M = mature readers, ages eighteen and older

These designations are based on the ratings assigned by the respective publishing companies, recommendations by fellow librarians and readers, and personal reviews of the titles. Readers should keep in mind that these ratings are subjective. I can't overemphasize that readers should read what they are comfortable with and find exciting, regardless of a designated age range.

Please note that graphic novel titles that some may consider to be appropriate for mature readers (typically ages eighteen and over) due to content can very well be enjoyed and appreciated by younger readers. What constitutes a "mature reader" can be very subjective and not limited only to a set age of eighteen. I have known many younger readers who can handle mature content better than many adult readers. In fact certain titles, including *Swamp Thing, John Constantine: Hellblazer,* and *Sandman*—all published by DC Comics' mature reader imprint Vertigo—I myself began to read and enjoy when I was around fifteen years old.

I have also listed titles in this publication that are for young readers. What is interesting about graphic novels is that they share very similar qualities in their all-ages appeal to other popular culture media such as movies, with films ranging from features such as Wallace and *Gromit: The Curse of the Wererabbit* and the *Star Wars* films having great appeal for all ages. Just because a graphic novel was created for a specific age group does not mean an audience younger or older than the target audience cannot enjoy it. Many popular series, such as Jeff Smith's award-winning Bone (listed in the fantasy chapter), were written for a target audience of comic book readers in their twenties and thirties, yet librarians have hailed the series as an ideal title for middle-school children, and Scholastic Books' graphic novel imprint, Graphix, has featured the series as one of its biggest launch titles for its imprint.

The annotations are specifically designed to be descriptive rather than critical due to the philosophy of this book to support readers in their choices of books as opposed to pointing out what I consider to be good literature. The annotations focus mainly on the story line, details of the main protagonist, main plot points, and other basic descriptions. The same philosophy holds in regard to why content indicators such as violence, sex, language, and others are not included.

How to Use This Guide

This guide can be used in a number of ways. First, it can be used as a source for readers' advisory and to help patrons find read-alike titles. Since the titles are broken down according to a wide variety of genres and subgenres, the readers' advisor need only consult the similar works on the page to find like titles. Librarians can use this publication to build more genre-specific collections and to browse titles that may be more popular for their specific collection. This book can also be used as a genre guide to graphic novel literature for those unfamiliar with the medium or just looking for another good book or hidden treasure to read.

As mentioned previously, this book examines just a small fraction of the variety of graphic novels being published today. I have attempted to include major works for each genre as well as significant works by a wide variety of authors and illustrators, but many titles are not listed to due space constraints. Many of the titles listed in this book have gone out of print or may have recently been reprinted. With over 2,600 titles published in the span of just one year, there are many titles that could not be listed, and many more new wonderful titles are appearing on the horizon. I apologize if I have excluded anyone's favorite title.

Regardless of how you wish to use this book (though I would prefer that you not use this publication as kindling or a door stop), it is my hope that this book is used to spread the love of reading and enjoying graphic novels. Happy reading.

Chapter 1

Super-Heroes

    The super-hero genre has continued to be one of the most popular and enduring genres of the comic book and graphic novel in the United States. The genre's popularity began with the appearance of the first super-hero, Superman, in the pages of DC Comics' *Action Comics* #1 in 1938. Created by Joe Shuster and Jerry Siegel, the hero was inspired by the pulp fiction heroes of the 1930s and featured strong ties to the heroes and gods of the ancient Greek, Roman, and Norse myths. As the popularity of Superman soared, DC Comics and a slew of other publishers introduced other superpowered characters to the industry's pantheon of heroes, and a genre was born. Most super-hero characters exhibit certain universal traits, including strong moral ideals, a willingness to confront and battle evil in the world, a heroic-sounding code name to hide their secret identity, a brightly colored costume with optional mask, and extraordinary powers that help to make the hero stand out. The powers can include flight, heat vision, or speed, as well as countless others. Some characters, such as Batman, do not have any super powers per se, but have honed their bodies to the peak of human perfection. Other traits include unique weapons of choice, a large cast of supporting characters and loved ones, an arch-nemesis or rogues' gallery for the hero, as well as the occasional sidekick. The genre is closely tied to the genres of action/adventure and fantasy, in which many of the titles below could easily be placed. Due to the flexible nature of the super-hero tales, often the titles can also cross over into the genres of romance, drama, humor, science fiction, horror, adventure, and more action-oriented genres. Listed below are examples of the super-hero genre from approximately the last fifteen years from a wide variety of publishers. They include tales of heroics from the most popular heroes of today, classic heroes of yesterday, super-teams, villains, deconstructionist works on the genre, and much more. Please note that super-hero titles featuring a healthy dose of humor are listed in the "Genreblends" section of chapter 8. The titles in this chapter are listed by the main code name of the hero or super-hero team, and listings with more than one title featuring the characters are listed below the heroes' code names if applicable. Titles that do not have a featured hero or team are listed according to the main title of the graphic novel.

Super-Hero Icons

Superman, Batman, and Spider-Man are some of the most recognizable super-hero characters in the world today and have set the standard for the plethora of heroes that have appeared over the decades. Television series, movies, and merchandising have also helped to make these protagonists the best-known characters ever published in comic books. Listed below is a wide range of titles that represent a small sample of graphic novel collections about these super-hero icons. Note that the iconic characters appear elsewhere in this chapter, including sections on team-ups, epic events that typically involve a multitude of super-heroes, and tales of alternative histories, which can feature the iconic heroes reinterpreted in a whole new light.

Superman

Created by Joel Siegel and Jerry Schuster. DC Comics, 1993– . ▤ ▢ 🎮

Created by Clevelanders Jerry Siegel and Joe Shuster in 1938, Superman has become one of the best-recognized characters in fiction worldwide. He helped to usher in the age of the super-heroes with his first appearance in *Action Comics* #1. Born as Kal-El on the doomed planet Krypton, he was sent to Earth in a rocketship by his Kryptonian parents, Jor-El and Lara, before the planet was destroyed. The last survivor of Krypton, he crash-landed in his ship in Smallville, Kansas, and was taken in by John and Martha Kent, who named him Clark. The yellow sun of Earth, much different than the red sun that Krypton orbited, results in Clark Kent's having powers beyond those of people from Earth: flight, super-strength, invulnerability, X-ray vision, heat vision, acute hearing, and super-breath. He uses these gifts to fight the never-ending battle for truth and justice on Earth as the hero known as Superman. Now married to his longtime crush Lois Lane, Clark continues to work as a reporter for the *Daily Planet* in the city of Metropolis and faces adversaries from his rogues' gallery, including Lex Luthor, Doomsday, Brainiac, Bizarro, Mr. Mxyzptlk, Metallo, the Parasite, Gog, and many more. Superman has also proved to be a franchisable character and has appeared in feature films, television shows, animated cartoons, video games, and more. Following are popular collected comic book stories and graphic novel collections of the greatest American hero. Please note that many more Superman titles have been published than are included in this list. Please visit DC Comics' Web site (http://www.dccomics.com) for more titles.

Collected Comic Book Titles Featuring Superman

Listed below are recommended Superman stories that were originally published in the variety of monthly comic book titles published by DC Comics. The titles are collected editions of the ongoing Superman comic books, including *Superman*, *Action Comics*, *Adventures of Superman*, and *Superman: The Man of Steel*.

Superman: Critical Condition. **Written by Jeph Loeb, J. M. DeMatteis, Joe Kelly, and Mark Schultz. Illustrated by Doug Mahnke, Mike McKone, and various.** 2003. 192pp. 1-56389-949-3. **Y**

When it's discovered that the arch-villain the Parasite has been disguised as Lois but has died from Kryponite poisoning, Superman will stop at nothing to find out where his wife has been taken. The collection also features an appearance by Batman.

The Death and Return of Superman/Superman vs. Doomsday Collections. Written by Dan Jurgens and various. Illustrated by Dan Jurgens. 1993–2006. **Y ◎**

© 2006 DC Comics

Superman has faced many villains and evildoers, but what happens when the Man of Steel dies? After confronting Doomsday, a behemoth beast from Krypton that has been buried deep in the earth and is now rampaging across the United States, Superman must make the ultimate sacrifice to defeat his greatest foe. As citizens around the world mourn Superman and his sacrifice, four mysterious heroes are claiming to be Superman—a man in forged armor, a teenage clone of Superman, a cyborg Superman, and a dark and brooding vigilante who closely resembles Superman. Can any of the four heroes really be Superman, back from the dead? When the arch-villain Mongul plans to invade Earth, secret enemies are revealed and once again the real Superman proves that not even death can stop justice. *Hunter/Prey* and *The Doomsday Wars* continue Superman's struggles against the diabolical Doomsday, and Day of Doom recounts the anniversary of the day Metropolis's favorite son died to save the world. Note that the *Superman/Doomsday Omnibus* collects the series Superman/Doomsday: Hunter/Prey, The Doomsday Wars, as well as key Superman comic book issues about their battles.

The Death of Superman. 1993. 168pp. 1-56389-097-6.
World Without a Superman. 1993. 240pp. 1-56389-118-2.
The Return of Superman. 1993. 480pp. 1-56389-149-2.
Superman/Doomsday: Hunter/Prey. 1995. 160pp. 1-56389-201-4.
The Doomsday Wars. 1999. 142pp. 1-56389-562-5.
Day of Doom. 2003. 96pp. 1-4012-0086-9.
Superman/Doomsday Omnibus. 2006. 416pp. 1-4012-1107-0.

Superman: The Greatest Stories Ever Told. **Written and illustrated by various.** 2004–2006. **Y**

A collection of some of the best Superman stories published in the last sixty-five years. Includes stories by such creators as Jerry Siegel, Joe Shuster, Jim Steranko, John Byrne, Joe Kelly, Curt Swan, Dick Giordano, and Mike Mignola.

Vol. 1. 2004. 192pp. 1-4012-0339-6.
Vol. 2. 2006. 192pp. 1-4012-0956-4.

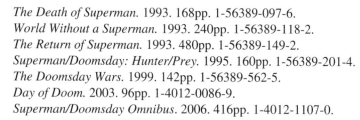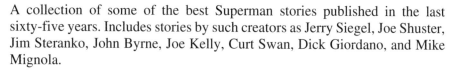

***Superman: Emperor Joker.* Written by Jeph Loeb, J.M. DeMatteis, Joe Kelly and Mark Schultz. Illustrated by Ed McGuinness, Doug Mahnke, Todd Nauck, and others.** 2007. 224pp. **Y**

When the Joker receives 99 percent of the power of Mr. Mxyzptlk, the imp from the fifth dimension, the Clown Prince of Crime re-creates the world in his image and declares himself emperor. In this twisted reality Superman is the most dangerous villain and Bizarro is the world's greatest hero. Superman must join with the criminal organization known as the JLA to help them remember their true selves and to defeat the Joker.

***Superman: Endgame.* Written by Jeph Loeb, Mark Millar, Joe Kelly, and various. Illustrated by Ed McGuinness and various.** 2000. 176pp. 1-56389-701-6. **Y**

After Brainiac 13 siphons the energy from Metropolis to upgrade its systems, Superman must team up with Lex Luthor, Green Lantern, and the Martian Manhunter to take on Brainiac 13 before it drains the entire planet of all its energy.

***Superman: Eradication!* Written by Dan Jurgens, Roger Stern, and various. Illustrated by Dan Jurgens, Jerry Ordway, George Pérez, Kerry Gammill, and various.** 1995. 160pp. 1-56389-193-X. **Y**

Kryptonian technology is slowly transforming Superman into an emotionless Kryptonian, and he is losing his humanity. The story is a precursor to the popular *Return of Superman* story line, since this tale features the first appearance of the being known as the Eradicator.

***Superman: Exile.* Written and illustrated by various.** 1998. 308pp. 1-56389-438-6. **Y**

Superman exiles himself into outer space to protect humanity and ends up a prisoner of the villainous Mongul on his gladiator planet called Warworld. Superman must rely on his skills in gladiator combat to survive; along the way he discovers more about his Kryptonian heritage.

Superman: For Tomorrow. Written by Brian Azzarello. Illustrated by Jim Lee. 2004–2006. **Y** ◉

Featuring artwork by fan-favorite artist Jim Lee. When millions of people disappear after a cataclysmic event, how does Superman cope with his own personal loss when Lois Lane is among those who disappeared? Can Superman find a way to bring back the missing, and could he have been part of the cause of the disaster?

> *Vol. 1.* 2004. 128pp. 1-4012-0351-5, hardcover.
> *Vol. 2.* 2006. 128pp. 1-4012-0715-4, hardcover.

***Superman: Healing Touch.* Written by Greg Rucka and Geoff Johns. Illustrated by Matthew Clark and Rags Morales.** 2005. 168pp. 1-4012-0453-8. **Y**

Ruin's plan is revealed when two twins he has kidnapped have been turned into the next generation of Superman's foe the Parasite. Now there are two Parasites, and Superman may be in for more than he bargained for.

Superman in the . . . . Written and illustrated by various. 1999–2005. **Y**

Collecting highlights of stories of the Man of Steel from each decade from the 1940s through the 1980s.

> *Forties*. 2005. 192pp. 1-4012-0457-0.
> *Fifties*. 2002. 190pp. 1-56389-826-8.
> *Sixties*. 1999. 224pp. 1-56389-522-6.
> *Seventies*. 2000. 214pp. 1-56389-638-9.
> *Eighties*. 2006. 192pp. 1-4012-0952-1.

Superman: In the Name of Gog. **Written by Chuck Austen. Illustrated by Ivan Reis, Joe Prado, Marc Campos and John Sibal.** 2005. 160pp. 1-4012-0757-X.

Superman must face off against not only the power Gog, but also the return of Doomsday—the only villain ever to kill the Man of Steel.

Superman: The Man of Steel. Written by John Byrne, Marv Wolfman, and various. Illustrated by John Byrne, Jerry Ordway, and various. 2003– . **Y**

In 1986, following the maxi-series <u>Crisis on Infinite Earths</u>, DC Comics relaunched the <u>Superman</u> series under the care of writer/illustrator John Byrne. Restarted back at square one, gone were classic characters including Supergirl, Superboy, Super-Woman, the Super-pets, and the various versions of Kryptonite. Lex Luthor was re-imagined as a shrewd businessman instead of a mad scientist, and Clark Kent's adopted parents, Jonathan and Martha Kent, were still alive. Collected here are the original issues of the relaunch, including the works by John Byrne, Marv Wolfman, Jerry Ordway, and others, in a fresh take on the all-new Superman.

> *Vol. 1*. 2003. 160pp. 0-930289-28-5.
> *Vol. 2*. 2003. 224pp. 1-4012-0005-2.
> *Vol. 3*. 2004. 208pp. 1-4012-0246-2.
> *Vol. 4*. 2005. 192pp. 1-4012-0455-4.
> *Vol. 5*. 2006. 192pp. 1-4012-0948-3.

Superman: No Limits. **Written by Jeph Loeb, Mark Millar, Joe Kelly, and various. Illustrated by Mike McKone, German Garcia, and Doug Mahnke.** 2000. 208pp. 1-56389-699-0. **Y**

Superman takes on Eradicator, Mongul, and Imperiex, as well as a brand-new nemesis, La Encantadora. Can Superman take such a nonstop beating? Meanwhile, Clark Kent's personal life is getting more and more complicated.

Superman: President Lex. **Written by J. M. DeMatteis, Joe Kelly, Jeph Loeb, Greg Rucka, Mark Schultz, and Karl Kesel. Illustrated by Ed McGuinness, Duncan Rouleau, Paco Medina, Doug Mahnke, and various.** 2003. 230pp. 1-56389-974-4. **Y**

The unthinkable has happened—the most evil man on planet Earth is president of the United States. What happens when Lex Luthor becomes President Luthor, and how can Superman, a symbol of freedom in the United States, work under the command of the vilest person on the planet?

***Superman: Sacrifice*. Written by Greg Rucka, Mark Verheiden, and Gail Simone. Illustrated by John Byrne, Rags Morale**s, Tony Daniel, and various. 2006. 192pp. 1-4012-0919-X. **Y** ◉

> A tie-in with the epic event called *Infinite Crisis* (see section in this chapter). Superman has been mind-controlled by Max Lord, and Wonder Woman must take the ultimate course of action to free Superman before he hurts more JLA members and other innocent bystanders.

***Superman: They Saved Luthor's Brain*. Written by Roger Stern and John Byrne. Illustrated by John Byrne, Jackson Guice, and Kieron Dwyer.** 2000. 160pp. 1-56389-601-X. **Y**

> A story too shocking to be true! When Lex Luthor is dying from cancer caused by Kryptonite poisoning, he seemingly commits suicide in a fiery plane crash. Meanwhile, a youthful heir to Lex's money, named Lex Luthor II, suddenly appears and charms everyone, including Supergirl. Little do people realize that Lex Luthor II is really just a clone of Lex's body, containing the brain and cunning of the real Lex Luthor!

***Superman: 'Til Death Do Us Part*. Written and illustrated by various.** 2002. 220pp. 1-56389-862-4. **Y**

> Superman faces many adversaries and dangers of all kinds, but can he handle losing the one he loves? When Lois Lane inexplicably is becoming distant from Clark, what can Clark do to save his marriage—or it is really Lois after all?

***Superman: The Trial of Superman*. Written by Louise Simonson. Illustrated by Dan Jurgens**. 1997. 264pp. 1-56389-331-2. **Y**

> Superman is held by an intergalactic tribunal for the destruction of Krypton, and all signs point to his Kryptonian family having played a role in the planet's destruction.

***Superman: Unconventional Warfare*. Written by Greg Rucka. Illustrated by Matthew Clark and various.** 2005. 160pp. 1-4012-0449-X. **Y**

> Superman must face a new villain named Ruin, who has more up his sleeve for the Man of Steel.

***Superman: The Wedding and Beyond*. Written and illustrated by various.** 1998. 192pp. 1-56389-392-4. **Y**

> A collection of stories featuring the wedding of Clark Kent and Lois Lane and other adventures.

***Superman: The Wrath of Gog*. Written by Chuck Austen. Illustrated by Ivan Reis, Joe Prado, Marc Campos and John Sibal.** 2005. 160pp. 1-4012-0450-3. **Y**

> The return of Gog, the villain from the future, as seen in the highly praised *Kingdom Come* (see section in this chapter).

Superman Miniseries and Graphic Novel Titles

Listed below are recommended Superman stories that were originally published as a comic book miniseries or as an original graphic novel title by DC Comics.

🎗 *Superman: Birthright—the Origin of the Man of Steel.* Written by Mark Waid. Illustrated by Leinil Yu and Gerry Alanguilan. 2004. 304pp. 1-4012-0251-9. **T** ◎

A mythic retelling of Superman's early years, from his birth on Krypton and his perilous journey to Earth, to his youth in Smallville and Clark Kent's early days as reporter for the *Daily Planet,* to his first public appearance as Superman. Beneath all the powers and super-heroic strength is a lonely young man, Clark Kent, struggling to find the answers to questions about where he belongs and what his role is on his adopted homeworld, Earth. YALSA's Best Books for Young Adults committee recognized the story in 2006 on their list.

🎗 *Superman: For All Seasons.* Written by Jeph Loeb. Illustrated by Tim Sale. 2002. 208pp. 1-56389-529-3. **T** ◎

The book that helped to inspire the WB network's *Smallville* television series. Clark Kent, a high school student in Smallville, Kansas, is just beginning to discover his extraordinary powers. Clark discovers his true origins and takes his first steps into a larger world that will eventually lead him to become the hero known as Superman. Tim Sale won an Eisner Award in 1999 for Best Artist/Penciller/Inker for his illustrations on this series.

Superman: Infinite City. Written by Mike Kennedy. Illustrated by Carlos Meglia. 2005. 96pp. 1-4012-0067-2. **Y**

Superman and Lois, hot on the trail of a weapon used in Metropolis, come across a deserted city named Infinite City—but it is not entirely abandoned. There is a doorway that transports people to the real Infinite City—a beautiful city where science and magic coexist. Meanwhile the robot architect of the city claims to be made up of what remains of Jor-El, Superman's Kryptonian father.

🎗 *Superman: Peace on Earth.* Written by Paul Dini. Illustrated by Alex Ross. 1998. 64pp. 1-56389-464-5. **Y** ◎

An oversized, fully painted, inspirational story in which Superman tackles one of the worst threats on the planet: world hunger. Despite naysayers and disbelievers, Superman travels across the globe, helping to turn the tide on this devastating disaster with a message of hope and peace during the holiday season. The story won several Eisner Awards in 1999 for Best Graphic Album: New and Best Painter/Multimedia Artist (Interior).

Superman: The Animated Series Tie-in Titles, 1998–2006 ▯

Hot on the heels of the hit *Batman: The Animated Series* cartoon show in 1992, creators Paul Dini and Bruce Timm created a similar show featuring the Man of Steel. Titled *Superman: The Animated Series*, the cartoon debuted in 1996. The comic book collections are based on the characters and situations featured in the animated series and include the indelible art style of Bruce Timm's designs from the cartoon show.

Superman: *Adventures of the Man of Steel*. Written by Paul Dini and Scott McCloud. Illustrated by Rick Burchett, Bret Blevins, and Terry Austin. 1998. 144pp. 1-56389-429-7. **A**

<u>Superman Adventures.</u> Written by Mark Millar. Illustrated by Aluir Amancio and Terry Austin. A
> *Vol. 1: Up, Up and Away!* 2004. 112pp. 1-4012-0331-0.
> *Vol. 2: The Never-Ending Battle.* 2004. 112pp. 1-4012-0332-9.
> *Vol. 3: Last Son of Krypton.* 2006. 112pp. 1-4012-1037-6.
> *Vol. 4: The Man of Steel.* 2006. 112pp. 1-4012-1038-4.

Superman Returns Tie-in Titles, 2006 🎬

In 2006 Warner Bros. released a brand new Superman movie titled *Superman Returns,* starring Brandon Routh as Superman/Clark Kent. DC Comics adapted the well-received movie into a graphic novel as well as a collection featuring prequel tales set before the film.

Superman Returns: *The Movie and More Tales of the Man of Steel*. Written and illustrated by various. 2006. 168pp. 1-4012-0950-5. **Y**
> A tie-in with the hit summer movie *Superman Returns*, released in 2006. The collection features the adaptation of the film which has revitalized the Superman movie franchise as well as features classic Superman tales that have helped to inspire the movie.

Superman Returns: *The Prequels*. Written and illustrated by various. 2006. 128pp. 1-4012-1146-1. **T**
> Collects four comic book stories set before the film *Superman Returns,* titled "Krypton to Earth," "Ma Kent," "Lois Lane," and "Lex Luthor." The tales expand the characters and situations seen in the summer blockbuster film.

Batman

Created by Bill Finger and Bob Kane. DC Comics, 1988– . 🎬 ▯ 🎮

Created by Bill Finger and Bob Kane in 1939, Batman has continued to be one of the most popular comic book characters ever, branching out into hit movies, television shows, cartoons, action figures, and more. Billionaire Bruce Wayne spends his nights as the Dark Knight Detective called Batman. Though he does not have super powers per se, he is a highly skilled detective and crime fighter, and night after night Batman fights a never-ending battle trying to save his beloved Gotham City from the rampant crime that took his parents away from him at a young age. Vowing after the brutal death of his parents to strike fear into the hearts of criminals, he trained for years in a variety of martial arts and detective skills, but all those skills still failed to instill fear in the cowardly and superstitious criminals. After an encounter with a bat, Bruce found just what he needed to fight against crime, and Batman was born. Draped in a long, dark cape, bat-eared mask concealing his face, matching black and grey costume, and belt carrying an amazing array of gadgets and weapons including gas bombs, Batarangs, and grapple guns, Bruce now was able to to instill fear in the criminals of Gotham City. Benefiting from a large bat cave located beneath his mansion, Bruce also had his own lair in which to run a state-of-the-art crime lab with the aid of his trusted butler, Alfred Pennyworth. Batman's war on crime has also expanded to include allies including Robin, Nightwing, Huntress, Batgirl, and the Gotham City Police Department. Together with Batman, they're out to save Gotham from common criminals and Batman's rogues' gallery, including such adversaries as the Joker, Mr. Freeze, Clayface, The Ventriloquist, Two-Face, The Penguin, The Riddler, and Catwoman. Many more Batman titles have been published than are included in this list and can be found at DC Comics' Web site (http://www.dccomics.com).

Collected Comic Book Titles Featuring Batman

Listed below are recommended Batman stories that were originally published in the variety of monthly comic book titles published by DC Comics. The titles are collected editions of the ongoing Batman comic books, including *Batman, Detective Comics, Batman: Legends of the Dark Knight*, and more. The collections are listed by title.

Batman: Broken City. Written by Brian Azzarello. Illustrated by Eduardo Risso. DC Comics, 2004. **Y**

Written and illustrated by the team behind the critically acclaimed *100 Bullets*. Batman investigates the homicide of a young girl found in a landfill and will stop at nothing—even working his way through his rogues' gallery of enemies to find the killer.

> *Vol. 1*. 2004. 144pp. 1-4012-0133-4.
> *Vol. 2*. 2004. 144pp. 1-4012-0214-4.

Batman: Bruce Wayne—Murderer?/Bruce Wayne—Fugitive. Written by Ed Brubaker, Chuck Dixon, Greg Rucka, Devin Grayson, and Kelly Puckett. Illustrated by Rick Burchett, Rick Leonardi, Steve Lieber, Trevor McCarthy, Scott McDaniel, and various. DC Comics, 2002–2003 **Y**

When all signs point to Bruce Wayne as the killer of Vesper Fairchild, he's on the run from the law and from his friends, too. Did he really commit murder, or has someone set Bruce Wayne up to take the fall?

> Batman: Bruce Wayne, Murderer? 2002. 264pp. 1-56389-913-2.
> Batman: Bruce Wayne, Fugitive. 2002–2003.
> > *Vol. 1*. 2002. 160pp. 1-56389-933-7.
> > *Vol. 2*. 2003. 176pp. 1-56389-947-7.
> > *Vol. 3*. 2003. 176pp. 1-4012-0079-6.

Batman: Cataclysm/No Man's Land. Written by Bob Gale and Greg Rucka. Illustrated by various. DC Comics, 1999–2001 **Y** ◎

Following an earthquake that destroys a majority of Gotham City, the U.S. government declares martial law and temporarily annexes the city. Now with chaos and crime running rampant, Bruce Wayne (Batman) and his team of heroes must find a way to save the city before the situation spirals out of control. Features the first appearance of the new Batgirl.

> *Batman: Cataclysm.* 1999. 320pp. 1-56389-527-7.
> Batman: No Man's Land. 1999–2001.
> > *Vol. 1.* 1999. 200pp. 1-56389-564-1.
> > *Vol. 2.* 2000. 208pp. 1-56389-599-4.
> > *Vol. 3.* 2000. 208pp. 1-56389-634-6.
> > *Vol. 4.* 2000. 224pp. 1-56389-698-2.
> > *Vol. 5.* 2001. 208pp. 1-56389-709-1.

Batman Chronicles. **Written by Bob Kane and Bill Finger. Illustrated by Bob Kane.** 2005–2006. **Y**

A collection of the original Batman stories in chronological order, beginning with his first appearance in 1939 in *Detective Comics* #27.

> *Vol. 1.* 2005. 192pp. 1-4012-0445-7.
> *Vol. 2.* 2006. 192pp. 1-4012-0790-1.

Batman: A Death in the Family. **Written by Jim Starlin. Illustrated by Jim Aparo.** DC Comics, 1995. 144pp. 0-930289-44-7. **T**

A gripping tale that culminates with the death of Jason Todd, the second teen hero to take on the mantle of Robin. When Jason's mother is kidnapped by the Joker, Jason heads to in to rescue her but instead is captured and beaten, bruised, and ultimately killed by the Joker. Batman, after finding his partner's tattered corpse, vows with Superman at his side to make sure the Joker pays with his life.

Batman: Gothic. **Written by Grant Morrison. Illustrated by Klaus Janson.** DC Comics, 1998. 128pp. 1-56389-028-3. **T**

A supernatural villain by the name of Mr. Whisper is murdering the crime bosses of Gotham City. Mr. Whisper casts no shadow and is unkillable. Batman is asked by the mob families to help them stop the mystical menace in exchange for a reprieve from illegal activities for a short period of time. When Batman discovers that Mr. Whisper is really a horrific individual from his own schoolboy past who was killed years ago, he finds himself up against an immortal villain who has brought back some of Batman's own childhood fears.

Batman: The Greatest Stories Ever Told, Vol. 1. **Written and illustrated by various.** DC Comics, 2005. 192pp. 1-4012-0444-9. **Y**

A collection looking back at some of the best-known Batman stories since the character's creation in 1939. The stories feature works spanning the Dark Knight's appearances from almost every decade, including from the twenty-first century.

Batman: Hush. **Written by Jeph Loeb. Illustrated by Jim Lee.** DC Comics, 2003–2005. **T** ◎

Someone is out to toy with Batman, someone who knows his deepest, darkest secrets and has hired a legion of Batman's enemies to push the Dark Knight over the edge. Killer Croc, the Joker, the Riddler, Poison Ivy, Ra's al Ghul, and even Superman are out to stop him. Who is this mysterious foe, and what vendetta does he have against Batman? Will he succeed in bringing Bruce Wayne to his biggest defeat? *Absolute Hush* collects both volumes in a deluxe format, including extra features such as sketch artwork, scripts, and more.

> *Vol. 1.* 2003. 128pp. 1-4012-0061-3, hardcover; 1-4012-0060-5, softcover.
> *Vol. 2.* 2004. 176pp. 1-4012-0084-2, hardcover; 1-4012-0092-3, softcover.
> *Absolute Hush.* 2005. 360pp. 1-4012-0426-0.

Batman: Hush Returns. **Written by A. J. Lieberman. Illustrated by Al Barrionuevo, Lee Bermejo, Javier Pina, and various.** 2006. 208pp. 1-4012-0900-9. **T**

A sequel to the popular *Batman: Hush* story. The masked enemy of Batman, a man responsible for so much torture and pain in Bruce Wayne's life, has come back. What is really his motivation, and is he really who Batman thinks he is?

Batman: Knightfall. **Written and illustrated by various.** 1993–1995. **Y**

After having his back broken by the venom-induced villain called Bane, Bruce Wayne temporarily passes the mantle of the bat to Jean Paul Valley (Azrael). While Bruce heals, the new Batman adopts a new costume and resumes patrolling Gotham with his own brand of vengeance, including a rematch with Bane. When Jean Paul's violent style of crime-fighting goes too far and costs a villain's life, a rejuvenated Bruce must come out of retirement to have a confrontation with Jean Paul to settle who will wear the cape and cowl.

> *Part 1: Broken Bat.* 1993. 264pp. 1-56389-142-5.
> *Part 2: Who Rules the Night.* 1993. 264pp. 1-56389-148-4.
> *Part 3: Knightsend.* 1995. 298pp. 1-56389-191-3.

Batman: A Lonely Place of Dying. **Written by Marv Wolfman. Illustrated by George Pérez and various.** DC Comics, 1998. 128pp. 0-930289-63-3. **Y**

After the death of Jason Todd, the second Robin (as seen in *Batman: Death in the Family*), Batman has become reckless in his grief, and it may cost him his own life. A young teenage boy named Tim Drake discovers Batman's true identity and seeks out Dick Grayson, the original Robin, to try to convince him to once again become a team with Batman before it is too late.

Batman: Officer Down. **Written by Greg Rucka, Ed Brubaker and others. Illustrated by Rick Burchett, Jacob and Arnold Pander, and various.** DC Comics, 2001. 168pp. 1-56389-787-3. **Y**

When Commissioner James Gordon is found shot in the back three times, Batman will do whatever it takes to find the culprit. The only eyewitness to the crime is Catwoman. Does she know who really did it, or did she pull the trigger?

***Batman: Strange Apparitions.* Written by Steve Englehart and Len Wein. Illustrated by Marshall Rogers, Terry Austin and Walter Simonson.** DC Comics, 1999. 176pp. 1-56389-500-5. **Y**

> A collection of classic Batman stories from the late 1970s comics featuring the Dark Knight's battle against Dr. Hugo Strange, a white-collar criminal who blackmails and drugs the rich into doing his bidding and who has discovered Batman's true identity. Also included is Bruce Wayne's bittersweet romance with a woman named Silver St. Cloud, a love who also discovers Bruce's secret, as well as classic tales about Batman's arch-nemeses the Joker, the Penguin, and a new Clayface.

***Batman: The Tales of the Demon.* Written by Dennis O'Neil. Illustrated by Neal Adams and others.** DC Comics, 1998. 208pp. 0-930289-94-3. **Y**

> A collection featuring highlights of conflicts the Dark Knight has with a James Bond-type mastermind called Ra's al Ghul. A near immortal with the ability to bring himself back from the dead via his Lazarus Pits, Ra's al Ghul has been trying to save humanity from itself for hundreds of years, but his extreme measures result in a dramatic loss of human life, and he soon becomes Batman's main adversary.

***Batman: Ten Nights of the Beast.* Written by Jim Starlin. Illustrated by Mike Zeck.** DC Comics, 1994. 96pp. 1-56389-155-7. **Y**

> Anatoli Knyazev, known as the KGBeast, is one of the deadliest assassins from the former Soviet Union. Having gone rogue, he's arrived in Gotham City to eliminate ten key people involved in the Strategic Defense Initiative program. As his targets are picked off one by one, the assassin runs afoul of Batman, who doesn't take kindly to Soviet assassins killing innocent victims, and Batman does whatever it takes to protect the citizens of Gotham and the president of the United States. But how can Batman defeat an assassin who feels no pain?

Batman: Under the Hood. Written by Judd Winick. Illustrated by Doug Mahnke, Tom Nguyen, and various. 2005–2006. **Y**

> Previously the Joker was known as the Batman villain called the Red Hood, but he discarded the old identity after falling into a vat of acid. Now there's a new Red Hood in Gotham City to challenge the crime lord called the Black Mask. When Batman discovers there's a new Red Hood in town, he sets out to stop him. Who Batman finds under the mask will shock him forever.

>> *Vol. 1.* 2005. 176pp. 1-4012-0756-1.
>> *Vol. 2.* 2006. 192pp. 1-4012-0901-7.

***Batman: Venom.* Written by Dennis O'Neil. Illustrated by Trevor Von Eeden and various.** DC Comics, 1993. 136pp. 1-56389-101-8. **T**

> After failing to save the life of a kidnapped child due to his own human limitations, Batman resorts to performance-enhancing drugs that improve his strength and stamina. Over time, as the steroids begin to affect his sense of judgment and morality, Batman must decide to either save his life or succumb to his drug addiction.

Batman: War Drums/War Games. **Written by Ed Brubaker, Chuck Dixon, Devin Grayson, Dylan Horrocks, Bill Willingham, and various. Illustrated by Pete Woods, Damion Scott, Brad Walker, Cam Smith and Troy Nixey.** DC Comics, 2004–2005. **Y**

> When the crime lords of Gotham City vie for supremacy, the citizens of Gotham are defenseless, and it's up to Batman and his caped allies, including a new Robin (formerly the Spoiler), as well as Nightwing, Oracle, Batgirl, and others, to save the city.

> Batman: War Drums. 2004. 256pp. 1-4012-0341-8.
> Batman: War Games. 2005.
>> *Act One.* 2005. 208pp. 1-4012-0429-5.
>> *Act Two.* 2005. 192pp. 1-4012-0430-9.
>> *Act Three.* 2005. 208pp. 1-4012-0431-7.

Batman: Year One. **Written by Frank Miller. Illustrated by David Mazzucchelli.** DC Comics, 1997. 104pp. 0-930289-33-1. deluxe ed., 2005. 144pp. 1-4012-0690-5. **Y** ◉

© 2006 DC Comics

> A young Bruce Wayne traveled the world after the death of his parents, seeking to learn all the martial arts and detective skills he could to become the man he is today. After he returns to Gotham City, a fight with street criminals nearly takes his life, and he knows that something's wrong with his approach: the criminals don't fear him. He adopts the identity of Batman, but he has a long way to go to become the feared vengeance of the night. Then he forges a friendship of sorts with police officer James Gordon, and together they fight to bring down the corruption that's rampant in Gotham City. Batman has taken his first steps as the protector of Gotham City. The basis for the story also served as the inspiration for the 2006 film *Batman Begins*.

Batman in the . . . . **Written and illustrated by various.** DC Comics, 1999–2004. **Y**

> A collection of the best Batman tales from each decade. Though the writers and artists have changed, the thrilling tales of Batman continue to thrive decade after decade, proving that he remains one of the most popular heroes of all time.

> *Forties.* 2004. 192pp. 1-4012-0206-3.
> *Fifties.* 2002. 192pp. 1-56389-810-1.
> *Sixties.* 1999. 224pp. 1-56389-491-2.
> *Seventies.* 2000. 192pp. 1-56389-565-X.
> *Eighties.* 2004. 192pp. 1-4012-0241-1.

Batman Miniseries and Graphic Novel Titles

Listed below are recommended Batman stories that were originally published as a comic book miniseries or as an original graphic novel title by DC Comics.

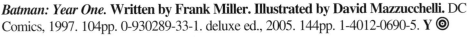

All-Star Batman. **Written by Frank Miller. Illustrated by Jim Lee.** DC Comics, 2007. **T** ◎

A retelling of the origin of Batman from two of the comic book industry's best-known creators—Frank Miller and Jim Lee. The story re-creates the familiar tale of how Bruce Wayne became the legendary hero known as Batman and dedicated his life to fighting a war on crime.

Vol. 1. 2007. 144pp. 1-4012-0895-9.

🗪 *Batman: Arkham Asylum.* **Written by Grant Morrison. Illustrated by Dave McKean.** DC Comics, 2004. 216pp. 1-4012-0424-4. **O**

When the Gotham City asylum has been taken over by the insane inmates, the criminals want only one person to negotiate with: Batman. Now a walking bargaining chip with the deadliest infestation of villains, Batman must try to save the captured Arkham employees from the murderous rampage of his rogues' gallery, including the Joker, Killer Croc, and more. The story won a Harvey Award Special Award for Excellence in Production/Presentation in 1990 when it was originally released.

🗪 **Batman: Black and White.** **Written and illustrated by various.** DC Comics, 2000–2002. **T** ◎

Short stories by a variety of writers and artists, including Neil Gaiman, Simon Bisley, Walter Simonson, Paul Dini, Chris Claremont, Alex Ross, Jim Lee, Tim Sale, and others each reinterpret Batman in a unique way: by stories that are only told in black and white. The short story "Heroes," written by the late Archie Goodwin and illustrated by Gary Gianni, won an Eisner Award for Best Short Story in 1997. The story appears in *Volume 1. Volume 2* received an Eisner in 2003 for Best Graphic Album: Reprint. *Volume 1* received a Harvey Award in 1998 for Best Graphic Album of Previously Published Work.

Vol. 1. 2000. 232pp. 1-56389-439-4.
Vol. 2. 2002. 176pp. 1-56389-828-4.

Batman: The Dark Knight Returns. **Written and illustrated by Frank Miller.** DC Comics, 1997–2006. **T** ◎

Ten years after Batman has retired, the world's heroes, except Superman, have all left, and Bruce Wayne is haunted by the death of Robin (Jason Todd). As Gotham City plunges further into despair with the rise of a mutant gang and Batman's old foes still running loose in the city, Bruce Wayne must don the cape and cowl, and the Dark Knight returns again. Allied with a new Robin (Carrie Kelly), Batman must face Two-Face, the leader of the mutants, a vengeful Joker, and (in this story) the government-sanctioned Superman to restore freedom to Gotham City by any means necessary. Once of the most highly regarded Batman stories ever told. In 2006 DC Comics released a deluxe <u>Absolute</u> edition of the series, which includes a deluxe slip-case for the collection and features revised coloring and behind-the-scenes information such as concept sketches and Frank Miller's scripts for the series.

*Batman: The Dark Knight Returns.*1997. 224pp. 1-56389-342-8. *T*
Absolute Dark Knight. 2006. 512pp. 1-4012-1079-1.

Batman: The Dark Knight Strikes Again. **Written and illustrated by Frank Miller.** DC Comics, 2002. 256pp. 1-56389-844-6. **T**

> Several years after the events in the classic tale *Batman: The Dark Knight Returns*, Batman reemerges from hiding to right the wrongs committed by a corrupt government secretly under the control of Lex Luthor and Brainiac. Joined by Catgirl (formerly known as Robin) and his army of Bat-soldiers, Batman is out to bring back the DC Universe heroes of old for one last strike against a world that banished them.

Batman: Death and the Maidens. **Written by Greg Rucka. Illustrated by Klaus Janson.** 2004. 224pp. 1-4012-0234-9. **T**

> Ra's al Ghul, one of Batman's greatest enemies, lies near final death, with no hope in the fires of his Lazarus Pits that have kept him alive for centuries. Fearful of a woman called Nyssa, with whom he shares a secret centuries-old past, he asks the Dark Knight tohelp him track her down. In return Ra's will give Batman a chance to speak with his dead parents, and Bruce Wayne may be shocked at what his deceased parents have to say to him.

Batman: Harley Quinn. **Written by Paul Dini. Illustrated by Yvel Guichet.** DC Comics, 2000. 48pp. 1-56389-773-3. **Y** ◎

> Batman faces a new adversary: Harley Quinn, the Joker's new clown-faced lover, who's just as crazy as "Mistah J" himself. Based on the popular character that first made her debut in the hit cartoon series *Batman: The Animated Series*.

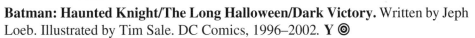

Batman: Haunted Knight/The Long Halloween/Dark Victory. Written by Jeph Loeb. Illustrated by Tim Sale. DC Comics, 1996–2002. **Y** ◎

> The team of Jeph Loeb and Tim Sale have created several memorable Batman stories. Listed below are their highly praised works.

Batman: Haunted Knight. 1996. 192pp. 1-56389-273-1. **T**

> Collects three dark Halloween-themed short stories in which Batman faces off against some of his greatest enemies, including Scarecrow, the Mad Hatter, the Penguin, Poison Ivy, and the Joker, on the spookiest night of the year.

🏵 *Batman: The Long Halloween.* 1999. 368pp. 1-56389-469-6. **T**

> During the earlier days of Batman's crime-fighting career, a mysterious killer is striking only on holidays and taking out members of the Falcone mob family. It's up to Batman, Lieutenant James Gordon, and District Attorney Harvey Dent to find the culprit before more lives are lost. Meanwhile, the murderous events are tied into a traumatic event in Dent's life, who is transformed into the duality-based Batman villain called Two-Face. The story won an Eisner Award in 1998 for Best Finite Series/Limited Series and in 1999 for Best

Graphic Album: Reprint. The collection received recognition from YALSA's Popular Paperbacks for Young Adults committee in 2002 on the "Graphic Novels: Superheroes and Beyond" list.

🏵 *Batman: Dark Victory.* 2002. 392pp. 1-56389-868-3. **T**

Sequel to *Batman: The Long Halloween*. Batman investigates a new series of holiday killings and police officers affiliated with Harvey Dent. Is the original Holiday killer still at large? Meanwhile, a brooding Bruce Wayne is losing more and more of himself in his night alter ego. Will he find his humanity again after taking in his new ward, Dick Grayson? Meanwhile, Batman's rogues' gallery, including the Joker, Poison Ivy, and Mr. Freeze, threatens the safety of Gotham City once again. The collection won an Eisner Award in 2002 for Best Graphic Album: Reprint.

🏵 *Batman: The Killing Joke.* **Written by Alan Moore. Illustrated by Brian Bolland.** DC Comics, 1988. 48pp. 0-930289-45-5. **O** ◎

© 2006 DC Comics

The Joker, Batman's insane arch-nemesis, goes on a rampage across Gotham City in a bid to drive Commission Gordon insane. After shooting and crippling Barbara Gordon (Batgirl) and kidnapping the Commissioner, the Dark Knight seeks to put an end to the Joker's madness. All the while, the origin of the Joker is revealed as a young man who takes a plunge into toxic waste and has never stopped maniacally laughing since. The powerful short story won many awards in the comic book industry in 1989, including three Eisner Awards for Best Graphic Album, Best Writer, and Best Artist/Penciller/Inker, as well as Harvey Awards for Best Artist or Penciller, Best Single Issue or Story, and Best Graphic Album.

Batman: Sword of Azrael. **Written by Dennis O'Neil. Illustrated by Joe Quesada.** DC Comics, 2000 112pp. 1-56389-100-X. **Y**

The origin of Jean Paul Valley, a man who would temporarily replace Bruce Wayne as Batman in the classic *Knightfall* story line. Jean Paul's ancestors were from an ancient cult called the Order of St. Dumas, and his family bloodline has served for generations as Azrael, the avenging angel of the order. After befriending Bruce Wayne, Jean Paul accepts the powers and becomes the latest Azrael. When the order decrees that Batman is the enemy of their cult, Jean Paul's faith is shattered. When an ancient demon rises up to destroy the Order of St. Dumas, Azrael and Batman together take it on, and Jean Paul must decide where his true allegiance lies: with the Order or with the Dark Knight.

🏵 *Batman: War on Crime.* **Written by Paul Dini. Illustrated by Alex Ross.** DC Comics, 1999. 64pp. 1-56389-576-5. **Y** ◎

Beautifully painted, oversized story retelling of the origin of Batman and why he wages his one-man war on crime protecting citizens of Gotham City from evil. The story won an Eisner Award in 2000 for Best Painter/Multimedia Artist (Interior) and a Harvey Award for Best Graphic Album or Original Work in 2000.

Year One: Batman/Ra's Al Ghul. **Written by Devin Grayson. Illustrated by Paul Gulacy.** 2006. 104pp. 1-4012-0904-1. **Y**

> A year has passed since Batman's enemy Ra's Al Ghul died (as seen in *Batman: Death and the Maidens*). When Batman receives a mysterious letter sent by Ra's Al Ghul, he must delve into the mysterious origin of his most cunning enemy in order to save the world from the reanimated dead.

🏆 *Batman: The Animated Series Tie-in Titles* ◎ 🖵

In 1992, Warner Bros. animation ventured to tell the tales of the Dark Knight in the instant cult-hit show *Batman: The Animated Series,* created by Bruce Timm and Paul Dini. Mixing solid writing with a 1930s-style artwork, it became an instant classic and has been considered by fans to be the definitive version of Batman on television and the silver screen (*Batman: Mask of the Phantasm*). The show's enduring popularity spawned a successful comic book series and introduced the character Harley Quinn to the regular DC Comics continuity. Listed below are the various collections of titles inspired by the series. *The Batman Adventures: Dangerous Dames and Demons* includes the short story "Mad Love," the 1994 Eisner Award-winning story for Best Single Issue/Single Story that retells the origin of Harley Quinn. The story also won a Harvey Award in 1994 for Best Single Issue or Story. The hit story was adapted for an animated episode. The series also won Eisner Awards in 1996, 1998, and 1999 in the category Best Title for Younger Readers/Best Comics Publication for a Younger Audience. *Batman and Superman Adventures: World's Finest* won an Eisner in 1998 for Best Graphic Album: New. *The Batman Adventures: Dangerous Dames and Demons* won an Eisner Award in 2004 for Best Graphic Album: Reprint.

The Batman: Adventures. Written by Kelley Puckett. Illustrated by various. DC Comics, 1993. 144pp. 1-56389-098-4. **A**.

Batman: Dark Knight Adventures. Written by Kelley Puckett. Illustrated by Rick Burchett and Mike Parobeck. 1994. 144pp. 1-56389-124-7. **A**

Batman: Mask of the Phantasm. **Written by Kelley Puckett. Illustrated by Mike Parobek and Bruce Timm.** DC Comics, 1993. 64pp. 1-56389-122-0. **A**

<u>Batman Adventures.</u> **Written and illustrated by various.** 2004. **A**
> *Vol. 1: Rogues' Gallery.* 2004. 112pp. 1-4012-0329-9.
> *Vol. 2: Shadows and Masks.* 2004. 112pp. 1-4012-0330-2.

🏆 *The Batman Adventures: Dangerous Dames and Demons.* **Written by Paul Dini. Illustrated by Bruce Timm, et al.** DC Comics, 2003. 192pp. 1-56389-973-6. **T**

🏆 *Batman and Superman Adventures: World's Finest.* **Written by Paul Dini. Illustrated by Joe Staton and Bruce Timm.** DC Comics, 1997. 64pp. 1-56389-386-X. **A**

Batman Movie Adaptations, 1997–2005

Adaptations of the hit <u>Batman</u> movies beginning with the 1989 film and ending with the 2005 summer blockbuster *Batman Begins*.

Batman: The Movies. **Written and illustrated by various.** DC Comics, 1997. 208pp. 1-56389-326-6. **T**

Batman Begins: The Movie & Other Tales of The Dark Knight. **Written by Scott Beaty. Illustrated by Killian Plunkett.** DC Comics, 2005 160pp. 1-4012-0440-6. **T**

Spider-Man

Created by Stan Lee and Steve Ditko. Marvel Comics, 1988– .

When teenage junior scientist and bookworm Peter Parker was bitten by a radioactive spider during a high school field trip, little did he know that he would gain the proportionate strength of a spider, the ability to climb walls, and a kind of "spider-sense" that warns him of coming danger. Peter also created his own spider-web cartridges and a red and blue costume complete with a mask that completely covered his face, and with that the wise-cracking wall-crawler, Spider-Man, was born! After losing his beloved Uncle Ben to a common thief whom Peter had failed to stop, he has vowed to remember his uncle's words that "with great power comes great responsibility," and he will always protect the streets of New York City from common criminals as well as superpowered villains, including the Green Goblin, Doctor Octopus, Venom, the Lizard, Electro, and more. Since his first appearance in 1962, Spider-Man has continued to be one of the most popular super-hero characters ever created.

Amazing <u>Spider-Man</u>. Written by J. Michael Straczynski. Illustrated by John Romita, Jr. and Mike Deodato, Jr. Marvel Comics, 2002–. **Y** ◎

Peter Parker is reunited once again with his estranged wife, Mary Jane, and discovers that he's not the only one with spider powers when he meets an enigmatic man named Ezekiel. In the midst of battling a seemingly unbeatable foe called Morlun, Peter also reveals to Aunt May his secret identity. Collected in *Volume 2: Revelations* is the poignant tribute to 9/11, which asks what a super-hero can do in the midst of devastating tragedy. The first volume, *Coming Home*, won an Eisner Award in 2002 in the category Best Serialized Story and also received recognition from YALSA's Quick Picks for Reluctant Readers committee in 2003.

© 2006 Marvel Comics

> *Vol. 1: Coming Home.* 2002. 152pp. 0-7851-0806-8.
> *Vol. 2: Revelations.* 2002. 96pp. 0-7851-0877-7.
> *Vol. 3: Until the Stars Turn Cold.* 2002. 144pp. 0-7851-1075-5.
> *Vol. 4: The Life and Death of Spiders.* 2003. 144pp. 0-7851-1097-6.
> *Vol. 5: Unintended Consequences.* 2003. 144pp. 0-7851-1098-4.
> *Vol. 6: Happy Birthday.* 2004. 160pp. 0-7851-1343-6.
> *Vol. 7: The Book of Ezekiel.* 2004. 144pp. 0-7851-1525-0.
> *Vol. 8: Sins of the Past.* 2005. 144pp. 0-7851-1509-9.
> *Vol. 9: Skin Deep.* 2005. 96pp. 0-7851-1642-7.

Vol. 10: New Avengers. 2005. 144pp. 0-7851-1764-4.
Vol. 11. 2006. 144pp. 0-7851-1974-4.

***Amazing Spider-Man: The Death of Gwen Stacy.* Written by Stan Lee and Gerry Conway. Illustrated by Gil Kane, John Romita, and Frank Giacoia.** Marvel Comics, 2002. 112pp. 0-7851-1026-7. **Y** ◎

Reprints the classic 1973 story line originally published in the comic book *The Amazing Spider-Man.* Harry Osborn, Spider-Man/Peter Parker's nemesis the Green Goblin, captures Peter's girlfriend Gwen Stacy as a ploy to kill Spider-Man. In the battle atop a bridge, Gwen falls, and even Spider-Man's webbing isn't able to save her; she breaks her neck and dies. Enraged by his beloved's death, Spider-Man has a final confrontation with the Green Goblin from which only one of them will walk away.

***Amazing Spider-Man: Saga of the Alien Costume.* Written by Tom DeFalco, Roger Stern, and various. Illustrated by Rick Leonardi, Mike Zeck, and various.** Marvel Comics, 1988. 192pp. 0-87135-396-2. **Y**

When Spider-Man's costume is damaged while on an alien planet (see listing for *Secret Wars* in this chapter), he receives a solid black costume of alien origin. Now with just a thought Peter Parker can transform into Spider-Man in the blink of an eye. But as Peter soon finds out, there's more to this costume than meets the eye—something sinister and deadly.

***Amazing Spider-Man: The Wedding.* Written by Stan Lee, Jim Shooter, and David Michelinie. Illustrated by various.** Marvel Comics, 2002. 144pp. 0-7851-0904-8. **Y**

A collection reprinting the 1987 wedding of Peter Parker with his longtime girlfriend Mary Jane Watson. The collection also includes the newspaper *Spider-Man* comic strip featuring the wedding.

The Best of Spider-Man. Written by J. Michael Straczynski, Paul Jenkins, and various. Illustrated by John Romita, Jr., Mike Deodato, Jr., and various. Marvel Comics, 2003– . **Y**

An anthology collection collecting recent story lines from several monthly Spider-Man comic books, including *Amazing Spider-Man* and *Peter Parker: Spider-Man,* in a hardcover format.

Vol. 1. 2003. 336pp. 0-785-10900-5, hardcover.
Vol. 2. 2003. 368pp. 0-785-11100-X, hardcover.
Vol. 3. 2004. 336pp. 0-785-11827-6, hardcover.
Vol. 4. 2005. 336pp. 0-785-11339-8, hardcover.
Vol. 5. 2006. 248pp. 0-785-12128-5, hardcover.

Essential Spider-Man Collections. Written by Stan Lee and various. Illustrated by Steve Ditko and various. Marvel Comics, 1997– .

Black & white reprints of the best Spider-Man stories, for those with a limited budget. The collections include the *Amazing Spider-Man* issues starting from his first appearance in 1962 as well as the monthly series Peter Parker: The Spectacular Spider-Man, which launched in 1976.

The Essential Amazing Spider-Man. 1997– . Y
> *Vol. I.* 1997. 528pp. 0-7851-0286-8.
> *Vol. II.* 1998. 528pp. 0-7851-0299-X.
> *Vol. III.* 1998. 528pp. 0-7851-0658-8.
> *Vol. IV.* 2000. 528pp. 0-7851-0760-6.
> *Vol. V.* 2002. 528pp. 0-7851-0881-5.
> *Vol. VI.* 2004. 576pp. 0-7851-1365-7.
> *Vol. VII.* 2005. 560pp. 0-7851-1879-9.

Essential Peter Parker: The Spectacular Spider-Man. Written by Gerry Conway, Archie Goodwin, and various. Illustrated by Sal Buscema and various. 2005– . Y
> *Vol. 1.* 2005. 568pp. 0-7851-1682-6.
> *Vol. 2.* 2006. 592pp. 0-7851-2042-4.

Friendly Neighborhood Spider-Man. Written by Peter David. Illustrated by Mike Wieringo. Marvel Comics, 2006– . Y
Collecting issues 5 through 10 of the newest ongoing Spider-Man monthly comic book. Spider-Man discovers that the Hobgoblin may be back in town; a woman claims that Spider-Man has been stalking her for years; and Spider-Man finds himself in a brand-new costume created by Tony Stark (Iron Man).
> *Vol. 1: Derailed.* 2006.144pp. 0-7851-1766-0.

Marvel Age/Marvel Adventures Spider-Man. Based on the stories created by Stan Lee and Steve Ditko. Written by Todd DeZago, Mike Raicht, and various. Illustrated by various. Marvel Comics, 2004–. A
A retelling of the very first Spider-Man stories from the 1960s, issue-for-issue, and bringing the story into the twenty-first century. The stories focus on a young high school student, Peter Parker, who after being bitten by a radioactive spider gains the powers of a spider and becomes a hero following the death of his Uncle Ben. The series was first published under the Marvel Age banner but was relaunched under the series title of Marvel Adventures.
> Marvel Age Spider-Man. 2004–2005.
> > *Vol. 1: Fearsome Foes.* 2004. 96pp. 0-7851-1439-4.
> > *Vol. 2: Everyday Hero.* 2004. 96pp. 0-7851-1451-3.
> > *Vol. 3: Swingtime.* 2004. 96pp. 0-7851-1632-X.
> > *Vol. 4: The Goblin Strikes.* 2004. 96pp. 0-7851-1549-8.
> > *Vol. 5: Spidey Strikes Back.* 2005. 96pp. 0-7851-1632-X.
> Marvel Adventures Spider-Man. 2005– .
> > *Vol. 1: The Sinister Six.* 2005. 96pp. 0-7851-1739-3.
> > *Vol. 2: Power Struggle.* 2005. 96pp. 0-7851-1903-5.
> > *Vol. 3: Doom with a View.* 2006. 96pp. 0-7851-2000–9.
> > *Vol. 4: Concrete Jungle.* 2006. 96pp. 0-7851-2005-X.
> > *Vol. 5: Monsters on the Prowl.* 2007. 96pp. 0-7851-2309-1.

Marvel Knights Spider-Man. Written by Mark Millar with Reginald Hudlin. Illustrated by Terry Dodson, Frank Cho, and various. Marvel Comics, 2004– . **T** ◎

The collected volumes of a new monthly Spider-Man comic book series under the banner of Marvel Comics' Marvel Knights series of titles. The collection gas a slightly harder edge in terms of storytelling approach. In the epic story line from *Volumes 1–3*, Aunt May is abducted and feared dead. A downtrodden and devastated Peter Parker must figure out who the real culprit is behind Aunt May's kidnapping while dealing with all of Spider-Man's greatest foes and a public out to collect the *Daily Bugle*'s reward for his identity. The hardcover collection reprints *Volumes 1–3*. *Volume 4* begins a brand new story line.

> *Vol. 1: Down Among the Dead Men.* 2004. 96pp. 0-7851-1437-8.
> *Vol. 2: Venomous.* 2005. 96pp. 0-7851-1675-3.
> *Vol. 3: The Last Stand.* 2005. 96pp. 0-7851-1676-1.
> *Vol. 4: Wild Blue Yonder.* 2005. 144pp. 0-7851-1761-X.
> *Vol. 1.* 2005. 304pp. 0-7851-1842-X, hardcover.

Spectacular Spider-Man. Marvel Comics, 2004–2005. **Y**

The collected monthly issues of Spectacular Spider-Man, a comic book series published by Marvel Comics from 2003 to 2005.

> *Vol. 1: The Hunger.* Written by Paul Jenkins. Illustrated by Humberto Ramos. 2004. 120pp. 0-7851-1169-7.
> *Vol. 2: Countdown.* Written by Paul Jenkins. Illustrated by Humberto Ramos. 2004. 120pp. 0-7851-1313-4.
> *Vol. 3: Here There Be Monsters.* Written by Paul Jenkins. Illustrated by Damion Scott. 2005. 96pp. 0-7851-1333-9.
> *Vol. 4: Disassembled.* Written by Paul Jenkins. Illustrated by Michael Ryan. 2005. 144pp. 0-7851-1626-5.
> *Vol. 5: Sins Remembered.* Written by Samm Barnes. Illustrated by Scot Eaton. 2005. 96pp. 0-7851-1628-1.
> *Vol. 6: The Final Curtain.* Written by Paul Jenkins. Illustrated by Mark Buckingham. 2005. 144pp. 0-7851-1950-7.

Spider-Man: Blue. **Written by Jeph Loeb. Illustrated by Tim Sale.** Marvel Comics, 2004. 144pp. 0-7851-1071-2. **T** ◎

Peter reminisces about his first love, the late Gwen Stacy, after unearthing a journal he had kept about her. In flashback sequences, Peter revisits the bittersweet days when he first met Gwen and tries to reconcile the pain that he still feels following her death at the hands of the Green Goblin.

Spider-Man: The Cosmic Adventures. **Written by David Michelinie. Illustrated by Todd McFarlane and Erik Larsen.** Marvel Comics, 1993. 192pp. 0-87135-963-4. **Y**

When the villains of the Marvel Universe switch opponents to defeat their heroic enemies, Spider-Man finds himself outnumbered; foes including The Trapster, Titania, Graviton, the Rhino, Magneto, the Incredible Hulk, the Shocker, the Brothers Grimm, Hydro-Man, the Super Soldier Eliminator, Goliath, and Dragon Man come after him. Meanwhile, after a strange, mysterious burst of energy, Spider-Man discovers that he has now received the superpowers of a god. The villains are sure in trouble now that Spider-Man has received the powers of Captain Universe! For other tales of Captain Universe, please see that section in this chapter.

Spider-Man: Hobgoblin Lives. **Written by Roger Stern. Illustrated by Ron Frenz, George Pérez, and various.** Marvel Comics, 1998. 112pp. 0-7851-0585-9. **Y**

Many people thought that Ned Leeds was really the Hobgoblin—a reporter for the *Daily Bugle* who was killed while on assignment in Germany. But now the Hobgoblin has resurfaced again—and Spider-Man discovers that everything he thought he knew about his deadly enemy is wrong.

Spider-Man: Kraven's Last Hunt. **Written by J. M. Dematteis. Illustrated by Mike Zeck.** Marvel Comics, 2006 160pp. 0-7851-2330-X. hardcover. **T** ◎

The tale was originally published in 1987 in the pages of the Spider-Man comic books *Web of Spider-Man* #32-33, *Amazing Spider-Man* #393-394, and *Spectacular Spider-Man* #131-132 and tells of the climactic final confrontation between Spider-Man and Kraven the Hunter. When Kraven does the unthinkable and actually captures and buries Spider-Man alive, he dons the Spider-Man costume to see what it is like to be his prey. Meanwhile, underneath New York, a humanoid, ratlike creature called Vermin stalks the sewers seeking revenge on Spider-Man.

Spider-Man: Maximum Carnage. **Written by Tom DeFalco and various. Illustrated by Mark Bagley and various.** Marvel Comics, 2005. 336pp. 0-7851-0987-0. **Y**

Spider-Man finds himself in a deadly game between his archenemy Venom and Carnage—an even deadlier symbiote spawn of Venom inhabiting the body of killer Kletus Cassiday. Can Spider-Man work together with Venom and stop Carnage from killing before it's too late?

Spider-Man: The Other. **Written and illustrated by various.** Marvel Comics, 2006. 144pp. 0-7851-1765-2. **T**

Spider-Man finds himself up against the dreaded Morlun once again and discovers that he is going through a metamorphosis. Will Spider-Man ever be the same again, and how can he defeat an immortal, vampirelike creature that will never stop hunting for Peter?

Spider-Man/Doctor Octopus: Negative Exposure. **Written by Brian K. Vaughan. Illustrated by Staz Johnson.** Marvel Comics, 2004. 120pp. 0-7851-1330-4. **Y**

Jealous of Peter Parker's success at taking photographs of Spider-Man for the *Daily Bugle,* Jeffrey Haight will do anything to one-up Peter—even if it means doing business with one of the deadliest of Spider-Man's enemies, Doctor Octopus.

Spider-Man Visionaries: Kurt Busiek. **Written by Kurt Busiek. Illustrated by Pat Olliffe.** Marvel Comics, 2006. 176pp. 0-7851-0263-9. **Y** ◎

Features the stories of Spider-Man that occurred early in his crime-fighting career shortly after his first appearance in *Amazing Fantasy* #15 in 1962 and set before the events of *Amazing Spider-Man* #1. The tales take place when Peter Parker is still in high school and trying to balance life as a high school student, new super-hero, and junior photographer while keeping his identity a secret from his Aunt May. The collection was originally published as a short-lived comic book series from 1995 called the Untold Tales of Spider-Man.

Spider-Man Visionaries: Todd McFarlane. Written by David Michelinie. Illustrated by Todd McFarlane. Marvel Comics, 2003–2004. Y

In 1988 Todd McFarlane joined writer David Michelinie with *Amazing Spider-Man* #298 and became an instant hit with fans. McFarlane's artwork created a spider-like hero with long, thin arms and large eyes—an influence that lasts to this day. Reprinted are the first major arcs of their work, including the first appearance of Venom, one of Spider-Man's most deadly enemies.

> *Book I.* 2003. 208pp. 0-7851-0800-9.
> *Book II.* 2003. 224pp. 0-7851-1037-2.
> *Book III.* 2004. 264pp. 0-7851-1039-9.

Ultimate Spider-Man. Written by Brian Michael Bendis. Illustrated by Mark Bagley. Marvel Comics, 2002– . Y ◎

© 2006 Marvel Comics

In 2001, Marvel Comics reimagined the world of the Marvel Universe with the "Ultimate" line of titles that reinterprets some of their most popular characters for a new generation and starts them back at the basics. In Ultimate Spider-Man, good teen characterization and plenty of web-swinging action go hand-in-hand as Peter Parker, an awkward teenager, deals with school bullies, homework problems, and first-love woes. After a bite by a super-spider at Osborn Labs has given him spiderlike powers, he's learned the importance of being responsible with his great power and is out to protect New York City as the costumed hero Spider-Man. But life isn't easy for the teen. He's trying to hold onto a secret identity (although his girlfriend, Mary Jane Watson, knows) and work a part-time job at the *Daily Bugle,* and he's the target of villains including the Green Goblin, Doctor Octopus, Venom, Carnage, and more. The collections featured below are in paperback format except for those listed as hardcover. They are reprint collections of the series and contain several story lines in each volume. Several volumes have received recognition from YALSA, including the Popular Paperbacks for Young Adults committee in 2002 and 2003 for *Volumes 1* and *3,* respectively, as well as Quick Picks for Reluctant Readers in 2002 and 2004 for *Volumes 1* and *2,* respectively.

> *Vol. 1: Power and Responsibility.* 2002. 192pp. 0-7851-0786-X.
> *Vol. 2: Learning Curve.* 2002. 192pp. 0-7851-0820-3.
> *Vol. 3: Double Trouble.* 2002. 176pp. 0-7851-0879-3.
> *Vol. 4: Legacy.* 2002. 160pp. 0-7851-0968-4.
> *Vol. 5: Public Scrutiny.* 2003. 120pp. 0-7851-1087-9.
> *Vol. 6: Venom.* 2003. 168pp. 0-7851-1094-1.
> *Vol. 7: Irresponsible.* 2003. 144pp. 0-7851-1092-5.
> *Vol. 8: Cats and Kings.* 2004. 152pp. 0-7851-1250-2.
> *Vol. 9: Ultimate Six.* 2004. 208pp. 0-7851-1312-6.

Vol. 10: Hollywood. 2004. 144pp. 0-7851-1402-5.
Vol. 11: Carnage. 2005. 144pp. 0-7851-1403-3.
Vol. 12: Superstars. 2005. 144pp. 0-7851-1629-X.
Vol. 13: Hobgoblin. 2005. 144pp. 0-7851-1647-8.
Vol. 14: Warriors. 2005. 168pp. 0-7851-1680-X.
Vol. 15: Silver Sable. 2006. 168pp. 0-7851-1681-8.
Vol. 16: Deadpool. 2006. 144pp. 0-7851-1927-2.
Vol. 17: Clone Saga. 2007. 168pp. 0-7851-1928-0.
Vol. 1. 2002. 352pp. 0-7851-0898-X, hardcover.
Vol. 2. 2003. 336pp. 0-7851-1061-5, hardcover.
Vol. 3. 2003. 304pp. 0-7851-1156-5, hardcover.
Vol. 4. 2004. 304pp. 0-7851-1249-9, hardcover.
Vol. 5. 2004. 360pp. 0-7851-1401-7, hardcover.
Vol. 6. 2005. 288pp. 0-7851-1841-1, hardcover.
Vol. 7. 2006. 344pp. 0-7851-2148-X, hardcover.

Spider-Man Movie Adaptations, 2002– 🎬

Adaptations of the box office hit films *Spider-Man* and *Spider-Man 2* directed by Sam Raimi and featuring Tobey Maguire as Spider-Man/Peter Parker and Kirsten Dunst as Mary Jane Watson.

***Spider-Man: The Movie.* Written by Stan Lee, Greg Rucka, and Paul Jenkins. Illustrated by Alan Davis.** Marvel Comics, 2002. 112pp. 0-7851-0903-X. **Y**

***Spider-Man 2: The Official Comic Book Adaptation.* Written and illustrated by various.** Marvel Comics, 2004. 120pp. 0-7851-1411-4. **Y**

Other Classic and Contemporary Crime Fighters

Since their first appearances in the late 1930s, super-heroes have come in all shapes and sizes. Included below are a variety of heroes and their respective collected editions of their stories available from publishers in the last fifteen years. The list features heroes who have been popular for decades as well as modern heroes, and the main listings are by the name of the character. Please note that many of the titles featuring the characters are from the collected editions of the characters' serial comic book titles. Due to space limitations, not every volume featuring a character has been annotated. Unless otherwise noted, each main listing features a brief write-up of the character, the recommended titles from the collected comic book series, as well as specific graphic novel titles.

General

Animal Man. Written by Grant Morrison. Illustrated by Steve Dillon et al. Vertigo/ DC Comics, 2001–2003. **O** ◉

Buddy Baker has one of the most unusual super-hero powers: he can temporarily adopt the powers and skills of any animal that is within reach by tapping into the animal spirit world. After living a life of middle-class prosperity with a loving wife and two children, he's trying to find his way in the world. After deciding to dust off the costume once again, Buddy comes out of inactive duty to help make the world a better place for all life on the planet. His journey takes him on the trail of animal experimentation on gorillas in Africa, stopping a foxhunt, alien invasions, what really happens to heroes who fade from popularity, an enormous egg that hatches a triceratops, as well as helping a cartoon coyote looking for a way out of all the animated violence in his Toon world. A second-rate super-hero, Animal Man proves to his family and the world that you don't need first-rate powers to stand up for what you believe in, no matter what odd adventures await you.

> *Vol. 1.* 2001. 240pp. 1-56389-005-4.
> *Vol. 2.* 2002. 224pp. 1-56389-890-X.
> *Vol. 3: Deus Ex Machina.* 2003. 232pp. 1-56389-968-X.

Araña. **Written by Fiona Avery. Illustrated by Mark Brooks.** Marvel Next/ Marvel Comics, 2005– . **Y**

A new teen female hero in the Marvel Universe, Araña is Anya Corazon, a Hispanic teenager from Brooklyn, New York, living with her father, Gil Corazon, an investigative reporter. Recruited by a mysterious organization called the Spider Society to fight a criminal organization called the Wasps, she is given spiderlike abilities to help her fight. Araña is learning what it takes to be a hero while battling the Wasp's young assassin, Amun, for the Spider Society. Along the way Anya discovers a family secret tied into the Spider Society and her mother.

© 2006 Marvel Comics

> *Vol. 1: Heart of the Spider.* 2005 144pp. 0-7851-1506-4.
> *Vol. 2: In the Beginning.* 2005 144pp. 0-7851-1719-9.
> *Vol. 3: Night of the Hunter.* 2006 144pp. 0-7851-1853-5.

Batgirl. DC Comics, 2001–2006.

Batman and Robin aren't the only heroes who protect Gotham City at night. The original Batgirl was Barbara Gordon, the daughter of Gotham Police Commissioner Jim Gordon. A mild-mannered librarian by day, she fought crime at night as Batgirl. After she was crippled by the Joker, a girl named Cassandra Cain took over the mantle for a short period of time but has since given up the costume. Recommended titles featuring both young ladies as the masked heroine are listed below.

Batgirl. 2001–2006. **Y**

Long after Barbara Gordon was crippled by the Joker and has retired as Batgirl, a new heroine has risen to take her place. Cassandra Cain, a silent, mute girl, was trained by her assassin father to be the deadliest assassin and fighter in the world. Rescued by Barbara Gordon, Cassandra is allowed to enter Batman's circle as the new Batgirl and has continued to prove her worth as one of the best fighters in the world. The series concluded in 2006.

Silent Running. Written by Kelley Puckett and Scott Peterson. Illustrated by Damion Scott and Robert Campanella. 2001. 144pp. 1-56389-705-9.

A Knight Alone. Written by Kelley Puckett and Scott Peterson. Illustrated by Damion Scott and Coy Turnbull. 2001. 160pp. 1-56389-852-7.

Death Wish. Written by Kelley Puckett and Chuck Dixon. Illustrated by Damion Scott and Robert Campanella. 2003. 176pp. 1-56389-981-7.

Fists of Fury. Written by Kelly Puckett and Scott Peterson. Illustrated by Damion Scott, Phil Noto, Vincent Giarrano, and Robert Campanella. 2004. 144pp. 1-4012-0205-5.

Kicking Assassins. Written by Andersen Gabrych. Illustrated by Alé Garza, Pop Mhan. 2006. 128pp. 1-4012-0439-2.

Destruction's Daughter. Written by Andersen Gabrych. Illustrated by various. 2006. 144pp. 1-4012-0896-7.

Batgirl: Year One. Written by Scott Beatty and Chuck Dixon. Illustrated by Marcos Martin and Alvaro Lopez. 2003. 224pp. 1-4012-0080-X. **Y** ◉

Featuring the first challenges that Barbara Gordon faced as the new heroine called Batgirl. See just what made ordinary librarian Barbara Gordon into the heroine known as Batgirl as she takes on Killer Moth, befriends the Dark Knight, and tries to hide her secret identity from Commissioner James Gordon—her father!

© 2006 DC Comics

Black Panther. Marvel Comics, 2001– . **Y**

The ruler of the African kingdom of Wakanda, T'Challa has served as the guardian hero for his kingdom in the guise of the Black Panther after ingesting a mystical, heart-shaped herb that has given him enhanced strength. His costume is woven with Vibranium, a special metal that comes from his country. It makes his costume bullet-proof and allows T'Challa to absorb the impact from falling from great heights as well as the ability to run up walls. He is a leader, hero, and scientist,and under his rule, Wakanda has become one of the most technologically advanced nations on the planet. Black Panther has served for a time as an Avenger, but his heart and his home are in Wakanda.

Vol. 1: The Client. Written by Christopher Priest. Illustrated by Mark Texeira. 2001. 128pp. 0-7851-0789-4.

Vol. 2: Enemy of the State. Written by Christopher Priest. Illustrated by Mike Manley. 2002. 160pp. 0-7851-0829-7.

Who Is the Black Panther. Written by Reginald Hudlin. Illustrated by John Romita, Jr. 2005. 152pp. 0-7851-1748-2.

Bad Mutha. Written by Reginald Hudlin. Illustrated by Scot Eaton. 2006. 96pp. 0-7851-1750-4.

Captain America. Created by Joe Simon and Jack Kirby. Marvel Comics, 1996– .

During World War II, Steve Rogers was a scrawny, would-be-soldier who was unfit to serve in the military, but instead served his country as a volunteer for the Operation: Rebirth super-soldier program. When injected with the super-soldier serum, he was transformed into the ultimate human, gaining enhanced muscle mass, strength, physical endurance, and a keen sense of agility. After months of training in hand-to-hand combat, military strategy, gymnastics, and more, Rogers was given a red, white, and blue, lightweight chain-mail uniform, and was christened Captain America, the symbolic leader of the United States. His only weapon is his shield, a disc forged from Vibranium-Adamantium, making it one of the hardest known substances on Earth. Still a hero today as he was in World War II, the Sentinel of Liberty from the Greatest Generation continues to fight for freedom on his own, partnered with the winged ally the Falcon, or as an Avenger in his battle against villains including his arch-nemesis the Red Skull, Baron Zemo, and foreign terrorists that threaten America. Since first appearing in comic books in 1941, Captain America has been a leading symbol for democracy and one of the most recognizable and noble of Marvel Comics' heroes. Listed below are a variety of recommended Captain America titles from his various monthly series collections as well as an anthology collection.

Captain America: The Bloodstone Hunt. **Written by Mark Gruenwald. Illustrated by Kieron Dwyer.** 1993. 176pp. 0-8713-5972-3. **Y**

Captain America is in a race against time to collect all six segments of an object of great occult powers: the Bloodstone. The collection also features the first appearance of the villain Crossbones. The collection reprints *Captain America* #357-364.

Captain America: Marvel Knights. Written by John Ney Reiber, Chuck Austin, Dave Gibbons, and Robert Morales. Illustrated by John Cassaday, Trevor Hairsine, Jae Lee, Lee Weeks, and Chris Bachalo. Marvel Comics, 2003–2004. **T**

© 2006 Marvel Comics

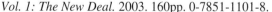

Following the events of September 11, 2001, Marvel Comics relaunched Captain America with the grittier Marvel Knights imprint. The tone was darker than previous stories, with a Tom Clancy-like tone, and featured real-world terrorists as villains.

Vol. 1: The New Deal. 2003. 160pp. 0-7851-1101-8.
Vol. 2: The Extremists. 2003. 128pp. 0-7851-1102-6.
Vol. 3: Ice. 2003. 128pp. 0-7851-1103-4.
Vol. 4: Cap Lives. 2004. 112pp. 0-7851-1318-5.
Vol. 5: Homeland. 2004. 192pp. 0-7851-1396-7.

Captain America: Red Menace. Written by Ed Brubaker. Illustrated by Mike Perkins. Marvel Comics, 2006. **T**

> Crossbones has kidnapped the Red Skull's daughter, Sin, from a secret government rehabilitation center, and together they're out take on the organization known as A.I.M. Little do they realize that Captain America and S.H.I.E.L.D. Agent 13 are tracking them down to foil their plan.
>
> *Vol. 1*. 2006. 112pp. 0-7851-2321-0.

***Captain America: Red, White & Blue.* Written by Bruce Jones, Paul Dini and various. Illustrated by various.** Marvel Comics, 2002. 192pp. 0-7851-1033-X. **T** ◉

> An anthology of works, old and new, celebrating fifty years of Captain America stories. Featured works include brand-new work by Paul Dini, Mark Waid, Bruce Timm, Evan Dorkin, and many others.

Captain America: Winter Soldier. Written by Ed Brubaker. Illustrated by Steve Epting. Marvel Comics, 2006. **T** ◉

> Featuring the hit story line that had comic book fans buzzing in 2005–2006. When a mysterious masked figure named the Winter Soldier enters Steve (Captain America) Rogers's life, old ghosts long thought dead are uncovered. Can Captain America's young sidekick from World War II, the boy-soldier named Bucky, still be alive?
>
> *Vol. 1*. 2006. 176pp. 0-7851-1920-5.
> *Vol. 2*. 2006. 144pp. 0-7851-1708-3.

***Captain America by Jack Kirby: Bicentennial Battles.* Written and illustrated by Jack Kirby.** 2005. 184pp. 0-7851-1726-1. **Y**

> A collection of stories featuring the classic Jack Kirby tales of Captain America and the Falcon. The collection reprints *Captain America* ##201–205 and *Bicentennial Battles* #1 from 1976.

Essential Captain America. Written by Stan Lee. Illustrated by Jack Kirby. Marvel Comics, 2000–2002. **Y**

> A black-and-white collection of the classic Captain America stories created by Stan Lee and Jack Kirby.
>
> *Vol. 1*. 2000. 528pp. 0-7851-0740-1.
> Vol. 2. 2002. 512pp. 0-7851-0827-0.

Mark Waid's Captain America. Written by Mark Waid. Illustrated by Ron Garney. Marvel Comics, 1996–1999. **Y**

Collecting the highly regarded stories of Captain America by writer Mark Waid and artist Ron Garney created from 1996 to 1999. The stories feature appearances by Captain America's archenemy the Red Skull, Captain America's former lover Sharon Carter, and plenty of action against the villainous agents of Hydra.

> *Captain America: Operation Rebirth.* 1996. 96pp. 0-7851-0219-1.
> *Captain America: Man without a Country.* 1998. 112pp. 0-7851-0594-8.
> *Captain America: To Serve and Protect.* 1999. 176pp. 0-7851-0838-6.

Truth: Red, White, and Black. **Written by Rags Morales. Illustrated by Kyle Baker.** Marvel Comics, 2004. 168pp. 0-7851-1072-0. **O**

Before weakling army soldier Steve Rogers was given the super-soldier serum that transformed him into the Sentinel of Liberty, Captain America, the serum was tested on those considered to be less than men: the brave African American enlisted men of the army. This is the story of the brave men who were the first true super-soldiers fighting for freedom, even if they weren't respected or treated as equals because of their skin color.

Captain Britain. **Written by Alan Moore. Illustrated by Alan Davis.** Marvel Comics, 2002. 208pp. 0-7851-0855-6. **Y**

Gifted by Merlin the Magician and the Goddess of the Northern Skies with great power and stamina, Brian Braddock became the champion of Great Britain as the mystical hero called Captain Britain. While training with Merlin, Brian discovered that he and his twin sister Betsy share a family from Earth and extradimensional origins. After journeying to the land of Otherworld—a nexus of realities—Brian finds that he's one of many who are known as Captain Britain, a corps of science/super-heroic warriors created by Merlin to defend all the infinite realms from evil. This is where Brian's father, Sir James Braddock, also served as the most noble of the Captain Britain Corps. Brian has a proud tradition to uphold and will serve his country in the name of the queen against the villains of both Earth and Otherworld.

Captain Marvel. Created by C. C. Beck and Bill Parker. DC Comics, 1995–2000.

The young boy Billy Batson was given the powers of ancient biblical and mythological heroes by an ancient wizard called Shazam. When he says aloud the wizard's name, "SHAZAM!" a bolt of magic lightning strikes and he's transformed into the caped red-and-gold-costumed hero Captain Marvel. With super speed, great strength, flight, and more, he's one of the most powerful heroes in the universe, equal to Superman—and he's able to retain a childlike innocence since he really is a young boy in the body of an adult. Billy is also joined on his adventures by some other of his Marvel family, including his twin sister Mary who becomes Mary Marvel, as well as crippled newsboy Freddie Freeman, who transforms into Captain Marvel Jr. Captain Marvel's foes include Black Adam, Dr. Sivana, Mister Mind, and many more. The hero was originally created by Fawcett Comics in 1940 in *Whiz Comics* #2 and was one of the most popular in the 1940s and 1950s. As a result of a copyright infringement suit brought by DC Comics, the series ended in 1953, and DC Comics began publishing *Captain Marvel* in the 1970s. Note that because Marvel Comics owns the trademark to the title Captain Marvel even after the series was canceled, all of DC Comics' titles featuring Captain Marvel cannot have the hero's' name in the title; most titles featuring Captain Marvel include the word "Shazam."

***Power of Shazam*. Written by Jerry Ordway. Illustrated by Jerry Ordway and Mike Wieringo.** DC Comics, 1995. 96pp. 1-56389-153-0. **Y**

A painted graphic novel by Jerry Ordway that retells the origin of Captain Marvel and features the villain Black Adam.

***Shazam!: Power of Hope*. Written by Paul Dini. Illustrated by Alex Ross.** DC Comics, 2000. 64pp. 1-56389-745-8. **Y**

An oversized, fully painted story about Captain Marvel and his adolescent alter ego, Billy Batson. When Billy receives a letter in the mail from a terminally ill boy in the local children's hospital, Captain Marvel makes a surprise appearance at the hospital and takes the kids on an adventure, telling them tales of his amazing exploits. Billy learns that there can be happiness and powerful hope in times of great sorrow.

Catwoman. DC Comics, 2002– .

Femme fatale Selena Kyle has been a thorn in Batman's side since her first appearance in the comic book *Batman* #1 in 1940. Walking a fine line and playing neither hero or villain, Catwoman is a talented thief and occasional lover of Batman who is out to make it rich, looking out for what matters most: herself. Following a rough upbringing and a life of crime, Selena became enamored of Batman and the other costumed characters and adopted her own identity as Catwoman. Rich from her thefts, Selena became well known as a wealthy socialite, but as Catwoman she robs from the rich and gives to herself. Now a little older and wiser, Selena has become a guardian of sorts in Gotham City for those in need, living outside the law and helping those society has cast off, who remind her of herself when she was a lost teenage girl. Catwoman currently has a monthly series, and the collected volumes of it as well as several miscellaneous titles featuring Catwoman are listed below. Note that the highly regarded graphic novel *Catwoman: Selena's Big Score* by Darwyn Cooke is not includedhere but is listed in the crime and mysteries chapter (chapter 5) because the tale features Selena Kyle on a noncostumed adventure on one of the biggest heists of her career.

Catwoman. Written by Ed Brubaker. Illustrated by various. 2002–. T

© 2006 DC Comics

Following are the currently published collected titles from the monthly Catwoman comic book series. The series is still being published.

Vol. 1: The Dark End of the Street. Written by Ed Brubaker. Illustrated by Darwyn Cooke and Mike Allred. 2002. 136pp. 1-56389-908-6.

Vol. 2: Crooked Little Town. Written by Ed Brubaker. Illustrated by Brad Rader, Cameron Stewart, and Rick Burchett. 2003. 168pp. 1-4012-0008-7.

Vol. 3: Relentless. Written by Ed Brubaker. Illustrated by Cameron Stewart and Javier Pulido. 2004. 192pp. 1-4012-0218-7.

Vol. 4: Wild Ride. Written by Ed Brubaker. Illustrated by Cameron Stewart, Guy Davis and Nick Derington. 2005. 128pp. 1-4012-0436-8.

Catwoman: Nine Lives of a Feline Fatale. Written and illustrated by various. 2004. 208pp. 1-4012-0213-6. T

Anthology collection features highlights of Catwoman's adventures, from her first appearance in comic books in *Batman* #1 in 1940 to the present.

Catwoman: When in Rome. Written by Jeph Loeb. Illustrated by Tim Sale. 2005. 160pp. 1-4012-0432-5. T

Following the events of *Batman: Dark Victory*, Selena Kyle goes on a mysterious trip to Rome. What is Selena's connection with crime boss Carmine Falcone's family, and will the league of Bat-villains uncover the greatest secret of all: Batman's identity?

Daredevil. Marvel Comics, 1987–. T

Matt Murdock has always had a life that was full of challenges. Growing up in Hell's Kitchen in New York City was tough enough, but Matt learned to roll with the punches. As a young boy he was blinded by a canister of nuclear waste. Although it stole his vision, the substance gave the boy a heightened sense akin to super-radar, and Matt was forever changed. He was trained by a mysterious man named Stick and was able to use his heightened skills to his advantage. He also went to college, where he got a law degree. He fell in love with Elektra Natchios, but after she disappeared and his boxing father was killed, Matt lost faith in the judicial system and decided to take matters into his own hands. By day he serves as a lawyer for those less fortunate, and by night he protects Hell's Kitchen when the law can't and is known as the masked crimson hero called Daredevil. Included here first are the classic works of Frank Miller, who was instrumental in redefining the character in the 1980s; followed by the works of Ann Nocenti from the late 1980s as well as the latest writings by Brian Michael Bendis, David Mack, Kevin Smith, and Jeph Loeb, who have all been influenced by Frank Miller's storytelling.

Frank Miller's Daredevil.

Writer/artist Frank Miller has been credited for reviving interest in Daredevil after taking over the title in the late 1970s. Through his art and writing he infused a noir style into the series and introduced popular characters, including Elektra Natchios, a love interest of Matt Murdock as well as a highly trained assassin, and Matt Murdock's mentor, called Stick. Miller also revived classic Marvel characters such as the Kingpin and Bullseye into top-class villains, and his influence is still felt today. Following are all of Frank Miller's collected tales of Daredevil published by Marvel Comics.

© 2006 Marvel Comics

Daredevil Visionaries: Frank Miller. **Written and illustrated by Frank Miller.** 2000–2001. **T**

> *Vol. 1.* 2000. 176pp. 0-7851-0757-6.
> *Vol. 2.* 2001. 368pp. 0-7851-0771-1.
> *Vol. 3.* 2001. 272pp. 0-7851-0802-5.

Daredevil: Born Again. **Written by Frank Miller. Illustrated by David Mazzucchelli.** 1987. 176pp. 0-87135-297-4. **T**

Daredevil: Love and War. **Written by Frank Miller. Illustrated by Bill Sienkiewicz.** 1986. 64pp. 0-87135-172-2. **T**

Daredevil: The Man Without Fear. **Written by Frank Miller. Illustrated by John Romita Jr.** 1994. 160pp. 0-7851-0046-6. **T**

***Daredevil by Frank Miller Omnibus*.** **Written by Frank Miller and various. Illustrated by Frank Miller.** 2007. 816pp. 0-7851-2343-1. **T**

🐾 **Daredevil** (current series). **T** ◎

Inspired and heavily influenced by Frank Miller's take on Daredevil, filmmaker Kevin Smith and writer Brian Michael Bendis have continued to work in the playground that Miller created and have used it as a springboard for more adventures of Matt Murdock. The volumes listed include Kevin Smith's highly regarded collection as well as the collected monthly editions of the comic book written by Bendis and David Mack. The recent Daredevil stories written by Bendis and Maleev won an Eisner Award in 2003 for Best Continuing Series. *Volume 1: Guardian Devil* received recognition from YALSA's Popular Paperbacks for Young Adults committee in 2002.

> *Vol. 1: Guardian Devil.* Written by Kevin Smith. Illustrated by Joe Quesada. 2001. 192pp. 0-7851-0737-1.
> *Vol. 2: Parts of a Hole.* Written and illustrated by David Mack. 2003. 176pp. 0-7851-0808-4.
> *Vol. 3: Wake Up.* Written by Brian Michael Bendis. Illustrated by David Mack. 2002. 96pp. 0-7851-0948-X.
> *Vol. 4: Underboss.* Written by Brian Michael Bendis. Illustrated by Alex Maleev. 2002. 144pp. 0-7851-1024-0.

Vol. 5: Out. Written by Brian Michael Bendis. Illustrated by Alex Maleev. 2002. 208pp. 0-7851-1074-7.

Vol. 6: Lowlife. Written by Brian Michael Bendis. Illustrated by Alex Maleev. 2003. 120pp. 0-7851-1105-0.

Vol. 7: Hardcore. Written by Brian Michael Bendis. Illustrated by Alex Maleev. 2003. 120pp. 0-7851-1168-9.

Vol. 8: Echo—Vision Quest. Written and illustrated by David Mack. 2004. 120pp. 0-7851-1232-4.

Vol. 9: King of Hell's Kitchen. Written by Brian Michael Bendis. Illustrated by Alex Maleev. 2004. 120pp. 0-7851-1337-1.

Vol. 10: The Widow. Written by Brian Michael Bendis. Illustrated by Alex Maleev. 2004. 160pp. 0-7851-1394-0.

Vol. 11: Golden Age. Written by Brian Michael Bendis. Illustrated by Alex Maleev. 2005. 120pp. 0-7851-1395-9.

Vol. 12: Decalogue. Written by Brian Michael Bendis. Illustrated by Alex Maleev. 2005. 144pp. 0-7851-1644-3.

Vol. 13: The Murdock Papers. Written by Brian Michael Bendis. Illustrated by Alex Maleev. 2006. 120pp. 0-7851-1810-1.

***Daredevil: The Movie.* Written by Bruce Jones. Illustrated by Manuel Garcia.** Marvel Comics, 2002. 128pp. 0-7851-0959-5. **T** ▪

Adaptation of the movie based on Daredevil starring Ben Affleck and Jennifer Garner as Daredevil and Elektra, respectively.

***Daredevil: Yellow.* Written by Jeph Loeb. Illustrated by Tim Sale.** Marvel Comics, 2002. 144pp. 0-7851-0840-8. **T** ◎

Following the death of Matt Murdock's former love, Karen Page, at the hands of his enemy Bullseye (as seen in *Daredevil, Vol. 1: Guardian Devil*), Matt tries to come to terms with her death. He reminisces about an earlier time when he started his career as both a lawyer and Hell's Kitchen's hero, when Daredevil wore a costume both yellow and red and a girl named Karen Page first walked into his life and stole his heart.

***Ultimate Daredevil and Elektra.* Written by Greg Rucka. Illustrated by Salvador Larroca.** 2002. 128pp. 0-7851-1076-3. **T**

A retelling of the origins of Matt Murdock and Elecktra Natchios, lovers in college, who have a similar nightlife activity in common. He's known as the crimson-colored hero Daredevil, and she's a ninja-trained assassin known simply as Elecktra.

***Doctor Spectrum: Full Spectrum.* Written by Sara "Samm" Barnes. Illustrated by Travel Foreman.** 2005. 144pp. 0-7851-1586-2. **M**

A spin-off from the pages of <u>Supreme Power</u> detailing the sad and abusive life of Joe Ledger and the events that led him to take up one of the most powerful weapons in the galaxy. A disciplined soldier for the U.S. armed forces, he was recruited to handle black-op assassinations and has become the perfect killer. When the government gets hold of a prism that accompanied the infant Hyperion to Earth, Joe is the only one with the discipline and focus to handle the power. Now known as Doctor Spectrum, the only limit to his power is his imagination and focus. Now with the ability to fly and to create anything out of thin air, he's become one of the most powerful forces on the planet. A reinterpretation of the hero Green Lantern published by DC Comics. For other stories featuring the Squadron Supreme team, please see the Supreme Power listing in this chapter.

Elektra. Marvel Comics, 2002–2004.

The beautiful Greek ninja assassin Elektra, who made her first appearance in the pages of Frank Miller's classic Daredevil in 1981, was killed in a climactic battle against the villain Bullseye, but she got better. Resurrected from the dead, Elektra has worked as an agent-for-hire, and she's dispensing justice and trying to control the dark side that still resides within her. Included below are various Elektra collected miniseries, including the cult-hit *Elektra: Assassin* originally published in comic book form in 1986, her monthly series that began in 2001, and mature-reader MAX imprint collections. *Elektra Lives Again* received an Eisner Award in 1991 for Best Graphic Album: New when it was originally released.

Elektra Graphic Novels by Frank Miller.

Frank Miller, the creator of Elektra, has revisited the character on several occasions. The titles created by him are listed below.

> *Elektra: Assassin.* 3d ed. Written by Frank Miller. Illustrated by Bill Sienkiewicz 2000. 264pp. 0-87135-309-1. **O**
>
> 🎗 *Elektra Lives Again.* Written and illustrated by Frank Miller. 2002. 80pp. 0-7851-0890-4.

Elektra. 2002–2005. **T**

A highlight of titles reprinting the monthly issues of the Elektra comic book series from the 2002 to 2005.

> *The Scorpio Key.* Written by Brian Michael Bendis and Chuck Austen. Illustrated by Chuck Austen.2002. 160pp. 0-7851-0843-2.
>
> *Vol. 1: Introspect.* Written by Greg Rucka. Illustrated by Carolo Pagulayan. 2002. 160pp. 0-7851-0973-0.
>
> *Vol. 2: Everything Old Is New Again.* Written by Greg Rucka. Illustrated by Carolo Pagulayan. 2002. 160pp. 0-7851-1108-5.
>
> *Vol. 3: Relentless.* Written by Robert Rodi. Illustrated by Sean Chen. 2004. 168pp. 0-7851-1222-7.
>
> *Vol. 4: Frenzy.* Written by Robert Rodi. Illustrated by Sean Chen. 2004. 168pp. 0-7851-1398-3.
>
> *Elektra: The Hand.* Written by Akira Yoshida. Illustrated by Christian Gossett. Marvel Comics, 2005. 120pp. 0-7851-1594-3. **T**

***Elektra: The Official Movie Adaptation.* Written by Sean McKeever. Illustrated by Mike Perkins.** Marvel Comics, 2005. 136pp. 0-7851-1713-X. **T**

In 2005 a movie starring Jennifer Garner as Elektra was released and was also collected as a graphic novel.

Ultimate Elektra: Devil's Due. **Written by Mike Carey. Illustrated by Salvador Larroca.** Marvel Comics, 2005. 120pp. 0-7851-1504-8. **T**

This series takes place in Marvel Comics' Ultimate universe, which features familiar Marvel characters but without a decade's worth of continuity and no ties with mainstream Marvel history. In this sequel to the *Ultimate Daredevil and Elektra*, Elektra must make a tough choice and becomes the Kingpin's top assassin.

The Escapist.

🏅 **The Amazing Adventures of the Escapist. Written by Michael Chabon, Brian K. Vaughan, and various. Illustrated by various.** Dark Horse Comics, 2004–2006. **O** ◎

Based on the fictional comic book character in the best-selling novel by Michael Chabon, *The Amazing Adventures of Kavalier and Clay*, these are the comic book exploits of the Escapist! Features a look back at more than sixty years' worth of fictionalized adventures of one of the most beloved heroes that never really existed. Includes work by such creators as Michael Chabon, Will Eisner, Brian K. Vaughan, Marv Wolfman, Scott Morse, Howard Chaykin, and many more. The series won an Eisner Award in 2005 for Best Anthology and a Harvey Award for Best New Series and Best Anthology in 2005.

> *Vol. 1.* 2004. 152pp. 1-59307-171-X.
> *Vol. 2.* 2004. 160pp. 1-59307-172-8.
> *Vol. 3.* 2006. 160pp. 1-59307-492-1

🏅 **Ex Machina. Written by Brian K. Vaughan. Illustrated by Tony Harris.** WildStorm Productions/DC Comics, 2005– . **M** ◎

In a world where super-heroes are only make-believe, civil engineer Mitchell Hundred received in an accident the amazing power to control machinery and became New York City's first super-hero. Calling himself the Great Machine, Mitchell soon grows tired of risking his life vigilante-style and does the unthinkable: he runs for mayor of New York City and wins in a landslide. Now Mitchell has traded in one dangerous job for another. When snowplow drivers are being murdered during the biggest snowstorm of the century and controversial decisions must be made, it's time for Mitchell Hundred to save the day. The series won several Eisner Awards in 2005, including Best New Series and Best Writer for Vaughan's body of work.

© 2006 WildStorm Productions/ DC Comics.

> *Vol. 1: The First Hundred Days.* 2005. 136pp. 1-4012-0612-3.
> *Vol. 2: Tag.* 2005. 128pp. 1-4012-0626-3.
> *Vol. 3: Fact vs. Fiction.* 2006. 144pp. 1-4012-0988-2.
> *Vol. 4: March to War.* 2006. 128pp. 1-4012-0997-1.

The Flash. DC Comics, 1992– .

Wally West is the fastest man alive. Splashed by lighting-charged chemicals when he was a youth, he's now the third hero to take on the mantle of scarlet speedster, after Jay Garrick (Flash I) and the late Barry Allen (Flash II). Tied into the Speed Force, a mystical plane that all speed-induced heroes and villains can tap into and draw power from, Wally can easily run nearly as fast as light, can transfer speed to and from others, and can even vibrate fast enough to travel through solid objects. As the guardian of Keystone City, he's a formidable hero, but he still finds himself and the city under constant threat from his rogues' gallery, including Captain Cold, Captain Boomerang, Professor Zoom, Savitar, and more. Frequently teamed up with several of his fellow speedster heroes, including Jay Garrick, Max Mercury, Kid Flash (formerly Impulse), and Green Lantern Kyle Rayner, Wally has proudly carried the mantle of the Flash. With the support of his loving wife Linda, he's proven that he has what it takes to be the fastest hero on Earth.

The Flash, 1992– . **Y**

Recommended The Flash titles that have been collected by DC Comics from the original comic book issues originally published from 1992 through 2006. Some titles listed may be out of print, but they are listed here according to when the collections were published. The collections feature the highly regarded writing of Mark Waid and Geoff Johns. Writer Mark Waid produced one of the best-received runs on the Scarlet Speedster, which was originally published in the pages of the monthly *Flash* comic book from 1992 to 2000. The series helped to bring Wally West out of the shadow of the late Barry Allen and also introduced the young teenager from the future, Bart Allen, who took on the costumed name of Impulse. The series helped to bring Wally West out of the shadow of the late Barry Allen and also introduced the young teenager from the future, Bart Allen, who took on the costumed name Impulse and who most recently has taken over the mantle of the Flash after Wally West's retirement. Geoff Johns succeeded Mark Waid as the writer on The Flash comic book series until 2006. The titles are listed in chronological order of the series.

> *Terminal Velocity.* Written by Mark Waid. Illustrated by Mike Wieringo, Salvador Larroca, Oscar Jimenez, and Carlos Pacheco. 1995. 192pp. 1-56389-249-9.
> *The Return of Barry Allen.* Written by Mark Waid. Illustrated by Greg LaRocque and Roy Richardson. 1996. 192pp. 1-56389-268-5.
> *Born to Run.* Written by Mark Waid. Illustrated by Tom Peyer and Humberto Ramos. 1999. 128pp. 1-56389-504-8.
> *Dead Heat.* Written by Mark Waid. Illustrated by Humberto Ramos. 2000. 144pp. 1-56389-623-0.

© 2006 DC Comics

> *Race Against Time.* Written by Mark Waid and Brian Augustyn. Illustrated by Oscar Jimenez and various. 2001. 168pp. 1-56389-721-0.
> *Blood Will Run.* Written by Geoff Johns. Illustrated by Scott Kolins and Doug Hazlewood. 2002. 192pp. 1-56389-879-9.
> *Rogues.* Written by Geoff Johns. Illustrated by Scott Kolins. 2003. 144pp. 1-56389-950-7.
> *Crossfire.* Written by Geoff Johns. Illustrated by Scott Kolins, Doug Hazlewood, and various. 2004. 224pp. 1-4012-0195-4.
> *Blitz.* Written by Geoff Johns. Illustrated by Scott Kolins, Doug Hazlewood and Phil Winslade. 2004. 224pp. 1-4012-0335-3.
> *Ignition.* Written by Geoff Johns. Illustrated by Alberto Dose, Howard Porter and Livesay. 2005. 144pp. 1-4012-0463-5.

The Secret of Barry Allen. Written by Geoff Johns. Illustrated by Howard Porter and Livesay. 2005. 240pp. 1-4012-0723-5.

Rogue War. Written by Geoff Johns. Illustrated by Howard Porter and Livesay. 2006. 208pp. 1-4012-0924-6.

The Greatest Flash Stories Ever Told. **Written and illustrated by various.** 1992. 288pp. 0-930289-84-6. **Y**

A collection of titles highlighting DC Comics' The Flash. The stories feature both Jay Garrick as the Golden Age Flash and Barry Allen as the Silver Age Flash.

Life Story of the Flash. **Written by Mark Waid and Brian Augustyn. Illustrated by Gil Kane and various.** DC Comics, 1998. 96pp. 1-56389-365-7. **Y**

The life of the late Barry Allen (Flash II) is played out in a combined graphic novel and prose work "written" by Iris Allen, Barry's beloved wife. From his youthful beginnings as the Flash, to his marriage to Iris, and ultimately to his sacrificial death that helped to save the universe, Barry's life reveals the true heroic character that was loved by many.

<u>**Go Girl.**</u> **Written by Trina Robbins. Illustrated by Anne Timmons.** Dark Horse Comics, 2002–2006. **Y**

The adventures of Lindsay Goldman, the teenage daughter of the retired super-heroine Go-Go Girl. Now calling herself Go Girl, she has inherited her mom's power of flight and has dusted off her mom's old costume ready for a life ranging from adventures in high school, to fighting crime, to battling dinosaurs in the past.

Go Girl!. 2002 136pp. 1-56971-798-2.
The Time Team. 2004. 96pp. 1-59307-230-9.
Robots Gone Wild!. 2006. 184pp. 1-59307-409-3.

Gravity: Big-City. **Written by Sean McKeever. Illustrated by Mike Norton.** Marvel Next/Marvel Comics, 2005. 120pp. 0-7851-1798-9. **Y**

All wide-eyed college freshman Greg Willis wanted to be was a super-hero, and in the Marvel Universe there's no place better than New York City to realize your dreams. Packing his bags and moving from his small hometown in the Sheboygan, Wisconsin area, he's now balancing life as a college student with life as the new hero called Gravity. Having the ability to control the forces of gravity ever since an accident many years back, Greg is trying to use his gift to help save the day, but in a city where heroes like the Fantastic Four and Spider-Man steal the headlines every day, will anyone care? The trials and tribulations of being a young new super-hero in New York City.

Green Arrow. DC Comics, 1991– .

Oliver Queen is an archer like none other. An outspoken, liberal, billionaire playboy, he became proficient with a bow and arrow after being stranded on a deserted island, and then took on the name Green Arrow and served as the protector of Star City and founding member of the Justice League of America. Listed below are the volumes collected from the monthly *Green Arrow* comic book titles that have been collected by DC Comics from 2003 as well as the miniseries *Green Arrow: The Longbow Hunters* from 1991.

Green Arrow: The Longbow Hunters. **Written and illustrated by Mike Grell.** 1991. 144pp. 0-930289-38-2. **O**

An aging Oliver Queen relocates to Seattle with Dinah Lance, the heroine known as Black Canary. There they take on drug lords, serial killers, and a Japanese assassin known as Shado. The miniseries is a darker-in-tone departure from Green Arrow stories in the past, and features a well-rounded, complex hero reevaluating his role in the world.

🌹 <u>Green Arrow.</u> 2003– . **O**

Listed below are volumes collected from the monthly *Green Arrow* comic book titles that have been collected by DC Comics from 2003. Some titles listed may be out of print, but they are listed below according to when the collections were published. Thinking of himself as a modern-day Robin Hood, this JLA member fought the good fight but was killed in action. Now he's been brought back to life by his former friend, Hal Jordan, using with his godlike powers. Now Green Arrow is catching up with the twenty-first century and learning the ropes all over again as the avenging archer. Joined by his son, Connor, who also has carried on his father's name of Green Arrow, his on-and-off girlfriend Black Canary (Dinah Lance), and the reformed street girl called Arrowette, Oliver is settling back into life just fine and is being a guardian for the downtrodden. YALSA's Best Books for Young Adults committee recognized n *Volume 1: Quiver* in their 2003 list.

> *Vol. 1: Quiver.* Written by Kevin Smith. Illustrated by Phil Hester and Ande Parks. 2003. 232pp. 1-56389-965-5.
> *Vol. 2: Sounds of Violence.* Written by Kevin Smith. Illustrated by Phil Hester. 2004. 128pp. 1-4012-0045-1.
> *Vol. 3: The Archer's Quest.* Written by Brad Meltzer. Illustrated by Phil Hester. 2004. 176pp. 1-4012-0044-3.
> *Vol. 4: Straight Shooter.* Written by Judd Winick. Illustrated by Phil Hester. 2004. 144pp. 1-4012-0200-4.
> *Vol. 5: City Walls.* Written by Judd Winick. Illustrated by Phil Hester. 2005. 160pp. 1-4012-0464-3.
> *Vol. 6: Moving Targets.* Written by Judd Winick. Illustrated by Phil Hester. 2006. 256pp. 1-4012-0930-0.

Green Lantern. DC Comics, 1998– . **T** ◎

With their oath, "In brightest day, in blackest night, no evil shall escape my sight. Let those who worship evil's might, beware my power, Green Lantern's light!" the Green Lantern Corps have served for over 3 billion years as the guardians of the galaxy and the protectors of peace. Each member wields an emerald power ring that is powered by the Central Power Battery on planet Oa, and the sheer will of the bearer is the only limitation on what they can do. All sectors of the galaxy are assigned a Green Lantern, and for Earth (Sector 2814) there have been many men who have honored the title with their skill and courage, including Alan Scott, Hal Jordan, John Stewart, Guy Gardner, and most recently Kyle Rayner. Like the men before him, Kyle was given the power ring when the previous bearer, Hal Jordan, was no longer able to carry on. Jordan relinquished the title after his home, Coast City and his loved ones were obliterated by Mongul and the cyborg Superman in an explosion. Jordan snapped and tried to rebuild Coast City and his loved ones by using the power rings of his fellow Green Lantern Corps members. Seduced by the power of the rings, he relinquished his title of Green Lantern, destroyed the central power battery on Oa, killed his longtime arch-nemesis Sinestro, and became known as Parallax. Meanwhile, the Oans needed to choose a new Green Lantern for Sector 2814, and they selected Kyle Rayner, a comic book artist who knows nothing about being a hero. Currently Hal Jordan (as seen in the *Rebirth* story line) has been given a second chance at life and has retaken the mantle alongside fellow Green Lantern John Stewart as the protector of Earth.

Green Lantern. 1998– . Y

Listed below are recommended Green Lantern titles that have been collected by DC Comics from the original comic book issues from 1998 to the present. They feature the fall of Hal Jordan, the rise of Kyle Rayner as a hero, and the return of Hal Jordan as a Green Lantern member. Some titles listed may be out of print but are listed below according to when the collections were published. The collections feature the writing of Ron Marz, Judd Winick, Brian K. Vaughan, and others, with art by Darryl Banks and various other illustrators. *Brother's Keeper* received recognition from YALSA's Popular Paperbacks for Young Adults committee in 2006 for dealing with the subject of hate crimes against homosexuals.

© 2006 DC Comics

Emerald Twilight/New Dawn. Written by Ron Marz. Illustrated by Darryl Banks. 2003. 192pp. 1-56389-999-X.

Emerald Knights. Written by Ron Marz and Chuck Dixon. Illustrated by Darryl Banks. 1998. 194pp. 1-56389-475-0.

Baptism of Fire. Written by Ron Marz. Illustrated by Darryl Banks. 1999. 198pp. 1-56389-524-2.

Emerald Allies. Written by Chuck Dixon and Ron Marz. Illustrated by Rodolfo Damaggio, Doug Braithwaite, Darryl Banks, and various. 2000. 208pp. 1-56389-603-6.

New Journey, Old Path. Written by Judd Winick. Illustrated by Darryl Banks. 2001. 192pp. 1-56389-729-6.

Circle of Fire. Written by Brian K. Vaughan and others. Illustrated by various. 2002. 224pp. 1-56389-806-3.

The Road Back. Written by Gerard Jones. Illustrated by Pat Broderick and Bruce Patterson. 2003. 192pp. 1-56389-045-3.

Brother's Keeper. Written by Judd Winick. Illustrated by Dale Eaglesham and Rodney Ramos. 2003. 128pp. 1-4012-0078-8.

Passing the Torch. Written by Judd Winick. Illustrated by Dale Eaglesham and Rodney Ramos. 2004. 128pp. 1-4012-0237-3.

Rebirth. Written by Geoff Johns. Illustrated by Ethan Van Sciver and Prentis Rollins. 2005. 176pp. 1-4012-0465-1, hardcover.

No Fear. Written by Geoff Johns. Illustrated by Carlos Pacheco, Ethan Van Sciver, Darwyn Cooke and others. 2006. 176pp. 1-4012-0466-X, hardcover.

Revenge of the Green Lanterns. Written by Geoff Johns. Illustrated by Carlos Pacheco, Ivan Reis, Ethan Van Sciver and others. 2006. 168pp. 1-4012-0960-2.

Green Lantern: Fear Itself. Written by Ron Marz. Illustrated by Brad Parker. DC Comics, 1999. 80pp. 1-56389-310-X. **Y**

Three generations of Green Lanterns—Alan Scott, Hal Jordan, and Kyle Rayner—face off against an ancient demon that has been released and feeds on the fear of others.

Green Lantern: The Greatest Stories Ever Told. Written by various. Illustrated by various. DC Comics, 2006. 192pp. 1-4012-0961-0. **Y**

A collection spanning from the Golden Age of comic books to today, featuring tales of the brave men who have carried the title Green Lantern. From Alan Scott, to Hal Jordan, to John Stewart, to Kyle Rayner, all have proudly borne the name Green Lantern in the fight against the forces of evil.

Green Lantern Corps: Recharge. Written by Dave Gibbons. Illustrated by Patrick Gleason. DC Comics, 2006. 128pp. 1-4012-0962-9. **Y**

After the events seen in *Green Lantern: Rebirth,* including the return of the Guardians of the Galaxy, the time has come again to ignite the torch and recruit members both old and new back into the ranks of the Green Lantern Corps. The series collection focuses on popular favorite Green Lanterns, including Guy Gardner, Kilowog, and Kyle Rayner.

Hawkman. Written by Geoff Johns. Illustrated by Rags Morales and various. DC Comics, 2003–. **T**

Carter Hall, the hero known as Hawkman, has lived a lifetime over and over again, in each one serving the forces of good in their struggle against evil. Once known as Prince Khufu in Ancient Egypt in the Fifteenth Dynasty, he and his beloved lover Chay-Ara were murdered by Hath-Set near the crash site of an alien spacecraft. The metal of the ship was Thanagarian Nth Metal, which miraculously gave their souls the ability to be reincarnated time and time again, unaware of their past lives. In the 1940s the latest reincarnation of Khufu, Carter Hall, adopted the winged warrior identity of Hawkman and was reunited with a reincarnated Chay-Ara, who adopted the guise of Hawkwoman. Wearing hawk-faced masks and wearing alien Nth Metal armor on their wings, they soared through the skies at terrific speeds as they battled the forces of evil. After a temporal anomaly seemingly erased Hawkman and Hawkwoman off the face of the earth, Hawkman triumphantly returned to the Justice Society of America and now remembers all of his past lives. He has been joined once again by the latest reincarnation of Chay-Ara, a woman named Kendra Saunders who doesn't remember her past lives, and they're both active members ofh the reactivated Justice Society of America team.

Vol. 1: Endless Flight. 2003. 176pp. 1-56389-952-3.

Vol. 2: Allies and Enemies. 2004. 192pp. 1-4012-0196-2.
Vol. 3: Wings of Fury. 2005. 192pp. 1-4012-0467-8.
Vol. 4: Rise of the Golden Eagle. 2006. 208pp. 1-4012-1092-9.

***H-E-R-O: Powers and Abilities.* Written by Will Pfeifer. Illustrated by Kano.**
DC Comics, 2003. 144pp. 1-4012-0168-7. **Y**

What would you do if you could become a super-hero with the push of a button and could instantly have the power of flight, X-ray vision, super-strength, and more? When Pennsylvanian fast-food employee Jerry Feldon finds a mysterious round disc abandoned in the restaurant, he finds that if he holds the disc and pushes the buttons labeled "H-E-R-O," he receives a brand-new super-power, complete with a costume. Now he believes that his luck has changed, but do heartache and pain come with great power? As Jerry finds, no matter what hero he is on the outside, it's really the hero on the inside that counts. Meanwhile, hidden in the shadows, the original bearer of the disc wants it back and will stop at nothing to get it. As the dial changes hands with some of the most unlikely people ever to be considered as super-heroes, they all face the one tough question: what are they going to do with all that power and responsibility?

The Hulk. Created by Stan Lee and Jack Kirby. Marvel Comics, 1991–.

Irradiated with gamma ray particles after being exposed to a gamma bomb, Doctor Bruce Banner miraculously survived and was amazingly transformed into something less than human but phenomenally strong. Nicknamed the "Hulk" by the military, Banner transforms into the green-skinned monster whenever he releases his repressed rage, making him one of the most powerful forces on the planet, able to leap great distances and crush anything that stands in his way. At various times Banner's transformation into the Hulk has created variations of Hulks, each with a different psyche of sorts. Sometimes Banner's transformation releases a mindless brute with the mind of a child, or a grey-colored "Joe Fixit" Hulk who is a semi-intelligent tough guy, or an intelligent "Professor" Hulk who retains Banner's intelligence. Though not a team player, the Hulk has been known to be an occasional member of such super-teams as the Avengers and the Defenders.

Essential Incredible Hulk. **Written by Stan Lee. Illustrated by Jack Kirby.**
2002– . **Y**

Reprints the classic original issues of the *Incredible Hulk* in one inexpensive black-and-white format.

Vol. 1. 2002. 512pp. 0-7851-0993-5.
Vol. 2. 2003. 520pp. 0-7851-0795-9.
Vol. 3. 2005. 576pp. 0-7851-1689-3.
Vol. 4. 2006. 608pp. 0-7851-2193-5.

Hulk: Destruction. **Written by Peter David. Illustrated by Jim Muniz.** Marvel Comics, 2006. 96pp. 0-7851-1824-1. **Y**

> In a tie-in to the popular video game *Incredible Hulk: Ultimate Destruction*, the Hulk faces one of his greatest foes: the gamma-powered Abomination, who is now in league with General Ross to capture or eliminate the Hulk.

Hulk: Grey. **Written by Jeph Loeb. Illustrated by Tim Sale.** Marvel Comics, 2004. 160pp. 0-7851-1314-2, hardcover; 2005. 144pp. 0-7851-1346-0, paperback. **T**

> A look back at the first time that Bruce Banner transformed into the grey-skinned (yes, grey-skinned) behemoth following an experiment gone wrong. As General Ross seeks out the humanoid monster, his daughter, Betty, finds that there may be more than just a monster inside the tortured soul: a man she loves called Bruce Banner.

Hulk: The Movie. **Written by Bruce Jones. Illustrated by Mark Bagley.** Marvel Comics, 2003. 128pp. 0-7851-1155-7. **Y**

> Adaptation of the 2003 summer film based on the Marvel Comics Jade Giant and directed by Ang Lee.

Hulk, Vol. 1: Incredible. **Written by Mike Raicht. Illustrated by Alex Sanchez, Ryan Odagawa, and Patrick Scherberger.** Marvel Age/Marvel Comics, 2005. 96pp. 0-7851-1616-8. **A**

> A retelling of the original *Hulk* issues created by Stan Lee and Jack Kirby, for a younger audience.

Hulk Visionaries: Peter David. **Written by Peter David.** 2005–. **Y**

© 2006 Marvel Comics

A collection highlighting writer Peter David's contribution to the Jade Giant from his run on the monthly Incredible Hulk comic book series from 1986 to 1998. The collections also feature the artwork of Todd McFarlane, Gary Frank, Dale Keown, and others. Peter David's stories have been regarded by many fans as the definitive treatment of the Hulk. In 1992 the work by Peter David and artist Dale Keown won an Eisner Award for Best Writer/Artist.

> *Vol. 1.* Illustrated by Todd McFarlane. 2005. 224pp. 0-7851-1541-2.
> *Vol. 2.* Illustrated by Todd McFarlane and Erik Larsen. 2005. 232pp. 0-7851-1878-0.
> *Vol. 3.* Illustrated by various. 2006. 192pp. 0-7851-2095-5.
> *Vol. 4.* Illustrated by various. 2006. 216pp. 0-7851-2096-3.

The Incredible Hulk. Marvel Comics, 1991– . **T**

> A highlight of titles reprinting the monthly issues of *The Incredible Hulk* comic book series from the 1990s to today.

> *Ground Zero.* Written by Peter David. Illustrated by Todd McFarlane. 1991. 176pp. 0-87135-792-5.
> *Ghost of the Past.* Written by Peter David. Illustrated by Dale Keown. 1997. 112pp. 0-7851-0261-2.
> *Transformations.* Written by Stan Lee, Peter David, and various. Illustrated by Jack Kirby and various. 1997. 176pp. 0-7851-0262-0.

Beauty and the Beast. Written by Peter David and Steve Englehart. Illustrated by Adam Kubert, Mark Farmer, and Herb Trimpe. 1998. 176pp. 0-7851-0659-6.

Dogs of War. Written by Paul Jenkins. Illustrated by Ron Garney. 2001. 224pp. 0-7851-0790-8.

Vol. 1: Return of the Monster. Written by Bruce Jones. Illustrated by John Romita Jr. and Lee Weeks. 2002. 144pp. 0-7851-0943-9.

Vol. 2: Morning After. Written by Bruce Jones. Illustrated by John Romita Jr. and Lee Weeks. 2002. 96pp. 0-7851-0905-6.

Vol. 3: Transfer of Power. Written by Bruce Jones. Illustrated by John Romita Jr. and Lee Weeks. 2003. 144pp. 0-7851-1065-8.

Vol. 4: Abominable. Written by Bruce Jones. Illustrated by Mike Deodato Jr. 2003. 136pp. 0-7851-1113-1.

Vol. 5: Hide in Plain Sight. Written by Bruce Jones. Illustrated by Leo Fernandez. 2003. 120pp. 0-7851-1151-4.

Vol. 6: Split Decisions. Written by Bruce Jones. Illustrated by Mike Deodato Jr. 2004. 144pp. 0-7851-1238-3.

Vol. 7: Dead Like Me. Written by Bruce Jones and Garth Ennis. Illustrated by Doug Braithwaite. 2004. 144pp. 0-7851-1399-1.

Vol. 8: Big Things. Written by Bruce Jones. Illustrated by Mike Deodato Jr. 2004. 192pp. 0-7851-1533-1.

Vol. 9: Tempest Fugit. Written by Peter David. Illustrated by Lee Weeks. 2005. 144pp. 0-7851-1543-9.

Vol. 11: Planet Hulk Prelude. Written by Daniel Way. Illustrated by Keu Cha. 2006. 144pp. 0-7851-1953-1.

The Incredible Hulk: Future Imperfect. Written by Peter David. Illustrated by George Pérez. Marvel Comics, 1994. 96pp. 0-7851-0029-6. **Y**

The Hulk is sent to the far future by his longtime friend Rick Jones to battle the toughest foe he's ever faced: himself. The heroes of the world are long gone, and the future is ruled by the psychotic but familiar green-skinned beast called the Maestro. When it comes to a battle between brawn and brains, the Hulk has finally met his match. How can the Hulk defeat the only person who knows him better than he knows himself?

© 2006 Marvel Comics

Startling Stories: Banner. Written by Brian Azzarello. Illustrated by Richard Corben. 2001. 112pp. 0-7851-0853-X. **O**

A shaken Bruce Banner wakes up after transforming from the beast inside him and witnesses the destruction, death, and devastation he has caused. Now on the run from himself as well as a military unit led by the gamma-powered Doc Sampson, when Banner releases the Hulk inside him, no one stands a chance against the rampaging beast.

Icon: A Hero's Welcome. **Written by Dwayne McDuffie. Illustrated by M. D. Bright.** DC Comics, 1996. 192pp. 1-56389-339-8. **T**

> Living secretly on Earth as a black man since 1839, the almost invulnerable alien named Augustus Freeman learns that there are other ways of making things right in the city of Dakota. Joined by teenager Raquel Ervin, he reluctantly takes on the super-hero identity called Icon, and she becomes his sidekick, Rocket. The true main character in the series is Raquel, a teenager who is learning to find her true voice in the world in-between being a hero and life's other challenges, including teenage pregnancy.

Impulse: Reckless Youth. **Written by Mark Waid. Illustrated by Mike Wieringo and Humberto Ramos.** DC Comics, 1997. 192pp. 1-56389-276-6. **Y**

> Bart Allen, the grandson of the late Barry Allen (Flash II), comes back from the the the thirtieth century to learn how to deal with his powers from his "uncle," Wally West (the Flash III). Teamed up with old-time speedster Max Mercury, Bart is learning to take things a little slower as he learns to control his speed powers while overcoming the equally challenging but humorous life in a high school in Alabama.

Invincible. **Written by Robert Kirkman. Illustrated by Cory Walker and Ryan Ottley.** Image Comics, 2003– . **T** ◉

© 2006 Robert Kirkman and Cory Walker.

Mark Grayson, average teenage son, is going through some changes. His voice is changing, he's starting to get interested in girls, and . . . he's gained his father's super-hero powers! Just what can you do when you're the son of Omni-Man, the most powerful hero in the universe? Anything! Now he's following in his dad's footsteps living the life of schoolbooks, super-villains, and plenty of action as the hero known as Invincible. *The Ultimate Collection* titles reprint several volumes of the softcover editions in a hardcover format and include extra DVD-style bonus material from Robert Kirkman. *Invincible: The Ultimate Collection, Volume 1* received recognition from YALSA's Quick Picks for Reluctant Readers committee in 2006.

> *Vol. 1: Family Matters.* 2003. 120pp. 1-58240-320-1.
> *Vol. 2: Eight Is Enough.* 2003. 128pp. 1-58240-347-3.
> *Vol. 3: Perfect Strangers.* 2004. 144pp. 1-58240-391-0.
> *Vol. 4: Head of the Class.* 2005. 168pp. 1-58240-440-2.
> *Vol. 5: The Facts of Life.* 2005. 176pp. 1-58240-554-9.
> *Vol. 6: A Different World.* 2006. 168pp. 1-58240-579-4.
> *Vol. 7: Three's Company.* 2006. 144pp. 1-58240-656-1.
> *Vol. 8: My Favorite Martian.* 2007. 128pp. 1-58240-683-9.
> *The Ultimate Collection, Vol. 1.* 2005. 400pp. 1-58240-500-X, hardcover.
> *The Ultimate Collection, Vol. 2.* 2006. 352pp. 1-58240-594-8, hardcover.
> *The Complete Invincible Library, Vol. 1.* 2006 768pp. 1-58240-718-5.

Iron Man. Marvel Comics, 1990– .

> Tony Stark has been known to be many things to many people, including billionaire, ladies' man, inventor, and owner of Stark Industries, the leading provider of some of the

greatest technologies the world has ever seen. Unknown to most, however, he is secretly best known as the golden-plated, armored Avenger called Iron Man. After an accident in Asia that left shrapnel lodged in his chest, Tony created an exoskeletal suit of armor that would help sustain his damaged heart, and the high-tech hero Iron Man was born. Creating a front that Iron Man was his own private bodyguard, Tony as Iron Man has served as one of the founding members of the super-team called the Avengers and to this day fights against high- and low-tech villains, including the Mandarin, the dragon Fing-Fang-Foom, and Ultimo. Recently going public with his identity, Tony Stark has entered a new world as one of the only heroes to reveal his identity to the world at large. A film adaptation starring Robert Downey Jr. as Iron Man will be released in 2008.

Iron Man. Marvel Comics, 1990– . **T**

Following are a variety of trade collections of the monthly Marvel Comics <u>Iron Man</u> series. The best-known stories include *Demon in a Bottle,* in which Tony Stark succumbs to perhaps his greatest weakness: alcohol, and *Armor Wars,* in which Tony Stark discovers that his technology has been misused by heroes and villains and sets out to destroy the illegal technology.

> *The Armor Wars.* Written by David Michelinie. Illustrated by Bob Layton. 1990. 208pp. 0-87135-627-9; 2d ed., 2006. 208pp. 0-7851-2506-x.
> *Mask in the Iron Man.* Written by Joe Quesada. Illustrated by Sean Chen. 2001. 128pp. 0-7851-0776-2.
> *Demon in a Bottle.* Written by David Michelinie and Bob Layton. Illustrated by Carmine Infantino. 2006. 176pp. 0-7851-2043-2.
> *Extremis.* Written by Warren Ellis. Illustrated by Adi Granov. 2006. 160pp. 0-7851-1612-5, hardcover; 2007, 160pp. 0-7851-2258-3, softcover.
> *Inevitable.* Written by Joe Casey. Illustrated by Frazer Irving. 2006. 144pp. 0-7851-2084-X.
> *Execute Program.* Written by Daniel Knauf. Illustrated by Patrick Zircher. 2007. 144pp. 0-7851-1671-0.

<u>Ultimate Iron Man.</u> Written by Orson Scott Card. Illustrated by Andy Kubert. Marvel Comics, 2006– . **T** ◉

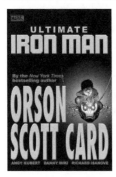

© 2006 Marvel Comics

Set in the "Ultimate" version of the Marvel Comics Universe, which reinterprets the classic Marvel Universe, a young Tony Stark finds that he has a talent for working with machinery. He was infected by a deadly virus that his mother passed to him before she died in childbirth, and his father coated him in experimental bio-armor. Years later, Tony has adapted to living with the bio-armor on, enhancing his every move, thought, and skill. With the bio-armor he has the skills and means to build an invincible suit of armor to fight the injustices of the corporate and public as the heroic Ultimate Avenger, Iron Man.

> *Vol. 1.* 2006. 136pp. 0-7851-2125-0, hardcover.

Judgment Day

Alan Moore's Judgment Day. **Written by Alan Moore. Illustrated by Gil Kane, Rob Liefeld, and Chris Sprouse.** Checker Book Publishing Group, 2003. 168pp. 0-9741664-5-6. **T**

> Super-hero work by Alan Moore following his acclaimed <u>Watchmen</u> series and his America's Best Comics imprint from WildStorm Productions. When Riptide, a member of the super-hero team Youngblood, is killed, her teammate, Knightsabre, stands trial for her murder because he has no alibi. What unfolds is a great adventure celebrating the history and genres of comic books, when it's discovered that the details of the crime date back to the dawn of time. Who is really the culprit?

Longshot. **Written by Ann Nocenti. Illustrated by Arthur Adams.** Marvel Comics, 1989. 176pp. 0-87135-568-X. **Y** ◉

© 2006 Marvel Comics

Gifted with the powers of luck and agility after being artificially created on the other-dimensional world called Mojoworld, the amnesiac blonde-haired hero, nicknamed "Longshot" for his superhuman gift of uncanny luck, is trying his best to get by in a strangest of worlds: New York City. After falling from his home dimension, a media-minded dimension ruled by Mojo, Longshot is trying to find out who he was and where he came from. A rebel from Mojoworld, he was inflicted with amnesia by Mojo for trying to instigate a rebellion and was chased to Earth by Mojo's soldiers—the father and son team of Gog and Magog—and Spiral, the six-armed, sword-wielding villainess and former lover of Longshot. After encountering heroes including Spider-Man, She-Hulk, Doctor Strange, the fellow Mojoworld ram-headed rebel named Quark, and a feisty stuntwoman named Ricochet Rita, Longshot learns that even though he doesn't have his memory back, he will continue the rebellion and destroy Mojo no matter what the cost.

Manhunter: The Special Edition. **Written by Archie Goodwin and Walter Simonson. Illustrated by Walter Simonson.** DC Comics, 1999. 104pp. 1-56389-374-6. **Y**

> Reprinted from the original backup stories in *Detective Comics* from 1973. Former solider-of-fortune Paul Kirk has had a hard time retiring, but after a near-fatal accident, he's found that he's been mended by a secret organization geared for world peace. Retrained in the martial arts and discovering that he's much stronger and can heal faster than a normal man, his world shatters as he discovers that the organization is secretly set to take over the world and that he's been genetically cloned. Now the perfect specimen of man is on the run, pursued by his cloned agents, and only with the aid of the Dark Knight Detective, Batman, will he be able to truly find peace of mind.

<u>Nightwing</u>. DC Comics, 1997– . **Y**

> Dick Grayson was the first person to take up the role of Robin, the lighthearted sidekick of Batman. After years of following in the Dark Knight's footsteps, a now grown-up Dick Grayson has gone on to be known as Nightwing. Setting up residence

in Blüdhaven, he's working as a police officer as well as a crime fighter in a brand-new city that needs his help.

© 2006 DC Comics

Ties That Bind. Written by Dennis O'Neil and Alan Grant. Illustrated by Greg Land. 1997 144pp. 1-56389-328-2.

A Knight in Blüdhaven. Written by Chuck Dixon. Illustrated by Scott McDaniel. 1998. 192pp. 1-56389-425-4.

Rough Justice. Written by Chuck Dixon. Illustrated by Scott McDaniel. 1999. 222pp. 1-56389-523-4.

Love and Bullets. Written by Chuck Dixon. Illustrated by Scott McDaniel. 2000. 144pp. 1-56389-613-3.

A Darker Shade of Justice. Written by Chuck Dixon. Illustrated by Scott McDaniel and Karl Story. 2000. 256pp. 1-56389-703-2.

The Hunt for Oracle. Written by Chuck Dixon. Illustrated by Greg Land, Butch Guice, and various. 2003. 192pp. 1-56389-940-X.

Nightwing/Huntress. Written by Devin Grayson. Illustrated by Greg Land and Bill Sienkiewicz. 2004. 96pp. 1-4012-0127-X.

Big Guns. Written by Chuck Dixon. Illustrated by Greg Land, et al. 2004. 186pp. 1-4012-0186-5.

Nightwing: Year One. Written by Chuck Dixon and Scott Beatty. Illustrated by Scott McDaniel and Andy Owens. 2005. 144pp. 1-4012-0435-X.

On the Razor's Edge. Written by Chuck Dixon. Illustrated by Greg Land, Rick Leonardi, and various. 2005. 192pp. 1-4012-0437-6.

Mobbed Up. Written by Devin Grayson. Illustrated by Phil Hester. 2006. 128pp. 1-4012-0907-6.

Renegade. Written by Devin Grayson. Illustrated by Phil Hester. 2006. 144pp. 1-4012-0908-4.

Phantom Jack: The Collected Edition. Written by Mike SanGiacomo. Illustrated by various. Speakeasy Comics, 2005. 200pp. 0-9737039-2-X. **T**

Jack Baxter is a news reporter like no other—he has the secret power to turn himself invisible. Using his "fade" powers for personal gain, he's risen to the top of the newspaper world, winning accolades for his daring reporting when in actuality he's had the upper hand all along. Reluctant to play the role of hero, he does just that when he does the unthinkable and must go inside Iraq to rescue his captured brother. The collected edition publication features all-new material made exclusively for the trade paperback collection.

Power Girl. Written by Geoff Johns, Paul Levitz, and Paul Kupperberg. Illustrated by Amanda Conner and various. DC Comics, 2006. 176pp. 1-4012-0968-8. **Y**

The beautiful blonde hero named Power Girl thought she knew where she was from—she was the descendant of the Atlantean sorcerer Arion, frozen in suspended animation and revived in the present day. What she soon discovers is that she's been living a lie thanks to the machinations of a villain called Psycho Pirate. She soon discovers that she is really Kara Zor-L, the cousin of the original Superman of Earth-Two—a parallel world similar to ours where all the original Golden Age-era heroes of the DC Comics universe came from. When Krypton was about to be destroyed, like her cousin she was sent by her parents in a rocketship to Earth, where after a while she became known as the hero Power Girl. A prequel tie-in to the events in the DC Comics epic series <u>Infinite Crisis</u>.

<u>The Punisher.</u> MAX/Marvel Comics, 1990– . **T M** 🎬 🔫

The vigilante anti-hero of the Marvel Comics universe. Originally created in 1974, he has remained an enduring character in the Marvel Comics Universe. Special Black Ops specialist Frank Castle lost his entire family when they were assassinated after witnessing a mafia-ordered murder in Central Park. The only one to survive the experience, the former Vietnam vet fell back on his wartime experience as a Marine captain and focused his rage to seek revenge on organized crime for the death of his wife and children. Frank created an identity called the Punisher, a fearful vigilante who shows no mercy to the criminals. Swearing bloody vengeance on organized crime, Frank now wears an all-black Kevlar uniform with a large image of a skull on his chest and is a master in armed and unarmed combat. Now armed to the teeth with the latest high-tech weaponry and utilizing the deadliest of force, the Punisher will never rest until he's killed those responsible for his family's death. The story line for *Welcome Back, Frank* was adapted as the plot for the 2004 Punisher film. Please note that the Marvel <u>MAX</u> titles feature graphic violence and language and are made for older, mature readers. The titles listed below are in chronological order beginning with the Punisher's first appearance.

    The Essential Punisher. Written and illustrated by various. 2004. 568pp. 0-7851-1364-9. **T**

© 2006 Marvel Comics

Circle of Blood. Written by Steven Grant. Illustrated by Mike Zeck. 1990. 144pp. 0-87135-394-6. **T**

Vol. 1: Welcome Back, Frank. Written by Garth Ennis. Illustrated by Steve Dillon. 2001. 272pp. 0-7851-0783-5. **O** ◎

Vol. 2: Army of One. Written by Garth Ennis. Illustrated by Steve Dillon. 2005. 160pp. 0-7851-0839-4. **O**

Vol. 3: Business as Usual. Written by Garth Ennis. Illustrated by Steve Dillon. 2005. 144pp. 0-7851-1014-3. **O**

Vol. 4: Full Auto. Written by Garth Ennis. Illustrated by Steve Dillon. 2005. 168pp. 0-7851-1149-2. **O**

Vol. 5: Streets of Laredo. Written by Garth Ennis. Illustrated by Steve Dillon. 2003. 168pp. 0-7851-1096-8. **O**

MAX Vol. 1: In the Beginning. Written by Garth Ennis. Illustrated by Lewis Larosa. 2004. 144pp. 0-7851-1391-6. **M**

MAX Vol. 2: Kitchen Irish. Written by Garth Ennis. Illustrated by Leandro Fernandez. 2004. 144pp. 0-7851-1539-0. **M**

MAX Vol. 3: Mother Russia. Written by Garth Ennis. Illustrated by Doug Braithwaite. 2005. 144pp. 0-7851-1603-6. **M**

MAX Vol. 4: Up Is Down and Black Is White. 2005. Written by Garth Ennis. Illustrated by Leo Fernandez. 144pp. 0-7851-1731-8. **M**

MAX Vol. 5: The Slavers. Written by Garth Ennis. Illustrated by Leo Fernandez. 2006. 144pp. 0-7851-1899-3. **M**

Robin. 1993– .

© 2006 DC Comics

The Boy Wonder sidekick to Batman, the mantle of Robin has been worn by many young men and a few good women, too. Dick Grayson, Jason Todd, and Tim Drake have all taken on the responsibility and the role, sometimes at the cost of their lives. The title's main focus is on the third Robin, Tim Drake, as he continues to fight crime in Gotham City alongside Batman, as well as other heroes including Nightwing, Batgirl, and the Spoiler, while tackling homework and a teenage social life.

<u>Robin</u>, 1993– . **Y**

Listed below are a variety of titles that feature teenager Tim Drake as Robin, the Boy Wonder. The collections were published by DC Comics and appeared as miniseries collections and from the ongoing monthly comic book series, too.

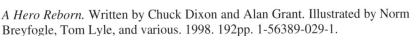

> *A Hero Reborn.* Written by Chuck Dixon and Alan Grant. Illustrated by Norm Breyfogle, Tom Lyle, and various. 1998. 192pp. 1-56389-029-1.
> *Tragedy & Triumph.* Written by Chuck Dixon and Alan Grant. Illustrated by Norm Breyfogle, Tom Lyle and various. 1993.192pp. 1-56389-078-X.
> *Flying Solo.* Written by Chuck Dixon. Illustrated by Tom Grummett. 2000. 144pp. 1-56389-609-5.
> *Unmasked.* Written by Bill Willingham. Illustrated by Rick Mays, Francisco Rodriguez de la Fuente, and Aaron Sowd. 2004. 128pp. 1-4012-0235-7.
> *Robin/Batgirl: Fresh Blood.* Written by Bill Willingham and Andersen Gabrych. Illustrated by Damion Scott, Alé Garza, and Jesse Delperdang. 2005. 144pp. 1-4012-0433-3.
> *To Kill a Bird.* Written by Bill Willingham. Illustrated by Damion Scott, Giuseppe Camuncoli, Scott McDaniel, and Pop Mhan. 2006. 144pp. 1-4012-0909-2
> *Days of Fire and Madness.* Written by Bill Willingham. Illustrated by Scott McDaniel and Andy Owens. 2006. 144pp. 1-4012-0911-4.

Robin: Year One. **Written by Chuck Dixon and Scott Beatty. Illustrated by Javier Pulido and Robert Campanella.** DC Comics, 2002. 200pp. 1-56389-805-5. **Y** ◎

A look back at the first year that Dick Grayson, the first Robin, underwent while training to be the crime-fighting sidekick to Batman.

<u>The Rocketeer.</u> Written and illustrated by Dave Stevens and various. Eclipse Books and Dark Horse Comics, 1991–1996. **T**

In 1938, test pilot Cliff Secord discovers a top-secret, experimental bullet-shaped jetpack hidden in the seat of his stunt plane. The engine can go over 200 miles per hour and seems like an answer to Cliff's prayers for the upcoming stunt show. With his pal Peevy, he designs a futuristic helmet, and the

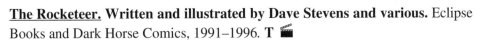

Rocketeer is born. But the government, organized crime, the creepy Marco, and the brute called Lothar are all after the experimental rocket. When Cliff's stunning and sexy girlfriend Betty is kidnapped by Marco and Lothar, Cliff dons the rocketpack to rescue his love no matter the cost. The graphic novel inspired the 1991 Disney cult movie.

> *The Rocketeer.* Written and illustrated by Dave Stevens. Eclipse Books, 1991. 72pp. 0-913035-06-8.
>
> *The Rocketeer: Cliff's New York Adventure.* Written by Dave Stevens. Illustrations by Dave Stevens, Arthur Adams, and Sandy Plunkett. Dark Horse Comics, 1996. 96pp. 1-56971-092-9.

Savage Dragon. Written and illustrated by Erik Larsen. Image Comics, 1992– . **O**

The city of Chicago was under the ruthless control of the superpowered crimelord, the OverLord, and his gang of mutant freaks, and the cops barely stood a chance against the brutal and vicious criminals. When police Lieutenant Frank Darling discovered a hulking green humanoid man with a large crest on his head, it seemed as if his prayers had been answered. An amnesiac without a memory of his past, the man is taken in by Frank and trained to become a police officer the likes of which the Windy City has never seen before. Now here comes Dragon, and the villains don't stand a chance. This is one of Image Comics' longest-running series and is published by cofounder Erik Larsen.

> *Vol. 1: Baptism of Fire.* 2002. 160pp. 1-58240-165-9.
> *Vol. 2: A Force to Be Reckoned With.* 1996. 160pp. 1-887279-12-1.
> *Vol. 3: The Fallen.* 1998. 128pp. 1-887279-83-0.
> *Vol. 4: Possessed.* 1998. 144pp. 1-58240-031-8.
> *Vol. 5: Revenge.* 1999. 128pp. 1-58240-101-2.
> *Vol. 6: Gang War.* 2001. 144pp. 1-58240-138-1.
> *Vol. 7: A Talk with God.* 1997. 176pp. 1-887279-59-8.
> *Vol. 8: Terminated.* 2004. 176pp. 1-58240-336-8.
> *Vol. 9: Worlds at War.* 2003. 144pp. 1-58240-324-4.
> *Vol. 10: End Game.* 2004. 144pp. 1-58240-346-5.
> *Vol. 11: Resurrection.* 2005. 144pp. 1-58240-523-9.
> *Vol. 12: Last Rites.* 2005. 152pp. 1-58240-592-1.

Shadow Lady. Written and illustrated by Masakazu Katsura. Dark Horse Comics, 1999–2001. **O Japanese manga.**

In Gray City, a reckless and beautiful thief called Shadow Lady is out to make the city her personal playground. With her little demon friend De-Mo, the sexy thief is out to steal everything the city has, just for the fun of it. When she rouses the ire of young police officer Bright Honda, he'll stop at nothing to bring the sassy thief to justice. Little does Bright know that there's less to Shadow Lady than meets the eye. In reality she's really a shy and demure eighteen-year-old café waitress named Aimi Komori who is able to transform into the thief when she puts on her magic eye shadow. Will Bright discover Shadow Lady's true identity and bring her in, justice or will love intervene?

> *Vol. 1: Dangerous Love.* 1999. 200pp. 1-56971-408-8.
> *Vol. 2: The Awakening.* 2000. 184pp. 1-56971-446-0.
> *Vol. 3: Sudden Death.* 2001. 176pp. 1-56971-477-0.

***Sidekicks: The Transfer Student.* 2d ed. Written by J. Torres. Illustrated by Takeshi Miyazawa.** Oni Press, 2003. 144pp. 1-929998-76-7. **Y**

© 2006 Oni Press.

Shuster Academy is the premiere school for teens with super-powers. Terry Highland's father was a famous sidekick hero, and her dad's hoping she will follow in his footsteps. Sure, there might be teens who can fly and have heat vision and all that, but at the academy, there's one rule: no powers! When three mysterious rule-breakers named "Biff," "Bam," and "Pow" appear on the scene at school, both the students and administration want the masquerade to end. Can Terry and her friends solve the mystery of their secret identities without breaking the school rule?

***Smax.* Written by Alan Moore. Illustrated by Zander Cannon and Andrew Currie.** America's Best Comics/WildStorm Productions/DC Comics, 2004. 128pp. 1-4012-0325-6. **M**

Jeff Smax, an eight-foot-tall, invulnerable blue giant, works at a super-hero police department called Precinct 10 in the city of Neopolis with his partner, Toybox. When he gets word that his uncle has died, he reluctantly goes back home to his own parallel fantasy world with Toybox in tow to take care of some unfinished business. Toybox finds out more than she ever dreamed about Smax as they walk through a fairy tale-type world with dwarves, elves, and humorous parodies of the realm of fantasy, and embark on an unfinished quest that Smax abandoned: to vanquish a dragon called MorningBright. Will Smax turn his back again on the home world he abandoned, and will he finally find true love with his sister? A humorous and offbeat super-hero/fantasy parody featuring characters from Alan Moore's <u>Top Ten</u> series.

***The Spectre: Crime and Punishments.* Written by John Ostrander. Illustrated by Tom Mandrake.** DC Comics, 1993. 104pp. 1-56389-127-1. **T**

The Spectre is one of the most powerful beings in the universe and one of the original members of the Justice Society of America. The Wrath of God merged with a human soul, he has roamed Earth for thousands of years smiting evil by avenging those who have died unavenged and punishing evil-doers as penance for his past misdeeds. The current human host of the Spectre is Jim Corrigan, a hard-nosed police officer who died at the hands of the mob in the 1930s. Now as the Spectre, he must avenge the deaths of the innocent and learn the true nature of evil. Only then will the Spectre be free of his task and be given peace in Heaven.

<u>Spider-Girl.</u> Written by Tom DeFalco. Illustrated by Pat Olliffe and Ron Frenz. Marvel Comics, 2004– . **Y**

Set in an alternate future in which May "Mayday" Parker, the daughter of Peter Parker and Mary Jane Watson-Parker, finds that she has inherited her father's powers and sets out to save the day as Spider-Girl. Like her father before her, May finds that her great powers come at a great price, as she's constantly under threat by the next generation of Spider-Man foes, including Ladyhawk, the Kingpin of Crime, Lady Octopus, Mr. Nobody, and Crazy Eight. How will May be able to balance school, a social life, and a night life of fighting villains and the worst enemies of all—her parents?

> *Vol. 1: Legacy.* 2004. 144pp. 0-7851-1441-6.
> *Vol. 2: Like Father, Like Daughter.* 2004. 144pp. 0-7851-1657-5.
> *Vol. 3: Avenging Allies.* 2005. 152pp. 0-7851-1658-3.
> *Vol. 4: Turning Point.* 2005. 152pp. 0-7851-1871-3.
> *Vol. 5: Endgame.* 2006. 144pp. 0-7851-2034-3.
> *Vol. 6: Too Many Spiders!* 2006. 144pp. 0-7851-2156-0.

Spider-Woman: Origin. Written by Brian Michael Bendis. Illustrated by Joshua Luna and Jonathan Luna. 2006. 128pp. 0-7851-1965-5. **T**

The origin of Jessica Drew, the hero known as Spider-Woman and current Avenger. Poisoned at a young age by radiation, she was given an experimental serum of irradiated spider blood. After a time she discovered that she had gained spiderlike powers, including super-human strength, immunity to toxins, pheromones that have a powerful effect on the opposite sex, and the ability to climb walls. Brainwashed by the terrorist organization called HYDRA, Jessica became an agent of evil, but soon she renounced her terrorist ways and used her skills as a superpowered spy for S.H.I.E.L.D., the sworn enemy of HYDRA. Now going by the alias Spider-Woman, Jessica is out to face the ghosts of her past and to destroy HYDRA once and for all.

Starman. Written by James Robinson. Illustrated by Tony Harris et al. DC Comics, 1996–2005. **T** ◉

© 2006 DC Comics

The epic story of Jack Knight, the youngest son of the Golden Age hero known as Starman. Jack couldn't care less about his father's alter ego and proud history, considering it a job for his older brother, David. When David is killed by the son of an old foe of his father called The Mist, Jack takes up his father's cosmic rod and in time learns to proudly carry on his family's legacy as the guardian of Opal City. *Volume 3: A Wicked Inclination* includes the 1997 Best Serialized Story Eisner Award-winning story "Sand & Stars," and *Volume 1: Sins of the Father* received recognition from YALSA's Popular Paperbacks for Young Adults committee in 2004.

> *Vol. 1: Sins of the Father.* 1996. 160pp. 1-56389-248-0.
> *Vol. 2: Night and Day.* 1997. 240pp. 1-56389-270-7.
> *Vol. 3: A Wicked Inclination.* 1998. 240pp. 1-56389-409-2.
> *Vol. 4: Times Past.* 1999. 176pp. 1-56389-492-0.
> *Vol. 5: Infernal Devices.* 2000. 208pp. 1-56389-633-8.
> *Vol. 6: To Reach the Stars.* 2001. 224pp. 1-56389-712-1.
> *Vol. 7: A Starry Knight.* 2002. 180pp. 1-56389-797-0.
> *Vol. 8: Stars My Destination.* 2004. 144pp. 1-4012-0011-7.
> *Vol. 9: Grand Guignol.* 2004. 296pp. 1-4012-0257-8.
> *Vol. 10: Sons of the Father.* 2005. 176pp. 1-4012-0473-2.

Supergirl. DC Comics, 1998– . **T**

The adventures of Supergirl, a protoplasm matrix from another dimension that Superman brought home and who assumed the guise of a blonde-haired female cousin of Superman. To save the life of a woman, Supergirl merged with Linda Danvers, a young brunette girl with a sordid past. Now Supergirl has to re-discover life co-inhabiting a body with a woman who was a murderer with less-than-noble life. The second collection, *Many Happy Returns*, features an exiting conclusion to the series as Supergirl discovers a rocketship that carries inside of it another Supergirl: Kara Zoe-El, Superman's Kryptonian cousin. The third Supergirl collection, called *Power*, features the recently collected adventures of Kara Zor-el, the true cousin of Superman in her brand-new adventures on Earth. <<Editor: The three Supergirl titles—though they feature variations on the character, they are not inter-related.]

Supergirl. **Written by Peter David. Illustrated by Gary Frank.** DC Comics, 1998. 224pp. 1-56389-410-6.

Supergirl: Many Happy Returns. **Written by Peter David. Illustrated by Ed Benes and Alex Lei**. DC Comics, 2003. 144pp. 1-4012-0085-0.

Supergirl: Power. **Written by Jeph Loeb. Illustrated by Ian Churchill**. DC Comics, 2006. 160pp. 1-4012-0915-7.

Supreme

🖋 **Alan Moore's Supreme. Written by Alan Moore. Illustrated by Joe Bennett, Rick Veitch, and Chris Sprouse.** Checker Book Publishing Group, 2002–2003. **T**

A blonde-haired hero and champion of the city Omegapolis, he's lost his memory and must rediscover who he is by retracing his life, family, and hometown of Little Haven, as well as his place with the super-team known as the Allied Supermen. A mild-mannered comic book artist by day, Supreme traces his history and the history of comic books from the Golden Age and Silver Age in a delightful tribute to the Fawcett Comics hero Captain Marvel and DC Comics' Superman titles of yesterday. The writer, Alan Moore, won a Harvey Award in 1999 for Best Writer for his body of work including this series.

> *Vol. 1: Story of the Year.* 2002. 332pp. 0-9710249-5-2.
> *Vol. 2: The Return.* 2003. 258pp. 0-9710249-6-0.

Supreme Power. Written by J. Michael Straczynski. Illustrated by Gary Frank. MAX/Marvel Comics, 2004– . **T M**

A reimagination of Marvel's classic hero team from another dimension: the Squadron Supreme. Formerly a riff on DC Comics' Justice League of America, this new retelling presents a hard-edged, mature, and deeply personal saga of a world about to give birth to its first generation of super-heroes! As the anti-heroes including Hyperion, Dr. Spectrum, Nighthawk, and Blur learn to use their powers and skills, a vastly changing world is arriving with the dawn of the super-heroes. Note that the series was originally intended for mature readers, but has since been published for teen readers and up. The collection Nighthawk focuses on Kyle Richmond, a Batman-inspired hero who must defeat a dark force killing innocent people in the streets of Chicago. For other titles featuring these characters, please see the listing for *Doctor Spectrum* in this chapter.

Vol. 1: Contact. 2004. 144pp. 0-7851-1224-3. **M**
Vol. 2: Power and Principalities. 2004. 144pp. 0-7851-1456-4. **M**
Vol. 3: High Command. 2005. 144pp. 0-7851-1474-2. **M**
Vol. 1: The Hyperion Project. 2005. 216pp. 0-7851-1369-X, hardcover. **M**
Hyperion. 2006. 120pp. 0-7851-1895-0. **T**
Nighthawk. 2006. 144pp. 0-7851-1897-7. **T**

Wonder Woman. DC Comics. 1995– . 🖥

Princess Diana is from the Amazon tribe of female warriors and was born from clay on the magical Greek island of Themyscira. The innocent reincarnation of an unborn child who died in her mother's womb over 30,000 years ago, she was blessed by the Greek gods with great powers to combat the warrior-god Ares, including flight, great strength, and super-speed. She also carries a magic lasso that was made from the girdle of Aphrodite and will force a fiend to tell the truth when in its grasp. The ambassador of her culture to the world, she earned the moniker of "Wonder Woman" by the press when she first appeared and to this day is an ally of Superman, Batman, and the Justice League of America. Listed are titles published since 1995 from the monthly comic book series as well as several graphic novels.

***Wonder Woman: The Hiketeia.* Written by Greg Rucka. Illustrated by Grawbadger Jones.** DC Comics, 2003. 96pp. 1-56389-914-0. **O**

Wonder Woman performs an ancient Greek ritual called a Hiketeia with a young woman called Danielle Wellys. Now Wonder Woman is honor bound to protect her charge at all costs. When Danielle is discovered to have murdered the drug dealers who murdered her sister, Wonder Woman is caught in the middle against the one person who has come to bring Danielle to justice: Batman. Now Wonder Woman is caught between an honor-bound oath and justice.

***Wonder Woman: Spirit of Truth.* Written by Paul Dini. Illustrated by Alex Ross.** DC Comics, 2001. 64pp. 1-56389-861-6. **Y**

A fully painted, oversized story featuring Wonder Woman as she tries to find her true role as the ambassador of peace from Amazonia. Many men either fear her or don't take her message in earnest due to her femininity. She decides to try a new way and blends in with society to get a view of the true nature of humanity from their vantage point and to see their hopes, dreams, and fears up close. She will learn something about herself in the process.

Wonder Woman. DC Comics, 1995– . **Y**

Listed below are highlights of recommend *Wonder Woman* titles that have been collected by DC Comics from the original comic book issues from the 1980 through mid-2000s. Some titles listed may be out of print, but are listed below according to when the collections were published. Highlights from the collection include *The Contest* in which the mantle of Wonder Woman is temporarily given to another warrior—an Amazonian named Artemis.

> *The Contest.* Written by William Messner-Loebs. Illustrated by Mike Deodato, Jr. 1995. 120pp. 1-56389-194-8.
>
> *The Challenge of Artemis.* Written by William Messner-Loebs. Illustrated by Mike Deodato, Jr. 1996. 192pp. 1-56389-264-2.
>
> *Paradise Lost.* Written by Phil Jimenez, J.M. DeMatteis, Joe Kelly, George Pérez and Devin Grayson. Illustrated by Phil Jimenez and Andy Lanning. 2002. 176pp. 1-56389-792-X.
>
> *Paradise Found.* Written by Phil Jimenez. Illustrated by Phil Jimenez and Andy Lanning. 2003. 192pp. 1-56389-956-6.
>
> *Gods and Mortals.* Written by George Pérez, Greg Potter and Len Wein. Illustrated by George Pérez and Bruce Patterson. 2004. 192pp. 1-4012-0197-0.
>
> *Down to Earth.* Written by Greg Rucka. Illustrated by Drew Johnson, Ray Snyder, Eric Shanower, Brian Stelfreeze, Steve Rude, Stuart Immonen and Eduardo Risso. 2004. 160pp. 1-4012-0226-8.
>
> *Challenge of the Gods.* Written by George Pérez. Illustrated by George Pérez and Bruce Patterson. 2004. 176pp. 1-4012-0324-8.
>
> *Bitter Rivals.* Written by Greg Rucka. Illustrated by Drew Johnson, Shane Davis, and various. 2005. 128pp. 1-4012-0462-7.
>
> *Beauty and the Beasts.* Written by George Pérez, John Byrne and Len Wein. Illustrated by George Pérez, John Byrne, and various. 2005. 168pp. 1-4012-0484-8.
>
> *Eyes of the Gorgon.* Written by Greg Rucka. Illustrated by Rags Morales and Mark Propst. 2005. 192pp. 1-4012-0797-9.
>
> *Land of the Dead.* Written by Greg Rucka. Illustrated by Rags Morales. 2006. 128pp. 1-4012-0938-6.
>
> *Mission's End.* Written by Greg Rucka. Illustrated by Rags Morales. 2006. 208pp. 1-4012-1093-7.

Cosmic Heroes

Many tales feature heroes whose powers and origins are derived from outer space. The hero may be an alien from outer space or have powers that originate from a cosmic source that is not Earth.

Battle Girlz, Pocket Manga. Written and illustrated by Rod Espinosa. Antarctic Press, 2004. 160pp. 1-932453-45-8. **T Neo-manga.**

On the planet Arlan, located just on the edge of the universe, Sasa Rai Desperado, a beautiful warrior goddess, has recruited a powerful group of superpowered women warriors from all over the galaxy into a fighting force known as the Battle Girlz. Called by their code names—Mech Girl, Super Mighty Girl, Powerful Priestess, Nerdy Gadgeteer, and Seductive Temptress —they're the best fighters from their worlds and ready to fight alongside

"Saintly Perfect Goddess," a.k.a. Sasa Rai herself, to take on any evil that dares to threaten the galaxy. When an ancient evil called Geneszorr and his armies rise to defeat the Battle Girlz, some of the newest recruits must see if they've got what it takes to be the saviors of the galaxy.

Captain Marvel. Marvel Comics, 2002–2005.

Several men have worn the mantle of Captain Marvel. The first was Mar-Vell, a captain of the humanoid alien race called the Kree. After arriving on Earth, he shared the physical body of Rick Jones, a frequent companion to Captain America, the Hulk, ROM the Spaceknight, and more Marvel Comics heroes. They are bonded by a pair of Nega-Bands so that when clasped together they are psionically linked but able to trade physical places. Given the title "Protector of the Universe" by the extraterrestrial called Eon, Mar-Vell became the archenemy of the villain Thanos, who wished to destroy the universe as a tribute to Death, whom he loved. After battling the nuclear villain called Nitro, Mar-Vell became a victim of carcinogenic fumes from Nitro's attack and was diagnosed with cancer. He died a short time later, surrounded by friends and loved ones. The second Captain Marvel is Genis-Vell, the son of the original Captain Marvel. Also forming a bond with Rick Jones via the Nega-Bands, Genis continues his father's legacy as the heroic galactic guardian, fighting to save the galaxy from danger with the aid of Rick Jones. Recently Genis was killed in battle against the villain Baron Zemo in the pages of the monthly comic book series <u>Thunderbolts</u>. A new hero, the daughter of Genis-Vell, named Phyla-Vell, has recently taken on the mantle of Captain Marvel.

<u>Captain Marvel.</u> Written by Peter David. Illustrated by Chriscross and Ivan Reis. 2003–2004. **Y**

    Vol. 1: First Contact. 2003. 160pp. 0-7851-0791-6.
    Vol. 2: The Coven. 2003. 136pp. 0-7851-1306-1.
    Vol. 3: Crazy Like a Fox. 2004. 136pp. 0-7851-1340-1.
    Vol. 4: Odyssey. 2004. 160pp. 0-7851-1530-7.

***The Life and Death of Captain Marvel.* Written and illustrated by Jim Starlin.** 2002. 304pp. 0-7851-0837-8. **Y**

<u>Captain Universe.</u> Marvel Comics, 2005–2006. **T**

Collecting the adventures of the hero who could be anyone, including you. In times of trouble, a mysterious Uni-Force power can be bestowed upon an individual, transforming that person into the costumed hero Captain Universe. The Uni-Power is derived from a power source called the Enigma Force, which originated from a microscopic universe called the Microverse. The person given the power of Captain Universe can for a period of time have enhanced strength, flight, X-ray vision, psychic awareness, telekinesis, and many other powers, until the danger has passed and the power is given to another individual in need.

    Power Unimaginable. Written and illustrated by various. 2005. 168pp. 0-7851-1891-8.
    Universal Heroes. Written by Jay Faerber, Jeff Parker. Illustrated by various. 2006. 136pp. 0-7851-1857-8.

Marvel Boy. **Written by Grant Morrison. Illustrated by J. G. Jones.** Marvel Comics, 2001. 144pp. 0-7851-0781-9. **O**

> The intense adventures of Noh-Varr, a member of the human-looking, superpowered alien race called the Kree. When his diplomatic team arrives on Earth and is immediately destroyed by Earth forces, Noh-Varr is the only survivor. He is captured and tortured by the mysterious Midas Organization, run by Dr. Midas, a criminal mastermind in golden Iron Man armor who bathes in cosmic radiation. When Noh-Varr escapes from the facility, he declares war on humanity and even the enforcers of Dr. Midas, including the Exterminatrix, Hexus, and the Bannermen, can't stop him.

Orion: The Gates of Apokolips. **Written and illustrated by Walter Simonson.** DC Comics, 2001. 144pp. 1-56389-778-4. **T**

> The adventures of Orion, the son of the evil despot Darkseid, the dark ruler of the planet Apokolips. A warrior since his birth, Orion has lived on the peaceful planet New Genesis in the company of the race of beings called the New Gods and has renounced his family's dark past. When Darkseid discovers an ultimate power in the form of the Anti-Life Equation, Orion must find a way to defeat his unbeatable father while the fate of the universe hangs in the balance.

Silver Surfer. Created by Stan Lee and Jack Kirby. Marvel Comics, 1991–2005. **Y**

> The silver-skinned man known as Norrin Radd, from the utopian planet Zenn-La, saved his planet from the ravages of the planet-devouring Galactus by becoming his herald. Powered by the awesome might of Galactus's Power Cosmic, the Silver Surfer soars the spaceways on his cosmic surfboard, trying to redeem his crimes against the universe for serving Galactus and inadvertently causing the deaths of billions across the universe. The Silver Surfer has also been a powerful ally of the Fantastic Four and other Marvel heroes in times of crisis. The Silver Surfer was created by Stan Lee and Jack Kirby and first appeared in the pages of *Fantastic Four* #48 in 1965. The short story "Parable" by Stan Lee and Moebius won an Eisner Award in 1989 for Best Short Story and tells a futuristic tale in which the Silver Surfer comes out of retirement to combat the threat of Galactus once more. The titles featuring the galactic hero are listed below by publication date.

🔖 *Parable.* **Written by Stan Lee. Illustrated by Moebius.** 1988. 72pp. 0-87135-491-8.

Homecoming. **Written by Jim Starlin. Illustrated by Bill Reinhold.** 1991. 64pp. 0-87135-855-7.

Essential Silver Surfer. **Written by Stan Lee. Illustrated by John Buscema.** Marvel Comics, 1998. 528pp. 0-7851-0271-X.

<u>**Silver Surfer.**</u> **Written by Stacy Weiss and Dan Chariton. Illustrated by Lan Medina.** 2004–2005.

> *Vol. 1: Communion.* 2004. 136pp. 0-7851-1319-3.
> *Vol. 2.* 2005. 192pp. 0-7851-1575-7.

The Rebirth of Thanos. **Written by Jim Starlin. Illustrated by Ron Lim.** 2006. 224pp. 0-7851-2046-7.

Stormbreaker: The Saga of Beta Ray Bill. **Written by Michael Avon Oeming and Daniel Berman. Illustrated by Andrea DiVito.** Marvel Comics, 2005. 144pp. 0-7851-1720-2. **Y** ◉

© 2006 Marvel Comics.

Beta Ray Bill is an honorable, horse-faced Korbinite alien who was biologically altered to be a protector of his people and was worthy to carry the hammer of the thunder god Thor. In return for saving his son's life, the Norse god Odin bestowed upon Beta Ray Bill a mystical uru hammer called Stormbreaker to aid his people and protect Earth in time of need. Now following the climactic events that devastated Asgard, he is the sole survivor of all that remains of Asgard. Beta Ray Bill heads off into space to help aid his Korbinite people. In space he encounters Stardust, a powerful creature composed of vast cosmic power sent by his master to destroy Beta Ray Bill and his people. Will the wielder of the hammer of Stormbreaker and last remaining savior of Asgard fall before the cosmic might of Stardust?

Mutant Heroes

Not all super-heroes receive their special powers by accident or chance. Some people are born with them. Born with a power that they did not choose, mutants are humans who after puberty have exhibited strange powers that they have used either to either humanity or for evil. They are the next evolution of humankind. Graphic novels such as the popular X-Men series of books and books that feature specific X-Men characters such as Wolverine are excellent examples of this subgenre. Following are titles featuring specific characters made popular by their appearances in the X-Men.

Bishop. Marvel Comics, 1995–1996. **Y**

A mutant from the future, he has come to the present to hunt for a fugitive criminal. Well aware that he has no way to go back home, he has become a valuable member of the X-Men. Bishop has the ability to absorb kinetic energy and reflect it back through his hands in concussive blasts. Bishop is also featured in the series District X, listed elsewhere in this chapter.

> *X-Men: The Coming of Bishop.* Written by John Byrne. Illustrated by Whilce Portacio and Art Thibert. 1995. 96pp. 0-7851-0099-7.
> *Bishop: The Mountjoy Crisis.* Written by John Ostrander. Illustrated by Carlos Pacheco. 1996. 96pp. 0-7851-0191-8.

Colossus. Marvel Comics, 1994–2006. **Y**

Piotr (Peter) Nikolaievitch Rasputin is a Russian-born powerhouse able to convert his skin into an organic, steel-like substance by his own will. One of the first multicultural mutants featured in the X-Men, he is an X-Man dedicated to Xavier's cause.

> *Colossus: God's Country.* 1994. Written by Ann Nocenti. Illustrated by Rick Leonardi. 64pp. No ISBN.

X-Men: Colossus—Bloodline. 2006. Written by David Hine. Illustrated by Jorge Lucas. 120pp. 0-7851-1900-0.

Cyclops. Marvel Comics, 1994–2002. **Y**

One of the original team members and leader of the X-Men, Cyclops is able to shoot optic beams from his eyes and wears a protective visor because he is unable to control the blasts. Married to Jean Grey up until her death, he is currently dating fellow X-Man the White Queen.

> *Cyclops: Retribution*. Written by Bob Harras. Illustrated by Ron Lim. 1994. 64pp. No ISBN.
> *X-Men Icons: Cyclops*. Written by Brian K. Vaughan. Illustrated by Mark Texeira. 2002. 192pp. 0-7851-0871-8.

Cyclops and Phoenix. Marvel Comics, 1996–1997. **Y** ◎

After their wedding, Jean Grey-Summers (Phoenix) and Scott Summers (Cyclops) are mystically sent far into the future by a familiar friend who was banished there. Now in an age where the ancient evil of Apocalypse reigns supreme, a young boy infected by a techno-organic virus just may be the key to defeating this ruler. His name is Nathan Christopher Summers, and he is the son of Scott and Jean. Able to live with him in the future, they raise him to be the strong leader of tomorrow known as Cable. *The Further Adventures of Cyclops and Phoenix* focuses on Scott's and Jean's trip to the past, where they encounter Mr. Sinister, and *Askani'Son* tells the further tales of Nathan in the far future.

> *The Adventures of Cyclops and Phoenix*. Written by Scott Lobdell. Illustrated by Gene Ha. 1996. 96pp. 0-7851-0171-3.
> *The Further Adventures of Cyclops and Phoenix*. Written by Peter Milligan. Illustrated by John Paul Leon. 1997. 96pp. 0-7851-0556-5.
> *Askani'Son*. Written by Scott Lobdell. Illustrated by Gene Ha. 1997. 96pp. 0-7851-0565-4.

Emma Frost. **Written by Karl Bollers. Illustrated by Carlo Pagulayan and Randall Green.** Marvel Age/Marvel Comics, 2004–2005. **T**

© 2006 Marvel Comics.

Before she became known as the White Queen, the platinum-blonde, voluptuous reformed villain from the Hellfire Club and now X-Men coleader Emma Grace Frost was the middle child of three girls and an older brother in one of the wealthiest families in New England. Her father, a ruthless businessman, chose Emma to be the heir to the family fortune, passing over her brother Christian and her two sisters. A frail, flat-chested brunette and a B-average student, she is now attending the best school in Boston, and now things are finally changing for her: her mutant powers are just now kicking in. Now able to read minds, control thoughts, and more, Emma proves to the world that she's got what it takes to climb up the corporate ladder with or without her father's inheritance, using the new mutant power she has been given.

> *Vol. 1: Higher Learning*. 2004. 144pp. 0-7851-1434-3.

> *Vol. 2: Mind Games.* 2005. 144pp. 0-7851-1413-0.
> *Vol. 3: Bloom.* 2005. 144pp. 0-7851-1473-4.

Gambit. Marvel Comics, 1995–2005. **Y**

Gambit is a mischievous thief able to take any object and convert it into kinetic energy. His real name is Remy LeBeau, and in his days away from the X-Men he spends his time in the Big Easy, where the Rajun' Cajun tackles all types of problems in the seedy underworld of New Orleans, where his mutant powers just might come in handy.

> *Gambit.* Written by Howard Mackie. Illustrated by Lee Weeks. 1995. 96pp. 0-7851-0109-8.
> Gambit (2d series). 2005. Written by John Layman. Illustrated by Georges Jeanty.
>> *Vol. 1: House of Cards.* 2005. 144pp. 0-7851-1522-6.
>> *Vol. 2: Hath No Fury.* 2005. 144pp. 0-7851-1747-4.

***Madrox: Multiple Choice.* Written by Peter David. Illustrated by Pablo Raimondi.** Marvel Comics, 2005. 120pp. 0-7851-1500-5. **Y**

James Madrox is a mutant with the ability to create an infinite number of identical duplicates of himself with just the slightest touch of kinetic energy. By touching any object he can easily become his own army. Once a member of the mutant team X-Factor, he now works as a private detective in the "mutant town" area of New York, known as District X, alongside his former X-Factor team of Wolfsbane and Strong Guy.

Mystique. Written by Brian K. Vaughan. Illustrated by Jorge Lucas. Marvel Comics, 2004–2005. **T**

A spy series in which Mystique, the mysterious shape-shifting, blue-skinned mutant and former member of the Brotherhood of Evil Mutants, reluctantly works undercover for Professor Xavier. *Volumes 3 and 4* were written by Sean McKeever and illustrated by Manuel Garcia.

> *Vol. 1: Drop Dead Gorgeous.* 2004. 144pp. 0-7851-1240-5.
> *Vol. 2: Tinker, Tailor, Mutant, Spy.* 2004. 168pp. 0-7851-1555-2.
> *Vol. 3: Unnatural.* 2005. 144pp. 0-7851-1376-2.
> *Vol. 4: Quiet.* 2005. 144pp. 0-7851-1475-0.

© 2006 Marvel Comics.

***Nightcrawler: The Devil Inside.* Written by Roberto Aguirre-Sacasa. Illustrated by Darick Robertson.** Marvel Comics, 2005. 144pp. 0-7851-1428-9. **Y**

Nightcrawler (Kurt Wagner) was one of the second generation of recruits to join the X-Men. Naturally born with a devil-like appearance, he has the ability to teleport great distances. In this collection, Nightcrawler must try to solve the mysterious deaths of thirteen children and must delve further into a supernatural darkness that even he may not be strong enough to withstand.

***Ororo: Before the Storm.* Written by Marc Sumerak. Illustrated by Carlos Barberi.** 2005. 96pp. 0-7851-1819-5. Marvel Comics, 2005. **Y**

Born with the mutant ability to control the weather, the African-born mutant Ororo Munroe (alias Storm) has been a longstanding member of the X-Men. With the ability to use the weather to create lightning, wind, rain, and more, she's a formidable X-Men leader. The 2005 miniseries takes a look at her youth growing up in Cairo as a street urchin.

Phoenix. Marvel Comics, 2005–2006. **T**

© 2006 Marvel Comics.

Once known as Marvel Girl, and one of the original X-Men, Jean Grey became something more than a telepath when she was merged with a powerful cosmic entity called the Phoenix. Transformed, she was a powerful entity feared by many across the galaxies. Although she died at the hands of Magneto at the conclusion of Grant Morrison's *New X-Men* storyline, it is only a matter of time until the Phoenix rises from the ashes and is reborn. The story continues in *Phoenix —Warsong*.

Phoenix—Endsong. Written by Greg Pak. Illustrated by Greg Land. Marvel Comics, 2005. 128pp. 0-7851-1641-9.
Phoenix—Warsong. Written by Greg Pak. Illustrated by Tyler Kirkham. Marvel Comics, 2006. 128pp. 0-7851-1930-2.

Rogue. Marvel Comics, 1995–2005. **Y**

Stories featuring the solo adventures of Rogue, a female mutant with the power to temporarily rob other mutants of their power with the slightest touch. Her mutant power is also her curse, since the slightest touch—even a warm embrace—can drain whomever she touches, and extended contact can even kill.

Rogue. **Written by Howard Mackie. Illustrated by Mike Wieringo.** 1995. 96pp. 0-7851-0140-3. **Y**

X-Men Icons: Rogue. **Written by Fiona Avery. Illustrated by Aaron Lopresti.** 2002. 224pp. 0-7851-0876-9. **Y**

Rogue: Going Rogue. **Written by Robert Rodi. Illustrated by Cliff Richards.** 2005. 144pp. 0-7851-1336-3. **Y**

Sabretooth. Marvel Comics, 1994–2005.

One of the X-Men's greatest nemeses, Victor Creed (a.k.a. Sabretooth) first appeared in 1977, and much like the mutant hero Wolverine, he has enhanced senses, speed, and strength, as well as a mutant healing factor that can repair almost any wound, including a broken back, a slice to the throat, and even a Wolverine claw to the brain. With longtime ties to Wolverine dating back to when they were young in the late nineteenth century and continuing through when they worked together in a black-ops unit, the killer works as a professional assassin, killing ruthlessly for the highest bidder and the adversaries of Wolverine and the X-Men.

Sabretooth. **Written by Larry Hama. Illustrated by Mark Texeira.** 1994. 96pp. 0-7851-0050-4. **T**

Sabretooth: Open Season. **Written by Daniel Way. Illustrated by Bart Sears.** 2005. 128pp. 0-7851-1507-2. **T**

Wolverine. Marvel Comics, 1990– . **T**

> The enigmatic anti-hero known as Wolverine first appeared in the pages of *The Incredible Hulk* #181 in 1974, and since that time he has become one of the most popular comic book characters ever. One of the toughest mutants on the planet, the man known as Logan is the best at what he does, but what he does isn't very nice. Born James Howlett in the late nineteenth century, he's been gifted with a mutant healing factor and sharp, retractable claws, and his entire bone structure is laced with adamantium, the hardest known metal substance on the planet. All three of these factors help to make Wolverine a one-mutant fighting force. One of the most popular of the X-Men characters, there are a significant number of titles featuring the enigmatic anti-hero. Listed below are recommended collections of graphic novel titles featuring the famous X-Men. The titles tend to be collected editions of a variety of story lines from the ongoing <u>Wolverine</u> comic book series and various miniseries; they are listed in order by release date of the graphic novels.

Wolverine. **Written by Chris Claremont. Illustrated by Frank Miller.** 1990. 96pp. 0-87135-277-X; rev ed. 2007. 144pp. 0-7851-2329-6, hardcover. **T** ◉

In the first-ever Wolverine miniseries, Logan travels to Japan to protect Lady Mariko Yashida, a daughter of a crime lord and the woman he loves. As his honor is tested, Logan must follow the code of the Samurai and protect Mariko from the attacks of the Hand, a secret society of ninja.

© 2006 Marvel Comics.

<u>**Essential Wolverine.**</u> **Written by Chris Claremont, Larry Hama, and various. Illustrated by John Buscema, Bill Sienkiewicz, John Byrne, Marc Silvestri, and various.** 1997– . **T**

> An inexpensive collection reprinting in black and white the solo adventures of Wolverine in his first monthly comic book series, originally published starting in 1989.
>
> > *Vol. 1.* 2005, new printing. 544pp. 0-7851-1867-5.
> > *Vol. 2.* 1997. 544pp. 0-7851-0550-6.
> > *Vol. 3.* 1998. 528pp. 0-7851-0595-6.
> > *Vol. 4.* 2006. 528pp. 0-7851-2059-9.

Wolverine: Not Dead Yet. **Written by Warren Ellis. Illustrated by Leinil F. Yu.** 1998. 96pp. 0-7851-0704-5. **T**

Logan takes on an old enemy, a deadly assassin called McLeish (a.k.a. the White Ghost), whom Wolverine thought he had killed. A skillful and deadly assassin, McLeish has come back to do the unthinkable and kill Logan. Has the White Ghost really come back from the dead, or is it something more?

🌑 ***Origin: The True Story of Wolverine.*** **Written by Paul Jenkins. Illustrated by Andy Kubert.** Marvel Comics, 2002. 208pp. 0-7851-0866-1. **T**

Presenting for the first time the true origin of one of Marvel's most popular mutants, Wolverine! Born James Howlett in Canada in the late nineteenth century, the boy who would become Wolverine was born sick and frail and was constantly hindered by his allergies while growing up. His mutant powers manifested themselves early in life while protecting his mother shortly after his father was killed by Thomas Logan, an alcoholic groundskeeper. After fleeing to British Columbia with a red-haired girl he adored called Rose, James adopts the name Logan to conceal his identity, but evil never does sleep. The collection received recognition from YALSA's Quick Picks for Reluctant Readers committee in 2003.

Best of Wolverine. **Written by Chris Claremont and Mark Gruenwald. Illustrated by Frank Miller, Len Wein, Barry Windsor-Smith and Mike Zeck.** 2004. **T**

A highlight of tales featuring the popular mutant from some of his earliest appearances by some of the best writers and artists, including Frank Miller and Barry Windsor-Smith.

Vol. 1. 2004. 320pp. 0-7851-1370-3.

Wolverine. **Written by Greg Rucka. Illustrated by Darick Robertson and Leo Fernandez.** 2004. **T**

Tales of Wolverine featuring the writing of crime novelist Greg Rucka. Wolverine befriends a down-and-out waitress, who is brutally gunned down, and then sets out to solve her murder; Wolverine sets out to exact revenge on the killers of two migrant workers; and an enigmatic ghost from Wolverine's past revisits him. The tales were originally published in the monthly comic book <u>Wolverine</u> (2d series), nos. 1–19.

Vol. 1: The Brotherhood. 2004. 144pp. 0-7851-1136-0.
Vol. 2: Coyote Crossing. 2004. 120pp. 0-7851-1137-9.
Vol. 3: Return of the Native. 2004. 184pp. 0-7851-1397-5.

Wolverine Legends: Marc Silvestri. **Written by Larry Hama. Illustrated by Marc Silvestri.** 2004. **T**

Stories featuring the artwork by comic book illustrator Mark Silvestri, a popular artist on the <u>X-Men</u> series during the late 1980s and founder of Top Cow Productions. The stories feature appearances by Wolverine's archenemy Sabretooth as well.

Book I. 2004. 216pp. 0-7851-0952-8.

Wolverine Classic. **Written by Chris Claremont and Peter David. Illustrated by John Buscema.** 2005– . **T**

Collects the first issues of the original ongoing Wolverine comic book series. Written by Chris Claremont and Peter David (beginning with *Volume 3*) and illustrated by John Buscema, the series featured Logan in his "off duty" time as an X-Man lying low in the Asian country of Madripoor.

> *Vol. 1.* 2005. 120pp. 0-7851-1797-0.
> *Vol. 2.* 2005. 120pp. 0-7851-1877-2.
> *Vol. 3.* 2006. 144pp. 0-7851-2053-X.

Wolverine: Enemy of the State. **Written by Mark Millar. Illustrated by John Romita Jr.** 2005. **T** ◉

Wolverine, one of the deadliest living weapons in the world, has just been brainwashed by the Hand, a secret sect of ninja. Now Wolverine strikes a deadly path through the heroes of the Marvel Universe, and nothing can stop him.

> *Vol. 1.* 160pp. 0-7851-1492-0, softcover; 0-7851-1815-2, hardcover.
> *Vol. 2.* 176pp. 0-7851-1627-3, softcover; 0-7851-1926-4, hardcover.

Wolverine: Origins and Endings. **Written by Daniel Way. Illustrated by Javier Saltares and Mark Texeira.** 2006. 128pp. 0-7851-1977-9. hardcover. **T**

After the events from the epic called *House of M* (see listing in this chapter), Wolverine, a man who did not know his past, now remembers every single moment of his life. Every good and bad deed he's ever done he fully remembers—and God help anyone who gets in his way.

Wolverine: Weapon X. **Written and illustrated by Barry-Windsor Smith.** 2006. 120pp. 0-7851-0033-4. **T**

A mysterious organization creates perfect soldiers, and their first test subject is a feral wildman they've captured called Logan. After bonding adamantium to his bones and claws, the test subject, whom they designate Weapon X, has become one of the deadliest men on the planet. After they've created an unstoppable, vicious killing machine, can they control it? The series was originally published in comic book form in 1990.

X-Men: Kitty Pryde—Shadows and Flame. **Written by Akira Yoshida. Illustrated by Paul Smith.** Marvel Comics, 2006. 120pp. 0-7851-1816-0. **Y**

One of the third generation of X-Men, Kitty Pryde has the mutant ability to phase through solid objects like a ghost, as well as disrupt any electrical component with her phasing powers. Kitty and her small pet dragon Lockheed must go to Japan to rescue Lockheed's former girlfriend dragon. Along the way they must take on the ninja clan called the Path as well as face the possible return of an old adversary thought to be dead.

X-Men Icons: Iceman. **Written by Dan Abnett. Illustrated by Karl Kerschl.** Marvel Comics, 2002. 128pp. 0-7851-0889-0. **Y**

The solo adventures of Bobby Drake (Iceman), one of the very first X-Men. Able to convert his entire body into ice, he's one of the most powerful mutants and a carefree member of the X-Men. He travels to Hong Kong, where he meets his ex-girlfriend, who has a surprise for him. Meanwhile, an evil corporation seeks to recruit Iceman to make use of his powers to augment humans into super-beings.

Super-Hero Teams

Although many super-heroes fight crime individually, there are many super-hero teams. A staple in comic books since the formation of the DC Comics' Justice Society of America back in *All-Star Comics #3* in 1940, they have continued to be popular to this day. The teams can be made up of heroes who have common origins, such as the Fantastic Four and X-Men, or be composed of a group of heroes from various origins, such as the Justice League of America and the Avengers. Below are listed a variety of super-hero teams from a wide range of publishers including DC Comics, Marvel Comics, Image Comics, and many more.

The Authority. WildStorm Productions/DC Comics, 2000– . **M**

One of the hardest-hitting super-teams on the planet, the group known as the Authority was founded by 100-year-old seemingly immortal Jenny Sparks from the ashes of her former team called the Stormwatch. Seeking to find a way to protect Earth from global battles as well as enemies from parallel worlds, Jenny recruited Jack Hawksmoor, Shen Li-Min, the Doctor, the Engineer, Apollo, and the Midnighter, as the toughest fighting force ever to take on evil and dole out justice, using the most extreme measures possible.

> *Relentless.* Written by Warren Ellis. Illustrated by Bryan Hitch .2000 192pp. 1-56389-661-3.

© 2006 WildStorm Productions/
DC Comics.

> *Under New Management.* Written by Warren Ellis and Mark Millar. Illustrated by Frank Quitely. 2000. 192pp. 1-56389-756-3.
> *Jenny Sparks: The Secret History of the Authority.* Written by Mark Millar. Illustrated by John McCrea. 2001. 128pp. 1-56389-769-5.
> *Earth Inferno and Other Stories.* Written by Mark Millar. Illustrated by Frank Quitely and Chris Weston. 2002. 192pp. 1-56389-854-3.
> *Transfer of Power.* Written by Mark Millar and Tom Peyer. Illustrated by Frank Quitely. 2002. 192pp. 1-4012-0020-6.
> *Harsh Realities, Vol. 1.* Written by Robbie Morrison. Illustrated by Dwayne Turner. 2004. 160pp. 1-4012-0278-0.
> *Human on the Inside.* Written by John Ridley. Illustrated by Ben Oliver. 2004. 96pp. 1-4012-0070-2, hardcover; 1-4012-0069-9, softcover.

> *Fractured Worlds.* Written by Robbie Morrison. Illustrated by Dwayne Turner. 2004. 192pp. 1-4012-0300-0.
> *The Kev.* Written by Garth Ennis. Illustrated by Glenn Fabry. 2005. 144pp. 1-4012-0614-X.
> *Revolution—Book One.* Written by Ed Brubaker. Illustrated by Dustin Nguyen. 2005. 144pp. 1-4012-0623-9.
> *Revolution—Book Two.* Written by Ed Brubaker. Illustrated by Dustin Nguyen. 2006. 144pp. 1-4012-0947-5.

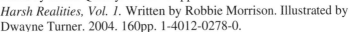

The Avengers. Created by Stan Lee and Jack Kirby. Marvel Comics, 1992– . 🖥 🦇

The Avengers are one of Marvel Comics' best-known super-hero teams and first appeared in *The Avengers* #1 in 1963. Over the last forty-plus years the team has consisted of some of the best-known and most popular super-heroes from Marvel Comics, including Captain America, Thor, Iron Man, The Wasp, Giant-Man, Vision, Hawkeye, Wonder Man, and others. Working with the full support of the U.S. government, they're one of the best fighting forces America has against common foes, including Ultron, Morgan Le Fay, Kang, and other forces of evil. Following are highlights of Avengers titles over the last several decades, recently published collections, and miscellaneous recommended titles.

The Avengers (1st series). Marvel Comics, 1990– . **Y**

Following are classic Avengers collections from the Avengers monthly comic book series, various miniseries stories, and occasional graphic novels. The stories run the gamut from their first appearance in 1963 to popular stories from the 1980s and early 1990s, and are listed by release date of the collection, then by title if applicable.

> *Emperor Doom.* Written by David Michelinie. Illustrated by Bob Hall. 1990. 64pp. 0-87135-256-7.
> *The Kree-Skrull War.* Written by Roy Thomas. Illustrated by Neal Adams. 2000. 208pp. 0-7851-0745-2.
> *The Serpent Crown.* Written by Steve Englehart. Illustrated by George Pérez. 2005. 136pp. 0-7851-1700-8.
> *Vision and the Scarlet Witch.* Written by Steve Englehart and Bill Mantlo. Illustrated by Don Heck and Rick Leonardi. 2005. 128pp. 0-7851-1770-9.
> *Avengers West Coast: Vision Quest.* Written and illustrated by John Byrne. 2005. 216pp. 0-7851-1774-1.
> *Kang Time and Time Again.* Written by Stan Lee and various. Illustrated by Jack Kirby and various. 2005. 176pp. 0-7851-1820-9.

Essential Avengers. **Written by Stan Lee and various. Illustrated by Jack Kirby and various.** Marvel Comics, 2000– . **Y**

Collects the earliest issues of the Avengers in an inexpensive black-and-white format in phone book-sized collections.

> *Vol. 1.* 2005. 536pp. 0-7851-1862-4.
> *Vol. 2.* 2000. 528pp. 0-7851-0741-X.
> *Vol. 3.* 2001. 528pp. 0-7851-0772-X.
> *Vol. 4.* 2004. 640pp. 0-7851-1485-8.
> *Vol. 5.* 2006. 600pp. 0-7851-2087-4.

The Avengers (2d series). Marvel Comics, 2000– . **Y**

Beginning with a relaunch of the series by acclaimed writer Kurt Busiek and artist George Pérez in 1997, the Avengers once again received critical praise. The series was published through 2005. The entire comic book series was collected, and the trade collections are listed below. Story line highlights include *The Morgan Conquest,* in which the villainous Morgan Le Fay has transformed Earth into a medieval state and there are alternative takes on the Avengers team and *Ultron Unlimited,* the penultimate tale of the Avengers and their sentient robot, Ultron. Currently the series has been relaunched as The New Avengers following the events in the *Avengers: Disassembled* story line listed below. Note that *Avengers Assemble* titles collect the Kurt Busiek and George Pérez stories in a beautiful hardcover format.

© 2006 Marvel Comics.

Avengers: Heroes Return. Written by Kurt Busiek. Illustrated by George Pérez. 2000. 112pp. 0-7851-0728-2.

The Morgan Conquest. Written by Kurt Busiek. Illustrated by George Pérez. 2000. 112pp. 0-7851-0728-2. ◉

Ultron Unlimited. Written by Kurt Busiek. Illustrated by George Pérez. 2001. 96pp. 0-7851-0774-6. ◉

Supreme Justice. Written by Kurt Busiek. Illustrated by George Pérez. 2001. 176pp. 0-7851-0773-8.

Clear and Present Dangers. Written by Kurt Busiek. Illustrated by George Pérez. 2001. 208pp. 0-7851-0798-3.

The Kang Dynasty. Written by Kurt Busiek. Illustrated by Alan Davis and Kieron Dwyer. 2004. 384pp. 0-7851-0958-7.

Living Legends. Written by Kurt Busiek. Illustrated by George Pérez and Stuart Immonen. 2004. 208pp. 0-7851-1561-7.

World Trust. Written by Geoff Johns. Illustrated by Kieron Dwyer. 2003. 152pp. 0-7851-1080-1.

Red Zone. Written by Geoff Johns. Illustrated by Olivier Coipol. 2004. 160pp. 0-7851-1099-2.

Search for She-Hulk. Written by Geoff Johns. Illustrated by Scott Kolins. 2004. 136pp. 0-7851-1202-2.

Avengers Assemble, Vol. 1. Written by Kurt Busiek. Illustrated by George Pérez and Stuart Immonen. 2005. 232pp. 0-7851-1845-4, hardcover. ◉

Avengers Assemble, Vol. 2. Written by Kurt Busiek. Illustrated by Jerry Ordway, John Francis Moore, George Pérez, Stewart Immonen, and Leonardo Manco. 2005. 336pp. 0-7851-1773-3, hardcover.

Avengers Assemble, Vol. 3. Written by Kurt Busiek. Illustrated by various. 2006. 432pp. 0-7851-2130-7, hardcover.

Avengers Assemble, Vol. 4. Written by Kurt Busiek. Illustrated by various. 2007. 416pp. 0-7851-2347-4, hardcover.

Avengers Disassembled. 2004–2005. T

A deconstruction of the Avengers by writer Brian Michael Bendis. As several Avenger heroes are killed in battle and their mansion is destroyed, the heroes discover that the true culprit behind all the terrible occurrences is one of their own members, the Scarlet Witch. She has now grown unstable with her mutant hex powers, and the remaining Avengers must try to take her down before more disasters befall the team. The series crossed over into the monthly comic book series of longtime Avengers including Thor, Captain America, and Iron Man. Other super-hero books also tied into the series are Spider-Man and the Fantastic Four; they are listed in their own sections in this chapter.

Avengers Disassembled: Thor. Written by Michael Avon Oeming. Illustrated by Andrea Divito. 2004. 152pp. 0-7851-1599-4.

Avengers Disassembled: Iron Man. Written by Mark Ricketts. Illustrated by Tony Harris. 2004. 144pp. 0-7851-1653-2.

Avengers Disassembled: Captain America. Written by Robert Kirkman. Illustrated by Scot Eaton. 2004. 168pp. 0-7851-1648-6.

Avengers Disassembled. Written by Brian Michael Bendis. Illustrated by David Finch. 2005. 128pp. 0-7851-1482-3, softcover; 2007. 184pp. 0-7851-2294-x, hardcover.

New Avengers. Written by Brian Michael Bendis. Illustrated by David Finch. 2005– . **T** ◎

After the fallout from the <u>Avengers: Disassembled</u> story line, a new Avengers team is formed and now includes veterans Captain America and Iron Man, joined by Spider-Man, Luke Cage, Spider-Woman, Wolverine, Sentry, and a new mysterious hero called Ronin.

> *Vol. 1: Breakout.* 2005. 160pp. 0-7851-1814-4, hardcover.
> *Vol. 2: Sentry.* 2006. 176pp. 0-7851-1924-8, hardcover.
> *Vol. 3: Secrets and Lies.* 2006. 128pp. 0-7851-1939-6, hardcover.
> *Vol. 4: The Collective.* 2006. 128pp. 0-7851-1986-8, hardcover.

Avengers Miniseries Collections

Listed below are several recommended self-contained stories featuring the super-hero team called the Avengers.

***Avengers: Earth's Mightiest Heroes.* Written by Joe Casey. Illustrated by Scott Kolins.** 2005. 192pp. 0-7851-1438-6. **Y**

A look back at the earliest days of the Avengers, when the team was created and each of the heroes, including Captain America, Iron Man, the Hulk, and Hawkeye, are trying to find their place on the team as well as with themselves.

***Avengers Forever.* Written by Kurt Busiek. Illustrated by Carlos Pacheco.** 2001. 264pp. 0-7851-0756-8. **Y** ◎

With the fate of longtime Avengers friend Rick Jones on the line, Avengers from different timelines converge to take on the threat from Immortus, the Lord of Time.

***The Last Avengers Story.* Written by Peter David. Illustrated by Ariel Olivetti.** 1996. 96pp. 0-7851-0218-3. **Y** ◎

A look far into the possible future of Marvel's favorite super-hero team. The future version of Ultron seeks to take out his "father," Henry Pym, and the aging super-heroes. As heroes and villains die, the final fate of the Avengers is revealed.

Birds of Prey. DC Comics, 1999–2005. **T**

Batman's not the only hero of Gotham City. After being paralyzed from the waist down by the Joker, Barbara Gordon retired as Batgirl and became the information cyber-broker Oracle. Joined by her longtime hero and friend, Black Canary (Dinah Lance), and most recently the Huntress (Helena Bertinelli), she's out to make Gotham City and the world safe from evil. *Volume 1* collection received recognition from YALSA's Popular Paperbacks for Young Adults committee in 2002.

> 🌷 *Vol. 1.* Written by Chuck Dixon. Illustrated by Gary Frank and various. 1999. 208pp. 1-56389-484-X.
> *Vol. 2: Old Friends, New Enemies.* Written by Chuck Dixon and Jordan Gorfinkel. Illustrated by various. 2003. 216pp. 1-56389-939-6.

Vol. 3: Of Like Minds. Written by Gail Simone. Illustrated by Ed Benes. 2004. 138pp. 1-4012-0192-X.

Vol. 4: Sensei and Student. Written by Gail Simone. Illustrated by Ed Benes and various. 2005. 168pp. 1-4012-0434-1.

Fantastic Four. Created by Stan Lee and Jack Kirby. Marvel Comics, 1992– .

Created in 1961 by Stan Lee and Jack Kirby, the Fantastic Four are one of the first Marvel Comics science heroes. An experimental flight into outer space is bombarded by cosmic rays. Reed Richards, genius scientist and the leader of the four-person crew, knew there would be risks involved in the flight. But when the crew crashes safely back to Earth, they find that each of them has been transformed by the cosmic rays into something a little more than human. Reed Richards discovers that he now has the ability to stretch his skin into any shape and calls himself "Mr. Fantastic." Reed's girlfriend, Susan Storm, finds that she can become invisible and can project invisible force bubbles and calls herself the "Invisible Girl." Her younger brother, the hot-headed Johnny Storm, now controls the power of fire and calls himself the "Human Torch." And Ben Grimm, the pilot of the crew, has gained super strength as well as a thick, rocklike skin and aptly calls himself "The Thing." Together the superpowered family use their unique gifts to explore the unknown and to protect New York City, Earth, and beyond from the forces of evil, including Reed's arch-nemesis, the metal-armored villainous dictator of the country of Latveria, Doctor Doom, the world-eating devourer Galactus, and many more. Below are listed highlights of the Fantastic Four's collected comic book adventures since the late 1980s. The classic tales are listed first, then the modern tales, followed by miscellaneous.

Essential Fantastic Four. Written by Stan Lee. Illustrated by Jack Kirby. Marvel Comics, 1999– . **Y**

Black-and-white reprints of the original *Fantastic Four* comic book stories in an affordable format.

> *Vol. 1.* 2005. 528pp. 0-7851-0666-9.
> *Vol. 2.* 1999. 528pp. 0-7851-0731-2.
> *Vol. 3.* 2001. 528pp. 0-7851-0782-7.
> *Vol. 4.* 2005. 536pp. 0-7851-1484-X.
> *Vol. 5.* 2006. 568pp. 0-7851-2162-5.

Fantastic Four Visionaries: John Byrne. Written and illustrated by John Byrne. Marvel Comics, 2001– . **Y**

Collects the highly popular run by writer/illustrator John Byrne that was originally published from 1981 through 1986 and included the trial of Galactus, the loss of Reed and Sue's second child, the introduction of the She-Hulk as a Fantastic Four team member, and a classic battle between Galactus's former heralds Terrax and the Silver Surfer that was manipulated by Doctor Doom.

> *Vol. 1.* 2001. 224pp. 0-7851-0779-7.
> *Vol. 2.* 2004. 248pp. 0-7851-1464-5.

> *Vol. 3.* 2005. 248pp. 0-7851-1679-6.
> *Vol. 4.* 2005. 280pp. 0-7851-1710-5.
> *Vol. 5.* 2005. 248pp. 0-7851-1844-6.

***Fantastic Four: Monsters Unleashed.* Written by Walter Simonson. Illustrated by Arthur Adams.** Marvel Comics, 1992. 80pp. 0-87135-877-8. **T** ◉

When the original Fantastic Four team has gone missing, a new team, made up of Wolverine, Ghost Rider, the Hulk, and Spider-Man, try to rescue them.

***Fantastic Four Visionaries: Jim Lee.* Written and illustrated by Jim Lee.** Marvel Comics, 2005. 160pp. 0-7851-1635-4. **Y**

Fan-favorite artist Jim Lee's 1990s take at reimagining the Fantastic Four.

Fantastic Four. Marvel Comics, 2003– . **Y** ◉

Listed below are the currently published Fantastic Four titles that were originally published as comic books. The collections feature the well-received run by Mark Waid and Mike Wieringo as well as the recently collected stories written by J. Michael Straczynski.

© 2006 Marvel Comics.

Vol. 1: Imaginauts. Written by Mark Waid. Illustrated by Mike Wieringo. 2003. 192pp. 0-7851-1063-1.

Vol. 2: Unthinkable. Written by Mark Waid. Illustrated by Mike Wieringo. 2003. 192pp. 0-7851-1111-5.

Vol. 3: Authoritative Action. Written by Mark Waid. Illustrated by Mike Wieringo. 2004. 136pp. 0-7851-1198-0.

Vol. 4: Hereafter. Written by Mark Waid. Illustrated by Mike Wieringo. 2004. 120pp. 0-7851-1526-9.

Vol. 5: Disassembled. Written by Mark Waid. Illustrated by Mike Wieringo. 2005. 136pp. 0-7851-1536-6.

Vol. 6: Rising Storm. Written by Mark Waid. Illustrated by Mike Wieringo and Howard Porter. 2005. 120pp. 0-7851-1598-6.

Vol. 1. Written by Mark Waid. Illustrated by Mike Wieringo. 2004. 368pp. 0-7851-1486-6, hardcover.

Vol. 2. Written by Mark Waid. Illustrated by Mike Wieringo and Howard Porter. 2005. 264pp. 0-7851-1775-X, hardcover.

Vol. 3. Written by Mark Waid. Illustrated by Mike Wieringo. 2005. 256pp. 0785120114, hardcover.

Vol. 1: Premiere. Written by J. Michael Straczynski. Illustrated by Mike McKone. 2005. 144pp. 0-7851-2029-7, hardcover.

***Best of the Fantastic Four.* Written and illustrated by various.** Marvel Comics, 2005. 360pp. 0-7851-1782-2. hardcover. **Y**

A collection highlighting some of the best stories from the Fantastic Four covering four decades. Includes *Fantastic Four* #1, ##39–40, #51, #100, #116, #176, #236, #267; *Fantastic Four* (Vol. 3) #56 and #60; *Marvel Fanfare* #15; *Marvel Two-In-One* #50; and *Marvel Knights 4* #4.

***Fantastic Four: Foes.* Written by Robert Kirkman. Illustrated by Cliff Rathburn.** Marvel Comics, 2005. 144pp. 0-7851-1662-1. **Y**

A unique look at the Fantastic Four from the perspective of their greatest foes.

Fantastic Four: Unstable Molecules. **Written by James Sturm. Illustrated by Guy Davis and Bob Sikoryak.** Marvel Comics, 2005. 128pp. 0-7851-1112-3. **T**

A unique premise featuring the "true" story of the people who inspired Stan Lee and Jack Kirby to create the comic book characters known as the Fantastic Four. Set in the 1950s, it's the story of Susan Sturm, her bitter younger brother Johnny, Susan's aloof boyfriend scientist Reed Richards, and Benjamin Grimm. The short story won an Eisner Award in 2004 for Best Finite Series/Limited Series.

The Thing: Idol of Millions. **Written by Dan Slott. Illustrated by Andrea DiVito.** Marvel Comics, 2006. 144pp. 0-7851-1813-6. **Y**

Featuring the adventures of the beloved Fantastic Four rocky bruiser enjoying life as a billionaire. Thanks to Reed Richards investing Ben's money, he finds out that he's now become super rich. Will Ben trade in Yancy Street for Park Avenue?

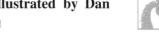

Fantastic Four: The Movie. **Written by Mike Carey. Illustrated by Dan Jurgens.** Marvel Comics, 2005. 120pp. 0-7851-1809-8. **Y** 🎬

An adaptation of the summer 2005 movie featuring Michael Chiklis as the Thing.

Marvel Age/Marvel Adventures: Fantastic Four. Written by Sean McKeever, Marc Sumerak, and Jeff Parker. Illustrated by Udon and Carlo Pagulayan. Marvel Age and Marvel Adventures/Marvel Comics, 2004– . **A**

A reinterpretation of the classic Stan Lee/Jack Kirby Fantastic Four series as well as a series featuring the Fantastic Four's Benjamin Grimm (a.k.a. The Thing). All the stories have been rewritten for a younger audience. The series was originally titled Marvel Age: Fantastic Four, but was renamed and relaunched as Marvel Adventures: Fantastic Four. A spin-off series featuring Fantastic Four member Ben Grimm was also released in 2005 and is listed below.

Marvel Age: Fantastic Four. 2004–2005.
    Vol. 1: All For One. 2004. 96pp. 0-7851-1468-8.
    Vol. 2: Doom. 2004. 96pp. 0-7851-1550-1.
    Vol. 3: The Return of Doom. 2005. 96pp. 0-7851-1622-2.
Marvel Adventures Fantastic Four. 2006– .
    Vol. 1: Family of Heroes. 2006. 96pp. 0-7851-1858-6.
    Vol. 2: Fantastic Voyages. 2006. 96pp. 0-7851-1859-4.
    Vol. 3: World's Greatest. 2006. 96pp. 0-7851-2002–5.
Marvel Adventures: The Thing. 2005.
    Vol. 1: Clobberin' Time. 2005. 96pp. 0-7851-1738-5.

Ultimate Fantastic Four. Marvel Comics, 2004– . **T** ◉

© 2006 Marvel Comics.

An updated retelling of the team of heroes known as the Fantastic Four, set in the Ultimate Universe. Join Reed Richards, Susan Storm, Johnny Storm, and Benjamin Grimm as they set out to explore the stars and come back literally changed by the experience, with strange new powers. Together the science adventurers become the Fantastic Four and find an enemy in the mad aristocratic scientist Victor Van Damme, a.k.a. Doctor Doom; the Mole Man; and the Atlantean ruler called Namor. The hardcover collections, listed below, reprint several of the softcover editions in one volume.

Vol. 1: The Fantastic. Written by Brian Michael Bendis and Mark Millar. Illustrated by Adam Kubert. 2004. 144pp. 0-7851-1393-2.

Vol. 2: Doom. Written by Warren Ellis. Illustrated by Stuart Immonen. 2004. 144pp. 0-7851-1457-2.

Vol. 3: The N-Zone. Written by Warren Ellis. Illustrated by Andy Kubert. 2005. 144pp. 0-7851-1495-5.

Vol. 4: Inhuman. Written by Mike Carey. Illustrated by Jae Lee. 2005. 96pp. 0-7851-1667-2.

Vol. 5: Crossover. Written by Mark Millar. Illustrated by Greg Land. 2006. 144pp. 0-7851-1802-0.

Vol. 6: Frightful. Written by Mark Millar. Illustrated by Greg Land. 2006. 144pp. 0-7851-2017-3.

Vol. 1. Written by Brian Michael Bendis, Mark Millar, and Warren Ellis. Illustrated by Adam Kubert and Stuart Immonen. 2005. 320pp. 0-7851-1458-0, hardcover.

Vol. 2. Written by Warren Ellis and Mike Carey. Illustrated by Andy Kubert and Jae Lee. 2006. 240pp. 0-7851-2058-0, hardcover.

The Foot Soldiers. Written by Jim Krueger. Illustrated by Michael Avon Oeming, Phil Hester, and Bill Sienkiewicz. AiT/Planet Lar, 2001–2002. **T**

In a fallen society where the heroes are dead and the people are illiterate, a small band of superpowered teenage fighters have risen up and have taken over as the next generation of heroes. Story, one of the young heroes, has faked his illiteracy, and it just might be that he holds a secret that may one day help save the planet. An inspirational tale of hope for humanity in a post-apocalyptic world, the series also pays tribute to the characters of the Silver Age of comic books.

Vol. 1. 2001. 156pp. 0-9676847-7-3.
Vol. 2. 2001. 156pp. 0-9709360-1-X.
Vol. 3. 2002. 144pp. 1-932051-03-1.

Justice League of America (JLA). DC Comics, 1996–2006. ▭ 🎮

The greatest heroes of the DC Comics universe—Superman, Batman, Wonder Woman, Martian Manhunter, Green Lantern, Flash, and Aquaman—are also part of the greatest super-hero team. Joined by a rotating cast of teammates, including Plastic

Man, Orion, Green Arrow, Zauriel, Huntress, Oracle, and Steel, they're a dedicated force out to fight for truth and justice whenever Earth is threatened. See chapter 6 for titles featuring a more humorous take on the heroic Justice League. Following are listed the collected graphic novel editions of the extremely popular monthly comic book series as well as a variety of graphic novel stories and miniseries featuring the heroes.

JLA (Justice League of America). DC Comics, 1996–2006. **Y**

Published in comic book form from 1996 to 2006, the collection reprints the monthly serialized comic book titled *JLA* and features the writings of Grant Morrison, Mark Waid, and Kurt Busiek. The series ended in 2006 but was recently relaunched in serial form as the nonabbreviated Justice League of America, written by Brad Meltzer and illustrated by Ed Benes. *Tower of Babel* received recognition by YALSA's Quick Picks for Reluctant Readers committee in 2003.

© 2006 DC Comics.

Justice League: A Midsummer's Nightmare. Written by Mark Waid and Fabian Nicieza. Illustrated by various. 1996. 116pp. 1-56389-338-X.

Vol. 1: New World Order. Written by Grant Morrison. Illustrated by Howard Porter. 1997. 96pp. 1-56389-369-X.

Vol. 2: American Dreams. Written by Grant Morrison. Illustrated by Howard Porter. 1998. 112pp. 1-56389-394-0.

Vol. 3: Rock of Ages. Written by Grant Morrison. Illustrated by Howard Porter. 1998. 160pp. 1-56389-416-5.

Vol. 4: Strength in Numbers. Written by Grant Morrison and Mark Waid. Illustrated by Howard Porter and Christopher Priest. 1998. 224pp. 1-56389-435-1.

Vol. 5: Justice for All. Written by Grant Morrison. Illustrated by Howard Porter. 1999. 192pp. 1-56389-511-0.

Vol. 6: World War III. Written by Grant Morrison. Illustrated by Howard Porter and various. 2000. 208pp. 1-56389-618-4.

Vol. 7: Tower of Babel. Written by Mark Waid. Illustrated by Howard Porter and various. 2001. 160pp. 1-56389-727-X.

Vol. 8: Divided We Fall. Written by Mark Waid. Illustrated by Bryan Hitch and various. 2002. 208pp. 1-56389-793-8.

Vol. 9: Terror Incognita. Written by Mark Waid. Illustrated by Bryan Hitch and various. 2002. 144pp. 1-56389-936-1.

Vol. 10: Golden Perfect. Written by Joe Kelly. Illustrated by Doug Mahnke and Tom Nguyen. 2003. 128pp. 1-56389-941-8.

Vol. 11: Obsidian Age, Book I. Written by Joe Kelly. Illustrated by Doug Mahnke and Tom Nguyen. 2003. 160pp. 1-56389-991-4.

Vol. 12: Obsidian Age, Book II. Written by Joe Kelly. Illustrated by Doug Mahnke and Tom Nguyen. 2003. 160pp. 1-4012-0043-5.

Vol. 13: Rules of Engagement. Written by Joe Kelly. Illustrated by Doug Mahnke and Tom Nguyen. 2004. 144pp. 1-4012-0215-2.

Vol. 14: Trial By Fire. Written by Joe Kelly. Illustrated by Doug Mahnke and Tom Nguyen. 2004. 144pp. 1-4012-0242-X.

Vol. 15: The 10th Circle. Written by Chris Claremont. Illustrated by John Byrne. 2004. 144pp. 1-4012-0346-9.

Vol. 16: Pain of the Gods. Written by Chuck Austen. Illustrated by Ron Garney. 2005. 144pp. 1-4012-0468-6.

Vol. 17: Syndicate Rules. Written by Kurt Busiek. Illustrated by Ron Garney. 2005. 200pp. 1-4012-0477-5.

Vol. 18: Crisis of Conscience. Written by Geoff Johns and Allan Heinberg. Illustrated by Chris Batista and Mark Farmer. 2006. 128pp. 1-4012-0963-7.

Vol. 19: World Without a Justice League. Written by Bob Harris. Illustrated by Tom Derenick. 2006. 144pp. 1-4012-0964-5.

Vol. 20: Mixed Signals. Written by Geoff Johns and Keith Champagne. Illustrated by Don Kramer, Dale Eaglesham, and various. 2006. 144pp. 1-4012-0967-x.

🐝 *JLA: Earth 2.* **Written by Grant Morrison. Illustrated by Frank Quitely.** DC Comics, 2000. 96pp. 1-56389-631-1. **T** ◎

Alex Luthor is the only hero alive on an alternate version of Earth. The planet is ruled by a merciless group of villains called the Injustice Gang, mirror-universe versions of the Justice League of America. Comprising Ultraman, Superwoman, Owlman, Power Ring, and Johnny Quick, they run a hellish utopian society where their power controls all. After traveling to "Earth 2" (our Earth) to recruit the JLA, Lex has a plan to go back to his world and, with the aid of the JLA, defeat the Injustice Gang and save the planet. As the heroes face off against bizarre mirror images of themselves, the fate of both planets is at stake when the chain of events that brought them there just might be their undoing. The collection received recognition from YALSA's Quick Picks for Reluctant Readers committee in 2001.

JLA: Heaven's Ladder. **Written by Mark Waid. Illustrated by Bryan Hitch and Paul Neary.** DC Comics, 2000. 72pp. 1-56389-753-9. **Y**

The JLA must save Earth and countless other planets when a godlike race has captured it and other planets in a massive alien craft.

JLA: A League of One. **Written and illustrated by Chris Moeller.** DC Comics, 2002. 112pp. 1-56389-923-X. **Y** ◎

Wonder Woman, after hearing a prophecy that the JLA are to die at the hands of an ancient dragon, defeats all of her comrades and then vows to defeat the golden dragon by herself, even if it costs her life.

JLA: Liberty and Justice. **Written by Paul Dini. Illustrated by Alex Ross.** DC Comics, 2003. 96pp. 1-56389-911-6. **Y** ◎

The fully painted adventures of the JLA as they tackle a deadly space virus that is creating mass panic and hysteria around the world. Can the JLA defeat this alien danger, and what connection does it have to the League?

JLA: Year One. **Written by Mark Waid. Illustrated by Barry Kitson.** DC Comics, 1999. 312pp. 1-56389-512-9. **Y** ◎

A look at the origins of the Justice League of America, when The Flash, Green Lantern, Martian Manhunter, Black Canary, and Aquaman first teamed up together. Joined by new members Superman and Batman, they're a fighting force fast on their way to being the best team ever.

Justice. Written by Jim Krueger and Alex Ross. Illustrated by Doug Braithwaite and Alex Ross. 2006– . **Y**

Collecting the first four issues of a planned twelve-volume maxiseries. The Justice League discovers that they're not the only ones well organized. A league of the greatest villains has set a plan in motion that may achieve more good than the JLA could ever accomplish. Can the heroes actually trust the criminal masterminds, and is their plan really that benevolent, or is there a hidden agenda to their reform?

Vol. 1. 2006. 160pp. 1-4012-0969-6, hardcover.

Justice League Cartoon Show Tie-ins. Written and illustrated by various. DC Comics, 2004–2006.

These are based on the hit Cartoon Network animated show, *Justice League,* which aired on the Cartoon Network from 2001 to 2004 and *Justice League Unlimited,* which aired from 2004 to 2006. When the world finds itself in jeopardy, only a group of the world's best heroes—Batman, Superman, Green Lantern, The Flash, Wonder Woman, Hawkwoman, and the Martian Manhunter—can save the day. The Justice League Unlimited collections are based on the latest release of the show featuring a wide range of DC Comics characters outside the typically featured JLA members. The stories are a little more simplified than the ongoing Justice League of America series, and the artwork is reminiscent of the style of the cartoon show.

Justice League Adventures. 2004. **A**

Vol. 1: The Magnificent Seven. 2004. 112pp. 1-4012-0179-2.
Vol. 2: Friends and Foes. 2004. 112pp. 1-4012-0180-6.

Justice League Unlimited. 2005–2006. **A**

Vol. 1: United They Stand. 2005. 104pp. 1-4012-0512-7.
Vol. 2: World's Greatest Heroes. 2006. 104pp. 1-4012-1014-7.
Vol. 3: Champions of Justice. 2006. 104pp. 1-4012-1015-5.

Justice Society of America (JSA). DC Comics, 2000– . **Y** ◎

Before the JLA, the first super-hero team was the Justice Society of America. Created by. DC Comics in 1940 in the pages of *All-Star Comics #3*, the JSA's original members included the Flash, Green Lantern, Dr. Fate, the Atom, Black Canary, Hawkman, the Sandman, Starman, and others. Fast-forward sixty years, and the JSA is still as popular as ever. Featuring a mix of original founding members as well as the newest generation of classic JSA members, they're still out fighting evil in the name of Justice.

Justice Be Done. Written by James Robinson and David S. Goyer. Illustrated by Scott Benefiel, Stephen Sadowski, Derec Aucoin and various. 2000. 144pp. 1-56389-620-6.
Vol. 1: Darkness Falls. Written by Geoff Johns and David Goyer. Illustrated by Stephen Sadowski, Michael Bair and various. 2001. 232pp. 1-56389-739-3.

© 2006 DC Comics.

Vol. 2: Return of Hawkman. Written by Geoff Johns and David Goyer. Illustrated by Stephen Sadowski. 2002. 256pp. 1-56389-912-4.

Vol. 3: Fair Play. Written by Geoff Johns and David Goyer. Illustrated by Peter Snejbjerg and Rags Morales. 2003. 176pp. 1-56389-959-0.

Vol. 4: Stealing Thunder. Written by Geoff Johns and David Goyer. Illustrated by Leonard Kirk. 2003. 176pp. 1-56389-994-9.

Vol. 5: All Stars. Written by Geoff Johns and David Goyer. Illustrated by Sal Velluto, Bob Almond, and various. 2004. 192pp. 1-4012-0219-5.

Vol. 6: Savage Times. Written by Geoff Johns and David Goyer. Illustrated by Leonard Kirk, Patrick Gleason, and various. 2004. 168pp. 1-4012-0253-5.

Vol. 7: Prince of Darkness. Written by Geoff Johns and David Goyer. Illustrated by Leonard Kirk, Don Kramer, Sal Velluto, and various. 2005. 256pp. 1-4012-0469-4.

Vol. 8: Black Reign. Written by Geoff Johns. Illustrated by Don Kramer, Keith Champagne, Rags Morales, and Michael Blair. 2005. 144pp. 1-4012-0480-5.

Vol. 9: Lost. Written by Geoff Johns. Illustrated by Dave Gibbons, Jerry Ordway, Sean Phillips, and various. 2005. 208pp. 1-4012-0722-7.

Vol. 10: Black Vengeance. Written by Geoff Johns. Illustrated by Don Kramer. 2006. 208pp. 1-4012-0966-1.

Vol. 11. Written by Geoff Johns. Illustrated by various. 2006. 128pp. 1-4012-0967-X.

League of Extraordinary Gentlemen. Written by Alan Moore. Illustrated by Kevin O'Neill. America's Best Comics/WildStorm Productions/DC Comics, 2001–2005. **M** ◎ 🎞

© 2006 America's Best Comics.

Set at the dawn of the twentieth century, when grave danger arises from those who wish to threaten England, a team made up of some of the most extraordinary individuals is there. Called the League of Extraordinary Gentlemen, the team is composed of the heroes and oddities from some of English literature's finest Victorian-age fiction: Mina Murphy, the Invisible Man, Alan Quartermain, Dr. Jekyll/Mr. Hyde, and Captain Nemo. Together the misfit team of beasts, oddities, and drug abusers must use their talents to save England from its most deadly enemies both on Earth and in outer space. The *Absolute Edition* volumes of the series are slipcased collections of each volume including the entire scripts as well as a sketchbook by Kevin O'Neill in a separate volume included with each. Beginning in 2006 the next volume in this highly regarded series will be published by Top Shelf Productions. The series has won multiple awards, including Eisner Awards for Best Writer (2000–2001, 2004), Best Artist/Penciller/Inker (2003), and Best Finite/Limited Series (2003). The series has also won Harvey Awards for Best Writer (2000), Best Continuing or Limited Series (2003–2004), and Best Single Issue or Limited Series (2003). The graphic novel was also adapted into a dreadful motion picture in 2004 that many comic book fans have tried to forget.

Volume 1. 2001. 176pp. 1-56389-665-6, hardcover; 2002, 1-56389-858-6, softcover.
Volume 2. 2003. 228pp. 1-4012-0117-2, hardcover; 2004, 1-4012-0118-0, softcover.
Absolute Edition, Vol. 1. 2003. 416pp. 1-40120-052-4, slipcased hardcover.
Absolute Edition, Vol. 2. 2005. 448pp. 1-40120-611-5, slipcased hardcover.

The Legion of Super-Heroes. DC Comics, 1991–2006. **Y**

The adventures of a team of super-heroes in the thirtieth century. Since their first appearance in 1958, they have remained popular with a steady fan base for almost fifty years. After saving the life of the wealthiest man on the planet, the team is made up of three teen heroes from Earth, other planets, and beyond: Saturn Girl, Cosmic Boy, and Live Wire. The Legion of Super-Heroes patrols the galaxy, protecting against threats to the United Planets.

> *The Great Darkness Saga.* Written by Paul Levitz. Illustrated by Keith Giffen and various. 1991. 176pp. 0-930289-43-9.
> *The Beginning of Tomorrow.* Written by Mark Waid. Illustrated by Tom McCraw. 1999. 240pp. 1-56389-515-3.
> *The Legion: Foundations.* Written by Dan Abnett and Andy Lanning. Illustrated by Dave Cockrum and various. 2004. 176pp. 1-4012-0338-8.
> *Teenage Revolution.* Written by Mark Waid. Illustrated by Barry Kitson. 2005. 200pp. 1-4012-0482-1.
> *Death of a Dream.* Written by Mark Waid. Illustrated by Barry Kitson. 2006. 200pp. 1-4012-0971-8.
> *Supergirl and the Legion of Super-Heroes.* Written by Mark Waid. Illustrated by various. 2006. 144pp. 1-4012-0916-5.

Less Than Heroes. **Written and illustrated by David Yurkovich.** Top Shelf Productions. 2004. 150pp. 1-891830-51-1. **T**

They're not in the super-hero union. Sure, they have powers, but they're not really that powerful. They're a super group more interested in snack foods and cookies than in tackling super-villains. Meet Cosmopolitan, Meridian, Mr. Malevolence, and Recoil, Philadelphia's "finest" super-heroes. Called Threshold, they're Philadelphia's finest non-union contracted heroes, ready to save the day when the law isn't enough. If only there were any decent super-villains attacking the rather peaceful city! Lucky for them, work is picking up, and soon they find themselves on the trail of a mysterious electrical man from outer space and a new villain called The Stamp.

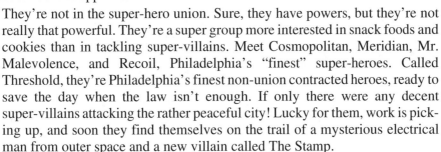

Noble Causes. **Written by Jay Faeber. Illustrated by Patrick Gleason and various.** Image Comics, 2003– . **T**

Life turns from ordinary to extraordinary when Georgetown bookstore owner Liz Donnelly gets engaged to Race Noble, the handsome super-hero speedster from the famous Noble family. Most of Race's superpowered family and friends take a liking to Liz, but as she finds out, nothing is peaceful and calm with the world's most famous super-heroic family. Following Race's tragic murder on their honeymoon, Liz ends up living with her in-laws. As she soon learns, the facade of an idyllic family is a front for the terrible secrets the family and close friends are keeping, including murder, jealousy, infidelity, unexpected teenage pregnancy, and more. Welcome to the family, Liz.

> *Vol. 1: In Sickness and in Health.* 2003. 144pp. 1-58240-293-0.
> *Vol. 2: Family Secrets.* 2004. 120pp. 1-58240-348-1.
> *Vol. 3: Distant Relatives.* 2005. 120pp. 1-58240-481-X.
> *Vol. 4: Blood and Water.* 2005. 144pp. 1-58240-536-0.
> *Vol. 5: Betrayals.* 2006. 168pp. 1-58240-578-6.
> *Vol. 6: Hidden Agendas.* 2006. 176pp. 1-58240-706-1.

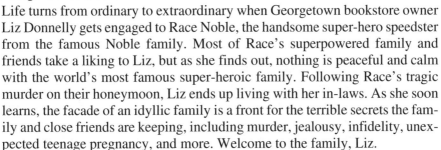

Planetary. **Written by Warren Ellis. Illustrated by John Cassaday.** WildStorm Productions/DC Comics, 2000–2005. **O** ◉

© 2006 WildStorm Productions/
DC Comics.

The adventures of Elijah Snow, a 100-year-old man; Jakita Wagner, a superpowered, bored woman; and The Drummer, a man who has the innate ability to speak with machines. Together they're the Planetary, a group of super-archaeologists out to explore the unexplained mysteries of the world, including an island of giant radioactive monsters, a computer that can access alternate universes, a government compound where humans were treated like guinea pigs in radioactive experiments, and an evil group known as "The Four." Funded by a secret individual known only as the "Fourth Man," they're out to find out the truths that are out there, including their own. The concluding chapters to the series have yet to be published at the time of this writing.

Vol. 1: All Over the World and Other Stories. 2000. 160pp. 1-56389-648-6.
Vol. 2: The Fourth Man. 2001. 144pp. 1-56389-764-4.
Vol. 3: Leaving the 20th Century. 2005. 144pp. 1-4012-0294-2.
Crossing Worlds. 2004. 192pp. 1-4012-0279-9.
Absolute Planetary. 2005. 320pp. 1-4012-0327-2, hardcover.

Power Pack. **Written by Marc Sumerak. Illustrated by GuriHiru.** Marvel Comics, 2005–2006. **A**

The first preteen heroes of the Marvel Comics universe, the team known as Power Pack are actually four siblings from the Powers family: Alex, Julie, Jack, and Katie. The kids were each given a power by a dying alien member of a horselike race called the Kymellians to help combat the evil reptilian alien race called Snarks. Alex received the power of gravity control (code name Gee), Julie received the power of flight (Lightspeed), Jack received the power to control his molecular mass (Mass Master), and Katie received the power to absorb energy and focus it back as an energy ball (Energizer). The first series features a guest appearance by the Fantastic Four; while the second series features a guest appearance by the mutant hero group the X-Men. Other collections featuring guest appearances by Spider-Man and other Marvel Comics heroes with the Power Pack team are forthcoming.

Pack Attack! 2005. 96pp. 0-7851-1736-9.
X-Men and Power Pack: The Power of X. 2006. 96pp. 0-7851-1955-8.
Avengers and Power Pack Assemble!. 2006. 96pp. 0-7851-2155-2.

🎗 **Rising Stars.** **Written by J. Michael Straczynski. Illustrated by Keu Cha and Christian Zanier.** Top Cow Productions/Image Comics, 2001–. **T** ◉

John Simon, also known as Poet, is the last of the Specials, one of 113 people born—or some say cursed—with super-human powers at birth. Sixty years after a mysterious falling star struck the town of Pederson, Illinois, John tells in backstory the true stories behind each of those given the varying powers of flight, invulnerability, pyrokinetic abilities, great strength, and more. Though they appear to be heroes in the public eye, sometimes having super-human powers isn't all it's cracked up to be. And sometimes it's the most wonderful gift of them all. As the years pass and the Specials dwindle in numbers, the true nature of their powers will be revealed, and in the end only the Poet will remain to tell their tales. *Volume 1: Born in Fire* received recognition from YALSA's Popular Paperbacks for Young Adults committee in 2003. *Volume 4* is a continuation of the completed three-volume series written by Straczynski's protégé Fiona Avery, with art by Dan Jurgens.

> *Vol. 1: Born in Fire.* 2001. 192pp. 1-58240-172-1.
> *Vol. 2: Power.* 2002. 192pp. 1-58240-226-4.
> *Vol. 3: Fire and Ash.* 2005. 208pp. 1-58240-491-7.
> *Vol. 4.* 2006. 224pp. 1-58240-613-8.
> *Visitations.* 2002. 64pp. 1-58240-268-X.
> *Rising Stars.* 2005. 624pp. 1-58240-488-7, hardcover.

Runaways. Written by Brian K. Vaughan. Illustrated by Adrian Alphona and Takeshi Miyazawa. Marvel Comics, 2004– . **T**

© 2006 Marvel Comics.

All teenagers think that their parents are evil—but what if they really were? That's what a group of teenagers find out when they accidentally discover that their parents are secretly a group of superpowered villains known as The Pride. When the teens receive the shock of their lives, they must find the courage, strength, and power within themselves to strike out on their own and ultimately confront their parents. The hardcover collection includes *Volumes 1–3* as well as supplemental material including sketches. YALSA's Best Books for Young Adults list featured the hardcover edition in their top ten titles for 2006. *Volume 1: Pride and Joy* was also featured by the Popular Paperbacks for Young Adults committee on their 2006 "Books That Don't Make You Blush, No Dirty Laundry Here" list.

> *Vol. 1: Pride and Joy.* 2004. 144pp. 0-7851-1379-7.
> *Vol. 2: Teenage Wasteland.* 2004. 144pp. 0-7851-1415-7.
> *Vol. 3: The Good Die Young.* 2005. 144pp. 0-7851-1684-2.
> *Vol. 4: True Believers.* 2005. 144pp. 0-7851-1705-9.
> *Vol. 5: Escape to New York.* 2006. 144pp. 0-7851-1901-9.
> *Vol. 6: Parental Guidance.* 2006. 144pp. 0-7851-1952-3.
> *Vol. 1.* 2005. 448pp. 0-7851-1876-4, hardcover.
> *Vol. 2.* 2006. 312pp. 0-7851-2358-x, hardcover.

Sailor Moon. Written by and Illustrated by Naoko Takeuchi. TOKYOPOP, 1998–2001. **Y Japanese manga.** あ

A schoolgirl and her friends turn into a super-hero group called the Sailor Warriors and high school will never be the same again! Klutzy fourteen-year-old junior high school student Usagi Tsukino is recruited by a talking black cat to be a fighter for love and justice against the dark, ever-evil that is reemerging. Usagi also discovers that she is the reincarnation of Princess Serenity, a princess of the ancient moon kingdom and defender against evil. As the protector of the solar system, Usagi calls herself Sailor Moon when in costume. Along the way she meets other reincarnations of female sailor warriors like herself, including Rei Hino (Sailor Mars), Makoto Kino (Sailor Jupiter), Ami Mizuno (Sailor Mercury), and Minako Aino (Sailor Venus), and they work together as a team to defeat evil at all costs. There is one other mysterious savior of Sailor Moon, a dashing young man known as Tuxedo Mask. In reality he is Usagi's boyfriend Mamoru Chiba, and they find they have a lot more in common than they thought: they're both the reincarnations of each other's true love. The manga inspired a hit anime television series, movies, and other spin-offs.

> Sailor Moon. 1998–2001.
>> *Vol. 1*. 1998. 200pp. 1-892213-01-X.
>> *Vol. 2*. 1999. 184pp. 1-892213-05-2.
>> *Vol. 3*. 1999. 184pp. 1-892213-06-0.
>> *Vol. 4*. 1999. 192pp. 1-892213-15-X.
>> *Vol. 5*. 1999. 184pp. 1-892213-20-6.
>> *Vol. 6*. 2000. 192pp. 1-892213-35-4.
>> *Vol. 7*. 2000. 176pp. 1-892213-42-7.
>> *Vol. 8*. 2001. 216pp. 1-892213-47-8.
>> *Vol. 9*. 2001. 190pp. 1-892213-68-0.
>> *Vol. 10*. 2001. 168pp. 1-892213-98-2.
>> *Vol. 11*. 2001. 184pp. 1-892213-99-0.
> Sailor Moon SuperS. 1999–2000.
>> *Vol. 1*. 1999. 184pp. 1-892213-12-5.
>> *Vol. 2*. 1999. 176pp. 1-892213-24-9.
>> *Vol. 3*. 1999. 160pp. 1-892213-26-5.
>> *Vol. 4*. 2000. 168pp. 1-892213-39-7.
> Sailor Moon StarS. 2001.
>> *Vol. 1*. 2001. 184pp. 1-892213-48-6.
>> *Vol. 2*. 2001. 176pp. 1-892213-70-2.
>> *Vol. 3*. 2001. 192pp. 1-892213-97-4.

Stormwatch. **Written by Warren Ellis. Illustrated by Tom Raney, Bryan Hitch, and various.** WildStorm Productions/DC Comics, 1999–2001. **T**

Once a super-hero police force for the United Nations Special Crisis Intervention Team, the Stormwatch was restructured into a strike team that later paved the way for the proactive super-hero squadron called the Authority. Founded by the Weatherman (a.k.a. Henry Bendix), the team members include the neo-human Jack Hawksmoor; the mysteriously homicidal Rose Tattoo; a youthful chain-smoking blonde; Jenny Sparks, the ninety-six-year-old "Spirit of the 20th Century" who controls electrical energy, and others. Stormwatch members are broken into several superpowered strike teams capable of handling all sorts of tough situations, ranging from international crises to terrorist organizations to covert operations to alien invasions. Meanwhile, all may not be well with the Weatherman, and the organization he created may very well be destroyed from within if its enemies don't get to it first. *Volume 1: Force of Nature* received recognition from YALSA's Quick Picks for Reluctant Readers committee in 2001.

> *Vol. 1: Force of Nature*. 2000. 160pp. 1-56389-646-X.
> *Vol. 2: Lightning Strikes*. 2000. 144pp. 1-56389-650-8.
> *Vol. 3: Change or Die*. 1999. 160pp. 1-56389-534-X.
> *Vol. 4: A Finer World*. 1999. 144pp. 1-56389-535-8.
> *Vol. 5: Final Orbit*. 2001. 96pp. 1-56389-788-1.

Teen Titans

Teen Titans. DC Comics, 1991–. **Y**

One of the most popular teen team books in the 1980s alongside Marvel Comics' *X-Men* and the inspiration for the hit anime-inspired cartoon television show on Cartoon Network. A team of young teen heroes, the Teen Titans first appeared in the Silver Age of comics in 1964 and has featured many youth-oriented heroes, including Robin, Starfire, Cyborg, Aqualad, Speedy, Kid Flash, Troia, Beast Boy, Raven, Terra, Wonder Girl, Nightwing, and Superboy. Together they have battled villains over the years, the most popular being the mercenary-for-hire Deathstroke the Terminator. *A Kid's Game* received recognition from YALSA's Quick Picks for Reluctant Readers committee in 2005.

> *New Teen Titans, Archive Editions.* Written by Marv Wolfman. Illustrated by George Pérez. 2004. 240pp. 1-56389-951-5. ◎
>
> *The Judas Contract.* Written by Marv Wolfman. Illustrated by George Pérez. 1991. 192pp. 0-930289-34-X. ◎
>
> *The Terror of Trigon.* Written by Marv Wolfman. Illustrated by George Pérez. 2003. 144pp. 1-56389-944-2.
>
> *A Kid's Game.* Written by Geoff Johns. Illustrated by Mike McKone, Tom Grummett, and various. 2004. 192pp. 1-4012-0308-6.
>
> *Family Lost.* Written by Geoff Johns. Illustrated by Mike McKone, Tom Grummett, and various. 2004. 176pp. 1-4012-0238-1.
>
> *Beast Boys and Girls.* Written by Geoff Johns. Illustrated by Ben Raab. 2005. 168pp. 1-4012-0459-7.
>
> *The Future Is Now.* Written by Mark Waid and Geoff Johns. Illustrated by various. 2005. 224pp. 1-4012-0475-9.
>
> *Who Is Donna Troy?.* Written by Marv Wolfman and Phil Jimenez. Illustrated by George Pérez and Phil Jimenez. 2005. 224pp. 1-4012-0724-3.
>
> *Life or Death.* Written by Geoff Johns, Bill Willingham and Marv Wolfman. Illustrated by Tony Daniel, Scott McDaniel, and various. 2006. 208pp. 1-4012-0978-5.

Teen Titans Go. **Written by J. Torres. Illustrated by Todd Nauck, Tim Smith and Lary Stucker.** DC Comics, 2004–2005. **A** 🖳 🎮

Adapted from the hit animated series that aired for three seasons on the Cartoon Network. Robin, the Boy Wonder, along with his teammates Cyborg, Beast Boy, Starfire, Raven, and others, are out to fight evil, just as soon as they're done eating a slice of pizza.

> *Vol. 1: Truth, Justice, Pizza!* 2004. 112pp. 1-4012-0333-7.
>
> *Vol. 2: Heroes on Patrol.* 2004. 112pp. 1-4012-0334-5.
>
> *Vol. 3: Bring It On!* 2005. 104pp. 1-4012-0511-9.
>
> *Vol. 4: Ready for Action.* 2006. 104pp. 1-4012-0985-8.
>
> *Vol. 5: On the Move.* 2006. 104pp. 1-4012-0986-6.

Terra Obscura. Written by Alan Moore and Peter Hogan. Illustrated by Yannick Paquette and Karl Story America's Best Comics/WildStorm Productions/DC Comics 2004–2005. **T**

> On the parallel Earth planet called Terra Obscura, the world is populated by science heroes who help save the day, and chief among them in Invertica City are the Black Terror, Tom Strange, Captain Future, and other members of the Society of Major American Science Heroes (SMASH). When the Black Terror is killed, his consciousness is transferred into a computer called the Terror 2000, which begins to enforce its own crime prevention program utilizing a robotic version of the Black Terror. When the Terror 2000 has gone too far, there's only one hero who can save the day: the real Black Terror! Based on the original comic book characters created by Nedor Comics in 1941 that have become part of the public domain.

> *Vol. 1.* 2004. 160pp. 1-4012-0286-1.
> *Vol. 2.* 2005. 144pp. 1-4012-0622-0.

🏆 **The Ultimates. Written by Mark Millar. Illustrated by Bryan Hitch.** Marvel Comics, 2002– . **O** ◎ 💻

> A reimagined and deconstructed version of Marvel's classic super-hero team the Avengers, the Ultimates are the top group of super-heroes brought together by Nick Fury, leader of S.H.I.E.L.D., and funded by the U.S. government, to take on the worst bad guys on the planet. The team is led by World War II super-soldier Steve Rogers (Captain America), and is also composed of billionaire Tony Stark (Iron Man), Janet Van Dyne (Wasp), Hank Pym (Giant Man), the Norse thunder god Thor, Pietro Maximoff (Quicksilver), Wanda Maximoff (Scarlet Witch), Clint Barton (Hawkeye), and the meek Dr. Robert Bruce Banner (the Hulk). They're out protecting the world from potential villains, but they soon find that the biggest danger to the world may be one of their own, as the Ultimates take on a rampaging and vile-tempered Hulk. Meanwhile, Janet takes on an abusive Hank, and following an alien invasion come the worst villains of all: the press. The *Volume 1* collected hardcover edition collects the first two volumes of the first series. The third installment of the Ultimates was released in 2007 and features Jeph Loeb as writer and Joe Madureira as illustrator. *Volume 1: Super-Human* received recognition from YALSA's Popular Paperbacks for Young Adults committee in 2004. In 2006 Marvel Comics began several direct-to-DVD animated adaptations of the Ultimates, which are listed under *Ultimate Avengers*.

> *Vol. 1: Super-Human.* 2002. 160pp. 0-7851-0960-9.
> *Vol. 2: Homeland Security.* 2004. 192pp. 0-7851-1078-X.
> *Ultimates 2, Vol. 1: Gods and Monsters.* 2005. 152pp. 0-7851-1093-3.
> *Ultimates 2, Vol. 2.* 2006. 144pp. 0-7851-1790-3.
> *Volume 1 Hardcover Edition.* 2004. 320pp. 0-7851-1082-8, hardcover.

🖋 **The Watchmen.** **Written by Alan Moore. Illustrated by Dave Gibbons.** DC Comics, 1994–2005. **O** ◉

In an alternate world where the threat of the Cold War still looms over an America still run by President Nixon, the super-heroes of old have all but have been outlawed, and only vigilante heroes and registered heroes remain. When the soldier-of-fortune hero known as The Comedian is murdered, a complex plot to eliminate heroes and murder innocent humans is uncovered by the vigilante hero known as Rorschach. After reuniting his old Watchmen teammates from retirement and self-banishment, not even the combined powers of Rorschach, Ozymandias, Nite Owl, and Dr. Manhattan can solve the mystery of their murdered companion and stop Armageddon. The story has been regarded by many fans as one of the most influential comic book stories from the 1980s. *The Absolute Watchmen* is a deluxe slipcased, oversized publication including sketches, scripts, and more. The series has won multiple awards, including Eisner Awards for Best Finite/Limited Series (1988), Best Graphic Album (1988), Best Writer (1988), Best Writer/Artist (1988), and Best Archival Collection/Project—Comic Books (2006); Harvey Awards for Best Writer (1988), Best Artist or Penciller (1988), Special Award for Excellence in Production/Presentation (1988), Best Continuing or Limited Series (1988), Best Single Issue of Story (1988), and Best Graphic Album (1988); and recognition in YALSA's Popular Paperbacks for Young Adults in 2002.

> *Watchmen.* 1994. 334pp. 0-930289-23-4.
> *The Absolute Watchmen.* 2005. 464pp. 1-4012-0713-8, hardcover.

WildC.A.T.S. WildStorm Productions/DC Comics 2001–2004. **T**

Created in 1991 by Image Comics' founder Jim Lee, the team has evolved over the years since its first appearance. Originally the super-hero strike team was composed of humanoid alien half-breeds called Kherubim, who were out to protect Earth from an invading race of aliens called Daemonites. Team members included the leader, Spartan, Zealot, Void, Voodoo, Grifter, Maul, and Warblade. *Version 2.0* showcases the team following a botched rescue mission that may have cost Zealot her life. *Version 3.0* features Spartan (now called Jack Marlowe) leading a mostly brand-new team of heroes, including Mr. Majestic, Savant, Condition Red, and others as they take on a proactive war against criminals.

> *Vol. 1: Street Smart.* Written by Scott Lobdell. Illustrated by Travis Charest. 2002. 160pp. 1-56389-685-0.
> *Vol. 2: Vicious Circles.* Written by Joe Casey. Illustrated by Sean Phillips. 2001. 144pp. 1-56389-761-X.
> *Vol. 3: Serial Boxes.* Written by Joe Casey. Illustrated by Sean Phillips. 2001. 144pp. 1-56389-766-0.
> *Vol. 4: Battery Park.* Written by Joe Casey. Illustrated by Sean Phillips. 2003. 224pp. 1-4012-0035-4.
> *Version 2.0: Brand Building.* Written by Joe Casey. Illustrated by Dustin Nguyen. 2003. 128pp. 1-4012-0119-9.
> *Version 3.0: Full Disclosure.* Written by Joe Casey. Illustrated by Dustin Nguyen. 2004. 160pp. 1-4012-0276-4.

***Wildguard: Casting Call.* Written and illustrated by Todd Nauck.** Image Comics, 2005. 200pp. 1-58240-470-4. **T**

> Reality television for comic books has finally arrived. Hundreds of super-heroes are trying out for the made-for-TV super-team called Wildguard, but only five will make the final cut. Who will make the team, and will they survive the grueling competition and voting by the mysterious Producer X?

<u>Young Avengers.</u> Written by Allan Heinburg. Illustrated by Jim Cheung. Marvel Comics, 2005–2006. **Y**

> The Avengers are in disarray following the events of the <u>Avengers: Disassembled</u> story line. A young group of heroes, each reminiscent of an Avenger, have mysteriously appeared: Iron Lad, the Asgardian, Patriot, and Hulkling. When Captain America and Iron Man investigate the strange appearance of these four young heroes, their connection to the original Avengers is revealed. Meanwhile, several more members, including Titan and Knightress, join this fledgling team as they continue to take on villains under the guidance of an Avenger once believed to be dead.
>
> *Vol. 1: Sidekicks.* 2005. 144pp. 0-7851-1470-X
> *Vol. 2: Family Matters.* 2006. 144pp. 0-7851-2021-1.

<u>Young Justice.</u> Written by Peter David. Illustrated by Todd Nauck. DC Comics, 2000. **Y**

> When the adults in the Justice League aren't around, a "junior JLA" made up of teen heroes Impulse, Robin, Superboy, Wonder Girl, Arrowette, and others are ready to take on any challenge and adventure with good humor and the power to back it up. From saving Earth from the extradimensional antics of Mr. Mxyzptlk, a magical power that has transformed all the adults in the world into children, or from the villain called Harm, the team is ready to prove they're just as good as their big JLA counterparts.
>
> *A League of Their Own.* 2000. 192pp. 1-56389-626-5.
> *Sins of Youth.* 2000. 320pp. 1-56389-748-2.

X-Men

X-Men. Created by Stan Lee and Jack Kirby. Marvel Comics, 1984– . 🎬 🖥 🎮

> In a world where a genetic evolution is on the horizon, *Homo sapiens'* time is ending and the dawn of the *Homo superior*—the mutants—is now upon us. Born with strange powers, the mutants live in a world that both hates and fears them for their differences and powers. In these troubling times of racial unrest, Professor Charles Xavier (Professor X) created a school for children of the atom where they could live and learn to accept their powers, control them, and use them for good. The original team was made up of Cyclops (Scott Summers), Marvel Girl (Jean Grey), Iceman (Bobby Drake), Angel (Warren Worthington), and Beast (Hank McCoy). Called X-Men, they're protectors of humanity against evil in its many forms, including such villains as the evil Magneto, Apocalypse, and the Brotherhood of Evil Mutants. Created in 1961, the <u>X-Men</u> has continued to be one of the most popular comic book series in the United States since the late 1970s, when the second generation of X-Men, including Wolverine, Colossus, Storm, Nightcrawler, and others, joined the team. Though the roster of team members

has changed continuously over the years, their popularity has persisted. Currently the adventures of the X-Men are published by Marvel Comics through three main comic book monthly titles—*Astonishing X-Men*, *Uncanny X-Men*, and adjectiveless *X-Men*—plus numerous spin-offs, miniseries, and more. Recommended trade paperback collections and various titles featuring tales of the X-Men are listed below. Specific adventures featuring individual X-Men members are listed in the section on mutant heroes earlier in this chapter. Visit Marvel Comics' Web site (http://www.marvel.com) for many more titles featuring this extremely popular team of heroes.

***X-Men: The Dark Phoenix Saga*. Written by Chris Claremont. Illustrated by John Byrne.** Marvel Comics, 2006. 200pp. 0-7851-2213-3. **Y**

The epic *Dark Phoenix Saga* focuses on Jean Grey (a.k.a. Marvel Girl) who, after nearly dying while saving New York, is merged with a mysterious cosmic entity called the Phoenix force. Now Jean, like the myth of the firebird, is reborn with augmented power, and she rejoins the X-Men as Phoenix. When she's played as a pawn by the mysterious mutant organization the Hellfire Club, the dark side of the Phoenix force is unleashed. After rampaging throughout the galaxy and destroying a planet, the Phoenix is put on trial for her crimes, and the X-Men must try to save her life in a contest of might. Ultimately, Jean Grey knows she can't hold on to the destructive power of the Phoenix and sacrifices herself to save the entire solar system. The *Dark Phoenix Saga* is one of the most highly regarded X-Men story lines.

***X-Men: Days of Future Past*. Written by Chris Claremont. Illustrated by John Byrne.** Marvel Comics, 2004. 144pp. 0-7851-1560-9. **Y**

© 2006 Marvel Comics.

Collecting the epic story line from *Uncanny X-Men* ##141–142 from 1981. The X-Men collection was the first to feature a look at a possible bleak future for mutantkind, in which the world is under the control of the mutant-hunting Sentinels, and most heroes—including the X-Men—are dead. Kitty Pryde's mind is taken over by a time-traveling Katherine Pryde from the future, and she warns the X-Men that the only way to prevent this dark and foreboding future for mutants and the world is to thwart the assassination of Senator Robert Kelly by Mystique and the new Brotherhood of Evil Mutants. The X-Men must try to stop Mystique from killing the senator and try to change the future for the better at all costs.

***X-Men: God Loves, Man Kills*. Written by Chris Claremont. Illustrated by Brent Anderson.** Marvel Comics, 1994. 64pp. 0-7851-0039-3. **Y**

A classic graphic novel in which a mutant-hating man known as Reverend William Stryker begins a crusade against mutantkind. After capturing Professor X, the racial bigot wants to utilize Professor X's mental powers to attack mutantkind. The X-Men must ally themselves with their greatest enemy, Magneto, to rescue Xavier. The story line was the inspiration for the *X-Men 2* movie released in 2003.

***X-Men Legends, Vol. 1: Mutant Genesis.* Written by Chris Claremont. Illustrated by Jim Lee.** Marvel Comics, 2002. 176pp. 0-7851-0895-5. **Y** ◎

> A collection reprinting the popular launch of the second X-Men monthly comic book series, the adjectiveless <u>X-Men</u>, in 1991 by Chris Claremont and Jim Lee. The X-Men members divide into two teams, Blue and Gold, to better fight for the rights of mutants and the preservation of humanity. The first adventure the Blue team (comprising Beast, Psylocke, Rogue, Gambit, Cyclops, and Wolverine) faces is a grand battle against Magneto and his minions, the Acolytes.

***X-Men Legends, Vol. III: Arthur Adams, Book I.* Written by Chris Claremont. Illustrated by Arthur Adams.** Marvel Comics, 2003. 272pp. 0-7851-1049-6. **Y** ◎

> Arthur Adams is regarded as one of the premiere artists today. His first major work in comic books was in the <u>Longshot</u> miniseries, and he penciled several classic story lines for the X-Men in the late 1980s and early 1990s. Collected are highlights from several comic book issues, including a rousing fantasy-like story line in which the New Mutants and the X-Men travel to the Thunder god Thor's world of Asgard and a temporarily depowered Storm is tempted to become the goddess of thunder by the god of lies, Loki. Another feature is a reprint of the lighthearted *Uncanny X-Men* Annual #10 from 1987, in which the X-Men help Longshot in his struggle against the maniacal spineless villain called Mojo and the team is unexpectedly transformed by Mojo's magic into the cute but still heroic group called the X-Babies.

🎗 <u>**Astonishing X-Men (3rd series).**</u> **Written by Joss Whedon. Illustrated by John Cassaday.** Marvel Comics, 2005– . **Y** ◎

© 2006 Marvel Comics.

> Written by popular *Buffy the Vampire Slayer* creator Joss Whedon. Professor X has left the school to help rebuild the mutant haven island of Genosha, and the School for Gifted Students is now in the hands of Scott Summers (Cyclops) and Emma Frost (White Queen). The X-Men have formed three squads, ironically with Wolverine being in all three of them at the same time. The core group of X-Men—Cyclops, White Queen, Kitty Pryde, Wolverine, and Beast—are both teaching the students how to control their powers and saving the world. Back in spandex costumes, the X-Men are out to quell the fear that they're a "mutant menace" and prove to the world at large that they're heroes. Meanwhile, a new menace threatens to destroy mutantkind. When a doctor announces she has devised a cure for mutantkind, what effect will it have on mutants, and does it really work? The series also features the much-welcomed return of a fan-favorite X-Man. The hardcover *Volume 1* edition reprints the entire original twelve issues of the first series. In 2006 the series received several Eisner Awards, including Best Continuing Series and Best Artist, for John Cassaday's artwork.

> > *Vol. 1: Gifted.* 2005. 144pp. 0-7851-1531-5.
> > *Vol. 2: Dangerous.* 2005. 144pp. 0-7851-1677-X.
> > *Vol. 3: Torn.* 2007. 144pp. 0-7851-1759-8.
> > *Vol. 1.* 2005. 320pp. 0-7851-1733-4, hardcover.

Essential X-Men. Marvel Comics, 1996–. **Y**

The collections reprint classic X-Men stories at an inexpensive price and in black and white. The series began by reprinting the more popular X-Men issues, including the first adventures of Storm, Colossus, Nightcrawler, and others as a team, but it has also gone back in the <u>Essential Uncanny X-Men</u> to reprint the classic Stan Lee and Jack Kirby issues from 1963.

> <u>Essential Uncanny X-Men.</u> 1999.
>> *Vol. I.* Written by Stan Lee. Illustrated by Jack Kirby. 1999. 528pp. 0-7851-0991-9.
>
> <u>Essential X-Men.</u> Marvel Comics, 1996– .
>> *Vol. I.* Written by Chris Claremont. Illustrated by Dave Cockrum, John Byrne. 1997. 528pp. 0-7851-0256-6.
>>
>> *Vol. II.* Written by Chris Claremont. Illustrated by John Byrne. 1996. 528pp. 0-7851-0298-1.
>>
>> *Vol. III.* Written by Chris Claremont. Illustrated by Dave Cockrum and Paul Smith. 1998. 528pp. 0-7851-0661-8.
>>
>> *Vol. IV.* Written by Chris Claremont. Illustrated by Paul Smith, and John Romita, Jr. 2006. 568pp. 0-7851-2295-8.
>>
>> *Vol. V.* Written by Chris Claremont. Illustrated by John Romita Jr., and various. 2004. 576pp. 0-7851-1366-5.
>>
>> *Vol. VI.* Written by Chris Claremont. Illustrated by John Romita Jr. 2005. 656pp. 0-7851-1727-X.
>>
>> *Vol. VII.* Written by Chris Claremont. Illustrated by Marc Silvestri and various. 2006. 560pp. 0-7851-2055-6.

New X-Men. Written by Grant Morrison. Illustrated by various. Marvel Comics, 2002–2004. **T ◉**

Professor X's long-lost twin sister Cassandra Nova destroys the mutant island nation of Genosha and takes over his body for a short while, exposing to the world that he is a mutant. Meanwhile the X-Men learn that some of the mutants are undergoing secondary mutations, including the Beast and the White Queen, and *Homo superior* is becoming extinct. Wolverine finds more information about his past thanks to the genetically advanced mutant thief known as Fantomex, and Cyclops is having a psychic affair with the White Queen, who finds herself at the mercy of Cyclops's wife, Phoenix. The Master of Magnetism, Magneto, has a final reign of terror in New York City with his less-than-capable new Brotherhood and loses his head in the heat of battle. Meanwhile, 150 years in the future, when humankind is waging its final battle against the vile Beast and his genetic X-Men hybrid clones, the last group of X-Men (Wolverine, Cassandra Nova, Beak, a Sentinel, and others) wage a last-ditch effort to retrieve the Phoenix egg.

> *Vol. 1: E Is for Extinction.* Illustrated by Frank Quitely. 2002. 144pp. 0-785-10811-4.
>
> *Vol. 2: Imperial.* Illustrated by Frank Quitely and Ethan Van Sciver. 2002. 224pp. 0-7851-0887-4.
>
> *Vol. 3: New Worlds.* Illustrated by Igor Kordey and Ethan Van Sciver. 2002. 176pp. 0-7851-0976-5.
>
> *Vol. 4: Riot at Xavier's.* Illustrated by Frank Quitely. 2003. 120pp. 0-7851-1067-4.

Vol. 5: Assault on Weapon Plus. Illustrated by Chris Bachalo. 2003. 168pp. 0-7851-1119-0.

Vol. 6: Planet X. Illustrated by Phil Jimenez. 2004. 128pp. 0-7851-1201-4.

Vol. 7: Here Comes Tomorrow. Illustrated by Marc Silvestri. 2004. 112pp. 0-7851-1345-2.

Vol. 1. Illustrated by Frank Quitely and Ethan Van Sciver. 2002. 384pp. 0-7851-0964-1, hardcover.

Vol. 2. Illustrated by Frank Quitely, Phil Jimenez, John Paul Leon, and Igor Kordey. 2003. 288pp. 0-7851-1118-2, hardcover.

Vol. 3. Illustrated by Marc Silvestri, Phil Jimenez, and Chris Bachalo. 2004. 336pp. 0-7851-1200-6, hardcover.

Ultimate X-Men. Written by Mark Millar, Brian Michael Bendis, and Brian K. Vaughan. Illustrated by Adam Kubert, Chris Bachalo, David Finch, and Stuart Immonen. Marvel Comics, 2001– . **T** ◉

© 2006 Marvel Comics.

A reinvention of the X-Men updated for the twenty-first century. Humanity is at a crossroads in evolution, and an offshoot of humanity has arrived: *Homo superior.* Gifted with strange and wondrous powers at birth that are revealed at the onset of puberty, they're hated and feared by the population at large. To combat the ever-growing threat of increased mutant activity, the government has commissioned giant mutant-hunting robots called Sentinels to quell the genetic uprising, but there are two resistance forces growing in the ranks of mutantkind who are out to stop the senseless slaughter of mutants. On one side, Eric Lensherr (known as Magneto, the master of magnetism) leads a group of mutants dedicated to toppling the U. S. government. Called the Brotherhood, they will not stop their war against humankind, who have tortured and killed many innocent mutants. Eric's longtime friend and now adversary, Professor Charles Xavier, a mutant gifted with the power of mind control, has created a school called Professor Xavier's School for Gifted Students as a haven for mutants to learn to control their powers and hope to peacefully coexist with humanity. Young mutants Jean Grey (Phoenix), Scott Summers (Cyclops), and Hank McCoy (Beast) are part of Xavier's fighting force squadron called the X-Men. Ready to rescue and protect mutants and humans from those who would harm either of them, they're the only mutant strike team ready to take on Magneto and his Brotherhood. After recruiting new mutants such as Bobby Drake (Iceman), Ororo Munroe (Storm), Peter Rasputin (Colossus), and the deadly and feral Logan (Wolverine), the X-Men have continued to prepare for the coming war that could decide the fate of all humanity. *Volume 1: The Tomorrow People* received recognition from YALSA's Popular Paperbacks for Young Adults committee as well as the Quick Picks for Reluctant Readers committee in 2002.

Vol. 1: The Tomorrow People. Written by Mark Millar. Illustrated by Adam Kubert. 2001. 176pp. 0-7851-0788-6.

Vol. 2: Return to Weapon X. Written by Mark Millar. Illustrated by Adam Kubert. 2002. 144pp. 0-7851-0868-8.

Vol. 3: World Tour. Written by Mark Millar. Illustrated by Adam Kubert and Chris Bachalo. 2002. 192pp. 0-7851-0961-7.

Vol. 4: Hellfire and Brimstone. Written by Mark Millar. Illustrated by Adam Kubert. 2003. 144pp. 0-7851-1089-5.

Vol. 5: Ultimate War. Written by Mark Millar. Illustrated by Chris Bachalo. 2003. 112pp. 0-7851-1129-8.

Vol. 6: Return of the King. Written by Mark Millar. Illustrated by Adam Kubert and David Finch. 2003. 192pp. 0-7851-1091-7.

Vol. 7: Blockbuster. Written by Brian Michael Bendis. Illustrated by David Finch. 2004. 144pp. 0-7851-1219-7.

Vol. 8: The New Mutants. Written by Brian Michael Bendis. Illustrated by David Finch. 2004. 144pp. 0-7851-1161-1.

Vol. 9: The Tempest. Written by Brian K. Vaughan. Illustrated by Brandon Peterson. 2004. 112pp. 0-7851-1404-1.

Vol. 10: Cry Wolf. Written by Brian K. Vaughan. Illustrated by Andy Kubert. 2005. 96pp. 0-7851-1405-X.

Vol. 11: Most Dangerous Game. Written by Brian K. Vaughan. Illustrated by Andy Kubert. 2005. 144pp. 0-7851-1659-1.

Vol. 12: Hard Lessons. Written by Brian K. Vaughan. Illustrated by Stuart Immonen and various. 2005. 128pp. 0-7851-1801-2.

Vol. 13: Magnetic North. Written by Brian K. Vaughan. Illustrated by Stuart Immonen and various. 2006. 128pp. 0-7851-1906-X.

Vol. 1. Written by Mark Millar. Illustrated by Adam Kubert. 2002. 352pp. 0-7851-1008-9, hardcover.

Vol. 2. Written by Mark Millar. Illustrated by Adam Kubert and Chris Bachalo. 2003. 336pp. 0-7851-1130-1, hardcover.

Vol. 3. Written by Mark Millar. Illustrated by Adam Kubert, Chris Bachalo, and David Finch. 2004. 304pp. 0-7851-1131-X, hardcover.

Vol. 4. Written by Brian Michael Bendis. Illustrated by David Finch. 2005. 304pp. 0-7851-1251-0, hardcover.

Vol. 5. Written by Brian K. Vaughan. Illustrated by Brandon Peterson, Andy Kubert, and Stuart Immonen. 2006. 296pp. 0-7851-2103-X, hardcover.

Vol. 6. Written by Brian K. Vaughan. Illustrated by Stuart Immonen and various. 2006. 256pp. 0-7851-2104-8, hardcover.

X-Treme X-Men. Written by Chris Claremont. Illustrated by Salvador Larroca, Igor Kordey, and various. Marvel Comics, 2002–2004. **Y**

Veteran X-Men members Storm, Bishop, Psylocke, Thunderbird, Rogue, and Beast are joined by former Hellfire Club member Sage. Together they're on a quest to find the mysterious Books of Destiny, written by the late mutant called Destiny. The X-Men team must try to recover the books before they fall into the wrong hands. The series is noted for featuring a sequel to Chris Claremont's classic X-Men graphic novel *God Loves, Man Kills*.

Vol. 1: Destiny. 2002. 192pp. 0-7851-0841-6.
Vol. 2: Invasion. 2002. 224pp. 0-7851-1018-6.
Vol. 3: Schism. 2003. 160pp. 0-7851-1084-4.
Vol. 4: Mekanix. 2003. 160pp. 0-7851-1117-4.
Vol. 5: God Loves, Man Kills II. 2003. 216pp. 0-7851-1254-5.
Vol. 6: Intifada. 2004. 120pp. 0-7851-1230-8.
Vol. 7: Storm—the Arena. 2004. 152pp. 0-7851-0936-6.
Vol. 8: Prisoner of Fire. 2004. 216pp. 0-7851-1351-7.
Savage Land. 2002. 96pp. 0-7851-0869-6.

Miscellaneous Recommended X-Men Collections

A selection of recommended X-Men titles published within the past decade by Marvel Comics.

***Astonishing X-Men* (2d series). Written by Howard Mackie. Illustrated by Brandon Peterson.** Marvel Comics, 2000. 160pp. 0-7851-0754-1. **T**

A miniseries tale pitting the Cyclops, Cable, Nate Grey, Archangel, Wolverine, and Jean Grey against Apocalypse's newest Fourth Horseman, called Death.

Uncanny X-Men: The New Age. Written by Chris Claremont. Illustrated by Alan Davis. Marvel Comics, 2005–. **Y**

Chris Claremont returns to write the adventures of the X-Men. The team includes Wolverine, Storm, Bishop, Sage, Nightcrawler, Marvel Girl, and Cannonball, who take on the mysterious adversary called the Fury. There is also a return to the villain from Arcade's realm called Murderworld, a trip to the Savage Land, the return of Psylocke, and much more. Note that *Volume 4* is a tie-in to the miniseries titled *House of M* and is listed in the epic events section of this chapter.

> *Vol. 1: The End of History.* 2005. 144pp. 0-7851-1536-6.
> *Vol. 2: The Cruelest Cut.* 2005. 120pp. 0-7851-1645-1.
> *Vol. 3: On Ice.* 2005. 168pp. 0-7851-1649-4.
> *Vol. 5: First Forsaken.* 2006. 120pp. 0-7851-2323-7.

***X-Men: The Blood of Apocalypse*. Written by Peter Milligan and Fabian Nicieza. Illustrated by Salvador Larroca and Lan Medina.** Marvel Comics, 2006. 216pp. 0-7851-2334-2. **Y**

The immortal mutant Apocalypse has returned from the dead to ensure that only the strong mutants of the world reign supreme over the weak. Who will join Apocalypse's ranks as his new Four Horsemen?

***X-Men: Children of the Atom*. Written by Joe Casey. Illustrated by Steve Rude.** Marvel Comics, 2001. 160pp. 0-7851-0805-X. **Y**

An early look at the first year that Professor X recruited five teenagers with mutant powers and formed them into the original team of X-Men, made up of Cyclops, Marvel Girl, Beast, Angel, and Iceman.

***X-Men: Crossroads*. Written by Chris Claremont. Illustrated by Jim Lee, Marc Silvestri and Rob Liefeld.** Marvel Comics, 1998. 128pp. 0-7851-0662-6. **T**

Collects the comic book issues from *Uncanny X-Men* nos. 273–277 and features the penultimate tale of the X-Men against their arch-nemesis Magneto.

***X-Men: Deadly Genesis*. Written by Ed Brubaker. Illustrated by Trevor Hairsine.** Marvel Comics, 2006. 160pp. 0-7851-1961-2. **Y**

A thirtieth-anniversary series of *Giant-Size X-Men* #1 (1976), which introduced the second generation of X-Men. While the X-Men search for Professor Xavier (following the events of the series House of M), Scott Summers (Cyclops) discovers that Alex (Havok) Summers is not his only brother. There is another Summers brother: a powerful and dangerous mutant named Gabriel Summers, a.k.a. Vulcan. After a former

X-Men member is killed by Vulcan, a strike team of X-Men try to stop him before he locates the missing Professor X.

X-Men: Dream's End. **Written by Scott Lobdell. Illustrated by Salvador Larroca and Leinil Francis Yu.** Marvel Comics, 2005. 192pp. 0-7851-1551-X. **Y**

When a cure for the deadly Legacy virus—a plague that has killed many mutants and those close to them—is found, what X-Men member will make the ultimate sacrifice so that mutantkind will be saved?

X-Men: Eve of Destruction. **Written by Scott Lobdell. Illustrated by Salvador Larroca and Leinil Francis Yu.** Marvel Comics, 2005. 152pp. 0-7851-1552-8. **Y**

Written before Grant Morrison's highly regarded series <u>New X-Men.</u> When the X-Men are trapped on the mutant island of Genosha, a new team led by Phoenix faces off against Magneto.

X-Men: Evolution. **Written by Devin Grayson. Illustrated by UDON Studios.** Marvel Comics, 2003. 96pp. 0-7851-1359-2. **Y**

Adaptation of the hit cartoon show featuring a young cast of X-Men including Cyclops, Jean Grey, Rogue, Iceman, and others as they battle both teen high school pressures and the adversaries Magneto, Mystique, and the Brotherhood of Mutants.

X-Men: Fatal Attractions. **Written by Fabian Nicieza. Illustrated by Andy Kubert, John Romita Jr., and various.** Marvel Comics, 1994. 256pp. 0-7851-0065-2. **Y**

When Magneto and his Acolytes wage war on humankind, the various X-Men teams set out to stop them. The series is best known for featuring Magneto painfully removing Wolverine's adamantium out of his body and the final showdown between Professor X and Magneto.

X-Men: From the Ashes. **Written by Chris Claremont. Illustrated by Paul Smith with Walt Simonson and John Romita Jr.** Marvel Comics, 1990. 226pp. 0-87135-615-5. **Y**

Scott Summers, still grieving over the death of Jean Grey (Phoenix), meets Madeline Pryor—a woman who looks uncannily like Jean Grey. Has the Phoenix really risen from the ashes? Meanwhile, the young mutant named Rogue seeks help from the X-Men, and Logan (Wolverine) prepares for his upcoming marriage to his Japanese lover, Mariko.

X-Men: Mutations. **Written by Chris Claremont and Louise Simonson. Illustrated by Walt Simonson, Jim Lee, and various.** Marvel Comics, 1996. 176pp. 0-7851-0197-7. **Y**

A collection of stories featuring the further mutations of three popular X-Men. Hank McCoy transforms into the blue-furred Beast; Angel is transformed by the evil Apocalypse into the razor-winged Archangel; and Psylocke is transformed by the Siege Perilous from a British woman into a deadly Japanese assassin and pawn of the evil Mandarin.

X-Men: The Origin of Generation X. **Written by Larry Hama. Illustrated by Joe Madureira.** Marvel Comics, 1996. 336pp. 0-7851-0196-9. **Y**

When a techno-organic alien race called the Phalanx arrive on Earth, they set out to destroy the mutant race before assimilating the weaker humans. Little did they realize they were up against the X-Men. The series also features the first appearance of the teen group called Generation X as well as the heroine called Blink.

X-Men: Phoenix Rising. **Written by John Byrne, Bob Layton, and Roger Stern. Illustrated by John Buscema, John Byrne, and Jackson Guice.** Marvel Comics, 1999. 112pp. 0-7851-0711-8. **Y**

When Phoenix died (as chronicled in *X-Men: The Dark Phoenix Saga* in this chapter) while on the moon to save the universe, Jean Grey died with her that fateful day, right? Everything the X-Men thought they knew turns out to be untrue when they discover that the real Jean Grey is still alive. The collection was a launching point in 1986 for the debut of the super-hero team called X-Factor—a team composed of the original five X-Men. See the subsection on X-Factor (below) for more titles featuring that team.

X-Men: Vignettes. **Written by Chris Claremont. Illustrated by John Bolton.** Marvel Comics, 2001–2005.

A collection of short stories featuring the X-Men, beautifully illustrated by John Bolton. The stories originally appeared in the X-Men title *Classic X-Men*, which reprinted the original comic book issues of the X-Men at an affordable price.

> *Vol. 1.* 2001. 160pp. 0-7851-0797-5.
> *Vol. 2.* 2005. 152pp. 0-7851-1728-8.

X-Men vs. the Brood: Day of Wrath. **Written by Chris Claremont and John Ostrander. Illustrated by Marc Silvestri and Bryan Hitch.** Marvel Comics, 1997. 176pp. 0-7851-0558-1. **Y**

A collection of tales featuring the X-Men against the Alien-like creatures from outer space called the Brood.

X-Men Visionaries. Marvel Comics, 1996–2002. **T**

The X-Men series has long been written and illustrated by some of the most talented creators in the comic book industry. Below are listed a variety of titles that focus on the artwork or writing of individual X-Men creators.

> *X-Men Visionaries: The Art of Andy and Adam Kubert.* Written by Fabian Nicieza. Illustrated by Adam Kubert and Andy Kubert. 1996. 96pp. 0-7851-0178-0.
> *X-Men Visionaries: Chris Claremont.* Written by Chris Claremont. Illustrated by various. 1998. 240pp. 0-7851-0598-0.
> *X-Men Visionaries: Jim Lee.* Written by Chris Claremont and Ann Nocenti. Illustrated by Jim Lee. 2002. 304pp. 0-7851-0921-8.
> *X-Men Visionaries: Joe Madureira.* Written by Scott Lobdell. Illustrated by Joe Madureira. 2000. 176pp. 0-7851-0748-7.
> *X-Men Visionaries: Neal Adams.* Written by Roy Thomas. Illustrated by Neal Adams. 1996. 160pp. 0-7851-0198-5.

X-Men Spin-Offs

The success of the X-Men has spun off into a wide variety of series featuring X-Men characters and other mutants branching off into their own team of heroes. Below are some highlights of the spin-offs published by Marvel Comics.

District X. Written by David Hine. Illustrated by David Yardin. Marvel Comics, 2005. **T**

A dark crime drama spin-off of the X-Men featuring Bishop taking on the ghetto slums of Manhattan, nicknamed District X. He's assigned to work with nonmutant NYPD policeman Ismael Ortega, and they're out to investigate the rising crime rate in the city among the humans and second-tier mutants and to take on the crime lords and others who threaten the city, including a mysterious individual known as Mr. M.

> *Vol. 1: Mr. M.* 2005. 144pp. 0-7851-1444-0.
> *Vol. 2: Underground.* 2005. 200pp. 0-7851-1602-8.

Excalibur. Written by Chris Claremont. Illustrated by Aaron Lopresti. Marvel Comics, 2004–2005. **T**

When the mutant haven, Genosha, was decimated by the mutant-hunting Sentinels, it was thought that the country would never rise again. Hope comes in the form of two great mutant adversaries: Professor Charles Xavier (Professor X) and Eric Lensherr (Magneto). Setting aside their differences, they must try to build a safer and more stable Genosha that can rise from the ashes and thrive once again as a haven for mutants.

> *Vol. 1: Forging the Sword.* 2004. 96pp. 0-7851-1527-7.
> *Vol. 2: Saturday Night Fever.* 2005. 144pp. 0-7851-1476-9.

Excalibur Classic. Written by Chris Claremont. Illustrated by Alan Davis. Marvel Comics, 2005– . **Y**

A reprinting of the X-Men spin-off title originally published from 1988 to 1998. The first Excalibur team was a spin-off branch of the X-Men based in England and mixed humor and adventure. The team members included Captain Britain (Brian Braddock), his lover Meggan, as well as several X-Men team members, including Nightcrawler (Kurt Wagner), Phoenix (Rachel Summers), Shadowcat (Kitty Pryde), and her pet dragon, Lockheed.

> *Vol. 1: The Sword Is Drawn.* 2005. 176pp. 0-7851-1888-8.
> *Vol. 2: Two-Edged Sword.* 2006. 200pp. 0-7851-2201-X.

Exiles. Marvel Comics, 2002– . Y ◎

When the world needs fixing, it's up to the Exiles to make it right. A mysterious entity called the Timebroker has recruited six X-Men heroes from alternate timelines to right the cosmic wrongs in the many variations of Earth that they visit. Each world is different than the next and in need of the Exiles' help to right the wrongs of that world. Should a member of the team fail in his mission, he is expelled and permanently sent back to his own alternate Earth, and a new team member from another world is called forth. Led by Blink, the lone survivor of a world where Apocalypse ruled the Earth, the team includes

Mimic, Morph, Nocturne, Warpath, and Magnus, all attempting to correct the timelines of other Earth realities or die trying.

© 2006 Marvel Comics.

Vol. 1: Down the Rabbit Hole. Written by Judd Winick. Illustrated by Mike McKone and Mark McKenna. 2002. 112pp. 0-7851-0833-5.

Vol. 2: A World Apart. Written by Judd Winick. Illustrated by Mike McKone and Mark McKenna. 2003. 160pp. 0-7851-1021-6.

Vol. 3: Out of Time. Written by Judd Winick. Illustrated by Jim Calafiore and Mike McKone. 2003. 192pp. 0-7851-1085-2.

Vol. 4: Legacy. Written by Judd Winick. Illustrated by Jim Calafiore and Jon Holdredge. 2003. 144pp. 0-7851-1109-3.

Vol. 5: Unnatural Instincts. Written by Chuck Austen. Illustrated by Jim Calafiore and Jon Holdredge. 2003. 144pp. 0-7851-1110-7.

Vol. 6: Fantastic Voyage. Written by Judd Winick. Illustrated by Jim Calafiore. 2004. 168pp. 0-7851-1197-2.

Vol. 7: A Blink in Time. Written by Chuck Austen. Illustrated by Jim Calafiore. Marvel Comics, 2004 144pp. 0-7851-1235-9.

Vol. 8: Earn Your Wings. Written by Tony Bedard and Chuck Austen. Illustrated by Mizuki Sakakibara. 2004. 144pp. 0-7851-1459-9.

Vol. 9: Bump in the Night. Written by Tony Bedard. Illustrated by Mizuki Sakakibara and Jim Calafiore. 2005. 168pp. 0-7851-1673-7.

Vol. 10: Age of Apocalypse. Written by Tony Bedard. Illustrated by Mizuki Sakakibara and Jim Calafiore. 2005. 128pp. 0-7851-1674-5.

Vol. 11: Time Breakers. Written by Tony Bedard. Illustrated by Mizuki Sakakibara and Jim Calafiore. 2005. 168pp. 0-7851-1730-X.

Vol. 12: World Tour, Book 1. Written by Tony Bedard. Illustrated by Mizuki Sakakibara and Jim Calafiore. 2006. 144pp. 0-7851-1854-3.

Vol. 13: World Tour, Book 2. Written by Tony Bedard. Illustrated by Jim Calafiore. 2006. 216pp. 0-7851-1855-1.

New Excalibur. Written by Chris Claremont. Illustrated by Michael Ryan. Marvel Comics, 2006. **Y**

A relaunch of the <u>Excalibur</u> title, once again featuring a team led by Captain Britain and set in London. The series also features a team composed of Pete Wisdom, the re-formed villain the Juggernaut, Sage, Dazzler, and Nocturne—an alternative universe daughter of the X-Man called Nightcrawler.

Vol. 1: Defenders of the Realm. 2006. 168pp. 0-7851-1835-7.

New Mutants. Marvel Comics, 1990–2004. **Y**

Recruited after the success of the X-Men, Professor Xavier opened the doors to his School for Gifted Youngsters to the next generation of mutants and the New Mutants were born. Originally debuting in 1982, one of the most popular adventures for the team was the *Demon Bear Saga,* which was reprinted. In time a second generation of New Mutants came to attend Professor Xavier's Institute for Higher Learning. Taught by the X-Men as well as Moonstar, Karma, Magma, and Wolfsbane, members of the original band of New Mutants, the latest teens are about to find out what a difficult life they have ahead of them, being feared for who they are and what powers they can control. The original series was renamed <u>X-Force</u> in the early 1990s and was a best-selling title for Marvel Comics. Recently the series started up again in 2004, but was re-launched with the title <u>New X-Men: Academy X</u> in 2005.

New Mutants: The Demon Bear Saga. Written by Chris Claremont. Illustrated by Bill Sienkiewicz. 1990. 120pp. 0-87135-673-2.
New Mutants. Written by Chris Claremont. Illustrated by Bob McLeod. 1994, reprint edition 64pp. 0-7851-0041-5.
New Mutants, Vol. 1: Back to School. Written by Nunzio DeFilippis and Christina Weir. Illustrated by Keron Grant. 2004. 144pp. 0-7851-1242-1.

New X-Men: Academy X. Marvel Comics, 2005– . **Y**

Continuing the events from New Mutants, the latest generation of teen mutant heroes are being trained by the X-Men and former New Mutants to control their powers, as well as getting a proper education. The series also features the new breakout character X-23, who is a female clone of Wolverine approximately the age of a teenager.

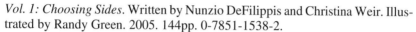

Vol. 1: Choosing Sides. Written by Nunzio DeFilippis and Christina Weir. Illustrated by Randy Green. 2005. 144pp. 0-7851-1538-2.
Vol. 2: Haunted. Written by Nunzio DeFilippis and Christina Weir. Illustrated by Michael Ryan and Paco Medina. 2005. 144pp. 0-7851-1615-X.
Hellions. Written by Nunzio DeFilippis and Christina Weir. Illustrated by Clayton Henry. Marvel Comics, 2005. 96pp. 0-7851-1746-6.

Vol. 3: X-posed. Written by Nunzio DeFilippis and Christina Weir. Illustrated by Michael Ryan and Rick Ketchum. 2006. 120pp. 0-7851-1791-1.
Childhood's End, Vol. 1. Written by Craig Kyle and Chris Yost. Illustrated by Mark Brooks. 2006. 104pp. 0-7851-1831-4.

Childhood's End, Vol. 2. Written by Craig Kyle and Chris Yost. Illustrated by Mark Brooks. 2006. 96pp. 0-7851-2024-6.
X-23: Innocence Lost. Written by Craig Kyle and Chris Yost. Illustrated by Billy Tan. 2006. 144pp. 0-7851-1502-1.

NYX. **Written by Joe Quesada. Illustrated by Joshua Middleton.** Marvel Comics, 2004. 176pp. 0-7851-1243-X. **Y**

A look at the underbelly of the mutant population: teens who have been born with uncontrollable power but haven't found a safe haven with Professor Xavier. Struggling to survive on the rough side of New York City, they only have each other for companionship, shelter, and love.

X-Factor. Marvel Comics, 2005– . **Y**

Originally launched in 1985 and published until 1998, the series originally featured all five original members of the X-Men: Cyclops (Scott Summers), Beast (Hank McCoy), Iceman (Bobby Drake), Angel (Warren Worthington III), and a resurrected Marvel Girl (Jean Grey). The series featured the return of Jean Grey, the first appearance of the X-Men villain Apocalypse, and the dark transformation of Angel into Apocalypse's minion Death and subsequently Archangel. The series was relaunched in 1991 by writer Peter David and featured a second string of Marvel mutant heroes, including Havok, Polaris, Strong Guy, Wolfsbane, Madrox the Multiple Man, and Quicksilver, who worked for the Pentagon, and has been highly regarded by X-Men fans for Peter David's use of humor in the series. Recently the series was relaunched, featuring the core members from Peter David's run, including

Madrox the Multiple Man, Wolfsbane, Strong Guy, Siryn, Rictor, and Monet working as an investigative mutant agency in the heart of the mutant town called District X. The first collection from the new series, The Longest Night, is listed below.

Essential X-Factor. Written by Louise Simonson and various. Illustrated by Walter Simonson, Marc Silvestri, and various. Marvel Comics, 2005. **Y**

The collection reprints in an inexpensive black-and-white format the first sixteen issues of *X-Factor* as well as *X-Factor Annual* #1, *Avengers* #263, *Fantastic Four* #286, and *Thor* ##373–374. The story features the original X-Men Cyclops, Jean Grey, Iceman, Beast, and Angel.

    Vol. 1. 2005. 568pp. 0-7851-1886-1.

X-Factor: The Longest Night. **Written by Peter David. Illustrated by Ryan Sook.** Marvel Comics, 2006. 144pp. 0-7851-2351-2. hardcover; 144pp. 0-7851-1817-9. softcover. **Y**

Jamie Madrox, the Multiple Man, recruits Wolfsbane, Strong Guy, Siryn, Rictor, and Monet to work at his detective agency in the heart of mutant town, called District X.

X-Factor Visionaries: Peter David. Written by Peter David. Illustrated by Larry Stroman. Marvel Comics, 2005. **Y** ◉

The collection features the second team to be called X-Factor. The team was composed of Havok, Polaris, Multiple Man, Wolfsbane, Strong Guy, and Quicksilver as a government-run mutant agency. It was well-received by fans in part because of Peter David's trademark sense of humor and excellent character development.

    Vol. 1. 2005. 144pp. 0-7851-1872-1.

X-Force. Marvel Comics, 1992–2005. **Y**

In the early 1991, the New Mutants series was relaunched as the team book *X-Force*. The team served as a proactive military-like strike team led by the enigmatic Cable—the time-displaced son of Cyclops, leader of the X-Men. The group included team members Domino, Cannonball, Shatterstar, Warpath, Feral, Boom Boom, Siryn, Rictor, and Sunspot. Collected below are several books reprinting some of the original stories from the comic book series as well as recent miniseries that reunited the original team and featured the X-Force member Shatterstar. In 2001 Peter Milligan and Mike Allred relaunched an all-new, all-different team called *X-Force*, subsequently renamed X-Statix. See the listing below for more information on X-Statix. Also included are reprints of the first appearances of Cable.

    Cable and the New Mutants. Written by Louise Simonson. Illustrated by Rob Liefeld. 1992. 176pp. 0-87135-937-5.
    X-Force: Big Guns. Written by Fabian Nicieza. Illustrated by Rob Liefeld. 2004. 136pp. 0-7851-1483-1.
    X-Force and Cable, Vol. 1: The Legend Returns. Written by Fabian Nicieza. Illustrated by Rob Liefeld. 2005. 144pp. 0-7851-1429-7.
    X-Force: Shatterstar. Written and illustrated by Rob Liefeld. 2005. 160pp. 0-7851-1633-8.

X-Statix. Written by Peter Milligan. Illustrated by Mike Allred. Marvel Comics, 2001–2006. **O**

> Welcome to a brand-new group of mutants. Meet The Orphan, Doop, Venus Dee Milo, and more. They're the quirky pop-star mutant heroes of the twenty-first century called X-Statix. Formerly called X-Force, until the copyright police wanted them to change their name, they're a group of mutants hired to form a glitzy paparazzi-friendly fighting force. Though the job is tough, deadly and dangerous, the reward of fame, fortune, and glamour is almost too much to resist. Can they handle the pressure of being in the spotlight as well as each other's egos before it costs another member of the team's life? In 2006 the X-Statix member Dead Girl was featured in her own miniseries.

> > X-Force. 2001–2002.
> > > *Vol. 1: New Beginnings.* 2001. 128pp. 0-7851-0819-X.
> > > *Vol. 2: The Final Chapter.* 2002. 224pp. 0-7851-1088-7.
> > X-Statix. 2003–2006.
> > > *Vol. 1: Good Omens.* 2003. 128pp. 0-7851-1059-3.
> > > *Vol. 2: Good Guys and Bad Guys.* 2003. 176pp. 0-7851-1139-5.
> > > *Vol. 3: Back from the Dead.* 2004. 192pp. 0-7851-1140-9.
> > > *Vol. 4: X-Statix vs. the Avengers.* 2005. 192pp. 0-7851-1537-4.
> > > *X-Statix Presents: Dead Girl.* 2006. 120pp. 0-7851-2031-9.

X-Men Movie Adaptations

Marvel Comics, 2000–2003. **Y**

> Adaptations of the hit X-Men movies released in 2000 and 2003. The third movie, *X-Men 3*, was released in summer 2006.

X-Men: Beginnings. Written by various. Illustrated by various. 2000. 144pp. 0-7851-0750-9. **Y**

X-Men: The Movie. Written by Ralph Macchio. Illustrated by Anthony Williams. 2000. 144pp. 0-7851-0749-5. **Y**

X-Men 2: The Movie. Written by Chuck Austen. Illustrated by Patrick Zircher. 2003. 144pp. 0-7851-1162-X. **Y**

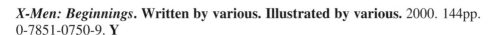

Team-Ups and Epic Events

Team-Ups

When a large-scale threat occurs, often heroes and super teams join together to face the common enemy or adversary in what is called a crossover or a team-up. The team-ups can be made up of normally lone crime-fighters working together (such as Batman and Superman) or can be large-scale team-ups featuring several heroes or a team working alongside another team (such as when the JLA teams up

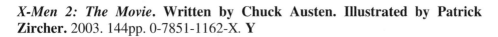

with the JSA). Part of the fun of the team-up crossovers is for readers to see how their favorite heroic characters interact with each other, especially in publications featuring heroes from several publishing companies.

***Batman and Superman: World's Finest.* Written by Karl Kesel. Illustrated by various.** DC Comics, 2003. 288pp. 1-4012-0082-6. **Y**

> A look at the first ten years of two of the most polar opposite heroes: the vigilante Batman and the noble Superman. As they meet each year to remember a tragic event from their past, their friendship is put to the test throughout a decade of change, including the loss of Robin at the hands of the Joker, the death of Superman, and the temporary reign of Jean-Paul Valley as a much different Dark Knight.

♠ ***The Batman/Judge Dredd Files.* Written by John Wagner and Alan Grant. Illustrated by Simon Bisley and various.** DC Comics and 2000 A.D. 2004. 208pp. 1-4012-0420-1. **T**

> A collection of three tales in which Mega City One's toughest policeman from the future has teamed up with the legendary Batman. The crossover collection features the two antiheroes teaming up against fan-favorite arch-villains, including the Joker, Judge Death, and the Riddler. The collection includes the story "Batman: Judgment in Gotham," for which Simon Bisley won an Eisner Award in 1992 for Best Artist.

***Batman/Superman/Wonder Woman: Trinity.* Written and illustrated by Matt Wagner.** DC Comics, 2004. 208pp. 1-4012-0187-3. **T** ◎

> A look at the first team-up of all three heroes as they take on Batman villain Ra's al Ghul and his odd assortment of allies, including Bizarro and an Amazon warrior. As the heroes try to stop the madman in his bid for global chaos, the heroes first have to reconcile their own differences and biases to work together as a team.

<u>Cable/Deadpool</u>. Written by Fabian Nicieza. Illustrated by Mark Brooks. Marvel Comics, 2004– . **T**

> The bullets and the black humor fly in this series lampooning the "big gun" comic books of the 1990s, in which every hero was armed to the teeth, carrying impossibly large weaponry. Featuring Cable, the son of Scott Summers (Cyclops) and a clone of Jean Grey, a powerful mutant with psychokinetic powers. Following the death of his adversary Apocalypse, he has lost his place in the world. Luckily he's taken up a new role of savior of Earth. He is reluctantly teamed up with Wade Wilson (Deadpool), a mentally unstable masked mercenary for hire with an odd sense of humor, and together they're taking a proactive stance against the evils in the world, with guns ablaze.
>
> > *Vol. 1: If Looks Could Kill.* 2004. 144pp. 0-7851-1374-6.
> > *Vol. 2: The Burnt Offering.* 2005. 144pp. 0-7851-1571-4.
> > *Vol. 3: The Human Race.* 2006. 144pp. 0-7851-1763-6.
> > *Vol. 4: Bosom Buddies.* 2006. 144pp. 0-7851-1869-1.

<u>Captain America and the Falcon</u>. Written by Christopher Priest. Marvel Comics, 2004–2005. **Y**

> The adventures of Captain America and his occasional partner in crime fighting, the winged hero called the Falcon. Together they're tackling current issues, including terrorism and a possible plot by a rogue Navy Intelligence unit that has created an

"Anti-Cap" Super-Sailor, and all signs are leading them to the deformed villain M.O.D.O.K.

> *Vol. 1: Two Americas*. Illustrated by Bart Sears. 2004. 144pp. 0-7851-1424-6.
> *Vol. 2: Brothers and Keepers*. Illustrated by Joe Bennett. 2005. 168pp. 0-7851-1568-4.

Daredevil vs. Punisher. **Written and illustrated by David Lapham.** Marvel Comics, 2006. 144pp. 0-7851-1745-8. **T**

Daredevil, the red-costumed defender of Hell's Kitchen, and the Punisher, the black-clad vigilante, both have their own ways of seeking justice and redeeming Hell's Kitchen after New York's deposed Kingpin of Crime, Wilson Fisk, was toppled. Now in a power vacuum, the criminals of the city are vying for Fisk's former top spot. When blood is being spilled, the two heroes have to redeem their city with their own brand of justice—even though their ways of fighting crime are very different.

<u>DC/Marvel Crossover Classics.</u> **Written and illustrated by various.** DC Comics and Marvel Comics, 1992–2003. **Y**

Since the late 1970s, Marvel Comics and DC Comics have copublished comic book tales featuring heroes from both publishers teaming up. The stories typically feature the popular heroes interacting and working together against a common adversary and even against each other. Starting with *Superman vs. the Amazing Spider-Man* in 1976, this popular team-up of the two best-selling comic book companies continues to this day, the latest being the long-awaited tale that teamed up the superteams the JLA and the Avengers in 2003.

© 2006 DC Comics.

> *Vol. 1*. Marvel Comics, 1992. 320pp. 0-87135-858-1.
> *Vol. 2*. DC Comics, 1998. 224pp. 1-56389-399-1.
> *Vol. 3*. Marvel Comics, 2002. 320pp. 0-7851-0818-1.
> *Vol. 4*. DC Comics, 2003. 224pp. 1-4012-0169-5.

Doctor Strange and Doctor Doom: Triumph and Torment. **Written by Roger Stern. Illustrated by Mike Mignola.** Marvel Comics, 1989. 0-87135-559-0. **T**

Doctor Strange reluctantly accompanies Doctor Doom, the villainous ruler of Latveria, as Doom participates in a contest of the Vishanti. The winner of the magical contest is to receive a gift from the Strange, the Sorcerer Supreme. After winning the tournament, Doom's wish is to travel to Hell to free his mother's soul from the clutches of Mephisto, but it's a perilous journey that might cost both of them their lives.

Essential Marvel Team-Up. **Written by Roy Thomas. Illustrated by Sal Buscema.** Marvel Comics, 2004. 496pp. 0-7851-0828-9. **Y**

A collection of black-and-white reprints of the classic Marvel Comics series originally published from 1972 to 1985, featuring the adventures of Spider-Man and a rotating cast of Marvel Comic book heroes as they take on the bad guys. In each issue a new hero appeared alongside Spider-Man.

Essential Super-Villain Team-Up. **Written and illustrated by various.** Marvel Comics, 2004. 552pp. 0-7851-1545-5. **Y**

An ultimate collection of the classic comic book series of the same name with a villain working alongside another villain. Sometimes evil can't stand an accomplice, as when Dr. Doom teams up with the Sub-Mariner. Also featured are Red Skull, Magneto, Attuma, Diablo, Arnim Zola, and many more.

Fantastic Four vs. the X-Men. **Written by Chris Claremont. Illustrated by Jon Bogdanove.** Marvel Comics, 1990. 96pp. 0-87135-650-3. **Y**

Following the battle against the murdering Marauders in the Morlock tunnels, Kitty Pryde's wounds have gotten worse, and the X-Men fear she's slowly dissipating. Unable to free her from her ghostly form, the X-Men turn to Reed Richards, leader of the Fantastic Four, for help. When a journal from Reed's past describing the space flight during which the Fantastic Four gained their powers is revealed, the X-Men lose trust that Reed can save Kitty, and the sinister ruler of Latveria, Doctor Doom, makes a deal to save Kitty's life that might cost the X-Men more than they ever bargained for.

Fantastic Four/Spider-Man. **Written by Stan Lee. Illustrated by various.** Marvel Comics, 2005. 152pp. 0-7851-1803-9. **Y**

A collection of some of the earliest meetings between the Fantastic Four and the Amazing Spider-Man from the original issues of the *Fantastic Four* and *Amazing Spider-Man* comic books.

Greatest Spider-Man and Daredevil Team-Ups. **Written by Stan Lee and various. Illustrated by various.** Marvel Comics, 1996. 176pp. 0-7851-0223-X. **Y**

Daredevil and Spider-Man have long fought crime together in New York City. The collection features some of the highlights from the earlier Marvel titles, in which the wall-crawler and old "horn head" have teamed-up.

Greatest Team-Up Stories Ever Told. **Written and illustrated by various.** DC Comics, 1998. 284pp. 0-930289-61-7. **Y**

A look back at some of the best-known team-up stories by DC Comics. Highlights include tales of Batman and Superman, Green Lantern and Green Arrow, the Golden Age Flash and Silver Age Flash, Adam Strange and Hawkman, and Superman and Swamp Thing.

<u>Green Lantern/Green Arrow Collection.</u> Written by Dennis O'Neil. Illustrated by Neal Adams. DC Comics, 2000–2004. **T**

Classic stories from the 1970s reprinted, about the socially responsible Green Arrow teaming up with the brave but naïve Green Lantern. The stories covered topical issues including race relations, pollution, and even drug abuse.

Vol. 1: Hard Traveling Heroes. 2004. 176pp. 1-4012-0224-1.
Vol. 2: More Hard Traveling Heroes. 2004. 200pp. 1-4012-0230-6.

Hulk and Thing: Hard Knocks. **Written by Bruce Jones. Illustrated by Jae Lee.**
Marvel Comics, 2005. 96pp. 0-7851-1576-5. **Y**

When a man made of rock and a jade giant get together for coffee, anything
can happen. The Thing and the Hulk, two of the biggest bruisers in the Marvel
Comics universe, have long been both friends and hard-hitting adversaries.
Ben Grimm (the Thing) has traveled to the desert to seek out Bruce Banner
(the Hulk) for advice, to see if he has experienced the same frustrations being
known only as a monster. The Thing tells in flashback about their earliest encounter, and in typical fashion, the Thing and the Hulk do what they do best
when they meet and beat the living daylights out of each other as in the old
days.

JLA/Avengers: The Collector's Edition. **Written by Kurt Busiek. Illustrated by**
George Pérez. DC Comics/Marvel Comics, 2004. 288pp. 1-4012-0207-1. **Y** ◉

A crossover of epic proportions as Marvel Comics and DC
Comics' favorite super-teams team up in one of the most eagerly awaited company crossovers of all time. The Avengers
and the Justice League of America are brought together by
two cosmic entities from different realities, using the teams in
a contest that will decide the fate of one of the realities. Featuring appearances by every member of both teams, including
Superman, Captain America, Batman, Iron Man, Wonder
Woman, Thor, and many others in an astonishing battle. Both
teams must set aside their differences to defeat the schemes of
Krona and his devious ally, the Grandmaster. The special
hardcover edition also collects Kurt Busiek's scripts as well

© 2006 DC Comics.

as the original artwork from a failed 1980s JLA/Avengers crossover that was
never printed due to company differences.

JLA/JSA: Virtue and Vice. **Written by Geoff Johns and David S. Goyer. Illus-**
trated by Carlos Pacheco. DC Comics, 2003. 96pp. 1-4012-0040-0. **Y**

Two super-teams, the JSA and JLA, team up to tackle a psionic threat that is
turning hero against hero and threatens to tear apart the entire planet if not
stopped. Can the combined power of Superman, Sentinel, Batman, Mr. Terrific, and others be enough to take on the combined might of JLA villain
Despero and JSA arch-nemesis Johnny Sorrow before it's too late and they
lose their team members and President Lex Luthor?

Marvel Team-Up. **Written by Robert Kirkman. Illustrated by Scott Kolins.**
Marvel Comics, 2005– . **Y**

A new ongoing Marvel Team-Up series written by fan-favorite writer Robert
Kirkman (*Invincible, Walking Dead*). Unlike previous Marvel Team-Up series, the collection of stories focuses not only on Spider-Man and his adventures with a rotating cast of Marvel heroes; it now features many Marvel
Comics characters, including Captain America, the Punisher, Blade, the Fantastic Four, Wolverine, Moon Knight, the Hulk, Daredevil, and the Black
Widow, each teaming up with another hero to take on the bad guys.

Vol. 1: The Golden Child. 2005. 144pp. 0-7851-1595-1.
Vol. 2: Master of the Ring. 2005. 144pp. 0-7851-1596-X.
Vol. 3: League of Losers. 2006. 120pp. 0-7851-1946-9.
Vol. 4. 2006. 144pp. 0-7851-1990-6.

Medieval Spawn/Witchblade. **Written by Garth Ennis. Illustrated by Brandon Peterson.** Top Cow Productions/Image Comics, 1997. 96pp. 1-887279-44-X. **T**

In the year 1175 in Ireland, when the realm of the Faerie folk comes under attack by the forces of the Darkness-powered Lord Cardinale, two unlikely heroes come together to fight the evil forces: this time period's champions, Medieval Spawn and a young woman who has just discovered she wields the power called the Witchblade. Former lovers from times past, an army of two is all they need to defeat the hordes of Cardinale's Darkness Army and to free the Fairie land from the grasp of evil.

Savage Dragon: Greatest Team-Ups. **Written and illustrated by Erik Larsen and various.** Image Comics, 1999. 176pp. 1-58240-047-4. **T**

A collection highlighting the team-ups that the super-strong, green-skinned Chicago policeman known as Dragon has encountered. The featured heroes who team up with Dragon include many from the Image Comics line, including Spawn, Super-Patriot, and Velocity.

Spider-Man and the Uncanny X-Men. **Written by Roy Thomas. Illustrated by various.** Marvel Comics, 1996. 176pp. 0-7851-0200-0. **Y**

A collection featuring a few highlights in comic book history in which the favorite wall-crawler has worked alongside the mutant team of heroes called the X-Men.

Spider-Man Team-Up. **Written by Todd DeZago. Illustrated by various.** Marvel Age/Marvel Comics, 2005. 96pp. 0-7851-1611-7. **A**

A collection for younger readers retelling the classic team-up stories of Spider-Man with some of Marvel's more popular heroes, including the Fantastic Four, Thor, Captain America, Kitty Pryde, and Storm.

Spider-Man/Human Torch: I'm with Stupid. **Written by Dan Slott. Illustrated by Ty Templeton.** Marvel Comics, 2005. 120pp. 0-7851-1723-7. **Y**

Five short stories highlighting friendship and humor, from the high school days to the present of Spider-Man and the Fantastic Four's Human Torch.

🎭 **Superman/Batman. Written by Jeph Loeb.** DC Comics, 2004– . **Y** ◉

For years DC Comics has featured story lines teaming up their classic characters Superman and Batman. This newest series, written by fan-favorite Jeph Loeb, continues that trend. After accusing Superman of crimes against humanity, U.S. President Lex Luthor sends a squadron of heroes against Superman and Batman, including Captain Atom, Hawkman, Captain Marvel, Power Girl, Green Lantern John Stewart, and others. But the team of Superman and Batman is more than a match for the heroes, and they expose President Luthor for the fraud he's always been. When President Luthor falls from grace, just what depths will he go to get revenge on Superman and Batman? In the second collection, a girl claiming to be Superman's cousin comes to Earth. Is she really who she claims to be, and what does the Darkseid, the fascist ruler of the planet

Apokolips, want with her? *Volume 3* is a glimpse into what the world would be like if Batman and Superman ruled it. *Public Enemies* received recognition from YALSA's Quick Picks for Reluctant Readers committee in 2006.

Vol. 1: Public Enemies. Illustrated by Ed McGuinness. 2004. 160pp. 1-4012-0323-X, hardcover; 1-4012-0220-9, softcover.

Vol. 2: The Return of Supergirl. Illustrated by Michael Turner. 2005. 160pp. 1-4012-0347-7, hardcover.

Vol. 3: Absolute Power. Illustrated by Carlos Pacheco. 2005. 128pp. 1-4012-0447-3, hardcover.

Vol. 4: Vengeance. Illustrated by Ed McGuinness. 2006. 160pp. 1-4012-0921-1, hardcover.

Vol. 5. Illustrated by Ed McGuinness. 2006. 144pp. 1-4012-0922-X, hardcover.

© 2006 DC Comics.

Superman/Madman: Hullabaloo. **Written and illustrated by Mike Allred.** Dark Horse Comics, 1998. 96pp. 1-56971-301-4. **Y** ◎

The world's snappiest hero from Snap City meets up with the Man of Steel! When a freak accident merges the two heroes of different dimensions, Madman and Superman wind up teaming up, literally! Now they've become two blended versions of both heroes, and they're in a world of adventure trying to get used to each other's powers. Can they find a way get things back to normal before it's too late? Along the way they're on the lookout for mutant street beatniks, a super-zombie, and other groovy freaks. For other titles featuring Madman, see the chapter 6.

<u>Ultimate Marvel Team-Up.</u> **Written by Brian Michael Bendis. Illustrated by various.** Marvel Comics, 2001–2003. **T**

From Marvel's Ultimate Universe, the adventures of Spider-Man with other denizens of justice, including Wolverine, Fantastic Four, Man-Thing, Iron Man, Doctor Strange, and many others.

Vol. 1. 2001. 144pp. 0-7851-0807-6.
Vol. 2. 2002. 120pp. 0-7851-1299-5.
Vol. 3. 2003. 136pp. 0-7851-1300-2.

Ultimate X-Men/Fantastic Four. **Written by Mike Carey. Illustrated by Pasqual Ferry.** 2006. 136pp. 0-7851-2292-3. **T**

From Marvel Comics' Ultimate Universe, the first team-up of the Ultimate X-Men and the Ultimate Fantastic Four. When Rhona Burchill, the villain called the Mad Thinker, steals the X-Men's mutant-detecting device called Cerebro and frames the Fantastic Four, the stage is set for a confrontation between the two teams as Wolverine, Iceman, and Shadowcat face the Fantastic Four.

WildC.A.TS./Cyberforce: Killer Instinct. **Written and illustrated by Jim Lee and Marc Silvestri.** Image Comics, 2004. 160pp. 1-4012-0322-1. **T**

Features the first appearance of the cybernetic team of heroes called Cyberforce, including Stryker, Heatwave, Cyblade, Ballistic, Impact, Velocity, and Ripclaw as they meet with the half-alien WildC.A.T.S. team in their quest to vanquish the villainous Daemonites.

WildC.A.TS./X-Men. **Written by Warren Ellis, Scott Lobdell, and James Robinson. Illustrated by Travis Charest, Jim Lee,** Adam Hughes and Matt Broome. WildStorm Productions/Image Comics and Marvel Comics, 1998. 184pp. 1-58240-022-9. **T** ◉

Spanning four ages in comic book history—the Golden Age, Silver Age, Modern Age, and Dark Age (the future)—this is a look at the adventures of the uncanny X-Men as they encounter another team of half-breed alien heroes called the WildC.A.T.S. Wolverine and Zealot meet during World War II to take on Daemonite-Nazi soldiers and their alien queen, and Grifter and Jean Grey take on a horde of Daemonite-Brood hybrids. More stories are featured as the heroes meet in different decades throughout the twentieth and twenty-first century.

Wolverine/Nick Fury: The Scorpio Connection. **Written by Archie Goodwin. Illustrated by Howard Chaykin.** Marvel Comics, 1989. 120pp. 0-7851-1491-2. **T**

A mutual friend of Wolverine and Nick Fury is killed by an imposter pretending to be Fury's brother, Scorpio. Wolverine and Fury work together to discover the identity of the new Scorpio and the real mastermind who is trying to snare Nick Fury into a deadly trap.

Wolverine/Punisher. Marvel Comics, 1989–2004. **T**

The Punisher and Wolverine, both vicious killers and hard-core fighters, have had a colorful history of team-ups through the years as both allies and antagonists.

> *Punisher-Wolverine: The African Saga.* Written by Carl Potts. Illustrated by Jim Lee. 1989. 64pp. 0-87135-611-2.
> *Wolverine/Punisher, Vol. 1.* Written by Peter Milligan. Illustrated by Lee Weeks. 2004. 120pp. 0-7851-1432-7.
> *Wolverine-Punisher: Revelation (Marvel's Finest).* Written by Christopher Golden. Illustrated by Pat Lee and Alvin Lee. 2000. 96pp. 0-7851-0729-0.

X-Men—Avengers: Bloodties. **Written by Fabian Nicieza, Scott Lobdell, and Roy Thomas. Illustrated by Adam Kubert and various.** Marvel Comics, 1995. 128pp. 0-7851-0103-9. **Y**

The Acolytes, mutant followers of the teachings of Magneto, have decided to take his teachings in a whole new direction and purify the world. Exodus, the new leader of the Acolytes, wants to purify the bloodline of Magneto by "cleansing" the world of Magneto's children Quicksilver and the Scarlet Wish, as well as his granddaughter Luna. Can the combined might of the Avengers and the X-Men be enough to defeat the Acolytes before they release a bomb capable of turning the entire island into a mutant haven by killing all nonmutant humans?

X-Men & The Amazing Spider-Man: Savage Land. **Written by Chris Clare-mont. Illustrated by Michael Golden.** Marvel Comics, 2002. 80pp. 0-7851-0891-2. **Y**

> A collection of tales featuring characters from the X-Men team and Spi-der-Man and the Tarzan-like adventurer known as Ka-Zar, facing off against the Pterodactyl-humanoid known as Sauron and other monstrous creatures in the mystic realm where dinosaurs still roam, called the Savage Land.

X-Men vs. the Avengers. **Written by Roger Stern. Illustrated by Marc Silvestri.** Marvel Comics, 1993. 96pp. 0-87135-967-7. **Y**

> When a giant chunk of Magneto's former asteroid base falls to Earth, the X-Men and then-current leader the mutant Master of Magnetism, Magneto, investigate the crash site. The Avengers, meanwhile, have also been sent by the government to check the site, and they attempt to bring Magneto to justice for war crimes. Soon Magneto is captured, and the U.S. government discovers that it isn't the only one wanting to try Magneto for his crimes against humanity.

X-Men/Fantastic Four. **Written by Akira Yoshida. Illustrated by Pat Lee.** Mar-vel Comics, 2005. 120pp. 0-7851-1520-X. **Y**

> The Fantastic Four and the X-Men must take on a race of vicious buglike aliens called the Brood before the aliens threaten Earth. Can the two teams set aside their differences and work together, or will they each become their own worst enemy? When a cosmic storm strikes that is similar to the one that cre-ated the Fantastic Four years before, several X-Men members temporarily re-ceive the powers of the Fantastic Four, and now members of both teams must work alongside each other to defeat not just the temporarily crazed members of the X-Men with the powers of the Fantastic Four, but the threat of the Brood as well.

Epic Events

Epic events are crossovers that feature a massive group of heroes working to-gether against a typically grand-scale threat such as a deadly villain, a worldwide crisis, or a galaxy-shaking event. Highlights from the past several years of epic events include DC Comics' *Crisis on Infinite Earths* and Marvel Comics' *Secret Wars*. Below are listed some of the better-known crossover team-ups collections. Note that epic events featuring Marvel Comics' mutant heroes, the X-Men, are listed in their own section in this chapter.

Cosmic Odyssey. **Written by Jim Starlin. Illustrated by Mike Mignola.** DC Comics, 1992. 200pp. 1-56389-051-8. **Y**

> The villainous Darkseid of Apokolips recruits Superman, Batman, Starfire, Green Lantern, the Demon Etrigan, Starfire, and several members of the New Gods to join him on a quest of cosmic proportions to save the galaxies from a worthy foe made from anti-life. As the fate of worlds hangs in the balance, only the heroes reluctantly teamed up with the vilest of enemies can rescue the universe.

Coup D'Etat. **Written by Ed Brubaker, Joe Casey, Robbie Morrison and Micah Wright. Illustrated by Jim Lee and various.** WildStorm Productions/DC Comics, 2004. 112pp. 1-4012-0570-4. **T**

> Set in the WildStorm comics universe, the proactive vigilante super-hero team called the Authority has finally had enough after a disaster in Florida and has decided to take over the United States. Can one team be allowed to do this, and who could even try to stop them? Features appearances by other WildStorm teams including Force Stormwatch: Team Achilles and the Wildcats.

<u>Crisis on Infinite Earths.</u> Written by Marv Wolfman. Illustrated by George Pérez. DC Comics, 2001–2005. **T ◎**

© 2006 DC Comics.

Our planet Earth is just one of many other infinite Earths, each with its own separate history and protected by its own brand of heroes. One by one the Earths are being systematically destroyed by a planet-killing wave of Anti-Matter being culled by the vicious being known as the Anti-Monitor. As Earth after Earth is destroyed, the heroes of all the Earths are called by the mysterious man known only as the Monitor to combine forces against the Anti-Monitor and his legion of para-demons. Together in one monumental book, all the heroes of the DC Universe join in a massive battle to save the multiple Earths against the most dangerous adversary their worlds have ever seen. As sacrifices are made and heroes die, the fate of the multiple Earths will be decided by the strength and determination of Superman of Earth 1, the original Man of Steel, and all the brave heroes who were inspired by him. Originally published in comic book form in 1985–1986, the series was a monumental story line that helped to clean house at DC Comics of many characters. The *Absolute Edition* features a slipcased edition as well as a ninety-six-page supplement on the making of this monumental story.

> *Crisis on Infinite Earths.* 2001. 368pp. 1-56389-750-4.
> *Crisis on Infinite Earths—The Absolute Edition.* 2005. 468pp. 1-4012-0712-X.

<u>Crisis on Multiple Earths.</u> Written by Gardner Fox. Illustrated by Mike Sekowsky and various. DC Comics, 2002–2006. **Y**

> Reprints the classic DC Comics stories in which the concept of multiple parallel Earths was first introduced. On each planet different super-heroes exist. The collections feature the best team-ups between the JSA of Earth 1 and the JLA from Earth 2.
>
> *Vol. 1.* 2002. 208pp. 1-56389-895-0.
> *Vol. 2.* 2003. 192pp. 1-4012-0003-6.
> *Vol. 3.* 2004. 192pp. 1-4012-0231-4.
> *Vol. 4.* 2006. 168pp. 1-4012-0957-2.
> *The Team-Ups.* 2005. 192pp. 1-4012-0470-8.

Day of Vengeance. **Written by Bill Willingham. Illustrated by Justiniano.** DC Comics, 2005. 224pp. 1-4012-0840-1. **Y ◎**

> When the Spectre, the wrath of God, seeks to destroy magic alongside a new incarnation of the villain called Eclipso, it's up to a band of unlikely magical-based heroes called the Shadowpact—including Ragman, Enchantress, Blue Devil, Nightmaster,

Detective Chimp, and Nightshade—to try to stop them, with the aid of Captain Marvel. A prelude to the 2006 mega-DC Comics event called <u>Infinite Crisis</u>.

***DC Comics Versus Marvel Comics*. Written by Ron Marz, Peter David, Dan Jurgens and various. Illustrated by various.** DC Comics/Marvel Comics, 1996. 192pp. 1-56389-294-4. **Y**

In 1995, the worlds of the DC Universe and Marvel Universe collided, and as the fates of both worlds hung in the balance, the super-hero companies' characters were pitted against each other, with the fans voting on the winners. Superman battled the Hulk, Captain America fought Batman, Wonder Women took on Thor, and so on. The series is also noted for being the first introduction of the Amalgam Universe, a fun blending of the characters that created brand-new characters who were different yet familiar. Superman and Captain America became the Super-Soldier; Spider-Man and Superboy merged to become Spider-Boy; Batman and Wolverine merged to become Dark Claw; and so on. The heroes were fresh and excited and were brought back in several sequels that were collected as well.

<u>Earth X.</u> **Written by Jim Krueger and Alex Ross. Illustrated by John Paul Leon and Doug Braithwaite.** Marvel Comics, 2000–2006. **T**

A massive story featuring a dystopian look at the Marvel Universe several decades into the future. All humankind is now genetically mutated due in part to an experiment-gone-wrong by Reed Richards, and all individuals are superpowered. The world is in shambles as the mutated Marvel heroes and villains experience a rapidly changing world in which new versions of old enemies are destroying America, and Captain America must try to find a way to defeat the brand-new Red Skull from taking over the United States. Meanwhile, Richards and the Inhumans discover the true reason for humanity's mutation, and the fates of many Marvel heroes and villains are revealed. The series was concluded in the sequels *Universe X* and *Paradise X*.

> *Vol. 1: Earth X.* 2d ed. 2006. 472pp. 0-7851-2325-3.
> *Vol. 2: Universe X, Book I.* 2002. 384pp. 0-7851-0867-X.
> *Vol. 3: Universe X, Book II.* 2002. 320pp. 0-7851-0885-8.
> *Vol. 4: Paradise X, Book I.* 2003. 304pp. 0-7851-1120-4.
> *Vol. 5: Paradise X, Book II.* 2003. 352pp. 0-7851-1121-2.
> *Earth X Hardcover, Vol. 1.* 2005. 592pp. 0-7851-1875-6.

***The Final Night*. Written by Karl Kesel and Ron Marz. Illustrated by Stuart Immonen, Mike McKone, and others.** DC Comics, 1998. 134pp. 1-56389-419-X. **Y**

When the sun is extinguished by the villain called the Sun-Eater, Earth is forced into a perpetual state of cold and total darkness. As the heroes and villains of the planet band together to devise a way to reignite the sun, the former Green Lantern, Hal Jordan (Parallax), makes peace with his demons and makes the ultimate sacrifice for the sake of the entire planet.

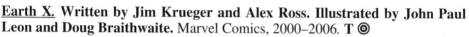

House of M/Decimation. Marvel Comics, 2005–2006 **T** ◉

Following the events of the <u>Avengers: Disassembled</u> story line, in which Wanda Maximoff (the Scarlet Witch) has gone insane, her father, the mutant Magneto, Master of Magnetism, uses her powers to rebuild a reality in which everyone's dreams have come true. Magneto's dream was for mutants to rule the world, and he is now the ruler over humankind. Peter Parker is happily married to Gwen Stacy; Kitty Pryde is a schoolteacher; Steve Rogers (Captain America) has lived a normal life and is now a senior citizen; Scott Summers and Emma Frost are married; and Hawkeye is still alive. In a dramatically changed world, the heroes of the universe are happy and content with the lives they've been living. When one hero, Wolverine, discovers the truth of their existence, can he convince the heroes to give up their dream lives and knock down the House of Magnus foundations to let it crumble under the lies that it has been built upon? The series <u>House of M</u> was followed up by the miniseries <u>Decimation</u>, and the multiple tie-in titles are listed below.

<u>House of M.</u> 2005. **T**

> *House of M: Excalibur—Prelude.* Written by Chris Claremont. Illustrated by Aaron Lopresti. 2005. 96pp. 0-7851-1812-8.
> *House of M.* Written by Brian Michael Bendis. Illustrated by Olivier Coipel. 2006. 200pp. 0-7851-1721-0.
> *House of M: Uncanny X-Men.* Written by Chris Claremont. Illustrated by Alan Davis. 2005. 96pp. 0-7851-1663-X.
> *House of M: Spider-Man.* Written by Mark Waid. Illustrated by Salvador Larroca. 2005. 120pp. 0-7851-1753-9.
> *House of M: Incredible Hulk.* Written by Peter David. Illustrated by Jorge Lucas. 2005. 120pp. 0-7851-1834-9.
> *House of M: Mutopia X.* Written by David Hine. Illustrated by Lan Medina. 2006. 120pp. 0-7851-1811-X.
> *House of M: Wolverine.* Written by Daniel Way. Illustrated by Javier Saltares and Mark Texeira. 2006. 128pp. 0-7851-1829-2.
> *House of M: World of M.* Written and illustrated by various. 2005. 184pp. 0-7851-1922-1.
> *House of M: Fantastic Four/Iron Man.* Written by John Layman and Greg Pak. Illustrated by Scot Eaton. 2005. 144pp. 0-7851-1923-X.
> House of M: New X-Men. Written by Nunzio DeFilippis and Christina Weir. Illustrated by Aaron Lopresti. 2005. 96pp. 0-7851-1941-8.

<u>Decimation.</u> 2006. **T**

> *Decimation: X-Men—the Day After.* Written by Chris Claremont and Peter Milligan. Illustrated by Salvador Larroca and Randy Green. 2006. 168pp. 0-7851-1984-1.
> *Decimation: Generation M.* Written by Paul Jenkins. Illustrated by Ramon Bachs. 2006. 120pp. 0-7851-1958-2.
> *Decimation: Son of M.* Written by David Hine. Illustrated by Roy Martinez. 2006. 144pp. 0-7851-1970-1.

Identity Crisis. **Written by Brad Meltzer. Illustrated by Rags Morales and Michael Bair.** DC Comics, 2005. 288pp. 1-4012-0688-3. **T**

When the spouse of a former JLA member is found savagely murdered and raped, the super-heroes fan out to find the real culprit behind this horrendous act. Superman, Batman, Wonder Woman, and a large cast of DC Comics heroes join in the search, fearing that their own loved ones might be next.,Secrets long-hidden are revealed, which might tear the allies apart before the murderer is caught. The ramifications of this event continue into the titles *Day of Vengeance*, *OMAC Project*, *Villains United*, and <u>Infinite Crisis</u>.

<u>Infinite Crisis.</u> **Written by Geoff Johns. Illustrated by Phil Jimenez and Andy Lanning.** DC Comics, 2006. **T**

A groundbreaking event borne from the ashes of the classic DC Comics' story *Crisis on Infinite Earths* as well as the story lines of *Day of Vengeance*, *OMAC Project*, *The Rann-Thanagar War*, and *Villains United*. When the original Superman, a grey-haired aging hero, re-enters our world, he finds the current heroes in disarray and the JLA disbanded, and he intends to fix it and return the world to the more peaceful Earth-2 of old from before the original Crisis. What happens when the Superman of Earth-2 finally confronts the much-younger Man of Steel of Earth-1? Meanwhile, a new disaster is coming that will forever change the heroes of the DC Comics' universe as heroes die, lives are changed, and a world will never be the same again. *Superman: Infinite Crisis* features the backstory of the original Superman and the events that lead into the series *Infinite Crisis*.

> *Infinite Crisis.* 2006. 272pp. 1-4012-0959-9, hardcover
> *Superman: Infinite Crisis.* 2006. 128pp. 1-4012-0953-X.

The Infinity Gauntlet. **Written by Jim Starlin. Illustrated by George Pérez and Ron Lim.** Marvel Comics, 2000. 256pp. 0-87135-944-8. **Y**

Thanos, the power-hungry servant of Death, has acquired the Infinity Gems, six gems that give the wielder of the gauntlet seemingly godlike powers. As Thanos destroys nearly half of the universe, the Silver Surfer races to Earth to warn the heroes about the danger, especially Doctor Strange. With an army of Marvel heroes aligned with the Silver Surfer, including Spider-Man, Thor, and Captain America, the heroes must try to wrest the gauntlet from Thanos before more innocent lives are destroyed by his devotion to Death. But there is only one man who can defeat Thanos and take possession of the glove, the resurrected hero known as Adam Warlock. For other stories featuring Thanos, please see the section above on villains.

JLA: One Million. **2d ed. Written by Grant Morrison. Illustrated by various.** DC Comics, 2004. 208pp. 1-4012-0320-5. **Y**

> The JLA is asked by their counterparts 1 million years in the future to visit the 853rd century. Superman, still alive after all these years and living in the sun, is going to once again visit Earth, and the Justice Legion A, future variations on Batman, the Flash, Green Lantern, and the like, are the heroes guarding the future. When the ancient immortal Vandal Savage plots a dangerous scheme with Solaris, the Tyrant Sun super-computer, a plan is set in motion that can destroy the festivities and be the end for the JLA teams of both the past and the future.

JLA: World Without Grown-ups. **Written by Todd DeZago. Illustrated by Mike McKone and various.** DC Comics, 1998. 128pp. 1-56389-473-4. **Y**

> When everyone on the planet younger than the age of seventeen is transported to another reality, apart from the adults, the kids must fend for themselves. Luckily for them the teen heroes Robin, Impulse, Superboy, and the rest of DC Comics' young heroes are there to find a way to get the kids back home.

<u>The Kingdom.</u> Written by Mark Waid. Illustrated by various. DC Comics, 2000. 232pp. 1-56389-567-6. **T**

> Spin-off from the hit fully painted story *Kingdom Come* by Mark Waid and Alex Ross. In the future, the villain Gog is slowly going back in time, killing Superman in order to prevent the past event from the hit series occurring. It's up to the heroes from the future and the heroes from the present to stop Gog from killing the Man of Steel and changing history.

🎖 *Kingdom Come.* **Written by Mark Waid. Illustrated by Alex Ross.** DC Comics, 1997. 232pp. 1-56389- 330-4. **T** ◉

© 2006 DC Comics.

> Gorgeous fully painted story of the last days of the DC Comics super-heroes by writer Mark Waid and illustrator Alex Ross. Many years in the future, the classic DC Comics heroes of old are retiring and making way for a new generation. When rebellion strikes the hearts of the young and corruptible, Superman and other heroes of old return to instill order and put them back in their place. Two camps, one led by Batman and the other by Superman, must decide the best way to handle the crisis. As a war breaks out, old allies must take on the armies of the young and corrupt, and an elderly Protestant minister named Norman McCay is caught up in the event to witness the end of the reign of the super-heroes. The story won several Eisner Awards in 1997 for Best Finite Series/Limited Series and Best Cover Artist and Best Painter/Multimedia Artist (Interior), as well as two Harvey Awards in 1997 for Best Penciller or Artist and Best Cover Artist.

Legends: The Collected Edition. **Written by John Ostrander and Len Wein. Illustrated by John Byrne.** DC Comics, 1993. 144pp. 1-56389-095-X. **Y**

> Darkseid, the ruler of Apokolips, finds a unique way to turn the tables on the super-heroes: to make them into hated adversaries of the people they save. After the president of the United States bans all meta-human activity, the heroes, including Bat-

man, Superman, Captain Marvel, Wonder Woman, the Flash, and Green Lantern, must try to reverse this diabolical scheme and bring order to the United States once again.

Marvel 1602. Marvel Comics, 2004–2006. **T** ◎

© 2006 Marvel Comics.

In the year 1602, Europe is at a crossroads as enemies of England vie for the crown and seek to end Queen Elizabeth's life. In England, Sir Nicholas Fury and Doctor Stephen Strange, both servants of Queen Elizabeth, have been instructed by the queen to retrieve a holy relic en route from Jerusalem and to solve the mystery of the strange storms in the sky. Meanwhile the Spanish Inquisition is executing individuals with strange powers, including an angel with wings and other "witchbreed," and Virginia Dare, the first-born child of the Colonies, is en route to England with her Native American protector on an important mission. A unique chain of seemingly unrelated events is imploding: the Marvel Universe has arrived 400 years earlier and the world might not survive another day. Written by *Sandman* creator Neil Gaiman. A sequel to the series, called *New World*, was released in 2006, but was not written by Gaiman.

> *Marvel 1602.* Written by Neil Gaiman. Illustrated by Andy Kubert. 2004. 248pp. 0-7851-1070-4.
> *Marvel 1602: New World.* Written by Greg Pak. Illustrated by Greg Tocchini. 2006. 120pp. 0-7851-1494-7.

The OMAC Project. **Written by Greg Rucka. Illustrated by Jesus Saiz.** DC Comics, 2005. 256pp. 1-4012-0837-1. **T**

A prelude to the 2006 mega-DC Comics event called <u>Infinite Crisis</u>. The heroes of the DC Universe are under attack by a robotic army of Observational Meta-human Activity Constructs (O.M.A.C.) under the control of Maxwell Lord, a one-time friend of the heroes and current leader of the international group known as Checkmate. Now the hero Blue Beetle is dead by Lord's hand, and Wonder Woman is forced to destroy Lord by any means necessary. When the O.M.A.C. protocol is unleashed following Lord's death, can the heroes save themselves and the world from the robot menace?

The Rann-Thanagar War. **Written by Dave Gibbons. Illustrated by Ivan Reis.** DC Comics, 2006. 192pp. 1-4012-0839-8. **T**

A prelude to the 2006 epic event in DC Comics called <u>Infinite Crisis</u>. When the planet of Rann, home to the Earthborn space hero Adam Strange, is teleported into the same solar system as the world of Thanagar, home to the race of Hawkmen, the unthinkable happens: Thanagar spirals out of orbit and is destroyed by the nearby sun. When the planet of Thanagar is obliterated, evacuees make their home on Rann, but it's only a matter of time before strife and chaos take over, and it seems that not even Hawkman, Hawkgirl, and the Green Lanterns Kilowog and Kyle Rayner can keep the peace.

***Secret War.* Written by Brian Michael Bendis. Illustrated by Gabriele Dell'Otto.** Marvel Comics, 2005. 256pp. 0-7851-1837-3. hardcover. **T**

One year ago Nick Fury of S.H.I.E.L.D. sent a covert group of heroes composed of Spider-Man, Daredevil, Captain America, Wolverine, Black Widow, Luke Cage, and S.H.I.E.L.D. agent Daisy Johnson to the country of Latveria to thwart the Tinkerer's plot. After the mission was over, all of the heroes' minds were wiped clean of the event. Now one year later, Luke Cage is in the hospital and the mystery deepens—what was their mission, did it succeed, and why don't they remember anything about it?

***Secret Wars.* Written by Jim Shooter. Illustrated by Mike Zeck.** Marvel Comics, 1999. 336pp. 0-7851-0727-4. **Y** ◎

A mysterious godlike being called The Beyonder whisks away the Marvel heroes and villains to fight a battle for the ultimate prize. When allegiances are tested and the battle lines have been drawn, only one is triumphant, and it isn't the heroes. When Doctor Doom carries within himself the power of a god, what hero can stop him?

***Superman: Our Worlds at War Complete Edition.* Written and illustrated by various.** DC Comics, 2006. 512pp. 1-4012-1129-1. **T**

Superman and other DC Comics heroes must make a stand to save Earth from the invading force of Imperiex, a ruthless leader of a vast galactic empire and destroyer of galaxies. A reluctant alliance is made when the heroes align themselves with Lex Luthor, then president of the United States, and Darkseid, the vicious ruler of the planet Apokolips. As heroes and villains fight alongside each other, many die under the brutal assault of Imperiex and his armies. Meanwhile, Superman's old nemesis Braniac seeks to tap into the vast powers of Imperiex for his own dark purpose.

<u>Ultimate Galactus.</u> Written by Warren Ellis. Marvel Comics, 2005–2007. **T**

The stage is set introducing the Ultimate universe to the greatest threat from outer space ever known: Galactus, devourer of planets. A strange anomaly is found in a region of Russia that attracts the attention of both the U.S.-sanctioned team the Ultimates and Charles Xavier's X-Men. As both teams investigate the crash site for something foreboding, the stage is set for an epic conflict with an unbeatable enemy and planet Earth will never be the same. Also features the first appearance of the Captain Marvel in the Ultimate universe.

> *Vol. 1: Nightmare.* Illustrated by Trevor Hairsine. 2005. 120pp. 0-7851-1497-1.
> *Vol. 2: Secret.* Illustrated by Steve McNiven. 2005. 96pp. 0-7851-1660-5.
> *Vol. 3: Extinction.* Illustrated by Brandon Peterson. 2006. 144pp. 0-7851-1496-3.
> *Ultimate Galactus Trilogy.* Written by Warren Ellis. Illustrated by various. 2007. 344pp. 0785121390, hardcover.

***Underworld Unleashed.* Written by Mark Waid and Harry Peterson. Illustrated by Howard Porter, Phil Jimenez and various.** DC Comics, 1998. 176pp. 1-56389-447-5. **T**

Neron, a demon from Hell, offers the greatest villains in the universe their heart's desire in exchange for one item in their possession: their souls. Soon the villains' powers are amplified, making their archenemies, the heroes, that much easier to defeat. The villains are just a pawn in Neron's game to control the universe, and the salvation of Earth falls not into the hands of the heroes, but into those of a reformed villain called the Trickster. Can a reformed criminal outsmart the devil?

Zero Hour: Crisis in Time. **Written and illustrated by Dan Jurgens.** DC Comics, 2004. 160pp. 1-56389-992-2. **T**

> After Green Lantern Hal Jordan becomes a villain called Parallax, he attempts to re-create the universe in his own image. As some heroes die in the battle, a team of heroes attempts to appeal to Hal's humanity before the universe is destroyed. When all else fails, it comes down to Parallax against the unstoppable wrath of God called the Spectre to avenge the deaths of trillions that he caused. Mainly done to clean up some continuity errors in DC comic books following the events of <u>Crisis on Infinite Earths</u>.

X-Men Epic Events

The X-Men, due to their plethora of titles, routinely feature epic story lines that cross over into several monthly series. Featured below are some of the highlights and a brief description of each crossover series. They are featured in this section due to the crossovers featuring mostly mutant characters. Epic event titles that including most major Marvel Comics characters, including the X-Men, Spider-Man, the Fantastic Four, the Avengers, and the like, are listed above.

X-Men: Fall of the Mutants. **Written by Chris Claremont and Louise Simonson. Illustrated by Walter Simonson.** Marvel Comics, 2002. 272pp. 0-7851-0825-4. **Y** ◎

> A dark period in X-Men history, during which tragedy strikes all three X-Men teams, comprising the X-Men, X-Factor, and New Mutants. The New Mutants battle against Cameron Hodge and lose one of their own in the battle; X-Factor faces betrayal by the former X-Men member called Angel, who is now the fourth horseman of the Apocalypse called Death; and the X-Men battle an ancient evil called the Adversary and pay the ultimate cost of their own lives.

X-Men: Inferno. **Written by Chris Claremont and Louise Simonson. Illustrated by Marc Silvestri and Walter Simonson.** Marvel Comics, 1996. 352pp. 0-7851-0222-1. **Y** ◎

> Realizing that she's been a pawn of the villain Mr. Sinister, Madelyne Pryor, a genetic clone of Jean Grey created by Sinister and the wife of Scott Summers (a.k.a. Cyclops), aligns herself with a demonic realm called Limo that has been infected with a techno-organic virus. As hell on Earth erupts, the forces of the X-Men, X-Factor, and New Mutants try to save New York from this demonic menace and prevent Madelyne from sacrificing her infant son, Nathan Christopher Summers, in a plot to become the Goblin Queen of Limbo and Earth.

X-Men: Mutant Massacre. **Written by Chris Claremont. Illustrated by John Romita Jr.** Marvel Comics, 1996. 256pp. 0-7851-0224-8. **Y** ◎

When the villain Mister Sinister sends a group of hunters called the Marauders into the Morlock tunnels to destroy the mutants living in the sewers, the X-Men are all that stand in their way. As Morlocks are brutally hunted down by the Marauders, the X-Men members will never be the same again after fighting such vicious villains. Also features a guest appearance by Power Pack and Thor.

© 2006 Marvel Comics.

X-Men: X-Cutioner's Song. **Written by Fabian Nicieza, Scott Lobdell, and Peter David. Illustrated by Andy Kubert and Adam Kubert.** Marvel Comics, 1994. 272pp. 0-7851-0025-3. **Y**

Stryfe, the mad genetic clone of Cable, seeks revenge on the villain Apocalypse as well as Cyclops and Jean Grey for abandoning their son to the far future. Meanwhile, several X-teams, including the X-Men, X-Force, and X-Factor, rush in to rescue Scott and Jean.

X-Men: X-Tinction Agenda. **Written by Chris Claremont and Louise Simonson. Illustrated by Jim Lee, Rob Liefeld, and Jon Bogdanove.** Marvel Comics, 1992. 224pp. 0-87135-922-7. **Y**

The X-Men, X-Factor, and New Mutants must fight against a biomechanical foe called Cameron Hodge on the island of Genosha, a place where mutants are being herded like cattle in concentration camps. Hodge's plan is to destroy all the mutants on Earth, and the X-Men are all that stand in his way.

Villains: Archenemies and Rogues' Galleries

A continuing theme in comic books as well as most heroic tales is an archenemy for the hero. Every hero needs a good villain as a foible for the character as well as a rogues' gallery of colorful villains. Sherlock Holmes had his Professor Moriarty, and in the super-hero world Superman has his Lex Luthor, Batman has his Joker, and Spider-Man has his Green Goblin. Below are listed the collected stories featuring the villains in the spotlight. Many more titles featuring appearances of the villains can be found in the titles listed throughout this chapter.

Bullseye: Greatest Hits. **Written by Daniel Way. Illustrated by Steve Dillon.** Marvel Comics, 2005. 120pp. 0-7851-1512-9. **T**

The origin of one of Daredevil's greatest foes. A killer with the ability to use any item as a weapon, his background is revealed when he's interrogated by U.S. Intelligence operatives looking for two missing nuclear arms, and only Bullseye knows the location. Also features cameos by Elektra, Daredevil, the Kingpin, and the Punisher.

Doctor Doom. Marvel Comics, 1994–2002. **Y**

© 2006 Marvel Comics.

All heroes have great villains as their archenemies. In the Marvel Universe, Doctor Doom, originally introduced in 1962 in *Fantastic Four* #5, is the premiere villain and is the iron-masked ruler of the country of Latveria After losing his parents at a young age, Victor Von Doom feverishly studied both the sciences and the mystic arts and became friends with Reed Richards and Ben Grimm (now members of the Fantastic Four). After an accident that disfigured Doom and scarred his face, he focused his energies on revenge for all of his life's tragedies. He constructed a suit of body armor with a faceplate, and then he overthrew the monarchy of Latveria. To this day he continues to strive to one day rule the world through the power of his tiny but powerful country and his schemes of seeking unlimited power. The collections include tales featuring the ruthless monarch as well as encounters with Marvel Comics heroes, including the Fantastic Four, Iron Man, Spider-Man, and others

> *Iron Man vs. Doctor Doom.* Written by David Michelinie. Illustrated by Bob Layton. 1994. 128pp. 0-7851-0062-8.
>
> *Spider-Man vs. Doctor Doom.* Written by David Michelinie. Illustrated by Eric Larsen. 1995. 64pp. 0-7851-0110-1.
>
> *The Villainy of Doctor Doom.* Written by Stan Lee, et al. Illustrated by Jack Kirby, et al. 1999. 176pp. 0-7851-0732-0.
>
> *Doom.* Written by Chuck Dixon. Illustrated by Leonardo Manco. 2002. 144pp. 0-7851-0835-1.
>
> *Fantastic Four: Books of Doom.* Written by Ed Brubaker. Illustrated by Pablo Raimondi. 2006. 144pp. 0-7851-2271-0.

Empire. **Written by Mark Waid. Illustrated by Barry Kitson.** DC Comics, 2004. 208pp. 1-4012-0212-8. **T**

The gold-armored tyrant called Golgoth has done the unthinkable: he's defeated his planet's heroes and has conquered Earth. In a bleak society where deception rules the day, what does a villainous monarch do after he's already accomplished all he can? A look at a world in which the villains do win, from the perspective of Golgoth's superpowered lieutenants as the monarch is surrounded by conspirators and back-stabbers who fear him.

The Greatest Joker Stories Ever Told. **Written and illustrated by various.** Reprint ed. DC Comics, 1997. 288pp. 0-930289-36-6. **Y**

© 2006 DC Comics.

Considered by many to be Batman's archenemy, the Joker is highlighted in a collection of over five decades' worth of the insane Clown Prince of Crime's stories.

***The Hench*. Written by Adam Beechen. Illustrated by Manny Bello.** AiT/Planet Lar, 2004. 80pp. 1-932051-17-1. **O**

> Most super-hero stories focus on the heroes or the villains, but this is the life of Mike Fulton, a henchman for some of the worst criminal super-villains. Told from the perspective of a low man on the criminal totem pole, Mike looks back at his life: how a college football player fell in league with the most vile of villains and has spent time in jail countless times to help out his ailing son and to put food on the table. Mike realizes that over time there really isn't that much difference between the good guys and the bad guys—they're all "men in funny pants." In the end Mike must cross a deadly decision that he has never faced before that will forever blur the lines of hero, villain, killer, and savior.

***The Hood: Blood from Stones*. Written by Brian K. Vaughan. Illustrated by Kyle Hotz.** MAX/Marvel Comics, 2003. 144pp. 0-7851-1058-5. **M**

> Nineteen-year-old Parker Robbins is taking the easy way out and following a life of crime. A high school dropout with a pregnant girlfriend, a mistress on the side, and an ill mother in an institution, Parker's only option is to follow in his late father's footsteps and become a member of the Kingpin's crime syndicate. When he finds a mystical cloak and boots that give him powers of invisibility and flight, Parker's road to crime takes a new turn as a costumed super-villain.

***Identity Disc*. Written by Robert Rodi. Illustrated by John Higgins.** Marvel Comics, 2005. 120pp. 0-7851-1567-6. **T**

> A group of the most ruthless villains—Vulture, Sandman, Deadpool, Bullseye, Sabretooth, and the Juggernaut—have been blackmailed by a mysterious person called Silver to retrieve a disc of vast importance. The disc belongs to the high-tech criminal organization called A.I.M. and is purported to carry the secret identities of the world's heroes. Can the villains trust each other enough to locate the disc together?

Thanos. Marvel Comics, 1990–2004. **Y**

> Thanos, the mad Titan, is a nihilistic ancient born on Saturn's moon, called Titan. A purple-skinned brute with unlimited strength, Thanos is a tyrant obsessed with the concept and physical personification of Death and has been a companion to her. For years the enemy of the late Captain Marvel, Thanos, in his quest to please his lover, Death, sought greater cosmic power to please his mistress. The culmination was the Infinity Gauntlet, a golden glove with six gems that gives the owner mastery of one part of the universe, including time, space, power, soul, mind, and reality. After losing the glove (as seen in *Infinity Gauntlet* in this chapter), Thanos gains introspection in his exile and spends his time planning ways to conquer the universe. Below is listed the miniseries Thanos Quest as well as the continuing volumes in the series featuring the mad Titan.

> > Thanos Quest. Written by Jim Starlin. Illustrated by Ron Lim.1990. Thanos sets out to find the pieces of the Infinity Gems to make the gauntlet of power and give him the power of a god.
> > > *Book I.* 1990. 48pp. 0-87135-681-3.
> > > *Book II.* 1990. 48pp. 0-87135-682-1.

Thanos. Written by Jim Starlin. 2003–2004.

> *Vol. 2: Infinity Abyss.* Illustrated by Jim Starlin. 2003. 176pp. 0-7851-0985-4.
>
> *Vol. 3: Marvel Universe—The End.* Written and illustrated by Jim Starlin. 2003. 160pp. 0-7851-1116-6.
>
> *Vol. 4: Epiphany.* Written and illustrated by Jim Starlin. 2004. 144pp. 0-7851-1355-X.
>
> *Vol. 5: Samaritan.* Written by Keith Giffen. Illustrated by Ron Lim. 2004. 144pp. 0-7851-1540-4.

Venom. Marvel Comics, 1995–2005. T

© 2006 Marvel Comics.

One of Spider-Man's greatest foes, the alien symbiote known as Venom was a sentient alien creature that bonded with Eddie Brock, a newspaper reporter dying of cancer, with only three months to live. After being chased away from its former host, Spider-Man, the shadowy alien symbiote found refuge in Brock, who had a personal vendetta against Spider-Man. Now a creature with the proportionate strength of Spider-Man, Venom is able to mimic all of Spider-Man's powers, is also able to camouflage itself in any appearance, and can evade Spider-Man's spider-sense and remain undetected by the wall-crawler. At times a villain with a conscience, Eddie Brock will not kill, and has at times been considered an anti-hero rather than a villain. Recently Eddie Brock found peace with faith and sold Venom to the highest bidder (as seen in the Marvel Knights: Spider-Man series in this chapter). Now the symbiote resides within Mac Gargan, the villain formerly known as Scorpion, and Eddie Brock is presumed dead. For now.

> *Venom: Lethal Protector.* Written by David Michelinie. Illustrated by Ron Lim. 1995. 144pp. 0-7851-0107-1.
>
> *Venom: Carnage Unleashed.* Written by Larry Hama. Illustrated by Andrew Wildman, and Art Nichols. 1996. 96pp. 0-7851-0199-3.
>
> Venom. Written by Daniel Way. Illustrated by Francisco Herrera. 2003–2004.
>
> > *Vol. 1: Shiver.* 2003. 120pp. 0-7851-1252-9.
> >
> > *Vol. 2: Run.* 2003. 192pp. 0-7851-1553-6.
> >
> > *Vol. 3: Twist.* 2004. 120pp. 0-7851-1554-4.
>
> *Venom vs. Carnage.* Written by Peter Milligan. Illustrated by Clayton Crain. 2005. 96pp. 0-7851-1524-2.

Villains United. **Written by Gail Simone. Illustrated by Dale Eaglesham and Wade von Grawbadger**. DC Comics, 2006. 144pp. 1-4012-0838-X. T ◉

There is victory in working as a team, and Superman's arch-nemesis Lex Luthor has decided to unite the villains of the DC Universe to combine their might into a group called the Society, made up of founding members Luthor, Black Adam, Deathstroke, Talia al Ghul, Dr. Psycho, and Calculator. Those villains who qualified were made an offer they couldn't refuse: join us or die. Those who turned down Luthor's proposal—including Catman, Cheshire, Scandal, Ragdoll, Deadshot, and Parademon—are recruited by a mysterious individual codenamed "Mockingbird" to oppose the Society—or else their loved ones would be killed. As the villains soon discover, there is a mounting crisis at hand, and the mysterious "Mockingbird" is someone no one could have guessed.

Wanted. **Written by Mark Millar. Illustrated by J. G. Jones.** Top Cow Productions/Image Comics, 2005. 192pp. 1-58240-480-1. **M**

© 2006 Top Cow Productions.

A brutal and bloody romp through the dark underworld of super-villains. Wesley Gibson's life really never counted for anything. Always being taken advantage of by people, including his cheating girlfriend, Wesley's life is turned upside down when he discovers that there really are super-villains controlling the world, super-heroes really do exist, and his real father was a mastermind criminal assassin called The Killer. Now Wesley is following in his father's footsteps as a member of the worldwide criminal organization called The Fraternity. No longer a putz, but a man who takes what he wants, he's living the high life on his father's vast fortune and learning the ropes of taking revenge and the art of being a bastard, and developing the skill to be the best assassin in the world as he takes on the legacy of The Killer.

Secret Origins of Heroes and Villains

Among the very first graphic novel anthologies in the 1970s were classics like *Origins of Marvel Comics* and *Bring on the Bad Guys,* which collected the tales of how the heroes and villains of popular Marvel Comics and DC Comics stories came to be. The trend continues to this day and is a great entry point for new fans. Please note that origin titles for some popular characters, including Batman, Superman, and Wolverine, are listed in their own individual sections in this chapter. Listed below are only anthology collections of super-hero and super-villain origins.

Bring Back the Bad Guys. **Written by Stan Lee and various. Illustrated by various.** Marvel Comics, 1998. 256pp. 0-7851-0591-3. **Y**

A collection of the most vile villains in the Marvel Universe of characters, including Magneto, The Kingpin, Kang, the Mandarin, and the dreaded Fing Fang Foom.

Bring on the Bad Guys. **Written and illustrated by various.** Marvel Comics, 1998. 256pp. 0-7851-0591-3. **Y**

Origins of Marvel Comics villains, including Dr. Doom, the Green Goblin, Mephisto, Dormammu, the Red Skull, and Loki.

Grandson of Origins of Marvel Comics. **Written and illustrated by various.** Marvel Comics, 1999. 256pp. 0-7851-0593-X. **Y**

Features the origins of classic Marvel Comics heroes, including Captain America, Ka-Zar, Nick Fury, the Sub-Mariner, and Professor X.

JLA: Secret Origins. **Written by Paul Dini. Illustrated by Alex Ross.** DC Comics, 2002. 48pp. 1-4012-0021-4. **Y**

> An oversized title featuring the origins of some of the greatest heroes in the DC Universe: Batman, Superman, Wonder Woman, Aquaman, Martian Manhunter, the Green Lantern, and the Flash.

Origins of Marvel Comics. **Written by Stan Lee and various. Illustrated by various.** Marvel Comics, 1997. 240pp. 0-7851-0551-4. **Y**

> A look at the first appearances of many classic Marvel Comics heroes and villains, including Spider-Man, the Hulk, the Fantastic Four, Thor, and Dr. Strange. One of the very first collected comic book publications, it was first printed in 1974.

Secret Origins Featuring the JLA. **Written and illustrated by various.** DC Comics, 1999. 150pp. 1-56389-542-0. **Y**

> A look at some of the backstories of popular JLA members, including Batman, Superman, Wonder Woman, Aquaman, Green Lantern, Martian Manhunter, and the Flash.

Son of Origins of Marvel Comics. **Written by Stan Lee and various. Illustrated by various.** Marvel Comics, 1999. 272pp. 0-7851-0559-X. **Y**

> The origin of classic Marvel Comics characters, including the X-Men, the Silver Surfer, Iron Man, Daredevil, Ant-Man, and the Wasp.

Weird Secret Origins. **Written and illustrated by various.** DC Comics, 2004. 80pp. 1-4012-0239-X. **Y**

> A look at some of the stranger heroes and villains from DC Comics, including Animal Man, Congorilla, the Spectre, Dr. Fate, Metamorpho, and Bizarro World.

Alternate Timelines, Elseworlds, and What-If Worlds

Many people have wondered what life would be like if they hadn't made the choices they've made in life, and it's the same for super-heroes, too. What would happen to our heroes and villains if they did one thing different? How would that one decision have affected them? It could be a small change or something larger—but the possibilities of these situations are endless, and the end result can sometimes be more entertaining than the stories of the mainstream hero. For years Marvel Comics had a comic book title called <u>What If</u>, which explored these ideas, and DC Comics has published similar works under their <u>Elseworlds</u> banner, most of which feature Batman and Superman. The ideas for the stories are virtually unlimited and include such scenarios as "What if Batman fought Jack the Ripper" or "What if Peter Parker's Aunt May died instead of his Uncle Ben?" and "What if Superman was raised in the U.S.S.R. instead of the United States?" Please note that some stories based on speculative events of the future or alternative time lines—such as *Batman: the Dark Knight Returns*, *The Incredible Hulk: Future Imperfect*, *Marvel: 1602*, *Kingdom Come*, and *Exiles*—are not listed here and are featured elsewhere in this chapter. DC Comics' Elseworlds titles are listed. For a complete list of Elseworlds and What If? titles, please visit DC Comics' Web site (http://www.dccomics.com) and Marvel Comics' Web site (http://www.marvel.com).

The Amalgam Age of Comics. Written and illustrated by various. DC Comics and Marvel Comics, 1996–2002. **Y**

A unique crossover event—*DC Versus Marvel* (1997)—resulted in these spin-offs blending familiar characters from both publishers into heroes and villains both familiar and brand new, such as Super Soldier (Captain America and Superman), Dark Claw (Wolverine and Batman), and Amazon (Storm and Wonder Woman).

> *The Amalgam Age of Comics: The DC Comics Collection.* DC Comics, 1996. 132pp. 1-56389-295-2.
> *The Amalgam Age of Comics: The Marvel Comics Collection.* Marvel Comic, 1996. 160pp. 0-7851-0240-X.
> *Return to the Amalgam Age of Comics: The DC Comics Collection.* DC Comics, 1997. 160pp. 1-56389-382-7.
> *Return to the Amalgam Age of Comics: The Marvel Comics Collection.* Marvel Comics, 1997. 160pp. 0-7851-0561-1.

***Batman: Dark Knight Dynasty*. Written by Mike W. Barr. Illustrated by Scott Hampton, Gary Frank, Cam Smith, Scott McDaniel, and Bill Sienkiewicz.** DC Comics, 1998. 124pp. 1-56389-390-8. **T**

A look at the legacy of Batman and his family's struggle for generations to destroy the immortal madman Vandal Savage. From Joshua Wainwright, a holy knight during the crusades of the fourteenth century, to Batman in the year 2500, the Batmen will not stop until Savage is defeated.

Batman: Gotham by Gaslight. Written by Brian Augustyn. Illustrated by Mike Mignola, Eduardo Barreto, and P. Craig Russell. DC Comics, 1990–2006. **T ◉**

One of DC Comics' first experiments with the Elseworlds line of titles, the story is an alternate look at what might have happened if Bruce Wayne became Batman during the late nineteenth century. The collection reprints the two graphic novels originally published as *Gotham by Gaslight* (1990) and *Batman: Master of the Future* (1991). In *Gotham by Gaslight,* when Bruce Wayne begins his crusade against evil as the masked vigilante called Batman, the notorious Jack the Ripper is terrorizing Gotham City. When Bruce Wayne is falsely convicted of being the murderer, only Batman can bring the true killer to justice. The tales of the nineteenth-century Batman continued in *Batman: Master of the Future*, which follows the exploits of Batman set at the end of the nineteenth century, as he must foil a plot by a madman who will stop at nothing to prevent Gotham City from entering the new century.

> *Gotham by Gaslight: A Tale of the Batman.* Written by Brian Augustyn. Illustrated by Mike Mignola and P. Craig Russell. DC Comics, 1990. 48pp. 0-930289-67-6. **T**
> *Batman: Master of the Future.* Written by Brian Augustyn. Illustrated by Eduardo Barreto. DC Comics, 1991 64pp. 1-56389-015-1. **T**
> *Batman: Gotham by Gaslight.* Written by Brian Augustyn. Illustrated by Mike Mignola, Eduardo Barreto, and P. Craig Russell. DC Comics, 2006. 112pp. 1-4012-1153-4. **T**

Batman: Thrillkiller. **Written by Howard Chaykin. Illustrated by Dan Brereton.** DC Comics, 1998. 128pp. 1-56389-424-6. **T** ◎

> Alternate world in which the dynamic duo is Batgirl and Robin. Set in the 1960s, as social unrest and political corruption stalk the streets of Gotham, police detective Bruce Wayne forges an uneasy truce with the two vigilantes after he is framed for murder.

The Best of What If. **Written and illustrated by various.** Marvel Comics, 1991. 192pp. 0-87135-857-3. **Y**

> A collection of some of Marvel's classic <u>What If?</u> stories, including "What If Spider-Man Joined the Fantastic Four?," "What If Phoenix Had Not Died?," "What If Daredevil Became an Agent of Shield?," "What If Gwen Stacy Had Lived?," "What If the Avengers Had Become the Pawns of Korvac?," "What If the Spider Had Been Bitten by a Radioactive Human?," and "What If the Fantastic Four Had Not Gained Their Powers?"

✦ <u>**DC: The New Frontier.**</u> **Written and illustrated by Darwyn Cooke.** DC Comics, 2004–2006. **T** ◎

© 2006 DC Comics.

> Even before the heroes of old put on costumes, they were always heroes. Joined together in an epic adventure starting during World War II and lasting until the dawn of the Cold War, the heroes of the Silver Age of comics must face an ancient foe threatening to take over the entire world. Hal Jordan (Green Lantern), The Flash, Martian Manhunter, Superman, Aquaman, Wonder Woman, Batman, Adam Strange, the Challengers of the Unknown, the Blackhawks, the Suicide Squad, and many more—the Silver Age heroes of yesterday —must work together to save humankind from extermination. The series won several Eisner Awards in 2005, for Best Finite Series/Limited Series and Best Colorist/Coloring, as well as Harvey Awards for Best Artist or Penciller (2005) and Best Continuing or Limited Series (2005). In 2006 the two-volume story was also collected in one hardcover edition.
>
> > *Vol. 1.* 2004. 208pp. 1-4012-0350-7.
> > *Vol. 2.* 2005. 208pp. 1-4012-0461-9.
> > *Absolute DC: The New Frontier.* 2006. 464pp. 1-4012-1080-5, hardcover.

Elseworld's Finest: Supergirl and Batgirl. **Written by Barbara Kesel. Illustrated by Matt Haley.** DC Comics, 1998. 64pp. 1-56389-375-4. **T**

> In a world in which Batman and Superman never existed, Gotham City is protected by the dark avenger Batgirl (Barbara Gordon), and Supergirl is the protector of Lex Luthor, the brainchild of the superteam known as the Justice League. As a venom-juiced Joker roams the streets, the heroines have to reconcile their differences to save Gotham City from the Joker and discover the true secret of Lex Luthor.

🎖 *JSA: The Golden Age.* **Written by James Robinson. Illustrated by Paul Smith.** DC Comics, 2005. 200pp. 1-4012-0711-1. **T** ◎

After winning World War II, what happens to the heroes when they might not be needed anymore? Now that the real evil has been conquered, is there anything left for the Classic Golden Age heroes to fight for? Meanwhile, a new hero with a shocking secret may change how heroes are perceived in the world. The nation is falling for Dynaman's fascist agenda, and the heroes of old find that evil is lurking within their ranks and is more powerful than all of them combined. An <u>Elseworlds</u> title. The story received recognition from YALSA's Popular Paperbacks for Young Adults committee in 1997.

JSA: The Liberty Files. **Written by Dan Jolley. Illustrated by Tony Harris.** DC Comics, 2004. 208pp. 1-4012-0203-9. **T** ◎

Alternate retelling of the Justice Society of America and their dealings with Jack the Grin (the Joker) and his connections to a plot by the Nazis to develop their own "super-man" weapon.

Just Imagine Stan Lee . . . . Written by Stan Lee with Michael Uslan. Illustrated by various. DC Comics, 2002–2004. **Y**

Marvel Comics' creator Stan Lee's reinterpretations of classic DC Comics characters as he would create them. A creative reimagination of heroes and characters including Superman, Batman, Sandman, and others.

> *Creating the DC Universe Book 1.* 216pp. 1-56389-891-8.
> *Creating the DC Universe Book 2.* 238pp. 1-56389-987-6.
> *Creating the DC Universe Book 3.* 224pp. 1-4012-0228-4.

Justice League of America: Another Nail. **Written and illustrated by Alan Davis.** DC Comics, 2004. 160pp. 1-4012-0265-9. **T**

Sequel to *JLA: The Nail.* As the JLA get accustomed to a team with Superman playing a major role, a galactic war breaks out between the New Gods that may change the face of the universe forever.

Justice League of America: The Nail. **Written and Illustrate by Alan Davis.** DC Comics, 2000. 160pp. 1-56389-480-7. **T**

A world of the DC Comics' universe without Superman to guide them. The rocketship that carried the infant Kal-El (Superman) is never rescued by Martha and Jonathan Kent due to a flat tire caused by a nail. What will become of the Justice League of America and their heroes without the greatest symbol of American freedom.

Marvel Knights 2099. **Written by Robert Kirkman. Illustrated by Steve Epting, Kyle Hotz, Cliff Rathburn, and Pop Mhan.** Marvel Comics, 2005. 120pp. 0-7851-1613-3. **T**

Set at the tail end of the twenty-first century comes the future generation of Marvel Comics heroes. Meet the future of Marvel heroes including Daredevil, the Punisher, the Black Panther, the Inhumans, and a mutant known only as Mutant 2099.

Marvel Mangaverse. Written and illustrated by Ben Dunn. Marvel Comics, 2002–2006. **Y Neo-manga.**

© 2006 Marvel Comics.

A reimagination of what the classic Marvel characters would be like anime-style, complete with all new backgrounds and origins. Meet Spider-Man, a ninja from the legendary Spider Clan; a Godzilla-sized Hulk; a mecha-style Iron Man; and many more manga reinterpretations of your favorite Marvel characters.

> *Vol. 1.* Written by Ben Dunn, Ken Siu-Chong, Adam Warren, Chuck Austen, Peter David, Kaare Andrews, and C. B. Cebulski. Illustrated by Ben Dunn, Udon, Keron Grant, Chuck Austen, Kaare Andrews, Jeff Matsuda, and Lea Hernandez. 2002. 224pp. 0-7851-0935-8.
>
> *Vol. 2.* Written and illustrated by Ben Dunn. 2002. 144pp. 0-7851-1006-2.

Vol. 3: Spider-Man—Legend of the Spider Clan. Written by Kaare Andrews. Illustrated by Skott Young. 2003. 128pp. 0-7851-1114-X.

Vol. 4: X-Men—Ronin. Written by J. Torres. Illustrated by Makoto Nakatsuka. 2004. 128pp. 0-7851-1115-8.

New Mangaverse: Rings of Fate. Written by C. B. Cebulski. Illustrated by Tommy Ohtsuka. 120pp. 0-7851-2001-7.

Son of Superman. **Written by Howard Chaykin and David Tischman. Illustrated by J. H. Williams III and Mick Gray.** DC Comics, 2000. 96pp. 1-56389-596-X. **T**

Fifteen years after the mysterious disappearance of Superman, teenager Jon Kent finds out that not only was the Man of Steel his father, he has inherited all of his father's powers as well. After rescuing his father from an underground prison created by President Lex Luthor, the Supermen are on the run from Luthor's corrupt government. When the president's personal squadron of fighters, the old Justice League of America, stand between peace and corruption, can the father and son Superman family take on their own friends and free the country from Lex's grasp?

Spider-Man: India. **Written by Suresh Seetharaman and Jeevan J. Kang. Illustrated by Jeevan J. Kang.** Marvel Comics, 2005. 104pp. 0-7851-1640-0. **T**

A unique twist on the legend of Spider-Man. In the city of Mumbai in India, Pavitr Prabhakar is given the proportionate abilities of a spider and fights crime as Spider-Man.

Superman: Red Son. **Written by Mark Millar. Illustrated by Dave Johnson and Killian Plunkett.** DC Comics, 2004. 160pp. 1-4012-0191-1. **T**

What if Superman's rocket hadn't crashed in Kansas, but instead in a region of Ukraine in the Soviet Union? As the Cold War between the United States and the Soviet Union dissolves with the emergence of Superman, a desperate United States turns to scientist Lex Luthor to succeed where they have failed and destroy the Man of Soviet Steel. Meanwhile, as Superman brings peace to the Soviet Union and much of the world, a revolution is starting, led by the terrorist known as Batman.

***Superman: Secret Identity.* Written by Kurt Busiek. Illustrated by Stuart Immonen.** DC Comics, 2004. 208pp. 1-4012-0451-1. **T** ◉

Set in the real world. A young man from Kansas named Clark Kent is teased for years about being Superman. Amazingly, he discovers that he really has mysteriously inherited the powers of the comic book hero Superman and begins to make a name for himself as a hero across the world. Can he keep his identity a secret, or will he fall prey to those trying to expose his identity and capture him?

© 2006 DC Comics.

***Superman: Speeding Bullets.* Written by J. M. DeMatteis. Illustrated by Eduardo Barreto.** DC Comics, 1993. 48pp. 1-56389-117-4. **T**

An alternate setting in which Superman has been raised in Gotham City by Thomas and Martha Wayne. After enduring the loss of his parents at the hands of a common criminal whom he burns in anger, a superpowered and very much bullet-proof young Bruce Wayne grows up to seek vengeance on those who prey on the good people of Gotham. He adopts the identity of the Batman and dispenses justice as the Bat of Steel. Will Bruce Wayne finally meet his match against the mastermind Lex Luthor?.

***Superman: True Brit.* Written by Kim "Howard" Johnson and John Cleese. Illustrated by John Byrne.** DC Comics, 2004. 96pp. 1-4012-0022-2. **T**

What if Superman's rocketship, instead of landing in Kansas, had landed in a town in England even smaller than Smallville? Raised by his parents, the Clarks, young Collin is taught to hide his awesome powers and not cause a scene. It's not very British, you know, and what will the neighbors think? After Collin grows up and works as a mild-mannered reporter for the *Daily Smear* tabloid, a paper known for uncovering the biggest stories of the century, he decides to reveal his secrets to the world, and the Superman legend is born. Co-written by the classic British sketch comedy troupe Monty Python alumnus John Cleese.

***Superman: Whatever Happened to the Man of Tomorrow.* Written by Alan Moore. Illustrated by Curt Swan.** DC Comics, 1997. 64pp. 1-56389-315-0. **T** ◉

When Superman was about to be revised and relaunched in 1986 by John Byrne, fan-favorite writer Alan Moore and longtime Superman artist Curt Swan created a tale featuring the last story ever of the Man of Steel's never-ending battle. Originally published in 1986, the story tells of the final adventure of Superman, the death of Clark Kent, the last stand of the *Daily Planet* staff, a Bizarro on the rampage, and the deadly duo of Lex Luthor and Brainiac. Can Superman defeat a hybrid Lex Luthor and Brainiac while the lives of his loved ones hang in the balance? A loving tribute to the history of Superman.

Superman/Batman: Alternate Histories. **Written and illustrated by various.** DC Comics, 1996. 224pp. 1-56389-263-4. **T**

A collection of alternate tellings of Batman and Superman set in different time periods. Bruce Wayne sails the high seas as a pirate known as Leatherwing; a predecessor to Superman, Gar-El, rules colonial America, and his grandson, Kal-El, questions his authority; John Henry Irons is a slave in the 1800s who fashions a suit of armor to free his people; and Harvey Dent adopts the identity of Batman to fight crime in Gotham City, and the only one who can bring him in is Bruce Wayne.

Superman/Batman: Generations—an Imaginary Tale. **Written and illustrated by John Byrne.** DC Comics, 2000–2003. **T** ◎

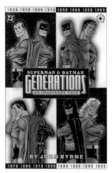

© 2006 DC Comics.

Have you ever wondered what would really have happened if Superman and Batman had aged in normal years since their first appearances in the comic books in the 1930s? How would life go on for them, their loved ones, and their bitter enemies? Old heroes would retire and be replaced by the younger generation of heroes, and family members would live and die. As an elderly Bruce Wayne treks the Himalayas in search of the fabled Lazarus Pit, which can bring youth back into a frail body, a disheartened Superman finds solace after tragedy has struck his peaceful family. Can the two archetypes of heroism rediscover the strength they need to battle their earliest of foes, or will they become lost in the perils of old age and the ravages of time.

Vol. 1. 208pp. 1-56389-605-2.
Vol. 2. 200pp. 1-56389-990-6.

Superman & Batman: World's Funnest. **Written by Evan Dorkin. Illustrated by various.** DC Comics, 2000. 64pp. No ISBN. **T** ◎

When dimensional imps Bat-Mite and Mr. Mxyzptlk accidentally kill Batman and Superman, they go on a hilarious, dimension-hopping jaunt through a variety of. DC Comics' worlds to see whose favorite hero really is better, and along the way destroy the various incarnations of Batman and Superman throughout the years. Includes artwork by a huge variety of Batman and Superman artists, including Frank Miller, Alex Ross, and others.

What If . . . , Vol. 1: Why Not. **Written by Brian Michael Bendis, Kevin Smith, Peter David, Karl Kesel, Chris Claremont and Ed Brubaker.** Illustrated by various. Marvel Comics, 2005. 144pp. 0-7851-1593-5. **Y**

A collection of brand-new <u>What If?</u> stories including "What If Jessica Jones Had Joined the Avengers?," "What If Aunt May Had Died Instead of Uncle Ben?," "What If Karen Page Had Lived?," "What If Magneto Had Formed the X-Men with Professor X?," and others.

What If?: Mirror Mirror. **Written by Daniel Way, Greg Pak, Robert Kirkman, Rick Veitch, and various. Illustrated by Michael Avon Oeming and various.** Marvel Comics, 2006. 144pp. 0-7851-1902-7. **Y**

> A collection of brand-new <u>What If?</u> stories including What If Captain America Fought in the Civil War?," "What If Daredevil Had Lived in Feudal Japan?," "What If the Fantastic Four Were Cosmonauts?," and others.

<u>**What If? Classic.**</u> **Written by Roy Thomas, Jim Shooter, and Don Glut. Illustrated by Herb Trimpe, Gil Kane, and various.** 2004–2005. **Y**

> A classic collection of imaginary stories, including "What If Spider-Man Joined the Fantastic Four?," "What If the Hulk Had Always Had Bruce Banner's Brain?," "What If the Avengers Had Never Been?," "What If the Invaders Had Stayed Together After World War Two?," "What If Captain America and Bucky Had Both Survived World War II?," and "What If the Fantastic Four Had Different Super-Powers?"
>
> > *Vol. 1.* 2004. 216pp. 0-7851-1702-4.
> > *Vol. 2.* 2005. 216pp. 0-7851-1843-8.

Wolverine Legends: The End. **Written by Paul Jenkins. Illustrated by Claudio Castellini.** Marvel Comics, 2004. 144pp. 0-7851-1349-5. **T**

> The last Wolverine story. One hundred years in the future, Logan runs wild in the woods of Canada. As the limits of his healing factor set in, an aging and reclusive Logan is still haunted by a hidden past that evades him to this day. Determined to find the truth, he spans the globe in search of answers, and his world will never be the same.

<u>**X-Men: The Age of Apocalypse.**</u> **Written by Scott Lobdell, Jeph Loeb, and various. Illustrated by various.** Marvel Comics, 1995–2006. **Y** ◎

© 2006 Marvel Comics.

In an alternate timeline in which Professor X was accidentally killed before he could form the X-Men, the evil genetic villain Apocalypse has the entire world in his grasp and humanity has been nearly exterminated. Only Erik Lensherr (Magneto) continues to fulfill Professor X's dreams, and with his team of X-Men and the help of the time-displaced Bishop, they're out to set things right: to change the past to make sure that this abomination of a world never happened. A tenth anniversary of the reality-warping story was published in 2005 as the *New Age of Apocalypse*, which continues the adventures of the alternate universe X-Men. In 2005 and 2006 Marvel Comics reprinted the out-of-print series in four collected editions.

> *Legionquest.* 1996. 96pp. 0-7851-0179-9.
> *Dawn of the Age of Apocalypse.* 1996. 96pp. 0-7851-0180-2.
> *Astonishing X-Men (1st series).* 1995. 96pp. 0-7851-0127-6.
> *X-Man.* 1995. 96pp. 0-7851-0133-0.
> *Generation Next.* 1995. 96pp. 0-7851-0130-6.
> *X-Calibre.* 1995. 96pp. 0-7851-0132-2.
> *Weapon X.* 1995. 96pp. 0-7851-0131-4
> *Factor-X.* 1995. 96pp. 0-7851-0128-4.
> *Gambit and the X-Ternals.* 1995. 96pp. 0-7851-0129-2.
> *Amazing X-Men.* 1995. 96pp. 0-7851-0126-8
> *Twilight of the Age of Apocalypse.* 1996. 128pp. 0-7851-0181-0.

Tales from the Age of Apocalypse. 1997. 48pp. 0-7851-0289-2.
Tales from the Age of Apocalypse: Sinister Bloodlines. 1998. 48pp. 0-7851-0584-0.
X-Men: The Complete Age of Apocalypse Epic. 2005–2006.
>   *Book 1.* 2005. 376pp. 0-7851-1714-8.
>   *Book 2.* 2005. 376pp. 0-7851-1874-8.
>   *Book 3.* 2006. 376pp. 0-7851-2051-3.
>   *Book 4.* 2006. 376pp. 0-7851-2052-1.

X-Men: The New Age of Apocalypse. Written by Akira Yoshida, Scott Lobdell, and Tony Bedard. Illustrated by Chris Bachalo. 2005. 192pp. 0-7851-1583-8

X-Men: Alterniverse Visions. **Written and illustrated by various.** Marvel Comics, 1996.144pp. 0-7851-0194-2. **Y**

A collection of What If? stories featuring alternate takes on the X-Men, including the tales "What If Wolverine Led Alpha Flight?" "What If Storm Remained a Thief?" "What If Rogue Possessed the Power of Thor?" "What If Stryfe Killed the X-Men?" and "What If Wolverine Battled Weapon X?"

X-Men: The End. **Written by Chris Claremont. Illustrated by Sean Chen.** Marvel Comics, 2005–2006. **Y** ◉

An epic trilogy featuring a possible final future for the X-Men. As the X-Men revel in their newfound families, tragedy strikes the team via a plot by Mister Sinister. As the X-Men ranks fall and casualties rise, will they by able to handle the crisis, or is this really the end for the mutants? Meanwhile the Phoenix is returning from the dead once again.

>   *Vol. 1: Dreamers and Demons.* 2005. 144pp. 0-7851-1690-7.
>   *Vol. 2: Heroes and Martyrs.* 2005. 144pp. 0-7851-1691-5.
>   *Vol. 3: Men and X-Men.* 2006. 144pp. 0-7851-1692-3.

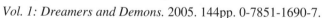

Slice-of-Life/Common Man Perspectives

These are stories that tell what it's like to live in a city where super-heroes walk Earth, from the perspective of an average person on the street to that of police officers working alongside the costumed heroes. The stories can also focus on the heroes before or after they became super-heroes.

✦ Astro City. **Written by Kurt Busiek. Illustrated by Brent Anderson. Covers by Alex Ross.** Homage Studios/WildStorm Productions/DC Comics, 1999– . **T** ◉

Welcome to Astro City, a city unlike any other, where everyday folks and the fantastic world of super-heroes interact and work together in the shining silver city. Rebuilt in 1947, Astro City has been protected by an ever-changing array of heroes, including the super-strong Samaritan, the female warrior-hero Winged Victory, the dark and brooding vampire The Confessor, the buffoonish Crackerjack, the clown-themed Jack-in-the-Box, the mythic Old Soldier, the super-team the First Family, the Honor Guard, the Christian-based team the Crossbreed, and the Irregulars. The boroughs of Astro

City, including City Center, Old Town, Chesler, Shadow Hill, and more, are protected by their own neighborhood guardian hero from any evil that would dare to commit a crime in the city. When villains such as Steeljack, Demolitia and the Unholy Alliance, Mock Turtle, Looney Leo, and the Living Nightmare attack, the heroes of Astro City will be there. Each "slice of life" story in <u>Astro City</u> is told through a unique and personal view, varying each time in perspective, showing the city through the eyes of a hero, a citizen of the city, a down and out reformed criminal, and others. The series has won numerous awards, including several Eisner Awards for Best Single Issue/Single Story (1996–1998), Best Serialized Story (1998), Best Continuing Series (1997–1998), Best New Series (1996), and Best Writer (1999). The series has also won several Harvey Awards for Best Single Issue or Story (1996), Best Writer (1997) for Kurt Busiek's body of work including this series as well as Best New Series (1996), Best Graphic Album of Previously Published Work (1997), and Best Continuing or Limited Series (1998). *Volume 1: Life in the Big City* received recognition from YALSA's Popular Paperbacks for Young Adults committee in 2002.

> *Vol. 1: Life in the Big City.* 1999. 192pp. 1-56389-551-X.
> *Vol. 2: Confession.* 1999. 192pp. 1-56389-550-1.
> *Vol. 3: Family Album.* 1999. 224pp. 1-56389-552-8.
> *Vol. 4: Tarnished Angel.* 2001. 224pp. 1-56389-663-X.
> *Vol. 5: Local Heroes.* 2005. 256pp. 1-4012-0284-5.

***Common Grounds.* Written by Troy Hickman. Illustrated by Dan Jurgens, George Pérez, Chris Bachalo, Angel Medina and Michael Avon Oeming.** Top Cow Productions/Image Comics, 2004. 144pp. 1-58240-436-4. **T**

The Common Grounds coffee and donut shop is neutral territory for heroes and villains in need of a place to relax and share their stories. Meet the colorful cast of costumed characters, including Man-Witch, Mental Midget, Speeding Bullet, Captain Gallant, Commander Power, and even gargantuan beasts such as Grondar, Crittor, Kkrapp, and a dragon named Wang Dang Doodle, who all just need a little coffee and donuts and someone to listen to them.

***The Factor.* Written by Nat Getler. Illustrated by Nat Getler and various.** About Comics, 2004. 128pp. 0-9716338-5-1. **T**

When a hero by the name of the Factor comes to town, he changes the lives of everyone in the city. These are their stories: a young girl with a dull boyfriend who has a crush on the hero; what happens to trick-or-treaters who dress up as the hero; how an actor's life is changed when he plays the hero in an unauthorized movie; and how the criminal underworld thinks of the hero. It's a look at how super-heroes affect the average person on the street and how one life can make a difference. Features more than twenty short stories. Illustrated by various artists, including Joe Staton, Justine Shaw, Carla Speed McNeil, Adam Rex, Janine Johnston, Alex Grecian, Ted Slampyak, and many more.

<u>**Hero Happy Hour.**</u> **Written by Dan Taylor and various. Illustrated by Chris Fason and various.** GeekPunk. 2003–2004. **O**

Where do all the heroes of First City go after a hard day's work of fighting crime? They all go to The Hideout Bar and Grill watering hole for the best drinks in town. Run by retired hero Rupert "Rusty" Russell, it's the best place to go when you're in the mood to drown your blues. Capes and tights are more than welcome. As "regulars," including Guardian, Night Ranger, and his sidekick Scout, Feline, Knightingale, and others stop in for a brew or two, find out what it's like when the heroes are off-duty and the trials, tribulations, and hilarities of being a hero in First City. *Hero Happy Hour Super Special* includes short stories by artists including Scott Morse, Tom Beland, Neil Vokes, and others that tell more tales from The Hideout Bar and Grill.

> *Super Hero Happy Hour.* 2003. 134pp. 0-9746743-0-3.
> *Hero Happy Hour Super Special.* 2004. 64pp. 0-9746743-1-1.

🎖 *Marvel's 10th Anniversary Edition.* **Written by Kurt Busiek. Illustrated by Alex Ross.** Marvel Comics, 2004. 240pp. 0-7851-1388-6. **T** ◎

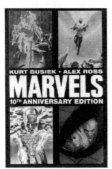

See the Marvel Universe in a whole new way—through the eyes of the average man on the street in New York City. This is a look at over thirty-five years of Marvel Comics' history, told from the perspective of *Daily Bugle* newspaper photographer Phil Sheldon. From the earliest days during World War II with Captain America and the Invaders, to the salvation of the world by the Fantastic Four and the Silver Surfer from the world-devouring giant called Galactus, to the persecution of an innocent little mutant girl who is protected by the X-Men, to Spider-Man's greatest heartache, the Marvel Universe will never look the same way again. The story won Eisner Awards

© 2006 Marvel Comics.

in 1994 for Best Finite Series/Limited Series, Best Painter/Multimedia Artist (Interior), and Best Publication Design, as well as Harvey Awards for Best Artists or Penciller (1994), Special Award for Excellence in Production/Presentation (1994), Best Continuing or Limited Series (1994), Best Single Issue or Story (1994), and Best Graphic Album of Previously Published Work (1995).

🎖 Powers. **Written by Brian Michael Bendis. Illustrated by Michael Avon Oeming.** Image Comics, Volumes 1–5, and Marvel Comics, Volumes 6– . 2001– . **M** ◎

Detectives Christian Walker and his new partner, the no-nonsense and loud-spoken Deena Pilgrim, work in a homicide department that handles cases involving "Powers" (people with superpowers). Walker himself used to be the Power known as Diamond, but he gave it up long ago when he lost his superpowers. Today he walks a beat with a badge but still maintains close tie to the Powers community. Their first case together involves the murder of the media darling known as Retro Girl, a close friend of Walker. As they continue their investigations into the world of Powers, they're exposed to the gritty, violent, and seedier aspects of the lives of these so-called heroes, including cases involving stalkers, role-playing fans, kinky sex acts, spontaneous combustion, and the obligatory scene of monkeys fighting and fornicating. After a hero goes insane and destroys most of the world, the opposition to Powers grows, resulting in the president declaring a ban on all superpowered activity. What side will Walker take, and where does his allegiance lie—with his hero friends from his past or the officers and his partners on the force? The series won an Eisner Award in 2001 for Best New Series as well as Eisners in 2002–2003 for Best Writer.

© 2006 Jinxworld.

Vol. 1: Who Killed Retro Girl? 2001. 208pp. 1-58240-183-7.
Vol. 2: Roleplay. 2002. 112pp. 1-58240-232-9.
Vol. 3: Little Deaths. 2003. 224pp. 1-58240-269-8.
Vol. 4: Supergroup. 2003. 184pp. 1-58240-309-0.
Vol. 5: Anarchy. 2004. 128pp. 1-58240-331-7.
Vol. 6: The Sellouts. 2004. 208pp. 1-58240-344-9.
Vol. 7: Forever. 2004. 272pp. 0-7851-1656-7.
Vol. 8: Legends. 2005. 208pp. 0-7851-1742-3.
Vol. 9: Psychotics. 2006. 200pp. 0-7851-1743-1.
Vol. 10: Cosmic. 2006. 200pp. 0-7851-2260-5.
Definitive Hardcover Collection, Vol. 1. 2005. 488pp. 0-7851-1805-5.

Top 10. **Written by Alan Moore. Illustrated by Gene Ha and Zander Cannon.** America's Best Comics/WildStorm/DC Comics, 2001–2003. **M** ◎

© 2006 Jinxworld.

The city of Neopolis was built as a haven for science heroes and villains shortly after World War II. Since that time more and more superpowered individuals, gods, and space aliens have come to call Neopolis their home. In order to police the powered populace, the city agreed to be under the jurisdiction of a multidimensional peacekeeping force spread across many parallel Earths. Located in Neopolis is precinct 10 (nicknamed Top 10), workplace to a colorful cast of cops. Enter Robyn "Toybox" Slinger, a rookie on the force, with partner Jeff Smax, a sulky and gruff blue-skinned giant. Other colorful cops include a near-retirement classic hero, Captain "Jetman" Traynor; a dog desk sergeant named Caesar;, a lesbian ghost girl, Jackie Phantom; the armored walking weapon Irma Geddon; a Satanist named King Peacock; and high-tech cowboy, Duane Dust Devil. The cases are fantastic and often humorous, ranging from an alien serial killer who murders prostitutes and bar brawls fought by gods, to a giant Godzilla-sized drunken lizard named Gograh. You can be sure that the streets are much safer with the team on the beat. Also features numerous inside jokes and appearances from many popular culture icons. *The Forty-Niners* presents for the first time the origins of Neopolis: a young science hero named Jetman and heroic companions create the beginnings of what will later come to be known as Precinct 10. *Beyond the Farthest Precinct* is a spin-off written by Paul Di Filippo and illustrated by Jerry Ordway. The original series received an Eisner Award in 2001 for Best Continuing Series, and *Top Ten: The Forty-Niners* received several Eisner Awards in 2006 for Best Graphic Album: New and Best Writer.

Book 1. 2001. 208pp. 1-56389-668-0.
Book 2. 2003. 144pp. 1-56389-966-3.
The Forty-Niners. 2005. 112pp. 1-56389-757-1.
Beyond the Farthest Precinct. 2006. 128pp. 1-4012-0991-2.

Ultra: Seven Days. **Written and illustrated by Joshua Luna and Jonathan Luna.** Image Comics, 2005. 232pp. 1-58240-483-6. **O**

© 2006 The Luna Brothers.

The life and adventures of three super-hero female crime-fighters in the city of Spring City, a place where fighting crime is only one of part of the multi-lucrative career of being a hero. Pearl Penalosa is Ultra, a beautiful super-hero who just happens to be unlucky in love as well as able to toss cars over her head. While things may be going well for her with plenty of fame and fortune and a "Best Heroine of the Year" nomination, Pam is just trying to find Mr. Right. When Pam and her two best friends (and super-heroes) Jen and Liv all visit a fortune teller, the woman says that each of them will have something occur to them within a week, and Pam is told she will find true love. Will their fortunes all come to pass, and will Pam really find true love?

Anthologies

Collections of super-hero stories featuring highlights from one creator's career or stories. Written by a showcase of creators for the super-hero genre.

DC Universe: The Stories of Alan Moore. **Written by Alan Moore. Illustrated by various.** DC Comics, 2006. 304pp. 1-4012-0927-0. **T**

Alan Moore has been highly praised in the comic book industry for his outstanding writing and creativity for decades. Collected together for the first time are some of his best-known stories created for DC Comics. Highlights include "Batman: The Killing Joke," "Superman: Whatever Happened to the Man of Tomorrow?" as well as stories featuring Swamp Thing, the Vigilante, the Omega Men, and the Green Lantern Corps.

Marvel Visionaries. Marvel Comics, 2002–2005. **Y**

A hardcover series by Marvel Comics, each book focusing on a legendary writer or artist who had a significant impact on Marvel Comics throughout its history. The stories feature a wide range of heroes and other characters written and/or illustrated by the featured creator.

> *Gil Kane.* Written by various. Illustrated by Gil Kane. 2002. 256pp. 0-7851-0888-2.
>
> *Jim Steranko.* Written by various. Illustrated by Jim Steranko. 2002. 128pp. 0-7851-0944-7.
>
> Jack Kirby. Written by Stan Lee and Jack Kirby. Illustrated by Jack Kirby. 2004–2006.
>
> > *Vol. 1.* 2004. 336pp. 0-7851-1574-9.
> >
> > *Vol. 2.* 2006. 344pp. 0-7851-2094-7.
>
> *Stan Lee.* Written by Stan Lee. Illustrated by Jack Kirby, Steve Ditko, and various. 2005. 336pp. 0-7851-1693-1.
>
> *John Romita Sr.* Written by Stan Lee, Tom DeFalco, Roy Thomas, and Roger Stern. Illustrated by John Romita Sr. 2005. 336pp. 0-7851-1780-6.

Steve Ditko. Written by Bill Mantlo, Stan Lee, Michael Fleisher, Tom DeFalco, and Roger Stern. Illustrated by Steve Ditko. 2005. 344pp. 0-7851-1783-0.

Chris Claremont. Written by Chris Claremont. Illustrated by various. 2005. 376pp. 0-7851-1887-X.

John Romita Jr. Written by various. Illustrated by John Romita Jr. 2005. 360pp. 0-7851-1964-7.

Roy Thomas. Written by Roy Thomas. Illustrated by various. 2006. 352pp. 0-7851-2088-2.

***Project Superior*. Written and illustrated by various.** Adhouse Books, 2004. 288pp. 0-9721794-8-8. **O**

An independent publishing look at the world of super-heroes from indy creators, animators, and mainstream comic book creators. Features the work of Gregory Benton, Jeffrey Brown, Dean Haspiel, Scott Morse, Joel Priddy, Paul Pope, Paul Rivoche, and others.

Tomorrow Stories. Written by Alan Moore. Illustrated by various. America's Best Comics/WildStorm Productions/DC Comics, 2002–2004. **T** ◉

An anthology collection by creator Alan Moore. The series features the humorous adventures of the child genius inventor Jack B. Quick, the crime-fighter ex-con Greyshirt, the patriotic antics of The First American, and the exploits of the 1940s femme-fatale investigator The Cobweb. The series won an Eisner Award in 2000 for Best Anthology as well as for Best Artist/Penciller/Inker and a Harvey Award in 2000 for Best Anthology.

Collected Edition, Book 1. 2002. 176pp. 1-56389-660-5.
Collected Edition, Book 2. 2004. 160pp. 1-4012-0165-2.

Ultimate Annuals. Written by Mark Millar, Brian Michael Bendis, and Brian K. Vaughan. Illustrated by Steve Dillon, Mark Brooks, Tom Raney, and Jae Lee. Marvel Comics, 2006–2007. **T**

Featuring four stories set in Marvel Comics' Ultimate line of comic book titles, including Ultimate Spider-Man, The Ultimates, Ultimate X-Men, and Ultimate Fantastic Four. The four stories are set in an alternate universe to the traditional Marvel Universe and take a new approach to classic Marvel characters, including Spider-Man, the X-Men, and others. For other titles set in the Ultimate Universe, please see the listings for Ultimate Spider-Man, The Ultimates, Ulimate X-Men, Ultimate Fantastic Four, and others in this chapter.

Vol. 1. 2006. 160pp. 0-7851-2035-1.
Vol. 2. 2007. 160pp. 0-7851-2371-7.

The World's Greatest Super-Heroes. **Written by Paul Dini. Illustrated by Alex Ross.** DC Comics, 2005. 404pp. 1-4012-0254-3. **Y**

A collection of beautifully painted, oversized stories featuring the classic heroes of the DC Comics universe. The titles include *Superman: Peace on Earth*, *Batman: War on Crime*, *Shazam!: Power of Hope*, *Wonder Woman: Spirit of Truth*, *JLA: Secret Origins*, and *JLA: Liberty and Justice*.

Chapter 2

Action and Adventure

The action and adventure genre in comic books and graphic novels finds its roots in the classic tales of adventure prose from nineteenth-century adventure writers such as Robert Louis Stevenson, from speculative fiction writers Jules Verne, H.G. Wells, Sir Arthur Conan Doyle, and from the pulp fiction novels of the early twentieth century, describing the exploits of such colorful heroes as Tarzan, Doc Savage, Conan the Barbarian, and the Shadow. With the expansion of the comic book industry the original action and adventure tales were reprints of newspaper comic strips including such popular characters as Terry and the Pirates, Little Orphan Annie, Dick Tracy, Flash Gordon, and Tarzan. Publishers also began to create all-new adventure stories with such characters as Dr. Occult, created by Jerry Siegel and Joe Shuster, the creators of Superman, the most popular super-hero character ever created.

Very similar to the prose action and adventure books and movies, the graphic novels in this genre feature themes such as classic tales of good guys versus bad guys, exotic locations, brave heroes, dastardly villains, and plenty of danger. The stories feature heroes as rugged adventurers, jungle warriors, cowboys, samurai, spies, fighters, soldiers, and more. Due to the illustrated nature of the format, unlike prose adventure fiction, the medium of the comic book readily lends itself to showing more heroic feats and is more closely related to motion pictures in this respect. Other traditional prose adventure themes, including political intrigue and industrial adventure, have not been widely published in a comic book or graphic novel format. Note that though the super-hero genre is directly related to this genre, the colorful heroes are featured in their own chapter in this publication.

Prehistoric Adventure

What was life like in prehistoric times? These stories sometimes accurately and sometimes inaccurately portray prehistoric life from the age of the dinosaurs and the age of prehistoric mammals onward. They feature worlds where dinosaurs, prehistoric mammals, and humans interact together. The protagonist may even be a dinosaur, prehistoric animal, or cave person. Although usually set in the past, some of these tales are set in the present or even the future. Scientific accuracy is optional, with some authors taking liberties for the sake of a good story. Film and television examples of this subgenre include the Jurassic Park series of movies, *King Kong*, *Beast from 20,000 Fathoms*, the television classic *Land of the Lost*, and even the BBC television documentary *Walking with Dinosaurs*. This theme closely borders and overlaps the realms of science fiction, horror, and historical fiction.

Age of Reptiles. Written by and Illustrated by Ricardo Delgado. Dark Horse Comics, 1996-1997. **Y** ◎

© 2006 Dark Horse Comics.

The ancient world of the dinosaurs comes alive again in two silent tales (there are no word balloons or dialogue; the pictures alone tell the story). In *Tribal Warfare*, a carnivorous Tyrannosaurus rex must fight for survival against the quick-footed scavenging pack of Deinonychus. In *The Hunt*, an orphaned Allosaurus must trek across the desert of Jurassic Period North America or share the fate of his mother: a bloody death at the hands of a ferocious pack of Ceratosaurs. In 1997, Ricardo Delgado received an Eisner Award in the category Talent Deserving of Wider Recognition.

Tribal Warfare. 1996. 128pp. 1-56971-101-1.
The Hunt. 1997. 128pp. 1-56971-199-2.

Cave-In. **Written and illustrated by Brian Ralph.** Highwater Books, 1999. 144pp. 0-9665363-3-9. **Y**

This is the silently told adventure of a cave-dwelling mole man as he struggles through an eerie underground world in search of food. Past giant worms, a friendly mummy, zombie mole-men, and more, the mole man won't stop on his quest underground until his belly is full.

Cavewoman: Missing Link. **Written by Bradley Walton. Illustrated by Jim Schumaker.** Basement Comics, 1998. 98pp. No ISBN. **T**

The citizens of the town of Marshville, Oregon, are on the trail of the legendary Bigfoot, but when the entire city is mysteriously teleported 70 million years into the past, things become much more complicated for the citizens of Marshville. Now the dinosaurs from the Cretaceous period are out to ensure that no one will make it out alive. Luckily they have a guide through these treacherous times: Meriem Cooper, a young woman who was also transported to the past over a decade earlier and can hold her own against any T rex.

Dinosaurs: A Celebration. **Edited by Steve White. Illustrated by various.** Marvel Comics, 1997. 192pp. 0-7851-0562-X. **Y**

A collection of short stories and scientific facts about the most famous extinct land and sea animals our world has ever known.

The Collected Paleo: Tales of the Cretaceous. **Written and illustrated by Jim Lawson.** Empty Sky/Zeromayo Productions, 2003. 172pp. 0-9661985-3-0. **Y** ◎

© 2006 Jim Lawson.

The savage and deadly ancient past comes alive in this exciting look at the Cretaceous period, a time when real monstrous beasts roamed the land. From the traumatic experience of a female Triceratops chased out of her herd by a pack of flesh-eating Daspletosaurs, to that of a pack of Dromeosaurs looking for a new leader after the death of the herd's alpha male, to a day in the life of an Albertasaur, and more. Take a journey back to the past, where the eaters and the eaten battle for survival and where day-to-day life was a struggle between the jaws of death of a fierce carnivorous dinosaur and the ever-changing landscape in a dangerous world.

Shanna, the She-Devil. **Written and illustrated by Frank Cho.** Marvel Comics, 2005. 168pp. 0-7851-1972-8. hardcover. **O** ◎

Stranded on a dinosaur-infested land, a platoon of rugged U.S. soldiers discover a secret Nazi base on the island. Inside the base they find a beautiful blonde in suspended animation. A product of German engineering, when she's freed the soldiers discover that she's been created by the Nazis to be strong enough to take on the bloody Velociraptors with her bare hands. Named by the soldiers after the pulp heroine Shanna, the She-Devil, the woman and the soldiers must learn to work together to survive against the most bloodthirsty of dinosaurs until help can finally arrive to rescue them. The story is written and illustrated by fan-favorite artist Frank Cho, best known for the beautiful women he draws in his comic strip Liberty Meadows. Please see chapter 8 for the listing for Liberty Meadows.

Tommysaurus Rex. **Written and illustrated by Doug TenNapel.** Image Comics, 2004. 112pp. 1-58240-395-3. **Y** ◎

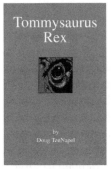

© 2006 Doug TenNapel.

Ten-year-old Ely is spending the summer at his grandfather's farm to help with the chores and to recuperate following the tragic death of Tommy, his pet golden retriever. After being chased by Randy, the local school bully, Ely finds a real Tyrannosaurus rex buried in a cave behind his grandfather's farm. Soon, Ely and Tommysaurus Rex are inseparable and are the best of friends; but after Tommysaurus Rex makes a brief rampage through town, the mayor declares that the dinosaur must be declared "safe" or else he'll have to leave. In no time Ely trains Tommysaurus rex, and after some trial and error the dinosaur becomes a genuine hero to the community, saving cats, helping to rebuild homes, making unwanted cattle "disappear," and making grandpa rich. During the mayor's reelection campaign, Tommysaurus Rex and Ely are the main stars at a big event and attract media attention from far and wide, much to the dismay of the school bully, Randy, who seeks revenge. When tragedy strikes, can two enemies find friendship with the healing power of forgiveness? The graphic novel also features a guest appearance by stop-motion animation legend Ray Harryhausen.

Tor. Written and illustrated by Joe Kubert. DC Comics, 2001–2003. **T**
   In a collection of classic tales from the 1950s, the caveman called Tor lives in a prehistoric world where people and dinosaurs share Earth. An outsider even among men, he travels the land accompanied by his pet lemur Chee-Chee, encountering vicious beasts, devious tribal humans, and natural disasters.

> *Vol. 1.* 2001. 144pp. 1-56389-781-4.
> *Vol. 2.* 2002. 144pp. 1-56389-830-6.
> *Vol. 3.* 2003. 144pp. 1-56389-998-1.

🏵 <u>**Xenozoic Tales.**</u> **Written by and Illustrated by Mark Schultz.** Dark Horse Comics, 2003. **O** ⓒ

Xenozoic Tales® © 2006
Mark Schultz.

In a future where a catastrophe has destroyed Earth, humanity's remnants have been forced into tribes and the world of old has come back. Man-eating dinosaurs and prehistoric beasts once again roam the planet and conquer the flooded seas. Now Shaman Jack "Cadillac" Tenrec, who spends his days fixing cars and technology of old, and Hannah Dundee, a scientist and Jack's potential love interest and sparring partner, are constantly on the run from dinosaurs, corrupt men, and dangers at every turn. The series received an Eisner Award in 1991 for Best Black and White Series and in 1993 for Best Short Story. The series also received a Harvey Award for Best Artist or Penciller (1990, 1992–1993) and for Best Single Issue or Story (1992).

> *Vol. 1: After the End.* 2003. 128pp. 1-56971-690-0.
> *Vol. 2: The New World.* 2003. 176pp. 1-56971-691-9.

Heroic Adventure

These are tales of high adventure featuring true heroes against unbeatable odds in settings ranging from the Seven Seas, to desert wastelands, to sparse jungles, to urban jungles. The heroes include classics such as Tintin, aquatic heroes of the sea, and bad-boy heroes stuck in dangerous environments and lifestyles. The stories in this genre at times may closely resemble those in the super-hero genre (see chapter 1), but these heroes exhibit subtle differences. Like the super-heroes, they have a high moral code, but typically these heroes do not have secret identities, a staple in super-hero stories. The heroes may have skills or powers that help to make them stand out above the common man to help them reach their goal. Typically the adventurous heroes are the common person striving to be the best he or she can be under trying times, on a quest to receive an item or object, or even to solve a mystery.

The Adventures of Tintin. **Written and illustrated by Hergé.** Little Brown & Company, 1994–1997. **A** ◎

One of the most popular European comics, published worldwide and in more than forty-seven languages. <u>Tintin</u> was created by Belgian writer and artist Georges Remi (his pen name is Hergé). The main character, a young traveling reporter named Tintin, travels with his faithful dog companion, Snowy, around the world and even into outer space out to solve many mysteries. He's also joined in his adventures by his friend Tchang, the gruff but loyal Captain Haddock, and others.

> *Collected Vol. 1.* 1994. 192pp. 0-316-35940-8.
> *Collected Vol. 2.* 1994. 192pp. 0-316-35942-4.
> *Collected Vol. 3.* 1994. 192pp. 0-316-35944-0.
> *Collected Vol. 4.* 1995. 192pp. 0-316-35814-2.
> *Collected Vol. 5.* 1995. 192pp. 0-316-35816-9.
> *Collected Vol. 6.* 1997. 192pp. 0-316-35724-3.
> *Collected Vol. 7.* 1997. 192pp. 0-316-35727-8.

The Amazing Joy Buzzards. **Written by Mark Andrew Smith. Illustrated by Mark Andrew Smith and Dan Hipp.** Image Comics, 2005–2006. **T**

Band mates Biff, Steve and Gabe are The Amazing Joy Buzzards, one of the biggest bands ever—but that's just their gig at night. While on tour they find themselves solving strange mysteries as they take on giant robots, witch doctors, and the spooky unknown alongside their mystical Mexican wrestler friend El Campeon. There's nothing too strange for the Amazing Joy Buzzards to handle.

> *Vol. 1.* 2005. 160pp. 1-58240-498-4.
> *Vol. 2.* 2006. 190pp. 1-58240-615-4.

© 2006 Mark Andrew Smith and Dan Hipp.

The Boss. **Written and illustrated by Jae Lim Won.** ADV Manga, 2004. **T Japanese manga.**

When the Woo Sang High School is under attack by a group of bullies recently released from juvenile detention, there's one boy they didn't count on to stand his ground. Saang Ti, a tough and strong teenager, can take on the juvie delinquents. He's got the might to stand up to the bullies since in school there's only one man who can be the boss.

> *Vol. 1.* 2004. 184pp. 1-4139-0069-0.
> *Vol. 2.* 2004. 184pp. 1-4139-0075-5.
> *Vol. 3.* 2004. 184pp. 1-4139-0083-6.

Chrono Crusade. **Written and illustrated by Daisuke Moriyama.** ADV Manga, 2004–2006. **T Japanese manga.** あ

In 1920s America, exorcist specialist Sister Rosette Christopher works for the Magdalan Order to bring down the demons causing destruction and to save innocent souls. She's joined in her quest by a reformed demon named Chrono.

Sister Rosette and Chrono share a pact in which Sister Rosette's life is literally in Chrono's hands. She wears a clock around her neck that contains her life force—which she willingly gives to Chrono to boost his strength in a time of need, but it also drains Sister Rosette of her life span. Armed with holy water bullets and demon hellfire, they're a deadly combination—especially when sometimes the duo does more damage than the demons! The series helped to inspire a Japanese anime series of the same name.

Vol. 1. 2004. 190pp. 1-4139-0084-4.
Vol. 2. 2004. 200pp. 1-4139-0104-2.
Vol. 3. 2004. 198pp. 1-4139-0045-3.
Vol. 4. 2004. 182pp. 1-4139-0239-1.
Vol. 5. 2005. 200pp. 1-4139-0273-1.
Vol. 6. 2005. 184pp. 1-4139-0309-6.
Vol. 7. 2006. 184pp. 1-4139-0339-8.
Vol. 8. 2006. 232pp. 1-4139-0343-6.

Climbing Out. **Written and illustrated by Brian Ralph.** Highwater Books, 2002. 88pp. 0-9700858-5-0. **Y**

A monkey decides to explore beyond the confines of his cave and discovers a world of adventure. Armed with science and curiosity, he tries to find out the meaning of life.

Digital Graffiti. **Written by Gez Fry. Illustrated by Gez Fry and Alex Frith.** AP Comics, 2004. 96pp. 1-905071-06-X **T**

In the twenty-third century, London is divided. Only those of privilege and class reside in the high-rise towers above the city, while the filth and gutter-trash squabble and get by in the lower levels. Teenage gangs rule the lower streets of London, marking their territories with graffiti on the digital billboards. Meanwhile, one gang member longs to leave the confines of the streets and decides to find a way to live the life of luxury that he's been denied.

Divine Right: The Adventures of Max Faraday. **Written by Scott Lobdell. Illustrated by Jim Lee.** WildStorm Productions/DC Comics, 2002. **T**

College student and part-time pizza delivery boy Max Faraday downloads a mysterious file from the Internet called the "Creation Equation." It's an instrument that both the forces of good and evil would kill to get, and it gives the user powers as well as unlocking the secrets of the universe. Now Max has more power than he's ever dreamed of, and it's only a matter of time before he discovers its secrets and what unlimited potential he really has. Max forwarded the file secrets to his online girlfriend Suzanne Caste—someone he's never even met in person! Now the evil Doctor Lazerous and his demonic minions, who want the "Creation Equation" back in their hands, have captured her. With his team of allies, Max is out to rescue her, and his problems have only just begun.

Vol. 1. 2002. 176pp. 1-56389-875-6.
Vol. 2. 2002. 192pp. 1-56389-652-4.

Duklyon: CLAMP School Defenders. **Written and illustrated by CLAMP.** TOKYOPOP, 2003. **Y Japanese manga.**

In a parody of typical Shonen (boy comics) from Japan, Kentarou and Takeshi are two freshmen ready to help save their CLAMP School campus from the forces of evil—whether it involves rescuing pets from trees or saving the school from super-villains from outer space. When their mysterious general plays a certain song over the intercom, they're ready to don their armor and protect the campus at all costs. Kept in line by the beautiful but tough Eri Chusonji, they're ready to save the day from Sinister Kotobuki, a space alien with a dark agenda to take over the planet.

> *Vol. 1.* 2003. 192pp. 1-59182-301-3.
> *Vol. 2.* 2003. 168pp. 1-59182-302-1.

Eat-Man. **Written and illustrated by Akihito Yoshitomi.** VIZ Media, LLC, 1997–1998. **T Japanese manga.**

Meet Bolt Crank, a cool and collected explorer. He's a charming but calculating man with the most bizarre appetite: whatever he eats—nuts, bolts, guns—can be retransformed back through his arms as a deadly weapon of his choosing. This special gift makes him one of the best and most expensive for-hire explorers. In a world with monsters, dragons, Devil Kings, and brigands, one man is all you need to take out the trash.

> *Vol. 1: Full Course Meal.* 1997. 192pp. 1-56931-292-3.
> *Vol. 2: Second Course.* 1998. 200pp. 1-56931-338-5.

Fathom. **Written by Michael Turner and Bill O'Neil. Illustrated by Michael Turner.** Top Cow Productions/Image Comics, 2002. 224pp. 1-58240-210-8. **T**

Aspen Matthews has always felt a calling to be near the sea. That's why she chose to become a marine biologist. After a terrible accident, she finds out that there is more to her calling than she ever thought possible: she is a water nymph with amazing control of the living seas. Discovering that she's not entirely human, Aspen is on a quest to find out more about her true origin and to discover if she really belongs with the humans or with the denizens of the deep.

© Michael Turner.

Firefighter! Daigo of Fire Company M. **Written and illustrated by Masahito Soda.** VIZ Media, LLC, 2003. **T ◎ Japanese manga.**

A slacker in high school with seemingly no future, eighteen-year-old Daigo Asahina has a new lease on life as a first-year firefighter at the relatively peaceful central Medaka-Ga-Hama fire station. Overconfident and proud of his position but an embarrassment to his team, he's out to prove to his fellow firefighters that he's got what it takes to get the job done and to be the best firefighter in Japan. The series was originally published in Japan and ran for twenty volumes.

Vol. 1. 2003. 200pp. 1-56931-955-3.
Vol. 2. 2003. 192pp. 1-56931-879-4.
Vol. 3. 2003. 200pp. 1-56931-880-8.
Vol. 4. 2003. 200pp. 1-56931-991-X.
Vol. 5. 2003. 192pp. 1-59116-093-6.
Vol. 6. 2004. 200pp. 1-59116-137-1.
Vol. 7. 2004. 200pp. 1-59116-315-3.
Vol. 8. 2004. 200pp. 1-59116-634-9.
Vol. 9. 2004. 200pp. 1-59116-634-9.
Vol. 10. 2005. 208pp. 1-59116-635-7.
Vol. 11. 2005. 200pp. 1-59116-795-7.
Vol. 12. 2005. 200pp. 1-59116-980-1.
Vol. 13. 2005. 200pp. 1-4215-0130-9.
Vol. 14. 2006. 200pp. 1-4215-0318-2.
Vol. 15. 2006. 200pp. 1-4215-0451-0.
Vol. 16. 2006. 200pp. 1-4215-0452-9.
Vol. 17. 2006. 200pp. 1-4215-0453-7.

🍴 **Fullmetal Alchemist. Written and illustrated by Hiromu Arakawa.** VIZ Media, LLC, 2005– . **T** ◎ 🐾 **Japanese manga.** あ

© Hiromu Arakawa/
SQUARE ENIX.

In a city where steam power still exists, two teenage brothers, Edward and Alphonse Elric, are apprentices inalchemy, the art of manipulating matter and transforming it into another state. After a tragic mistake, Edward lost a leg and an arm, but his younger brother lost much more: his entire body. Now Alphonse's soul is grafted into a suit of armor and Edward has mechanical appendages. They both work for the state as military alchemists on dangerous missions as they continue their search for the Philosopher's Stone, a magical item with the power to restore Edward's body and even return something more precious to them both: their mother. The popular series so far has been collected into fourteen volumes in Japan and is still being published. The series received recognition from YALSA's Quick Picks for Reluctant Readers list in 2006. Recently a Japanese anime series of the same name was released in North America, and both have become huge hits with anime and manga fans of all ages.

Vol. 1. 2005. 192pp. 1-59116-920-8.
Vol. 2. 2005. 192pp. 1-59116-923-2.
Vol. 3. 2005. 192pp. 1-59116-925-9.
Vol. 4. 2005. 200pp. 1-59116-929-1.
Vol. 5. 2006. 192pp. 1-4215-0175-9.
Vol. 6. 2006. 208pp. 1-4215-0319-0.
Vol. 7. 2006. 208pp. 1-4215-0458-8.
Vol. 8. 2006. 208pp. 1-4215-0459-6.
Vol. 9. 2006. 208pp. 1-4215-0460-x.
Vol. 10. 2006. 208pp. 1-4215-0461-8.

The Gift. **Written by Raven Gregory. Illustrated by Tyler Kirkham and various.** Image Comics, 2005– . **T**

There walks among us an ancient being who bestows upon random individuals a gift of incredible power. Depending on each individual's personality, the powers may be used for good or evil, and each one must decide how to use it. While the actions by the Ancient One may seem random, his true reasons for bestowing the powers will ultimately be revealed as more are given the gift.

Vol. 1: Choices. 2005. 144pp. 1-58240-416-X.
Vol. 2: Consequences. 2005. 128pp. 1-58240-528-X.

Go Boy 7. **Written by Tom Peyer and Brian Augustyn. Illustrated by Jon Sommariva.** Dark Horse Comics, 2004. **T**

En route with his parents to his reclusive uncle's secret Go Base facility, tragedy strikes teenager Jonny when their plane is shot down and both his parents are killed. Revived by his uncle, Jonny has been cybernetically enhanced with a nanoplasm that now runs in his blood and gives him an advantage over any obstacle. Now his uncle's archenemy, a humorous being called the Cultist who's out to destroy all logic, wants the secrets of Jonny and his new powers. With the aid of his uncle's sexy but levelheaded security chief, Jett Girl, there's nothing that Jonny can't handle.

Vol. 1: Ready Set Go. 2004. 96pp. 1-56971-937-3.
Vol. 2: The Human Factor. 2004. 96pp. 1-59307-264-3.

Hikaru no Go. **Written and illustrated by Yumi Hotta.** VIZ Media, LLC, 2004– . **A Japanese manga** あ

Sixth-grader Hikaru Shindo was never one for his grandfather's board games, but when he finds a blood-stained board of the classic Japanese game GO, that's all about to change. Hikaru unknowingly releases the spirit of Fujiwara-no-Sai, the ghost of an ancient GO master who was instructor to the Emperor of Japan many centuries ago and has not been able to ascend to Heaven until he achieves the "Divine Move." Fujiwara teams up with Hikaru and together they make a formidable team, taking on the best GO players the world has ever seen, to free Fujiwara's spirit. The hit manga series has also spawned an anime series, released in 2001 in Japan.

Vol. 1. 2004. 192pp. 1-59116-222-X.
Vol. 2. 2004. 194pp. 1-59116-496-6.
Vol. 3. 2005. 208pp. 1-59116-687-X.
Vol. 4. 2005. 200pp. 1-59116-688-8.
Vol. 5. 2005. 208pp. 1-59116-689-6.
Vol. 6. 2006. 208pp. 1-4215-0275-5.
Vol. 7. 2006. 208pp. 1-4215-0641-6.
Vol. 8. 2006. 208pp. 1-4215-0642-4.

Immortal Rain. **Written and illustrated by Kaori Ozaki.** TOKYOPOP, 2004–2006. **O Japanese manga.**

Fourteen-year-old Machika Balfaltin is a young and energetic bounty hunter who's trying hard to follow in her late grandfather's, the legendary Grim Reaper Zol, footsteps. She's out to kill the one man her grandfather could never capture: Rain Jewlett, the 624-year-old man also known as the Methuselah. His bounty is the highest in the land, and everyone is out to learn the secret of this eccentric man's youthful appearance and incredible immortality. When Rain saves Machika over and over from competing bounty hunters, a strange friendship is created. Machika vows that when she finds a way to end Rain's immortality, she'll be his grim reaper. When Yucca, a dark archenemy of Rain's hidden past, is reborn, Machika may not be able to fulfill her promise if he kills Rain first.

Vol. 1. 2004. 232pp. 1-59182-722-1.
Vol. 2. 2004. 200pp. 1-59182-723-X.
Vol. 3. 2004. 208pp. 1-59182-724-8.
Vol. 4. 2005. 192pp. 1-59182-990-9.
Vol. 5. 2005. 216pp. 1-59182-991-7.
Vol. 6. 2005. 192pp. 1-59532-799-1.
Vol. 7. 2006. 192pp. 1-59532-798-7.

Initial D. **Written and illustrated by Shuichi Shigeno.** TOKYOPOP, 2002– . **T Japanese manga.** あ

In the world of street racing, only those with nerves of steel can survive the dangerous, winding roads of Mt. Akina. Takumi Fujiwara couldn't care less about street racing. Sure, his skills as a driver are unequalled, but he's got to deliver tofu down Mt. Akina for his dad's restaurant in his Trueno Eight Six. When he inadvertently enters a race, Tak finds that he just may have the skills to become the best race car driver ever. The series was published in thirty volumes in Japan and was also the inspiration for an anime series.

Vol. 1. 2002. 200pp. 1-931514-98-4.
Vol. 2. 2002. 200pp. 1-59182-035-9.
Vol. 3. 2002. 200pp. 1-59182-036-7.
Vol. 4. 2003. 192pp. 1-59182-037-5.
Vol. 5. 2003. 240pp. 1-59182-038-3.
Vol. 6. 2003. 240pp. 1-59182-039-1.
Vol. 7. 2003. 240pp. 1-59182-040-5.
Vol. 8. 2003. 240pp. 1-59182-041-3.
Vol. 9. 2003. 240pp. 1-59182-109-6.
Vol. 10. 2004. 240pp. 1-59182-110-X.
Vol. 11. 2004. 240pp. 1-59182-174-6.
Vol. 12. 2004. 232pp. 1-59182-462-1.
Vol. 13. 2004. 240pp. 1-59182-463-X.
Vol. 14. 2004. 240pp. 1-59182-464-8.
Vol. 15. 2004. 240pp. 1-59182-465-6.
Vol. 16. 2005. 240pp. 1-59182-992-5.
Vol. 17. 2005. 240pp. 1-59182-993-3.
Vol. 18. 2005. 232pp. 1-59182-994-1.
Vol. 19. 2005. 192pp. 1-59182-995-X.
Vol. 20. 2005. 192pp. 1-59182-996-8.
Vol. 21. 2006. 192pp. 1-59182-997-6.
Vol. 22. 2006. 192pp. 1-59182-998-4.
Vol. 23. 2006. 198pp. 1-59532-000-8.
Vol. 24. 2006. 192pp. 1-59532-001-6.

Invincible Ed. **Written and illustrated by Ryan Woodward.** Dark Horse Comics, 2004. 112pp. 1-59307-194-9. **T**

> When the peaceful planet of Quanda senses that Earth needs a hero, they send Nod, the Earth scientist, to deliver a power called "The Right" to a lone human champion. When the power is accidentally split between Lance Lungrin, the bullish high school football hero, and Ed, a local high school freshman geek who's constantly bullied by Lance, they both must share a portion of "the Right." Now Lance has the power to channel blasts of energy, and Ed is invincible, sort of. Though he is gifted with an insanely high level of pain tolerance, Ed can feel every blow, explosion, and crack to the head. He's going to learn the hard way how to beat Lance and see if he's got what it takes to be a true hero, even though it hurts like hell.

Isaac the Pirate. **Written and illustrated by Christophe Blain.** NBM Publishing, 2003–2005. **O**

> In eighteenth-century France, Isaac is a talented artist with a captivating girlfriend but no steady income to marry her. When a wealthy captain offers him a lucrative job as an artist aboard a ship, little does he realize what he's gotten himself into. The Captain, as it turns out, is a pirate, and now what was to be a quick way to earn money has led Isaac across the globe and farther and farther away from his beloved, with no end in sight.

> > *Vol. 1: To Exotic Lands.* 2003. 96pp. 1-56163-366-6.
> > *Vol. 2: The Capital.* 2005. 96pp. 1-56163-418-2.

The Jungle Book. **Written by Rudyard Kipling. Adapted by P. Craig Russell.** NBM Publishing, 1997. 88pp. 1-56163-152-3. **Y**

> Adaptation of the classic adventure book by Rudyard Kipling about the abandoned "man cub," Mowgli, who is raised in the wilderness by wolves in the Indian jungle. The collection features the three short stories "The King's Ankus," "Red Dog," and "The Spring Running."

Junior Pirates: Beginnings. **Created by Eduardo Alpuente and Eric Mahr with Chuck Dixon. Written by Chuck Dixon. Illustrated by Guillermo Mendosa.** Mahrwood Press, 2004. 64pp. 1-58330-782-6. **Y**

> The legendary pirate Blackbeard and his men are dead, but their children live on to continue their legacy! In England in 1635, hard-luck orphans Eddie, Caesar, John, Joe, and Felicity discover that their parents were none other than the legendary pirate Blackbeard and his crew. When they discover that their parents left them a treasure of gold, nothing can keep them from claiming their destiny and the treasure that awaits them on the high seas.

© 2006 Eduardo Alpuente, Eric Mahr and Mahrwood Press Ltd.

Legal Drug. Written and illustrated by CLAMP. TOKYOPOP, 2004– . **O Japanese manga.**

Kazahaya and Rikuo are pharmacists who work at the unique Green Drug pharmacy. By day they fill normal prescriptions, but by night their manager has them filling prescriptions and taking on tasks for the most unusual clients. Luckily, they both have powers that help them with their clients: Kazahaya has been given the gift of visions, while Rikuo has control over telekinesis. Together they have the ability to take on the most unusual jobs. The series was never fully completed by CLAMP, and the concluding story line has yet to be published.

> *Vol. 1*. 2004. 184pp. 1-59182-485-0.
> *Vol. 2*. 2005. 176pp. 1-59532-421-6.
> *Vol. 3*. 2005. 184pp. 1-59532-422-4.

Poppie's Adventures: Serpents in Paradise. **Written by Julie Yeh. Illustrated by Jack Hsu.** Way Out Comics, 2002. 48pp. 0-9742386-0-0. **T**

A new writer for *Traveler Magazine,* perky and inquisitive seventeen-year-old Poppie Field is joined by photographer James "Ham" Hamamura for an average article on Hawaii vacation spots. But when they discover a conspiracy that involves snakes, a snake-worshipping cult of Kebechet, and a plot to use Mt. Kilauea to destroy the environment, Poppie and Ham are there to save the day.

R^2. Written and illustrated by Maki Hakoda. ADV Manga, 2004–2005. **Y Japanese manga.**

Teenager Kenta Akagi knows the Palpatin city of Lutzheim like the back of his hand. He's been there his whole life, secluded from the rest of the world, spending his days daydreaming, delivering pizzas, and wandering the back alleys and hidden paths in the sprawling ancient city. Lately he's been having dreams about a young girl whom he knows he must protect at all costs. After a terrorist attack occurs at a cathedral in the city, Kenta discovers that the girl of his dreams is real and that they're both keys in a plot far bigger than he ever imagined.

> *Vol. 1*. 2004. 184pp. 1-4139-0056-9.
> *Vol. 2*. 2005. 184pp. 1-4139-0321-5.

Rave Master. Written and illustrated by Hiro Mashima. TOKYOPOP, 2003– . **T Japanese manga.** あ

Fifty years ago a dark, evil power known as the Dark Bring was vanquished with the aid of the fabled Rave stones. The blast was so powerful that the Rave stones were scattered into five pieces all around the globe. Now a sinister society called the Demon Card plans to harness the power of the Dark Bring stones, and the only one who can save the world is Haru Glory, a fun-loving, adventurous sixteen-year-old boy living on peaceful Garage Island. He's the only one who can wield the power of the Rave stones and the Rave-powered sword called the "Ten Commandments." Joined by the bizarre-looking snowman dog called Plue, who is the only one capable of detecting the missing Rave stones, he's out to retrieve the missing pieces of the Rave stones to prevent the powers of Demon Card and the Dark Bring engulfing the world. The series was originally published in thirty-two volumes in Japan. An anime series was also released and was based on the manga.

Vol. 1. 2003. 176pp. 1-59182-064-2.
Vol. 2. 2003. 200pp. 1-59182-065-0.
Vol. 3. 2003. 192pp. 1-59182-210-6.
Vol. 4. 2003. 200pp. 1-59182-211-4.
Vol. 5. 2003. 200pp. 1-59182-212-2.
Vol. 6. 2003. 208pp. 1-59182-213-0.
Vol. 7. 2004. 200pp. 1-59182-517-2.
Vol. 8. 2004. 192pp. 1-59182-518-0.
Vol. 9. 2004. 208pp. 1-59182-519-9.
Vol. 10. 2004. 224pp. 1-59182-520-2.
Vol. 11. 2004. 208pp. 1-59182-521-0.
Vol. 12. 2004. 208pp. 1-59182-522-9.
Vol. 13. 2005. 192pp. 1-59532-018-0.
Vol. 14. 2005. 200pp. 1-59532-019-9.
Vol. 15. 2005. 192pp. 1-59532-020-2.
Vol. 16. 2005. 192pp. 1-59532-021-0.
Vol. 17. 2005. 192pp. 1-59532-022-9.
Vol. 18. 2005. 192pp. 1-59532-023-7.
Vol. 19. 2006. 192pp. 1-59532-024-5.
Vol. 20. 2006. 200pp. 1-59532-025-3.
Vol. 21. 2005. 192pp. 1-59532-026-1.
Vol. 22. 2006. 192pp. 1-59532-626-X.
Vol. 23. 2007. 200pp. 1-59532-627-8.

Ray. **Written and illustrated by Akihito Yoshitomi.** ADV Manga, 2004–2005. **O Japanese manga.**

A surgeon extraordinaire, Ray was originally bred to be a living organ donor at a facility called the Farm. After her eyes are taken from her in the body banks, a mysterious individual gives her back her sight and more: X-ray vision! Ten years later, Ray has used her gift as an underground surgeon, able to accomplish any emergency surgery for the right price. When an old friend from "The Farm" comes back into her life, she decides to dedicate her life to destroying the Farm forever.

Vol. 1. 2004. 208pp. 1-4139-0204-9.
Vol. 2. 2004. 208pp. 1-4139-0237-5.
Vol. 3. 2005. 208pp. 1-4139-0290-1.

Shaman King. **Written and illustrated by Hiroyuki Takei.** VIZ Media, LLC, 2003– . **T Japanese manga.** あ

In our world there are a select few individuals called shamans who are able to speak with the dead. The shamans also have the gift to have their bodies temporarily inhabited by the spirits of the dead. Yoh Asakura, a recent transfer student to Shinra Private Junior High, is a shaman-in-training. Though he appears to be a careless slacker, he's anything but. Joined by hyper but inquisitive fellow student Manta Oyamada, his fiancée Anna Kyoyama, and the spirit of the fallen samurai Amidamaru, Yoh is ready to take on his archenemy, the Chinese shaman Ren, and to participate in the Great Shaman Fight in Tokyo to decide who can communicate with the Great Spirit and become the Shaman

King. The series was published originally in Japan, where it ran for thirty-two volumes, and has also been adapted as an anime series.

Vol. 1. 2003. 208pp. 1-56931-902-2.
Vol. 2. 2004. 208pp. 1-59116-182-7.
Vol. 3. 2004. 192pp. 1-59116-252-1.
Vol. 4. 2004. 200pp. 1-59116-253-X.
Vol. 5. 2004. 200pp. 1-59116-254-8.
Vol. 6. 2005. 192pp. 1-59116-788-4.
Vol. 7. 2005. 192pp. 1-59116-996-8.
Vol. 8. 2006. 208pp. 1-4215- 0198-8.
Vol. 9. 2006. 208pp. 1-4215-0676-9.
Vol. 10. 2006. 208pp. 1-4215-0677-7.
Vol. 11. 2006. 192pp. 1-4215-0678-5.
Vol. 12. 2007. 200pp. 1-4215-1100-2.

***Sticks and Stones.* Written and illustrated by Peter Kuper.** Crown Publishing Group/Random House, 2004. 128pp. 1-4000-5257-2. **T**

On a barren wasteland a volcano gives birth to a large rock creature that demands that the small stone creatures worship and pay homage to him, building him a castle made of stone. Later he sets his sights on the village, made entirely of wood. As the corruption of the rock-god continues, a resistance front from the stone and wood villages appears to challenge the self-made god and to take down his small empire.

***Treasure Island.* Written by Robert Louis Stevenson. Adapted and illustrated by Tim Hamilton.** Penguin Graphics/Penguin Group, 2005. 176pp. 0-14-240470-5. **Y**

Adaptation of the classic adventure novel first published in 1883. In the eighteenth century, young Jim Hawkins becomes entangled in a quest for buried treasure after discovering a map from an old sea captain named Billy Bones. The map is rumored to tell the whereabouts of the buried treasure of the infamous pirate Captain Flint. An expedition is put together to find the treasure, and Jim discovers that the cook, Long John Silver, was actually a shipmate of Flint's, and most of the crew on board were, too. Will the pirate mutineers get Flint's treasure before Jim and Captain Smollet's crew does, and what other secrets lie on the island?

***William Shakespeare's Macbeth.* Written by William Shakespeare. Adapted by Arthur Byron Cover. Illustrated by Tony Leonard Tamai.** Penguin Graphics/Penguin Group, 2005. 176pp. 0-14-240409-8. **T**

On a massive ringworld that encircles a sun, Macbeth, the Thane of Glamis, is a general for the army of King Duncan. When he encounters three witches, they foretell a time when Macbeth will be king. When he tells his wife, Lady Macbeth, about the witches' prophecy, they scheme to make the witches' vision a reality and become king and queen, setting out on a bloody and tragic path of betrayal and guilt. A futuristic setting for a classic tale.

YuYu Hakusho. Written and illustrated by Yoshihiro Togashi. VIZ Media, LLC, 2003– . **T Japanese manga.** あ

When delinquent fourteen-year-old Yusuke Urameshi is killed while saving a child from a speeding car, he's given a new lease in the afterlife as a reward for his honorable, selfless act. Under the guidance of Botan, the cute guide to the river Styx, and Koenma, the junior Lord of the Underworld, he's been given a second chance, to act as a guardian spirit guide helping those in need. Meanwhile, his body has been brought back from the dead and kept in a coma, and Yusuke can become human for one day a month. If Yusuke can save enough lives—both the living and the dead—through good deeds, he can earn a permanent reunion with his body. The popular series is still ongoing in Japan and was also adapted into an anime series.

> *Vol. 1.* 2003. 200pp. 1-56931-904-9.
> *Vol. 2.* 2003. 200pp. 1-59116-082-0.
> *Vol. 3.* 2004. 200pp. 1-59116-183-5.
> *Vol. 4.* 2004. 192pp. 1-59116-325-0.
> *Vol. 5.* 2004. 200pp. 1-59116-521-0.
> *Vol. 6.* 2004. 200pp. 1-59116-668-3.
> *Vol. 7 .*2005. 200pp. 1-59116-812-0.
> *Vol. 8.* 2005. 192pp. 1-4215-0026-4.
> *Vol. 9.* 2006. 208pp. 1-4215-0278-X.
> *Vol. 10.* 2006. 208pp. 1-4215-0695-5.
> *Vol. 11.* 2006. 208pp. 1-4215-0696-3.
> Vol. 12. 2007. 192pp. 1-4215-1118-5.

Adventurers, Explorers, and Soldiers of Fortune

In these adventure stories the main character, typically portrayed as the ideal male or female, searches for an item as part of a quest for noble reasons, or is hired for his or her exceptional skills. Traps, hidden dangers, and deadly archenemies are commonplace in these gripping stories, and they owe a lot of their storytelling technique to pulp adventure stories. Comedy and romance sometimes alleviate the plot pressure. Movies like the <u>Indiana Jones</u> films exemplify this genre. Stories may also include influences from other genres, including science fiction and super-heroess.

Alison Dare, Little Miss Adventures. **Written by J. Torres. Illustrated by J. Bone.** Oni Press, 2002–2005. **Y**

© 2006 Oni Press.

Twelve-year-old Alison isn't your typical 'Tweener. She's the daughter of a famous archaeologist/adventurer. Her dad's a hero known as the Blue Scarab, so adventure is in her blood whether her divorced parents like it or not. Unfortunately for her, her parents want something a little bit more normal for her, so she's been enrolled at the strict St. Joan of Arc Academy for Girls. But curfews and rules aren't enough to keep Alison and her friends Wendy and Dot from globe-trotting the world and finding magic lamps (with wish-granting genies), confronting her parents' archenemies, hanging out with her super-spy uncle, and more.

Vol. 1. 2002. 96pp. 1-929998-20-1.
Vol. 2. 2005. 104pp. 1-932664-25-4.

Blackjack: Blood and Honor. Written and illustrated by Alex Simmons. Dark Angel Productions, 1999. 104pp. 0-9676341-0-5. **T**

In 1935, African American soldier of fortune and gentleman Arron Day is hired to protect a Japanese dignitary who has been targeted for assassination by his countrymen, bent on plunging Japan into war. Spies, ninjas, and the armies of Japan will stop at nothing to achieve their goal, but they didn't count on Arron Day, a.k.a. Blackjack. A suave but rough and tough warrior, Arron is out to fight the good fight even though he's a stranger in a strange land.

Captain Nemo. Written by Jason DeAngelis. Illustrated by Aldin Viray. Seven Seas Entertainment, 2006. **T Neo-manga.**

The adventures of a young Captain Nemo and his crew a aboard the *Nautilus II.* Set in the year 1893, after Napoleon IV has conquered not just France, but the entire world, creating a vast empire. Now Captain Nemo and his crew are all that stand in the way of the world conqueror.

Vol. 1. 2006. 192pp. 1-933164-08-5.

Gold Digger. Written and illustrated by Fred Perry. Antarctic Press, 2003– . **T Neo-manga.**

Gina Diggers comes from a family that is slightly different than most: her father was a powerful mage and her mother was a warrior from another world. Her adopted sister Brittany is her were-cheetah bodyguard, and their sister Brianna is a hybrid clone of both of them and a weapons genius. Together the sisters travel the globe in search of treasure and fortune, from down in the depths of Atlantis to other realms, always on the run from whatever evil they've unearthed. The series has been published since 1991 and is being reprinted in a pocket-sized edition.

© 2006 Antarctic Press.

Pocket Manga Vol. 1. 2003. 158pp. 1-932453-00-8.
Pocket Manga Vol. 2. 2003. 128pp. 1-932453-07-5.
Pocket Manga Vol. 3. 2004. 128pp. 1-932453-35-0.
Pocket Manga Vol. 4. 2005. 128pp. 1-932453-61-X.
Pocket Manga Vol. 5. 2005. 144pp. 1-932453-71-7.
Pocket Manga Vol. 6. 2005. 128pp. 1-932453-81-4.
Pocket Manga Vol. 7. 2006. 144pp. 1-932453-94-6.
Pocket Manga Vol. 8. 2006. 200pp. 0-976804-30-1.
Pocket Manga Vol. 9. 2003. 128pp. 0-966358-82-1.
Pocket Manga Vol. 10. 2003. 124pp. 0-972897-87-9.
Pocket Manga Vol. 11. 2003. 124pp. 1-932453-29-6.
Gold Digger Max Pocket Manga, Vol. 1. 2006. 152pp. 0-977642-41-0.

***High Roads.* Written by Scott Lobdell. Illustrated by Leinil Francis Yu.**
WildStorm Productions/DC Comics, 2003. 224pp. 1-4012-0033-8. **T**

At the end of World War II, a comical misfit band of fighters—a naïve U.S. army sergeant, a midget Hitler impersonator, a sultry former concubine of Hitler, and a shamed kamikaze Japanese fighter pilot—take on the Nazis in a quest for Hitler's treasured jewel, known as Morpheus's Necklace. When there's more to the fabled necklace than they knew, the uncommon heroes find themselves inadvertently saving the world from Nazi ninjas and Hitler's final solution.

© 2006 WildStorm Productions.

***Indiana Jones and the Fate of Atlantis.* Written by William Messner-Loebs.**
Illustrated by Dan Barry. Dark Horse Comics, 1992. 128pp. 1-878574-36-1. **T**

In 1939, archaeologist Dr. Henry "Indiana" Jones has seen a lot of strange things in his lifetime. He's discovered the Lost Ark of the Covenant and even the Holy Grail, but as an adventurer/explorer, but he's never believed that the ancient continent of Atlantis ever existed . . . until now. Joined by former colleague Sophia Hapgood, he's traveling the globe on a race against time and the Nazis to put together the missing pieces of the puzzle and find out what happened to Atlantis and its legendary advanced technology, before it falls into the hands of the Third Reich.

<u>Liling-Po</u>. Written and illustrated by Ako Yutenji. TOKYOPOP, 2005– . **T**
Japanese manga.

When the near-legendary master thief Liling-Po is captured, he's given a chance for freedom, on one condition: he must "recover" treasures that, when assembled, can grant wishes. Working with two agents from the government, Bu-cho and Mei-toku, Liling-Po's skills are put to the ultimate test as they journey to recover the mysterious artifacts. Seven volumes were originally published in Japan.

> *Vol. 1.* 2005. 208pp. 1-59532-519-0.
> *Vol. 2.* 2005. 200pp. 1-59532-520-4.
> *Vol. 3.* 2005. 192pp. 1-59532-521-2.
> *Vol. 4.* 2006. 184pp. 1-59532-522-0.
> *Vol. 5.* 2006. 192pp. 1-59532-523-9.
> *Vol. 6.* 2007. 184pp. 1-59532-524-7.

***Rex Steele: Nazi Smasher.* Written by Matt Peters. Illustrated by Bill Presing.**
Monkeysuit Press, 2004. 134pp. 0-9673289-1-8. **O**

When the evil Nazis from World War II are ready to strike against the Allies with yet another insane plot to take over the world, there's only one true-blue American hero who can take them on: Rex Steele, Nazi Smasher! He and his trusted gal Friday, Penny Thimble, are ready to fight their way American-style against the Nazi femme-fatale assistant Greta Schultz and her leader, Eval Schnitzler. The "Ratzis" don't stand a chance against Rex.

☕ Tom Strong. Written by Alan Moore. Illustrated by Chris Sprouse. America's Best
Comics/WildStorm Productions/DC Comics, 2000–2006. **T ◎**

© 2006 America's Best Comics.

Born more than 100 years ago at the dawn of the twentieth century on
the remote island of Attabar Teru and raised by the indigenous Ozu
people, pulp "science-hero" Tom Strong is one of the most brilliant
minds and strongest men our world has ever seen. Settled with his
family in 1950s-inspired Millennium City, his family, made up of his
wife Dhulua, their hero-in-training daughter Tesla, as well as their as-
sistants the robot butler Pneumann and the bow-tied talking gorilla
King Solomon, are ready for adventure wherever it may take them.
From alien invaders, to parallel universes, to dimension-hopping
hordes of the half-dead, the science/adventurer Strong family is ready
to take hold and accomplish the impossible and the unbelievable in a
world where anything can happen. The series has won multiple
awards, including an Eisner Award for Best Single Issue/Single Story (2002), Best Serialized Story (2002), and Best Writer (2000-2001, 2004). *Tom Strong, Book 1* received recognition from YALSA's Quick Picks for Reluctant Readers committee in
2001.

> *Book 1.* 2000. 208pp. 1-56389-654-0, hardcover; 2001. 1-56389-664-8, softcover.
> *Book 2.* 2002. 192pp. 1-56389-874-8, hardcover; 2003. 1-56389-880-2, softcover.
> *Book 3.* 2004. 144pp. 1-4012-0282-9, hardcover; 1-4012-0285-3, softcover.
> *Book 4.* 2005. 176pp. 1-4012-0571-2, hardcover; 1-4012-0572-0, softcover.
> *Book 5.* 2005. 144pp. 1-4012-0624-7, hardcover; 2006. 1-4012-0625-5, softcover.
> *Book 6.* 2006. 160pp. 1-4012-1108-9, hardcover.

**☕ Tom Strong's Terrific Tales. Written by Alan Moore and Steve Moore. Illustrated
by Arthur Adams, Sergio Aragones, and various.** America's Best Comics/WildStorm
Productions/DC Comics, 2005. **T ◎**

Spun off from the Tom Strong main series, this anthology series follows the exploits of
the Tom Strong family, including Tom's daughter Tesla, the intelligent ape King Solomon, and flashbacks of the life of a young Tom Strong on the island of Attabar Teru.
The stories also presents tales set in the far future featuring the fantastic exploits of the
heroine called Jonni Future. Alan Moore received an Eisner Award for Best Writer for
his collective body of work, including this series, in 2004.

> *Book 1.* 2005. 176pp. 1-4012-0030-3, hardcover.
> *Book 2.* 2005. 160pp. 1-4012-0615-8, hardcover.

**Tomb Raider. Written by Dan Jurgens, Michael Turner, and various. Illustrated by
Andy Park and Michael Turner.** Image Comics/Top Cow Productions, 2000–2002;
Bandai Entertainment, Inc and Top Cow Productions, 2006. **T 🎬 🎮**

Based on the popular adventure video game phenomenon, Lara Croft is an extraordinary young woman. With a thirst for high adventure and travel, the captivating Lara is
trained in archaeology, martial arts, hand-to-hand combat, and firearms to become one
of the most dangerous and highly skilled adventurers. Coming from a British family of
great wealth and aristocracy, she's dedicated her life to searching for the most unat-
tainable treasures and antiquities from the ancient world. Naturally her search for adventure and treasures has pitted her against terrifying dangers, including ancient

mythical forces, heavily armed opponents, and more, yet she has always returned victorious. The title *Tomb Raider/Witchblade: Trouble Seekers* features a team-up adventure with NYPD police officer Sara Pezzini, the wielder of the dark weapon called the Witchblade. In 2006 Bandai Entertainment, Inc. and Top Cow Productions joined together to reprint in digest size black-and-white format highlights from the Top Cow monthly comic book series, and Top Cow has reproduced the entire fifty comic book issues in a massive collection called the *Tomb Raider Compendium*.

> *Vol. I: The Saga of the Medusa Mask.* 2000. 112pp. 1-58240-164-0.
> *Vol. II: Mystic Artifacts.* 2001. 136pp. 1-58240-202-7.
> *Vol. III: Chasing Shangri-La* 2002. 128pp. 1-58240-267-1.
> *Tomb Raider/Witchblade: Trouble Seekers.* 2002. 80pp. 1-58240-279-5.
> *Vol. 1: Digest Edition.* 2006. 220pp. 1-59409-666-X.
> *Vol. 2: Digest Edition.* 2006. 220pp. 1-59409-667-8.
> *Tomb Raider Compendium.* 2006. 1248pp. 1-58240-637-5.

Treasure Hunter. Written and illustrated by Hitoshi Tomizawa. CPM Manga, 2004. **T Japanese manga.**

Young Jubei is the best thief in the entire world. There's no treasure he can't retrieve, no trap he can't escape, no door he can't unlock, and no request he can turn down. Joined with his friend and magic carpet, named Carpet, and his magical genie, he's out to hunt any treasure that he's asked to find, and no matter what it takes, you can bet that Jubei will find it.

> *Vol. 1: Eternal Youth.* 2004. 200pp. 1-58664-921-3.
> *Vol. 2: Figurehead of Souls.* 2004. 200pp. 1-58664-922-1.

Fists of Fury and Swords of Steel—Fighting Adventure Stories

Pure action defines this subgenre. The stories in this section involve a main character or characters testing their skills either in a combat competition as a rite of passage, for monetary goals, for personal glory, or to survive. Combat may consist of bare-knuckle brawls, weapons combat, or even inexplicable superpowers as a natural extension of fighting prowess or mysterious powers the combatant has received. Romance and comedy may be involved but typically aren't the main focus of the story line, where action remains supreme and characters are reduced to the sum of their own strengths—pure fighting machines.

***Battle Gods: Warriors of the Chaak.* Written and illustrated by Francisco Ruiz Velasco.** Dark Horse Comics, 2001. 240pp. 1-56971-562-9. **O**

In the year A.D. 2065, the best and deadliest enhanced fighters of the world are gathered together at the no-holds-barred contest known as the Lucha Libre to decide who the ultimate fighter is. When the dust settles, only the victors are advanced into a mysterious tournament, known only as the Chaak, held in a secret Mayan temple where the stakes are higher than any of the combatants realize. When the ancient evil of the Mayan gods is released on Earth, the warriors must learn to set aside their differences and personal vendettas while the fate of the entire planet hangs in the balance.

Battle Vixens. **Written and illustrated by Yuji Shiozaki.** TOKYOPOP, 2004–2005. **O Japanese manga.** あ

The beautiful but air-headed Hakufu Sonsaku has always felt the urge to fight, but her mother has always discouraged it. But Hakufu is a Toushi, a person who possesses a jewel that carries the souls of ancient warriors, and all Toushi feel the call of battle within them. When another Toushi at school threatens a friend of Hakufu, Hakufu's mother reluctantly lets her daughter follow the ways of the fighter and go to Tokyo to learn the ways of the Toushi at the prestigious Yoshuu School. A thirteen-episode anime series, loosely based on the manga, was released in Japan in 2003.

Vol. 1. 2004. 168pp. 1-59182-743-4.
Vol. 2. 2004. 168pp. 1-59182-744-2.
Vol. 3. 2004. 176pp. 1-59182-745-0.
Vol. 4. 2004. 176pp. 1-59182-746-9.
Vol. 5. 2004. 168pp. 1-59182-947-X.
Vol. 6. 2005. 168pp. 1-59182-948-8.
Vol. 7. 2005. 192pp. 1-59532-602-2.
Vol. 8. 2005. 176pp. 1-59532-902-1.

Beyblade. **Written and illustrated by Takao Aoki** VIZ Media, LLC, 2004– . **A Japanese manga.** 🎮 あ

Tied in with the hit Japanese game and anime series of the same name. Tyson wants nothing else but to be the best Beyblader in all of Japan. His enemies, the Blade Sharks, are tough, but with his secret Beyblade given to him by a mysterious individual, Tyson is practically unstoppable. Jealous of his new Beyblade, the Blade Sharks will use every dirty trick in the book to get it from Tyson.

Vol. 1. 2004. 200pp. 1-59116-621-7.
Vol. 2. 2004. 192pp. 1-59116-697-7.
Vol. 3. 2005. 192pp. 1-59116-705-1.
Vol. 4. 2005. 192pp. 1-59116-719-1.
Vol. 5. 2005. 192pp. 1-59116-793-0.
Vol. 6 .2005.192pp. 1-59116-857-0.
Vol. 7 .2005.192pp. 1-4215-0019-1.
Vol. 8 .2005.192pp. 1-4215-0129-5.
Vol. 9 .2005.192pp. 1-4215-0249-6.
Vol. 10 .2006.192pp. 1-4215-0380-8.
Vol. 11 .2006.192pp. 1-4215-0437-7.
Vol. 12. 2006. 208pp. 1-4215-0438-3.

Bulletproof Monk. **Written by Brett Lewis and R. A. Jones. Illustrated by Michael Avon Oeming.** Image Comics, 2002. 80pp. 1-58240-244-2. **O** 🎬

Years ago a Tibetan village was saved by a "Bulletproof Monk," a Mongolian hero who rescued the villagers from the Nazis during World War II and mysteriously vanished once the village was safe. Legend has it that he will return again in their time of need when summoned with an amulet by the villagers. Now the descendants of that village live in San Francisco's Chinatown district, and Kar, a young Asian American working for the Chinese Mafia, finds that he needs the aid of the Bulletproof Monk more than ever. Little does Kar know that the power of the Monk lies far closer than he realizes.

Dragon Ball. Written and illustrated by Akira Toriyama. VIZ Media, LLC, 2004–2005. **T Japanese manga.** あ

A loose retelling of the Chinese folktale "Journey to the West." Son Goku is a monkey-tailed boy, and the <u>Dragon Ball</u> series follows his youthful adventures through when he becomes a father. Throughout Goku's lifetime he fights many battles and over time becomes the most powerful martial artist in the universe in his quest for the Dragon Balls of power as well as his true origin as a powerful force of destruction as a member of the superpowered group of aliens known as Saiyans. The series has also featured a large and colorful cast of supporting characters of heroes and villains to supply the conflict of the story, which was originally published in Japan from 1984 to 1995 and spun off a wildly popular animated series. In the VIZ Media translations, the series was divided into the <u>Dragon Ball</u> and <u>Dragon Ball Z</u> titles.

Dragon Ball. 2003–2004.

The adventures of Son Goku from youth through early adulthood as he hones his martial arts skills and searches for the legendary Dragon Balls that are able to grant wishes.

Vol. 1. 2003. 192pp. 1-56931-920-0.
Vol. 2. 2003. 200pp. 1-56931-921-9.
Vol. 3. 2003. 192pp. 1-56931-922-7.
Vol. 4. 2003. 192pp. 1-56931-923-5.
Vol. 5. 2003. 192pp. 1-56931-924-3.
Vol. 6. 2003. 192pp. 1-56931-925-1.
Vol. 7. 2003. 192pp. 1-56931-926-X.
Vol. 8. 2003. 192pp. 1-56931-927-8.
Vol. 9. 2003. 192pp. 1-56931-928-6.
Vol. 10. 2003. 192pp. 1-56931-848-4.
Vol. 11. 2003. 192pp. 1-56931-919-7.
Vol. 12. 2003. 200pp. 1-59116-155-X.
Vol. 13. 2003. 192pp. 1-59116-148-7.
Vol. 14. 2004. 200pp. 1-59116-169-X.
Vol. 15. 2004. 192pp. 1-59116-297-1.
Vol. 16. 2004. 192pp. 1-59116-457-5.

Dragon Ball Z. 2003–2006.

Five years after the events in the first series, Goku is married and has a son named Gohan. When an adversary arrives from outer space, Goku's true origin is revealed, and he must team up with his old enemy, Piccolo, to save Earth from Goku's own brother.

Vol. 1. 2003. 192pp. 1-56931-930-8.
Vol. 2. 2003. 192pp. 1-56931-931-6.
Vol. 3. 2003. 192pp. 1-56931-932-4.
Vol. 4. 2003. 192pp. 1-56931-933-2.
Vol. 5. 2003. 192pp. 1-56931-934-0.

Vol. 6. 2003. 192pp. 1-56931-935-9.
Vol. 7. 2003. 192pp. 1-56931-936-7.
Vol. 8. 2003. 192pp. 1-56931-937-5.
Vol. 9. 2003. 192pp. 1-56931-938-3.
Vol. 10. 2003. 192pp. 1-56931-939-1.
Vol. 11. 2003. 192pp. 1-56931-807-7.
Vol. 12. 2003. 192pp. 1-56931-985-5.
Vol. 13. 2003. 200pp. 1-56931-986-3.
Vol. 14. 2004. 200pp. 1-59116-180-0.
Vol. 15. 2004. 192pp. 1-59116-186-X.
Vol. 16. 2004. 192pp. 1-59116-328-5.
Vol. 17. 2004. 184pp. 1-59116-505-9.
Vol. 18. 2004. 192pp. 1-59116-637-3.
Vol. 19. 2005. 184pp. 1-59116-751-5.
Vol. 20. 2005. 192pp. 1-59116-808-2.
Vol. 21. 2005. 200pp. 1-59116-873-2.
Vol. 22. 2005. 192pp. 1-4215-0051-5.
Vol. 23. 2005. 192pp. 1-4215-0148-1.
Vol. 24. 2006. 208pp. 1-4215-0273-9.
Vol. 25. 2006. 208pp. 1-4215-0404-9.
Vol. 26. 2006. 208pp. 1-4215-0636-X.

Gadirok: Requiem Chorus. **Written and illustrated by Hwang Jeong-Ho.** ADV Manga, 2004. **O Korean manhwa.**

The cruel General Hae-Mo-Soo has taken control of the lands of Korea and China from the reigning king of the Jew-Shin Empire and has imprisoned and broken the Prince Chi-Woo. When Gat, a lowly but loyal peasant skilled in the ways of fighting, rescues the mentally broken Chi-Woo, together they forge a bloody path of destruction against the minions of Hae-Mo-Soo to ensure that Chi-Woo will sit on the throne.

Vol. 1. 2004. 192pp. 1-4139-0068-2.
Vol. 2. 2004. 184pp. 1-4139-0082-8.

Jing: King of Bandits. **Written and illustrated by Yuichi Kumakura.** TOKYOPOP, 2003–2005. **T Japanese manga.** あ

In a world of wonder called Aquavitae, where ghost ships fly the skies carrying zombies stuffed with gold, buses are shaped like crocodiles, and there are many more oddities, a young master thief called Jing is the best in the land, capable of stealing any item no matter how difficult it is to attain. Accompanied by his sidekick, Kir, a lecherous talking bird, there's nothing that the two of them can't steal as they go on adventure after adventure to steal the impossible. An anime series based on the manga was released in Japan in 2002.

Jing: King of Bandits (1st series). 2003–2004.
Vol. 1. 2003. 224pp. 1-59182-176-2.
Vol. 2. 2003. 232pp. 1-59182-177-0.
Vol. 3. 2003. 216pp. 1-59182-178-9.
Vol. 4. 2004. 232pp. 1-59182-179-7.
Vol. 5. 2004. 224pp. 1-59182-466-4.
Vol. 6. 2004. 216pp. 1-59182-467-2.

> *Vol. 7.* 2004. 208pp. 1-59182-468-0.
>
> Jing: King of Bandits—Twilight Tales. 2004–2005.
>> *Vol. 1.* 2004. 180pp. 1-59182-469-9.
>> *Vol. 2.* 2004. 184pp. 1-59182-470-2.
>> *Vol. 3.* 2005. 184pp. 1-59182-471-0.
>> *Vol. 4.* 2005. 188pp. 1-59532-417-8.
>> *Vol. 5.* 2005. 192pp. 1-59532-418-6.
>> *Vol. 6.* 2005. 192pp. 1-59532-419-4.

Juline. **Written and illustrated by Narumi Kakinouchi.** TOKYOPOP, 2001–2002. **Y Japanese manga.**

Juline Kenga, Bakuya Houkyo, and Seika Suisho, warrior princesses of the top three martial arts schools in the valley of the Sleeping Dragon Mountain, must join together on a quest to solve the mystery of the clan known as the Black Pearl Guardians, which has recently come to their valley and has attracted fighters from the other three dojos, including Juline's long-lost father, Seika's brother, and Bakuya's fiancée. Now three precious dojo artifacts—a Water Crystal of the Suisho, the Jeweled Mirror of the Houkyo, and the Ivory Sword of the Kenga—have been taken from the clans for some darker purpose. Juline, accompanied by her friends, including Juline's best friend Kio, must stop the Black Pearl Guardians and their mysterious leader from unleashing an ultimate power that will bring about the destruction of their clans.

> *Vol. 1.* 2001. 168pp. 1-892213-63-X.
> *Vol. 2.* 2001. 168pp. 1-892213-85-0.
> *Vol. 3.* 2002. 168pp. 1-931514-03-8.
> *Vol. 4.* 2002. 168pp. 1-931514-04-6.
> *Vol. 5.* 2002. 176pp. 1-931514-05-4.

Mega Dragon and Tiger: Future Kung-Fu Action. **Written and illustrated by Tony Wong.** ComicsOne, 2002–2004. **T Chinese manhua.**

Ten years after a near world-destroying asteroid attack in 1999, a cruel new world order has arrived. It's a brutal world, where only the strong survive and are given superpowers, while the weak are cast out. In 2020, two fighters have risen to right the wrongs committed by the corrupted strong: Mega Dragon and Tiger. ComicsOne reprinted the series in the United States, but it has yet to be completed because the company folded.

> *Vol. 1.* 2002. 120pp. 1-58899-190-3.
> *Vol. 2.* 2002. 120pp. 1-58899-238-1.
> *Vol. 3.* 2002. 120pp. 1-58899-239-X.
> *Vol. 4.* 2003. 120pp. 1-58899-240-3.
> *Vol. 5.* 2003. 120pp. 1-58899-237-3.
> *Vol. 6.* 2003. 120pp. 1-58899-236-5.
> *Vol. 7.* 2004. 160pp. 1-58899-251-9.

Project Arms. **Written by Ryoji Minagawa. Illustrated by Kyoichi Nanatsuki.** VIZ Media, LLC, 2003– . **O Japanese manga.**

Ryo Takahashi's normal life as a high school student takes an unexpected and dramatic turn when he discovers that a cybernetic arm has actually replaced his right arm, which he injured when he was young. Utilizing the latest in nanotechnology, his arm can transform into nearly any deadly shape at will, and soon he finds that he's being hunted by a mysterious fellow student and a secret organization for the secret that he carries inside of him. The series was originally published in Japan in twenty-two volumes.

Vol. 1: The Awakening. 2003. 208pp. 1-56931-889-1.
Vol. 2: Egrigori. 2003. 224pp. 1-59116-058-8.
Vol. 3: Jabberwock. 2004. 216pp. 1-59116-101-0.
Vol. 4: The Evil Eye. 2004. 216pp. 1-59116-165-7.
Vol. 5: The X-Army. 2004. 200pp. 1-59116-338-2.
Vol. 6: Knight. 2004. 202pp. 1-59116-488-5.
Vol. 7: White Rabbit. 2004. 200pp. 1-59116-522-9.
Vol. 8: Gallow's Bell. 2005. 216pp. 1-59116-732-9.
Vol. 9: Mars. 2005. 216pp. 1-59116-733-7.
Vol. 10: Agni. 2005. 216pp. 1-4215-0073-6.
Vol. 11. 2006. 216pp. 1-4215-0194-5.
Vol. 12. 2006. 208pp. 1-4215-0386-7.
Vol. 13. 2006. 208pp. 1-4215-0502-9.
Vol. 14. 2006. 208pp. 1-4215-0503-7.
Vol. 15. 2007. 208pp. 1-4215-0504-5.
Vol. 16. 2007. 216pp. 1-4215-0916-4.

Ranma ½. Written and illustrated by Rumiko Takahashi. VIZ Media, LLC, 2003–2006. **T** ◎ 🎮 **Japanese manga.** あ

RANMA ½ © 1988 Rumiko TAKAHASHI/Shogakukan Inc.

When highly skilled martial artist teenager Ranma Saotome and his father Ganma journeyed to China for training for their dojo, they accidentally landed in some cursed springs. Now whenever they come in contact with cold water, Ranma transforms into a girl and his father changes into a panda! The only way to return them to normal is a nice splash of warm water. To makes things even more awkward, Ranma gets engaged in an arranged marriage to the ultra-spunky fighter Akane, and she's a little shocked to find out that her fiancé is also a girl half of the time! With a large and ever-expanding cast of cursed characters, including the Chinese maiden Shampoo, the clueless Ryoga, and others, their dojo will never be the same, in one of the funniest and most action-packed stories from Japan. The series was originally published starting in 1987 in Japan and was first published in the United States in 1993 by VIZ. Since then volumes 1 through 21 have been reissued in the traditional right-to-left reading style. The series will conclude with volume 38 in late 2006. Be sure to go to VIZ Media's Web site (http://www.viz.com) for more information on this extremely popular series. *Volume 1* received recognition from YALSA's Popular Paperbacks for Young Adults committee in 2002 on the "Graphic Novels: Superheroes and Beyond" list. The popular manga was also adapted into a hit anime series.

Vol. 1. 2003. 304pp. 1-56931-962-6.
Vol. 2. 2003. 224pp. 1-56931-963-4.
Vol. 3. 2003. 224pp. 1-59116-062-6.
Vol. 4. 2003. 224pp. 1-59116-063-4.

Vol. 5. 2003. 224pp. 1-59116-064-2.
Vol. 6. 2003. 224pp. 1-59116-065-0.
Vol. 7. 2004. 200pp. 1-59116-129-0.
Vol. 8. 2004. 200pp. 1-59116-130-4.
Vol. 9. 2004. 200pp. 1-59116-283-1.
Vol. 10. 2004. 200pp. 1-59116-284-X.
Vol. 11. 2004. 200pp. 1-59116-285-8.
Vol. 12. 2004. 200pp. 1-59116-286-6.
Vol. 13. 2004. 200pp. 1-59116-287-4.
Vol. 14. 2004. 200pp. 1-59116-288-2.
Vol. 15. 2005. 200pp. 1-59116-289-0.
Vol. 16. 2005. 200pp. 1-59116-290-4.
Vol. 17. 2005. 192pp. 1-59116-291-2.
Vol. 18. 2005. 192pp. 1-59116-292-0.
Vol. 19. 2005. 184pp. 1-59116-293-9.
Vol. 20. 2005. 200pp. 1-59116-294-7.
Vol. 21. 2005. 192pp. 1-59116-295-5.
Vol. 22. 2003. 184pp. 1-56931-890-5.
Vol. 23. 2003. 224pp. 1-59116-060-X.
Vol. 24. 2003. 224pp. 1-59116-061-8.
Vol. 25. 2004. 184pp. 1-59116-128-2.
Vol. 26. 2004. 184pp. 1-59116-296-3.
Vol. 27. 2004. 200pp. 1-59116-459-1.
Vol. 28. 2004. 200pp. 1-59116-584-9.
Vol. 29. 2005. 200pp. 1-59116-681-0.
Vol. 30. 2005. 192pp. 1-59116-776-0.
Vol. 31. 2005. 200pp. 1-59116-860-0.
Vol. 32. 2005. 192pp. 1-4215-0072-8.
Vol. 33. 2006. 208pp. 1-4215-0256-9.
Vol. 34. 2006. 208pp. 1-4215-0505-3.
Vol. 35. 2006. 208pp. 1-4215 -0506-1.

Samurai Deeper Kyo. **Written and illustrated by Kamijyo Akimine.**
TOKYOPOP, 2003– . **O Japanese manga.**

Four years after the bloody Battle of Sekigahara at the dawn of the seventeenth
century, a peaceful medicine peddler named Kyoshiro is joined by a young female bounty hunter named Yuya to hunt down criminals after she mistakes
him for Demon Eyes Kyo, a vicious samurai whom Kyoshiro resembles. But
after bandits attack Kyoshiro, his eyes turn red and the man of peace gives way
to Demon Eyes Kyo, the slayer of a thousand men. Now Kyoshiro is out to discover the mystery of the two souls inhabiting his body, and Yuya is waiting for
the right time to claim her reward on Kyo, the man who killed her brother.
Thirty-three volumes of the series were published in Japan and are being
republished by TOKYOPOP.

Vol. 1. 2003. 208pp. 1-59182-225-4.
Vol. 2. 2003. 208pp. 1-59182-226-2.
Vol. 3. 2003. 208pp. 1-59182-227-0.
Vol. 4. 2003. 208pp. 1-59182-249-1.
Vol. 5. 2004. 200pp. 1-59182-541-5.

Vol. 6. 2004. 208pp. 1-59182-542-3.
Vol. 7. 2004. 208pp. 1-59182-543-1.
Vol. 8. 2004. 200pp. 1-59182-544-X.
Vol. 9. 2004. 216pp. 1-59182-545-8.
Vol. 10. 2004. 216pp. 1-59532-450-X.
Vol. 11. 2005. 192pp. 1-59532-451-8.
Vol. 12. 2005. 200pp. 1-59532-452-6.
Vol. 13. 2005. 200pp. 1-59532-453-4.
Vol. 14. 2005. 192pp. 1-59532-454-2.
Vol. 15. 2005. 192pp. 1-59532-455-0.
Vol. 16. 2005. 192pp. 1-59532-456-9.
Vol. 17. 2006. 192pp. 1-59532-457-7.
Vol. 18. 2006. 192pp. 1-59532-458-5.
Vol. 19. 2006. 192pp. 1-59532-459-3.
Vol. 20. 2006. 192pp. 1-59532-460-7.
Vol. 21. 2007. 192pp. 1-59532-461-5.

Samurai Girl: Real Bout High School. Written by Reiji Saiga. Illustrated by Sora Inoue. TOKYOPOP, 2002–2004. **T Japanese manga.** あ

Welcome to Daimon High, where organized K-fights are part of the school curriculum and they're the only way to prove who's on top. In a school where even student and teacher can duke it out for bragging rights, and rivals for someone's affection can solve their differences in the ring, there's only room for one champ. Ryoko Mitsurugi is a sixteen-year-old sophomore at Daimon High School, but she's not an ordinary girl. She's the toughest fighter in the entire school and thinks of herself as a modern-day samurai, wandering the school halls and streets dispensing justice. Enter Shimizuma Kusanagi, a tough but talented sixteen-year-old transfer student, who has just enrolled in Daimon High on a fighting scholarship and has become enamored of Ryoko's fighting abilities. It's pretty clear that one day they'll be sparring to see who's the best. The manga was adapted into an anime series.

Vol. 1. 2002. 200pp. 1-931514-95-X.
Vol. 2. 2002. 192pp. 1-931514-46-1.
Vol. 3. 2002. 184pp. 1-59182-020-0.
Vol. 4. 2002. 184pp. 1-59182-021-9.
Vol. 5. 2003. 192pp. 1-59182-107-X.
Vol. 6. 2004. 256pp. 1-59182-913-5.

Shaolin Sisters. Written by Narumi Kakinouchi. Illustrated by Toshiki Hirano. TOKYOPOP, 2003–2006. **T Japanese manga.**

A spin-off of the manga series Juline, set in an alternative setting. Fifteen-year-old Juline Kenga has always thought that she was an only child. She's lived her entire life at Fighting Fang Hall, a kung-fu dojo run by Master Yoh, along with her childhood friend Kio and other orphans. Then the evil White Lotus Clan breaks into Fighting Fang Hall and their leader, the Bai Wang—the White Queen—defeats Master Yoh in combat. Dying, he reveals to Juline before he dies that she has two other half-sisters, and that the three sisters each carry a small golden bell that will ring when they are close to one another. The three bells are part of a great power called the Secret of Shaolin that can unleash a powerful and deadly force that Bai Wang and others want for their own use. Now the three Shaolin sisters must band together to make sure that the power of the Shaolin bells will never fall into the hands of the evil White Lotus Clan, or die trying. The series continued with <u>Shaolin Sisters Reborn</u>, released in 2005–2006.

<u>Shaolin Sisters (1st series).</u> 2003.
Vol. 1. 2003. 192pp. 1-59182-024-3.
Vol. 2. 2003. 192pp. 1-59182-025-1.
Vol. 3. 2003. 192pp. 1-59182-026-X.
Vol. 4. 2003. 192pp. 1-59182-027-8.
Vol. 5. 2003. 192pp. 1-59182-233-5.
<u>Shaolin Sisters Reborn.</u> 2005–2006.
Vol. 1. 2005. 224pp. 1-59532-507-7.
Vol. 2. 2005. 192pp. 1-59532-508-5.
Vol. 3. 2005. 216pp. 1-59532-509-3.
Vol. 4. 2006. 216pp. 1-59532-510-7

<u>Sky Blade: Sword of the Heavens.</u> Written and illustrated by Kang Suk Hyung. ADV Manga, 2004. **T Korean manhwa.**

It has been prophesied that Jin-Ro will become ruler of the land, and that one other person born at the same time on the same day will become ruler after his death. When Jin-Ro meets Il-Geum, a possible rival for his future, will they become the best of friends or bitter rivals for the future of a kingdom and can one man escape his fate but keep his destiny?

Vol. 1. 2004. 184pp. 1-4139-0081-X.
Vol. 2. 2004. 184pp. 1-4139-0102-6.

***Southpaw.* Written and illustrated by Scott Morse.** Adhouse Books, 2004. 128pp. 0-9721794-4-5. **T**

The tale of a robot-fighting boxing tiger named Southpaw, who was too proud to give up his title. The champion fighter in the illegal circuit, when his robot manager asks him to take a fall, the feline with a mean left hook decides not to take a dive, and then his troubles really begin.

***Xin: Legend of the Monkey King.* Written and illustrated by Kevin Lau.** Anarchy Studios, 2003. 88pp. 0-910692-97-1. **T**

Xin is the most powerful warrior in the realm of light and darkness—at least, he thinks so! Arrogant and boastful, Xin is one of the Saints of Heaven and a protector of the Torch of Light—a post he abandoned when he deemed it beneath him. Years later, Xin has come back to claim the title Guardian of the Light even if he has to take on the other Saints by himself. A loose retelling of the Chinese fable of the Monkey King, with a futuristic kung-fu kick.

War Stories

War stories have long been a part of comic book history, especially during World War II and shortly thereafter, when comic book readership among GIs was at an all-time peak. Though the genre has declined in popularity over the years, like the Western genre, a variety of titles have focused on all aspects of war, from battles in ancient times up to and including the Iraq war. War, with its stories of life and death, intense action, and high visual impact, provides a dramatic backdrop for heroics and has historically been a common theme in comic books and graphic novels. The first comic book devoted entirely to war stories was Dell's *War Comics* (May 1940), which appeared a year before America's entry into World War II. Since the 1940s, the genre's popularity has drifted, but some excellent collections on the subject have been released within the last decade. Tales here are broken down into ancient and modern warfare.

Ancient Warfare

These tales of battles from ancient times include stories of the great warriors of Sparta, the battlefields of Troy, and the Crusades.

Age of Bronze. Written and illustrated by Eric Shanower. Image Comics, 2001– . O ◎

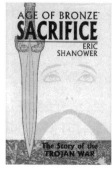

© 2006 Eric Shanower.

A retelling of the epic saga of the Trojan War, based on the poet Homer's epic poem *The Iliad* as well as a wide range of researched sources. Paris, the son of King Priam of Troy long thought to be dead, discovers that he truly is a prince of Troy. To thwart a prophecy that Paris would destroy Troy someday, the king and queen had left the infant Paris to die in order to save their kingdom. Now Paris has been reunited with his father, but the prophets once again foresee that the kingdom is doomed at Paris's hand. Paris unwillingly sets in motion a chain of events that will doom the entire kingdom when, on a mission to return King Priam's sister from the kingdom of Salamis, he decides to capture someone even more fair than his aunt: the beautiful wife of Menelaus of Sparta, Helen. Agamemnon, Menelaus's brother, intends to attack Troy to free his brother's wife, and he will amass the greatest army ever seen, combining the might of the other Achaean kingdoms. As the expedition is prepared to rescue Helen, the stage is set for a classic tale of ancient warfare. The epic series is planned to be released in a total of seven collected volumes. Eric Shanower won an Eisner Award in 2001 and 2003 in the category of Best Writer/Artist for his work on this series.

Vol. 1: A Thousand Ships. 2001. 224pp. 1-58240-200-0.
Vol. 2: Sacrifice. 2005. 224pp. 1-58240-399-6.

***Horns of Hattin*. Written by Shane L. Amaya. Illustrated by Bruno D'Angelo.** Terra Major, 2004. 120pp. 0-9704149-1-9. **M**

In the twelfth century, on the eve of the climactic battle in Jerusalem called the Horns of Hattin, God's emissary, Death, summons a carefree crusader called Everyman. The message is that he and his fellow men from the army of the King of Jerusalem will be defeated and he will die. A man who until now has had no need for faith, Everyman now arrives at a personal crossroads when given the knowledge of his impending doom in the battle against the armies of the Babylonian sultan Saladin. In one night Everyman must find his faith and reconcile his past deeds before the coming of the Lord. A graphic adaptation of the classic morality play *The Summoning of Everyman.*

♦ *300*. Written and illustrated by Frank Miller. Dark Horse Comicsm, 1999. 88pp. 1-56971-402-9. **O**

The center of intellectualism, Greece is about to be crushed by the vast armies of Prince Xerses of Persia. The only defense until the Greek armies can gather is 300 brave Spartan warriors. Too bad for the Persian army. A fictionalized account of the Battle of Thermopylae, which occurred in 481 B.C., *300* tells of how a small army of 300 Spartan warriors was able to hold its ground against King Xerses of Persia's grand army of hundreds of thousands in his grand quest to conquer Greece. The sacrifice of these valiant Spartan warriors gave the Greek army enough time to gather and to ultimately defeat Persia and is a powerful reminder that sometimes we have to lose a battle to win a war. The tale won an Eisner Award in 1999 for Best Finite Series/Limited Series and a Harvey Award in 1999 for Best Continuing Series or Limited Series. A film version of the graphic novel will be released in 2007.

Modern Warfare

Tales of combat and bravery from the point of view of the soldiers during modern-era conflicts, including the world wars, Vietnam, and Iraq.

***Adventures in the Rifle Brigade.* Written by Garth Ennis. Illustrated by various.** Vertigo/DC Comics, 2005. 144pp. 1-4012-0353-1. **M**

© 2006 DC Comics.

Meet the "finest" soldiers from Great Britain in World War II: the Rifle Brigade! Six World War II commandos make up the group: the stereotypically heroic Captain Hugo Darcy; Second Lieutenant Cecil Milk, the limp-wristed marksman and pilot; Hank the Yank, a demolitions expert from the United States who joined before Pearl Harbor; Sergeant Crumb, an enormous man capable of snapping necks with his pinky fingers; Corporal Geezer, a man who has 413 counts of murder against him as a civilian; and the Piper, a Scotsman with bagpipes that will kill any man within earshot. There's nothing they can't handle from "Ol' Jerry," no matter how bawdy, bloody, and outrageous the mission. The collection is a parody of classic flag-waving British military adventures.

Adolf. Written and illustrated by Osamu Tezuka. VIZ Media, LLC, 1995–1996. **O Japanese manga.**

With World War II looming closer and closer, two children living in Tokyo, a Jewish boy named Adolf Kamil and a German Japanese boy named Adolf Kaufmann, become the best of friends despite the differences in their religions and upbringing. Once tensions increase, with Adolf Hitler in Germany and the Third Reich setting in motion World War II, can their friendship survive the terrible atrocities committed in Adolf's name, the terrors of nuclear destruction, and a world-spanning conflict?

> *Vol. 1: 1945 and All That Remains.* 1995. 264pp. 1-56931-058-0.
> *Vol. 2: An Exile in Japan.* 1996. 256pp. 1-56931-057-2.
> *Vol. 3: The Half-Aryan.* 1996. 278pp. 1-56931-133-1.
> *Vol. 4: Days of Infamy.* 1996. 238pp. 1-56931-124-2.
> *Vol. 5: A Tale of the Twentieth Century.* 1996. 254pp. 1-56931-162-5.

Apocalypse Meow. Written and illustrated by Motofumi Kobayashi. ADV Manga, 2004. **O Japanese manga.**

An anthropomorphized but authentic look at the Vietnam War in which the Americans are portrayed as rabbits, Vietnamese are cats, Koreans are dogs, Russians are bears, Japanese are monkeys, Chinese are pandas, and French are pigs. Seen through the eyes of the U.S. Army's three-rabbit squad "Cat Shit One," composed of Par, White, and Bota. They're on dangerous mission after mission trying to help win the difficult and bloody war against the North Vietnamese Army through the superior firepower of the United States and the aid of local cat pro-American sympathizers.

> *Vol. 1.* 2004. 146pp. 1-4139-0017-8.
> *Vol. 2.* 2004. 144pp. 1-4139-0046-1.
> *Vol. 3.* 2004. 138pp. 1-4139-0047-X.

Barefoot Gen. Written and illustrated by Keiji Nakazawa. Last Gasp, 2003–2004. **T Japanese manga.** あ

A harrowing and humbling account of one family's struggle to survive following the dropping of the atomic bomb over the city of Hiroshima on August 6, 1945. Though this is a mostly fictionalized account, the creator of the series was a survivor of the bombing and gives a personal history of how people survived the tragic event and eventually rose from the ashes. Two anime adaptations of the manga were originally released in Japan in 1982–1983.

> *Vol. 1: A Cartoon Story of Hiroshima.* 2003. 286pp. 0-86719-602-5.
> *Vol. 2: The Day After.* 2004. 240pp. 0-86719-619-X.
> *Vol. 3: Life After the Bomb.* 2d ed. 2004. 284pp. 0-86719-594-0.

Combat Zone: True Tales of GIs in Iraq. **Written by Karl Zinsmeister. Illustrated by Dan Jurgens.** Marvel Comics, 2005. 120pp. 0-7851-1516-1. **T**

True stories of the 82nd Airborne during three months of the battle for Iraq during Operation Iraqi Freedom. The story is told through the eyes of a soldier, a viewpoint seldom seen today.

Enemy Ace. DC Comics, 1998–2003. **T**

Debuting in 1965 in DC Comics' *Our Army at War* #151 was an unusual hero: a German fighter pilot from World War I named Baron Hans von Hammer, the Enemy Ace. Loosely inspired by the real-life Rittmeister Manfred von Richthofen, the Red Baron, von Hammer was portrayed as a brave and noble aristocrat who cared little about sending honorable men to their graves. *War Idyll* tells the story of a dying von Hammer in 1969 recounting to a Vietnam veteran the troubles of war, while *War in Heaven* tells the tale of a forty-six-year-old von Hammer reluctantly taking to the skies again after being asked by Nazi Germany to fight against the Russians at the height of World War II. Though he despises Hitler and the Third Reich, he will not betray his homeland.

> *Archives, Vol. 1.* Written by Bob Kanigher. Illustrated by Joe Kubert. 2002. 224pp. 1-56389-896-9.
> *War Idyll.* Written and illustrated by George Pratt. 1998. 120pp. 0-930289-78-1, 2d printing.
> *War in Heaven.* Written by Garth Ennis. Illustrated by Chris Weston, Russ Heath, and Joe Kubert. 2003. 128pp. 1-56389-982-5.

G.I. Joe: A Real American Hero! **Written by Josh Blaylock and various. Illustrated by Steve Kurth and Jamal Ingle.** Devil's Due Publishing, 2002– . **Y**

© 2006 Devil's Due Publishing.

When the evil forces of COBRA are ready to strike against the free people of the world, there's only one force that can take them on and win the day: G.I. Joe! The United States, the soldiers all use code names to protect their identities. Join Duke, Snake Eyes, and the rest as they wage their battle against COBRA Commander, Destro, Serpentor and the rest of COBRA. The popular toy line has spawned many other titles in this series, which can be found at Devil's Due Publishing's Web site (http://www.devilsdue.net).

> *Vol. 1: Reinstated.* 2002. 112pp. 1-58240-252-3.
> *Vol. 2: Reckonings.* 2002. 96pp. 1-58240-284-1.

Gulf War Journal. **Written and illustrated by Don Lomax.** ibooks, inc., 2004. 216pp. 0-7434-8669-2. **O**

A look at the first Gulf War through the eyes of Scott "Journal" Neithammer, a reporter who comes out of retirement to cover the war. Covering both sides of the war, Neithammer gets a firsthand account of the dangers of war from the soldiers and civilians caught in the crossfire and the terrible consequences for all sides. Also includes a preface and afterword on Operation Iraqi Freedom and the Palestinian/Israeli conflict.

🖋 *Last Day in Vietnam: A Memory.* **Written and illustrated by Will Eisner.** Dark Horse Comics, 2000. 80pp. 1-56971-500-9. **O**

A collection of six war stories featuring tales of U.S. soldiers during the Korean and Vietnamese conflicts. The spotlight is not on the battlefield, but on the personal conflicts and consequences and internal minefields of the soldiers. Taken from Will Eisner's personal accounts of camp life while serving as an artist for *P.S. Magazine,* the stories focus on the human soul as the soldiers experience gut-wrenching fear, humor, and courage while near the front lines of battle. The story won a Harvey Award in 2001 for Best Graphic Album of Original Work and was recognized by YALSA's Popular Paperbacks for Young Adults committee on the 2002 "War: Causes and Consequences" list.

***The Light Brigade*. Written by Peter Tomasi. Illustrated by Peter Snejbjerg.** DC Comics, 2006. 200pp. 1-4012-0795-2. **M** ◉

Set during the horrific days of World War II, a band of U.S. soldiers fighting against a horde of Nazis find out that their struggle against the Nazi evil is anything but ordinary. The U.S. soldiers discover that they've been recruited by an immortal Roman centurion to rescue the sword of God from the hands of the supernatural Nazis, being led by a fallen angel. Soon the band of brothers find themselves deputized as the Light Brigade and vow to save the sword of God from falling into the enemy's hands, at all costs.

© 2006 DC Comics.

The Losers. Written by Andy Diggle. Illustrated by Jock. Vertigo/DC Comics, 2004–2006. **M**

A covert Special Forces Unit working for the C.I.A. witnessed one too many atrocities and were eliminated in a helicopter crash. At least that's what the C.I.A. is supposed to believe. Now the squad is taking down the dirty operations of the C.I.A., one job at a time.

> *Vol. 1: Ante Up.* 2004. 160pp. 1-4012-0198-9.
> *Vol. 2: Double Down.* 2004. 144pp. 1-4012-0348-5.
> *Vol. 3: Trifecta.* 2005. 168pp. 1-4012-0489-9.
> *Vol. 4: Close Quarters.* 2005. 144pp. 1-4012-0719-7.
> *Vol. 5: Endgame.* 2006. 168pp. 1-4012-1004-X.

***The 'Nam*. Written by Doug Murray. Illustrated by Michael Golden.** Marvel Comics, 1999. 96pp. 0-7851-0718-5. **T**

In 1966 Private Ed Marks, a green soldier in the army, is sent on his first tour of duty in Vietnam. It's a whole new world for him, and his life is forever changed by what he sees and endures with his fellow soldiers in their bloody fight against the Vietnamese. As each month passes, the reader relives through Private Marks's eyes one of the most grueling wars ever fought by the United States.

***The Pride of Baghdad*. Written by Brian K. Vaughan. Illustrated by Niko Henrichon.** Vertigo/DC Comics, 2006. 136pp. 1-4012-0314-0. **M** ◉

Based on a true story. In the early days of the Iraq war in 2003 a pride of lions escaped from the Baghdad Zoo. Confused and hungry, they wandered around the streets of the decimated city searching for food and struggling to survive. Told as a metaphor for the cost of freedom: Is it better to live in the security of captivity or to die free of tyranny?

The Punisher: Born. **Written by Garth Ennis. Illustrated by Darick Robert-son.** MAX/Marvel Comics, 2004. 120pp. 0-7851-1231-6. **M**

© 2006 Marvel Comics.

Before he became known as the vigilante called The Punisher, Frank Castle served as a Marine in Vietnam. There his trau-matic experiences helped mold the soldier who would later dedicate his life to being a one-man reign of terror on crime. Set near the end of the war in 1971 at Valley Forge Firebase on the Cambodian border. Castle is one of only twenty-nine Marines ready to defend the firebase in a war they can't possi-bly win. With an impending attack by the Viet Cong army, what can Frank do that will turn the tide of the battle and change his outlook forever?

Sgt. Rock. **Written by Brian Azzarello and various. Illustrated by Joe Kubert.** DC Comics, 2002–2004. **T M**

Debuting in <u>Our Army at War</u> comics in 1959, Sgt. Rock is one of the most iconic war heroes in comic books. He was the platoon leader of Easy Com-pany, an outfit that faced some of the most dangerous action in World War II. Joining Rock was an ever-changing cast of soldiers in the Easy Company pla-toon, including Ice Cream, Wild Man, Solider, and Four Eyes, who trudged on through the front lines experiencing firsthand the cost of freedom. *Sgt. Rock: Between Hell & a Hard Place* is a Vertigo title that reunited famed artist Joe Kubert with the iconic character he illustrated. The story tells of Rock and Easy Company trying to solve a mystery after four high-ranking German offi-cials they captured are found murdered.

> *Archives, Vol. 1.* 2002. 240pp. 1-56389-841-1 **T**
> *Archives, Vol. 2.* 2003. 216pp. 1-4012-0146-6 **T**
> *Archives, Vol. 3.* 2004. 224pp. 1-4012-0410-4 **T**
> *Sgt. Rock: Between Hell & a Hard Place.* Vertigo/DC Comics, 2003. 140pp. 1-4012-0053-2. **M**
> *Sgt. Rock's Combat Tales.* 2005. 128pp. 1-4012-0794-4. **T**

Stephen Crane's The Red Badge of Courage. **Written by Stephen Crane. Adapted and Illustrated by Wayne Vansant.** Penguin Graphics/Penguin Group, 2005. 176pp. 0-14-240410-1. **T**

The story of Henry Fleming, a young boy who enlisted in the Civil War. He had always dreamed about the glory of battle, but after witnessing the brutal realities of war, he would gladly give anything to be back home. Will he be a coward and run away to safety, or will he come through the war a hero, either dead or alive?

Vietnam Journal. **Written and illustrated by Don Lomax.** ibooks, inc., 2001. 192pp. 0-7434-5894-X. **T**

War correspondent Scott "Journal" Neithammer is sent to Southeast Asia on a tour of duty to cover the Vietnam conflict, but the real truths of the war aren't found in the barracks and officer headquarters—they're in the trenches and in the muddy fields with the grunts. These young men, who are trying to fight a war that they don't understand but are willing to sacrifice their lives for, share their experiences and the brutal realities of war.

War Stories. Written by Garth Ennis. Illustrated by Dave Gibbons and various. Vertigo/DC Comics, 2004–2006. **M** ◉

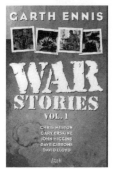

© 2006 DC Comics.

Collection of short stories that tell of both the horrors and heroics of World War II from all fronts of the brutal conflict. With the war as a backdrop to smaller skirmishes, the more personal conflicts show that both sides of the war were not made up of ranks and files, but of individuals making their own choices during one of the darkest periods in human history in the twentieth century. Stories range from tales of the famous Screaming Eagles, to exploits of the British Navy in the dark and cold European seas, to other accounts that personalize the conflicts and consequences of the soldiers.

Vol. 1. 2004. 240pp. 1-4012-0328-0.
Vol. 2. 2006. 240pp. 1-4012-1039-2.

***White Death.* Written by Robbie Morrison. Illustrated by Charles Adlard.** AiT/Planet Lar, 2002. 96pp. 0-9709360-6-0. **M**

In the Italian hills during the height of World War I in 1916, a young Italian soldier returns to his home of Trentino to find a much-changed countryside. Memories of adventure and excitement have been replaced by death and decay and the horrors of trench warfare. As the weapons blast into the night, there is one thing that both camps dread more than any other—the white death that comes in the form of avalanches. Caused by deliberate gun fire, if an avalanche hits it will destroy everything in its path . . . if there is anything not already consumed by the war.

***Witness to War.* Written and illustrated by Chuck Bordell.** Tome Press, 2000. 88pp. 0-941613-10-0. **O**

A fictionalized account of the last days of World War II leading up to the Battle of the Bulge. Anna Kreig is a female war correspondent on the front lines of battle. She's assigned to cover the daily life of a grunt on the front lines. As she witnesses a night attack in the Ardennes Forest, she sees firsthand the best and worst that war can bring.

Far East Adventure—Code of the Warrior: Samurai, Ninja, and Other Asian Influences

The samurai, ninja, and other aspects of Asian culture have been explored in great detail in comic books, especially in Japanese manga, which has crossed into American markets and inspired American creators, too. The quintessential samurai epic is the twenty-eight-volume *Lone Wolf and Cub*, which has inspired Western illustrators and writers for many years. In typical samurai stories, the main character or characters fight according to a code of honor or a sense of discipline. This is exemplified in the samurai code of Bushido, as created by samurai legend Miyamoto Musashi. Thus, the subgenre can be compared to the American Western, where the cowboy code of honor is integral to the story.

The samurai or ninja adventure usually takes the protagonist on a quest of discovery or search for hidden truths, but of utmost importance is that the character retains his sense of discipline throughout the task. Because of the discipline of the character, the personality may even be considered by others as arrogant or out of touch with the rest of humanity, but it is the strict adherence to his principles that enables the protagonist to succeed. In the end the hero's discipline and teamwork with his companions overcome all obstacles. Of course, fighting and swordplay are musts in these tales. Though the settings typically are feudal Japan or other ancient Asian countries, the story may take place as well during current times, the far future, or even in a fantasy-like Asia that may have elements of the fantastic as part of the plot. Romance may be involved but is not usually essential to the plot. Film comparisons include *Seven Samurai*, *Hidden Fortress*, *Crouching Tiger, Hidden Dragon*, and *Hero*.

***Bastard Samurai: Samurai Noir.* Written by Michael Avon Oeming and Miles Gunter. Illustrated by Kelsey Shannon.** Image Comics, 2003. 112pp. 1-58240-283-3. **O**

© 2006 Michael Avon Oeming,
Miles Gunter and Kelsey Shannon.

High above the rooftops of Manhattan, Bushido—the ancient code of the samurai—lives again in a deadly gambling tournament run by the Japanese Yukaza. Two men from schools disciplined in the ancient code of the Samurai test their swords and skill in battle, and only one warrior will walk away. Jiro has been raised since he was an orphan in the ways of the Samurai. He's unbeatable with a katana and is the best killer. When he finds that the last combatant he killed was in actuality his older brother, Jiro, with the aid of a healer named Toshi, vows to end the corrupt tournaments that destroyed his life and took his family away from him.

***Blade of Kumori.* Written by Ron Marz. Illustrated by Dub and Grafiksismik.** Aftermath/Devil's Due, 2005. 144pp. 1-932796-35-5. **T**

Kumori Ashina, a skilled member of the secret samurai Ashina clan, has never questioned her loyalty to the code of Bushido and carrying on the traditions of the samurai . . . until now. After not following through on her assignment to assassinate a U.S. vigilante called Great White, Kumori finds herself on a precarious road trying to balance the code of a warrior with the responsibilities to her family, her clan, and the one she loves. When Kumori also discovers that she's more than human, she'll need the skills of a warrior and the powers of her true potential just to survive against the mysterious assassin called Synth, while the fates of her loved ones hang in the balance.

Blade of the Immortal. Written and illustrated by Hiroaki Samura. Dark Horse Comics 1997– . **O ◎ Japanese manga.**

Blade of the Immortal © 2006 by Hiroaki Samura. All rights reserved. New and adapted artwork and text copyright 2005 Dark Horse Comics, Inc.

In feudal Japan, Manji, a fallen Ronin (wandering Samurai), has been cursed with life everlasting by mystical bloodworms that will heal his every wound. The curse will end on one condition: he must slay 1,000 evil men in battle. Now immortal, no matter how many times he gets cut, stabbed, slit, burnt, or gouged, he will always heal. He and Rin, a female companion who is out to seek revenge on those who killed her parents, are on the path to redeem Rin's family honor and to give her eternal rest. The series is still currently published in Japan, with more than seventeen volumes collected so far. The series won an Eisner Award in 2000 in the category Best U.S. Edition of Foreign Material.

Vol. 1: Blood of a Thousand. 1997. 136pp. 1-56971-239-5.
Vol. 2: Cry of the Worm. 1998. 176pp. 1-56971-300-6.
Vol. 3: Dreamsong. 1999. 208pp. 1-56971-357-X.
Vol. 4: On Silent Wings. 1999. 176pp. 1-56971-412-6.
Vol. 5: On Silent Wings II. 2000. 184pp. 1-56971-444-4.
Vol. 6: Dark Shadows. 2000. 192pp. 1-56971-469-X.
Vol. 7: Heart of Darkness. 2001. 192pp. 1-56971-531-9.
Vol. 8: The Gathering. 2001. 208pp. 1-56971-546-7.
Vol. 9: The Gathering II. 2001. 216pp. 1-56971-560-2.
Vol. 10: Secrets. 2002. 232pp. 1-56971-746-X.
Vol. 11: Beasts. 2002. 192pp. 1-56971-741-9.
Vol. 12: Autumn Frost. 2003. 232pp. 1-56971-991-8.
Vol. 13: Mirror of the Soul. 2004. 256pp. 1-59307-218-X.
Vol. 14: Last Blood. 2005. 256pp. 1-59307-321-6.
Vol. 15: Trickster. 2006. 224pp. 1-59307-468-9.
Vol. 16: Shortcut. 2006. 200pp. 1-59307-723-8.

Crouching Tiger, Hidden Dragon. Adapted and Illustrated by Andy Seto, based on the story by Wang Du Lu. Hong Kong Comics, Ltd., 2004–2005. **T 🀄 Chinese manhua.**

Inspired by the hit movie from 2000 and based on the story by Wang Du Lu, the kung-fu martial arts epic tells the tale of hidden love against the background of ancient China. When Grand Yu is targeted for assassination by a rival clan, he's helped by the wise and powerful martial arts master Li Mu Bai. He meet's Yu's daughter Shu Lien, and they instantly fall in love. Shu Lien is already engaged to another man, and Li Mu Bai will not admit his feelings for her. Humbled, but not deterred, Li Mu Bai aligns himself with Shu Lien's family and they continue their quest for the legendary Green Sword while fighting the most dangerous masters of the deadly martial arts.

Vol. 1—Revised & Expanded Edition. 2005. 128pp. 988-97972-7-5.
Vol. 2—Revised & Expanded Edition. 2005. 128pp. 988-97972-8-3.
Vol. 3—Revised & Expanded Edition. 2005. 128pp. 988-97972-9-1.
Vol. 4—Revised & Expanded Edition. 2005. 128pp. 988-97972-0-8.
Vol. 5. 2004. 105pp. 962-85278-3-5.
Vol. 6. 2004. 120pp. 962-85278-4-3.
Vol. 7. 2004. 120pp. 962-85278-5-1.
Vol. 8. 2004. 120pp. 962-85278-6-X.

Vol. 9. 2004. 120pp. 962-85278-7-8.
Vol. 10. 2004. 128pp. 962-85278-8-6.
Vol. 11. 2005. 120pp. 962-85278-9-4.
Vol. 12. 2005. 128pp. 962-85278-0-0.
Vol. 13. 2005. 128pp. 988-97972-2-4.

Flame of Recca. Written and illustrated by Nobuyuki Anzai. VIZ Media, LLC, 2003– . **O Japanese manga.** あ

Recca Hanabishi is a typical high school student. He lives with his father, he's a tough scrapper of a fighter, he enjoys playing with fireworks—and he's also a ninja with the mysterious ability to shoot fire! Maybe he's not so typical. With his friends, including the dumb-but-strong brute Domon, the pretty-boy Mikagami, and the ninja girl Fuuko, who has the ability to control the wind, he must rescue Yanagi Sakoshita, his "princess," whom he has sworn to protect. Yanagi has the magical power to heal and has been kidnapped by an evil madman who wants to harness her powers for immortality and more. When another villain with powers similar to Recca's control of flames offers the group a chance to participate in a tournament of death, they begrudgingly accept, and through the fighting they learn more about themselves, the price of friendship, and the true secret of Recca's past. The series was originally published in Japan and collected into thirty-three volumes and also inspired a hit Japanese anime television show.

Vol. 1. 2003. 180pp. 1-59116-066-9.
Vol. 2. 2003. 184pp. 1-59116-067-7.
Vol. 3. 2003. 184pp. 1-59116-094-4.
Vol. 4. 2004. 200pp. 1-59116-125-8.
Vol. 5. 2004. 200pp. 1-59116-193-2.
Vol. 6. 2004. 200pp. 1-59116-316-1.
Vol. 7. 2004. 200pp. 1-59116-448-6.
Vol. 8. 2004. 200pp. 1-59116-480-X.
Vol. 9. 2004. 192pp. 1-59116-481-8.
Vol. 10. 2005. 200pp. 1-59116-636-5.
Vol. 11. 2005. 200pp. 1-59116-741-8.
Vol. 12. 2005. 192pp. 1-59116-796-5.
Vol. 13. 2005. 192pp. 1-59116-858-9.
Vol. 14. 2005. 184pp. 1-4215-0014-0.
Vol. 15. 2005. 200pp. 1-4215-0131-7.
Vol. 16. 2006. 208pp. 1-4215-0250-X.
Vol. 17. 2006. 208pp. 1-4215-0381-6.
Vol. 18. 2006. 208pp. 1-4215-0454-5.
Vol. 19. 2006. 208pp. 1-4215-0455-3.
Vol. 20. 2006. 208pp. 1-4215-0456-1.
Vol. 21. 2006. 192pp. 1-4215-0457-X.
Vol. 22. 2007. 192pp. 1-4215-0893-1.
Vol. 23. 2007. 192pp. 1-4215-0894-X.

The Four Constables. **Written by Rui-An Wen. Illustrated by Andy Seto.** ComicsOne and DrMaster Publications Inc., 2004– . **T Chinese manhua.**

In Ancient China, four fighters of great strength and courage have banded together as a brotherhood of detective-assassins in a land gone corrupt. Nicknamed Emotionless, Iron Hands, Life Snatcher, and Cold Blooded after their particular specialized training in the martial arts, they have been brought together under the guidance of the Emperor's bodyguard, Master Zhuge Zhen-Wo (The Little Flower). They are the ultimate upholders of the law and defenders of the innocent in a time when assassination is rampant and plots to destroy the Empire are commonplace. Now, when a secret society of assassins or murderers roams the land, they'll be facing the wrath of the Four Constables.

> *Vol. 1.* 2004. 128pp. 1-58899-383-3.
> *Vol. 2.* 2004. 128pp. 1-58899-384-1.
> *Vol. 3.* 2004. 128pp. 1-58899-385-X.
> *Vol. 4.* 2006. 128pp. 1-59796-092-6.
> *Vol. 5.* 2006. 128pp. 1-59796-093-4.

Frank Miller's Ronin. **Written and illustrated by Frank Miller.** DC Comics, 1995. 192pp. 0-930289-21-8. **T**

A masterless and dishonored samurai from thirteenth-century Japan is given a second chance at restoring his honor and avenging his master's death. Suddenly reborn in a futuristic, twenty-first-century New York City where technology reigns, the samurai must kill the reincarnation of his master's killer—a demon called Agat—in order to conclude his road to redemption. Now trapped in a strange world that's foreign and repulsive to him, the Ronin must fight for his life and his soul against the most vicious of enemies in a bloody battle to the death.

Hero. **Written and illustrated by Wing Shing Ma with Zhang Yimou.** ComicsOne, 2004. 128pp. 1-58899-374-4. **T** 🎬 **Chinese manhua.**

Adaptation of the hit 2003 martial arts film about a plot to assassinate Qin, the most powerful ruler in the northern province of China's Six Kingdoms, by other warring factions. When a minor official miraculously defeats the Qin's three principal enemies and takes revenge on those who destroyed his home, he's sent to the palace to recount to Qin the story of what really happened, and a plot to overthrow the Empire is revealed.

Kaze Hikaru. **Written and illustrated by Taeko Watanabe.** VIZ Media, LLC, 2006– . **T Japanese manga.**

During the Bakumatsu revolution at the end of the Tokugawa era and the beginning of the Meiji era, a young woman named Sei Tominaga seeks to avenge the deaths of her father and brother. Disguising herself as a young boy, Sei—now called Seizaburo Kamiya—joins the special police force called the Shinsengumi to seek revenge, but also finds true love with Okita Souji, one of the premiere Shinsengumi swordsmen. The series was originally published in Japan and in seventeen collected volumes.

> *Vol. 1.* 2006. 200pp. 1-4215-0189-9.
> *Vol. 2.* 2006. 208pp. 1-4215-0581-9.
> *Vol. 3.* 2006. 208pp. 1-4215-0582-7.

Vol. 4. 2007. 200pp. 1-4215-1017-0.
Vol. 5. 2007. 208pp. 1-4215-1018-9.

Lady Snowblood. Written by Kazuo Koike. Illustrated by Kazuo Kamimura. Dark Horse Comics, 2005–2006. **M** **Japanese manga.**

During the Meiji period in Japan, when the old ways of the age of Edo are being replaced by a new sensibility, there is one woman who walks the bloody path of vengeance. Called Yuki, Japanese for "snow," she is a master assassin, born of a woman who was raped by bandits. Now skilled in the deadly arts, she seeks revenge on those who murdered and violated a family she never knew, and for 1,000 yen, she will seek revenge for those not skilled enough to do it on their own. The character also spawned two film adaptations, in 1973 and 1974, respectively, and was the inspiration for the lead role of The Bride played by Uma Thurman in Quentin Tarantino's films *Kill Bill I* and *II*.

> *Vol. 1.* 2005. 288pp. 1-59307-385-2.
> *Vol. 2: The Deep-Seated Grudge.* 2005. 224pp. 1-59307-443-3.
> *Vol. 3: Retribution, Part 1.* 2006. 224pp. 1-59307-458-1.
> *Vol. 4: Retribution, Part 2.* 2006. 288pp. 1-59307-532-4.

The Legendary Couple. Written by Louis Cha. Illustrated by Tony Wong. ComicsOne, 2002– . **T Chinese manhua.**

In Ancient China, an orphan named Kuo Yung is raised under the watchful eye of Fong Ouyang, the Poison of the West, as an apprentice. Quick thinking, kindhearted, and wise, Kuo Yung is an excellent martial arts student. When he meets the equally talented martial artist Xiao Longu, they fall madly in love, and as time passes, they grow up and get married. When Longu mysteriously disappears, Kuo Yung will do whatever it takes to get her back, including perfecting his martial arts skills to prepare for the coming battle. It will be an agonizing sixteen years until they'll be reunited. Can love stand the test of time, and how will their love change? Meanwhilee, the Seven Great Masters of the Circle of Warriors (where Fong Ouyang is a member) compete in battles to prove who is the best fighter. One day Kuo Yung may have to face each of them in battle to rescue Xiao Longu, and he can only pray that he is ready. The series was never completed because the publisher folded.

> *Vol. 1.* 2002. 128pp. 1-58899-191-1.
> *Vol. 2.* 2003. 128pp. 1-58899-229-2.
> *Vol. 3.* 2003. 128pp. 1-58899-230-6.
> *Vol. 4.* 2003. 128pp. 1-58899-231-4.
> *Vol. 5.* 2003. 128pp. 1-58899-231-2.
> *Vol. 6.* 2003. 128pp. 1-58899-232-2.
> *Vol. 7.* 2004. 120pp. 1-58899-234-9.

❦ Lone Wolf and Cub. Written by Kazuo Koike. Illustrated by Goseki Kojima. Dark Horse Comics, 2000–2002. **O**   **Japanese manga.**

The classic and epic journey of widowed and disgraced Ronin (wandering samurai) Itto Ogami and his infant son Daigoro, on their long and bloody road to revenge and redemption by the sword. Set firmly within the code of Bushido and honor, they sell their "special services" to people in need as "assassins-for-hire" while traveling the Japanese countryside to confront those who framed Itto and to destroy the assassins who killed his wife. As the body count rises, Itto will walk the path of the assassin to become the perfect killer-for-hire, but after miles and miles of wandering, can Itto finally clear his name and find a way out of the darkness and bloodshed? The series won an Eisner Award in 2001 in the category Best U.S. Edition of Foreign Material and Harvey Awards for Best Graphic Album of Previously Published Work (2002) and Best American Edition of Foreign Material (2001-2003). The manga series was adapted into six live action films and released between 1972 and 1974.

    Vol. 1: The Assassin's Road. 2000. 296pp. 1-56971-502-5.
    Vol. 2: The Gateless Barrier. 2000. 296pp. 1-56971-503-3.
    Vol. 3: The Flute of the Fallen Tiger. 2000. 304pp. 1-56971-504-1.
    Vol. 4: The Bell Warden. 2000. 304pp. 1-56971-505-X.
    Vol. 5: Black Wind. 2001. 288pp. 1-56971-506-8.
    Vol. 6: Lanterns for the Dead. 2001. 288pp. 1-56971-507-6.
    Vol. 7: Cloud Dragon, Wind Tiger. 2001. 320pp. 1-56971-508-4.
    Vol. 8: Chains of Death. 2001. 304pp. 1-56971-509-2.
    Vol. 9: Echo of the Assassin. 2001. 288pp. 1-56971-510-6.
    Vol. 10: Hostage Child. 2001. 320pp. 1-56971-511-4.
    Vol. 11: Talisman of Hades. 2001. 320pp. 1-56971-512-2.
    Vol. 12: Shattered Stones. 2001. 304pp. 1-56971-513-0.
    Vol. 13: The Moon in the East, the Sun in the West. 2001. 320pp. 1-56971-585-8.
    Vol. 14: The Day of the Demons. 2001. 320pp. 1-56971-586-6.
    Vol. 15: Brothers of the Grass. 2001. 352pp. 1-56971-587-4.
    Vol. 16: The Gateway into Winter. 2001. 320pp. 1-56971-588-2.
    Vol. 17: The Will of the Fang. 2002. 320pp. 1-56971-589-0.
    Vol. 18: Twilight of the Kurokuwa. 2002. 320pp. 1-56971-590-4.
    Vol. 19: The Moon in Our Hearts. 2002. 320pp. 1-56971-591-2.
    Vol. 20: A Taste of Poison. 2002. 320pp. 1-56971-592-0.
    Vol. 21: Fragrance of Death. 2002. 320pp. 1-56971-593-9.
    Vol. 22: Heaven and Earth. 2002. 288pp. 1-56971-594-7.
    Vol. 23: Tears of Ice. 2002. 320pp. 1-56971-595-5.
    Vol. 24: In These Small Hands. 2002. 320pp. 1-56971-596-3.
    Vol. 25: Perhaps in Death. 2002. 320pp. 1-56971-597-1.
    Vol. 26: Struggle in the Dark. 2002. 312pp. 1-56971-598-X.
    Vol. 27: Battle's Eve. 2002. 300pp. 1-56971-599-8.
    Vol. 28: The Lotus Throne. 2002. 320pp. 1-56971-600-5.

Lone Wolf 2100. **Written by Mike Kennedy. Illustrated by Francisco Ruiz Velasco.** Dark Horse Comics, 2003–2004. **O**

Over 100 years in the future, when humanity is facing extinction at the hands of a deadly virus, a young girl named Daisy Ogami is wanted by a corrupt organization for the secrets she carries inside her. Itto, the rogue humanoid EmCon bodyguard warrior who killed her father, accompanies Daisy, and together they're on the run from the evil organization and its well-armed warriors. Seeking to clear their names and vowing to protect Daisy at all costs, Itto walks the path of the warrior with Daisy, following the code of Bushido and cleaving a path of justice with his sword. Inspired by the original *Lone Wolf and Cub* Japanese manga.

> *Vol. 1: Shadows on Saplings.* 2003. 104pp. 1-56971-893-8.
> *Vol. 2: The Language of Chaos.* 2003. 120pp. 1-56971-997-7.
> *Vol. 3: Pattern Storm.* 2004. 104pp. 1-59307-079-9.

Naruto. **Written and illustrated by Masashi Kishimoto.** VIZ Media, LLC, 2003– . **T** ◎ 🎮 **Japanese manga.** あ

In a world much like our own, where ninja clans and their magic are commonplace, a nine-tailed demon fox appeared twelve years earlier in the Konohagakure village and was defeated only after one Shinobi—the Fourth Hokage—sacrificed his life to seal the demon inside an infant boy named Uzumaki Naruto. Years later, Naruto has grown into a twelve-year-old orphan ruffian who is reckless adn obscene, but skilled and confident that he will be the greatest Hokage ever. Though the village is fearful that one day his powers as the nine-tailed fox may one day return, the village elder Hokage has faith in him. Together with the help of his teachers, Iruka and Kakashi, and newfound friends (and sometimes

NARUTO © 1999 by Masashi Kishimoto/SHUEISHA Inc.

rivals) Sasuke and Sakura, Naruto continues to fight the prejudices of the townsfolk and to do whatever it takes to prove he's going to be the best Hokage ever. The series is still being published in Japan and has been collected in over thirty volumes. The manga series also inspired a hit Japanese anime television show currently airing in North America.

> *Vol. 1: The Tests of the Ninja.* 2003. 192pp. 1-56931-900-6.
> *Vol. 2: The Worst Client.* 2003. 216pp. 1-59116-178-9.
> *Vol. 3: Bridge of Courage.* 2004. 208pp. 1-59116-187-8.
> *Vol. 4: Next Level.* 2004. 200pp. 1-59116-358-7.
> *Vol. 5: The Challengers.* 2004. 200pp. 1-59116-359-5.
> *Vol. 6: The Forest of Death.* 2005. 192pp. 1-59116-739-6.
> *Vol. 7: Orochimaru's Curse.* 2005. 192pp. 1-59116-875-9.
> *Vol. 8: Life-And-Death Battles.* 2005. 192pp. 1-4215-0124-4.
> *Vol. 9: Turning the Tables.* 2006. 208pp. 1-4215-0239-9.
> *Vol. 10.* 2006. 208pp. 1-4215-0240-2.
> *Vol. 11.* 2006. 208pp. 1-4215-0241-0.
> *Vol. 12.* 2006. 208pp. 1421502429.
> *Vol. 13.* 2007. 192pp. 1-4215-1087-1.

Ninja Boy: Faded Dreams. **Written by Allen Warner. Illustrated by Alé Garza with Dan Norton.** WildStorm Productions/DC Comics, 2002. 160pp. 1-4012-0102-4. **T**

Young Nakio is the youngest of three brothers training to be Mugen-style ninja in a mythical world similar to Japan. He is constantly picked on by his brothers, and only his grandfather can see the potential that lies within Nakio. He sends Makio on his first mission. When his elder brothers are brutally killed by the crimelord Amatsu Mikaboshi's men, Nakio vows revenge, but even though he's found an unlikely ally in the short, fuzzy, and heavily intoxicated creature called Sake, they might not be enough to take on Mikaboshi and his horde of assassins.

Ninja High School. Written and illustrated by Ben Dunn. Antarctic Press, 2003– . **T Neo-manga.**

© 2006 Antarctic Press.

All teenager Jeremy Feeple wanted to do was pass his next Advanced Algebra test, but all that is about to change when two lovely ladies enter his life and vie for his affection. Enter ninja Ichikun "Ichi Koo" Ichinohei and Princess Asrial of the planet Salusia—both with their own reasons for wanting to marry Jeremy. Now Jeremy's fending off the affections of an alien and a ninja and the small but not-so-quiet town of Quagmire, USA, will never be the same! The series was originally published starting in 1986 and continues to this day.

Pocket Manga Vol. 1. 2003. 128pp. 1-932453-08-3.
Pocket Manga Vol. 2. 2004. 128pp. 1-932453-39-3.
Pocket Manga Vol. 3. 2004. 136pp. 1-932453-52-0.
Pocket Manga Vol. 4. 2004. 136pp. 1-932453-62-8.
Pocket Manga Vol. 5. 2005. 144pp. 1-932453-70-9.
Pocket Manga Vol. 6. 2005. 144pp. 1-932453-84-9.
Pocket Manga Vol. 7. 2005. 144pp. 1-932453-95-4.
Pocket Manga Vol. 8. 2006. 144pp. 0-97680-432-8.
Pocket Manga Vol. 9. 2006. 128pp. 0-97764-246-1.

No Honor. **Written by Fiona Kai Avery. Illustrated by Clayton Crain.** Image Comics, 2003. 112pp. 1-58240-321-X. **T**

When art thief Random Chance steals an ancient Samurai sword, he accidentally cuts himself and unwittingly releases the soul of a samurai named Tannen who's been trapped in the sword. Now Tannen is sharing Random's body and mind, and the two must learn to settle their differences and work with one another. Gifted with the power to speak to other spirits, Tannen and Random journey to Japan to try to solve the mystery of who really killed Tannen and to avenge his master's death. Meanwhile police officer Brit Morrigan, a former thief turned cop, is trying to track Random down and capture the most wanted thief in the world.

🏵 **The Path. Written by Ron Marz. Illustrated by Bart Sears with Walter Simonson.** CrossGen Comics, 2002–2003. **T**

On the island nation of Nayado, on a world that resembles feudal Japan, a lone warrior seeks the path of vengeance. Obo-San is a monk who has lost his faith after witnessing the death of his brother at the hands of those he and his people once thought of as gods. Armed with a mystical sigil-brand "Weapon of Heaven" that gives him great power, a once-peaceful monk is accompanied by two unusual warrior companions on a quest to overthrow their gods, even if it puts him at odds with the mad Emperor Mitsumune. The otherworld samurai epic was never completed following the company CrossGen's financial bankruptcy. The collection *Crisis of Faith* received recognition from YALSA's Quick Picks for Reluctant Readers committee in 2004.

Vol. 1: Crisis of Faith. 2002. 160pp. 1-931484-32-5.
Vol. 2: Blood on Snow. 2003. 160pp. 1-931484-60-0.

Peacemaker Kurogane. **Written and illustrated by Nanae Chrono.** ADV Manga, 2004–2005. **T Japanese manga.** あ

> In feudal Japan, Tetsunosuke Ichimura is now a member of the imperial capital of Kyoto's samurai police force, the Shinsengumi. As a page to Vice-Commander Hijikata, he's a witness to the comings and goings of the highest-ranking officials in the land. Tetsunosuke finds that he must not only defend the capital from attackers, but also be a protector of its darkest secrets as well. The series was also released as a twenty-four-episode anime series in Japan.

> *Vol. 1.* 2004. 192pp. 1-4139-0161-1.
> *Vol. 2.* 2004. 184pp. 1-4139-0192-1.
> *Vol. 3.* 2005. 184pp. 1-4139-0197-2.
> *Vol. 4.* 2005. 184pp. 1-4139-0325-8.

Ronin Hood of the 47 Samurai. **Written by Jeff Amano. Illustrated by Craig Rousseau.** Image Comics, 2005. 96pp. 1-58240-555-7. **T**

> In the early eighteenth century in Japan, a rogue group of samurai plot to avenge their fallen master. After the death of their master, Lord Asano Takuminokami, his loyal samurai subjects become ronin (masterless samurai) and plot against Lord Kira Hozukenosuke, the one behind their master's death. In hiding for almost two years, Oishi, leader of the forty-seven ronin, knows that soon it is time to strike back and claim vengeance in the name of their beloved master. Honor must be preserved, and to be victorious they must die.

© 2006 Jeff Amano and
Craig Rousseau.

Rurouni Kenshin. **Written and illustrated by Nobuhiro Watsuki.** VIZ Media, LLC, 2003–2006. **O ◎ Japanese manga.** あ

> In the Meiji period of Japan (the late 1800s), when swords and killing were outlawed, wandering Samurai Kenshin Himura, formerly one of the most brutal executioners, strives to keep his honor as a swordsman alive in the new era. He now fights with a Sakabato blade (a sword with the blade upside down), so his strikes are not lethal, but his blows with his sword still dole out justice. Joined by companions, including Kamiya Kaoru, a young woman who's taken over her father's dojo and Kenshin's future love interest, and youthful Myojin Yahiko, who dreams of becoming the most powerful samurai ever, Kenshin is on a path to discover just where he truly belongs in a new age of Japan. The manga series also inspired a hit Japanese anime television show that was renamed as *Samurai X* in North America.

> *Vol. 1.* 2003. 208pp. 1-59116-220-3.
> *Vol. 2.* 2003. 200pp. 1-59116-249-1.
> *Vol. 3.* 2004. 208pp. 1-59116-250-5.
> *Vol. 4.* 2004. 192pp. 1-59116-251-3.
> *Vol. 5.* 2004. 192pp. 1-59116-320-X.
> *Vol. 6.* 2004. 200pp. 1-59116-356-0.

Vol. 7. 2004. 200pp. 1-59116-357-9.
Vol. 8. 2005. 200pp. 1-59116-563-6.
Vol. 9. 2004. 200pp. 1-59116-669-1.
Vol. 10. 2004. 192pp. 1-59116-703-5.
Vol. 11. 2005. 192pp. 1-59116-709-4.
Vol. 12. 2005. 200pp. 1-59116-712-4.
Vol. 13. 2005. 192pp. 1-59116-713-2.
Vol. 14. 2005. 192pp. 1-59116-767-1.
Vol. 15. 2005. 192pp. 1-59116-810-4.
Vol. 16. 2005. 192pp. 1-59116-854-6.
Vol. 17. 2005. 208pp. 1-59116-876-7.
Vol. 18. 2005. 200pp. 1-59116-959-3.
Vol. 19. 2005. 192pp. 1-59116-927-5.
Vol. 20. 2005. 200pp. 1-4215-0064-7.
Vol. 21. 2005. 192pp. 1-4215-0082-5.
Vol. 22. 2006. 208pp. 1-4215-0196-1.
Vol. 23. 2006. 208pp. 1-4215-0276-3.
Vol. 24. 2006. 208pp. 1-42150-338-7.
Vol. 25. 2006. 208pp. 1-4215-0407-3.
Vol. 26. 2006. 208pp. 1-4215-0673-4.
Vol. 27. 2006. 208pp. 1-4215-0674-2.
Vol. 28. 2006. 208pp. 1-4215-0675-0.

Samurai: Heaven and Earth. **Written by Ron Marz. Illustrated by Luke Ross.** Dark Horse Comics, 2006– . **T** ◎

In the year 1704, when his beloved is captured by his enemies, a lone samurai warrior risks everything to rescue her. Traveling from his native Japan to distant lands in the empire of China, across Europe, to the streets of Paris, his swords are tested against the best blades of the lands, but neither Heaven nor Earth can stop him from his epic journey to be reunited with his beloved.

Vol. 1. 2006. 120pp. 1-59307-388-7.

© 2006 Ron Marz.

Samurai Executioner. **Written by Kazuo Koike. Illustrated by Goseki Kojima.** Dark Horse Comics, 2004–2006. **M Japanese manga.**

Before his death at the hands of Itto Ogami (as seen in the epic samurai series <u>Lone Wolf and Cub</u>), Kubikiri Asa was the chief tester of the swords for his shogun and a beheader of men. Feared across feudal Japan for his skill with the blade Onibocho, he lived in the world of cutthroats and killers lurking in every corner of the land. In these troubling times of feudal Japan, one man tries to not stray from the path and to do the honorable work that his skill calls for. This series was created by Kazuo Koike and Goseki Kojima before their monumental work on <u>Lone Wolf and Cub</u>.

Vol. 1. 2004. 328pp. 1-59307-207-4.
Vol. 2. 2004. 304pp. 1-59307-208-2.

Vol. 3. 2005. 312pp. 1-59307-209-0.
Vol. 4. 2005. 304pp. 1-59307-210-4.
Vol. 5. 2005. 304pp. 1-59307-211-2.
Vol. 6. 2005. 304pp. 1-59307-275-9.
Vol. 7. 2006. 304pp. 1-59307-276-7.
Vol. 8. 2006. 304pp. 1-59307-277-5.
Vol. 9. 2006. 304pp. 1-59307-278-3.
Vol. 10. 2006. 224pp. 1-59307-279-1.

Samurai Legend. **Written by Kan Furuyama. Illustrated by Jiro Taniguchi.** CPM Manga, 2003. 240pp. 1-58664-856-X. **O Japanese manga.**

Based on the true life of the legendary samurai swordsman Yagyu Jubei and set in 1649 Japan. The brave samurai warrior is charged by his family with protecting the Yagyu Secret Chronicles—texts that might topple the empire if their secrets were revealed. When the Chronicles are stolen, Jubei must uncover the plot behind the theft and restore them to their proper place before the land falls into a bloody civil war—even if it costs him his life.

Teenage Mutant Ninja Turtles. **Written and illustrated by Kevin Eastman, Peter Laird, and various.** Mirage Studios et al., 1986– . **Y** 🎞 🖥 🎮

When four baby turtles are splashed by radioactive waste, they mutate into humanoid-like reptiles. Named after the masters of art—Leonardo, Donatello, Michelango, and Raphael—by their wise master Splinter, a sewer rat who was also mutated by the goo, they're also known as the Teenage Mutant Ninja Turtles. Trained in the martial arts and each skilled in the ways of a specialized weapon of choice, the Turtles are a fierce and disciplined fighting force against their archenemy Oroku Saki—otherwise known as the Shredder—and his ninja clan, known as The Foot, as well as against other villains, including the dinosaurlike Triceratons. Their adventures take them to different realms, worlds, time lines, and more as they team up with characters such as the masked vigilante Casey Jones, the robot Fugitoid, samurai rabbit ronin Usagi Yojimbo, and even the aardvark warrior called Cerebus.

Book 1. First Publishing 1986. 124pp. 0-915419-09-2.
Book 2. First Publishing 1989. 126pp. 0-915419-22-X.
Book 3. First Publishing 1989. 126pp. 0-915419-28-9.
Book 4. First Publishing 1989. 108pp. 0-915419-43-2.
Body Count: Casey Jones and Raphael. Written and illustrated by Kevin Eastmen and Erik Larsen. Image Comics, 1996. 112pp. 1-887279-36-9.
A New Beginning. Written by Gary Carlson. Illustrated by Frank Fosco. Image Comics, 1997. 112pp. 1-887279-56-3.
Vol. 1: Things Change. Written by Peter David. Illustrated by LeSean Thomas. Dreamwave Productions, 2004. 104pp. 0-9732786-8-4.

🎌 Usagi Yojimbo. **Written and illustrated by Stan Sakai.** Fantagraphics (Vols. 1–7), Dark Horse Comics (Vols. 8–up), 1987– . **Y** ◎

In a story loosely based on the life of Miyamoto Musashi, one of Japan's best-known and beloved samurai, Miyamoto Usagi is a rabbit ronin (masterless samurai) warrior roaming an anthropomorphized feudal Japan following the death of his lord. Kindhearted and noble as the most honorable samurai yet deadly with a blade, Usagi is on a journey across Japan that is marked by death, suffering, danger, and heartache, yet also by great humor and joy. His journey is not easy. It's lined with conspirators, mysteries, murder, deceptive ninja clans, demonic assassins, and more. But with a colorful cast of companions, including the stubborn rhinoceros samurai Gen, the fox thief Kitsune, Usagi's lionlike Master Katsuichi, Chizu of the Neko Ninja clan, the doglike Inspector Ishida, and Usagi's "nephew," the young and brave Jotaro, it is not a lonely road but one paved with friendship. *Space Usagi* is the adventures of Usagi Yojimbo's descendant in the far future. The series has won numerous awards, including Eisner Awards for Best Lettering (1993), Talent Deserving of Wider Recognition (1996), and Best Serialized Story (1999). *Grasscutter* and *Duel at Kitanoji* received recognition from YALSA's Popular Paperbacks for Young Adults committee in 2002 and 2004, respectively.

Usagi Yojimbo™ © 2006
Stan Sakai.

Book 1: Samurai. 1987. 152pp. 0-930193-35-0.
Book 2: Ronin. 1989. 144pp. 0-930193-88-1.
Book 3: The Wanderer's Road. 1989. 152pp. 1-56097-009-X.
Book 4: The Dragon Bellow Conspiracy. 1990. 179pp. 1-56097-063-4.
Book 5: Lone Goat and Kid. 1992. 160pp. 1-56097-088-X.
Book 6: Circles. 1994. 144pp. 1-56097-146-0.
Book 7: Gen's Story. 1996. 184pp. 1-56097-304-8.
Book 8: Shades of Death. 1997. 200pp. 1-56971-259-X.
Book 9: Daisho. 1998. 200pp. 1-56971-292-1.
Book 10: The Brink of Life and Death. 1998. 208pp. 1-56971-297-2.
Book 11: Seasons. 1999. 208pp. 1-56971-375-8.
Book 12: Grasscutter. 1999. 256pp. 1-56971-413-4.
Book 13: Grey Shadows. 2000. 208pp. 1-56971-459-2.
Book 14: Demon Mask. 2001. 224pp. 1-56971-523-8.
Book 15: Grasscutter II—Journey to Atsuta Shrine. 2002. 184pp. 1-56971-660-9.
Book 16: The Shrouded Moon. 2003. 184pp. 1-56971-883-0.
Book 17: Duel at Kitanoji. 2003. 224pp. 1-56971-973-X.
Book 18: Travels with Jotaro. 2004. 208pp. 1-59307-220-1.
Book 19: Fathers and Sons. 2005. 184pp. 1-59307-319-4.
Book 20: Glimpses of Death. 2006. 184pp. 1-59307-549-9.
Space Usagi. 1998. 296pp. 1-56971-290-5.

Vagabond. Written and illustrated by Takehiko Inoue. VIZ Media, LLC, 2002– . **M** ◎
Japanese manga.

The epic life of Miyamoto Musashi (1584–1645), one of Japan's best-known and beloved samurai and creator of Bushido, the code of the samurai. From his humble beginnings as a dishonored seventeen-year old soldier named Takezô, he's on a long, violent, and bloody path to find spiritual enlightenment by the sword. Based on the Japanese fictionalized biography *Musashi* by Eiji Yoshikawa, so far only twenty-one volumes of this highly regarded series have been published in Japan, and it is estimated that the series may be completed around the fortieth volume.

Vol. 1. 2002. 248pp. 1-59116-034-0.
Vol. 2. 2002. 240pp. 1-59116-035-9.
Vol. 3. 2002. 228pp. 1-59116-049-9.

Vol. 4. 2002. 228pp. 1-56931-854-9.
Vol. 5. 2002. 208pp. 1-56931-893-X.
Vol. 6. 2002. 216pp. 1-56931-894-8.
Vol. 7. 2003. 200pp. 1-59116-073-1.
Vol. 8. 2004. 200pp. 1-59116-119-3.
Vol. 9. 2004. 216pp. 1-59116-256-4.
Vol. 10. 2004. 208pp. 1-59116-340-4.
Vol. 11. 2004. 224pp. 1-59116-396-X.
Vol. 12. 2004. 216pp. 1-59116-434-6.
Vol. 13. 2004. 216pp. 1-59116-451-6.
Vol. 14. 2004. 200pp. 1-59116-452-4.
Vol. 15. 2004. 200pp. 1-59116-453-2.
Vol. 16. 2004. 200pp. 1-59116-454-0.
Vol. 17. 2004. 192pp. 1-59116-455-9.
Vol. 18. 2004. 200pp. 1-59116-642-X.
Vol. 19. 2005. 200pp. 1-59116-643-8.
Vol. 20. 2005. 224pp. 1-59116-583-0.
Vol. 21. 2006. 208pp. 1-4215-0741-2.

***Way of the Rat: The Walls of Zhumar.* Written by Chuck Dixon. Illustrated by Jeff Johnson.** CrossGen Comics, 2003. 160pp. 1-931484-51-1. **T**

A lighthearted martial arts adventure set on a planet very similar to our own. In the city of Zhumar, a place reminiscent of ancient China, the city's ruler, Judge X'ain, has sold the fate of the city to a barbarian horde led by Bhuto Khan, giving him several mystical artifacts that will make him invincible. When the happy-go-lucky young master thief Boon Sai Hong, alias "the Jade Rat," accidentally steals the mystic Ring of Staffs before Bhuto receives it, Boon discovers that he's in over his head; the ring gives him the ability to be a martial arts expert. Accompanied by his newfound companion, a talking monkey named Po Po, on the run, he carries one of the deadliest weapons on the planet. The series unfortunately was never completed due to the publisher's bankruptcy.

Religious Heroes

These stories feature religious heroes from Jewish, Christian, Buddhist, and other religions. They can be adaptations of religious sources, retellings, or fictional stories.

Buddha. **Written and illustrated by Osamu Tezuka.** Vertical, Inc., 2003–2005. **T © Japanese manga.**

An epic retelling of the life of Gautama Buddha, known by Buddhists as the Supreme Buddha. Born in South Asia around the middle of the fifth century B.C. as Siddhartha Gautama, he found spiritual enlightenment at the age of twenty-nine and became a key figure in Buddhism. The retelling is by the legendary Ozama Tezuka and features many characters whom Tezuka infused into the story for dramatic effect and humor. The stories were originally published from 1974 to 1984 in Japan. The series has won several Eisner Awards, for Best U.S. Edition of Foreign Material in 2004–2005, and a Harvey Award in 2005 for Best American Edition of Foreign Material.

> *Vol. 1: Kapilavastu.* 2003. 400pp. 1-932234-43-8.
> *Vol. 2: The Four Encounters.* 2003. 408pp. 1-932234-44-6.
> *Vol. 3: Devadatta.* 2004. 320pp. 1-932234-45-4.
> *Vol. 4: The Forest of Uruvela.* 2004. 366pp. 1-932234-46-2.
> *Vol. 5: Deer Park.* 2005. 352pp. 1-932234-47-0.
> *Vol. 6: Ananda.* 2005. 360pp. 1-932234-48-9.
> *Vol. 7: Prince Ajatasattu.* 2005. 414pp. 1-932234-49-7.
> *Vol. 8: Jetavana.* 2005. 368pp. 1-932234-50-0.

The Chosen. **Written by Mark Millar. Illustrated by Peter Gross.** Dark Horse Comics, 2005. 80pp. 1-59307-213-9. **M**

What would you do if you discovered that instead of being just a normal twelve-year old boy, you're destined for greatness: you're Jesus Christ reborn? Now you can raise the dead, change water into wine, and bring affect the destiny of humanity over 2,000 years in the making.

Graphic Bible. **Written by Mike Maddox. Illustrated by Jeff Anderson.** Broadman & Holman, 1998. 256pp. 0-8054-1813-X. **T**

A comprehensive collection of Old and New Testament stories from the Bible, from the story of Adam and Eve to the crucifixion and resurrection of Jesus Christ. Originally published in England as the *Lion Graphic Bible.*

!Hero. **Adapted from the original story by Eddie DeGarmo and Bob Farrell. Written by Stephen R. Lawhead and Ross Lawhead. Illustrated by Ross Lawhead.** TH1NK books, a division of NavPress, 2003. 96pp. 1-57683-5000-6. **T**

A modern retelling of the life and death of Jesus Christ, set on an alternate Earth where humans live under a totalitarian, world-dominating government known as the International Confederation of Nations (I.C.O.N.), and Christ is an African American man named Hero born in Bethlehem, Pennsylvania. Alex Hunter, an agent from I.C.O.N,. is sent to report on the rumors of a miracle maker but finds himself drawn in to the miracles Hero performs and is a witness to his teachings, death, and resurrection.

King David. **Written and illustrated by Kyle Baker.** Vertigo/DC Comics, 2002. 158pp. 1-56389-866-7. **M**

A fictionalized retelling of the life of David of Israel, a peaceful but dim shepherd in th eeleventh-century B.C. Devoted to God, he faces his most famous opponent, the giant called Goliath, with comic carnage. Unknown to David, King Saul has deemed David to be a risk and will try to eliminate him at all costs, regardless of whether David is favored by the God of Israel.

***The Lone and Level Sands*. Written by A David Lewis. Illustrated by Marvin Mann.** Archaia Studio Press, 2006. 160pp. 1-932386-12-2. hardcover. **T**

> The historical retelling of the Book of Exodus from the Old Testament as seen through the eyes of Pharaoh Ramses II, the ruler of the Egyptians. As a proud ruler of his people, Ramses II must deal with his long-lost kinsman, Moses, and try to grasp the impossible demands of a deity that he does not worship.

***Samson: Judge of Israel*. Written by Jerry Novick. Illustrated by Mario Ruiz.** Metron Press/American Bible Society, 2002. 72pp. 1-58516-647-2. **T**

> In flashback from inside a Philistine prison, the former hero called Samson recounts the days in which his mighty strength was a gift from God. As the judge soon realizes while contemplating his faith, Samson's own inability to control his lust, pride, and anger caused him to lose all that he had been given by Heaven.

***Testament*. Written by Jim Krueger. Illustrated by various.** Metron Press, 2003. 120pp. 1-58516-765-7. **T**

> At a bar named J.J.'s, all of your questions are answered—even questions you might have never thought to ask. A lonely man is told lessons from one of the oldest books in history, the Bible. A collection of stories from the Bible featuring artwork by Bill Sienkiewicz, Steve Rude, George Pratt, Kent Williams, Sergio Aragonés, Rudy Nebres, Teddy Kristiansen, Vince Locke, John Van Fleet, Ray Lago, Scott Hampton, Phil Hester, Zach Howard, Bill Koeb, Greg Spalenka, Yvonne Gilbert, Tommy Lee Edwards, Mario Ruiz, Jason Alexander, and Mark Texeria. Presents stories from the Old and New Testament, some better known than others, that are as still as relevant today as when they were originally written.

Spies/Espionage

These graphic novel tales involve spies, secret agents, and more, typically out to stop some fiendish James Bond-type villain aiming to control the world. Like the prose tales, spy films, and television shows such as the James Bond film series and the television show *Alias* and *24* that have helped to inspire the subgenre, the tales feature fast pacing, suspense, dangerous escapes, exotic locations, a dash of romance, and a heaping amount of dastardly villains.

***The Agents*. Written and illustrated by Ben Dunn and Kevin Gunstone.** Antarctic Press, 2004. 136pp. 1-932453-64-4. **T Neo-manga.**

> Thirty years after Washington, D.C., and Moscow were devastated by nuclear fallout by a super-villain, a worldwide group called the Agency has emerged from the ashes to better protect the world from global emergencies. Based in Britain, the group takes on oncoming threats by using counterterrorism and espionage, but world peace is a difficult task, and many smaller countries are out to destroy all that the Agency stands for.

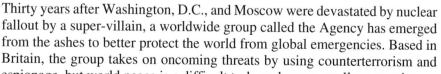

Amazing Agent Luna. **Written by Nunzio Defilippis and Christina Weir. Illustrated by Shiei.** Seven Seas Entertainment, LLC, 2005– . **T** ◉

The world's best spy has just taken on her most difficult case: high school! Meet Luna, a fifteen-year-old secret agent who was created from the best genetic material to be the ultimate spy for the United States. Sent to a prestigious high school to uncover a plot by the devious Count Von Brucken, she's finding that being a typical teen isn't as easy as it sounds, especially when she finds herself falling for Jonah, the Count's son!

> *Vol. 1.* 2005. 192pp. 1-933164-00-X.
> *Vol. 2.* 2005. 192pp. 1-933164-04-2.
> *Vol. 3.* 2006. 192pp. 1-933164-10-7.

© 2006 Seven Seas Entertainment.

Assassin School. **Written by Phil Littler and Richard Emms. Illustrated by Edu Francisco and Enrique Corts.** APComics, 2004–2005. **T**

Sixteen-year-old Emma Lee is getting an education like no other. Though she's a little accident prone, the beautiful blonde is one of many recruits trained as super-assassins at a special military school. Now determined to save the day by any means necessary, she'll take on terrorists as well as a mad scientist aiming to destroy the world with his robot army.

> *Vol. 1.* 2004. 88pp. 1-905071-05-1.
> *Vol. 2.* 2005. 140pp. 1-905071-09-4.

Athena Inc. **Written by Brian Haberlin. Illustrated by Jay Anacleto.** Image Comics, 2002. 240pp. 1-58240-303-1. **O**

What if you were engineered to be the ultimate black ops agent, with no memory of your dark deeds? Mary was created by the organization Athena, Inc., to escape capture by switching personalities. For a while she was their best agent, but now that the genetic trigger to change personalities has eroded, she's become a dangerous threat to the organization and to herself as well.

Barnum! In Secret Service to the USA. **Written by Howard Chaykin and David Tischman. Illustrated by Niko Henrichon.** Vertigo/DC Comics, 2003. 128pp. 1-4012-0072-9. **T**

When the big-top promoter and entrepreneur P. T. Barnum saves the life of President Grover Cleveland, the showman becomes a secret agent for the United States to help foil a plot by the mad genius Nikola Tesla to conquer the United States. Accompanying Barnum is his Congress of Anomalies from his beloved circus, including a human fly, a sword-swallowing rubber man, and the Siamese twins Chang and Eng; they cover the continent to save the Union.

Beautiful Killer. **Written by Jimmy Palmiotti. Illustrated by Phil Noto.** Black Bull Entertainment, 2003. 80pp. 0-9672489-9-X. **T**

> Raised on a remote island by her former secret-agent parents, nineteen-year-old Brigit Cole is thrust into the world of espionage and double deals after her parents' enemies finally track them down. Trained by her parents as the ultimate weapon, she's a one-woman force out for revenge, taking on those who stole from her the most precious thing she ever had.

<u>**Danger Girl.**</u> **Written by Andy Hartnell and J. Scott Campbell. Illustrated by J. Scott Campbell.** Cliffhanger!/WildStorm Productions/DC Comics, 2002–2005. **O** ◉

© 2006 WildStorm Productions.

Who says that spying is only for dashing men like James Bond? Enter the Danger Girls, a sexy trio of lady super-spies guaranteed to break men's hearts and save the world at the same time. Join up with explorer Abbey Chase and her fellow Danger Girl team of Sydney Savage, Natalia Kassle, and Silicon Valerie as they fight the evil Hammer Empire, a neo-fascist regime with delusions of world conquest, with plenty of Indiana Jones-like treasure hunts, car chases, gun fights, kung-fu, and lighthearted humor. Led by the mysterious elder spy named "Deuce," there's nothing the ultra-secret spy group can't do.

> *The Ultimate Collection.* 2002. 256pp. 1-56389-549-8.
> *Absolute Danger Girl.* 2003. 326pp. 1-4012-0096-6.
> *Odd Jobs.* Illustrated by Joe Chiodo. 2005. 136pp. 1-4012-0108-3 **M**

F5. **Written and illustrated by Tony Daniel.** Dark Horse Comics, 2002. 128pp. 1-56971-760-5. **O**

> F5, a super-elite team of twelve operatives led by Penny Hurst, are out to stop a madman from unleashing a biological germ from another planet called the Saturn Germ that will have terrible global repercussions on Earth. One by one the agents are being eliminated, and it becomes all too clear that a traitor is in their midst. How can F5 save the world when one of their own agents is out to steal the Saturn Germ for his or her own dire purpose?

<u>**Full Metal Panic!**</u> **Written by Shouji Gatou. Illustrated by Retsu Tateo.** 2003–2005. **T Japanese manga.** あ

> Young secret agent Sosuke Sagara has been assigned to protect Kaname Chidori from international terrorists, and he's one of the best agents around, fully trained in all forms of combat. So why is a pretty, all-around successful, sixteen-year-old schoolgirl in need of a bodyguard? She's one of "the whispered," owner of a special power that men would die to take from her. Now with her life on the line, Sosuke is the best at what he does—but can a soldier survive the treacherous life of a high schooler? The manga was adapted from an original series of novels from Japan and was also turned into an anime series.

> *Vol. 1.* 2003. 168pp. 1-4139-0001-1.

Vol. 2. 2003. 200pp. 1-4139-0006-2.
Vol. 3. 2004. 178pp. 1-4139-0007-0.
Vol. 4. 2004. 160pp. 1-4139-0039-9.
Vol. 5. 2004. 168pp. 1-4139-0051-8.
Vol. 6. 2004. 172pp. 1-4139-0198-0.
Vol. 7. 2005. 172pp. 1-4139-0200-6.
Vol. 8. 2005. 184pp. 1-4139-0322-3.

Full Metal Panic: Overload! **Written and illustrated by Tomohiro Nagai.** 2005– . **T Japanese manga**

A retelling of the <u>Full Metal Panic</u> story with more emphasis on comedy and explosions. Secret agent Sosuke Sagara is out to protect Kaname from international terrorists. Too bad that his training didn't prepare him for the tortures of high school!

Vol. 1. 2005. 192pp. 1-4139-0315-0.
Vol. 2. 2005. 184pp. 1-4139-0326-6.
Vol. 3. 2005. 184pp. 1-4139-0331-2.
Vol. 4. 2006. 192pp. 1-4139-0340-1.

Global Frequency. **Written by Warren Ellis. Illustrated by Glenn Fabry and various.** Vertigo/DC Comics, 2004. **M**

© 2006 Warren Ellis.

A thousand and one secret operatives are hidden around the world, ready and on call for a catastrophe to strike. No matter whether the danger is from terrorists releasing deadly viruses, bomb threats, man-made black holes, deployed nuclear weapons, biofeedback terrorism, or even kidnappings, the Frequency will be there. With a phone call from Miranda Zero, the director of the Global Frequency, a specialist with expertise in the disaster at hand will tackle the mission . . . though sometimes operatives are picked out of sheer desperation to get the job done at all costs.

Vol. 1: Planet Ablaze. 2004. 144pp. 1-4012-0274-8.
Vol. 2: Detonation Radio. 2004. 144pp. 1-4012-0291-8.

Gunslinger Girl. **Written and illustrated by Yu Aida.** ADV Manga, 2003–2005. **O Japanese manga.** あ

The Social Welfare Agency is not what it seems—it's a place where injured and battered young girls are given a second chance at life . . . and are programmed to be lethal assassins. Henrietta is one such girl. Given a second chance at life, she's now a cyborg killer with the mind of a young girl. Assigned a handler named Giuseppe to whom she is devoted, will Henrietta be able to balance being a cold-blooded killer with her emotions? The manga was also adapted into an anime, which originally aired in Japan.

Vol. 1. 2003. 184pp. 1-43139-0020-8.
Vol. 2. 2005. 186pp. 1-4139-0233-2.
Vol. 3. 2005. 186pp. 1-4139-0274-X.

The Interman. **Written and illustrated by Jeff Parker.** Octopus Books, 2003. 128pp. 0-9725553-0-7. **T**

© 2006 Jeff Parker.

Van Meach is an adventurer like no other, and he's the most wanted man in the world! He's The Interman, the result of a top-secret experimental project started in the 1960s. Created by five NATO nations searching to help humanity survive nuclear fallout, Van was genetically created from birth to survive in the world's most harsh conditions. With his talents, he can learn any language, mimic other animals' traits, grow gills to breathe under water, and survive in extremes of temperature and weather. But the CIA wanted to use the project to create the perfect killer. Now in his early thirties, Van uses his talents for a fee. Someone wants him dead to close the Interman project files once and for all, and Van wants to know why he's suddenly become a target. While traveling around the world evading assassins, he's out to solve the mystery of how he came to be, whether he can really adapt to becoming a cold-blooded killer, and whether he is really the only Interman.

James Bond 007. **Adapted from the novels by Ian Fleming.** Titan Books, 2003–2004. **T**

James Bond—the suave secret agent 007 for British Intelligence with a license to kill—remains one of the most famous secret agents in modern fiction. Bond travels the globe and uses his wits, fighting skills, and high-tech gadgets to prevent criminal masterminds from taking over the world. Though his popularity is due in part to the hit movies, James Bond continues to be one of the best-known and beloved spy characters created in the twentieth century, and the success translates into graphic novel adaptations of Fleming's classic novels.

> *On Her Majesty's Secret Service.* Adapted by Henry Gammidge. Illustrated by John McLusky. 2003. 128pp. 1-84023-674-4.
> *The Man with the Golden Gun.* Adapted by Jim Lawrence Illustrated by Yaroslav Horak. 2004. 80pp.1-84023-690-6.
> *Octopussy.* Adapted by Jim Lawrence. Illustrated by Yaroslav Horak. 2004. 96pp. 1-84023-743-0.
> *James Bond 007: Goldfinger.* Adapted by Henry Gammidge. Illustrated by John McClusky. 2005. 130pp. 1-84023-908-5.
> *James Bond: Casino Royale.* Adapted by Henry Gammidge. Illustrated by John McClusky. 2005. 96pp. 1-84023-843-7.

Killer Princesses. **Written by Gail Simone. Illustrated by Lea Hernandez.** Oni Press, 2004. 104pp. 1-929998-31-7. **O Neo-manga.**

Faith, Hope, and Charity are three members of the Tri-Omega Sorority. To most of the boys, they're the most beautiful (but dim-witted) gals on campus, but those who get to know the real side of them know that they're the most dangerous (dim-witted) assassins in the world. Will they be able to save the world at night and still look good for class in the morning?

Lupin III. Written and illustrated by Monkey Punch (Katou Kazuhiko). TOKYOPOP, 2002–2004. **O Japanese manga.** あ

Master thief extraordinaire Lupin III is a man of many talents. Part spy, thief, and ladies' man, he's always knee-deep in trouble and two steps ahead of the game of any opponent, especially Interpol's Inspector Zenigata. Along with his companions, including Fujiko, Jigen, and Goemon, his humorous adventures have continued to be popular in Japan since 1967. The series was also adapted into a series of anime television episodes and films. The original fourteen-volume series from Japan was followed by the equally popular series <u>Lupin III—World's Most Wanted</u>, which ran for seventeen volumes in Japan and is currently being reprinted in North America.

<u>Lupin III (1st series)</u>. 2002–2004.
    Vol. 1. 2002. 176pp. 1-59182-252-1.
    Vol. 2. 2003. 200pp. 1-59182-104-5.
    Vol. 3. 2003. 192pp. 1-59182-121-5.
    Vol. 4. 2003. 200pp. 1-59182-122-3.
    Vol. 5. 2003. 192pp. 1-59182-123-1.
    Vol. 6. 2003. 192pp. 1-59182-124-X.
    Vol. 7. 2003. 184pp. 1-59182-125-8.
    Vol. 8. 2003. 192pp. 1-59182-126-6.
    Vol. 9. 2003. 168pp. 1-59182-127-4.
    Vol. 10. 2003. 176pp. 1-59182-128-2.
    Vol. 11. 2004. 176pp. 1-59182-489-3.
    Vol. 12. 2004. 176pp. 1-59182-490-7.
    Vol. 13. 2004. 176pp. 1-59182-491-5.
    Vol. 14. 2004. 208pp. 1-59182-492-3.
<u>Lupin III—Worlds Most Wanted</u>. 2004– .
    Vol. 1. 2004. 240pp. 1-59532-070-9.
    Vol. 2. 2004. 184pp. 1-59532-071-7.
    Vol. 3. 2005. 240pp. 1-59532-072-5.
    Vol. 4. 2005. 240pp. 1-59532-073-3.
    Vol. 5. 2005. 232pp. 1-59532-074-1.
    Vol. 6. 2006. 192pp. 1-59532-075-X.
    Vol. 7. 2006. 192pp. 1-59532-076-8.

Metal Gear Solid. Written by Kris Oprisko. Illustrated by Ashley Wood. IDW Publishing, 2005. **M**

© 2006 IDW Publishing.

When the threat of global destruction is near, there's only one soldier, a retired agent known as Solid Snake, who can save the world from annihilation. At his side against the former wetworks agents known as the FOXHOUND, Solid Snake has his team of agents, including Ninja, Master Miller, Octagon, and Meryl, to take down the enemy using infiltration, espionage, and counterterrorism to save the day from the villainous Liquid Snake and his band of genetically enhanced terrorists. Based on the extremely popular video game series created by Konami.

    Vol. 1. 2005. 152pp. 1-932382-81-X.
    Vol. 2. 2005. 144pp. 1-933239-30-1.
    Sons of Liberty, Vol. 1. 2006. 148pp. 1-933239-78-6.
    The Complete Metal Gear Solid. 2006. 288pp. 1-600100-31-7, hardcover.

Musashi #9. **Written and illustrated by Takahashi Miyuki.** CMX/DC Comics, 2005– . **T Japanese manga.**

When the world is in danger and there's a job too tough for any man, send a woman to do it. Sixteen-year-old field operative Number Nine is an agent for the secret Universal Blue organization, a group set up to be the last line of defense against the hordes of terrorists and criminals around the world. An enigmatic and cool individual, when Number Nine arrives on the scene, the bad guys don't stand a chance. The series was originally published in fifteen volumes in Japan.

> *Vol. 1.* 2005. 208pp. 1-4012-0540-2.
> *Vol. 2.* 2005. 192pp. 1-4012-0541-0.
> *Vol. 3.* 2005. 192pp. 1-4012-0542-9.
> *Vol. 4.* 2005. 208pp. 1-4012-0543-7.
> *Vol. 5.* 2005. 192pp. 1-4012-0544-5.
> *Vol. 6.* 2006. 192pp. 1-4012-0857-6.
> *Vol. 7.* 2006. 192pp. 1-4012-0858-4.
> *Vol. 8.* 2006. 192pp. 1-4012-0859-2.
> *Vol. 9.* 2006. 192pp. 1-4012-0860-6.

Najica Blitz Tactics. **Written by Sakura Kinoshita. Illustrated by Kazuko Higashiyama.** ADV Manga, 2004. **O Japanese manga.** あ

By day CRI Cosmetics is known worldwide as a leading perfume company, and the beautiful Najica is one of the most famous jet-setting perfumers for the company. By night the company is a front for a secret intelligence agency, and Najica is their leading operative. With guns blazing and the latest technology at her disposal, there's nothing Najica can't handle as she fights against terrorists and other bad guys. Together, she and her android "Humaritt" partner named Lila are out to take down the original creator of the Humaritts and safely retrieve as many Humaritts as they can before they're destroyed. The manga is adapted from the hit twelve-episode anime series, which originally aired in Japan in 2001.

> *Vol. 1.* 2004. 200pp. 1-4139-0018-6.
> *Vol. 2.* 2004. 192pp. 1-4139-0042-9.
> *Vol. 3.* 2004. 200pp. 1-4139-0140-9.

Nick Fury, Agent of S.H.I.E.L.D. **Written by Jim Steranko and Roy Thomas. Illustrated by Jim Steranko**. Marvel Comics, 2001. 248pp. 0-785107479. **T**

Originally published in the Marvel 1960s title *Strange Tales,* Nick Fury, the one-eyed cigar-chomping former super-soldier from World War II, is now an agent for the Supreme Headquarters, International Espionage, Law-Enforcement Division (S.H.I.E.L.D), the United States' premiere department of espionage. In their floating Helicarrier in the sky, they're constantly thwarting the terrorist organizations of HYDRA and A.I.M. and playing the spy game one bullet at a time.

Queen and Country. Written by Greg Rucka. Illustrated by Steve Leiber and various. Oni Press, 2002– . O ◎

There's a top-secret organization in the United Kingdom dedicated to handling worldwide espionage in the name of the queen. Lead agent/operative Tara Chace is the best sharpshooter in the agency, and she and her crew are the best offense defending England. Every action has a consequence, and for every hit they perform, another more dire circumstance can rise in its place and cost them their very lives. The series won an Eisner Award in 2002 for Best New Series.

Vol. 1: Operation: Broken Ground. 2002. 128pp. 1-929998-21-X.
Vol. 2: Operation: Morningstar. 2003. 88pp. 1-929998-35-X.
Vol. 3: Operation: Crystal Ball. 2003. 152pp. 1-929998-49-X.
Vol. 4: Operation: Blackwall. 2003. 88pp. 1-929998-68-6.
Vol. 5: Operation: Stormfront. 2004. 168pp. 1-929998-84-8.
Vol. 6: Operation: Dandelion. 2004. 128pp. 1-929998-97-X.
Vol. 7: Operation: Saddlebag. 2005. 144pp. 1-932664-14-9.
Declassified, Vol. 1. 2003. 88pp. 1-929998-58-9.
Declassified, Vol. 2. 2006. 96pp. 1-932664-28-9.
Declassified, Vol. 3. 2006. 96pp. 1-932664-35-1.

R.O.D: Read or Die. Written by Hideyuki Kurata. Illustrated by Shutaro Yamada. VIZ Media, LLC. 2006. **O Japanese manga.** あ

R.O.D -READ OR DIE- © 2000 by Hideyuki Kurata (Studio Orphee) Aniplex, Shutaro Yamada/ SHUEISHA Inc.

Yomiko Readman is not your average bookworm. She has the unique ability to manipulate paper into whatever shape she desires, from a super-sharp dagger to a super-dense shield. The only limit to Yomiko's powers is her imagination. An agent for the British Empire's Special Operations Division, Yomiko (a.k.a. "The Paper") and the other specially gifted agents, including Miss Deep, are on the lookout for rare books that are to be rescued by the agency before any criminal organizations can get their hands on them. Can Yomiko save the world from evil and still find the time to curl up with a good book? The four-volume manga series is based on the novels originally published in Japan, which has also spawned an anime series.

Vol. 1: Mr. Woo's Woes. 2006. 232pp. 1-4215-0248-8.
Vol. 2: Ancient Chinese Secrets. 2006. 208pp. 1-4215-0257-7.
Vol. 3. Reading Can Be Deadly. 2006. 208pp. 1-4215-0508-8.
Vol. 4. 2006. 208pp. 1-4215-0509-6.

Silke. **Written and illustrated by Tony Daniel.** Dark Horse Comics, 2002. 96pp. 1-56971-667-6. **O**

The secret Ministry of Genetics was out to create the perfect spy, and they succeeded with the creation of Sandra Silke. They manipulated her genetic structure to make her the perfect weapon: someone who can change her appearance into anything. After the government shuts down the organization, all evidence of the project is to be terminated —including Silke—but she's not going down without a fight.

Sleeper. **Written by Ed Brubaker. Illustrated by Sean Phillips.** WildStorm Productions/ DC Comics, 2003–2004. **M**

Holden Carver is a double agent working for the vicious, superpowered criminal organization called Tao. Tired of the escalating body count, Holden longs to cut his ties, but the only man who can acquit him is in a coma. What can Holden do to escape the game when it becomes harder and harder to differentiate the good guys from the bad guys?

> *Vol. 1: Out in the Cold.* 2003. 160pp. 1-4012-0115-6.
> *Vol. 2: All False Moves.* 2004. 144pp. 1-4012-0288-8.

🗡 <u>**SpyBoy.**</u> **Written by Peter David. Illustrated by Pop Mhan.** Dark Horse Comics, 2001–2005. **T**

What if in the blink of an eye you could have martial arts skills and cool gadgets to save the world, like the super-spies in the books and movies? For teenager Alex Fleming, this life isn't fiction. With the flick of a switch he can go from humdrum homework to being an international super-spy. Joined by other teammates including the beautiful spy Bombshell, Spygirl, and his super-spy family, Alex has his hands full, thwarting the evil schemes of super-villains out to conquer the world and still finding the time to go out on a date. The series also featured a team-up with the super-hero team called

SpyBoy™ & © 2006
Dark Horse Comics, Inc.

Young Justice—led by Robin, the sidekick to Batman. *The Deadly Gourmet Affair* received recognition from YALSA's Quick Picks for Reluctant Readers committee in 2002.

> *Vol. 1: The Deadly Gourmet Affair.* 2001. 80pp. 1-56971-463-0.
> *Vol. 2: Trial and Terror.* 2001. 80pp. 1-56971-501-7.
> *Vol. 3: Bet Your Life.* 2001. 80pp. 1-56971-617-X.
> *Vol. 4: Undercover, Underwear!* 2002. 88pp. 1-56971-664-1.
> *Vol. 5: Spy-School Confidential.* 2003. 96pp. 1-56971-834-2.
> *Vol. 6: The M.A.N.G.A. Affair.* 2003. 80pp. 1-56971-984-5.
> *Vol. 7: Final Exam.* 2005. 96pp. 1-59307-017-9.
> *SpyBoy/Young Justice: Young Spies Like Us.* Published with DC Comics, 2003. 80pp. 1-56971-850-4.

Striker. **Written by Hiroshi Takashige. Illustrated by Ryoji Minagawa.** VIZ Media, LLC, 1998–1999. **T Japanese manga.**

Yu Ominae isn't your typical Japanese high school student. Code-named Striker, he's a one-man army for the Arcam Foundation, a secret organization of the Japanese government that's out to prevent dangerous artifacts and technology, including a resurrected ancient "Berserker" warrior, the recipe for eternal life, and other sources of power, from falling into the wrong hands. Outfitted with a special combat suit that magnifies his strength thirty-fold, Yu Ominae is an unstoppable fighting force guaranteed to save the day no matter what the cost, and he still makes time for his high school track team.

> *Vol. 1: The Armored Warrior.* 1998. 248pp. 1-56931-286-9.
> *Vol. 2: The Forest of No Return.* 1998. 208pp. 1-56931-290-7.

Vol. 3: Striker vs. the Third Reich. 1999. 160pp. 1-56931-353-9.

24. Written by J. C. Vaughn and Mark L. Haynes. Illustrated by Renato Guedes. IDW Publishing, 2005. 152pp. 1-932382-71-2. **O** ⌨

> Based on the hit Fox Network television show of the same name. The stories tell the continuing adventures of federal agent Jack Bauer and his colleagues of the Counter Terrorist Unit (CTU) in Los Angeles. The collection features three short stories as federal agent Jack Bauer and CTU take on Chechen separatists, drug dealers, and plots destined to destroy freedom, featuring the same fast-paced, urgent plotting that has made the television series so popular.

***21 Down: The Conduit.* Written by Justin Gray and Jimmy Palmiotti. Illustrated by Jesus Saiz.** WildStorm Productions/DC Comics, 2003. 176pp. 1-4012-0120-2. **M**

> Preston Kills is a twenty-year-old tattoo artist from Coney Island with an unusual gift: when he was thirteen he was granted a power by a mysterious figure called Herod to see the last few moments before and after a person's death. Other teenagers recently have also had this power bestowed on them by Herod, and they have not lived past their twenty-first birthdays. Meanwhile, an attractive FBI Agent named Mickey Rinaldi is on the trail of those with the "gift" of Herod. Together with Preston they try to solve the mystery of Herod and to stop the murder of innocents.

Westerns

The American cowboy has been a major entertainment figure ever since nineteenth-century pulp magazines first dramatized the untamed setting of the Old West. Tales featuring rugged cowboys roaming a wild landscape and settling their differences with fists and guns were instantly popular with readers. Tales of good and evil, in which the good guys wore white hats and the bad guys wore black, were in such demand that their popularity continued into other media, including films, television, and comic books. Western comic books were in their heyday from the late 1930s through the mid-1960s, with tie-ins to popular television shows and musicians, including the Lone Ranger, Roy Rogers, Gene Autry, the Durango Kid, and many others. Today publishers occasionally revisit the genre, but not with the frequency or zest of earlier days. Some of the most recent Westerns are about old once-popular DC Comics (Jonah Hex) and Marvel Comics characters (Blaze of Glory/Apache Skies/Rawhide Kid), and the genre-crossing horror/Western series called Desperadoes by WildStorm Productions and IDW Publishing. Note that several of the titles, including Blazin' Barrels and Daisy Kutter, combine elements of science fiction to make them futuristic Western stories, while titles such as Desperadoes, No Man's Land, and Wicked West blend the horror genre with tales set in the Old West.

Blaze of Glory/Apache Skies. Written by John Ostrander. Illustrated by Leonardo Marco. Marvel Comics, 2002–2003. **O**

> The original Marvel heroes of the Wild West—the Rawhide Kid, Kid Colt, the Ghost Rider, Gunhawk, Red Wolf, and the Two-Gun Kid—fought their last battle together in the summer of 1885. Some heroes lived and some died, but they went out in a blaze of glory. The story is continued in *Apache Skies,* in which Johnny Bart, the Rawhide Kid,

seeks to avenge the cowardly murder of the Apache Kid and make the murderers pay. But someone else is after the murderers . . . someone with the right to the mantle of the Apache Kid.

> *Blaze of Glory: The Last Ride of the Western Heroes.* 2002. 96pp. 0-7851-0906-4.
> *Apache Skies.* 2003. 112pp. 0-7851-1086-0.

© 2006 Marvel Comics.

Blazin' Barrels. **Written and illustrated by Min-Seo Park.** TOKYOPOP, 2005– . **Y Korean manhwa.**

In a futuristic Old West, a fumbling and awkward man named Sting wants nothing more than to be a bounty hunter. Already a deadly fighter, he's on the verge of becoming something great. When he rescues Chuck Black, a professional bounty hunter, he's found a friend and a mentor who can show him the way to reach his dreams. As they take on more and more jobs, Sting is out to prove to everyone that he's the best bounty hunter the Old West has ever seen. The series was published in eighteen volumes in Korea.

> *Vol. 1.* 2005. 176pp. 1-59532-558-1.
> *Vol. 2.* 2005. 196pp. 1-59532-559-X.
> *Vol. 3.* 2005. 192pp. 1-59532-560-3.
> *Vol. 4.* 2006. 192pp. 1-59532-561-1.
> *Vol. 5.* 2006. 192pp. 1-59532-562-X.

The Blueberry Saga: Confederate Gold. **Written by Jean-Michel Charlier. Illustrated by Jean "Moebius" Giraud.** Mojo Press, 1996. 288pp. 1-885418-08-6. **T**

An enigmatic soldier of fortune in the rough-and-tough American West, Lieutenant Mike S. Blueberry of the U.S. Calvary is assigned to locate hidden Confederate gold in the Old West. After being falsely accused of the stealing the gold, he's sent to a penitentiary, but no prison could hold Blueberry for long. After escaping from jail and now on the run, he's once again falsely accused—this time of attempting to assassinate President Grant. Now Blueberry's out to clear his wronged name. One step ahead of the game, with his six-shooter in hand, he's kindhearted and coolheaded and out to make a name for himself on the plains of the Old West.

Bouncer: Raising Cain. **Written by Alexandro Jodorowsky. Illustrated by François Boucq.** Humanoids/DC Comics, 2005. 128pp. 1-4012-0388-4. **M**

Welcome to Jurytown, a place where at the Inferno Bar it's kill or be killed, the one-armed Bouncer at the bar is the fastest gun in the West, and it's not a place for a kid. When his fifteen-year-old nephew arrives in town seeking revenge against a one-eyed man who killed his mother, father, and dog, the Bouncer finds himself on the same path of violence that has plagued the family for several generations, against a most vicious enemy: his own brother.

***Comanche Moon.* Written by Jack Jackson. Illustrated by T. R. Fehrenbach.** Reed Press, 2004. 128pp. 1-59429-003-2. **T**

Three vignettes abour the birth, life, and slow dissolution of the warrior-chief Quanah of the Comanche. Born of Cynthia Ann Parker, a white woman taken into the Comanche tribe when she was very young, he becomes warrior-chief, but the Texas military force defeats his tribe. As the conquest of his people destroys the spirit of a once-proud race, he succumbs to his own failure as a leader to prevent the western expansion. A reprint of the classic 1979 graphic novel.

***The Kents.* Written by John Ostrander. Illustrated by Tim Truman and Tom Mandrake.** DC Comics, 1999. 272pp. 1-56389-513-7. **T**

Before there was a Superman, there were other famous Kents other than Clark. This is the story of Silas Kent and his sons, Nathaniel and Jebediah, who lived the American adventure. After settling in Lawrence, Kansas, the Kents help to fan the flames of the Abolitionist movement, are affected by the eruption of the Civil War, and in the later 1800s, deal with the chaos and danger of the legendary Wild West.

***The Long Haul.* Written by Anthony Johnson. Illustrated by Eduardo Barreto.** Oni Press, 2004. 176pp. 1-932664-05-X. **T**

In the year 1871, Cody Plummer has been trying to lie low after serving time in prison. When he gets wind that there's a train headed west carrying $1.9 million, old habits die hard, and he soon is planning the heist of his life. As an added bonus, the same agent who brought him in is the head of security on the train, and Cody would like nothing better than to even the score. With a team of aging-but-skilled professionals at Cody's side, the crime of the century is underfoot.

© 2006 Anthony Johnson
and Eduardo Barreto.

***Rawhide Kid: Slap Leather.* Written by Ron Zimmerman. Illustrated by John Severin.** MAX/Marvel Comics, 2002. 120pp. 0-7851-1069-0. **M**

A humorous reimagining of the classic Marvel hero Johnny Bart, a.k.a. the Rawhide Kid, as a flamboyant gay gunfighter. When the town of Wells Junction is being overrun by a group of thugs with nothing but debauchery and drinking on their minds, the Rawhide Kid steps in to save the day. He's a hero in the eyes of the boys, a dreamboat to the women, and a creampuff in the eyes of the men, who snicker at his brightly colored outfit. As those who make fun of him soon realize, sexual preference has nothing to do with how you can handle a six-shooter, and the Rawhide Kid shows why he's one of the fastest guns in the West.

Showcase Presents: Jonah Hex, Vol. 1. **Written by John Albano and Michael Fleischer. Illustrated by Tony DeZuniga, Doug Wildey, José Luís García-López and various.** DC Comics, 2005. 528pp. 1-4012-0760-X. **T**

> A reprinting of the classic Western tales of the scarred bounty hunter called Jonah Hex. During a tough upbringing in the Old West, where his own father sold him into slavery at the age of thirteen to an Apache chief, Hex eventually learned to ride horses, shoot a gun, and become the best hunter of the tribe. Jonah joined the Confederate army and on his return after the war to his tribe, he was given a terrible brand on the right side of his face to represent the "Mark of the Demon" after killing the chief's son in combat. Now, years later, Jonah has used what he's learned from his harsh upbringing to become the best bounty hunter in the West.

 2

Spaghetti Western. **Written and illustrated by Scott Morse.** Oni Press, 2004. 136pp. 1-929998-91-0. **O**

> "Horses? Check. Authentic cowboy hats? Check. Ponchos? Check. Boots with spurs? Check? Vintage six-shooters? Check. Time to rob a bank!" Missing the days of long ago, when men were no-nonsense and cowboys roamed the romantic West in the classic cowboy films of John Wayne and Clint Eastwood, two men decide to live the life of the Old Western cowboys. Riding into town dressed like cowboys and carrying authentic six-shooters, they ride up to the local bank and rob it old-school style. A tribute to the cowboy stories of old, with a modern twist.

© 2006 Scott Morse.

Western Genreblends

These tales of the Old West have a twist. Some of the most popular takes on Westerns involve blending other genres with the common themes found in Western tales. Two of the most popular blended genres of Westerns are Western horror and science fiction Westerns.

Western Horror

Stories of the Old West with a horror slant. The hero, typically a mysterious cowboy, comes to a town that has been overrun by an evil presence, and only a six-shooter can take care of the horrific menace. Readers who enjoy this subgenre may also enjoy titles listed in chapter 6.

Desperadoes. Written by Jeff Mariotte. Image Comics, 1998; WildStorm Productions/ DC Comics, 1999–2002; IDW Publishing, 2005–present. **T** ◉

> Welcome to the American West of the late 1800s, where the supernatural mingles with the everyday, powerful magical forces roam the plains, and a six-shooter can keep the monsters at bay. Meet Gideon Brood, Jerome Alexander Betts, Abby DeGrazia, and Race Kennedy, outlaws on the run with a penchant for taking on whatever supernatural force they encounter. From

zombies, to ancient evils buried under churches, to murderers who feed off the energy of the dead, the close-knit band of desperadoes will do whatever it takes to banish evil and clear their names.

> *A Moment's Sunlight.* Illustrated by John Cassiday. 1998. 144pp. 1-58240-013-X.
> *Epidemic!* Illustrated by John Cassiday. 1999. 48pp. 1-56389-554-4.
> *Quiet of the Grave.* Illustrated by John Severin. 2002. 128pp. 1-4012-0018-4.
> *Banners of Gold.* Illustrated by Jeremy Haun. 2005. 120pp. 1-932382-96-8.

No Man's Land. Written by Jason DeAngelis. Illustrated by Jennyson Rosero. Seven Seas Entertainment, 2005– . O ◎ **Japanese manga.**

© 2004 Seven Seas Entertainment LLC and Jason DeAngelis.

John Parker seemed to have it all—a decorated sharpshooter in the Civil War, he had a beautiful wife and an infant son, but they were taken from him in a demonic conspiracy created by the Bakerton Detective Agency, and he's lost everything. Now John wanders the Old West as a rogue demon-killing gun-for-hire called "No Man." Killing demons is his only solace as he takes on the demonkind that he accidentally set free, with his modified sixteen-inch Buntine Special in hand, and tries to right the wrongs of his past or at least escape them. Publisher synopsis: "John Parker had it all. A decorated sharpshooter in the Civil War, he had a promising career ahead of him, a beautiful wife, and a newborn son. But after becoming embroiled in a dark and demonic conspiracy engineered by the Bakerton Detective Agency, he lost everything. Fleeing to the West, a broken man, Parker reinvents himself as "No Man," a heartless gun-for-hire whose only solace comes from hunting and killing the demons who he helped set loose. With Buntline Special in hand, a deadly revolver with a sixteen inch barrel, he blasts his way through a different kind of Old West, where strange and evil beings lurk."

> *Vol. 1.* 2005. 192pp. 1-933164-03-4.
> *Vol. 2.* 2005. 192pp. 1-933164-07-7.

Wicked West. **Written by Todd Livingston and Robert Tinnell. Illustrated by Neil Vokes.** Image Comics, 2004. 96pp. 1-58240-414-3. **T** ◎

All gunfighter Cotton Coleridge wanted was a peaceful place to lie low for a while. But after taking a job as a schoolteacher in the frontier town of Javer's Tanks in Texas, he discovers that an ancient evil has been released and the bodies of the innocent are starting to pile up, drained of their blood. The local residents blame the deaths on Coleridge, but when the dead come back to life, they realize that they have a much bigger problem. Six-shooters don't work too well on vampires.

Science Fiction Western

These tales of the Old West are planted firmly in the far future, where robots, spaceships, and aliens are commonplace among the cowboys. Readers of this subgenre may enjoy titles listed in chapter 3.

🐾 *Daisy Kutter: The Last Train.* **Written and illustrated by Kazu Kibuishi.** Viper Comics, 2005. 192pp. 0-9754193-2-3. **T** ◎

© 2006 Kazu Kibuishi.

In a futuristic Old West where bandits, robots, and bounty hunters roam the land, Daisy Kutter, ex-bandit extraordinaire of the town of Middleton, has been plagued by boredom. A former gunfighter, she's put away her six-shooters for a legitimate lifestyle and a lonely, dead-end job at a general store. When she loses her store in a game of cards, she's offered one last chance to win back her money and her pride—all she has to do is rob her very last train. Are the cards in her favor this time—or has Daisy's luck just run out? YALSA's Best Books for Young Adults list recognized the story in 2006.

Et Cetera. Written and illustrated by Tow Nakazaki. TOKYOPOP, 2004–2007. **Y Japanese manga.**

Dim-witted Mingchao is a young Chinese orphan dead-set on becoming a legendary Hollywood actress who will cross the plains of the Wild West on her quest to find fame and fortune in California. Luckily for her, she has the powerful Eto Gun, a legendary weapon that her grandfather once owned that can absorb the spirits of the Zodiac animals to fire special bullets of immense power. With her on the trip is a priest named Baskerville, a man of peace who has secret intentions for the Eto Gun. Will Mingchao make it big in Hollywood, and will she get there before someone nefarious steals the rare weapon?

> *Vol. 1.* 2004. 224pp. 1-59532-130-6.
> *Vol. 2.* 2004. 208pp. 1-59532-131-4.
> *Vol. 3.* 2004. 208pp. 1-59532-132-2.
> *Vol. 4.* 2005. 200pp. 1-59532-133-0.
> *Vol. 5.* 2005. 208pp. 1-59532-134-9.
> *Vol. 6.* 2005. 192pp. 1-59532-135-7.
> *Vol. 7.* 2006. 192pp. 1-59532-136-5.
> *Vol. 8.* 2006. 192pp. 1-59532-137-3.
> *Vol. 9.* 2007. 192pp. 1-59532-138-1.

Iron West. **Written and illustrated by Doug TenNapel.** Image Comics, 2006. 160pp. 1-58240-630-8. **T**

© 2006 Doug TenNapel.

Outlaw Preston Struck was never one to call himself a hero. Whenever danger reared its ugly head, Struck bravely turned his heel and fled. But when a mysterious army of metal men set out to destroy central California, he reluctantly rises to the cause and is deputized. Struck will need all the help he can get from a crusty old shaman, Sasquatch, and even the Loch Ness Monster, to save the town of Twain Harte from the massing army of metal men and a train transformed into a giant iron monster.

2

Chapter 3

Science Fiction

Ever since the days of such classic prose authors such as Mary Shelley and Jules Verne, Ray Bradbury and Robert Heinlein, readers have long been interested in speculative fiction tales. With the release of the comic strip adventures of Buck Rogers in 1929, the comic book format soon proved to be an excellent vehicle for this genre. For the first time a science fiction story could be told visually, and the only limit was the writer's and illustrator's imagination. Since that time, comic books—and later graphic novels—have been a popular format for telling speculative fiction. Stories ranging from humanity's future on this planet, space exploration, and contacts with alien life, to concepts including mind control and telepathy, space operas, robots, science fiction action, and even the funny side of science fiction, have all appeared in comic books for decades. Featured here are some of the most recent popular science fiction tales for all ages including the subjects mentioned above as well as the equally popular variety of media tie-ins such as the <u>Star Wars</u> films and toy properties such as the *Transformers*. Note that titles that are a mix of humor and science fiction are listed in chapter 8.

Space Opera/Space Fantasy

Space opera/fantasy cience fiction stories feature epic adventure, romance, action, space battles, and grand interstellar conflicts. The central characters' relationships with each other, and a conflict that the protagonists must face, are more central to the plot than scientific accuracy. The subgenre is a blending of s the science fiction and fantasy genres. Science fiction tales, including starships, strange new worlds, and space exploration, can easily be found alongside themes common in fantasy tales, such as wizards, heroes, dragons, quests, and other fantastic elements. This unique vision of a fantastic future or of a technological long ago readily appeals to many for its unique ability to combine the best of both genres. The <u>Star Wars</u> movies and Frank Herbert's classic <u>Dune</u> series of novels are some of the best examples of the space opera/space fantasy subgenre.

<u>A Distant Soil.</u> Written and illustrated by Colleen Doran. Image Comics, 1997– . **T** ◎

© 2006 Colleen Doran.

Teenage siblings Jason and Liana have always known they were special even without their parents in their lives. After escaping from an unusual orphanage that forced experiments on the teens to tap into their growing psionic powers, they find out that they're not quite human. Their father was a humanoid alien named Aeren, a fugitive from the planet Ovanan, which is the center of the grand Ovanan Empire and home planet to almost immortal psionic beings of great greed and malice. Jason and Liana also have powers that have been passed down from Ovanan history: Jason is a Disrupter—he can short-circuit machinery as well as living beings. Liana is an Avatar—one who can siphon all of the Ovanan race's psionic energy into a deadly weapon. Only one Avatar can live at a time, and the Ovanan Empire is out to eliminate Liana after her power is revealed. A large cast of colorful characters help Liana and Jason in their quest to topple the Ovanan Hierarchy, including the D'Mer and Rieken, emissaries from the Ovan resistance movement, and companions; Sergeant Tony Minetti, an Earth police officer; teenage tough-guy Brent Donewitz; Bast, a beautiful and seductive shape-shifting Ovanan exiled on Earth; and Galahad, a temporally displaced knight of the fabled Round Table from the mystic realm of Avalon. But as they reach their destination, will they be ready to take on the Hierarchy and bring freedom to the galaxy, when the odds definitely are not in their favor and there's already dissention in the rebellion's ranks?

> *Vol. 1: The Gathering.* 1997. 240pp. 1-887279-51-2.
> *Vol. 2: The Ascendant.* 1998. 240pp. 1-58240-018-0.
> *Vol. 3: The Aria.* 2001. 164pp. 1-58240-201-9.
> *Vol. 4: Coda.* 2006. 164pp. 1-58240-525-5.

Galaxion: Volume One. **Written and illustrated by Tara Tallan.** Helikon Comics, 1998. 158pp. 0-9684228-0-2. **T**

The starship Galaxion is only the third ship to attempt the experimental jump to hyperspace. Following their successful jump, the crew discover that Earth has mysteriously become a seemingly uninhabited planet. The captain and crew, all lovingly portrayed by the series creator, begin to sort out the mystery of the desolate planet and the sudden reappearance of a long-lost sister starship. A second volume has yet to be released.

Masamune Shirow's Orion. **3d ed. Written and illustrated by Masamune Shirow.** Dark Horse Comics, 2001, 272pp. 1-56971-572-6 **O Japanese manga.**

In a future where science and magic walk hand-in-hand and space travel is assisted by the powers of the mind and psycho-science, the bloated and corrupt Yamata People's Empire rules the land. The powerful empire has decided to destroy all the negative karma in the world, but Master Fuzen, the leader of a rogue clan of spellmasters, has foreseen that the spell will fail and will destroy the world instead. Now Seska, a dim-witted and sarcastic daughter of Master Fuzen, has merged with a spell to cleanse the world of delusions of grandeur and power, and it's going to take the help of the tough but hilarious Susano, the God of Darkness, to stop the bloated Nine-Headed Naga from consuming Earth.

The Metabarons. Written by Alexandro Jodorowsky. Illustrated by Juan Gimenez. Humanoids Publishing/DC Comics, 2002– . **M**

In a universe where greed, corruption, and terror rule the day, there exist ruthless warriors called the Metabarons, a clan that values blood, self-sacrifice, cybernetic implants, and defeating one's own father in battle to secure a right of title as a Metabaron. An epic story line spanning generations of the Metabarons as they battle against each other for supremacy and the right of title, might, and power.

> *Vol. 1: Othon & Honorata.* 2004. 136pp. 1-4012-0362-0.
>
> *Vol. 2: Aghnar & Oda.* 2004. 136pp. 1-4012-0381-7.
>
> *Vol. 3: Steelhead & Dona Vicenta.* 2005. 136pp. 1-4012-0642-5.

Alpha/Omega. Illustrated by Travis Charest. 2002. 48pp. 1-930652-41-0.

Outlanders. Written and illustrated by Johji Manabe. Dark Horse Comics, 1989–2000. **O Japanese manga.**

They say that love conquers all, but the love between Tetsuya Wakatsuki, a Tokyo news photographer from Earth, and the alien Princess Kahm will tear apart the galaxy. When Princess Kahm's father, the Emperor Quevas of the Santovasku Empire, hears from his daughter of her forbidden love with an Earthling, tensions break out between the planets, and war is only threads away. Can the princess betray her own people in the name of love even if it costs her her beloved homeworld, the Santovasku Empire?

> *Vol. 1.* 1989 148pp. 1-56971-161-5.
>
> *Vol. 2.* 1990. 184pp. 1-56971-162-3.
>
> *Vol. 3.* 1994. 168pp. 1-56971-163-1.
>
> *Vol. 4.* 1995. 168pp. 1-56971-069-4.
>
> *Vol. 5.* 1998. 216pp. 1-56971-275-1.
>
> *Vol. 6.* 1999. 200pp. 1-56971-423-1.
>
> *Vol. 7.* 1999. 184pp. 1-56971-424-X.
>
> *Vol. 8.* 2000. 176pp. 1-56971-425-8.

Phoenix. Written and illustrated by Osamu Tezuka. VIZ Media, LLC, 2002– . **O Japanese manga.**

From the legendary manga creator Osamu Tezuka comes an epic tale planned to span twelve volumes that was started in 1954 and was never completed; Tezuka died in 1989. Phoenix is a moral parable spanning centuries, dipping far into the future and then into the past and back again in an exploration of humanity's quest for immortality, the struggles and strengths of faith, the ridiculousness of war, and the enduring hope for humanity. At the time of this printing, the remaining volumes have yet to be reprinted.

> *Vol. 1: Dawn.* 2002. 200pp. 1-59116-608-X.
>
> *Vol. 2: A Tale of the Future.* 2002. 200pp. 1-59116-026-X.
>
> *Vol. 3: Yamato/Space.* 2003. 336pp. 1-59116-100-2.

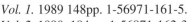

> *Vol. 4: Karma.* 2004. 368pp. 1-59116-300-5.
> *Vol. 5: Resurrection.* 2004. 200pp. 1-59116-593-8.
> *Vol. 6.* 2006. 208pp. 1-4215-0258-5.
> *Vol. 7.* 2006. 208pp. 1-4215-0517-7.
> *Vol. 8.* 2006. 208pp. 1-4215-0518-5.

The Red Star. Written by Christian Gossett and Bradley Kayl. Illustrated by Christian Gossett and Team Red Star. Archangel Studios, 2001– . **T**

An epic science fiction and sorcery story set in an alternate earth version of the Soviet Union and Afghanistan conflict. Struggling to free their country of the legacy of the insane wizard Imbohl, the heroes of the Red Star continue on after their personal losses and the deaths of millions of their countrymen. Little do they know that there is something more in play here, and the ghosts of the living still participate in a grand battle for the soul of a nation. A complex and awe-inspiring look at a future world where technology and magic go hand-in-hand and the horrors of war are ever-present. The books also include URL links to more background information on the company's Web site.

> *Vol. 1: The Battle of Kar Dathra's Gate.* Image Comics, 2001. 144pp. 1-58240-197-7.
> *Vol. 2: Nokgorka.* Archangel Studios, LLC 2002. 172pp. 0-9714714-1-X.
> *Vol. 3: Prison of Souls.* Archangel Studios, LLC 2004. 142pp. 0-9714714-3-6.
> *The Red Star Collected Edition.* Archangel Studios, LLC 2003. 312pp. 0-9714714-2-8.

***Saga of the Seven Suns: Veiled Alliances.* Written by Kevin J. Anderson. Illustrated by Robert Teranishi.** WildStorm Productions/DC Comics, 2004. 96pp. 1-56389-901-9. **T**

A prequel to the events seen in novelist Kevin J. Anderson's continuing prose series. Eleven starships from Earth left the planet generations ago and have encountered the space-faring Ildaran Empire. Now joined with the new race, who have shared with them the secrets of Faster Than Light travel, the children of the original voyagers have been granted permission to populate uninhabited worlds within the Empire. Meanwhile, ambassadors of the Ildaran Empire are sent to Earth to make first contact.

Seikai Trilogy. Adapted by Aya Yoshinaga, Based on the works of Hiroyuki Morioka. Illustrated by Toshihiro Ono and Wasoh Miyakoshi. TOKYOPOP, 2004. **T Japanese manga.** あ

Love and understanding set behind the backdrop of a galactic war. The Abh, a space-faring race of long-living, elf-like aliens, have conquered the galaxy with little bloodshed and have formed the Humankind Empire Abh. But there are those who are resisting the Abh, and a coalition of the United Mankind Triple Alliance are determined to prevent any more planets from falling into Abh hands. Meanwhile, Jinto Lin has long been saddened and disgraced by his father's cowardice and easy surrender of the planet Martine to the Abh for personal gain and power. Now an outcast among his own people, he has joined with Lafiel, the granddaughter of the Abh Empress. Lafiel is nothing like what Jinto had expected: she's strong-minded, beautiful, tough, and a born leader. As time passes, Lafiel has earned the command of her own ship, with Jinto serving onboard as an advisor and friend. Will the ongoing conflagration between the two empires force Lafiel to choose between the love and friendship of Jinto and the fate of her ship? An anime series based on the original novels was also released in Japan.

Vol. 1: Crest of the Stars. 2004. 248pp. 1-59182-857-0.

Vol. 2: Banner of the Stars I. 2004. 200pp. 1-59182-858-9.

Vol. 3: Banner of the Stars II. 2004. 240pp. 1-59182-859-7.

Serenity. Written by Joss Whedon and Brett Mathews. Illustrated by Will Conrad. Dark Horse Comics, 2006. 104pp. 1-59307-449-2. **T** 🎬 💻

A prequel to the cult-hit 2005 science fiction movie based on the television show *Firefly* (2004) from Joss Whedon, creator of *Buffy the Vampire Slayer* and *Angel*. In the far future, Captain Malcolm Reynolds is a hardened veteran from the losing side of a galactic civil war. He makes a living as a smuggler and transporter of goods aboard his ship, *Serenity*. At his side is a loyal crew that is the closest thing he has to family. When Mal takes on two new passengers, a young doctor and his telepathic younger sister, the crew finds theyn have taken on more than they bargained for. Caught between both the Universal Alliance's military might and the cannibalistic fury of a space-faring humanoid race called the Reavers, the crew of the *Serenity* find that the biggest threat to the galaxy may be a passenger in their own ship.

Star Wars

Dark Horse Comics, 1993– . 🎬 💻 🎮

In 1977, George Lucas' *Star Wars: Episode IV: A New Hope* was released in theaters to an enthusiastic audience. The space fantasy film series continues to be as popular today as ever with the release of the final *Star Wars* movie, *Star Wars: Episode III—Revenge of the Sith,* in 2005, shattering box office records. The future also looks bright with the release of the <u>Clone Wars</u> animated series in 2004–2005, as well as two upcoming television series. The further adventures of Luke Skywalker, Darth Vader, Obi-Wan Kenobi, and others have also been successfully continued in comic book form by both Marvel and Dark Horse Comics. Due to the high volume of recommended titles, those not listed below can be viewed at Dark Horse Comics' Web site at www.darkhorse.com. Titles that are highly recommended are listed with brief annotations.

Star Wars Film Adaptations—North American Editions

Following are the adaptations of the <u>Star Wars</u> films in comic book format as published in the United States.

Star Wars: A New Hope—the Special Edition. **Written by Bruce Jones. Illustrated by Eduardo Barreto.** 1997. 104pp. 1-56971-213-1. **Y**

Star Wars: The Empire Strikes Back—the Special Edition. **Written by Archie Goodwin. Illustrated by Al Williamson.** 1997. 104pp. 1-56971-234-4. **Y**

Star Wars: Return of the Jedi—the Special Edition. **Written by Archie Goodwin. Illustrated by Al Williamson.** 1997. 104pp. 1-56971-235-2. **Y**

Star Wars: Episode I: The Phantom Menace. **Written by Henry Gilroy. Illustrated by Rodolfo Damaggio.** 1999. 112pp. 1-56971-359-6. **Y**

Star Wars: Episode II: The Attack of the Clones. **Written by Henry Gilroy. Illustrated by Jan Duursema.** 2002. 144pp. 1-56971-609-9. **Y**

Star Wars: Episode III: Revenge of the Sith. **Written by Miles Land. Illustrated by Doug Wheatley.** 2005. 96pp. 1-59307-309-7. **Y**

Star Wars Film Adaptations—Japanese Editions

Folllowing are the adaptations of the Star Wars films in comic book format as published in Japan and reprinted by Dark Horse Comics. At the time of this writing, no adaptations have been released for *Attack of the Clones* or *Revenge of the Sith* from Japan. Star Wars: A New Hope—Manga received an Eisner Award in 1999 for Best U.S. Edition of Foreign Material as well as a Harvey Award in 2000 for Best American Edition of Foreign Material.

❀ **Star Wars: A New Hope—Manga. Adapted and Illustrated by Hisao Tamaki.** 1998. **Y Japanese manga.**
>   *Vol. 1.* 1998. 96pp. 1-56971-362-6.
>   *Vol. 2.* 1998. 96pp. 1-56971-363-4.
>   *Vol. 3.* 1998. 96pp. 1-56971-364-2.
>   *Vol. 4.* 1998. 96pp. 1-56971-365-0.

Star Wars: The Empire Strikes Back—Manga. Written by Adapted and Illustrated by Toshiki Kudo. 1999. **Y Japanese manga.**
>   *Vol. 1.* 1999. 96pp. 1-56971-390-1.
>   *Vol. 2.* 1999. 96pp. 1-56971-391-X.
>   *Vol. 3.* 1999. 96pp. 1-56971-392-8.
>   *Vol. 4.* 1999. 96pp. 1-56971-393-6.

Star Wars: Return of the Jedi—Manga. Written by Adapted and Illustrated by Shin-ichi Hiromoto. 1999. **Y Japanese manga.**
>   *Vol. 1.* 1999. 96pp. 1-56971-394-4.
>   *Vol. 2.* 1999. 96pp. 1-56971-395-2.
>   *Vol. 3.* 1999. 96pp. 1-56971-396-0.
>   *Vol. 4.* 1999. 96pp. 1-56971-397-9.

Episode I: The Phantom Menace—Manga. Written by Adapted and Illustrated by Kia Asamiya. 1999–2000. **Y Japanese manga.**
>   *Vol. 1.* 1999. 88pp. 1-56971-483-5.
>   *Vol. 2.* 2000. 88pp. 1-56971-484-3.

Star Wars Novel Adaptations, 1996–2000

Star Wars has spun off into many other media, including novels. Included are comic book collections in which the stories are adapted from and inspired by the novels. Included is Timothy Zahn's popular Heir to the Empire Trilogy of Star Wars novels originally published by Random House from 1992 to 1994.

Star Wars: Splinter of the Mind's Eye. **Written by Terry Austin. Illustrated by Chris Sprouse.** 1996. 112pp. 1-56971-223-9.

Star Wars: Shadows of the Empire. 1997–2000.
> *Shadows of the Empire.* Written by John Wagner. Illustrated by Kilian Plunkett. 1997. 160pp. 1-56971-183-6.
> *Shadows of the Empire—Evolution.* Written by Steve Perry. Illustrated by Christopher Moeller. 2000. 120pp. 1-56971-441-X.

Heir to the Empire Trilogy. 1996–1999. **Y**
> *Heir to the Empire.* Written by Timothy Zahn. Adapted by Mike Baron. Illustrated by Oliver Vatine and Fred Blanchard. 1996. 160pp. 1-56971-202-6.
> *Dark Force Rising.* Written by Timothy Zahn. Adapted by Mike Baron. Illustrated by Terry Dodson. 1998. 160pp. 1-56971-269-7.
> *The Last Command.* Written by Timothy Zahn. Adapted by Mike Baron. Illustrated by Edvin Biukovic. 1999. 144pp. 1-56971-378-2.

Star Wars Prequel Trilogy Era Titles

Following are miscellaneous recommended <u>Star Wars</u> titles that take place during and after the events seen in the prequel-era films *Star Wars: Episode I: The Phantom Menace* and *Star Wars: Episode II: Revenge of the Sith*. Titles are listed chronologically.

Jedi Council—Acts of War. **Written by Randy Stradley. Illustrated by Davide Fabbri.** 2001. 96pp. 1-56971-539-4. **Y**

Darkness. **Written by John Ostrander. Illustrated by Jan Duursema.** 2002. 96pp. 1-56971-659-5. **Y**

Cover art of Star Wars: Rite of Passage © 2004 Lucasfilm Ltd. & ™. All Rights Reserved. Used under authorization.

Rite of Passage. **Written by John Ostrander. Illustrated by Jan Duursema.** 2004. 120pp. 1-59307-042-X. **Y**

Twilight. **Written by John Ostrander. Illustrated by Jan Duursema**. 2001. 96pp. 1-56971-558-0. **Y**

Jango Fett. **Written by Ron Marz. Illustrated by Tom Fowler**. 2002. 64pp. 1-56971-650-1. **Y**

Zam Wesell. **Written by Ron Marz. Illustrated by Ted Naifeh.** 2002. 64pp. 1-56971-624-2. **Y**

General Grievous. **Written by Chuck Dixon. Illustrated by Rick Leonardi.** 2005. 96pp. 1-59307-442-5. **Y**

Honor and Duty. **Written by John Ostrander. Illustrated by C.P. Smith**. 2006. 96pp. 1-59307-546-4. **Y**

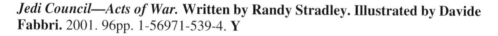

Star Wars Original Trilogy Era Titles

Following are miscellaneous recommended <u>Star Wars</u> titles that take place during and after the events seen in *Star Wars: Episode IV: A New Hope* and *Star Wars: Episode VI: Return of the Jedi*. The tales feature such familiar characters as Luke Skywalker, Han Solo, Princess Leia, Chewbacca, Darth Vader, Boba Fett, and many more. The series <u>Legacy</u> takes place 100 years after the events in the movie *Return of the Jedi* and focuses on the last-remaining Skywalker heir, Cade Skywalker

***Boba Fett—Death, Lies, & Treachery*. Written by John Wagner. Illustrated by Cam Kennedy.** 1998. 144pp. 1-56971-311-1.

***Boba Fett—Enemy of the Empire*. Written by John Wagner. Illustrated by Ian Gibson.** 1999. 112pp. 1-56971-407-X.

***Chewbacca.* Written by Darko Macan. Illustrated by various.** 2001. 96pp. 1-56971-515-7.

***Union*. Written by Michael Stackpole. Illustrated by Robert Teranishi.** 2000. 96pp. 1-56971-464-9.

<u>Empire,</u> 2003–2007 **Y**

> *Vol. 1: Betrayal*. Written by Scott Allie. Illustrated by Ryan Benjamin. 2003. 104pp. 1-56971-964-0.
> *Vol. 2: Darklighter*. Written by Paul Chadwick. Illustrated by Doug Wheatley. 2004. 144pp. 1-56971-975-6.
> *Vol. 3: The Imperial Perspective*. Written by Ron Marz and various. Illustrated by Davidé Fabbri. 2005. 144pp. 1-59307-128-0.
> *Vol. 4: The Heart of the Rebellion*. Written by Judd Winick, Ron Marz, and Randy Stradley. Illustrated by Paul Chadwick, Davidé Fabbri, and various. 2005. 152pp. 1-59307-308-9.
> *Vol. 5: Allies and Adversaries*. Written by Jeremy Barlow and Ron Marz. Illustrated by Brandon Badeaux, Jeff Johnson, Joe Corroney, Adriana Melo, and Nicola Scott. 2006. 120pp. 1-59307-466-2.
> *Vol. 6: In the Shadows of Their Fathers*. Written by Thomas Andrews and Scott Allie. Illustrated by Adriana Melo, Michael Lacombe, and Joe Corroney. 2006. 144pp. 1-59307-627-4.
> *Vol. 7: The Wrong Side of the War*. Written by Welles Hartley. Illustrated by Davidé Fabbri. 2007. 120pp. 1-59307-709-2.

<u>Legacy.</u> **Written by John Ostrander. Illustrated by Jan Duursema.** 2007– . **Y**

> *Vol. 1: Broken*. 2007. 160pp. 1-59307-716-5.

***Mara Jade—By the Emperor's Hand*. Written by Timothy Zahn and Michael Stackpole. Illustrated by Carlos Ezquerra.** 1999. 144pp. 1-56971-401-0.

<u>Omnibus: X-Wing Rogue Squadron.</u> **Written by Hayden Blackmen, Michael Stackpole, Mike Baron, and various. Illustrated by various.** 2006.

> *Vol. 1*. 2006. 296pp. 1-59307-572-3.
> *Vol. 2*. 2006. 288pp. 1-59307-619-3.

<u>Rebellion.</u> 2007– . **Y**

> *Vol. 1: My Brother, My Enemy*. Written by Rob Williams. Illustrated by Brandon Badeaux and Michael Lacombe. 2007. 128pp. 1-59307-711-4.

Star Wars Infinities. 2002–2004. **Y**

A collection of imaginary stories showcasing what could have happened in the original trilogy movies if one thing had changed. What if Luke Skywalker had not destroyed the Death Star in *A New Hope*; what if Luke had died on Hoth and Leia instead became a Jedi Knight in *The Empire Strikes Back*; and what if C-3PO never was able to serve as a translator droid for Jabba the Hutt? The stories are similar to the big screen counterparts but create a unique opportunity for events wished for but never before seen.

> *Infinities: A New Hope.* Written by Chris Warner. Illustrated by Drew Johnson. 2002. 96pp. 1-56971-648-X.
> *Infinities: The Empire Strikes Back.* Written by Dave Land. Illustrated by Davide Fabri. 2003. 96pp. 1-56971-904-7.
> *Infinities: Return of the Jedi.* Written by Adam Gallardo. Illustrated by Ryan Benjamin. 2004. 104pp. 1-59307-206-6.

Classic Star Wars: A Long Time Ago . . . . Written by various. Illustrated by various. 2002–2003. **Y**

A collection of the entire Marvel Comics series that was published originally in comic book form from 1977 to 1987. The stories feature the adventures of Luke, Han, and Leia and the Rebel Alliance in their struggle against the Sith Lord Darth Vader and the evil Galactic Empire.

> *Vol. 1: Doomworld.* 2002. 336pp. 1-56971-754-0.
> *Vol. 2: Dark Encounters.* 2002. 336pp. 1-56971-785-0.
> *Vol. 3: Resurrection of Evil.* 2002. 344pp. 1-56971-786-9.
> *Vol. 4: Screams in the Void.* 2003. 376pp. 1-56971-787-7.
> *Vol. 5: Fool's Bounty.* 2003. 376pp. 1-56971-906-3.
> *Vol. 6: Wookie World.* 2003. 360pp. 1-56971-907-1.
> *Vol. 7: Far, Far Away.* 2003. 312pp. 1-56971-908-X.

Star Wars: Clone Wars. Written by John Ostrander, Haden Blackman, and various. Illustrated by Jan Duursema, Brian Ching, and various. 2003–2006. **Y** ◉

Set between the events of the films *Episode II: Attack of the Clones* (2002) and *Episode III: Revenge of the Sith* (2005), the Clone Wars are the civil war period that will eventually lead to the rise of the evil Galactic Empire, as seen in the original trilogy of Star Wars films. The Separatists, led by the fallen Jedi Count Dooku and the cyborg General Grievous, battle against the Old Republic's clone army, commanded by the Jedi Knights Yoda, Mace Windu, Obi-Wan Kenobi, and Anakin Skywalker. Meanwhile, the real manipulator of the plot, the Sith Lord called Darth Sidious, waits for the right time to strike and achieve his goal of destroying the Jedi Knights and creating a Galactic Empire. The final volume takes place during and immediately after the events of the hit movie *Episode III: Revenge of the Sith*.

> *Vol. 1: The Defense of Kamino.* 2003. 128pp. 1-56971-962-4.
> *Vol. 2: Victories and Sacrifices.* 2003. 120pp. 1-56971-969-1.
> *Vol. 3: Last Stand on Jabiim.* 2004. 120pp. 1-59307-006-3.
> *Vol. 4: Light and Dark.* 2004. 112pp. 1-59307-195-7.
> *Vol. 5: The Best Blades.* 2004. 144pp. 1-59307-273-2.

Vol. 6: On the Fields of Battle. 2005. 168pp. 1-59307-352-6.

Vol. 7: When They Were Brothers. 2005. 144pp. 1-59307-396-8.

Vol. 8: The Last Siege, The Final Truth. 2006. 144pp. 1-59307-482-4.

Vol. 9: Endgame. 2006. 144pp. 1-59307-553-7.

Star Wars: Clone Wars Adventures. Written by Haden Blackman and Welles Hartley. Illustrated by Ben Caldwell, Matt Fillbach, and Shawn Fillbach. 2004– . **A**

Cover art of Star Wars: Clone Wars
Adventures: Vol. III © 2006
Lucasfilm Ltd. & ™. All Rights
Reserved. Used under authorization.

These are short stories from the battlefields as the Republic's army of clone troopers and Jedi Knights battles against Count Dooku, General Grievous, and the Separatist's droid armies during the epic struggle known as the Clone Wars. Based on the Emmy Award-winning cartoon series by Genndy Tartovsky of the same name.

Vol. 1. 2004. 96pp. 1-59307-243-0.

Vol. 2. 2004. 96pp. 1-59307-271-6.

Vol. 3. 2005. 96pp. 1-59307-307-0.

Vol. 4. 2005. 96pp. 1-59307-402-6.

Vol. 5. 2006. 96pp. 1-59307-483-2.

Vol. 6. 2006. 96pp. 1-59307-567-7.

Vol. 7. 2007. 80pp. 1-59307-678-9.

🏵 **Star Wars: Dark Empire. Written by Tom Veitch. Illustrated by Cam Kennedy with Jim Baikie.** Dark Horse Comics, 1992–2006. **Y** ◎

Five years after the destruction of the second Death Star, Luke Skywalker turns to the dark side of the Force to see why his father, Anakin Skywalker, was seduced by it. While embraced in the shadow of the dark side, he joins the reborn Sith Master, Emperor Palpatine, as his new Sith apprentice. The collection *Dark Empire* received recognition by YALSA's Quick Picks for Reluctant Readers committee in 1996 and was the first graphic novel fiction title ever recognized by YALSA. The second edition of Dark Empire II also includes the long out-of-print finale titled *Empire's End.*

Dark Empire. 3d ed. 2003. 152pp. 1-59307-039-X.

Dark Empire II. 1st ed. 1995. 168pp. 1-56971-119-4. 2nd edition, 2006. 208pp. 1-59307-526-X.

Empire's End. 1997. 56pp. 1-56971-306-5.

***Star Wars: Darth Maul.* Written by Ron Marz. Illustrated by Jan Duursema.** Dark Horse Comics, 2001. 96pp. 1-56971-542-4. **Y** ◎

The vicious Dark Lord of the Sith, apprenticed to Darth Sidious, is sent on a mission to infiltrate the Black Sun criminal organization and destroy it from within. The story takes place before the events of *Episode I: The Phantom Menace.*

***Star Wars: Tag & Bink Were Here.* Written by Kevin Rubio. Illustrated by Lucas Marangon.** Dark Horse Comics, 2007. 104pp. 1-59307-641-X. **Y** ◎

When Tag Greenley and Bink Otauna, two Rebels trapped on a captured freighter carrying a certain Princess Leia, chose life over death and disguised themselves as Stormtroopers, little did they know the trouble they'd see. Now they're reluctant Stormtroopers for the Empire, getting into one fine mess after another. Relive the greatest moments from the original trilogy of Star Wars films as the heroes in disguise get into one disastrous adventure after another. A comical take on William Shakespeare's Rosencrantz and Guildenstern, two background characters from *Hamlet*.

Star Wars: Tales of the Jedi. 1994–2001. Y

Four thousand years before the rise of the Empire, a young Jedi Knight named Ulic Quel-Droma falls to the Dark Side of the Force, and a galaxy is changed forever as the epic Sith War erupts. The series inspired the hit Xbox RPG LucasArts games *Knights of the Old Republic I and II*. A new monthly comic book series called Knights of the Old Republic was released in early 2006 and the first story arc will be collected in 2007. Inspired by the Xbox game, the series continues the adventures of the Jedi Order thousands of years before Luke Skywalker and focuses on a young Jedi Padawan named Zayne Carrick, who must clear his name after being accused of murdering all his fellow Jedi-in-training. *Jedi vs. Sith* features a story set 1,000 years ago in which Lord Kaan, ruler of the Sith Brotherhood of Darkness, seeks the destruction of the Jedi Master Hoth and the army of Jedi Knights, and a young girl falls prey to the dark side.

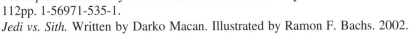

> *Knights of the Old Republic.* Written by Tom Veitch. Illustrated by Chris Gossett, Janine Johnston, David Roach. 1994. 136pp. 1-56971-020-1.
>
> *The Freedon Nadd Uprising.* Written by Tom Veitch. Illustrated by Tony Atkins and Denis Rodier. 1997. 56pp. 1-56971-307-3.
>
> *Dark Lords of the Sith.* Written by Tom Veitch and Kevin J. Anderson. Illustrated by Chris Gossett and Art Wetherell. 1996. 160pp. 1-56971-095-3.
>
> *The Sith War.* Written by Kevin J. Anderson. Illustrated by Dario Carrasco, Jr. 1996. 152pp. 1-56971-173-9.
>
> *Redemption.* Written by Kevin J. Anderson. Illustrated by Chris Gossett. 2001. 112pp. 1-56971-535-1.
>
> *Jedi vs. Sith.* Written by Darko Macan. Illustrated by Ramon F. Bachs. 2002. 144pp. 1-56971-649-8.
>
> *Knights of the Old Republic, Vol. 1: Commencement.* Written by John Jackson Miller. Illustrated by Brian Ching. 2007. 144pp. 1-59307-640-1.

Star Wars: Visionaries. **Written and illustrated by Iain McCaig, Warren Fu, Derek Thompson, and various.** 2005. 136pp. 1-59307-311-9. **T**

These are short stories created by the Lucasfilm art department, designers of the Star Wars prequels. Highlights include a rematch between Obi-Wan Kenobi and a cyborg, Darth Maul, and a short story featuring the origin of the cyborg villain General Grievous.

Star Wars Tales. **Written by various. Illustrated by various.** 2002–2006. **Y**

An anthology series featuring the work of some of the comic book industry's best talents telling stories within the Star Wars world, featuring tales of high adventure, comedy, and much more. Highlights include "Resurrection" (volume 3), in which Darth Vader duels a cloned Darth Maul in a fierce fight to the finish.

> *Vol. 1.* 2002. 224pp. 1-56971-619-6.
>
> *Vol. 2.* 2002. 224pp. 1-56971-757-5.

Vol. 3. 2003. 224pp. 1-56971-836-9.
Vol. 4. 2004. 224pp. 1-56971-989-6.
Vol. 5. 2005. 248pp. 1-59307-286-4.
Vol. 6. 2006. 232pp. 1-59307-447-6.

Technopriests, Vol. 1. **Written by Alexandro Jodorowsky. Illustrated by Zoran Janjetov.** Humanoids Publishing/DC Comics, 2004. 160pp. 1-4012-0359-0. **M**

In a world where virtual entertainment is the dominant form of entertainment and culture, Albino, an elder high technopriest, recounts his brutal upbringing and the trials that he faced to become master of games and virtual reality. Also told in flashbacks is the tale of Albino's cruel mother and her brutal but dark-humored road to revenge against her three abusers.

Tenchi Muyo! Written and illustrated by Hitoshi Okuda. VIZ Media, LLC, 1997–. **T Japanese manga.** あ

Spun off from the hit Japanese science fiction/comedy anime. Tenchi Masaki is definitely not your average teenage boy. His grandfather is the crown prince of the planet Jurai, who crashed on Earth many years ago. Tenchi is now an heir to the Jurai throne, wielder of an hierloom laser-sword and a mystic power called the Light Hawk Wings. He's also surrounded by a legion of the cutest females ever from outer space who happen to live with Tenchi and his grandfather in their home. From the ill-mannered, super-powered female demon pirate Ryoko, to the kind-hearted and easily jealous Princess Ayeka, to Ayeka's young sister Sasame, to the clueless Galaxy Policewoman Mihoshi, to the 5,000-year-old genius Washu, and even the bio-organic living ship (and part-time space rabbit) Ryo-oh-ki, all are in love with Tenchi and practically fighting over him, while adventure and plenty of comedy await both on and off planet. Beginning in 2004, the original series No Need for Tenchi has begun to be reprinted in the traditional right-to-left format.

No Need for Tenchi. 1st ed., 1997–2002; 2d ed., 2004– .

NO NEED FOR TENCHI ©
HITOSHI OKUDA 1994 ©
AIC/VAPNTV.

Vol. 1. 1997. 184pp. 1-56931-180-3; 2d ed., 2004. 184pp. 1-59116-610-1.
Vol. 2: Sword Play. 1997. 176pp. 1-56931-254-0; 2d ed., 2005. 200pp. 1-59116-611-X.
Vol. 3: Magical Girl Pretty Sammy. 1998. 184pp. 1-56931-288-5; 2d ed., 2005. 176pp. 1-59116-783-3
Vol. 4: Samurai Space Opera. 1998. 176pp. 1-56931-339-3; 2d ed., 2005. 184pp. 1-59116-870-8
Vol. 5: Unreal Genius. 1999. 176pp. 1-56931-365-2; 2d ed., 2005. 176pp. 1-4215-0106-6.
Vol. 6: Dream a Little Scheme. 1999. 173pp. 1-56931-429-2; 2d ed., 2006. 208pp. 1-4215-0590-8.
Vol. 7: Tenchi in Love. 2000. 178pp. 1-56931-470-5; 2d ed., 2006. 208pp. 1-4215-0590-8.
Vol. 8: Chef of Iron. 2000. 184pp. 1-56931-535-3.
Vol. 9: Quest for More Money. 2001. 184pp. 1-56931-559-0.
Vol. 10: Mother Planet. 2001. 184pp. 1-56931-648-1.

Vol. 11: Ayeka's Heart. 2002. 184pp. 1-56931-709-7.
Vol. 12: No Need for Endings. 2002. 188pp. 1-56931-741-0.

The All-New Tenchi Muyo! 2003– .

Vol. 1: Alien Nation. 2003. 176pp. 1-56931-825-5.
Vol. 2: Sasami Stories. 2003. 192pp. 1-59116-156-8.
Vol. 3: Dark Washu. 2003. 176pp. 1-56931-971-5.
Vol. 4: Girls Get Busy. 2004. 208pp. 1-59116-302-1.
Vol. 5: Point and Shoot. 2005. 200pp. 1-59116-494-X.
Vol. 6: Pet Peeves. 2005. 184pp. 1-42150-011-6.
Vol. 7: Picture Book. 2005. 184pp. 1-4215-0105-8.
Vol. 8: Brain Drain. 2006. 208pp. 1-4215-0315-8.
Vol. 9: Family Affair. 2006. 184pp. 1-4215-0748-X.
Vol. 10. 2007. 208pp. 1-4215-1127-4.

ALL-NEW TENCHI MUYO ©
HITOSHI OKUDA 1994 ©
AIC/VAPNTV.

Wandering Star. Written and illustrated by Teri Sue Wood. Sirius Entertainment, Inc., 2003. T

In a tale of bravery, sacrifice, hardship, and friendship, Cassandra Andrews, the daughter of the President of Earth and the first human to attend a galactic college, is asked by an interviewer to recount a time when she was the young and naïve captain of the ship *The Wandering Star* and their battle against the vicious Bono Kirian empire. From her days at the Academy, where she met friends Mekon, Graikor, Elli, and the psychic Madison—some of whom would pay the ultimate price in the war—to the antics of the crew she commanded, the invasion by the Bono Kiri, Earth's tragic truce, and the Galactic Alliance's last stand, Cassandra tells all. What could one woman do after her father has betrayed their planet and the Galactic Alliance and aligned himself with the Boni Kirian empire?

Vol. 1. 2003. 160pp. 1-57989-010-5.
Vol. 2. 2003. 160pp. 1-57989-011-3.
Vol. 3. 2003. 176pp. 1-57989-012-1

Space Exploration

These stories tell the tales of humanity's urge to explore the stars as well as what speculative wonders people find while in outer space. The stories tend to focus on a time near the present as the explorers have just invented the technology to explore outer space, or they may be set in the far future as humans explore outer space and colonize other worlds. This subgenre has much in common with the science action subgenre, but the focus is more on a spaceship crew or specific crew members as they explore the unknown.

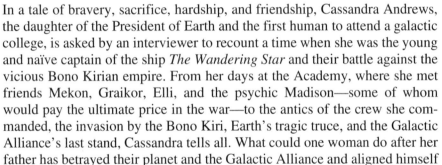

Astronauts in Trouble. Written by Larry Young. Illustrated by Matt Smith and Charlie Adlard. AiT/Planet Lar, 1999–2005. **O**

© 2006 Larry Young.

In the year 2019, Ishmael Hayes, the world's richest man, declares that he wants to go to the moon for the fiftieth anniversary of the moon landing. It's a much-changed world from today, in which the mob has nuclear capabilities, and to help celebrate the event, the Channel 7 news team is invited to cover the story. Accidental astronauts cameraman Heck Allen, news anchor Dave Archer, and producer Annie Franklin discover that they're in over their heads after Hayes declares the moon his own personal property and other parties, including the government and the eco-terrorist organization Green Sleeves, decide to get involved in a high-stakes battle for the fate of the moon and the Channel 7 news team. *Space: 1959* is a look back at the culture of 1959 at the beginning of the Cold War as a Channel 7 team is on the heels of an arms-race story to put the first man on the moon. *One Shot, One Beer* is an anthology of short stories surrounding the first bar on the moon and its wide variety of inhabitants relaxing after a long journey into outer space. *Masterplan* is a hardcover collection of all three stories.

> *Live from the Moon*. 1999. 144pp. 0-9676847-1-4.
> *Space 1959*. 2000. 72pp. 0-9676847-3-0.
> *One Shot, One Beer*. 2000. 72pp. 0-9676847-5-7.
> *Masterplan*. 2005. 288pp. 1-932051-16-3, hardcover.

Babylon 5: Price of Peace. **Written by J. Michael Straczynski, Mark Moretti, and Tim DeHaas. Illustrated by John Ridgway, Carlos Garzon, and various.** DC Comics, 1998. 128pp. 1-56389-467-X. **T** 🖰

Continuation of the cult-phenomenal television series that featured the fragile coexistence of humans and various aliens living together in the year 2250 on the space station called Babylon 5. It takes place during the series' second season. The station's first commander, Jeffrey Sinclair, is recalled to Earth to become the ambassador to the planet Minbar, and the crew of the station must try to stop an unknown assassin.

Infinite Ryvius. Written by Hajime Yatate. Illustrated by Shinsuke Kurihashi. DR Master, 2004–2005. **T Japanese manga.** あ

In the year A.D. 2225, when Earth has been devastated by solar flames, humanity has reached out and colonized the solar system. On one of the space stations, a catastrophe occurs while a group of teenagers are on board training to become astronauts. All the adults are killed, and the teens must try to survive on a ship called *Ryvius*. In a power vacuum, a struggle ensues for control of the group, and the teens must face horrendous odds in the blackness of space and against their own personal struggles if they're to survive. Based on the hit anime.

> *Vol. 1*. 2004. 200pp. 1-58899-008-7.
> *Vol. 2*. 2005. 200pp. 1-58899-228-4.

Iron Empires. Written and illustrated by Chris Moeller. Dark Horse Comics, 2004. **T**

In a distant future when humans have reached the stars, eight nations of humanity struggle against an alien invasion from the parasitic worms that have corrupted and destroyed them from the inside out through mind control and motor function manipulation. In *Volume 1*, a soldier-priest is assigned to the farthest region of the galaxy and finds a corrupt class of priests ruled by the worms, with plenty of ammunition to repel them. In *Volume 2*, a tough and beautiful warrior woman disenchanted with her marriage finds the odds stacked against her on a mission to protect her planet from a horde of soul-sucking aliens controlled by the worms. Humanity's last stand is now, but they're not going down without a fight.

> *Vol. 1: Faith Conquers.* 2004. 160pp. 1-59307-015-2.
> *Vol. 2: Sheva's War.* 2004. 168pp. 1-59307-110-8.

***The Masterplan*. Written and illustrated by Scott Mills.** Top Shelf Productions, 2003. 352pp. 1-891830-39-2. **T**

In A.D. 2040, Professor Carter Zacharias, a legendary brilliant scientist, embarks on a journey that takes him to the edge of the galaxy and back to save the universe from its continuing expansion. Joined with his ex-wife Carolyn and his estranged brother, Father George Zacharias, the journey takes them to the year A.D. 18,000,000,042,041 to save the universe. When sabotage occurs and Carolyn becomes time-displaced, together Carter and George must try to find a way to save the galaxy as well as Carolyn.

***Ministry of Space*. Written by Warren Ellis. Illustrated by Chris Weston and Laura Martin.** Image Comics, 2005. 96pp. 1-58240-423-2. **O**

What would have happened if Great Britain rather than the United States was at the forefront in the space race? An alternate history of the space race in which Great Britain is the first country to begin the steps to space exploration. Shortly after the fall of the Third Reich in World War II, British troops extract German scientists before the U.S. troops arrive, and soon Britain creates a Ministry of Space under the command of John Dashwood to conquer the stars in the queen's name. Will the flag carrying the Union Jack be the first to wave proudly on the moon, or will the United States and Russia give Great Britain a run for its money in the space race?

***Orbiter*. Written by Warren Ellis. Illustrated by Colleen Doran.** Vertigo/DC Comics, 2003. 104pp. 1-4012-0056-7. **M**

Ten years after it mysteriously disappeared and was presumed to have been destroyed, the U. S. space shuttle *Venture* returns to Earth with only one of the original crew members on board. The pilot is in catatonic shock, and a small group of U.S.-led scientists set out to solve the mystery of the shuttle, which has been refitted with an organic outer shell, rewired with alien technology, and appears to have been to Mars.

© 2006 Warren Ellis
and Colleen Doran.

Planet Blood. Written and illustrated by Kim Tae-Hyung. TOKYOPOP, 2005– . **T Korean manhwa.**

> After the fallout from World War V, Earth is a wasteland and over 46 percent of humanity has been killed in the battle. When Earth is no longer habitable, the planet must be abandoned to give it time to heal and be cleansed before it can be purified. Mars and the moon are soon colonized and serve as temporary homes for humans. Now the year is Universal Century 0091, Earth has been cleansed, and the two colonies can come back—but the struggle to find the best land to repopulate Earth takes an unexpected turn when members of both colonies end up in a foreign land. Sinan is a mecha pilot for the Mars Colonies. After an explosion, he wakes up on an entirely different planet—an archaic medieval-like planet called Horai. He becomes embroiled in an attempt to take back the dual Horai kingdoms of Gaia and Pratria with the aid of Noodles, the twin brother of the overlord Zetsos. As Sinan discovers, there's more to this planet than he realized, as he finds that there are others like him from the Mars and moon colonies stranded on this backward planet that seems to defy time and space. More than eleven volumes have been published in Korea, and they are currently being published in North America.

> *Vol. 1*. 2005. 192pp. 1-59532-537-9.
> *Vol. 2*. 2005. 200pp. 1-59532-538-7.
> *Vol. 3*. 2005. 192pp. 1-59532-539-5.
> *Vol. 4*. 2006. 192pp. 1-59532-540-9.

🌳 **Planetes. Written and illustrated by Makoto Yukimura.** TOKYOPOP, 2003–2005. **T**
◎ **Japanese manga.** あ

> In a time when humanity has reached for the stars, the spaceways around Earth are littered with debris. It's up to the crew of the *Toy Box* to help clean the spaceways free of space junk, but crew members Yuri, Hachimaki, Fee, and Pops all have their reasons for being in one of the worst jobs in the galaxy. Sure, it's not the most glamorous of jobs in outer space, but who else will clean up the space junk? The series was adapted into an anime series in Japan. *Volume 1* received recognition by YALSA's Popular Paperbacks for Young Adults committee in 2004 on the "Simply Science Fiction" list.

> *Vol. 1*. 2003. 240pp. 1-59182-262-9.
> *Vol. 2*. 2004. 268pp. 1-59182-509-1.
> *Vol. 3*. 2004. 240pp. 1-59182-510-5.
> *Vol. 4, Part 1*. 2004. 192pp. 1-59532-208-6. *T*
> *Vol. 4, Part 2*. 2005. 200pp. 1-59532-467-4. *T*

Star Trek. DC Comics, 1992-2002. **T** 🎬 🖥

> One of the most enduring science fiction television and film franchises, the popular television/movie series featured many well-written stories published throughout the years. Listed below are highly recommended titles featuring the adventures of original series heroes, including Captain Kirk, Spock, and Dr. McCoy, as well as *Star Trek: The Next Generation's* Captain Jean-Luc Picard, Commander William Riker, Lieutenant Worf, and more in the trek into outer space aboard the starship *Enterprise*.

> *Star Trek: Debt of Honor*. Written by Chris Claremont. Illustrated by Adam Hughes. 1992. 96pp. 1-56389-031-3.

Star Trek: Ashes of Eden. Written by William Shatner with Judith Reeves-Stevens. Illustrated by Steve Erwin. 1995. 94pp. 1-56389-235-9.

Star Trek: The Modala Imperative. Written by Michael Jan Friedman and Peter David. Illustrated by Pablo Marcos. 1992. 192pp. 1-56389-040-2.

Star Trek: The Next Generation: Forgiveness. Written by David Brin. Illustrated by Scott Hampton. 2002. 96pp. 1-56389-918-3.

Star Trek: The Next Generation: The Gorn Crisis. Written by Kevin J. Anderson and Rebecca Moesta. Illustrated by Igor Kordey. 2002. 96pp. 1-56389-926-4.

***The Starjammers: The Cadet and the Corsairs.* Written by Kevin J. Anderson. Illustrated by Ale Garza.** Marvel Comics, 2005. 120pp. 0-7851-1409-2. **T**

When an all-human empire with xenophobic tendencies crushes an all-alien opposition, a rag-tag group of aliens from different races form a team to take down the empire. Tolo Hawk, a young space cadet, and the beautiful Princess Sabra of the Union of Intelligent Races, become entangled with the plant-like Captain Kalyx and his shipmates. Called the Starjammers, they are a rogue group of aliens out to defeat the Union of Intelligent Races. Will they be able to pull Tolo and Princess Sabra to their cause and help bring freedom to the galaxy? A revision of the classic space pirate team from the pages of Marvel Comics' <u>X-Men</u> series.

Science Action

Action is the main focus of these stories, with science fiction settings that can include the far future, tales of alien civilizations, and even a slightly tweaked look at current life on Earth with a dash of future technology thrown in. Readers who enjoy these titles will also enjoy those listed in the action and adventure genre.

<u>**Adam Strange.**</u> **Created by Gardner Fox.** DC Comics, 2003–2005. **T**

© 2006 DC Comics.

Adam Strange, a scientist from Earth, was transported by "Zeta Ray" beam to the planet Rann. There he became a hero with his spacesuit, jet-pack, and laser pistols, and he saved the planet from countless threats, including space invaders, monsters, and other galactic evil-doers. Strange, after his time on Rann was up, would be transported back to Earth when the effects of the Zeta Beam wore off. *Adam Strange Archives* reprints the classic science fiction stories from the late 1950s, while *Man of Two Worlds* sheds some light on his life on Earth and his future on Rann with his wife, Alanna, and their daughter Aleena.

Adam Strange: The Man of Two Worlds. Written by Richard Bruning. Illustrated by Andy Kubert. 2003. 144pp. 1-4012-0065-6.

Adam Strange Archives, Vol. 1. Written by Gardner Fox. Illustrated by Carmine Infantino. 2004. 224pp. 1-4012-0148-2.

Adam Strange: Planet Heist. Written by Andy Diggle. Illustrated by Pascal Ferry. 2005. 192pp. 1-4012-0727-8.

Adrenalynn: Weapon of War. **Written by Tony Daniel. Illustrated by Martin Egeland.** Dark Horse Comics, 2001. 96pp. 1-56971-621-8. **O**

> During the Cold War, the Soviet Union made the perfect weapon out of human and machine in the form of a girl named Sabina Nikoli. Capable of stealth, superior strength, and speed, she is the ultimate weapon of destruction. Now she's been sent to the United States to deactivate her renegade prototypes, which have mutated into flesh-eating monsters—but once her job is done she must be deactivated as well.

Angelic Layer. Written and illustrated by CLAMP. TOKYOPOP, 2002–2003. **A Japanese manga.**

> The favorite game in the future is a battle competition between lifelike dolls nicknamed "Angels." Sixth-grade Angelic Layer prodigy Misaki Suzuhara may win the championship, but the path to victory will be paved with obstacles. Luckily Misaki's doll, a tough Angel named Hikaru, has what it takes to get her to victory.
>
> > *Vol. 1.* 2002. 200pp. 1-931514-47-X.
> > *Vol. 2.* 2002. 200pp. 1-59182-003-0.
> > *Vol. 3.* 2002. 200pp. 1-59182-004-9.
> > *Vol. 4.* 2003. 200pp. 1-59182-086-3.
> > *Vol. 5.* 2003. 192pp. 1-59182-152-5.

Baby Birth. Written by Sukehiro Tomita. Illustrated by Haruhiko Mikimoto. TOKYOPOP, 2002–2003. **T Japanese manga.**

> An ancient mystical seal has been broken, and demons have made their way into our world. Only the combined powers of a teenage figure skater and a musician can save it. Hizuru Oborozuki is a skater who doesn't have confidence in her ability to succeed. When she meets music prodigy Takuya Hijou, he sees the potential in her to fight the demons, because they come from the same bloodline. Both descendants of a powerful demon-fighting warrior, when Takuya plays his music, Hizuru transforms into a beautiful winged warrior. Can she handle the power and the responsibility before the entire earth is doomed?
>
> > *Vol. 1.* 2002. 208pp. 1-59182-372-2.
> > *Vol. 2.* 2003. 232pp. 1-59182-373-0.

Battle of the Planets. Written by Munier Sharrieff, David Wohl, and various. Illustrated by Wilson Tortosa. Top Cow Productions/Image Comics, 2003–2004. **T あ**

> In the near future, humanity has spread its wings and colonized other planets, but an alien race from the planet Spectra has invaded Earth. To protect the planet is G-Force, a teenage group of heroes made up of Mark, Jason, Princess, Keyop, and Tiny, who travel in their ship *The Phoenix* to battle the evil forces of Zoltar from Planet Spectra. Guided by Chief Anderson and 7-Zark-7, the cybernetically enhanced teens are based on Center Neptune, far beneath the sea on the west coast of the United States. Together they must take on Zoltar's minions and giant beasts of destruction. Based on the imported classic Japanese anime *Gatchaman*, released in the United States as *Battle of the Planets* and *G-Force*.
>
> > *Vol. 1: Trial by Fire.* 2003. 80pp. 1-58240-289-2.
> > *Vol. 2: Blood Red Sky.* 2003. 144pp. 1-58240-323-6.
> > *Vol. 3: Destroy All Monsters.* 2004. 208pp. 1-58240-332-5.

> *Vol. 1: Trial by Fire Digest.* 2004. 244pp. 1-58240-337-6.
> *Vol. 2: Destroy All Monsters Digest.* 2004. 248pp. 1-58240-384-8.

Bio-Booster Armor Guyver. **Written and illustrated by Yoshiki Takaya.** VIZ Media, LLC, 1995–1998. **O Japanese manga.** あ

Teenager Sho Fukamachi finds himself embroiled in a struggle to save humanity when he finds a mysterious device of alien origin called a Guyver Unit. When he accidentally triggers the unit, he's transformed into an armored killing machine called the Guyver. A high-tech costume with the ability to manipulate gravity, use telepathic energies, and equipped with deadly weapons, it's one of the deadliest weapons on the planet. He discovers an enemy in a worldwide domineering organization called Chronos, which is bent on transforming humans into monstrous beasts called Hyper-Zoanoids to use as soldiers. Chronos lost control of the Guyver Unit and will stop at nothing to get it back. The manga was also adapted into an anime series as well as a series of live-action films.

3

> *Vol. 1.* 1995. 196pp. 1-56931-032-7.
> *Vol. 2: Revenge of Chronos.* 1995. 192pp. 1-56931-091-2.
> *Vol. 3: Dark Masters.* 1996. 200pp. 1-56931-067-X.
> *Vol. 4: Escape from Chronos.* 1996. 192pp. 1-56931-136-6.
> *Vol. 5: Guyver Reborn!* 1997. 184pp. 1-56931-192-7.
> *Vol. 6: Heart of Chronos.* 1997. 192pp. 1-56931-205-2.
> *Vol. 7: Armageddon.* 1998. 192pp. 1-56931-242-7.

Blue Inferior. **Written and illustrated by Kyoko Shitou.** ADV Manga, 2004. 208pp. 1-4139-0086-0. **T Japanese manga.**

After most of the world has been destroyed by environmental pollution, humanity has been broken into smaller civilizations living along the coastlines, with little trust of subhuman outsiders. When a girl with no past and no memories washes ashore, only a curious young boy named Kazuya has the courage to go against the wishes of the village and try to find the girl's true origin, even if the penalty is being ostracized from civilization.

Buster's Neighbourhood: Kid Comet vs. the Agents of Doom. **Written by Kaja Blackley. Illustrated by Alex Hawley.** Mutant Toast Productions, Inc., 2002. 112pp. 0-9731395-0-1. **Y**

When the world needs saving, there's only one man for the job: Buster Jones! He's an inventor, scientist, and secret agent rolled into one, and to top it off, he's only an eleven-year-old kid. While others are in school, Buster's an agent of the Headquarters Investigating Visiting Evil (H.I.V.E.), where he designs weapons for the government in their new space race against potential alien invaders. Along with his best friend Zoe, fellow H.I.V.E. agent Sgt. Jack Crypt, and Buster's giant robot Titan, he's out to save the world even though the cost might be Buster's innocence.

Cain. **Written by Ricardo Barreiro. Illustrated by Eduardo Risso.** Strip Art Features, 2003. 90pp. 1-931724-24-5. **O**

> In a near-future society, an infant boy named Cain was discarded by his mother and left in a garbage dump for dead. Rescued and raised by gypsies and then the brought up in a harsh correctional institution, mental hospitals, and worse, Cain has grown angry about the injustice and tragedy of his life. Even with the odds against him, he's able to discover something about his past: his own mother abandoned him at birth in order to prevent him becoming an heir to the fortunes that she has shared with Cain's older brother. Cain can take no more, and vengeance will be his.

<u>**Caravan Kidd.**</u> **Johji Manabe.** Dark Horse Comics, 1997–1999. **O Japanese manga.**

> When the citizens under the rule of cruel Princess Shion of the Helgebard Empire need a revolution, the beautiful fox-tailed android Mian Toris is there. Formerly a warrior for the empire, she's a one-android fighting force out to save the galaxy. One of her companions, Wataro, is madly in love with her, and the other, Babo, will do anything for a profit. With the fate of the galaxy at hand, will Mian be able to save the day?

> > *Vol. 1.* 1997. 312pp. 1-56971-260-3.
> > *Vol. 2.* 1998. 304pp. 1-56971-324-3.
> > *Vol. 3.* 1999. 292pp. 1-56971-338-3.

Chronicles of the Universe: Desperado Brothers Pocket Manga. **Written and illustrated by Rod Espinosa.** Antarctic Press, 2005. 188pp. 1-932453-87-3. **T Neo-manga.**

> After the devastating Universal Wars, during which technological abuse, corruption, and violence nearly destroyed humanity, from the ashes comes the Desperado family. Once part of a bloodline that helped usher in the devastating war, they've become a precautionary fighting force to prevent the same mistakes their precursors made and to keep evil at bay.

<u>**Cowboy Bebop.**</u> **Written by Hajime Yatate. Illustrated by Yutaka Nanten.** TOKYOPOP, 2002–2003. **T Japanese manga.** あ

> Set in Universe Century 2071, when Earth is a ruined planet and humanity has spread out among the stars, cowboy-like bounty hunters roam the planets in starships, trying to capture criminals who have slipped through the arms of the law. Spike Spiegel and Jet Black are the best bounty hunters in the galaxy, and they're always out for the next capture in their starship *Bebop*. Joined by the mysterious, beautiful, and tough Faye Valentine and Ed, a goofy but talented preteen cyber-sleuth, they're in search of their next meal and cash in their quest to capture criminals. Meanwhile, the ghosts of the past of Spike, Jet, and Faye haunt them as they travel the galaxy. Based on the hit anime series. The <u>Shooting Star</u> series is an alternate take on the events seen in the television show.

> > <u>Cowboy Beebop.</u> 2002.
> > > *Vol. 1.* 2002. 184pp. 1-931514-91-7.
> > > *Vol. 2.* 2002. 184pp. 1-931514-48-8.
> > > *Vol. 3.* 2002. 184pp. 1-59182-033-2.
> > <u>Cowboy Beebop: Shooting Star.</u> 2003.
> > > *Vol. 1.* 2003. 192pp. 1-59182-297-1.
> > > *Vol. 2.* 2003. 176pp. 1-59182-298-X.

Fire Proves Iron. **Written by Page Malbrough. Illustrated by Michael Malbrough and G. W. Fisher.** Dodd Street Studios, 2004. **T**

In the dystopian, technologically advanced industrial city of New Promise, cybernetically enhanced Mechans, mutants, and robots are part of the ruling class of society, while the human Precarians (or "skimps") are exploited and oppressed in a slave working caste. Rex Creedon is a young laborer Precarian working as a miner deep in the bowels of the earth below New Promise City. When he discovers a way out of his mundane and dire circumstances, he soon finds himself wanted by those in power. Though Rex never imagined himself a revolutionary hero, he finds that this is his one chance for freedom from an existence that could be so much more than it is. Meanwhile Madeline, a young Precarian girl, is forced to be assimilated into the Mechan class. Can she find a way to escape her dire predicament and leave her Mechan life behind?

Vol. 1: Grounded Stars. 2004. 80pp. 0-9758883-0-7.

Gate Keepers. **Written and illustrated by Keiji Gotoh.** TOKYOPOP, 2003. **Y** **Japanese manga.** あ

Set in 1969, when alien invaders attack Japan and the rest of the world, there's a group of teens to save the day—the Gate Keepers of. A.E.G.I.S.! With the power to channel energies from other dimensions, they're the best chance of defeating the aliens from conquering Earth. Shun Ukiya, a reluctant teenager who has just realized that he has these strange powers, is recruited by the mysterious director of the global organization A.E.G.I.S. to lead the all-girl squadron of Gate Keepers to defend Japan and the world. Based on the hit anime series.

Vol. 1. 2003. 200pp. 1-59182-164-9.
Vol. 2. 2003. 192pp. 1-59182-165-7.

Grey. **Written and illustrated by Yoshihisa Tagami.** VIZ Media, LLC, 1997. **T** **Japanese manga.**

In a world where humanity is constantly at war with itself, a caste system is in place. The "People" of the cities live in slums, and the only way to move up and out of the caste is to fight as a "Trooper." Once your time as a soldier is completed, you can earn the right to be a "Citizen" and live in luxury. One man, the cold-hearted "Trooper" Grey, is determined to make it no matter what the cost and become a "Citizen." Constantly reminded of the death of his lover, Lips, who died in battle as a fellow "Trooper," he's the only one of his platoon to survive many dangerous assignments. Now that a fellow soldier, Red, has been captured, he'll do whatever it takes to free him, even if it costs Grey his own life.

Perfect Collection Vol. 1. 1997. 296pp. 1-56931-208-7.
Perfect Collection Vol. 2. 1997. 296pp. 1-56931-209-5.

***The HALO Graphic Novel*. Written by various. Illustrated by various.** Marvel Comics, 2006. 128pp. 0-7851-2372-5. **O** ⊚ 🦊

Based on the characters and events from the cult hit Xbox video game series *HALO: Combat Evolved* and *HALO 2*. It is an anthology of short stories featuring the armor-clad Spartan warrior called the Master Chief who, with the Marines, takes on the alien warrior race empire called the Covenant as well as the mutating killing parasites called the Flood. The main story line and three short stories are created by artists and writers including Moebius, Phil Hale, Ed Lee, Tsutomo Nihei, Jay Faerber, Andrew Robinson, Simon Bisley, and Lee Hammock.

© 2006 Marvel Comics
and Bungie Studios.

Judge Dredd. Titan Books Limited and DC Comics, 2002– . **T** 🎬

In a post-nuclear world, Earth's population has been crammed into sprawling, crime-ridden Mega-Cities. A new breed of justice—the Judges—were created to police the cities and render verdicts on the spot, even executions. In Mega-City One, one Judge stands above all others and takes no prisoners: Judge Dredd! The adventures of Dredd and other characters, including Psi-Judge Anderson, Judge Death, and more, have been told since Dredd's first appearance in the pages of *2000 AD* in 1977. Many more graphic novel collections of Judge Dredd and his oddball cast of Judges, oddballs, and mutants can be found at Titan Book Limited's Web site (www.titanbooks.com). Dredd has also appeared in a number of crossovers with a variety of U.S. comic book characters, including Batman, Aliens, and Predators; these are listed throughout this publication.

> *Cursed Earth.* Written by Pat Mills and John Wagner. Illustrated by Mike McMahon and Brian Bolland. Titan Books Limited, 2004. 160pp. 1-84023-774-0.
> *Judge Dredd Featuring Judge Death.* Written by John Wagner. Illustrated by Brian Bolland. Titan Books Limited, 2002. 96pp. 1-84023-386-9.
> *Judge Dredd: Necropolis Book 1.* Written by John Wagner. Illustrated by Carlos Ezquerra. Titan Books Limited, 2003. 144pp. 1-84023-601-9.
> *Judge Dredd: Necropolis Book 2.* Written by John Wagner. Illustrated by Carlos Ezquerra. Titan Books Limited, 2003. 144pp. 1-84023-635-3.
> *Dredd vs. Death.* Written by Alan Grant and John Wagner. Illustrated by Brian Bolland. 2005.112pp. 1-4012-0580-1.

Junk Force. Written by Hideki Kakinuma and Sword Yuusuke. Illustrated by Yusuke Ken.** ComicsOne, 2004. **T Japanese manga.**

In the year 2100, Earth's resources have dried up. Following a world war that split Earth into two ideologies, one advocating repairing Earth (Earth Regeneration) and the other wanting to salvage what they can and colonize Mars (Mars Pioneer), the Mars Pioneer faction won, taking the last few precious resources with them to Mars. They left a mechanized system behind called the Z.P.T., with promises to purify Earth. Thirty years later the Z.P.T. malfunctioned and began a new form of purifying: killing humanity and massacring millions. Now a group of upbeat teens, Mill, Liza, Wooty, and Louis, are out to destroy the Z.P.T. and purify Earth by any means necessary. A rag-tag group of three girls and one lucky boy, when they recover an android that was sent by the Mars Pioneers, they find they may have the key to taking on the Z.P.T. and turning the tide of humanity's fate on Earth.

Vol. 1. 2004. 208pp. 1-58899-364-7.
Vol. 2. 2004. 200pp. 1-58899-365-5.
Vol. 3. 2004. 200pp. 1-58899-366-3.

Kin: Descent of Man. **Written and illustrated by Gary Frank**. Image Comics, 2002. 160pp. 1-58240-224-8. **T**

What if Neanderthal man really never became extinct 35,000 years ago and had a much more evolved technology than ours? Considered a threat by the S.I.A. and marked for extinction, the last of the Neanderthals escapes and is rescued by a forest ranger and former S.I.A. executive. Now "Bob" has vowed to get revenge for his people and to make sure the secrets of his people do not fall into enemy hands.

Little White Mouse. **Written and illustrated by Paul Sizer.** Café Digital Comics, 2001–2003; Fiery Studios, 2006. **T**

Sixteen-year-old Loo has been stranded on remote, deserted mining satellite facility 713 after her ship was destroyed in a meteor storm. Her sister P'heng did not survive the crash but her brainwave patterns were saved. With nothing but automated computer systems, maintenance droids Boris and Dieter, and even a ghost called Pascal as companions, can Loo's resourcefulness keep her alive until help arrives? She manages to keep her cool dealing with automated CyberDogs, space pirates, and a dwindling oxygen supply. Now all she needs is a way home to bring back the stored memories of her sister and to be reunited with her family.

© 2006 Paul Sizer.

Perfect Collection #1: Dream of the Ghost. 2001. 144pp. 1-888429-07-0.
Perfect Collection #2: Into the Blue. 2002. 128pp. 1-888429-11-9.
Perfect Collection #3: Entroy Dreaming. 2004. 144pp. 1-888429-23-2.
Little White Mouse Omnubus Edition. Fiery Studios, 2006. 448pp. 0-9768565-5-7.

Micronauts: Revolution. **Written by Scott Wherle. Illustrated by Eric Wolfe Hanson and E. J. Su.** Image Comics, 2003. 112pp. 1-58240-311-2. **T**

Abducted from Earth, Ryan Archer is thrust into the diminutive world known as the Microcosm, a futuristic realm that is under the rule of the tyrannical black-armored Baron Karza. Can Archer and his newfound companions Acroyear, the insect-like Vaerian, and Biotron defeat Karza and restore freedom to the Microcosm? Based on the popular 1970s toy property and inspired by the hit Marvel Comics series that was originally published from 1979 to 1986.

***Mighty Tiny: Tales of the Old Empire.* 2d ed. Written and illustrated by Ben Dunn.** Antarctic Press, 2005. 174pp. 1-932453-86-5. **T**

> In a future where humanity is extinct and the stuff of legend, the mice and rats have evolved. In a setting reminiscent of late nineteenth- and early twentieth- century technology, when the peace treaty of the nations Mosputa and Ratveria is nearly destroyed by an assassination plot, a great war is about to be started by a secret organization bent on destruction, known only as The Triad. Only two orphaned best friends, a mouse and a rat, and the friends they make on the way can foil the fiendish plot to destroy peace and take on the mysterious Triad.

***Monkeyman & O'Brien.* Written and illustrated by Arthur Adams.** Dark Horse Comics, 1997. 136pp. 1-56971-232-8. **T**

> In a San Francisco laboratory, a dimensional barrier searching for space-space life-forms accidentally targets an unknown object pulled from the space-time continuum. To scientist Ann O'Brien's surprise, a very large humanoid in a spacesuit emerges from the field. From another dimension comes Axwell Tiberius, alias Monkeyman—a super-intelligent gorilla from another dimension. Ann also has gone through some changes due to the interdimensional rift, and she has gained super strength, too. Trapped on Earth until they can relocate his home dimension, Tiberius and Ann use their skills of science and strength to save the world from the evil of the nefarious frog-men from outer space, the terror called Quash and the Shewmanoid, and his behemoth minions from beneath Earth's crust.

Monkeyman & O'Brien™ & © 2006
Dark Horse Comics, Inc.

***Moped Army.* Written and illustrated by Paul Sizer.** Café Digital Comics, 2005. 138pp. 0-9768565-4-9. **O**

> In the year 2277, gasoline is now an illegal substance, and air-powered cars fly through the city of Bolt Harbor. Simon, a rich high school girl disenfranchised by the partying life she lives and her bullish rich boyfriend, sets out to decide just where her heart belongs—to the sprawling high-rise metropolis city of Bolt Harbor or in the decaying lower underbelly that serves as the foundation for Rust City. Nicknamed 'Rust City,' the seedy ruins of a fallen city are home to the low-lifes, gangs, and a unique geek squad of moped riders called the Moped Army. The gang is made up of many moped enthusiasts, including Dingle, Chu-Toi, Crank, and others, who ride 250-year-old mopeds and have their headquarters based in an abandoned library. When Simone's boyfriend and his rich-boy gang decide to take on the Moped Army in their air cars, a war is about to explode in the streets of Rust City, and Simone must decide where her loyalties truly lie.

<u>Negation.</u> Written by Tony Bedard. Illustrated by Paul Pelletier. Cross Generation Comics, 2002–2003. **T**

> People from planets all across the universe—both superpowered and nonpowered—find themselves prisoners of the godlike Charon and the sinister Negation Empire. Now trapped in another dimension, the prisoners can either rebel or duel against each other to the death. Only Obregon Caine, a brilliant wartime strategist, has guessed the rules of the game the empire is playing, and he decides that the only way to

truly win is to unite the quarrelling prisoners and take on the Negation empire. Further collected volumes were planned but never published because the publisher went bankrupt.

> *Vol. 1: BOHICA.* 2002. 192pp. 1-931484-30-9.
> *Vol. 2: Baptism of Fire.* 2003. 160pp. 1-931484-59-7.

100 Girls. Written by Adam Gallardo. Illustrated by Todd Demong. Arcana Studio, 2005–2006. T ◉

© 2006 Adam Gallardo and Todd Demong.

Thirteen-year-old Sylvia Mark always knew she didn't quite fit in. It's not only that she's two grades ahead of anyone her age—she's also tremendously strong, too. At night Sylvia constantly has dreams about other girls who look exactly like her. In reality, Sylvia is one of 100 girls cloned in a genetics breeding experiment to give normal humans super-human powers. Thirteen years ago, four of the cloned girls were kidnapped from the facility where they were created and sent to families around the country. Now Sylvia is on a journey to find her other counterparts and find out why she was kidnapped all those years ago. Meanwhile the organization that created the girls will stop at nothing to retrieve Sylvia and her counterparts.

> *The First Girl, Vol. 1.* 2005. 56pp. 0-9763095-3-X.
> *The First Girl, Vol. 2.* 2006. 56pp. 0-9763095-1-3.

Planet Racers. Written and illustrated by Jim Lawson and Peter Laird. Zeromayo Studios, 1997–2000. T

The United Systems Planet Racers Association (USPRA) Championships are the biggest events in the galaxy in the year 2999, with over a trillion fans from thousands of star systems. The events comprise two-man pilot and navigator teams in monstrous two-wheeled vehicles. The most famous team is the Koyoshada riders team of Tripper Nitro and the pompous racing sensation Godman Falcon. When Godman causes an accident his career is in ruins, but after a chance encounter with Methania Fitts of the Fitts Racing team, he's given a second chance. Can this new team take on his old partner and rivals and become the best planet racers in the universe?

> *Vol. 1: Life Cycle.* 1997. 276pp. 0-9661985-0-6.
> *Vol. 2: Off Season.* 1998. 176pp. 0-9661985-1-4.
> *Vol. 3: Janus Rising.* 2000. 294pp. 0-9661985-2-2.

Psy-Comm. Written by Jason Henderson and Tony Salvaggio. Illustrated by Shane Granger. TOKYOPOP. 2005–. T Neo-manga.

Mark Leit is one of the best of the Psychic Commandoes, a unique fighting force for the Electromedia Corp, a corporation state in the year 2261 that uses the "Psy-Comms" battles as a form of entertainment. Mark can't shake the past and is obsessed by an accident that occurred six years earlier and cost the life of Raven, a fellow Psy-Comm. When a mission brings Mark face-to-face with an enemy who reminds him of the long-dead Raven, Mark finds himself on the wrong side of the law. Now a fugitive, he must discover where his true loyalties lie and where he truly belongs.

> *Vol. 1.* 2005. 192pp. 1-59816-269-1.

Rocketo. Written and illustrated by Frank Espinosa. Image Comics, 2006–. T ◎

© 2006 Frank Espinosa.

Set 2,000 years in humanity's future after the earth that we know is gone and its magnetic field shattered by a deadly alien life-form, fragments are all that remain. Only the Mappers, heroic men who have compasses fused onto their right arms, can help rebuild and map the planet. There's only one Mapper brave enough to navigate through the remnants of Earth—Rocketo Garrison! An explorer of the unknown and mapmaker, he's following in his missing father's footsteps as he remaps Earth in search of adventure. A new graphic novel series reminiscent of classic science fiction pulp stories, including *Flash Gordon* and *Buck Rogers.*

> *Vol. 1: Journey to the Hidden Sea.* 2006. 256pp. 1-58240-585-9.

Rogue Trooper. Written by Gerry Finley-Day. Illustrated by Dave Gibbons, Cam Kennedy, and various. 2000 A.D./DC Comics, 2005. T 🎮

A futuristic parable about the dehumanization of soldiers and the grim nature of war. On the planet Nu-Earth, the Norts and the Southers battle for control of the planet. Chemical warfare has made the planet inhospitable, but both sides struggle for control. The Souther Genetic Infantrymen are soldiers genetically engineered to thrive in the toxic wonderland of Nu-Earth. When all but one of the G.I.s is killed, he continues a lone battle as a Rogue Trooper, cutting through the ranks of the armored Norts. The Rogue Trooper carries with him the semi-organic memory chips of several lost souls, so he is never alone. Carrying the memories of Trooper Gunnar, Bagman, and Helm, he struggles in his battle to defeat the Norts. The collection reprints the classic British series from the early 1980s.

> *Vol. 1: The Future of War.* 2005. 160pp. 1-4012-0577-1.
> *Vol. 2: Fort Neuro.* 2005. 192pp. 1-4012-0589-5.
> *Vol. 3: Fort Neuro—@Ulist = Vol. 2.* 2005. 192pp. 1-4012-0589-5.

Runners. Written and illustrated by Sean Wang. Serve Man Press, 2005–. T ◎

© 2006 Sean Wang.

In the ungoverned sectors of intergalatic space called "Roguespace," smuggler Roka Nostaco and his alien crew have had a tough time making it as runners of all sorts of cargo. When a simple cargo pickup goes wrong, they discover that pirates have hijacked their rendezvous freighter ship, and Roka's crew has to protect the goods. After chasing the pirates away, they discover that the freighter crew is dead, the cargo is mostly intact, and one canister has released something they're not prepared to deal with: a beautiful young girl lying unconscious on the cargo hold floor. Are they really running slaves? They hate to think of it, but a job is a job. Meanwhile, the crew find themselves in more danger than they ever imagined after finding the girl as they take on bounty hunters, revenge-seeking pirates, local galactic police, a possible blossoming romance, and cliffhanger escapes.

Vol. 1: Bad Goods. 2005. 168pp. 0-9768517-0-9.

Scryed. Written by Yosuke Kuroda. Illustrated by Yasunari Toda. TOKYOPOP, 2003. O Japanese manga. あ

Over two decades earlier the Yokohama region experienced massive seismic activity that raised it miles above the rest of Japan. Years later some of the newest generation of Yokohama infants developed extraordinary powers, each different from the rest. Called Alters, they devastated Yokohama as their powers grew and turned it into a wasteland. Now a battle for the fate of Yokohama has erupted in which two factions of Alters have emerged from the ashes: the HOLY, those who want to return Yokohama to order and peace through dogmatic control, and those who want to rule over the nonpowered humans. Alter and mercenary-for-hire Kazuma Torisuma, along with his young ward Kanami Yuta, may be the only ones capable of finding a middle ground of peace among the ruins of what is now called the Lost Grounds. The first rule of order is to take on HOLY, even if Kazuma Torisuma has to do it by himself, one superpowered Alter at a time. The series was also adapted as a Japanese anime.

Vol. 1. 2003. 192pp. 1-59182-228-9.
Vol. 2. 2003. 192pp. 1-59182-229-7.
Vol. 3. 2003. 192pp. 1-59182-230-0.
Vol. 4. 2003. 200pp. 1-59182-231-9.
Vol. 5. 2003. 192pp. 1-59182-232-7.

Shockrockets: We Have Ignition. Written by Kurt Busiek. Illustrated by Stuart Immonen. Dark Horse Comics, 2004. 160pp. 1-59307-129-9. T

In the year 2071, Earth is rebuilding after defeating an alien invasion. The skies above Earth are protected by the Shockrockets, a group of flying fighters made from captured alien technology and human ingenuity and flown by the best pilots on the planet. Alejandro Cruz, a daredevil teenager who's always wanted to become a Shockrocket, accidentally becomes bonded with a Shockrocket ship. Although he's reluctantly accepted into the elite fighter pilot squadron, his unique skills may be the key to defeating the Shockrocket's most deadly adversary: a military genius who helped win the war against the alien invaders over ten years ago.

Sigil. Written by Mark Waid and Chuck Dixon. Illustrated by Scot Eaton. Cross Generation Comics, 2002–2003. T

Ex-soldier Samandahl Rey is just trying to get by in life following the Human/Saurian war, but when he's been selected to be a Sigil-Bearer by a god-like entity, he finds out that when you're carrying one of the most powerful weapons in the universe, you become one of the deadliest and most wanted men in the galaxy. Joined with Sam are the crew of his ship, *The BitterLuck,* including a hologram/computer simulation of his dead best friend Roiya Sintor, an escaped concubine named Zanni, and the rogue JeMerik. They wander the galaxy and fight off constant threats from the Saurian Empire and the Negation Empire, as Sam slowly discovers the limits of his new power. Meanwhile Tchlusarud, Sam's archenemy from the dinosaurlike Saurians, has also been gifted with Sigil-like powers, and the Negation Empire makes its bid to control the universe.

> *Vol. 1: Mark of Power.* 2002. 192pp. 1-931484-01-5.
> *Vol. 2: The Marked Man.* 2002. 208pp. 1-931484-07-4.
> *Vol. 3: The Lizard God.* 2002. 160pp. 1-931484-28-7.
> *Vol. 4: Hostage Planet.* 2003. 160pp. 1-931484-53-8.

Silent Möbius. Written and illustrated by Kia Asamiya. VIZ Media, LLC, 1999–2003. **O Japanese manga.**

In the year 2026, the A.M.P. (Abnormal Mystery Police) are the best line of defense for a rebuilt Tokyo against the otherworldly Lucifer Hawks, vicious and demonic entities with a craving for human flesh. And as if the Lucifer Hawks weren't bad enough, the group also has to take on other nasty monstrosities like killer cyborgs, robotic megadynes, and destructive dragons. The A.M.P. is made up of seven female members, each of whom has a unique power. Together the A.M.P. are a powerful fighting force combining futuristic technology and ancient magic to fight evil. Led by Chief Rally Cheyenne and Mana Isozaki, the A.M.P. must set aside the ghosts from their own troubled pasts and work as a team to defeat the dimension-hopping monsters and save the citizens of Tokyo.

> *Vol. 1.* 1999. 256pp. 1-56931-364-4.
> *Vol. 2.* 1999. 248pp. 1-56931-367-9.
> *Vol. 3.* 1999. 248pp. 1-56931-370-9.
> *Vol. 4.* 2000. 200pp. 1-56931-472-1.
> *Vol. 5.* 2001. 248pp. 1-56931-545-0.
> *Vol. 6.* 2001. 192pp. 1-56931-630-9.
> *Vol. 7.* 2002. 232pp. 1-56931-712-7.
> *Vol. 8.* 2002. 192pp. 1-56931-743-7.
> *Vol. 9: Turnabout.* 2002. 184pp. 1-56931-852-2.
> *Vol. 10: Blood.* 2003. 184pp. 1-56931-891-3.
> *Vol. 11: Hell.* 2003. 176pp. 1-59116-070-7.
> *Vol. 12.* 2003. 184pp. 1-59116-118-5.

***The Surrogates*. Written by Robert Venditti. Illustrated by Brett Weldele.** Top Shelf Productions, 2006. 208pp. 1-891830-87-2. **O**

By the year A.D. 2054, humanity has developed the ultimate in cybernetics and virtual reality with the release of the personal surrogates. Now the surrogate can do all of life's tasks, and humans never have to leave the home ever again. To help this perfect world to continue to run smoothly, Detectives Harvey Greer and Pete Ford of the Metro Police Department are there to keep things in line. When a techno-terrorist strikes who is bent on returning humanity to a time when people lived their own lives instead of experiencing them vicariously, Greer and Ford must try to stop the madman—or should they?

***TechJacket: Lost and Found.* Written by Robert Kirkman. Illustrated by E. J. Su.** Image Comics, 2003. 144pp. 1-58240-314-7. **T**

© 2006 Robert Kirkman
and E. J. Su.

A war has been raging for years between the peaceful Geldarians and the violent Kresh. To compensate for their weak frames, the superiorly intelligent Geldarians have created a TechJacket, a lightweight vest that each Geldarian wears from birth. The suit enhances their strength and over time focuses on the needs of the bearer of the suit. When teenager Zack Thompson comes across a crashed Geldarian spaceship, he receives the TechJacket from the dying alien. Can a teenage boy handle one of the most powerful weapons in the universe and help the Geldarians defeat the Kresh invasion in time to catch up on his schoolwork?

3

***The Tenth: Blackout.* Written by Tony Daniel and Beau Smith. Illustrated by Tony Daniel.** Dark Horse Comics, 2001. 128pp. 1-56971-616-1. **O**

Victor DeLeon was a CIA agent who was abducted and transformed by the mad scientist Rhazes Darkk into The Tenth, a hulking, genetically enhanced monster who becomes the ultimate hunter when he gets a taste of his prey's blood. DeLeon is the latest creation by Darkk; in fact, he's the tenth in the line of monsters, hence his name. Now he will stop at nothing to ensure that there never is an eleventh monster and that his predecessors are eliminated. He's joined in his quest for vengeance by the telekinetic teen Esperanza del Toro and her friend Zorina Fine as they try to locate Zora's missing mom, Jaena, who was also a covert agent investigating Darkk. Along the way they discover that they aren't the only ones looking for Darkk. Will these powered opponents be allies or adversaries in their quest to conquer evil?

Trigun. Written and illustrated by Yasuhiro Nightow. Dark Horse Comics, 2003–. **T Japanese mango.** あ

In the far future on a desert planet walks a man nicknamed the "Humanoid Typhoon." Meet Vash the Stampede, a spikey-blonde-haired man known for his trademark red coat and for being an expert marksman. A slightly goofy and lighthearted man, he's become known as a walking one-man human disaster, bringing trouble wherever he goes. There's a $60,000,000,000 bounty on his head, which guarantees that he'll always be chased by those foolish enough to try to bring him in. Those who try to bring him all soon find out that they don't stand a chance against Vash, as he wanders across a dusty western landscape in search of understanding and helping those in need while reconciling with his enigmatic past. The series was renamed Trigun Maximum and was published in Japan in eleven volumes. The manga was adapted into a twenty-six-episode anime series in Japan.

Trigun. 2003.
    Vol. 1. 2003. 360pp. 1-59307-196-5.
    Vol. 2. 2003. 344pp. 1-59307-053-5.

Trigun Maximum. 2003–.
> *Vol. 1: The Hero Returns.* 2004. 192pp. 1-59307-196-5.
> *Vol. 2: Death Blue.* 2004. 200pp. 1-59307-197-3.
> *Vol. 3: His Life As a . . . .* 2004. 192pp. 1-59307-266-X.
> *Vol. 4: Bottom of the Dark.* 2005. 192pp. 1-59307-314-3.
> *Vol. 5: Break Out.* 2005. 208pp. 1-59307-344-5.
> *Vol. 6: The Gunslinger.* 2005. 208pp. 1-59307-351-8.
> *Vol. 7: Happy Days.* 2005. 192pp. 1-59307-395-X.
> *Vol. 8: Silent Run.* 2006. 224pp. 1-59307-452-2.
> *Vol. 9.* 2006. 200pp. 1-59307-527-8.
> *Vol. 10.* 2006. 240pp. 1-59307-556-1.

***The Vanishers.* Written by Chuck Dixon. Illustrated by Andres Klacik.** Idea and Design Works, LLC, 2002. 80pp. 0-9712282-6-4. **T**

Junior high student Andy discovers that his friends are disappearing—literally! One by one they're vanishing, and no one except Andy remembers that they even existed. Andy finds that another student, Arnold Voltz, also is noticing the disappearances, and together they embark on an adventure across time, from medieval England, to the dawn of the twentieth century, to the far future, to find their friends and return home.

Zendra. Written by Stuart Moore. Illustrated by Martin Montiel Luna and Jose Carlos Buelna. Penny-Farthing Press, Inc., 2002–2003. **T**

In the far future, as three galaxies are in turmoil from the ruthless Jakkaran Empire, a curious race of aliens are in search of the mythological planet Zendra. The planet is rumored to be the home of a perfect race of beings called Humans, and as the legends state, there will be one Human who will lead the rebellion against the Jakkarans. The humans are believed to be extinct, destroyed by the Jakkaran warlord Abathor. Hoping to jump-start the prophecy, the alien scientist Dr. Forcilia has succeeded in creating a test-tube human: a girl named Halle. Over time she becomes aware of her powers, and she soon finds herself on the run from Abathor. As she travels across the galaxies, the nineteen-year-old, half-human, superpowered teenager is in search of the legendary planet Zendra, where she can be reunited with humanity and one day be the protector of the last remaining colony of humans.

> *1.0: Collocation.* 2002. 160pp. 0-9673683-9-1.
> *2.0: Heart of Fire.* 2003. 216pp. 0-9719012-1-X.

New Wave Science Fiction

This subgenre takes a radical, alternative look at science fiction. Prose pioneers in the field include Ray Bradbury, Phillip K. Dick, Ursula LeGuin, Harlan Ellison, and Michael Moorcock. In new wave science fiction the literate writing quality of the story tends to be more important than the scientific accuracy of occurrences in the plot. Generally difficult to categorize, this subgenre can include facets of religion, thought-provoking topics on the nature of the soul, and psychological rides of fantasy that flow alongside common science fiction themes including—but not limited to—time travel, alien races, space travel to other planets, and alternative looks into the far future. Carla Speed McNeil's genre-busting series Finder is an excellent example of this subgenre.

***The Best of Ray Bradbury: The Graphic Novel.* Written by Ray Bradbury. Illustrated by various.** ibooks, Incorporated, 2003. 160pp. 0-7434-7476-7. **T**

A collection of works based on short stories by award-winning science fiction author Ray Bradbury. The highlight of the collection is the classic tale "The Sound of Thunder," in which a time-travel safari visit to the age of dinosaurs accidentally brings about changes that affect the future—no matter how small.

***The Compleat Moonshadow.* Written by J. M. DeMatteis. Illustrated by Jon J. Muth.** Vertigo/DC Comics, 1998. 464pp. 1-56389-343-6. **M**

A strange life journey through the birth, adolescence, adulthood, senior years, and death of a man called Moonshadow, the child of hippie parents, who is a round, ball-sized alien from a race called the G'l-Doses. Moonshadow was born in an intergalactic zoo and raised on the classic literature of William Blake, Lord Byron, Samuel Beckett, and others. He is kicked out of his home at age fourteen to explore the galaxy alongside his mother and pseudo-surrogate father Ira, a foul-mouthed, lecherous, furry creature. Moonshadow learns about love, life, despair, death, and other emotions as he travels from planet to planet on his journey of self-discovery.

Finder. Written and illustrated by Carla Speed McNeil. Lightspeed Press, 1999–. **M** ◉

© 2006 Carla Speed McNeil.

In the domed city of Anvard, where various alien and familiar cultures coexist, are Finders, mysterious hunters and trackers who are able to eat the sin from someone's life before he or she dies. Jaeger Ayers is one such Finder. A shaman-like, charming rogue, he's come to the city to help Emma Grosvenor and her three children. Her ex-husband is Brig, a member of the Medawar clan and a vicious homicidal maniac, and Jaegar once served in the army under his command. Can Jaeger resolve the family conflict without causing any bloodshed? Through each story line, Jaeger and other Finders travel around the planet in search of a connection with other humans and aliens, taking on their sins for the good of the world. The complex science fiction story was awarded an Ignatz Award in 2004 and 2005 for Outstanding Series and is still ongoing.

> *Vol. 1: Sin-Eater, Part I.* 1999. 168pp. 0-9673691-0-X.
> *Vol. 2: Sin-Eater, Part II.* 2000. 184pp. 0-9673691-1-8.
> *Vol. 3: King of Cats.* 2001. 120pp. 0-9673691-2-6.
> *Vol. 4: Talisman.* 2002. 104pp. 0-9673691-3-4.
> *Vol. 5: Dream Sequence.* 2003. 104pp. 0-9673691-4-2.
> *Vol. 6: Mystery Date.* 2004. 160pp. 0-9673691-5-0.
> *Vol. 7: The Rescuers.* 2005. 160pp. 0-9673691-6-9.
> *Vol. 8: Five Crazy Women.* 2006. 136pp. 0-9673691-7-7.

***Second Soul.* Written by Scott O. Brown. Illustrated by Amin Amat.** Cyberosia, 2003. 88pp. 0-9742713-1-4. **O**

When you're a rock star and you die, you get out of your contract, right? Wrong. The clone of the musician Mtukubwa finds out the hard way that contracts and a second chance at life cost a hefty price, when not even death can keep him out of the spotlight.

Aliens from Outer Space

Ever since science fiction classic novels such as H.G. Wells's *War of the Worlds*, writers have been telling tales of alien visitors from outer space as well as the impending invasion of aliens from outer space. The stories listed below focus on tales of alien races, both benign and monstrous, and their interaction with humanity. The aliens can be portrayed as the protagonists, antagonists, or supporting characters.

Alien Legion. Created by Carl Potts. Written by Chuck Dixon, Alan Zelenetz, and various. Illustrated by Larry Stroman, Frank Cirocco, and various. Checker Book Publishing Group, 2001–2005. **T**

Soldiers for the Tophan Galactic Union, a rag-tag group of misfits, outcasts, criminals, and soldiers of fortune, are the main fighting force against the ruthless and hostile race known as the Harkilon Empire. Led by the blue-skinned, snakelike humanoid Major Sarigar, the Legion is the best there is when it comes to taking on the toughest assignments in the galaxy. The Checker Books collections reprint the original Epic Comics series. Created by Carl Potts.

Force Nomad. 2001. 212pp. 0-9710249-0-1.
Piecemaker. 2002. 212pp. 0-9710249-4-4.
Footsloggers. 2005. 200pp. 0-9753808-7-7.

Alien Nine. Written and illustrated by Hitoshi Tomizawa. CPM Manga, 2003. **O Japanese manga.**

After aliens have begun to infest the planet, three girls are chosen to protect their school, Elementary School #9, from the daily rigors of the alien infestation. Each girl shares a symbiotic relationship with her froglike, alien companion as they sweep the school halls on patrol. The job isn't easy, and even the best of the girls isn't prepared for the horrors from outer space that lurk in the hallways. *Emulators* features the same three girls after they graduate from sixth grade and attend junior high school.

Vol. 1. 2003. 224pp. 1-58664-891-8.
Vol. 2. 2003. 224pp. 1-58664-892-6.
Vol. 3. 2003. 224pp. 1-58664-893-4.
Emulators. 2004. 240pp. 1-58664-924-8.

Aliens. Dark Horse Comics, 1996– . **T O** 🎬

These acid-spewing, insectoid Aliens first appeared in Ridley Scott's film *Alien* in 1979 and have been scaring audiences ever since with three sequels, as well as the 2004 *Aliens versus Predator* film. Dark Horse Comics tales of the Aliens delve deeper into the science fiction world of facehuggers, chestbursters, Alien Queens, and the unlucky humans who find themselves face-to-face with the deadliest species in the galaxy. Note that other tie-ins featuring the Aliens and popular characters from other comic books, including Superman, Green Lantern, Judge Dredd, and others, are also listed below.

Aliens. 1996–. **O**

Tales spun off directly from the events seen in the <u>Alien</u> quadrilogy of films. The stories feature a variety of characters from the movies, including Ripley, and plenty of acid-spewing Aliens and deadly facehuggers.

> *Vol. 1: Outbreak.* Written by Mark Verheiden. Illustrated by Mark A. Nelson. 1996. 176pp. 1-56971-174-7.
> *Vol. 2: Nightmare Asylum.* Written by Mark Verheiden. Illustrated by Denis Beauvais. 1996. 112pp. 1-56971-217-4.
> *Vol. 3: Female War.* Written by Mark Verheiden. Illustrated by Sam Kieth. 1996. 112pp. 1-56971-190-9.
> *Vol. 4: Genocide.* Written by Mike Richardson. Illustrated by Damon Willis. 1997. 112pp. 1-56971-196-8.
> *Vol. 5: Harvest.* Written by Jerry Prosser. Illustrated by Kelley Jones. 1998. 120pp. 1-56971-198-4.
> *Salvation and Sacrifice.* Written by Dave Gibbons and Peter Milligan. Illustrated by Mike Mignola and Paul Johnson. 2001. 112pp. 1-56971-561-0.

Batman/Aliens. DC Comics and Dark Horse Comics, 1997–2003. **T**

When a secret vault under Gotham city is unearthed, its hidden secrets include four Alien embryos and a vicious Alien drone loose in the city. When a secret organization is found to be harvesting the aliens for a deadly experiment, the armor-protected dark knight detective, having faced the enemy before, is the only hero who knows how deadly acid-spewing creatures from outer space can truly be.

> *Batman/Aliens.* Written by Ron Marz. Illustrated by Bernie Wrightson. 1997. 128pp. 1-56971-305-7.
> *Batman/Aliens 2.* Written by Ian Edginton. Illustrated by James Hodgkins. 2003. 160pp. 1-4012-0081-8.

Green Lantern vs. Aliens. **Written by Ron Marz. Illustrated by Rick Leonardi.** DC Comics and Dark Horse Comics, 2001. 96pp. 1-56971-538-6. **T**

Years earlier Hal Jordan, once the Green Lantern, vowed to preserve all life—including those of the vicious Aliens. Now years later a new Green Lantern, Kyle Rayner, investigates a gruesome scene that could have been prevented years earlier had Hal not vowed to preserve all life and destroyed the Aliens. Can Kyle undo the damage that Hal unknowingly inflicted, or will he lose his life trying to defeat the acid-spewing Alien menace?

Judge Dredd vs. Aliens: Incubus. **Written by John Wagner and Andy Diggle. Illustrated by Henry Flint.** Dark Horse Comics, 2004. 104pp. 1-56971-983-7. **T**

In Mega City One, the law is enforced by the toughest lawman on Earth: Judge Dredd. When a deadly infestation of Aliens threatens to destroy the city,

Dredd and a team of bug-hunters called the Verminators are there to take on the vicious killing machines from outer space.

Superman/Aliens. DC Comics and Dark Horse Comics, 1996–2003. **T** ◎

While investigating a possible signal that deviated from his home planet Krypton, a depowered Superman finds himself face-to-face with one of the deadliest creatures in space. In the sequel, the villain Darkseid of the planet Apokolips has use for the deadly Aliens, and Superman and his allies must try to defeat the horde of Apokolips-Alien hybrids.

> *Superman/Aliens.* Written by Dan Jurgens. Illustrated by Kevin Nowlan. 1996. 152pp. 1-56971-167-4.
>
> *Superman/Aliens 2: Godwar.* Written by Chuck Dixon. Illustrated by Jon Bogdanove. 2003. 96pp. 1-56971-963-2.

Aliens vs. Predator. Dark Horse Comics, 1991– . **T O** 🎬

A science fiction movie fan's dream come true, the first collection pairing up two of Hollywood's most horrific aliens appeared in 1991, thirteen years before the long-awaited Fox film based on the premise of the two alien races' battle against each other was released in 2004. Many film buffs feel that the graphic novel stories featuring the Aliens against the Predators were better done treatments than the film could ever hope to be.

> *Aliens vs. Predator.* Written by Randy Stradley. Illustrated by Phil Norwood. 1991. 176pp. 1-56971-125-9. **T** ◎
>
> *Aliens/Predators: War.* Written by Randy Stradley. Illustrated by Ricardo Villagran and Richard Corben. 1996. 200pp. 1-56971-158-5. **O**
>
> *Aliens vs. Predator: Deadliest of the Species.* Written by Chris Claremont. Illustrated by Jackson Guice. 1996. 320pp. 1-56971-184-4. **T**
>
> *Aliens vs. Predator: Eternal.* Written by Ian Edginton. Illustrated by Alex Maleev. 1999. 88pp. 1-56971-409-6. **O**
>
> *Aliens vs. Predator: Thrill of the Hunt.* Written by Mike Kennedy. Illustrated by Roger Robinson. 2004. 96pp. 1-59307-257-0. **T**
>
> *Alien vs. Predator: Civilized Beasts.* Written by Mike Kennedy. Illustrated by Roger Robinson. 2006. 96pp. 1-59307-342-9. **T**

Aliens vs. Predator vs. The Terminator. **Written by Mark Schultz. Illustrated by Mel Rubi.** 2001. 96pp. 1-56971-568-8. **T** 🎬

Set as a sequel of sorts to the last <u>Alien</u> film *Alien: Resurrection,* another popular movie character, the cyborg Terminators from the movies of the same name, are resurrected after centuries of silence. The Terminators' skeletal frames bonded with the genetics of the acid-spewing Aliens, and humanity's last stand is in the hands of the Alien-human clone of Ellen Ripley and a battalion of Predators.

Chocolate and French Fries. **Written by Carlos Trillo. Illustrated by Juan Bobillo.** SAF, 2004. 48pp. 1-59396-003-4. **Y**

Six young brothers, all living in a tiny apartment complex, discover that their parents were abducted by Martians! Smart kids that they are, they must try to extirpate the alien menace and rescue their parents. Along the way, they've got to figure out how to run the household, and one of the boys, Lorenzo, discovers he's a great cook. His signature dish? Why chocolate and french fries, of course! Can the kids prepare in time for the return of the Martian invasion and rescue their parents?

Cloudburst. **Written by Justin Gray and Jimmy Palmiotti. Illustrated by Christopher Shy and Eliseu Gouvei.** Image Comics, 2004. 64pp. 1-58240-368-6. **O**

Lauren Moore is a beautiful and brilliant scientist onboard a ship carrying hundreds of families and mercenary soldiers to an uninhabitable planet being prepared for colonization. She's about ready to release the Cloudburst, a satellite program designed to control the climates of uninhabitable worlds and make them safe for humans. The only problem is that she discovers the planet is already inhabited, and the mercenaries are hired men paid to exterminate the current inhabitants. Her only help is a mysterious nomad whom many consider to be only myth and legend. Can Lauren find a way to save the lives of those who have peacefully lived on the planet before they are permanently evicted?

🏵 ***Creature Tech.*** **Written and illustrated by Doug TenNapel.** Top Shelf Productions, 2002. 208pp. 1-891830-34-1. **T** ◎

Creature Tech

by Doug TenNapel

© 2006 Doug TenNapel.

Some 150 years ago the evil Dr. Jameson wanted to destroy the world by using giant space eels. He messed up and died—but that didn't stop him. Resurrected by the Shroud of Turin, the now zombified doctor wants to set his evil scheme in motion again. Only Dr. Ong, a young scientist at the top-secret "Creature Tech" facility, and the strangest assortment of allies, including a CIA-trained praying mantis, rednecks, alien symbiotes, and a little Christian faith, can save the day. The collection received recognition by YALSA's Popular Paperbacks for Young Adults committee in 2004 on the "Simply Science Fiction" list.

Decoy. **Written by Buddy Scalera. Illustrated by Courtney Huddleston.** Penny Farthing Press, Inc., 2000–2003. **T**

Bobby Luck, a rookie police officer for the waterlogged Dolphin City, has found an unlikely friend from another planet: a cute, fluorescent-green, shape-shifting alien named Decoy, who is stranded on Earth. After Officer Luck's near-fatal shooting in the line of duty, he and Decoy form a symbiotic relationship, and now they're practically inseparable. While Dolphin City continues to be consumed by a flood orchestrated by the sinister Dr. Alloy, Officer Luck and Decoy have to find a way to stop the evil doctor. But how can you stop an evil genius who's got three aliens like Decoy in his thrall and wants to add Decoy to his twisted team? Though the odds are against them, never underestimate what a comedic symbiotic crime-fighting duo can do.

> *Vol. 1.* 2000. 112pp. 0-9673683-2-4.
> *Vol. 2: Storm of the Century.* 2003. 160pp. 0-9719012-0-1.

***Earthboy Jacobus.* Written and illustrated by Doug TenNapel.** Image Comics, 2005. 272pp. 1-58240-492-5. **T** ◉

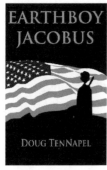

© 2006 Doug TenNapel.

Chief Edwards is an ex-marine who has just retired from the Modesto Police Department. While driving home from his final night of work, he literally drives into a whale on the road. The whale is actually a transdimensional Terra-Whale, and inside the mouth of the beast is a young boy called Jacobus. The young boy with strange markings on his right hand is being hunted by an insectoid race of creatures called Ectoids who assimilate others into their collective. Chief takes Jacobus into his home to keep him safe and treats him as if he were his own son. As time passes and Jacobus ages from a small boy to a slacker teenager to a hero, the Ectoids have never given up their desire to eliminate him. It's up to Jacobus to enter the belly of the beast, literally, to conquer his fears and save Earth from a conquering race of Ectoids, even if it costs him a part of himself.

<u>Gunparade March.</u> Written and illustrated by Hiroyuki Sanadura. ADV Manga, 2004–2005. **O Japanese manga.** あ

In 1945, World War II was disrupted when an alien invasion force of Phantom Beasts landed on Earth and quickly started destroying human life. Humanity picked up the pieces and has continued to fight to this day. In 1999, fifty-four years after the invasion began, Japan has created a strong perimeter, but due to the lack of recruits the Japanese government has drafted teens from ages fourteen to seventeen to serve on the front line. Giant mecha robots called Shikon, each commanded by a squadron of teens, watch over the borders of Japan for the Phantom Beasts. One such squadron, the 5121st Army Unit, is run by kindhearted Atsushi Hayami. What will their command become when he is joined by Mai Shibamura, a bratty daughter of a powerful family in Japan? Can these two awkward teens learn to work together—and perhaps learn to love each other—while Japan's fate hangs in the balance? The series was based on a video game originally released in Japan for the Playstation game system and has also been turned into an animated series.

> *Vol. 1.* 2004. 216pp. 1-4139-0035-6.
> *Vol. 2.* 2005. 200pp. 1-4139-0141-7.
> *Vol. 3.* 2005. 248pp. 1-4139-0142-5.

***Invasion '55.* Written by Chuck Dixon. Illustrated by Lito Fernández.** Idea and Design Works, LLC, 2002. 80pp. 0-9719775-1-8. **Y**

A washed-up alcoholic Air Force lieutenant, a tough biker, a determined female reporter, and a six-year-old boy are all that's left to save the city of Hidalgo Well, New Mexico, from an alien invasion from outer space. A homage to the classic science fiction B-movies of the 1950s.

***Nemesis the Warlock: Death to All Aliens.* Written by Pat Mills. Illustrated by Kevin O'Neill and Jesus Redondo.** Titan Books, 2003. 176pp. 1-84023-475-X. **O**

From the pages of the British publication *2000 AD* comes a science fiction story that mixes dark humor with a different take on the concept of a savior. In the far future, the aliens of the galaxy have been persecuted and downtrodden by humans of the mighty

Termight Empire. The Grand Inquisitor Torquemada, the leader of the alien hunters known as Terminators and scourge of all aliens, has spread his vicious teachings of intolerance and has declared death to all nonhumans. From the ashes of rebellion has come a savior of sorts: a horselike, insectoid alien known as Nemesis. Neither good nor evil, he's come to rescue the aliens from the cruelty of humanity and to destroy his arch-nemesis, Torquemada.

Parasyte. Written and illustrated by Hitoshi Iwaaki. TOKYOPOP, 1998–2002. **M Japanese manga.**

Shin seems to be a typical high school student and an all-around normal boy, but he discovers a plot by parasitic aliens to dominate the world. The aliens take over the human body and appear on the outside to blend in well with other humans, but their faces detach to reveal a sharp-toothed horror. How does Shin know of this invasion? He's got one living inside his body! He was able to trap his own attacker in his left arm before it could take over the rest of his body. Now the parasite, nicknamed "Lefty," has become an inquisitive sort, and Shin must decide what he can do to prevent the invasion. Should he go public with this startling information, or will it place him in even more danger, and will more innocents be killed by the vicious and gory aliens before it's too late?

> *Vol. 1.* 1998. 192pp. 1-892213-02-8.
> *Vol. 2.* 1999. 190pp. 1-892213-07-9.
> *Vol. 3.* 1999. 176pp. 1-892213-21-4.
> *Vol. 4.* 2000. 184pp. 1-892213-44-3.
> *Vol. 5.* 2000. 176pp. 1-892213-53-2.
> *Vol. 6.* 2001. 176pp. 1-892213-67-2.
> *Vol. 7.* 2001. 192pp. 1-892213-71-0.
> *Vol. 8.* 2001. 192pp. 1-892213-86-9.
> *Vol. 9.* 2002. 184pp. 1-931514-09-7.
> *Vol. 10.* 2002. 192pp. 1-931514-10-0.
> *Vol. 11.* 2002. 184pp. 1-931514-11-9.
> *Vol. 12.* 2002. 184pp. 1-931514-12-7.

Predator. Dark Horse Comics, 1990-2001. **T**

Continuing the success of Dark Horse Comics' treatment of Fox's *Aliens* license, the hunter warriors from another world that originally plagued Arnold Schwarzenegger in the 1987 *Predator* film also successfully translated into the comic book format. The Predators are a race of warriors who hunt the deadliest known prey across the galaxy for their own sport. The tales serve as sequels of sorts to the first *Predator* film and expand on the original concept. For other tales featuring the Predator, please see the series <u>Aliens vs. Predator</u> listed previously in this chapter.

> <u>Predator.</u> Dark Horse Comics, 1990–1993. **T**
>
> > *Concrete Jungle.* Written by Mark Verheiden. Illustrated by Chris Warner. 1990. 112pp. 1-56971-165-8.
> > *Big Game.* Written by John Arcudi. Illustrated by Evan Dorkin. 1992. 96pp. 1-56971-166-6.

Cold War. Written by Mark Verheiden. Illustrated by Ron Randall. 1993. 112pp. 1-87857-479-5.

🎗 Batman vs. Predator. DC Comics and Dark Horse Comics, 1993–1998. **T**

The series features the greatest Predators from outer space pitted against the greatest crime-fighting detective, with the backdrop of Gotham City. The first series, Batman vs. Predator, received an Eisner Award in 1992 for Best Artist/Penciller/Inker for Andy Kubert's artwork.

Batman vs. Predator. Written by Dave Gibbons. Illustrated by Andy Kubert. 1993. 124pp. 1-56389-092-5.◉

Batman vs. Predator II: Bloodmatch. Written by Doug Moench. Illustrated by Paul Gulacy. 1995. 144pp. 1-56389-221-9.

Batman vs. Predator III: Blood Ties. Written by Chuck Dixon. Illustrated by Rodolfo Damaggio. 1998. 129pp. 1-56389-418-1.

Tarzan vs. Predator at the Earth's Core. Written by Walter Simonson. Illustrated by Lee Weeks. 1997. 104pp. 1-56971-231-X. **T**

The feared Predators come to the savage land of Pellucidar, the last known free jungle, where dinosaurs still roam and prehistoric beasts still walk the earth. When the ruler of Pellucidar, David Innes, has gone missing, Tarzan travels to the realm to find his lost friend. There in Pellucidar, the Predators meet their match in the might of Tarzan, Lord of the Jungle.

Predator vs. Judge Dredd. Written by John Wagner. Illustrated by Enrique Alcatena. Dark Horse Comics and DC Comics, 1998. 80pp. 1-56971-345-6. **T**

When a rogue Predator find it's way to the far-future world of Mega City One, it's out for the biggest trophy of all—the head of Judge Dredd, the toughest lawman of Mega City One.

Superman vs. Predator. Written by Dave Michelinie. Illustrated by Alex Maleev. Dark Horse Comics and DC Comics, 2001. 160pp. 1-56389-732-6. **T**

When a suddenly depowered Superman finds himself pitted against a fearsome Predator, he must use his wits to survive a deadly game of cat and mouse with a cold-hearted warrior. When the fate of the world is in play, Superman finds that his best ally could be the one trying to kill him.

Red Rocket 7. **Written and illustrated by Mike Alred.** Dark Horse Comics, 1997. 208pp. 1-56971-347-2. **T**

A science fiction journey though the history of rock 'n' roll. After fleeing his home planet to escape the conquering alien race called Enfinites, the Celestonian called the Original crash lands on Earth. To preserve his race, he's cloned six times over, with the last clone called Red Rocket 7. The clone brothers are on the run and have been evading the Enfinites, who have followed them to Earth. Red and his clone brothers become intertwined with rock 'n' roll history. Starting with Elvis Presley and Little Richard and moving on to the Beatles, Rolling Stones, and David Bowie, the clones experience music history and find their own identities along the way.

Scarlet Traces. **Written by Ian Edginton. Illustrated by D'Israeli.** Dark Horse Comics, 2003. 88pp. 1-56971-940-3. **T**

> At the dawn of the twentieth century, spiderlike machines roam the dark streets of London. It's been ten years since the failed Martian invasion when the invaders were infected by Earth germs (as seen in the classic H. G. Wells novel *War of the Worlds*), and now England is the ultimate superpower and in control of the Martian technology. When girls begin turning up dead with their throats punctured, Major Robert Autumn and his manservant Sergeant Archibald Currie are on the hunt to solve to the murders. At first the culprits are thought to be vampires, but the truth is far, far worse.

<u>**Shadow Star.**</u> **Written and illustrated by Mohiro Kitoh.** Dark Horse Comics, 2001– . **O Japanese manga.** あ

> While visiting her grandparents on their small island, sixth-grader Shiina Tamai nearly drowns but is rescued by a silent, star-shaped creature. She brings the creature back to her grandparents' house and names it Hoshimaru. To her surprise, Hoshimaru can also transform and allows Shiina to stand on it, and together they can fly up high in the clouds. Soon, though, their magic experience ends as Shiina discovers that Hoshimaru is part of an alien society that is at war with the Shadow Dragons, deadly, sword-shaped extraterrestrials who have bonded with some of the most malevolent teens who have hate in their hearts. As Shiina and Hoshimaru find more and more human/alien bonded creatures and discover the true nature of the Shadow Dragons, it's apparent that a war is brewing between the bonded teens, who feel nothing but hate, and those with good in their hearts, and there's no escaping the coming conflict. Twelve volumes of the series were published in Japan. An anime series was released in Japan in 2003 and based off on the manga.

>> *Vol. 1.* 2001. 192pp. 1-56971-548-3.
>> *Vol. 2: Darkness Visible.* 2002. 182pp. 1-56971-740-0.
>> *Vol. 3: Shadows of the Past.* 2002. 144pp. 1-56971-743-5.
>> *Vol. 4: Nothing but the Truth.* 2003. 160pp. 1-56971-920-9.
>> *Vol. 5: A Flower's Fragrance.* 2004. 208pp. 1-56971-990-X.
>> *Vol. 6: What Can I Do For You Now?* 2005. 224pp. 1-59307-212-0.
>> *Vol. 7: Victim's Eyes, Assailant's Hands.* 2005. 232pp. 1-59307-363-1.

Starship Troopers. **Written by Warren Ellis, Bruce Jones, and various. Illustrated by Tommy Lee Edwards, Mitch Byrd, and various.** Dark Horse Comics, 1998. 152pp. 1-56971-314-6. **O** 🎬

> Invading arachnids from space have declared war on Earth, and the Federation's Mobile Infantry force is there to take on the bugs with plenty of gunfire and high-tech weapons. When the Mobile Infantry force invades the bugs' home planet of Klendathu, they discover that the brutal bugs are a lot smarter then they thought. Can there be a more powerful bug in control? Meanwhile, on the planet Dantana a teacher leads an untrained crew of civilians against an army of bugs. Can they hold out long enough for the Mobile Infantry to arrive? Loosely based on the classic science fiction novel by Robert. A. Heinlein and adapted and inspired by the 1997 movie.

<u>Unearthly.</u> Written by Ted Naifeh. Illustrated by Elmer Damaso. Seven Seas Entertainment, 2006– . **T Neo-manga.**

Bookish Ann never thought she'd find true love in high school, but when she heard Jem, the school pretty boy, speak in class, she instantly fell in love with him. The only problem is that Ann isn't the only one with the hots for Jem. Rae, one of the most popular, beautiful, and athletic girls in school, also has a crush on Jem and neither she nor Ann will give him up without a fight. Meanwhile Jem is the only witness to an alien ship crash-landing in the middle of the woods, and in an instant his identity is swapped by a runaway shape-shifting alien. Now the alien has assumed Jem's identity, and the real Jem has been captured by those out to kidnap the alien. After Ann and Rae discover the alien's secret, the three of them must reluctantly work together and travel across space to rescue the real Jem.

> *Vol. 1.* 2006. 1-933164-09-3.

***Virus.* Written by Chuck Pfarrer. Illustrated by Howard Cobb.** Dark Horse Comics, 1998. 144pp. 1-56971-317-0. **O** 🎬

Stranded following a storm, a commercial tug boat's crew find a seemingly deserted Chinese ship, only to discover that the ship's crew are dead or missing. The crew could salvage the ship and make a profit, but there's still something on the Chinese ship—something that might be from outer space. The story inspired the not-so cult-classic movie starring Jamie Lee Curtis in 1999.

***Zed: Volume One.* Written and illustrated by Michel Gagné.** Gagné International Press, 2002. 104pp. 0-9719053-0-4, hardcover; 0-9666404-8-9, softcover. **T**

When Zed, a young inventor from the planet Gallos, exhibits his energy-saving device to the peaceful planet Xandria at the annual Nob-L prize celebration, catastrophe inexplicably occurs when his device destroys the entire peaceful planet, including Zed's parents. The only one to survive the planet explosion, and shattered by what he's inadvertently done, Zed finds that there's a sinister plot behind the destruction of the planet—a secret that could cost his life and those of the people on his own planet. The follow-up to the story has yet to be released.

Alternate Worlds and Dimensions

This subgenre features stories about the adventures of explorers from our world transported to other worlds or dimensions. The worlds or dimensions can be very similar to our own, with subtle differences that may not even be perceptible to the human eye, or they can be vastly different and seem almost like an alien planet. The plots can even involve the protagonists exploring alternate histories of famous historical events, alternate pasts and futures, and even worlds so abstract that they defy common thought. The Marvel Super-Hero series <u>Exiles</u>—which prominently features the group of X-Men heroes from a variety of alternate worlds traveling from one parallel world to the next—is listed in chapter 1.

Abenobashi: Magical Shopping Arcade. **Written and illustrated by Satoru Akahori.** TOKYOPOP, 2004. **O Japanese manga.** あ

When teenager Sasshi's Osaka neighborhood is demolished in the name of progress, he discovers that the town is above a portal to an unlimited number of parallel universes. Joined by his girl-next-door friend Arumi, he hops world to world in search of adventure in settings that seem to spoof popular manga, anime, video games, and movies and are populated by voluptuous vixens and outlandish comedic situations. An anime series was released simultaneously in Japan.

> *Vol. 1.* 2004. 192pp. 1-59182-790-6.
> *Vol. 2.* 2004. 208pp. 1-59182-791-4.

Dead Enders: Stealing the Sun. **Written by Ed Brubaker. Illustrated by Warren Pleece.** Vertigo/DC Comics, 1999. 104pp. 1-56389-706-7. **M**

Bartholomew Beezenbach ("Beezer") is a twenty-something living in the squalor of Sector 5, a practically lawless encampment where the poor and downtrodden have been relegated by the upper class, from which no one can escape, and where the only key to survival is friendship. Even the drugs on the streets can't hide the depression and gloom of Sector 5. Beezer has a strange gift—he can experience hallucinations of a better world before the catastrophe that they live in today: a place reminiscent of our world. Though his friends think he's just making up the stories to pass time, someone on the outside is taking notice of people having visions and is gathering them for a secret agenda.

Last Hope. **Written by Michael Dignan. Illustrated by Kriss Sison.** Seven Seas Entertainment, 2005. **T ◎ Neo-manga.**

© 2004 Seven Seas Entertainment LLC and Michael Dignan.

Students from all over the world have come to study at the Maunaloa Institute for International Studies in Hawaii. One of the students, the lonely and brooding Hiroto Nakadai, has come much farther than anyone else—he's actually a prince from another dimension! Hiroto has come to Earth to escape from the madman who killed his family to take over the throne. Now after accidentally revealing his true identity to Ikuko, a girl who has a crush on him, as well as some of her friends, they're on the run, hopping dimension to dimension to flee from Hiroto's enemies, with the hope of someday being able to return home.

> *Vol. 1.* 2005. 192pp. 1-933164-02-6.
> *Vol. 2.* 2006. 192pp. 1-933164-26-3.

Misplaced: Somewhere Under the Rainbow. **Written and illustrated by Josh Blaylock.** Devil's Due Publishing, 2005. 128pp. 1-932796-04-5. **T**

Have you ever felt that there are some places where you just will never fit in? Alyssa feels this way all the time and has ever since she was a child. She's from the high-tech utopian dimension of Realm 77, a beautiful place where no one stretches out with their imagination or goes outside of the box, and where large flying portal dragons gently rule the skies. There, Alyssa's an outcast among her own people. She says what she thinks, means what she says, and has also been developing strange powers recently. When she accidentally is swallowed by a portal dragon, she ends up on Earth, where she finally feels like she's at home. She quickly befriends Billy Rocko, an owner of a clothing store, and party-girl Jezebelle. They show Alyssa how to have a good time and enjoy life. Alyssa's party is soon over, though, when the forces from Realm 77 arrive to take her back home—but that may be easier said than done.

Nextworld. Written and illustrated by Osamu Tezuka. Dark Horse Comics, 2003. **T Japanese manga.**

Classic tale originally published in the 1940s in Japan. Set in the Atomic Age, where nuclear power has created new creatures and every nation wants to harness atomic energy, the power struggle for world dominance and World War III seem inevitable. An odd team of oddball scientists, blustery politicians, and young heroes is the last line of defense to save Earth from corrupt government officials, shadowy secret societies, robots, and more. Meanwhile, a supernatural creature called Fumoon discovers that Earth is doomed and wants to rescue all life on the planet. Can the team save all the inhabitants of Earth before it's too late?

> *Vol. 1.* 160pp. 1-56971-866-0.
> *Vol. 2.* 168pp. 1-56971-867-9.

***Overtime.* Written by Marc Bryant. Illustrated by Mal Jones.** Cyberosia, 2002. 76pp. 0-9709474-2-9. **O**

On an Earth where immortality was accidentally unleashed over 400 years ago, the biggest crime anyone can commit is procreation. Capital punishment has been abolished, and in its place prisoners are sentenced to serve years in a virtual reality, trapped in an orbiting coffin. Nativity Detective DeSoto has just been assigned her first case: a baby has been born and she has to track down the birth parents for committing such a heinous crime. The road to exposing the truth is an uphill battle, and DeSoto's first case may turn out to be her last.

Steampunk. Written by Joe Kelly. Illustrated by Chris Bachalo. Cliffhanger! Studios/ WildStorm Productions/DC Comics, 2001–2003. **T**

In England in 1738, a fisherman by the name of Cole Blaquesmith will do anything to save the life of his beloved, Fiona. He accepts Dr. Mortimer Absinthe's offer to make him a guinea pig in his experimental time machine in exchange for medical treatment for Fiona. When Cole returns from his visit to 1950, Absinthe instead uses the knowledge from the future to remake Victorian-era England into his own twisted image. Cole, meanwhile, wakes up 100 years later in a coffin to find a much-changed England and himself equally changed. In place of his right arm is a large metal arm, there is a steam-powered furnace where his heart should be, and England is a world in which Absinthe is a mad immortal with death as his righthand man. Can a steam-powered hero reclaim part of himself and repair the damage done to the citizens of England?

> *Vol. 1: Manimatron.* 2001. 160pp. 1-56389-762-8.
> *Vol. 2: Drama Obscura.* 2003. 176pp. 1-4012-0047-8.

Texas Steampunk. Written and illustrated by Lea Hernandez. Cyberosia Publishing, 2002. **T Neo-manga.**

© 2006 Lea Hernandez.

These are stories of lives and loves in Texas in 1897, where steam technology and old magic still exist. In *Cathedral Child* Parrish Stuart, a man corrupted by his own brilliance, has created a steam-powered, analytical engine called Cathedral. The Cathedral is so named because it is stored in the local church. Cathedral is able to learn through the user interface of the church organ via programming tutors, including the young lovers Glory and Sumner. When they wish that Glory's virtual friend Camille could be freed, they get far more than they ever expected. In *Clockwork Angels* the villainous Doctor Sacerdote returns and is accompanied by his assistant Milly in New Orleans. Temperance, a female magician with the ability to "read" the dead, is called on to investigate another of Sacerdote's murders. Her companion, Amy, who amazingly shares a striking resemblance to Milly, joins her. When Temperance reads the last thoughts of Sacerdote's last victim, a man known as the "Mad Machinist," she and Amy find themselves trapped in the same pact that binds Milly to Sacerdote, and the truth of evil and destinies foretold are revealed. A third volume in the trilogy, *Ironclad Petals*, has yet to be published.

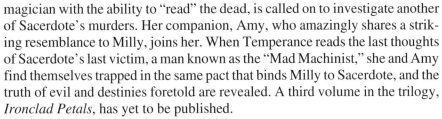

> *Cathedral Child.* 2002. 120pp. 0-9709474-5-3.
> *Clockwork Angels.* 2002. 120pp. 0-9709474-9-6.

Dystopian and Utopian Worlds

These are stories in which society has peaked and things seem perfect—or do they? Utopian fiction focuses on the idea of a perfect world as the basis of the plot. Dystopian fiction showcases an alternate look at the world, with the protagonist trying to cope with a totalitarian form of government—typically a fascist state. A good example of this is the graphic novel *V for Vendetta,* which transports readers to a bleak and moody fascist England where a masked vigilante stirs up the citizens from their somber life to bring freedom and individuality back to the masses.

Appleseed. Written and illustrated by Masamune Shirow. Dark Horse Comics, 1995. **O Japanese manga.** あ

In the postwar setting of Olympus, a self-declared utopia, everyone's desires are catered to thanks to a supercomputer system called Gaia and the humanlike bioroids that make up part of the city's populace. From the ashes of World War III, peace has arrived and there is no pollution, crime, or unemployment—but there is a need to prepare for these things. There is a squadron of ESWAT (Extra Special Weapons and Tactical) that patrols the perfect city, and Deunan Knute is one of the best. After being rescued from the badlands, she's been reunited with her former lover and fellow soldier Briareos Hecatonchires. Briareos is no longer human and has become more machine than man, but their love for each other is still apparent. Together they must

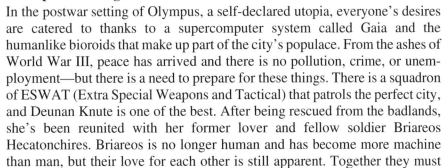

protect the city from outside terrorists and inner turmoil and preserve the city's peace at all costs. The series inspired two separate anime adaptations in Japan.

> *Book 1: The Promethean Challenge.* 1995. 132pp. 1-56971-070-8.
> *Book 2: Promethean Unbound.* 1995. 132pp. 1-56971-071-6.
> *Book 3: The Scales of Prometheus.* 1995. 132pp. 1-56971-072-4.
> *Book 4: The Promethean Balance.* 1995. 216pp. 1-56971-074-0.
> *Appleseed Databook.* 1995. 128pp. 1-56971-103-8.

ARIA. Written and illustrated by Kozue Amano. ADV Manga, 2004. **A Japanese manga.**

By the year A.D. 2301, Mars has become an inhabitable planet and has been renamed Aqua. Many of the citizens live in the city of Neo-Venezia, a replication of the beautiful city Venice, and young Akari Mizunashi has just come to the city to realize her dream. A likeable girl who enjoys the ancient and more calm ways of life, Akari has always wanted to be the best gondolier (called a prima undine) in the city. As she works her way up from a trainee to a prima for the ARIA Company, she's an enthusiastic, hard worker but always finds time to relax and enjoy life. As she learns the tricks of the trade with the help of Alicia, her prima undine and teacher, Akari explores the city and culture of Neo-Venezia in the midst of the ever-changing climates on Aqua. The manga is a follow-up to the manga called *Aqua*. The series has yet to be released in North America.

> *Vol. 1.* 2004. 184pp. 1-4139-0040-2.
> *Vol. 2.* 2004. 194pp. 1-4139-0071-2.
> *Vol. 3.* 2004. 188pp. 1-4139-0089-5.

Black Magic. **Written and illustrated by Masamune Shirow.** Dark Horse Comics, 1998. 204pp. 1-56971-360-X. **O Japanese manga.**

In the far future, humanity is at the brink of annihilation in the fight between two warring synthetic life-form races, the bioroids and the warriorlike cyborgs. When the galaxy is on the verge of imploding, the last hope of humanity is a female bioroid sorceress, Duna Typhon. With her magic, and with her sword that contains the will of the life-creating supercomputer Nemesis, she might be the one to bring utopia back to Venus.

Channel Zero. Written and illustrated by Brian Wood. AiT/Planet Lar, 2000–2003. **O** ◉

In a near future, the U.S. government has caved in to the pressures of special interest groups and condescending religious ideologues rule the government. Free speech and all forms of expression have been silenced, but Jennie 2.5 is there to send the country a wake-up call. A self-described info-terrorist, she's hijacking the media with only a camera and a determination to remind the country of the right of free speech and freedom of the press. *Jennie One* follows the life of Jennie, the girl who would become known as the legendary Jennie 2.5.

> *Vol. 1.* 2000. 144pp. 0-9676847-4-9.
> *Vol. 2: Jennie One.* 2003. 72pp. 1-932051-07-4.

© 2006 Brian Wood.

Metropolis. **Written and illustrated by Osamu Tezuka.** Dark Horse Comics, 2003. 168pp. 1-56971-864-4. **T Japanese manga.** あ

Originally published in Japan in 1949, in the near future when humanity has reached its summit and towers soar into the sky, the city is on the lookout for the fiendish Duke Red, a criminal mastermind who has forced the scientist Dr. Lawson to create a superpowered artificial life-form. Dr. Lawson's creation, Michi, must find her way in life after Dr. Lawson is killed by Duke Red. But Michi discovers that Dr. Lawson wasn't her real father, and that in fact no one is. Her new friend Kenichi, the nephew of Japanese detective Mustachio, helps her try to figure out just where she belongs. But Duke Red will stop at nothing to get back the synthetic girl. A loose anime adaptation of the classic manga was released in Japan and worldwide in 2001.

Neotopia. **Written and illustrated by Rod Espinosa.** Antarctic Press, 2004–2005. **Y** ◎ **Neo-manga.**

© 2006 Antarctic Press.

A thousand years in the future in the kingdom of Mathenia, civilization has learned to live in peace and coexist with the surrounding nature without the conveniences of technology. The mythological beings of old have come back, airships fly high in the sky, and large sailing ships rule the high seas. The ruler of Mathenia is the Grand Duchess Nadia, a wise and pleasant ruler. However, not all is what it seems: Nadia is in actuality a servant girl called Nalyn, who plays the part of the ruler, while the real Nadia is a spoiled woman. When the dark, alienlike Krossians seek to return to the excesses of technology, Mathenia is the last line of defense. The good citizens need a strong ruler in these trying times, and Nadia isn't up to the task—but Nalyn is. Joined by her crew, including a young tech-savvy mechanic, a dolphin in an exoskeleton suit, and others, the forces of Mathenia are sure to win under Nalyn's reluctant but strong command.

> *Vol. 1.* 2004. 168pp. 1-932453-57-1.
> *Vol. 2: The Perilous Winds of Athanon.* 2004. 168pp. 1-932453-58-X.
> *Vol. 3: The Kingdoms Beyond.* 2005. 168pp. 1-932453-75-X.
> *Vol. 4: The New World.* 2005. 188pp. 1-932453-85-7.

Transmetropolitan. **Written by Warren Ellis. Illustrated by Darick Robertson.** Vertigo/DC Comics, 1998–2004. **M** ◎

Spider Jerusalem, the no-holds-barred, foul-mouthed vigilante journalist of tomorrow, comes back from exile to cover the filth and desperation of the City and the impending U.S. presidential election. He's a voice of reason (and anarchistic lunacy) in a frantic world, in search of the truth—even if it gets him killed.

> *Vol. 1: Back on the Street.* 1998. 72pp. 1-56389-445-9.
> *Vol. 2: Lust for Life.* 1999. 208pp. 1-56389-481-5.
> *Vol. 3: Year of the Bastard.* 1999. 144pp. 1-56389-568-4.
> *Vol. 4: The New Scum.* 2000. 144pp. 1-56389-627-3.
> *Vol. 5: Lonely City.* 2001. 144pp. 1-56389-722-9.

Vol. 6: Gouge Away. 2002. 144pp. 1-56389-796-2.

Vol. 7: Spider's Thrash. 2002. 144pp. 1-56389-894-2.

Vol. 8: Dirge. 2003. 144pp. 1-56389-953-1.

Vol. 9: The Cure. 2003. 144pp. 1-56389-988-4.

Vol. 10: One More Time. 2004. 144pp. 1-4012-0217-9.

Vol. 11: Tales of Human Waste. 2004. 112pp. 1-4012-0244-6.

V for Vendetta. **Written by Alan Moore. Illustrated by David Lloyd.** Vertigo/DC Comics, 1990. 286pp. 0-930289-52-8. **M** ◉ 🎬

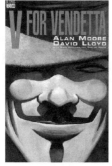

In an alternate future in which Britain lost World War II and has become a fascist totalitarian state under the rule of the Norsefire, a mysterious masked figure known as "V" haunts the streets of London in 1997 to remind England of what it once was. Evey Hammond, a young girl who lost her father years ago, is rescued by the vigilante from a corrupt policeman about to rape her for selling herself for money. After she witnesses V dispatching the officer and destroying Parliament, she is drawn into the mysterious world of this masked anarchist and his treasure trove of lost art, long banned by the Norsefire. As V dispatches more high-government officials, Evey finds that she too has a role to play in this drama to once again wake Britain from its long slumber and to ignite the flames of freedom. In 2006 a film adaptation based on the graphic novel was released starring Natalie Portman and Hugo Weaving.

© 2006 DC Comics.

Post-Apocalypse

This subgenre examines what life would be like if a planetwide disaster struck Earth. In the tales there may be an ecological change, civilization may nearly be made extinct, and strange life-forms may now inhabit Earth. The subgenre is closely related to dystopian science fiction, but goes one step further by showcasing the entire collapse of society following a nuclear holocaust or other devastating event.

<u>Eden: It's an Endless World!</u> **Written and illustrated by Hiroki Endo.** Dark Horse Comics, 2006–2007. **M Japanese manga.**

In the near future, a virus has devastated much of humanity. The terrible disease has killed untold millions of people by hardening the skin and eventually turning the innards to mush. Those who were not immune to the virus survived only by replacing their organs with cybernetic robotic parts. Meanwhile, in this barren landscape a paramilitary organization known as Propater has toppled the crumbling United Nations, and a young boy named Elijah, who is immune to the virus, is joined on his travels by an artificial intelligence combat robot. Together the two of them roam the crumbling, run-down cities in search of love and companionship in a dog-eat-dog world of tomorrow. Five volumes of this series were originally published in Japan.

Vol. 1. 2006. 216pp. 1-59307-406-9.

Vol. 2. 2006. 208pp. 1-59307-454-9.

Vol. 3. 2006. 224pp. 1-59307-529-4.

Vol. 4. 2006. 208pp. 1-59307-544-8.

Vol. 5. 2006. 216pp. 1-59307-634-7.
Vol. 6. 2007. 240pp. 1-59307-702-5.

Just a Pilgrim. **Written by Garth Ennis. Illustrated by Carlos Ezquerra.** Black
Bull Entertainment, L.L.C., 2001. 128pp. 0-9672489-3-0. **O**

When the world's oceans have been dried by an expanding sun, humanity's
few survivors are either at war with one another or banding together in hope of
surviving. When bandits and mutated monsters from the depths of the dry
ocean floor terrorize what's left of humanity, a man of faith (who might be
slightly insane) is there with a gun in one hand and the Bible in his other to
help lead a boy and his family to safety through the treacherous dry ocean.

The Legend of Mother Sarah: Tunnel Town. **Written by Katsuhiro Otomo. Illustrated by Takumi Nagayasu.** Dark Horse Comics, 1996. 224pp.
1-56971-145-3. **T Japanese manga.**

When Earth is an uninhabitable wasteland following a nuclear war, humanity's remnants have reached the stars in large space colonies, biding their time
until Earth can be repopulated. After a terrorist attack that forces the colonists
to land on Earth, a lone mother is separated from her children in the ensuing
confusion. Lost but not without hope, Sarah embarks on a quest across the
charred landscape in search of her lost children.

Lone. **Written by Stuart Moore. Illustrated by Jerome Opená, Alberto
Ponticelli, and Ben Templesmith.** Dark Horse Comics, 2004. 152pp.
1-59307-265-1. **T**

When irradiated mutant zombies have taken over the run-down town of
Desolation, the town's last hope is to locate the legendary gunman known as
Lone to take care of the problem. Traveling for two weeks to the west, sharpshooter Luke and her older brother Mark battle zombies and a giant mutant
boar and find their man. A Clint Eastwood-esque loner with a cool head who
has lived through Armageddon and Hell, he accepts Luke's offer to take care
of the zombies and their green-armored leader, who bleeds yellow blood. For
Lone, the tale of a yellow-blooded zombie can mean only one thing: the
GunFathers have returned and only Lone, armed to the gills, can take them
out.

🌳 **Nausicaa of the Valley of the Wind. 2d ed.** **Written and illustrated by Hayao
Miyazaki.** VIZ Media, LLC, 2004. **T ◎ Japanese manga.** あ

Created by the famous anime director of such wonderful animated films as
Princess Mononoke, *Spirited Away*, *Kiki's Delivery Service*, and *My Neighbor
Totoro*, this is a seven-volume epic environmental story of Earth's future, in
which the air has been poisoned and humanity shares the planet with giant insects and deadly mutant fungus. Nausicaa, a young princess who is empathic
with the mutated insects of the ecosystem, must negotiate peace between kingdoms and preserve the last natural resources of the world before the Sea of
Corruption destroys the planet. Hayao Miyazaki released an anime adaptation
of the manga in 1984. The *Volume 1* collection received recognition by

YALSA's Popular Paperbacks for Young Adults committee in 2002 on the "Graphic Novels: Superheroes and Beyond" list.

Vol. 1. 2004. 136pp. 1-59116-408-7.
Vol. 2. 2004. 136pp. 1-59116-350-1.
Vol. 3. 2004. 160pp. 1-59116-410-9.
Vol. 4. 2004. 144pp. 1-59116-352-8.
Vol. 5. 2004. 160pp. 1-59116-412-5.
Vol. 6. 2004. 168pp. 1-59116-354-4.
Vol. 7. 2004. 232pp. 1-59116-355-2.

Rain Dogs. **Written by Gordon Rennie. Illustrated by Colin Wilson.** Dark Horse Comics, 2002. 52pp. 1-56971-697-8. **T**

After her reconnaissance airship has been downed over New York City, Eve must learn to survive in a post-flood world. She'll need the help of Holly, an eighteen-year-old scavenger who can outsmart and outfight any Time Square Troglodytes, Flying Dragon gangs, and the sinister religious zealot, Rainmaker.

Sand Land. **Written and illustrated by Akira Toriyama.** VIZ Media, LLC, 2003. 224pp. 1-59116-181-9. **T Japanese manga.**

In a post-apocalyptic future in which the most precious commodity is water, the king of Japan has greedily stored all of it and sells it at a high price, while the humans barely survive in the heat of the desert. Disgruntled by the king's miserly ways, a war veteran acts on a hunch and treks across the desert by dune buggy and tank with several of the most unlikely allies, in a quest for a new water source that may save humans as well as demons. Joined by the short and immature son of Lucifer, the 2,500-year-old, childlike demon Beezelbub, as well as the elderly demon named Thief, the veteran will face sand dragons, scavengers, and even the grand army of the king in the quest for water.

Vic and Blood: The Continuing Adventures of a Boy and His Dog. **Written by Harlan Ellison. Illustrated by Richard Corben.** ibooks, Inc., 2002. 128pp. 0-7434-5903-2. **T**

The classic characters of Harlan Ellison's science fiction story "A Boy and His Dog" return in a short story format combined with prose chapters. In the year 2048, Vic, a fourteen-year-old teenager, and his "pet," the super-smart telepathic dog Blood, continue their journey across a post-apocalyptic United States. In search of food, shelter, entertainment, and love, they're the best of friends, struggling to get by in a world without hope and filled with dangers, including criminals, fungus-laden screamers, and giant mutant spiders.

Wolf's Rain. **Written by BONES and Keiko Nobumoto. Illustrated by Toshitsugu Iida.** VIZ Media, LLC, 2004–2005. **T Japanese manga.** あ

In a post-apocalyptic world, four wolves travel in search of a mythical haven they call Paradise: majestic Kiba, the always-sneering Tsume, voracious Hige, and naïve Toboe. After having been pushed practically to the point of extinction nearly 200 years before, the wolves have adapted in order to blend in with humans by mentally cloaking their wolf forms and appearing to most in human guise. Now the wolf pack follows Kiba in his quest to find the scent of the Lunar Flower, a special smell that will lead them all to Paradise. The manga was released simultaneously with the twenty-six-episode anime series of the same name.

> *Vol. 1*. 2004. 184pp. 1-59116-591-1.
> *Vol. 2*. 2005. 200pp. 1-59116-718-3.

Wonderland. Written by Derek Watson. Illustrated by Kit Wallis. Image Comics, 2004. 64pp. 1-58240-415-1. **T**

Generations from now, when the world has been ravaged by nuclear and biological warfare, cannibalistic mutants walk Earth, and humanity is on the verge of extinction. Sarah, Edison, and Poncho are three children in search of their father, a once highly regarded scientist, five months after he disappeared. Their father left to look for fuel for the house's generators and never came back. Now the children have left the safety of their controlled environment to go out into the dangerous world and find their missing father. Has their father really survived all these months, and will they even find him before the mutants get to them?

★ **Y the Last Man. Written by Brian K. Vaughan. Illustrated by Pia Guerra.** Vertigo/DC Comics, 2003– . **M** ◎

© 2006 Brian K. Vaughan and Pia Guerra.

A deadly plague instantaneously kills every single male human and animal on the entire planet with a Y chromosome, except for one young man and his male pet monkey. How does society survive when 48 percent of Earth's population has died? Joined by a mysterious female African American agent known only as Agent 355, young Yorrick must travel the United States in search of the mysterious cause of the man-killing plague and try to find out why he and his pet monkey Ampersand were the only males to survive in a world now ruled by women. The writer of the series, Brian K. Vaughan, received an Eisner Award for Best Writer in 2005 for his body of work, including this series. *Unmanned* received recognition by YALSA's Popular Paperbacks for Young Adults committee in 2006 on the "What Ails You" list.

> *Vol. 1: Unmanned*. 2003. 128pp. 1-56389-980-9.
> *Vol. 2: Cycles*. 2003. 128pp. 1-4012-0076-1.
> *Vol. 3: One Small Step*. 2004. 168pp. 1-4012-0201-2.
> *Vol. 4: Safeword*. 2004. 144pp. 1-4012-0232-2.
> *Vol. 5: Ring of Truth*. 2005. 192pp. 1-4012-0487-2.
> *Vol. 6: Girl on Girl*. 2005. 128pp. 1-4012-0501-1.
> *Vol. 7: Paper Dolls*. 2006. 144pp. 1-4012-1009-0.
> *Vol. 8: Kimono*. 2006. 144pp. 1-4012-1010-4.

Computers and Artificial Intelligence

In these science fiction stories computers play a pivotal role in the plot. Typically the fictionalized computers are much more sophisticated than any type of computer currently available in the real world. In the fictionalized world of computers, artificial intelligence (AI) is commonplace, and surfing the Internet or online gaming can literally be a life and death situation. The tales can range from the humorous, to the lighhearted, to a struggle for survival against an evil computer. Films such as Walt Disney's *Tron* and the *Matrix* trilogy are excellent examples of the type of stories found in the subgenre.

Corrector Yui. Created by Kia Asamiya. Written and illustrated by Keiko Okamoto. TOKYOPOP, 2002. **A Japanese manga.** あ

In the year 2020, when almost everything is computer-operated, fourteen-year-old Yui Kasuga has been chosen to save the computers of the world from the deadliest of viruses. Not a problem, except that Yui is completely computer illiterate! With the aid of her Corrector robot companion I.R., she surfs cyberspace in search of the missing corrector robots who can help cure the Grosser computer virus and make cyberspace safe for surfing. An anime series was released simultaneously in Japan when the manga was released and ran for fifty-two episodes.

> *Vol. 1: Corrector Initialize.* 2002. 192pp. 1-931514-28-3.
> *Vol. 2: Lost in Cyberspace.* 2002. 200pp. 1-931514-29-1.
> *Vol. 3: A Song for Yui.* 2002. 192pp. 1-931514-30-5.
> *Vol. 4: Double Trouble.* 2002. 200pp. 1-931514-31-3.
> *Vol. 5: How the Web Was Won.* 2002. 200pp. 1-931514-32-1.

Gamerz Heaven. Written and illustrated by Maki Murakami. ADV Manga, 2004–2005. **T Japanese manga.**

High school student Kaito Suzuki has always been obsessed with video games. When he receives a game called *Gamerz Heaven,* he discovers that it is much more than an average game. When the game is turned on, Kaito is greeted by a small boy named Nata, who is a mysterious connection between the real world and the video game world. When a girl from school disappears from everyone's memory when Kaito kills her demonic boss counterpart, Kaito discovers after a mission inside the fantasy-based video game that the world inside the game affects real life as well. Now, with their own lives hanging in the balance, Kaito as well as several of his schoolmates enter the world of the video game to rescue Nata from certain doom and hoping to not lose their own lives in the process.

> *Vol. 1.* 2004. 184pp. 1-4139-0202-2.
> *Vol. 2.* 2005. 184pp. 1-4139-0199-9.
> *Vol. 3.* 2005. 184pp. 1-4139-0323-1.

Junction 17, Pocket Manga Vol. 1. **Written and illustrated by David Hutchison.** Antarctic Press, 2004. 128pp. 1-932453-50-4. **T Neo-manga.**

In the near future when online gaming is as real as everyday life, people are dying, literally, in the neural game called *Black Wave.* Now the best players are being eliminated by an obsessed fan, who appears in the game as a skull-faced visage of death called the "Ghost." Is it a real person, or an artificial intelligence taken over by the ghost in the machine? Time is running short for the top players, as one by one they're becoming victims of the "Ghost."

The Matrix Comics. Written and illustrated by various. Burlyman Entertainment, Inc., 2003–2005. **O**

Further tales set in the world of Neo and his followers, based on the stories and scenarios from the hit science fiction <u>Matrix</u> trilogy of films (1999–2003). The stories are created by trilogy creators Andy and Larry Wachowski and a host of comic book talent, including Neil Gaiman, Tim Sale, and Bill Sienkiewicz.

    Vol. 1. 2003. 160pp. 1-932700-00-5.
    Vol. 2. 2005. 160pp. 1-932700-09-9.

MegaMan NT Warrior. Written and illustrated by Ryo Takamisaki. VIZ Media, LLC, 2004–2005. **A** 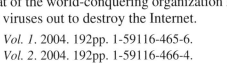 **Japanese manga.**

Based on the popular video game character. Set in a near future where everyone is connected to the Internet Cyber Network via their PET (Personal Terminal) and an artificial intelligence program called NetNavi. Though on the outside the world seems peaceful, danger in the Internet is always only a step away. To save the day is Lan Hikari, an active fifth-grader with a talent for surfing the Internet. Joined by his NetNavi, he becomes known as MegaMan, a dynamic, superpowered fighting force in cyberspace against the continuous threat of the world-conquering organization known as World Three and rampant viruses out to destroy the Internet.

    Vol. 1. 2004. 192pp. 1-59116-465-6.
    Vol. 2. 2004. 192pp. 1-59116-466-4.
    Vol. 3. 2004. 200pp. 1-59116-414-1.
    Vol. 4. 2004. 200pp. 1-59116-501-6.
    Vol. 5. 2004. 200pp. 1-59116-561-X.
    Vol. 6. 2005. 200pp. 1-59116-755-8.
    Vol. 7. 2005. 184pp. 1-4215-0003-5.
    Vol. 8. 2005. 192pp. 1-59116-981-X.
    Vol. 9. 2005. 192pp. 1-4215-0132-5.

World of Hartz. **Written and illustrated by Terrence Walker.** TOKYOPOP, 2004. 192pp. 1-59182-410-9. **T Neo-manga.**

Gamers Han and T have always had a hard time putting the game control down and living in the real world. Han becomes engrossed in a new super-game called *World of Hartz,* and after meeting Makiko, the cyber-girl of his dreams, and saving the day, he's hooked. Now T has to enter the highly addictive game to free Han, but he doesn't want to go. Why would you go back to the real world if the cyber-world was the only place that you ever got the respect and the admiration that the real world couldn't possibly provide? When it's friend versus friend, who will win, and will Han ever find true love with Machiko?

Psychic Powers and Mind Control

The ability to control thoughts and manipulate matter is also a common theme in science fiction. The ability endows the characters with extraordinary power, allowing them to read minds and use telekinesis, clairvoyance, and other powers. Typically the characters receive their powers through experimental procedures or genetically at birth. The appeal of these stories centers on the protagonist or antagonist, an extraordinary being who uses the powers given to him or her for either good or evil purposes. See chapter 1, featuring mutant heroes such as the X-Men, for more tie-ins to characters born with strange powers.

Akira. Written and illustrated by Katsuhiro Otomo. Dark Horse Comics, 2000–2002. **O Japanese manga.** あ

In the year 2019, Neo-Tokyo stands on the ashes of a city destroyed in a mysterious, annihilating blast whispered by the government as "Akira." Meanwhile, streetwise teens Tetsuo and Kaneda find their friendship pushed to its limits after Tetsuo develops latent psychic powers and is targeted by a secret government organization, whom they believe will bring about the return of Akira and the destruction of the world. In 2002 the series won several Eisner Awards in the categories of Best U.S. Edition of Foreign Material and Best Archival Collection/Project as well as Harvey Awards in the categories of Best American Edition of Foreign Material (1990, 1992–1993, 1996) for the original editions translated by Marvel Comics' short-lived Epic imprint. The manga served as the inspiration for the cult-hit anime movie released in 1988.

> *Vol. 1.* 2000. 364pp. 1-56971-498-3.
> *Vol. 2.* 2001. 304pp. 1-56971-499-1.
> *Vol. 3.* 2001. 288pp. 1-56971-525-4.
> *Vol. 4.* 2001. 400pp. 1-56971-526-2.
> *Vol. 5.* 2001. 416pp. 1-56971-527-0.
> *Vol. 6.* 2002. 440pp. 1-56971-528-9.

Clover. Written and illustrated by CLAMP. TOKYOPOP, 2001–2002. **T Japanese manga.**

In a futuristic society where shady political machinations are everywhere are Clovers, people genetically engineered for their supernatural powers, who are highly coveted. One such Clover, a mysterious girl named Sue, is to be escorted to Fairy Park to discover the truth behind her powers and what they are meant to be used for. Led by Kazuhiko, an ex-soldier and private eye, Sue finds that she's one of the most special Clovers ever created. Sue finds she's an object of interest to government officials called the Parliament as well as the Azaien army, and together with Kazuhiko and his friends, she's out to discover the truth behind her powers. Meanwhile Kazuhiko discovers why he's been selected for the mission, as well as Sue's relationship to his long-lost wife, Oruha.

> *Vol. 1.* 2001. 128pp. 1-892213-66-4.
> *Vol. 2.* 2001. 128pp. 1-892213-94-X.
> *Vol. 3.* 2001. 128pp. 1-892213-95-8.
> *Vol. 4.* 2002. 128pp. 1-892213-96-6.

Icaro. **Written by Moebius. Illustrated by Jiro Taniguchi.** ibooks, Incorporated, 2003–2004. **M Japanese manga.**

In the near future a Japanese boy is born blessed with the gift of flight; since his birth he has gracefully floated in the sky. Poked and prodded like a guinea pig, Icaro has been quarantined for over twenty years in a secret complex by a top secret scientific organization. Only Yukiko, a beautiful young woman who works for the secret organization, has the courage to free Icaro from his cagelike surroundings. They form a close bond, and Icaro learns to love for the first time. Meanwhile, the organization that held him in captivity is looking to get him back and to imprison the one human who can soar like the birds.

> *Vol. 1.* 2003. 160pp. 0-7434-7538-0.
> *Vol. 2.* 2004. 144pp. 0-7434-7980-7.

�**Mai the Psychic Girl.** **Written by Kazuya Kudo. Illustrated by Ryoichi Ikegami.** VIZ Media, LLC, 1996. **O Japanese manga.**

Mai Kuju, a gentle fourteen-year-old Japanese schoolgirl, has a rather unique power: she's an unparalleled psychic and can move objects with her mind. Her father reveals to her that she's from a long line of psychics who used their power to protect a special region of Japan. But after an attack by a hidden force, she soon realizes that her special gift makes her the target of a secret world organization called the Wisdom Alliance. A hidden society whose rule of the world goes beyond borders, they've already used other young psychics to their own advantage to create a small army of psychics to better rule the world, and they're not afraid to use the children to attack Mai. Now on the run with her father, Mai must learn to use her skills to fight those who would come between them and in the end find out just how much power she truly wields. *Perfect Collection Volume 1* received recognition by YALSA's Popular Paperbacks for Young Adults committee in 2002 on the "Graphic Novels: Superheroes and Beyond" list.

> *Perfect Collection Vol. 1.* 1996. 368pp. 1-56931-070-X.
> *Perfect Collection Vol. 2.* 1996. 360pp. 1-56931-066-1.
> *Perfect Collection Vol. 3.* 1996. 360pp. 1-56931-059-9.

Miracle Girls. **Written and illustrated by Naomi Akimoto.** TOKYOPOP, 2000–2003. **A Japanese manga.**

Fourteen-year-old identical twins Mika and Toni are nothing alike. Mika is shy and quiet, while Toni is outgoing, popular, and athletic. They do have one special thing in common—they're both gifted with the powers of telepathy and teleportation, which can get them into a load of trouble. When their teacher, Mr. Kageura, hopes to cash in on the girls' secret, what can the girls do to prove to him that they really don't have any powers at all?

> *Vol. 1.* 2000. 184pp. 1-892213-64-8.
> *Vol. 2.* 2001. 194pp. 1-892213-69-9.
> *Vol. 3.* 2001. 192pp. 1-892213-81-8.
> *Vol. 4.* 2002. 192pp. 1-892213-82-6.
> *Vol. 5.* 2002. 192pp. 1-892213-83-4.
> *Vol. 6.* 2002. 192pp. 1-892213-84-2.

Vol. 7. 2003. 192pp. 1-59182-073-1.
Vol. 8. 2003. 192pp. 1-59182-193-2.
Vol. 9. 2003. 192pp. 1-59182-194-0.

Seraphic Feather. Written by Yo Morimoto. Illustrated by Hiroyuki Utatane. Dark Horse Comics, 2001– . **O Japanese manga.**

In the near future, humans have discovered an intact alien starship beneath the surface of the moon and hope to harness the potentially incredible power it may carry. The starship is somehow connected to three mysterious "Emblem Seeds" that have been found on Earth and may be the key to unleashing its powers. Sunao Oumi, a young man stranded on the moon taking odd jobs to earn enough money to get back home after visiting the site where his girlfriend Kei died, is working as an escort for two U.N. secret agents from Earth who have brought several of the "Emblem Seeds" with them to the station. When shadowy agents try to take the "Emblem Seeds," the two agents easily dispatch them, and Sunao discovers that they are the beautiful and enigmatic Attim M-Zak and Kei, Sunao's girlfriend! What sort of secrets are contained in the ship, and are they really meant to be unleashed?

Vol. 1: Crimson Angel. 2001. 232pp. 1-56971-555-6.
Vol. 2: Seeds of Chaos. 2002. 240pp. 1-56971-739-7.
Vol. 3: Target Zone. 2003. 240pp. 1-56971-912-8.
Vol. 4: Dark Angel. 2005. 240pp. 1-56971-913-6.
Vol. 5: War Crimes. 2005. 240pp. 1-59307-198-1.

Robots, Androids, and Cyborgs

Humans have long been fascinated by robots, androids, cyborgs, and other robotic life-forms. Tales featuring metal men who were created to serve humanity but have the capability for so much more—even one day to surpass huhumanity—have long been a staple in science fiction books and films. Listed here are a wide variety of titles featuring robots from both Western and Eastern cultures, from human-sized robots to pint-sized cyborg saviors.

Man-sized Robots

These are stories featuring robots, cyborgs, and others that are roughly the size of humans. Central themes in titles featuring human-sized robots include humanity's paranoia about nonhuman life-forms, as exhibited in such titles as *AD Police*; whether a robot can be more than just wiring and become human, as told in such tales as *Astro Boy* and *Battle Angel Alita*; and tales of killer robots from the future, as seen in the Terminator graphic novels, which expanded on the events from the trilogy of Terminator films.

AD Police. **Written by Toshimichi Suzuki. Illustrated by Tony Takezaki.** VIZ Media, LLC, 1994. 144pp. 1-56931-005-X. **O Japanese manga.** あ

A prequel to the manga series called Bubblegum Crisis. In the year 2027, Tokyo is recuperating from a devastating earthquake, and the corporation called Genom is aiding in the reconstruction of NeoTokyo. With their biomechanical androids called Boomers, cleanup time has been greatly reduced. Unfortunately, new problems arise when rogue Boomers begin committing crimes against the citizens of NeoTokyo. The Armored Defense Police (AD Police) is created to take on the Boomers and re-store peace. Leon McNichol, a rookie in the police squad, learns the hard way that there's a thin line between man and machine. An anime series was also re-leased in Japan.

Aphrodite IX. **Written by David Wohl. Illustrated by David Finch and Clarence Lansang.** Top Cow Productions/Image Comics, 2004. 142pp. 1-58240-372-4. **T**

The perfect assassin has been created—one who can perform a wetwork oper-ation (assassination) and then immediately erase all knowledge of the mission and its former life. Called Aphrodite IX, she appears as a beautiful woman and is able to easily blend into society once a job is done. When she begins to in-vestigate her own true identity and why she doesn't remember anything, she's chased by unknown operatives out to keep her true identity under wraps, and she's also blamed for murders that she didn't commit—or did she? Will she discover her true origins before she's shut down permanently?

<u>**Astro Boy.**</u> **Written and illustrated by Osamu Tezuka.** Dark Horse Comics, 2002–2004. **T Japanese manga.** あ

Created by the legendary manga creator Osama Tezuka in 1952, <u>Astro Boy</u> has been considered by many to be the launching point of the manga craze, in-spiring artists and storytellers for years to come. Astro Boy is also one of the most recognizable characters from Japan. In a future where androids coexist with humans, Astro Boy was created in the year 2003 by the Ministry of Sci-ence's Dr. Tenma in Japan. His designs were based on Tobio, Dr. Tenma's son, who was killed in a car accident. The good doctor loved Astro Boy as if he were his own son, but realized that he could never truly replace Tobio. Though his upbringing was hard and sometimes cruel, Astro Boy was rescued by Pro-fessor Ochanomizu, the new Minister of Science, from a life in the circus. In Dr. Ochanomizu, Astro Boy finds a new father figure and proves to all of Ja-pan that he is a hero with a 100,000-horsepower motor. Commonly facing off against bad guys ranging from robot-hating humans, to giant evil robots, to in-vaders from outer space, with his super strength, jet-powered books, la-ser-tipped fingers, and more, Astro Boy is sure to win the day. The manga inspired the popular anime series, which first aired in Japan in 1963.

Vol. 1. 2002. 224pp. 1-56971-676-5.
Vol. 2. 2002. 208pp. 1-56971-677-3.
Vol. 3. 2002. 208pp. 1-56971-678-1.
Vol. 4. 2002. 216pp. 1-56971-679-X.
Vol. 5. 2002. 216pp. 1-56971-680-3.
Vol. 6. 2002. 232pp. 1-56971-681-1.
Vol. 7. 2002. 216pp. 1-56971-790-7.
Vol. 8. 2002. 200pp. 1-56971-791-5.
Vol. 9. 2002. 216pp. 1-56971-792-3.
Vol. 10. 2002. 216pp. 1-56971-793-1.
Vol. 11. 2003. 216pp. 1-56971-812-1.
Vol. 12. 2003. 224pp. 1-56971-813-X.

Vol. 13. 2003. 224pp. 1-56971-894-6.

Vol. 14. 2003. 224pp. 1-56971-895-4.

Vol. 15. 2003. 232pp. 1-56971-896-2.

Vol. 16. 2003. 256pp. 1-56971-897-0.

Vol. 17. 2003. 216pp. 1-56971-898-9.

Vol. 18. 2003. 216pp. 1-56971-899-7.

Vol. 19. 2003. 208pp. 1-56971-900-4.

Vol. 20. 2003. 224pp. 1-56971-901-2.

Vol. 21. 2003. 232pp. 1-56971-902-0.

Vol. 22. 2003. 216pp. 1-56971-903-9.

Vol. 23. 2004. 192pp. 1-59307-135-3.

🔥 **Battle Angel Alita. Written and illustrated by Yukito Kishiro.** VIZ Media, LLC, 2003–2005. **O ◉ Japanese manga.** あ

GUNNM © 1991 by Yukito
Kishiro/SHUEISHA Inc.

In a post-apocalyptic world, Doctor Ido discovers a badly damaged cyborg in a junk heap beneath the floating city of Tiphares and renames her "Alita." Now reactivated with no memory of her past life, she discovers that she is much more than meets the eye and must seek out her hidden past. Working part-time with Ido as "hunter-warrior" bounty hunters, she's out to find the truth about her past amid the fighting and bloodshed. The hit series' second editions were reprinted in the traditional right to left format, and the follow-up to the first series, <u>Battle Angel Alita—Last Order</u>, is printed in that format as well. The second series is still being published in Japan, with more than seven volumes published at the time of this writing. The manga helped to inspire an anime series as well as a forthcoming live-action film from director James Cameron. *Volume 1: Rusty Angel* received recognition by YALSA's Popular Paperbacks for Young Adults committee in 2004 on the "Simply Science Fiction" list.

<u>Battle Angel Alita (1st series, 2d ed.).</u> 2004–2005.

Vol. 1: Rusty Angel. 2004. 240pp. 1-56931-945-6.

Vol. 2: Tears of an Angel. 2004. 216pp. 1-56931-951-0.

Vol. 3: Angel of Victory. 2004. 216pp. 1-59116-274-2.

Vol. 4: Killing Angel. 2004. 216pp. 1-59116-275-0.

Vol. 5: Angel of Redemption. 2004. 208pp. 1-59116-276-9.

Vol. 6: Angel of Death. 2004. 200pp. 1-59116-277-7.

Vol. 7: Angel of Chaos. 2004. 216pp. 1-59116-278-5.

Vol. 8: Fallen Angel. 2005. 232pp. 1-59116-280-7.

Vol. 9: Angel's Ascension. 2005. 256pp. 1-59116-280-7.

<u>Battle Angel Alita: Last Order.</u> 2003– .

Vol. 1: Angel Reborn. 2003. 200pp. 1-56931-824-7.

Vol. 2: Angel of the Innocents. 2003. 206pp. 1-56931-976-6.

Vol. 3: Angel Eternal. 2004. 200pp. 1-59116-135-5.

Vol. 4: Angel of Protest. 2005. 200pp. 1-59116-281-5.

Vol. 5: Haunted Angel. 2005. 200pp. 1-59116-282-3.

Vol. 6: The Angel and the Vampire. 2005. 192pp. 1-4215-0057-4.

Vol. 7: Guilty Angel. 2006. 192pp. 1-4215-0433-2.
Vol. 8. 2006. 208pp. 1-4215-0865-6.

❧ *Big Guy and Rusty the Boy Robot.* **Written by Frank Miller. Illustrated by Geof Darrow.** Dark Horse Comics, 1996. 80pp. 1-56971-201-8. **A** ◎ ▭

The adventures of a tiny Japanese-made robot named Rusty and the ironclad man-in-suit powerhouse called Big Guy. For over a decade the world has been protected by BGY-11 (Big Guy), a robot built like a tank and capable of taking on any giant Godzilla-sized kaiju monsters, and programmed not to harm any humans. Secretly, the artificial intelligence portion of the project was a failure, and a human pilot has really been in control all this time. Big Guy was decommissioned after Japan released the pint-sized artificially intelligent robot named Rusty to take on the monsters. As Rusty soon finds out, he's in need of some help, so once again Big Guy is called in after being mothballed. Combined they're the best fighting force in the world. Too bad Big Guy doesn't want to hurt Rusty's feelings and tell him that he's really human. The artist, Geoff Darrow, received an Eisner Award in 1996 in the category of Best Artist/Penciller/Inker. The graphic novel helped to inspire the short-lived animated series, which originally aired in North America in 1999.

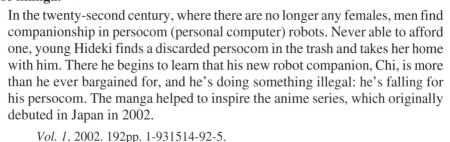

Chobits. **Written and illustrated by CLAMP.** TOKYOPOP, 2002–2003. **O Japanese manga.** あ

In the twenty-second century, where there are no longer any females, men find companionship in persocom (personal computer) robots. Never able to afford one, young Hideki finds a discarded persocom in the trash and takes her home with him. There he begins to learn that his new robot companion, Chi, is more than he ever bargained for, and he's doing something illegal: he's falling for his persocom. The manga helped to inspire the anime series, which originally debuted in Japan in 2002.

Vol. 1. 2002. 192pp. 1-931514-92-5.
Vol. 2. 2002. 184pp. 1-59182-005-7.
Vol. 3. 2002. 184pp. 1-59182-006-5.
Vol. 4. 2003. 200pp. 1-59182-007-3.
Vol. 5. 2003. 192pp. 1-59182-153-3.
Vol. 6. 2003. 192pp. 1-59182-257-2.
Vol. 7. 2003. 192pp. 1-59182-258-0.
Vol. 8. 2003. 128pp. 1-59182-409-5.

E.V.E. Protomecha: Sins of the Daughter. **Written by Aron Lusen and Christian Lichtner. Illustrated by Alé Garza.** Image Comics, 2001. 168pp. 1-58240-204-3. **T**

In the near future, an elderly scientist has put the final touches on his greatest creation—a female android known as E.V.E. Lifelike, but not sentient, when a mysterious heavenly power not from this Earth bestows life on E.V.E., what originally seemed like a gift from Heaven is anything but, as E.V.E. discovers the true reason she's been given life. Now to win her own freedom it will cost her the lives of all she holds dear, as she must take on those with the power of gods.

Fused. **Written by Steve Niles. Illustrated by Paul Lee, Ben Templesmith, Brad Rader, Josh Medors, and Peter Repovski.** Dark Horse Comics, 2004. **O**

Robotics engineer Mark Haggerty was working on a prototype Cy-Bot suit originally planned to be a rescue suit for paramedics and firefighters. In a freak accident, Mark gets fused with the robot exoskeleton. His skin is melding with metal and he finds himself trapped in a suit of armor. Unless something is done soon, it could be permanent! Now he's on the run from the government's superpowered enforcers, the Implementers, as well as the law for appearing to accidentally kill himself. Luckily Mark is in a fully equipped suit of armor, and he's not afraid to fight for his freedom. Will he be able to one day get out of the suit, and more important, does the government really want him to?

Vol. 1: Canned Heat. 2004. 96pp. 1-59307-192-2.
Vol. 2: Think Like a Machine. 2004. 112pp. 1-59307-263-5.

🦋 *Geisha: The Complete Geisha.* **Written and illustrated by Andi Watson.** Oni Press, 2003. 160pp. 1-929998-51-1. **T** ◎

© 2006 Andi Watson.

Jomi is an android like no other. In a future world that is prejudiced against artificial life, she's been blessed to be raised as a human and has lived with a supportive adoptive father and three very protective brothers who work as professional bodyguards with Jomi. She's also been given something special: the freedom to choose her own path in life. She's chosen to become a painter. Along the path to find a patron to support her, she becomes involved with the criminal underworld, the high-fashion world of supermodels, giant robots, and a scheme to have a famous painting forged. How can Jomi make it in a world that has lumped all synthetic output as undesirable and uncreative, even though she knows she has the talent for something as humanly creative as a career in art? The collection received recognition by YALSA's Popular Paperbacks for Young Adults committee in 2002 on the "Graphic Novels: Superheroes and Beyond" list.

Ghost in the Shell. **Written and illustrated by Masamune Shirow.** Dark Horse Comics, 1995–2005. **M** ◎ **Japanese manga.** あ

One of the most influential manga cyberpunk stories. By 2029, humanity has begun to rely so heavily on the assistance of computer technology that the lines between man and machine have blurred to the point that humans now use cybernetic implants and androids now wear human skin. Major Mokoto Kusanagi is a female military cyborg agent for Section 9. She's in charge of a covert ops unit of fellow cyborgs, including the hulking Batau and a half-human rookie named Togusa. Their unit handles everything from hostage recovery situations, to hacking jobs, to black market ghost thieves, to antiterrorism missions. Their toughest mission entails taking on a hacker known only as the Puppeteer, a cyber-criminal who makes the team question their loyalty to one another, their mission, and their preconceptions about what it means to be a human being. The second edition of the book includes a cyber-sex scene that was missing from the original edition. The sequel takes place in the year 2035 and explores similar themes of the soul as Motoko Aramaki, a cyborg counterespionage officer for the global Poseidon International organization, questions what's reality and what makes someone truly alive.

> *Vol. 1.* 1st ed. 1995. 352pp. 1-56971-081-3; 2d ed. 2004. 368pp. 1-59307-228-7.
> *Vol. 2: Man-Machine Inferface.* 2005. 312pp. 1-59307-204-X.

***Livewires: Clockwork Thugs, Yo!* Written by Adam Warren. Illustrated by Rick Mays.** Marvel Comics, 2005. 144pp. 0-7851-1519-6. **T**

Hollowpoint Ninja, Gothic Lolita, Cornfed, Stem Cell, and Social Butterfly are the best in robotic technology. A team of nanobuilt robots (semiautonomous, artificially intelligent, limited-nanofunction, human-form mecha constructs), they so closely resemble teenagers that you'd swear they were real. Funded by S.H.I.E.L.D. in a project code-named Protect: LIVEWIRE, they're the latest in counterespionage technology and programmed to hunt down other rogue black-ops programs like themselves, out to destroy the world. They're ready to save the day—even if it costs them their own "lives."

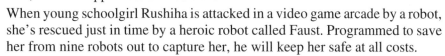

***Metal Guardian Faust.* Written and illustrated by Tetsuro Ueyama.** VIZ Media, LLC, 1998. 272pp. 1-56931-263-X. **T**

When young schoolgirl Rushiha is attacked in a video game arcade by a robot, she's rescued just in time by a heroic robot called Faust. Programmed to save her from nine robots out to capture her, he will keep her safe at all costs.

***Frank Miller's RoboCop.* Written by Frank Miller. Adapted by Steven Grant. Illustrated by Juan Jose Ryp.** Avatar Press, 2007. 216pp. 1-59291-036-X, hardcover; 1-59291-035-1, softcover. **M**

When superstar comic book creator Frank Miller wrote the screenplays for the two sequels to the cult-classic science fiction film *RoboCop* (1987), his scripts were cut apart by Hollywood, and *RoboCop 2* (1990) and *RoboCop 3* (1993) bore little resemblance to his original drafts. Now for the first time Frank Miller's original scripts have been adapted by Steven Grant and Juan Jose Ryp, and fans can finally see what could have been. The story features RoboCop (Officer Murphy) as Frank Miller has always intended, combining the violence, humor, and robotic action that made the original movie a cult classic.

***RoboCop: Prime Suspect.* Written by John Arcudi. Illustrated by John Paul Leon.** Dark Horse Comics, 1993. 112pp. 1-878574-87-6. **O**

Based on the characters from the science fiction classic film *RoboCop* (1987). Officer Murphy must clear his name when ballistics tests link a murder to a gun only the cyborg cop can fire. Murphy maintains his innocence, but did RoboCop really pull the trigger?

***RoboCop vs. Terminator.* Written by Frank Miller. Illustrated by Walter Simonson.** Dark Horse Comics/Diamond Comics, 1992. 128pp. No ISBN. **T** ◎

A crossover of two of the most popular cyborgs in science fiction motion picture history! Cyborg Detroit police officer Murphy (RoboCop) learns a terrible secret from a time-traveler from the future: humanity will be hunted down like dogs by the year 2029 by Skynet and their killer robots, called Terminators, and he's the reason for it. In the bleak future, the human-killing Terminators are the grunts, created by the evil computer system known as Skynet. It becomes clear to Murphy that the only way to make sure the future never happens is that he must die to ensure the secrets of his cyborg mind are never revealed. But the Terminators from the future are sent back to the past to prevent Murphy from dying again and again. Each time Murphy destroys himself, another horde of Terminators jumps back to the past to rescue him. How can the robotic supercop of today outsmart the evil technology of the future and save humanity?

Rumble Girls: Silky Warrior Tansie. **Written and illustrated by Lea Hernandez.** NBM Publishing, 2003. 176pp. 1-56163-370-3. **T**

Raven Tansania Ransom is one of the best Hardskin fighters-in-training (a large robotic suit of armor that the fighter merges with) at the Juliet Academie for Girls. She's in love with her coach, who in secret is the hunky-but-villainous Crimson August on the popular corporate-created fighting show. His ratings as the Crimson August are slumping, and the corporate suits want some new blood to play the heroine—someone just like Raven. Now Raven's stuck in an almost unbreakable contract with the manipulative corporate suits, and there's only one way out of the contract: to kill Crimson.

© 2006 Lea Hernandez.

<u>**Saber Marionette J.**</u> **Written by Satoru Akahori. Illustrated by Yumisuke Kotoyoshi.** TOKYOPOP, 2003–2004. **O Japanese manga.**

On the planet Terra II, where women are extinct, humanity has created emotionless androids called "marionettes" for companionship and to share the workload. Love is a foreign word, since the androids can't feel love, anger, or other common emotions. In the city of Japoness, a re-creation of nineteenth-century Japan, a boy named Otaru Mamiya discovers a marionette named Lime. Unlike any other marionette, Lime has a full range of emotions, and she soon bonds with Otaru as her master. Otaru reactivates several other marionettes, including Cherry and Bloodberry, both of whom also take a liking to Otaru. Together they're out to prevent war from erupting, and fighting over Otaru as they try to save Japoness from Faust, the villainous ruler of the attacking city of Gartland

Vol. 1. 2003. 168pp. 1-59182-386-2.
Vol. 2. 2003. 192pp. 1-59182-387-0.
Vol. 3. 2003. 192pp. 1-59182-388-9.
Vol. 4. 2004. 168pp. 1-59182-539-3.
Vol. 5. 2004. 208pp. 1-59182-540-7.

Semantic Lace Vol. 1: Ghost Story. **Written and illustrated by Sherard Jackson.** Image Comics, Inc., 2003. 112pp. 1-58240-313-9. **M**

In the year 2190, the war in Israel rages on, but the technology has changed dramatically and robots and cyber-powered suits of armor are now commonplace on the battle-filled streets. When thousands of people are killed in a bombing at a shopping mall in Tel Aviv, Israeli Intelligence Agency Mossad agent Illuatha Assad must fight the terrorists and search for survivors with the aid of her armored Harlequin model, Automaton. When she finds that some of her loved ones are caught in the battlefield, she must separate the machine from man and reclaim her humanity after the technology has taken her soul.

Steel Angel Kurumi. **Written and illustrated by Kaishaku.** ADV Manga, 2003–2004. **O Japanese manga.**

In the roaring 1920s, a shy boy named Nakahito Kagura, an eleven-year-old mystic, discovers a strange, life-sized doll attached to a machine in an abandoned facility. He gives the attractive-looking doll a kiss, and to his amazement it awakens. The doll is really a Steel Angel named Kurumi, and according to her programming, whoever wakens her will be her master forever. Created by Dr. Ayanokoji, Kurumi was to be a last-resort weapon for peace and was put into storage until the time she was needed. Now due to being imprinted by Nakahito, she's a gentle and loving fighter for peace, able to take on giant robots with great ease. Meanwhile, the villainous Dr. Amagi and the government have plans of their own to use the Steel Angels as instruments of death. Dr. Amagi is able to recover Saki, a second Steel Angel, to use for destruction and war, and they will stop at nothing to recover Kurumi whether she likes it or not.

> *Vol. 1*. 2003. 180pp. 1-4139-0011-9.
> *Vol. 2*. 2004. 172pp. 1-4139-0012-7.
> *Vol. 3*. 2004. 172pp. 1-4139-0013-5.
> *Vol. 4*. 2004. 172pp. 1-4139-0059-3.
> *Vol. 5*. 2004. 172pp. 1-4139-0078-X.
> *Vol. 6*. 2004. 188pp. 1-4139-0099-2.
> *Vol. 7*. 2004. 180pp. 1-4139-0117-4.
> *Vol. 8*. 2004. 180pp. 1-4139-0152-2.
> *Vol. 9*. 2004. 188pp. 1-4139-0153-0.

Superman vs. The Terminator: Death to the Future. **Written by Alan Grant. Illustrated by Steve Pugh.** Dark Horse Comics and DC Comics, 2000. 96pp. 1-56971-476-2. 🎬

A crossover published by both DC Comics and Dark Horse Comics. When Sara Connor and her young son John, the future resistance fighter, are attacked by two robotic Terminator robots at a mall in Metropolis, they're rescued by Superman, who quickly dispatches the fiendish robotic foes. Skynet, the robot network that will stop at nothing to destroy John Connor, teleports Superman into the future, where the robots rule the day. Can Superman and some old friends help an aged John Connor fight against the Terminators, and can Superman find a way back home to the present?

The Terminator. Dark Horse Comics, and ibooks, inc. 1991-2003. T 🎬

Ever since Arnold Schwarzenegger first played the role of the unrelenting robot assassin sent from the future to kill Sarah and her son John Connor in James Cameron's 1984 science fiction/action film *The Terminator*, the movie and its sequels have inspired graphic novel stories that further propel the reader into a world where humanity has been crushed by the sinister Skynet and killer robots are out to destroy humans, even by transporting to the past.

The Terminator: Tempest. Written by John Arcudi. Illustrated by Chris Warner. Dark Horse Comics, 1991. 112pp. 1-878574-21-3.

The Terminator: Secondary Objectives. Written by James Robinson. Illustrated by Paul Gulacy. Dark Horse Comics, 1992. 112pp. 1-878574-31-0.

The Terminator: The Enemy Within. Written by Ian Edginton. Illustrated by Vince Giarrano. Dark Horse Comics, 1992. 112pp. 1-878574-33-7.

The Terminator: Endgame. Written by James Robinson. Illustrated by Jackson Guice. Dark Horse Comics, 1999. 80pp. 1-56971-373-1.

The Terminator: Rewired. Written by James Robinson, Alan Grant, Adam Warren, Toren Smith, and Chris Warner. Illustrated by Matt Wagner, Bill Jaaska, Dan Panosian, Guy Davis, and Jeff Albrecht. ibooks, inc., 2003. 168pp. 0-7434-9303-6.

Terminator: The Burning Earth. Written by Ron Fortier. Illustrated by Alex Ross. ibooks, inc., 2003. 128pp. 0-7434-7927-0.

T2: Judgment Day: The Graphic Novel. Written by Gregory Wright. Illustrated by Klaus Janson. ibooks, inc., 2003. 176pp. 0-7434-7992-0.

***Tokyo Knights.* Written by Robert Place Napton. Illustrated by Ph.** Top Cow Productions/Image Comics, 2005. 128pp. 1-58240-428-3. **T**

In the vast mega-city known as Tokyo 2, a shy teenager called Kenny, while looking for some excitement, meets a beautiful girl called Sharon, a member of a thrill-seeking gang. For kicks the gangs participate in a fight like no other, with eight-foot-tall piloted mechs called Tokyo Knights. The pilots of the mechs during the battle feel every punch and blow dealt by the robots. Soon Kenny puts his life on the line as a Tokyo Knight pilot to impress Sharon, but will he last long in the live-fast, die-hard ring of robot death?

***WE3.* Written by Grant Morrison. Illustrated by Frank Quitely.** Vertigo/DC Comics, 2005. 104pp. 1-4012-0495-3. **M** ◉

The U.S. Air Force has created the most lethal weapons to annihilate the small-time drug cartels—the Animal Weapon 3 project. Code-named WE3, three stray pets—a dog, cat, and rabbit—are enhanced with cybernetic components, giving them the ability to use a variety of lethal weapons and even the ability to speak basic English. Working as a close-knit team, WE3 were created as the perfect prototype weapons to fight in the future wars of America. When the project is terminated and the pets are ordered to be destroyed, the animals escape into a confusing outside world, with the only thing leading them on a place they distantly remember, called "home."

© 2006 Grant Morrison and Frank Quitely.

Mecha and Giant Robots

These stories focus on giant robots (mecha) that protect huhumanity on Earth or other civilizations from alien invaders. The robots usually are humanoid in shape but sometimes take the shape of familiar animals, including dinosaurs, lions, and horses. In most cases giant mecha are typically not sentient and are usually piloted by a person or team. Many Japanese manga and anime series feature stories with this popular theme.

***Assembly Pocket Manga.* Written and illustrated by Sherard Jackson.** Antarctic Press, 2004. 142pp. 1-932453-51-2. **T**

> In a bleak future in a totalitarian state, the only way out of poverty is to join the army and fight in a suit of mech armor against a terrorist group of mech pilots. Young Shon and her sister Elaine just try to get by in the war-torn place they call home. Their family all dead and gone, Elaine wants nothing but for her younger sister to go to college and become someone, but Shon wants to follow in the family tradition and enlist in the military. Shon enlists and is soon put to work as a medical surgeon treating wounded soldiers, but her skills catch the eye of the military leadership, who are looking for capable young pilots for their mech warriors. The war is tough, but she proves that she's a talented and dedicated pilot. But when she finds herself up against a tough mech enemy, her world comes crashing down as she discovers who her enemy really is.

Big O. Written by Hitoshi Ariga. Illustrated by Hajime Yatate. VIZ Media, LLC, 2003–2004. **T Japanese manga.** あ

> Forty years ago the people of Paradigm City lost their memory, and since then they have tried to rebuild their lives. Roger Smith, a rich young man known as the city's negotiator, has an ace up his sleeve: he's also the controller of the giant robot savior of the city known as the Big. O. Based on the anime series co-produced by the Cartoon Network.

> > *Vol. 1*. 2003. 208pp. 1-56931-953-7.
> > *Vol. 2*. 2003. 216pp. 1-56931-806-9.
> > *Vol. 3*. 2003. 216pp. 1-56931-827-1.
> > *Vol. 4*. 2003. 216pp. 1-56931-977-4.
> > *Vol. 5*. 2003. 192pp. 1-59116-108-8.
> > *Vol. 6*. 2004. 208pp. 1-59116-219-X.

Brigadoon. Written and illustrated by Nozomi Watase. TOKYOPOP, 2003. **T Japanese manga.**

> Tokyo, 1969: A mysterious city named Brigadoon has appeared in the sky and covers as far as the eye can see. Marin, a thirteen-year-old orphan, finds that her life is in danger from a presence up there that has come just for her—and that the robotic hero the Blue Swordsman, whom she'd always thought of as something in her imagination, just might be real after all and here to save her. It's bad enough that Marin is being teased at school by her classmates, let alone being attacked by alien monsters. What secret could she possibly carry that would make her a target for assassination, and what is the secret of Brigadoon?

> > *Vol. 1*. 2003. 208pp. 1-59182-377-3.
> > *Vol. 2*. 2003. 200pp. 1-59182-378-1.

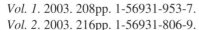

B'tX. Written and illustrated by Masami Kurumada. TOKYOPOP, 2004– . **T Japanese manga.**

When computer inventor Kotaro Takamiya is captured by the Machine Empire, a ruthless organization that has existed in the desert for hundreds of years, they want him for his skills at creating robots with extremely powerful artificial intelligence. Kotaro's younger brother Teppei sets out to rescue him, but Teppei can't do it alone. With the help of the horselike robot B't called X, a creation of the Machine Empire long thought to be dead, he sets out to rescue Kotaro from the Machine Empire's grip. The sixteen-volume series was originally published in Japan.

> *Vol. 1.* 2004. 192pp. 1-59182-639-X.
> *Vol. 2.* 2004. 200pp. 1-59182-640-3.
> *Vol. 3.* 2004. 192pp. 1-59182-641-1.
> *Vol. 4.* 2004. 192pp. 1-59182-642-X.
> *Vol. 5.* 2004. 192pp. 1-59182-643-8.
> *Vol. 6.* 2004. 192pp. 1-59182-644-6.
> *Vol. 7.* 2005. 192pp. 1-59532-377-5.
> *Vol. 8.* 2005. 192pp. 1-59532-378-3.
> *Vol. 9.* 2005. 192pp. 1-59532-379-1.
> *Vol. 10.* 2005. 192pp. 1-59532-380-5.
> *Vol. 11.* 2006. 192pp. 1-59532-381-3.

The Candidate for Goddess. Written and illustrated by Yukiru Sugisaki. TOKYOPOP, 2004. **T Japanese manga.**

A thousand years ago, four planetary systems of huhumanity were wiped out by the Giseisha, a mysterious alien race, and humans were driven out to the stars to form space colonies. To battle the Giseisha, humanity's greatest weapons are the five giant humanoid warriors called the Goddesses. Each one piloted by a fully trained pilot, they're out to ensure that Zion, the last known habitable planet, is never destroyed. Now in the year 4088, the G.O.A. (Goddess Operator Academy) has been created to train the highly selective group of men to be the next generation of Goddess pilots. Zero Enna, a young teen whose life was once save by the White Goddess, is out to prove, along with four other teen boys, that he's got what it takes to be the best of the next generation of Goddess pilots. And the G.O.A. just might need their skills soon, before Zion falls at the hands of the Giseisha.

> *Vol. 1.* 2004. 208pp. 1-59182-747-7.
> *Vol. 2.* 2004. 184pp. 1-59182-748-5.
> *Vol. 3.* 2004. 176pp. 1-59182-749-3.
> *Vol. 4.* 2004. 176pp. 1-59182-750-7.
> *Vol. 5.* 2004. 192pp. 1-59182-751-5.

Cannon God Exaxxion. Written and illustrated by Kenichi Sonoda. Dark Horse Comics, 2002– . **O Japanese manga.**

Ten years ago the Riofaldians came to Earth from another planet and brought peace and salvation. While they've coexisted with huhumanity, one man, a brilliant inventor/scientist and grandfather of teenager Hoichi Kano, has never trusted the aliens and knew that it was just a matter of time until the aliens showed their true nature. He went into hiding to prepare for war, and judgment day is now: the Riofald colony is now showing their true colors and are bent on enslaving Earth. And now thanks to Hoichi

Kano's grandfather, Hoichi is ready to reclaim Earth with the coolest gadgets and weapons. Now Hoichi has a state-of-the-art battle suit and a sexy shape-changing robot assistant who also transforms into his speeder bike, and is the pilot of the mega-robot known as Exaxxion. He may be humanity's last hope against an alien colony, and Hoichi is saving the world in style. The series was originally published in Japan in seven volumes.

> *Stage 1.* 2002. 208pp. 1-56971-745-1.
> *Stage 2.* 2003. 184pp. 1-56971-966-7.
> *Stage 3.* 2004. 224pp. 1-59307-087-X.
> *Stage 4.* 2005. 208pp. 1-59307-338-0.
> *Stage 5.* 2006. 208pp. 1-59307-571-5.

***Doug TenNapel's Gear.* Written and illustrated by Doug TenNapel.** Image Comics, 2007. 160pp. 1-58240-680-4. **T**

Welcome to a darkly humorous and violent world, where cats from the "armpit" state of Newton fight for dominance in a four-way struggle against the dogs from Dogtown, their alliance with the cats from North Plate, and preying mantis-like insects from South Plate. Utilizing their giant robot Guardians as weapons, all sides are on the brink of war to retrieve a fabled secret gear called the Forbidden Mechanism. The gear, once placed inside a Guardian, will give the user omnipotent power, and its secret location in Newton has brought all the enemies together on one battlefield. Meanwhile, four bumbling cats from the state of Newton are sent on an important mission to steal a giant robot Guardian from the enemy state of Dogtown. When one of the cats accidentally gets squashed by the Guardian, the three remaining team members carry out the mission and return to Newton, but the clumsy cat named Waffle, as well as an enemy insect named Chee, undergo a strange metamorphosis, and they are both transformed into living Guardians. When the Forbidden Mechanism is unlocked improperly outside of a Guardian, the creature is revealed to be the most dumb-tarded creature that the animal kingdoms could ever have imagined. As the battle escalates and more lives are lost, Gear's true purpose is revealed as Heaven and Hell play a role in the final battle.

***Frontier Line.* Written and illustrated by Yoshihisa Tagami.** CPM Manga, 2002. 240pp. 1-56219-936-6. **T Japanese manga.**

On the planet Sodom, civil war has broken out between the humans who have made the world their home. The north and south colonies have discovered giant mech warriors left behind by an ancient race. Brought back into working condition, the giant robots can help turn the tide of the war, reunite the colonies, or help bring about total annihilation. Told in six short stories focusing on different sides of the war. Will humanity survive, or has it sealed its own fate?

***Giant Robot Warriors.* Written by Stuart Moore. Illustrated by Ryan Kelly.** AiT/Planet Lar, 2003. 120pp. 1-932051-19-8. **T**

When the president needs it, the U.S. Department of Giant Robot Warriors strikes out to defend the United States from foreign countries developing Gi-

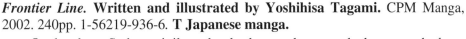

ant Robot technology capability. In this political satire, can the underfunded, motley crew work together long enough to get the job done in a robot not yet ready for combat? And what's the secret behind the president's odd behavior?

Jason and the Argobots. Written by J. Torres. Illustrated by Mike Norton. Oni Press, **2003. A**

© 2006 J. Torres and Mike Norton.

Jason and his little sister Juni live with their inventor grandfather in the secluded desert near the metropolis of Shimmer City. One day after an earthquake hits the area, Jason spots an amazing site: a robot of immense size stuck in the sand. Taking control of the robot, named Chiron, he unwittingly helps to stop a prison break in Shimmer City and becomes a citywide hero. Now Jason is a celebrity of sorts, much to the dismay of his family, and he's stuck in the media's spotlight. Meanwhile, the government that originally built the robot with the help of an alien race for a coming battle wants Chiron back in their possession before the coming war—but it might already be too late.

Vol. 1: Birthquake. 2003. 112pp. 1-929998-55-4.
Vol. 2: Machina Ex Deus. 2003. 88pp. 1-929998-56-2.

Jinki: Extend. Written and illustrated by Sirou Tunasima. ADV Manga, 2004. **O Japanese manga.**

After a strange explosion occurs in the city of La Gran Sabana, Venezuela, in 1989, people are found murdered and entire civilizations just vanish. Dubbed the "lost life phenomenon" (LLP), these occurrences begin to happen all over the globe, and a shadowy organization and its giant mech robots, called "jinki," appear to be behind the occurrences. Three years later, heroine Akao Hiiragi has had amnesia ever since the first LLP. For an unknown reason, she's being targeted for a power she doesn't remember she has: the power to control the jinki. With the fate of Japan and the world at stake, Akao has to find the power within herself to control the giant robots and save the world.

Vol. 1. 2004. 186pp. 1-4139-0052-6.
Vol. 2. 2004. 186pp. 1-4139-0090-9.
Vol. 3. 2004. 186pp. 1-4139-0108-5.

Mobile Police Patlabor. Written and illustrated by Masami Yuki. VIZ Media, LLC, **1998. T Japanese manga.** あ

When the "Labors," large robotic exoskeletons used for construction purposes, fall into the hands of criminals, it's up to the police to fight fire with fire with their own brand of Labors. Though not respected by the rest of the police department, the comedically misfit "Special Vehicles Division 2" force is ready to take on the cybernetic criminals. Led by the sweet but determined Noa Izumi, they'll prove that they're the best police department ever. The manga inspired a hit television series as well as feature-length movies.

Vol. 1. 1998. 192pp. 1-56931-287-7.
Vol. 2: Basic Training. 1998. 192pp. 1-56931-337-7.

Mobile Suit Gundam. Created by Yoshiyuki Tomino and Hajime Yadate. TOKYOPOP and Del Rey Manga, 1999– . **T Japanese manga.** あ

In a world where Earth is overcrowded and humanity has relocated into separate orbiting colonies, a brutal civil war erupts for control of Earth. Each colony's army of giant robots fights for dominance of Earth, where there is no clear-cut good versus evil—only people trying to survive. Created as an anime series by Yoshiyuki Tomino and Hajime Yadate in Japan, the now-successful series has spawned a variety of "alternate world" versions of the basic premise of the series, including G Gundam, Gundam Wing, Gundam X, and many more series published by TOKYOPOP and Del Rey in the United States. For a complete list of Gundam titles, check with their respective Web sites. The series is inspired by the anime series, which originally debuted in 1979.

Gundam Wing. TOKYOPOP, 1999–2002.
    Vol. 1. 2000. 184pp. 1-892213-41-9.
    Vol. 2. 2001. 184pp. 1-892213-51-6.
    Vol. 3. 2001. 184pp. 1-892213-60-5.
    Battlefield of the Pacifists. 2002. 176pp. 1-931514-71-2.
    Endless Waltz. 2002. 208pp. 1-931514-72-0.
    Blue Destiny. 1999. 220pp. 1-892213-10-9.
The Last Outpost (G-Unit). TOKYOPOP, 2003.
    Vol. 1. 2002. 184pp. 1-931514-81-X.
    Vol. 2. 2003. 192pp. 1-931514-82-8.
    Vol. 3. 2003. 192pp. 1-931514-83-6.
G Gundam. TOKYOPOP, 2003.
    Vol. 1. 2003. 200pp. 1-59182-166-5.
    Vol. 2. 2003. 192pp. 1-59182-167-3.
    Vol. 3. 2003. 216pp. 1-59182-168-1.
SEED Astray. TOKYOPOP, 2004.
    Vol. 1. 2004. 188pp. 1-59182-938-0.
    Vol. 2. 2004. 188pp. 1-59182-939-9.
    Vol. 3. 2004. 208pp. 1-59532-416-X.
SEED Astray R. TOKYOPOP, 2005.
    Vol. 1. 2005. 184pp. 1-59532-576-X.
    Vol. 2. 2005. 192pp. 1-59532-577-8.
    Vol. 3. 2005. 192pp. 1-59532-578-6.
    Vol. 4. 2005. 232pp. 1-59532-997-8.
Gundam Seed. Del Rey Manga/Random House, 2004–2005.
    Vol. 1. 2004. 208pp. 0-345-47045-1.
    Vol. 2. 2004. 208pp. 0-345-47179-2.
    Vol. 3. 2004. 192pp. 0-345-47230-6.
    Vol. 4. 2005. 176pp. 0-345-47794-4.
    Vol. 5. 2005. 208pp. 0-345-47795-2.

Myth Warriors. **Written by Robert Place Napton. Illustrated by Ph.** Top Cow Productions/Image Comics, 2004, 128pp. 1-58240-427-5. **T**

Skateboarding teenage trouble-maker Eric Volker lives for excitement. He's a quick-thinking daredevil and a petty thief, and he's discovered that an amulet

he swiped from the Los Angeles Art Museum is more than just a trinket. The amulet is a port key for Ares, an ancient giant mecha warrior built by the Roma Imperium. By accidentally bonding with Ares, Eric has rekindled an ancient war with the Empires of the Kemet Sphere and Maya Empire. Bringing their ancient Egyptian and Mayan mechs to Earth, Eric must rely on his skills as a skateboarder and do the impossible to save Earth from annihilation.

Neon Genesis Evangelion. 2d ed. Written and illustrated by Yoshiyuki Sadamoto. VIZ Media, LLC, 2004. **O Japanese manga.** あ.

In the year A.D. 2015, Earth is still suffering from the aftereffects of a devastating meteor attack fifteen years earlier, which destroyed half of the human race and spun Earth's axis out of control. Now humanity is facing extinction at the hands of an alien race of giants called the Angels. To combat the aliens, in Tokyo-3 a secret organization called NERV has trained a small group of teenage pilots to pilot the giant biomechanical mechas to combat the aliens at all costs. The series is also tied in with an animated series from Japan that debuted in 1995.

> *Vol. 1.* 2004. 184pp. 1-59116-400-1.
> *Vol. 2.* 2004. 176pp. 1-59116-390-0.
> *Vol. 3.* 2004. 176pp. 1-59116-401-X.
> *Vol. 4.* 2004. 192pp. 1-59116-402-8.
> *Vol. 5.* 2004. 200pp. 1-59116-403-6.
> *Vol. 6.* 2004. 200pp. 1-59116-404-4.
> *Vol. 7.* 2004. 200pp. 1-59116-405-2.
> *Vol. 8.* 2004. 200pp. 1-59116-415-X.
> *Vol. 9.* 2004. 200pp. 1-59116-707-8.

RahXephon. Created by Yutaka Izubuchi and Takeaki Momose. VIZ Media, LLC, 2004. **O Japanese manga.** あ.

In the year A.D. 2015, teenager Ayato Kamina's comfortable life in Tokyo is about to be shattered, and his entire life will become a lie. After mysterious agents from an organization known as MU try to capture Ayato and his close friend Reika, they're rescued by a secret agent from the organization known as TERRA. The agent reveals to him the shocking truth: it really is the year A.D. 2033, and the entire city is a time-displaced fortress for MU. Also, Ayato is the only human capable of controlling the ancient god-protector robot that MU desperately want in their control: the RahXephon. Knowing that he will do anything to protect Reika, Ayato joins with TERRA to rescue Tokyo from MU's time-displaced influence, with the aid of one of the most powerful weapons on the planet. The manga is based on the anime series, which originally debuted in Japan in 2002.

> *Vol. 1.* 2004. 192pp. 1-59116-407-9.
> *Vol. 2.* 2004. 200pp. 1-59116-427-3.
> *Vol. 3.* 2004. 200pp. 1-59116-428-1.

Robotech. Written by Jack Herman and Markalan Joplin. Illustrated by various. WildStorm Productions/DC Comics, 2003. **Neo-manga.** あ

Macross Saga is a collection reprinting the classic *Comico* comic books originally published from 1984 to 1989. The story focuses on the 70,000-member crew of the *Super Dimensional Fortress One* (*SDF-1*), a ship made from the remnants of crashed alien technology, as they try to struggle back to Earth after being accidentally flung out into space near Pluto. Earth's enemy are the Zentraedi, an engineered alien race sent to retrieve the stolen alien technology by their creators, the Robotech Masters.

> *Macross Saga 1*. 2003. 176pp. 1-4012-0024-9.
> *Macross Saga 2*. 2003. 144pp. 1-4012-0025-7.
> *Macross Saga 3*. 2003. 176pp. 1-4012-0026-5.
> *Macross Saga 4*. 2003. 176pp. 1-4012-0027-3.

***Robotech: From the Stars*. Written by Tommy Yune and Jay Faerber. Illustrated by various.** WildStorm Productions/DC Comics, 2003. 176pp. 1-4012-0144-X. **T Neo-manga.** あ

Based on the classic hit anime from Japan. The origin of the Veritech Robotech technology (planes that can transform into robotic warriors) is revealed for the first time. When an abandoned alien vessel crashes to Earth, humanity discovers that it truly isn't alone in the universe. With a treasure-trove of newfound technology for the taking, humans are learning to utilize this find and transform it to our specs, and must prepare for the inevitable confrontation with an alien race. Old soldiers are called back into service, including test pilot Roy Fokker, to try to understand the full potential of the Veritech program technology and decide whether it's worth the price of so many lives.

Sentinel. Written by Sean McKeever. Illustrated by UDON. Marvel Age/Marvel Comics. 2004–2006. **Y**

© 2006 Marvel Comics.

Life's been tough on teenager Juston Seyfert. A sophomore at Antigo High School, he's still picked on by the jocks at school, and his family's never been the same since his mother left them. While scavenging in his father's junkyard, he spots something mysterious—the remains of an old robot programmed to exterminate mutants: a thirty-foot-tall Sentinel. What can a downtrodden boy possibly do with a giant robot? Anything he wants, that's what! A story about a boy and his robot and what it really means to be a hero.

> *Vol. 1: Salvage*. 2004. 136pp. 0-7851-1380-0.
> *Vol. 2: No Hero*. 2004. 144pp. 0-7851-1368-1.
> *Vol. 3: Past Imperfect*. 2006. 120pp. 0-7851-1914-0.

Transformers. Titan Books, Dreamwave Productions, and IDW Publishing, 2002– . **Y**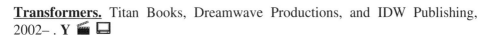

On the distant planet Cyberton, where all life is computer-based, a never-ending battle for the planet rages between two races of cybernetic, giant-sized robots called Transformers, which are more than meets the eye. Each robot can transform into another form such as a car, dinosaur, gun, and more. After a long and weary battle between the good Autobots led by Optimus Prime and the evil Decepticons ruled by the vicious Megatron, the Autobots have fled to Earth to evade slavery by the Decepticons. Sworn to fight to the end to defeat the Decepticons and ultimately to reclaim Cybertron, the Autobots fight on against the Decepticons as well as other foes, including the planet-devouring transformer known as Unicron. Inspired by the hit action figure line by Hasbro that's been popular since the 1980s, the stories feature a huge cast of characters. The series is currently published by both IDW Publishing in the United States as well as Titan Books in the United Kingdom. A short-lived publisher named Dreamwave Productions had the license from 2002 to 2004, but the Canadian company folded in 2004 and lost the license. IDW Publishing received the license for <u>Transformers</u> in late 2005. A feature film produced by Steven Spielberg will be released in theaters in 2007.

<u>Transformers (1st series).</u> Titan Books Limited, 2002– . **Y**

Titan Books from England reprinted the classic Marvel Comics series that began in 1984, but reached new ground and the respect of many <u>Transformers</u> fans by continuing to tell well-written stories that continued past Marvel Comics' run. The series was the launching point for Simon Furman, one of the best-known <u>Transformers</u> writers.

Vol. 1: Beginnings. Written by Ralph Macchio and Bob Budiansky. Illustrated by Jim Salicrup. 2003. 144pp. 1-84023-623-X.

Vol. 2: New Order. Written by Bob Budiansky. Illustrated by Herb Trimpe. 2003. 144pp. 1-84023-624-8.

Vol. 3: Cybertron Redux. Written by Bob Budiansky. Illustrated by Don Perlin. Titan Books, 2004. 144pp. 1-84023-657-4.

Vol. 4: Showdown. Written by Bob Budiansky. Illustrated by Herb Trimpe and Don Perlin. 2004. 144pp. 1-84023-681-7.

Vol. 5: Breakdown. Written by Bob Budiansky. Illustrated by Ian Akin. Titan Books, 2004. 144pp. 1-84023-791-0.

Vol. 6: Treason. Written by Bob Budiansky. Illustrated by Don Perlin and Jose Delbo. 2005. 128pp. 1-84023-844-5.

Vol. 7: Trial By Fire. Written by Bob Budiansky. Illustrated by Jose Delbo and Frank Springer. 2005. 144pp. 1-84023-950-6.

Vol. 8: Maximum Force. Written by Bob Budiansky. Illustrated by Frank Springer and Jose Delbo. 2005. 128pp. 1-84023-955-7.

Vol. 9: Dark Star. Written by Bob Budiansky. Illustrated by Jose Delbo. 2005. 128pp. 1-84023-960-3.

Vol. 10: Last Stand. Written by Bob Budiansky. Illustrated by Jose Delbo. 2005. 144pp. 1-84576-008-5.

Vol. 11: Primal Scream. Written by Simon Furman. Illustrated by Geoff Senior and Jose Delbo. 2002. 142pp. 1-84023-401-6.

Vol. 12: Matrix Quest. Written by Simon Furman. Illustrated by Geoff Senior and Jose Delbo. 2002. 142pp. 1-84023-471-7.

Vol. 13: All Fall Down. Written by Simon Furman. Illustrated by Andrew Wildman and Stephen Baskerville. 2002. 142pp. 1-84023-300-1.

Vol. 14: End of the Road. Written by Simon Furman. Illustrated by Andrew Wildman, Geoff Senior and Stephen Baskerville. 2002. 142pp. 1-84023-372-9.

Dark Designs. Written by Simon Furman. Illustrated by Derek Yaniger and Manny Galan. Titan Books, 2003. 160pp. 1-84023-525-X.

Rage in Heaven. Written by Simon Furman. Illustrated by Geoff Senior and Manny Galan. 2003. 160pp. 1-84023-528-4.

Target 2006. Written by Simon Furman. Illustrated by Geoff Senior et al. Titan Books, 2003. 136pp. 1-84023-510-1.

Fallen Angel. Written by Simon Furman. Illustrated by Geoff Senior. Titan Books, 2003. 136pp. 1-84023-511-X.

Time Wars. Written by Simon Furman. Illustrated by Dan Reed, Andrew Wildman and Lee Sullivan. Titan Books, 2003. 136pp. 1-84023-647-7.

Legacy of Unicron. Written by Simon Furman. Illustrated by Geoff Senior and Bryan Hitch. Titan Books, 2003. 136pp. 1-84023-578-0.

Space Pirates. Written by Simon Furman. Illustrated by Dan Reed and Bryan Hitch. 2003. 136pp. 1-84023-619-1.

City of Fear. Written by Simon Furman. Illustrated by Jeff Anderson, Dan Reed and Robin Smith. Titan Books, 2004. 136pp. 1-84023-671-X.

Dinobot Hunt. Written by Simon Furman. Illustrated by Barry Kitson. Titan Books, 2004. 144pp. 1-84023-789-9.

Second Generation. Written by Simon Furman. Illustrated by Jeff Anderson and Barry Kitson. 2005. 128pp. 1-84023-935-2.

Prey. Written by Simon Furman. Illustrated by Jeff Anderson and Dan Reed. 2004. 128pp. 1-84023-831-3.

Aspects of Evil. Written by Simon Furman. Illustrated by Andrew Wildman. 2005. 80pp. 1-84576-055-7.

Way of the Warrior. Written by Simon Furman. Illustrated by Simon Colby and Andrew Wildman. 2005. 80pp. 1-84576-059-X.

Fallen Star. Written by Simon Furman. Illustrated by Andrew Wildman. 2005. 80pp. 1-84576-060-3.

Earthforce. Written by Simon Furman. Illustrated by Andrew Wildman. 2006. 80pp. 1-84576-061-1.

Perchance to Dream. Written by Simon Furman. Illustrated by Andrew Wildman. 2006. 80pp. 1-84576-062-X.

Transformers (2d series). Dreamwave Productions, 2002–2004. **Y**

Published through Dreamwave Productions, the *Transformers* line was reinvigorated with the dynamic drawing style of Pat Lee and other artists, as well as the writing of Simon Furman. The various *Transformers* mini-series are based on recent animated cartoons such as *Energon*, as well as tales involving the classic characters including Optimus Prime, Megatron, the Dinobots, and even cross-overs with the Hasbro toy series G.I. Joe.

Generation One, Vol. 1. Written by Chris Sarrachini. Illustrated by Pat Lee. 2002. 168pp. 0-9730837-2-7.

Generation One, Vol. 2. Written by Brad Mick. Illustrated by Pat Lee. 2002. 160pp. 0-9733817-0-1.

Energon, Vol. 1: Pocket Edition. Written by Simon Furman. Illustrated by Guido Guidi. 2004. 112pp. 0-9733817-3-6.

Armada, Vol. 1: First Contact. Written by Chris Sarracini. Illustrated by James Raiz. 2003. 144pp. 0-9732786-1-7.

Armada, Vol. 2. Written by Simon Furman. Illustrated by Pat Lee. 2003. 160pp. 0-9732786-4-1.

Armada, Vol. 3. Written by Simon Furman. Illustrated by Guido Guidi and Don Figueroa. 2004. 184pp. 0-9733817-4-4.

The War Within, Vol. 1. Written by Simon Furman. Illustrated by Don Figueroa. 2003. 168pp. 0-9732786-0-9.

The War Within, Vol. 2: The Dark Ages. Written by Simon Furman. Illustrated by Andrew Wildman. 2004. 168pp. 0-9733817-5-2.

Transformers/G.I. Joe. Written by John Ney Reiber. Illustrated by Jae Lee. 2004. 168pp. 0-9733817-9-5.

G.I. Joe vs. the Transformers. Written by Josh Blaylock and various. Illustrated by various. Devil's Due Publishing, 2004. 160pp. 1-932796-09-6.

Transformers (3d series). IDW Publishing, 2006–. **Y**

At the time of printing, Dreamwave Productions closed down and the *Transformers* license has been awarded to IDW Publishing. IDW Publishing has begun to reprint Dreamwave's recent publications that are now out of print under their banner as well as create new *Transformers* ongoing stories of the Autobots and Decepticons.

Generation One, Vol. 1. Written by Chris Sarrachini. Illustrated by Pat Lee. 2006. 160pp. 1-933239-81-6.

Generation One, Vol. 2. Written by Brad Mick. Illustrated by Pat Lee. 2006. 176pp. 1-933239-82-4.

Generation One, Vol. 3. Written by James McDonough and Adam Patyk. Illustrated by Don Figueroa. 2006. 160pp. 1-933239-83-2.

Infiltration. Written by Simon Furman. Illustrated by E. J. Su. 2006. 160pp. 1-600100-10-4.

Stormbringer Written by Simon Furman. Illustrated by Don Figueroa. 2006. 104pp. 1-600100-18-X.

Ultraman Tiga. Written by Tony Wong. Illustrated by Khoo Fuk Lung. Dark Horse Comics, 2004–2005. **O** ⌨

In the year 2049, when the fate of the world hangs in the balance and giant monsters once again roam Earth in search of destruction, there's only one giant robot warrior with martial arts moves ready to take them on: Ultraman Tiga. After saving the world 30 million years in the past, he's been called again to save Earth. Bonded with the hotshot human pilot, he's out to fight the good fight against the horde of horrors attacking Earth. Based on the hit Japanese television and movie series that originally debuted in 1966.

Vol. 1: Return of the Warrior. 2004. 128pp. 1-59307-119-1.
Vol. 2: Past Sins, Present Dangers. 2005. 200pp. 1-59307-315-1.

Voltron: Defender of the Universe. Written by Dan Jolley. Illustrated by Mike Norton. Devil's Due Publishing, 2004–2005. **T** あ.

Based on the popular Japanese anime series and toy line. In the future the planets Arus and Earth are under the constant threat of the evil King Zarkon and his gigantic beasts. The best defense is the Voltron Force—five courageous pilots from the interplanetary Galaxy Garrison—who patrol the skies of Arus and beyond in five giant lion robots that were recovered by ancient magics. Each lion robot is powered by a different elemental magic: the Black Lion by Lightning, the Red Lion by Fire, the Green Lion by Cyclone, the Blue Lion by Water, and the Yellow Lion by Magma. When the struggle is too great, the five lion robots transform into one giant sword-wielding defender known as Voltron: The Defender of the Universe.

Vol. 1: Revelations. 2004. 144pp. 1-932796-00-2.
Vol. 2: Paradise Lost. 2004. 128pp. 1-932796-03-7.
Vol. 3: Warpath. 2005. 144pp. 1-932796-19-3.

Chapter 4

Fantasy

Fantasy is commonly understood as literature that portrays a fanciful realm where magic and imagination are commonplace. Many people consider a fantasy to be a story about a world where dragons, orcs, goblins, and wizards reside and where fair maidens in kingdoms languish in need of rescue. In comic books and graphic novels, the genre is no different, except that the medium aids visually in conjuring up the setting and the creatures that inhabit it. Over the last decade, a renewed interest in fantasy fiction has erupted with the release of the <u>Harry Potter</u> novels, as well as the big-screen adaptations of that series and the <u>Lord of the Rings</u>. Graphic novels, too have had their share of fantasy titles, with the release and completion of several major fantasy series, including Neil Gaiman's <u>Sandman</u> and Jeff Smith's <u>Bone</u>; fresh new takes on fantasy including Linda Medley's <u>Castle Waiting</u>, DC Comics' <u>Fables</u>, the late CrossGen's <u>Sojourn</u>, and Image Comics' <u>Tellos</u>; foreign reprints of titles including ADV's <u>Culdcept</u>, and CPM Press's <u>Record of Lodoss War</u>. There is renewed interest in classic fantasy titles such as Richard Pini and Wendy Pini's <u>ElfQuest</u> and Robert E. Howard's *Conan the Barbarian,* published by Dark Horse Comics.

The chapter is organized according to subgenres and common themes, which include adaptations, dark fantasy, high fantasy, and many more. Fantasy is difficult to divide into specific subgenres, and opinions about where titles should be placed vary widely. For the subgenre humorous fantasy, see chapter 8 for a list of highlighted titles.

Sword and Sorcery Fantasy

One of the most popular subgenres of fantasy, tales of sword and sorcery generally feature battles between good and evil, as well as an individual or fellowship undertaking a monumental task or quest. Plenty of action with swordplay and magic is common and practically required. The subgenre is further broken down into subcategories of epic, heroic, and quest.

Epic/Quest Fantasy

The epic or quest tale is archetypal of traditional fantasy. Set in a timeless ancient world, these sweeping tales feature strong characters, fantastical settings, and a quest or journey that needs to be undertaken to save the realm from certain doom. The <u>Lord of the Rings</u> books and movies are excellent examples of this theme in fantasy.

<u>**Bastard!! 2d ed.**</u> **Written and illustrated by Kazushi Hagiwara.** VIZ Media, LLC, 2003–present. **M Japanese manga.** あ

> When the magical kingdom of Metallicana is under attack by the forces of Osbourne, a secret weapon can save the day. One kiss from the virgin girl named Tia on the lips of fifteen-year-old Lucien transforms him into the banished, foul-mouthed wizard known throughout the land as Dark Schneider. One more kiss will turn him back. When the attacking army is defeated with the help of the wizard, is the solution to Metallicana's problems worse than the invading army? Loaded with references to classic heavy metal bands as well as fantasy role-playing games (the "Bastard" in the title refers to a weapon called a "Bastard Sword") , the series is still being published in Japan in the manga publication <u>Ultra Jump</u>, with more than twenty-three volumes in print. A six-part anime was also released to tie in with the manga when it debuted in Japan in 1992.
>
> > *Vol. 1.* 2003. 200pp. 1-56931-952-9.
> > *Vol. 2.* 2003. 208pp. 1-56931-968-5.
> > *Vol. 3.* 2003. 208pp. 1-56931-861-1.
> > *Vol. 4.* 2003. 208pp. 1-56931-826-3.
> > *Vol. 5.* 2004. 208pp. 1-59116-506-7.
> > *Vol. 6.* 2004. 208pp. 1-59116-134-7.
> > *Vol. 7.* 2005. 192pp. 1-59116-742-6.
> > *Vol. 8.* 2005. 200pp. 1-59116-837-6.
> > *Vol. 9.* 2005. 184pp. 1-4215-0050-7.
> > *Vol. 10.* 2006. 184pp. 1-4215-0219-4.
> > *Vol. 11.* 2006. 208pp. 1-4215-0379-4.
> > *Vol. 12.* 2006. 208pp. 1-4215-0434-0.
> > *Vol. 13.* 2006. 208pp. 1-4215-0435-9.
> > *Vol. 14.* 2007. 208pp. 1-4215-0436-7.

Battle Chasers: A Gathering of Heroes. **Written and illustrated by Joe Madureira.** Cliffhanger!/WildStorm Productions/DC Comics, 1999. 160pp. 1-56389-538-2. **T**

> The quest of nine-year-old Gully to find her missing father. Set in a traditional fantasy world populated by monsters and wizards. Young Gully takes her missing father's oversized gauntlets of strength and sets out to find him. Along the way she is joined in her quest by a wise and sarcastic old wizard called Knolan, an outlawed War Golem called Calibretto, a legendary swordsman named Garrison who is still mourning the death of his wife, and a busty thief called Red Monika.

🐾 **Bone.** Written and illustrated by Jeff Smith. Cartoon Books, 1996–2004; Graphix/Scholastic Books 2005– . **Y** ◎ 🎮

Jacket art copyright © 2005 Jeff Smith.

After being run out of Boneville, the Bone cousins—Fone Bone, Phoney Bone, and Smiley Bone—are lost in a mysterious valley far from home. Stuck in a strange land, they befriend the tough and craggy Grandma Ben, her beautiful and tough granddaughter Thorn, Grandma Ben's friend—a burly tavernkeeper named Lucius, and a giant red dragon. Together the three Bone cousins become embroiled in an epic and sometimes humorous journey to end the reign of the mysterious Hooded One, the Lord of Locusts, and the fierce-but-stupid Rat Creatures. A blend of Tolkien-esque adventure with loads of charm, humor, and a dash of <u>Star Wars</u> as inspiration, Jeff Smith's award-winning <u>Bone</u> series was well received by

4

comic book readers from its creation in 1992 through its completion in 2004. The series has won numerous awards over the years, including Eisner Awards for Best Humor Publication (1993–1995), Best Serialized Story (1994), Best Continuing Series (1994–1995), Best Writer/Artist (1994), Best Writer/Artist: Humor (1995, 1998), and Best Graphic Album—Reprint (2005). The series has also been awarded many Harvey Awards, including Best Cartoonist (1994–1997, 1999–2000, 2003, 2005), Best Graphic Album of Previously Published Work (1994, 2005), and a Special Award for Humor in 1994 for Jeff Smith. *Out from Boneville* received recognition from YALSA's Popular Paperbacks for Young Adults committee in 2002 on the "Graphic Novels: Superheroes and Beyond" list. The series has also spun off into two books, *Stupid, Stupid Rat Tales*, which tells the humorous tale of why rat creatures don't have tails, and *Rose*, a look at the youth of Grandma Ben and her sister. The series has also been adapted into a PC video game series created by Tell-Tale Games and launched in 2005.

Bone (Original Black and White Graphic Novels). Cartoon Books, 1996–2004. **Y**

A collection of the classic fantasy titles in their original black-and-white format. The one volume edition released in 2004 collects the entire nine-volume arc in one inexpensive volume with over 1,300 pages of revised text and illustrations

Vol. I: Out from Boneville. 1996. 144pp. 0-9636609-9-3, hardcover; 0-9636609-4-2, softcover.

Vol. II: The Great Cow Race. 1996. 144pp. 0-9636609-8-5, hardcover; 0-9636609-5-0, softcover.

Vol. III: Eyes of the Storm. 1996. 184pp. 0-9636609-7-7, hardcover; 0-9636609-6-9, softcover.

Vol. IV: The Dragonslayer. 1997. 184pp. 1-888963-01-8, hardcover; 1-888963-00-X, softcover.

Vol. V: Rock Jaw, Master of the Eastern Border. 1998. 128pp. 1-888963-02-6, hardcover; 1-888963-03-4, softcover.

Vol. VI: Old Man's Cave. 1999. 128pp. 1-888963-04-2, hardcover; 1-888963-05-0, softcover.

Vol. VII: Ghost Circles. 2002. 160pp. 1-888963-08-5, hardcover; 1-888963-09-3, softcover.

Vol. VIII: Treasure Hunters. 2002. 144pp. 1-888963-12-3, hardcover; 1-888963-13-1, softcover.

Vol. IX: Crown of Thorns. 2004. 184pp. 1-888963-15-8, hardcover; 1-888963-16-6, softcover.

One Volume Edition. 2004. 1300pp. 1-888963-14-X, softcover.

Bone (Full Color Edition Graphic Novels). Graphix/Scholastic Books, 2005– . **Y**

Beginning in 2005, Scholastic Books' new Graphix imprint has begun reprinting the entire nine-volume series in full color, with an estimated two volumes printed each year.

Vol. 1: Out from Boneville (full color edition). 2005. 144pp. 0-439-70623-8, hardcover; 0-439-70640-8, softcover.

Vol. 2: The Great Cow Race (full color edition). 2005. 144pp. 0-439-70624-6, hardcover; 0-439-70639-4, softcover.

Vol. 3: Eyes of the Storm (full color edition). 2006. 192pp. 0-439-70625-4, hardcover; 0-439-70638-6, softcover.

Vol. 4: Dragonslayer (full color edition). 2006. 176pp. 0-439-70626-2, hardcover; 0-439-70637-8, softcover.

Bone Spin-offs, 2000–2002

The <u>Bone</u> series has spun off several other stories featuring a look at the world of Bone from other inhabitants of the past. The tales include familiar characters, such as the rat creatures and Grandma Ben as a young woman known as Rose.

***Stupid, Stupid Rat Tales: The Adventures of Big Johnson Bone, Frontier Hero.* Written by Tom Sniegoski. Illustrated by Jeff Smith and Stan Sakai.** Cartoon Books, 2000. 104pp. 1-888963-06-9. **Y**

A <u>Bone</u> spin-off, the book features tall tales of Boneville settler Big Johnson Bone and a tall-tale reason why the rat creatures don't have any tails. A humorous fantasy tale full of adventure, humor, and one big giant rat creature. Though this tale could be included in the humorous fantasy section, it is included as a follow-up listing to Jeff Smith's fantasy works.

🌸 *Rose.* **Written by Jeff Smith. Illustrated by Charles Vess.** Cartoon Books, 2002. 160pp. 1-888963-10-7, hardcover; 1-888963-11-5, paperback. **T**

A spin-off of Jeff Smith's <u>Bone</u> series detailing the early years of Grandma Ben. After inadvertently releasing a vile water dragon that is laying siege to small towns in the Northern Valley, Princess Rose vows to defeat the dragon and undo the evil she's accidentally unleashed. Unable to defeat the monster at first, Rose seeks the advice of the great Red Dragon, who tells the princess that to balance the water dragon's death requires a terrible sacrifice: the life of her elder sister, Briar. Can Rose make the ultimate sacrifice to save the town? Meanwhile, the vile Lord of the Locusts has been released from the dreaming world prison and finds a willing host. Charles Vess was awarded

ROSE is a ® and © 2006 Jeff Smith.

an Eisner Award in 2002 for Best Painter/Multimedia Artist for his artwork in the series.

By the Sword. **Written and illustrated by Sanami Matoh.** ADV Manga, 2005. **T Japanese manga.**

The demon hunter Asagi is cursed with a special power: every sword he ever touches is easily shattered. He's out to find a special sword called the Moegi, which carries the power of 101 demons within it. Asagi hopes that Moegi may be the one blade that is unbreakable in his hands. He spots the sword being carried by a half-demon girl named Kaede and her demon father, Kurenai. There is a catch, though: it can only be drawn by Kurenai's nephew. Little does Asagi realize that the power is within his grasp when he is able to unsheath and wield Moegi, and discovers that he shares a bloodline with demons.

Vol. 1. 2005. 192pp. 1-4139-0213-8.
Vol. 2. 2005. 180pp. 1-4139-0214-6.

Chronicles of the Cursed Sword. **Written by Park Hui-Jin. Illustrated by Yuy Beop-Ryong.** TOKYOPOP, 2003– . **T Korean manhwa.**

An orphan boy named Rayan steals a cursed PaSa blade forged from the bones of a demon king and discovers that with the blade he now has the power to be a great hero. Meanwhile, others want the sword for their own evil purposes, including the vile Prime Minister Shiyan, who seeks the blade he created to release his dark ancestor, the demon king, from his banished entombment. The ongoing series is still being printed in Korea.

Vol. 1. 2003. 176pp. 1-59182-254-8.
Vol. 2. 2003. 192pp. 1-59182-255-6.
Vol. 3. 2003. 184pp. 1-59182-256-4.
Vol. 4. 2004. 176pp. 1-59182-421-4.
Vol. 5. 2004. 176pp. 1-59182-422-2.
Vol. 6. 2004. 176pp. 1-59182-423-0.
Vol. 7. 2004. 176pp. 1-59182-424-9.
Vol. 8. 2004. 168pp. 1-59182-425-7.
Vol. 9. 2004. 176pp. 1-59182-426-5.
Vol. 10. 2005. 192pp. 1-59532-387-2.
Vol. 11. 2005. 192pp. 1-59532-388-0.
Vol. 12. 2005. 192pp. 1-59532-389-9.
Vol. 13. 2005. 192pp. 1-59532-645-6.
Vol. 14. 2006. 192pp. 1-59532-646-4.
Vol. 15. 2006. 192pp. 1-59532-647-2.
Vol. 16. 2006. 192pp. 1-59532-648-0.
Vol. 17. 2006. 192pp. 1-59816-204-7.

The Circle Weave: Apprentice to a God, Vol. 1. **Written and illustrated by Indigo Kelleigh.** Abalone Press, 2003. 112pp. 1-58898-927-5. **T**

The last survivor of the bloody siege at the town of Maplehead, young Rowan must race to the kingdom of Iscia and warn the king of the coming doom. With his fellow soldiers killed in battle at the hands of a mysterious and dark army

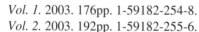

of warriors, the soldier must brave a treacherous journey. With the aid of his new allies, including the wizard Morrim, Phiteas, and Reyna, can Rowan make it to Iscia before the dark mystic Forx and his legion of Carrion Knights lay siege to the kingdom? A collection of the ongoing online comic book is available to view at http://www.circleweave.com.

Culdcept. Written and illustrated by Shinya Kaneko. TOKYOPOP, 2004–2006. **T** 🎮 **Japanese manga.**

When the magical book called *Culdcept* that chronicled the creation of the universe and all of its secrets was shattered into hundreds of cards with the power to summon magical creatures, men and women across the land of Bablashca became Cepters, those trained to handle the cards and call forth the creatures to do their bidding. The hope is that one day all of the cards will be collected by one master through combat matches, and the ancient book will once again be made whole, and the master of all Cepters will gain godlike powers. Enter Narajan, a young woman who has been sent by her master, Horowitz, to learn more about the Black Cepters, a group who are using the cards for ill gain. Soon, though, her skills as a Cepter are put to the test when she is forced into combat in the tournaments and must prove she has the skills to save a town on the verge of destruction by the Black Cepters. Is she talented enough to win all the cards through combat and rebuild the Culdcept? Based on the popular video game from Japan.

> *Vol. 1.* 2004. 236pp. 1-59182-782-5.
> *Vol. 2.* 2004. 210pp. 1-59182-783-3.
> *Vol. 3.* 2004. 200pp. 1-59182-954-2.
> *Vol. 4.* 2005. 192pp. 1-59532-447-X.
> *Vol. 5.* 2006. 232pp. 1-59816-553-4.

Dark Angel. 2d ed. Written and illustrated by Kia Asamiya. CPM Press, 2003–2005. **T Japanese manga.**

The epic story of Dark, a young and powerful swordsman with a mysterious background from the mystic land of the Four Winds. A powerful fighter, he is on a quest to earn the right to the title Phantom Saint of the Red Phoenix. With his winged spirit guide, Kyo, he embarks on the dangerous quest to prove his title, battling opponents who want to keep him from his destiny. Meanwhile, the Phantom Saint Leen's battles Nie, the Black Dragon, in an epic struggle for survival against a jealous and cunning foe.

> *Book 1: The Path to Destiny.* 2003. 200pp. 1-58664-899-3.
> *Book 2.* 2004. 224pp. 1-58664-926-4.
> *Book 3.* 2004. 176pp. 1-58664-927-2.
> *Book 4: Legend of the Sacred Beast I.* 2004. 184pp. 1-58664-942-6.
> *Book 5: Legend of the Sacred Beast II.* 2005. 208pp. 1-58664-978-7.

Demon Diary. Written by Jee-Hyung Lee. Illustrated by Kara Lim. TOKYOPOP, 2003–2004. **T Korean manhwa.**

In a ancient time when demons and gods battle for power, young Raenef is a boy destined to be a demon lord who will unite the land and bring peace, but he has a lot to learn, and he's is definitely not considered courtly material. Tutored by the demon

Eclipse, he forms a bond of friendship that surpasses that of teacher and student, and the two are soon joined on their journey by a young knight and a god-blessed priest to find their true destiny.

> *Vol. 1.* 2003. 192pp. 1-59182-154-1.
> *Vol. 2.* 2003. 192pp. 1-59182-155-X.
> *Vol. 3.* 2003. 192pp. 1-59182-156-8.
> *Vol. 4.* 2003. 192pp. 1-59182-157-6.
> *Vol. 5.* 2004. 208pp. 1-59182-430-3.
> *Vol. 6.* 2004. 192pp. 1-59182-431-1.
> *Vol. 7.* 2004. 192pp. 1-59182-432-X.

***Diablo: Tales of Sanctuary.* Written by Dave Land and Philip Amara. Illustrated by Francisco Ruiz Velasco.** Dark Horse Comics, 2001. 64pp. 1-56971-682-X. **O**

A tie-in to the extremely popular fantasy-adventure role-playing game series *Diablo,* created by Blizzard Entertainment. A moody, dark fantasy setting in which the monsters and beasts from nightmares walk the earth and a demon named Diablo sets out to create his own hell on Earth. In two short stories, a barbarian named Renit and a necromancer named Cairo must work together to find the fabled "Hand of Naz" artifact while battling an attacking demon horde. Meanwhile, a druid called Azgar must learn to defend his village from his own personal and literal demons.

Dragon Arms. Written and illustrated by David Hutchison. Antarctic Press, 2004– . **T Neo-manga.**

When the heroes of old have become corrupted by their power and arrogance, new heroes have risen to oppose them. Over a thousand years ago, the dreaded Dragon Kings ruled the land with cruelty and humans were crushed under their reign. The strongest men rose to the cause and freed humanity. Now the heroes of old have become as corrupt and ruthless as the Dragon Kings of old, and five new heroes have risen to oppose them, armed with the deadly Dragon Arms weaponry. Under the tutelage of the ancient wizard Anrack, they're ready to fight for the freedom of humanity against an ancient and ruthless empire.

> *Pocket Manga Vol. 1: Blood and Steel.* 2d ed. 2005. 192pp. 1-932453-89-X.
> *Pocket Manga Vol. 2: Chaos Blade.* 2004. 128pp. 1-932453-66-0.

Dragon Knights. Written and illustrated by Mineko Ohkami. TOKYOPOP, 2002–2006. **T Japanese manga.**

Japanese manga fantasy/comedy about three bickering and wise-cracking heroes. An elf named Rune, a human thief named Thatz, and a humanoid demon named Rath are anything but a Fellowship. The chosen Dragon Knights of Water, Earth, and Fire, they've been called by the Dragon Lord Lykouleon and his Dragon Tribe to travel across the land of Dusis to end the reign of the vicious Demon Horde. Before they save the land, they'll have to face off against the worst enemy of all—themselves! The series is still published in Japan, with more than twenty-four volumes, and has yet to be completed.

Vol. 1. 2002. 192pp. 1-931514-40-2.
Vol. 2. 2002. 200pp. 1-931514-41-0.
Vol. 3. 2002. 208pp. 1-931514-42-9.
Vol. 4. 2002. 200pp. 1-931514-43-7.
Vol. 5. 2002. 200pp. 1-591820-69-3.
Vol. 6. 2003. 208pp. 1-59182-109-2.
Vol. 7. 2003. 208pp. 1-59182-111-8.
Vol. 8. 2003. 208pp. 1-59182-112-6.
Vol. 9. 2003. 192pp. 1-59182-113-4.
Vol. 10. 2003. 200pp. 1-59182-114-2.
Vol. 11. 2003. 208pp. 1-59182-115-0.
Vol. 12. 2004. 184pp. 1-59182-440-0.
Vol. 13. 2004. 216pp. 1-59182-441-9.
Vol. 14. 2004. 208pp. 1-59182-442-7.
Vol. 15. 2004. 192pp. 1-59182-443-5.
Vol. 16. 2004. 208pp. 1-59182-444-3.
Vol. 17. 2004. 192pp. 1-59182-445-1.
Vol. 18. 2005. 192pp. 1-59182-961-5.
Vol. 19. 2005. 192pp. 1-59182-962-3.
Vol. 20. 2005. 192pp. 1-59182-963-1.
Vol. 21. 2005. 192pp. 1-59532-634-0.
Vol. 22. 2006. 192pp. 1-59532-635-9.
Vol. 23. 2006. 200pp. 1-59816-184-9.

DragonLance: The Legend of Huma. Written by Brian Augustyn, Richard Knaak, Trampus Whiteman, and Sean Jordan. Illustrated by Mike S. Miller and Rob Stotz. Devil's Due Publishing, Inc., 2004. 160pp. 1-932796-07-X. **T**

Adaptation of the *DragonLance* story by Richard Knaak featuring the origin of the mysterious Hero of the Lance, Huma, joined by the minotaur to stop the treacherous Knights of Solamnia and the Queen of Darkness. With the aid of the beautiful Silver Dragon, Huma may just have a chance to save the realm.

Dungeon Siege: The Battle for Aranna. Written by Paul Alden. Illustrated by Al Rio. Dark Horse Comics, 2005. 88pp. 1-59307-425-5. **T**

Based on the magical world featured in the hit PC computer game series from Gas Powered Games. The vile Zaramoth the Unmaker has claimed the magical River of Souls, the center of magic power in the kingdom of Aranna, for himself. When the brave human chieftain Azunai arrives to challenge Zaramoth because he believes that the river is for all of Aranna, a mighty battle erupts and the fate of the kingdom hangs in the balance.

ElfQuest. Written by Wendy and Richard Pini. Illustrated by Wendy Pini. DC
Comics, 2003– . **T**

© 2006 WARP Graphics.

Created in 1978, Wendy and Richard Pini's ElfQuest series
was one of the first independent comic book series and has become one of the best-loved fantasy series of the past
twenty-five years. Spanning centuries, the series tells the tales
of the Wolfrider clan of elves and how they came to be a part
of Earth from their extraterrestrial origins. Elves who have a
close relationship with the native wolves of the region, the
Wolfriders, led by tribe leader Cutter, must learn to live
among the fearful humans, the cave-dwelling troll civilizations, and various other tribes of elves that populate the land.
Soon the Wolfrider clan discovers that what they thought of
humans, trolls, and the other tribes is put to the ultimate test.
Recently DC Comics has agreed to reprint the stories in a manga-sized format
as well as hardcover collections while publishing new ElfQuest tales, too.

> Archives.
>> *Vol. 1.* 2003. 216pp. 1-4012-0128-8.
>> *Vol. 2.* 2005. 224pp. 1-4012-0129-6.
>> *Vol. 3.* 2005. 240pp. 1-4012-0412-0.
>> *Vol. 4.* 2006. 228pp. 1-4012-0773-1.
> Wolfrider.
>> *Vol. 1.* 2003. 200pp. 1-4012-0131-8.
>> *Vol. 2.* 2003. 216pp. 1-4012-0132-6.
> The Grand Quest.
>> *Vol. 3.* 2004. 192pp. 1-4012-0140-7.
>> *Vol. 4.* 2004. 192pp. 1-4012-0141-5.
>> *Vol. 5.* 2004. 224pp. 1-4012-0142-3.
>> *Vol. 6.* 2004. 224pp. 1-4012-0270-5.
>> *Vol. 7.* 2005. 208pp. 1-4012-0503-8.
>> *Vol. 8.* 2005. 224pp. 1-4012-0504-6.
>> *Vol. 9.* 2005. 208pp. 1-4012-0505-4.
>> *Vol. 10.* 2005. 224pp. 1-4012-0506-2.
>> *Vol. 11.* 2005. 224pp. 1-4012-0507-0.
>> *Vol. 12.* 2006. 224pp. 1-4012-0508-9.
>> *Vol. 13.* 2006. 224pp. 1-4012-0935-1.
>> *Vol. 14.* 2006. 224pp. 1-4012-0979-3.
> *The Searcher and the Sword.* 2004. 96pp. 1-4012-0183-0, hardcover; 2005
> 96pp. 1-4012-0184-9, softcover.
> The Hidden Years.
>> *Vol. 1.* 2006. 224pp. 1-4012-0980-7.

**Forgotten Realms: The Dark Elf Trilogy. Written by R.A. Salvatore. Adapted
by Andrew Daab. Illustrated by Tim Seeley.** Devil's Due Publishing, 2005– . **T**

Adaptation of the Forgotten Realms series' most popular characters, the dark
elf called Drizzt Do'Urden. A drow (dark elf) who has abandoned his people's

dark ways and his home in the cavernous realm of the Underdark, Drizzt Do'Urden is armed with his two scimitars, Icingdeath and Twinkle, and sets out to live an honorable life as a ranger in the world of Faerûn. The third volume in the trilogy, *Sojourn*, has yet to be collected at the time of press.

  Part I—Homeland. 2005. 160pp. 1-932796-40-1.
  Part II—Exile. 2006. 160pp. 1-932796-46-0.

***George R. R. Martin's The Hedge Knight.* Written by George R. R. Martin. Adapted by Ben Avery. Illustrated by Mike S. Miller.** Devil's Due Publishing, 2004. 160pp. 1-932796-06-1. **T**

An adaptation of the fantasy novel of the same name. Dunk, the young squire of an elderly knight, sets off to find recognition and fame after his master's passing. Calling himself Ser Duncan the Tall and now with a young squire of his own called Egg, the young knight enters the Ashford tournament in hopes of becoming a champion. The path of the hero is less golden than he realizes, and the code of chivalry that he has upheld proudly for years may be his undoing.

© 2006 Devil's Due Publishing, Inc.

***The Hobbit: An Illustrated Edition of the Fantasy Classic.* By J. R. R. Tolkien, adapted by Chuck Dixon. Illustrated by David Wenzel.** Ballantine Books/Del Rey/Random House, 2001. 144pp. 0-345-44560-0. **T**

An adaptation of the classic fantasy tale and prequel to the <u>Lord of the Rings</u>. A young hobbit named Bilbo Baggins embarks on a quest that will change him forever and have dire consequences for the fate of the world. In the realm of Middle Earth, Bilbo Baggins's life at Bag's End is never the same again when he, Gandalf the Grey, and twelve dwarves go on a quest to reclaim dwarven treasure from the dreaded dragon Smaug.

***JLA: Riddle of the Beast.* Written by Alan Grant. Illustrated by various.** DC Comics, 2002. 104pp. 1-56389-873-X. **T**

A young hero sets out to defeat the dark Beast that is ravaging the land, but it is no simple task. Only with the aid of the other heroes of the land can the kingdom be united and the evil vanquished. A beautifully painted reinterpretation of familiar DC Comics superheroes in a imaginative sword and sorcery setting.

Legendz. Written by Rin Hirai. Illustrated by Makoto Haruno. VIZ Media, LLC, 2005–2006. **A** 🎮 **Japanese manga.** あ

Master trainer Ken Kazaki and Shiron, his loyal Windragon, are players of the ultimate live-action role-playing game. Set in a world where mermaids, dragons, werewolves, and other fantasy creatures, called Legendz, exist, Ken is one of many gamers who compete using the Legendz in battle. Raising the Legendz to compete and taking care of them is the only way for Shiron to grow and become more powerful. Will Ken be able to take on his high school and become the best Legendz player of all? Based on the popular game and animated series of the same name from Japan.

Vol. 1. 2005. 208pp. 1-59116-772-8.
Vol. 2. 2005. 208pp. 1-59116-773-6.
Vol. 3. 2005. 224pp. 1-59116-994-1.
Vol. 4. 2006. 208pp. 1-4215-0149-X.

Madara. Written by Eiji Otsuka. Illustrated by Tajima Sho-u. CMX Manga/DC Comics, 2004–2005. **O Japanese manga.**

In a land where evil comes in the form of Emperor Miroku and his eight demon generals, a lone young man called Madara may just be the key to salvation. Rescued when he was an infant, he was discovered with various parts of his natural body replaced by mechanical parts. With each missing part in the possession of the demon generals, Emperor Miroku will stop at nothing to destroy what humanity remains in Madara, while Madara will stop at nothing to get his humanity back from the Emperor. Now Madara, trained in the mystic arts, is joined on his journey with Kirin, a young girl from Madara's village, and the bumbling Haku Tuku and his trained pet monkeys. Together they'll take on an empire.

4

Vol. 1. 2004. 200pp. 1-4012-0529-1.
Vol. 2. 2005. 176pp. 1-4012-0530-5.
Vol. 3. 2005. 200pp. 1-4012-0531-3.
Vol. 4. 2005. 198pp. 1-4012-0532-1.
Vol. 5. 2005. 184pp. 1-4012-0533-X.

Magic: The Gathering—Gerrard's Quest. **Written by Mike Grell. Illustrated by Pop Mhan.** Dark Horse Comics, 1999. 112pp. 1-56971-403-7. **T**

Inspired by the popular customizable card game *Magic: The Gathering*, featuring many characters, creatures, and settings straight from the game. When the captain of the flying ship Weatherlight is kidnapped, it's up to the swashbuckling hero called Gerrard to face his destiny and rescue the captain. Now with the Weatherlight's crew, Gerrard must try to rescue the captain from the clutches of Volrath, the ruler of the plane of Rath. Only with the aid of the Skyshroud elves can he ensure the safety of the realm of Dominaria and face his true destiny.

Monster Collection: The Girl Who Can Deal with Magical Monsters. Written and illustrated by Itoh Sei. CMX Manga/DC Comics, 2005–2006. **M Japanese manga.**

In the realm called the World of the Six Gates, great mythological beasts of legend still roam. Only powerful sorcerers called summoners can bring them forth into the real world. Kasche Arbadel is a summoner-in-training. Bold but reckless, she's highly skilled at summoning, but she still has a lot to learn to become a master of the art. Charged by her master with a quest to return a stolen relic called the Guardian of Knowledge, she must ally herself with humans and beasts and prevent the relic from falling into the wrong hands. The Guardian of Knowledge is a key to unlocking the *Encyclopedia Verum,* a tome capable of unlocking the most dangerous beasts from the World of the Six Gates. If it should fall into the hands of a wicked summoner, the results would be disastrous. Now Kasche and her allies must recover the Guardian of Knowledge and defeat the horrendous monsters at all costs. The series is composed of six volumes.

Vol. 1. 2005. 174pp. 1-4012-0650-6.
Vol. 2. 2005. 176pp. 1-4012-0651-4.
Vol. 3. 2005. 162pp. 1-4012-0652-2.
Vol. 4. 2006. 162pp. 1-4012-0653-0.
Vol. 5. 2006. 168pp. 1-4012-0654-9.
Vol. 6. 2006. 168pp. 1-4012-0655-7.

R. A. Salvatore's DemonWars: Trial by Fire. **Written by R. A. Salvatore and Scott Ciencin. Illustrated by Ron Wagner.** Code 6/CrossGen Comics, 2003. 160pp. 1-931484-62-7. **T**

Fan-favorite fantasy writer R. A. Salvatore's epic world of Corona comes to the realm of comics. In the first volume, Salvatore's enigmatic barbarian ranger Andacanavar is joined by a quarreling band of fighters, including the capable Abellican Sister Moira and the redcap dwarf Grave Mungo. Together they form an odd fighting force to thwart a plot by the frost giants of Alpinador to destroy humanity with the aid of the demon Managarm. Also included is a short story by R. A. Salvatore.

Record of Lodoss War. **Written by Ryo Mizuno.** CPM Press, 2001–2004. **T** 🎮 **Japanese manga.** あ

© 2006 Central Park Media.

An epic adventure on the medieval-like fantasy isle of Lodoss, a cursed continent where kings and warlords continue the 1,000-year-old stalemate battle of good versus evil to claim the continent for their own. As a mysterious force gathers an army of monstrous beasts to offset the balance, six warriors combine their skills to free the land of evil. Parn, a Holy Knight of Lodoss, is accompanied by the cleric Etoh, the magician Slayn, the elf Deedlit, dwarf Ghim, and a thief called Woodchuck to take on the Grey Witch Karla, Ashram the black knight warlord of Marmo. The series has spawned other adventures as well as a hit anime series and is strongly influenced by the role-playing game *Dungeons and Dragons*. The series Welcome to Lodoss Island! is a spoof created by Rei Hyakuyashiki and is listed in t chapter 8. The volumes are listed below according to chronological order. The series has spawned not just the manga series, but a series of novels, an anime series, as well as computer games.

Record of Lodoss War: The Grey Witch. Illustrated by Yoshihiko Ochi. 2004.
 Book 1: A Gathering of Heroes. 2004. 224pp. 1-58664-925-6.
 Book 2: Birth of a New Knight. 2004. 224pp. 1-58664-928-0.
 Book 3: The Final Battle. 2004. 224pp. 1-58664-945-0.
Record of Lodoss War: The Lady of Pharis Collector's Edition. Illustrated by Akihiro Yamada. 2003–2004.
 Book One. 2003. 288pp. 1-58664-894-2.
 Book Two. 2004. 208pp. 1-58664-897-7.

Record of Lodoss War: Chronicles of the Heroic Knight. Illustrated by Masato Natsumoto. 2001–2003.

> *Book 1.* 2001. 176pp. 1-56219-945-5.
> *Book 2.* 2002. 176pp. 1-58664-850-0.
> *Book 3.* 2002. 192pp. 1-58664-861-6.
> *Book 4.* 2003. 192pp. 1-58664-862-4.
> *Book 5.* 2003. 192pp. 1-58664-895-0.
> *Book 6.* 2003. 248pp. 1-58664-896-9.

Record of Lodoss War: Deedlit's Tale. Illustrated by Setsuko Yoneyama. 2002–2003.

> *Book 1: Choices.* 2002. 192pp. 1-58664-863-2.
> *Book 2: Forest of No Return.* 2003. 192pp. 1-58664-875-6.

❀ <u>Ring of the Nibelung.</u> Written and illustrated by P. Craig Russell. Adapted from the operas by Richard Wagner. Dark Horse Comics, 2002. **O**

© 2006 P. Craig Russell.

An adaptation of the four epic operas composed by Richard Wagner between 1848 and 1874. The gold of the Rhinemaids is stolen and forged into a mighty ring of power by the dwarf Alberich. As the Norse gods, brave heroes, and mythological beasts battle for control of the ring, the fate of the world is in the hands of whoever controls it. As generations pass, Wotan's (Odin) and other gods' quest to possess the ring will destroy heroes, including the brave Siegfried; estrange the daughter of Wotan, the Valkyrie Brünhilde, from her father; and ultimately be the cause of the death of the Norse gods. The collection received an Eisner Award in 2001 for P. Craig Russell's work in the category of Best Artist/Penciller/Inker.

> *Vol. 1: The Rhinegold & the Valkyrie.* 2002. 200pp. 1-56971-666-8.
> *Vol. 2: Siegfried & Gotterdammerung.* 2002. 200pp. 1-56971-734-6.

<u>Saiyuki.</u> Written and illustrated by Kazuya Minekura. TOKYOPOP, 2004– . **O** **Japanese manga.** あ

A retelling of the classic Chinese legend. In the land of Togenkyo in the paradise of Shangri-la, it's a time on Earth when magic and modern technology go hand in hand and humans and demons work together in peace. But evil never rests, and to the west in India the demon lord Gyumaoh is being resurrected in a horrible union between science and magic and is causing a destructive wave of negative matter across the land, morphing the demons of the land into mindless minions of evil. Now four brave but unlikely men—Genjyo Sanzo, Son Goku, Sha Gojyo, and Cho Hakkai—must begin their journey to the West by any means necessary to confront and destroy the evil. The series continues in <u>Saiyuki Reload</u>, which has been published in six volumes in Japan. The series has also been adapted as an anime series in Japan.

<u>Saiyuki.</u> 2004–2005.

> *Vol. 1.* 2004. 208pp. 1-59182-651-9.
> *Vol. 2.* 2004. 204pp. 1-59182-652-7.
> *Vol. 3.* 2004. 204pp. 1-59182-653-5.

> *Vol. 4.* 2004. 208pp. 1-59182-654-3.
> *Vol. 5.* 2004. 208pp. 1-59182-655-1.
> *Vol. 6.* 2005. 192pp. 1-59532-431-3.
> *Vol. 7.* 2005. 208pp. 1-59532-432-1.
> *Vol. 8.* 2005. 208pp. 1-59532-433-X.
> *Vol. 9.* 2005. 200pp. 1-59532-434-8.

Saiyuki Reload. 2005–.
> *Vol. 1.* 2005. 192pp. 1-59816-025-7.
> *Vol. 2.* 2005. 192pp. 1-59816-026-5.
> *Vol. 3.* 2006. 192pp. 1-59816-027-3.
> *Vol. 4.* 2006. 200pp. 1-59816-028-1.

Shidima. **Written by Adrian Stang. Illustrated by Arnold Stang.** DreamWave Productions, Incorporated, 2003. 176pp. 0-9732786-6-8. **O**

In the realm of Shidima, where all battles of status, land, power, and more are decided by combat in the mystic art of warfare by fighting with the dual skill of the sword and magik, empires have been raised and brought down by the fighting clans of Shidima known as Zirushi. The realm has been under the rule of a bloody, brutal, and vicious leader, Emperor Gurakai, who has inflicted torture and pain across the land. The blonde-haired, legendary swordsman Aldaran vows that with his blades he'll bring down the emperor; he recruits the best warriors and scoundrels in the land to confront and eliminate the ruler by any means necessary.

Sleeping Dragons, Book One: Becca's Scarecrow. **Written by Kevin Mason. Illustrated by Alex Szewczuk.** Too Hip Gotta Go, 2004. 176pp. 0-9735161-0-0. **T**

When the good knight Philip Escaladine comes to the walled city of Gan to commemorate the end of a great war, he finds happiness and a warm welcome from the town's leaders as well as potential romance with Becca, the champion archer and daughter of one of the men of the village. As the historical battle is retold in verse, an ancient beast threatens the town again, and it's up to Philip and Becca to use the sword and arrows to save the city from the rampaging attacks of a dragon. Will it cost them their lives to save the city they've sworn to protect?

<u>Sojourn.</u> **Written by Ron Marz. Illustrated by Greg Land.** CrossGen Comics, 2002–2004. **T**

When the evil wizard called Mordath is reborn and destroys all that she loved, Arwyn, a widowed archer, vows revenge and sets out to kill the dark wizard. Eons ago Mordath was first killed by a weapon of great power, and Arwyn is given the task of locating the five fragments of the weapon. Accompanied by the rogue archer Gareth, she battles Mordath's minions, orcs, and one red dragon. She'll stop at nothing to get revenge against Mordath. The collected series is incomplete because the publisher folded.

> *Vol. 1: From the Ashes.* 2002. 192pp. 1-931484-15-5.
> *Vol. 2: The Dragon's Tale.* 2002. 160pp. 1-931484-34-1.
> *Vol. 3: The Warrior's Tale.* 2003. 160pp. 1-931484-65-1.
> *Vol. 4: The Thief's Tale.* 2004. 160pp. 1-931484-91-0.

<u>Sorcerer Hunters</u>. Written by Satoru Akahori. Illustrated by Ray Omishi. TOKYOPOP, 2000–2002, 1st ed. 2005–present, 2d ed. **O Japanese manga.** あ

In a world of magic and sorcery called Spoolner, black magic users subjugate the Parsoners (i.e., those without magic). One team of magic users, the Sorcerer Hunters, has united to right these wrongs and fight the evil magicians. Led by Big Momma, a holy woman of the Stella Church, the team is made up of some very talented but off-beat heroes: Carrot Glaces, a lusty young man who transforms into one of twelve giant, uncontrollable monsters; Marron Glaces, Carrot's younger and prettier brother, who is a specialist of Eastern magic and the sword; Gateau Mocha, a super-strong martial artist immune to magic; Tira Misu, a quiet girl in love with Carrot who transforms into a dominatrix when the time calls for her to whip Carrot back into human form; and Chocolate Misu, Tira's older sister, who is also in love with Carrot, and an expert with the wire threads. Together the tightly knit group use their unique magical powers to save the world in a fun, farcical adventure full of romance, girl (and boy) chasing, comedy, fighting, magic, and plenty of odd food references. The series has recently been republished by TOKYOPOP in the traditional right-to-left format and the in-print volumes of the second edition are listed below. The series was also adapted into a twenty-six-episode anime series in Japan.

Sorcerer Hunters, 1st edition.

Vol. 1. 2000. 192pp. 1-892213-22-2.
Vol. 2. 2000. 192pp. 1-892213-54-0.
Vol. 3. 2001. 200pp. 1-892213-55-9.
Vol. 4. 2001. 200pp. 1-892213-93-1.
Vol. 5. 2001. 200pp. 1-892213-92-3.
Vol. 6. 2001. 216pp. 1-892213-91-5.
Vol. 7. 2001. 192pp. 1-892213-87-7.
Vol. 8. 2002. 192pp. 1-931514-23-2.
Vol. 9. 2002. 184pp. 1-931514-24-0.
Vol. 10. 2002. 176pp. 1-931514-25-9.
Vol. 11. 2002. 200pp. 1-931514-26-7.
Vol. 12. 2002. 184pp. 1-931514-27-5.
Vol. 13. 2002. 192pp. 1-59182-066-9.

Sorcerer Hunters—100% Authentic Format.

Vol. 1. 2005. 208pp. 1-59532-494-1.
Vol. 2. 2005. 208pp. 1-59532-495-X.
Vol. 3. 2005. 208pp. 1-59532-496-8.
Vol. 4. 2005. 192pp. 1-59532-497-6.
Vol. 5. 2006. 192pp. 1-59532-498-4.
Vol. 6. 2006. 192pp. 1-59532-499-2.

Soulwind. Written and illustrated by Scott Morse. Oni Press, 2000–2003. **T**

© 2006 Scott Morse.

An epic fantasy adventure spanning space and time. A young boy named Nick is abducted by aliens, whisked away, and transported to another planet to retrieve a legendary sword called Soulwind so he can save the planet's inhabitants from a cruel dictator. Nick's strange journey becomes even stranger as it takes him and his furry, talking alien companion Poke on a journey back in time and back again in a never-ending tale blending ancient myths, Japanese culture, fairy tales, and futuristic adventure in one all-encompassing story. The series was collected in one complete edition in 2003.

Vol. 1: The Kid from Planet Earth. 2000. 128pp. 0-9667127-4-9.
Vol. 2: The Day I Tried to Live. 2000. 128pp. 0-9667127-6-5.
Vol. 3: The Infamous Transit Vagrants. 2000. 96pp. 0-9667127-7-3.
Vol. 4: The Way Things Never Happened. 2000. 96pp. 1-929998-01-5.
Vol. 5: The August Ones. 2001. 96pp. 1-929998-02-3.
The Complete Soulwind. 2003. 522pp. 1-929998-73-2.

Suikoden III: The Successor of Fate. Written and illustrated by Shimizu Aki. TOKYOPOP 2004–2006. **T** 🏔 **Japanese manga.**

Based on the popular role-playing video game from Japan, the fantasy world of Suikoden has been caught up in a tribal war with no end in sight. Six tribes of the Grasslands, including the region of Karaya, went to war with the Zexen Federation, and after a much-needed truce failed, only a war legend called the Flame Champion can save the peace. A reluctant core group of warriors from the warring regions, including Zexen knight Chris Longfellow; a proud and determined female soldier; Hugo, a Karayan boy who is learning the path to manhood along with his pet gryphon Fubar; Geddoe, a one-eyed mercenary, and others must join together to find the Flame Champion and help restore peace to the Grasslands.

Vol. 1. 2004. 176pp. 1-59182-765-5.
Vol. 2. 2004. 180pp. 1-59182-766-3.
Vol. 3. 2004. 180pp. 1-59182-767-1.
Vol. 4. 2004. 180pp. 1-59182-768-X.
Vol. 5. 2005. 176pp. 1-59532-435-6.
Vol. 6. 2005. 180pp. 1-59532-436-4.
Vol. 7. 2005. 180pp. 1-59532-437-2.
Vol. 8. 2005. 180pp. 1-59182-433-8.
Vol. 9. 2006. 192pp. 1-59816-181-4.

Tales of Colossus. **Written and illustrated by Mark Andrews.** E-Ville Press/Image Comics, 2006. 220pp. 1-58240-591-3. **O**

A deceased knight's spirit is reborn in the shell of a giant metal colossus. Now more powerful than any mortal man, the knight must rescue a kingdom and a princess from a corrupt paladin who has tarnished the good name of knighthood. Can a fallen knight who is trapped in a juggernaut-sized suit of armor find a way to defeat the corrupt paladin and reclaim his own stolen humanity? From the award-winning storyboard artist of the cult-classic animated film *The Iron Giant.* Also includes pin-ups by Mike Mignola, Troy Nixey, Scott Morse, and others.

Tellos. **Written by Todd DeZago. Illustrated by Mike Wieringo.** Image Comics, 2001–2002. **Y**

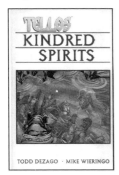

A swashbuckling young boy named Jarek finds himself in the role of savior to the entire kingdom, up against the evil might of Malesur. Joined by his tiger warrior friend Koj, as well as their newfound friends Serra, Hawke, and Rikk, he heads out on an adventure across the land to stop Malesur, with the entire realm hanging precariously on the verge of annihilation. As the battle ensues, a dark secret that controls the realm of Tellos is released, and the realm will never be the same again.

Vol. 1: Reluctant Heroes. 2001. 152pp. 1-58240-186-1.
Vol. 2: Kindred Spirits. 2002. 136pp. 1-58240-231-0.

© 2006 Todd DeZago
and Mike Wieringo.

Warcraft: The Sunwell Trilogy. **Written by Richard Knaak. Illustrated by Jae Hwan Kim.** TOKYOPOP, 2005– . **T** 🀄 **Korean manhwa.**

Based on the best-selling fantasy role-playing PC games by Blizzard Entertainment, the <u>Sunwell Trilogy</u> focuses on the adventures of Kalec, a shape-shifting blue dragon able to assume human form, in the battle-ravaged land of Azeroth. Together with the young maiden Anveena, he's on a quest to ensure that the fabled weapon of destruction, the dreaded Sunwell, is destroyed before it can fall into the wrong hands. As they travel through the Elvin kingdom of Quel'Thalas, they must battle armies of orcs, goblins, and the armies of the Undead to reach their destiny. At the time of this writing the third volume of the trilogy has not yet been published. Visit TOKYOPOP's Web site (http://www.tokyopop.com) for updated information on this fantasy series.

Vol. 1: Dragon Hunt. 2005. 176pp. 1-59532-712-6.
Vol. 2: Shadows of Ice. 2006. 192pp. 1-59532-713-4.

🎗 *The Wizard's Tale.* **Written by Kurt Busiek. Illustrated by David Wenzel.** WildStorm Productions/DC Comics, 1999. 126pp. 1-56389-589-7. **A** ◎

A charming and beautifully illustrated story about an evil wizard from a long line of really evil wizards, who really wasn't that evil after all. In the land of Ever-Night, evil ruled and good had been driven out. But before the good left, they had managed to steal and hide the spell book called the *Book of Worse,* and prevented the casting of the spell that would ensure evil's supremacy forever. Bafflerog Rumplewhisker, the last in a long line of evil wizards, is really one of the nicest evil old wizards imaginable. Charged to find the *Book of Worse* and to ensure the ultimate supremacy of evil, he reluctantly leaves his comfortable castle and journeys with Muddle, the third son of a woodcutter, to find the book and complete the

© 2006 Kurt Busiek
and David Wenzel.

spell to destroy all the good from Ever-Night. The collection received recognition from YALSA's Popular Paperbacks for Young Adults committee in 2003 on the "Flights of Fantasy: Beyond Harry and Frodo" list.

Heroic Fantasy

Though very similar to epic fantasy, heroic fantasy focuses on a main protagonist who typically relies on his own brain and brawn in a fantasy world full of deadly creatures, sorcerers, and more. The hero may have some magical skills, but this is not typically the case. Though the hero may live in a world of sorcery and magical beasts, the focus is on a hero who lives and dies by the sword, and the bloody path of vengeance that he cleaves with it. The character of the hero—his upbringing, pure (or even less-than-pure) motives, and behavior—also plays a role in forging the hero into the man he is and the man he will become. The hero, from sometimes humble and naïve beginnings, sets out to discover who he really is. The journey is difficult, and the reward is humbling on the road to discovery. The Conan the Barbarian books and movies fit in this subgenre.

Aqua Knight. Written and illustrated by Yukito Kishiro. VIZ Media, LLC, 2001–2002. **T Japanese manga.**

> In the aquatic land of Marmundo, ocean-riding Aqua Knights patrol the seas and protect the kingdom islands. A young boy named Ashika and his father, the strong but possibly insane lighthouse keeper Arrabaras, rescue the Aqua Knight Ruliya after finding her trapped under the water near their tranquil oceanic home. Arrabaras is the keeper of a sacred light in the lighthouse called Niselle. He refers to the sacred light as his wife and Ashika's mother. The light itself is a revered covenant between the living and the dead. As a sign of thanks, Ruliya promises that she will make Ashika a knight one day, and he, in his eagerness to prove his worth, makes a foolish journey that takes him to the end of the ocean and into the mouth of a sea dragon. Ruliya discovers that Arrabaras is really one of the legendary Twelve Knights of Neptune and fought alongside her father. When the pompous and mad scientist Alcantara steals both Ashika and Niselle, Arrabaras, defeated by his double loss, becomes resigned to his fate and is reclaimed by the skeletal Knight of Parca (the underworld). Before they descend to the depths, Parca gives Ruliya a magic sword of the underworld, which she takes on the quest to rescue Ashika and Niselle from Alcantara's evil grasp and to restore the covenant between life and death.
>
> > *Vol. 1.* 2001. 232pp. 1-56931-634-1.
> > *Vol. 2.* 2002. 232pp. 1-56931-635-X.
> > *Vol. 3.* 2002. 216pp. 1-56931-694-X.

Basara. Written and illustrated by Yumi Tamura. VIZ Media, LLC, 2003–. **O Japanese manga.** あ

In a post-apocalyptic Japan, a young girl must find the strength and courage to avenge her twin brother's death and to fulfill an ancient prophecy as the "child of destiny." For years, many of her people believed that Basara's brother was the promised one who would free their people from the tyranny of the land's cruel kingdoms. Now that he's dead, who will lead them? Disguised as her late brother, Basara is finding out that she just might have what it takes to be the prophesied one and be the hero of legend. An epic twenty-six-volume series from Japan, which features a bold female hero in a genre-bending setting,

BASARA © 1991 Yumi TAMURA/Shogakukan Inc.

mixing fantasy, science fiction, action, and romance. A thirteen-episode anime series based on the manga was released in Japan.

> *Vol. 1.* 2003. 192pp. 1-56931-974-X.
> *Vol. 2.* 2003. 192pp. 1-56931-975-8.
> *Vol. 3.* 2003. 200pp. 1-59116-091-X.
> *Vol. 4.* 2003. 200pp. 1-59116-123-1.
> *Vol. 5.* 2004. 200pp. 1-59116-246-7.
> *Vol. 6.* 2004. 200pp. 1-59116-313-7.
> *Vol. 7.* 2004. 200pp. 1-59116-367-6.
> *Vol. 8.* 2004. 200pp. 1-59116-368-4.
> *Vol. 9.* 2004. 200pp. 1-59116-369-2.
> *Vol. 10.* 2005. 200pp. 1-59116-628-4.
> *Vol. 11.* 2005. 200pp. 1-59116-746-9.
> *Vol. 12.* 2005. 200pp. 1-59116-800-7.
> *Vol. 13.* 2005. 200pp. 1-59116-864-3.
> *Vol. 14.* 2005. 200pp. 1-4215-0017-5.
> *Vol. 15.* 2005. 200pp. 1-4215-0135-X.
> *Vol. 16.* 2006. 208pp. 1-4215-0261-5.
> *Vol. 17.* 2006. 208pp. 1-4215-0391-3.
> *Vol. 18.* 2006. 208pp. 1-4215-0528-2.
> *Vol. 19.* 2006. 208pp. 1-4215-0529-0.
> *Vol. 20.* 2006. 208pp. 1-4215-0530-4.
> *Vol. 21.* 2006. 208pp. 1-4215-0531-2.
> *Vol. 22.* 2007. 192pp. 1-4215-0979-2.
> *Vol. 23.* 2007. 208pp. 1-4215-0980-6.

***The Black Dragon.* Written by Chris Claremont. Illustrated by John Bolton.** Dark Horse Comics, 1996. 184pp. 1-56971-042-2. **T**

In A.D. 1193, James Dunreith, the Duke of Ca'rynth, returns home to Britain after fighting in the brutal battlefields of Palestine during the Crusades. Branded a sorcerer and exiled by his king, Henry II, James has now come back home and finds a much changed England that has close ties with the realm of the Faerie. Now in the service of the new queen, James must seek out a potential rebellion against the crown while battling enemies both human and fantastic.

***The Collected Beowulf.* Retold by Gareth Hinds. Thecomic.com, 2000. 120pp.** 1-89313-104-1. **T**

The epic poem of Beowulf, King of the Geats, is retold in a graphic novel format. The mead hall of Hrothgar the Dane lies empty at night, and no warrior dares to set foot outside for fear of the swamp-fiend monster known as Grendel. But there's one man from the north, a Viking of legend, who will defeat the monster. Without weapons or armor Beowulf comes, and Grendel doesn't stand a chance.

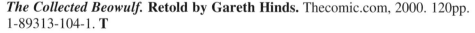

Conan the Barbarian. Dark Horse Comics, 2003– . **T O**

© 2006 Conan Properties International, LLC. Used with permission.

No other barbarian in pulp fiction history can compare with Robert E. Howard's Conan. Created in the 1930s, Conan has become one of the most popular characters in literature. A brutal and cunning Cimmerian warrior born on the fields of battle, Conan was consumed by wanderlust at an early age and encountered many beasts, monsters, damsels, and wizards in his adventures as a thief, warrior, mercenary, and ultimately king. The character found renewed popularity in the monthly comic book series <u>Conan the Barbarian</u> by Marvel Comics in the early 1970s. Written by Roy Thomas, with art by such illustrators as Barry Windsor-Smith, John Buscema, and others, these are some of the most memorable fantasy stories inspired by Howard's novels focusing on the early years of Conan. The classic stories are now being reprinted in the Dark Horse Comics series called <u>Chronicles of Conan</u>, with all new coloring and text corrections. Dark Horse has also begun retelling and embellishing the classic Robert E. Howard stories in both a monthly comic book series and several miniseries projects. Featuring the Eisner Award-winning team of writer Kurt Busiek and the illustrator Cary Nord as well as such creators as P. Craig Russell and Akira Yoshida, these series have helped to revitalize the Conan legacy, to the delight of older fans and a new generation.

<u>The Chronicles of Conan.</u> Written by Roy Thomas. Illustrated by Barry Windsor Smith, John Buscema, Gil Kane, and various. Dark Horse Comics, 2003– . **T**

Reprints and recolors the classic Marvel Comics series that began in 1970. The character was published regularly by Marvel until early 2001.

Vol.1: Tower of the Elephant & Other Stories. 2003. 144pp. 1-59307-016-0.
Vol. 2: Rogues in the House & Other Stories. 2003. 160pp. 1-59307-023-3.
Vol. 3: The Monster of the Monoliths and Other Stories. 2004. 168pp. 1-59307-024-1.
Vol. 4: The Song of Red Sonja and Other Stories. 2004. 160pp. 1-59307-025-X.
Vol. 5: The Shadow in the Tomb and Other Stories. 2004. 160pp. 1-59307-175-2.
Vol. 6: The Curse of the Golden Skull and Other Stories. 2004. 160pp. 1-59307-274-0.
Vol. 7: The Dweller in the Pool and Other Stories. 2005. 160pp. 1-59307-300-3.
Vol. 8: The Tower of Blood and Other Stories. 2005. 160pp. 1-59307-349-6.
Vol. 9: Riders of the River-Dragons and Other Stories. 2005. 160pp. 1-59307-394-1.
Vol. 10: When Giants Walk the Earth and Other Stories. 2006. 168pp. 1-59307-490-5.
Vol. 11: The Dance of the Skull and Other Stories. 2007. 168pp. 1-59307-636-3.

🎐 <u>Conan.</u> Written by Kurt Busiek and various. Illustrated by Cary Nord and various. 2005–present. **O ◉**

The below-listed titles are currently published by Dark Horse Comics. The monthly series is currently written by Kurt Busiek and illustrated by Cary Nord. In 2006, P. Craig Russell was the writer/illustrator for a self-contained story. The adventures are adaptations of Robert E. Howard's pulp adventures. The comic book issue #0, reprinted in *Volume 1,* received an Eisner Award for Best Single Issue/Single Story in 2004.

© 2006 Conan Properties International, LLC. Used with permission.

Vol. 1: The Frost Giant's Daughter and Other Stories. Written by Kurt Busiek. Illustrated by Cary Nord. 2005. 192pp. 1-59307-301-1.

Vol. 2: The God in the Bowl and Other Stories. Written by Kurt Busiek. Illustrated by Cary Nord. 2005. 176pp. 1-59307-403-4.

Vol. 3: The Tower of the Elephant and Other Stories. Written by Kurt Busiek. Illustrated by Cary Nord. 2006. 168pp. 1-59307-547-2.

Conan and the Jewels of Gwahlur. Written and illustrated by P. Craig Russell. 2006. 88pp. 1-59307-491-3.

Conan and the Demons of Khitai. Written by Akira Yoshida. Illustrated by Pat Lee. Written by Kurt Busiek. Illustrated by Cary Nord. 2006. 96pp. 1-59307-543-X.

Conan: Book of Thoth. Written by Kurt Busiek and Len Wein. Illustrated by Kelley Jones. Written by Kurt Busiek. Illustrated by Cary Nord. 2006. 192pp. 1-59307-648-7.

Deicide. Written by Carlos Portela. Illustrated by Das Pastoras. Humanoids Publishing/DC Comics, 2004. 112pp. 1-4012-0363-9. **M**

In a fantasy world reminiscent of ancient Mayan culture, gods walk the lands, sacrifices to the gods must be honored, and a young warrior named Agon walks the path of destruction, vowing revenge on his god, the prince of darkness called Madorak, for the unnecessary sacrifice by the village elder of his beloved fiancée, Aldara. Her body has been preserved by magic but her soul has been taken by their god as a sacrifice. Agon is joined on his quest to reclaim Aldara's soul by the half-man, half-lion beast named Beluch—even if they must kill a god for it.

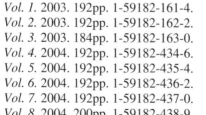

Dragon Hunter. Written and illustrated by Hong-Seock Seo. TOKYOPOP, 2003– . **T Korean manhwa.**

In the kingdom of Kayla (an alternate world version of Korea circa A.D. 500), bigger pests than ants are roaming the kingdom: dragons! Enter Seur-Chong, one of the best Dragon Hunters in the business. Infected with dragon's blood, the curse has given him enhanced strength and stamina but is slowly killing him. Along with his friend, shaman Hyung-Ho, he will solve anyone's pest problem for a hefty price. The series was published in eighteen volumes in Korea.

Vol. 1. 2003. 192pp. 1-59182-161-4.
Vol. 2. 2003. 192pp. 1-59182-162-2.
Vol. 3. 2003. 184pp. 1-59182-163-0.
Vol. 4. 2004. 192pp. 1-59182-434-6.
Vol. 5. 2004. 192pp. 1-59182-435-4.
Vol. 6. 2004. 192pp. 1-59182-436-2.
Vol. 7. 2004. 192pp. 1-59182-437-0.
Vol. 8. 2004. 200pp. 1-59182-438-9.
Vol. 9. 2004. 176pp. 1-59182-439-7.
Vol. 10. 2005. 192pp. 1-59182-958-5.
Vol. 11. 2005. 192pp. 1-59182-959-3.
Vol. 12. 2005. 176pp. 1-59182-960-7.

Vol. 13. 2005. 196pp. 1-59532-649-9.
Vol. 14. 2006. 192pp. 1-59532-650-2.

***Dragon Wars: The Tale of Lufiak Duell.* Written and illustrated by Ryukihei.** I.C. Entertainment, 2000. 234pp. 1-929090-03-X. **T Japanese manga.**

In a magical land which humans and dragons, both good and evil, share, young Lufiak is given the task of bringing back a dragon scale to his clan to prove that he is a man. On his road to self-discovery, Lufiak finds the true secret of his clan's connections to the dragons that share their world, and after forming an alliance with the techno-savvy dragons, he sets out to defeat an evil force of dragonkind darkness, while the fate of the world hangs in the balance.

***Ezra: The Egyptian Exchange.* Written by Sean O'Reilly. Illustrated by Alfonso Ruiz.** Arcana Studios, 2005. 120pp. 0-9763095-4-8. **T**

© 2005 Arcana Studios.

A spin-off of the series <u>Kade</u>. After watching her parents die at the hands of a barbarian and his men, a young girl called Ezra tried to fight back but was severely beaten and left for dead. Her near brush with death changed her both physically and mentally: her skin became chalky white, and her strength and stamina increased significantly. Over time she also learned the ways of magic from a cruel mystic named Pediot of the Order of the Black Sun. Now Ezra is a mercenary-for-hire, stealing artifacts and other goods in exchange for a few coins. When she is hired by Barak, the head of the local thieves' guild, she soon finds she is in way over her head. A simple quest to exchange the Sword of Turin for the equally powerful amulet called Eye of the Serpent becomes much more difficult when she must take on the Egyptian goddess called Nephilila and her cadre of cat-warriors.

***Kade: Identity.* Written by Sean O'Reilly. Illustrated by Allan Otero.** Arcana Studios, 2005. 132pp. 0-9763095-1-3. **T**

Abandoned in a world ruled by the dark lord Apollyon, the ebony-skinned and dark-haired infant with strange tattoos on his body was rescued from death and raised in a monastery by monks. There his rescuers learned that Kade has been cursed not to feel anything physical, from the blade of a sword to the soft caress of a woman's touch. Prophesied to be the Lord of the Order of the Black Sun, who will endn Apollyon's dark reign, following the murder of the monks he searches out those who can aid him in his quest to destroy Apollyon once and for all.

🐦 **Leave It to Chance. Written by James Robinson. Illustrated by Paul Smith.** Image Comics, 2002–2003. **Y**

Fourteen-year-old Chance Falconer, the daughter of the mystical city of Devil's Echo's greatest wizard, Lucas Falconer, is ready to take on the family business as the city's protector, but her father will have nothing to do with it. Naturally, in Nancy Drew-fashion, she, along with her dragon sidekick, gets into one adventure after another in the magical city to prove that she's the true heir to her father's work. The series won several Eisner Awards, including Best New Series (1997) and Best Title for Younger Readers/Best Comics Publication for a Younger Audience (1997). The series also received a Harvey Award in 1997 for Best New Series.

Vol. 1: Shaman's Rain. 2002. 112pp. 1-58240-253-1.
Vol. 2: Trick or Threat and Other Stories. 2003. 112pp. 1-58240-278-7.
Vol. 3: Monster Madness. 2003. 112pp. 1-58240-298-1.

Les Bijoux. **Written by Eun-Ha Jo. Illustrated by Park Sang Sun.** TOKYOPOP, 2004. **O Korean manhwa.**

In a world divided into twelve island nations, the ruler class called "Habit" rule over the lower-class "Spar," who serve them. A young man called Lapis, the son of a dwarf and a hunchback, is prophesied to overthrow the Habit, but he is cursed as well. Lapis has the unique ability to transform into a woman at any given moment. Calling his female identity Lazuli, he must try to fend off the advances of the vile Lord Daimon, a ruler of the Habit in love with Lazuli, but who despises Lapis. Will Lapis be able to change a world without letting anyone know that he and Lazuli are one and the same?

Vol. 1. 2004. 192pp. 1-59182-690-X.
Vol. 2. 2004. 192pp. 1-59182-691-8.
Vol. 3. 2004. 192pp. 1-59182-692-6.
Vol. 4. 2004. 184pp. 1-59182-693-4.
Vol. 5. 2004. 200pp. 1-59182-694-2.

Louie the Rune Soldier. **Written by Ryo Mizuno. Illustrated by Jun Sasameyuki.** ADV Manga, 2004–2005. **T Japanese manga.** あ

The adventures of one of the most unlikely of sorcerers. When three gorgeous female adventurers—Genie the warrior, Merrill the thief, and Melissa the priestess—are in need of a wizard, Louie is the last person they think could help them. A lecherous wizard who thinks with his fists instead of his head—and lives for drinking beer and chasing women—Louie is definitely not their first choice for a mission. When Mylee the war god selects Louie to be a hero, divine providence brings the four of them together, and together they roam the countryside, taking on goblins, ice giants, stone golems, and more in their quest to change Louie from a zero to a hero. A twenty-four-episode anime series was released in Japan in 2001.

Vol. 1. 2004. 182pp. 1-4139-0085-2.
Vol. 2. 2004. 174pp. 1-4139-0105-0.
Vol. 3. 2004. 190pp. 1-4139-0123-9.
Vol. 4. 2005. 180pp. 1-4139-0236-7.

Meridian. **Written by Barbara Kesel. Illustrated by Joshua Middleton, Steve McNiven, and various.** CrossGen Comics, 2001–2002. **T**

On the planet of Demetria, where floating sailing vessels soar in the skies, young Sephie's world is changed forever by the death of her father Turos, the minister of the island city of Meridian, and the appearance of a mysterious brand of power that appears on her forehead. Now the new Minister of Meridian, she must protect her beloved city from the clutches of her manipulative uncle Ilahn, the Minister of the neighboring island of Cadador. When she discovers that he also has been given a sigil of power, but for destruction, they wage a battle of wits and strength as Sephie struggles to ensure the freedom of the world of Demetria. The series was never completed due to CrossGen's

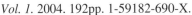

bankruptcy. The title is now owned by Hyperion Press, but it appears the highly regarded series will never conclude.

> *Vol. 1: Flying Solo.* 2001. 192pp. 1-931484-03-1.
> *Vol. 2: Going to Ground.* 2002. 208pp. 1-931484-09-0.
> *Vol. 3: Taking the Skies.* 2002. 160pp. 1-931484-21-X.
> *Vol. 4: Coming Home.* 2002. 160pp. 1-931484-38-4.

Red Sonja. **Written by Michael Avon Oeming and Mike Carey. Illustrated by Mel Rubi, Caesar Roderiguez, and Richard Isanove.** Dynamite Entertainment, 2006. 150pp. 1-93330-511-8. **O**

Loosely based on the original creation by *Conan the Barbarian* creator Robert E. Howard, the famed "She-Devil with a Sword" is a warrior woman from the lands of Hyrkania. When she was seventeen, her parents were murdered after her father refused to join the army, and Sonja was raped by the leader of the soldiers. Crying for revenge, Sonja prayed to the goddess Scathach, and she was blessed with superior skill of all weapons, with which she could exact her revenge on mankind.

Scion. **Written by Ron Marz. Illustrated by Jim Cheung and various.** CrossGen Comics, 2002–2003. **T**

In a world where magic and technology blend together, where computer-guided dragons soar the skies and ritual combat has replaced warfare, young Prince Ethan of the kingdom of Heron seeks revenge against the Eastern land enemies of Raven for the death of his elder brother at the hands of cruel tyrant Prince Bron. Now venturing into enemy territory, Ethan finds an unlikely ally and perhaps more in a beautiful woman called Ashleigh, who's also driven by hatred of the leadership of Raven and of Bron. As they seek to bring about the freedom of the slaves held captive by the rule of Raven, Ethan finds out that he's been given a gift of mysterious power—a sigil—that just save the kingdoms from total annihilation and defeat Raven. The series has not been completed due to CrossGen's bankruptcy.

> *Vol. 1: Conflict of Conscience.* 2002. 160pp. 1-931484-02-3.
> *Vol. 2: Blood for Blood.* 2002. 160pp. 1-931484-08-2.
> *Vol. 3: Divided Loyalties.* 2002. 160pp. 1-931484-26-0.
> *Vol. 4: Sanctuary.* 2003. 160pp. 1-931484-50-3.

Thieves & Kings. **Written and illustrated by Mark Oakley.** I Box Publishing, 1997– . **Y**

The hero's journey of a fourteen-year-old thief called Rubel and his adventures in the city state of Oceansend. Since his childhood he's been the young Princess Katara's personal thief, and everything he has done has been devoted to her. An everyman's young hero, he comes home after five years at sea to find his kingdom in turmoil, taken over by a scheming prince, Princess Katara's brother. Resolving to do what he can to change things, he's soon joined by the eleven-year-old proper apprentice sorceress Heath Wingwit, the youthful-looking immortal wizard Quinton Zempfester, and Rubel's imp friend Varkias. They set out to battle the coming storm of darkness across the land. All the while Rubel is pursued by the immortal beauty Soracia, the Shadow Lady, for reasons as yet unknown, and the fate of the fair young Princess Katara is revealed. The epic series combines prose with comic book-style paneling and is part of a planned nine-volume series still in production.

Vol. 1: The Red Book. 1998. 154pp. 0-9681025-0-6.
Vol. 2: The Green Book. 1997. 210pp. 0-9681025-1-4.
Vol. 3: The Blue Book. 1998. 184pp. 0-9681025-2-2.
Vol. 4: The Shadow Book. 1998. 272pp. 0-9681025-3-0.
Vol. 5: The Winter Book. 2004. 208pp. 0-9681025-4-9.

Fairy Tales and Folklore

For generations, fairy tales have been a traditional source of fantasy for children. Presented here are adaptations, reinterpretations, and brand new fairy tales. In addition, some stories take the traditional fairy tales and expand on them to show what happened after "happily ever after" or create variations and reinterpretations of tales for a new generation. Note that other titles that play on the familiar characters and settings of fairy tales and folklore can be found in chapters 5 and 8.

Castle Waiting. Written and illustrated by Linda Medley. Olio Press and Fantagraphics, 2002– . **T** ◎

© 2006 Linda Medley.

The tales of what happened after everyone "happily ever after." *The Curse of Brambley Hedge* is a retelling of *Sleeping Beauty*. In *The Lucky Road*, a pregnant princess leaves her abusive prince to be with her true lover—an ogre, and the third collection, *Solicitine*, features the origin of the bearded nun Sister Peace. *Castle Waiting* collects the fourteen issues of the ongoing series, including a previously uncollected story line, and sets the stage for future tales from Linda Medley. The series has won many awards, including Eisner Awards for Best New Series (1998), and Linda Medley received an Eisner for Talent Deserving of Wider Recognition (1998). The collection *The Lucky Road* received recognition from YALSA's Popular Paperbacks for Young Adults committee in 2002 on the "Graphic Novels: Superheroes and Beyond" list.

The Curse of Brambley Hedge. 3d ed. Olio Press, 2002. 96pp. 0-9651852-2-2.
Vol. 1: The Lucky Road. 2d printing. Olio Press, 2002. 184pp. 0-9651852-3-0.
Vol. 2: Solicitine. Olio Press, 2003. 192pp. 0-9651852-4-9.
Castle Waiting, Vol. 1. Fantagraphics, 2006. 450pp. 1-56097-747-7.

***The Courageous Princess: Masterpiece Edition.* Written and illustrated by Rod Espinosa.** Antarctic Press, 2003. 240pp. 0-9728978-6-0. hardcover; 2004, 1-932453-36-9, softcover. **A Neo-manga.**

The adventures of the spunky, smart, and self-reliant young Princess Mabelrose. The daughter of the king and queen from the small, fairy tale kingdom of New Tinsley, she's beloved by the people. Though she's a little clumsy and not the fairest of the land, she's not one to accept things the way they are. When a dragon captures her, she doesn't wait for a dashing knight to rescue her—she does it herself! Having escaped from the dragon but a long way from home, Princess Mabelrose and her friend Spikey, a talking porcupine, find themselves in even more adventures.

Fables. Written by Bill Willingham. Illustrated by various. Vertigo/DC Comics, 2002– . **M** ◎

The characters from our fairy tales are alive and well and living in New York City in Fabletown. After being thrown out of their world by an enemy called the Adversary, the fairy tale characters are doing what they can to survive. When Rose Red is killed, only the Big Bad Wolf can find her killer, and all of the former residents of Fabletown are suspects. The series features a large cast of fairy tale characters, including Snow White, Prince Charming, the Big Bad Wolf, Boy Blue, Bluebeard, Pinocchio, and many more, in genre-defying story arcs featuring murder, suspense, and more, with classic fairy tale characters in more realistic and adult situations since their time away from Fabletown. The series has won many awards, including Eisner Awards for Best Serialized Story (2003, 2005) and Best New Series (2003). *Legends in Exile* and *Animal Farm* received recognition from YALSA's Quick Picks for Reluctant Readers committee in 2004 as well as the Popular Paperbacks for Young Adults committee's 2005 "Gateway to Faerie" list for *Legends in Exile*.

> *Vol. 1: Legends in Exile.* 2002. 128pp. 1-56389-942-6.
>
> *Vol. 2: Animal Farm.* 2003. 128pp. 1-4012-0077-X.
>
> *Vol. 3: Storybook Love.* 2004. 192pp. 1-4012-0256-X.
>
> *Vol. 4: March of the Wooden Soldiers.* 2004. 192pp. 1-4012-0222-5.
>
> *Vol. 5: The Mean Seasons.* 2005. 168pp. 1-4012-0486-4.
>
> *Vol. 6: Homelands.* 2006. 192pp. 1-4012-0500-3.
>
> *Vol. 7: Arabian Nights (and Days).* 2006. 144pp. 1-4012-1000-7.
>
> *Vol. 8: Wolves.* 2006. 160pp. 1-4012-1001-5.
>
> *1001 Nights of Snowfall.* 2006. 144pp. 1-4012-0367-1.

Fairy Tales of Oscar Wilde. Adapted by P. Craig Russell from the works of Oscar Wilde. NBM Publishing, 1992–2004. **A** ◎

© 2006 P. Craig Russell.

Adaptations of the classic fairy tales by Oscar Wilde. Each volume includes two tales, adapted by P. Craig Russell for children. The series has won several Eisner Awards, including Best Artist/Penciller/Inker for P. Craig Russell's body of work in 1993, and for Best Graphic Album: New for *Volume 2* in 1995. The series also received a Harvey Award in 1993 for Best Graphic Album of Original Work for *Volume 1*.

> *Vol. 1: The Selfish Giant and the Star Child.* 1992. 32pp. 1-56163-056-X.
>
> *Vol. 2: The Young King and the Remarkable Rocket.* 1994. 32pp. 1-56163-085-3.
>
> *Vol. 3: The Birthday of the Infanta.* 1998. 32pp. 1-56163-213-9.
>
> *Vol. 4: The Devoted Friend, The Nightingale, and the Rose.* 2004. 32pp. 1-56163-391-7.

Fairy Tales of the Brothers Grimm. **Adapted from the tales created by Jacob and Wilhelm Grimm. Script by Doug Wheeler. Illustrated by Dave Wenzel.** NBM Publishing, 1994. 48pp. 1-56163-130-2. **A**

Illustrated by *The Wizard's Tale* artist Dave Wenzel are adaptations of the classic fairy tales "Little Snow White," "The Three Sluggards," and "The Shoemaker & The Elves.".

The Legend of Chun Hyang. **Written and illustrated by CLAMP.** TOKYOPOP, 2004. 232pp. 1-59182-763-9. **T Japanese manga.**

A reinterpretation of one of Korea's best-loved folklores. In an era of ancient Korea when tyrants ruled the land with an iron fist, Chun Hyang is a lively martial artist and headstrong daughter of a shaman of a small Korean village. When the Ryanban, the warlord of the region, tries to illegally take over her city and capture one of her friends, Chun Hyang sets out to free her village and rescue her mother, who was captured by the Ryanban, with the aid of a young lecherous local man called Mong Ryong.

<u>Lullaby.</u> **Written by Mike S. Miller and Ben Avery. Illustrated by Hector Sevilla.** Alias Enterprises, 2005– . **T**

The heroes from children's fiction, including Jim Hawkins (Treasure Island), Alice (from Wonderland), Pinocchio, Little Red Riding Hood, and the Pied Piper, have joined together to battle a dark evil tainting their storybook land. When Alice senses that something is amiss in the magical world, she forms an alliance with some of literature's greatest characters to solve the mystery of the growing darkness and to uncover its identity.

Vol. 1: Wisdom Seeker. 2005. 96pp. 1-933428-62-7.
Vol. 2: Power Grabber. 2006. 104pp. 1-600390-13-7.

© 2006 Alias Enterprises.

The Princess and the Frog. **Written and illustrated by Will Eisner.** NBM Publishing, 2003. 32pp. 1-56163-346-1. **A**

The legendary writer-artist Will Eisner adapts the classic tale in which a good prince is turned into a frog by a spiteful wizard. The princess makes a promise to the frog that she is reluctant to fulfill despite his kindness and her desire not to hurt him.

Sei: Death & Legend. **Written and illustrated by Sho Murase.** Image Comics, 2004. 64pp. 1-58240-334-1. **O**

Set in the ancient world of Japanese Shinto mythology is the possible origin of Sei, the Japanese equivalent of Death and the Grim Reaper. Tsuchi, the fire goddess, recounts her birth and how it cost her mother, Izanami, her life. Enraged by her death, her husband Izanagi, the god of light and heaven, sets out on a treacherous journey to the realm of the netherworld to reclaim his lost love.

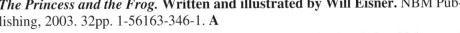

Sundiata: A Legend of Africa. **Written and illustrated by Will Eisner.** NBM Publishing, 2002. 32pp. 1-56163-332-1. **A**

> A retelling of the classic African tale in which a young crippled boy named Sundiata grows up to become the liberator of the region of old Mali from Sumanguru, a corrupt mage-king determined to rule by fear.

Mythological Fantasy

Fantasy tales that are highly influenced by the traditional world myths and legends are enjoyed by many graphic novel fans. Some tales include and feature the gods of old, while others are merely inspired by ancient myths. Tales feature prominent heroes, villains, gods, and goddesses from ancient and modern mythologies from all over the world.

Ancient Joe: el bizarron. **Written and illustrated by C. Scott Morse.** Dark Horse Comics 2002, 120pp. 1-56971-795-8. **T**

> A century in the life of Ancient Joe, an enigmatic, Aztec-like god who learns what life and love are all about by wandering the earth as a barroom brawler and finally settling down. After his beloved human wife dies, Joe fears the worst: that his wife's soul is trapped in Hell as payback for his tricking El Diablo years ago. So he travels to Hell to rescue her soul from the clutches of the devil. Along with the help of a retired repairman and a little girl with a hidden secret, Joe will do anything for true love, even if it means going to Hell and back.

Camelot 3000. **Written by Mike W. Barr. Illustrated by Brian Bolland.** DC Comics, 1997. 312pp. 0-930289307. **O**

> In the year 3000, the world has been conquered by insectlike aliens from Chiron, the farthest known planet in the universe, but the heroes of old have come back from the dead as prophesied, and King Arthur has returned. Reunited with Merlin in new and strange world, they're helped by Tom, a young man from Britain, who helps them become reunited with the current but changed reincarnations of Guenivere, Lancelot, Galahad, Tristan, Percival, and others. As the reincarnated heroes of the Round Table try to save Earth and unite its people against an alien race, the true puppet master of the Chiron army is none other than the dreaded and immortal Morgan le Fay. As King Arthur and his knights find betrayal within their ranks, can they learn to resolve their past-life mistakes and foibles to defeat Moran for the final time?

Hammer of the Gods. **Written by Michael Avon Oeming and Mark Wheatley. Illustrated by Michael Avon Oeming.** Image Comics, 2002–2005. **T**

After his parents made a deal with the Norse Valkyries, Modi has been blessed with phenomenal strength since birth. But every deal has a catch: if Modi should ever use a weapon, he would lose his soul. Modi sets sail for a life of adventure and excitement and to travel the world to become a hero. After returning home to find his parents murdered by frost giants, he must confront the Norse gods of old to ask them why his parents were allowed to die at the hands of such vile beasts and why the gods of old seemingly abandoned him.

> *Vol. 1: Mortal Enemy.* 2002. 176pp. 1-58240-271-X.
> *Vol. 2: Back from the Dead.* 2005. 160pp. 1-58240-508-5.

© 2006 Michael Avon Oeming.

The Life Eaters. **Written by David Brin. Illustrated by Scott Hampton.** WildStorm Productions/DC Comics, 2003. 144pp. 1-4012-0098-2. **O**

As World War II rages, the Nazis have the greatest secret weapon on their side: the Norse gods of old! Brought back to the present, the gods are seemingly unbeatable, and Germany's victory is practically assured. Meanwhile, the Allies and a few renegade gods have formed a resistance front to the rule of the Norse-led Nazis. Years later, humanity is under the rule of a Nazi-controlled government, but the gods of fire and ice are destroying the world. Will humanity be able to rise up and take on the gods of old?

Ragnarok. Written and illustrated by Myung-Jin Lee. TOKYOPOP, 2002–2004. **T Korean manhwa.**

The age of the Norse myths lives again. Ragnarok, the all-ending twilight of the Norse gods, is fast approaching and the age of man draws near. Fenris Fenrir, the wolf-god, has been reborn in the guise of a sorceress woman with one goal: to find the reincarnated god Balder the Brave on Midgard (Earth). The goddess Freya and her Valkyries will stop at nothing to keep Fenris from her task, and to ensure that the gods will rule for another thousand years. The amnesiac swordsman Chaos and Iris Irine, a chief's daughter from the city of Fayon, join Fenris on her quest to start the end of the gods. With plenty of action and sorcery, this is a final fantasy-style reinterpretation of the Norse myths.

Vol. 1. 2002. 192pp. 1-931514-73-9.
Vol. 2. 2002. 192pp. 1-931514-74-7.
Vol. 3. 2002. 192pp. 1-931514-75-5.
Vol. 4. 2002. 192pp. 1-931514-76-3.
Vol. 5. 2003. 192pp. 1-931514-77-1.
Vol. 6. 2003. 200pp. 1-931514-78-X.
Vol. 7. 2003. 200pp. 1-59182-206-8.
Vol. 8. 2003. 200pp. 1-59182-207-6.
Vol. 9. 2004. 192pp. 1-59182-208-4.
Vol. 10. 2004. 192pp. 1-59182-209-2.

Shirahime-Syo: Snow Goddess Tales. **Written and illustrated by CLAMP.** TOKYOPOP, 2004. 192pp. 1-59182-304-8 **T Japanese manga.**

A collection of three sorrowful short stories and a book-end tale surrounding Japanese mythology of the legendary snow princess, a popular character in Japanese folklore. A traveler discovers a beautiful woman in the middle of a snowstorm; a young maiden warrior seeks revenge on a wolf that killed her father; young lovers vow to wait for one another when the young man must leave their village; and a young warrior who is trapped in a great snowstorm en route to his beloved back home discovers a pair of herons in the most unlikely of places.

Thor. Created by Stan Lee and Jack Kirby. Marvel Comics, 1992–2005. **T**

The thunder god of Norse mythology and the son of Odin, the lord of Asgard, home of the Norse gods, giants, and dwarves. With his enchanted hammer Mjolner, Thor is one of the strongest and most powerful warriors who has ever lived and a defender of both Midgard (Earth) and Asgard. For times, Thor has assumed multiple identities when on Earth, including Dr. Donald Blake, EMS Technician Jake Olson, and construction worker Sigurd Jarlson, but the identities have been only temporary. The thunder god also is a founding and still active member of the super-hero team called The Avengers and has defended both Asgard and Earth against threats, including his half-brother Loki, the god of lies, the goddess Hel, the demon Surtur, the Enchantress, the Midgard Serpent, and human foes including the Absorbing Man and others. Alongside allies from Asgard, including Thor's beloved Sif, the Warriors Three, Balder the Brave, and the alien Beta Ray Bill and his equally powerful hammer called Storm Breaker, Thor is ready to protect the realms from evil. Since the death of Odin, Thor has assumed the mantle of Lord of Asgard and continues to watch over both Earth and Asgard. Marvel Comics' version of Thor first appeared in *Journey into Mystery* #83 in 1963. Below are listed highlights of Marvel's take on the thundergod as well as spin-offs featuring other denizens of Asgard.

Essential Thor. Written by Stan Lee and various. Illustrated by Jack Kirby and various. 2005. **Y**

Black-and-white reprints of the classic Thor stories, starting with the original *Journey into Mystery* issues from 1963 created by Stan Lee and Jack Kirby.

Vol. 1. 2005. 536pp. 0-7851-1866-7.
Vol. 2. 2005. 584pp. 0-7851-1591-9.

© 2006 Marvel Comics.

Thor. 2000–2005 **T**

Beginning in 1998, the Thor series from Marvel was relaunched and featured the writing of Dan Jurgens as well as Michael Ovon Oeming, and covered the death of Odin and Thor's new place among the gods of Asgard as ruler. The series concluded in 2004 for the time being and culminated with the apparent death of Thor and all Asgardians, with Beta Ray Bill the only non-Asgardian to survive the conflict. It is inevitable that the thundergod will rise again. Collected here are the monthly issues of the series until its conclusion in the *Avengers Disassembled: Thor* collection.

The Dark Gods. Written by Dan Jurgens. Illustrated by John Romita Jr. 2000. 128pp. 0-7851-0739-8.

Across All Worlds. Written by Dan Jurgens. Illustrated by John Romita Jr. 2001. 160pp. 0-7851-0796-7.

Vol. 1: The Death of Odin. Written by Dan Jurgens. Illustrated by Stuart Immonen. 2002. 144pp. 0-7851-0925-0.

Vol. 2: The Lord of Asgard. Written by Dan Jurgens. Illustrated by Tom Raney and Joe Bennett. 2002. 176pp. 0-7851-1020-8.

Vol. 3: Gods on Earth. Written by Dan Jurgens. Illustrated by Tom Raney and Joe Bennett. 2003. 240pp. 0-7851-1126-3.

Vol. 4: Spiral. Written by Dan Jurgens. Illustrated by Ben Lai and Ray Lai. 2003. 192pp. 0-7851-1127-1.

Vol. 5: The Reigning. Written by Dan Jurgens. Illustrated by Scot Eaton. 2004. 192pp. 0-7851-1247-2.

Vol. 6: Gods and Men. Written by Dan Jurgens. Illustrated by Scot Eaton. 2004. 120pp. 0-7851-1528-5.

Avengers Disassembled: Thor. Written by Michael Avon Oeming. Illustrated by Andrea DiVito. 2005. 144pp. 0-7851-1599-4.

Thor: Alone Against the Celestials. **Written by Tom DeFalco. Illustrated by Ron Frenz.** 1992. 64pp. 0-87135-934-0. **T**

Thor faces his greatest challenge yet when the godlike, towering, 2,000-foot-tall cosmic beings called Celestials pass judgment on the alien planet of Pangoria and the thundergod must battle against the juggernaut Celestial Exitar the Executioner for the fate of a planet.

Thor Visionaries/Thor Legends: Walter Simonson. Written by Walt Simonson. Illustrated by Walt Simonson with Sal Buscema. 2001–2004. T

A collection reprinting the classic stories from the 1980s of one of the most popular chapters in Thor's history. Written and illustrated by Walt Simonson. Many fans of the Marvel series consider Walt Simonson's tale of Thor to be the definitive take on the character, blending stories and characters from Norse myths and introducing the character Beta Ray Bill. The god of thunder meets his match in a monstrous, cybernetically enhanced horse-faced alien called Beta Ray Bill. After defeating Thor in battle, Beta Ray Bill claims Thor's hammer and Thor's power, to save his space-faring people from a demonic menace. There are very few who are pure in heart and mind and therefore can lift the hammer of Thor, and Thor discovers a unique ally in the alien. Odin, proud of Beta Ray Bill and his honorable character, forges a new Uru hammer, Stormbreaker, for Bill, and together with Thor and the Lady Sif they set out to save Bill's alien race from a horde of demons. Other highlights from Walt Simonson's tales include the epic battle against Surtur the giant fire demon and his army, the coming of the dark elf Kurse, Thor's magical transformation into a frog, and the epic battle against the Midgard Serpent. At the time of this writing Marvel Comics has yet to complete this highly regarded collection of tales by Walt Simonson.

Thor Visionaries: Walter Simonson, Book 1. 2001. 288pp. 0-7851-0758-4.
Thor Legends: Walter Simonson, Book 2. 2003. 240pp. 0-7851-1046-1.
Thor Legends: Walter Simonson, Book 3. 2004. 232pp. 0-7851-1047-X.

Thor Mini-Series and Spin-Offs

Tales of Asgard featuring characters from outside the monthly comic book series as well as other Asgardians. Note that the only exception is the graphic novel *Stormbreaker: The Saga of Beta Ray Bill.* It is listed in chapter 1 and features the alien hero called Beta Ray Bill, who has been imbued with the power of Thor.

***Loki.* Written by Rob Rodi. Illustrated by Esad Ribic.** 2005. 96pp. 0-7851-1652-4.

A tale of Asgard from the perspective of Thor's archnemesis and half-brother, the trickster god known as Loki. For thousands of years Loki the deceiver has attempted to overthrow his father, Odin; defeat his half-brother, Thor; and rule over all of Asgard. After all these years he has finally succeeded. Now with Thor shackled and in chains and the Lady Sif imprisoned, Loki begins his rule over Asgard and discovers the truth about himself and his destiny.

© 2006 Marvel Comics.

***Thor: Blood Oath.* Written by Michael Avon Oeming. Illustrated by Scott Kolins.** 2006. 144pp. 0-7851-2274-5. hardcover. **T**

Thor and his companions from Asgard, the Warriors Three, are sent to recover several magical items to make up for the accidental killing of a giant.

Thor: Son of Asgard. Written by Akira Yoshida. Illustrated by Greg Tocchini. 2004–2005. **T**

The adventures of a young Thor, Sif, and Balder the Brave set before the days when Thor was worthy to carry the mighty hammer Mjolnir. Sent by Odin to retrieve four elements to be used to forge a powerful sword, they travel across the lands of Asgard, encountering danger from the elements, monsters, and Thor's evil half-brother, Loki.

> *Vol. 1: The Warriors Teen.* 2004. 144pp. 0-7851-1335-5.
> *Vol. 2: Worthy.* 2005. 144pp. 0-7851-1572-2.

***Thor: Vikings.* Written by Garth Ennis. Illustrated by Glenn Fabry.** MAX, 2004. 120pp. 0-7851-1175-1 **M**

Thor must try to stop a horde of cursed immortal Viking zombies who will stop at nothing to destroy New York City. With the aid of Dr. Strange, Thor must ally himself with time-displaced ancestors of the original man who cursed the Vikings 1,000 years ago in order to defeat them before they annihilate the entire city.

***Thundergod.* Written by Christopher Golden. Illustrated by Albert Debnam.** Digital Webbing, 2005. 112pp. 0-9728567-8-1. **O**

For over a 100 years the Norse god of thunder, Thor, has been imprisoned by the darkling race of beings that have poisoned Earth. The evil beings have taken over the planet in the form of corrupt world leaders, drug manufacturers, and CEOs, and are out to destroy humanity. Only Thor and his wife Sif can see the vile darklings for who they really are and take vengeance on them; to normal humans it appears that Thor is killing innocent world leaders. Will Asgard intervene against the thundergod, or will they side with their once-lost brother and show humanity what the face of evil truly is?

Magic Portal Fantasy/Parallel Worlds

This is fantasy in which the main protagonists are typically from our current world and are magically transported to the magic realm. The realm can be in the past or can be an alternate reality that coincides with our time line. The lead character typically goes to the world in question, but on occasion, the fantasy world's elements interact with our world.

Alice 19th. Written and illustrated by Yû Watase. VIZ Media, LLC, 2003–2004. **T Japanese manga.**

Alice Seno is a typical young teenage girl. She and her older, pretty sister, Mayura, both have a crush on the same upperclassman, Kyo, and Alice quietly gives her sister a chance and demurely backs away. One day Alice sees a rabbit caught in the middle of traffic. She saves the rabbit, and Kyo ends up saving Alice, too. The rabbit has left behind a bracelet for Alice with the ancient magical Lotus Word "courage" written on it. Alice discovers that there's more to the rabbit than she originally thought when the rabbit transforms into a cute rabbit girl named Nyozuka. She tells Alice about the Lotus Words and that words, rather than deeds and violence, have more power. Alice soon realizes that Nyozuka spoke the truth when, after a fight with her sister, Mayura magically disappears! Now Alice must learn the ancient Lotus Words of power and bring back her sister. Meanwhile, there are others like Alice who are also learning the ways of the mysterious Lotus Words.

> *Vol. 1: Lotus Master.* 2003. 192pp. 1-59116-215-7.
> *Vol. 2: Inner Heart.* 2003. 192pp. 1-59116-229-7.
> *Vol. 3: Chained.* 2004. 192pp. 1-59116-230-0.
> *Vol. 4: Unrequited Love.* 2004. 192pp. 1-59116-241-6.
> *Vol. 5: Jealousy.* 2004. 192pp. 1-59116-242-4.
> *Vol. 6: Blindness.* 2004. 200pp. 1-59116-243-2.
> *Vol. 7: The Lost Word.* 2004. 200pp. 1-59116-244-0.

***Baron: The Cat Returns.* Written and illustrated by Aoi Hiiragi.** VIZ Media, LLC., 2005. 224pp. 1-59116-956-9. **T Japanese manga.** あ

A shy young schoolgirl named Haru is having the absolute worst day of her life. She's late for school, stepping in puddles, and has just embarrassed herself in front of the boy she has a crush on. When she rescues a cat on her way home from school one day, she's astonished when the cat stands up and thanks her for the help! As a thank you for rescuing a member of the cat royal family, she's given a chance to marry the cat prince, whom she rescued. Haru finds herself magically spirited away to the Kingdom of Cats, and with the help of the suave adventurer cat called the Baron and the fat cat Muta, she's determined to avoid marrying the Prince and to find a way back home. An anime based on the manga was released in Japan in 2002 by Studio Ghibli, as *The Cat Returns.*

Cardcaptor Sakura. Written and illustrated by CLAMP. TOKYOPOP, 2003–2005. **A Japanese manga.** あ

> When fourth-grader Sakura Kinomoto finds an enchanted book in her father's library called *Clow,* she discovers that the book is designed to contain magical Clow Cards, which are missing. Both she and her friend begin a quest to recover the missing cards from the book so that the cards will not become evil and create chaos and destruction. The second series continues the adventures of Sakura and her battle against the creator of the Clow Cards. The first series is the second edition of the series reprinted in the correct right-to-left Japanese format. An anime series was also released in Japan that adapts the manga.

> > Cardcaptor Sakura, 100% Authentic Manga edition. 2004–2005.
> > > *Vol. 1.* 2004. 200pp. 1-59182-878-3.
> > > *Vol. 2.* 2004. 192pp. 1-59182-879-1.
> > > *Vol. 3.* 2004. 200pp. 1-59182-880-5.
> > > *Vol. 4.* 2005. 200pp. 1-59182-881-3.
> > > *Vol. 5.* 2005. 192pp. 1-59182-882-1.
> > > *Vol. 6.* 2005. 192pp. 1-59182-883-X.
> > Cardcaptor Sakura: Master of the Clow. 2002–2003.
> > > *Vol. 1.* 2002. 192pp. 1-892213-75-3.
> > > *Vol. 2.* 2002. 192pp. 1-892213-76-1.
> > > *Vol. 3.* 2003. 192pp. 1-892213-77-X.
> > > *Vol. 4.* 2003. 192pp. 1-892213-78-8.
> > > *Vol. 5.* 2003. 192pp. 1-892213-79-6.
> > > *Vol. 6.* 2003. 192pp. 1-892213-80-X.

Desert Coral. Written and illustrated by Wataru Murayama. ADV Manga, 2004. **A Japanese manga.**

> High school student Naoto Saki has been dreaming vivid dreams lately. He dreams of a world called Orgos and a small group of fighters called Desert Coral, led by a beautiful pink-haired girl called Lusia. As Naoto soon finds out, his dreams are very more real; Luisa casts a spell and summons him to the world of Orgos to fight a monster. Now when Naoto sleeps he's magically transported to Orgos and is in the company of Lusia and her teammates, including Epsilon, Levinus, and Euro, a cute little cat-girl. Now able to jump between both worlds, Naoto reluctantly finds himself fighting alongside the crew of Desert Coral against the vicious Elphis, who want them dead. What is Naoto's connection with Orgos and a strange power called the Flame Spirit, which he and Lusia share?

> > *Vol. 1.* 2004. 186pp. 1-4139-0050-X.
> > *Vol. 2.* 2004. 186pp. 1-4139-0088-7.
> > *Vol. 3.* 2004. 186pp. 1-4139-0107-7.

Dream Saga. Written and illustrated by Megumi Tachikawa. TOKYOPOP, 2004–2005. **Y Japanese manga.**

> After she catches a red magic stone that fell from the sky, fifth-grader Yuuki Wakasa discovers that there's more to our world than meets the eye. . When she looks in the mirror, she sees a reflection of a dark-haired girl, who tells her the secret of the stone: it allows people to magically transport to the dream world known as Takamagahara. Yuuki discovers that she's one of the chosen few who must save the sun in the magical

realm to prevent dire consequences for both worlds. Now Yuuki must try to locate the others who also caught the magic red stone pieces, and together they can save both worlds.

> *Vol. 1.* 2004. 216pp. 1-59182-774-4.
> *Vol. 2.* 2004. 208pp. 1-59182-775-2.
> *Vol. 3.* 2005. 192pp. 1-59182-776-0.
> *Vol. 4.* 2005. 208pp. 1-59532-210-8.
> *Vol. 5.* 2005. 192pp. 1-59532-211-6.

El-Hazard: The Magnificent World. Written and illustrated by Hidetomo Tsubura. VIZ Media, LLC., 2001–2002. **T Japanese manga.** あ

When high school student Makoto Mizuhara finds himself magically transported to an alternate world where there are beautiful princesses, a fierce female priestesses warrior, giant bugs, and more, aside from the bugs, why would he ever want to go home? Based on the hit anime from the creators of *Tenchi Muyo*.

> *Vol. 1.* 2001. 168pp. 1-56931-628-7.
> *Vol. 2.* 2002. 168pp. 1-56931-771-2.
> *Vol. 3.* 2002. 184pp. 1-56931-847-6.

Faeries' Landing. Written and illustrated by You Hyun. TOKYOPOP, 2004– . **T Korean manhwa.**

After inadvertently helping the faerie mischief-maker Robin Goodfellow, cocky sixteen-year-old Ryang Jegal's world just got more complicated, and he discovers that the mysterious world of the Faerie Realm is more than make believe. Now the guardian of a 176-year-old beautiful faerie named Fanta, Ryang has it good, right? Wrong. After Fanta discovers that Ryang is doomed to experience 108 failed relationships, it will take both the mortal and fantasy realm (and a whole lot of guests from the Faerie Realm living with Ryang) to set things right and get him through his ordeal.

> *Vol. 1.* 2004. 176pp. 1-59182-609-8.
> *Vol. 2.* 2004. 176pp. 1-59182-610-1.
> *Vol. 3.* 2004. 176pp. 1-59182-611-X.
> *Vol. 4.* 2004. 176pp. 1-59182-612-8.
> *Vol. 5.* 2004. 192pp. 1-59182-613-6.
> *Vol. 6.* 2004. 192pp. 1-59182-614-4.
> *Vol. 7.* 2005. 192pp. 1-59532-395-3.
> *Vol. 8.* 2005. 192pp. 1-59532-396-1.
> *Vol. 9.* 2005. 192pp. 1-59532-397-X.
> *Vol. 10.* 2005. 192pp. 1-59532-398-8.
> *Vol. 11.* 2005. 192pp. 1-59532-399-6.
> *Vol. 12.* 2006. 192pp. 1-59532-400-3.
> *Vol. 13.* 2006. 192pp. 1-59532-401-1.
> *Vol. 14.* 2006. 192pp. 1-59532-655-3.

From Far Away. **Written and illustrated by Kyoko Hikawa.** VIZ Media, LLC, 2004–2007. **T Japanese manga.**

High school girl Noriko finds herself magically transported to a hostile fantasy world. Trapped in a world alien to her with a language barrier preventing her from speaking with the local inhabitants, she's rescued by a brave young man called Izark. But appearances can be deceiving, and a prophecy foretells that a woman will bring doom and destruction. Will Izark have to kill Noriko to save his land? The series was collected into fourteen volumes in Japan.

Vol. 1. 2004. 200pp. 1-59116-599-7.
Vol. 2. 2005. 184pp. 1-59116-601-2.
Vol. 3. 2005. 192pp. 1-59116-603-9.
Vol. 4. 2005. 192pp. 1-59116-770-1.
Vol. 5. 2005. 200pp. 1-59116-835-X.
Vol. 6. 2005. 184pp. 1-59116-972-0.
Vol. 7. 2005. 184pp. 1-4215-0088-4.
Vol. 8. 2006. 200pp. 1-4215-0220-8.
Vol. 9. 2006. 208pp. 1-4215-0537-1.
Vol. 10. 2006. 208pp. 1-4215-0322-0.
Vol. 11. 2006. 208pp. 1-4215-0538-X.
Vol. 12. 2006. 208pp. 1-4215-0539-8.
Vol. 13. 2006. 208pp. 1-4215-0540-1.
Vol. 14. 2007. 208pp. 1-4215-0541-X.

Fushigi Yugi: The Mysterious Play. **Written and illustrated by Yû Watase.** VIZ Media, LLC, 2003–2006. **T Japanese manga.** あ

Schoolmates Miaka Yûki and Yui Hongo discover a magical Chinese book in the National Library that transports Miaka to the Universe of the Four Gods, a fictionalized version of ancient China. There they find that they can go back home only after Miaka, who has been declared the shrine maiden of Suzaku, fulfills a prophecy by finding and befriending seven celestial warriors and summoning the god Suzaku with a treasure called the Shentso-Pao. When Miaka meets Tamahome, a seventeen-year-old celestial warrior, and they fall in love, will she ever want to go back? The manga series is one of the most popular Shojo manga in all of Japan. An anime series based on the manga was originally released in Japan.

Vol. 1: Priestess. 2003. 200pp. 1-56931-957-X.
Vol. 2: Oracle. 2003. 200pp. 1-56931-958-8.
Vol. 3: Disciple. 2004. 200pp. 1-56931-992-8.
Vol. 4: Bandit. 2004. 200pp. 1-56931-993-6.
Vol. 5: Rival. 2004. 200pp. 1-59116-097-9.
Vol. 6: Summoner. 2005. 200pp. 1-59116-098-7.
Vol. 7: Castaway. 2005. 200pp. 1-59116-139-8.
Vol. 8: Friend. 2005. 200pp. 1-59116-087-1.
Vol. 9: Lover. 2003. 200pp. 1-59116-096-0.
Vol. 10: Enemy. 2004. 200pp. 1-59116-138-X.
Vol. 11: Veteran. 2004. 200pp. 1-59116-107-X.
Vol. 12: Girlfriend. 2004. 192pp. 1-59116-201-7.
Vol. 13: Goddess. 2004. 200pp. 1-59116-086-3.

Vol. 14: Prophet. 2005. 200pp. 1-59116-737-X.

Vol. 15: Guardian. 2005. 200pp. 1-59116-843-0.

Vol. 16: Assassin. 2005. 200pp. 1-4215-0023-X.

Vol. 17: Demon. 2006. 200pp. 1-4215-0180-5.

Vol. 18: Bride. 2006. 200pp. 1-4215-0393-X.

<u>Fushigi Yugi: Genbu Kaiden</u>. Written and illustrated by Yû Watase. VIZ Media, LLC, 2005–2006. **T Japanese manga.**

<u>Fushigi Yugi: Genbu Kaiden</u> is a prequel to the hit series and focuses on the origins of the Universe of the Four Gods book and the origins of the priestess of Genbu, who was drawn into the book that was written by her father.

Vol. 1. 2005. 200pp. 1-59116-896-1.

Vol. 2. 2005. 200pp. 1-59116-911-9.

Vol. 3. 2006. 200pp. 1-4215-0288-7.

<u>.hack/Legend of the Twilight</u>. Written by Tatsuya Hamazaki. Illustrated by Rei Izumi. TOKYOPOP, 2003. **T Japanese manga.** あ

When fraternal twins Shugo and Rena win a contest to play "The World," the most advanced online game ever created, they soon realize that this is more than a game. Armed with a powerful weapon called the Twilight Bracelet, the twins try to solve the mystery of the rampaging monsters that are trying to destroy a fantasy world that seems just as real as their own. The manga series was released to coincide with both a Playstation 2 role-playing game series and an anime series, each telling a bigger piece of the puzzle.

Vol. 1. 2003. 192pp. 1-59182-414-1.

Vol. 2. 2003. 192pp. 1-59182-415-X.

Vol. 3. 2004. 280pp. 1-59532-369-4.

<u>InuYasha</u>. Written and illustrated by Rumiko Takahashi. VIZ Media, LLC, 2003– . **O Japanese manga.** あ

© 1997 Rumiko
TAKAHASHI/Shogakukan, Inc.

Junior high schoolgirl Kagome Higurashi travels to the distant past through a well in her own backyard and ends up in a fictionalized Sengoku period in Japan, in which demons roam Earth alongside people. She finds the strangest companion bound to a tree: InuYasha, a half-man/half-wolf demon, whom she frees, much to the chagrin of the local village. The village priestess, Kaede, is shocked that Kagome is the spitting image of her oldest sister Kikyo, who died protecting a mystical jewel called the Jewel of Four Souls. Kikyo also was the one who had bound InuYasha to the tree fifty years before. Kagome, it is revealed, is the reincarnation of Kikyo, and now Kaede gives her the task of relocating the lost pieces of the Jewel of Four Souls after Kagome accidentally shatters it. Together Kagome and InuYasha set out on their quest to prevent the power of the jewel from falling into the hands of monsters, which would result in the destruction of feudal Japan. Along the way they are joined by an ever-expanding cast of fantastic characters, including a talking flea named Myoga, Shippo the seven-year-old fox demon, and a Buddhist priest named Miroku. The series is still ongoing and has been printed in Japan in more than forty-three volumes and is being reprinted in the United States by VIZ Media. Visit their Web site (http://www.viz.com) for updates and the latest volumes. An anime series based on the manga was originally released in Japan and is still running. The series is a huge hit in North America as well.

Vol. 1. 2003. 178pp. 1-56931-947-2.
Vol. 2. 2003. 192pp. 1-56931-948-0.
Vol. 3. 2003. 192pp. 1-56931-960-X.
Vol. 4. 2003. 184pp. 1-56931-961-8.
Vol. 5. 2003. 192pp. 1-59116-052-9.
Vol. 6. 2003. 192pp. 1-59116-053-7.
Vol. 7. 2004. 192pp. 1-59116-114-2.
Vol. 8. 2004. 192pp. 1-59116-115-0.
Vol. 9. 2004. 192pp. 1-59116-236-X.
Vol. 10. 2004. 192pp. 1-59116-237-8.
Vol. 11. 2004. 192pp. 1-59116-332-3.
Vol. 12. 2004. 192pp. 1-59116-333-1.
Vol. 13. 2003. 192pp. 1-56931-808-5.
Vol. 14. 2003. 192pp. 1-56931-886-7.
Vol. 15. 2003. 192pp. 1-56931-999-5.
Vol. 16. 2004. 192pp. 1-59116-113-4.
Vol. 17. 2004. 192pp. 1-59116-238-6.
Vol. 18. 2004. 192pp. 1-59116-331-5.
Vol. 19. 2004. 200pp. 1-59116-678-0.
Vol. 20. 2004. 200pp. 1-59116-626-8.
Vol. 21. 2005. 200pp. 1-59116-740-X.
Vol. 22. 2005. 192pp. 1-59116-840-6.
Vol. 23. 2005. 192pp. 1-4215-0024-8.
Vol. 24. 2006. 192pp. 1-4215-0186-4.
Vol. 25. 2006. 208pp. 1-4215-0383-2.
Vol. 26. 2006. 208pp. 1-4215-0466-9.
Vol. 27. 2006. 208pp. 1-4215-0467-7.
Vol. 28. 2007. 208pp. 1-4215-0468-5.

Jax Epoch and the Quicken Forbidden. Written by Dave Roman. Illustrated by John Green. AiT/Planet Lar, 2003–2004. **Y**

© 2006 Dave Roman
and John Green.

Teenager Jackie "Jax" Epoch has a problem. After accidentally falling into the surprisingly barren fantasy realm called Realmsend, she has "borrowed" some magical items from that dimension. Now back in the real world, she finds that she has accidentally let Realmsend's world into our own, starting a chain reaction of events apocalyptically called the "Quicken Forbidden." Now the fantasy realm is coming alive in the real world as dragons, knights, and other strange creatures try to adjust to our society, and Jax has to get over not only invading monsters, but being dumped by her boyfriend and being put on trial for trying to destroy all reality. Some days you're just better off staying in bed.

Vol. 1: Borrowed Magic. 2003. 152pp. 1-932051-11-2.
Vol. 2: Separation Anxiety. 2004. 144pp. 1-932051-24-4.

Kingdom Hearts. **Written and illustrated by Shiro Amano.** TOKYOPOP, 2005–2006. A **Japanese manga.**

Based on the hit *Kingdom Hearts* video games. When King Mickey from the realm of Disney has gone missing, Donald Duck and Goofy set out to rescue him. Along the way they befriend fourteen-year-old Sora, who has left his peaceful island home in search of his two lost friends. As they travel from magical realm to realm (featuring some of Walt Disney's most beloved worlds and characters), Sora discovers that the mystical artifact he is carrying, the "Keyblade," may be the key to solving King Mickey and Sora's friends' disappearances and will end the reign of the wicked Maleficent and her vile minions, called the Heartless.

> *Vol. 1.* 2005. 144pp. 1-59816-217-9.
> *Vol. 2.* 2006. 144pp. 1-59816-218-7.
> *Vol. 3.* 2006. 96pp. 1-59816-219-5.
> *Vol. 4.* 2006. 96pp. 1-59816-220-9.

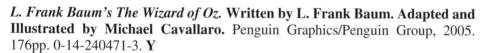

Kore: Lost in Abaddon. **Written by Josh Blaylock. Illustrated by Tim Seeley.** Devil's Due Publishing, 2004. 128pp. 1-932796-13-4. **T**

Alex Crane, a down-on-his-luck stock boy, is having the worst day possible. His girlfriend just dumped him, and his gambling debts are piling up—and then it gets worse! When a mystical spell transforms him into a red-skinned, bull-horned, monstrous Mantikore, he lands in the mystical realm of Abaddon, a world where magic has run dry. Now stuck in a nonmagical realm where elves, dwarves, goblins, fairies, and more live in a modern society reminiscent of Earth, Kore is out to find out how to become human again and to find a way to get back home before wizards seeking his power kill him first.

L. Frank Baum's The Wizard of Oz. **Written by L. Frank Baum. Adapted and Illustrated by Michael Cavallaro.** Penguin Graphics/Penguin Group, 2005. 176pp. 0-14-240471-3. **Y**

When her Kansas house is caught in a tornado, young Dorothy Gale and her dog Toto find themselves transported from Kansas to the magical land of Oz. Heralded as a hero for accidentally killing the Wicked Witch of the East when her house drops on the witch, Dorothy is given the witch's magical silver shoes as a reward for saving the munchkins. Hoping to return home, she heads to the Emerald City to seek the Wizard of Oz. Along the way she is joined by Tin Woodsman, Cowardly Lion, and Scarecrow, who are also seeking something that the wizard can provide. The four companions will have their wishes granted only if one of them can kill the Wicked Witch of the West, who rules in Winkle County. Adapted from the classic 1900 children's novel.

***The Land of Sokmunster.* Written and illustrated by Mike Kunkel and Randy Heuser.**
The Astonish Factory, 2004. 60pp. 0-9721259-2-2. **A**

> The mystery of what really happens to missing socks, keys, and more is finally revealed! Twelve-year-old Sam needs to learn about responsibility, so his parents have him take care of a rare buffalo nickel. If Sam succeeds in taking care of it, he'll be able to go with his friends to the new waterpark. When Sam's nickel is stolen by a sock that escapes through the lint screen, Sam has no choice but to get his nickel back, and he follows the sock to the incredible Land of Sokmunster. There he meets the soks—most notably Spike, the lost sok, and King Jacque, the ruler of all soks. Together Sam and Spike journey across the wondrous land to Mothgonia to retrieve the nickel from the Moth King, the enemy of the soks.

<u>Lions, Tigers, and Bears.</u> Written by Mike Bullock. Illustrated by Jack Lawrence. Image Comics, 2006– . **Y**

© 2006 Mike Bullock and Jack
Lawrence.

> Young Joey Price hated when his mother had to move away to take a job in a neighboring town. The move took him away from his best friends at school, and most important, far away from his loving grandmother. Before saying good-bye, his grandmother gave Joey four stuffed animals: a lion, two tigers, and a panther. Called the Night Pride, like the stories she told, they would protect Joey with their magical powers should he ever need them. When his worst nightmares, the Beasties, come out of the closet at night, the Night Pride, now transformed into huge regal-looking beasts, are ready to protect Joey. After journeying to the Stuffed Animal Kingdom, Joey learns that the fate of all children hangs in the balance, and he must find his own destiny with the help of the Night Pride.

> *Vol. 1: Fear and Pride*. 2006. 112pp. 1-933428-41-4.

<u>Magic Knight Rayearth.</u> Written and illustrated by CLAMP. TOKYOPOP, 2003–2004 **Y Japanese manga.** あ

> Schoolgirls Hikaru, Umi, and Fuu are transported to the magical realm of Cephiro to free the Princess Emeraude. The girls discover that they are the revered Magic Knights who, it has been foretold, will free the land. Each is given a special power tied into the elements. Hikaru is the Magic Knight of Fire, Umi is the Magic Knight of Water, and Fuu is the Magic Knight of Wind. Together they begin their quest, along with the cute blobbish creature called Makona, to free the Princess from the evil entity called Zagato. The sequel takes the girls back to Cephiro again a year later to save the mystical realm when other nearby countries claim it in their names. Will they be able to save Cephiro before it is reduced to ashes? The series was adapted into an anime series that originally aired in Japan.

> <u>Magic Knight Rayearth I.</u> 2003.
> > *Vol. 1*. 2003. 208pp. 1-59182-082-0.
> > *Vol. 2*. 2003. 208pp. 1-59182-083-9.
> > *Vol. 3*. 2003. 208pp. 1-59182-084-7.
> <u>Magic Knight Rayearth II.</u> 2004.
> > *Vol. 1*. 2004. 224pp. 1-59182-266-1.
> > *Vol. 2*. 2004. 224pp. 1-59182-267-X.
> > *Vol. 3*. 2004. 232pp. 1-59182-268-8.

<u>Mar.</u> Written and illustrated by Nobuyuki Anzai. VIZ Media, LLC, 2005– . **Y Japanese manga.**

Ginta Toramizu, a short fourteen-year-old boy who is nearsighted and not the best athlete in school, would much rather spend time dreaming of the same fantasy world he has dreamt of over 102 times. In his dreams he's a hero able to do things he wishes he could in real life. When a mysterious figure at Ginta's school summons him to the world from his own dreams, it really is a dream come true. Now Ginta is the hero, strong, agile, and without the need for glasses. He's also on a quest to recover mystical artifacts called Arms, one of which may have the power to return him back home. Ginta is joined on his adventure by his companion Jack, as well as the talking iron-ball weapon called Babbo, a weapon that many are after but only Ginta can wield.

> *Vol. 1.* 2005. 208pp. 1-59116-902-X.
> *Vol. 2.* 2005. 200pp. 1-59116-903-8.
> *Vol. 3.* 2005. 200pp. 1-59116-904-6.
> *Vol. 4.* 2005. 192pp. 1-4215-0053-1.
> *Vol. 5.* 2006. 192pp. 1-4215-0190-2.
> *Vol. 6.* 2006. 208pp. 1-4215-0320-4.
> *Vol. 7.* 2006. 208pp. 1-4215-0489-8.
> *Vol. 8.* 2006. 208pp. 1-4215-0490-1.

Once in a Blue Moon. **Written by Nunzio DeFilippis and Christina Weir. Illustrated by Jennifer Quick.** Oni Press, 2004. 120pp. 1-929998-83-X. **T Neo-manga.**

© 2006 Nunzio DeFilippis, Christina Weir, and Jennifer Quick.

When Aeslin Finn was just a child, every part of her life was perfect, from her two loving parents to the home they lived in. Every night her parents read her the latest fantasy adventures of the *Avalon Chronicles,* in which the dashing Dragon Knight and the prince saved the day. One day the stories shifted from innocent and magical to dark and disturbing. Before the story could be completed, Aeslin's parents went on a trip. After her father died on that trip, her mother never again read from the *Avalon Chronicles.* Years later, Aeslin is now a teenager living a fairly normal life, dealing with school and a boy, Michael, on whom she has a crush. When she and her friend Samantha find in a strange bookstore a book called *Once in a Blue Moon,* the sequel to the *Avalon Chronicles,* Aeslin can't wait to read what happened after the Dragon Knight was defeated. Devastated by the loss Avalon endured, Aeslin wishes she could be there to help save Avalon and finds herself magically transported to the realm from her favorite childhood book. Now trapped in a fantasy world that is deadly and much more dangerous than she has imagined, Aeslin is out to save Avalon and get back home before she is grounded by her mother.

<u>Pakkins' Land.</u> Written and illustrated by Gary and Rhonda Shipman. Illustrated by Gary Shipman. Pakkins' Presents, 1997–2003. **Y**

A young boy named Paul finds himself in a fantastic world called Pakkins' Land, where animals can talk. He befriends a giant eagle made of pure light,

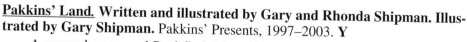

which gives him a feather as a sign of friendship and then vanishes into thin air. Realizing that he is lost and far from home, he is befriended by Gus, a talking lion, and Mr. Brambles, a grizzly bear. Together with the help of the other creatures from the forests, they set out to locate King Aryah, the lost ruler of Pakkins' Land. In 2005 the series was printed in full color through Alias Enterprises.

> *Vol. 1: Paul's Adventure.* 1997 128pp. 0-9700241-1-8.
> *Vol. 2: Quest for Kings.* 2001 128pp. 0-9700241-2-6.
> *Vol. 3: Forgotten Dreams.* 2001 128pp. 0-9700241-3-4.
> *Vol. 4: Tavitah.* 2003 128pp. 0-9700241-4-2.

Planet Ladder. Written and illustrated by Yuri Narushima. TOKYOPOP, 2002–2005. **T Japanese manga.**

Schoolgirl Kaguya never knew much about her youth, and has only distant memories of a young boy. Adopted at a very young age by the Haruyamas, Kaguya has lived with them ever since. When the boy from her dreams appears to her in real life, he alone knows the truth about her: she is an orphaned princess from another world that desperately needs her help. The boy is actually an android named Gold, who serves as her protector as she grows from school girl to savior of a land she doesn't remember.

> *Vol. 1.* 2002. 208pp. 1-931514-62-3.
> *Vol. 2.* 2002. 208pp. 1-931514-63-1.
> *Vol. 3.* 2002. 208pp. 1-931514-64-X.
> *Vol. 4.* 2003. 208pp. 1-59182-063-4.
> *Vol. 5.* 2003. 208pp. 1-59182-199-1.
> *Vol. 6.* 2004. 200pp. 1-59182-507-5.
> *Vol. 7.* 2005. 256pp. 1-59182-508-3.

Prétear: The New Legend of Snow White. Written and illustrated by Kaori Naruse. Created by Junichi Satou. ADV Manga, 2004–2005. **A Japanese manga.** あ

In contemporary Japan, freshman high school student Himeno Awayuki is trying to adjust to her new life. After her father, a famous but washed-up children's book author, remarries, Himeno lives in a mansion with an evil and manipulative stepmother and two cruel stepsisters. While walking to school one day, Himeno strolls down a different path through the woods and finds herself in the company of seven young men, who tell her that she's the prophesied Prétear, a force for the planet to defeat the Princess of Disaster, who wishes to destroy Leafe, the power of life on Earth. The men are actually the seven Knights of Leafe, protectors of all plants, water, light, wind, cold, heat, and sound, who live in both Earth and the kingdom of Leafeania and can share their power with the Prétear. Now Himeno must adjust to her new role as the world's savior and still try to get along with her new family as well as the brooding Hayate, the Knight of Wind, who isn't sure he believes Himeno is up to the challenge that awaits her. An anime series was also released in Japan and ran for thirteen episodes.

> *Vol. 1.* 2004. 188pp. 1-4139-0144-1.
> *Vol. 2.* 2004. 196pp. 1-4139-0145-X.
> *Vol. 3.* 2004. 172pp. 1-4139-0146-8.
> *Vol. 4.* 2005. 180pp. 1-4139-0147-6.

The Queen's Knight. **Written and illustrated by Kim Kang Won.** TOKYOPOP, 2004– . **T Korean manhwa.**

Fifteen-year-old Yuna Lee is the youngest sister of three overprotective older brothers. She spends the summer visiting her mother, who is studying in Germany for a music degree. One day while up in the hills in Germany, Yuna Lee falls off a cliff and is rescued by Rieno, an eighteen-year-old knight from the realm of Phantasma. In exchange for saving her life, Rieno asks that she spend the rest of her days with him as her queen. Now Yuna is torn between living a dreamlike life as a queen of Phantasma or being reunited with her loved ones at home.

Vol. 1. 2004. 200pp. 1-59532-257-4.
Vol. 2. 2005. 192pp. 1-59532-258-2.
Vol. 3. 2005. 192pp. 1-59532-259-0.
Vol. 4. 2005. 192pp. 1-59532-260-4.
Vol. 5. 2006. 192pp. 1-59532-261-2.
Vol. 6. 2006. 192pp. 1-59532-262-0.
Vol. 7. 2006. 184pp. 1-59532-263-9.

Red River. **Written and illustrated by Chie Shinohara.** VIZ Media, LLC, 2004– . **O Japanese manga.**

4

Fifteen-year-old Yuri Suzuki's life has never seemed so good. She just passed her college entrance exams and just kissed her boyfriend, Himuro, for the first time. Little does she know that her life will make a drastic change, to the past! Magical hands appear out of a puddle and drag her straight down into the water. She awakens to find herself in the year 1500 B.C. in the heart of the Hittite Empire, Anatolia, in the ancient Middle East. Captured by the queen of Anatolia, she is to be sacrificed in a ritual that will curse five princes who come before her son in the line of succession, so that one day he may sit on the throne. Yuri manages to escape from the queen and is rescued by Prince Kail, third in line for the throne. Now Yuri is safe under Kail's protection, and as they look for a way to return Yuri to the present, Yuri finds that she may have a true purpose for being there in the past—a purpose that can change the fate of the war and overthrow an empire. The epic series was originally published in twenty-eight volumes in Japan.

Vol. 1. 2004. 192pp. 1-59116-429-X.
Vol. 2. 2004. 188pp. 1-59116-430-3.
Vol. 3. 2004. 200pp. 1-59116-431-1.
Vol. 4. 2004. 200pp. 1-59116-432-X.
Vol. 5. 2005. 200pp. 1-59116-433-8.
Vol. 6. 2005. 192pp. 1-59116-780-9.
Vol. 7. 2005. 192pp. 1-59116-847-3.
Vol. 8. 2005. 200pp. 1-59116-988-7.
Vol. 9. 2005. 192pp. 1-4215-0066-3.
Vol. 10. 2006. 208pp. 1-4215-0195-3.
Vol. 11. 2006. 208pp. 1-4215-0327-1.
Vol. 12. 2006. 208pp. 1-4215-0554-1.
Vol. 13. 2006. 208pp. 1-4215-0555-X.
Vol. 14. 2006. 208pp. 1-4215-0556-8.

Vol. 15. 2006. 208pp. 1-4215-0557-6.
Vol. 16. 2007. 208pp. 1-4215-0558-4.
Vol. 17. 2007. 192pp. 1-4215-0997-0.

Scrapped Princess. Written by Ichiro Sakaki. Illustrated by Yabuki Go. TOKYOPOP, 2005–2006. **T Japanese manga.** あ

Fifteen years ago, in the kingdom of Linevan, a boy and a girl were born to the king. Shortly after their birth, a prophecy foretold that at the age of sixteen the girl would destroy all of humanity. To preserve humanity from destruction, the daughter was to be eliminated. Having miraculously survived the murder attempt, the girl, called Pacifica Casull, is now fifteen. When the kingdom of Linevan receives word that the princess is indeed still alive, the kingdom of Linevan will do whatever it takes to make sure that the prophecy is not fulfilled and Pacifica is eliminated for good. Now Shannon and Raquel, her adopted brother and sister, who are skilled in the ways of the sword and magic, respectively, protect Pacifica from the constant threat of assassination. An anime series was also released. Both the manga and the anime are based on thirteen novels created by Ichiro Sakaki and Yukinobu Asami.

Vol. 1. 2005. 184pp. 1-59532-981-1.
Vol. 2. 2006. 192pp. 1-59532-982-X.
Vol. 3. 2006. 192pp. 1-59532-983-8.

Sokora Refugees. Written and illustrated by Segamu and Melissa DeJesus. TOKYOPOP, 2005– . **T Neo-manga.**

© 2006 TOKYOPOP.

Flat-chested slacker teenager Kana hasn't quite yet developed like some of her other friends from school have, but other than the teasing, she gets along with them just fine. When a new student at her school, a perverted elf-in-hiding named Tien, creates a portal to his homeworld of Sokora in, of all places, a bathroom stall in the girls' locker room, Kana finds herself transported to a world where goblins, demons, nymphs, and elves roam the land. Trapped by a marauding demon army, Kana accidentally finds herself time-sharing her body with a buxom elf from the realm called Veila. Back in school, Kara shows an all-new side when she shares the same body as a beautiful elf part of the time. Can the odd team of Kana/Veila, a gargoyle named Griever, a half-raccoon girl named Salome, Tien, the warrior-elf Tristan, and Kana's friends from school find a way to save the kingdom and get some homework done for once?

Vol. 1. 2005. 192pp. 1-59532-736-3.
Vol. 2. 2006. 192pp. 1-59816-551-8

Those Who Hunt Elves. Written and illustrated by Yu Yagami. ADV Manga, 2003– . **O Japanese manga.** あ

In a fantasy world where goblins, demons, and elves exist, a small group of people from Earth are trying to find a way back home. Airi, a talented actress; Ritsuko, a weapons fanatic; and Junpei, a martial arts expert, find themselves stranded in this strange world along with Airi's fully functional T-74 military tank, now possessed by the spirit of a cat. Their only hope of getting back to Japan lies with the hot-tempered elf sorceress Celcia's spell of restoration. When the ancient spell is retranslated into modern language, an accident happens, and instead of the spell forming on the body of Celcia like a tattoo, it shatters into five pieces across the fantasy land onto the bodies of five other elves! Now in order to return home the group has to find out who has the five shards of the spell, and the only way to do that is to have the elves strip naked for them! An anime series was released in Japan that adapts the manga series.

> *Vol. 1*. 2003. 216pp. 1-4139-0014-3.
> *Vol. 2*. 2003. 192pp. 1-4139-0015-1.
> *Vol. 3*. 2004. 202pp. 1-4139-0034-8.
> *Vol. 4*. 2004. 200pp. 1-4139-0063-1.
> *Vol. 5*. 2004. 202pp. 1-4139-0077-1.
> *Vol. 6*. 2004. 202pp. 1-4139-0098-4.
> *Vol. 7*. 2004. 202pp. 1-4139-0116-6.
> *Vol. 8*. 2005. 202pp. 1-4139-0155-7.
> *Vol. 9*. 2005. 200pp. 1-4139-0158-1.
> *Vol. 10*. 2005. 202pp. 1-4139-0160-3.

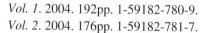

Threads of Time. **Written and illustrated by Mi Young Noh.** TOKYOPOP, 2004– . **T Korean manhwa.**

High school student Moon Bin Lee has been having the same reccurring dream—that he is trapped in the thirteenth century in Korea, in the Koryo Dynasty. Named Sa Kyoung Kim, Moon dreams that he's the son of a prominent warrior family, and a pretty young woman from the past consumes his dreams. Soon the dreams turn into nightmares that he can't escape from, and he wakes up to find that he's really in ancient Korea. He is told that he is really Sa Kyoung Kim, and that he has been in a coma for several years. Now as Sa Kyoung, he's living the life he's always dreamed of, as a warrior fighting for the Koryo Dynasty, and he has possibly found true love in Altanhads, the young woman from his dreams. Meanwhile, in the present Moon Bin Lee's body lies in a coma in Seoul, and his kendo team is struggling without him. Which life will Moon Bin Lee choose—and which one is his real life? The series was originally published in Korea and collected into eleven volumes.

> *Vol. 1*. 2004. 192pp. 1-59182-780-9.
> *Vol. 2*. 2004. 176pp. 1-59182-781-7.
> *Vol. 3*. 2005. 192pp. 1-59532-034-2.
> *Vol. 4*. 2005. 192pp. 1-59532-035-0.
> *Vol. 5*. 2005. 192pp. 1-59532-036-9.
> *Vol. 6*. 2006. 192pp. 1-59532-037-7.
> *Vol. 7*. 2006. 192pp. 1-59532-038-5.

Tsubasa: RESERVoir CHRoNiCLE. **Written and illustrated by CLAMP.** Del Rey Manga/Random House, 2004– . **T Japanese manga.** あ

In the magical Kingdom of the Clow, young archaeologist Syaoran Li is in love with Sakura, the princess of the Clow, and master of a magical and so-far untapped potential. When a mysterious artifact found at a dig knocks Sakura unconscious, no science or magic can heal her—except one. Syaoran takes her to the king's magical advisor, who transports Syaoran and Sakura across dimensions and worlds to the magic shop owned by the time-space witch Yuko. Joined with Fai D. Flowright, the Wizard of Serusu, and Kurogane, a cursed ninja from ancient Japan, who each have a separate desire to be fulfilled by Yuko, Syaoran journeys across dimensions to retrieve the small fragments of Sakura's memories so prevent her from dying. There is a cost for Yuko's aid: they must all give up their most precious item. For Fai it's his tattoo of power, for Kurogane it's his sword, but Syaoran must give up what matters to him the most: his relationship with Sakura. The cost is high, but Syaoran will do anything to get her back. Now accompanied by the magical rabbitlike creature Mokona, he travels dimension after dimension in search of shards of Sakura's memories, along the way meeting up with other popular characters from many CLAMP titles. The manga has recently been adapted into a hit anime series, currently airing in Japan.

> *Vol. 1.* 2004. 208pp. 0-345-47057-5.
> *Vol. 2.* 2004. 208pp. 0-345-47182-2.
> *Vol. 3.* 2004. 208pp. 0-345-47183-0.
> *Vol. 4.* 2005. 208pp. 0-345-47791-X.
> *Vol. 5.* 2005. 208pp. 0-345-47792-8.
> *Vol. 6.* 2005. 208pp. 0-345-47793-6.
> *Vol. 7.* 2005. 208pp. 0-345-47797-9.
> *Vol. 8.* 2006. 208pp. 0-345-48428-2.
> *Vol. 9.* 2006. 208pp. 0-345-48429-0.
> *Vol. 10.* 2006. 208pp. 0-345-48430-4.
> *Vol. 11.* 2006. 208pp. 0-345-48528-9.
> *Vol. 12.* 2007. 208pp. 0-345-48532-7.

<u>Vision of Escaflowne.</u> Written and illustrated by Katsu Aki. TOKYOPOP, 2003–2004. **O Japanese manga.** あ

After dabbling with tarot cards, high school student Hitomi Hoshino is magically transported to the mystical planet Gaea. There she discovers that she has mysteriously gained precognitive abilities and can see the future. Together with Van Fanel, the prince of the war-torn kingdom of Fanelia, Hitomi joins the fight against the evil Zaibach Empire. With the aid of the Fanelian deity known as Escaflowne, a powerful robotlike weapon that only she can power and Van can pilot, they just might have an edge in the conflict. As the battle rages for control of the land, Van and Hitomi must combine their might to defeat Dornkirk, the leader of the Zaibach Empire. What is the final price for victory, and will Hitomi ever return home? The manga series was inspired by the original anime series, which debuted in Japan in 1996.

> *Vol. 1.* 2003. 192pp. 1-59182-366-8.
> *Vol. 2.* 2003. 192pp. 1-59182-367-6.
> *Vol. 3.* 2003. 192pp. 1-59182-368-4.
> *Vol. 4.* 2004. 192pp. 1-59182-449-4.
> *Vol. 5.* 2004. 192pp. 1-59182-450-8.
> *Vol. 6.* 2004. 208pp. 1-59182-451-6.
> *Vol. 7.* 2004. 192pp. 1-59182-452-4.
> *Vol. 8.* 2004. 216pp. 1-59182-453-2.

Contemporary Fantasy

Contemporary fantasy titles involve stories set on Earth or a very similar world, where the influence of magic is very subtle. The stories usually take place in modern or contemporary times, but also can be set in the recent past.

<u>Alichino.</u> **Written and illustrated by Kouyu Shurei.** TOKYOPOP, 2005. **T Japanese manga.**

There exist beautiful androgynous creatures called Alichino who can grant wishes to those who discover them, but a price must be paid for this wish. When a young woman wants to save the life of her dying brother, she mistakes a beautiful man, Tsugiri, for an Alchino. The Alchino aren't what they seem: beautiful on the outside, their souls are wicked and scarred and they feast on the souls of the living. The brighter the soul, the better. Tsugiri is no ordinary man. His memory lost, he's being pursued by the Alchino, who would like to feast on his soul. What is Tsugiri's connection with the Alichino, and why do they want him dead? A fourth and final volume of the series has yet to be released.

Vol. 1. 2005. 192pp. 1-59532-478-X.
Vol. 2. 2005. 164pp. 1-59532-479-8.
Vol. 3. 2005. 192pp. 1-59532-480-1.

Arrowsmith: So Smart in Their Fine Uniforms. **Written by Kurt Busiek. Illustrated by Carlos Pacheco and Jesús Mérino.** WildStorm Productions/DC Comics, 2004. 160pp. 1-4012-0299-3. **T**

© 2006 Kurt Busiek and Carlos Pacheo.

On an alternate Earth in the year 1915, magic rules the land and World War I has erupted in Europe. The battle is being fought not with biplanes, but with flying dragons and magic spells, as fantastic monsters and humans are enlisted soldiers roaming the battlefields of Gallia. Across the globe in the United States of Columbia, young Fletcher Arrowsmith runs away to join the elite squadron of Overseas Aero Corps to fight with their dragons and magic spells against the fiendish Prussian armies. When the harsh realities of war destroy his squadron leaders, can Arrowsmith find the courage to lead his small band of soldiers to safety from the attacking the Prussian army and their soldiers of vampires, werewolves, and fire demons?

The Forbidden Book. **Written and illustrated by various.** Renaissance Press, 2001. **T**

An anthology of short fantasy stories by some of comic books' best talent, including Charles Vess, Colleen Doran, Marv Wolfman, Rick Veitch, David Wenzel, Frank Brunner, Michael Cohen, Eric Taillefer, Eric Shanower, Al Williamson, and others. Each volume contains eleven dissimilar short stories, all connected by the element of magic.

Vol. 1: Journeys into the Mystic. 2001. 128pp. 0-9712169-0-8.

Vol. 2: Into the Uncharted Realm. 2001. 128pp. 0-9712169-1-6.

Mage. **Written and illustrated by Matt Wagner.** Image Comics, 2004–2006. **T**
The adventures of Kevin Matchstick, the man who discovers that he is really the reincarnated King Arthur. Armed with his magical baseball bat, called Excalibur, he and
his band of reborn heroes, including Hercules and Coyote, battle the coming darkness
that threatens all of reality. The conclusion to the epic trilogy, *The Hero Denied*, is
planned but has yet to be released. The original issues of *The Hero Discovered* were released in 1984 and have been recollected by Image Comics.

> *The Hero Discovered.* 2004. 464pp. 1-58240-356-2, hardcover; 2005, 1-58240-388-0,
> softcover.
> *The Hero Defined, Vol. 1.* 2005. 432pp. 1-58240-535-2, hardcover.
> *The Hero Defined, Vol. 2.* 2006. 432pp. 1-58240-510-7, hardcover.

More Than Mortal. **Written by Steve Firchow, Walden Wong, and Robin Spehar.**
Illustrated by Sharon Scott. Image Comics, 2001. 128pp. 1-58240-191-8. **T**
Eighteen-year-old Irish maiden Derde dreams of a female warrior protector of Ireland's medieval days, but the dreams are more real than she thinks. Accused of killing
a local priest, she leaves her orphanage in search of the truth with the aid of a
Witchfinder and a local boy, Connor, to protect Ireland from the evil spirits that walk
the land.

Mystic. **Written by Ron Marz and Tony Bedard. Illustrated by various.** CrossGen
Comics, 2001–2003. **T**
On the planet Ciress, where magic is a part of everyday life, partygoer Gizelle Villard
could care less about magic. Magic was something that her older sister, Genevieve,
dedicated her life to, and after years of practicing the rituals and spells, Genevieve was
slated to become one of the great masters of magic of their world. But when a spell
goes awry, Gizelle unwittingly becomes the champion sorceress for the land, taking in
not just the powers intended for Genevieve, but also those of the other four grand
mages attending the ceremony. Now Gizelle can become the greatest mage in the
world—if she can survive the experience. The series was incomplete when the
publisher folded.

> *Vol. 1: Rite of Passage.* 2001. 192pp. 1-931484-00-7.
> *Vol. 2: The Demon Queen.* 2002. 184pp. 1-931484-06-6.
> *Vol. 3: Siege of Scales.* 2002. 160pp. 1-931484-24-4.
> *Vol. 4: Out All Night.* 2003. 160pp. 1-931484-46-5.
> *Vol. 5: Master Class.* 2003. 160pp. 1-931484-79-1.

Tokyo Babylon. **Written and illustrated by CLAMP.** TOKYOPOP, 2004–2005. **T Japanese manga.** あ
For generation after generation, the Sumeragi clan has been the leading group of
Onmyoujis, who guard the souls and spirits. Now the sixteen-year-old leader of the
clan, Subaru, is the best person to call for hauntings and supernatural events, joined by
his flamboyantly dressed twin sister, Hokuto. They're also joined by Seishirou
Sakurazuka, a twenty-three-year-old male veterinarian who is also a mysterious
onmyouji and professes to be in love with Subaru. The three of them travel in the new

Babylon of the world, the great city of Tokyo, seeking to save humanity from its darker side and the demons and spirits that are trapped in the city. An anime based on the manga was released in Japan.

> *Vol. 1.* 2004. 160pp. 1-59182-871-6.
> *Vol. 2.* 2004. 168pp. 1-59182-872-4.
> *Vol. 3.* 2004. 160pp. 1-59182-873-2.
> *Vol. 4.* 2004. 184pp. 1-59182-874-0.
> *Vol. 5.* 2005. 176pp. 1-59532-049-0.
> *Vol. 6.* 2005. 176pp. 1-59532-050-4.
> *Vol. 7.* 2005. 160pp. 1-59532-051-2.

W.I.T.C.H. Graphic Novel. Written and illustrated by TK. Volo/Hyperion Books for Children, 2005–2006. **Y**

Five girls—Will, Irma, Taranee, Cornelia, and Hay Lin (W.I.T.C.H.)—are much more than ordinary schoolgirl friends. The girls have been given magical powers by the Guardians of the Veil to protect Earth. Each has been given one power, over the elements of air, water, earth, fire, and the power of energy, and together the girls must battle the villainous Elyon and travel to the magical world called Metamoon. Now going to school, homework, boyfriends, and using their magical powers to save the world are all part of a good day's work. The graphic novel series is an adaptation of the chapter books series of the same name.

> *Vol. 1: The Power of Friendship.* 2005. 128pp. 0-7868-3674-1.
> *Vol. 2: Meridian Magic.* 2005. 128pp. 0-7868-0974-4.
> *Vol. 3: The Revealing.* 2005. 128pp. 0-7868-3655-5 .
> *Vol. 4: Between Light and Dark.* 2006. 128pp. 0-7868-3656-3.
> *Vol. 5: Legends Revealed.* 2006. 128pp. 0-7868-4876-6.
> *Vol. 6: Forces of Change.* 2006. 128pp. 0-7868-4877-4.

X/1999. Written and illustrated by CLAMP. VIZ Media, LLC, 2003–2005. **T Japanese manga.** あ

In the year 1999, the fate of Earth depends on the decision of Kamui Shiro, a twenty-one-year-old man who, it has been prophesied by angels, will be either its savior or its destroyer. He and six other young individuals with magical powers are out to battle a rival gang of powered individuals bent on destroying the human race. A complex and beautifully illustrated adaptation of the biblical apocalypse by the all-female manga team called CLAMP, the series has yet to be completed. An anime series based on the manga was released in Japan.

> *Vol. 1: Prelude.* 2003. 184pp. 1-56931-949-9.
> *Vol. 2: Overture.* 2003. 184pp. 1-56931-950-2.
> *Vol. 3: Sonata.* 2003. 184pp. 1-56931-966-9.
> *Vol. 4: Intermezzo.* 2003. 184pp. 1-56931-967-7.
> *Vol. 5: Serenade.* 2003. 184pp. 1-59116-079-0.
> *Vol. 6: Duet.* 2003. 184pp. 1-59116-080-4.
> *Vol. 7: Rhapsody.* 2003. 184pp. 1-59116-121-5.
> *Vol. 8: Crescendo.* 2003. 184pp. 1-59116-122-3.
> *Vol. 9: Requiem.* 2004. 184pp. 1-59116-341-2.

Vol. 10: Fugue. 2003. 184pp. 1-56931-896-4.

Vol. 11: Interlude. 2003. 184pp. 1-56931-897-2.

Vol. 12: Movement. 2003. 184pp. 1-59116-078-2.

Vol. 13: Lament. 2004. 184pp. 1-59116-120-7.

Vol. 14: Concerto. 2004. 208pp. 1-59116-204-1.

Vol. 15: Waltz. 2004. 184pp. 1-59116-349-8.

Vol. 16: Nocturne. 2004. 184pp. 1-59116-596-2.

Vol. 17: Suite. 2005. 184pp. 1-59116-682-9.

Vol. 18: Inversion. 2005. 176pp. 1-59116-782-5.

Yu-Gi-Oh! Written and illustrated by Kazuki Takahashi. VIZ Media, LLC, 2003– . **T Japanese manga. 🐾 Japanese manga.** あ

Tenth-grader Yugi has always loved puzzles. There's never been a time when he wasn't solving games at his grandfather's puzzle shop. He decides to finally finish the unsolvable Millennium Puzzle, an ancient Egyptian puzzle that has been rumored to contain the spirit of a master gambler and that gives the solver of the puzzle the powers and knowledge of darkness. After Yugi sets the final piece, he is possessed by the so-called King of Games and sets out to play a duel of Shadow Games with those who are evil. He and his new friends Honda, Jonouchi, and Anzu become embroiled in a new high-stakes card game that is played with monsters who come to life, played against Seto Kaiba, a rich and arrogant fellow high school student. When all is said and done, there can only be one King of Games. The series was continued in 2005, with the series title changing to <u>Yu-Gi-Oh! Duelist</u> and <u>Yu-Gi-Oh! Millennium World</u>.

Vol. 1. 2003. 192pp. 1-56931-903-0.

Vol. 2. 2003. 200pp. 1-59116-081-2.

Vol. 3. 2003. 200pp. 1-59116-179-7.

Vol. 4. 2004. 200pp. 1-59116-185-1.

Vol. 5. 2004. 200pp. 1-59116-324-2.

Vol. 6. 2004. 200pp. 1-59116-471-0.

Vol. 7. 2004. 200pp. 1-59116-613-6.

<u>Yu-GI-Oh! Duelist.</u>

Vol. 1. 2005. 200pp. 1-59116-614-4.

Vol. 2. 2005. 208pp. 1-59116-716-7.

Vol. 3. 2005. 216pp. 1-59116-771-X.

Vol. 4. 2005. 208pp. 1-59116-759-0.

Vol. 5. 2005. 200pp. 1-59116-811-2.

Vol. 6. 2005. 208pp. 1-59116-856-2.

Vol. 7. 2005. 208pp. 1-59116-877-5.

Vol. 8. 2005. 224pp. 1-59116-998-4.

Vol. 9. 2005. 208pp. 1-4215-0052-3.

Vol. 10. 2005. 200pp. 1-4215-0078-7.

Vol. 11. 2005. 200pp. 1-4215-0150-3.

Vol. 12. 2006. 208pp. 1-4215-0207-0.

Vol. 13. 2006. 208pp. 1-4215-0277-1.

Vol. 14. 2006. 208pp. 1-4215-0339-5.

Vol. 15. 2006. 208pp. 1-4215-0408-1.

<u>Yu-Gi-Oh!: Millennium World.</u>

Vol. 1. 2005. 192pp. 1-59116-878-3.

Vol. 2. 2005. 192pp. 1-4215-0151-1.
Vol. 3. 2006. 208pp. 1-4215-0409-X.

Dark Fantasy

An overshadowing, almost gothic darkness sets the mood for these atmospheric stories. Realms of angels, demons, and faerie can all interact with the protagonist, and magic is the overall presiding force at work. This subgenre is closely akin to horror and can often be indistinguishable from it. Standout titles in this subgenre include Neil Gaiman's <u>Sandman</u> series.

<u>Angel Sanctuary.</u> Written and illustrated by Kaori Yuki. VIZ Media, LLC, 2004– . **O Japanese manga.** あ

Setsuna is definitely not your average teenager, and his life has just become a little more complex. He's madly in love with a woman near and dear to him—his own sister! As disturbing as that is, Setsuna also has discovered that he's the reincarnation of a rebellious female angel named Alexial, who it was foretold would cleanse Earth of humans. Are these two issues related to some darker past? Setsuna is finding it harder and harder to separate the good and the evil in this world, as friends are turning into deadly enemies and those he considered enemies are offering help. Allied with a pair of demons whom Alexial saved millennia ago, he's out to stop a mad angel from distributing a deadly computer game called "Angel Sanctuary," which will have deadly consequences for humanity should the game be released. The series was collected in twenty volumes in Japan and was adapted into an anime series as well.

Vol. 1. 2004. 192pp. 1-59116-245-9.
Vol. 2. 2004. 192pp. 1-59116-312-9.
Vol. 3. 2004. 192pp. 1-59116-392-7.
Vol. 4. 2004. 192pp. 1-59116-495-8.
Vol. 5. 2004. 192pp. 1-59116-576-8.
Vol. 6. 2005. 200pp. 1-59116-627-6.
Vol. 7. 2005. 200pp. 1-59116-745-0.
Vol. 8. 2005. 200pp. 1-59116-799-X.
Vol. 9. 2005. 200pp. 1-59116-862-7.
Vol. 10. 2005. 200pp. 1-4215-0058-2.
Vol. 11. 2005. 200pp. 1-4215-0126-0.
Vol. 12. 2006. 208pp. 1-4215-0259-3.
Vol. 13. 2006. 208pp. 1-4215-0389-1.
Vol. 14. 2006. 208pp. 1-4215-0520-7.
Vol. 15. 2006. 208pp. 1-4215-0521-5.
Vol. 16. 2006. 208pp. 1-4215-0522-3.
Vol. 17. 2006. 208pp. 1-4215-0523-1.
Vol. 18. 2007. 200pp. 1-4215-0976-8.
Vol. 19. 2007. 200pp. 1-4215-0977-6.

Aria. **Written by Brian Holguin. Illustrated by Jay Anacleto and Lan Medina.** Image Comics, 2000–2004. **M**

> Lady Killdare, a magical being from the land of Faerie, would much prefer spending her immortal days in New York City, but a killer of immortals may change that. Elegantly drawn. The second volume delves into the mystery that beckons Killdare back to the Faerie realm.
>
> > *Vol. 1: The Magic of Aria.* 2001. 140pp. 1-58240-139-X.
> > *Vol. 2: The Soulmarket.* 2002. 144pp. 1-58240-339-2.
> > *Vol. 3: The Uses of Enchantment.* 2004. 144pp. 1-58240-361-9.

Berserk. **Written and illustrated by Kentaro Miura.** Dark Horse Comics, 2003– . **M Japanese manga.** あ

> When demons and their ilk begin to destroy the medieval land of Midland and terrorize the countryside, only a fearless lone warrior named Guts, alias the Black Swordsman, is tough enough to take on the monsters and send them back to Hell in a casket. Carrying his long black sword and wearing the scars of many bloody battles and a rough and abusive upbringing, Guts is the only one capable of taking the beasts down, even if the cost is his own soul. Reluctantly accompanied by the wisecracking but kind fairy named Puck, he roams the land in search of the beasts, which shed innocent blood, and no one will stand in Guts' way as he walks the path of death, mutilation, and destruction. Thirty-one volumes have been published to date in Japan. The manga was adapted into an anime series that aired from 1997 to 1998 in Japan.
>
> > *Vol. 1.* 2003. 224pp. 1-59307-020-9.
> > *Vol. 2.* 2004. 240pp. 1-59307-021-7.
> > *Vol. 3.* 2004. 240pp. 1-59307-022-5.
> > *Vol. 4.* 2004. 240pp. 1-59307-203-1.
> > *Vol. 5.* 2004. 240pp. 1-59307-251-1.
> > *Vol. 6.* 2005. 224pp. 1-59307-252-X.
> > *Vol. 7.* 2005. 232pp. 1-59307-328-3.
> > *Vol. 8.* 2005. 232pp. 1-59307-329-1.
> > *Vol. 9.* 2005. 240pp. 1-59307-330-5.
> > *Vol. 10.* 2006. 240pp. 1-59307-331-3.
> > *Vol. 11.* 2006. 240pp. 1-59307-470-0.
> > *Vol. 12.* 2006. 232pp. 1-59307-484-0.
> > *Vol. 13.* 2006. 240pp. 1-59307-500-6.
> > *Vol. 14.* 2006. 240pp. 1-59307-501-4.
> > *Vol. 15.* 2007. 240pp. 1-59307-577-4.

The Books of Faerie. **Written by Bronwyn Carlton and John Ney Rieber. Illustrated by Peter Gross.** Vertigo/DC Comics, 1998–1999. **M**

> The lives of the Faerie are revealed in two volumes that serve as companion books to the Books of Magic series. In the first collection, Titania, Queen of the Faerie realm, reflects on her life and thinks back to how as a young mortal girl she became the Queen of the Faeries. The second collection focuses on the early life of Auberon. Both volumes feature a Tim Hunter short story at the end of the collection.
>
> > *The Books of Faerie.* 1998. 144pp. 1-56389-401-7.
> > *The Books of Faerie: Auberon's Tale.* 1999. 128pp. 1-56389-502-1.

The Books of Magic. Vertigo/DC Comics, 1993–2005. **M**

Tim Hunter will someday be the most powerful wizard of all—if he chooses to. To help him decide, four of DC Comics' mages—the Phantom Stranger, Dr. Occult, Mister E, and John Constantine—form a "trenchcoat brigade" and show Tim the many worlds of magic and the wonders that await him if he accepts his destiny. Written by award-winning author Neil Gaiman and featuring the art of Charles Vess, John Bolton, and others. The continuing adventures of Tim Hunter as he learns the ways of magic were collected in several series from Vertigo, listed below, including The Books of Magic (1994–2002), The Names of Magic, and the most recent series, called The Books of Magick (2005–present). The issues are listed below in chronological order.

The Books of Magic. **Written by Neil Gaiman. Illustrated by various.** Vertigo/DC Comics, 1993, 196pp. 1-56389-082-8. **M**

 **The Books of Magic. Written by Jon Rey Nieber. Illustrated by various.** Vertigo/DC Comics, 1994–2002. **M**

The continuing adventures of 14-year-old Tim Hunter, following the original series by Neil Gaiman. The collection *Bindings* received recognition by YALSA's Popular Paperbacks for Young Adults committee in 1997.

Vol. 1: Bindings. 1995. 112pp. 1-56389-187-5.
Vol. 2: Summonings. 1996. 240pp. 1-56389-265-0.
Vol. 3: Reckonings. 1997. 192pp. 1-56389-321-5.
Vol. 4:Transformations. 1998. 128pp. 1-56389-417-3.
Vol. 5: Girl in the Box. 1999. 192pp. 1-56389-539-0.
Vol. 6: The Burning Girl. 2000. 224pp. 1-56389-619-2.
Vol. 7: Death After Death. 2001. 232pp. 1-56389-740-7.

The Books of Magick: Life During Wartime Book 1. **Written by Si Spencer. Illustrated by Dean Ormston.** Vertigo/DC Comics, 2005. 128pp. 1-4012-0488-0. **M**

Fifteen months after the events in *The Names of Magic*, war has been started on Earth between the Bred (humans who acquired magic) led by John Constantine, and the Born (magical beings who serve Titania, the faerie queen). When a coalition of humanity places their faith in Tim Hunter, he's nowhere to be found. He is in a self-created parallel Earth, where magic doesn't exist and he has no memory of his destiny.

The Names of Magic. **Written by Dylan Horrocks. Illustrated by Richard Case.** Vertigo/DC Comics, 2002. 128pp. 1-56389-888-8. **M**

Tim Hunter, fourteen-year-old sorcerer-in-training, travels to the land of Faerie to discover his origin and his true name. His quest is soon in peril when a league of wizards aim to capture him and use his power for their sinister purposes. This volume chronologically takes places after the events of *Books of Magic, Volume 7: Death After Death.*

🏮 **Courtney Crumrin.** **Written and illustrated by Ted Naifeh.** Oni Press, 2002–2004. **T**
◎

© 2006 Ted Naifeh.

Courtney isn't like all those stuck-up girls who like to play with their dolls and talk about fashion and boys—she likes the creepier side of things. When she and her family move in with her elderly Uncle Aloysius in his old mansion, she's bored silly. She hates the town and the kids at school, and misses her old life. But after meeting the odd denizens of the Night Things, a dark world that her uncle is quite familiar with, where witches, fairies, trolls, werewolves, and other monsters roam, the precocious twelve-year-old Goth finds that maybe things aren't so bad here after all. *Courtney Crumrin and the Night Things* received recognition from YALSA's Popular Paperbacks for Young Adults committee in 2005 on the "Own Your Freak" list.

> *Vol. 1: Courtney Crumrin and the Night Things.* 2002. 128pp. 1-929998-60-0.
> *Vol. 2: Courtney Crumrin and the Coven of Mystics.* 2003. 128pp. 1-929998-59-7.
> *Vol. 3: Courtney Crumrin in the Twilight Kingdom.* 2004. 128pp. 1-932664-01-7.

Darkblade. **Written by Dan Abnett. Illustrated by Kev Hopgood.** Black Library, 2000–2003. **O**

A dark elf from the harsh realm of Naggaroth, Malus Darkblade, and his clan's ancestors broke off from the Elven land of Ulthuan 5,000 years ago following a civil war. Raised in a vicious land, Malus and his elven brothers are not the noble elves of legend. They are dark, twisted, and vicious fighters who live and die by the sword, and Malus is the most cunning of them all. Riding astride his dinosaurlike mount, Malus scours the land in his quest for treasure and to battle the daemons that roam the dark realm.

> *Book I: Born of Blood.* 2000. 108pp. 1-84154-124-9.
> *Book II: World of Blood.* 2001. 96pp. 1-84154-147-8.
> *Book III: Throne of Blood.* 2003. 96pp. 1-84154-241-5.

Death: At Death's Door. **Written and illustrated by Jill Thompson.** Vertigo/DC Comics, 2003. 192pp. 1-56389-938-8. **T Neo-manga.**

The Endless entities known as Death, Delirium, and Despair, sisters of Dream, must find a way to keep the dead from coming out after the gates of Hell are opened. Set during the <u>Sandman</u> story line "Season of Mists," in which Dream receives the key to Hell, this manga-style graphic novel is a funny look at what the Sandman's sisters did to save the world from the undead, drawn in a manga style by Jill Thompson.

🏮 ***Death: The High Cost of Living.*** **Written by Neil Gaiman. Illustrated by Chris Bachalo, Mark Buckingham, and Dave McKean.** Vertigo/DC Comics, 1994. 104pp. 1-56389-133-6. **M** ◎

In this spin-off of Neil Gaiman's award-winning <u>Sandman</u> series, Dream's older sister Death takes the spotlight. In between the here and the hereafter, each century she walks the earth for one day to better understand those whom she must take. In the guise of a girl named Didi, she helps Mad Hattie, a 250-year-old homeless woman, find her missing heart. The collection received recognition from YALSA's Popular Paperbacks for

Young Adults committee in 2002 on the "Graphic Novels: Superheroes and Beyond" list.

***Death: The Time of Your Life*. Written by Neil Gaiman. Illustrated by Chris Bachalo, Mark Buckingham, and others.** Vertigo/DC Comics, 1997. 96pp. 1-56389-333-9. **M**

Death of the Endless intervenes in the life of a rising music star who is wrestling with revealing her sexual orientation to the world just as her lover is lured into the realm of Death.

© 2006 DC Comics.

<u>**The Demon Ororon.**</u> **Written and illustrated by Mizuki Hakase.** TOKYOPOP, 2004. **T Japanese manga.**

Chiaki is the fifteen-year-old orphaned daughter of the archangel Michael and a human woman. Being half angel, she's been ostracized by Heaven for her father's affair and is finding that there are many out there who want her dead. Secluded in her home, she finds comfort in Ororon, the son of the Devil Lord Oz. An outcast as well, Ororon is the youngest of his father's demon children and a threat to his other brothers, who seek the crown of Hell. One a powerful fighter and the other a powerful listener, Chiaki and Ororon have a lot to learn about each other. Maybe a demon can learn what makes life so precious and a half-angel can learn a thing or two from a demon. When the armies and assassins of Heaven come to eliminate Chiaki, there's no person better for the job of protecting her than a powerful young demon from Hell. Can Ororon learn something from a pacifist half-angel?

Vol. 1. 2004. 240pp. 1-59182-725-6.
Vol. 2. 2004. 208pp. 1-59182-726-4.
Vol. 3. 2004. 200pp. 1-59182-727-2.
Vol. 4. 2004. 232pp. 1-59182-728-0.

<u>**The Dreaming.**</u> **Written by Caitlin Kiernan, Peter Hogan and Jeff Nicholson. Illustrated by Peter Doherty, Jeff Nicholson, and others.** Vertigo/DC Comics, 1998–1999. **M**

Following the completion of Neil Gaiman's <u>The Sandman</u> (see entry in this chapter), DC Comics published a spin-off comic book series focusing on the denizens of the mystical realm of *The Dreaming*. The series focused on a variety of popular characters, including Merv Pumpkinhead, the Corinthian, Matthew the Raven, Lucien, and Cain and Abel, and was collected in two volumes.

Beyond the Shores of Night. 1998. 208pp. 1-56389-393-2.
Through the Gates of Horn & Ivory. 1999. 224pp. 1-56389-493-9.

Evenfall. Written and illustrated by Pete Stathis. Amaze Ink/Slave Labor Graphics. 2004. **O**

© 2006 Pete Stathis.

Feeling lost and alone following the death of her mother, and hating her job as an apartment building superintendent, nineteen-year-old Phoebe Shankar has dreams of a world in which her mother is still alive, but when she wakes, the pain and loneliness continue to torment her until something really strange happens. Now Phoebe is shifting back and forth between reality and a mystical realm that combines her memories and fantasy. Is Phoebe really in a supernatural/fantasy realm, or is this dark, monster-filled alternate-reality world that she keeps falling in and out of just a product of her imagination?.

Vol. 1: Lay Me Down. 2004. 96pp. 0-943151-86-4.

Gloom Cookie. Written by Serena Valentino. Illustrated by Ted Naifeh and various. Slave Labor Graphics, 2001– . **O**

Dressed all in black, Goth girl Lex is a wreck when it comes to true love. When love does unexpectedly come her way, he actually is a monster—a gargoyle who has loved Lex in many other past lives and who has been cursed by the demonic dark queen Isabella. Meanwhile, a young Goth boy named Chrys discovers more about his mysterious past and his connections to Isabella and a freakish traveling circus. Welcome to a world of gothic despair, unrequited love, black humor, bad Goth poetry, and spooky monsters under the bed.

Vol. 1. 2001. 240pp. 0-943151-34-1.
Vol. 2. 2002. 224pp. 0-943151-61-9.
Vol. 3. 2004. 144pp. 0-943151-88-0.
Vol. 4. 2005. 208pp. 1-59362-022-5.

King of Hell. Written by Ra In-Soo. Illustrated by Kim Jae-Hwan. TOKYOPOP, 2003–. **T Korean manhwa.**

When a rift between Hell and the mortal world is opened, the spirits of the underworld have been unleashed on Earth to torture and haunt the living. In order to right this wrong, the King of Hell sends Majeh, the greatest swordsman in the underworld and formerly of Earth, to capture the evil spirits before the rifts are permanently opened. His role changing from reaper of souls to capturer of demon spirits, the 300-year-old Majeh is joined on his quest to cleanse our world from evil by the boy Chung-Poong and the mooching young woman Dohwa Baik. Meanwhile, on Earth the body of Majeh is guarded by his mortal lover as it is peacefully submerged in an enchanted lake. Will he be reunited with his long-preserved body, and how will it affect his mission for the King of Hell?

Vol. 1. 2003. 192pp. 1-59182-187-8.
Vol. 2. 2003. 192pp. 1-59182-188-6.
Vol. 3. 2003. 192pp. 1-59182-189-4.
Vol. 4. 2004. 192pp. 1-59182-482-6.
Vol. 5. 2004. 192pp. 1-59182-483-4.
Vol. 6. 2004. 192pp. 1-59182-484-2.
Vol. 7. 2004. 200pp. 1-59182-867-8.

Vol. 8. 2005. 200pp. 1-59182-914-3.

Vol. 9. 2005. 192pp. 1-59532-597-2.

Vol. 10. 2005. 192pp. 1-59532-598-0.

Vol. 11. 2005. 192pp. 1-59816-059-1.

Vol. 12. 2006. 192pp. 1-59816-060-5.

Vol. 13. 2006. 192pp. 1-59816-061-3.

Vol. 14. 2006. 208pp. 1-59816-867-3.

Vol. 15. 2007. 192pp. 1-59816-868-1.

Legends from Darkwood. Written by Christopher Reid. Illustrated by John Kantz. Antarctic Press, 2004– . **T Neo-manga.**

The fairy tale land called Unicorn Town is known for serving a special delicacy that is available nowhere else in the land: unicorn meat! Now the town is on the map, prosperous and wealthy thanks to the ingenious decision by the mayor to find a way to hunt and harvest this special creature with the aid of the virtuous hunter called Raynd. When the mayor's daughter, the young and also virtuous Rose, witnesses the violent demise of a unicorn at the hands of Raynd, will she still follow in her father's footsteps and become the next unicorn hunter? Meanwhile, a reporter finds the true origin of Unicorn Town, and a male unicorn makes a deal with the devil to defeat Raynd.

© 2006 Antarctic Press.

Pocket Manga Vol. 1. 2004. 142pp. 1-932453-49-0.

Lucifer. Written by Mike Carey. Illustrated by Scott Hampton, Peter Gross, and various. Vertigo/DC Comics, 2001–2007. **M**

A smart and well-written spin-off from the events in Neil Gaiman's award-winning <u>Sandman</u> series (see entry). Lucifer Morningstar, the former Lord of Hell, is called back from semiretirement by Heaven and is promised a prize of his own choosing upon completion of a task that only he can accomplish. The Prince of Darkness's request for the completion of the task rocks the foundations of Heaven and Hell and reignites Lucifer's role in the universe.

Vol. 1: Devil in the Gateway. 2001. 160pp. 1-56389-733-4.

Vol. 2: Children and Monsters. 2002. 208pp. 1-56389-800-4.

Vol. 3: A Dalliance with the Damned. 2002. 160pp. 1-56389-892-6.

Vol. 4: The Divine Comedy. 2003. 192pp. 1-40120-009-5.

Vol. 5: Inferno. 2004. 168pp. 1-4012-0210-1.

Vol. 6: Mansions of the Silence. 2004. 144pp. 1-4012-0249-7.

Vol. 7: Exodus. 2005. 168pp. 1-4012-0491-0.

Vol. 8: The Wolf Beneath the Tree. 2005. 160pp. 1-4012-0502-X.

Vol. 9: Crux. 2006. 168pp. 1-4012-1005-8.

Vol. 10: Morningstar. 2006. 192pp. 1-4012-1006-6.

Vol. 11: Evensong. 2007. 224pp. 1-4012-1200-x.

🐾 *Michael Moorcock's Elric: Stormbringer.* **Adapted by P. Craig Russell with Neil Gaiman, based on the story by Michael Moorcock. Illustrated by P. Craig Russell.** Dark Horse Comics, 1998. 224pp. 1-56971-336-7. **T**

> Michael Moorcock's pale warrior and the last emperor of Melniboné, Elric, lives again in this adaptation of the climactic battle of Law and Chaos. Armed with the deadly runeblade called Stormbringer, Elric is caught in a penultimate battle between Law and Chaos and must destroy his enemies with his soul-swallowing sword before he can meet his own fate. The adaptation also features a short story written by <u>Sandman</u> creator Neil Gaiman. The artist, P. Craig Russell, received in Eisner Award in 1998 in the category of Best Artist/Penciller/Inker for his work on this collection and a Harvey Award in 1998 for Best Artist or Penciller.

Murder Mysteries. **Written and illustrated by P. Craig Russell, adapted from the short story by Neil Gaiman.** Dark Horse Comics, 2002. 64pp. 1-56971-634-X. **O**

> Adapted from the short story by Neil Gaiman. An elderly man recounts an old tale to a young Englishman while sharing a park bench in the city of Los Angeles. Borrowing a cigarette from the young man, he tells him a story of God's city of angels and the first death that ever occurred. Raguel, the Angel of Vengeance, is sent to investigate the brutal murder of the angel Carasel, who was in charge of handling the concept of death. The angel was stabbed in the back, and God has assigned Raguel to discover who committed the crime. Like any good crime detective, Raguel questions several suspects, including the angels Seraquel, Phanuel, and Lucifer, the Captain to the Host, to solve the crime. Will the Angel of Vengeance be able to exact revenge, or was the murder of Carasel preordained by someone in the city of angels?

🐾 <u>**PhD: Phantasy Degree.**</u> **Written and illustrated by Son Hee-Joon.** TOKYOPOP, 2005– . **T Korean manhwa.**

> There exists a Demon School Hades, a place where young monsters learn how to scare humans. Four slacker students skipping school—Dev, a demon with small horns; Mordicus, the half-blood vampire; Lukan the werewolf; and Pannus the mummy—encounter a spunky human girl named Sang. She wants to join the school any way possible, but the school's policy is strictly not for humans. She agrees to have Mordicus turn her into a vampire, and afterward she's welcomed into the halls of Demon School Hades. Before long she sees what it's like for demons, when she and her new friends are bullied by an older group of more powerful demon students, and a mysterious cult of humans called the Madosa Guild attack the school. The leader of the group recognizes Sang—is there more to this newly transformed vampire girl than meets the eye? The series received recognition from YALSA's Quick Picks for Reluctant Readers committee on the 2006 list. Ten volumes have been published in Korea to date.
>
> > *Vol. 1.* 2005. 192pp. 1-59532-319-8.
> > *Vol. 2.* 2005. 192pp. 1-59532-320-1.
> > *Vol. 3.* 2005. 192pp. 1-59532-321-X.
> > *Vol. 4.* 2005. 192pp. 1-59532-322-8.
> > *Vol. 5.* 2006. 192pp. 1-59532-323-6.
> > *Vol. 6.* 2006. 192pp. 1-59532-324-4.
> > *Vol. 7.* 2006. 192pp. 1-59532-325-2.

★ Promethea. Written by Alan Moore. Illustrated by J. H. Williams III. America's Best Comics/WildStorm Productions/DC Comics, 2000–2006. **O**

Drawn into the mystery of the mythical warrior called Promethea, college student Sophie Bangs uncovers its secret and is magically transformed into Promethea, the living embodiment of imagination. One in a long line of women bonded through the magical realm called the Immateria, she must learn to focus her power and to fight the ancient evil that has plagued Prometheas before her for centuries. The short story "Sex, Stars, and Serpents" (collected in *Volume 2*) received an Eisner Award for the category Best Single Issues/Best Short Story. The series also won a Harvey Award for Best Writer in 2001 and 2003. *Book 1* received recognition from YALSA's Popular Paperbacks for Young Adults committee in 2002 on the "Graphic Novels: Superheroes and Beyond" list.

© 2006 America's Best Comics.

> *Collected Edition Book 1.* 2000. 176pp. 1-56389-667-2, hardcover; 2001, 176pp. 1-56389-667-2, softcover.
> *Collected Edition Book 2.* 2001. 176pp. 1-56389-784-9, hardcover; 2003, 1-56389-957-4, softcover.
> *Collected Edition Book 3.* 2000. 160pp. 1-56389-655-9, hardcover; 2003, 1-4012-0094-X, softcover.
> *Collected Edition Book 4.* 2003. 192pp. 1-4012-0032-X, hardcover; 2005, 1-4012-0031-1, softcover.
> *Collected Edition Book 5.* 2005. 200pp. 1-4012-0619-0, hardcover; 2006, 1-4012-0620-4, softcover.

★ The Sandman. Written by Neil Gaiman. Illustrated by various. Vertigo/ DC Comics, 1991–1999. **M** ◉

Dream, the lord of the mystical dream realm we all share at night time (aptly called "The Dreaming") , is one of the few godlike beings known as The Endless. His brothers and sisters are Death, Destruction, Delirium, Destiny, Despair, and Desire. Morpheus, as Dream is also called, rebuilds his realm after a 100-year imprisonment and then takes the path of redemption, rescuing his once-beloved from Hell and saving his only son, Orpheus, from a fate far worse than death. All the while other sacrifices are made, hard decisions are handed down, and Dream must make a choice in the end that will shake his realm. Gaiman's series is a literate and groundbreaking exercise in story telling and one of the most highly praised graphic novel series published. The series was originally published in comic book form from 1989 to 1995. It has won numerous awards and recognition, including Eisner Awards for Best Continuing Series (1991–1993), Best Single Issue/Single Story (1992), Best Graphic Album—Reprint (1991) for *The Doll's House*, and Best Writer (1991–1994) and Best Artist/Penciller/Inker (1993, 1997) for P. Craig Russell's and Charles Vess's work. The series has also won Harvey Awards for Best Writer (1991–1992) and for Best

© 2006 DC Comics.

Continuing or Limited Series (1993). It has been recognized by YALSA's Popular Paperbacks for Young Adults committee in 1997 for *Dream Country* and *World's End*. Beginning in 2006, DC Comics is reprinting the series in their Absolute hardcover format, which includes new coloring and a slipcase for all four volumes. The first collection reprints the first original twenty comic book issues.

Vol. 1: Preludes and Nocturnes. Illustrated by Sam Kieth, Mike Dringenberg, and Malcolm Jones III. 1998. 256pp. 1-56389-227-8, hardcover; 1993, 1-56389-011-9, paperback.

Vol. 2: The Doll's House. Illustrated by Mike Dringenberg and Malcolm Jones III. 1999. 256pp. 1-56389-225-1, hardcover; 1991, 0-93028-959-5, paperback.

Vol. 3: Dream Country. Illustrated by Kelley Jones, Colleen Doran, Charles Vess, and Malcolm Jones III. 1999. 160pp. 1-56389-226-X, hardcover; 1991, 1-56389-016-X, paperback.

Vol. 4: Season of Mists. Illustrated by Kelley Jones and others. 1999. 224pp. 1-56389-035-6, hardcover; 1994, 1-56389-041-0, paperback.

Vol. 5: A Game of You. Illustrated by Shawn McManus, Colleen Doran and others. 1999. 192pp. 1-56389-093-3, hardcover; 1993, 1-56389-089-5, paperback.

Vol. 6: Fables and Reflections. Illustrated by P. Craig Russell, Bryan Talbot, Shawn McManus, Jill Thompson and others. 1999. 264pp. 1-56389-106-9, hardcover; 1994, 1-56389-105-0, paperback.

Vol. 7: Brief Lives. Illustrated by Jill Thompson and Vince Locke. 1999. 256pp. 1-56389-137-9, hardcover; 1995, 1-56389-138-7, paperback.

Vol. 8: Worlds' End. Illustrated by Mike Allred, Gary Amano, Mark Buckingham, Dick Giordano, Tony Harris, Steve Leialoha, Vince Locke, Shea Anton Pensa, Alec Stevens, Bryan Talbot, John Watkiss, and Michael Zulli. 1999. 168pp. 1-56389-170-0, hardcover; 1995, 1-56389-171-9, paperback.

Vol. 9: The Kindly Ones. Illustrated by Marc Hempel. 1999. 352pp. 1-56389-204-9, hardcover; 1996, 1-56389-205-7, paperback.

Vol. 10: The Wake. Illustrated by Michael Zulli, John J. Muth, and Charles Vess. 1999. 192pp. 1-56389-287-1, hardcover; 1997, 1-56389-279-0, paperback.

Absolute Sandman, Vol. 1. 2007. 612pp. 1-40121-082-1, hardcover.

🏆 ***The Sandman: Endless Nights.*** **Written by Neil Gaiman. Illustrated by various.** 2003. 160pp. 1-40120-089-3 **M** ◉

A collection of short stories, each focusing on a member of The Endless. Features the work of Glenn Fabry, Milo Manara, Dave McKean, Miguelanxo Prado, Frank Quitely, P. Craig Russell, Bill Sienkiewicz, and Barron Storey. Each artist was hand-picked by Neil Gaiman to match the corresponding Endless family member, with breathtaking results. The short story "Death" won several Eisner Awards for Best Short Story and Best Anthology in 2004.

The Sandman Presents. Vertigo/DC Comics, 2003–2005. **M**

A spin-off series of tales that focus on the denizens of the mystical realm of the Dreaming as featured in Neil Gaiman's award-winning <u>The Sandman</u> series. *The Furies* focuses on the character Lyta Hall and what happens to her after her loss in the events of <u>The Sandman</u>. *Taller Tales* includes a variety of short-story collections, including Mervyn Pumpkinhead's role as a James Bond-like secret spy out to save the Dreaming, as well as the adventures of Danny Nod, Heroic Library Assistant. *Thessaly* is the continuing tales of the Thessalian, one of the oldest and most powerful witches and former lover of Dream, as she becomes embroiled in a monster-hunting business with her former nemesis, Fetch.

> *The Furies.* Written by Mike Carey. Illustrated by John Bolton. 2003. 96pp. 1-4012-0093-1.
> *Taller Tales.* Written by Bill Willingham. Illustrated by Shawn McManus and Mark Buckingham. 2003. 224pp. 1-40120-100-8.
> *Thessaly: Witch for Hire.* Bill Willingham. Illustrated by Shawn McManus. 2005. 96pp. 1-4012-0497-X.

Under the Glass Moon. **Written and illustrated by Ya-Seong Ko.** TOKYOPOP, 2003. **O Korean manhwa.**

Luka Reinhardt is this century's greatest dark wizard. Hot-tempered and sometimes cruel, he lives with his shy brother, Luel, who is now an alchemist. Luka and Luel are living next door to a mother-daughter witch family, the beautiful Madame Batolli and her witch-apprentice daughter, eighteen-year-old Nell. The lives of the residents become much more complex when Nell has a crush on Luka, Luel has a crush on Nell, and other players enter the game, including Luka's ex-girlfriend, Sage Claudia Maxillion, who is still determined to marry Luka, as well as Luka's apprentice Neo, in this gothic fantasy with touches of romance, comedy, magic, and mistaken identities. The series is still being published in Korea.

> *Vol. 1.* 2003. 192pp. 1-59182-240-8.
> *Vol. 2.* 2003. 192pp. 1-59182-241-6.

Chapter 5

Crime and Mysteries

Crime and mystery graphic novels feature stories—both fiction and nonfiction—about criminals, police detectives, mysterious cases of murder, disappearances, and much more. Crime and mystery stories have long been some of the most maligned of comic-book genres. In the mid-1950s, along with the horror genre, crime comics were singled out as a possible cause for juvenile delinquency. The claim came from Dr. Frederick Wertham, a noted psychiatrist and author of the notorious anti-comic book nonfiction title *Seduction of the Innocent,* which described the harmful effects of the mass media on children, and the comic book industry was subsequently subjected to a congressional investigation. Despite the accusations that portrayed crime comics as little more than "how to" manuals for murder and mayhem, no clear connection ever was established between reading crime comics and deviant social behavior. After the Comic Code Authority's crackdown on crime and horror titles, the majority of titles slowly faded from popularity, unlike other media, including fictional works, television, and film. Within the last decade, interest in crime comic books has been renewed. With suspenseful titles such as <u>Sin City</u>, *Torso*, <u>100 Bullets</u>, and <u>Gotham Central</u>, the Victorian age true crime stories by Rick Geary, and many more, it seems that the crime genre is back in full form and here to stay.

Detectives

These crime stories focus on the police departments, detectives, and special crime units that take on criminal elements, showing how they solve cases and catch ruthless criminals with finesse, brute force, or any other means necessary. As in mystery fiction, the emphasis here is generally on the character of a single detective or team of investigators.

Professional Detectives and Police Officers

Public investigators and city police forces that take on the criminal element play central roles in these stories. The focus may be on several partners in a police department, a specific division of the police department, or a single detective investigating a case.

Banana Fish. 2d ed. Written and illustrated by Akimi Yoshida. VIZ Media, LLC, 2004– . **O Japanese manga.**

In New York City in the 1980s, Ash was adopted years ago by crime lord "Papa" Dino Golzine after his brother died in Vietnam and Ash was surviving on the streets as a runaway. Now Ash is heir to the crime syndicate but wants nothing of that life. He is on the run from the mafia and his past life after discovering that his brother's death is linked to "Papa" and the mysterious mind-controlling drug called banana fish. Meanwhile, a young photographer from Japan named Eiji Okamura has befriended Ash and gets caught up in the cycle of violence. Can they make it out before it's too late? Nineteen volumes of this Shonen-ai (girls' boy-boy light romance) manga were originally published in Japan.

> *Vol. 1.* 2004. 200pp. 1-56931-972-3.
> *Vol. 2.* 2004. 192pp. 1-56931-973-1.
> *Vol. 3.* 2004. 192pp. 1-59116-106-1.
> *Vol. 4.* 2004. 192pp. 1-59116-133-9.
> *Vol. 5.* 2004. 200pp. 1-59116-417-6.
> *Vol. 6.* 2005. 192pp. 1-59116-418-4.
> *Vol. 7.* 2005. 192pp. 1-59116-419-2.
> *Vol. 8.* 2005. 200pp. 1-59116-420-6.
> *Vol. 9.* 2005.192pp. 1-59116-863-5.
> *Vol. 10.* 2005. 192pp. 1-4215-0048-5.
> *Vol. 11.* 2005. 192pp. 1-4215-0134-1.
> *Vol. 12.* 2006. 208pp. 1-4215-0260-7.
> *Vol. 13.* 2006. 208pp. 1-4215-0390-5.
> *Vol. 14.* 2006. 208pp. 1-4215-0524-X.
> *Vol. 15.* 2006. 208pp. 1-4215-0525-8.
> *Vol. 16.* 2006. 208pp. 1-4215-0526-6.
> *Vol. 17.* 2006. 208pp. 1-4215-0527-4.
> *Vol. 18.* 2007. 192pp. 1-4215-0876-1.
> *Vol. 19.* 2007. 192pp. 1-4215-0877-X.

Complex City: All in a Day's Work. **Written and illustrated by J. E. Smith.** Better Comics, 2003. 120pp. 0-9728070-0-4. **T**

Complex City is no ordinary city, and the number one crime-fighter in it is no ordinary cop, either. The streets are safe due to Bulldog Malone, a six-foot-tall, cigar-chomping, talking bulldog and the toughest cop on the beat. Also aiding Bulldog are the scientists Fidge Dextro and Dr. Martin Handsome, the super-hero team of Bulletproof and Ubermodel, as well as reporter Rebecca Shultz. Together they're up against the toughest and strangest crimes by vampires, the amphibious-like Shadowling, and an urban-legend vigilante called the Crazy Quilt.

Dead to Rights: Vapor Trails in the Afterglow. **Written by Mike Kennedy. Illustrated by Francisco Paronzini.** Dark Horse Comics, 2002. 64pp. 1-56971-853-9. **M**

> The stories of undercover cop Jack Slate, knee-deep in his mission to fight the crime in seedy Grant City. He's on the run, trying to clear his name and to discover who really murdered his father. A supplemental graphic novel tied in directly with the hit video game of the same name.

<u>FAKE.</u> **Written and illustrated by Sanami Matoh.** TOKYOPOP, 2003–2004. **O Japanese manga.**

> The hit Shonen ai (boy-boy light romance) manga from Japan. NYPD officers Randy "Ryo" MacClean and Dee Laytner are partners at the 27th precinct, where they routinely take care of perps and other dangers every day. Randy is soft-spoken but has a real soft spot for kids, having taken in two of them, including a street punk named Bikky and a young girl named Carol. Dee is charismatic but cocky, dedicated to the ones he cares about,—especially Ryo. Together they're partners on the police force and perhaps a little bit more.
>
> *Vol. 1.* 2003. 216pp. 1-59182-326-9.
> *Vol. 2.* 2003. 216pp. 1-59182-327-7.
> *Vol. 3.* 2003. 192pp. 1-59182-328-5.
> *Vol. 4.* 2003. 176pp. 1-59182-329-3.
> *Vol. 5.* 2004. 192pp. 1-59182-330-7.
> *Vol. 6.* 2004. 200pp. 1-59182-331-5.
> *Vol. 7.* 2004. 168pp. 1-59182-332-3.

🌶 <u>Gotham Central.</u> **Written by Greg Rucka and Ed Brubaker. Illustrated by Michael Lark and various.** DC Comics, 2004– . **T** ◎

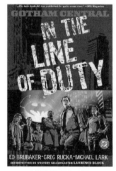

© 2006 DC Comics.

> Batman may get all the glory as the defender of corrupt Gotham City, but the Gotham City Police Department is there to help clean up. Led by Commissioner Akins and his Major Crimes Unit commander Maggie Sawyer, the streets are kept safe with the aid of dedicated officers including Detectives Renee Montoya and Harvey Bullock. They inevitably find themselves on the lookout for some of Batman's villains, including a deadly Mr. Freeze, the pyrotechnic Firebug, and The Penguin. In *Volume 2,* Montoya's past comes back to haunt her while trying to take in a common drug lord, and the secret that he spills about her may cost her her career when he ends up murdered. *Half a Life* received an Eisner Award in 2004 for Best Serialized Story, a Harvey Award in 2004 for Best Single Issue or Story, as well as recognition from YALSA's Popular Paperbacks for Young Adults selection list in 2005.

> *Vol. 1: In the Line of Duty.* 2004. 128pp. 1-4012-0199-7.
> *Vol. 2: Half a Life.* 2005. 168pp. 1-4012-0438-4.
> *Vol. 3: Unresolved Targets.* 2006. 192pp. 1-56389-995-7.
> *Vol. 4: The Quick and the Dead.* 2006. 168pp. 1-4012-0912-2.

Iron Wagon. **Adapted and Illustrated by Jason.** Fantagraphics, 2003. 72pp. 1-56097-541-5. **O**

> In the quiet Norwegian countryside, when game warden Blinde is found dead of an apparent blow to the head, the game is afoot to find out who murdered him. Legend says that it was an "Iron Dragon"—an invisible metal chariot—that claimed the life of old man Gjaernes four years earlier, but Detective Krag thinks it might be something else. When ghosts seemingly come back from the dead to haunt the living and citizens are hiding dark secrets, a culprit will be discovered and truths will be revealed. Based on a novel published over a century ago by Stein Riverton, the book features anthropomorphic characters in the roles of humans.

<u>Kane.</u> **Written and illustrated by Paul Grist.** Image Comics, 2004– . **O**

© 2006 Paul Grist.

> Detective Kane is back on active duty at the New Eden Police Department after shooting his corrupt partner, Dennis Harvey, six months before. Kane is being welcomed back to the 39th Precinct with unopened arms and two bullets with his name engraved on them, because Harvey's friends want revenge. Teamed up with his new partner, Kate Felix, Kane is back on duty and has to watch his back for both his fellow officers and crime boss Oscar Darke, who is running the once vibrant city of New Eden into the ground.
>
> > *Vol. 1: Greetings from New Eden.* 2004. 120pp. 1-58240-340-6.
> > *Vol. 2: Rabbit Hunt.* 2004. 144pp. 1-58240-355-4.
> > *Vol. 3: Histories.* 2004. 144pp. 1-58240-382-1.
> > *Vol. 4: Thirty Ninth.* 2005. 200pp. 1-58240-468-2.
> > *Vol. 5: Untouchable Rico Costas and Other Stories.* 2005. 168pp. 1-58240-551-4.
> > *Vol. 6: Partners.* 2006. 200pp. 1-58240-704-5.

<u>Remote.</u> **Written by Seimaru Amagi. Illustrated by Tetsuya Koshiba.** TOKYOPOP, 2004–2006. **M Japanese manga.**

> Officer Kurumi Ayaki was a distinguished traffic cop before she quit her job. With her upcoming wedding, though, she's been hard-pressed for money and is allowed to return to the police department on one condition: she must work with the reclusive and emotionless Inspector Kouzaburou Himuro in the Special A Class Pending Case Investigation Division, solving unsolvable crimes. Together they tackle the most baffling crimes committed in Japan: serial clown murders, bomb threats, beheadings, and more.
>
> > *Vol. 1.* 2004. 208pp. 1-59182-740-X.
> > *Vol. 2.* 2004. 224pp. 1-59182-741-8.
> > *Vol. 3.* 2004. 224pp. 1-59182-742-6.
> > *Vol. 4.* 2005. 216pp. 1-59532-031-8.
> > *Vol. 5.* 2005. 216pp. 1-59532-032-6.
> > *Vol. 6.* 2005. 216pp. 1-59532-033-4.
> > *Vol. 7.* 2005. 224pp. 1-59532-810-6.
> > *Vol. 8.* 2006. 192pp. 1-59532-811-4.
> > *Vol. 9.* 2006. 240pp. 1-59532-812-2.
> > *Vol. 10.* 2006. 192pp. 1-59532-813-0.

Ruse. **Written by Mark Waid. Illustrated by Butch Guice et al.** CrossGen Comics, 2002–2004. **T**

On the world of Arcadia, a planet similar to our own, in late nineteenth-century Victorian England, batlike gargoyles fly high above the streets of the city called Partington. Master sleuth Simon Archard has become bored with the criminals of the day. A brilliant but abrasive and distant detective able to infer clues from the ordinary to solve crimes, Archard and his assistant, the lovely Emma Bishop, can solve any mystery. When a new nemesis, the striking, raven-haired Baroness Mirando Cross, comes to take control of the city, Archard is invigorated by the challenge she presents, and the game is afoot. When Archard is framed for murder, help is closer than he ever expected: there's more to Emma than he dared dream. She's not some stodgy sidekick—she has the power to stop time. The series was not completed because of CrossGen's bankruptcy in 2004.

> *Vol. 1: Enter the Detective.* 2002. 160pp. 1-931484-19-8.
> *Vol. 2: The Silent Partner.* 2003. 160pp. 1-931484-48-1.
> *Vol. 3: Criminal Intent.* 2004. 160pp. 1-931484-74-0.

Sam and Twitch: The Brian Michael Bendis Collection, Vol. 1. **Written by Brian Michael Bendis. Illustrated by Angel Medina.** Image Comics, 2006. 224pp. 1-58240-583-2. **M**

2006 Todd McFarlane.

New York City detectives Sam Burke and Max "Twitch" Williams have seen a lot of strange cases in their time on the force, but when they investigate the first of many mafia murders in the Sangiacomo mob family, they find something odd left behind at the scene of the crime: four severed thumbs, none belonging to any of the victims. Even more strange, the thumbs are all genetically identical, except that each one is more and more genetically unstable. As the body count rises and more genetically engineered body appendages pop up, Sam and Twitch need to figure out who or what the mysterious Udaku is and what its connection is to a bio-engineered virus, before more innocents die.

Sherlock Holmes Mysteries. **Written by Martin Powell. Illustrated by Seppo Makinen.** Moonstone, 2003–2004. **T**

A collection of Sherlock Holmes's adventures as he faces off against some of the best-known horror characters from literature and folklore, including Dracula, the Invisible Man, and the Loch Ness Monster. In *Volume 1* Dr. Watson and Dr. Van Helsing must prevent Moriarty from unleashing the power of Dracula. In a separate mystery, Holmes is called to Scotland Yard to help solve the riddle of the Invisible Man. In *Volume 2* Holmes encounters the mystic Aleistar Crowley trying to resurrect a long-slumbering evil in Loch Ness as well as battling his own inner demon of drug dependency.

> *Vol. 1.* 2003. 216pp. 0-9721668-6-6.
> *Vol. 2.* 2004. 142pp. 0-9748501-4-4.

The Shield: Spotlight. **Written by Jeff Mariotte. Illustrated by various.** IDW Publishing, 2004. 128pp. 1-932382-23-2. **M** 🖵

Based on the hit television show. When a TV journalist is murdered, the spotlight is turned on the tough cops of the Barn. When Captain Aceveda orders his officers to be on their best behavior, how will this affect Detective Vic Mackey and his corrupt-but-effective Strike Team?

<u>**Steam Detectives.**</u> **Written and illustrated by Kia Asamiya.** VIZ Media, LLC, 1999–2004. **T Japanese manga.** あ

Steam City, a gaslit city powered by steam engines, is overrun by rampant crime committed under the ever-present blanket of mist. Never fear, Detective Narutaki is on the case, solving crimes with help from his assistant, nurse Ling Ling Hsu, and Goriki, a megamaton robot with the brain of Dr. Hsu in him. An orphaned son of a prominent detective, Narutaki is out to save the city and honor his fallen father. With his gang of crime-fighters he takes on criminals such as the Phantom Knight, the Machine Baron, the diabolical Dr. Guilty, steam-powered robots, and more, to help rid the city of evil. The manga series was adapted into a twenty-sixepisode anime series in Japan.

> *Vol. 1.* 1999. 200pp. 1-56931-317-2.
> *Vol. 2.* 1999. 192pp. 1-56931-405-5.
> *Vol. 3.* 2000. 208pp. 1-56931-527-2.
> *Vol. 4.* 2001. 192pp. 1-56931-674-0.
> *Vol. 5.* 2002. 200pp. 1-59116-032-4.
> *Vol. 6.* 2003. 192pp. 1-56931-892-1.
> *Vol. 7.* 2004. 200pp. 1-59116-208-4.
> *Vol. 8.* 2004. 184pp. 1-59116-321-8.

Violent Messiahs: The Book of Job. **Written by Joshua Dysart. Illustrated by Tone Rodriguez.** Image Comics, 2002. 224pp. 1-58240-236-1. **M**

In the isolated city of Rankor Island, police officer Cheryl Major's case involving the masked and nearly invulnerable vigilante known as "Citizen Pain" takes a surprising turn. When "Citizen Pain" tips Major to the latest murder scene, of another high-profile case involving the "Family Man"—a serial killer who murders drug dealing parents and orphans their children—Major discovers that the cases are mysteriously connected. Major finds that Citizen Pain and Family Man are just puppets in a show controlled by a secret organization specializing in genetic manipulation and the future of Rankor Island.

© 2006 Joshua Dysart
and Tone Rodriguez.

🏵 <u>**Whiteout.**</u> **Written by Greg Rucka. Illustrated by Steve Lieber.** Oni Press, 1999–2000. **O** ◎

U.S. Marshall Deputy Carrie Stetko works in the most desolate location on Earth: Antarctica. A year-round resident, she was banished to the South Pole after having killed a prisoner in her custody. When a lone body at the McMurdo Station is discovered and five other men disappear, she's called to investigate the case as a killer walks among them. She's teamed up with a colleague from British Intelligence to find out who did it before the base personnel ship out for winter or the body count rises. In *Whiteout: Melt*, Stetko returns to the South Pole to investigate an explosion at a Russian Research Station and to recapture stolen nuclear missiles before an international incident escalates out of control. The first volume won an Eisner Award in 2000 for Best Finite Series/Best Limited Series

> *Vol. 1.* 1999. 128pp. 0-9667127-1-4.
> *Vol. 2: Melt.* 2000. 128pp. 1-929998-03-1.

Private Detectives

These stories feature a detective-for-hire like those in the classic noir fiction stories by Raymond Chandler and Mickey Spillane. The private detective is generally a tougher type than the typical "armchair detective" (or amateur) and handles tougher crimes in seedier places.

Alias. **Written by Brian Michael Bendis. Illustrated by Bill Sienkiewicz, Michael Gaydos, and various.** MAX/Marvel Comics, 2002–2004. **M** ◎

© 2006 Marvel Comics.

Jessica Jones is barely making a living as a private investigator for her own company Alias Investigations, but it's much more fulfilling than what she used to do. She used to be a small-time super-hero, but she's outgrown the costume and the spotlight and has a hard time dealing with her temper and her super-strengths. Now working out of a crummy office with some of the crummiest cases around, Jessica's taking on jobs that deal with infidelity, missing persons, and more, in the back alleys in a seedier part of the Marvel Universe. Features guest appearances by some of Marvel's heroic characters, including Captain America, Luke Cage, and Daredevil.

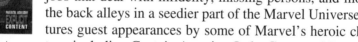

> *Vol. 1.* 2002. 224pp. 0-7851-1141-7.
> *Vol. 2: Come Home.* 2002. 128pp. 0-78511-123-9.
> *Vol. 3: The Underneath.* 2003. 160pp. 0-7851-1165-4.
> *Vol. 4: The Secret Origins of Jessica Jones.* 2004. 176pp. 0-7851-1167-0.
> *Alias Omnibus.* 2006. 720pp. 0-7851-2121-8.

Blacksad. **Written by Juan Diaz Canales. Illustrated by Guarnido.** I Books, Inc., 2003–2004. **M** ◎

Set in an anthropomorphized crime noir setting. Private Investigator John Blacksad, a humanoid black panther, finds that his past has just caught up to him as an old flame, a movie starlet, has been murdered. John decides to get to the bottom of Natalia's murder despite urgings by the police department to drop the case. The hard-boiled alley cat soon uncovers a trail of betrayal, intrigue, sex, and violence. In *Volume 2: Arctic Nation,* John investigates a child's disappearance in a racially divided small town. As tempers flare and a race war erupts, a dark conspiracy is revealed that engulfs the entire town, with John stuck in the middle. *Arctic Nation* received a Harvey Award in 2005 for Best Graphic Album of Original Work.

> *Vol. 1: Somewhere Within the Shadows.* 2003. 56pp. 0-7434-7991-2.
> *Vol. 2: Arctic Nation.* 2004. 56pp. 0-7434-7935-1.

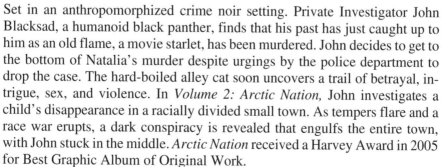

Vol. 3: The Sketch Files. 2005. 96pp. 0-7434-9838-0.

Hawaiian Dick. **Written by B. Clay Moore. Illustrated by Steven Griffen.** Image Comics, 2003–2006. **O** ◎

© 2006 B. Clay Moore.

In 1953 Hawaii, exiled detective Byrd is trying to get over a dark past that drove him to the island with some Mai Tai drinks and odd jobs on the side. When Byrd's been asked to retrieve a stolen car with something very valuable inside, he needs help on the case. Joined by Honolulu detective Mo Kalama, he finds that this is no simple retrieval—it's a kidnapping case involving the girlfriend of the eccentric crime lord Bishop Masaki. Just when things couldn't get any worse, a trip to the psychic Madame Chan, zombies, the ghosts of ancient Hawaiian warriors, and more stand in the way of solving one of the strangest cases Byrd's ever seen. *Volume 1* also collects several short strips originally featured online. In the second volume Byrd is caught between two warring gangs as well as encountering a few ghosts along the way.

Vol. 1: Byrd of Paradise. 2003. 136pp. 1-58240-317-1.
Vol. 2: The Last Resort. 2006. 144pp. 1-5824-0664-2.

Heavy Liquid. **Written and illustrated by Paul Pope.** Vertigo/DC Comics, 2001. 240pp. 1-56389-635-4. **M**

In the late twenty-first century, there's a substance that everyone is out to get, a mysterious metal known as Heavy Liquid. "S," a worn-down former drug agent, small-time criminal, and part-time private investigator, has discovered something special about it: when it's heated into a liquid form and injected into your ear canal, it's an experience that's far better than any drug or alcohol could ever provide. Now hooked on Heavy Liquid, he's caught in the middle of a battle for it. A reclusive art collector wants a sculpture made from it by S's ex-girlfriend, criminals want to use it for its explosive nature, and a government agent knows of its origin. When S's overdose on it reveals the true nature of the substance, is it just a massive hallucination, or has humanity finally made contact with an entity that could be extraterrestrial?

Max Hamm, Fairy Tale Detective. **Written and illustrated by Frank Cammuso.** Nite Owl Comix, 2005. 208pp. 0-9720061-4-1. **T** ◎

The gumshoe adventures of the ace detective in Storybookland, Max Hamm, Fairy Tale Detective. He and his partner, Humpty Dumpty, are the Hamm and Eggs Detective Agency, but when Humpty's egg gets scrambled, it's up to Max to solve the fairy tale crimes alone. Storybookland sounds wonderful, but it's a seedy, 1940-ish town where the Grimm Brothers and Mother Goose fight for control of the crime syndicate, and the damsels in distress are tough. Includes four short stories featuring hard-boiled riffs on Little Bo Peep, Cinderella, and other fairy tale classics. A spoof of the hard-boiled crime dramas and fairy tales.

Pistolwhip. **Written by Matt Kindt and Jason Hall. Illustrated by Matt Kindt.** Top Shelf Productions, 2001–2003. **O**

In typical crime-noir fashion, a triple shoot-out occurs between private eye Mitch Pistolwhip, femme fatale Charlie Minks, and her prey: a carefree European musician named Mr. Vogel. But as the story progresses before and after the shootings of each of the characters, nothing is quite what it seems. Mitch isn't quite the hard-boiled P.I., Mr. Vogel does not exude evil, and Charlie is not quite the femme fatale one would have thought. Meanwhile, a wheel-chair-bound man known only as Pretzel is a witness to the shooting (or is he secretly the mastermind?) and translates it into a ridiculous radio drama. The sequel, *The Yellow Menace,* sees the return of Mitch Pistolwhip trying to make ends meet when events in the fantasy world of radio and comics start occurring in the real world and a famed radio star, the voice actor of radio show action hero Jack Peril, has been murdered in the name of "The Yellow Menace." Soon others are being murdered in real life just as in the comic book stories. Meanwhile, someone claiming to be the real Jack Peril (a fictional character) appears to stop the murders, and Matt realizes that the real world has become a lot more complicated.

> *Vol. 1.* 2001. 128pp. 1-891830-23-6.
> *Vol. 2: The Yellow Menace.* 2003. 144pp. 1-891830-35-X.

Sandman Mystery Theatre. **Written by Matt Wagner. Illustrated by Guy Davis et al.** Vertigo/DC Comics, 1995–2005. **M**

© 2006 DC Comics.

For years Wesley Dodds served as a member of the Justice Society of America as the crime-fighting hero known as the Sandman. A young man tormented by dreams, with the aid of his sleeping gas and gas mask he solves crimes in a gritty New York City in the dangerous 1930s. He's also grown fond of Dian Belmont, a daughter of the district attorney and a natural investigator, and together they take on villains, including The Tarantula, The Face, and others. Written in the style of pulp novels, collected here are mystery tales featuring the Sandman against a backdrop of the changing times reflected in the depiction of the gangland warfare, racism, sexuality, and brutality of the time period.

 5

> *Vol. 1: The Tarantula.* 1995. 112pp. 1-56389-195-6.
> *Vol. 2: The Face and the Brute.* 2004. 208pp. 1-4012-0345-0.
> *Vol. 3: The Vamp.* 2005. 104pp. 1-4012-0718-9.
> *Vol. 4: The Scorpion.* 2006. 104pp. 1-4012-1040-6.

Scene of the Crime: A Little Piece of Goodnight. **Written by Ed Brubaker. Illustrated by Sean Phillips.** Vertigo/DC Comics, 2000. 112pp. 1-56389-670-2. **M**

What started out as a simple missing persons case for private detective Jack Herriman has just become a lot more complicated. When the woman in question ends up murdered, Jack has to revisit some of his personal ghosts and past failures to solve the supposedly simple case and has left a trail of adultery, murder, and revenge.

Amateur Detectives

Mysteries featuring a novice detective protagonist are popular with many fans. Like their mainstay fictional counterparts, amateur detectives can be someone who has stumbled onto a case by accident and tries to solve the mystery, or an up-and-coming detective or detective agency out to prove they can handle any case that co-mes their way. These stories tend to have less in common with traditional "cozies" in fiction due to the visual medium showcasing more action and gore and tend to be more brutal, along the lines of hard-boiled detective novels.

***Batman: Detective No. 27.* Written by Michael Uslan. Illustrated by Peter Snejbjerg.** DC Comics, 2003. 96pp. 1-4012-0185-7. **T**

> A secret society of detectives known only by their numbers is created by legendary detective Allan Pinkerton shortly following the assassination of Abraham Lincoln. Their goal is to fight a secret battle against a nihilist organization called the Knights of the Golden Circle, who have been working for seventy-five years on a plot that began with Lincoln's murder. Flash forward to the late 1920s and a young Bruce Wayne, trained in all the arts to claim revenge for the murder of his parents, is recruited by the secret society. Instead of becoming the legendary Batman, he becomes known as Detective 27 (a play on the first issue that Batman appeared in, *Detective Comics* #27, 1939), and is continuing Pinkerton's legacy to take down the Knights of the Golden Circle. Part of DC Comics Elseworld series, which reinterprets classic DC Comics heroes.

***The Bogie Man.* Written by John Wagner and Alan Grant. Illustrated by Robin Smith.** Paradox Press/DC Comics, 1998. 224pp. 1-56389-450-5. **O**

> Every guy likes to think he's as cool and suave as Humphrey Bogart. When evil lurks in dark alleys, the citizens of Glasgow have nothing to fear since Bogie's still on the case solving crimes and roughing up the criminals. As Bogie searches for the legendary Black Bird and tries to evade the criminal mastermind called the Fat Man, there's just one problem: "Bogie" is really an escaped mental patient named Francis Forbes Clunie, who really does think he's Humphrey Bogart. Too bad for the criminals of the underworld—even if they're all really innocent bystanders—Bogie's back!

***Codeflesh.* Written by Joe Casey and Charlie Adlard. Illustrated by Richard Starkings.** AiT/Planet Lar, 2003. 144pp. 1-932051-15-5. **M**

> A gritty look at what it takes to become a vigilante. Anti-hero Cam Daltrey is a bail bondsman who takes his job a little too seriously. When he severely injures a super-villain who skipped out on his court date, he's court-ordered to stop and proceeds to take out his frustration and anger as the barcode-masked vigilante known as Codeflesh. As both his private and public lives are being destroyed by his crime-fighting, he steps back and sees the villains for what they truly are: individuals with hopes, dreams, responsibilities, and families just like him. Has Cam done the right thing striking back at these people and losing touch with what really matters in life?

The Dare Detectives. Written and illustrated by Ben Caldwell. Dark Horse Comics, 2004–2005. **T**

> Maria Dare is a young and tough reformed crook out to redeem her name. She's created the Dare Detective Agency, a group made up of the oddest assortment of crime-fighters, including Toby, the naive and ignorant muscle, and Jojo, the irritable and sarcastic talking rabbit. Together the energetic team takes on the most bizarre cases in the world. After destroying half the city in their reckless pursuit of the simian criminal Furious George, with their license suspended and rent due, they inadvertently find themselves on a new case chasing Madame Bleu, a new villain with a dastardly

plot to steal the city's supply of snow peas. Can they stop Madame Bleu and her snow pea-swiping gang of abominable snowmen and panda bears before it's too late?

> *Vol. 1: The Snowpea Plot.* 2004. 96pp. 1-59307-176-0.
> *Vol. 2: The Royal Treatment.* 2005. 96pp. 1-59307-340-2.

Deadline. **Written by Bill Rosemann. Illustrated by Guy Davis.** Marvel Comics, 2002. 96pp. 0-7851-1010-0. **O**

Katherine "Kat" Ferrell, a young rookie reporter for the *Daily Bugle,* is tired of covering the beats on "the capes." Writing about super-heroes is not what Kat had in mind as a career. A new front-page story lands in her lap when several random "capes" are found murdered. When the serial killer appears as a ghost-like apparition known as "The Judge," Kat wonders if she will be able to make it out alive, much less make her deadline.

Dodge's Bullets. **Written by Jay Faerber. Illustrated by James Francis.** Image Comics, 2004. 80pp. 1-58240-373-2. **O**

Webster Dodge doesn't want to follow in his father's footsteps and become a police officer—he wants to play music with his rock band. But the gigs aren't coming in, so he reluctantly works a day job as a private eye handling all sorts of odd cases, with his office being a computer terminal at a cyber-café in Seattle. When he's asked by a client to locate his missing father, it's a seemingly easy task . . . until the father ends up missing again. Now Dodge is thrust into a deadly game that might claim more victims unless he solves the case.

5

© 2006 Jay Faerber and James Francis.

Fort: Prophet of the Unexplained! **Written by Peter Lenkow. Illustrated by Frazer Irving.** Dark Horse Comics, 2003. 96pp. 1-56971-781-8. **T**

In the late nineteenth century, when fish fall from the sky and citizens disappear mysteriously, one man is up to the task of saving New York City: mild-mannered librarian Charles Hoy Fort. With the help of a strange visitor from another world, he tries to solve the murders and discover the identity of the killer. An expert researcher on the occult and strange, Charles is the champion for discovering the mysterious truths that are out there.

The Mystery Play. **Written by Grant Morrison. Illustrated by Jon J. Muth.** Vertigo/DC Comics, 1995. 80pp. 1-56389-189-1. **M**

In the recession-riddled English village of Townely, someone has murdered God. In actuality, someone has murdered the actor who plays God in a touring company that interprets stories from the Bible on stage. As police detective Frank Carpenter tries to solve the case, the citizens of Townely are suspects, including the mayor, the reverend, the town reporter, and Satan. Did the Devil really do it? The clues are scattered throughout the dense work. Can you guess the real murderer before the conclusion—or is there really a killer at all?

The Pulse. Written by Brian Michael Bendis. Illustrated by Michael Gaydos. Marvel Comics, 2005– . **T** ◉

© 2006 Marvel Comics.

The continuing adventures of Jessica Jones, the featured character from the book *Alias*. With her detective agency closed, Jessica goes to the *Daily Bugle* for a job and is assigned by J. Jonah Jameson to a supplement called "The Pulse," which will focus on the "costumed vigilantes." Jameson doesn't want Jones to write it, that's for top *Bugle* reporter Ben Urich. Instead, she'll be the poster child for the book due to her past as a hero as well as the scoop on her impending pregnancy, (the father is Luke "Power Man" Cage). When a drowned female *Bugle* reporter washes ashore in the waters of Central Park, Jessica, Ben, and young reporter Kat Farrell investigate the case and find that Norman Osborn, the corporate head of Oscorp and archenemy of Spider-Man, is most likely the culprit. Can three reporters bring down the Green Goblin before more innocents are killed?

> *Vol. 1: Into Thin Air.* 2005. 144pp. 0-7851-1332-0.
> *Vol. 2: Secret War.* 2005. 96pp. 0-7851-1478-5.

Rex Mundi. Written by Arvid Nelson. Illustrated by Eric Johnson. Dark Horse Comics, 2006– . **M**

In an alternate version of 1933, where the Catholic Church controls much of Europe with an iron fist, in Paris a secret manuscript entrusted to Father Gerard Martin by the Church has gone missing, and the priest can only turn to his good friend Doctor Julien Saulniere for help. When Father Martin and a prostitute who knew of his secret are found ritualistically murdered, all signs point to something more disturbing than just a common theft: someone or something using magic is behind all of this. Meanwhile, the French government has its own plans for conquest, and Julien discovers the identity of Father Martin's murderer: a white-suited man with magical powers. Meanwhile, the scroll and its secrets are still lost.

> *Vol. 1: The Guardian of the Temple.* 2d ed. 2006. 176pp. 1-59307-652-5.
> *Vol. 2: The River Underground.* 2d ed. 2007. 176pp. 1-59307-682-7.
> *Vol. 3: The Lost Kings.* 2006. 176pp. 1-59307-651-7.

🐛 *Shutterbug Follies.* **Written and illustrated by Jason Little.** Doubleday/Random House, 2002. 160pp. 0-385-50346-6. **O**

Eighteen-year-old Bee has the best job at Mulberry Photo. When you're a photo developer, you can sure see some interesting things that people capture on film. When the Russian shock photographer Oleg Khatchatourian comes in to have his film developed for his exhibit on recent atrocities, Bee finds that the roll of film contains pictures of recently murdered people. Intrigued by Oleg's odd behavior, Bee discovers that one more victim might have paid the price for his shocking exhibit of atrocities: his own wife. Determined to gather the facts before calling the police, Bee and her taxi driving friend Rodney are on the case trying to solve the mystery surrounding the death of Oleg's wife and the shocking truth of how Oleg gets his pictures. In 2003 Jason Little received an Ignatz Award for Outstanding Artist for his work on the graphic novel. The story also received recognition from YALSA's Quick Picks for Reluctant Readers committee as well as the Best Books for Young Adults committee in 2004.

Junior Sleuths

Adults aren't the only ones capable of solving crimes. Listed here are some of the best junior sleuths in print, including adaptations of Nancy Drew and the Hardy Boys and other young detectives. They are listed separately from the amateur detectives subcategory because many of the junior detectives are more skilled at solving the murders and crimes than their adult amateur detective counterparts, and, of course, they're younger.

Case Closed. Written and illustrated by Gosho Aoyama. VIZ Media, LLC, 2004–. **O ◎ Japanese manga.** あ

High school student Jimmy Kudo is an eleventh-grade legend around Japan. He's a brilliant crime-solver, handling disturbing cases that have perplexed the Japanese police. His hero is the fictional creation of Sir Arthur Conan Doyle, the super-sleuth Sherlock Holmes. Like Holmes's character, Jimmy uses the art of deduction and reasoning to be one step ahead of the crime. When he is one day poisoned from behind, the poison doesn't kill him but mysteriously turns him into a grade schooler. The school and police (and Jimmy's would-be girlfriend, Rachel) all believe that Jimmy has vanished. Determined to still fight crime, he takes on the pseudonym Conan Edogawa and continues to live up to his personal hero in his pint-sized adventures with the hopes of one day finding a cure for his condition. The series is a huge hit in Japan, has been collected into over fifty volumes, and has also spawned a hit animated series.

Vol. 1. 2004. 192pp. 1-59116-327-7.
Vol. 2. 2004. 184pp. 1-59116-587-3.
Vol. 3. 2005. 200pp. 1-59116-589-X.
Vol. 4. 2005. 200pp. 1-59116-632-2.
Vol. 5. 2005. 200pp. 1-59116-633-0.
Vol. 6. 2005. 184pp. 1-59116-838-4.
Vol. 7. 2005. 184pp. 1-59116-978-X.
Vol. 8. 2005. 192pp. 1-4215-0111-2.
Vol. 9. 2006. 184pp. 1-4215-0166-X.
Vol. 10. 2006. 194pp. 1-4215-0316-6.
Vol. 11. 2006. 208pp. 1-4215-0441-3.
Vol. 12. 2006. 208pp. 1-4215-0442-1.
Vol. 13. 2006. 208pp. 1-4215-0443-X.
Vol. 14. 2006. 208pp. 1-4215-0444-8.
Vol. 15. 2007. 208pp. 1-4215-0445-6.
Vol. 16. 2007. 192pp. 1-4215-0881-8.
Vol. 17. 2007. 208pp. 1-4215-0882-6.

CLAMP School Detectives. Written and illustrated by CLAMP. TOKYOPOP, 2003. **A Japanese manga.** あ

When the women of Japan are in need of a problem solver, they should look no further than the CLAMP School Elementary Division's Class Chairman, Secretary, and Treasurer. Sixth-grader Nokoru Imonoyama, fifth-grader Suoh Takamura, and fourth-grader Akira Ijyuin, three noble young boys from the prestigious school, are breaking the hearts of all the girls and tackling any crime, unsolved mystery, or injustice done to a damsel in distress. The series was adapted as an anime in Japan.

> *Vol. 1.* 2003. 208pp. 1-59182-294-7.
> *Vol. 2.* 2003. 208pp. 1-59182-295-5.
> *Vol. 3.* 2003. 208pp. 1-59182-296-3.

The Dead Boy Detectives. **Written and illustrated by Jill Thompson.** Vertigo/DC Comics, 2005. 144pp. 1-4012-0313-2. **T ◉ Neo-manga.**

© 2006 DC Comics.

Charles Rowland and Edwin Paine are the ghosts of two young English schoolboys who have a knack for solving crimes. They travel to Chicago at the request of Annika Abernathy, a pretty young schoolgirl at the Chicago International Academy, who wants the ghostly detectives to help solve the mysterious disappearance of her best friend, Elizabeth Parker. Fearing the worst and that some or all of the teachers are behind her disappearance, the boys must infiltrate the all-girls school in drag to get to the bottom of the mystery. Meanwhile, Charles has become rather smitten with Annika. Does a ghost stand a ghost of a chance with a live girl? Features a guest appearance by Neil Gaiman's popular <u>The Sandman</u> character, Death. Charles and Edwin's first appearance is in the <u>The Sandman</u> volume *Season of Mists,* listed in chapter 4.

The Hardy Boys. Written by Scott Lobdell. Illustrated by Lea Hernandez and Daniel Rendon. Papercutz, 2005– . **Y**

Frank and Joe Hardy are America's best teen detectives. Members of a secret organization called ATAC (American Teens Against Crime), there's no mystery they can't solve: stolen art, diamond smuggling skydivers, identity thefts, murders, and more. Now the classic series of teen novels is back in all-new graphic novel stories.

> *Vol. 1: The Ocean of Osyria.* 2005. 96pp. Paperback, 1-59707-001-7; Hardcover 1-59707-005-X.
> *Vol. 2: Identity Theft.* 2005. 96pp. paperback, 1-59707-003-3; hardcover, 1-59707-007-6.
> *Vol. 3: Mad House.* 2005. 96pp. paperback, 1-59707-010-6; hardcover, 1-59707-011-4.
> *Vol. 4: Malled.* 2006. 96pp. paperback, 1-597-07014-9; hardcover, 1-59707-015-7.
> *Vol. 5: Sea You, See Me!.* 2006. 96pp. paperback, 1-59707-022-X ; hardcover, 1-59707-023-8.
> *Vol. 6: Hyde & Shriek.* 2006. 96pp. paperback, 1-59707-028-9; hardcover, 1-59707-029-7.

The Kindaichi Case Files. Written by Kanari Yozaburo. Illustrated by Satoh Fumiya. TOKYOPOP, 2003–2005. **T ◉ Japanese manga. あ**

Hajime Kindaichi is a seventeen-year-old high school student with a knack for solving mysteries even though he's a bit of a slacker. Really no idiot, he's quite a perceptive young man and he's following in the footsteps of his grandfather, Kousuke, a famous Japanese detective, as he assists Inspector Isamu Kenmochi of the local Japanese police department. Each volume contains a separate mystery case in which Hajime, accompanied on occasion by his next-door neighbor and blossoming love interest, Miyuki Nanase, travels to the site of an inexplicable airtight murder and only he can solve the crime. The murders vary from case to case, involving mythological beasts, reality shows, campfire legends, slasher-film fanatics, deadly secrets, and even someone being framed for murder. The hit series from Japan was adapted into a 148-episode anime series.

> *Vol. 1: The Opera House Murders.* 2003. 240pp. 1-59182-354-4.
> *Vol. 2: The Mummy's Curse.* 2003. 256pp. 1-59182-355-2.
> *Vol. 3: Death TV.* 2003. 232pp. 1-59182-356-0.
> *Vol. 4: Smoke and Mirrors.* 2003. 232pp. 1-59182-357-9.
> *Vol. 5: Treasure Isle.* 2004. 224pp. 1-59182-359-5.
> *Vol. 6: The Legend of Lake Hiren.* 2004. 232pp. 1-59182-360-9.
> *Vol. 7: The Santa Slayings.* 2004. 280pp. 1-59182-478-8.
> *Vol. 8: No Noose is Good Noose.* 2004. 288pp. 1-59182-479-6.
> *Vol. 9: The Headless Samurai.* 2004. 288pp. 1-59182-480-X.
> *Vol. 10: Kindaichi the Killer, Part 1.* 2004. 176pp. 1-59182-481-8.
> *Vol. 11: Kindaichi the Killer, Part 2.* 2005. 168pp. 1-59532-695-2.
> *Vol. 12: Playing the Fool.* 2005. 192pp. 1-59532-696-0.

The Mythical Detective Loki Ragnarok. Written and illustrated by Sakura Kinoshita. ADV Manga, 2004–2005. **Y Japanese manga.** あ

The Norse gods of old have been mystically transformed into young Japanese kids. Loki, the god of lies, is now a rather likeable boy detective who still retains the knowledge of his past while running a detective agency from his home. With a keen eye for crime and the criminal mind since he is the god of lies, Loki is a natural at solving crimes and riddles. His son, the giant wolf Fenrir, is now a cute puppy dog, and the muscle-bound god of thunder, Thor, is also a young boy, who carries his hammer, Mjornir, as a bokken. Odin, the lord of the Norse gods who transformed them as a punishment, is not content just to have Loki exiled and will do what he can to cause trouble for him and his friends. The series was adapted into a twenty-six-episode anime series in Japan.

> *Vol. 1.* 2004. 184pp. 1-4139-0055-0.
> *Vol. 2.* 2005. 184pp. 1-4139-0184-0.
> *Vol. 3.* 2005. 184pp. 1-4139-0320-7.
> *Vol. 4.* 2005. 200pp. 1-4139-0324-X.

Nancy Drew. Written by Stefan Petrucha. Illustrated by Sho Murase. Papercutz, 2005– . **Y**

© 2006 NBM Publishing.

Based on the original series created seventy-five years ago by Carolyn Keene, America's favorite girl detective is back. From tackling cases involving urban legends and a stolen child, to a mysterious doll house that predicts murder, there's not a case that Nancy, with the aid of some of her best friends from River Heights, can't handle.

> *Vol. 1: The Demon of River Heights.* 2005. 96pp. paperback, 1-59707-000-9; hardcover, 1-59707-004-1.
> *Vol. 2: Writ in Stone.* 2005. 96pp. paperback, 1-59707-002-5; hardcover, 1-59707-006-8.
> *Vol. 3: The Haunted Dollhouse.* 2005. 96pp. paperback, 1-59707-008-4; hardcover, 1-59707-009-2.

> *Vol. 4: The Girl Who Wasn't There.* 2006. 96pp. paperback, 1-59707-012-2; hardcover, 1-59707-013-0.
>
> *Vol. 5: The Fake Heir.* 2006. 96pp. paperback, 1-59707-024-6; hardcover, 1-59707-025-4.
>
> *Vol. 6: Mr. Cheeters Is Missing.* 2006. 96pp. paperback, 1-59707-030-0;hardcover, 1-59707-031-9.

Zachary Holmes. Written by Carlos Trillo. Illustrated by Juan Bobillo. Dark Horse Comics/Strip Art Features, 2001. **T** ◉

When there's a mystery to be solved there's only one Holmes you should call: kid sleuth Zachary Holmes! He and his faithful assistant, an intelligent mouse named Watson, can take on any case no matter how difficult or dangerous. *Case 1* involves Zachary coming to the defense of the Frankenstein Monster after an apparent rampage through London. Can he, Watson, and his friend Diana find out who really is to blame before it is too late? In *Case 2,* Holmes is charged by the legendary mage Merlin with saving the life of Queen Victoria from the ghost of the sorcerer Lord Moriarty. How can Holmes stop a ghost?

> *Case 1: The Monster.* 2001. 48pp. 1-56971-702-8.
>
> *Case 2: The Sorcerer.* 2001. 48pp. 1-56971-703-6.

Zodiac P. I. Written and illustrated by Natsumi Ando. TOKYOPOP, 2003. **Y Japanese manga.**

Thirteen-year-old Lili Hoshizawa is a cute and energetic high school student with a unique hobby: she enjoys reading horoscopes. She's popular at school for her skills and she's just the latest in a long line of fortune tellers. After her mother disappeared years ago, she's taken on the family profession. Secretly she is also known as Spica, an ace private investigator. With a magical ring, as Spica she can tap into the zodiac and ask them for clues to aid her in solving crimes. Lila is also aided by an old friend, a boy named Hiromi, who wants to be as good a detective as Spica. His first task to prove he's as great a detective as Spica is to uncover her secret identity, while he helps Lili with her own murder mysteries.

> *Vol. 1.* 2003. 184pp. 1-59182-383-8.
>
> *Vol. 2.* 2003. 184pp. 1-59182-384-6.
>
> *Vol. 3.* 2003. 208pp. 1-59182-385-4.
>
> *Vol. 4.* 2003. 184pp. 1-59182-412-5.

Crime and the Criminal Underworld

Graphic novel stories focusing on the criminal element include tales of murder and the world of ex-cons, thieves, pimps, gangsters, hitmen, and more. Here the focus is on the darker side of crime, with the antagonist in the spotlight instead of the police and detectives. The tales can range from life as a gang member on the streets, to a group of criminals planning to steal the biggest payload of their lives, to other, darker looks at the criminal element. The stories are reminiscent of television shows such as *The Sopranos* and movies such as *Pulp Fiction.* The comic books have also inspired movies, as seen in the 2005 release of Frank Miller's *Sin City*, which is adapted from his graphic novel series.

***Abel.* Written by William Harms. Illustrated by Mark Bloodworth.** AiT/Planet Lar, 2002. 96pp. 1-932051-01-5. **O**

During the height of World War II in 1944, the small town of Friend, Nebraska, has its share of murder and betrayal. Thirteen-year-old John Vitosh is constantly harassed by his bullish older brother, Phillip. The latest incident culminates with John helplessly watching Phillip shoot the neighbor's dog just for kicks. Shockingly, Phillip turns the now empty rifle on John, and John resigns himself to fate in that his brother will always have the upper hand, or else he will die. Later, he befriends Mr. Mar, a nice Chinese man who works for Mr. Harrison. The air of racism, especially against the Asian community, is rampant, and when Phillip and a gang of boys rape and murder a retarded girl, they put the blame on Mr. Mar. It's up to John to tell the truth and save Mr. Mar—but will he?

***Catwoman: Selina's Big Score.* Written and illustrated by Darwyn Cooke.** DC Comics, 2003. 96pp. 1-56389-922-1. **T**

© 2006 DC Comics.

Selina Kyle, better known as the thief called Catwoman, has temporarily put away her costume and is lying low in Gotham City after being presumed dead. Desperate for some serious money after a failed international heist and her personal accounts being closed, she hears of a money train loaded with $24 million in mob money heading north. She recruits a team of specialists, including her ex-lover Stark, and together they're going to take that train. Sounds like an easy job, right? Meanwhile a private eye by the name of Slam Bradley has figured out that Selina isn't as dead as was rumored and is determined to catch her any way he can. See chapter 1 for more title recommendations featuring Catwoman.

5

The Couriers. Written by Brian Wood. Illustrated by Rob Goodridge. AiT/Planet Lar, 2003–2005. **M**

Spin-off of the hit book *Couscous Express.* When you absolutely need something dangerous delivered around New York City, there's only one group you can trust: the Couriers. Anything you need done, they can do—assassinations, money transactions, protection, or intelligence gathering. In *Volume 1,* Mustafa and Special reluctantly deal with an odd biological package: a deaf/mute Nepalese girl. When the Chinese Red Army Brigade will stop at nothing to get her back, it's up to them to finish the job. In *Volume 2,* when a gun run goes wrong, Mustafa and Special travel to upstate New York to get what's coming to them: money.

Vol. .1. 2003. 88pp. 1-932051-06-6.
Vol. 2: Dirtbike Manifesto. 2004. 88pp. 1-932051-18-X.
Vol. 3: Ballad of Johnny Funwrecker. 2005. 88pp. 1-932051-31-7.

Couscous Express. **Written by Brian Wood. Illustrated by Brett Weldele.** AiT/Planet Lar, 2001. 80pp. 0-9709360-2-8. **O**

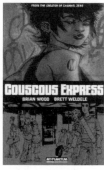

© 2006 Brian Wood.

Sixteen-year old Olive Yassin is a spoiled brat, but on her motor scooter, she's the best courier for her parents' New York City Middle Eastern restaurant, called Couscous Express. She hates her job, but Olive has Moustafa, her twenty-two-year-old boyfriend, who makes the job of working for her parents not so bad. When her parents are being strong-armed by the Turkish scooter mafia, she and her boyfriend will do whatever it takes to get back at the mafia. Luckily, Moustafa is a contracted armed courier for less legal types of transfers like cash and the occasional gun-running, because the bullets will fly and nothing will keep Olive from her family.

Gangland. **Written and illustrated by various.** Vertigo/DC Comics, 2000. 112pp. 1-56389-608-7. **M**

Fourteen short stories, both humorous and brutal, about life in organized crime. Includes stories written by Brian Azzarello, Dave Gibbons, and more as well as art by Frank Quitely, Richard Corben, Killian Plunkett, and others.

Goldfish: The Definitive Collection. **Written and illustrated by Brian Michael Bendis.** Image Comics, 2001. 272pp. 1-58240-195-0. **M** ◉

A con artist named David "Goldfish" Gold has realized that sometimes you can't come back home, but he's not about to leave without his young son. After returning to his home town of Cleveland, the grifter discovers that things have drastically changed since he left. His former partner-in-crime Izzy is now a detective, and his ex-girlfriend Lauren is leading the city's crime bosses. All he wants to do is get out of town with his young son, but will they let him leave?

Greyshirt: Indigo Sunset. **Written by Rick Veitch. Illustrated by Dave Gibbons.** America's Best Comics/WildStorm Productions/DC Comics, 2002. 224pp. 1-56389-909-4. **O**

The origin of Greyshirt, the "science hero" crime-busting savior of Indigo City. Frank LaFayette and his childhood buddy Johnny Apollo were always troublemakers, and as they got older they decided to take over the crime syndicate of Indigo City. But Frank had a change of heart, and after he's presumed dead in an explosion that Johnny helped to cause, he now fights crime as the masked hero. Meanwhile, a legendary entity called "The Lure" is haunting the sapphire mines of the city. What is the deadly secret of the creature, and can anyone survive who encounters it? A tribute to Will Eisner's *The Spirit* crime stories and 1950s horror stories.

🏆 **Hitman.** **Written by Garth Ennis. Illustrated by John McCrea.** DC Comics, 1997–2001. **O**

Ex-mercenary Tommy Monaghan has come back home to Gotham City to set himself up as a gun-for-hire. Hired for the oddest jobs you can imagine, Tommy's got an ace up his sleeve: he's been gifted by aliens with telepathy and X-ray vision so he can now read his opponents' minds and see them from a whole new perspective. Now with an edge that has saved his life more than once, he's got a lot of peculiar characters after him, including the mafia with a two-headed mob boss, Western outlaws, an army of zombie sea animals, and a six-armed gun-toting demon named Mawzir. He and his friend and fellow hitman Natt have the world against them, and they'll gladly go out in a blaze of glory with bullets and bad humor all the way. The series won an Eisner Award for Best Writer (1998) and Best Single Issue/Single Story (1999) for the story "Of Thee I Sing" in issue #34 of the series. The award-winning issue has yet to have been collected in a graphic novel format at the time of this writing.

> *Vol. 1.* 1997. 144pp. 1-56389-314-2.
> *Vol. 2: 10,000 Bullets.* 1998. 112pp. 1-56389-404-1.
> *Vol. 3: Local Heroes.* 1999. 192pp. 1-56389-509-9.
> *Vol. 4: Ace of Killers.* 2000. 144pp. 1-56389-614-1.
> *Vol. 5: Who Dares Wins.* 2001. 144pp. 1-56389-718-0.

Jinx: The Definitive Collection. **Written and illustrated by Brian Michael Bendis.** Image Comics, 2001. 480pp. 1-58240-179-9. **M**

Bounty hunter Jinx Alameda has had it rough being one of the only female headhunters in a male-dominated business. Capturing bail jumpers hasn't been quite the romantic life she imagined, and it's starting to wear her down. Petty criminal David Gold, a.k.a. "Goldfish," can't stand his partner-in-crime, the chrome-domed Columbia, and they're at each other's throats following a nearly botched game of dice. When a dying man gives them clues to where $3 million is hidden somewhere in the dark alleys of Cleveland, the two must try to work together one last time to find the stolen mob cash. After a chance meeting in a diner, Jinx and David find themselves attracted to each other even though he's a criminal and she could take him in at any time for a cash reward. But when David dumps Colombia and tells Jinx about the hidden cash, they have to learn to trust each other so they both can leave their pasts behind and recover the mob money. A film adaptation of the graphic novel, written by Bendis and starring Charlize Theron, is forthcoming.

5

Kissing Chaos. **Written and illustrated by Arthur Dela Cruz.** Oni Press, 2002–2003. **O**

© 2006 Arthur Dela Cruz.

Angela, Raevyn, and Damien, three teens from different walks of life, are on the run from the law in a stolen car and trying to escape their tumultuous past to find out where they belong. Angela's madly in love with Damien, her savior, Damien's on the run from a shooting crime, and Raevyn, who's carrying a laptop with something on it that someone will kill to get, was caught by Damien trying to hotwire the same car he was going to steal. Now they're driving across the United States, running away from the law, criminals, and maybe even themselves.

> *Vol. 1.* 2002. 208pp. 1-929998-32-5.
> *Vol. 2: Nonstop Beauty.* 2003 112pp. 1-929998-64-3.

Last of the Independents. **Written by Matt Fraction. Illustrated by Kieron Dwyer.**
AiT/Planet Lar, 2003. 104pp. 1-932051-14-7. **M**

> Cole Claudle was just looking to make some retirement money on a simple bank rob-
> bery. What he and his two friends found instead was a stash of mob money that was too
> good to pass up. Now he's on the run from the mob, who want their money back, but
> there's one thing the mob didn't count on—that Cole would be prepared to fight back.

🏆 **100 Bullets. Written by Brian Azzarello. Illustrated by Eduardo Risso.** Vertigo/DC
Comics, 2000– . **M** ◎

© 2006 Brian Azzarello
and DC Comics.

If you were given 100 forensically untraceable bullets to exact revenge and get away with it, would you do it? The mysterious Agent
Graves is in a position to give any person this gift and to place the user
above the law. Handling personal conflicts isn't his only concern—
there are much bigger fish to fry. Graves is out to put an end to a
shadow organization called The Trust, a wealthy and powerful thir-
teen-family organization with connections to nearly all of organized
crime. At his aid are the Minutemen, a squad of specialists trained to beat
the odds and to get the job done no matter how many bullets it takes. As
the bullets, bloodshed, double-crosses, morality issues, and street lingo
fly, Agent Graves's plan is put in motion for revenge, but can the Minutemen and their new recruits really take down The Trust? The series has
won several Eisner Awards, including Best Serialized Story (2001) for *Hang Up on the
Hang Low* and Best Continuing Series (2002, 2004), and Best Artist/Penciller/Inker
(2002) for Eduardo Risso's illustrations. The series has also won Harvey Awards for Best
Writer (2002), Best Artist (2002–2003), and Best Continuing or Limited Series (2002).

> *Vol. 1: First Shot, Last Call.* 2000. 128pp. 1-56389-645-1.
> *Vol. 2: Split Second Chance.* 2000. 224pp. 1-56389-711-3.
> *Vol. 3: Hang Up on the Hang Low.* 2001. 128pp. 1-56389-855-1.
> *Vol. 4: A Forgone Tomorrow.* 2002. 264pp. 1-56389-827-6.
> *Vol. 5: The Counterfifth Detective.* 2003. 144pp. 1-56389-948-5.
> *Vol. 6: Six Feet Under the Gun.* 2003. 144pp. 1-56389-996-5.
> *Vol. 7: Samurai.* 2004. 168pp. 1-4012-0189-X.
> *Vol. 8: The Hard Way.* 2005. 224pp. 1-4012-0490-2.
> *Vol. 9: Strychnine Lives.* 2006. 224pp. 1-4012-0928-9.
> *Vol. 10: Decayed.* 2006. 192pp. 1-4012-0998-x.

🏆 *The Originals.* **Written and illustrated by Dave Gibbons.** DC Comics, 2004. 160pp.
1-4012-0355-8. **M** ◎

© 2006 Dave Gibbons.

In a near-future, the streets of England are ruled by street gangs: the
clean-cut Originals and the greasers called the Dirts. All seventeen-year-old Lel and his best friend Bok ever wanted was to become
Originals and to someday get the bikes, the girls, and the street cred.
When the opportunity arises, they earn their way into the group, and in
no time Lel soon gets what he feels he's earned and rises up the Originals ladder. He's now selling and doing drugs, he's got the girl, the
bike, the clothes, and the attitude. When a gang clash between the
Originals and the Dirts results in the death of a Dirt gang member, the

blame is mistakenly placed on Lel. The Dirt members are out to seek revenge, and it will cost Lel something more dear than he ever expected. The story won an Eisner Award in 2005 for Best Graphic Novel: New.

Road to Perdition. Written by Max Allan Collins. Illustrated by Richard Piers Rayner, Jose Luis Garcia-Lopez, and Steve Lieber. Simon & Schuster and Paradox Press/DC Comics, 2002–2004. **M** 🎬

At the dawn of the 1930s, Michael O'Sullivan is a top mob enforcer for John Looney, the local Illinois Irish godfather in the Midwest town of Rockwell. For years he has been the "Angel of Death," taking care of loose ends for the Looneys as well as mobsters Al Capone and Frank Nitti. When O'Sullivan's eldest son one day spies on his dad and inadvertently witnesses his father and others killing a crooked cop, the Looneys fear what the boy has seen, and they set up O'Sullivan. His wife and youngest child having been killed, a frazzled but determined O'Sullivan walks a deadly path of vengeance with his eldest son by his side. Loosely inspired by the <u>Lone Wolf and Cub</u> series and adapted into the acclaimed film staring Tom Hanks in 2002. *Volume 2: On the Road* is set during the six-month period in which Michael O'Sullivan and his son were on the run.

> *Vol. 1.* Simon & Schuster, 2002. 304pp. 0-7434-4224-5.
> *Vol. 2: On the Road.* Paradox Press/DC Comics, 2004. 296pp. 1-4012-0357-4.

🖊 **Frank Miller's Sin City. 2d ed. Written and illustrated by Frank Miller.** Dark Horse Comics, 2005. **M** 🎬

 5

If you like your crime hard-boiled, then welcome to Sin City, the toughest, seediest city ever, where everyone's a cutthroat or worse. Each volume, in black and white with accentuated colors, tells a different hard-hitting crime noir story guaranteed to shock the reader with tales of revenge, over-the-top violence, and occasional nudity. Featuring a strong cast of tough guys, killers, strippers, and prostitutes, including Marv, Goldie, Dwight, and many more unforgettable noir characters. The series has won numerous awards, including Eisner Awards for Best Writer/Artist (1993), Best Artist/Penciller/Inker (1993), Best Graphic Album: Reprint for *The Hard Goodbye* (1993) and *That Yellow Bastard (*1998), Best Short Story (1995), and Best Finite Series/Limited Series for *A*

Dame to Kill For (1995) and *The Big Fat Kill* (1996). In 2005 director Robert Rodriguez and Frank Miller released a film version of Miller's stories, adapting the stories included in *The Hard Goodbye*, *The Big Fat Kill*, and *That Yellow Bastard*. A sequel is planned to tell other tales of Sin City. The series also won a Harvey Award in 1996 for Best Continuing or Limited Series and Best Graphic Novel of Original Work for *Sin City: Family Values* in 1998.

> *Vol. 1: The Hard Goodbye.* 2005. 208pp. 1-59307-293-7.
>> Tough-but-simple Marv finds true love in a hooker named Goldie, but when she's found murdered he'll stop at nothing to take on a serial killer and get his revenge.

Vol. 2: A Dame to Kill For. 2005. 208pp. 1-59307-294-5.

Dwight McCarthy, a down-on-his-luck photojournalist, can't resist his femme fatale ex-girlfriend's pleas for help and is drawn back into her world of corruption, deceit, and lies.

Vol. 3: Big Fat Kill. 2005. 184pp. 1-59307-295-3.

Dwight and a group of Old City prostitutes try to salvage the red light district from the corrupt mob and the police.

Vol. 4: That Yellow Bastard. 2005. 240pp. 1-59307-296-1.

Hartigan, a cop on the verge of retirement, must save an eleven-year-old girl from the clutches of a lunatic before it's too late.

Vol. 5: Family Values. 2005. 128pp. 1-59307-297-X.

Dwight and Miho take on the mob after a hooker is killed and her lover demands revenge.

Vol. 6: Booze, Broads, and Bullets. 2005. 160pp. 1-59307-298-8.

A vignette collection of short stories in Sin City, including stories of Marv, Dwight, and Delia.

Vol. 7: Hell and Back. 2005. 320pp. 1-59307-299-6.

Wallace, a brooding artist with a knack for hurting people, saves a beautiful actress from killing herself. A tale of true love with twists and turns and deadly conspiracies.

🏅 <u>**Stray Bullets.**</u> **Written and illustrated by David Lapham.** El Capitan Books, 2005– . **M** ◎

Begun originally in comic book format in 1995, David Lapham's series spans from the 1980s through the mid-1990s and features a sprawling cast of lowlifes, con artists, deadbeats, criminals, and other people caught in circumstances beyond their control and the repercussions that follow upon their actions. The graphic novels were recently reprinted, in 2005. In 1996 David Lapham won an Eisner for Best Writer/Artist, and in 1997 the first collection received an Eisner Award for Best Graphic Album: Reprint. The series has continued to be published, but on an irregular schedule.

Vol. 1: Innocence of Nilhilism. 224pp. 0-9727145-6-1.
Vol. 2: Somewhere Out West. 224pp. 0-9727145-7-X
Vol. 3: Other People. 224pp. 0-9727145-8-8.
Vol. 4: Dark Days. 224pp. 0-9727145-9-6.

Three Strikes. **Written by Nunzio Defilippis and Christina Weir. Illustrated by Brian Hurtt.** Oni Press, 2004. 160pp. 1-929998-82-1. **O**

In this grey morality tale, Rey Quintana is a good college kid who got into some trouble and has three strikes against him under California law. Noah Conway is an ex-cop who became a bail bondsman in a failed attempt to save his marriage and who is desperate to learn to communicate with his estranged teenage daughter. When Rey skips bail, it sets up a chain of events destined to destroy one of them.

<u>**Tokyo Tribes.**</u> **Written and illustrated by Santa Inoue.** TOKYOPOP, 2004– . **O Japanese manga.**

A hard-hitting look at the influence of hip-hop/gangsta rap in Japanese culture. Tokyo's districts are ruled by two rival gangs—the Musashinokuni Saru gang and the Bukuro Wu-Ronz gang. Kai and Hasheem are best friends and members of the Saru gang, while Kai's former best friend, Mera, is the leader of the Wu-Ronz tribe. When battle lines are drawn and blood is spilled, old friendships and family are forfeit as the gangs decide who will rule the streets of Tokyo. More than eleven volumes were originally published in Japan.

    Vol. 1. 2004. 208pp. 1-59532-186-1.
    Vol. 2. 2005. 192pp. 1-59532-187-X.
    Vol. 3. 2005. 192pp. 1-59532-188-8.
    Vol. 4. 2005. 192pp. 1-59532-189-6.
    Vol. 5. 2006. 208pp. 1-59532-190-X.

True Crime

Whether it is the historical aspects, morbid details, or the psychological questions surrounding the crime, tales of real-life murders have fascinated people for ages. Listed here is a small but excellent collection of true-life crime in a graphic novel format.

Brownsville. **Written by Neil Kleid. Illustrated by Jake Allen.** NBM Publishing, 2006. 208pp. 1-56163-458-1. hardcover. **O**

A unique look at the 1930s in the central Brooklyn neighborhood of Brownsville, where the Jewish gangsters ran organized crime. Focuses on the lives of Albert "Tick Tock" Tannenbaum and Abe "Kid Twist" Reles, two Jewish gangsters who rose up in the ranks of the Mafia's ranks to become hit men in one of the biggest hits in Mafia history. Brought into the Mafia from different walks of life, they each became one of the most feared hitmen of Murder, Inc., the enforcement arm of the National Crime Syndicate, and eventually became "stool pigeons" when the chips fell against them.

🎭 *From Hell*. **Written by Alan Moore. Illustrated by Eddie Campbell.** Eddie Campbell Comics, 1999. 560pp. 0-9585783-4-6. **M** ◎ 🎬

From Hell © 2006 Alan Moore
& Eddie Campbell.

"Jack the Ripper" is one of the most infamous murderers in modern history. From 1888 to 1891 he terrorized London's East End through London's highly publicized Whitechapel murders, where five prostitutes were brutally murdered. To this day no one really knows his true identity. In this in-depth, well-researched, and annotated tome, writer Alan Moore surmises who the killer was—Queen Victoria's personal physician Dr. William Gull. By compiling facts, rumors, and speculation along with detailed information about the gruesome murders, Moore sets up a fantastical story in which the doctor is portrayed as a leader of a Masonic plot to eliminate Queen Victoria's illegitimate grandson's prostitute mother. Though it is never certain who "Jack the Ripper" really was, it makes for a thrilling and well-researched, bloody tale that also helped to inspire the 2001 movie starring Johnny Depp. The series won an Eisner Award for Best Serialized Story (1993), Best Writer (1995–1997), and

Best Graphic Novel: Reprint (2000). The series also received several Harvey Awards, including Best Writer (1995–1996, 1999), Best Continuing or Limited Series (1995), and Best Graphic Album of Previously Published Work (2000).

***Torso: The Definitive Collection.* Written by Brian Michael Bendis and Marc Andreyko. Illustrated by Brian Michael Bendis.** Image Comics, 2001. 280pp. 1-58240-174-8. **M** ◎ 🎬

© 2006 Brian Michael Bendis and Marc Andreyko.

Heavily researched by Bendis and Andreyko, the story is based on the true unsolved mystery of the very first serial killer in the United States, who claimed at least twelve and possibly thirty murder victims in Cleveland in the mid-1930s. Elliot Ness, fresh from his success at cleaning out notorious gangster Al Capone from Chicago, became the safety director in Cleveland to clamp down on corruption on the streets and in his own police force. When body parts wash ashore that are so badly mutilated that the victims' remains are mostly headless torsos, there are few clues to go on. As the body count rises by the media-dubbed "Torso Murderer," Ness does what he can to catch the real killer. A feature film adaptation of the graphic novel is forthcoming and will be directed by David Fincher.

🌺 **A Treasury of Victorian Murder.** **Written and illustrated by Rick Geary.** NBM Publishing, 1990– . **T** ◎

A collection of true crime graphic novels, each focusing on a particular event in crime history, from Lincoln's assassination, to the mystery of Jack the Ripper, to the murders by Lizzy Borden. Geary takes the reader on a meticulously researched journey to each well-known murder and includes minute-by-minute accounts of the famous murders, the events leading up to the events, and what happened afterward. *Jack the Ripper* was featured on YALSA's Best Books for Young Adults list in 1996.

Vol. 1. Reprint ed. 2002. 64pp. 1-56163-309-7.

An anthology collection looking at three different murders that occurred during the Victorian era. After an introduction that sets the stage of the time period, the reader is taken on an accurate and uncomfortable journey into the dark recesses of the criminal mind and how they committed murder.

Vol. 2: Jack the Ripper. 1995. 64pp. 1-56163-308-9.

At look at the notorious butcher of Whitechapel, known as "Jack the Ripper," told from the perspective of an English commoner fascinated by the horrendous killings in 1888–1889. Five women, all prostitutes, were horrifically mutilated by a mysterious murderer whose identity remains unknown to this day.

Vol. 3: The Borden Tragedy. 1997. 80pp. 1-56163-189-2.

The tale of Lizzy Borden, famous for being accused of committing the double murder in her own home in 1892 of her father and stepmother. Through the meticulous notes of a friend of Lizzie, Geary attempts to figure out what led up to and what occurred after this family tragedy.

Vol. 4: The Fatal Bullet: The Assassination of President Garfield. 1999. 80pp. 1-56163-228-7.

On July 2, 1881, popular U.S. President James A. Garfield was shot by con-man Charles Guiteau, and the president died from complications on September 19. Takes a look at the lives of both James and Charles, two men of very similar upbringing but who walked very different paths in life, showing how a man can rise so high and yet sink so low.

Vol. 5: The Mystery of Mary Rogers. 2001. 80pp. 1-56163-288-0.

A detailed look at the 1840 disappearance and murder of New York City native Mary Cecilia Rogers, who sold cigars and tobacco in a shop frequented by many of the era's authors, including Edgar Allan Poe. Her bruised and broken body was found in the Hudson River, and many people have never fully accepted the official cause of her death.

Vol. 6: The Beast of Chicago. 2003. 80pp. 1-56163-362-3.

The tale of H. H. Holes, a seemingly mild-mannered young man who was in actuality a con-man murderer who became one of America's first serial killers. His brutal murders in Chicago from 1886 to 1891 in his "murder castle," a boarding house where people checked in but never checked out. shocked the nation.

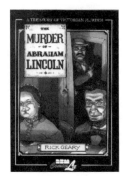

© 2006 Rick Geary.

Vol. 7: The Murder of Abraham Lincoln. 2005. 80pp. 1-56163-425-5.

An in-depth look at the events leading up to and after the assassination of Abraham Lincoln, as well as the life of his murderer, John Wilkes Booth.

Vol. 8: The Case of Madeleine Smith. 2006. 80pp. 1-56163-467-0.

A look at the life of Madeleine Smith, a Glasgow socialite whom some people were convinced was a murderess who killed her lover with arsenic. Though she was proven not guilty, many believed that she escaped the noose by the shear luck that there were no witnesses to the murder.

Chapter 6

Horror

The horror comic book, the crown prince of comic books in the 1950s, has recently reemerged. Publishers, writers, and artists are once again delving into that bloody, rich pool of horrific inspiration that was once one of the most popular genres in comic book history. Meanwhile, many popular horror comics from previous decades are still around, such as DC Comics' *Swamp Thing*, and classic titles of old are being reprinted in paperback collections. Comic book horror stories have even inspired such television shows as *Buffy the Vampire Slayer* and its spin-off, *Angel*. Some comic books are being made into hit horror movies. Theaters showcasing horror comic book characters, including the <u>Blade</u> trilogy of films and Mike Mignola's 2004 cult-hit *Hellboy* have done well at the box office, and many more movie adaptations are being released, including *Dark Water*, *Ghost Rider*, and *30 Days of Night*.

Note that the horror genre has much in common with the dark fantasy subgenre of chapter 4, and many titles listed in that subgenre will easily appeal to horror readers. Also note that tales featuring genreblending titles are listed in other chapters. A section on Western horror is listed in the Westerns section of chapter 2, and chapter 8 features a genreblend subgenre, humorous horror.

Supernatural Heroes

Heroes can come in all shapes and sizes. Some heroes even are vampires, devils, demons, ghosts, or other beasties from the supernatural world. Despite how they may appear on the outside, their hearts are still pure and good. Below are listed titles featuring paranormal fighters who battle against the forces of evil. Though tied closely to the super-hero genre, the tales focus on individuals or a group of heroes who typically are either born or gifted with superhuman or even inhuman power and use it to fight monsters, ghosts, the forces of the occult, common criminals on occasion, and more. Mike Mignola's <u>Hellboy</u> series is an excellent example of this genre.

Angel. **Created by Joss Whedon. Written and illustrated by various.** Dark Horse Comics, 2000-2002; IDW Publishing, 2006– . **T** 🖵

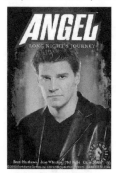

Adaptation of the hit TV series. Who says vampires have no souls? Angelus, a vampire feared like no other, was cursed by gypsies with the return of his soul. Now he lives in torment over the pain he caused countless innocent people while he was enjoying the art of the kill. Still with vampire strength and immortality, his new mission is to save as many victims of demonic crime as he can, and possibly himself as well. In 2006, IDW Publishing took over the license.

The Hollower. 2000. 88pp. 1-56971-450-9.
Surrogates. 2000. 80pp. 1-56971-491-6.
Earthly Possessions. 2001. 80pp. 1-56971-533-5.
Hunting Ground. 2001. 80pp. 1-56971-547-5.
Autumnal. 2002. 80pp. 1-56971-559-9.
Strange Bedfellows and Other Stories. 2002. 104pp. 1-56971-753-2.
Long Night's Journey. 2002. 104pp. 1-56971-752-4.
The Curse. 2006. 120pp. 1-933239-79-4.
Old Friends. 2006. 120pp. 1-922329-76-X.

B.P.R.D. **Written by Mike Mignola. Illustrated by various.** Dark Horse Comics, 2003– . **T** ◎ 🎬 🖵

When things go bump in the night, the Bureau for Paranormal Research and Defense is a secret government organization there to bump back. Spun off from the pages of Mike Mignola's <u>Hellboy</u>, the team features aquatic creature Abe Sabien, Roger the Homunculus, firestarter Liz Sherman, psychic Johann Kraus, Lobster Johnson, and other odd agents, ready to confront the mysterious paranormal and monstrous evil. The Bureau was featured in the *Hellboy* (2004) motion picture and in the 2006 *Hellboy Animated* cartoon.

Vol. 1: Hollow Earth and Other Stories. 2003. 120pp. 1-56971-862-8.
Vol. 2: The Soul of Venice and Other Stories. 2004. 128pp. 1-59307-132-9.
Vol. 3: A Plague of Frogs. 2005. 144pp. 1-59307-288-0.
Vol. 4: The Dead. 2005. 152pp. 1-59307-380-1.
Vol. 5: The Black Flame. 2006. 168pp. 1-59307-550-2.
Vol. 6: The Universal Machine. 2006. 144pp. 1-59307-710-6.

🎗 <u>**Buffy the Vampire Slayer.**</u> **Created by Joss Whedon. Written and illustrated by various.** Dark Horse Comics, 1998–2004. **T** 🖵

Adaptation of the hit TV series that aired from 1997 to 2003. "In every generation there is a Chosen One. She alone will stand against the vampires, the demons, and the forces of darkness. She is the Slayer." In this generation, the Slayer is Buffy Summers, a hip high school cheerleader now saddled with a bigger responsibility than setting fashion trends. She puts her life on the line every night to save the world from bloodsuckers and other demons, while trying to be a normal teenager by day. *Ring of Fire* received recognition from YALSA's Popular Paperbacks for Young Adults committee in 2002 on the "Graphic Novels: Superheroes and Beyond" list.

The Dust Waltz. 1998. 80pp. 1-56971-342-1.
The Remaining Sunlight. 1999. 88pp. 1-56971-354-5.
The Origin. 1999. 80pp. 1-56971-429-0.
Uninvited Guests. 1999. 96pp. 1-56971-436-3.
Bad Blood. 2000. 88pp. 1-56971-445-2.
Crash Test Demons. 2000. 80pp. 1-56971-461-4.
Ring of Fire. 2000. 80pp. 1-56971-482-7.
Pale Reflections. 2000. 88pp. 1-56971-475-4.
Blood of Carthage. 2001. 128pp. 1-56971-534-3.
Spike and Dru. 2001. 96pp. 1-56971-541-6.
Food Chain. 2001. 168pp. 1-56971-602-1.
Past Lives. 2001. 96pp. 1-56971-552-1.
Autumnal. 2001. 80pp. 1-56971-554-8.
Tales of the Slayers. 2002. 96pp. 1-56971-605-6.
Out of the Woodwork. 2002. 112pp. 1-56971-738-9.
Oz. 2002. 80pp. 1-56971-569-6.
False Memories. 2002. 96pp. 1-56971-736-2.
Ugly Little Monsters. 2002. 104pp. 1-56971-750-8.
Haunted. 2002. 96pp. 1-56971-737-0.
The Death of Buffy. 2002. 120pp. 1-56971-748-6.
Note from the Underground. 2003. 104pp. 1-56971-888-1.
Willow and Tara. 2003. 80pp. 1-56971-905-5.
Viva Las Buffy. 2003. 96pp. 1-56971-980-2.
Slayer, Interrupted. 2003. 120pp. 1-59307-011-X.
Stake to the Heart. 2004. 104pp. 1-59307-012-8.

The Cal McDonald Mysteries. Written by Steve Niles. IDW Publishing and Dark Horse Comics, 2003–2005. O

Cal MacDonald, an L.A. private eye with a knack for handling supernatural cases and an equal knack for booze and drugs, finds himself in a world of trouble when a simple job of trailing a vagrant vampire leads to a bigger problem than he ever expected: a secret pact between the demonic races and a mystery involving a stolen vial of the deadly bubonic plague, and many more hard-boiled horrific adventures. Cal, a skeptical police officer, and the undead ghouls who live in the sewers, are all that stand in the way of the total annihilation of humanity. When vampires, zombies, werewolves, and more are at war with humans, there's only one way out: a 12-gauge shotgun, plenty of silver bullets, and a wooden cross.

Dial M for Monster: A Cal McDonald Collection. Illustrated by various. IDW Publishing, 2003. 200pp. 1-932382-05-4.
Criminal Macabre: A Cal McDonald Mystery. Illustrated by Ben Templesmith. Dark Horse Comics, 2004. 168pp. 1-56971-935-7. O

Last Train to Deadsville: A Cal McDonald Mystery. Illustrated by Kelley Jones. Dark Horse Comics, 2005. 144pp. 1-59307-107-8.

***Crush.* Written by Jason Hall. Illustrated by Sean Murphy.** Dark Horse Comics, 2004. 96pp. 1-59307-214-7. **T**

Goth girl outsider Liz Mason has had a rough life with her abusive father and alcoholic mother. The only good thing in her life is her best friend, Jen. On her eighteenth birthday, Liz finds out that there's something even worse than her monsterlike parents: herself! Now whenever Liz bleeds, she transforms into a super-strong, brutal beast called "Crush." This new dark side of Liz instantly begins to seek vengeance for any wrongs done her, and she realizes that the curse of "Crush" may be the best thing that ever happened to her. Meanwhile, a mysterious agent and his pack of teenage werewolves are on Crush's trail. Wait until they get a taste of Liz's new "softer" side!

Darkham Vale. Written and illustrated by Jack Lawrence. AP Comics, 2004–2005. **T**

Teenager Ryan Harris and his father have just moved into the seemingly quiet and cozy British town of Darkham Vale following the divorce of Ryan's parents. Ryan had always been fascinated by stories of ghosts, demons, goblins, vampires, and werewolves, but he never thought they were real. He soon discovers that the town has a dark and haunting past as well as creatures of the night. Ryan suddenly finds himself a believer when he is caught in the middle of a long-standing battle between the forces of good (magically imbued humans and dinosaurlike lizard-dogs called Kankrollin) and an ancient evil demon and his army of darkness, led by the mysterious Tarnas Kerith. As Ryan finds allies in fellow teenager Troy Brendis and Halka of the defenders of Darkham, he must also find out the reason for Lord Kerith's vendetta against him and find his place in the battle of good versus evil.

Vol. 1. 2004. 140pp. 1-905071-00-0.
Vol. 2. 2004. 140pp. 1-905071-01-9.
The Complete Darkham Vale. 2005. 244pp. 1-905071-06-X.

The Darkness. Written by Garth Ennis and Malachy Coney. Illustrated by various. Top Cow Productions/Image Comics, 2001–2006. **T**

New York hit man Jackie Estacado's life as a member of the mafia was going well. He was an orphan adopted into a life of crime, and now fame, fortune, and women are in his cards. After his twenty-first birthday, Jackie inherits an unholy power called The Darkness. It gives him almost unstoppable power during the night, but there's a terrible curse on him if he wants to retain the power of The Darkness. Now a powerful occult anti-hero, his very own desire may be what destroys him unless his enemies from the Angelus, the Brotherhood of the Darkness, the Witchblade, or the mob do it first.

Vol. 1. 2001. 176pp. 1-58240-032-6.
Vol. 2. 2001. 144pp. 1-58240-205-1.
Vol. 3: Spear of Destiny. 2000. 106pp. 1-58240-147-0.
Resurrection. 2004. 176pp. 1-58240-349-X.
Vol. 5. 2006. 272pp. 1-58240-646-4.

The Gunwitch: Outskirts of Doom. **Written by Dan Brereton. Illustrated by Ted Naifeh.** Oni Press, 2002. 104pp. 1-929998-22-8. **T**

The popular silent scarecrow-like golem from <u>The Nocturnals</u> series by Dan Brereton takes center stage with Doc Horror's daughter Eve in the city of Heliopolis. There they find themselves in the middle of a gang war between two vampire clans fighting over an ancient Egyptian vampire mummy. Facing nearly impossible odds, Gunwitch and his two six-shooters are all that stand between the vampires and the humans.

✦ <u>Hellboy.</u> Written and illustrated by Mike Mignola. Dark Horse Comics, 2003– . **T ◉ ▦**

Hellboy™ © 2006 Mike Mignola.

Near the end of World War II, the Nazis were trying desperately to gain ground and win the war by any means necessary—including using the occult. Brought to Earth in 1944 to carry out a fiendish plot by the Nazis and a resurrected Rasputin to bring forth chaos and destroy the world, the infant demon was rescued by American soldiers and named "Hellboy." A true red-tailed devil, horns and all, but raised on Earth by humans, Hellboy is a unique champion—a paranormal hunter with the ethics of a working-class bruiser. With his shaved horn look (to better fit in) and a large stone right hand, Hellboy fights the good fight for the secret government organization known as the Bureau for Paranormal Research and Defense, tackling oddities, monsters, mysteries, ancient myths, and more alongside his fellow B.P.R.D. companions Liz Sherman, Abe Sapien, Roger the Homunculus, and others. The series has won numerous awards and recognition, including several Eisner Awards, for Best Graphic Album: Reprint (1995) for *Seed of Destruction*, Best Writer/Artist (1995, 1997–1998), Best Anthology (1998) for the *Hellboy Christmas Special* (reprinted in the collection *The Chained Coffin and Other Stories*), and Best Finite Series/Limited Series for the collection *Conqueror Worm*. The series has also received Harvey Awards for Best Artist or Penciller (1995–1996, 2000) and Best Graphic Album of Previously Published Work (1996). For a twisted take on Hellboy in his youth, see the *Hellboy Junior* graphic novel in chapter 8.

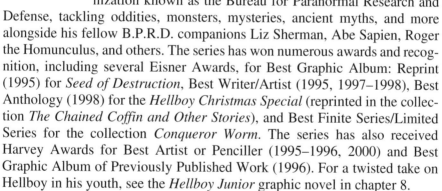

6

> *Seed of Destruction.* 3d ed. 2003. 128pp. 1-59307-094-2.
> *Wake the Devil.* 2003. 144pp. 1-59307-095-0, 2nd edition.
> *The Chained Coffin and Other Stories.* 2d ed. 2003. 176pp. 1-59307-091-8.
> *The Right Hand of Doom.* 2d ed. 2003. 144pp. 1-59307-093-4.
> *Conqueror Worm.* 2d ed. 2003. 144pp. 1-59307-092-6.
> *Strange Places.* 2006. 128pp. 1-59307-475-1.

✦ <u>Hellboy: Weird Tales.</u> Written by Mike Mignola and various. Illustrated by various. Dark Horse Comics, 2003–2004. **T**

Featuring the work of the best in the comic book industry, <u>Hellboy: Weird Tales</u> is an anthology series of short stories about Hellboy and his teammates, told by writers and artists other than Hellboy creator Mike Mignola. Creators in *Volume 1* include John Cassaday, Andi Watson, Eric Powell, Sara Ryan,

Steve Lieber, and others. *Volume 2* includes works by P. Craig Russell, Scott Morse, Jill Thompson, Evan Dorkin, Kia Asamiya, and others. Artist John Cassaday received an Eisner Award in 2004 for his body of work, including the short story in *Volume 1*.

> *Vol. 1*. 2003. 128pp. 1-56971-622-6.
> *Vol. 2*. 2004. 144pp. 1-56971-953-5.

Hellboy Animated. Written by Jim Pascoe and Tad Stones. Illustrated by Rick Lacy, Fabio Laguna, and Mike Mignola. Dark Horse Comics, 2007-. **T** 🖵

Hellboy Animated is inspired by a direct-to-DVD animated series featuring Hellboy, a demon raised by humankind, and other members of the Bureau for Paranormal Research, including Liz Sherman, Abe Sapien, and Dr. Broom. The team is an unlikely but determined group of agents who must investigate and eliminate the evil beasts and dark forces that haunt our world. The animated series was produced by Hellboy creator Mike Mignola and *Hellboy* movie director Guillermo del Toro.

> *Vol. 1: The Black Wedding*. 2007. 80pp. 1-59307-700-9.

I Hunt Monsters. Written by Rod Espinosa. Illustrated by Craig Babiar. Antarctic Press, 2004– . **T Neo-manga.**

© 2006 Antarctic Press.

For generations the Warlock clan guarded an ancient seal preventing the Queen of the Undead and her monstrous minions from being released. Enter young William Warlock, the last of the clan and clueless about his role in the ultimate struggle of good versus evil. He was supposed to recharge the ancient seal and ensure that evil was locked away for another generation, but now it's too late and the monsters have been unleashed upon Earth once again. Only William and his group of misfit heroes—the beautiful sorceress Aarna, the vampire Delilah, and William's ghostly ancestors—can save the world from being conquered by the wicked Queen. Can William clean up the mess he made before it's too late?

> *Pocket Manga Vol. 1*. 2004. 144pp. 1-932453-67-9.
> *Pocket Manga Vol. 2*. 2005. 144pp. 1-932453-74-1.
> *Pocket Manga Vol. 3: Hunting Season*. 2006. 144pp. 1-932453-97-0.

The Irregulars . . . in the Service of Sherlock Holmes. Written by Steven-Elliot Altman and Michael Reaves. Illustrated by Bong Dazo. Dark Horse Comics, 2005. 128pp. 1-59307-303-8. **T**

A slasher stalks the streets of London in 1885. All signs point to Dr. Watson as the murderer, and famed detective Sherlock Holmes is on the case to exonerate his comrade. When duty calls Holmes out of London, the youthful street urchins called the Baker Street Irregulars, his eyes and ears on the street, are called in to help find clues to clear Watson's good name. What they find is an ancient dark evil in league with Professor Moriarty that will destroy all of known existence unless the Irregulars can save the day.

Jack the Lantern. **Written by Tim Vigil. Illustrated by Scott Lee.** Castle Rain Entertainment, 2004. 136pp. No ISBN. **T**

> Haunted his entire life by his own personal demons, Jack Gordon Corby sought experimental treatment from his psychiatrist, Dr. Frank Casper. The treatment may be worse than the symptoms as Jack finds that he's tapped into a destiny he never knew existed. With a dash of magic he becomes the vessel for an otherworldly pumpkin demon. A secret war is being played out with knights, demons, and wizards, and now Jack finds himself front and center in the coming climax of the battle.

🏆 *Joss Whedon's Fray: Future Slayer.* **Written by Joss Whedon. Illustrated by Karl Moline.** Dark Horse Comics, 2003. 216pp. 1-56971-751-6. **T** ◎ ⌨

> A spin-off of the cult-hit television series *Buffy the Vampire Slayer.* "In every generation there is a Chosen One. She alone will stand against the vampires, the demons, and the forces of darkness. She is the Slayer." In the far future, after all the demons have been vanquished from Earth, a new Chosen One has been called after centuries of silence: evil has returned. Melaka Fray, a tough professional thief who thought she had no real future, has been chosen to be the new Slayer. With a demon as her guardian Watcher and her scythe in hand, she's out to take on the reborn evil nest of vampires and their mysterious leader before they summon an ancient dragon that's threatening to destroy a decaying Manhattan if unleashed. Both YALSA's Best Books for Young Adults list and Quick Picks for Reluctant Readers featured the story in 2005.

The Magdalena. **Written by Marcia Chen. Illustrated by Joe Benitez.** Top Cow Productions/Image Comics, 2006. 248pp. 1-58240-645-6. **O**

> The Magdalena is a warrior-priestess from the bloodline of Mary Magdalene who has for generations served as the guardian for the Roman Catholic Church. With sword in hand, this beautiful bloodline continues its struggle against the vampires and other evils that plague Earth. The current Magdalena faces a crisis of faith while investigating a murder case. All signs lead her directly into a battle against a vampire horde, who tell her tales too unbelievable to be true—or are they? Are the vampires really telling the truth about their origins, and will this change her attitude toward her faith forever?

Monster Club. **Written by Richard Emms and Phil Littler. Illustrated by Kit Wallis and Matthew Sleaford.** AP Comics, 2003–2005. **T**

> Many years ago the DNA of an alien race was combined with the DNA of humans by an evil scientist. From his hideous experiments, a new, fast-multiplying, shape-shifting race of monstrous aliens was born, and slowly but surely they're eliminating the human race. They have infiltrated society in sleeper cells, blending in perfectly with human society, waiting for the right moment to strike. Enter a covert group called The Organization. Hovering high above the clouds in their self-contained secret base that's home to more than 10,000 members, they're out to protect England and the world from the alien forces. In order to infiltrate and disable the menace, teams within The Organization have been created to curb the recent rise in monster activity wherever they're

needed. One such squadron is led by Mia, a tough-fighting, bubble-gum-chewing teenage girl with a knack for good-humored sarcasm. Her squad and many others like it are out to make the world a safer place, using an arsenal of deadly weapons, big guns, katanna swords, and giant robots.

> *Collected Vol. 1*. 2003. 136pp. 1-905071-03-5.
> *Collected Vol. 2*. 2004. 160pp. 1-905071-04-3.
> *Collected Vol. 3*. 2005. 100pp. 1-905071-11-6.

Nobody. Written by Alex Amado and Sharon Cho. Illustrated by Charlie Adlard. AiT/Planet Lar, 2000. 128pp. 0-9676847-2-2. **O**

Jessica Drake is a street-tough woman who's a Nobody, an unseen warrior on the side of the angels. The latest in a long line of Nobodies, she's another soldier waging war against the hordes of Hell in a Cold War-like espionage struggle for supremacy on Earth. A loner, she has the most unusual weapon on her side: the ability to look like anyone. After a botched rescue attempt in which Jessica accidentally killed the sacrificial person she was to save as well as the people making the sacrifice, she enters a downward spiral, trying to focus on the next job. The struggle to redeem herself may cost her something more precious than she realized: her own identity. Can she regain her ground in the battle, or will nobody care?

Nocturnals. Written and illustrated by Dan Brereton. Oni Press, 1998–2002. **T**

© 2006 Dan Brereton.

In the pitch black of Pacific City, the creatures of the night roam free. It's time for the Nocturnals. Led by Doc Horror, a refugee scientist from another planet, they're a horror-fest of ghouls, genejoke freaks, and abominations bound together to rid the world of the darker side of humanity. Doc's seen evil—the same kind that's about ready to pounce on humanity—and nothing can stop his crusade. Joined with Polychrome, The Gunwitch, Starfish, Firelion, Komodo, the Raccoon, and his own daughter, Halloween Girl, he's ready to take on the monsters when no one else can.

> *Black Planet*. 1998. 184pp. 0-9667127-0-6.
> *The Dark Forever*. 2002. 96pp. 1-929998-23-6.
> *Unhallowed Eve*. 2002. 96pp. 1-929998-43-0.

Ogre Slayer. Written and illustrated by Kei Kusunoki. VIZ Media, LLC, 1997–1998. **T** **Japanese manga.**

An ogre is born in human form as a handsome young man carrying a curse: he will forever walk Earth as an ogre until he destroys all other ogres. Only then will he have earned his humanity and be fully human. Until then, he roams Japan in search of his kin and has taken on no name, only the name of the sword he carries, "Ogre Slayer."

> *Vol. 1*. 1997. 184pp. 1-56931-198-6.
> *Vol. 2: Love's Bitter Fruit*. 1998. 184pp. 1-56931-261-3.

The Perhapanauts. Written by Todd DeZago. Illustrated by Craig Rousseau. Dark Horse Comics, 2006. 128pp. 1-59307-607-X. **T**

When the fabric of reality on Earth shatters and great beasts beyond description break free of their dimensions and enter ours, the organization called Bedlam is there to save the day. Lucky for us Earth's own monsters—Bigfoot, Ghosts, Aliens, Faeries, and Chupacabras—are on our side. Working for Bedlam, they're called The Parhapanauts, and they're ready to save Earth one monster at a time.

Priest. **Written by Ra In-Soo. Illustrated by Min-Woo Hyung.** TOKYOPOP, 2002–2006. **O** **Korean manhwa.**

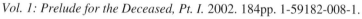

On the frontier of the old American Wild West, Hell has arrived on Earth, and there's only one man who can send the demons back to Hell: a cursed man of the cloth. That man is Ivan Isaacs, a somber and determined man of God, who made a deal with the demon Belial after he and his love were massacred. Now the demon owns half of his soul, and Ivan has been given a second chance at life along with super-human strength and stamina. Traveling across the West with a gun loaded with silver bullets, his Bible, and a journal to record his journey, Ivan must go where the hordes of the undead roam. He's on an unholy mission from Belial to prevent the resurrection of the fallen archangel Temozarela and to eradicate Temozarela's minions on Earth—and pray that no demon tries to get in Ivan's way. The manhwa is being adapted into a live-action film to be released in 2007.

> *Vol. 1: Prelude for the Deceased, Pt. I.* 2002. 184pp. 1-59182-008-1.
> *Vol. 2: Prelude for the Deceased, Pt. II.* 2002. 176pp. 1-59182-009-X.
> *Vol. 3: Requiem for the Damned.* 2002. 176pp. 1-59182-010-3.
> *Vol. 4: Harbinger's Song.* 2003. 200pp. 1-59182-088-X.
> *Vol. 5: Ballad of a Fallen Angel.* 2003. 192pp. 1-59182-201-7.
> *Vol. 6: Symphony of Blood.* 2003. 192pp. 1-59182-202-5.
> *Vol. 7.* 2003. 184pp. 1-59182-203-3.
> *Vol. 8.* 2003. 184pp. 1-59182-204-1.
> *Vol. 9: Hallelujah of the Beast.* 2003. 184pp. 1-59182-205-X.
> *Vol. 10: Traitor's Lament.* 2004. 192pp. 1-59182-511-3.
> *Vol. 11.* 2004. 192pp. 1-59182-512-1.
> *Vol. 12: Choir of Wolves.* 2004. 176pp. 1-59182-513-X.
> *Vol. 13: Strain of the Dispossessed.* 2004. 192pp. 1-59182-514-8.
> *Vol. 14: Stygian Mode.* 2005. 176pp. 1-59182-515-6.
> *Vol. 15.* 2006. 240pp. 1-59182-516-4.

R.I.P.D. **Written by Peter Lenkov. Illustrated by Lucas Marangan.** Dark Horse Comics, 2003. 96pp. 1-56971-928-4. **O**

Nick Cruz was killed in the line of duty and is looking to find the perp who did it. Luckily he's in Heaven and took a job with the R.I.P.D. (Rest in Peace Department). Now in exchange for 100 years of service he has a chance to go back to Earth and solve the mystery of who murdered him. He's not going to like what he finds there: his wife is being consoled by his ex-partner and his murderer is in Hell, literally! Now Nick has to travel to the fiery pits of Hell to solve his murder, and somehow stop a rebellion led by a demon carrying Archangel Michael's flaming sword! They never covered this in the training manual at R.I.P.D. The graphic novel has been optioned to become a film directed by David "Wedding Crashers" Dobkin and will be at a theater near you in 2008.

Sister Red. Written and illustrated by Shizuru Hayashiya. ComicsOne, 2004. **T Japanese manga.**

Teenager Mahito was hit by a car, her body shredded by the hit-and-run driver's vehicle, and she was left for dead. Now she's mysteriously still alive and all her wounds have healed, thanks to an enigmatic girl named Alice. Even stranger, Mahito has now become like Alice and is a Median—an undead—gifted with extraordinary senses, an uncanny healing ability, and the ability to transform her body into a deadly weapon. She's become a pawn in a deadly game played by a violent and bloodthirsty rogue group of Medians who are seeking the gift of immortality. Now Alice and Mahito—who share the relic known as the Sacred Heart—are all that stand between humanity and an uncaring mob of Medians who are out to cheat death even if it costs the lives of innocent humans.

Vol. 1. 2004. 200pp. 1-58899-405-8.
Vol. 2. 2004. 200pp. 1-58899-406-6.

The Skull Man. Created by Shotaro Ishinomori. Written and illustrated by Kazuhiko Shimamoto. TOKYOPOP, 2002–2003. **T Japanese manga.**

Brought back from the dead after losing his loved ones, his face, and more, the Japanese anti-hero known only as Skull Man returns to seek revenge on the evil men who destroyed his life, as well as the monsters under their control. Born Tatsuo Kagura, his parents experimented on him as a boy, and through them he received amazing powers and skills. Following their deaths, he took the name Skull Man to seek revenge upon their murderers. Accompanying Skull Man on his path of revenge is shape-shifter Goro, his longtime protector. Together they fight such as enemies as Spider-Man, Parasite Green, Queen Bee, Cobra Man, and Vulture Man. Although all vicious mutant monstrosities, they are being controlled by the crime lord Rasputin, who will stop at nothing to discover the secrets of Skull Man.

Vol. 1. 2002. 224pp. 1-931514-65-8.
Vol. 2. 2002. 200pp. 1-931514-66-6.
Vol. 3. 2002. 208pp. 1-931514-67-4.
Vol. 4. 2002. 208pp. 1-931514-68-2.
Vol. 5. 2003. 200pp. 1-931514-69-0.
Vol. 6. 2003. 248pp. 1-931514-70-4.
Vol. 7. 2003. 240pp. 1-59182-235-1.

Spawn. Written by Todd McFarlane. Illustrated by Todd McFarlane, Greg Capullo, and various. Image Comics, 1995– . **O** 🎬 🖳

Al Simmons was a soldier for the U.S. government but was killed in the line of duty and found his soul in Hell. Given a second chance at life, he made a pact with a devil called Malbolgia and was able to roam Earth, but at a great cost. Now a Hellspawn, a soldier with demonic powers and superior strength, he's back on Earth to try to right wrongs of his own past while resisting the temptations of a throne in Hell made for him. Spawn debuted in 1992 and remains one of the most popular independent comics. The character also branched out in a live-action film in 1997 as well as a cartoon series, which aired on HBO from 1997 to 1999.

Book 1: Beginnings. 1995. 116pp. 1-887279-01-6.
Book 2. 1997. 116pp. 1-887279-18-0.
Book 3. 1997. 96pp. 1-887279-54-7.
Book 4. 1997. 120pp. 1-887279-52-0.
Book 5. 1999. 128pp. 1-887279-71-7.
Book 6: Book of the Dead. 1999. 120pp. 1-58240-001-6.
Book 7: Deadman's Touch. 1999. 96pp. 1-58240-020-2.
Book 8: Betrayal of Blood. 1999. 96pp. 1-58240-021-0.
Book 9: Urban Jungle. 1999. 96pp. 1-58240-111-X.
Book 10: Vengeance of the Dead. 2000. 120pp. 1-58240-131-4.
Book 11: Crossroads. 2000. 96pp. 1-58240-132-2.
Book 12: Immortality. 2001. 96pp. 1-58240-198-5.
Spawn: Simony. Written by Alex Nikolavitch. Illustrated by Jeff Porcherot. 68pp. 1-58240-365-1.

Spawn: Angela's Hunt. 2d ed. Written by Neil Gaiman. Illustrated by Mark Pennington and Greg Capullo. Image Comics, 2000. 112pp. 1-58240-168-3. **O**

© 2006 Todd McFarlane.

Since the beginning of time, hellspawns and angels have been on opposing sides in the battle of Heaven versus Hell, and the greatest of all the angels is the fierce hunter Angela, a vanquisher of all evil creatures. While celebrating her 100,000th birthday, Angela is placed under arrest by her fellow beautiful angel warriors. She's put on trial in Heaven for treason and for conspiring with the hellspawn Al Simmons, the dark vigilante hero known as Spawn. Soon it becomes clear that Angela is being framed by the angel Gabrielle, who has held a grudge against Angela for centuries. The only person who can help clear Angela's name is Spawn—a creature who is definitely not welcome in Heaven and is the sworn enemy of angels. Can a hellspawn be trusted to testify for his sworn enemy, and will Angela ever put her trust in angels again?

The Tomb. Written by Nunzio DeFilippis and Christina Weir. Illustrated by Christopher Mitten. Oni Press, 2004. 152pp. 1-929998-95-3. **T**

Artifact-hunter and archaeologist Jessica Parrish has seen her share of odd things. When she's asked to lead a team of explorers to retrieve stolen Egyptian artifacts from an abandoned house formerly owned by someone affected by King Tut's curse, they encounter more than they could have expected. One by one the cursed house is killing the team, and Jessica must discover whether the house is just booby-trapped against intruders or really haunted.

© 2006 Nunzio DeFilippis, Christina
Weir, and Christopher Mitten.

6

***Very Big Monster Show.* Written by Steve Niles. Illustrated by Butch Adams.** IDW Publishing, LLC, 2005. 56pp. 1-932382-59-3. **A**

> The monsters of old just aren't scary anymore to the kids of today. Vampires, werewolves, mummies, and swamp monsters have lost their appeal to more gruesome and outlandish creatures, and classic monsters have relocated and retired in the town of Creepyville. One resident of Creepyville, a young boy named Theo, still believes in the classic creatures' power to scare. He finds them living together and decides to take the monsters to Hollywood to find themselves and their audiences again. Can he reinvigorate the out-of-work monsters so they can learn to scare us all once again?

<u>Witchblade.</u> Written by Christina Z., David Wohl, Fiona Avery, and various. Illustrated by Michael Turner and various. Top Cow Productions/Image Comics, 1998–2003. **O** 🖵

> New York police officer Sara Pezzini is a tough and beautiful cop just trying to save life wherever she can. When one day she is bonded with an ancient weapon called the Witchblade, which grants her immeasurable power, she has found a new way to conquer her foes and still serve as New York's Finest. Now the forces of darkness from demons, secret organizations, and men of corporate power are out to destroy Sara and claim the Witchblade for their own, but Sara's not giving up without a fight.

>> *Vol. 1: Origins.* 2001. 192pp. 1-887279-65-2.
>> *Vol. 2: Revelations.* 2000. 224pp. 1-58240-161-6.
>> *Vol. 3: Prevailing.* 2000. 160pp. 1-58240-175-6.
>> *Vol. 4: Distinctions.* 2001. 160pp. 1-58240-199-3.
>> *Vol. 5.* 2003. 208pp. 1-58240-235-3.
>> *Vol. 7: Blood Relations.* 2003. 128pp. 1-58240-315-5.
>> *Vol. 10: Witch Hunt.* 2006. 144pp. 1-58240-590-5.

***Witchblade: Obakemono.* Written by Fiona Avery. Illustrated by Billy Tan.** Image Comics, 2002. 80pp. 1-58240-259-0. **O**

> In feudal Japan, a young woman named Shiori seeks revenge for the deaths of her lord and husband. Her journey will take her past demons, gods, bandits, and more and will put in her hands the ultimate source of power to grant her vengeance: the Witchblade. This is Volume 6 in the <u>Witchblade</u> series.

<u>The Wretch.</u> Written and illustrated by Phil Hester. Amaze Ink/Slave LaborGraphics, 2003. **T**

> In Glass City, extraordinary occurrences are part of an ordinary day. UFOs, Bigfoot, flesh-eating viruses, and satanic cults are par for the course in this paranormal haven for urban legends. The only thing stranger than the paranormal is the silent hero known only as the Wretch. No one in the city seems to know what he is. Is he a hero? An alien? Is he even human? As long as he's here to protect the city from the strange and unknown, he's fine with the citizens of Glass City.

>> *Vol. 1: Everyday Doom.* 2003. 120pp. 0-943151-68-6.
>> *Vol. 2: Devil's Lullaby.* 2003. 120pp. 0-943151-72-4.
>> *Vol. 3: From Cradle to Grave.* 2003. 64pp. 0-943151-73-2.

A Bestiary

A primary focus in horror are the mysterious creatures and monsters featured in the stories. Listed here according to type are the various graphic novel tales of vampires, werewolves, the undead, muck monsters, and giant monsters from the movies. Note that humorous takes on these popular creatures can also be found in the humorous horror subgenre in chapter 8.

Vampires and Werewolves

Vampires and werewolves are one of the universally recognized creatures of the night. Featured here are graphic novel tales focusing both on creatures of the night and on the beasts as protagonists, antagonists, and anti-heroes.

***Anne Rice's The Vampire Lestat.* Based on the novel by Anne Rice. Adapted by Faye Perozich. Illustrated by Daerick Gross.** Ballantine Books, 1991. 384pp. 0-345-37394-4. **M**

> After over a half century underground, the blonde-haired vampire Lestat is drawn to the world of today and its music. Breaking the vampire oath of silence, he is adored as a rock star and vows to tell the world his tale. With pen in hand, he recounts his life, from his days as a human living in France to his turning into a vampire. His retelling of his life still leaving him feeling incomplete, Lestat searches the Earth for the true origins of his race. It's a quest that will alienate him from the other vampires and plunge him into a dark, long-held secret that longs to be set free. The graphic novel is an adaptation of the cult novel by Anne Rice.

Batman & Dracula. Written by Doug Moench. Illustrated by Kelley Jones. DC Comics, 1991–1995. **T**

> When the most fearsome vampire of all—Dracula—comes to Gotham City, only the Dark Knight Detective Batman (Bruce Wayne) can prevent the undead from taking over Gotham. When Batman pays the ultimate price to save his city, how long can the city last when its protector is one of the undead and a bloodthirsty vampire? The trilogy was originally printed from 1991 to 1995.

> > *Red Rain.* 2d ed.1997. 96pp. 1-56389-036-4.
> > *Crimson Mist.* 2d ed. 2001. 96pp. 1-56389-495-5.
> > *Bloodstorm.* 1994. 96pp. 1-56389-177-8, hardcover; 1995, 1-56389-185-9, softcover.

The Black Forest. Written by Todd Livingston and Robert Tinnell. Illustrated by Neil Vokes. Image Comics, 2004–2005. **T**

> During World War I, the Germans are conducting a secret program called Project Prometheus to win the war and break the front lines. Now daredevil American pilot Jack Shannon and Britain's greatest stage magician Archie Caldwell must go behind enemy lines to the mysterious Black Forest and stop the plans to reanimate the dead using the secrets of the captured Frankenstein

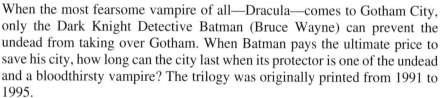

Monster. The odds are definitely stacked against them. What can two men do to stop a project that is heavily protected by Frankenstein's Monster, werewolves, Nosferatu, and the dark sorcerer known as Avery Dye? In the second collection, Hack and Archie must take on the mad scientist Dr. Bosch, who is looking for the secrets of Dr. Frankenstein and will stop at nothing to get them.

> *Vol. 1.* 2004. 104pp. 1-58240-350-3.
>
> *Vol. 2: The Castle of Shadows.* 2005 64pp. 1-58240-561-1.

Blade. Created by Marv Wolfman and Gene Colan. Marv Comics, 1998– . **T** 🎞 ▭

Since his first appearance in 1973, Blade has continued to be a popular underground character in Marvel Comics. His mother was bitten by a vampire at the moment of his birth, and since then he has been a daywalker: a living vampire who can walk among the living in sunlight. Half man and half vampire, he will not rest until every vampire is dead. He often hunts with the aid of other vampire hunters, including Quincy Harker, Rachael Van Helsing, Morbius the Living Vampire, Frank Drake, and others. The character appeared in a hit trilogy of Blade movies from 1998 to 2004, with Wesley Snipes in the lead role as the vampire hunter and a new cable series.

> *Sins of the Father.* Written by Marc Andreyko. Illustrated by Bart Sears. 1998. 46pp. 0-7851-0707-X.
>
> *Black & White.* Written by Marv Wolfman and Chris Claremont. Illustrated by Tony DeZuniga and Gene Colan. 2004. 144pp. 0-7851-1469-6.

***Blood + Water.* Written by Judd Winick. Illustrated by Tomm Coker.** Vertigo/DC Comics, 2004. 128pp. 1-4012-0175-X. **M**

Adam Heller was the darling of high school, but after graduating he came down with a debilitating disease that hasn't given him much longer to live. Now his two best friends, Joshua and Nicole, have a secret that just may save his life: they're vampires. Now Adam has a new lease on "life," but when a dark presence disrupts his happiness, Adam discovers some hard truths about what it really means to be a vampire.

***The Book of Jack.* Written by D. P. Filippi. Illustrated by O. G. Boiscommun.** Humanoids Publishing, 2001. 48pp. 1-930652-19-4. **T**

When initiation into a street gang involves breaking into a supposedly haunted mansion, kindhearted and cautious young Jack steals the first thing he sees—a dusty old book. But it's no ordinary book. Strangely enough, it tells Jack his entire life story, and even worse, a curse is set loose on him and he's transformed into a werewolf. With no cure in sight, Jack and his friend Sam must search for one before it's too late.

Boy Vampire. Written by Carlos Trillo. Illustrated by Eduardo Risso. Strip Art Features, 2003–2004. **M**

For more than 5,000 years, a nameless boy vampire has roamed Earth and has been unable to die. Every time he has been injured, the next morning he has been magically healed, with no evidence of any wounds. Since the time of ancient Egypt and the pharaohs, there has been one other immortal been pursuing the boy: Ahmasi, a vengeful woman from his past who will stop at nothing to destroy him. Though many years have passed since they first met, her adamant resolve to destroy him has never waned. They prepare for their final conflict.

Vol. 1: The Resurrection. 2003. 132pp. 1-931724-33-4.
Vol. 2: The Curse. 2003. 156pp. 1-593960-05-0.
Vol. 3: Destruction. 2004. 98pp. 9-076752-54-0.
Vol. 4: Resolution. 2004. 86pp. 9-076752-56-7.

Bram Stoker's Dracula: Graphic Album. Written by Roy Thomas. Illustrated by Mike Mignola. Topps, Inc., 1993. 180pp. No ISBN. **M**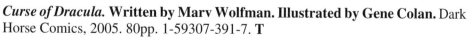

Adaptation of the 1992 movie. Jonathan Harker, a young lawyer, finds himself assigned to a gloomy village in Europe. When he meets Count Dracula, the vampire is entranced by a picture of Harker's fiancée, Mina Murray, and travels to London to seduce her. Once in his thrall, Mina's life hangs in the balance, and only a rescue attempt by Harker and Professor Van Helsing can save her soul.

Castlevania: The Belmont Legacy. Written by Marc Andreyko. Illustrated by E. J. Su. IDW Publishing, 2005. 128pp. 1-933239-19-0. **M**

Based on the cult-hit video game series by Konami. The Belmont family has for generations been at war with Dracula, the lord of the vampires. Young Christopher Belmont is the latest generation to continue the hunt for Dracula. The grandson of the fabled vampire hunter Simon Belmont, like his family before him he will not rest until Dracula is once again returned to the grave.

<u>**Crimson.**</u> **Written by Brian Augustyn. Illustrated by Humberto Ramos.** Cliffhanger!/WildStorm Productions/DC Comics ,1999–2001. **T**

© 2006 Humberto Ramos.

Alex Elder is a typical angst-ridden teen, but after an attack by vampires that leaves him dead, he finds himself reborn as a vampire with a thirst for blood. Alex is rescued by an ancient vampire elder named Eskimus, who believes Alex is the chosen one—a vampire who will play a pivotal role in the ultimate battle of good versus evil. There have been other "chosen ones" before him, but they have all become demonic pawns of the vampire queen Lisseth. Now Alex must fight the evil within him and find out what his true calling is. Is he the chosen one, or will his thirst for blood overcome him and send him to the dark side?

Tome 1: Loyalty and Loss. 1999. 160pp. 1-56389-532-3.
Tome 2: Heaven and Earth. 2000. 160pp. 1-56389-647-8.
Tome 3: Earth Angel. 2001. 160pp. 1-56389-768-7.
Tome 4: Redemption. 2001. 160pp. 1-56389-790-3.

Curse of Dracula. Written by Marv Wolfman. Illustrated by Gene Colan. Dark Horse Comics, 2005. 80pp. 1-59307-391-7. **T**

The original creative team of the Marvel Comics series <u>The Tomb of Dracula</u>, Marv Wolfman and Gene Colan, reunited here with their unique spin on the legend of Count Dracula. Jonathan Van Helsing and his team of vampire hunters scour Los Angeles for signs of the vampire lord's return after a mysterious figure is seen among the higher-class politicians of the city. When the blood-drained bodies begin to appear, it's only a matter of time before the hunters become the hunte.

CVO. Written by Alex Garner and Jeff Mariotte. Illustrated by Gabriel Hernandez and Antonio Vazquez. IDW Publishing, 2004–2005. **M**

When there is a global threat that's too tough to handle, it's time to contact the one branch of the U.S. government with the fangs to do it: Covert Vampiric Operations (CVO). Agents Cross, Bools, and Britt, all blood-sucking vampires, take on global espionage with their own brand of prejudice. Fromtaking down a mad Latin American dictator who has acquired nukes, to a quest across Italy, Iraq, and Russia to locate an arcane and ancient relic of considerable power, the CVOs are ready for any job.

Vol. 1: Covert Vampiric Operations. 2004. 116pp. 1-932382-40-2.
Vol. 2: Rogue State. 2005. 120pp. 1-932382-93-3.

***Damn Nation.* Written by Andrew Cosby. Illustrated by J. Alexander.** Dark Horse Comics, 2005. 104pp. 1-59307-389-5. **M**

The United States has been shut off from the world following a vampire plague that devastated the country, and now barbed wire and concrete barricades keep the plague from spreading to other countries. When a small group of scientists outside Buffalo, New York, discover a cure, the president of the United States' current office at the U.S. Embassy in London sends a Special Ops team to infiltrate the infested nation and retrieve the cure. Meanwhile, there are others out there who would prefer not to see the United States rise again.

Essential Tomb of Dracula. Written by Marv Wolfman, Archie Goodwin and various. Illustrated by Gene Colan. Marvel Comics, 2003–2005. **T**

Collects the classic 1970s Tomb of Dracula series, which features Dracula battling against a vampire-hunting group, including Dr. Quincy Harker, Rachel Van Helsing, Dracula ancestor Frank Drake, vampire Hannibal King, and the half-vampire hunter Blade. Together the hunters take on the Prince of Darkness as well as other fiendish foes. Dracula also battles against demons, other vampires, ghosts, elemental spirits, Marvel Comics heroes, and more in his quest to quench his thirst for blood.

Vol. 1. 2003. 560pp. 0-7851-0920-X.
Vol. 2. 2004. 592pp. 0-7851-1461-0.
Vol. 3. 2004. 584pp. 0-7851-1558-7.
Vol. 4. 2005. 576pp. 0-7851-1709-1.

♣ Hellsing. Written and illustrated by Kohta Hirano. Dark Horse Comics, 2003–2005. **T Japanese manga.** あ

There's a secret Protestant organization in England called Hellsing that's ready to take down the minions of darkness and the creatures of the night. A centuries-old group that has passed down its leadership to the youngest Van Hellsing, Integral Van Hellsing, they are all that can stop the vampires overtaking England. Integral is tough as nails and so is her organization, but no one is as tough as Alucard, a centuries-old vampire with the skill and wit needed to eradicate evil. With his shotgun in hand and accompanied by his newly turned vampire Victoria Ceres as backup, he's the only weapon they'll ever need to take out the trash and rescue the world from evil. YALSA's Quick

Picks for Reluctant Readers list featured the series in 2005. The hit manga, which is still being published, was adapted into a hit thirteen-episode anime series in Japan.

> *Vol. 1.* 2003. 208pp. 1-59307-056-X.
> *Vol. 2.* 2004. 180pp. 1-59307-057-8.
> *Vol. 3.* 2004. 192pp. 1-59307-202-3.
> *Vol. 4.* 2004. 192pp. 1-59307-259-7.
> *Vol. 5.* 2004. 208pp. 1-59307-272-4.
> *Vol. 6.* 2005. 192pp. 1-59307-302-X.
> *Vol. 7.* 2005. 192pp. 1-59307-348-8.

Lament of the Lamb. **Written and illustrated by Kei Toume.** TOKYOPOP, 2004–2005. **O Japanese manga.**

High school student Kazuna Takashiro doesn't have much of an appetite now-adays, and oddly enough he has become enamored of the color red that the girl he likes paints. He still misses his mother, who died from a mysterious disease when he was very young, and he has had a tough upbringing living with his parents' friends after his father left. When his older sister Chizuna unexpect-edly comes back into his life, she reveals to him the family secret: that they're from a family of vampires. Now Kazuna is dealing with an insatiable thirst for blood, and both he and his sister descend further into madness, becoming in-creasingly less human. How much longer can they prevent the inevitable, when they succumb to their now-basic urge for crimson red blood?

> *Vol. 1.* 2004. 216pp. 1-59182-814-7.
> *Vol. 2.* 2004. 196pp. 1-59182-815-5.
> *Vol. 3.* 2004. 200pp. 1-59182-862-7.
> *Vol. 4.* 2004. 200pp. 1-59182-863-5.
> *Vol. 5.* 2005. 192pp. 1-59532-004-0.
> *Vol. 6.* 2005. 200pp. 1-59532-005-9.
> *Vol. 7.* 2005. 192pp. 1-59532-006-7.

Lycanthrope Leo. **Written by Kengo Kaji. Illustrated by Kenji Okamura.** VIZ Media, LLC, 1998. 272pp. 1-56931-237-0. **T Japanese manga.**

Leo is not your normal teenager in high school: he's secretly a lycanthrope—and he can transform into a werelion. His powers manifested af-ter his seventeenth birthday, and he's become something much more than man. When the bullies at school are ganging up on a friend of his, can Leo re-sist the blood-letting urges rising up in him? Can he really unleash the animal inside him and slaughter the taunters?

Model. **Written and illustrated by So-young Lee.** TOKYOPOP, 2004–2005. **T Korean manhwa.**

Jae, a Korean student studying art in Europe, isn't quiet sure she has what it takes to be the best painter possible, but she's sure going to try. When her roommate brings home a drunken man she picked up, Jae reluctantly lets him stay the night. After dreaming that he bites her, she awakens to discover that he really did! Fascinated by her, this beautiful and alluring vampire named

Michael has a proposition for Jae: if she comes to live with him in his castle and he can drink her blood, he will let Jae paint his portrait—something no one has done since Michael painted his own portrait centuries ago when he was human. Now Jae is in a castle with the strangest of roommates, including Michael's vampiric son Ken, who is seemingly infatuated with her, as well as Eva Rose, a former model who now works for Michael as his maid and housekeeper. Will this opportunity to live with Michael in his castle help her to become the best painter in the world, or has she damned herself to being a slave to a blood-sucking vampire?

Vol. 1. 2004. 216pp. 1-59182-711-6.
Vol. 2. 2004. 200pp. 1-59182-712-4.
Vol. 3. 2004. 200pp. 1-59182-713-2.
Vol. 4. 2004. 208pp. 1-59182-714-0.
Vol. 5. 2005. 192pp. 1-59532-007-5.
Vol. 6. 2005. 200pp. 1-59532-008-3.
Vol. 7. 2005. 192pp. 1-59532-009-1.

Neal Adams' Monsters. **Written and illustrated by Neal Adams.** Vanguard Productions, 2004. 68pp. 1-887591-55-9. **T**

Frankenstein's Monster! The Werewolf! Dracula! This is comic book legend Neal Adams's imaginary tale of what would happen if all three of the best-known monsters from literature and film were featured together in one story. One dark night a young couple find themselves pursued by wolves and are saved by the dashing Count Vlad. The rescued man is none other than the nephew of Baron Frankenstein, and Vlad holds the man's fiancée captive in his castle until the Baron's nephew can build a new monster to aid the vampire. Meanwhile, the fiancée is more than she seems, and transforms into a werewolf. When all three beasts collide, it's the ultimate tag team match between the greatest monsters.

New Vampire Miyu. **Written and illustrated by Narumi Kakinouchi.** Studio Ironcat, LLC., 1999–2001. **T Japanese manga.**

The Western Shinma have set their sights on invading the Miyu's spirit realm of Kakinouchi and punishing Miyu for banishing their kind. Carlua, a blood relation of Miyu's companion Larva, is consumed with destroying Miyu, but the first order is to cut the bond between Miyu and Larva. Following Miyu's death at the hands of Larva, he rejoins the Western Shinma, and a half-girl/half-vampire named Yui roams the realm of Kakinouchi in search of her destiny to resurrect Miyu. Meanwhile, the Shinma have taken over the realm, and only a reborn vampire can take on the Shinma and restore the balance.

Vol. 1: The Shinma Menace. 1999. 224pp. 1-929090-08-0.
Vol. 2: The Western Shinma Strike Back. 2000. 196pp. 1-929090-04-8.
Vol. 3: The Shinma Wars. 2000. 214pp. 1-929090-06-4.
Vol. 4: The Return of Miyu. 2000. 214pp. 1-929090-10-2.
Vol. 5: The Wrath of Miyu. 2001. 214pp. 1-929090-12-9.

Rebirth. Written and illustrated by Kang-Woo Lee. TOKYOPOP, 2003– . **T Korean manhwa.**

For over 300 years the Dark Magician vampire Deshwitat Lived Rudbich has been imprisoned in stone and has been contemplating revenge on Light Sorcerer Kalutika Maybus for the death of his beloved fiancée, Lilith. Now accidentally freed from his limbo exile created by Kalutika, the vampire once again walks the world of the living in the foreign world of the twenty-first century. Although his powers were originally meant for good, it has been prophesied that Kalutika will destroy Earth with his powers, and his reign must end. Now Deshwitat wants to claim vengeance for the death of Lilith and do whatever it takes to save Earth from Kalutika, and then let himself die. He's joined in his quest by Millenear Sheffield, a twenty-one-year-old excommunicated exorcist; Rett Buttler, a swordsman who knew Deshwitat 300 years before and is cursed with immortality; and Remi Do, a seventeen-year-old supernatural investigator. As Deshwitat soon realizes, he's going to need more than his vampire and Dark Magician skills to defeat Kalutika. Will a Dark Magician vampire be able to do the impossible and learn to harness the power of the Light? Twenty volumes have been published in Korea.

> *Vol. 1.* 2003. 176pp. 1-59182-216-5.
> *Vol. 2.* 2003. 176pp. 1-59182-217-3.
> *Vol. 3.* 2003. 176pp. 1-59182-218-1.
> *Vol. 4.* 2003. 176pp. 1-59182-219-X.
> *Vol. 5.* 2003. 176pp. 1-59182-220-3.
> *Vol. 6.* 2004. 184pp. 1-59182-524-5.
> *Vol. 7.* 2004. 184pp. 1-59182-525-3.
> *Vol. 8.* 2004. 184pp. 1-59182-526-1.
> *Vol. 9.* 2004. 192pp. 1-59182-527-X.
> *Vol. 10.* 2004. 192pp. 1-59182-528-8.
> *Vol. 11.* 2004. 192pp. 1-59182-529-6.
> *Vol. 12.* 2005. 192pp. 1-59532-027-X.
> *Vol. 13.* 2005. 200pp. 1-59532-028-8.
> *Vol. 14.* 2005. 200pp. 1-59532-029-6.
> *Vol. 15.* 2005. 192pp. 1-59532-030-X.
> *Vol. 16.* 2005. 192pp. 1-59532-660-X.
> *Vol. 17.* 2006. 192pp. 1-59532-661-8.
> *Vol. 18.* 2006. 192pp. 1-59532-662-6.
> *Vol. 19.* 2006. 192pp. 1-59816-211-x.

6

Renfield: A Tale of Madness. **Written by Gary Reed. Illustrated by Galen Showman.** Image Comics, 2006. 192pp. 1-58240-674x. **O**

A look at the life of Renfield, the bug-eating servant of Dracula in Bram Stoker's classic novel. Taken from the novel and adding more background characterization, it's a look at what makes a man become a servant of evil and what it ultimately costs him to be released. A man plagued by madness, Renfield is admitted to an insane asylum in England, where he spends his days catching flies and putting them in his pocket. He has been having visions of a mysterious Count from Transylvania, and his madness becomes more focused on this "true messiah," who will deliver him. When a Russian cargo ship delivering Transylvanian dirt arrives, seemingly deserted save for the dead captain, drained of his blood, Renfield discovers his true calling and realizes that his "Master," Count Dracula, has arrived. Will he stay in his Master's service, or will he rediscover his humanity in Mina, a lovely girl who is the object of Dracula's machinations?

Richard Matheson's I Am Legend. **Written by Steve Niles, Adapted from the work by Richard Matheson. Illustrated by Elman Brown.** IDW Publishing, 2003. 224pp. 1-932382-08-9. **M**

> How would you survive if you were the only one left alive—the only one in the world who isn't a vampire? For Richard Neville, life day-to-day is a struggle and a nightmare that is all too real. Haunted by the deaths of his family in the vampiric plague, he's the last human alive in a world overrun by vampires. Trapped all night in his boarded up, garlic-infested house, he waits and waits for the daylight to come. When the sun is out, he rules the streets of Inglewood, taking what he wants and needs, but when the night comes the vampires taunt him outside his home. How long can one man survive when the world is after his blood? The adaptation of the classic horror novel originally published in 1954.

<u>**Sea of Red.**</u> **Written by Rick Remender. Illustrated by Kieron Dwyer.** Image Comics, 2005–2006. **T**

© 2006 Rick Remender, Kieron Dwyer, and Max Douglas.

> The ancient Spanish vampire Marco Esperanza has spent nearly 500 years alone, adrift at the bottom of the sea. Tied to the bow of a sunken ship and barely alive, he's inadvertently rescued by a famous film director who was scouting for shooting locations for his next feature. Now freed of his prison, the vampire is out to seek revenge on Lesser Blackthroat, the man who brought this curse upon him. As Marco soon discovers, there's much more to the curse and why he became a vampire, as the truth of Lesser Blackthroat is revealed.
>
> > *Vol. 1: No Grave But the Sea.* 2005. 104pp. 1-58240-537-9.
> > *Vol. 2: No Quarter.* 2006. 104pp. 1-58240-541-7.
> > *Vol. 3: The Deadlights.* 2006. 120pp. 1-58240-666-9.

Spike. **Written by Peter David and Scott Tipton. Illustrated by Fernando Goni.** IDW Publishing, 2006. 152pp. 1-600100-30-9. **T** ▭

> Three short story collections featuring Joss Whedon's fan-favorite vampire, Spike. In "Old Times," Spike is out to get revenge on Halfrek, the vengeance demon who unwittingly set him on the path to becoming a vampire. In "Old Wounds," a retired L.A. detective arrives at Wolfram and Hart, and Spike attempts to solve a decades-old murder mystery. In "Lost and Found," Spike and Angel try to stop a vampire from killing innocents in broad daylight. The graphic novel is a spin-off from the cult-hit television shows *Buffy the Vampire Slayer* and *Angel*.

Spike vs. Dracula. **Written by Peter David. Illustrated by Joe Corroney.** IDW Publishing, 2006. 120pp. 1-600100-12-0. **T** ▭

> A spin-off of *Buffy the Vampire Slayer* and *Angel* featuring the bleached-blonde vampire Spike against the one and only Dracula. One hundred twenty years ago, the evil vampire Angelus was cursed by gypsies and given his soul back. In revenge for the

curse, the gypsies were slaughtered by Angelus's vampire family of Darla, Drusilla, and William the Bloody, a.k.a. "Spike." But the vampire Dracula was close to the gypsy clan, and he will stop at nothing to get revenge. From there began a decades-long rivalry between Spike and Dracula that is steeped in blood, vengeance, and eleven quid.

Supernaturalists. **Written by Patrick Neighly. Illustrated by Jorge Heufemann.** Mad Yak Press, 2004. 160pp. 0-9717995-4-7. **M**

In Manhattan in 1926, Detective Edgar Drake is out to solve a murder mystery that appears to permeate even the highest society. Truth is stranger than fiction, and Detective Drake finds out that vampires really do walk among us. Now Drake is caught on the opposite side of the law with a mysterious vampire socialite by his side as they try to solve a murder case before it's too late.

Sword of Dracula. **Written by Jason Henderson. Illustrated by Greg Scott, William Belk, and Terry Pallot.** IDW Publishing, 2005. 156pp. 1-932382-70-4. **M**

© 2006 Jason Henderson.

Ronnie Van Helsing, leader of a squad of vampire hunters from the horror-fighting organization called the Polidorium, will do anything it takes to bring Dracula to justice. One of the few immortal vampires of legend, his agile strength and powers over blood and the undead make him one of humanity's deadliest foes. When two fallen angels, the true creators of vampires, are accidentally released from their prison on the Dead Sea, Ronnie reluctantly makes a deadly pact with the dreaded "Vlad the Impaler" for the survival of humanity and vampires against the angelic onslaught and their zombie armies of the dead.

Tales of the Vampires. **Written by Joss Whedon, Sam Loeb, et al. Illustrated by Tim Sale, Scott Morse, and various.** Dark Horse Comics, 2004. 144pp. 1-56971-749-4. **T**

Based on the mythology of Joss Whedon's television cult-hit series *Buffy the Vampire Slayer* (1997–2003) and *Angel* (1999–2004). Enter a world where vampires and other demons freely roam Earth and the only enemy they fear is a girl called a Slayer. Told from the perspective of young Watchers-in-training having their first encounters with vampires, the stories cover a variety of time periods, from medieval times, to the Depression, to today, and also include a rematch encounter between Buffy and Dracula, how Drusilla was made, and a story featuring the vampiric hero Angel.

30 Days of Night. **Written by Steve Niles. Illustrated by Ben Templesmith.** IDW Publishing, 2003– . 104pp. 0-9719775-5-0. **M**

For thirty days a year, Barrow, Alaska, the northernmost town in North America, is covered in total darkness. When husband and wife sheriff team Eben and Stella investigate a bizarre crime wave involving a pile of burned cell phones, they connect the dots and realize it's a ploy by someone or something trying to disable all communication. They soon realize that, isolated in pitch

Story © Steve Niles; artwork, Ben
Templesmith. © 2006 Idea + Design
Works, LLC.

blackness, Barrow has become the prime hunting ground for vicious vampires, who savor the thirty days of eternal darkness in their hunt for blood. The self-titled collection received recognition from YALSA's Popular Paperbacks for Young Adults committee in 2005 on the "All Kinds of Creepy" list. A feature film based on the property will be coming from the production studio of Sam Raimi, director of the Spider-Man movies and the classic Evil Dead films. Listed below are the original titles as well as the sequels and spin-offs that continue and expand on the events in the *30 Days of Night* graphic novel. The stories are listed in chronological order and continue the tale of the fate of the vampires against the backdrop of the darkest corner of Earth in Barrow, Alaska.

30 Days of Night. 2003. 104pp. 0-9719775-5-0. **M**

Vicious vampires take on the town of Barrow, Alaska, the only place on Earth where it is dark for thirty days straight. Can any human survive against the vampire horde?

Dark Days: A 30 Days of Night Sequel. 2004. 144pp. 1-932382-16-X.

Following the tragic events in Barrow, Alaska, Stella Olemaun is prepared to tell the world the truth about vampires in a book she is publishing. Now, armed and prepared, she's determined to put an end to the undead bloodthirsty creatures and has declared all-out war on them.

30 Days of Night: Return to Barrow. 2004. 144pp. 1-932382-36-4.

One year later after the events in Barrow, Alaska, Wayne Kitka arrives four days before complete darkness envelopes the town to find the truth about his brother's death. As darkness covers the city, once again the vampires come out to claim the town for their own.

30 Days of Night: Bloodsucker Tales. 2005.

An anthology series featuring tales by Steve Niles, Matt Fraction, Ben Templesmith, and Kody Chamberlain, set in the world of *30 Days of Night,* where evil never rests and vampires never stop thirsting for blood.

Vol. 1. 2005. 200pp. 1-932382-78-X
Vol. 2. 2005. 144pp. 1-933239-44-1.

30 Days of Night: Three Tales. 2006. 132pp. 1-933239-92-1.

A collection of three short stories set in a world where vampires run rampant.

Underworld. **Written by Kris Oprisko. Illustrated by Nic Postic.** IDW Publishing, 2004. 128pp. 1-932382-26-7. **M** 🎬

Adaptation of the successful 2003 movie in which war is about to erupt between the werewolves and the vampires. Caught in the middle is Selena, a female vampire who has fallen in love with Michael, a werewolf who may be the key to their race's future. Also included is a prequel story set several hundred years before the events of the movie.

<u>Vampi.</u> Written by David Conway. Illustrated by Kevin Lau. Anarchy Studios, 2001–2002. **M**

Set in the near future, when technology consumes cities and the vices of greed and excess rule the day, there exists a vigilante vampire fighter called Vampi who will stop at nothing to take on those who abuse their power and prey on the weak. She hopes that one day she can regain her humanity and rediscover her hidden past. For now she's much more than human, transformed by science into a vampiric killing machine. Vampi is armed with two deadly blades, and she's not shy about using them to dismember and behead anyone who stands in her way. Everyone from the corrupt Archangel organization, to vicious child enslavers like Endura, to other vampires, to common criminals has to face the blades and bite of Vampi.

> *Vol. 1: Switchblade Kiss.* 2001. 128pp. No ISBN.
> *Vol. 2: Tainted Love.* 2002. 128pp. No ISBN.

<u>Vampire: The Masquerade.</u> Written by various. Illustrated by Vince Locke, Andy Bennett, and various. Moonstone Books, 2002–2003. **M**

Based on the popular role-playing game created by White Wolf. Each focuses on a different clan of vampires, ranging from the Toreador, Nosferatu, Ventrue, and other clans to character-focused stories including fan-favorite vampire Madeleine Giovanni, in the gothlike world where vampires reign supreme. Each story line differs, and they feature themes such as clan battles, assassinations, intrigue, treasure hunts, and more.

> *Vol. 1: Blood & Roses.* 152pp. 0-9726443-0-X.
> *Vol. 2: Blood & Shadows.* 208pp. 0-9726443-5-0.
> *Vol. 3: Blood & Loyalty.* 248pp. 0-9726443-8-5.

The Vampire Dahlia. **Written and illustrated by Narumi Kakinouchi.** Studio Ironcat, LLC., 2003. 216pp. 1-929090-25-0. **T Japanese manga.**

 6

By day the vampire called Dahlia masquerades as Lia D. Green, an English student studying in Japan. She lives by herself in an old mansion, searching for the reincarnated soul of her vampire lover, Ranan. Facing immortality alone, she's desperate to be with him once again. When she meets another foreign exchange student from England, has she finally found him after all this time?

Vampire Loves. **Written and illustrated by Joann Sfar.** First Second, 2006. 188pp. 1-59643-093-1. **O**

© 2006 Joann Sfar.

Ferdinand the vampire is no ordinary dark creature of the night. He doesn't bite his victims; instead he pricks them with only one tooth to pass himself off as a mosquito just out for a gentle taste of blood. When it comes to his dating life, Ferdinand has a devil of a time finding that special someone, be she alive or dead. Joined by his talking cat Imhotep, he goes from adventure to adventure, always in search of that special woman. From a cheating lover who is a plant elemental, to flings with ghosts, to a Goth vampire, to a witch, Ferdinand finds that love definitely doesn't get any easier when you're dead.

Vampire Princess Miyu. Written and illustrated by Narumi Kakinouchi. Studio Ironcat, LLC, 2001–2004. **T Japanese manga.** あ

A young vampire girl named Miyu must fulfill her destiny as Guardian of the Shinma (demons) to track down the stray manipulative Shinma, who have escaped their realm of origin, the Dark. The Shinma are crafty and have blended into human society, where they can use humans as they will. With the aid of her friend and servant Larva of the Western Shinma, Miyu is one of the only vampiric guardians able to flush the Shinma out and send them back to the Dark. The Western Shinma are growing in discord and seek to break Miyu's ties with Larva. The popular Shojo (girl's manga) series spawned many spin-off and sequel titles, including an anime series.

> *Vol. 1: Origins.* 2001. 216pp. 1-929090-16-1.
> *Vol. 2: Encounters.* 2002. 216pp. 1-929090-18-8.
> *Vol. 3: Déjà Vu.* 2002. 236pp. 1-929090-19-6.
> *Vol. 4: Pursuit.* 2003. 212pp. 1-929090-28-5.
> *Vol. 5: Nature.* 2003. 212pp. 1-929090-36-6.
> *Vol. 6: Capture.* 2003. 212pp. 1-929090-60-9.
> *Vol. 7: Vortex.* 2004. 216pp. 1-929090-82-X.
> *Vol. 8: Dissention.* 2004. 216pp. 1-929090-83-8.
> *Vol. 9.* 2004. 216pp. 1-932575-14-6.

Vampire Yui. Written and illustrated by Narumi Kakinouchi. IC Entertainment/ Studio Ironcat, LLC, 2001–2003. **T Japanese manga.**

A young girl named Yui discovers that something's not right with her—she's been sick for an awful long time and now has the oddest craving for blood. After having visions of a strange woman named Miyu, Yui learns that she is in fact half-human/half-vampire. Join Yui on her path of discovery with her companion Nagi as she finds out more about her full transformation into a vampire, her strange connections to Vampire Princess Miyu, and what happens when a vampire has the morals of a human while battling against a dark mysterious force that's out to manipulate her.

> *Vol. 1: A New Awakening.* 2d ed. 2003. 192pp. 1-929090-13-7.
> *Vol. 2: Currents of Life.* 2d ed. 2004.196pp. 1-929090-22-6.
> *Vol. 3: Eternal Dreams.* 2003. 196pp. 1-929090-33-1.
> *Vol. 4: Puppet Master.* 2003. 202pp. 1-929090-43-9.
> *Vol. 5: Heart of Truth.* 2003. 216pp. 1-929090-65-X.

Vampires. **Written by various. Illustrated by various.** Dark Horse Comics, 2002. 48pp. 1-56971-683-8. **O**

An anthology by some of the best comic book writers and artists, including Mike Mignola, Bryan Talbot, Gary Gianni, and Tommy Lee Edwards. Each shares his take on the bloodthirsty undead. From dark tales of families under the thrall of vampires to more humorous stories, the collection showcases a variety of pin-ups and short stories to haunt your dreams or tickle your funny bone.

Vamps. **Written by Elaine Lee. Illustrated by William Simpson.** Vertigo/DC Comics, 2000. 160pp. 1-56389-220-0. **M**

> Five alluring female vampires decide they've had enough of their abusive vampire master, who enthralled and turned them into what they are, so they do what any vampire female would do—they kill him. Now they're on the road heading out west on their Harleys in search of fun and a little blood, but some of the vampires' pasts are catching up with them, and their master might not be as dead as they thought.

The Wanderer. **Written and illustrated by Narumi Kakinouchi.** Studio Ironcat, LLC, 2004. **T Japanese manga.**

> Sei Kodo is a sixteen-year-old high school student studying music at the prestigious Japanese branch of the European Performing Arts Academy. He also is more than he appears: Sei is a vampire. Awakened by his lover, the vampire Yui, he's on a quest to find her even if he has to go all over Europe and Japan to do it. At school he discovers a music prodigy named Marie who seems to be much different than many of the high school students. Is Marie a fellow vampire, or something else? Is Marie the key to finding Yui? Sei had better find out soon, before he succumbs to something no vampire has ever survived: the pressures of high school!

> *Vol. 1: Full Moon.* 2004. 200pp. 1-929090-95-1.
> *Vol. 2: Quarter Moon.* 2004. 200pp. 1-929090-96-X.

Werewolf: The Apocalypse—Fang & Claw. **Written by Joe Gentile. Illustrated by Steve Ellis, Eddy Newell, and Jerry DeCaire.** Moonstone Books, 2003. **M**

> Werewolf stories based on and inspired by the cult-hit role-playing game of the same name. Werewolves (called "Garou") are not make-believe monsters: they truly exist. Divided into thirteen tribes all across the world, including the Bone Gnawers, the Black Furies, Children of Gaia, Fianna, and others, they try to protect Earth from the forces of those who seek to destroy it.

> *Vol. 1.* 2003. 168pp. 0-9721668-7-4.
> *Vol. 2.* 2003. 158pp. 0-9726443-4-2.

The Undead

Zombies, skeletons, golems, the reanimated dead—these are stories of those brought back to life from the land of the dead by humanity's own folley, mad scientists, or the dead's own will to continue to exist. The Walking Dead series, published by Image Comics, is an excellent example of this popular genre.

The Coffin. **Written by Phil Hester. Illustrated by Mike Huddleston.** Oni Press, 2001. 120pp. 1-929998-16-3. **O**

> Scientist Dr. Ashtar Ahmad has devised a suit of armor that can mysteriously trap the soul after death and give it eternal life in an iron coffin. Now the secrets of the soul can be revealed, and no one would ever have to die ever again. When terrorists seek to steal his technology, Ahmad is killed in the crossfire

and must become his own living experiment in a prototype suit of armor. Now dead but beyond death, he's out to save his daughter from a ruthless tycoon who has kidnapped her as a bargaining chip for the iron coffin.

Dark Edge. Written and illustrated by Yu Aikawa. DrMaster Publications, Inc., 2004– . T Japanese manga.

Following his mother's death, Kuro Takagi has been unsure what to do and where to go, since none of his other relatives wants to take him in. After his mother's cremation ceremony, he's summoned by his father—which is quite a shock to Kuro since he's always believed his father was dead. His father, it seems, is the headmaster at the Yotsuji Private High School, and Kuro transfers there to be reunited with him. The school has one main rule: no students are to be on campus after sunset. Kuro and some fellow students accidentally break this rule, and they quickly find out why the rule exists: the campus at night is teeming with zombies! What could possibly be worse than this? The zombies are part of the school faculty, and Kuro discovers that he has latent zombie abilities that have been dormant for far too long. The series originally ran for eleven volumes in Japan.

> *Vol. 1.* 2004. 200pp. 1-58899-039-7.
> *Vol. 2.* 2004. 200pp. 1-58899-040-0.
> *Vol. 3.* 2005. 200pp. 1-59796-030-6.
> *Vol. 4.* 2005. 200pp. 1-59796-024-1.
> *Vol. 5.* 2005. 208pp. 1-59796-025-X.
> *Vol. 6.* 2005. 200pp. 1-59796-026-8.
> *Vol. 7.* 2006. 200pp. 1-59796-027-6.
> *Vol. 8.* 2006. 200pp. 1-59796-028-4.
> *Vol. 9.* 2006. 200pp. 1-59796-029-2.

Dead@17. Written and illustrated by Josh Howard. Viper Comics, 2004– . O ◎

© 2006 Josh Howard.

Teenagers Nara Kilday and Hazy Foss are best friends stuck in the small town of Darlington Hills, going nowhere. Something dark and sinister is afoot as demonic zombies begin to tear apart the town, and Nara is horribly murdered inside her house by an intruder. Meanwhile, Hazy finds herself attacked by the zombies and rescued by the most unlikely hero: Nara. Now while the fate of the town hangs in the balance, an axe-wielding Nara finds herself a key figure in the climactic battle of good versus evil. Even worse, she might be prophesied to be on the bad guys' side! *Dead@17: The Complete Collection* collects the entire three volumes in a limited-edition slipcase.

> *Vol. 1: The Complete First Series.* 2004. 112pp. 0-9754193-0-7.
> *Vol. 2: Blood of Saints.* 2004. 112pp. 0-9754193-1-5.
> *Vol. 3: Revolution.* 2005. 112pp. 0-9754193-3-1.
> *Dead@17: The Complete Collection.* 2006. 336pp. 0-9754193-5-8.

***Essential Monster of Frankenstein.* Written by Gary Friedrich and Doug Moench. Illustrated by Mike Ploog, John Buscema, and various.** Marvel Comics, 2004. 496pp. 0-7851-1634-6. **T**

> Collects the classic 1970s horror stories from Marvel Comics featuring a retelling of Mary Shelley's classic monster as he battles against Dracula, Werewolf by Night, and others in the present day, where he hunts for the last remaining descendant of his creator, Victor Frankenstein, to exact his revenge.

***Frankenstein.* Based on the story by Mary Shelley. Adapted by Martin Powell. Illustrated by Pat Olliffe.** Moonstone, 2003. 88pp. 0-9712937-9-1. **T**

> The classic tale of the modern Prometheus, adapted as a graphic novel. In flashbacks, Victor Von Frankenstein tells the strange tale of how he, a man of science, played god and created a man from the dead reanimated. After tragedy strikes both man and monster, a final confrontation takes place in the frozen north between the patchwork creature and his equally fiendish creator.

***George A. Romero's Dawn of the Dead.* Written by Steve Niles. Illustrated by Chee.** IDW Publishing, 2004. 104pp. 1-932382-32-1. **M**

> Adaptation of the cult-classic 1978 zombie horror sequel to Romero's *Night of the Living Dead*. When the zombie plague takes over the city and pushes the survivors elsewhere, four people escape from the urban catastrophe and barricade themselves in a shopping mall. Can they survive there on their own, or will they perish at the hands of either the militant street bikers ruling the streets or the brain-eating living dead?

***Marvel Zombies.* Written by Robert Kirkman. Illustrated by Sean Phillips.** Marvel, 2006. 120pp., 0-7851-2277-X, hardcover; 120pp., 0-7851-2014-9, softcover. **O**

> A dark twist on fan-favorite heroes. In a world very similar to that the Marvel Comics heroes such as Spider-Man, Captain American, and the X-Men call home, an alien virus has turned the entire world into zombies. The super-heroes of the world are all still heroes . . . they're just dead zombies, too. As the zombies continue to crave human flesh, are there any heroes or villains who can repel the zombified costumed monstrosities, or are humanity's days numbered? An over-the-top romp through the Marvel Universe, with a dash of good old horror mixed in.

***Mary Shelley's Frankenstein.* Written by Mary Shelley. Adapted by Gary Reed. Illustrated by Frazer Irving.** Penguin Graphics/Penguin Group, 2005. 176pp. 0-14-240407-1. **T**

> Originally published in 1818, this is the story of Victor Frankenstein and his failed experiment to create life from the sewn together parts of cadavers. The end result of his quest is a patchwork monster, both cruel and misunderstood. Instead of unlocking the key to everlasting life and immortality, Victor and his creation's lives become intertwined in a harrowing tale of horror and sadness, resulting in suffering, pain, and death.

***Obergeist: Director's Cut.* Written by Dan Jolley. Illustrated by Tony Harris and Ray Snyder.** Image Comics/Top Cow Productions, 2002. 192pp. 1-58240-243-4. **O**

Dr. Jurgen Steinholtz was one of the most gruesome and cruel butchers in World War II. A German scientist working under the direction of Josef Mengele, he performed many experiments on Jews and was responsible for thousands of their deaths in the name of science. Cursed by a Jewish man with the gift of second sight who revealed to Jurgen what madness he had performed, he was silenced and executed for his blasphemy against Hitler and buried with those he tortured. Now a corpse reanimated in the year 2147, he has become a pawn in the final battle between Heaven and Hell, as a psionic being whose power a new Nazi-like force would like to harvest, but Jurgen is just looking for atonement and forgiveness.

Resident Evil. Written and illustrated by various. WildStorm Productions/DC Comics, 1999–2002. **M**

© 2006 WildStorm Productions/
DC Comics and Capcom.

Based on the popular video game series. The town of Raccoon City has been plagued by an epidemic of monstrous proportions. When a top-secret biotechnical experiment goes wrong, the town is turned into a haven for the undead. As zombies, mutant dogs, and evil mutations run amok in the city, a strike team has been authorized to contain and eliminate the evil. The Code Veronica series of titles was originally published in Hong Kong and reprinted in the United States.

Collection One. 1999. 160pp. 1-56389-572-2.
Code Veronica: Book 1. 2002. 144pp. 1-56389-899-3.
Code Veronica: Book 2. 2002. 144pp. 1-56389-919-1.
Code Veronica: Book 3. 2002. 144pp. 1-56389-920-5.
Code Veronica: Book 4. 2002. 144pp. 1-56389-921-3.

***Shaun of the Dead.* Written by Chris Ryall. Illustrated by Zach Howard.** IDW Publishing, 2005. 104pp. 1-933239-43-3. **O**

Slacker Londoner Shaun must try to turn his souring life around by saving his relationship with his ex-girlfriend, reconciling with his mother, and dealing with an entire city that's been turned into flesh-eating zombies. An adaptation of the cult-classic romantic zombie comedy movie released in 2004.

3x3 Eyes. Written and illustrated by Yuzo Takada. Dark Horse Comics, 2001–2004. **O Japanese manga.** あ

Pai is a Sanjiyan—a three-eyed, mystical immortal race and one of the last of her kind. She's come down from the Tibetan lands to find Yakumo, a reckless high school student from Tokyo, to tell him of his father's death and also to find a way to become human. When an accident takes Yakumo's life, his soul is absorbed into Pai, and he's given new life as her unkillable zombie servant. Now the two of them are joined together in their quest for Pai's humanity and to restore Yakumo's, but the road ahead of them is blocked by an almost unending legion of hellish fiends. Two anime series were released in Japan that were based on the manga.

Vol. 1: House of the Demons. 2003. 160pp. 1-56971-930-6.

Vol. 2: Curse of the Gesu. 2003. 152pp. 1-56971-931-4.
Vol. 3: Flight of the Demon. 2001. 208pp. 1-56971-553-X.
Vol. 4: Blood of the Sacred Demon. 2002. 144pp. 1-56971-735-4.
Vol. 5: Summoning of the Beast. 2002. 152pp. 1-56971-747-8.
Vol. 6: Key to the Sacred Land. 2003. 136pp. 1-56971-881-4.
Vol. 7: The Shadow of the Kunlun. 2003. 224pp. 1-56971-981-0.
Vol. 8: Descent of the Mystic City. 2004. 288pp. 1-59307-216-3.

Wake the Dead. **Written by Steve Niles. Illustrated by Chee.** IDW Publishing, 2004. 128pp. 1-932382-22-4. **M**

A retelling of the Frankenstein story set in modern times. College medical student Victor and his friends are searching for a way to cheat death and do what his medical school could never dream of. After a pig is resurrected, Victor yearns for more, and his patchwork man just might be it, no matter that it may cost Victor his girlfriend, his friends, and the lives of innocents. Once again man learns the price he pays for playing God, as something that should never have been born rises from the dead and lives again.

The Walking Dead. **Written by Robert Kirkman. Illustrated by Tony Moore and Charlie Adlard.** Image Comics, 2004– . **M**

© 2006 Robert Kirkman.

Police officer Rick Grimes was injured in the line of duty and woke from his coma to a world much harsher than the one he left. Civilization has been nearly destroyed by an unknown epidemic, and now flesh-eating zombies have overrun entire cities. It's unknown how far the damage has spread. Civilization as we know it has collapsed, and the streets are deserted. Lost and confused, Rick is rescued by a small band of humans who have escaped the collapse of civilization and are now hunkered down outside of Atlanta. Reunited with his family and his partner from the police force, Rick and the small band of brothers have formed a struggling family that must support itself or die. In a time when there's little hope for any rescue, a tragedy of epic proportions has done the impossible—brought people even closer to one another. But how long can they survive when the threat of zombies lurks around every corner?

6

Vol. 1: Days Gone Bye. 2004. 144pp. 1-58240-358-9.
Vol. 2: Miles Behind Us. 2004. 136pp. 1-58240-413-5.
Vol. 3: Safety Behind Bars. 2005. 136pp. 1-58240-487-9.
Vol. 4: The Heart's Desire. 2005. 136pp. 1-58240-530-1.
Vol. 5: The Best Defense. 2006. 136pp. 1-58240-612-X.
Vol. 6: This Sorrowful Life. 2007. 144pp. 1-58240-684-7.
Walking Dead Book 1. 2006. 304pp. 1-58240-619-7, hardcover.
Walking Dead Book II. 2006. 304pp. 1-58240-698-7, hardcover.

War on Flesh. **Written by Greg Hildebrandt and Justin Boring. Illustrated by Tim Smith.** TOKYOPOP, 2005– . **O Neo-manga.**

A voodoo curse is released in the bayou of Louisiana, and a plague of hornets has been released. Called the Ew Chott, the locusts carry a plague that turn the dead into zombies and rips the hearts out of living creatures, replacing them with a Black Heart Hive. With each new soul captured, the original curse maker becomes stronger and stronger. To stop this plague, five individuals have to set aside their personal differences and work together to conquer the zombie king and the army of the undead. Two other volumes in the series are forthcoming and have not been released at the time of writing.

> *Vol. 1.* 2005. 192pp. 1-59816-070-2.

ZombieWorld. Dark Horse Comics, 2005. **O**

A 42,000-year-old Hyberborean mummy has just moved into a small-town museum in Whistler, Massachusetts, and one by one the residents of the city are disappearing. The proprietor of the museum blames the disappearances on the mummy, but the dead can't hurt the living, right? Little do the townsfolk know that long-dead Azzul Gotha has returned from the dead and soon, with his zombie army, they'll bring forth a tribute to the worm gods of old. The residents of the city will face a final battle in the local cemetery against Azzul Gotha and the armies of the undead. *Winter's Dregs* collects the short mini-miniseries when New York City is infested by zombies living in the sewers under the city and are about to surface.

> *Champion of the Worms.* 2d ed. Written by Mike Mignola. Illustrated by Pat McEown. 2005. 80pp. 1-59307-407-7.
> *Winter's Dregs.* Written by Bob Fingerman, Kelley Jones, Pat Mills, and Gordon Rennie. Illustrated by Tommy Lee Edwards, J. Deadstock, and Gary Erskine. 2005. 240pp. 1-59307-384-4.

Rampant Animals and Other Eco-Monsters, Big and Small

These are stories about monsters and beasts, both large and small, other than the traditional vampire, werewolf, or undead zombie, that strike back against people. The beasts can be man-made, from unknown origins, or even created by Mother Nature to exact revenge on humanity.

Art Adams' Creature Features. **Written and illustrated by Arthur Adams.** Dark Horse Comics, 1996. 104pp. 1-56971-214-X. **T** ◎ 🎬

Creature Features™ © 2006
Art Adams.

Known for his magnificent talent as a comic book artist, Art Adams's personal passions have always been with the classic monsters of cinema such as King Kong, Godzilla, and the creatures from Universal Studios' monster movies. Now in one collection are some of best monster stories illustrated by Art Adams, including a Godzilla story in which the lizard king must face off against a guardian warrior statue, an adaptation of the classic Universal Studios monster movie *The Creature from the Black Lagoon*, and a short story from Art Adams's own *King Kong* tribute comic book *Monkeyman and O'Brien*. A real treat for monster fans.

Bigfoot. **Written by Steve Niles and Rob Zombie. Illustrated by Richard Corben.** IDW Publishing, 2005. 128pp. 1-933239-14-X. **M**

> In the woods of the Pacific Northwest there still lives the legendary ape-man known as Bigfoot or Sasquatch. Some people think it's a hoax, but after a campsite murder scene that has baffled authorities and left young Billy an orphan, Billy knows that Bigfoot is definitely real. Years later, Bigfoot has returned from hiding and is viciously attacking campers and drivers in the vicinity of Shadow Hills National Park, and a much-older Billy is ready for revenge. For years Bigfoot has walked the fringes of society and avoided humans, but no more. Lock your doors and hide your children, because the man-eating prehistoric relic called Bigfoot is coming for you.

Firebreather. **Written by Phil Hester. Illustrated by Andy Kuhn.** Image Comics, 2004. 144pp. 1-58240-380-5. **T**

> Duncan never liked the messy divorce his parents had gone through, but he's dealing with it. Life with his mom has been good, but his dad has been a real monster, literally! A 300-foot-tall, city-smashing dragon, to be more precise. Now all Duncan wants to do after high school is go to college, but his dad wants him to join the family business and help him destroy the world!

Giantkiller. **Written and illustrated by Dan Brereton.** Image Comics, 2006. 128pp. 1-58240-539-5. **T**

> When giant monsters from another dimension attack San Francisco, the U.S. government creates "Jack," a genetically engineered, super-strong hybrid man/monster, to destroy the beasts. Armed with a sword, Jack the giant monster killer is the only weapon humanity needs to save the day. When Jack delves deeper and deeper into his mission to destroy the monsters, he discovers that there's more to his job than he realized. A tribute to Japanese kaiju (giant monster) movies such as the <u>Godzilla</u> series of films.

© 2006 Dan Brereton.

<u>Godzilla.</u> Dark Horse Comics, 1995–1998; Marvel Comics, 2006. **T** ◎ 🎬

> One of the most famous and beloved monsters in Japanese film, the atomic-breathing tyrannosaur-like dinosaur Godzilla has been a constant threat to the world since his first appearance in 1954 in the film *Godzilla: King of the Monsters*. After he has nearly destroyed Japan numerous times and created a wake of destruction in his path, destroying entire cities with his atomic breath and brute strength, the world community is out to put an end to the giant behemoth. A G-Force strike team led by Noriko Yoshiwara has been created to try to tackle the threat of Godzilla and to scientifically study the monster. Meanwhile, other ancient monsters are appearing, including Bagorah, Gekido-Jin, and the G-Force-created Cybersaur. The highlight of this collection is the reprint of the 1992 Godzilla Color Special from the *Age of Monsters* collection, in

which Godzilla faces off against a reanimated Japanese guardian statue that houses the soul of a human who was crushed by Godzilla. The self-titled *Godzilla* collection is the adaptation from Japanese writer/artist Kazuhisa Iwata of the movie *Godzilla: 1985. Essential Godzilla* reprints in black and white the original twenty-four issues of Marvel Comics' short-lived comic book series from the late 1970s.

> *Godzilla.* Written and illustrated by Kazuhisa Iwata. Dark Horse Comics, 1995. 200pp. 1-56971-063-5.
>
> *Age of Monsters.* Written by Randy Stradley, Arthur Adams, et al. Illustrated by Steve Bissette, Arthur Adams, et al. Dark Horse Comics, 1998. 272pp. 1-56971-277-8.
>
> *Past, Present, and Future.* Written by Arthur Adams, et al. Illustrated by Tatsuya Ishida, et al. Dark Horse Comics, 1998. 272pp. 1-56971-278-6.
>
> *Essential Godzilla.* Written by Doug Moench. Illustrated by Herb Trimpe, Jim Mooney, and Tom Sutton. Marvel Comics, 2006. 432pp. 0-7851-2153-6.

<u>Gyo</u>. Written and illustrated by Junji Ito. VIZ Media, LLC, 2003–2004. **M** ◎ **Japanese manga.**

The terrors of the deep sea are doing the unthinkable: they're creeping, clanking, and walking in droves on land, spreading a path of undead stench, decay, and rotting flesh. The walking and rotting sea creatures infest the seaside town of Okinawa, infecting and killing the residents one-by-one and spreading the infection across Japan. When a teenage boy, Tadachi, finds himself seemingly immune to the disease, all he can do is watch in horror as his loved ones take a maddening turn from illness to transformation into walking, bloated, man-machine hybrid corpses.

> *Vol. 1.* 2003. 200pp. 1-56931-995-2.
>
> *Vol. 2.* 2004. 208pp. 1-59116-140-1.

***King Kong*. Written by Christian Gossett. Illustrated by Dustin Weaver.** Dark Horse Comics, 2006. 96pp. 1-59307-472-7. **T**

Adaptation of the hit 2005 Peter Jackson remake of the classic 1933 monster movie. When Carl Denham needs to make a big picture or face bankruptcy, he throws away his last chance by casting unknown, down-on-her-luck actress Ann Darrow, kidnapping his screenwriter Jack Driscoll, and sailing on a barge to mysterious Skull Island. There the natives kidnap Ann as a sacrifice to their god, a giant beast known only as Kong. Jack, Carl, and the crew hunt for Ann on a dangerous island that time has forgotten to rescue her from the clutches of Kong.

***Marvel Monsters*. Written by Steve Niles, Eric Powell, Peter David, Jeff Parker, and others. Illustrated by Duncan Fegredo, Eric Powell, and others**. 2006. 216pp. 0-7851-1893-4. **T** ◎

Before Marvel Comics became known as the home of Spider-Man, the publisher was known for its tales featuring giant monsters with such names as Fing Fang Foom, Devil Dinosaur, Droom, Grogg, Goom, Rombuu, and Grattu. Collected are four tales featuring the beasts and their encounters with some Marvel heroes, including the Avengers, Spider-Man, and the Hulk.

Muck Monsters

These are tales of horror and suspense featuring plantlike muck monsters and elementals. The legends of muck monsters date back to England's history, with the tales of the Jack-in-the-Green or bogie monsters. During the history of the American comic book there have been many tales of muck monsters, spawned from the popularity of horror titles; these include creatures such as The Heap, The Man-Thing, and Swamp Thing. Those collected in a graphic novel format are listed below. The most popular muck monster published in comic books and graphic novels is DC Comics' Swamp Thing.

Black Orchid. **Written by Neil Gaiman. Illustrated by Dave McKean.** Vertigo/DC Comics, 1991. 160pp. 0-930289-55-2. **M** ◉

A re-envisioning of an obscure DC Comics character by award-winning author Neil Gaiman. After awakening in a lab with the memories of a woman named Susan Linden, a luminous violet-colored plant creature is born in a humanlike form. Confused by her memories of Susan, the Black Orchid is joined by one more plant creature—a childlike exact duplicate of herself nicknamed "Suzy." On the run from those who killed the original Black Orchid, the Black Orchids try to understand their existence, with help from the plant elemental Swamp Thing, the villainess Poison Ivy, and the night vigilante Batman. The Black Orchids discover that they are the exact duplicates of Susan Linden, a woman created by a professor combining the cells of his dear friend and the black orchid plant. When the original Black Orchid was slain, her death triggered the release of both of her successors, and now the killers of the original Black Orchid's killers will stop at nothing to complete the job. When Suzy is captured, the older Black Orchid must find a way to free her young counterpart and stop the cycle of violence.

Man-Thing: Whatever Knows Fear . . . . **Written by Hans Rodionoff. Illustrated by Kyle Hotz.** Marvel Comics, 2005. 112pp. 0-7851-1488-2. **O** 🎬

A prequel to the straight-to-video movie based on the Marvel Comics muck monster who lives in the Florida Everglades, called the Man-Thing. Formerly a scientist named Ted Sallis, he was working on an experimental miracle serum but was accidentally dosed in it after being chased by evil agents. The combination of the serum and the mystical properties of the Everglades destroyed his body and mind, but he was reborn as the mindless entity called the Man-Thing.

<u>**Swamp Thing**</u>. **Created by Len Wein and Bernie Wrightson.** Vertigo/DC Comics, 1987– . **M** ◉ 🎬💻

Biologist Alec Holland died in a ball of flames after he was dosed in chemicals in the Louisiana swamps. As his body died, his consciousness encoded itself into something more. Alec became something else: a wandering muck man . . . a green monster . . . a plant elemental . . . a defender of the green . . . a creature known as Swamp Thing. The current plant elemental from a long line of guardians of the Green Earth, his journeys take him from the backwater greens of Earth to outer space, Heaven, and Hell, where werewolves, vampires, demons, his arch-nemesis Anton Arcane, and more are out there waiting in the hidden shadows of suspense. He is joined by his true love Abby Arcane, the dark grifter-magician John Constantine, and even DC Comics heroes including Batman and Green Lantern. The sophisticated suspense of Swamp Thing helped to make it one of the most influential comic book series in the 1980s, helped to make Alan Moore a premiere comic book writer, and paved the way for the Vertigo imprint from DC Comics. The character also appeared in two feature films as well as a television series. Below are listed in chronological order the tales of the muck monster called Swamp Thing both before and after Alan Moore's classic tales of the walking plant elemental.

> *Dark Genesis.* Written by Len Wein. Illustrated by Bernie Wrightson. 2003. 240pp. 1-56389-044-5.
>
> *Secret of the Swamp Thing.* Written by Len Wein. Illustrated by Bernie Wrightson. 2005. 232pp. 1-4012-0798-7.
>
> *Book 1: Saga of the Swamp Thing.* 2d ed. Written by Alan Moore. Illustrated by Steve Bissette and John Totleben. 1987. 176pp. 0-930289-22-6.
>
> *Book 2: Love and Death.* Written by Alan Moore. Illustrated by Steve Bissette and John Totleben. 1990. 208pp. 0-930289-54-4, 2nd edition.
>
> *Book 3: The Curse.* Written by Alan Moore. Illustrated by Steve Bissette and John Totleben. 2000. 192pp. 1-56389-697-4.
>
> *Book 4: A Murder of Crows.* Written by Alan Moore. Illustrated by Steve Bissette and John Totleben. 2001. 192pp. 1-56389-719-9.

© 2006 DC Comics.

> *Book 5: Earth to Earth.* Written by Alan Moore. Illustrated by Steve Bissette and John Totleben. 2002. 160pp. 1-56389-804-7.
>
> *Book 6: Reunion.* Written by Alan Moore. Illustrated by Steve Bissette and John Totleben. 2003. 176pp. 1-56389-975-2.
>
> *Regenesis.* Written by Rick Veitch. Illustrated by Rick Veitch, Alfredo Alcala, and John Totleben. 2004. 160pp. 1-4012-0267-5.
>
> *Spontaneous Regeneration.* Written by Rick Veitch. Illustrated by Rick Veitch, Alfredo Alcala and John Totleben. 2006. 160pp. 1-4012-0793-6.
>
> *Infernal Triangles.* Written by Rick Veitch, Jamie Delano and Stephen Bissette. Illustrated by Rick Veitch, Alfredo Alcala, Tom Mandrake, and others. 2006. 176pp. 1-4012-1008-2.
>
> *Bad Seed.* Written by Andy Diggle. Illustrated by Enrique Breccia. 2004. 144pp. 1-4012-0421-X.
>
> *Love in Vain.* Written by Joshua Dysart. Illustrated by Enrique Breccia. 2005. 144pp. 1-4012-0493-7.
>
> *Healing the Breach.* Written by Joshua Dysart. Illustrated by Enrique Breccia. 2006. 144pp. 1-4012-0934-3.

The Old Ones

This is horror based on or inspired by the writings of H. P. Lovecraft from his story "At the Mountains of Madness," originally published in 1936. The stories feature great ancient behemoths and gods of evil who existed before the age of man. The elder beings wait in the wings and bide their time to take over the world once again.

Alone in the Dark. **Written by Randy and Jean-Marc Lofficier. Illustrated by Matt Haley and Aleksi Vriciot.** Image Comics, 2003. 48pp. 1-58240-276-0. **O**

> Four explorers—academics Aline Cedrac and Frank Stone, a mysterious businessman named Ganeesha, and secret agent by the name of Carnby—journey to the treacherous mountains of Nepal in search of the hidden city of Aggartha. Past an army of Yetis, giant insects, and a Lovecraftian behemoth, they seek to find the mysterious Crown of Ghengis—an artifact that the fate of the entire world depends on for its recovery. Based on the popular video game series of the same name.

Before Dawn. **Written by Wesley Craig Green. Illustrated by Jason Whitley.** Green Fly Productions, 2003. 64pp. 0-9732468-0-4. **M**

> Tabby has inherited her grandfather's mansion, and she and four of her teenage friends, including her boyfriend Eugene, take a weekend trip there for a little rest and relaxation. Little do they know that for most of them, this will be their last weekend alive. An ancient evil that was trapped in the cellar has been reawakened, and the family graveyard next door has released the dead. Now zombies, demonic creatures, and more once again walk the earth, and Eugene and his friends have to try to stay alive. A tribute to cult horror films such as Sam Raimi's (*Evil Dead*) and Peter Jackson's (*Dead Alive*).

Clive Barker's Hellraiser. **Written and illustrated by various.** Checker Books Publishing, 2002–2004. **M**

> A collection of short stories inspired by the Clive Barker short story "The Hellbound Heart" and the hit series of Hellraiser horror movies. The stories, including works from such creators as Neil Gaiman, Mike Mignola, and Alex Ross, tell the further tales of unfortunate men and women who are looking for the ultimate pleasure and instead open a rift to a Hell-like dimension where the lucky puzzle-solvers are torn, tortured, and enslaved by the leather-clad demonic monstrosities called Cenobites and their leader, Pinhead.

> *Collected Best I.* 2002. 232pp. 0-9710249-2-8.
> *Collected Best II.* 2003. 200pp. 0-9710249-7-9.
> *Collected Best III.* 2004. 340pp. 0-9753808-0-X.

Deep Sleeper. **Written by Phil Hester. Illustrated by Mike Huddleston.** Image Comics, 2005. 136pp. 1-932664-04-1. **O**

> Cole Gibson is a writer who has been plagued by bad dreams so vivid and disturbing that he's been having trouble getting back to sleep. Other days he's fine, spending his time with his family and his fantastical writing. When he encounters a self-help guru who tells him that his dreams are much more than he realizes, Cole soon finds that his nightmares and his own stories are being played out in real life. Can Cole exist between these converged realities, and more important, will his own soul be saved when it becomes a prize for a horrific race of ancient horrors?

Lovecraft. **Written by Keith Giffen and Hans Rodionoff. Illustrated by Enrique Breccia.** Vertigo/DC Comics, 2004. 144pp. 1-4012-0110-5. **M**

> A fictional account of the life of one of the most influential horror writers of the early twentieth century. What if some of Howard Phillip Lovecraft's most famous creations, such as the Necronomicon, the dark town of Arkham, and Cthulhu the Leviathan, were real and not simply creations of the writer's imagination? From Lovecraft's days as a youth, when his mother dressed him up in girl's clothing, to the fallout of his marriage in adulthood, we see a dark underlying evil in Lovecraft's life. It killed his father, and it is slowly, surely out to corrupt the young writer. Something evil and many-tentacled from a dark place seeks to escape from its prison. H. P. is one of the only ones who can see it all around him.

Ghosts and Spirits

Curiosity about what lies after death is natural, and many people believe in spirits of the undead that have yet to find their way to the land of the dead. Graphic novel ghost stories tend to feature protagonists who can speak with the dead, spirits that have come back to exact revenge, or those that serve as guides to the recently deceased in the afterlife.

Bizenghast. Written and illustrated by M Alice LeGrow. TOKYOPOP, 2005– . **T Neo-manga.**

> After losing both of her parents, Dinah, a girl who suffers from schizophrenia, has reluctantly relocated to the run-down mill town of Bizenghast to live with her aunt in a gothic-looking house. Her only friend is Vincent, her personal hero, who bails her out of trouble and serves as her protector. Dinah is out of touch with reality and has been seeing ghosts and spirits for some time in this city, but no one has believed her. Even after the spirits have bruised her and worse, her aunt refuses to believe her stories. After witnessing an eerie conclave at the local cemetery with Vincent, Dinah discovers the ruins of the city and discovers that ghosts really do exist . . . and they want Dinah for their purpose. Now Dinah is embroiled in a deadly contract with a spider-woman named Bali-Lali and must find her true destiny, with Vincent at her side, or perish trying.
>
> *Vol. 1.* 2005. 192pp. 1-59532-743-6.
> *Vol. 2.* 2006. 192pp. 1-59532-744-4.

Bleach. Written and illustrated by Tite Kubo. VIZ Media, LLC, 2004– . **T Japanese manga.** あ

BLEACH © 2001 by Tite Kubo/SHUEISHA Inc.

> Red-haired high school student Ichigo Kurosaki has always had the ability to see ghosts and spirits, but his life changes forever when he meets Rukia Kuchiki, a member of the mysterious Soul Society. Rukia is a shinigami, or soul reaper, who has the power to fight against evil spirits called Hollowers as well as the power to send the wandering souls of the dead to the Soul Society. When Ichigo's family is threatened, Rukia attempts to lend him some of her power, but instead Ichigo absorbs all of her powers. Now a shinigami himself, he's able to see the Hollowers. Together with Rukia, who is slowly regaining her own powers, they're out to save the world from Hollowers and to allow the spirits of ghosts to find peace. The series is still ongoing in Japan and has been adapted as an anime series.

Vol. 1: Strawberry and the Soul Reapers. 2004. 192pp. 1-59116-441-9.
Vol. 2: Goodbye Parakeet, Good Night My Sister. 2004. 192pp. 1-59116-442-7.
Vol. 3: Memories in the Rain. 2004. 192pp. 1-59116-443-5.
Vol. 4: Quincy Archer Hates You. 2004. 192pp. 1-59116-444-3.
Vol. 5: Right Arm of the Giant. 2005. 192pp. 1-59116-445-1.
Vol. 6: Death Trilogy Overture. 2005. 200pp. 1-59116-728-0.
Vol. 7: The Broken Coda. 2005. 200pp. 1-59116-807-4.
Vol. 8: The Blade and Me. 2005. 200pp. 1-59116-872-4.
Vol. 9: Fourteen Days of Conspiracy. 2005. 200pp. 1-59116-924-0.
Vol. 10. 2005. 208pp. 1-4215-0081-7.
Vol. 11. 2006. 208pp. 1-4215-0271-2.
Vol. 12. 2006. 208pp. 1-4215-0403-0.
Vol. 13: The Undead. 2006. 208pp. 1-4215-0611-4.
Vol. 14: White Tower Rocks. 2006. 208pp. 1-4215-0612-2.
Vol. 15: Beginning of the Death of Tomorrow. 2006. 208pp. 1-4215-0613-0.
Vol. 16: Night of Wijnruit. 2006. 208pp. 1-4215-0614-9.
Vol. 17: Rosa Rubicundior, Lilio Candidior. 2007. 208pp. 1-4215-1041-3.
Vol. 18: The Deathberry Returns. 2007. 208pp. 1-4215-1042-1.

Death Note. **Written and illustrated by Tsugumi Ohba.** VIZ Media, LLC, 2005–2007. **O** **Japanese manga.**

The Shinigami all own notebooks called "Death Notes," which grant the grim reaper-like spirits the ability to decide the fate of humans. Whoever's name is written in the Death Notes will die within forty seconds. When the Shinigami named Ryuku misplaces his notebook on the earthly realm, it's recovered by a teenage boy named Raito. Now the teen has command over death, and being a quick study, Raito has decided to remake the world the way he wants it. Now one-by-one Raito is killing off all the criminals in the world. When the countries of the world notice the large loss of life of criminals, they hire a master detective to bring in the murderer. But is Raito really committing a crime, or will someone stop him from finishing the good he has accomplished? The series was collected into twelve volumes in Japan and was also adapted as a live-action film.

Vol. 1. 2005. 200pp. 1-4215-0168-6.
Vol. 2. 2005. 200pp. 1-4215-0169-4.
Vol. 3. 2006. 200pp. 1-4215-0170-8.
Vol. 4. 2006. 200pp. 1-4215-0331-X.
Vol. 5. 2006. 208pp. 1-4215-0626-2.
Vol. 6. 2006. 208pp. 1-4215-0627-0.
Vol. 7. 2006. 208pp. 1-4215-0628-9.
Vol. 8. 2006. 208pp. 1-4215- 0629-7.
Vol. 9. 2006. 208pp. 1-4215-0630-0.
Vol. 10. 2007. 208pp. 1-4215-1155-X.
Vol. 11. 2007. 208pp. 1-4215-1178-9.

Descendants of Darkness. **Written and illustrated by Yoko Matsushita.** VIZ Media, LLC, 2004–2006. **◑ Japanese manga.** あ

Tsuzuki Asato is a Guardian of Death. Serving the King of Hell, he's a charming and self-centered shinigami, a spirit of death, who has to make sure that all the spirits of the deceased find their place in the afterlife. He locates and sends lost souls trapped on Earth to find peace as well. He's joined by a new partner, Hisoka Kurosaki, a young recruit who doesn't seem too thrilled about his job in the afterlife. Can they work out their differences to solve the cases and make sure the souls find their way home? A unique and fun look at the corporate side of the afterlife. The manga was adapted into an anime series that debuted in Japan in 2000.

Vol. 1. 2004. 200pp. 1-59116-507-5.
Vol. 2. 2004. 208pp. 1-59116-597-0.
Vol. 3. 2004. 200pp. 1-59116-460-5.
Vol. 4. 2005. 184pp. 1-59116-702-7.
Vol. 5. 2005. 200pp. 1-59116-778-7.
Vol. 6. 2005. 192pp. 1-59116-842-2.
Vol. 7. 2005. 192pp. 1-59116-983-6.
Vol. 8. 2005. 184pp. 1-4215-0115-5.
Vol. 9. 2006. 192pp. 1-4215-0171-6.
Vol. 10. 2006. 208pp. 1-4215-0321-2.
Vol. 11. 2006. 208pp. 1-4215-0536-3.

Ghost Rider. Marvel Comics, 1991– . **T** 🎬

© 2006 Marvel Comics.

Johnny Blaze was a daredevil motorcycle stunt performer for a traveling circus. He made a deal with the devil Mephisto to save his brother's life, by means of which he was bound with the demon called Zarathos. After the merging of man and devil, at night Blaze's skin would magically melt away to reveal a leather-clad skeleton with a flaming skull, and his will could conjure a vehicle of vengeance: a motorcycle with flaming wheels that was conjured by hellfire. Now transformed into Ghost Rider, he is cursed to walk the earth as a spirit of vengeance. *Resurrected* and *Rise of the Midnight Sons* feature a young teen called Danny Ketch, another young man who also was temporarily cursed with the spirit of vengeance and called Ghost Rider. Ghost Rider first appeared in *Marvel Spotlight* #5 in 1972. A feature film version of the Ghost Rider will be released in 2007, starring Nicholas Cage as Johnny Blaze.

Resurrected. Written by Howard Mackie. Illustrated by Mark Texeira. 1991. 192pp. 0-87135-803-4.
Rise of the Midnight Sons. Written by Howard Mackie. Illustrated by Adam Kubert and Andy Kubert. 1993. 224pp. 0-87135-969-3.
The Hammer Lane. Written by Devin Grayson. Illustrated by Trent Kanuiga. 2002. 144pp. 0-7851-0910-2.
Essential Ghost Rider, Vol. 1. Written by Roy Thomas, Len Wein, and Marv Wolfman. Illustrated by Michael Ploog and various. 2005. 560pp. 0-7851-1838-1.
Road to Damnation. Written by Garth Ennis. Illustrated by Clayton Crain. 2006. 144pp. 0-7851-1592-7.

Kekkaishi. **Written and illustrated by Yellow Tanabe.** VIZ Media, LLC, 2005–2006. **O Japanese manga.** あ

While others his age are in bed fast asleep, junior high student Yoshimori Sumimura must follow in his family's footsteps as a "kekkaishi," a demon-hunter. His family skill is to create magical barriers around his prey of ghosts, or Ayakashi, and he is joined in the hunt by his family's faithful 500-year-old demon dog. Yoshimori would rather eat sweets and build life-sized castle cakes than chase spirits, but his strict grandfather Shigemori has pushed him to follow the traditional family practice. Though Yoshimori hates it, he's trying to become a better kekkaishi, so that he can one day win the heart of the girl of his dreams, sixteen-year-old neighbor and childhood friend Tokine Yukimura. Like him, she's also a kekkaishi, and she's better at it than he is. The two families have been feuding for years. If Yoshimori's family found out about his secret crush, he'd never hear the end of it! Who's got time for love anyway, when there are sweets to eat and ghosts to capture? The series was also released as an anime series in Japan.

Vol. 1. 2005. 192pp. 1-59116-968-2.
Vol. 2. 2005. 192pp. 1-59116-970-4.
Vol. 3. 2005. 192pp. 1-4215-0067-1.
Vol. 4. 2006. 192pp. 1-4215-0253-4.
Vol. 5. 2006. 192pp. 1-4215-0486-3.
Vol. 6. 2006. 192pp. 1-4215-0487-1.
Vol. 7. 2006. 208pp. 1-4215-0488-X.

Kwaïdan. **Written by Jung and Jee-Yun. Illustrated by Jung.** Dark Horse Comics, 2004. 144pp. 1-56971-841-5. **O**

A twelfth-century Japanese tale of true inner beauty and the spirits of the dead. Lady Akane, jealous of the love that the beautiful Lady Orin shares with the returning soldier Nanko, disfigures her own sister with acid before Nanko returns from battle. Saddened by her disfigured face, Lady Orin drowns herself in a nearby mystical lake. Nanko, after hearing about Orin's death, takes his own life in the same waters. Meanwhile Lady Akane is driven into hiding after an attack on their castle, and she roams the land as something a little more than human, given an extremely long life by the power of the lake and able to summon kwaïdan (ghosts). Now two centuries later, a girl named Setsuko is inhabited by the spirit of Lady Orin, carries the same facial disfigurations, wears a mask reminiscent of Lady Orin's once-beautiful face. Setsuko and a monk and spirit warrior must confront Lady Akane and the ghosts of her past to accept what is real beauty and to free the spirits of Orin and Nanko.

Legend of Sleepy Hollow. **Written by Washington Irving. Adapted and Illustrated by Bo Hampton.** Image Comics, 2004. 64pp. 1-58240-411-9. **T**

Adaptation of the classic Washington Irving short story. In a Dutch settlement in the late 1700s, Ichabod Crane, a schoolteacher in love with eighteen-year-old Katrina Van Tassel, is scared away from the town of Sleepy Hollow after an encounter with the legendary spirit called the Headless Horseman.

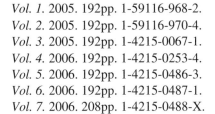

***Spooked.* Written by Antony Johnston. Illustrated by Ross Campbell.** Oni Press, 2004. 168pp. 1-929998-79-1. **O**

> Emily Spook is like no other painter. She gets her inspirations from the dead who temporarily inhabit her head. They've inhabited her for years, and Emily has just now started being recognized for her talent. But when the ghosts have long gone to the afterlife and her well of creativity has run dry, Emily discovers that without them she can barely create any form of art at all. Now a new ghost named Simon has taken residence in Emily's head, a man who was targeted for murder. When other members of Simon's coven are also targeted, can the two of them solve the mystery as well as save Emily's painting career?

Demonic Possession, Black Magic, and Mages

Here are tales featuring those who have made deals with the devil, those possessed or visited by demons, as well as witches, warlocks, and mages. Not all magicians portrayed in graphic novels are black magic users, though some may use the dark arts to defeat evil. These tales featuring magicians closely resemble those found in the fantasy subgenre, but here the focus is not on the more traditional aspects of magic, including the faerie realm. The anti-hero black magician John Constantine, from the <u>Hellblazer</u> series of books, is an excellent example of a dark magician.

***Bad Mojo.* Written by William Harms. Illustrated by Steve Morris.** AiT/Planet Lar, 2004. 88pp. 1-932051-23-6. **M**

> Bruce O'Connor is about to realize his childhood dream to play professional baseball. While driving with two other friends to spring training, he accidentally falls asleep behind the wheel and causes a collision with a witch with a grudge. Cursed by the witch, he dies every morning, only to be reanimated at dusk. If he is able to help her reclaim certain items, she'll lift the curse. Unfortunately, Bruce "dies" one morning at a diner in Oklahoma, and the residents don't take too kindly to zombies and witches in their neck of the woods.

***Blackburne Covenant.* Written by Fabian Nicieza. Illustrated by Stefano Raffaele.** Dark Horse Comics, 2003. 104pp. 1-56971-889-X. **O**

> Richard Kaine has written a best-selling fantasy/horror novel and is now the toast of the town. But someone out there knows one thing that Richard never expected: every word of his fictional story about a secret society known as the Blackburne Covenant is true. Now friends are being killed, and Richard is slowly being pulled into a world that he thought only existed in his head. Truth sometimes is stranger than fiction, and Richard's just about to find out how much.

***The Blair Witch Chronicles.* Written by Jennifer van Meter. Illustrated by Guy Davis, Bernie Mireault, and Tommy Lee Edwards.** Oni Press, 2000. 120pp. 1-929998-04-X. **O** 🎬

> The events from the hit 1999 independent movie *The Blair Witch Project* are expanded on in this collection of short stories focusing on the community of Blair and their strange connection with a vengeful witch who can still strike back from beyond the grave. All the stories are written as "true" events to help connect the events of the graphic novel with the film.

Cross. **Written and illustrated by Sumiko Amakawa.** TOKYOPOP, 2004–2006. **T Japanese manga.**

Takara Amakusa is a young Catholic priest who has followed in his father's footsteps to be a renowned exorcist. Given what many see as a blessing and a curse, when he makes the sign of the cross on his forehead, a cross miraculously appears. With this cross he's able to repel the demons, but his blessed power nearly causes madness and great pain each time he uses it. While on the hunt for demons he comes across a young woman named Matsuri Shizuha, who has the writings of the Scripture on her body and growing empathic powers. Her strange gift makes her a target for demons and a deadly cult out to capture her. As they grow closer together in their struggles against the demons, will she aid Takara and help share the burden, and will they be able to work together without falling in love?

Vol. 1. 2004. 184pp. 1-59532-227-2.
Vol. 2. 2005. 192pp. 1-59532-228-0.
Vol. 3. 2005. 200pp. 1-59532-229-9.
Vol. 4. 2005. 192pp. 1-59532-230-2.
Vol. 5. 2006. 192pp. 1-59532-231-0.

Diabolo. **Written and illustrated by Kaoru Ohashi and Kei Kusunoki.** TOKYOPOP, 2004–2005. **O Japanese manga.**

Two young men, Ren and Rai, sold their souls to the devil to save the life of Ren's seven-year-old cousin, Mio. Despite the deal, Mio died, and in exchange the two received "gifts": Ren has the power of ultimate defense and Rai the power of ultimate offense. Their powers are their own until their eighteenth birthdays, when they will become enslaved by Diabolo and transformed into monsters of Hell. Now seventeen years old, the friends find themselves trying to redeem themselves for failing Mio and their harsh upbringing and to find a way to trick Diabolo. Meanwhile, Diabolo is laying a trap to ensnare every seventeen-year-old in the world. Can the two best friends find a way to trap the Devil and reclaim a bit of their souls in the process?

Vol. 1. 2004. 208pp. 1-59532-232-9.
Vol. 2. 2004. 200pp. 1-59532-233-7.
Vol. 3. 2005. 216pp. 1-59532-594-8.

Doctor Strange. Marvel Comics, 2002–2005. **T**

© 2006 Marvel Comics.

Originally created by Stan Lee and Steve Ditko in 1963, Doctor Strange is the Sorcerer Supreme of Earth in the Marvel Comics universe. The protector of our world from supernatural villains including the dreaded Dormammu, Baron Mordo, and other evil magical threats, Doctor Stephen Strange is a man who rose from humble beginnings to become the chief magic user on the planet. Once an arrogant surgeon, he learned the art of magic from the fabled Ancient One and now uses his mastery over the mystic arts as a protector of Earth, a consultant to Marvel heroes in time of mystical catastrophes, and a member of the hero group called the Defenders. *The Essential Doctor Strange* and *A Separate Reality* highlight early stories from the 1960s and early 1970s. *Strange: Beginnings and Endings* is a retelling of the origin of Strange's emergence as the Sorcerer Supreme.

Doctor Strange: A Separate Reality. **Written by Steve Englehart. Illustrated by Frank Brunner.** 2002. 176pp. 0-7851-0836-X.

Essential Dr. Strange. 2002–2005.
> *Vol. 1.* Written by Stan Lee. Illustrated by Steve Ditko. 2002. 608pp. 0-7851-0816-5.
> *Vol. 2.* Written by Roy Thomas. Illustrated by Gene Colan. 2005. 608pp. 0-7851-1668-0.

Strange: Beginnings and Endings. **Written by J. Michael Straczynski. Illustrated by Gary Frank.** 2005. 144pp. 0-7851-1577-3.

The Drowned. **Written by Laini Taylor-Di Bartolo. Illustrated by Jim Di Bartolo.** Image Comics, 2004. 80pp. 1-58240-379-1. **O**

In the year 1800 in France, a young man named Theophile Finistre escapes from a mysterious five-year imprisonment in an insane asylum after being beckoned by some outside force to flee. His only comfort during his incarceration was the constant visitation of crows and a mysterious key that hangs around his neck. Upon his escape he heads back to his homeland of Breton in western France, and there he revisits the tragic death of his sister . . . or is she really dead? He thought that she had been tried and sentenced to death by drowning for being a witch, but here she is today, in front of him. Soon he is being chased by drowned witches and a secret society of priests, as well as by what may really be his dead sister. Is her appearance nothing more than a figment of his imagination or has he succumbed further and to madness and revenge?

Evil's Return. **Written by Jong-Kyu Lee. Illustrated by Hwan Shin.** TOKYOPOP, 2004–2005. **O Korean manhwa.**

Yumi Seo's normal life at high school is over when she finds out that she is cursed and is destined to become the wife and childbearer of Evil. Now that she has reached puberty, the evil of the world, converged in an organization called the "Heavenly Father," is emerging from the shadows to get the chance to be the father of evil. The side of good and right hasn't given up hope: they've sent defenders from the Buddhist and Catholic faiths to protect Yumi from those who wish to harm the world. Their chief emissary is the monk Hyun Sunwoo, who has infiltrated high school as a student to better protect Yumi. Yumi has found another protector, though, a heartthrob freshman named Chail Tae. After having a vision about Yumi, he feels compelled to protect her from evil at all costs.

> *Vol. 1: Heaven, Earth, and Mortal Men.* 2004. 184pp. 1-59182-784-1.
> *Vol. 2.* 2004. 184pp. 1-59182-785-X.
> *Vol. 3.* 2005. 176pp. 1-59182-967-4.
> *Vol. 4.* 2005. 192pp. 1-59182-968-2.

Faro Korbit. **Written by Mike Baron. Illustrated by Mel Rubi.** AP Comics, 2004. 100pp. 1-905071-03-5. **M**

Ancient evil never rests, but salvation comes in the guise of an ancient Egyptian mystic and former pharaoh, the 4,000-year-old sorcerer called Faro Korbit. A wizard who still uses ancient and unorthodox magic, his purpose is to prevent the ancient and evil Great Old Ones and their servants from returning to Earth. As he waits for the coming evil in the wastelands of a Nevada desert, Faro must recruit an odd assortment of allies to aid him in the coming battle. A stuntwoman named Audrey who is moonlighting as a cocktail waitress, a Grand Prix driver, Damian Lane, and a dancer called Blue all find that they have a role to play with the sorcerer supreme to prevent the world from ending.

The Festering Season. **Written by Kevin Tinsley. Illustrated by Tim Smith.** 3 Stickman Graphics, 2002. 240pp. 0-9675423-2-4. **O**

When her mother is gunned down in a brutal police shooting, Voodou priestess-in-training Rene DuBoise leaves her Haitian home to come to New York City to try to solve her mother's mysterious death. The police claim that it was an accident, that her mother appeared as a male monster to them, but when all leads take her to a drug-dealing Pateros sorcerer, Rene knows there's more to this than meets the eye. Amid social tensions erupting after her mother's death, Rene is joined by the sister of a fallen police officer and a cultural anthropologist, and together the three must stop the drug-dealing sorcerer's sinister spell before chaos reins.

Hellblazer. Vertigo/DC Comics, 1994– . **M**

© 2006 DC Comics.

A trench-coat-wearing, smooth-talking British grifter-magician, John Constantine is anything but a simple man. The Sting look-a-like first appeared in DC Comics' <u>Swamp Thing</u> series. Neck-deep in the occult ever since he was a teen in Newcastle, England, Constantine is not a powerful sorcerer by any means, but his presence alone can intimidate magic practitioners and humble the demons. Traveling all around the globe to wherever he's needed, he's smart enough to trick the Devil (even though he's been known to damn some of his friends in the process) and is one of the only men on Earth capable of confronting demons, devils, and horrors of the supernatural world and our own. In 2005 a feature film adaptation of the series was released as *Constantine*, starring Keanu Reeves and Rachel Weisz.

> *Dangerous Habits.* Written by Garth Ennis. Illustrated by William Simpson. 1994. 160pp. 1-56389-150-6.
> *Fear and Loathing.* Written by Garth Ennis. Illustrated by Steve Dillon. 1997. 160pp. 1-56389-202-2.
> *Original Sins.* Written by Jamie Delano. Illustrated by John Ridgway and Alfredo Alcala. 1997. 256pp. 1-56389-052-6.

Tainted Love. Written by Garth Ennis. Illustrated by Steve Dillon. 1998. 176pp. 1-56389-456-4.

Damnation's Flame. Written by Garth Ennis. Illustrated by Steve Dillon. 1999. 175pp. 1-56389-508-0.

Hard Time. Written by Brian Azzarello. Illustrated by Richard Corben. 2000. 125pp. 1-56389-696-6.

Good Intentions. Written by Brian Azzarello. Illustrated by Marcelo Frusin. 2002. 144pp. 1-56389-856-X.

Haunted. Written by Warren Ellis. Illustrated by John Higgins. 2003. 144pp. 1-56389-813-6.

Freezes Over. Written by Brian Azzarello. Illustrated by Marcelo Frusin. 2003. 144pp. 1-56389-971-X.

Rake at the Gate of Hell. Written by Garth Ennis. Illustrated by Steve Dillon. 2003. 224pp. 1-4012-0002-8.

Son of Man. Written by Garth Ennis. Illustrated by John Higgins. 2004. 128pp. 1-4012-0202-0.

Highwater. Written by Brian Azzarello. Illustrated by Marcelo Frusin, Giuseppe Camuncoli and Cameron Stewart. 2004. 264pp. 1-4012-0223-3.

Setting Sun. Written by Warren Ellis. Illustrated by Tim Bradstreet and various. 2004. 96pp. 1-4012-0245-4.

All His Engines. Written by Mike Carey. Illustrated by Leonardo Manco. 2005. 128pp. 1-4012-0316-7, hardcover; 2006. 128 pp. 1-4012-0317-5, softcover.

Constantine: The Hellblazer Collection. Written by Neil Gaiman, Garth Ennis, Jamie Delano, and Steven T Seagle. Illustrated by various. 2005. 168pp. 1-4012-0340-X.

Red Sepulchre. Written by Mike Carey. Illustrated by Steve Dillon and Marcelo Frusin. 2005. 144pp. 1-4012-0485-6.

Black Flowers. Written by Mike Carey. Illustrated by Jock, Lee Bermejo and Marcelo Frusin. 2005. 144pp. 1-4012-0499-6.

Staring at the Wall. Written by Mike Carey. Illustrated by Marcelo Frusin. 2006. 144pp. 1-4012-0929-7.

Lady Constantine. Written by Andy Diggle. Illustrated by Goran Sudzuka. 2006. 96pp. 1-4012-0942-4.

Stations of the Cross. Written by Mike Carey. Illustrated by various. 2006. 160pp. 1-4012-1002-3.

***Killing Demons.* Written by Peter Siegel. Illustrated by Brent White.** Engine Press, 2003. 88pp. 0-9743150-0-1. **M**

Joshua Brand is a special kind of hunter—he's a demon killer. Cursed since he was a child to be able to see demons when others can't, ever since they butchered his parents, he has dedicated his life to defeating them. Raised by a madman who helped him to hone his demon-hunting skills, he has grown up to be a formidable enemy of demonkind. Years later, when a grisly murder is discovered, Brand is asked by police detective Sarah Bentley to assist in the investigation. As more innocents are killed, the stage is set for a showdown with the demons and their human agent, who is skilled in the ways of the dark arts.

Lazarus Jack. **Written by Mark Ricketts. Illustrated by Horacio Domingues.** Dark Horse Comics, 2004. 128pp. 1-59307-097-7. **T**

> After losing his family in a tragedy, the magician Jackson Pierce dimension-hops in order to reclaim them. Landing in magical alternate realms that have each been touched by magic in good or evil ways—from mad sorcerers to worlds of zero gravity—Jack must finally confront the demons of his past.

Mark of the Succubus. Written and illustrated by Irene Flores and Ashley Raiti. TOKYOPOP, 2005– . **T Neo-manga.**

© 2006 TOKYOPOP.

> Easygoing seventeen-year-old Aiden Landis has had a difficult time finding what he wants out of life. His girlfriend, teachers, parents, and everyone else all have plans for him, butn Aiden would much rather play his guitar, write songs, and relax. Enter Maeve, a dim-witted, fledgling succubus—a demon seducer of men. She's not sure of her own powers and has been sent to this strange human world to seduce and kill for the first time. Maeve enrolls at the local high school and meets Aiden and his friends. Soon she brands him with her Mark, which claims that he is to be her target and will be killed. Sylene, the head succubus for the Demon World, has sent a spy to ensure that Maeve follows the path of demonkind, but when Maeve falls in love with Aiden, will the succubus-in-training follow her demon laws or her demon heart?

> *Vol. 1.* 2005. 192pp. 1-59816-266-7.
> *Vol. 2.* 2006. 208pp. 1-59816-267-5.

The Possessed. **Written by Geoff Johns and Kris Grimminger. Illustrated by Liam Sharp.** WildStorm Productions/DC Comics, 2004. 144pp. 1-4012-0292-6. **M**

6

> When a horde of demons roams Earth, the last salvation for humanity is a tough troupe of exorcists ready to send the demons back to Hell. Each has been possessed by a demon at one time, and they must band together to overcome the terror they experienced and use their spells and high-tech weapons to banish the demons from Earth.

Spellbinders: Signs and Wonders. **Written by Mike Carey. Illustrated by Mike Perkins.** Marvel Comics, 2005. 0-7851-1756-3. **T**

> Fifteen-year-old transfer student Kim Vesco knew that her new high school in Salem, Massachusetts, would have cliques—but nothing like what she encounters. When Kim meets the student body, she soon realizes that there is a war brewing between those with witch powers and those without them, and they both want Kim on their side. On top of that, some unknown force wants Kim dead. Will Kim be able to survive the mysterious attacks of her mystery assailant long enough to be able to decide which side of the high school mage-war she truly belongs on?

William Hope Hodgson's the House on the Borderland. Adapted by Richard Corben and Simon Revelstroke. Illustrated by Richard Corben. Vertigo/DC Comics, 2000. 96pp. 1-56389-860-8. **M**

> An adaptation of the classic 1908 atmospheric horror story. In the Irish countryside, two Oxford dropouts find a book that tells about a reclusive man named Byron Gault who lives with his sister Meg and their pet Mastiff in an old Irish mansion near the edge of a chasm. Gault's nightmares about the home being a gateway for a demonic darkness come true as an earthquake rips open a nearby ravine and unleashes monstrous were-boars into our world. Soon after, Meg falls victim to the bite of a were-boar, and it's only a matter of time before she turns into something far, far worse and destroys what's left of Byron's sanity.

The Occult

These stories deal with the unexplainable and mysterious supernatural forces and strange powers. Typically they feature characters with strange psychic powers and mysterious people with dark powers. Although their powers may be similar to people with psychic powers and mind control (such as those listed in chapter 3), here the focus is not on the scientific nature of the powers, but instead on pure supernatural evil. The Ring series of books from Japan, which also helped to inspire the hit movies of the same name, are an excellent example of this type of horror.

Aleister Arcane. **Written by Steve Niles. Illustrated by Breehn Burns.** IDW Publishing, 2004. 104pp. 1-932382-33-X. **M**

© 2006 Steve Niles and Breehn Burns.

> Aging television weatherman Aleister Green spends his days in semiretirement, playing the B-movie host Aleister Arcane, but his dream of pursuing his adolescent interests is cut short when locals protest the inappropriate creepiness of the show. Eventually the network caves in, and soon Aleister is out of a job, his sick wife dies, and he succumbs to the deepest corners of despair, descending fully into the identity of the mad hermit Aleister Arcane. Before Aleister dies, he curses the town with a dark arts spell wronging him. Soon the town's adults are transformed into monsters, while something special awaits its good children. Revenge is sweet.

The Awakening. **Written by Neal Shaffer. Illustrated by Luca Genovese.** Oni Press, 2004. 96pp. 1-932664-00-9. **O**

> Francesca, daughter of a wealthy family, is excited to be attending one of the most prestigious boarding schools in New England, but the joy is short-lived when she discovers the mutilated body of her girlfriend Rachel and is knocked unconscious by the killer. She wakes up traumatized by the event and now mute from shock. Francesca has begun to have psychic visions of who the killer will strike next, but she finds herself unable to communicate with anyone about it. Is there a killer on the prowl, or something more ancient and sinister walking the school grounds?

***Black Harvest*. Written and illustrated by Josh Howard.** Devil's Due Publishing, 2006. 144pp. 1-932796-54-1. **O**

Jericho, Texas, is not your average small town. Each year it's host to an unexplainable phenomenon known as the Jericho Lights. The lights draw in UFO aficionados and other tourists to the city each year. Nineteen-year-old Zaya Vahn disappeared in Jericho three years ago but now has mysteriously returned. A much different person than she was before her abduction, Zara inexplicably has the words "repent" carved in her abdomen. Meanwhile, Internet blogger Daniel Webster has become obsessed with discovering the truth of the Jericho Lights. What he finds will shake his very beliefs and change a small town forever.

Ceres, Celestial Legend. Written and illustrated by Yû Watase. VIZ Media, LLC, 2003–2006. **O Japanese manga.** あ

Aya and her twin brother Aki have just turned sixteen. What might have been a normal happy birthday turned bizarre when their grandfather gave them a severed hand as a present. The unusual gift unleashed a hidden power inside Aya—and she finds out that she's a "Celestial Maiden." In her bloodline lies the power of angels. Now Aya has been targeted for assassination by her own family, and her brother has been captured by their grandfather and hidden away in his mansion. All Aya wants is her normal life back, but instead she's a half-human descendant of an angel whom everyone wants dead. The series was adapted into a twenty-four-episode anime series.

Vol. 1. 2003. 200pp. 1-56931-980-4.
Vol. 2. 2004. 192pp. 1-56931-981-2.
Vol. 3. 2004. 200pp. 1-56931-982-0.
Vol. 4. 2004. 192pp. 1-59116-609-8.
Vol. 5. 2004. 192pp. 1-56931-979-0.
Vol. 6. 2004. 200pp. 1-59116-109-6.
Vol. 7. 2004. 200pp. 1-59116-259-9.
Vol. 8. 2004. 200pp. 1-59116-260-2.
Vol. 9. 2004. 200pp. 1-59116-261-0.
Vol. 10. 2005. 200pp. 1-59116-262-9.
Vol. 11. 2005. 200pp. 1-59116-263-7.
Vol. 12. 2005. 200pp. 1-59116-264-5.
Vol. 13. 2005. 200pp. 1-59116-265-3.
Vol. 14. 2006. 208pp. 1-4215-0263-1.

***Closer*. Written by Anthony Johnson. Illustrated by Mike Norton.** Oni Press, 2004. 160pp. 1-929998-81-3 **O**

Over thirty years ago a secret government experiment called Project Hermes, led by physicist Graham Butcher, failed disastrously, costing one scientist his life and injuring others. Since that time the project has been covered up and deemed unsafe. Although almost everyone has given up on the project, Butcher never has. Now destitute and dying, the physicist has invited six individuals with connections to the failed project to witness the realization of his work before he dies. Called Project Thoth, the experiment will rise from the failed ashes of Project Hermes, but also something ancient and evil will rise once again.

Dead End. Written and illustrated by Shohei Manabe. TOKYOPOP, 2005–2006. **O Japanese manga.**

Shirou is a slacker who works as a construction worker to make ends meet. His job is pretty dull and ordinary, but one day he rescues Lucy, a naked woman who literally falls out of the sky. He brings her to his apartment, nurses her back to health, and discovers that he's falling in love with her. He returns home one day to discover that three of his friends have been found murdered, and Lucy has disappeared. Now Shirou is stalked by a man named "Stitch Man," who will not die, and he is rescued by a large brute of a man who tells Shirou that he's more than what he appears. It seems that Shirou is suffering a form of amnesia and doesn't remember his real past. If he can rescue five of his long-lost mystical friends before he encounters Stitch Man again, his true memory will be returned to him.

Vol. 1. 2005. 224pp. 1-59532-161-6.

Vol. 2. 2005. 232pp. 1-59532-162-4.

Vol. 3. 2005. 192pp. 1-59532-163-2.

Vol. 4. 2006. 192pp. 1-59532-164-0.

Girls. Written and illustrated by Joshua Luna. Image Comics, 2005– . **O**

© 2006 Luna Brothers.

All Ethan Daniels wanted was a girlfriend, but he was unlucky in love. After getting into a fight at the local bar and insulting many of the town's population, he finds a nameless, mysterious girl on the road. Finding her naked and shaken, he takes her into his home, and in the blink of an eye the ordinary, sleepy town of Pennystown, population sixty-five, is the sight of the extraordinary, the mysterious, and the unexplainable. Soon the town's residents are in for the fight of their lives, and Ethan will never look at women the same way again.

Vol. 1: Conception. 2005. 152pp. 1-58240-529-8.

Vol. 2: Emergence. 2006. 152pp. 1-58240-608-1.

Vol. 3: Survival. 2006. 152pp. 1-58240-703-7.

***I Am Legion: The Dancing Faun.* Written by Fabian Nury. Illustrated by John Cassaday.** Humanoids Publishing/DC Comics, 2004. 64pp. No ISBN. **M**

During World War II, in December 1942, a different kind of war is being waged between Nazi Germany and the Allies that can decide the fate of the war in London and Bucharest. Under the shadow of espionage, Nazi Germany pursues a top-secret project code-named "Legion," involving a Romanian girl with supernatural powers able to turn the tide of the war. Meanwhile, in London Stanley Pilgrim leads a police investigation into the apparent murder of Victor Thorpe, a man whose blood was drained from his body and his mansion destroyed. His body was found, but did he really die? The conclusion to the series has not yet been published.

***Inferno.* Written by Mike Carey. Illustrated by Michael Gaydos.** Titan Books, 2004. 144pp. 1-84023-764-3. **O**

> Jack Travis was murdered on his thirtieth birthday and woke up in Hell, literally. But both his killer and the mage Nostradamus, who rescues him in Hell, are calling him "Terrence." Now, with a werewoman as his guide, Jack finds out that there's a darker secret to Hell: he's been here before, and he's back to reclaim his power—enough power to take on the demon lord Baal and rule Hell if he has to. The conclusion to the series has not yet been published because the original publisher, Caliber Press, folded.

***The Last Temptation.* Written by Neil Gaiman. Illustrated by Michael Zulli.** Dark Horse Comics, 2000. 104pp. 1-56971-455-X. **T**

> Young Steven is afraid of a lot of things in life, like girls, growing up, and ghosts. On a dare from his friends, Steven enters an odd theater and finds himself face-to-face with a spooky, top-hated Showman (who resembles rock star Alice Cooper), the master of the ghostly Theatre of the Real. The showman has an offer for Steven: he promises to take away all of Steven's fears if he will stay at the ghostly theater and give up his true potential to live forever with the other spirits and ghosts who reside at the show. Will Steven face his fears, or will he lose his soul forever to the Showman?

<u>The Malay Mysteries.</u> Written by Jai Sen. Illustrated by Rizky Wasisto Edi. Shoto Press, 2002–2003. **T**

> In 1910, a period of dramatic change in Indonesia, in a village where Dutch explorers threaten to take over the region, there are other more sinister changes taking place. A wise village shaman/midwife discovers a vampiric entity threatening her village when newborns begin to disappear and newborn mothers are found murdered. Can this once-peaceful village ever reclaim its peace again, or have the tides of modernization as well as superstitions destroyed the land and its people?

> *Book 1: Garlands of Moonlight.* 2002. 86pp. 0-9717564-0-6.
> *Book 2: The Ghost of Silver Cliff.* 2003. 96pp. 0-9717564-2-2.
> *Book 3: Island of Glass and Ashes.* 2003. 120pp. 0-9717564-3-0.

***Midnight Nation.* Written by J. Michael Straczynski. Illustrated by Gary Frank.** Image Comics, 2003. 288pp. 1-58240-272-8. **O**

LAPD Homicide Lieutenant David Grey has seen his share of disturbing crime scenes, but when he encounters a homicide that has been caused by a supernatural force like nothing he's ever seen, he loses something else—his very soul. David has "slipped through the cracks" in the world. He's lost his soul and can only be seen by people like him who have lost their way: the homeless, the hopeless, and the lost, as well as noncorporeal monsters called "Walkers" who skate between both realities in search of blood and corruption. Now David must make a cross-country trek on foot to New York City to reclaim his soul, or else he, too will become a vicious Walker.

His guide on the twelve-month journey is the enigmatic and beautiful Laurel, who has walked this road many times and knows it's only a matter of time before David succumbs, too.

***Orochi: Blood.* Written and illustrated by Kazuo Umezu.** VIZ Media, LLC, 2002. 200pp. 1-56931-787-9. **T Japanese manga.**

A mysterious young girl named Orochi saves the life of Lisa, a drunk driver, in a car crash. Though her sacrifice rescued Lisa, it accidentally put Orochi into a deep sleep for over two decades. Years later she awakens and finds herself living in a mansion owned by Lisa and her older sister, Kasuza. There Orochi finds herself trapped in a psychological power struggle between the two sisters and discovers that there's something more dark and chilling about them than she realized.

***Out There: The Evil Within.* Written by Brian Augustyn. Illustrated by Humberto Ramos.** Cliffhanger!/WildStorm Productions/DC Comics, 2002. 144pp. 1-56389-893-4. **T**

Behind the facade of the peaceful town of El Dorado City, something sinister walks among us. The town is secretly being infested by demonic hordes, and only four teenage kids—Zach Mullins, Casey Philips, Jessica Santiago, and Mark Wexler—have the ability to see them in their dreams and in real life. And even worse—the authorities seemingly are in league with the demons. Do four kids in a town overrun by a demonic invasion even have a chance to turn the tide and save El Dorado City?

The Ring. Based on the story by Koji Suzuki. Written by Hiroshi Takahashi. Illustrated by Misao Inagaki, Sakura Mizuki, and Meimu. Dark Horse Comics, 2003–2004. **T 🎬 Japanese manga.**

Adaptation of the hit series of horror novels by Japanese writer Koji Suzuki. The novels were also adapted into the cult hit Japanese movies *Ringu* (1998) and its sequels, as well as the U.S. movie in 2002. As do the hit movies, the manga story line centers around a deadly videotape that when watched will kill the viewer within a week. Reiko Asakawa, a young journalist, discovers that her cousin Tomoko has been found dead, with a look of pure shock on her face. After hearing about the mysterious tape, Reiko thinks it is merely as rumor, but when three of Tomoko's friends who watched the tape with her are also found to have died at the exact same time, that sounds rather sinister. Soon Reiko watches the tape, and with the help of her ex-husband, she tries to solve the mystery before her own life ends. The prequel and sequels expand on the theme of a videotape virus and also tell the backstory of the mysterious girl called Sadako and how the horror really started.

> *Vol. 0.* 2005. 160pp. 1-59307-306-2.
> *Vol. 1.* 2003. 304pp. 1-59307-054-3.
> *Vol. 2.* 2004. 192pp. 1-59307-055-1.
> *Vol. 3: Spiral.* 2004. 192pp. 1-59307-215-5.
> *Vol. 4: Birthday.* 2004. 160pp. 1-59307-267-8.

***Route 666: Highway of Horror.* Written by Tony Bedard. Illustrated by Karl Moline.** CrossGen, 2003. 160pp. 1-931484-56-2. **T**

In the world called Empyrean (which resembles 1950s America), Cassandra Starkweather is the only one who can see that their world has been invaded by shape-shifting creatures who are eating the population. No one believes Cassie, and she soon finds herself sent to a mental institution. After a murder at the institution caused by the shape-shifters, Cassie is falsely blamed, and she's on the run. Meanwhile the evil shape-shifters are seeking to take over positions of power to better prepare to take over the planet. How can Cassie save the world from evil when no one will believe her?

***Silent Hill: Dying Inside.* Written by Scott Ciencin. Illustrated by Ben Templesmith.** IDW Publishing, 2004. 128pp. 1-932382-24-0. **M**

Tie-in to the popular horror video games franchise. Dr. Troy Abernathy has never believed in anything even remotely supernatural. The only ghosts and demons that people see are their own personal demons, which they face every day. To prove this, he is taking patient Lynn DeAngelis to the horrific city of Silent Hill to face her fears. But as Dr. Abernathy discovers, the horror is for real, and in a town where your worst fears and personal demons are made real, there's little hope of staying alive.

***Skinwalker.* Written by Nunzio DeFilippis and Christina Weir. Illustrated by Brian Hurtt.** Oni Press, 2003. 120pp. 1-929998-45-7. **M**

In Navajo country, Reservation police officer Anne Adakai discovers a skinned body and believes that the corpse is that of an F.B.I. agent. Fearing that the body is a victim of an ancient Navajo practice of skinning a man and then assuming the corpse's identity, she investigates the murder, which leads to a trail of death and more skinned bodies across America. The hunt is on to find the real killer—but how can you find a criminal who is using an ancient magic to appear as anyone?

***Sleep, Little Girl.* Written and illustrated by Sergio Bleda.** SAF Comics, 2003. 48pp. 1-931724-31-8. **M**

Juan, a freelance reporter, discovers at a local hospital a mysterious chain of deaths of young couples. Healthy married couples are being found dead in their beds, with no sign of murder or foul play. Though that seems odd in itself, all of the people who died were foster parents who adopted the same autistic little girl and then died the night after taking the young girl in. Juan investigates the mysterious deaths further and uncovers a deep, dark secret that should have remained hidden forever, as well as the horrible fate of the little girl's biological parents.

Tomie. Written and illustrated by Junji Ito. ComicsOne, 2001. **O Japanese manga.**

An eerie collection of short stories that revolve around the mysterious girl known as Tomie. A young and pretty college girl, she has the effect on men of making them want to love her to pieces. Literally. No matter whether you hate her, love her, or wish to be rid of her—even no matter how many times you kill her—she keeps on coming back for more. She will kill you with her love.

Vol. 1. 2001. 256pp. 1-58899-084-2.
Vol. 2. 2001. 256pp. 1-58899-085-0.

Uzumaki: Spiral into Horror. **Written and illustrated by Junji Ito.** VIZ Media, LLC., 2002. **O ◎ Japanese manga.** 📽

In the provincial seaside town of Korozu-cho, the residents are slowly being seduced into the never-ending world of the spiral. Some curl up into self-made spirals and die, and some are slowly turned into human-sized snails. As the town slowly goes mad with their obsessions, teenager Kirie and her boyfriend must learn the terrible secret to survive a nightmarish world that no one can escape. The series was adapted into a live-action film in Japan.

   Vol. 1. 2002. 208pp. 1-56931-714-3.
   Vol. 2. 2002. 192pp. 1-59116-033-2.
   Vol. 3. 2002. 224pp. 1-59116-048-0.

Visitor. **Written and illustrated by Yi-Jung No.** TOKYOPOP, 2005– . **T Korean manhwa.**

Hyo-Bin Na is young and beautiful and instantly becomes popular at her new high school. The problem is that Hyo-Bin doesn't want to be popular—she just wants to be left alone. Cursed with paranormal abilities, she has seemingly caused every one of her loved ones to be killed, injured, or worse, and she is haunted by this every day. To protect herself and others, she has vowed to not get close to anyone. Is her promise easy to keep, or will someone else become the next victim? Five volumes were originally published in Korea.

   Vol. 1. 2005. 184pp. 1-59532-342-2.
   Vol. 2. 2005. 192pp. 1-59532-343-0.
   Vol. 3. 2006. 192pp. 1-59532-344-9.
   Vol. 4. 2006. 192pp. 1-59532-663-4.

The Wicked: Omnibus. **Written by Francis Takenaga. Illustrated by Roy Martinez, Lan Medina, and David Yardin.** Image Comics, 2003. 264pp. 1-58240-302-3. **M**

Nathan Ellstings is not your normal exorcist. He's been given a truly blessed power since birth: he can undo a deal with the Devil with a gift called The Forgiving. Though many welcome his power to break their unholy pacts, to some, he's their worst nightmare. Hidden within our own world is a secret society called the Wicked, a group of people who have sold their souls to the Devil in return for power, fame, fortune, and more. They walk among us as pop-star idols, politicians, etc., and they don't want their power to end or to be exposed. Can Nathan destroy this nightmare organization before they destroy him?

Slasher

This category is based on the film genre of the same name, in which people, especially young women, are violently killed, usually with knives, resulting in a bloody mess.

***Hack/Slash: First Cut.* Written by Tim Seeley. Illustrated by Stefano Casellia and Federica Manfredi.** Devil's Due Publishing, 2005. 160pp. 1-932796-42-8. **O**

© 2006 Tim Seeley.

Everyone has seen those slasher movies in which there's only one survivor. Cassie Hack is one such girl. Years ago she was the only one left alive after a deadly encounter with the Lunch Lady slasher—who turned out to be her own mother! She got away and has made it her personal mission to prevent anyone else from sharing the same fate,s by going after the Slashers before they can kill again. She is joined on her journey by Vlad, a monstrous beast of a companion, but she may have met her match in the form of an undead killer and the army of zombie killer pets, a killer who strikes college kids on spring break, and a comic book convention killer. Slashers beware: your days are numbered!

***Island.* Written by In-Wan Youn. Illustrated by Kyung-Il Yang.** TOKYOPOP, 2002–2003. **O Korean manhwa.**

Miho, a young female teacher, has come to the Korean island of Cheju to start over and to escape her spoiled life as the daughter of a wealthy family. When she discovers the mutilated body of a female on the island, we see that the old island superstitions turn are true, and the demons of the land are out for blood. Miho is rescued by a mysterious man known only as Pan. With his icy stare, skill in the mystic arts, and prowess with the blades, he's the only one capable of fighting the demons. When Miho reluctantly makes a bargain with the heartless Pan to destroy the demons, she finds herself making a deal with the devil, because Pan is in reality a serial killer and she's potentially his next victim.

Vol. 1. 2002. 170pp. 1-931514-33-X.
Vol. 2. 2002. 168pp. 1-931514-34-8.
Vol. 3. 2002. 168pp. 1-931514-35-6.
Vol. 4. 2002. 168pp. 1-931514-36-4.
Vol. 5. 2002. 176pp. 1-931514-37-2.
Vol. 6. 2002. 176pp. 1-931514-38-0.
Vol. 7. 2003. 192pp. 1-931514-39-9.

Anthologies and Short Story Collections

These collections of short stories and anthologies present the horror genre in a graphic novel format. The stories are either made for the collections or adapted from prose work.

***Clive Barker's Tapping the Vein.* Adapted from the works of Clive Barker by various. Illustrated by various.** Checker Book Publishing Group, 2002. 232pp. 0-9710249-3-6. **M**

A collection of short stories by famed writer Clive Barker based on his cult *Books of Blood* short stories. Highlights include works by John Bolton, P. Craig Russell, Klaus Janson, Tim Conrad, Bo Hampton, Stan Woch, Hector

Gomez, and others in such classic horror shorts as "Skins of the Fathers," "Human Remains," "In the Hills, In the Cities," "Down Satan," "How Spoilers Bleed," "The Madonna," "Pig Blood Blues," and "The Midnight Meat Train."

Creatures of the Night. **Written by Neil Gaiman. Illustrated by Michael Zulli.** Dark Horse Comics, 2004. 48pp. 1-56971-936-5. **M**

Adaptation of two Neil Gaiman short stories from the collection *Smoke and Mirrors: Short Fictions and Illusions*. In "The Price," a small black panther-like cat arrives at a home, and after each night's outing in the morning the owner spots mysterious wounds on it. What would do this to a cat, and why? In "The Daughter of Owls," a small newborn girl is left on the doorstep of a church with an owl pellet. Fourteen years later, many travel far and wide to see her rumored beauty, but there's a price to pay for those who would dare look at her.

Dark Horse Book of Hauntings. **Written and illustrated by Mike Mignola and various.** Dark Horse Comics, 2003. 96pp. 1-56971-958-6. **O**

A fresh sampling of horror by Dark Horse Comics featuring such talents as Mike Mignola, P. Craig Russell, Jill Thompson, Paul Chadwick, and more. The stories center on the theme of hauntings and range from a brand-new <u>Hellboy</u> short story involving a haunted house, to a haunted suit, and to a haunted doghouse. Two noncomic contributions are also included: a gothic short story by Perceval Landon (1869–1927) and an interview with a spiritualist medium.

Dark Horse Book of Hauntings ™ &
© 2006 Dark Horse Comics, Inc.
Cover © Gary Gianni.

Dark Horse Book of Monsters. **Written and Illustrated by Mike Mignola, Kurt Busiek, Evan Dorkin, Jill Thompson, and various.** Dark Horse Comics, 2006. 96pp. 1-59307-656-8. **O**

Anthology of stories based on the theme of beasts and other creatures from our darkest nightmares. The anthology is the fourth in its series and includes works by Mike Mignola, Kurt Busiek, Evan Dorkin, Sarah Dyer, Leah Moore, John Reppion, Scott Allie, William Hope Hodgson, Arvid Nelson, Keith Giffen, Timothy Green II, Jill Thompson, Paul Lee, Gary Gianni, Juan Ferreyra, and Brian Horton. Featured stories include a brand-new Hellboy story as well as the return of the dog crime solvers and a tribute to Jack Kirby.

Dark Horse Book of the Dead. **Written and illustrated by Mike Mignola, Evan Dorkin, Jill Thompson, Kelley Jones, Gary Gianni, and various.** Dark Horse Comics, 2005. 96pp. 1-59307-281-3. **O**

The third continuing anthology by Dark Horse Comics, featuring a brand new <u>Hellboy</u> short story, another canine occult adventure from the Eisner award-winning team of Jill Thompson and Evan Dorkin, and more.

✦ *Dark Horse Book of Witchcraft.* **Written and illustrated by Mike Mignola, Evan Dorkin, Jill Thompson, Scott Morse, and various.** Dark Horse Comics, 2004. 96pp. 1-59307-108-6. **O**

An anthology of stories centered around the theme of witches and warlocks, from comic book veterans Mike Mignola, Jill Thompson, Evan Dorkin, Scott Morse, and others. Highlights include another <u>Hellboy</u> installment by Mignola, Morse's story of the Salem witchcraft trials, and the return of the dogs from the "Stray" story by Thompson and Dorkin in the *Dark Horse Book of Hauntings* collection. A new adventure, called "Unfamiliar," won an Eisner Award in 2005 for Best Short Story as well as Best Painter/Multimedia Artist (Interior).

Dark Water. **Written by Koji Suzuki. Illustrated by Meimu.** ADV Manga, 2004. 144pp. 1-4139-0044-5. **T** 🎞 **Japanese manga.**

A collection of four short horror stories centered on the theme of water. The first story features a young mother living in an apartment complex with her young daughter. When she hears a story about a young girl who mysteriously disappeared, she feels compelled to solve the mystery and discovers a dark secret that threatens to claim her own life. The other stories involve a father who gets trapped in a cave and leaves his son a message; a corpse discovered in the water that might be a figment of someone's imagination; and a deadly creature trapped in a bottle stalking bikini-clad girls. The first story was adapted into the horror film *Dark Water,* released in 2005 and starring Jennifer Connelly.

Flesh-Colored Horror: The Junji Ito Horror Comic Collection. **Written and illustrated by Junji Ito.** ComicsOne, 2001. 220pp. 1-58899-086-9. **O Japanese manga.**

Anthology series by Japanese horror writer/artist Junju Ito. Stories included are "Long Hair in the Attic," "Approval," "Beehive," "Dying Young," "Headless Sculptures," and "Flesh-Colored Horror."

<u>Graphics Classics.</u> **Adapted and illustrated by various.** Eureka Productions, 2003–2004. **T**

Collected works retranslating horror prose works by classic horror authors in a graphic novel format. The collections feature tales by the authors in both prose and graphic novel formats. *Volume 10: Horror Classics* features stories by famous horror writers H. P. Lovecraft, Edgar Allan Poe, Saki, W. W. Jacobs, Jack London, and others.

> *Vol. 1: Edgar Allan Poe.* 2004. 144pp. 0-9712464-9-1.
> *Vol. 4: H. P. Lovecraft.* 2003. 144pp. 0-9712464-4-0.
> *Vol. 7: Bram Stoker.* 2004. 144pp. 0-9712464-7-5.
> *Vol. 10: Horror Classics.* 2004. 144pp. 0-9746648-1-2.

IDW Tales of Terror. **Written by Steve Niles and various. Illustrated by Ben Templesmith and various.** IDW Publishing, 2004. 96pp. 1-932382-31-3. **M**

An anthology collection of short stories based on several popular horror series, including <u>30 Days of Night</u>, <u>CVO</u>, <u>Wake the Dead</u>, <u>Wynonna Earp</u>, and

Singularity 7. Also included are several prose horror stories by Scott Ciencin, John Urbancik, and others.

***Mantis Woman.* Written and illustrated by Senno Knife.** Studio Iron Cat, 2003. 184pp. 1-929090-68-4. **O Japanese manga.**

Anthology of six frightening tales set in modern Japan, with a touch of dark humor and a few ironic endings. From a new teacher who severs the heads of teachers and students and attaches them to doll bodies, to a stuffed Koala bear that's hiding more than its stuffing, to strange neighbors who exact revenge on the locals, to a haunted pool, there's something to guarantee a fright.

<u>Mermaid Saga.</u> 2d ed. Written and illustrated by Rumiko Takahashi. VIZ Media, LLC, 2004. **O Japanese manga.**

A collection of short stories surrounding the Japanese myth of mermaids. It is said that those who consume the flesh of a mermaid will gain immortality. Some who have consumed the rare flesh and have become immortal have seen it as a gift, but others have been driven to madness, insanity, and depression, and have wished for the rarely granted gift of death.

> *Vol. 1.* 2004. 216pp. 1-59116-336-6.
> *Vol. 2.* 2004. 208pp. 1-59116-484-2.
> *Vol. 3.* 2004. 176pp. 1-59116-483-4.
> *Vol. 4.* 2004. 192pp. 1-59116-482-6.

***Neil Gaiman's Midnight Days.* Written by Neil Gaiman. Illustrated by various.** DC Comics, 1999. 160pp. 1-56389-517-X. **M**

A collection of tales by the author of <u>The Sandman</u>, including a <u>Swamp Thing</u> tale, "Jack in the Green"; the <u>Hellblazer</u> short story "Hold Me," in which grifter-mage John Constantine must deal with a ghost of a different sort; and a team-up of sorts featuring the Golden Age version of The Sandman and his encounter with Neil Gaiman's *Sandman—Morpheus, the Lord of Dreams.*

© 2006 DC Comics.

<u>Nightmares & Fairytales.</u> Written by Serena Valentino. Illustrated by Foo Swee Chin. Slave Labor Graphics, 2004–2005. **O**

Annabelle is a dark-haired doll like no other—hidden away for years, she's potentially the cause of or the witness to (she doesn't know which) a string of bloody tragedies that occur among her owners and their loved ones. From friends murdered by a vampire, to hidden monsters in attics at a convent, to the "real" story of Snow White and her evil aunt, to a young girl from an uncaring family who's terrified by the monsters in the closet, to what really happened to Cinderella and her cruel stepmother and stepsisters—Annabelle's a witness to them all.

> *Vol. 1: Once Upon a Time* . . . . 2004. 160pp. 0-943151-87-2.
> *Vol. 2: Beautiful Beasts.* 2005. 192pp. 1-59362-018-7.

***The Nightstand Chillers.* Written by Pat Boyette. Illustrated by various.** Vanguard Productions, 2003. 116pp. 1-887591-04-4. **T**

Late classic movie and television director Pat Boyette's tribute to the horror genre. Best known for his 1962 B-movie *The Dungeon of Harrow.* Many of Boyette's short stories for Charlton Comics and other publishers are showcased. Ghouls, demons, space travel, monsters, losers, witches, and even a trip to the guillotine are featured and bring out Boyette's love for the odd and macabre.

***Only the End of the World Again.* Based on a short story by Neil Gaiman. Adapted by P. Craig Russell. Illustrated by Troy Nixey.** Troy Oni Press, 2000. 48pp. 1-929998-09-0. **O**

When Lawrence Talbot comes to town to set up shop as an adjuster, his odd eating habits and the disappearance of the townsfolk are definitely connected: a werewolf has come to H. P. Lovecraft's town in Innsmouth. What happens when the townsfolk try to bring back the octopus-like Deep Ones from the depths of the ocean, and who's to stop them? It's the end of the world again, and only a werewolf is available to save the day or be the main sacrifice.

Pet Shop of Horrors. Written and illustrated by Akino Matsuri. TOKYOPOP, 2003–2005. **O Japanese manga.** あ

At the mysterious Count D's pet shop in Chinatown, no ordinary pets can be found, only magical creatures that can fulfill your wildest dreams and fantasies. But there's a line to cross should you ever break the contract that comes with each creature, as tragedy can follow those who stray from the rules. Each volume follows the stories of several creatures and the choices their owners have made. Meanwhile, an American cop has found a link between Count D's pet shop and a bizarre series of unexplainable murders. The manga series was also adapted into a Japanese anime.

> *Vol. 1.* 2003. 200pp. 1-59182-363-3.
> *Vol. 2.* 2003. 224pp. 1-59182-364-1.
> *Vol. 3.* 2003. 200pp. 1-59182-365-X.
> *Vol. 4.* 2004. 216pp. 1-59182-501-6.
> *Vol. 5.* 2004. 224pp. 1-59182-502-4.
> *Vol. 6.* 2004. 216pp. 1-59182-503-2.
> *Vol. 7.* 2004. 224pp. 1-59182-504-0.
> *Vol. 8.* 2004. 208pp. 1-59182-505-9.
> *Vol. 9.* 2004. 224pp. 1-59182-506-7.
> *Vol. 10.* 2005. 216pp. 1-59532-185-3.

Spookhouse. **Written by Scott Hampton and various. Illustrated by Scott Hampton.**
IDW Publishing, 2004. **M**

Ghosts and ghouls that go bump in the night are sure to bring a terrible fright. A collection of illustrated and prose ghost stories illustrated by Scott Hampton. Included are works by horror writers Liselotte Erlanger, Clive Barker, Robert E. Howard, and others, as well as adaptations of classic works by E. F. Benson and M. R. James, and W. W. Jacob's classic tale, "The Monkey's Paw."

Vol. 1. 2004. 136pp. 1-932382-15-1.
Vol. 2. 2004. 136pp. 1-932382-41-0.

© 2006 by Scott Hampton.

XxxHOLiC. **Written and illustrated by CLAMP.** Del Rey Manga/Random House, 2004– . **O Japanese manga.** あ

Watanuki Kimihiro has always been plagued by spirits. He can't seem to get rid of them, and they're starting to drive him crazy. By chance he stumbles into the beautiful and mysterious witch Yuko's store for a cure to his ailment but expectedly becomes her unpaid servant in the process. Now customer after customer comes into the store seeking that special aid that only Yuko knows, and it can cost someone their dearest possessions. But will being Yuko's assistant really solve his ghostly problem? Only time will tell. The manga was recently adapted as an anime film as well as an anime television series.

Vol. 1. 2004. 208pp. 0-345-47058-3.
Vol. 2. 2004. 192pp. 0-345-47119-9.
Vol. 3. 2004. 192pp. 0-345-47181-4.
Vol. 4. 2005. 208pp. 0-345-47788-X.
Vol. 5. 2005. 192pp. 0-345-47789-8.
Vol. 6. 2005. 208pp. 0-345-47790-1.
Vol. 7. 2006. 208pp. 0-345-48335-9.
Vol. 8. 2006. 208pp. 0-345-48336-7.

Chapter 7

Contemporary Life

While graphic novels featuring characters that readers can relate to are listed throughout this book (the most popular being the down-on-his-luck, real-life issues of teenager Peter Parker and his alter-ego Spider-Man), included here are stories that for the most part describe real-life situations involving teenagers, young adults, and adults. The focus is on common issues that readers can readily identify with, including romance, friendships, slice-of-life, teen issues, and even activities such as playing sports. This genre finds its origins in the romance comic book stories published by American comic book publishers from the golden age of comics through the early 1970s, as well as in the plethora of teen and adult prose fiction being published today. Though mainstream publishers, including Marvel Comics and DC Comics, have not published romance comic books and graphic novels on a regular basis for several decades, there has been a resurgence of graphic novels in the United States featuring slice-of-life tales. Many smaller publishing companies in North America, including Dark Horse Comics, Oni Press, Fantagraphics, Top Shelf Productions, and Abstract Studios, have published stories that deal with the everyday, but the current popular trend has been mostly spurred by the popularity of Japanese, Korean, and Chinese romance titles being reprinted in English. The tales from Asia are striking a chord with nontraditional U.S. graphic novel readers, mostly teenage girls and adults, drawn into the strong focus on romantic comedies, sympathetic characters, lighthearted romances, and heart-breaking stories of teenage and adult life.

Romance

Stories dealing with the love, confusion, heartache, hilarity, and ups-and-downs of teenage and young adult romance. Romance comic books have a long-standing history in the United States, from their inception in the 1940s through their decline in the 1970s. Within the last decade, with the popularity of Asian graphic novels and the rise of North American independent publishers, significant graphic novel titles have been published with a strong focus on teens and young adults. Like most teen romance fiction as well as adult romance, the focus in a graphic novel romance title is the blossoming relationship between two individuals. Romance knows no boundaries, so titles may include off-beat couples, same-sex couples, faraway settings, and even a heavy helping of comedy. Listed below are titles in several subgenres of romance, including romantic comedy and romantic fantasy.

***Aquarium.* 2d ed. Written and illustrated by Tomoko Taniguchi.** CPM Manga, 2003. 200pp. 1-58664-900-0. **A Japanese manga.**

> This collection of three heartwarming stories of innocent love includes the story of Naoka, a girl who has failed her entrance exam for a competitive school and is not attending the school of her choice. Heartbroken, she seeks solace at the local aquarium and meets a nice boy named Haruki, but Naoka isn't much in the mood for friends these days. Also included are the short stories "The Flying Stewardess" and "The Heart Is Your Kingdom."

Boys Be . . . . Written by Masahiro Itabashi. Illustrated by Hiroyuki Tamakoshi. TOKYOPOP, 2004– . **O Japanese manga.**

> Anthology series focusing on ordinary high school boys and their trials and tribulations in love, relationships, friendships, compromising situations, misunderstandings, and more. Each volume features several different short stories from a boy's point of view. Stories range from an otaku (an over-obsessed fan of manga and anime) falling in love for the first time, to a benched jock who gets a taste of the night life, to guys talking about what they like in girls, to screwball dating circumstances, to a boy overachieving to make sure he's the "perfect" boyfriend, to guys competing for the love of the same girl, and much more. Twenty volumes have been published in Japan and will be available in the United States from TOKYOPOP.
>
> > *Vol. 1.* 2004. 216pp. 1-59532-099-7.
> > *Vol. 2.* 2005. 216pp. 1-59532-100-4.
> > *Vol. 3.* 2005. 208pp. 1-59532-101-2.
> > *Vol. 4.* 2005. 208pp. 1-59532-102-0.
> > *Vol. 5.* 2005. 196pp. 1-59532-103-9.
> > *Vol. 6.* 2005. 196pp. 1-59532-104-7.
> > *Vol. 7.* 2005. 196pp. 1-59532-105-5.
> > *Vol. 8.* 2006. 196pp. 1-59532-106-3.
> > *Vol. 9.* 2006. 196pp. 1-59532-107-1.
> > *Vol. 10.* 2006. 196pp. 1-59532-108-X.
> > *Vol. 11.* 2006. 208pp. 1-59532-109-7.

Boys Over Flowers: Hana Yori Dango. **Written and illustrated by Yoko Kamio.** VIZ Media, LLC, 2003– . **T** **Japanese manga.** あ

Middle-class girl Tsukusi Makino has just been accepted to the prestigious Eitoku Academy, a school for the snobbish elite, but she is no meek conformist. The school is ruled by the "F4" (or Flower Four), a group of prissy and pompous rich boys who enjoy wreaking havoc and ruining lives at school. When a friend of hers accidentally trips into one of the F4, Tsukusi stands up to them and becomes their main target. Now no one at school wants to be her friend for fear of retribution from the F4, and she must try to stay one step ahead of the boorish bullies. Strangely, she does feel some attraction to Rui, a sometimes-helpful yet aloof member of the F4. Is there really some chemistry there? Does she even want to be a part of this horrid clique? The series was collected into thirty-six volumes originally published in Japan from 1992 to 2002 and was also adapted into an anime series.

Vol. 1. 2003. 216pp. 1-56931-996-0
Vol. 2. 2003. 184pp. 1-56931-997-9
Vol. 3. 2003. 192pp. 1-56931-998-7
Vol. 4. 2004. 192pp. 1-59116-112-6
Vol. 5. 2004. 192pp. 1-59116-141-X
Vol. 6. 2004. 192pp. 1-59116-314-5
Vol. 7. 2004. 200pp. 1-59116-370-6
Vol. 8. 2004. 200pp. 1-59116-371-4
Vol. 9. 2004. 200pp. 1-59116-372-2
Vol. 10. 2005. 176pp. 1-59116-629-2
Vol. 11. 2005. 184pp. 1-59116-747-7
Vol. 12. 2005. 176pp. 1-59116-801-5
Vol. 13. 2005. 176pp. 1-59116-865-1
Vol. 14. 2005. 192pp. 1-4215-0018-3
Vol. 15. 2005. 192pp. 1-4215-0136-8
Vol. 16. 2006. 208pp. 1-4215-0262-3
Vol. 17. 2006. 208pp. 1-4215-0392-1.
Vol. 18. 2006. 208pp. 1-4215-0532-0.
Vol. 19. 2006. 208pp. 1-4215-0533-9.
Vol. 20. 2006. 208pp. 1-4215-0534-7.
Vol. 21. 2006. 208pp. 1-4215-0535-5.
Vol. 22. 2006. 208pp. 1-4215-0985-7.
Vol. 23. 2006. 192pp. 1-4215-0986-5.

Call Me Princess. **Written and illustrated by Tomoko Taniguchi.** CPM Manga, 2002. 194pp. 1-58664-898-5. **T Japanese manga.**

Mako, a teenage girl, finds that appearances aren't everything when it comes to love. She is already involved in a burgeoning romance with her first love, a nice boy named Yo. But Mako has always wanted to have a loving relationship exactly like the kind her old sister has with her husband, Shin. When she finds out that Shin has a younger brother named Ryu who looks almost like him, she couldn't be more thrilled. But Mako finds that Ryu is cold and distant—nothing like her brother in law. Torn between her first love and a physical version of an ideal love, will Mako make the right decision?

Crazy Love Story. Written and illustrated by Vin Lee. TOKYOPOP, 2004–2005. T Korean manhwa.

Hae Jung Shin, who was at the top of her class in high school, is on a downward spiral after losing her mother, embittered by the unfairness of life. She's now a self-professed "ice queen" who steals when the opportunity strikes and seeks security in her psychotic boyfriend, Jimmy. Sung Moo has always admired Hae Jung from afar, and has been coasting through school until he reaches his goal of pop-idol stardom. When he meets Hae Jung and her best friend Bo Na in a bar, he's easy prey for Hae Jung. In no time the infatuated boy is wrapped around her finger. But in the end, who will Hae Jung choose—a boy who really loves her, or her dangerous, mafia-made boyfriend?

> *Vol. 1.* 2004. 192pp. 1-59182-772-8.
> *Vol. 2.* 2005. 192pp. 1-59182-773-6.
> *Vol. 3.* 2005. 208pp. 1-59182-949-6.
> *Vol. 4.* 2005. 192pp. 1-59182-950-X.
> *Vol. 5.* 2005. 192pp. 1-59182-951-8.

Gravitation. Written and illustrated by Maki Murakami. TOKYOPOP, 2003–2005. O Japanese manga. あ

A shonen-ai (light male-male romance) title. Shuichi Shindou is a good-natured high school senior who dreams of his band, Bad Luck, making it big in the music industry and top the charts in Japan. His only obstacle—or perhaps blessing—appears in the guise of Eiri Yuki, a rude and blunt, but honest, romance writer who becomes a critic of Shuichi's lyrics. Yuki helps to toughen Shuchi up for the cut-throat world of the music industry. With the help of Yuki, Shuichi just might have a chance of making it, and perhaps they may be much more than friends, if Bad Luck's good luck streak continues. The manga was also adapted into an anime in Japan.

> *Vol. 1.* 2003. 200pp. 1-59182-333-1.
> *Vol. 2.* 2003. 216pp. 1-59182-334-X.
> *Vol. 3.* 2003. 216pp. 1-59182-335-8.
> *Vol. 4.* 2004. 216pp. 1-59182-336-6.
> *Vol. 5.* 2004. 224pp. 1-59182-337-4.
> *Vol. 6.* 2004. 216pp. 1-59182-338-2.
> *Vol. 7.* 2004. 232pp. 1-59182-339-0.
> *Vol. 8.* 2004. 224pp. 1-59182-340-4.
> *Vol. 9.* 2004. 224pp. 1-59182-341-2.
> *Vol. 10.* 2005. 192pp. 1-59182-342-0.
> *Vol. 11.* 2005. 192pp. 1-59532-414-3.
> *Vol. 12.* 2005. 192pp. 1-59532-415-1.

Hot Gimmick. Written and illustrated by Aihara Miki. VIZ Media, LLC, 2003–2006. O Japanese manga.

When sixteen-year-old high schooler Hatsumi reluctantly goes to the pharmacy to pick up a pregnancy test for her "popular" younger sister who thinks she's pregnant, she inadvertently becomes the slave of Ryoki Tachibana in order to save face and not embarrass her younger sister. The son of the tyrannical company-housing supervisor, he's been a thorn in her side since childhood. Now she has to do anything he says, or he'll tell his manipulative mother about her sister. But she's also found out that her old friend—and possibly more—Azusa Odagiri, is back in town, and she's falling in love with both him and her "slave" role with Ryoki. When the pressures of her life prevent her from telling anyone what she really means, how can she find her own voice if she won't even voice her feelings?

> *Vol. 1*. 2003. 192pp. 1-59116-214-9.
> *Vol. 2*. 2004. 192pp. 1-59116-227-0.
> *Vol. 3*. 2004. 192pp. 1-59116-228-9.
> *Vol. 4*. 2004. 192pp. 1-59116-389-7.
> *Vol. 5*. 2004. 192pp. 1-59116-144-4.
> *Vol. 6*. 2004. 192pp. 1-56931-965-0.
> *Vol. 7*. 2004. 192pp. 1-59116-502-4.
> *Vol. 8*. 2005. 192pp. 1-59116-706-X.
> *Vol. 9*. 2005. 192pp. 1-59116-845-7.
> *Vol. 10*. 2005. 176pp. 1-4215-0109-0.
> *Vol. 11*. 2005. 176pp. 1-4215-0712-9.

Imadoki: Nowadays. **Written and illustrated by Yû Watase.** VIZ Media, LLC, 2004–2005. **O ◎ Japanese manga.**

IMADOKI!: NOWADAYS © 2000
Yuu WATASE/Shogakukan Inc.

Shy but outspoken Tampopo Yamazaki has just been accepted to the elitist Meio Academy. The students won't talk to her due to her middle-class background, and even the nice boy with whom she spoke the day before in the garden, the one tending to a dandelion, won't acknowledge her existence. The boy is Kouki Kugyou, the son of some of the wealthiest parents. Is he being cold to her on purpose, or is there something else going on? Hoping to make new friends, she starts up a horticulturist club. Is this really the best way to make new friends, or will it ensure that her social days at school are numbered?

> *Vol. 1*. 2004. 200pp. 1-59116-330-7.
> *Vol. 2*. 2004. 200pp. 1-59116-469-9.
> *Vol. 3*. 2004. 200pp. 1-59116-504-0.
> *Vol. 4*. 2004. 200pp. 1-59116-618-7.
> *Vol. 5*. 2005. 200pp. 1-59116-619-5.

I.N.V.U. **Written and illustrated by Kim Kang Won.** TOKYOPOP, 2003. **Korean manhwa.**

When teenager Sey's mom moves to Italy for five years, she's left to transfer to an all-new school and stay with her mom's friend Meja and her son Terry. Though the house is warm and cozy, there's something strange about Terry that intrigues Sey. Even more intriguing is that Sey's teacher, Hajun Cho, whom she (and every other girl at school) has a crush on, has a mysterious past with Terry. Even when things aren't what they seem to be and secrets are revealed, nothing can come between the loves and lives of four teenage girls.

> *Vol. 1*. 2003. 176pp. 1-59182-001-4.
> *Vol. 2*. 2003. 192pp. 1-59182-002-2.
> *Vol. 3*. 2003. 192pp. 1-59182-062-6.

I''s. **Written and illustrated by Masakazu Katsura.** VIZ Media, LLC, 2005– . ⊚ **Japanese manga.**

I''S © 1997 by Masakazu
Katsura/SHUEISHA Inc.

Sixteen-year-old Ichitaka Seto has been in love with his shy classmate, the cute Iori Yoshizuki, since the first time he saw her. Thanks to an unhappy incident from his past with another girl, he's too shy to tell her how he really feels. Suddenly, after posing in a bathing suit for a magazine, Iori is the most popular girl in school, and it looks like she's now way out of Ichitaka's league. But when the two of them are paired together to work on a school party, Iori calls the two of them I''s (due to the first letters of their names), and it seems that Ichitaka might have a chance after all. Unfortunately, thanks to the interference of well-meaning friends, innocent comedic accidents, and the return of an old childhood friend, Itsuki, who has a crush on Ichitaka, he may have lost Iori's heart forever. Fifteen volumes were published in Japan from 1997 to 1999 and are now being translated by VIZ Media for publication in North America.

Vol. 1: Iori. 2005. 192pp. 1-59116-952-6.
Vol. 2: Itsuki. 2005. 200pp. 1-59116-953-4.
Vol. 3: Bitter Summer. 2005. 184pp. 1-59116-969-0.
Vol. 4: October 3rd. 2005. 200pp. 1-4215-0054-X.
Vol. 5: Scorched Past. 2006. 200pp. 1-4215-0188-0.
Vol. 6: Bye Bye. 2006. 200pp. 1-4215-0333-6.
Vol. 7. 2006. 200pp. 1-4215-0648-3.
Vol. 8. 2006. 200pp. 1-4215-0649-1.
Vol. 9. 2006. 208pp. 1-4215-0650-5.
Vol. 10. 2006. 208pp. 1-4215-0651-3.
Vol. 11. 2006. 200pp. 1-4215-0652-1.
Vol. 12. 2006. 200pp. 1-4215-1074-X.
Vol. 13. 2006. 192pp. 1-4215-1075-8.

Land of the Blindfolded. **Written and illustrated by Tsukuba Sakura.** CMX/DC Comics, 2004–2006. **T** ⊚ **Japanese manga.**

MEKAKUSHI NO KUNI © 1998
Sakura Tsukuba/ HAKUSENSHA Inc.

High school girl Kaneda Outsuke has the ability to see the future when she touches people. She walks among the blindfolded (those without visions) and she finds it's a tricky path to walk, with many consequences if she tries to change the future. She wants to try to help people avoid having bad things happen to them, but it's not an easy task. She meets Arou, a boy who has the opposite power of hers and can see the past. While Kaneda wants to help people, Arou believes that she shouldn't change what is destined to happen. When they become closer, they find that their beliefs in their gifts are put to the test. When another clairvoyant, a possibly devious boy named Namiki, befriends them, Arou is horrified by his enjoyment of idly watching a horrible fate occur, and changes his ways. Namiki also finds out that since he's met Kaneda, she's made him rethink his beliefs in his powers. Meanwhile, both boys are finding that they are falling in love with Kaneda.

Vol. 1. 2004. 208pp. 1-4012-0524-0.
Vol. 2. 2005. 208pp. 1-4012-0525-9.

Vol. 3. 2005. 200pp. 1-4012-0526-7.
Vol. 4. 2005. 192pp. 1-4012-0527-5.
Vol. 5. 2005. 200pp. 1-4012-0528-3.
Vol. 6. 2006. 208pp. 1-4012-1016-3.
Vol. 7. 2006. 200pp. 1-4012-1017-1.
Vol. 8. 2006. 208pp. 1-4012-1018-X.
Vol. 9. 2006. 200pp. 1-4012-1052-X.

Love as a Foreign Language. Written by J. Torres. Illustrated by Eric Kim. Oni Press, 2004– . O Neo-manga.

© 2006 J. Torres and Eric Kim.

Joel is a stranger in a strange land. An English teacher in Korea, he's in a job he hates in a country he hates even more. Homesick and tired of the culture, he's eager to hand in his resignation at the end of his first year and return to Canada, until Hana, the new school secretary, comes into his life. Joel will now do anything to win her heart, even if it means staying in Korea for one more year. Now all he needs is the courage to ask her out.

Vol. 1. 2004. 72pp. 1-932664-06-8.
Vol. 2. 2005. 72pp. 1-932664-15-7.
Vol. 3. 2005. 72pp. 1-932664-18-1.
Vol. 4. 2005. 72pp. 1-932664-19-X.
Vol. 5. 2006. 64pp. 1-932664-39-4.
Vol. 6. 2006. 64pp. 1-932664-40-8.

MARS. Written and illustrated by Fuyumi Soryo. TOKYOPOP, 2002–2004. T ◎ Japanese manga.

Rei, a seemingly typical bad-boy teen with a dangerous streak and a fascination for fast motorcycles, has met an unlikely match: the shy and beautiful Kira, a teen painter who is finding a way to express her pent-up feelings through her art. Both with tragic pasts, they're finding out that even though on the outside they're nothing alike, with each painful revelation of their family history they have more in common than they imagined. Can Rei and Kira overcome their angst-filled, tragic pasts before old habits and dark secrets break them apart? *Horse with No Name* is a prequel to the events in the series featuring a younger bad boy Rei and an unexpected friendship.

7

Vol. 1. 2002. 200pp. 1-931514-58-5.
Vol. 2. 2002. 208pp. 1-931514-59-3.
Vol. 3. 2002. 198pp. 1-59182-054-5.
Vol. 4. 2002. 198pp. 1-591820-55-3.
Vol. 5. 2002. 198pp. 1-59182-056-1.
Vol. 6. 2002. 198pp. 1-59182-057-X.
Vol. 7. 2002. 198pp. 1-59182-072-3.
Vol. 8. 2003. 200pp. 1-59182-087-1.
Vol. 9. 2003. 200pp. 1-59182-105-3.
Vol. 10. 2003. 176pp. 1-59182-129-0.
Vol. 11. 2003. 184pp. 1-59182-130-4.

Vol. 12. 2003. 184pp. 1-59182-131-2.
Vol. 13. 2003. 184pp. 1-59182-132-0.
Vol. 14. 2003. 176pp. 1-59182-133-9.
Vol. 15. 2003. 200pp. 1-59182-134-7.
Horse with No Name. 2004. 208pp. 1-59182-864-3.

***Miss Me?* Written and illustrated by Tomoko Taniguchi.** CPM Manga, 2004. 184pp. 1-58664-905-1. **A Japanese manga.**

Emyu is a fashionable high school girl who has a crush on Shinkichi, the leader of a heavy metal band, but her love is unrequited. After one of their concerts she meets Yasu, the band's bass player, and he instantly falls in love with her, but she doesn't feel anything for him. Will Emyu find true love, or will no one's wishes of love come true? Sometimes love works in mysterious ways.

***The One I Love.* Written and illustrated by CLAMP.** TOKYOPOP, 2004. 128pp. 1-59182-764-7. **T Japanese manga.**

A short story collection by the premiere manga creators in Japan. The collection is a brief look at the lives of the artists, as well as their heartwarming concepts of love and romance and the tug of emotions that it carries. The twelve stories and prose each feature a nameless female protagonist as she experiences love, insecurity, vulnerability, loneliness, and second thoughts.

<u>Peach Girl.</u> Written and illustrated by Miwa Ueda. TOKYOPOP, 2003–2007. **T** ◎
Japanese manga. あ

Trials and tribulations of surviving in high school and the heartache of being misunderstood. Momo is a level-headed, beautiful blonde-haired girl with a natural tan whom everyone at school believes is a slut due to her appearance. She has a "friend" in the raven-tressed, pale-skinned Sae, a back-stabbing girl who only appears to be happy when Momo is going through the ringer in pain. Momo has a crush on Toji, a shy and easily manipulated boy in her school, and naturally Sae wants to steal whatever she can from Momo. Can Momo keep her crush a secret for long? Meanwhile, the hunky Kiley is starting to make moves on Momo. <u>Peach Girl Authentic</u> is the second edition of the first <u>Peach Girl</u> series, now being published in the traditional right-to-left format. The story continues in <u>Peach Girl: Change of Heart</u> and a three-volume spin-off called <u>Peach Girl: Sae's Story</u>. The series <u>Peach Girl</u> was also adapted as a twenty-five-episode anime series.

<u>Peach Girl Authentic.</u> 2004–2006.
Vol. 1. 2004. 192pp. 1-59532-171-3.
Vol. 2. 2004. 184pp. 1-59532-172-1.
Vol. 3. 2005. 192pp. 1-59532-173-X.
Vol. 4. 2005. 192pp. 1-59532-174-8.
Vol. 5. 2005. 192pp. 1-59532-175-6.
Vol. 6. 2005. 184pp. 1-59532-176-4.
Vol. 7. 2006. 192pp. 1-59532-177-2.
Vol. 8. 2006. 192pp. 1-59532-178-0.
<u>Peach Girl: Change of Heart.</u> 2003–2004.
Vol. 1. 2003. 192pp. 1-931514-19-4.
Vol. 2. 2003. 176pp. 1-59182-195-9.

Vol. 3. 2003. 184pp. 1-59182-196-7.
Vol. 4. 2003. 176pp. 1-59182-197-5.
Vol. 5. 2003. 176pp. 1-59182-198-3.
Vol. 6. 2004. 176pp. 1-59182-495-8.
Vol. 7. 2004. 176pp. 1-59182-496-6.
Vol. 8. 2004. 176pp. 1-59182-497-4.
Vol. 9. 2004. 176pp. 1-59182-498-2.
Vol. 10. 2004. 192pp. 1-59182-499-0.

Peach Girl: Sae's Story. 2006–2007.
Vol. 1. 2006. 216pp. 1-59816-517-8.
Vol. 2. 2006. 216pp. 1-59816-518-6.

Perfect Day for Love Letters. Written and illustrated by George Asakura. Del
Rey Manga/Ballantine Books, 2005– . **T Japanese manga.**

Anthology series showcasing how heartaches, love, friendship, loneliness,
and pain can be eased by love letters. The stories, which are not related, range
from the humorous, to the heart-wrenching, to the uplifting, and all feature the
strength of epistolary power. A librarian finds a love letter in a book from a secret admirer, a school bully accidentally sends a love letter and shows a different side of himself, a girl receives a love letter and has to figure out what boy
could have sent it. The series was originally published in Japan in three
volumes.

Vol. 1. 2005. 208pp. 0-345-48266-2.
Vol. 2. 2005. 208pp. 0-345-48267-0.

***Popcorn Romance.* Written and illustrated by Tomoko Taniguchi.** CPM
Manga, 2002. 192pp. 1-58664-901-9. **A Japanese manga.**

Zenta and Ryouta Yamazaki, two brothers in a heavy metal band, try to recuperate at their grandfather's farm in the countryside of Hokkaido after Zenta
collapses on stage. When the farm is about to be closed down and turned into a
golf course, the brothers decide to do what they can to save it. Will they give
up their hopes and dreams of making it big in the music world, or will they
turn their backs on their grandfather?

Saikano. Written and illustrated by Shin Takahashi. VIZ Media, LLC,
2004–2006. **M Japanese manga.** あ

Hokkaido high school sweethearts Chise, a shy and innocent girl, and Shuji,
an awkward boy, have just gotten back together after a rough patch in their relationship. While Shuji is visiting Sapporo for a shopping trip, the city is
bombed by unnamed ships and thousands die. Shuji spots a tiny fighter craft
taking down the enemy ships, which then lands next to him: it's Chise. Metal
wings are protruding from her back, and her right hand has been replaced by a
laser cannon. Chise's dark secret is revealed: she's not your average shy
girl—she's an engineered living weapon from the Japanese Self Defense
Force. And she's slowly gaining more and more destructive power. As their
relationship continues to grow, what will Chise do when she finds it difficult
to walk the path of a normal teenager, and what will Shuji do when his girl-

friend is a living ultimate weapon, built for destruction? The series was also adapted as an anime series and a live-action film.

> *Vol. 1*. 2004. 232pp. 1-59116-339-0.
> *Vol. 2*. 2004. 232pp. 1-59116-474-5.
> *Vol. 3*. 2004. 232pp. 1-59116-475-3.
> *Vol. 4*. 2005. 248pp. 1-59116-476-1.
> *Vol. 5*. 2005. 248pp. 1-59116-477-X.
> *Vol. 6*. 2005. 288pp. 1-59116-478-8.
> *Vol. 7*. 2006. 336pp. 1-4215-0197-X.

SOS. **Written and illustrated by Hinako Ashihara.** VIZ Media, LLC, 2005. 192pp. 1-59116-735-3. **T Japanese manga.**

A collection of humorous short stories set in Japan by Hinako Ashihara. Three high school students—Raku, Nono, and Yu—start a dating service in their high school. When a date goes wrong the three cupids have to rescue their client and wait until the teachers find out about the service! In 1920s Japan, a bookstore clerk and budding poet encourages her customer to follow his dreams and become a composer. Finally, Yohei is a male chauvinist who always takes his girlfriend for granted. When she tires of his behavior, she sets her sights on nice guy Horie. Will Yohei learn to change his ways, or has his girlfriend left him for good?

Strangers in Paradise. **Written and illustrated by Terry Moore.** Abstract Studio, Incorporated, 1994– . O ◉

© 2006 Terry Moore.

The complex story of three friends—Katina "Katchoo" Choovanski, Francine Peters, and David Qin—and their turbulent experiences of love, life, and sorrow with the people they fall in and out of love with—including each other. The emotional dynamite Katchoo and "All-American Girl" Francine have been best friends since high school, and Katchoo, despite her aggressive tendencies and dark past, loves Francine dearly. David loves Katchoo through all her highs and lows, and sweet Francine is caught awkwardly in the middle, not sure where or with whom she really belongs. The romantic triangle started in 1993, and *Strangers in Paradise* is regarded as one of the best-known independent comic books. The series has won multiple awards, including an Eisner Award for Best Serialized Story (1996), as well as recognition from YALSA's Popular Paperbacks for Young Adults in 2002 and 2005. Recently the creator has announced that the series will come to its conclusion in 2007. The pocket book editions of the titles include the contents of several normal-sized graphic novel collections.

> *Vol. 1: The Collected Strangers in Paradise.* 1994. 96pp. 1-892597-00-4.
> *Vol. 2: I Dream of You.* 1996. 208pp. 1-892597-01-2.
> *Vol. 3: It's a Good Life.* 1998. 152pp. 1-892597-02-0.
> *Vol. 4: Love Me Tender.* 1997. 120pp. 1-892597-03-9.
> *Vol. 5: Immortal Enemies.* 1996. 152pp. 1-892597-04-7.

© 2006 Terry Moore.

Vol. 6: High School!. 1999. 88pp. 1-892597-07-1.
Vol. 7: Sanctuary. 1999. 176pp. 1-892597-09-8.
Vol. 8: My Other Life. 2000. 120pp. 1-892597-11-X.
Vol. 9: Child of Rage. 2001. 154pp. 1-892597-13-6.
Vol. 10: Tropic of Desire. 2001. 104pp. 1-892597-15-2.
Vol. 11: Brave New World. 2002. 88pp. 1-892597-16-0.
Vol. 12: Heart in Hand. 2003. 120pp. 1-892597-20-9.
Vol. 13: Flower to Flame. 2003. 144pp. 1-892597-24-1.
Vol. 14: David's Story. 2004. 88pp. 1-892597-25-X.
Vol. 15: Tomorrow Now. 2004. 114pp. 1-892597-27-6.
Vol. 16: Molly & Poo. 2005. 80pp. 1-892597-32-2.
Vol. 17: Tattoo. 2005. 120pp. 1-892597-33-0.
Vol. 18: Love & Lies. 2006. 120pp. 1-892597-34-9.
Pocket Book 1. 2005. 360pp. 1-892597-26-8.
Pocket Book 2. 2005. 344pp. 1-892597-29-2.
Pocket Book 3. 2005. 372pp. 1-892597-30-6.
Pocket Book 4. 2005. 360pp. 1-892597-31-4.
Pocket Book 5. 2005. 376pp. 1-892597-38-1.

<u>Sweet and Sensitive.</u> Written and illustrated by Eun-Ah Park. ADV Manga, 2004. **A Korean manhwa.**

Freshman Ee-Ji has a problem: she's in love with two boys! One of them is the kind Han-Kyul, her sweetheart from elementary school. They lost touch after he moved away, but now he's come back into her life. The other is Sae-Ryun, a rowdy and rude boy with poor manners. To top it off, the boys are best friends. What can a girl do?

> *Vol. 1*. 2004. 200pp. 1-4139-0074-7.
> *Vol. 2*. 2004. 208pp. 1-4139-0095-X.

***Times Two.* Written and illustrated by Shouko Akira.** VIZ Media, LLC, 2005. 200pp. 1-59116-736-1. **O Japanese manga.**

Collects five romance short stories by creator Shouko Akira. Captured herein are stories that range from the touching to the humorous to the fantastic, as high school students experience the sometimes awkward but magical first moments of being in love. Stories are about secret crushes, rekindled love, what happens when opposites really do attract, what happens when a girl gains telepathic powers and can hear the mind of a boy, and the kinetic significance of a touch.

<u>Wild Act.</u> Written and illustrated by Rie Takada. TOKYOPOP, 2003–2005. **O Japanese manga.**

Fifteen-year-old Yuniko loves being a groupie and has vowed to collect one piece of memorabilia from each of her favorite stars, especially the belongings of the late actor Akira Nanae. She's decided to steal everything of his and bring the things to her sick mother to cheer her up. Her mother, once a famous actress/model who had a relationship with Akira Nanae when they were younger, now suffers from amnesia. While waiting to steal Akira's Academy Award, Yuniko inadvertently meets up with the incredible seventeen-year-old

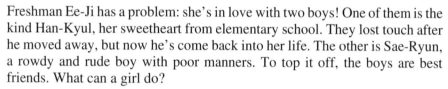

actor Ryu Eba, whom some people call the next Nanae. As their relationship grows, at first she hates him since he's always intervening in her plans to take Akira's possessions, but soon Ryu has stolen her heart and more. Together Yuniko and Ryo try to cure her mother's amnesia and to discover what Yuniko's real relationship with the late actor was.

Vol. 1. 2003. 200pp. 1-59182-374-9.
Vol. 2. 2003. 200pp. 1-59182-375-7.
Vol. 3. 2003. 200pp. 1-59182-376-5.
Vol. 4. 2004. 200pp. 1-59182-562-8.
Vol. 5. 2004. 208pp. 1-59182-563-6.
Vol. 6. 2004. 200pp. 1-59182-564-4.
Vol. 7. 2004. 200pp. 1-59182-565-2.
Vol. 8. 2004. 200pp. 1-59182-566-0.
Vol. 9. 2004. 208pp. 1-59182-567-9.
Vol. 10. 2005. 192pp. 1-59532-445-3.

Romantic Comedy

Like today's television and movies, the romantic comedy is one of the more common forms of romance stories being published as graphic novels. Typically the romance is depicted as a clumsy and awkward relationship that blossoms, falters, resurges, and then fully blooms by the conclusion of the story. The stories tend to be lighthearted, and though there usually is some conflict that could destroy the love relationship, there is almost always a happy ending.

Ai Yori Aoshi. Written and illustrated by Kou Fumizuki. TOKYOPOP, 2004– . O Japanese manga. あ

Kaoru Hanabishi is a good-natured junior in college living a fairly normal life, when he meets up with an old friend, the sweet and unfailingly faithful Aoi Sakuraba. She's more than an old friend—they were paired up for an arranged marriage by their parents eighteen years ago, and she has never stopped loving him. But times have changed, and after Kaoru left the Hanabishi family under less-than-pleasant circumstances, the marriage was dissolved. Though Aoi, the daughter of a wealthy dry goods family, was told to forget about him, she never has. Can anyone try to keep them apart once they find each other again? The series was originally published in seventeen volumes in Japan. The series was adapted into an anime series in Japan.

Vol. 1. 2004. 232pp. 1-59182-645-4.
Vol. 2. 2004. 208pp. 1-59182-646-2.
Vol. 3. 2004. 224pp. 1-59182-647-0.
Vol. 4. 2004. 208pp. 1-59182-648-9.
Vol. 5. 2004. 200pp. 1-59182-649-7.
Vol. 6. 2004. 216pp. 1-59182-650-0.
Vol. 7. 2005. 192pp. 1-59532-370-8.
Vol. 8. 2005. 192pp. 1-59532-371-6.
Vol. 9. 2005. 200pp. 1-59532-372-4.
Vol. 10. 2005. 192pp. 1-59532-373-2.
Vol. 11. 2005. 192pp. 1-59532-374-0.

Vol. 12. 2006. 200pp. 1-59532-375-9.
Vol. 13. 2006. 192pp. 1-59532-376-7.
Vol. 14. 2006. 192pp. 1-59816-2.

Club 9. **Written and illustrated by Makoto Kobayashi.** Dark Horse Comics, 2003–2005. **O Japanese manga.**

Beautiful and naïve eighteen-year-old Haruo Hattori is leaving behind her boyfriend, her eccentric family, and her rural life in Akita and going to the big city of Tokyo to college! The only things she's taking with her are her small-town charm and her promise to stay faithful to her boyfriend. Haruo finds out that she needs a quick way to earn some money to make ends meet, and her new friends at school have the perfect job for her: hostess at Club 9, the hottest bar in the Ginza! Soon Haruo finds herself charming the wealthiest and most handsome men in Tokyo with her fish-out-of-water appeal and natural clumsiness. After all she's seen and experienced, will Haruo remain true to her boyfriend, and will she ever want to go back to her small home town?

Vol. 1. 2003. 192pp. 1-56971-915-2.
Vol. 2. 2003. 192pp. 1-56971-968-3.
Vol. 3. 2005. 192pp. 1-59307-124-8.
Vol. 4. 2005. 200pp. 1-59307-359-3.

Couple. **Written and illustrated by Jae Sung Park.** CPM Manga, 2004. **O Korean manhwa.**

When Yu Mi Yu, a cute young college student, can't make her rent payments, she's thrown out on the streets of Seoul, Korea. Young Ho Han, a young ex-soldier who is going back to college, just moved into the same complex. He finds Yu Mi shivering out in the cold and takes her in after she catches a fever. Once Yu Mi has been nursed back to health, she has a great idea: for them to share the apartment. Young Ho and Yu Mi become unlikely roommates, but how long can a boy and a girl remain just co-habitants of an apartment?

Vol. 1. 2004. 192pp. 1-58664-951-5.
Vol. 2. 2004. 176pp. 1-58664-952-3.
Vol. 3. 2004. 168pp. 1-58664-953-1.

Doubt!! **Written and illustrated by Izumi Kaneyoshi.** VIZ Media, LLC, 2005–2006. **O Japanese manga.**

Ai Maekawa was never the most popular girl in junior high school. After finding out that the boy she had a crush on slept with a vindictive classmate named Yumi, Ai lashes out at her and in return is humiliated in class for being a frumpy ugly duckling. Ai vows to never again let this happen in high school. Six months later, Ai has transferred to a high school where no one knows the old Ai, and she transforms herself into a beauty queen. When she starts at her new high school she is swept off her feet by a cute boy named So. With his help she is made head girl in class, and she decides that she'd like to have So be her boyfriend. Unfortunately her actions earn the ire of the other girls, and it seems that Ai has traded in her problems from junior high for all new ones. More problems arise when a mysterious note threatens to expose Ai's past,

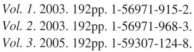

and a ghost from So's past comes to wreck their relationship. Who'd have thought being the popular girl in school would be this much trouble?

> *Vol. 1*. 2005. 192pp. 1-59116-908-9.
> *Vol. 2*. 2005. 184pp. 1-59116-909-7.
> *Vol. 3*. 2005. 200pp. 1-59116-910-0.
> *Vol. 4*. 2005. 192pp. 1-59116-984-4.
> *Vol. 5*. 2005. 192pp. 1-4215-0055-8.
> *Vol. 6*. 2006. 200pp. 1-4215-0172-4.

Dragon Voice. Written and illustrated by Yuriko Nishiyama. TOKYOPOP, 2004– . **T Japanese manga.**

Rin Amami is a talented fourteen-year-old t who has always wanted to be a pop singer. He's one of the best street dancers, but his singing voice scares people away. His voice doesn't sound like angels—it sounds like a frog bellowing! When he meets up with a boy-band called Beatmen (made up of Shino, Goh, Toshi, and Yuhgo), his odd-sounding voice inexplicably makes their harmonizing voices even better. This voice, some members of the band believe, is the legendary "dragon voice." Though some members of the band are against it, Rin makes the audition and becomes a member of the group. Will Beatmen finally make it big in the music world with the aid of Rin, and will Rin make his dream come true? The eleven-volume series is still being reprinted in North America from Japan.

> *Vol. 1*. 2004. 208pp. 1-59532-119-5.
> *Vol. 2*. 2004. 208pp. 1-59532-120-9.
> *Vol. 3*. 2005. 208pp. 1-59532-121-7.
> *Vol. 4*. 2005. 208pp. 1-59532-122-5.
> *Vol. 5*. 2005. 192pp. 1-59532-123-3.
> *Vol. 6*. 2006. 192pp. 1-59532-124-1.
> *Vol. 7*. 2006. 208pp. 1-59532-125-x.

Duck Prince. Written and illustrated by Ai Morinaga. CPM Manga, 2004. **T Japanese manga.**

Reiichi Swan was anything but a swan. He was a nerd with thick glasses, coarse hair, and a round face that even his mother couldn't love. His dream girl, Yumiko Itoh, loves him for who he is inside, but he can't believe it. When he's hit by a car while trying to rescue Yumiko's dog, he finds that the dog was no ordinary pooch but a magical prince in disguise who grants Reiichi his wish: he's now phenomenally handsome. Now the lame duck is a beautiful swan. When you're handsome, all of your troubles go away, right?

> *Vol. 1*. 2004. 176pp. 1-58664931-0.
> *Vol. 2*. 2004. 192pp. 1-58664-932-9.
> *Vol. 3*. 2004. 184pp. 1-58664-933-7.

Hana-Kimi: For You in Full Blossom. Written and illustrated by Hisaya Nakajo. VIZ Media, LLC, 2004– . **O Japanese manga.**

Teenager Mizuki Ashiya, a female Japanese American track-and-field star, will do anything to be close to her idol, high jump star Izumi Sano. Anything. So when the opportunity comes to be near him, she transfers to an exclusive school in Japan—an all-male high school. Now Izumi is closer than ever—he's in her classes and also her roommate! Can she be falling in love with Izumi? The series was originally published in Japan and collected in twenty-three volumes.

> *Vol. 1.* 2004. 184pp. 1-59116-329-3.
> *Vol. 2.* 2004. 200pp. 1-59116-398-6.
> *Vol. 3.* 2004. 200pp. 1-59116-399-4.
> *Vol. 4.* 2005. 188pp. 1-59116-458-3.
> *Vol. 5.* 2005. 200pp. 1-59116-497-4.
> *Vol. 6.* 2005. 200pp. 1-59116-498-2.
> *Vol. 7.* 2005. 200pp. 1-59116-499-0.
> *Vol. 8.* 2005. 192pp. 1-4215-0007-8.
> *Vol. 9.* 2005. 192pp. 1-4215-0138-4.
> *Vol. 10.* 2006. 208pp. 1-4215-0264-X.
> *Vol. 11.* 2006. 208pp. 1-4215-0394-8.
> *Vol. 12.* 2006. 208pp. 1-4215-0542-8.
> *Vol. 13.* 2006. 208pp. 1-4215-0543-6.
> *Vol. 14.* 2006. 208pp. 1-4215-0544-4.
> *Vol. 15.* 2006. 208pp. 1-4215-0545-2.
> *Vol. 16.* 2007. 184pp. 1-4215-0991-1.
> *Vol. 17.* 2007. 184pp. 1-4215-0992-X.

Happy Hustle High. **Written and illustrated by Rie Takada.** VIZ Media, LLC, 2005–2006. **O Japanese manga.**

Hanabi Oozora, a spunky, tomboy-ish sixteen-year-old girl, has made a name at the all-girls Uchino High School for rescuing her girlfriends from the rude and crude boys. Then she finds out that her school will be closing and integrating at Meibi, the local all-boys' high school with strict rules about dating. When she meets Yasuaki Garaku, a member of the Boys' Student Council and all-around dreamboat, she finds that he's uninterested in girls and would rather spend time surfing. Hanabi joins the Girls' Student Council to discover what his secret is and to perhaps change his mind about the "no dating" the school policy. As their romance blossoms, other girls are waiting in line and will stop at nothing to get a chance at Yasuaki, but will spitfire Hanabi let them?

> *Vol. 1.* 2005. 192pp. 1-59116-912-7.
> *Vol. 2.* 2005. 200pp. 1-59116-913-5.
> *Vol. 3.* 2005. 192pp. 1-59116-914-3.
> *Vol. 4.* 2005. 200pp. 1-4215-0083-3.
> *Vol. 5.* 2006. 208pp. 1-4215-0323-9.

Here Is Greenwood. **Written and illustrated by Yukie Nasu.** VIZ Media, LLC, 2004–2006. **O Japanese manga.** あ

One bad thing after another is happening to fifteen-year-old Kazuya Hasukawa. He's recuperating from a bad car accident that perforated his stomach, his brother has just married the girl Kazuya has been in love with, and they're coming to live at his house. Not wanting to live at home, his only option is to enroll at the all-male boarding school, Ryokuto Academy, a.k.a.

"Greenwood." He's in for the shock of his life in the dorm, with its colorful cast of playboys, tough guys (who live with their bikes), geeks, and even a female ghost that haunts the dorms. There Kazuya meets his roommate, Shun Kisaragi, the cutest girl to attend an all-boy's academy! While things are nutty and screwy, Kazuya just might find love and happiness amid the madness. The series was adapted into an anime series in Japan.

Vol. 1. 2004. 208pp. 1-59116-604-7.
Vol. 2. 2005. 216pp. 1-59116-605-5.
Vol. 3. 2005. 200pp. 1-59116-606-3.
Vol. 4. 2005. 232pp. 1-59116-779-5.
Vol. 5. 2005. 216pp. 1-59116-844-9.
Vol. 6. 2005. 216pp. 1-59116-985-2.
Vol. 7. 2005. 224pp. 1-4215-0071-X.
Vol. 8. 2006. 224pp. 1-4215-0183-X.
Vol. 9. 2006. 208pp. 1-4215-0324-7.

Instant Teen: Just Add Nuts. Written and illustrated by Haruka Fukushima. TOKYOPOP, 2004–2005. Y Japanese manga.

Fifth-grader Natsumi Kawashima is tired of being seen as a kid. She can't wait until she's an adult and gets the curves she's sorely lacking. When she happens to eat a packet of pink nuts, she wakes up the next morning to realize that her dream just came true! Now a stunning supermodel with the mind of a ten-year-old, she has exactly what she wanted, and she's turning lots of heads. But even though she looks like an adult, is she really ready to handle the responsibility that goes with all the glamour and fame?

Vol. 1. 2004. 192pp. 1-59532-146-2.
Vol. 2. 2004. 192pp. 1-59532-147-0.
Vol. 3. 2005. 192pp. 1-59532-148-9.
Vol. 4. 2005. 184pp. 1-59532-149-7.

Kare First Love. Written and illustrated by Kaho Miyasaka. VIZ Media, LLC, 2004– . T Japanese manga.

Sixteen-year-old Karin Karino is a typically bespectacled, shy, and awkward high school student who's never been in love before and never says what's on her mind. When she meets Kiriya, a handsome photography student, he sees the true beauty inside her. She doesn't know what he could possibly see in her, and he has an uphill battle to win her heart. Meanwhile, other girls who have their hearts set on Kiriya are about to strike—first on the list is Yuka, Karin's best friend!

Vol. 1. 2004. 200pp. 1-59116-394-3.
Vol. 2. 2005. 200pp. 1-59116-395-1.
Vol. 3. 2005. 192pp. 1-59116-701-9.
Vol. 4. 2005. 192pp. 1-59116-802-3.
Vol. 5. 2005. 192pp. 1-59116-986-0.
Vol. 6. 2005. 192pp. 1-4215-0139-2.
Vol. 7. 2006. 208pp. 1-4215-0325-5.
Vol. 8. 2006. 208pp. 1-4215-0546-0.
Vol. 9. 2006. 208pp. 1-4215-0547-9.
Vol. 10. 2006. 208pp. 1-4215-0548-7.

Kare Kano: His and Her Circumstances. **Written and illustrated by Masami Tsuda.** TOKYOPOP, 2003–2006. **T Japanese manga.** あ

All-around student Yukino Miyazawa has everything going for her. She's at the top of her class, pretty, and popular. She always wants to be the center of attention. When a new male student, the sincere and good-looking Soichiro Arima, ends up being better at her at almost everything, she vows to beat him. Little does she know how much they have in common and that Arima will steal her heart. The series was originally published in Japan and collected in twenty-one volumes. It was also adapted into a twenty-six-episode anime series in Japan.

Vol. 1. 2003. 192pp. 1-931514-79-8.
Vol. 2. 2003. 192pp. 1-931514-80-1.
Vol. 3. 2003. 192pp. 1-59182-058-8.
Vol. 4. 2003. 200pp. 1-59182-059-6.
Vol. 5. 2003. 208pp. 1-59182-180-0.
Vol. 6. 2003. 216pp. 1-59182-181-9.
Vol. 7. 2004. 224pp. 1-59182-472-9.
Vol. 8. 2004. 216pp. 1-59182-473-7.
Vol. 9. 2004. 224pp. 1-59182-474-5.
Vol. 10. 2004. 224pp. 1-59182-475-3.
Vol. 11. 2004. 216pp. 1-59182-476-1.
Vol. 12. 2004. 208pp. 1-59182-477-X.
Vol. 13. 2005. 208pp. 1-59532-587-5.
Vol. 14. 2005. 200pp. 1-59532-588-3.
Vol. 15. 2005. 200pp. 1-59532-589-1.
Vol. 16. 2005. 192pp. 1-59532-590-5.
Vol. 17. 2005. 192pp. 1-59532-591-3.
Vol. 18. 2005. 192pp. 1-59532-592-1.
Vol. 19. 2006. 192pp. 1-59816-182-2.
Vol. 20. 2006. 192pp. 1-59816-183-0.

Kill Me, Kiss Me. **Written and illustrated by Lee Young You.** TOKYOPOP, 2004–2005. **T Korean manhwa.**

Tae Yeon Im is madly infatuated with the rock star Kun Kung and would do anything to meet him or even marry him. Then she finds out that her male cousin, Jung-Woo Im, who looks almost identical to her, will be attending the same boys' high school as her idol. For one week they switch schools. Sounds like a fun plan, but the cousins soon find that it's not so easy playing the opposite sex, especially when people want to either beat you up or kiss you.

Vol. 1. 2004. 184pp. 1-59182-593-8.
Vol. 2. 2004. 192pp. 1-59182-594-6.
Vol. 3. 2004. 192pp. 1-59182-595-4.
Vol. 4. 2004. 192pp. 1-59182-596-2.
Vol. 5. 2005. 192pp. 1-59532-420-8.

Love Fights. **Written and illustrated by Andi Watson.** Oni Press, 2004. **T**

Love Fights

© 2006 Andi Watson.

After a chance encounter with a nice, normal girl named Nora, single and insecure Jack thinks he's found the right girl, but she's a reporter for *eXpose* magazine—the trash journal that's all about the one thing he despises: super-heroes. You see, when you live in a city that's home to godlike super-heroes who steal the hearts of women, it can be such a hassle to have to compete with gods just to get a date. Nora swears she's not into that kind of guy, but Jack's a little hard to convince. He's been the penciler for the comic book based on the Flamer, the most dashingly handsome hero in town, and Nora's exposé on the Flamer is shaping up to be a citywide super-hero scandal—what's the secret, and could it possibly be true? As their relationship blossoms, there's only one thing standing in their way: Jack's pet cat Guthrie. Not only can Guthrie talk, but he has mysterious powers! Why doesn't he like Nora, and how can Jack tell Nora that he's the owner of a super-cat?

　　Vol. 1. 2004. 168pp. 1-929998-86-4.
　　Vol. 2. 2004. 168pp. 1-929998-87-2.

Love Hina. **Written and illustrated by Ken Akamatsu.** TOKYOPOP, 2002–2003. **O** **Japanese manga.** あ

Keitaro Urashima has failed his entrance exams to Tokyo University twice, he's been unlucky at love, and his parents have kicked him out of their home! His grandmother has the perfect job to tide him over until he can pass his entrance exams: to be the landlord at the beautiful Hinata House. What his grandmother neglected to mention is that it's an all-girl college dorm, and now he's living a life that most men would kill for. But after spending time with five beautiful women, he's not sure he's going to survive the experience, much less have time to study for his entrance exams! Meanwhile, Keitaro finds out that Naru, one of the girls living at the dorm might be his very first crush when he was a child. Will they end up together, as they promised as kids, or will Keitaro's accidental antics destroy that chance forever? The series was adapted into an anime series in Japan.

　　Vol. 1. 2002. 198pp. 1-931514-94-1.
　　Vol. 2. 2002. 198pp. 1-931514-97-6.
　　Vol. 3. 2002. 192pp. 1-59182-014-6.
　　Vol. 4. 2002. 192pp. 1-59182-015-4.
　　Vol. 5. 2002. 192pp. 1-59182-016-2.
　　Vol. 6. 2002. 192pp. 1-59182-017-0.
　　Vol. 7. 2002. 192pp. 1-59182-018-9.
　　Vol. 8. 2003. 200pp. 1-59182-019-7.
　　Vol. 9. 2003. 200pp. 1-59182-103-7.
　　Vol. 10. 2003. 192pp. 1-59182-116-9.
　　Vol. 11. 2003. 192pp. 1-59182-117-7.
　　Vol. 12. 2003. 192pp. 1-59182-118-5.
　　Vol. 13. 2003. 192pp. 1-59182-119-3.
　　Vol. 14. 2003. 200pp. 1-59182-120-7.

Love or Money. **Written and illustrated by Sang-Eun Lee.** TOKYOPOP, 2004–2006. **T Korean manhwa.**

Money-obsessed Yenni is a fifteen-year-old financial guru. She's so into money, she has even started a very profitable loan shark business at school. Her wealthy grandmother tries to break her granddaughter's bad habits by stipulating in her will that in order for Yenni to receive her grandmother's fortune of $150 million, she has to give up the loan shark business forever and marry an honest man! If Yenni fails to change and is not able to marry an honest man, the money will be given instead to In-Young, a grandson of her grandmother's friend. When Yenni's grandmother dies accidentally, she now has to change her exorbitant ways or else she'll lose her grandmother's money forever. Meanwhile, In-Young is doing his best to squash Yenni's plans—but finds himself attracted to Yenni. At the time of this writing, the final volume of the series has not yet been published. Visit the publisher's Web site (http://www.tokyopop.com) for the latest information.

> *Vol. 1.* 2004. 192pp. 1-59532-248-5.
> *Vol. 2.* 2005. 192pp. 1-59532-249-3.
> *Vol. 3.* 2005. 192pp. 1-59532-250-7.
> *Vol. 4.* 2005. 192pp. 1-59532-251-5.

Maison Ikkoku. 2d ed. **Written and illustrated by Rumiko Takahashi.** VIZ Media, LLC, 2003–2005. **O ◎ Japanese manga.**

Yusaku Godai is a resident of Maison Ikkoku, a quaint but run-down boarding house in the middle of Tokyo. He's currently a ronin, a student who hasn't passed his entrance exams and is retaking them. Unfortunately it doesn't look like he's going to get much studying done, with all the racket his fellow tenants make. From the bar waitress Akemi, to the mysterious Yotsuya, to housewise Ichinose, he's had enough of them, especially when they all party in his room! But Yusaku has a change of heart when he finds his true love in Kyoko Otonashi, the beautiful widowed manager of Maison Ikkoku. Will he be able to win her heart and help her love again? The manga was adapted into an anime series in Japan.

> *Vol. 1.* 2003. 208pp. 1-59116-054-5.
> *Vol. 2.* 2003. 200pp. 1-59116-099-5.
> *Vol. 3.* 2004. 208pp. 1-59116-127-4.
> *Vol. 4.* 2004. 248pp. 1-59116-248-3.
> *Vol. 5.* 2004. 232pp. 1-59116-319-6.
> *Vol. 6.* 2004. 208pp. 1-59116-422-2.
> *Vol. 7.* 2004. 288pp. 1-59116-485-0.
> *Vol. 8.* 2004. 288pp. 1-59116-562-8.
> *Vol. 9.* 2005. 288pp. 1-59116-617-9.
> *Vol. 10.* 2005. 248pp. 1-59116-729-9.
> *Vol. 11.* 2005. 232pp. 1-59116-804-X.
> *Vol. 12.* 2005. 323pp. 1-59116-869-4.
> *Vol. 13.* 2005. 232pp. 1-4215-0141-4.
> *Vol. 14.* 2005. 240pp. 1-4215-0142-2.

7

Man of Many Faces. **Written and illustrated by CLAMP.** TOKYOPOP, 2003. **A Japanese manga.**

Akira, a third-grade boy who is attending CLAMP School, has a unique family. He has two mothers, and they love to have him cook and steal for them! When he's stealing, he wears a tuxedo and a mask and becomes the debonair 20 Faces, a master thief whom no one can catch. One day, while hiding from the police, 20 Faces hides in kindergartner Utako's bedroom. Although he is nine and she is six, they fall in love. Many years later their love is put to the ultimate test: If their love is real the master thief must steal his greatest conquest ever—Utaku's heart!

Vol. 1. 2003. 208pp. 1-59182-299-8.
Vol. 2. 2003. 176pp. 1-59182-300-5.

Midori Days. **Written and illustrated by Kazurou Inoue.** VIZ Media, LLC, 2005–2006. **T Japanese manga.** あ

High school punk Seiji "Mad Dog" Sawamura is one of the toughest fighters at school. With his devastating and almost-invincible right hand, he can punch through walls and take out any opponent. Unfortunately, having a reputation as a "Mad Dog" practically ensures that no girl would ever want to be with him. One morning Seiji wakes up to find that his right hand has transformed into a girl! Named Midori Kasugano, she's a carefree girl who's always had a crush on Seiji. She wished one day that she would always be by his side, and now she literally is! Can Seiji handle having a cute girl attached to him 24/7, and does this mean his fighting days are over? The manga series was adapted into an anime series in Japan.

Vol. 1. 2005. 192pp. 1-59116-905-4.
Vol. 2. 2005. 200pp. 1-59116-906-2.
Vol. 3. 2005. 192pp. 1-59116-907-0.
Vol. 4. 2006. 208pp. 1-4215-0254-2.
Vol. 5. 2006. 208pp. 1-4215-0287-9.
Vol. 6. 2006. 208pp. 1-4215-0495-2.
Vol. 7. 2006. 208pp. 1-4215-0496-0.
Vol. 8. 2006. 208pp. 1-4215-0497-9.

Mink. **Written and illustrated by Megumi Tachikawa.** TOKYOPOP, 2004–2005. **Y Japanese manga.**

Teenager Mink has always dreamed of being a pop star idol. When she accidentally purchases a CD from the future called *Wanna Be,* she finds out that it's actually a reality-changing device and that her wish to be a pop star has just come true. Now called Cyber Idol Mink, she has a hit album, the best clothes, adoring fans, and a robot sidekick. The downside is that the *Wanna Be* program is illegal, and someone wants to make sure her identity is permanently deleted. Will Mink give up the glamorous life of being in the spotlight and become "plain" schoolgirl Mink again?

Vol. 1. 2004. 184pp. 1-59182-715-9.
Vol. 2. 2004. 192pp. 1-59182-716-7.
Vol. 3. 2004. 184pp. 1-59182-717-5.
Vol. 4. 2004. 184pp. 1-59182-718-3.
Vol. 5. 2005. 192pp. 1-59532-423-2.
Vol. 6. 2005. 184pp. 1-59532-424-0.

More Starlight to Your Heart. **Written and illustrated by Hiro Matsuba.** ADV Manga, 2004– . **A Japanese manga.**

Set in the Heian period (794–1192) of Japan, this is the story of a charming princess who will do what she can to be with the one she loves. Princess Akane, daughter of the Nashinokami of the Inner Palace and the High Councilor of Japan, has lived a pampered life of luxury but will do anything to be reunited with Aogi, a childhood friend. Akane takes a job as a servant in the Inner Palace to see Aogi again, who is now a palace guard and once saved her life. When her father gets word of their relationship, he banishes Aogi to be a minor captain in the Inner Palace guard and forbids them to see each other. Joined by her cute kitten Hikoboshi, Akane, with the help of her mother, goes undercover as a servant in the hope of being reunited with Aogi.

Vol. 1. 2004. 184pp. 1-4139-0206-5.
Vol. 2. 2005. 184pp. 1-4139-0227-8.

My Sassy Girl. **Written by Ho Sik Kim. Illustrated by Dae Hong Min.** ComicsOne, 2002–2005. **O Korean manhwa.**

They say opposites attract, but when these two college students meet it's anything but true love—it's more like a comedy of errors. Based on the popular Korean movie of the same name, My Sassy Girl tells of clumsy and kind-hearted Geon-woo, who spots one of the most beautiful girls he's ever seen while on a train. She might be beautiful, but she's also a problem drinker who's crude, mean, cruel, and comically abusive to Geon-woo. It might turn out to be true love, but Geon-woo is going to go through some rings of fire for a girl who has him wrapped around her finger.

Vol. 1. 2002. 128pp. 1-58899-342-6.
Vol. 2. 2004. 128pp. 1-58899-343-4.
Vol. 3. 2004. 128pp. 1-58899-344-2.
Vol. 4. 2004. 128pp. 1-58899-345-0.
Vol. 5. 2004. 120pp. 1-58899-346-9.
Vol. 6. 2005. 128pp. 1-58899-311-6.

Neck and Neck. **Written and illustrated by Sun Hee Lee.** TOKYOPOP, 2004–2006. **T Korean manhwa.**

Jr. *Sopranos* in Seoul! Dabin Choi is the daughter of the famous Seoul crime boss, and she has a major crush on a boy named Eugene Sung, who happens to be the son of one of her father's closest business partners. Is the love returned? Oh no. Eugene thinks of Dabin as a little sister and couldn't be less interested in her. When Shihu Myoung, the son of her father's worst enemy, also becomes Dabin's classmate, the children take on the roles of the parents and soon a power struggle begins. But will this animosity last long when Dabin starts having feelings for Shihu? Meanwhile, an old schoolmate rival, Rose Shim (alias, the Black Rose) returns to continue her rivalry with Dabin. Will she steal Eugene from her, and at this point will Dabin even care? The final volume of this series has not yet been published.

Vol. 1. 2004. 196pp. 1-59532-253-1.
Vol. 2. 2005. 192pp. 1-59532-254-X.

Vol. 3. 2005. 192pp. 1-59532-255-8.

Vol. 4. 2005. 192pp. 1-59532-657-X.

Vol. 5. 2006. 192pp. 1-59816-099-0.

Rizelmine. Written and illustrated by Yukiru Sugisaki. TOKYOPOP, 2005. 192pp. 1-59532-901-3. **T Japanese manga.**

The Japanese government has just created its first artificial human from nanomachines, a humanoid named Rizel who appears to be a twelve-year-old grade school girl. Still learning every day, she needs to feel the emotion of love in order to continue her development, and what better way than to be married? Meanwhile, Tomonori Iwaki has a crush on his schoolteacher and is saddened to hear that she's getting married. Imagine his surprise when he comes home to find out that the government has something for him: his very own bride, named Rizel! Now she's totally devoted to him and will do anything for him. Will this be true love, or will Tomonori be embarrassed being married to what looks like a grade school girl? Meanwhile, the United States has created a counterpart to Rizel called LUX, and she also becomes attracted to Tomonori. Who will win in this battle for the awkward teen?

Tuxedo Gin. Written and illustrated by Tokihiko Matsuura. VIZ Media, LLC, 2003–2005. **O Japanese manga.**

Death can't kill love; it can only postpone it for a little while. Or so high school student and boxing contender Ginji Kusanagi hopes. Unfortunately, he was just killed before his big boxing debut, and before he ever got a chance to go on a date with Minoko, the girl of his dreams. He has been given a second chance at life: he's been reincarnated as a penguin! Can true love really blossom between a beautiful girl and a cute boxing penguin?

Vol. 1. 2003. 200pp. 1-59116-071-5.

Vol. 2. 2003. 192pp. 1-59116-072-3.

Vol. 3. 2003. 184pp. 1-59116-102-9.

Vol. 4. 2004. 184pp. 1-59116-131-2.

Vol. 5. 2004. 184pp. 1-59116-255-6.

Vol. 6. 2004. 200pp. 1-59116-322-6.

Vol. 7. 2004. 192pp. 1-59116-456-7.

Vol. 8. 2004. 200pp. 1-59116-489-3.

Vol. 9. 2004. 200pp. 1-59116-585-7.

Vol. 10. 2005. 192pp. 1-59116-695-0.

Vol. 11. 2005. 192pp. 1-59116-744-2.

Vol. 12. 2005. 184pp. 1-59116-798-1.

Vol. 13. 2005. 200pp. 1-59116-861-9.

Vol. 14. 2005. 184pp. 1-4215-0033-7.

Vol. 15. 2005. 240pp. 1-4215-0133-3.

<u>W Juliet.</u> Written and illustrated by Katsumi Emura. VIZ Media, LLC, 2004–2007. **T Japanese manga.**

Sixteen-year-old tomboy Ito Miura has been chosen to play Romeo in the school production of *Romeo and Juliet,* but she doesn't want to play a man! When a beautiful student named Makoto Amano enters the school, all the girls are in awe of how beautiful she is, and she ends up getting the part of fair Juliet. When Ito invites Makoto over, she accidentally discovers Makoto's secret: she's really a man! Makoto wanted to become an actor, but his father, the head of a prominent dojo, wouldn't allow it. His father made a bargain—if his son could pass as a girl for two years without anyone finding out, then he would be allowed to pursue his dream. If not, he'd have to take over the family dojo. Now Ito and Makoto have to keep the secret safe from everyone, and Ito agrees to be "partners" with Makoto. But when they really fall in love with each other, how long can they keep their love a secret?

Vol. 1. 2004. 184pp. 1-59116-598-9.
Vol. 2. 2005. 184pp. 1-59116-602-0.
Vol. 3. 2005. 200pp. 1-59116-600-4.
Vol. 4. 2005. 200pp. 1-59116-781-7.
Vol. 5. 2005. 200pp. 1-59116-848-1.
Vol. 6. 2005. 200pp. 1-59116-989-5.
Vol. 7. 2005. 208pp. 1-4215-0065-5.
Vol. 8. 2006. 208pp. 1-4215-0205-4.
Vol. 9. 2006. 208pp. 1-4215-0328-X.
Vol. 10. 2006. 208pp. 1-4215-0563-0.
Vol. 11. 2006. 208pp. 1-4215-0564-9.
Vol. 12. 2006. 208pp. 1-4215-0565-7.
Vol. 13. 2006. 208pp. 1-4215-0566-5.
Vol. 14. 2007. 208pp. 1-4215-0567-3.

Romantic Fantasy

These are romance titles in which magic or a fantasy-based incident plays a key role in giving the protagonist the means to finding true love, sometimes with someone that person least expects. The appeal of a fantasy-based romance is that it drops two lovers into the make-believe setting of a fantasy world, where magic is real and knights in shining armor do exist, as well as true love. The setting may take place in a fantasy world or in the present day, with subtle hints of science fiction, but it is through magic that love is possible. For other fantasy titles, see chapter 4.

<u>A.I. Love You.</u> Written and illustrated by Ken Akamatsu. TOKYOPOP, 2004–2005. **O Japanese manga.**

High school student Hitoshi Kobe has never had any luck with the ladies. He's always been awkward and nerdish and has focused his energy on creating artificially intelligent robots. When his latest project, a lifelike female android called "Thirty," amazingly comes to life, what's he to do with a beautiful girl living at his house? Soon, Thirty brings her "sisters," Twenty and Forty, to life as well, and Hitoshi's house will never be the same again.

Vol. 1. 2004. 224pp. 1-59182-615-2.
Vol. 2. 2004. 216pp. 1-59182-616-0.
Vol. 3. 2004. 240pp. 1-59182-617-9.
Vol. 4. 2004. 256pp. 1-59182-618-7.
Vol. 5. 2004. 264pp. 1-59182-619-5.
Vol. 6. 2004. 248pp. 1-59182-620-9.

Vol. 7. 2005. 192pp. 1-59182-943-7.
Vol. 8. 2005. 248pp. 1-59182-944-5.

Cheeky Angel. Written and illustrated by Hiroyuki Nishimori. VIZ Media, LLC, 2004–2007. **O Japanese manga.**

When Megumi was nine years old, he was already a martial arts champion and a bit of a headstrong bully, too. After he saves a wizard from a group of thugs (he was actually going to beat up the wizard but the thugs beat him to it), the old man gives him a book that releases a pint-sized genie who grants Megumi one wish. Naturally, Megumi wants to be the manliest man among men on Earth, but the genie mistakenly makes him the womanliest woman on Earth. Megumi, "trapped" in a beautiful girl's body, would have to endure ten years in this condition. Six years later, Megumi is still as bull-headed as ever, breathtakingly beautiful, and not afraid to beat up on the bullies. Too bad "she" has attracted the attention of Genzo, the biggest bully in town! Only four more years to go, and the curse will be lifted, but can Megumi stand being a girl any longer? The series was originally published in Japan and was collected in twenty volumes.

Vol. 1. 2004. 200pp. 1-59116-397-8.
Vol. 2. 2004. 200pp. 1-59116-467-2.
Vol. 3. 2004. 200pp. 1-59116-503-2.
Vol. 4. 2004. 200pp. 1-59116-620-9.
Vol. 5. 2005. 200pp. 1-59116-631-4.
Vol. 6. 2005. 192pp. 1-59116-774-4.
Vol. 7. 2005. 184pp. 1-59116-839-2.
Vol. 8. 2005. 192pp. 1-59116-979-8.
Vol. 9. 2005. 192pp. 1-4215-0069-8.
Vol. 10. 2006. 192pp. 1-4215-0167-8.
Vol. 11. 2006. 192pp. 1-4215-0317-4.
Vol. 12. 2006. 208pp. 1-4215-0446-4.
Vol. 13. 2006. 208pp. 1-4215-0447-2.
Vol. 14. 2006. 192pp. 1-4215-0448-0.
Vol. 15. 2006. 208pp. 1-4215-0449-9.
Vol. 16. 2007. 208pp. 1-4215-0450-2.

D.N. Angel. Written and illustrated by Yukiru Sugisaki. TOKYOPOP, 2004–2005. **T Japanese manga.** あ

Middle school student Daisuke Niwa is in love with Risa Harada, a girl in his school who couldn't care less about him. Instead, she's infatuated with the mysterious and gorgeously handsome Phantom Thief known as Dark. No one suspects that Dark is none other than Daisuke! In the Niwa clan, for over 400 years there has been a blood condition that, when the males turn fourteen, can transform them into the Phantom Thief. Now Daisuke will also be Dark, unless his true love returns his affection. But how can Daisuke get Risa to love him, when she barely gives him the time of day? Meanwhile, security at the museums has been tightened, and a determined police force will stop at nothing to capture the mysterious and legendary thief. The manga was adapted into a twenty-six-episode anime series in Japan.

Vol. 1. 2004. 184pp. 1-59182-799-X.

Vol. 2. 2004. 184pp. 1-59182-800-7.
Vol. 3. 2004. 184pp. 1-59182-801-5.
Vol. 4. 2004. 184pp. 1-59182-802-3.
Vol. 5. 2004. 184pp. 1-59182-803-1.
Vol. 6. 2005. 176pp. 1-59182-955-0.
Vol. 7. 2005. 176pp. 1-59182-956-9.
Vol. 8. 2005. 192pp. 1-59182-957-7.
Vol. 9. 2005. 192pp. 1-59532-794-0.
Vol. 10. 2005. 192pp. 1-59532-795-9.

Fruits Basket. Written and illustrated by Natsuki Takaya. TOKYOPOP, 2004– . **T Japanese manga.** あ

After losing her mother in a car accident, orphaned high school student Tohru Honda is living in a tent in a forest near her school. Headstrong and positive despite her family's misfortunes, she is neighbors with the odd but generous Sohma family, who have a special secret. The Sohma family members are possessed by the spirits of the Chinese Zodiac. When hugged by a member of the opposite sex, they will turn into the animal sign of the Zodiac that they represent. Taken in by the Sohma family in return for helping around the house, Honda has found a new family—but can she keep the animals running around the house from destroying it? The series received recognition from YALSA's Popular Paperbacks for Young Adults committee in 2006 as well as the Quick Picks for Reluctant Readers in 2005. Eighteen volumes were originally published in Japan. The twenty-one-volume manga was adapted into a twenty-six-episode anime series in Japan.

Vol. 1. 2004. 216pp. 1-59182-603-9.
Vol. 2. 2004. 200pp. 1-59182-604-7.
Vol. 3. 2004. 200pp. 1-59182-605-5.
Vol. 4. 2004. 216pp. 1-59182-606-3.
Vol. 5. 2004. 208pp. 1-59182-607-1.
Vol. 6. 2004. 208pp. 1-59182-608-X.
Vol. 7. 2005. 208pp. 1-59532-402-X.
Vol. 8. 2005. 208pp. 1-59532-403-8.
Vol. 9. 2005. 208pp. 1-59532-404-6.
Vol. 10. 2005. 192pp. 1-59532-405-4.
Vol. 11. 2005. 192pp. 1-59532-406-2.
Vol. 12. 2005. 192pp. 1-59532-407-0.
Vol. 13. 2006. 192pp. 1-59532-408-9.
Vol. 14. 2006. 192pp. 1-59532-409-7.
Vol. 15. 2006. 192pp. 1-59816-023-0.
Vol. 16. 2006. 192pp. 1-59816-024-9.

Guardian Angel Getten. Written and illustrated by Sakurano Minene. Gutsoon! Entertainment, 2003–2004. **T Japanese manga.** あ

Fourteen-year-old Junior high school student Shichir Tasuke has a lonely life at home. His archaeologist parents are always away on trips around the world, and he has the entire house to himself. One day he receives in the mail a magic ring that his father sent him from China. When Shichir puts the ring on, he summons Shao Lin, a Guardian Angel Getten who vows to always protect him, her new master. After being trapped in the ring for centuries, Shao Lin is not too used to this strange new world, and soon enough she's hindering more than she's helping. She enrolls in school with Shuchir, and as various school rivals vie for Shao Lin's affections, more calamity ensues with the appearance of sun guardian Ruulaun, Shao Lin's rival. Will Shao Lin and Shichir ever find true love with all these hi jinks going on? The manga was adapted into an anime series in Japan.

> *Vol. 1.* 2003. 190pp. 1-932454-06-3.
> *Vol. 2.* 2004. 192pp. 1-932454-19-5.
> *Vol. 3.* 2004. 190pp. 1-932454-37-3.
> *Vol. 4.* 2004. 190pp. 1-932454-28-4.

Heaven Sent. Written and illustrated by Ben Dunn. Antarctic Press, 2005. **T Neo-manga.**

© 2006 Antarctic Press.

Middle school student Kyle Taylor was killed in a traffic accident, but after he is sent to Heaven, he finds out that it's not quite his time. Sarah, Kyle's very own guardian angel, who is in love with him, makes a deal with the Angel of Death to spare his life. Kyle also finds out that he's somehow playing a major role in the upcoming battle between Heaven and Hell, and he has protection until this time from his very own guardian angel, Sarah! Meanwhile, Kyle trains in the afterlife for the coming battle as dark forces set their plan in motion to rule Heaven and Earth.

> *Pocket Manga Vol. 1.* 2005. 144pp. 1-932453-73-3.
> *Pocket Manga Vol. 2.* 2005. 144pp. 1-932453-83-0.

Onegai Teacher. Written by Yosuke Kuroda. Illustrated by Shizuru Hayashiya. ComicsOne, 2003. **T Japanese manga.** あ

After being in a mysterious coma for over two years, eighteen-year-old Kei Kusanagi has to finish up high school. Strangely enough, his condition makes him look like he's still only fifteen. One night while exploring the woods after a reported U.F.O. sighting, he spots a beautiful alien woman. The next day at school, Kei discovers that same woman, Mizuho Kazami, is his new homeroom teacher as well as his next-door neighbor! To get out of a jam after being caught in each other's arms after a mishap, Kei and Mizuho tell his aunt and uncle that they're actually married, since technically he's eighteen. He's moving in next door with an alien woman, to the disbelief of the school principal and others. And as their relationship grows, could it be that they're really in love after all? The manga was adapted into an anime series in Japan.

> *Vol. 1.* 2003. 200pp. 1-58899-196-2.
> *Vol. 2.* 2003. 200pp. 1-58899-294-2.

Onegai Twin. Written by Yosuke Kuroda. Illustrated by Shizuru Hayashiya. ComicsOne, 2004. **T Japanese manga.** あ

A sequel of sorts to the two-volume <u>Onegai Teacher</u>. Maiku Kamishiro is a teenage boy living alone at his house after the death of his parents, with the memory of a twin sister who disappeared from his life. One day at school he meets two girls, Miina

Miyafuji and Karen Onodera. Although they're totally different in personality and appearance, they have a secret—one of them is really his long-lost twin sister! Until he finds out which one is really his sister, they both get to live at his house, and that's where the fun really begins. The manga was adapted into an anime series in Japan.

Vol. 1: One and a Pair. 2004. 220pp. 1-58899-299-3.
Vol. 2. 2004. 220pp. 1-58899-002-8.

Pita-Ten. **Written and illustrated by Koge Donbo.** TOKYOPOP, 2004–2005. **T Japanese manga.** あ

What would you do if you found out that your cute next-door neighbor was an angel? Life has been hard on Kotarou Higuchi. His mother died, and his father is away on business trips all the time, so the sixth-grader has been spending time alone at his house. As if that weren't difficult enough, he's having a hard time studying for the entrance exam for middle school and is unlucky in love. When the cute angel Misha moves in next door, he finds that she too is cramming for an exam (for angels), and she promises to protect him always, even at school. Unfortunately Misha's not too up on the habits of the modern world, and Kotarou finds that having your own guardian angel isn't everything it's cracked up to be, as more angels, and demons, stop by. The manga was adapted into a twenty-six-episode anime series in Japan.

Vol. 1. 2004. 200pp. 1-59182-627-6.
Vol. 2. 2004. 192pp. 1-59182-628-4.
Vol. 3. 2004. 208pp. 1-59182-629-2.
Vol. 4. 2004. 192pp. 1-59182-630-6.
Vol. 5. 2004. 208pp. 1-59182-631-4.
Vol. 6. 2004. 208pp. 1-59182-632-2.
Vol. 7. 2005. 192pp. 1-59532-016-4.
Vol. 8. 2005. 208pp. 1-59532-017-2.

Please Save My Earth. **Written and illustrated by Saki Hiwatari.** VIZ Media, LLC, 2003–2007. **O Japanese manga.** あ

Schoolgirl Alice has moved from the countryside of Hokkaido to the busy congestion of Tokyo, and she has the unique gift of communicating with the plants and animals. One day she runs into two of her classmates, who have an amazing story to tell her. For years, male school friends Jinpachi and Issei have shared a dream in which they are lovers. In their dream Jinpachi is a man called Gyokuran, and Issei is a woman called Enju. In their dream they also are two of seven scientists based on the moon at a research station to observe Earth and collect data. Alice just thinks it's sort of odd that they still have this dream, but then Alice begins to have dreams about the scientists, too. Is there more at work than she realizes—is she a reincarnation of seven scientists reborn to live and love once more? The series was originally published in Japan and collected in twenty-one volumes and was also adapted as an anime.

Vol. 1. 2003. 192pp. 1-59116-059-6.
Vol. 2. 2004. 192pp. 1-59116-116-9.
Vol. 3. 2004. 192pp. 1-59116-142-8.

Vol. 4. 2004. 192pp. 1-59116-267-X.
Vol. 5. 2004. 208pp. 1-59116-268-8.
Vol. 6. 2004. 200pp. 1-59116-269-6.
Vol. 7. 2004. 200pp. 1-59116-270-X.
Vol. 8. 2004. 200pp. 1-59116-271-8.
Vol. 9. 2005. 184pp. 1-59116-272-6.
Vol. 10. 2005. 208pp. 1-59116-273-4.
Vol. 11. 2005. 208pp. 1-59116-846-5.
Vol. 12. 2005. 184pp. 1-59116-987-9.
Vol. 13. 2005. 192pp. 1-4215-0127-9.
Vol. 14. 2006. 192pp. 1-4215-0193-7.
Vol. 15. 2006. 208pp. 1-4215-0326-3.
Vol. 16. 2006. 208pp. 1-4215-0549-5.
Vol. 17. 2006. 208pp. 1-4215-0550-9.
Vol. 18. 2006. 208pp. 1-4215-0551-7.
Vol. 19. 2006. 208pp. 1-4215-0552-5.
Vol. 20. 2007. 208pp. 1-4215-0553-3.
Vol. 21. 2007. 208pp. 1-4215-0837-0.

Skeleton Key. Written and illustrated by Andi Watson. Slave Labor Graphics/Amaze Ink, 1996–2000. **T**

© 2006 Andi Watson.

Tamsin Mary Cates's time in high school just got a lot more interesting! She has received a mysterious skeleton costume and matching skeleton key. While dressed in the costume, the wearer can use the key to open any door into a gateway to another dimension. Using the key, Tamsin finds herself suddenly liberated from the Canadian town of Garfield. The key doesn't pinpoint where she will end up. Along the way she is joined by the fox-spirit called Kitsune, and soon the spirit, with an appetite for sweets, stays with Tamsin. But other people want the suit and key, and soon Tamsin's friend, Yale, is involved, too. What other trouble can they get into with the turn of a key?

Vol. 1: Beyond the Threshold. 1996. 96pp. 0-943151-12-0.
Vol. 2: The Celestial Calendar. 1997. 96pp. 0-943151-15-5.
Vol. 3: Telling Tales. 1998. 96pp. 0-943151-13-9.
Vol. 4: Cats & Dogs. 1998. 104pp. 0-943151-19-8.
Vol. 5: Roots. 2000. 104pp. 0-943151-26-0.

Sparks: An Urban Fairy Tale. **Written and illustrated by Lawrence Marvit.** Slave Labor Graphics, 2003. 424pp. 0-934151-62-7. **O**

Twenty-year-old Josephine may be the best grease monkey mechanic in town, but socially she's a very awkward young woman and has the worst experiences with men. She lives in a "castle" with an abusive father and a drug-addicted and distant mother who wears her down and makes her feel more unloved. Out of frustration, one night she builds her "ideal" man out of scrap metal in a junkyard; to her surprise it comes to life. Christened "Galahad" by a playful boy on the street, the robot learns how to live and how to love, but needs to learn from the ground up how to write, speak, and experience life with Josephine. When tragedy and misunderstanding nearly kill Galahad, both he and Josephine are caught in a downward spiral of events that will put their friendship and love to the ultimate test.

Ursula. **Written by Fabio Moon. Illustrated by Gabriel Ba.** AiT/Planet Lar, 2004. 72pp. 1-932051-22-8. **T**

A fable about the beauty and innocence of young love. When Prince Miro was young he was in love with a girl named Ursula, but she had to go away to school and he never saw her again. Now that he is older, the King declares that it is time for the Prince to take a bride, so Miro searches high and low and finally finds the elusive Ursula. It turns out that she is really a fairy, and fairies explode when they are in love. When she does explode, Miro and Ursula find themselves trapped in her subconscious, where fantasy and reality overlap. Can Miro still rescue Ursula from the curse? All it takes is a little love.

<u>Video Girl Ai.</u> **Written and illustrated by Masakazu Katsura.** VIZ Media, LLC, 2004–2005. **O ◎ Japanese manga.** あ

High school student Yota Moteuchi has never been lucky in love. Even the gentle girl he has a crush on, Moemi, likes his best friend, Takashi. One day he happens to stop by a video store and rents a movie featuring a girl called Ai Amano to cheer him up. The videotape malfunctions in his VCR, and the girl on the videotape materializes in the real world! Now he has a girl living at his house who is following her own programming to cheer him up and to give him the confidence to win Moemi's heart. But soon Ai falls in love with Yota. Can a boy and a program find love, or will Yota finally get the girl he's been eyeing all along? The hit series was originally published in Japan and collected in fifteen volumes. The last two

VIDEO GIRL AI © 1989 by Masakazu Katsura/SHUEISHA Inc.

volumes focuses on a Video Girl by the name of Len and how she helps a budding manga artist named Hiromu fall in love. The manga was adapted into an anime series in Japan.

Vol. 1: Preproduction. 2004. 200pp. 1-59116-074-X.
Vol. 2: Mix Down. 2004. 192pp. 1-59116-075-8.
Vol. 3: Recall. 2004. 184pp. 1-59116-103-7.
Vol. 4: Off-Line. 2004. 200pp. 1-59116-104-5.
Vol. 5: Spin-Off. 2004. 200pp. 1-59116-146-0.
Vol. 6: Cutting Room. 2004. 200pp. 1-59116-607-1.
Vol. 7: Retake. 2005. 192pp. 1-59116-748-5.
Vol. 8: Flashback. 2004. 200pp. 1-59116-303-X.
Vol. 9: Cut Scenes. 2004. 184pp. 1-59116-304-8.
Vol. 10: Rough Cut. 2004. 200pp. 1-59116-305-6.
Vol. 11: Farewell Scene. 2005. 200pp. 1-59116-306-4.
Vol. 12: Close Up. 2005. 192pp. 1-59116-307-2.
Vol. 13: Fade Out. 2005. 192pp. 1-59116-308-0.
Vol. 14: Len's Story. 2006. 200pp. 1-59116-309-9.
Vol. 15: Len's Story. 2006. 208pp. 1-4215-0295-X.

7

<u>Wish.</u> Written and illustrated by CLAMP. TOKYOPOP, 2002–2003. **T**

When Shuichiro, a successful medical doctor, rescues the simple-minded angel Kohaku from a tree, he is granted one wish. Shuichiro, a stern man of science, already has everything money can buy. So instead, Kohaku moves in with Shuichiro while she continues her search for the angel Hisui, who has left God's order. Now Kohaku appears during the day as an attractive woman, while by night she reverts to looking like a childlike cherub. Over time she grows more and more found of Shuichiro, but does he love her? When a demon named Koryu and his minions begin investigating why Kohaku is on the earthly plane, a forbidden love is revealed that will rock Heaven and Hell and may delay Kohaku from telling Shuichiro that she loves him.

Vol. 1. 2002. 192pp. 1-59182-034-0.
Vol. 2. 2002. 192pp. 1-59182-060-X.
Vol. 3. 2002. 192pp. 1-59182-061-8.
Vol. 4. 2003. 192pp. 1-59182-080-4.

***Your and My Secret.* Written and illustrated by Ai Morinaga.** ADV Manga, 2004. 186pp. 1-4139-0143-3. **T Japanese manga.**

Mild-mannered Akira Uehara has never been good at anything at all. From love to sports to an active social life, Akira has always been too shy for anything. The old saying that opposites attract really does hold true: Akira has a crush on Nanako Momoi, a brash, outspoken, no-nonsense tough girl. One day Akira finds out that Nanako's mad scientist grandfather is performing experiments on her, so Akira gets in the way and wakes up a whole new person, literally! Akira is now trapped in Nanako's body, while Nanako is now in Akira's body! Akira wants to be returned to normal before more of his friends hit on him. Will they be able to ever switch back, and more important, will Nanako even want to?

<u>Zero Girl.</u> Written and illustrated by Sam Kieth. Homage/WildStorm Productions/DC Comics, 2001–2003. **O**

© 2006 Sam Keith.

Amy Smootster, a fifteen-year-old bespectacled outcast, is having a difficult time adjusting to her new school. She's constantly taunted by three viciously vain girls, she lives in hiding and is homeless, and she has a major crush on Tim, her high school counselor. But that's just the beginning. Amy has a peculiar knack for being able to speak to a reincarnated Dr. Carl Jung (who is now a worm) and also has the odd power to use the geometric shapes of circles for the power of good. Squares, as proven by one of the bullish teen girls who is converted by its power, are evil and the nemesis of the circles. Ultimately the growing relationship between Amy and Tim is tested against the backdrop of a surrealistic setting and the frustrations, and the feelings that love can foster prove to be the most powerful weapon of all.

Zero Girl. 2001. 114pp. 1-56389-851-9.
Zero Girl: Full Circle. 2003. 128pp. 1-4012-0170-9.

Coming-of-Age/Slice-of-Life

Included here are interpersonal graphic novels focusing on the drama, relationships, love, hard choices, heartaches, and occasional humor of growing up as a teen and the choices they make.

American Born Chinese. **Written and Illustrated by Gene Yang.** First Second, 2006. 240pp. 1-59643-152-0. **T** ◎

Teenager Jin Wang, an American-born Chinese, has it hard enough being an outcast at school. He's awkward around Caucasian girls he likes, he regularly gets picked on by school bullies and jocks, and he's one of only a few Asian students at school. When he befriends another Asian student, they find a kindred link in their heritage, but soon their friendship is put to the ultimate test. Meanwhile, two parallel stories are played out that may be more closely related to Jin Wang's plight: the legend of the Monkey King and the stereotypical exploits of Chin-Kee, an embarrassing, buck-toothed relative visiting a young Caucasian boy. Can Jin Wang come to terms with himself and his heritage?

Anna Sewell's Black Beauty. **Written by Anna Sewell. Adapted and Illustrated by June Brigman and Roy Richardson.** Penguin Graphics/Penguin Group, 2005. 176pp. 0-14-240408-X. **Y**

Adaptation of the classic story, written by Anna Sewell in 1877. Black Beauty, a spirited but kind horse, has lived a life of peace in the countryside of England, but is sold into a life of hard work pulling a cab in the bleak conditions of nineteenth-century London. He is treated cruelly and his life is difficult, but he is able to rise above hardships and eventually receives the kindness he deserves.

B. B. Explosion. Written and illustrated by Yasue Imai. VIZ Media, LLC, 2004–2005. **A Japanese manga.**

The Okinawa Actors School's graduates, who appear on the talent show called *Boom Boom*, are destined to have a lasting on the music scene of Japan and the world. The show is the first true stepping stone to success. Young Airi Ishikawa wants nothing more than to be on that show and will do anything to prove she has what it takes; she wants make it like her idol, Issa, from the boy band called Da Pump. Even though her parents don't approve, with the help of her guardian lion-god Cesar and the support of her fellow stars-in-waiting, Airi is going to follow her dream of making it big on the stage, singing and dancing her heart out to the world.

Vol. 1. 2004. 192pp. 1-59116-384-6.
Vol. 2. 2004. 192pp. 1-59116-385-4.
Vol. 3. 2004. 192pp. 1-59116-386-2.
Vol. 4. 2004. 192pp. 1-59116-387-0.
Vol. 5. 2005. 192pp. 1-59116-388-9.

***Barefoot Serpent.* Written and illustrated by Scott Morse.** Top Shelf Productions, 2003. 128pp. 1-891830-37-6. **T** ◉

© 2006 Scott Morse.

Famed Japanese film director Akira Kurosawa's life and works are explored through the framework of a fictional girl and her family, who come to Hawaii to heal and rediscover themselves following the death of her older brother. While on the island, the girl befriends a young local boy who, though reluctantly at first, helps to show the girl true friendship and gives her a personal way of healing through grief. Through their story, Kurosawa's personal life and the characters he brought to life are honored to show how we can all overcome adversity and challenges to live life to the fullest.

***Berlin: City of Stones, Book One.* Written and illustrated by Jason Lutes.** Drawn & Quarterly, 2000. 212pp. 1-896597-29-7. **O** ◉

A poignant look at pre–World War II Germany and the citizens who helped to shape and define the struggle that the Weimar Republic faced during the reconstruction after World War I. As the shadow of the Third Reich rises from the ashes of a devastated Germany, the citizens struggle to find their voice in a country plagued by poverty and sadness. Seen through the eyes of the many citizens in the famous yet impoverished city of Berlin. College students, shipyard workers, cabaret singers, and others struggle with the harsh realities of life and love amid the ever-growing powder keg of politics in 1928 in Germany.

❦ *Black Hole.* **Written and illustrated by Charles Burns.** Knopf, 2005. 368pp. 0-375-42380-X. **M**

In the 1970s in Seattle, a sexually transmitted disease called the "bug" is having strange effects on the teenagers and mutating them. For some the mutation may be something easily covered up, such as a tiny mouth appearing on the body—but for others the mutation is much more revolting. Those with the most horrendous forms of the disease are exiled in shame as homeless vagrants, who stay away from normal society unless they have to venture into the city. Meanwhile, two teens, Keith and Chris, discover that they too have the bug. The alienation of high school, combined with the bug's amplification of emotions and puberty, sends the youths on a roller coaster of changes much worse than they could have imagined. This graphic novel, ten years in the making, is a masterful metaphor for the changes of youth in a tumultuous period in American history. In 2006 the graphic novel received an Eisner Award in the category Best Graphic Album: Reprint.

<u>Blue Monday.</u> **Written and illustrated by Chynna Clugston-Major.** Oni Press, 2000– . **T** **Neo-manga.**

© 2006 Chynna Clugston-Major.

Bleu L. Finnegan is a spunky and fun teenage girl who has a penchant for 1980s songs and has a crush on her history teacher, Mr. Bishop, as well as on her favorite rocker, Adam Ant. She spends her days hanging out with her best friend, tough girl Clover, and her two prankish guy friends, Alan and Victor, listening to their favorite songs, riding scooters, and participating in other fun, foolish teen shenanigans. A love quadrangle emerges when Adam and Victor find they're both in love with Bleu, Clover is in love with Victor, and Bleu still secretly pines for Mr. Bishop. Love, relationships, and high school are never easy, but good times, the occasional slapdash prank, and some good humor make it all worthwhile.

> *Vol. 1: The Kids Are Alright.* 2d ed. 2003. 136pp. 1-929998-62-7.
> *Vol. 2: Absolute Beginners.* 2001. 128pp. 1-929998-17-1.
> *Vol. 3: Inbetween Days.* 2003. 96pp. 1-929998-66-X.
> *Vol. 4: Painted Moon.* 2005. 128pp. 1-932664-11-4.

<u>Box Office Poison.</u> **Written and illustrated by Alex Robinson.** Top Shelf Productions, 2003–2005. **M**

The intertwining lives of a group of friends living in New York City. Sherman, a twenty-three-year-old bookstore clerk, is dating twenty-five-year-old Dorothy. Jane, age twenty-six, can't stand Dorothy (she thinks she's a slob), but she and her boyfriend, Stephen, are sharing an apartment with the others in Brooklyn, New York. Meanwhile, Sherman's lonely best friend Ed has always wanted to be a comic book artist. Ed has the chance of a lifetime to work under the tutelage of Mr. Flavor, a crusty artist from the Golden Age of comics. When Ed realizes that Mr. Flavor's former company, Zoom Comics, robbed Flavor of his best-known creation, he encourages Flavor, the most offensive man in New York, to go on the offensive. *BOP! More Box Office Poison* includes short stories featuring the characters.

> *Box Office Poison.* 4th ed. 2005. 608pp. 1-891830-19-8.
> *BOP! More Box Office Poison.* 2003. 88pp. 1-891830-46-5.

The Complete Copybook Tales. **Written by J. Torres. Illustrated by Tim Levins.** Oni Press, 2002. 240pp. 1-929998-39-2. **T**

© 2006 J. Torres and Tim Levins.

Jamie and Thatcher have always dreamt of making it big in the comic book industry, but they haven't a clue where to look for a story and inspiration. When Jamie finds his old copybook journals from high school, which detailed his misadventures growing up in the 1980s with his school friends, they find the inspiration in their younger days' ups and downs, the sad and hilarious times of school days, and friendships that seemed like they would never end. Jumping back and forth between the "then" and the "now," Jamie and Thatcher are soon on their way to making their comic book dreams come true. Based on the life of J. Torres.

🪶 **Concrete. Written and illustrated by Paul Chadwick.** Dark Horse Comics, 2005–2006. **O**

Ron Lithgow was just an ordinary man with a mundane job as a speechwriter for a senator, when one day the extraordinary happened: aliens abducted him. His brain was transplanted into a large and powerful alien body that was made of a substance resembling concrete, and he now finds himself with phenomenal strength, eyesight as keen as an eagle's, and limitless endurance. Now calling himself Concrete, the sentimental man with a formerly mundane life is living a life he could never have dreamed and doing the impossible. Joined by his assistant writer and a female scientist to monitor the alien body, Concrete now lives a wide variety of adventures. The series has received the Harvey Award for Best New Series in 1988, and Paul Chadwick won the award for Best Cartoonist (Writer/Artist) for 1989. The series won the Eisner Awards for Best Continuing Series for 1988 and 1989, Best Black-and-White Series for 1988 and 1989, and Best New Series for 1988, and Paul Chadwick won the Best Writer/Artist Award for 1989.

> *Vol. 1: Depths.* 2d ed. 2005. 208pp. 1-59307-343-7
> *Vol. 2: Heights.* 2d ed. 2005. 208pp. 1-59307-420-4.
> *Vol. 3: Fragile Creature.* 2d ed. 2006. 208pp. 1-59307-464-6.
> *Vol. 4: Killer Smile.* 2d ed. 2006. 184pp. 1-59307-469-7.
> *Vol. 5: Think Like a Mountain.* 2d ed. 2006. 208pp. 1-59307-559-6.
> *Vol. 6: Strange Armor.* 2d ed. 2006. 192pp. 1-59307-560-X.
> *Vol. 7: The Human Dilemma.* 2006. 160pp. 1-59307-462-X.

The Contract with God Trilogy: Life on Dropsie Avenue. **Written and illustrated by Will Eisner.** W. W. Norton, 2006. 498pp. 0-393-06105-1. **O** ◉

The Contract with God Trilogy: Life on Dropsie Avenue by Will Eisner. Copyright © 2006 by the Estate of Will Eisner. Used by permission of W.W. Norton & Company, Inc.

A collection featuring three of Will Eisner's highly praised works set in the fictionalized South Bronx community. Partly taken from Eisner's Jewish youth growing up in New York in the early twentieth century, the collections focus on a wide cross-section of cultures and span well over 100 years of life in the same neighborhood. As time goes by, many families from a variety of cultures and nationalities help to bring their own influences to a small part of South Bronx—both the good and the bad. In that small space called Dropsie Avenue, nationalities clash, lifelong friendships are forged, people fall in and out of love, and new communities continually rise from the ashes of old ones. In the end, though, the old brick buildings of Dropsie Avenue are just buildings; it is the people of the community who make a neighborhood. The collection includes *A Contract with God and Other Tenement Stories*, *A Life Force*, and *Dropsie Avenue: The Neighborhood*.

Cry Yourself to Sleep. **Written and illustrated by Jeremy Tinder.** Top Shelf Productions, 2006. 88pp. 1-891830-81-3. **O**

© 2006 Jeremy Tinder.

A simple and bittersweet look at the disappointing lives of three roommates: Andy, a failed twenty-something, single writer who just received another rejection letter; a rabbit named Jim who was just fired from his minimum wage job and is in search of money for rent; and The Robot, a machine who tired of being cold and cruel and wants to become a better person. Along the way they deal with the mundane heartaches of loneliness, failed relationships, horrid customers, and personal embarrassments. When Jim reluctantly takes a new job with his dad, little does he know that his life will change dramatically and the three friends will never be the same again.

David Boring. **Written and illustrated by Daniel Clowes.** Knopf, 2002. 136pp. 0-375-71452-9. **O**

The menial life of David—an affectless young man who is living with his lesbian friend Dot in the big city, spending his days recounting past sexual encounters. While trying to find the meaning of life and to better understand his father—a former comic book artist for a comic book called *The Yellow Streak*—David falls in love with a girl named Wanda, becomes the chief suspect in a murder after an acquaintance from his hometown is murdered, and is shot in the head. While recuperating from his injury on a resort island, he and many other vacationers become stranded there after a terrorist organization unleashes germ warfare on the mainland of the United States. Can love, murder, and warfare keep David from finding out just where he truly belongs?

🏵 *Days Like This*. **Written by J. Torres. Illustrated by Scott Chantler.** Oni Press, 2003. 104pp. 1-929998-48-1. **T**

© 2006 J. Torres and Scott Chantler.

A look back at the heyday of the Motown movement, when a young trio of female singers calling themselves "Tina & the Tiaras" rise to the top of the charts and surmount personal problems to make it big. The graphic novel received recognition from YALSA's Popular Paperbacks for Young Adults committee in 2003 on the "On That Note . . . Music and Musicians" list.

7

Deogratias: A Tale of Rwanda. **Written and illustrated by J. P. Stassen.** First Second, 2006. 80pp. 1-59643-103-2. **O**

A tale of heartbreak set during the horrendous Rwandan genocide committed in 1994, when almost a million native Tutsi people were slaughtered by rebel extremist Hutu groups and the world powers did nothing. The tale focuses on Deogratias, a young Hutu man who is looking for a little action with the local girls and a taste of the succulent banana beer. But soon Deogratias is drawn into the culture of violence that envelopes Rwanda and over time drives him into his own personal madness. Told through flashbacks between a more peaceful time and the events leading up to as well as following the genocide, the tale of Deogratias is a sorrowful look at the brutality that people can inflict on their fellow humans.

© 2006 Stassen.

The Devil Does Exist. Written and illustrated by Takanashi Mitsuba. CMX/DC Comics, 2005–. **T Japanese manga.**

Shy high school girl Kayano has been having a horrible time in school, and it's about to get much much worse. She has a crush on Yuichi, the captain of the basketball team. When the love letter she wrote to him is confiscated by Takeru, the school bully, she is mortified at how he manipulates the situation (his father is the school principal). Upset about Takeru's behavior, Kayano comes home to find that her mother is engaged to Takeru's father, making Takeru a live-in tormentor! Soon Takeru is manipulating events at school, even putting himself on the basketball team alongside Yuichi, with Kayano as the team manager. Can her life get much worse? The devil really does exist: he's her stepbrother! The series was published in eleven volumes in Japan.

> *Vol. 1.* 2005. 192pp. 1-4012-0545-3.
> *Vol. 2.* 2005. 192pp. 1-4012-0546-1.
> *Vol. 3.* 2005. 192pp. 1-4012-0547-X.
> *Vol. 4.* 2006. 192pp. 1-4012-0548-8.
> *Vol. 5.* 2006. 192pp. 1-4012-0549-6.
> *Vol. 6.* 2006. 192pp. 1-4012-1020-1.
> *Vol. 7.* 2006. 192pp. 1-4012-1021-X.
> *Vol. 8.* 2006. 192pp. 1-4012-1022-8.

Fade from Blue, Vol. 1. **Written by Myatt Murphy. Illustrated by Scott Dalrymple.** Second 2 Some Studios, 2003–. 144pp. 0-9725703-1-4. **O**

Nine years ago, when their mothers were mysteriously killed, Iya, Marit, Elisa, and Christa found out that they all had one thing in common: the same father! Now in hiding in New York City, the four half-sisters have forged a unique family, trying to overcome their personal struggles and to find their polygamist father, who has abandoned them. Together through bad relationships, unrequited love, a murder mystery, sarcastic comments, and a visit to the clinic, the four Shermot sisters must learn to ride the ups and downs of being a family in hiding and try to make the best of what they have before their father's hidden past brings their world crumbling down.

Fagin the Jew. **Written and illustrated by Will Eisner.** Doubleday Publishing/Random House, 2003. 128pp. 0-385-51009-8. **O**

The "true" life of fictional Jewish character Fagin from Charles Dickens's classic novel *Oliver Twist*. From his hard life as the son of an immigrant, learning from his father on the grim streets of London, to his encounter with the young boy named Oliver, to his sad incarceration and hanging, Moses Fagin's life is recounted in flashbacks. Fagin demands that Dickens portray the Jewish people in his books as more than just stereotypical thieves and money-lovers.

<u>Flowers and Bees.</u> Written and illustrated by Moyoco Anno. VIZ Media, LLC, 2003–2005. **M Japanese manga.**

High school student Masao Komatsu's out to make himself into a beautiful man so he can have his pick of the girls at school and stop being teased by the them for his looks. Not very good-looking or very bright, he's falling into a vicious trap by Kiyoko and Harumi, gorgeous manipulative owners of the World of Beautiful Men salon. With each visit he'll do anything they say no matter how odd, humiliating, or abusive, and no matter how much it costs—just as long as he gets recognition at school and the attention of a girl he's interested in.

Vol. 1. 2003. 216pp. 1-56931-978-2.
Vol. 2. 2004. 232pp. 1-59116-124-X.
Vol. 3. 2004. 216pp. 1-59116-298-X.
Vol. 4. 2004. 200pp. 1-59116-346-3.
Vol. 5. 2004. 200pp. 1-59116-347-1.
Vol. 6. 2004. 200pp. 1-59116-348-X.
Vol. 7. 2005. 200pp. 1-59116-777-9.

<u>Forbidden Dance.</u> Written and illustrated by Hinako Ashihara. TOKYOPOP, 2003–2004. **T Japanese manga.**

When ballet dancer Aya Fujii injures herself in a dancing mishap, her faith in herself is shattered, and she believes she'll never dance again. When she sees a show of an all-male rock ballet troupe called COOL, she's reenergized and will do anything to be a part of their troupe—even though she's just a girl. Akira, the cocky leader of COOL, will let her into the all-male troupe on one condition: she has to take first place in the national ballet competition. Will Aya step up to the plate and prove that she has what it takes to be COOL?

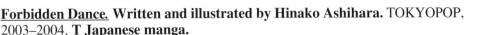

Vol. 1. 2003. 192pp. 1-59182-345-5.
Vol. 2. 2003. 200pp. 1-59182-346-3.
Vol. 3. 2004. 192pp. 1-59182-347-1.
Vol. 4. 2004. 200pp. 1-59182-348-X.

🐾 *Ghost World.* **Written and illustrated by Daniel Clowes.** Fantagraphics Books, 2001. 80pp. 1-56097-427-3. **O** ◉ 🎬

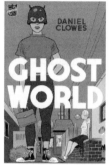

© 2006 Daniel Clowes.

The coming-of-age story of Enid and Rebecca, two sarcastic teenage friends who are facing their existence following high school. Enid is the more extroverted, doing the out-of-the-ordinary just for the sake of doing it (such as going to an adult book store and wearing a bondage mask in public), while Rebecca is the more prudent of the two. They spend their time after school talking about the mundane and teasing boys as well as awkward adults like Seymore, a secluded jazz collector. They know their behavior isn't nice, but they do it out of boredom and for fun. Enid is considering moving away from their working-class neighborhood to go to college, and Rebecca has different life goals in mind, inevitably creating a rift in their relationship that no bridge could ever cross. The graphic novel received recognition from YALSA's Popular Paperbacks for Young Adults committee in 2002 on the "Graphic Novels: Superheroes and Beyond" list. It was adapted as a live-action film in 2001.

Golden Vine. **Written by Jai Sen. Illustrated by Seijuro Mizu, Umeka Asayuki, and Shino Yotsumoto.** Shoto Press, 2003. 304pp. 0-9717564-1-4. **T Neo-manga.**

A fictionalized retelling of Alexander the Great's life from the point of view of his adopted son, Alexander. The young ruler must learn the secrets that his father took to his grave or else perish as a leader of what was once greatest civilization in the world.

Good-bye Chunky Rice. **Written and illustrated by Craig Thompson.** Pantheon Press/Random House, 2006. 128pp. 0-375-71476-6. **O**

A small turtle named Chunky Rice is leaving his seaside home behind as well as his best friend, a mouse named Dandel. Dandel tries to remain strong, though she misses her friend dearly and writes him long letters, which she places in bottles and sends out to sea. Chunky is on an adventure of his own on a sailing vessel with a married couple and two sisters joined at the head. Meanwhile, Chunky's old neighbor Solomon sees the separated friends as a reflection of his own past relationship with his pet. Can he rekindle what he lost with an injured bird named Merle and heal his broken heart? A poignant tale of the tests of true friendship, growing up, and the risks of going away from home for the first time.

High School Girls. **Written and illustrated by Towa Oshima.** DrMaster Publications Inc., 2004–2005. **O Japanese manga.**

A fictionalized account of creator Towa Oshima's life attending an all-girls private school in Japan. All the cliques, rivalries, humor, and drama are there, combined with tales of academic woes, relationships, sexual frustrations, and even time for a little fun in the sun with Eriko, Ayano and Yuma, three girls entering high school together.

Vol. 1. 2004. 200pp. 1-58899-200-4.
Vol. 2. 2004. 200pp. 1-58899-201-2.
Vol. 3. 2005. 200pp. 1-58899-202-0.
Vol. 4. 2005. 200pp. 1-58899-219-5.
Vol. 5. 2005. 200pp. 1-59796-058-6.
Vol. 6. 2005. 208pp. 1-59796-059-4.

🏆 <u>Hopeless Savages.</u> **Written by Jen Van Meter.** Oni Press, 2003–2004. **T** ◎

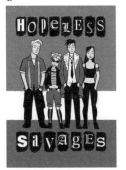

© 2006 Jen Van Meter.

Two punk rockers, who never quit the business or forgot about their ways, married and settled down. Their kids all have names like Arsenal, Skank, and Twitch. When the parents are kidnapped (*Volume 1*), the kids have to figure out how to save them, but they can't do it without the help of their estranged eldest brother, Rat. What did he do to rebel when his parents were the ultimate rebels? Become a businessman, that's what. In the continuing adventures, Skank, the youngest of the family, starts considering dating as well as forming her own band, the Dust Bunnies, in the midst of a video crew recording the family's every move for a television show. Meanwhile Twitch, the middle brother, is discovering his own sexual identity. Both he and Arsenal are dating the Shi brothers as well as participating in a kung fu tournament in Hong Kong, and the punk family follows them to Hong Kong to watch them compete, as well as to escape from their religious convert grandmother. A humorously touching look at an anti-establishment family. *Volume 1* received recognition from YALSA's Popular Paperbacks for Young Adults committee in 2003 on the "On That Note . . . Music and Musicians" list.

> *Vol. 1.* Illustrated by Christine Norrie and Chynna Clugston-Major. 2003, 2nd edition 136pp. 1-929998-75-9.
>
> *Vol. 2: Ground Zero.* Illustrated by Bryan Lee O'Malley. 2004, 2nd edition 128pp. 1-929998-99-6.
>
> *Vol. 3: Too Much Hopeless Savages.* Illustrated by Christine Norrie and Ross Campbell. 2004. 120pp. 1-929998-85-6.

🏆 *Jimmy Corrigan: The Smartest Kid on Earth.* **Written and illustrated by Chris Ware.** Knopf Publishing Group, 2003. 380pp. 0-375-71454-5. **O**

The sad lives of four generations of the Corrigan family. An Everyman in his mid-thirties who spends his days working in a cubicle as well as having a boxed-in home life, Jimmy's lonely tale of abandonment can be traced back generation after generation, to Jimmy's father, grandfather, and great-grandfather, who also had equally depressing childhoods. The main story is set in Chicago in the 1980s, when Jimmy receives an invitation and a plane ticket from his estranged and distant father for a Thanksgiving dinner. Can years of neglect, heartache, and missed breakfasts be mended over breakfast? The graphic novel received several Harvey Awards, including the Special Award for Excellence in Presentation and Best Graphic Album of Previously Published Work, as well as Eisner Awards for Best Publication Design and Best Graphic Album: Reprint.

7

Joan. **Written and illustrated by Yoshikazu Yasuhiko.** ComicsOne, 2001. **T Japanese manga.**

In medieval France following the death of Joan of Arc, a young woman named Emil, who was also raised by a man named Baudricourt as Joan was, sets out to find her own destiny and reunited France. Guided by visions of Joan of Arc, she follows in the footsteps of Joan and forges her own path to rebuild France despite the adversaries that stand in her way.

> *Vol. 1*. 2001. 192pp. 1-58899-090-7.
> *Vol. 2*. 2001. 224pp. 1-58899-091-5.
> *Vol. 3*. 2001. 224pp. 1-58899-092-3.

Just a Girl. Written and illustrated by Tomoko Taniguchi. CPM Manga, 2004. **A Japanese manga.**

Young Erica is finally on her own after she makes it to the boarding school of her choice. Taking her stuffed animals with her for companionship, she has no parents and total freedom. So why is she so lonely? Luckily she's soon joined by some old friends and makes some new ones, too, including Rena, an older girl whom she soon admires. Will Erica blossom at boarding school, or will she always be just a girl? In *Volume 2* she finds innocent love with Rocky, a young boy with dreams of making it big in Hollywood. Will she wait for him when he leaves, or will she learn to love again?

> *Vol. 1*. 2004. 184pp. 1-58664-911-6.
> *Vol. 2*. 2004. 176pp. 1-58664-912-4.

La Perdida. **Written and illustrated by Jessica Abel.** Pantheon Books/Random House, 2006. 288pp. 0-375-42365-6. **O**

Young half-Latina Carla, estranged from her Mexican father, abandons the security of the United States to find herself and her roots in Mexico. Now completely out of her element, she's an innocent lost among various characters, including her expatriate ex-boyfriend, a petty drug dealer and DJ-wannabe named Oscar, and eventually a drug don named el Gordo. Can Carla reconcile her lofty dreams of a mythical Mexico with the grim reality of life in Mexico as an impoverished youth before her cycle of hard living destroys her?

Lost at Sea. **Written and illustrated by Bryan Lee O'Malley.** Oni Press, 2003. 168pp. 1-929998-71-6. **O** ◎

Eighteen-year-old Raliegh hates crowds, people, and everything. So what is she doing on a road trip with three other teenagers from her private school? On the surface, it appears that she's just hitching a ride with classmates Stephanie, Dave, and Ian to get from California to her home in Vancouver, Canada. It's an uncomfortable trip for her, but she endures it as she writes in her journal that she believes she's lost her soul. As Raliegh sorts out her past, her personality, and just who she really is via epistolary letters, her stream of consciousness reveals a girl running away from herself and monsters largely of her own making.

Marmalade Boy. Written and illustrated by Wataru Yoshizumi. TOKYOPOP, 2002–2003. **T Japanese manga.** あ

Teenager Miki Koishikawa's life has just been turned upside down. When her loving parents announced they were getting divorced, that was one thing, but now her parents are swapping spouses with the Matsuuras and living in the same house! Now Miki is living with four parents, and though she is in love with her childhood friend Ginta, she thinks she might be falling for her new stepbrother, Yuu. Love and family could never be more complicated and funny than this. The manga was adapted into a seventy-six-episode anime series in Japan.

> *Vol. 1.* 2002. 198pp. 1-931514-54-2.
> *Vol. 2.* 2002. 176pp. 1-931514-55-0.
> *Vol. 3.* 2002. 192pp. 1-931514-56-9.
> *Vol. 4.* 2002. 192pp. 1-931514-57-7.
> *Vol. 5.* 2003. 192pp. 1-59182-071-5.
> *Vol. 6.* 2003. 192pp. 1-59182-190-8.
> *Vol. 7.* 2003. 184pp. 1-59182-191-6.
> *Vol. 8.* 2003. 192pp. 1-59182-192-4.

Mary Jane/Spider-Man Loves Mary Jane. Written by Sean McKeever. Illustrated by Takeshi Miyazawa. Marvel Comics, 2004– . **Y**

© 2006 Marvel Comics.

No matter where she goes, Mary Jane Watson is always the life of the party. But under that façade of pretentiousness lies a teen girl trying to escape the harsh realities of school and home. She'd rather daydream about someday becoming an actress or talk about the one mystery man she has a severe crush on, Spider-Man. She is joined by her best friend, Liz Allen, her somewhat faithful boyfriend Flash Thompson, wonderful-but-not-"Spider-Man wonderful" Harry Osborn, and even Harry's geeky friend Peter Parker. If only Spider-Man could take all of her problems away. The series was relaunched as Spider-Man Loves Mary Jane in 2006.

Mary Jane. 2004–2005.
> *Vol. 1: Circle of Friends.* 2004. 96pp. 0-7851-1467-X.
> *Vol. 2: Homecoming.* 2005. 96pp. 0-7851-1779-2.

Spider-Man Loves Mary Jane. 2006– .
> *Vol. 1: Super-Crush.* 2006. 120pp. 0-7851-1954-X.
> *Vol. 2: The New Girl.* 2007. 120pp. 0-7851-2265-6.

Minor Miracles. **Written and illustrated by Will Eisner.** DC Comics, 2000. 110pp. 1-56389-755-5 **O**

Short stories highlighting Jewish life set in Dropsie Avenue during the early part of the twentieth century. Lives young and old share their stories of the minor miracles in life, from good fortune, to how to earn dignity, to people who changed and bettered the lives of others, to the small things in life that can make it easier. The storytellers prove that even in times of tragedy, miracles do sometimes happen, even small ones.

Mirror, Window: An Artbabe Collection. **Written and illustrated by Jessica Abel.** Fantagraphics Books, 2001. 96pp. 1-56097-384-6. **O**

A collection of Jessica Abel's vibrant looks at twenty-something life in Chicago in the 1990s. The stories are an honest and hard-to-put down, honest look at life among the hip, the bar hoppers, college students, struggling musicians, clerks, art students, and more. The slice-of-life tales focus on how they struggle to find their way in life and fall in and out of love and bad relationships, the importance of friendship, and the uphill battle of just trying to get by in life. The series collects Abel's *Artbabe* comics, which were originally collected in comic books and mini-comics from 1992 to 1999.

One. **Written and illustrated by Vin Lee.** TOKYOPOP, 2004– . **T Korean manhwa.**

Jenny You, a spoiled and beautiful teenage actress turned pop diva, thinks she's the most talented student at Daewon High School. She has the boys all wanting to date her and she's the envy of all the girls. When Eumpa One, a former childhood prodigy in music, transfers to Daewon High from the United States, he's just trying to fit in and couldn't care less about Jenny. He's fallen for the plain but nice girl, Young-ju Chae. When a stolen composition that Eumpa creates becomes a hit theme song for a television soap opera called *Yesterday's Love,* will Eumpa reclaim what is his and once again enter the spotlight to take center stage, and what happens when two girls become attracted to the same boy? The final two volumes of the series have not yet been published in North America.

> *Vol. 1.* 2004. 192pp. 1-59182-752-3.
> *Vol. 2.* 2004. 200pp. 1-59182-753-1.
> *Vol. 3.* 2004. 208pp. 1-59182-754-X.
> *Vol. 4.* 2004. 200pp. 1-59182-755-8.
> *Vol. 5.* 2004. 192pp. 1-59182-756-6.
> *Vol. 6.* 2005. 192pp. 1-59532-010-5.
> *Vol. 7.* 2005. 192pp. 1-59532-011-3.
> *Vol. 8.* 2005. 192pp. 1-59532-012-1.
> *Vol. 9.* 2006. 192pp. 1-59532-013-X.

Othello. **Written and illustrated by Satomi Ikezawa.** Del Rey Manga/Random House, 2004–2006. **O Japanese manga.**

Sixteen-year-old Yaya Higuchi is a timid high school girl who never stands up for herself. Even girls she considers to be her friends, like Seri and Moe, taunt her and call her names. Some friends. Nana, on the other hand, is a tough, no-nonsense goth girl who puts Yaya's "friends" in their place with plenty of attitude to go around. Yaya and Nana are like day and night or more precisely, like two sides of the same coin. Through her goth cosplaying (dressing up as a manga/anime/video game character) Yaya inadvertently releases the pent-up side of herself and becomes a whole new person, ready to dole out revenge on Seri and Moe. When Nana leaves, Yaya wakes up with no memory at all of her dark-haired, aggressive side. Can the two of them survive in the same body without bad consequences?

> *Vol. 1.* 2004. 208pp. 0-345-47913-0.
> *Vol. 2.* 2004. 208pp. 0-345-47948-3.
> *Vol. 3.* 2005. 192pp. 0-345-47998-X.
> *Vol. 4.* 2005. 208pp. 0-345-48000-7.
> *Vol. 5.* 2005. 208pp. 0-345-47796-0.
> *Vol. 6.* 2005. 208pp. 0-345-48438-X.
> *Vol. 7.* 2006. 208pp. 0-34548-439-8.

Para Para. **Written and illustrated by Andy Seto.** Comicsone, 2004. 144pp. 1-58899-373-6. **T** Chinese manhua.

Yuki, the spoiled teenage daughter of a rich corporation president, is withdrawn from her fellow teens due to her status and a dark memory. Her older sister Mary died after being taken away by a man to Japan, and she's always missed her and hated the man for stealing her from her family. Meanwhile, a young man named Dennis, a leader of the dance craze called "Para Para" in Hong Kong, spots Yuki and they instantly feel the chemistry. What is Dennis's connection to Mary, and what tragic secret is he hiding from everyone?

Paradise Kiss. **Written and illustrated by Ai Yazawa.** TOKYOPOP, 2002–2003. **O Japanese manga. あ**

Yukari is a hard-working, pretty, but simple girl in her senior year in high school. She's accosted one day by Arashi, an Anglophile and member of the eccentric four-person fashion group from the Yazawa School for the Arts called Paradise Kiss. He thinks she's the perfect model for the line of high-fashion clothes they're designing, and with encouraged by the drag queen Isabella, Yukari reluctantly goes with them. There she meets George, the blue-haired, snobbish lead designer. Yukari soon finds herself drawn out of her shell and is introduced to the world of fashion modeling, catwalks, spotlights, and divas. She also finds herself in the arms of seemingly aloof George, a complex boyfriend who soon takes their relationship one step further. When Paradise Kiss's finals for graduation come up, what will happen to them—will they reach their dreams in the world of fashion and in love, and has Yukari found where she truly belongs? The manga series was adapted as a twelve-episode anime series in Japan.

> *Vol. 1*. 2002. 184pp. 1-931514-60-7.
> *Vol. 2*. 2002. 192pp. 1-931514-61-5.
> *Vol. 3*. 2002. 184pp. 1-59182-053-7.
> *Vol. 4*. 2003. 192pp. 1-59182-108-8.
> *Vol. 5*. 2003. 200pp. 1-59182-242-4.

Passion Fruit. **Written and illustrated by various.** TOKYOPOP, 2005. **O Japanese manga.**

An anthology collection of short stories created by some of the foremost manga legends. Each volume is by a different manga-ka and showcases a variety of dramatic genrebending tales about teenagers bridging the gap from youth to adulthood as they experience sensuality and maturity for the first time. The tales are not interrelated, and feature light fantasy, true love, friendships, fantastic tales, and more.

> *Vol. 1*. 2005. 208pp. 1-59182-797-3.
> *Vol. 2*. 2005. 192pp. 1-59182-798-1.

 ❦ *Pulpatoon Pilgrimage*. Written and illustrated by Joel Priddy. AdHouse Books, 2002. 160pp. 0-9721794-0-2. **O**

Three oddball friends—a Minotaur, a walking Delaware thistle, and a robot sailor named Rowbot—embark on a quest, along the way discovering more about themselves. Short vignettes give brief glimpses into the lives of the colorful characters as they share their stories of personal adventure, grief, love, sex, and their own quests for meaning. The collection won an Ignatz Award in 2002 for Outstanding Debut.

Saint Marie. **Written and illustrated by Yang Yeo-Jin.** ADV Manga, 2004–2005. **Korean manhwa.**

Beneath the façade of peace, the private school Saint Marie's is playing a deadly game of chess that can even cost you your life! Sophomore Dah-In Hyun has been best friends with her roommate Na-Na for years. She's a spunky and cheerful orphan and has a crush on bad boy Yoon-Ha. When she finds Na-Na oddly talking to herself, she becomes concerned for her friend—and then inexplicably Dah-In finds herself hearing voices, too! After Na-Na dies mysteriously, Dah-In becomes embroiled in a struggle between good and evil, and she's become a chosen soldier in the struggle for the school grounds against the schoolteachers.

Vol. 1. 2004. 190pp. 1-4139-0065-8.
Vol. 2. 2004. 192pp. 1-4139-0080-1.
Vol. 3. 2005. 208pp. 1-4139-0110-7.
Vol. 4. 2005. 200pp. 1-4139-0250-2.

🏵 *Same Difference and Other Stories.* **Written and illustrated by Derek Kirk Kim.** Top Shelf Productions, 2004. 144pp. 1-891830-57-0. **O** ◉

Best friends Simon and Nancy, both twenty-something Korean Americans, have had their share of humor, heartache, and regret. When Simon spots a former high school classmate whom he had treated badly, he shares his own personal insecurities about when he was in high school and was embarrassed to go to the school dance with a platonic and disabled friend. Meanwhile Nancy, a chain-smoking, nosy sleuth, confesses to Simon that she's been writing love letters to a man who lives in Simon's hometown. The man was sending love letters that were addressed to the previous owner of her apartment, and as a game, Nancy has been pretending to be the ex-girlfriend. As Nancy and Simon travel back to Simon's California hometown to find out just who this man is, Simon spots his old friend and gets the opportunity to tell her how he really feels. When true confessions and pent-up feelings are revealed, both Nancy and Simon find that though the truth hurts, the healing power of the heart can mend all wounds. In 2005 the creator received an Eisner Award in the category Talent Deserving of Wider Recognition as well as an Ignatz Award in 2003 for Promising New Talent.

Scooter Girl. **Written and illustrated by Chynna Clugston-Major.** Oni Press, 2004. 168pp. 1-929998-88-0. **O Neo-manga.**

© 2006 Chynna Clugston-Major.

Over-sexed and overconfident California high school student Ashton Archer has things made. He's from a long line of "studs" who have had their way with women and have had life handed to them on a silver platter: in sports, the arts, school, and more, he has always succeeded. When he spots mod newcomer Margaret Sheldon while riding his Vespa scooter, he loses control for the first time, and his bike is totaled. Whenever he sees her now he's suddenly tongue-tied and a klutz—and things go from bad to worse. Now no one likes him at school, his family is bankrupt, and all of his ladies no longer want to be with him. Cursed wherever he goes, even relocating after graduation to San Diego, it seems the only way that Ashton can get this beautiful bane of his existence to break his bad streak is to win her love, but he's going to have to learn how to treat a woman first.

Scott Pilgrim. **Written and illustrated by Bryan Lee O'Malley.** Oni Press, 2004– . **T** ◎

© 2006 Bryan Lee O'Malley.

Scott Pilgrim has it good. A twenty-three-year-old slacker, he's "in-between" jobs right now (i.e., unemployed) and on the side he plays in a so-so band called Sex Bob-omb and plays video games. He's sharing a tiny apartment with his roommate, who owns almost everything in it. He even has a girlfriend named Knives Chau, who's still in high school and is really nice. Basically Scott's not that bright a guy, but he's cool. Über cool. When he meets a rollerblading delivery girl named Ramona Flowers at several parties, is she worth having a relationship with and breaking his girlfriend's heart? And just why is it that Ramona's seven evil ex-boyfriends want to beat him up? Meanwhile, the inevitable happens after Scott's cheating results in Knives and Ramona have a confrontation kung-fu style, and there's plenty of drama, comedy, and action mixed in.

>*Vol. 1: Scott Pilgrim's Precious Little Life.* 2004. 168pp. 1-932664-08-4.
>*Vol. 2: Scott Pilgrim vs. the World.* 2005. 200pp. 1-932664-12-2.
>*Vol. 3: Scott Pilgrim and the Infinite Sadness.* 2006. 192pp. 1-932664-22-X.

Sensual Phrase. **Written and illustrated by Mayu Shinjo.** VIZ Media, LLC, 2004–2006. **M Japanese manga.** あ

When Aine, a blossoming teen lyricist/songwriter, almost literally has a run-in with Sakuya, the seductive lead singer of the band Lucifer, she realizes that he's stealing more than her heart: he's stolen her song, and now it's a hit single! Now Sakuya wants both a personal and professional relationship with the cute Aine, but does he really care for her, or is she just another girl he's seducing and a key to another hit song? The manga series was adapted as an anime series in Japan.

>*Vol. 1.* 2004. 192pp. 1-59116-205-X.
>*Vol. 2.* 2004. 192pp. 1-59116-334-X.
>*Vol. 3.* 2004. 192pp. 1-59116-449-4.
>*Vol. 4.* 2004. 192pp. 1-59116-411-7.
>*Vol. 5.* 2004. 192pp. 1-59116-560-1.
>*Vol. 6.* 2004. 192pp. 1-59116-671-3.
>*Vol. 7.* 2005. 200pp. 1-59116-734-5.
>*Vol. 8.* 2005. 200pp. 1-59116-803-1.
>*Vol. 9.* 2005. 200pp. 1-59116-867-8.
>*Vol. 10.* 2005. 192pp. 1-4215-0013-2.
>*Vol. 11.* 2005. 192pp. 1-4215-0107-4.
>*Vol. 12.* 2006. 208pp. 1-4215-0265-8.
>*Vol. 13.* 2006. 208pp. 1-4215-0395-6.
>*Vol. 14.* 2006. 208pp. 1-4215-0559-2.
>*Vol. 15.* 2006. 208pp. 1-4215-0560-6.
>*Vol. 16.* 2006. 208pp. 1-4215-0561-4.
>*Vol. 17.* 2006. 208pp. 1-4215-0562-2.

Serenity. Written by Buzz Dixon. Illustrated by Min Kwon. RealBuzz Studios/ Barbour Publishing, 2005–2006. **Y Neo-manga.**

Teenage rebel Serenity Harper has just transferred to James A. Madison High School after living in Los Angeles for her entire life. Rude, crude, and with an attitude that won't quit, she's already miserable at her new school, and her broken family life couldn't be much worse. When she is befriended by Derek, Kimberly, and Tim, members of the school's teen prayer club, Serenity can't believe how dorky and yet nice the teens are despite her attitude toward them. Soon Serenity is the prayer club's pet project, and no matter how crude or obnoxious she is to them, they're still going to be her friends. Can a bad girl learn what it's like to be a good girl again and become a good Christian? The series will be collected in six volumes.

> *Vol. 1: Bad Girl in Town.* 2005. 96pp. 1-59310-941-5.
> *Vol. 2: Stepping Out.* 2006. 96pp. 1-59310-942-3.
> *Vol. 3: Basket Case.* 2006. 96pp. 1-59310-872-9.
> *Vol. 4: Rave-N-Rant.* 2006. 96pp. 1-59310-873-7
> *Vol. 5: Snow Biz.* 2006. 96pp. 1-59310-874-5.
> *Vol. 6: You Shall Love.* 2006. 96pp. 1-59310-875-3.

Short Program. Written and illustrated by Mitsuru Adachi. VIZ Media, LLC, 2000–2004. **T Japanese manga.**

A collection of universal, unrelated short stories by creator Mitsuru Adachi. Stories cover all walks of life, from youth to adulthood, and focus on the quirks of life, love, humor, and more that make life so unique, including tales of high school love, life after high school, sports, and coming-of-age.

> *Vol. 1.* 2000. 288pp. 1-56931-473-X.
> *Vol. 2.* 2004. 280pp. 1-59116-301-3.

🦎 *Signal to Noise.* **Written by Neil Gaiman. Illustrated by Dave McKean.** Dark Horse Comics, 1992. 80pp. 1-56971-144-5. **O** ◎

A dying fifty-year-old filmmaker, known for always visualizing his movies in his mind before filming a single piece of footage, spends the last few months of his life on his masterpiece. His film revolves around the eve of the new year A.D. 999, when the villagers of a small community are dreading Armageddon. As death approaches, the filmmaker's masterpiece is finished in a touching and poignant way no one will ever see coming, except for the readers of the story. The story won an Eisner Award in 1993 for Best Graphic Novel—New.

Slow News Day. **Written and illustrated by Andi Watson.** Slave Labor Graphics, 2002. 160pp. 0-943151-59-7. **O**

Katharine Washington, an American fresh out of college, interns at a small-town newspaper in the British countryside for the summer in search of a change of pace to help her with her writing skills on a secret project. At the newspaper, the *Wheatstone Mercury,* she has her hands full with Owen, a cranky and overworked columnist coworker; Owen's girlfriend, who works at the paper; and a managing editor more into advertising than news stories on the front page.

Snow Drop. **Written and illustrated by Choi Kyung-ah.** TOKYOPOP, 2004–2006. **O Korean manhwa.**

Rich girl So-Na loves her Snow Drop nursery. It's her own personal refuge from the horror she faced as a young child, when she was kidnapped and raped. She and her friend, Ha-Da, a good-natured, spoiled tough guy, are starting their freshman year in a new high school together. She's stuck in class sitting next to Hae-Gi, a poor boy who works on the side as a model. Like So-Na, Hae-Gi has his own skeletons in his closet and is recuperating from the death of his older brother, Gae-Ri. When they meet, like Romeo and Juliet, they fall madly in love, but problems from their pasts may yet come back to haunt them.

> *Vol. 1*. 2004. 200pp. 1-59182-684-5.
> *Vol. 2*. 2004. 200pp. 1-59182-685-3.
> *Vol. 3*. 2004. 208pp. 1-59182-686-1.
> *Vol. 4*. 2004. 208pp. 1-59182-687-X.
> *Vol. 5*. 2004. 192pp. 1-59182-688-8.
> *Vol. 6*. 2004. 192pp. 1-59182-689-6.
> *Vol. 7*. 2005. 192pp. 1-59532-043-1.
> *Vol. 8*. 2005. 192pp. 1-59532-044-X.
> *Vol. 9*. 2005. 192pp. 1-59532-045-8.
> *Vol. 10*. 2005. 192pp. 1-59532-046-6.
> *Vol. 11*. 2005. 192pp. 1-59532-047-4.
> *Vol. 12*. 2006. 192pp. 1-59532-048-2.

Soundtrack: Short Stories 1989–1996. **Written and illustrated by Jessica Abel.** Fantagraphics Books, 2001. 96pp. 1-56097-430-3. **O**

A collection of short stories by creator Jessica Abel. The tales highlight Abel's unique skill at capturing the vibrancy of life in Chicago, where vignettes featuring slices of life from the poignant, to the heartbreaking, to the hilarious (and a visit to a Godzilla convention) are all succinctly and poetically told. The series collects Abel's *Artbabe* comics, which were originally collected in comic books and mini-comics from 1992 to 1999.

Stylish Vittles. **Written and illustrated by Tyler Page.** Dementian Comics, 2002–2005. **O**

The semiautobiographical story of Tyler, a senior college art design major who meets Nanette, a dark-haired woman who will change his life. As their relationship grows, they have to balance friends, past secrets, college life, and families if they're going to make it. Difficult topics of discussion come up, and they both speak frankly about the concerns they have in the relationship, such as religious differences, sex, and everything in between. As their relationship reaches its pinnacle, through Tyler's completion of grad school and Nanette leaving to spend her last semester of college abroad, they find out the ultimate test of a relationship and the heartache, pain, and catharsis it takes to let someone go.

> *Vol. 1: I Met a Girl*. 2002. 208pp. 0-9720801-0-4.
> *Vol. 2: All the Way*. 2003. 280pp. 0-9720801-1-2.
> *Vol. 3: Fare Thee Well*. 2005. 184pp. 0-9720801-2-0.

Suki. **Written and illustrated by CLAMP.** TOKYOPOP, 2004. **T Japanese manga.**

Hinata Asahi is a high school student who lives alone in a house. Her only companions at home are her giant stuffed teddy bears Tomo and Waka. A new next-door neighbor arrives, the handsome thirty-two-year-old Shirou Asou, whom Hinata instantly develops a crush on. Not only is he her neighbor, but he's also her new teacher at school! As their friendship grows, Asou accepts Hinata's invitations to keep her company for dinner, and word gets around fast in school about this taboo relationship. Is there something that Asou is hiding from Hinata, and is their something more to their "love and like" relationship?

> *Vol. 1.* 2004. 192pp. 1-59182-760-4.
> *Vol. 2.* 2004. 192pp. 1-59182-761-2.
> *Vol. 3.* 2004. 176pp. 1-59182-762-0.

Summer of Love. **Written and illustrated by Debbie Drechsler.** Drawn & Quarterly, 2003. 142pp. 1-896597-65-3. **O**

In 1967, after her family relocates to the small town of Woodland from Cleveland, ninth-grader Lilly Maier and her younger sister Pearl are trying to fit in with new friends, a new school, and learning the hard way about the secrets of love. When Pearl's relationship with a bright young teen boy intensifies over the summer and then abruptly dissolves, she's left feeling awkward and alone. Meanwhile, Lily sees her sister becoming intimately attracted to Kim, a local neighborhood seventh-grade girl. Confused by her sister's romantic interests, Lily herself rebounds right into the arms of an annoyingly parasitic boy who won't take no for an answer. When both of their relationships crumble before their eyes, Lily and Pearl find that there's more to life than fitting in and finding true love, and that Cleveland wasn't so bad after all.

Swan. **Written and illustrated by Ariyoshi Kyoko.** CMX/DC Comics, 2004– . **Y Japanese manga.**

The story of a sixteen-year-old ballet student passionate about her dancing who gets the chance of a lifetime to study ballet with the best dancers in Japan. After losing her first competition, Hijiri Masumi vows to come back to ballet dancing even better than ever. She's going to have to work her hardest in order to get where she wants to be: the best dancer in the company. The series was previously published in Japan in the 1970s and will be collected in a planned twenty-one volumes.

> *Vol. 1.* 2004. 200pp. 1-4012-0535-6.
> *Vol. 2.* 2005. 208pp. 1-4012-0536-4.
> *Vol. 3.* 2005. 208pp. 1-4012-0537-2.
> *Vol. 4.* 2005. 200pp. 1-4012-0538-0.
> *Vol. 5.* 2005. 192pp. 1-4012-0539-9.

Tramps Like Us. **Written and illustrated by Yayoi Ogawa.** TOKYOPOP, 2004– . **O Japanese manga.**

Sumire Iwaya is a strong and independent woman working in a man's world. After studying abroad in America, she returned to Japan to work at a local newspaper. Tired of all that she has to put up between her love life (or lack thereof) and work (where she's called "Sumire the Ice Princess") , one evening she takes a young homeless man into her apartment and nurses him back to health. After finding out the man has been living away from his own apartment because he is afraid that his gay landlord will hit on him again and that he has no money for the train, Sumire offers the young man a unique proposal: to be her pet! He agrees and she renames him "Momo" after a pet dog she once had. Now he's a loyal part of her life and all of Sumire's coworkers think is that she has a pet dog or cat. When Sumire starts dating again, can she handle having a human pet at home, ruining her love life? And is Sumire starting to fall for Momo—a "pet" who is a more ideal boyfriend than any of her other suitors? Twelve volumes were originally published in Japan and are being reprinted in North America.

> *Vol. 1.* 2004. 192pp. 1-59532-139-X.
> *Vol. 2.* 2004. 200pp. 1-59532-140-3.
> *Vol. 3.* 2004. 192pp. 1-59532-141-1.
> *Vol. 4.* 2005. 192pp. 1-59532-142-X.
> *Vol. 5.* 2005. 192pp. 1-59532-143-8.
> *Vol. 6.* 2005. 192pp. 1-59532-144-6.
> *Vol. 7.* 2005. 192pp. 1-59532-145-4.
> *Vol. 8.* 2006. 192pp. 1-59532-438-0.
> *Vol. 9.* 2006. 200pp. 1-59532-439-9.
> *Vol. 10.* 2006. 192pp. 1-59532-640-5.
> *Vol. 11.* 2007. 200pp. 1-59816-198-9.

Tricked. **Written and illustrated by Alex Robinson.** Top Shelf Productions, 2005. 352pp. 1-89183-073-2. **M** ◎

The dramatic lives of six people who all interconnect on one fateful and violent day: a reclusive rock star who has had writer's block for four years; an office temp who becomes more than a fling for the rock star; counterfeiter who has lost all his morals; a teenage runaway trying to better know her distant father; a waitress tired of dating jerks; and an obsessed fan who is slipping away from reality. In one brief moment at a restaurant their lives will forever change.

Violent Cases. **2d ed. Written by Neil Gaiman. Illustrated by Dave McKean.** Dark Horse Comics, 2002. 48pp. 1-56971-606-4. **O** ◎

A young man recounts his youth and recalls when he met Chicago mobster Al Capone's physician. With his aging mind not remembering events exactly, the story changes and fluctuates to show that truths can vary depending on time and one's personal point of view.

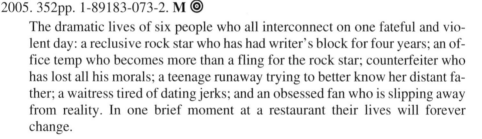

Visitations. **Written and illustrated by Scott Morse.** Oni Press, 1998. 96pp. 1-929998-34-1. **O**

A slice-of-life story set in a brownstone apartment complex in the Bronx. When an elderly woman goes to church to talk about her lack of faith, the priest tells her three random tales straight from the newspaper that help to prove that t God and faith still exist.

🎗 **The Waiting Place. Written by Sean Kelley McKeever. Illustrated by various.** Slave Labor Graphics/Amaze Ink, 2001–2003. **T** ◉

© 2006 Sean McKeever.

The story of a group of teens and one young adult trying to get by and get away from life in the mundane city of Northern Plains, USA. Jeffrey Dietz is a high school senior who has just moved with his parents from the big city. He's struggling to find his place in the world in a dead-end town with a new school and schoolmates, Lora, Jill, Scott, and Kyle. Together they seek friendship, companionship, love, and understanding while living in an empty town going nowhere. In 2005 Sean McKeever received an Eisner Award for Talent Deserving of Wider Recognition for his body of work, including this series.

Vol. 1. 2001. 152pp. 0-943151-36-8.
Vol. 2. 2002. 152pp. 0-943151-53-8.
Vol. 3. 2003. 160pp. 0-943151-76-7.

The Wallflower: Yamatonadeshiko Shichihenge. Written and illustrated by Tomoko Hayakawa. Del Rey Manga/Random House, 2004–2006. **O Japanese manga.**

High school student Sunako Nakahara seems like a lost cause—she could never be transformed from a social misfit into a Cinderella. With long black bangs dangling, she would rather spend her days watching horror movies and wearing the most unfashionable clothing possible while staying at her aunt's boarding house mansion. She'll need a miracle to become a whole new person. Her aunt has a solution to her niece's problem: she recruits four gorgeous, fashionable men and makes them an offer that sounds too easy to refuse. They must teach Sunako how to become a lady, keep her grades up, and have her start dating. In return the aunt will let them stay in her mansion rent-free for three years. Along the way to Sunako's transformation they encounter murder, possible rapists, impossible school classroom projects, gangs, and even a ghost. As the guys soon find out, this Herculean task to transform the socially inept niece keeps on getting worse and worse. The series was originally published in ten volumes in Japan.

Vol. 1. 2004. 216pp. 0-345-47912-2.
Vol. 2. 2004. 192pp. 0-345-47949-1.
Vol. 3. 2005. 224pp. 0-345-47999-8.
Vol. 4. 2005. 208pp. 0-345-48001-5.
Vol. 5. 2005. 192pp. 0-345-48094-5.
Vol. 6. 2005. 208pp. 0-34548-370-7.
Vol. 7. 2006. 208pp. 0-34548-371-5.
Vol. 8. 2006. 208pp. 0-34548-526-2.
Vol. 9. 2006. 208pp. 0-34548-527-0.
Vol. 10. 2006. 208pp. 0-34548-530-0.

X-Day. Written and illustrated by Setona Mizushiro. TOKYOPOP, 2003. **O Japanese manga.**

High school track star Rica has been sidelined, and to add insult to injury, her boyfriend just dumped her. Disgruntled and depressed, she meets online with several other disenfranchised students and forms a pact to blow up the school on a day when school is not in session. With the day fast approaching, will they continue with their plan, or has Rica found something worthwhile to make her want to stop it?

> *Vol. 1.* 2003. 200pp. 1-59182-379-X.
> *Vol. 2.* 2003. 200pp. 1-59182-380-3.

Social and Political Issues

Similar to the "problem novel" common in teen fiction, the focus of these stories is on contemporary issues that teens may struggle with, including rape, drug abuse, domestic issues, homelessness, and alcoholism. Although teens are the protagonists, adults may be featured as well. Typically the protagonist takes a strong stand to resolve the issue by the conclusion of the story.

The Bunker. **Written and illustrated by Bruce Mutard.** Image Comics, 2003. 90pp. 1-58240-296-5. **O**

Jason and Annie have been neighbors and friends for years, but time and maturity have brought on more complicated feelings, and their platonic teenage friendship may mean more to Jason. When Annie concocts the excuse of a ghost in her house to spend each night in Jason's room and sleep in his unused bunk bed, how can Jason say no to the girl he has a crush on? But as night after night of sleepovers pass, Annie's behavior tests and begins to destroy the very core of their odd relationship. When dark family secrets are revealed, not even the best-laid foundations of their friendship can survive.

Confidential Confessions. **Written and illustrated by Momochi Reiko.** TOKYOPOP, 2003–2005. **O Japanese manga.**

A hard-hitting anthology series in which each volume focuses on a hidden, embarrassing, and deadly situation that teens today find themselves in. Stories feature subjects such as teen sex, school bullies, HIV, suicide, sexual orientation, teen prostitution, rape, and sexual harassment.

> *Vol. 1.* 2003. 208pp. 1-59182-393-5.
> *Vol. 2.* 2003. 208pp. 1-59182-394-3.
> *Vol. 3.* 2003. 216pp. 1-59182-395-1.
> *Vol. 4.* 2004. 232pp. 1-59182-427-3.
> *Vol. 5.* 2004. 224pp. 1-59182-428-1 O
> *Vol. 6.* 2005. 224pp. 1-59532-165-9 O

Four Women. **Written and illustrated by Sam Kieth.** Homage Comics/ WildStorm Productions/DC Comics, 2002. 128pp. 1-56389-910-8. **O**

Four women en route to a wedding have car trouble and stop in an isolated area. They're accosted by two men with anything but help on their minds, and the women must decide what they can endure and do to survive. When it's all done, rape and murder have been committed, and a lasting friendship has been pushed to its ultimate limits.

♠ *The Tale of One Bad Rat.* **Written and illustrated by Bryan Talbot.** Dark Horse Comics, 1995. 136pp. 1-56971-077-5. **O** ◉

THE TALE OF
ONE BAD RAT

by
BRYAN TALBOT
DARK HORSE BOOKS

Entire contents of The Tale of One Bad Rat are copyright © 2002 Bryan Talbo. All prominent characters and their likenesses are trademarks of Bryan Talbot. All rights reserved.

A powerful tale of Helen Potter, a teenage runaway in London, who only has her collection of Beatrix Potter stories and her pet rat to keep her on the straight and narrow and prevent her from committing suicide. After running away from an uncaring mother and a sexually abusive father, she finds comfort in revisiting the places where Beatrix Potter once walked. Hiking to the hills of Lake District Historical Park, after time passes Helen finds the courage to confront her parents about their abuse. After the confrontation, Helen finds solace at Hill Top, the home of Beatrix Potter, and discovers that she and her favorite author have more in common than she realized. The title won an Eisner Award in 1996 for Best Graphic Novel: New. It also received recognition from YALSA's Popular Paperbacks for Young Adults committee in 1997.

Trailers. **Written and illustrated by Mark Kneece and Julie Collins-Rousseau.** NBM Publishing, 2005. 160pp. 1-56163-445-X. **O**

After teenager Josh Clayton's low-life, trailer-trash mother kills a man with a bat and has him dispose of the body, things go from bad to worse. Even after the body is buried, secrets are hard to keep down for too long, and soon everyone in the trailer park knows about the body. Guilty about what he has done and sickened by his sad devotion to his drug-addled mother, Josh descends further down a spiral of futility while trying to take care of his two younger brothers and sister. When Josh finds comfort with a cute girl named Michele, even though she doesn't come from the same walk of life, she must give him the strength he needs to confess his sins and confront his delinquent mother once and for all.

Sports

In these graphic novel tales sports play a central role in the story to hook the reader in. Often the sport itself serves to reinforce common values, including teamwork, working to one's full potential, and playing fair. The sport itself may also serve as a backdrop to teen-related issues such as relationships, friendship, and personal secrets.

Eyeshield 21. Written by Riichiro Inagaki. Illustrated by Yusuke Murata. VIZ Media, LLC, 2005– . **O Japanese manga.**

A look at the sport of football, Japanese-style! Sena Kobayakawa is a pencil-necked high school student just barely getting by, and being walked over by bullies. When he tries to make new friends, he reluctantly joins fellow student Kurita's American Football team (all two of them) and thinks he'll have no problem being the team's manager. When he is spotted running by the Hiruma, the team captain, he instantly gets bumped from the sidelines to the frontline. To protect his identity from rival schools and potential bullies, Sena wears a tinted eyeshield helmet so no one can see his face or know his identity. Can the "mysterious" Eyeshield 21 take the team to Japan's high school championships? The series was originally published in Japan in seventeen volumes.

Vol. 1. 2005. 208pp. 1-59116-752-3.
Vol. 2. 2005. 208pp. 1-59116-809-0.
Vol. 3. 2005. 200pp. 1-59116-874-0.
Vol. 4. 2005. 208pp. 1-4215-0074-4.
Vol. 5. 2005. 208pp. 1-4215-0113-9.
Vol. 6. 2006. 208pp. 1-4215-0274-7.
Vol. 7. 2006. 208pp. 1-4215-0405-7.
Vol. 8. 2006. 208pp. 1-4215-0637-8.
Vol. 9. 2006. 208pp. 1-4215-0638-6.
Vol. 10. 2006. 208pp. 1-4215-0639-4.
Vol. 11. 2006. 208pp. 1-4215-0640-8.

Girl Got Game. Written and illustrated by Shizuru Seino. TOKYOPOP, 2004–2005. T Japanese manga.

Teenager Kyo Aizawa has learned her father's love of the game of basketball, but thought it was all behind her. After she is accepted at the prestigious Seisyu High School, she's ready to wear the cute uniform of a female student. But when it turns out to be a boy's uniform, she finds out that her father, who had dreams of playing in the NBA until an injury ruined his career, had her enrolled as a boy so she could play on the very competitive basketball team. So now Aizawa is cutting her hair, wearing a strap around her chest, and living in the guys' dorm just so her dad can live his dream through her! Her roommate is Chiharu, who's also on the team but doesn't know that he's rooming with a girl. Their attitudes toward each other at first are hardly cordial. In fact, Chiharu is downright rude. But now Aizawa is playing basketball and being recognized as a great male athlete, and she's earning the respect and admiration—or is it love—of Chiharu both on and off the court. How long can this charade last before people find out her secret?

Vol. 1. 2004. 176pp. 1-59182-696-9.
Vol. 2. 2004. 192pp. 1-59182-697-7.
Vol. 3. 2004. 192pp. 1-59182-698-5.
Vol. 4. 2004. 200pp. 1-59182-699-3.
Vol. 5. 2004. 192pp. 1-59182-700-0.
Vol. 6. 2004. 176pp. 1-59182-701-9.
Vol. 7. 2005. 176pp. 1-59182-986-0.
Vol. 8. 2005. 192pp. 1-59182-987-9.
Vol. 9. 2005. 208pp. 1-59182-988-7.
Vol. 10. 2005. 192pp. 1-59182-989-5.

♣ Harlem Beat. Written and illustrated by Yuriko Nishiyama. TOKYOPOP, 1999–2002. Y Japanese manga.

Nate Torres was always the benchwarmer on his high school basketball team, and after blowing his school tryouts, the prospect of being a top-notch player is fading fast. When he discovers the no-holds-barred, back-alley game of half-court, Nate forms Team Scratch with Mizzy and Oz. Together they just might find the skills to take on the best basketball players and rekindle Nate's dream of playing on the high school team. *Volume 1* received recognition from YALSA's Popular Paperbacks for Young Adults committee in 2002 on the "Graphic Novels: Superheroes and Beyond" list.

Vol. 1. 1999. 200pp. 1-892213-04-4.
Vol. 2. 1999. 184pp. 1-892213-17-6.
Vol. 3. 2000. 184pp. 1-892213-23-0.
Vol. 4. 2000. 184pp. 1-892213-34-6.
Vol. 5. 2001. 192pp. 1-892213-38-9.
Vol. 6. 2001. 184pp. 1-892213-57-5.
Vol. 7. 2001. 184pp. 1-892213-58-3.
Vol. 8. 2001. 184pp. 1-931514-00-3.
Vol. 9. 2002. 184pp. 1-931514-01-1.

The Prince of Tennis. Written and illustrated by Takeshi Konomi. VIZ Media, LLC, 2004–. **Y Japanese manga.** あ

Ryoma Echizen, a freshman tennis player and four-time junior champion in the United States, has returned home to Japan and enrolled in the prestigious Seishun Gakuen Middle School. Allowing seventh graders to play on the varsity tennis squad has never been done before, but Ryoma knows he has the skills and the moves to prove he's one of the best. The popular sports series manga has been collected in more than thirty volumes in Japan and has inspired an anime spin-off as well as a live-action movie. The manga series was also adapted as a 178-episode anime series in Japan.

Vol. 1. 2004. 184pp. 1-59116-435-4.
Vol. 2. 2004. 200pp. 1-59116-436-2.
Vol. 3. 2004. 200pp. 1-59116-437-0.
Vol. 4. 2004. 200pp. 1-59116-438-9.
Vol. 5. 2004. 200pp. 1-59116-439-7.
Vol. 6. 2005. 200pp. 1-59116-440-0.
Vol. 7. 2005. 192pp. 1-59116-787-6.
Vol. 8. 2005. 184pp. 1-59116-853-8.
Vol. 9. 2005. 184pp. 1-59116-995-X.
Vol. 10. 2005. 184pp. 1-4215-0070-1.
Vol. 11. 2006. 176pp. 1-4215-0201-1.
Vol. 12. 2006. 208pp. 1-4215-0337-9.
Vol. 13. 2006. 208pp. 1-4215-0666-1.
Vol. 14. 2006. 208pp. 1-4215-0667-X.
Vol. 15. 2006. 208pp. 1-4215-0668-8.
Vol. 16. 2006. 208pp. 1-4215-0669-6.
Vol. 17. 2006. 208pp. 1-4215-0670-X.
Vol. 18. 2007. 208pp. 1-4215-1095-4.
Vol. 19. 2007. 208pp. 1-4215-1095-2.

Rebound. Written and illustrated by Yuriko Nishiyama. TOKYOPOP, 2003– . **T Japanese manga.**

Sequel to the hit manga series Harlem Beat. Nate Torres is now a member of the Johnan High School Varsity basketball team. Though he's second string, he and his team have set their sights on the ultimate prize: the National Basketball Championships pennant. Playing half-court as Team Scratch may have given Nate the skills to be a winner, but he'll need to step up to the plate and show the pros just what he has, or else Johnan High School will be eliminated in the fierce competition. Eighteen volumes were originally published in Japan.

Vol. 1. 2003. 192pp. 1-931514-02-X.
Vol. 2. 2003. 192pp. 1-59182-074-X.
Vol. 3. 2003. 192pp. 1-59182-221-1.
Vol. 4. 2003. 192pp. 1-59182-222-X.
Vol. 5. 2003. 208pp. 1-59182-223-8.
Vol. 6. 2004. 200pp. 1-59182-530-X.

Vol. 7. 2004. 200pp. 1-59182-531-8.
Vol. 8. 2004. 192pp. 1-59182-532-6.
Vol. 9. 2004. 192pp. 1-59182-533-4.
Vol. 10. 2004. 192pp. 1-59182-534-2.
Vol. 11. 2004. 200pp. 1-59182-535-0.
Vol. 12. 2005. 200pp. 1-59532-617-0.

Vol. 13. 2005. 192pp. 1-59532-618-9.
Vol. 14. 2005. 192pp. 1-59532-619-7.
Vol. 15. 2006. 192pp. 1-59532-620-0.

Shaolin Soccer. Written and illustrated by Andy Seto. ComicsOne, 2003. T 📽 Chinese manhua.

Sing, a fully trained Shaolin Temple graduate, is having a tough time in the real world trying to uphold his teachings to promote the philosophy and kung-fu training of Shaolin. Practically penniless, a chance encounter with a former soccer star gives Sing the idea and drive to promote his teachings through the world's most popular sport: soccer! Reuniting with his former brothers from the temple, he has formed a team that will break all the rules and show the world how kung fu can be a part of everyone's life through soccer. Based on the events from the hit movie of the same name.

Vol. 1. 2003. 128pp. 1-58899-318-3.
Vol. 2. 2003. 128pp. 1-58899-319-1.

Slam Dunk. Written and illustrated by Takehiko Inoue. Gutsoon! Entertainment, 2003–2004. T Japanese manga.

High school delinquent Sakuragi Hanamichi couldn't have cared less about the game of basketball, but when the girl of his dreams tells him that she's in love with the sport, he does the unthinkable and tries out for the team. After beating the captain in a one-on-one match, he's on the team, but he has a long way to go to become team captain and move up the ranks from benchwarmer. Will he ever learn the skills he needs, on and off the court, to win in the game of life?

Vol. 1. 2003. 190pp. 0-9725037-9-X.
Vol. 2. 2003. 190pp. 1-932454-04-7.
Vol. 3. 2003. 190pp. 1-932454-10-1.
Vol. 4. 2003. 190pp. 1-932454-16-0.
Vol. 5. 2004. 190pp. 1-932454-26-8.

Top Speed. **Written by Man Wai Cheung. Illustrated by Wai Kit Leung.** ComicsOne, 2004. **T Chinese manhua.**

When night falls over Hong Kong, the Pacific Road is ruled by the kings of speed. Fast cars, hot tempers, and high egos rule the night. When twenty-one-year-old taxicab driver Tian Ren nearly steals the scene one fateful night, all of the local street racers are out to beat this new devil behind the wheel. Little do they know that Tian is the son of a famous street racer who perished in a race years ago, and though he loathes the street racers who killed his father, he finds himself being pulled back into a world he wants nothing to do with.

  Vol. 1. 2004 208pp. 1-58899-402-3.
  Vol. 2. 2004 208pp. 1-58899-403-1.

Whistle! **Written and illustrated by Daisuke Higuchi.** VIZ Media, LLC, 2004–. **T Japanese manga.** あ

After being banned from his high school soccer team for being too short, teenager Sho Kazamatsuri still won't give up his dream of becoming a top-notch player, even after a few embarrassing mishaps. Now he and the other second-string soccer players at his new school will prove they have what it takes to be the best. A tale of David versus Goliath on the field of soccer! The manga also has an anime adaptation.

  Vol. 1. 2004. 208pp. 1-59116-685-3.
  Vol. 2. 2004. 208pp. 1-59116-686-1.
  Vol. 3. 2004. 208pp. 1-59116-692-6.
  Vol. 4. 2005. 200pp. 1-59116-727-2.
  Vol. 5. 2005. 208pp. 1-59116-789-2.
  Vol. 6. 2005. 200pp. 1-59116-836-8.
  Vol. 7. 2005. 200pp. 1-59116-973-9.
  Vol. 8. 2005. 208pp. 1-4215-0068-X.
  Vol. 9. 2006. 200pp. 1-4215-0206-2.
  Vol. 10. 2006. 208pp. 1-4215-0340-9.
  Vol. 11. 2006. 208pp. 1-4215-0685-8.
  Vol. 12. 2006. 208pp. 1-4215-0686-6.
  Vol. 13. 2006. 208pp. 1-4215-0687-4.
  Vol. 14. 2006. 208pp. 1-4215-0688-2.
  Vol. 15. 2006. 208pp. 1-4215-0689-0.
  Vol. 16. 2007. 208pp. 1-4215-1107-x.

Short Stories and Anthologies

A collection of general titles featuring a variety of works by many writers and illustrators. Highlights include the various 9/11 relief publications published in 2002. The anthology stories include tales of true love, adventure, humor, horror, and many other genres and showcase a wide variety of talent in the comic book industry.

Afterworks. **Written and illustrated by various.** Image Comics, 2006. **O**

An anthology title featuring a variety of writers and artists from PIXAR Studios and other animation companies. Based in Emeryville, California, the studio is called E-Ville Press and features a wide variety of works that will touch the soul and entertain your brain. The collections feature the work of Mark Andrews, Jason Boose, Jennifer Chang, Josh Cooley, Rob Gibbs, Louis Gonzales, Scott Morse, Bill Presing, Derek Thompson, Anthony Wong, and many others.

> *Vol. 1.* 2006. 152pp. 1-58240-626-X.
> *Vol. 2.* 2006. 200pp. 1-58240-627-8.

© 2006 E-Ville Press.

Comiculture Anthology. **Written and illustrated by various.** Comiculture Books/Mad Science Media, Inc., 2005. 92pp. 0-9749260-2-7. **T**

A collection of original short stories by the creators of *Comiculture* magazine. Tales include a werewolf story set in feudal Japan, the positives and negatives about dating a zombie, a fantasy adventure tale, sea monsters, geriatric crime-fighters, and much more.

🕯 **Drawn & Quarterly.** **Written and illustrated by various.** Drawn & Quarterly Publishing, 2002–2004. **T** ◎

An oversized anthology series by the Canadian publisher Drawn & Quarterly. The collection focuses on literary works from all genres for readers of comix and includes works from creators all across the world as well as reprints of classic comic strips. *Volume 3* was awarded an Eisner Award in 2001 for the category Best Anthology.

> *Vol. 3.* 2000. 176pp. 1-896597-30-0.
> *Vol. 4.* 2001. 160pp. 1-896597-40-8.
> *Vol. 5.* 2003. 192pp. 1-896597-61-0.

Flight. **Written and illustrated by various.** Image Comics, 2004–2005; Ballantine Books, 2006. **T** ◎

An anthology collection of short stories taking the reader to unique and creative settings, with imaginative characters brought to you by some of the comic book and animation industries' brightest talents, in a series edited by Kazu Kibuishi. The stories include the adventures of a boy and his dog building a kit plane, a flying whale courier service, a young man's sentimental journey back home to India, how two high school graduates find something in common while kite flying, and much more. A variety of subjects and themes are covered, including humor, sadness, adventure, inspired by the animated works and short stories of Hayao Miyazaki and Moebius. *Volumes 1* and *2* were published by Image Comics and *Volume 3* was published by Ballantine Books.

© 2006 Kazu Kibuishi.

    Vol. 1. Image Comics, 2004. 208pp. 1-58240-381-3.
    Vol. 2. Image Comics, 2005. 432pp. 1-58240-477-1.
    Vol. 3. Ballantine Books, 2006. 352pp. 0-345-49039-8.

***Friends of Lulu Presents: Broad Appeal.* Written and illustrated by various.** Friends of Lulu, 2003. 128pp. 0-9740960-1-6. **T**

A collection of works by women writers and artists to support the nonprofit organization "Friends of Lulu." The works cover a wide range of subjects, including mystery, fantasy, and humor, from such creators as Sara Varon, Rachel Hartman, and Donna Barr.

<u>**Komikwerks Presents.**</u> **Written and illustrated by various.** Komikwerks, LLC, 2003– . **T**

A continuing anthology series featuring a wide range of stories for young and old readers including funny animal, horror, humor, suspense, monsters, robots, and more. Features short stories by such creators as Keith Giffen, Dwayne McDuffie, Rick Parker, Tom Mandrake, and Cynthia Martin.

    Vol. 1. 2003. 120pp. 0-9742803-0-5.
    Vol. 2. 2003. 112pp. 0-9742803-1-3.
    Nuts and Bolts. 2004. 144pp. 0-9742803-2-1.
    Rockets and Robots. 2005. 160pp. 0-9742803-3-X.
    Thrills and Chills. 2005. 198pp. 0-9742803-4-8.

<u>**Monkeysuit.**</u> **Written and illustrated by Mike Foran, Ben Edlund, Bill Presing, and various.** Monkeysuit Press, 1999– . **O**

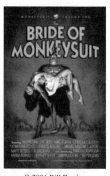

An anthology of artists from the New York City alternative comics and animation scene. The stories range from humor to action and everything in between, and include works by Mike Foran, Ben Edlund, Bill Presing, Mo Willems, and many others.

    Monkeysuit. 1999. 128pp. 0-9673289-0-X.
    Bride of Monkeysuit. 2000. 144pp. 0-9673289-2-6.
    Viva La Monkeysuit. 2001. 172pp. 0-9673289-3-4.
    In Search of Monkeysuit. 2003. 128pp. 0-9673289-8-5.
    Death Comes to Monkeysuit. 2005. 136pp. 0-9673289-9-3.

© 2006 Bill Presing.

<u>**More Fund Comics.**</u> **Written and illustrated by various.** Sky Dog Press, 2003–2004. **T**

An anthology series created for the Baltimore Comic-Con benefiting the Comic Book Legal Defense Fund. The collection features short stories, pin-ups, sketchbooks, and more from some of the best-known comic book creators today, including Frank Cho, Kurt Busiek, George Perez, Michael Avon Oeming, and many others. A follow-up was released in 2004 as *Even More Fund Comics*.

    More Fund Comics. 2003 192pp. 0-9721831-2-4.
    Even More Fund Comics. 2004. 192pp. 0-9721831-3-2.

9-11. Written and illustrated by various. Dark Horse Comics and DC Comics, 2002. **T**

© 2006 DC Comics.

A two-part anthology collection copublished by DC Comics and Dark Horse Comics, benefiting the American Red Cross. The stories range from personal accounts of the tragedy; to familiar comic book characters, including Death and Destruction from Neil Gaiman's <u>The Sandman;</u> to fictionalized stories of loss, suffering, pain, and ultimately of hope. *Volume 1* features works by Will Eisner, P. Craig Russell, Eric Powell, Kevin Nowlan, Paul Chadwick, Dave Gibbons, and many others. *Volume 2* features works by Neil Gaiman, Stan Lee, Will Eisner, Jill Thompson, Jim Lee, Sergio Aragones, and others.

> *Vol. 1: Artists Respond.* Dark Horse Comics. 192pp. 1-56389-881-0.
> *Vol. 2: The World's Finest Comic Writers and Artists Tell Stories to Remember.* DC Comics 224pp. 1-56389-878-0.

9-11: Emergency Relief. **Written and illustrated by various.** Alternative Press, 2002. 208pp. 1-891867-12-1. **T**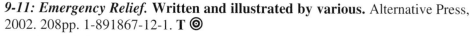

An anthology collection benefiting the American Red Cross. Features works by more than creators, including Jeff Smith, Frank Cho, James Kochalka, Will Eisner, Harvey Pekar, Jessica Abel, Mike Avon Oeming, and Scott Morse, telling fictional and true personal accounts of the tragic day in American history.

P. Craig Russell Library of Opera Adaptations. **Adapted by P. Craig Russell.** NBM Publishing, 2003–2004. **T**

© 2006 P. Craig Russell.

P. Craig Russell has always been a fan of opera and the classic stories of drama, love, betrayal, pathos, fantasy, and comedy that they're composed of. Featured herein are adaptations of some of opera's greatest musical works, translated into a comic book format.

> *Vol. 1: The Magic Flute.* 2003. 144pp. 1-56163-350-X.
> *Vol. 2: Parsifal, Ariane & Bluebeard, I Pigliacci, Songs by Mahler.* 2003. 128pp. 1-56163-372-0.
> *Vol. 3: Pelleas & Melisande, Salome, Ein Heldentraum, Cavalleria Rusticana.* 2004. 144pp. 1-56163-389-5.

Rising Stars of Manga. Written and illustrated by various. TOKYOPOP, 2003–2006. **T**

Features the winners of the biannual competition for fans to create their own manga. The grand prizewinner is awarded his or her own graphic novel series. The collections include stories from a whole range of writing styles, genres, and art styles, all with their own distinct manga style.

© 2006 TOKYOPOP.

> *Vol. 1.* 2003. 248pp. 1-59182-224-6.
> *Vol. 2.* 2003. 224pp. 1-59182-536-9.
> *Vol. 3.* 2004. 232pp. 1-59182-537-7.
> *Vol. 4.* 2004. 224pp. 1-59182-538-5.
> *Vol. 5.* 2005. 192pp. 1-59532-815-7.
> *Vol. 6.* 2006. 192pp. 1-59532-816-5.

Rumic World Trilogy. Written and illustrated by Rumiko Takahashi. VIZ Media, LLC, 1997. **T Japanese manga.**

A collection of short stories that helped pave the way for the creator of such hits as *Ranma ½, Maison Ikkoku,* and *InuYasha.* The stories feature the odd, eerie, and downright hilarious.

> *Vol. 1.* 1997. 192pp. 1-56931-126-9.
> *Vol. 2.* 1997. 216pp. 1-56931-194-3.
> *Vol. 3.* 1997. 192pp. 1-56931-206-0.

24 Hour Comics. Edited by Scott McCloud. Written and illustrated by various. About Comics 2004– . **T**

Most monthly twenty-four-page comic books take about a month to prepare. Acclaimed comic book historian Scott McCloud set up a challenge in 2004 to create a twenty-four-page comic book in twenty-four hours, now an annual event. From hundreds of entries each year, editor Scott McCloud has picked the best. Includes works by Neil Gaiman, Dave Sim, Sean McKeever, Paul Smith, and Josh Howard. For more information, check out http://www.24hourcomics.com.

> *24 Hour Comics.* 2004. 240pp. 0-9716338-4-3.
> *24 Hour Comics Day Highlights.* 2004. 496pp. 0-9753958-0-7.
> *24 Hour Comics All-Stars.* 2005. 240pp. 0-9753958-4-X.

24Seven. **Written and illustrated by various.** Image Comics, 2006. 200pp. 1-58240-636-7. **O**

An anthology collection featuring some of the best writers and artists in the industry, including Phil Hester, Adam Hughes, Jim Mahfood, Tony Moore, Mike Avon Oeming, Eduardo Risso, and many others. The stories run the gamut of genres: romance, horror, comedy, science fiction, and more.

Chapter 8

Humor

Consider the term "comic books." From its beginning, the comic book format has often featured comedy and humor. Though comic books can trace their origins back to the dawn of time, one of their closest forerunners, the comic strip, debuted in 1895 in newspapers with the first appearance of the comic strip cartoon character The Yellow Kid in Richard F. Outcault's strip called *Hogan's Alley*. The hit character was soon followed by the *Katzenjammer Kids* by Rudolph Dirks in 1897. Decades later, the very first comic book, *Funnies on Parade,* was published by the Eastern Color Printing Company, in 1933. It was a collection of reprinted comic strips and helped to launch the comic book in America. This chapter features a wide variety of graphic novels and trade collections with media tie-ins, including Walt Disney's Mickey Mouse, Uncle Scrooge, and Donald Duck; Matt Groening's The Simpsons and Futurama; comic strip collections published by comic book publishers, including *PVP, Liberty Meadows,* and Penny Arcade; black comedy titles including Judd Winick's Adventures of Barry Ween; classic comedy series collections including Archie; new comedy series, including Amelia Rules!; the classic works of Sergio Aragonés; and many more. Note that comedy plays some role in most other genres. Titles that are a genreblend of comedy and another genre are listed at the end of this chapter, including sections on romantic comedy, horror comedy, fantasy comedy, super-hero comedy, and more.

General Humor

These are stories of everyday life heavily interspersed with comedy. The plot lines typically border on the ridiculous, and the focus is on the absurdities of the protagonist's life and even on his or her surroundings, friends, and family. Included are reprints of classic comic books, stories featuring mostly young protagonists, and the tales typically tend to be appropriate for all ages. Included here are *Archie, Little Lulu*, as well as a variety of new titles from both the United States and Japan.

<u>Amelia Rules!</u> Written and illustrated by Jim Gownley. Renaissance Press, 2006. **A** ◎

© 2006 Jim Gownley.

After her parents' divorce, sarcastic and outspoken nine-year-old Amelia Louise McBride begins to adjust to a new life away from the hustle and bustle of Manhattan. She is settling into life in small-town America with her mom and her hip Aunt Tanner. She's starting at a new school and has formed a club with her three new quirky friends, Reggie, Rhonda, and Pajamaman, called G.AS.P. (Gathering of Awesome Superpals). Life sure is different in rural America when you're the only "normal" one and everyone around you is crazy.

> *Vol. 1: The Whole World's Crazy.* 2006. 176pp. 0-9712169-2-4, softcover; 0-9712169-3-2, hardcover.
> *Vol. 2: Whatever Makes You Happy.* 2006. 176pp. 0-9712169-4-0, softcover; 0-9712169-5-9, hardcover.
> *Vol. 3: Superheroes.* 2006. 176pp. 0-9712169-6-7, softcover; 0-9712169-7-5, hardcover.

<u>Archie.</u> Written and illustrated by various. Archie Comics Publications, 1991-2003. **A**
Archie Andrews, Betty Cooper, Veronica Lodge, Reggie Mantle, and Forsythe "Jughead" Jones and the rest of the gang at Riverdale High have been entertaining comic book readers ever since their first appearance in *Pep Comics* #22 in 1941. After sixty-five years, Archie still hasn't graduated from high school or decided whether he really loves Betty or Veronica the best, but Archie comics are as popular today as ever. Here you'll find highlights from the past decades as well as a collection featuring Betty and Veronica's summertime adventures through the years as they spend time on the beach relaxing while Archie and Reggie vie for their affection.

> *Archie Americana Series: Best of the Forties Book 1.* 1991. 128pp. 1-879794-00-4.
> *Archie Americana Series: Best of the Forties Book 2.* 2002. 96pp. 1-879794-09-8.
> *Archie Americana Series: Best of the Fifties Book 1.* 2002. 96pp. 1-879794-01-2.
> *Archie Americana Series: Best of the Fifties Book 2.* 2003. 96pp. 1-879794-15-2.
> *Archie Americana Series: Best of the Sixties.* 1995. 96pp. 1-879794-02-0.
> *Archie Americana Series: Best of the Seventies.* 1999. 96pp. 1-879794-05-5.
> *Archie Americana Series: Best of the Eighties.* 2001. 96pp. 1-879794-06-3.
> *Archie Classics: Betty and Veronica Summer Fun, Vol. 1.* 2003. 96pp. 1-879794-13-6.

Azumanga Daioh. **Written and illustrated by Kiyohiko Azuma.** ADV Manga, 2003–2004. **T ◎ Japanese manga.** あ

Chiyo-chan, Osaka, Tomo, Koyomi, Sakaki, Kaorin, and Kagura are a close group of high school gals from Japan suffering and succeeding in the rigors of school and beyond, from their sophomore year through graduation. From school sports, vacations, and pop quizzes, to cats who like to bite and more, the girls find true friendship as they try to survive dim-witted Miss Yukari's English class, learn to play sports with Yukari's rival Minamo, and ward off the lecherous advances of Mr. Kimura. The hit manga was adapted as an anime series.

> *Vol. 1.* 2003. 172pp. 1-4139-0000-3.
> *Vol. 2.* 2004. 172pp. 1-4139-0023-2.
> *Vol. 3.* 2004. 172pp. 1-4139-0030-5.
> *Vol. 4.* 2004. 206pp. 1-4139-0048-8.

The Baby-Sitters Club. **Written and illustrated by Raina Telgemeier.** Graphix/Scholastic Books, 2006. **Y**

When best friends Kristy, Mary, Anne, Claudia, and Stacey start up their own baby-sitting club, they have their hands full of dirty diapers and more. As best friends, they also have to deal with their own family lives, including keeping secrets, adjusting to a parent dating again following a divorce, and much more. Luckily they have each other to count on. Based on the best-selling series of novels for kids.

> *Vol. 1.* 2006. 192pp. 0-439-80241-5.
> *Vol. 2: The Truth about Stacy.* 2006. 144pp. 0-439-73936-5.

Bow Wow Wata. **Written and illustrated by Umekawa Kazumi. Gutsoon!** Entertainment, 2004. **T Japanese manga.**

Welcome to the Yashiro Animal Hospital, a place where animals can come in and tell the doctor what's bothering them. Lucky for them Dr. Yoshiro can talk to animals! Really a Shinto god in disguise, he has passed his gifts down to his son, Tasuke, who couldn't care less about this genetic ability. But when a beautiful woman named Funakoshi Misato comes into his life, he decides to adopt her pet dog Wata, and Tasuke finds that there are good and bad things about being able to talk to animals.

> *Vol. 1.* 2004. 192pp. 1-932454-18-7.
> *Vol. 2.* 2004. 200pp. 1-932454-29-2.

Brain Bomb: Comics and Creativity for Kids. **Written and illustrated by various.** Behemoth Books, 1999. 288pp. No ISBN. **A**

Designed to promote all-ages comics for students who are fans of drawing, *Brain Bomb* contains works by more than twenty-five comic book creators, including Scott Morse, Jay Hosler, and Chris Yambar. Short introductions by the creators are included as well as drawing tips and fun projects for students on how to create comic books, with sound effects, expressions, and more.

Chuck the Ugly American Book One: A Heck of an Adventure. **Written and illustrated by Mike Bocianowski.** Comic Library International, 2000. 128pp. 1-929515-10-3. **T**

Chuck hates everything. From his neighbors next door to life in Hell following a freak accident, he just hates it all. When Chuck unexpectedly falls in love with Persephone, the Queen of the Underworld, not even Hell, the devil, dragons, or a bomb can keep him from having a cranky day. Well, at least he's in love.

Comic Party. **Written and illustrated by various.** CPM Manga, 2004. **T Japanese manga.** あ

The annual doujinshi (fan-made manga) convention that draws thousands of manga-obsessed, self-published creators and fans is coming up soon. Can a fledgling group of crazy artists come up with their best ideas in time for the big show? And find out once and for all who's more insane: the creators, their manga, or the crazed manga fans they meet? Features actual doujinshi made by fans. The series was also adapted as an anime series in Japan.

Vol. 1: Party Time 2004 168pp. 1-58664-918-3.
Vol. 2: Another Round 2004 192pp. 1-59182-854-6.
Vol. 3: Last Time 2004 168pp. 1-58664-920-5.

Comic Party. **Written and illustrated by Sekihiko Inui.** TOKYOPOP, 2004–2006. **T Japanese manga.**

Inspired by the hit videogame and anime series from Japan. Kazuki Sendoh was just rejected by the art school of his choice. Determined not to fail as an artist, he has been introduced by his friend Taishi to the doujinshi exhibition of fan-made manga and finds his true calling in life: to be a manga artist! But Kazuki's girlfriend, Mizuki, may have some mixed feelings as he becomes more and more a manga otaku.

Vol. 1. 2004. 192pp. 1-59182-854-6.
Vol. 2. 2004. 176pp. 1-59182-855-4.
Vol. 3. 2004. 176pp. 1-59182-856-2.
Vol. 4. 2004. 192pp. 1-59532-584-0.
Vol. 5. 2006. 192pp. 1-59816-272-1.

Cosplay Koromo-Chan. **Written and illustrated by Mook.** ComicsOne, 2004. 160pp. 1-58899-321-3. **T Japanese manga.**

What happens when a cos-play (costume play) fan wears her costumes in public? The dress code at Koromo's high school has just gone casual, so now she's wearing her favorite manga and anime cos-play outfits to school, and she's turning a lot of heads and raising a lot of eyebrows, too. High school, college, and work will never be the same again!

Cromartie High School. **Written and illustrated by Eiji Nonaka.** ADV Manga, 2005– . **T** ◎ **Japanese manga.** あ

Takashi Kamiyama, a clean-cut, decent student with average grades, decides to enroll at the less-than-stellar Cromartie high school out of camaraderie with a friend. Cromartie has the worst reputation of all the high schools in Tokyo because of its low academic standards. When Takashi's friend turns out to be too stupid to even pass, Takashi finds himself a bookworm alone among an army of the toughest bullies, juvenile delinquents, and wild cards this side of Tokyo. Amazingly, he doesn't get killed by them, and he finds out that even the toughest guy has a soft side. The bullies are in awe of his ability to not get into a fight. With a growing cast of light-hearted, tough-guy students, including a robot named Mechazawa, a silent Freddie Mercury look-alike, a Mucha-Lucha wrestler, and a 400-pound gorilla, Takashi is going to have one strange experience getting an education at the toughest school in town. In Japan, the series was collected in thirteen volumes. The hilarious manga series was also adapted as a twenty-six-episode anime series.

> *Vol. 1.* 2005. 168pp. 1-4139-0257-X.
> *Vol. 2.* 2005. 208pp. 1-4139-0258-8.
> *Vol. 3.* 2005. 184pp. 1-4139-0259-6.
> *Vol. 4.* 2005. 168pp. 1-4139-0260-X.
> *Vol. 5.* 2006. 176pp. 1-4139-0261-8.
> *Vol. 6.* 2006. 176pp. 1-4139-0262-6.
> *Vol. 7.* 2006. 176pp. 1-4139-0263-4.
> *Vol. 8.* 2006. 176pp. 1-4139-0264-2.

50 Rules for Teenagers. **Written and illustrated by Na Ye-Ri.** ADV Manga, 2004– . **T Korean manhwa.**

All fifteen-year-old Mi-Roo wants is a normal life, but in her house she's the foundation that's supporting the family, with a father on the verge of losing his job; a slacker, pain-in-the-neck twin brother (who happens to have a very cute and crushworthy friend); and an overworked older sister who's a stressed-out manhwa artist. To top it off, Mi-Roo is baby-sitting her younger brother and doing all the shopping and errands while her mother is overseas. Mi-Roo's life is never easy, but her energetic and positive attitude helps to get her through each day, as long as her twin doesn't get in her way.

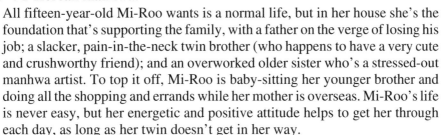

> *Vol. 1.* 2004. 200pp. 1-4139-0067-4.
> *Vol. 2.* 2005. 200pp. 1-4139-0094-1.

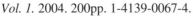

Gals! **Written and illustrated by Fujii Mihona.** CMX/DC Comics, 2005– . **T Japanese manga.** あ

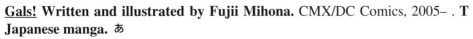

Tough girl Kotobuki Ran is a sixteen-year-old freshman whose keen fashion sense doesn't get in the way of any opportunity to get into a fight. Like most kogal girls (girls who like to shop and spend money on the latest material goods), Ran likes hanging out with her friends, trying on the latest fashions in the Shibuya shopping district of Tokyo, and even scamming guys young and old into buying her clothes, food, and more. Being the middle child of a family made up of police officers certainly has its benefits. She's learned to take care of herself and to make sure no one messes with her! Because of her no-nonsense attitude to bad people, she has to constantly fend off thugs, street gang members, creepy stalker boyfriends, vixen kogal rivals, and other bad guys both at school and while out shopping. Shibuya will be safe for shopping if Ran and her friends have anything to say about it! The ten-volume series was also adapted as an anime series in Japan.

> *Vol. 1.* 2005. 208pp. 1-4012-0550-X.
> *Vol. 2.* 2005. 192pp. 1-4012-0551-8.

Vol. 3. 2005. 192pp. 1-4012-0552-6.
Vol. 4. 2005. 192pp. 1-4012-0553-4.
Vol. 5. 2006. 192pp. 1-4012-0554-2.
Vol. 6. 2006. 192pp. 1-4012-0844-4.
Vol. 7. 2006. 192pp. 1-4012-0845-2.
Vol. 8. 2006. 176pp. 1-4012-0846-0.

Genshiken. Written and illustrated by Kio Shimoku. Del Rey Manga/Random House, 2005–2006. **T ⓒ Japanese manga.** あ

A tongue-in-cheek look at the world of otaku fandom. A group of fellow otaku at school have their own club called the Society for the Study of Modern Visual Culture. A new membership drive is underway, and new members are welcomed into the club, including Kanji Sasahara and Saki Kasukabe. Kanji has been a fanboy and has eagerly awaited being a part of the club, while Saki is a different beast all together. A surprisingly normal girl, she wanted her boyfriend, Kousaka, to stop watching anime and reading manga. So how the heck did she end up in a club with what she despises? Could it be she's starting to become an otaku, too? A fun look at all the stereotypes of otaku and the otaku lifestyle. The series was also adapted as an anime series in Japan.

Vol. 1. 2005. 192pp. 0-345-48169-0.
Vol. 2. 2005. 192pp. 0-345-48170-4.
Vol. 3. 2005. 176pp. 0-345-48171-2.
Vol. 4. 2006. 192pp. 0-345-48242-5.
Vol. 5. 2006. 208pp. 0-345-49153-X.
Vol. 6. 2006. 208pp. 0-345-49154-8.
Vol. 7. 2006. 208pp. 0-345-49155-6.

***Gordon Yamamoto and the King of the Geeks.* Written and illustrated by Gene Yang.** Slave Labor Graphics/Humble Comics, 2004. 104pp. 0-943151-95-3. **T**

Gordon, the big bully at school has, a small problem: he has a tiny UFO lodged in his left nostril! Now he needs the help of Miles, the latest "king" geek he has just crowned. The tiny aliens collect information on humans to help save and aid humanity, and they store it in certain humans, including Gordon and Miles. When Miles connects his nose to Gordon's with a VCR cable to transfer the information for the aliens, some of their memories get mixed up in the file-sharing! How in the world can big bully Gordon get Miles's memories out of him?

Grickle. Written and illustrated by Graham Annable. Alternative Comics, 2001–2003. **T**

The quirky, mundane, melancholy, and hilarious combine in short vignettes by Graham Annable. Drawn in a simple style, the characters emote sadness, regret, fear, infatuation, love, and more wrapped up in rich, dark humor.

Grickle. 2001. 128pp. 1-891867-01-6.
Further Grickle. 2003. 128pp. 1-891867-55-5.

© 2006 Graham Annable.

Halo and Sprocket: Welcome to Humanity. **Written and illustrated by Kerry Callen.** Slave Labor Graphics/Amaze Ink, 2003. 128pp. 0-943151-81-3. **T**

© 2006 Kerry Callen.

What happens when an angel from Heaven, a robot learning the ropes of humanity, and a young single woman share a house? Anything! In these humorous vignettes, Halo and Sprocket try to understand the everyday quirks of humanity, and Katie, with a good spoonful of humor, tries her best to live in a home with the strangest of roommates. From learning whether the glass is really half-empty or half-full, how to pronounce Halo's real name, who really killed the dinosaurs and what's missing from the statues of them, and what constitutes art, to the age-old question of whether cats are really highly intelligent (but aloof) or just plain stupid, the most unlikely trio of friends are out to learn more about the strange world around them as well as about themselves.

Hands Off! **Written and illustrated by Kasane Katsumoto.** TOKYOPOP, 2004– . **T Japanese manga.**

Effeminate fifteen-year-old Kotarou Oohira has always had an unusual type of ESP that is transferred by personal contact. He's always thought this strange power was normal in everyone. Years ago, when they were young, Kotarou accidentally gave his cousin Tatsuki the "gift" to see into the past, and to this day Tatsuki has never forgiven Kotarou. Years later, Kotarou has moved in with his grandpa in Tokyo and discovers that Tatsuki lives there as well. Along with their friend Yuuto, a boy with the power to see auras in people, they help the people in the community deal with odd occurrences and kidnappings. Both Tatsuki and Yuuto recognize that Kotarou is an ESP battery that supercharges their powers. Unfortunately physical contact—skin to skin—is needed to enhance their abilities. Oddly, Kotarou has no idea he has this power. He's just freaked out that his two friends like to touch him! Can they save the day from a variety of crimes and ESPers without freaking Kotarou out?

> *Vol. 1.* 2004. 192pp. 1-59532-153-5.
> *Vol. 2.* 2005. 184pp. 1-59532-154-3.
> *Vol. 3.* 2005. 176pp. 1-59532-155-1.
> *Vol. 4.* 2005. 192pp. 1-59532-156-X.
> *Vol. 5.* 2006. 192pp. 1-59532-157-8.
> *Vol. 6.* 2006. 192pp. 1-59532-158-6.
> *Vol. 7.* 2006. 192pp. 1-59532-159-4.

 8

Happy Lesson. **Written by Mutsumi Sasaki. Illustrated by Shinnosuke Mori.** ADV Manga, 2004. 170pp. 1-4139-0021-6. **O Japanese manga.**

Orphan Susumu Arisaka is eighteen years old and can now move back into his family home. But five comely teachers of his have unexpectedly moved in as well to help him out. For Susumu this can be a very good thing or a very bad thing, and with five ladies around the house, they're sure to show him a thing or two about life and love.

Hickee. **Written and illustrated by Paul Brown, Graham Annable, Joe White, Nathan Stapley, Razmig Mavlian, Marc Overney, Scott Campbell, Vamberto Maduro, Derek Sakai, and David Bogan.** Alternative Comics, 2003. 128pp. 1-891867-42-3. **T**

> Anthology of alternative comics created by a coffeehouse klatch of animators from the San Diego area. The styles and stories vary from the humorous to the mundane, but never suffer in creativity.

Iron Wok Jan. Written by Shinji Saijyo. Illustrated by ComicsOne and DR Publishing, 2002– . **T ◎ Japanese manga.**

> At Gobancho, the best Chinese restaurant in all of Tokyo, master chefs are wowing customers with their signature dishes and succulent masterpieces, and Kiriko Gobancho, granddaughter of the owner, is their most talented chef. When the arrogant but super-talented chef Jan Akiyama, grandson of Grandfather Gobancho's only real rival, is hired at Gobancho, Kiriko and Jan instantly become competitors, and the fried rice flies. As they try to outdo each other with their soy sauce skills and prove who's the better prodigy in cooking competitions, Kiriko is determined to show Jan that even though he's talented and arrogant, she can talk the talk and wok the wok. More than twenty-seven volumes of the hit manga series have been published in Japan.

> > *Vol. 1.* 2002. 190pp. 1-58899-256-X.
> > *Vol. 2.* 2002. 196pp. 1-58899-257-8.
> > *Vol. 3.* 2003. 200pp. 1-58899-258-6.
> > *Vol. 4.* 2003. 200pp. 1-58899-259-4.
> > *Vol. 5.* 2003. 200pp. 1-58899-260-8.
> > *Vol. 6.* 2003. 200pp. 1-58899-261-6.
> > *Vol. 7.* 2004. 200pp. 1-58899-262-4.
> > *Vol. 8.* 2004. 200pp. 1-58899-263-2.
> > *Vol. 9.* 2004. 200pp. 1-58899-264-0.
> > *Vol. 10.* 2004. 200pp. 1-58899-000-1.
> > *Vol. 11.* 2005. 200pp. 1-58899-303-5.
> > *Vol. 12.* 2005. 208pp. 1-58899-303-5.
> > *Vol. 13.* 2005. 200pp. 1-58899-309-4.
> > *Vol. 14.* 2005. 208pp. 1-59796-032-2.
> > *Vol. 15.* 2005. 208pp. 1-59796-033-0.
> > *Vol. 16.* 2005. 200pp. 1-58899-034-9.
> > *Vol. 17.* 2006. 200pp. 1-58899-035-7.
> > *Vol. 18.* 2006. 200pp. 1-58899-036-5.
> > *Vol. 19.* 2006. 200pp. 1-58899-037-3.
> > *Vol. 20.* 2006. 200pp. 1-58899-038-1.
> > *Vol. 21.* 2006. 200pp. 1-59796-039-X.
> > *Vol. 22.* 2006. 200pp. 1-59796-040-3.

Jetcat Clubhouse. **Written and illustrated by Jay Stephens.** Oni Press, 2002. 104pp. 1-929998-30-9. **A**

> Melanie, an elementary school-age girl, has a secret identity: she's the super-hero called JetCat, and she has her very own secret club! The other members of the Two Fisted Five are Tutenstein, a mummy/Frankenstein monster trying to adjust to modern life; Oddette, a rich punk girl who's out to be the coolest/strangest girl around; Teen Idol; and Ploppy, a space monkey with the urge to always go to the bathroom! To-

gether they're out to save the day from JetCat's arch-nemesis, the evil scientist Bela Kiss.

Kodocha: Sana's Stage. Written and illustrated by Miho Obana. TOKYOPOP, 2002–2003. **T Japanese manga.** あ

Eleven-year-old child star Sana Kurata is a very strong-willed girl and has an unusual life much different than that of most sixth-graders. She's been an actress since she was very young and is currently starring in a hit television show in Japan, *Kodomo No Omocha* (*Child's Toy*). She lives with her mother, an award-winning author (with a squirrel living in her hair), and Rei, her manager (on whom she has a crush). At school, there's trouble coming her way in the form of school bully Akito Hayama (dubbed "the Demon Child") and his gang. He's a terror to the whole school, and Sana decides to take matters into her own hands and straighten him out. After she gets to know him better, she finds that she really has a lot more in common with him than she would have ever thought. Could this really be true love? A humorous and touching look at the daily life of a child television star and all the ups and downs that go with it. The series was also adapted as an anime series in Japan.

> *Vol. 1.* 2002. 200pp. 1-931514-50-X.
> *Vol. 2.* 2002. 200pp. 1-931514-51-8.
> *Vol. 3.* 2002. 200pp. 1-931514-52-6.
> *Vol. 4.* 2002. 200pp. 1-931514-53-4.
> *Vol. 5.* 2003. 200pp. 1-59182-089-8.
> *Vol. 6.* 2003. 200pp. 1-59182-182-7.
> *Vol. 7.* 2003. 184pp. 1-59182-183-5.
> *Vol. 8.* 2003. 192pp. 1-59182-184-3.
> *Vol. 9.* 2003. 208pp. 1-59182-185-1.
> *Vol. 10.* 2003. 192pp. 1-59182-186-X.

Land of Nod. Written and illustrated by Jay Stephens. Dark Horse Comics and Oni Press, 1999–2001. **A**

The collected works of Jay Stephens, featuring an odd assortment of characters, short stories, and silly situations. *The Land of Nod Rockabye Book* features stories of JetCat as she tries to defeat the JetCat Haters Club. Help is on the way in the form of Space Ape Number Eight. *Land of Nod Treasury* includes characters such as Merv, Dave, mini-yetis, Jumbo Head, Coxwell the Badly Drawn Ghost, and more from the dreamland of Nod having offbeat adventures.

> *Land of Nod Rockabye Book.* Dark Horse Comics, 1999. 176pp. 1-56971-356-1.
> *Land of Nod Treasury.* Oni Press, 2001. 128pp. 1-929998-13-9.

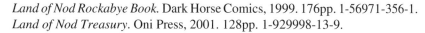

Little Lit. Edited by Art Spiegelman and Françoise Mouly. Written and illustrated by Art Spiegelman and various. Joanna Cotler Books/HarperCollins Children's Book Group, 2000–2003. **Y**

© 2006 RAW Junior LLC.

Geared for kids of all ages, the Little Lit anthology series created by Art Spiegelman and Françoise Mouly features a central theme and boasts a strong creative contribution by some of the comic book and prose book industries' best artists, as well as classic comic book tales from yesteryear. *Volume 1*'s theme of fairy tales features works by Spiegelman, Walt Kelly, Dan Clowes, Harry Bliss, and others. *Volume 2*'s theme of strange stories boasts work by Maurice Sendak, David Sedaris, Martin Handford, Paul Auster, Crockett Johnson, Spiegelman, and others. *Volumes 3*'s theme of darkly delightful stories to tell by candlelight, beginning with the opening line, "It was a dark and stormy night," includes works by Neil Gaiman and Gahan Wilson, Lemony Snickett, William Joyce, J. Otto Siebold, Spiegelman, and others.

> *Vol. 1: Folklore & Fairy Tale Funnies.* 2000. 64pp. 0-06-028624-5.
> *Vol. 2: Strange Stories for Strange Kids.* 2001. 64pp. 0-06-028626-1.
> *Vol. 3: It Was a Dark and Silly Night . . . .* 2003. 48pp. 0-06-028628-8.

Little Lulu. Written by John Stanley. Illustrated by Irving Tripp. Dark Horse Comics, 2004– . **A** ◉

Reprinted for the first time in a collected format, these are the humorous adventures of Little Lulu, the sassiest girl on the block and one of the most beloved comic book heroines ever. Hailed as one of the best all-ages series of comic book stories, these stories are once again available in an inexpensive format through Dark Horse Comics, which has been reprinting the classic tales that originally appeared starting in 1942.

> *Vol. 1: My Dinner with Lulu.* 2005. 200pp. 1-59307-318-6.
> *Vol. 2: Sunday Afternoon.* 2005. 208pp. 1-59307-345-3.
> *Vol. 3: In the Doghouse.* 2005. 208pp. 1-59307-345-3.
> *Vol. 4: Lulu Goes Shopping.* 2004. 200pp. 1-59307-270-8.
> *Vol. 5: Lulu Takes a Trip.* 2005. 200pp. 1-59307-317-8.
> *Vol. 6: Letters to Santa.* 2005. 200pp. 1-59307-386-0.
> *Vol. 7: Lulu's Umbrella Service.* 2005. 200pp. 1-59307-399-2.
> *Vol. 8: Late for School.* 2006. 200pp. 1-59307-453-0.
> *Vol. 9: Lucky Lulu.* 2006. 232pp. 1-59307-471-9.
> *Vol. 10: All Dressed Up.* 2006. 200pp. 1-59307-534-0.
> *Vol. 11: April Fools.* 2006. 200pp. 1-59307-557-X.
> *Vol. 12: Leave It to Lulu.* 2006. 208pp. 1-59307-620-7.
> *Vol. 13: Too Much Fun.* 2006. 200pp. 1-59307-621-5.
> *Vol. 14: Queen Lulu.* 2007. 240pp. 1-59307-683-5.
> *Color Special.* 2006. 208pp. 1-59307-613-4.

***Loyola Chin and the San Peligran Order.* Written and illustrated by Gene Yang.** Amaze Ink/Slave Labor Graphics, 2004. 104pp. 1-59362-005-5. **T**

A companion to the graphic novel *Gordon Yamamoto and the King of the Geeks*. A high school sophomore named Loyola Chin discovers that she's able to travel to different dimensions depending on what food she eats the night before. The more unique the food combination, the weirder the realm she visits. One such dimension leads her to encounter a mysterious man called Saint Danger. A man who has lost his faith, he has a grand plan for huhumanity, and Loyola must find true faith to overcome his plan to destroy 10 percent of the population to restore balance to the world.

Maniac Road. **Written and illustrated by Shinsuke Kurihashi.** Dr Master Publishing, 2004–2005. **T Japanese manga.**

In the backstreets of Akihabara, the electronics shopping capital of Japan, the run-down Ijima Electronics and Appliance store is destined to go out of business. Run by three sisters, the small store needs something new and fresh to attract customers. When they meet the eccentric Takezou, he has the perfect plan to save the store: make it an otaku paradise. Soon the girls are dressing up in cos-play outfits and money is starting to pour in. The girls meet for the first time the eccentric and overenthusiastic fans of anime, manga, and toy collectors as they try to sell their own manga, role-playing games, video games, and more. A hilarious look at the world of otaku.

> *Vol. 1.* 2004. 200pp. 1-58899-012-5.
> *Vol. 2.* 2004. 200pp. 1-58899-014-1.
> *Vol. 3.* 2005. 200pp. 1-58899-015-X.

Mister O. **Written and illustrated by Lewis Trondheim.** NBM, 2004. 32pp. 1-56163-382-8. **Y**

The silently told humorous attempts by Mister O, a round circle with stick arms and legs, to make it across a gorge. He tries jumping, pole-vaulting, flying an airplane, tossing rocks, and stealing some passerby's inventions, but he always fails spectacularly. Will he ever make it across and find out what lies on the other side?

Oddville. **Written and illustrated by Jay Stephens.** Oni Press, 2002. 88pp. 1-929998-25-2. **T**

In the town of Oddville, the extraordinary is the ordinary as the city is visited by a flying baby alien and the town develops a love–hate relationship with it. On the one hand it would like to cuddle the baby, since its cute, but on the other hand it's a stinky-diaper alien from outer space! What's a town to do? Also contains short-story adventures featuring the first appearance of Jetcat and the adventures of King Tutenstein.

One Pound Gospel. **Written and illustrated by Rumiko Takahashi.** VIZ Media, LLC, 1999. **T Japanese manga.**

Kosaku Hatanaka was the pride of the Mukaida Gym, but he always had a craving for foods and a voracious appetite. The more he ate, the more weight he'd gain, and the higher weight class he would have to enter. His coach is frustrated by Kosaku's weight gain, and a savior has come from one of the most unlikely sources: the convent! Sister Angelica, a novice nun, has taken it upon herself to cure Kosaku of his gluttony. Can she get him into shape and ignore the feelings they're starting to have for each other?

Vol. 1. 1999. 240pp. 1-56931-131-5.
Vol. 2: Hungry for Victory. 1999. 224pp. 1-56931-188-9.
Vol. 3: Knuckle Sandwich. 1999. 208pp. 1-56931-260-5.

Patty Cake & Friends. **Written and illustrated by Scott Roberts.** Amaze Ink/ Slave Labor Graphics, 2001–2003. **Y**

Follow the humorous daily life adventures of seven-year-old Patty Bakerman as she goes through all the fun, calamity, and touching moments of being a kid. A spunky all-American preteen living with her parents and older sister, she's learning about life, making friends (and rivals, too), and experiencing all the funs things we did as kids, such as playing games, school plays, meeting the new baby-sitter, singing songs, watching movies, and becoming engrossed in popular culture.

Vol. 1: Sugar and Spice. Mostly Spice. 2001. 112pp. 0-943151-44-9.
Vol. 2: And Everything Nice. 2001. 112pp. 0-943151-49-X.
Vol. 3: Love Is All Around. 2003. 112pp. 0-943151-69-4.

Peach Fuzz. **Written and illustrated by Lindsay Cibos and Jared Hodges.** TOKYOPOP, 2005. **A Neo-manga.**

Amanda Keller is a fourth-grader who has always wanted a pet. Her workaholic mom reluctantly agrees to let her pick an animal of her choice as long as Amanda promises to take care of it and that it never bites her. Of all the creatures in the pet shop, Amanda picks out a sleepy-looking ferret that she names Peach. Now the family of two has become a family of three and it's hard to tell who's in charge, especially since Peach likes to nibble on Amanda's fingers, which Peach thinks are "monsters." Will Amanda be able to keep Peach, and will their house ever be the same again?

Vol. 1. 2005. 160pp. 1-59532-599-9.

President Dad. **Written and illustrated by Ju-Yeon Rhim.** TOKYOPOP, 2004– . **Y Korean manhwa.**

Freshman Ami Won has never had many social graces. She's always been clumsy and sheltered, but her late mother always knew that her daughter would be a person of great distinction. Now it looks like her time has come: her dad, Won Ho-Chan, has just become the president of Korea. Now the First Lady in the eyes of many since her mother is gone, she arouses jealousy in her aunt Bi-Na. Struggling with the pressures of school and her scheming aunt and cousin, can Ami cope with the responsibilities of being a First Lady?

Vol. 1. 2004. 192pp. 1-59532-234-5.
Vol. 2. 2005. 192pp. 1-59532-235-3.
Vol. 3. 2005. 184pp. 1-59532-236-1.
Vol. 4. 2005. 192pp. 1-59532-237-X.
Vol. 5. 2006. 208pp. 1-59532-238-8.
Vol. 6. 2006. 192pp. 1-59532-658-8.

Queen Bee. **Written and illustrated by Chynna Clugston.** Graphix/Scholastic Books, 2005– . **Y**

© 2006 Chynna Clugston.

Haley Madison has had it tough trying to fit in at middle school. Like most kids her age she's a little awkward, but to top it off she has psychic powers! Gifted with the power of psychokinesis—the power to move objects with her mind—she has always embarrassed herself with her powers in school. When her mom gets a job working for a top teen magazine, Haley has to relocate to John F. Kennedy Intermediate School and she couldn't be more thrilled with a fresh chance to make it big in school. Haley quickly makes friends with the good girls in school, but she wants to be in with the popular crowd. Popular in no time, Haley soon finds she has a rival in Alexa Harmon—a new transfer student who has the same psychic powers as Haley! Can the school survive when the battle to be the most popular girl in school kicks in and the psychic powers fly? This is the first of many volumes in the series to be published through Scholastic Book's Graphix imprint. The graphic novel received recognition from YALSA's Quick Picks for Reluctant Readers committee for the 2006 list.

Vol. 1. 2005. 112pp. 0-439-70987-3.

The Rabbi's Cat. **Written and illustrated by Joann Sfar.** Pantheon Press/Random House, 2005. 152pp. **O** ◎

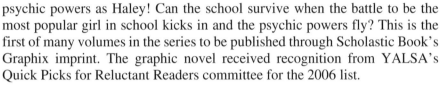

Set in the 1930s, the story focuses on a rabbi, his beautiful daughter Zlabya, and their talking cat. After gaining the ability to speak after eating the family parrot, the cat begins to tell lies, and the rabbi decides to teach the cat the ways of the Torah, but can a cat become Jewish? When Zlabya falls in love with a young rabbi from France, soon the master and his cat journey to Paris to meet the in-laws, who admit feeling jealous about losing their beloved Zlabya to a dashing young man. As the master and cat experience one adventure after another, they always have a chance to philosophize and discuss the important and trivial issues in life. A tender and humorous look at a most unique pet. The story won an Eisner award in 2006 for Best U.S. Edition of Foreign Material.

Ralph Snart Adventures. **Written and illustrated by Marc Hansen.** NOW Comics, 2003–2004. **T**

The insane comic adventures inside the head of a mild-mannered accountant who has gone completely wacko. When the evil Dr. Goot has captured Ralph for his powerful brain, Ralph escapes from his own realities into a world created by his imagination. It's a bizarre world where he spends his days drinking beer, hanging out with friends, drinking more beer, and going completely insane. A cult classic comic book that originally appeared in 1986.

Vol. 1: Let's Get Naked. 2003. 430pp. 0-9745205-1-9.
Vol. 2: Let's Be Good Citizens! 2004. 432pp. 0-9745205-7-8.

***Scatterbrain*. Written and illustrated by various.** Dark Horse Comics, 2001. 128pp. 1-56971-426-6. **O**

A collection of work by a variety of multitalented comic book and children's book writers and artists, including Mike Mignola, Sergio Aragonés, Killian Plunkett, Evan Dorkin, Jay Stephens, Scott Morse, James Kochalka, Craig Thompson, and others. Stories range from the humorous, to the silly, to the odd. Highlights of the collection include Mike Mignola's "Abu Gung and the Beanstalk" and "Fisher Price Theatre Presents: George Orwell's 1984," by Evan Dorkin and Sarah Dyer.

🏵 Sock Monkey. Written and illustrated by Tony Millionaire. Dark Horse Comics, 2000–2004. **T** ◉

The oddly endearing but unsettling adventures of a mischievous sock monkey called Uncle Gabby and his pal, a clumsy stuffed bird called Drinky Crow. Home alone among the various toys, the two stuffed animals discover adventures galore, sometimes with disastrous results for the chandelier, as they try to return a shrunken head to its home, burn down the house, and much more. The series won several Eisner Awards, including Talent Deserving of Wider Recognition (2000) and Best Humor Publication (2001), and creator Tony Millionaire received recognition as Best Writer/Artist: Humor (2001) for his work as well as a Harvey Award in 2004 for Special Award for Humor.

> *The Adventures of Tony Millionaire's Sock Monkey.* 2000. 96pp. 1-56971-490-8.
> *The Glass Door Knob.* 2002. 40pp. 1-56971-782-6.
> *Collected Works of Tony Millionaire's Sock Monkey.* 2004. 88pp. 1-59307-098-5.

Weird Melvin. Written and illustrated by Marc Hansen. NOW Comics, 2004. **O**

The adventures of a comic book-collecting kid and his über-muscled, monster-pummeling hero. The Kid has lived his whole life in fear of the vicious monsters under his bed. When he purchases a strange comic book about the exploits of a monster hunter called Weird Melvin, the Kid begins to idolize the hero with no fear of monsters. One night after the Kid reads the comic book adventures of Weird Melvin, he notices that life seems to be imitating the story in the comic books and soon discovers that reality and the comic book world have mixed and Weird Melvin is very real. Now his personal buddy, the hero Weird Melvin, is sealed inside the mint-condition covers of his comic book, ready to be released and pummel monsters until their skulls split open to save the Kid from any harm and to beat the living crap out of them. A humorous spoof on the comic book industry as well as a tribute to the classic monster comic books of the 1950s.

> *Vol. I: Origin Tales and Head-On Collisions.* 2004. 126pp. 0-9745205-3-5
> *Vol. II.* 2004. 128pp. 0-9745205-2-7.

***Where's It at, Sugar Kat? Vol. 1: The Thin of the Land*. Written by Ian Carney. Illustrated by Woodrow Phoenix.** Slave Labor Graphics/Amaze Ink, 2002. 120pp. 0-943151-56-2. **T**

Sugar and Rebecca Kat are fraternal twin sisters and co-owners of the Kat and Kat Detective Agency in Bumrush, Pennsylvania. They specialize in occult mysteries. Rebecca is the brains of the outfit, while Sugar is a super-model who's one of the most popular girls in the world, with her own clothing and action figure line. Together they're trying to solve mysteries involving missing hobos, overweight flatulating vampires, and more spooky things that go bump in the night. How can Sugar and Rebecca work as a team fighting vampires when they can't even stand each other?

WJHC. Written and illustrated by Jane Smith Fisher. Wilson Place Comics, Inc. 2003– . Y

After years of hearing boring school announcements through a PA system, Janey Wells, a headstrong student at Jackson Hill High, gets the idea to have the students run their very own radio station. With help from some of her best friends, including Ciel, Roland, Sandy, a boy called "The Skate," and even her rival, Tara, WJHC is born. Though things are a little shaky at first, the group proves that they have what it takes to run a radio station. And maybe Tara isn't so bad after all. Maybe. Join them as they continue their fun school adventures both on and off the air.

© 2006 Jane Smith Fisher.

Vol. 1: On the Air. 2003. 96pp. 0-9744235-0-5.
Vol. 2: Hold Tight! 2005. 96pp. 0-9744235-1-3.

Yotsuba&! Written and illustrated by Kiyohiko Azuma. ADV Manga, 2005– . Y ◉ Japanese manga.

These are the charming exploits of an innocent but odd four-year-old girl named Yotsuba and how she naively reacts to the world around her. Yotsuba and her adoptive father have just moved into a new neighborhood in Japan, but is the neighborhood really ready for Yotsuba? After settling in, the exuberant little girl discovers how a swing works, the wonders of air conditioners, the horrors of global warming, the proper way to catch cicadas, and even how to enjoy a beautiful skyline view of a city. The father and the three beautiful girls who live next door may have trouble keeping up with this little ball of energy, but there's nothing in the world that can get her down.

Vol. 1. 2005. 232pp. 1-4139-0317-7.
Vol. 2. 2005. 184pp. 1-4139-0318-5.
Vol. 3. 2005. 192pp. 1-4139-0329-0.

You're Under Arrest. Written and illustrated by Kosuke Fujishima. Dark Horse Comics, 1997–1999. O Japanese manga.

Miyuki and Natsumi are two crazy and beautiful Tokyo policewomen. Miyuki can turn any car into a high-performance speedster, and Natsumi has phenomenal strength. Together they—as well as the zany cast of the police department—can take on any criminal, no matter how absurd or dangerous. Handling a panty thief, extortion rings, counterfeit golf club memberships, and more, Myyuki and Natsumi will have a fun time while taking down the bad guys.

The Wild Ones. 1997. 120pp. 1-56971-319-7.
Lights and Sirens. 1999. 120pp. 1-56971-432-0.

Comic Strip Collections and the Secret Life of Gamers

The Internet has been a great tool for cartoonists to get their comic strips noticed. Featured here are collections of comic strips that come from gaming magazines, comic book publishers, and popular Web sites that have satirized the gaming and comic book world, popular culture, and more. It is a win-win situation for the artists, who might not have been noticed if not for the support of comic book publishers, and the publishers, who might not have gotten support if not for the fans of the original comic strips. Some of the most popular artists to be noticed for their comic book strips are Frank Cho and Scott Kurtz. Note that because of space limitations, only comic strips reprinted by comic book publishers are listed in this section. Collections of newspaper comic strips, including such highly regarded titles as *Foxtrot, Zits, Calvin and Hobbes,* and the *Far Side,* are not included in this publication.

Dork Tower. Written and illustrated by John Kovalic. Dork Storm Press, 2000– . **T**

Collects the hit Web comic strips featuring the antics of Matt, Igor, Ken, Gilly the Perky Goth, and Carson the Muskrat as they revel in all things in their subculture and embrace their inner dork. From comic book conventions, to Star Wars geekdom, to Lord of the Rings fanaticism, to role-playing dungeons, to action figure collecting, to Internet gaming, follow a group of nerds from the town of Mud Bay in their all-too-familiar dorkish adventures. The current online strips of *Dork Tower* can be seen at http://archive.gamespy.com/comics/dorktower/.

> *Vol. 1: Dork Covenant.* 2000. 160pp. 1-930964-40-4.
> *Vol. 2: Dork Shadows.* 2001. 164pp. 1-930964-41-2.
> *Vol. 3: Heart of Dorkness.* 2002. 160pp. 1-930964-43-9.
> *Vol. 4: Livin' la Vida Dorka.* 2002. 152pp. 1-930964-42-0.
> *Vol. 5: Understanding Gamers.* 2002. 144pp. 1-930964-44-7.
> *Vol. 6: 1D6 Degrees of Separation.* 2004. 160pp. 1-930964-74-9.
> *Vol. 7: Dork Side of the Goon.* 2004. 160pp. 1-930964-85-4.
> *Vol. 8: Go, Dork, Go!* 2005. 160pp. 1-930964-70-6.
> *Vol. 9: All Mod Cons.* 2006. 160pp. 1-933288-52-3.

Hsu and Chan: Too Much Adventure. **Written and illustrated by Norm Scott.** Slave Labor Graphics, 2004. 144pp. 0-943151-89-9. **T**

Originally featured in the monthly pages of *Electronic Gaming Monthly* magazine, now for the first time in their very own comic book collection! Meet Hsu and Chu, two video game designers just trying to get by in life as they peddle their programs at conventions, try their luck at picking up women, fight their arch-nemesis the Yammamoto Organization, contend with Cthuluesque monsters in their rec room, and on occasion fly into outer space to rescue the galaxy. Whoever said that being fanboys would be dull?

Knights of the Dinner Table. Written and illustrated by Jolly R. Blackburn. Kenzer and Company, 1998–2002. **T**

A humorous look at the world of gaming featuring a group of friends doing what they love best: staying indoors and playing their favorite role-playing games and customizable card games. Bob, Dave, Sara, Brian, and Game-Master B.A. Fenton might not see a lot of the outdoors, but the funny and odd world of gamers is fair game for humor and will make any gaming fan laugh.

Tales from the Vault I. 1999. 64pp. 1-889182-25-7.
Tales from the Vault II. 1999. 64pp. 1-889182-26-5.
Tales from the Vault III. 2000. 64pp. 1-889182-27-3.
Tales from the Vault IV. 2002. 64pp. 1-889182-85-0.
Bundle of Trouble I. 2002. 96pp. 1-889182-75-3.
Bundle of Trouble II. 2002. 96pp. 1-889182-76-1.

Bundle of Trouble III. 2003. 96pp. 1-889182-77-X.
Bundle of Trouble IV. 2001. 96pp. 1-889182-78-8.
Bundle of Trouble V. 2001. 96pp. 1-889182-79-6.
Bundle of Trouble VI. 2000. 96pp. 1-889182-80-X.
Bundle of Trouble VII. 2000. 96pp. 1-889182-81-8.

Bundle of Trouble VIII. 2002. 96pp. 1-889182-82-6.
Bundle of Trouble IX. 2002. 96pp. 1-889182-83-4.
Bundle of Trouble X. 2002. 96pp. 1-889182-84-2.

♣ <u>Liberty Meadows.</u> **Written and illustrated by Frank Cho.** Image Comics, 2006– . **O** ◉

© 2006 Frank Cho.

Welcome to Liberty Meadows, an animal sanctuary like no other. It's a scenic place where talking animals such as a hypochondriac bullfrog, a midget circus bear, a real male chauvinist pig, and more are cared for by the beautiful animal psychologist Brandy and her hapless co-worker Frank. As Brandy and Frank try to keep the animals out of trouble, catastrophe is just around the corner, and the peaceful animal sanctuary is anything but. In 1999 the first comic book issue (collected in *Vol. 1: Eden*) by Frank Cho received an Ignatz Award for Outstanding Artist.

Vol. 1: Eden. 2006. 144pp. 1-58240-624-3.
Vol. 2: Creature Comforts. 2006. 144pp. 1-58240-625-1.
Vol. 3: Summer of Love. 2006. 144pp. 1-58240-650-2
Vol. 4: Cold, Cold Heart. 2006. 144pp. 1-58240-502-6.

<u>Megatokyo.</u> **Written and illustrated by Fred Gallagher and Rodney Caston.** Dark Horse Comics, 2004–2005; CMX/DC Comics, 2006– . **T** ◉ **Neo-manga.**

The hilarious adventures of Piro, a true manga/anime otaku (fanboy), and Largo, a hardcore gamer, who find themselves stranded in a strange land. After deciding to fly to Japan on a whim, they find themselves stuck in Tokyo without enough money to get home or a place to sleep. Until they can find their way back, they'll experience Japanese culture from a unique perspective, as fanboys stuck in their own land of paradise. Beginning in 2006, <u>Megatokyo</u> is published through DC Comics' manga imprint, CMX.

Vol. 1. 2004. 152pp. 1-59307-163-9.
Vol. 2. 2004. 176pp. 1-59307-118-3.
Vol. 3. 2005. 224pp. 1-59307-305-4.
Vol. 4. 2006. 224pp. 1-4012-1126-7.

Penny Arcade. **Written by Jerry Holkins. Illustrated by Mike Krahulik.** Dark Horse Comics, 2006. **O**

A collection of cult online video game cartoon strips featuring the gaming gods Gabe and Tycho and their foul-mouthed adventures as representatives of the gaming community. As they stand up for the rights of video gamers, Gabe and Tycho experience the frustrations, delays, hype, and exhilaration of gaming with plenty of attitude, profanity, and a healthy dose of humor. The video gaming Webcomic has been online since 1998, and current episodes can be viewed at http://www.penny-arcade.com.

Vol. 1: Attack of the Bacon Robots! 2006. 120pp. 1-59307-444-1.
Vol. 2: Epic Legends of the Magic Sword Kings!. 2006. 120pp. 1-59307-541-3.
Vol. 3: The Warsun Prophecies. 2006. 136pp. 1-59307-635-5.

PVP. **Written and illustrated by Scott Kurtz.** Image Comics. 2004– . **T** ◉

© 2006 Scott Kurtz.

At the offices of *PVP (Player versus Player) Magazine,* every day is a laugh-out-loud fun fest where anything can happen. Join Cole, Brent, Jade, Francis, Robbie, Jase, and Skull the blue-skinned troll in the collected antics of their hit comic strip Web site http://www.pvponline.com. At *PVP* the average day of the employees is anything but work-related. The staff spend their time goofing off; playing plenty of video and role-playing games; talking about fanboy popular culture topics like movies, comic books, and other forms of geekdom; engaging in not-so-subtle office romances; and even combating old high school rivalries. The first collection, *The Dork Ages,* features the cast in a feature-length comic book-style adventure, while the other collections reprint the popular Webcomic. In 2006 the cartoon received an Eisner Award for the category of Best Digital Comic.

The Dork Ages. 2004. 128pp. 1-58240-345-7.
Vol. 1: At Large. 2004. 128pp. 1-58240-374-0.
Vol. 2: PVP Reloaded. 2005. 144pp. 1-58240-433-X.
Vol. 3: PVP Rides Again. 2006. 144pp. 1-58240-553-0.
Vol. 4: PVP Goes Bananas! 2006. 144pp. 1-58240-722-3.

Cartoons, Animation, and Media Tie-Ins

Humor that is adapted from popular animated films or from animated television shows. The titles include graphic novel collections based on the Cartoon Network's programming, classic cartoons including *Bugs Bunny* and *Mickey Mouse, The Simpsons,* and motion pictures including Dreamworks' *Shrek* and Pixar's *Monsters, Inc.*

Bugs Bunny and Looney Tunes. **Written and illustrated by various.** DC Comics, 1998–2005. **A**

© 2006 DC Comics.

A tribute in comic book form to one of the most popular cartoon characters and animation studios of all time. Join Bugs, Daffy Duck, Elmer Fudd, Yosemite Sam, Pepe LePew, Wile E. Coyote, and all the rest in a variety of Looney Tunes tales.

> *Bugs Bunny and Friends: A Comic Celebration.* 1999. 160pp. 1-56389-458-0.
> *Bugs Bunny: What's Up, Doc? Vol. 1.* 2005. 112pp. 1-4012-0516-X.
> *Daffy Duck: You're Despicable!* 2005. 112pp. 1-4012-0515-1.

Carl Barks' Greatest Ducktales Stories. **Written and illustrated by Carl Barks.** Gemstone Publishing, 2006. **A**

Regarded by many creators as one of the greatest comic book storytellers of all time, Carl Barks has inspired many Disney comic book storytellers as well as famed comic book creators including Jeff Smith and many more. The collection features highlights from Barks's tenure as a Disney storyteller and the adventures of Donald Duck, his uncle Scrooge McDuck, and Donald's nephews Huey, Louie, and Dewey, as they set off in search of high adventure. The original adventures and settings created by Carl Barks were eventually adapted into the hit animated series *Ducktales,* which aired from 1987 to 1990.

> *Vol. 1.* 2006. 144pp. 1-888472-36-7.
> *Vol. 2.* 2006. 144pp. 1-888472-38-3.

Cartoon Cartoons. **Written and illustrated by various.** DC Comics, 2004–2005. **A**

Comic book adaptations of some of the Cartoon Network's best cartoons. The stories feature such hits as *Dexter's Laboratory*, *Johnny Bravo*, *Cow & Chicken*, *Courage the Cowardly Dog*, *Ed, Edd n Eddy*, *I.M. Weasel*, and *Sheep in the Big City*.

> *Vol. 1: Name That Toon!* 2004. 112pp. 1-4012-0181-4.
> *Vol. 2: The Gang's All Here!* 2004. 112pp. 1-4012-0182-2.
> *Cartoon Network Block Party: Get Down! Vol. 1.* 2005. 112pp. 1-4012-0517-8.

Family Guy. **Written and Illustrated by various.** Devil's Due Publishing, 2006– . **O**

8

Based on the hit animated series created by Seth MacFarlane. The series features Peter Griffin, idiot blue-collar father of a middle-class family in fictional Quahog, Rhode Island, whose antics usually set the stage for each episode. Joining him is his stay-at-home and piano-teaching wife, Lois; slow-talking and equally moronic son, Chris; Meg, the ignored middle child; Stewie, the brilliant infant son determined to destroy Lois and to take over the world;

Brian, the talking family dog; and many of Peter's neighbors, including Joe Swanson, sex-crazed Glenn Quagmire, and Cleveland Brown.

A Big Book of Crap. 2006. 160pp. 1-932796-65-7.

Futurama. **Written and illustrated by Matt Groening, et al.** HarperPerennial, 2002–2006. **Y** ◎ 💻

© 2006 Matt Groening and HarperPerennial, a Division of HarperCollins Publishing.

The continuing humorous escapades of *Simpsons* creator Matt Groening's hilarious vision of the future. Meet Fry, a pizza delivery boy from the twentieth century who was cryogenically frozen by accident for 1,000 years; Leela, a female cyclops and captain of the Planet Express ship; Bender, an immoral robot with a penchant for beer, and others as they work for Planet Express, an intergalactic delivery service owned by Fry's great, great, great, great nephew, Professor Farnsworth. Join them as they fight intergalactic space pirates; rescue Zapp Branigan, the universe's "greatest" hero; save New New York City from the evil Robot Santa's slay ride; take on the Robot Devil; and save the day again as a super-hero team. The future has never been more fun.

Futurama-O-Rama. 2002. 120pp. 0-06-050598-2.
Futurama Adventures. 2004. 144pp. 0-06-073909-6.
Futurama: The Time-Bender Trilogy. 2006. 120pp. 0-06-111807-9.

Monsters, Inc. **Written and illustrated by Hiromi Yamafuji,** based on the movie by Walt Disney and Pixar Studios. TOKYOPOP, 2002. 104pp. 1-59182-075-8. **A** 🎬 **Japanese manga.**

The Japanese manga adaptation of the hit Pixar movie. The giant, blue-furred James P. "Sulley" Sullivan is the top scare-monster in the hidden world of Monstropolis, where his occupation is to collect the screams of human kids to power the city. When a two-year-old girl they call "Boo" accidentally gets trapped in their world, it's up to Sulley and his buddy, the one-eyed Mike Wazowski, to get her back to the real world before they get in trouble.

Shrek. **Written by Mark Evanier. Illustrated by Ramon F. Bachs.** Dark Horse Comics, 2003. 72pp. 1-56971-982-9. **Y** 🎬

The continuing fractured fairy tale adventures of a lovable ugly ogre named Shrek. Join Shrek, Donkey, and the gang as they set out to rescue Shrek's bride, Princess Fiona, who's been captured by Thelonius, the henchman of Lord Farquaad. It seems that not even death can keep him from marrying Fiona, but Shrek, Donkey, and Dragon have something to say about that! Also, Shrek and Donkey meet an old lady in a rotting gingerbread house. Little do they know that it's really a witch who has ogre on the menu. After a quick getaway, Shrek finds that his swamp home has been flooded to make way for a troll bridge.

The Simpsons/Futurama Infinitely Secret Crossover Crisis. **Written and illustrated by Matt Groening et al.** Bongo/HarperTrade/Perennial, 2006. 160pp. 0-06-089726-0. **Y** ◎ 💻

The comic crossover event of the century! When the casts of Matt Groening's two popular cartoon series, *The Simpsons* and *Futurama*, meet up, neither will ever be the same again. The collection features two crossover tales including Fry's battle with the Brain Spawn as he and the rest of the Planet Express crew are trapped in a *Simpsons* comic book as well as what happens when the citizens of Springfield are transported to New New York in the year 3005.

The Simpsons

Bart Simpson. Created by Matt Groening. Written and illustrated by various. HarperPerennial. 1995– . **A**

The comic book adventures of kid troublemaker and skateboarding under-achiever Bart Simpson. The ten-year-old son of Marge and Homer Simpson, the juvenile jokester's collected short stories revolve around daily fun life in Springfield, USA, where almost anything can happen. Bart's colorful cast of supporting characters include many of *The Simpsons* television staples, including his parents, Bart's sisters Lisa and Maggie, best friend Milhouse, and many more.

> *Bartman: The Best of the Best!* 1995. 128pp. 0-06-095151-6.
> *Big Book of Bart Simpson.* 2002. 120pp. 0-06-008469-3.
> *Big Bad Book of Bart Simpson.* 2003. 128pp. 0-06-055590-4.
> *Big Bratty Book of Bart Simpson.* 2004. 120pp. 0-06-072178-2.
> *Big Beefy Book of Bart Simpson.* 2005. 118pp. 0-06-074819-2.
> *Big Bouncy Book of Bart Simpson.* 2006. 128pp. 0-06-112455-9.

🖈 **The Simpsons Comics. Written and illustrated by Matt Groening et al.** Bongo/HarperTrade/Perennial, 1994– . **Y**

© 2006 Matt Groening and HarperPerennial, a Division of HarperCollins Publishing.

The longest-running television show in U.S. history (currently going into its seventeenth season), it debuted on December 17, 1989. Set in the fictional U.S. town of Springfield, the comic continues the hilarious lampooning antics of well-meaning buffoon Homer, his wife Marge, trouble-maker son Bart, brainiac daughter Lisa, baby Maggie, and Grampa Simpson. Drawing from the large cast of main and supporting characters, including Comic Book Guy, Barney Gumble, C. Montgomery Burns, and Bumble Bee Man, the satirical series continues to make light of middle-class living in America and popular culture topics including movies, music, and comic books. The series won an Eisner Award for Best Short Story in 1994 for "The Amazing Colossal Homer." The story is collected in *Simpsons Extravaganza.* The series also won an Eisner for Best Title for Younger Readers/Best Comics Publication for a Younger Audience in 2000. It has also received recognition from YALSA's Quick Picks for Reluctant Readers several years in a row for *Simpsons Comics a Go-Go* (2001), *Simpsons Comics Royale* (2002), *Simpsons Comics Unchained* (2003), and *Simpsons Comics Madness* (2004).

8

> *Simpsons Comics Extravaganza.* 1994. 128pp. 0-06-095086-2.
> *Simpsons Comics Spectacular.* 1995. 128pp. 0-06-095148-6.

Simpsons Comics Simpsorama. 1996. 128pp. 0-06-095199-0.
Simpsons Comics Strike Back. 1996. 128pp. 0-06-095212-1.
Simpsons Comics Wingding. 1997. 120pp. 0-06-095245-8.
Simpsons Comics on Parade. 1999. 120pp. 0-06-095280-6.
Simpsons Comics Big Bonanza. 1999. 120pp. 0-06-095317-9.
Simpsons Comics a Go-Go. 2000. 120pp. 0-06-095566-X.
Simpsons Comics Royale. 2001. 160pp. 0-06-093378-X.
Simpsons Comics Unchained. 2002. 176pp. 0-06-000797-4.
Simpsons Comics Madness. 2003. 176pp. 0-06-053061-8.
Simpsons Comics Belly Buster. 2004. 176pp. 0-06-058750-4.
Simpsons Comics Holiday Humdinger. 2004. 144pp. 0-06-072338-6.
Simpsons Comics Barn Burner. 2005. 160pp. 0-06-074818-4.
Simpsons Comics Jam-Packed Jamboree. 2006. 128pp. 0-06-087661-1.
Simpsons Comics Beach Blanket Bongo. 2007. 128pp. 0-06-123126-6.

The Simpsons Treehouse of Horror. Written and illustrated by Matt Groening et al.
Bongo/HarperTrade/Perennial, 1999– . **Y** ◉ ▢

An annual tradition since the first Halloween episode on October 25, 1990, the comic book *Treehouse of Horror* stories continue to spoof the scary and spooky things that go bump in the night and features the Simpsons cast in a gore-ific theme. Anything is lampooned in the collections, including tributes to giant monster movies, slasher films, classic horror novels, science fiction stories, and more. The compilations and their original issues have been nominated for comic book industry awards for years and won an Eisner Award in 2000 for Best Humor Publication. *Bart Simpson's Treehouse of Horror Spine-Tingling Spooktacular* received recognition from YALSA's Popular Paperbacks for Young Adults committee in 2002 on the "Graphic Novels: Superheroes and Beyond" list.

> *Bart Simpson's Treehouse of Horror Heebie-Jeebie Hullabaloo.* 1999. 144pp. 0-06-098762-6.
> *Bart Simpson's Treehouse of Horror Spine-Tingling Spooktacular.* 2001. 144pp. 0-06-093714-9.
> *The Simpsons Treehouse of Horror Fun-Filled Frightfest.* 2003. 128pp. 0-06-056070-3.
> *The Simpsons Treehouse of Horror: Hoodoo Voodoo Brouhaha.* 2006. 128pp. 0-06-114872-5.

Walt Disney Treasures: 75 Years of Disney Comics. Written and illustrated by various. Gemstone Publishing, 2006. **A** ◉

For seventy-five years Walt Disney comics have been in publication and now Gemstone Publishing presents a collection highlighting some of the best-loved characters and comic book creators from Walt Disney's collections. Highlights include Mickey Mouse adventures by Floyd Gottfredson and Paul Murry; Donald Duck and Uncle Scrooge adventures by Carl Barks and Don Rosa; plus other tales featuring a wide assortment of beloved Walt Disney characters. The collection also complements Walt Disney's limited edition *Walt Disney Treasures* DVDs series featuring classic cartoons and shows from Disney's long history.

> *Vol. 1.* 2006. 160pp. 1-888472-37-5.

Walt Disney's Donald Duck Adventures. Based on the cartoons created by Walt Disney and Carl Barks. Written and illustrated by various. Gemstone Publishing, 2002– . **A** ◎ ☐

© 2006 Walt Disney.

Comedic adventure stories featuring standard Walt Disney cartoon characters. The series features Donald Duck, Uncle Scrooge McDuck, and Donald's nephews Huey, Dewey and Louie. The stories also include other reoccurring characters of Duckburg, including the Beagle Boys, inventor Gyro Gearloose, the sorceress Magica De Spell, as well as Disney staples such as Mickey Mouse and Goofy. The stories continue the fun tradition as created by famous Donald Duck comic book artist Carl Barks and combine comedy, high adventure, daring escapes, treasure hunts, and suspense, all in a Disney package for all ages.

Vol. 1. 2002. 128pp. 0-911903-10-0.
Vol. 2. 2003. 128pp. 0-911903-11-9.
Vol. 3. 2003. 128pp. 0-911903-12-7.
Vol. 4. 2004. 128pp. 0-911903-26-7.
Vol. 5. 2004. 128pp. 0-911903-46-1.
Vol. 6. 2004. 128pp. 0-911903-27-5.
Vol. 7. 2004. 128pp. 0-911903-47-X.
Vol. 8. 2004. 128pp. 0-911903-52-6.
Vol. 9. 2004. 128pp. 0-911903-53-4.
Vol. 10. 2005. 128pp. 0-911903-66-6.
Vol. 11. 2005. 128pp. 0-911903-67-4.
Vol. 12. 2005. 128pp. 0-911903-68-2.
Vol. 13. 2005. 128pp. 0-911903-93-3.
Vol. 14. 2005. 128pp. 0-911903-94-1.
Vol. 15. 2005. 128pp. 0-911903-99-2.
Vol. 16. 2006. 128pp. 1-888472-11-1.
Vol. 17. 2006. 128pp. 1-888472-12-X.
Vol. 18. 2006. 128pp. 1-888472-30-8.
Vol. 19. 2006. 128pp. 1-888472-31-6.
Vol. 20. 2006. 128pp. 1-888472-49-9.
Vol. 21. 2006. 128pp. 1-888472-50-2.

Walt Disney's Mickey Mouse Adventures. Based on the cartoons created by Walt Disney. Written and illustrated by various. Gemstone Publishing, 2004– . **A** ◎ ☐

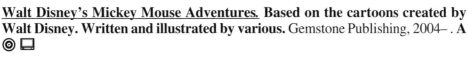

The collected adventures of Walt Disney's signature cartoon character, Mickey Mouse. Other characters from the Disney cartoon pantheon are also featured, including Donald Duck, Goofy, Minnie Mouse, and Pluto, in adventures that span the globe and travel back and forth through time, over the Internet, and more.

Vol. 1. 2004. 128pp. 0-911903-48-8.
Vol. 2. 2005. 128pp. 0-911903-69-0.
Vol. 3. 2005. 128pp. 0-911903-90-9.

Vol. 4. 2005. 128pp. 0-911903-91-7.
Vol. 5. 2005. 128pp. 0-911903-90-9.
Vol. 6. 2005. 128pp. 0-911903-91-7.
Vol. 7. 2006. 128pp. 0-911903-92-5.
Vol. 8. 2006. 128pp. 1-888472-09-X.
Vol. 9. 2006. 128pp. 1-888472-10-3.
Vol. 10. 2006. 128pp. 1-888472-32-4.
Vol. 11. 2006. 128pp. 1-888472-33-2.
Vol. 12. 2006. 128pp. 1-888472-51-0.

Funny Animals

Humorous stories in which the protagonist or supporting characters are animals. The animals may appear to be normal-looking, typically with the ability to speak, or may be anthropomorphized, with human qualities as well as the ability to speak. Anthropomorphized stories such as *Usagi Yojimbo* and the *Teenage Mutant Ninja Turtles* are not listed in this chapter, but are featured in chapter 2 because the main focus in the stories featuring those characters tends to be on action, though some humorous tales may appear. Other licensed anthropomorphized characters, including Walt Disney's Mickey Mouse and Donald Duck, are listed in the "Cartoons, Animation, and Media Tie-Ins" section of this chapter.

The Collected Sam & Max: Surfin' the Highway. **Written and illustrated by Steve Purcell.** Marlowe & Co./Avalon Publishing Group, 1995. 160pp. 1-56924-814-1. **T** ◎ ▢
🎮

© and ™ 2006 Steve Purcell.
Appears by permission of the
publisher, Marlowe & Company,
a division of Avalon Publishing
Group.

Holy jumping mother o' God in a sidecar with chocolate jimmies and a lobster bib! Collects the cult-hit hilarious antics of private investigators Sam the dog and his long-eared rabbit partner Max. The series also inspired a hit video game from both LucasArts and Telltale Games as well as a cartoon show. Sam is a canine version of Columbo and Max is pretty much just a naked rabbit wearing a maniacal grin and packing a Colt 45. Together they take on the most absurd cases and still know how to relax by playing a fun game of fizzball, which basically entails hitting cheap beer cans with a whacking object of one's choice.

Comic Adventures of Boots. **Written and illustrated by Satoshi Kitamura.** Farrar, Straus & Giroux, 2002. 32pp. 0-374-31455-1. **A**

Three short stories about Boots, a good-natured housecat, and his comic adventures. First, Boots must try to get some sleep on his favorite brick wall, which has been overrun by some neighborhood cats. Second, what on earth can a cat and a duck learn from each other? Third, it's time for charades, cat-style.

The Frank Book. **Written and illustrated by Jim Woodring.** Fantagraphics Books, 2003. 352pp. 1-56097-534-2. **T**

> The short adventures of a buck-toothed, anthropomorphic creature named Frank and his life in a world where the absurd and the psychedelic walk hand-in-hand. With a humanoid pig creature called Manhog and Frank's frequent companion Pupshaw, their nearly wordless journeys take them where imagination is the only limit.

Gon. **Written and illustrated by Masashi Tanaka.** Paradox Press/DC Comics, 1996–2001. **A**

© 2006 DC Comics.

> Though pint-sized, he's still king of the animals and the toughest little dinosaur you'll ever meet. He's Gon, a pygmy Tyrannosaurus rex and the last of his kind. He's a friend to the helpless animals of the world, and if you're a vicious predator, you've been warned: even though he's silent and a little on the short side, he'll clean your clock and help the helpless. From his travels all around the world to exotic locales and habitats, Gon is the true king of the animals. In each silent story, he roams a different part of Earth's landscape intermingling with the local animals. From Africa to Australia, he's befriending defenseless animals, looking for a good place to nap, and making the animal kingdom his own. *Gon Swimmin'* has won several Eisner Awards, including Best U.S. Edition of Foreign Material (1998) and Best Humor Publication (1998), as well as a Harvey Award for Best American Edition of Foreign Material (1997).

> > *Gon.* 1996. 112pp. 1-56389-296-0.
> > *Gon Again.* 1996. 112pp. 1-56389-297-9.
> > *Here Today, Gone Tomorrow.* 1996. 112pp. 1-56389-298-7.
> > *Going, Going, Gone.* 1996. 112pp. 1-56389-299-5.
> > *Gon Swimmin'.* 1997. 160pp. 1-56389-380-0.
> > *Gon Color Spectacular.* 1999. 48pp. 1-56389-381-9.
> > *Gon Wild.* 1999. 224pp. 1-56389-474-2.
> > *Gon Underground.* 1999. 176pp. 1-56389-591-9.
> > *Gon on Safari.* 2000. 176pp. 1-56389-669-9.
> > *Gon: Introducing the Dinosaur That Time Will Never Forget!* 2001. 224pp. 1-56389-749-0.

Howard the Duck. **Created and Written by Steve Gerber. Illustrated by John Buscema and various.** Marvel Comics, 2002. **M**

> Created in 1973 by Steve Gerber, Howard the Duck is a cigar-smoking three-foot tall anthropomorphic duck from another dimension. Trapped on our Earth, he's trying to make the best of it. As an outsider to our culture and way of life, he easily sees the absurdities of our lives with razor-sharp wit. *The Essential Howard the Duck* lampoons the tumultuous 1970s and even includes a run for the presidency of the United States. The self-titled series was a return by Steve Gerber to the character he created and continues to lampoon popular culture as well as Walt Disney's lawsuit because of a semi-resem-

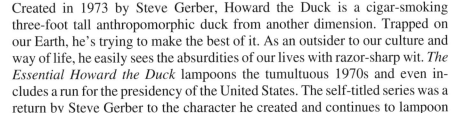

blance to another duck with no pants: Donald Duck. The series was collected under Marvel's mature-reader MAX imprint. And yes, *Howard the Duck* was also released as a movie in 1986.

> *The Essential Howard the Duck.* 2002. 528pp. 0-7851-0831-9.
>
> *Howard the Duck.* Illustrated by Phil Winslade. MAX/Marvel Comics, 2002. 144pp. 0-7851-0931-5.

Owly. Written and illustrated by Andy Runton. Top Shelf Productions, 2004– . **A** ◎

© 2006 Andy Runton.

The simple and kind adventures of an owl who is always on the lookout for new friends and fun. The simple yet beautiful stories earned creator Andy Runton an Ignatz Award for Promising New Talent in 2005 and an Eisner Award in 2006 in the category Best Title for Younger Readers/Best Comics Publication for a Younger Audience, for *Flying Lessons.*

> *Vol. 1: The Way Home and the Bittersweet Summer.* 2004. 160pp. 1-891830-62-7.
>
> *Vol. 2: Just a Little Blue.* 2005. 120pp. 1-891830-64-3.
>
> *Vol. 3: Flying Lessons.* 2005. 128pp. 1-891830-76-7.

***Peanutbutter and Jeremy's Best Book Ever!* Written and illustrated by James Kochalka.** Alternative Comics, 2003. 280pp. 1-891867-46-6. A ◎

Peanutbutter is your typical house cat who just likes to think she's an employee at her "boss's" business. Wearing a tie and a hat, she's ready to work on the Flumdummer account . . . after a nap. Enter Jeremy, a crow who lives outside Peanutbutter's home and is always out to cause her trouble, both indoors and out. Although he's usually up to no good and out to steal her nice hat, she considers Jeremy to be her best friend. Despite all the teasing and taunting, they have a slew of adventures around Peanutbutter's "office" and Jeremy's nest outside.

***Salmon Doubts.* Written and illustrated by Adam Sacks.** Alternative Comics, 2004. 128pp. 1-891867-71-7. **O**

The universal questions of life and death and the quest to find our own identity are asked by a salmon named Geoff. Why was he born? Why is he here? Why is he so shy and insecure? As we watch his life begin and move forward, Geoff decides to stray from the spawning pack and his best friend Henry. While many of his fellow salmon are spawning and dying, Geoff takes a significant and universal leap of faith, strays from the pack, and ventures out into the mysterious ocean.

Sky Ape. Written by Philip Amara, Tim McCarney, and Mike Russo. Illustrated by Richard Jenkins. AiT/Planet Lar 2001–2003. **M**

Kirk Madge is not your average 800-pound gorilla. He's a millionaire without a past, he likes making light and fluffy pancakes, and he flies a jet pack as Sky Ape! He's on the job to tackle the oddest of free-flowing adventures, including a quest to find the Suspense Jacket, a blazer that can make the wearer travel back in time. Along the way he is attacked by Spanish bicyclists, forced to make pancakes for hours on end, and more in his quest to find out who he really is. Other volumes tell more adventures in the absurd.

Vol. 1. 2001. 96pp. 0-9676847-8-1.
Vol. 2: Waiting for Crime. 2001. 56pp. 0-9709360-3-6.
Vol. 3: All the Heroes. 2003. 56pp. 1-932051-08-2.

🌱 *Spiral-Bound.* **Written and illustrated by Aaron Renier.** Top Shelf Productions, 2005. 144pp. 1-891830-50-3. **Y** ◎

© 2006 Aaron Renier.

The daily lives and adventures of several animal friends, including a depressed elephant named Turnip, a cheerful dog named Stucky Hound, and Ana and Em, a rabbit and a bird. The terminally depressed Turnip is coerced by Stucky into take a sculpting class, and the professor in charge of the class assigns the students to work on a sculpture garden by a haunted lake. When the professor disappears, Ana and Em, reporters for the local town newspaper, investigate the haunted lake in search of the professor as well as the truths about a monster rumored to live there. When the rumors of the monster turn out to be true, the four friends must find the courage to fight the beast and discover what really happened to the missing professor. In 2006 the creator, Aaron Renier, received an Eisner Award in the category Talent Deserving of Wider Recognition.

What's Michael? Written and illustrated by Makoto Kobayashi. Dark Horse Comics, 1997– . **Y** ◎ **Japanese manga.**

The slice-of-life humorous short stories of the most precocious cat in all of Japan, Michael, an orange tomcat with a penchant for doing just what cats do best—whatever they want! From curling up into a ball in summertime, to eating food too fast, using the litter box, finding a mate, and vying for attention against an even cuter adversary (a baby), Michael's tales are full of humor both subtle and slapstick. Stories also go for the absurd as Michael and his cast of animal friends take on anthropomorphized roles in sketches featuring cats and dogs as samurai, high school students, martial arts fighters, private detectives, and more.

Vol. 1: Michael's Album. 1997. 88pp. 1-56971-247-6.
Vol. 2: Living Together. 1997. 88pp. 1-56971-248-4.
Vol. 3: Off the Deep End. 1997. 88pp. 1-56971-249-2.
Vol. 4: Michael's Mambo. 1999. 88pp. 1-56971-250-6.
Vol. 5: Michael's Favorite Spot. 2002. 88pp. 1-56971-557-2.
Vol. 6: A Hard Day's Life. 2002. 88pp. 1-56971-744-3.
Vol. 7: Fat Cat in the City. 2003. 88pp. 1-56971-914-4.
Vol. 8: Show Time. 2003. 88pp. 1-56971-972-1.
Vol. 9: The Ideal Cat. 2004. 88pp. 1-59307-120-5.
Vol. 10: Sleepless Nights. 2005. 88pp. 1-59307-337-2.
Vol. 11: Planet of the Cats. 2006. 104pp. 1-59307-525-1.

Silent Humor

This is comedy in which no dialogue is spoken and humor is exhibited through body language and sight gags. Sergio Aragonés is a recognized master of this art form. This visual humor style was inspired by classic silent comedy films such as the early work of Charlie Chaplin, Laurel and Hardy, as well as mime artist extraordinaire Marcel Marceau, under whom Aragonés studied.

***Buzz and Bell: Space Cadets.* Written and illustrated by Sergio Aragonés.** Malibu Comics, 1991. 48pp. 1-56398-007-X. **Y**

> Silent, one-page skits featuring the comic misadventures of space astronauts Buzz and his chimpanzee partner Bell. Humanity's future in space exploration has never been this pitiful or this funny.

Li'l Santa. Written by Lewis Trondheim. Illustrated by Thierry Robin. NBM Publishing, 2003. **A**

> The silent comic misadventures of Santa Claus at the North Pole. In *Volume 1,* see just what Santa has to go through every year just to deliver toys and presents to all the good boys and girls around the world. In *Volume 2,* when an evil band of lumberjacks are cutting down all the trees, it's up to Santa to save the day, but he'll need the help of his friend the Abominable Snowman, and the creepy monsters from the vacationing Halloween town, too.
>
> > *Vol. 1: Li'l Santa.* 2003. 48pp. 1-56163-335-6.
> > *Vol. 2: Happy Halloween, Li'l Santa.* 2003. 48pp. 1-56163-361-5.

Sergio Aragonés' . . . . Written and illustrated by Sergio Aragonés. Dark Horse Comics, 1998–2002. **Y**

> In every issue of *MAD* magazine, Sergio's single-panel silent strips have humorously touched on all facets of life. Thought by many in the industry to be the master of silent comedy, Sergio Aragonés' silently told vignettes are sure to make you laugh. The short and sweet tales cover all walks of life, from lighthearted looks at everyday living to the absurd and fantastic.
>
> > *Sergio Aragonés' Louder Than Words.* 1999. 160pp. 1-56971-343-X.
> > *Sergio Aragonés' Actions Speak.* 2002. 160pp. 1-56971-758-3.

***Smokehouse Five.* Written and illustrated by Sergio Aragonés.** Malibu Comics, 1992. 48pp. 1-56398-024-X. **Y**

> Silently told comedy sketches featuring the finest firefighters: Smokehouse Five! Fighting fires was never this funny.

Black Humor

These stories feature toilet humor, dirty jokes, bawdy situations, and dark humor that sometimes teeters between comedy and tragedy. The humor may be crude, but the reader still finds the offensive and possibly inappropriate jokes quite funny. Readers' advisors beware: some people may not think these comics are humorous. Also, the titles in this section tend to be more appropriate for older audiences. Films in this genre include Mel Brooks's *Blazing Saddles*, Stanley Kubrick's *Dr. Strangelove*, as well as Matt Stone and Trey Parker's *Team America* film and their *South Park* television series.

The Adventures of Barry Ween, Boy Genius. Written and illustrated by Judd Winick. Oni Press, 1999–2002. **O**

© 2006 Judd Winick.

The smartest person on the planet is a ten-year-old, foul-mouthed boy named Barry. With an IQ of about 350, though he still has an awkward time talking to his crush, he's a mad scientist at home, inadvertently causing all sorts of misadventures. From opening up space–time continuum portals in his basement, to cloning himself to get along better at school, to helping stranded aliens get back home, to traveling back in time to the Old West, to turning his best friend Jeremy Ramirez into a T-rex (with an afro), science has never been this fun. The first graphic novel in the series received recognition from YALSA's Popular Paperbacks for Young Adults committee for the 2002 "Graphic Novels: Superheroes and Beyond" selection list.

Vol. 1. 1999. 88pp. 1-929998-00-7.
Vol. 2.0. 2000. 96pp. 1-929998-05-8.
Vol. 3: Monkey Tales. 2001. 96pp. 1-929998-18-X.
Vol. 4: Gorilla Warfare. 2002. 96pp. 1-929998-19-8.

Annotated Mantooth. **Written and illustrated by Matt Fraction.** AiT/Planet Lar, 2002. 96pp. 1-932051-05-8. **O**

The world's greatest super-spy is really . . . a talking gorilla who swears?!? Meet Rex Mantooth, the only secret agent capable of saving the world from the armies of the absurd whenever it's in danger (which is quite often). Joined by his sidekick, the sexy Honey Hamptonwick, he's out to stop super ninjas, crazed ducks, lesbian commandos, zombie scientists, and even Adolf Hitler in the most over-the-top way possible.

Bluntman and Chronic. **Written by Kevin Smith. Illustrated by Michael Avon Oeming and Pat Garrahy.** Image Comics, 2001. 96pp. 1-58240-208-6. **O**

From the warped mind of director/writer Kevin Smith come the "super-hero" aliases of his cult slackers Jay and Silent Bob. The actual *Bluntman and Chronic* comic book was seen in the hit Kevin Smith film *Chasing Amy* (1997) as created by the fictional characters Banky Edwards and Holden McNeil. Now fans of the film can finally read the off-color adventures of two of the most inept heroes of all, lampooning the world of the super-hero.

Clerks (The Comic Books). **Written by Kevin Smith. Illustrated by Ande Parks, Phil Hester, and Jim Mahfood.** Oni Press,2000. 96pp. 0-9667127-8-1. **O** 🎬

> The continuing adventures of Dante, Randal, Jay, Silent Bob, and all the customers of the Quick Shop Mini Mart. Spun off from Kevin Smith's cult-classic film *Clerks* (1994). They take on more pop culture in search of the rarest <u>Star Wars</u> action figure, the true secret of Santa Claus, as well as a cut scene never shown from the original *Clerks* film. Doing nothing has never been this fun.

<u>**Crayon Shinchan.**</u> **Written and illustrated by Yoshito Usui.** ComicsOne, 2002–2004. **O Japanese manga.**

> Shinchan is the world's worst five-year-old boy. He's rude, crude, and a constant annoyance to his parents with his outrageous behavior. Starring in his own hit comedy anime and then released as a manga, Shinchan has been called the "Bart Simpson of Japan," but that's too nice a comment. The manga stories are told in a short-story format similar to newspaper comic strips. A hilarious look at the not-so-subtle antics of a disobedient boy.
>
>> *Vol. 1.* 2002. 120pp. 1-58899-194-6.
>> *Vol. 2.* 2003. 200pp. 1-58899-266-7.
>> *Vol. 3.* 2003. 200pp. 1-58899-267-5.
>> *Vol. 4.* 2003. 200pp. 1-58899-270-5.
>> *Vol. 5.* 2003. 120pp. 1-58899-268-3.
>> *Vol. 6.* 2003. 120pp. 1-58899-269-1.
>> *Vol. 7.* 2004. 120pp. 1-58899-271-3.
>> *Vol. 8.* 2004. 120pp. 1-58899-272-1.
>> *Vol. 9.* 2004. 120pp. 1-58899-273-X.

🏮 *Fun with Milk & Cheese*. **Written and illustrated by Evan Dorkin.** Slave Labor Graphics/Amaze Ink, 1995. 96pp. 0-943151-07-4. **O**

> Meet the crankiest half-pint of milk (the self-titled "Hercules of Hate") and his friend, a wedge of cheese (the self-proclaimed "Sampson of Spite") . They're what happens when dairy products really do go bad. They're the most angry, foul-mouthed, alcoholic dairy products ever, and they have a "slight case" of the ultra-violent. Nothing's taboo as they go on mad tirades and hate everything, including this annotation. The creator, Evan Dorkin, received an Eisner Award for Talent Deserving of Wider Recognition in 1995, and in 1996 an issue of the title, "Milk & Cheese #666," won an Eisner Award for Best Humor Publication.

© 2006 Evan Dorkin.

Jay and Silent Bob: Chasing Dogma. **Written by Kevin Smith. Illustrated by Duncan Fegredo.** Oni Press,1999. 128pp. 0-9667127-3-0. **O** 🎬

> Set between the events of Kevin Smith's cult movies *Chasing Amy* (1997) and *Dogma* (1999), the book chronicles the further adventures of stoner slackers Jay and Silent Bob. Join them as they attempt to travel to Shermer, Illinois (the fictional setting of the classic John Hughes films). After getting kicked off the bus, they have to make it there by any means possible. Watch their off-color trek through the seedy side of America as

they try to reach their destiny. Too bad no one told them Shermer, Illinois, doesn't really exist.

🏅 ***Three Fingers.* Written and illustrated by Rich Koslowski.** Top Shelf Productions, 2002. 144pp. 1-891830-31-7. **O**

A behind-the-scenes, black-comedy parody of the animation business. When a "toon" makes it big in the real world, there's a dark secret that it follows in order to fit in. Everyone knows that a "toon" only has three fingers and a thumb—look at Mickey Mouse, Daffy Duck, and Homer Simpson. Join down-and-out toons Ricky Rat and others as they recount their days before the downward spiral of booze, drugs, smoking, and old age ravaged them. Both touchingly sad and darkly funny. Ricky remembers being discovered by mogul Dizzy Walters and how the toons, hoping to have the same success as Ricky, have paid the price of a digit to fit in. In 2003 the graphic novel received an Ignatz Award for Outstanding Graphic Novel or Collection.

***The Unauthorized Puffed Movie Adaptation.* Written by John Layman. Illustrated by David Crosland.** IDW Publishing, 2005. 132pp. 1-932382-94-1. **O**

Aaron Owens's job is to wear a ridiculous-looking, cumbersome "Puff the Dragon" costume for the local amusement park. It's embarrassing, it smells, and it can't be removed without the help of another person. When a jealous co-worker cold-cocks Aaron, he finds out that he's been dumped off late at night in the worst neighborhood possible. After witnessing a murder by gang bangers, he's now on the run from thugs, stuck hanging out among druggies, hookers, and thugs, trying desperately to get someone to help him take his costume off before his bladder explodes.

Satire

In these stories the humor makes light of current subjects from within our own culture, including government, entertainment, relationships, and our way of life.

***Birth of a Nation.* Written by Aaron McGruder and Reginald Hudlin. Illustrated by Kyle Baker.** Crown Publishers/Random House, 2004. 144pp. 1-4000-4859-1. **O**

The social satire tale of Fred Fredericks, the activist black mayor of East St. Louis, who decides to secede from the United States after constitutional problems with the U.S. government and a Bush-like presidency. With the financial backing of shady black billionaire John Roberts, Fredericks calls his new country the Republic of Black Land, an experiment in creating a country "for the people, by the people." Soon Black Land becomes a safe haven for knuckleheads, and the U.S. government isn't taking too kindly to its new neighboring country. When Black Land is about to collapse from the corruption and clashes from within, can the President of Blackland restore his country to hope, or will it fall to corruption and terrorism?

Catch As Catch Can. **Written and illustrated by Greg Cook.** Highwater Books, 2000. 88pp. 0-9665363-6-3. **O**

> A twisted take on familiar fairy tale characters and situations told in short vignettes. When a foul-mouthed gingerbread man working as an ice cream vendor buys cigarettes for kids, he soon finds himself on the run from the law. In the second tale the gingerbread man finds himself the imaginary love interest for a juvenile pig infatuated with him. Rounding out the collection is a darkly twisted short story in which the Big Bad Wolf takes up a job as the ice cream vendor to score something good to eat.

Cowboy Wally Show. **Written and illustrated by Kyle Baker.** DC Comics, 1996. 128pp. 1-4012-0050-8. **O** ◉

> A tongue-in-cheek look at the absurd, short-lived television and film career of Cowboy Wally, a stupid, lecherous, obese man in a ten-gallon cowboy hat who for some unexplainable reason became famous in showbiz. Interviewing him documentary-style in 1987, Oswald Stairs speaks with the churlish man at his mansion in Jeepersville, North Dakota, to try to get to know him better and see if there's a hint of humanity behind the stupidity, sarcasm, and vulgarity. There isn't. From his start as a kid's television host in 1974, to his *Sands of Blood* Foreign Legion film flop farce, to the only movie adaptation of *Hamlet* filmed in prison, it's clear that this boorish man doesn't have a clue. Cowboy Wally is a living legend . . . at least he thinks so.

Excel Saga. **Written and illustrated by Rikdo Koshi.** Viz Media, 2003–2006. **T** ◉ **Japanese manga.**

> Beneath the small northern province of Fukuoka in Japan there exists a secret ideological organization called ACROSS, with the lofty goal of ruling the world. Since they don't have enough financial resources, for the time being they're going to settle for taking over the city. The handsome, mysterious, and manipulative plotter Lord Il Palazzo's call for minions only brings in three bumbling recruits: Excel, an energetic-but-ditsy blonde; Hyatt, a shy female recruit who has the unfortunate habit of constantly dying during the missions; and Mince, the emergency food supply (actually just a stray dog). The only thing that stands in their way besides their own incompetence is the anti-ACROSS organization, the Safety Assurance Agency, that just so happens to be made up of the neighbors right across the hall from Excel and Hyatt's housing complex. As the absurdity escalates, nothing popular-culture related is taboo as ACROSS's goal to take over the city ramps up along with the humor.

> *Vol. 1.* 2003. 200pp. 1-56931-988-X.
> *Vol. 2.* 2003. 200pp. 1-56931-989-8.
> *Vol. 3.* 2003. 200pp. 1-56931-990-1.
> *Vol. 4.* 2004. 208pp. 1-59116-110-X.
> *Vol. 5.* 2004. 208pp. 1-59116-136-3.
> *Vol. 6.* 2004. 208pp. 1-59116-231-9.
> *Vol. 7.* 2004. 208pp. 1-59116-232-7.
> *Vol. 8.* 2004. 208pp. 1-59116-233-5.
> *Vol. 9.* 2004. 208pp. 1-59116-234-3.
> *Vol. 10.* 2004. 200pp. 1-59116-644-6.
> *Vol. 11.* 2005. 208pp. 1-59116-722-1.
> *Vol. 12.* 2005. 208pp. 1-59116-775-2.

Vol. 13. 2005. 208pp. 1-4215-0143-0.
Vol. 14. 2006. 208pp. 1-4215-0481-2.

***Mad About the Mob: A Look at Organized and Unorganized Crime.* Written and illustrated by The Usual Gang of Idiots.** MAD/DC Comics, 2002. 96pp. 1-56389-883-7. **Y**

A look at the funny side of organized crime. Collects *Mad Magazine* spoofs from some of the most famous popular culture films and television shows featuring the mob. Classic films and shows such as *The Godfather*, *The Untouchables*, *Analyze This*, *The Sopranos*, and *Scarface* don't stand a chance when Alfred E. Neuman and the Usual Gang of Idiots get hold of them.

***My Faith in Frankie.* Written by Mike Carey. Illustrated by Sonny Liew and Marc Hempel.** Vertigo/DC Comics, 2004. 112pp. 1-4012-0390-6. **M**

© 2006 DC Comics.

Frankie Moxon is a typical seventeen-year-old, ready for college and looking for the right boyfriend, who just so happens to have her own overprotective deity. She has found true love with Dean, a hunky former boyfriend who has come back into her life years after he was raised from the dead by Jerevin at Frankie's wish. Bad boy Dean looks like he's going to be her knight in dreamy armor, and Jerevin doesn't care for it. The young god has given her everything she ever has asked for and has been her guardian for years—and he doesn't take it too kindly when someone has stolen his only worshipper. But Dean has a demonic secret of his own, and a simple struggle over love escalates into a battle over a woman's soul. Who will choose: Dean or Jerevin, or does she have a third option?

***My Monkey's Name Is Jennifer.* Written and illustrated by Ken Knudsten.** Slave Labor Graphics/Amaze Ink, 2003. 152pp. 0-943151-71-6. **O**

Kaitlin's playtime friend is Jennifer, a male chimpanzee who's anything but nice. He's one angry and cranky "monkey" out to make his torturous tea-time play with Kaitlin more fun with his active imagination of spies, ninjas, pirates, peas up his nose, and more.

***Truer Than True Romance: Classic Love Comics Retold!* Written by Jeanne Martinet. Illustrated by Vince Colletta, Mike Sekowsky, Irv Novick, Bernard Sachs, Jack Sparling, Art Saaf, Tony Abruzzo, Howard Purcell, Bill Draut, Manny Stallman, and Seymour Barry.** Watson-Guptill Publications, Incorporated, 2001. 112pp. 0-8230-8438-8. **T**

The romance books from DC Comics were a staple of the comic book industry from the 1940s through the 1970s, and here are some highlights, as you've never seen them before! Reprinted in their entirety but reworded by humorist Jeanne Martinet, this is a whole new look at romance, thanks to just a few changes in text. For nonsatirical looks at romance, see chapter 7.

***Why I Hate Saturn.* Written and illustrated by Kyle Baker.** Vertigo/DC Comics, 1998. 208 pp 0-930289-72-2. **M**

> Cranky Anne Merkel is an overly analytic New York columnist for an obscure magazine in love with her whiskey and sick of being single in the city. When her seemingly crazy sister Laura, a health nut from the West Coast, comes to live with her, Anne's in for an even wilder ride, with a sister claiming to be "Queen of the Leather Astro-Girls of Saturn." Can Anne's life get any worse?

Genreblends

The popularity of humor continues to this day in a variety of forms and crosses a variety of genres. Most other genres have been touched by humor in some form, even those in which one might not think comedy could flourish, such as horror and science fiction. By adding a touch of humor to another genre, that genre can be reinterpreted in a new light and readers can laugh along at the plot points both familiar and new to them. The tales tend to feature mockeries of standard genre characters. Typically in a genreblending comedy, the main characters appear to be the opposite of that genre's traditions. Instead of being overly brave or heroic, they can appear clumsy or dim-witted, and standard plot points, locations, and more are fair game for spoofing.

Humorous Horror

Humor can best alleviate the dread and fright of horror, and the two are often paired. Best examples of this are the classic <u>Evil Dead</u> series of films by Sam Raimi as well as the 2004 zombie romantic comedy *Shaun of the Dead*. For other horror titles, see chapter 6.

<u>Army of Darkness</u>. Created by Sam Raimi and Ivan Raimi. Dynamic Forces, 2004– . **T**

> Adaptation of the cult-classic movie (and sequel to the *Evil Dead 2* film) in which Ash, the bumbling but stalwart S-Mart employee, is sent back in time to medieval England to fight the Skeleton King and his army of the undead. With his severed right hand replaced by a chainsaw and his "boomstick" (sawed-off shotgun) in his left, there's nothing that can stop Ash from defeating the skeletal soldiers and finding a way back to the future.
>
> > *Army of Darkness: The Official Movie Adaptation.* Written by Sam Raimi and Ivan Raimi. Illustrated by John Bolton. 2004. 88pp. 0-9749638-3-6.
> > *Ashes 2 Ashes.* Written by Andy Hartnell. Illustrated by Nick Bradshaw. 2004. 112pp. 0-9749638-9-5.
> > *Shop 'Til You Drop Dead Collection.* Written by James Anthony Kuhoric. Illustrated by Nick Bradshaw. 2005. 112pp. 1-933305-01-0.

***Bear, Vol. 1: Immortal.* Written and illustrated by Jamie Smart.** Amaze Ink/Slave Labor Graphics, 2004. 144pp. 1-59362-001-2. **O**

> The comic adventures of a sarcastic stuffed teddy bear called Bear, living at home with his owner, Karl, and a terribly deranged cat called Looshkin. Each vignette features ways in which Bear is humorously tormented, tortured, and worse by his mortal enemy Looshkin. Will Bear ever get revenge on the cat? Stay tuned for hijinks including inci-

dents with ninjas, a giant squid, lawnmowers, flammable aerosols, evil puppets, and more.

Boneyard. **Written and illustrated by Richard Moore.** NBM Publishing, 2002– . **T**

© 2006 by Richard Moore.

Michael Paris has inherited a plot of land in the town of Raven Hollow. And what a plot it is—it's a cemetery! The residents of the town want it razed, and for good reason—the graveyard is haunted by all sorts of monstrous creatures. But when Michael meets the denizens of his cemetery, they're anything but monstrous. In fact, they're all quite nice, especially the cute vampire girl. Now Michael has a humorous home full of monsters and is facing townspeople angry about the situation. In the end, who are the real monsters? Recently NBM Publishing has re-released the first volume in full color.

> *Vol. 1.* 2002. 96pp. 1-56163-316-X.
> *Vol. 2.* 2003. 96pp. 1-56163-369-0.
> *Vol. 3.* 2004. 96pp. 1-56163-405-0.
> *Vol. 4.* 2005. 104pp. 1-56163-424-7.
> *Vol. 5.* 2006. 104pp. 1-56163-479-4.
> *Boneyard in Color, Vol. 1.* 2005. 96pp. 1-56163-427-1.

Death, Jr. **Written by Gary Whitta. Illustrated by Ted Naifeh.** Image Comics, 2005–2007. 144pp. 1-58240-526-3. **T**

Like most young sons, lil' "DJ" has always looked up to his father and can't wait to help dad with the family business. But DJ's dad isn't like the other fathers—he has a special job: he's the grim reaper! When DJ and his odd assortment of fellow misfit friends from middle school attend a school field trip to the Museum of Supernatural History, they accidentally unleash a demon out to reclaim the grim reaper's title from DJ's dad. Can a little boy with a skull for a face and his odd friends fix what they've unleashed across the world? The series was adapted into a hit video game for the Playstation PSP.

> *Vol. 1.* 2005. 144pp. 1-58240-526-3.
> *Vol. 2.* 2007. 144pp. 1-58240-682-0.

Doctor Gorpon. **Written and illustrated by Marc Hansen.** NOW Comics, 2004. 80pp. 0-9745205-6-X. **O**

A dark comedy about a monster hunter whose methods of taking care of the vicious beasts of the night (i.e., ripping their heads off) is so extreme that even the monsters fear him and the police of Big City want to bring him in. The Doctor is not easily fazed, and no matter what it takes he'll make sure all the beasts, monsters, demons, and more are vanquished in the most vile way possible. The bill is in the mail.

✦ <u>**The Goon.**</u> **Written and illustrated by Eric Powell.** Dark Horse Comics, 2003– . **T** ◎

Goon™ © 2006 Eric Powell.

Set against a backdrop reminiscent of 1930–1940s gangster movies with a heaping mix of humor and horror. The Zombie Priest has come to Lonely Street to rule the neighborhood with his gang of zombies, and only one bruiser of a man is tough enough to handle the job and beat the living daylights out of the hordes of undead: the Goon. Goon and his longtime buddy Franky have seen their share of weird things in the neighborhood: zombies, ghosts, fish mobsters, spider cardsharks, reverse zombies, werewolves, harpies, and many other oddities. When you absolutely need someone to beat up the monsters, just ask for the Goon. *Volume 3* features a cameo appearance by Mike Mignola's Hellboy. The series has won multiple Eisner Awards, including Best Single Issue/Single Story (2004), Best Continuing Series (2005), and Best Humor Publication (2005). *Fancy Pants Edition* is a limited edition hardcover volume collecting key stories of the Goon.

> *Vol. 0: Rough Stuff.* 2004. 88pp. 1-56971-086-1.
> *Vol. 1: Nothin' But Misery.* 2003. 136pp. 1-56971-998-5.
> *Vol. 2: My Murderous Childhood (and Other Grievous Yarns).* 2004. 128pp. 1-59307-194-9.
> *Vol. 3: Heaps Of Ruination.* 2005. 128pp. 1-59307-292-9.
> *Vol. 4: Virtue and the Grim Consequences Thereof.* 2006. 144pp. 1-59307-456-5.
> *Vol. 5: Wicked Inclinations.* 2006. 136pp. 1-59307-646-0.
> *Fancy Pants Edition.* 2005. 184pp. 1-59307-426-3, hardcover.

Grumpy Old Monsters. **Written by Kevin J. Anderson and Rebecca Moesta. Illustrated by Paco Cavero and Guillermo Mendoza.** IDW Publishing, 2004. 96pp. 1-932382-35-6. **Y**

At the Rest In Peace retirement community, where their slogan is "retirement care facility for mature monsters with special needs," you'll find all of the classic movie monsters. Time hasn't been kind to them, but they're still dead and kicking. Dracula wears dentures, the Wolfman is losing all of his hair, and the Mummy is literally unraveling. When their beloved Castle Frankenstein is threatened to be torn down and made into high-rise condos by the Van Helsing Development Corporation, Frankenstein's monster, Dracula, the Wolf-Man, the Mummy, and other favorites break out of R.I.P. to save it.

Hellboy Junior. **Written by Mike Mignola, Bill Wray, et al. Illustrated by various.** Dark Horse Comics, 2004. 120pp. 1-56971-988-8. **O**

A dark, twisted spoof of the Harvey Comics stories of old. Featuring Hellboy Junior, a pint-sized version of Mike Mignola's popular horrific hero Hellboy in his youth. The stories feature vignettes of Hellboy Junior's youth growing up in Hell. Along for the ride in Hell are Hellboy Jr.'s pals Wheezy the Sick Little Witch, the Ginger Beef Boy, and Huge Retarded Duck. For more tales featuring a more serious look at Hellboy, see chapter 6.

I Luv Halloween. **Written by Keith Giffen. Illustrated by Ben Roman.** TOKYOPOP, 2005– . **O Neo-manga.**

© 2006 TOKYOPOP.

A series focusing on the scariest day of the year. No, not April 15, it's Halloween! In the first collection, a group of not-so-nice juvenile delinquents—Finch, Pig Pig, Devil Lad, Mr. Kitty, Spike, and Moochie—seek revenge on an old lady whom they think jinxed their Halloween haul by passing out fruit instead of candy to the trick-or-treaters. In the meantime, murders, flashing big-breasted neighbors, razorblade apples, sliced fingers, and more happen in one spooky night. In the second collection, the city is overrun by zombies. Will the kids still be able to get their candy when the undead are walking and ruining Halloween?

> *Vol. 1.* 2005. 192pp. 1-59532-831-9.
> *Vol. 2.* 2005. 192pp. 1-59532-832-7.

Johnny the Homicidal Maniac: Director's Cut. **Written and illustrated by Jhonen Vasquez.** Slave Labor Graphics, 1998. 168pp. 0-943151-16-3. **M**

Sadistic, brutal, but never taking itself too seriously, this is a cult-classic collection featuring a shockingly dark and disturbing look at the twisted life of Johnny (or "Nny" as he likes to call himself). Nny is not your typical goth teenager—he doesn't fit in and is constantly ridiculed. Nny deals with his detractors in a most unhealthy way: by either murdering, mutilating, or capturing them. Nny's room is painted red with blood, bunnies are nailed to the walls, and his own comic book, *Happy Noodle Boy,* is a hit with the comic-book-reading homeless. Nny definitely does not have the healthiest of hobbies, but he does need to apply fresh blood often to catch a monster that lives behind them. So that means that anyone, even those who annoy Nny in the slightest, is next on the chopping block.

Lenore. **Written and illustrated by Roman Dirge.** Slave Labor Graphics, 1999–2006. **T** ◎

© 2006 by Roman Dirge.

The dark-humored gothic adventures of a little dead girl named Lenore. She's sweet and innocent yet hysterically violent and twisted to all of her odd friends, both the living and the dead. Lenore lives alone in her own house, where the odd and bizarre are her next-door neighbors and she's chased by a love-sick sockpuppet-faced suitor who just doesn't know that they're not dating no matter how many times she kills him. He'll get it right one of these days.

> *Vol. 1: Noogies.* 1999. 112pp. 0-943151-03-1.
> *Vol. 2: Wedgies.* 2001. 112pp. 0-943151-31-7.
> *Vol. 3: Cooties!.* 2006. 120pp. 1-59362-024-1.

***Little Gloomy: It Was a Dark and Stormy Night* . . . . Written by Landry Walker. Illustrated by Eric Jones.** Slave Labor Graphics, 2002. 128pp. 0-943151-64-3. **Y**

© 2006 by Landry Walker
and Eric Jones.

In the Halloween-like town of Spooksville, everyone's out to get the girl named Gloomy—she's the seemingly only normal human in a town where everyone's a monster. Plant people want to hypnotize her and make her their leader, a girl wants to bathe in Gloomy's blood so she can remain young, and now her spurned ex-boyfriend has created an army of zombies to get revenge on her! Sometimes it pays to stay indoors. Now Gloomy and her pals Frank (a Frankenstein Monster who has a crush on her but is afraid to tell her), Larry (a sarcastic werewolf), and Carl Cthulhu (a shy astral projection of the great evil behemoth demi-god) must try to figure out how to stop Gloomy's ex-boyfriend from destroying Spooksville and then the rest of the world.

***Little Scrowlie Vol. 1.* Written by Todd Meister. Illustrated by Jen Feinberg.** Amaze Ink/Slave Labor Graphics, 2004. 120pp. 1-59362-000-4. **T**

The adventures of a scrowlie black cat named Little Scrowlie, her goth-girl owner Elisabeth, their live-in ghost, and Elisabeth's boyfriend James, as they go through the routines of life in California with an impending appearance of Cthulhu, Cthulhu's minions, and even mad plots to take over the world through an army of evil fashion zombies. Can Scrowlie get the job done and still have time to take a mid-afternoon nap?

***Outlook Grim, Vol. 1: The Dead Nasties.* Written and illustrated by Black Olive.** Amaze Ink/Slave Labor Graphics, 2005. 160pp. 1-59362-006-3. **T**

Spunky Wren and her best friend Chloe have accidentally invited unwelcome house guests from another realm into their lives. Now how the heck can they get the ghosts out of their house? With Ouijah boards, voo doo dolls, zombies, psychic gypsies, and more, Wren is trying her darndest to clean the house, but she may just have to go to the "other side" to solve her problem once and for all! Can she exorcise her house before she gets annoyed to death?

<u>Patrick the Wolf Boy.</u> Written by Art Baltazar and Franco Aureliani. Illustrated by Art Baltazar. Blind Wolf Studios and Devil's Due Publishing, 2004–2005. **A**

© 2006 by Art Baltazar
and Franco Aureliani.

Meet Patrick, a not-so normal young boy being raised by normal parents. Even though there's something not quite right about him, his parents don't seem to mind. Could it be the two fangs protruding from his mouth, the pointy ears, and the fact that he changes into a werewolf when the full moon rises? Yeah, that's probably it. Join Patrick the Wolf Boy as he spends his humorous days at school, in the playground, chasing squirrels, out camping with his father, trick-or-treating for Halloween night, going to see *Star Wars* at the movie theater, playing super-hero at home, and meeting aliens from outer space; there's plenty of fur-flying fun wherever he goes.

The Giant Size Collection Volume 1 & 2. 2004. 160pp. 0-9749941-0-3.
The Giant Size Collection Volume 3 & 4. 2004. 160pp. 0-9749941-1-1.

Patrick the Wolf Boy, Vol. 1. 2005. 144pp. 1-932796-27-4.
Patrick the Wolf Boy, Vol. 2. 2005. 144pp. 1-932796-29-0.

Preacher. Written by Garth Ennis. Illustrated by Steve Dillon and various.
Vertigo/DC Comics, 1996–2001. **M**

© 2006 by Garth Ennis
and Steve Dillon.

A black-humored and ultra-violent journey of one man given the power of God. Jesse Custer had dedicated his life to God as a preacher for a small town church in Texas. When he's unexpectedly joined by a half-angel/half-demon known as Genesis, he is given the gift of The Word. Now he can command anyone to do his bidding, even to kill. He joins up with his gun-toting tough ex-girlfriend Tulip and a hard-drinking Irish vampire named Cassidy, and the group begins a violent and dark-humored journey across America to find God, who has left his throne in Heaven in fear of Genesis. Pursued by a secret religious organization called the Grail and by an unkillable, ultra-violent force of nature known as the Saint of Killers, Jesse, Tulip, and Cassidy's friendship is all that they have to keep them together—but even that might not be enough to get them past the horrors awaiting them in the coming conflict. The series won several Eisner Awards, including Best Writer (1998) and Best Continuing Series (1999).

Vol. 1: Gone to Texas. 1996. 200pp. 1-56389-261-8.
Vol. 2: Until the End of the World. 1997. 256pp. 1-56389-312-6.
Vol. 3: Proud Americans. 1997. 232pp. 1-56389-327-4.
Vol. 4: Ancient History. 1999. 224pp. 1-56389-405-X.
Vol. 5: Dixie Fried. 1999. 224pp. 1-56389-428-9.
Vol. 6: War in the Sun. 1999. 240pp. 1-56389-490-4.
Vol. 7: Salvation. 1999. 256pp. 1-56389-519-6.
Vol. 8: All Hell's A-Coming. 2000. 256pp. 1-56389-617-6.
Vol. 9: Alamo. 2001. 232pp. 1-56389-715-6.

Reiko the Zombie Shop. Written and illustrated by Rei Mikamoto. Dark Horse Comics, 2005– . **O Japanese manga.**

When brutal murders are committed in the sleepy town of Shiraike and a culprit can't be found, there's only one woman for the job—Reiko the Zombie Shop! A beautiful and powerful young necromancer, she can bring back the dead for a hefty price and have them tell their deepest secrets—including how they died and who killed them. A word of caution—Reiko's not responsible for what the zombies say or do once they awaken! A zany horror comedy in the vein of the classic <u>Evil Dead</u> films. Eleven volumes were published in Japan.

 8

Vol. 1. 2005. 192pp. 1-59307-413-1.
Vol. 2. 2006. 200pp. 1-59307-459-X.
Vol. 3. 2006. 192pp. 1-59307-535-9.
Vol. 4. 2006. 192pp. 1-59307-609-6.
Vol. 5. 2006. 184pp. 1-59307-610-x.

🏵 <u>Scary Godmother.</u> **Written and illustrated by Jill Thompson.** Sirius Entertainment, 1997–2004. **A** ◎ ⌨

A charming series for all ages. Little Hannah Marie is spending Halloween with her rotten cousin Jimmy, who is sullen because he is stuck baby-sitting her on Halloween night. To make up for it, he's making sure Hannah's scared silly. To Hannah's rescue comes the oddest fairy of all—her Scary Godmother! Dressed in a witch's costume with white and red-striped stockings and bright red hair, Scary Godmother, with a little help from her spooky friends, will give Jimmy a fright he'll never forget. Further adventures take Hannah, Jimmy, Scary Godmother, and her ghastly monstrous friends to the realm of Fright Side (where Scary Godmother comes from—and where every day is Halloween) and more. The series has won several Eisner Awards, including Best Title for Younger Readers/Best Comics Publication for a Younger Audience (2001), and Jill Thompson won an Eisner for Best Painter/Multimedia Artist (Interior) (2001). The story has also been recently been adapted as a computer animated series of cartoons that have aired on the Cartoon Network.

Vol. 1. 1997. 48pp. 1-57989-015-6.
Vol. 2: The Revenge of Jimmy. 1999. 48pp. 1-57989-020-2.
Vol. 3: The Mystery Date. 2003. 48pp. 1-57989-026-1.
Vol. 4: The Boo Flu. 2003. 48pp. 1-57989-038-5.
Wild About Harry. 2003. 72pp. 1-57989-046-6.
Spooktacular Stories. 2004. 96pp. 1-57989-076-8.

Sergio Aragonés' Boogeyman. **Written by Mark Evanier and Sergio Aragonés. Illustrated by Sergio Aragonés.** Dark Horse Comics, 1999. 112pp. 1-56971-374-X. **T**

Sergio Aragonés spoofs the horror genre and classic shows like *The Twilight Zone* in short tales narrated by Mr. Dibbs, the gravedigging storyteller at the local boneyard. Mr. Dibbs narrates through rhyme his humorous tales of the fears and paranoia that we all carry inside us in their many manifestations, including ghosts, goblins, zombies, and movie critics.

Squee's Wonderful Big Giant Book of Unspeakable Horrors. **Written and illustrated by Jhonen Vasquez.** Slave Labor Graphics, 1998. 144pp. 0-943151-24-4. **O** ◎

What would you say if you lived next door to a serial killer? That's part of Todd's (Squee's) dilemma. This shy little boy lives next door to Johnny the Homicidal Maniac, and "Nny" takes great delight in making Todd nervous. When Nny speaks to Todd, the only sound he can make is a meager "squee." Todd's life just seems to go from bad to worse. His parents hate him. His dad says he ruined his life. His mom ignores him. To top if off, Todd's odd stuffed teddy bear constantly tries to scare him and eggs him on to hate his parents, and he has even been abducted by two different alien species in one night. Life sure is tough on the most high-strung six-year-old in town.

Supernatural Law. **Written and illustrated by Batton Lash.** Exhibit A Press, 1999– . **T**

When the creatures of the night are in dire need of help, there's only one place they can go: Alanna Wolff and Jeff Byrd, attorneys at law! At Wolf & Byrd, they can handle any case of the supernatural, including a "hexual harassment" case, a teenage vampire afraid of a vampire slayer, an ex-wife of a mad scientist, a famed horror author in a coma, and a man so negative that he repels everything. There's no case too strange for Wolff & Byrd to handle.

> *Sonovawitch! and Other Tales of Supernatural Law.* 1999. 176pp. 0-9633954-6-7.
> *The Vampire Brat and Other Tales of Supernatural Law.* 2001. 176pp. 0-9633954-7-5.
> *Mister Negativity and Other Tales of Supernatural Law.* 2003. 176pp. 0-9633954-8-3.

Van Helsing's Night Off and Other Tales. **Written and illustrated by Nicholas Mahler.** Top Shelf Productions, 2004. 112pp. 1-891830-38-4. **O**

Welcome to the haunting but hilarious world of vampires, werewolves, and mummies, and the heroes who fight them. In these short sketches, the absurd and the supernatural go hand in hand. See what Van Helsing does on his day off, laugh as the wolf-woman eats dinner with her husband, and find out just how Van Helsing, smooth man that he is, gets all the ladies in the room.

Humorous Science Fiction

A tongue-in-cheek look at what life could be like with androids, robots, and alien invaders. The stories can be set in the present day on Earth, in the far future, or a million miles away in outer space, but inclusion of the absurd or the off-beat is a must. Prose science fiction titles comparable to this subgenre include the late Douglas Adams's *Hitchhiker's Guide to the Galaxy* as well as the writing of Terry Pratchett. You may be glad to see that in the future there are plenty of laughs.

Akiko. **Written and illustrated by Mark Crilley.** Sirius Entertainment, Incorporated, 2004– . **Y**

© 2006 by Mark Crilley.

The out-of-this-world adventures of the spunky Japanese American fourth grader, Akiko, and her exciting exploits in outer space. Whisked away to the faraway planet Smoo, she is asked by the planet's ruler, King Froptoppit, to rescue the prince on several occasions and also has other odd adventures. Accompanying Akiko on her travels are her extraterrestrial companions: iPoog, a floating head; Spuckler Boach, a scruffy-looking mercenary; Mr. Beeba, a stodgy academic; and Gax, Spuckler's broken-down robot. Together they take on the menace of Alia Rellapor. A fun and whimsical series inspired by Frank L. Baum's Wizard of Oz series, Star Wars, and Monty Python.

> *Pocket-Size, Vol. 1: The Menace of Alia Rellapor part 1.* 2004. 192pp. 1-579890-67-9.

Pocket-Size, Vol. 2: The Menace of Alia Rellapor part 2. 2004. 128pp. 1-57989-068-7.
Pocket-Size, Vol. 3: The Menace of Alia Rellapor part 3. 2004. 128pp. 1-579890-69-5.
Pocket-Size, Vol. 4: The Story Tree. 2006. 144pp. 1-579890-78-4.
Pocket-Size, Vol. 5: Bornstone's Elixir. 2006. 112pp. 1-579890-79-2.
Vol. 6: Stranded in Komura/Moonshopping. 2005. 136pp. 1-579890-57-1.
Vol. 7: The Battle of Boach's Keep. 2005. 144pp. 1-57989-064-4.

A.L.I.E.E.E.N. Written and illustrated by Lewis Trondheim. First Second, 2006. 96pp. 1-59643-095-8. **Y**

© 2006 by Lewis Trondheim.

People have long pondered about life in outer space and whether aliens really do exist—what sort of comic books would they read? Though humanity has never seen aliens, we've now discovered the next best thing: a graphic novel made by aliens and accidentally left behind on Earth! Claimed to have been left behind by an alien race and found by the vacationing graphic novel creator Lewis Trondheim in the middle of the Catskills, the stories feature short Pokémon-like creatures gouging their eyes out, being eaten, making friends, and even having an occasional poop—which proceeds to flood an entire alien city. *AL.I.E.E.E.N.* (Archives of Lost Issues and Earthly Editions of Extraterrestrial Novelties) is a nonsensical and farcical look at what comic books would be like on other planets. The book also includes faux printing to make it look like an aged graphic novel.

***All Purpose Cultural Cat Girl Nuku Nuku.* Written and illustrated by Yuzo Takada and Yuji Moriyama.** ADV Manga, 2004. 104pp. 1-4139-0024-0. **T Japanese manga.**

When inventor Kyusaku Natsume places the brain of his son's pet cat in the body of a high-tech android he is building for Mishima Heavy Industries, the unexpected happens and Nuku Nuku is born! Now the family cat has enhanced strength, speed, and agility framed around a metal alloy that looks amazingly like a normal cute high school girl, and she's turning all the heads at school. She'll need all the strength she can muster as she tries to rescue her "brother" Ryunosuke from the attacks of Mishima Heavy Industries, a ruthless business company run by the most ruthless businessperson —his own mother!

***Astronauts of the Future.* Written by Lewis Trondheim. Illustrated by Manu Larcenet.** NBM Publishing, 2004. 96pp. 1-56163-407-7. **T**

Martina and Gil are elementary school-age kids full of imagination and secret conspiracies. For Martina, everyone else on Earth is a robot and pretending to be human. Gil believes that he's an astronaut sent to exterminate the aliens from outer space. Naturally, they become the best of friends as they try to uncover the truth of their own theories. Are both kids making up their stories, or is there really a truth to their seemingly wild imaginations?

***Bubblegum Crisis: Grand Mal.* Written and illustrated by Adam Warren.** Dark Horse Comics, 1995. 112pp. 1-56971-120-8. **O Neo-manga.** あ

Six years after the devastating Great Kanto earthquake, Tokyo was rebuilt into a symbol of wealth and power and rechristened MegaTokyo in 2031. Crime is still rampant and Boomers, deadly biomechanical humanoid constructs, rule the streets. When even the heavily equipped Armored Defense Police (AD Police) can't stop the Boomers, it's up to a shadowy organization called the Knight Sabers to save the day. Led by Sylia Stingray, the organization is made up of three other tough-but-good-natured female members, including musician Priss, fighting instructor Linna Yamazaki, and tech-support contact Nene Romanova. Their goal is to burst the bubble of the Boomers before the beleaguered city is over-run by the androids. The series was also released as an anime series in Japan.

DearS. Written and illustrated by Peach-Pit. TOKYOPOP, 2005–2006. **T Japanese manga.** あ

Aliens walk among us. The world has nicknamed them "DearS" due to their elegant appearance. They have come to Earth to learn about our culture and ways by being assigned to families across the globe. High-school student Takeya Ikuhara has it rough enough dealing with Neneko, his landlady's cute daughter, and Myu, a friend at school who is knowledgeable about the aliens; but when he inadvertently rescues a slave DearS named Ren, she becomes in-debted to him and now calls him "master" and stays with him in his apartment. Ren decides to learn the culture of Japan and enrolls in school alongside Takeya, but what will he do when he's surrounded by three beautiful women? Meanwhile, there are others out there looking for Ren who will stop at nothing to reclaim her. Eight volumes were originally published in Japan and the se-ries was also adapted into a thirteen-episode anime series.

Vol. 1. 2005. 200pp. 1-59532-308-2.
Vol. 2. 2005. 208pp. 1-59532-309-0.
Vol. 3. 2005. 192pp. 1-59532-310-4.
Vol. 4. 2005. 192pp. 1-59532-311-2.
Vol. 5. 2006. 192pp. 1-59532-797-5.
Vol. 6. 2006. 192pp. 1-59532-798-3.
Vol. 7. 2006. 200pp. 1-59816-185-7.
Vol. 8. 2006. 192pp. 1-59816-861-4.

The Dirty Pair. Written and illustrated by Adam Warren. Dark Horse Comics, 1998–2003. **O Neo-manga.** あ

When you absolutely need something destroyed overnight, send in the Lovely Angels, a.k.a. the Dirty Pair! Kei and Yuri are professional trouble consultants for the 3WA of the United Galactica, traveling around the galaxy solving crimes for the good of the universe and out for a good tan in their downtime. Two of the most reckless employees, they've battled hordes of murderers, a former co-worker-turned-assassin, gangsters, prisoners, a legion of Dirty Pair fans at their own convention, and even the dreaded employee review. Can the galaxy survive one more hazardous mission of mangafied action and comedy? The series was based on a series of novels by Haruka Takachiho and was also adapted as an anime series in Japan in 1985.

Biohazards. 2d ed. 1998. 120pp. 1-56971-339-1.
Fatal But Not Serious. 1996. 128pp. 1-56971-172-0.
Dangerous Acquaintances. 1997. 122pp. 1-56971-227-1.

> *Run from the Future.* 2002. 136pp. 1-56971-577-7.
> *Sim Hell.* 3d ed. 2004. 128pp. 1-56971-742-7.

Dominion. Written and illustrated by Masamune Shirow. Dark Horse Comics, 1997–2000. O Japanese manga. あ

The lighthearted adventures of a tank-driving police force in a future when the air is toxic and people must wear gas masks outside. When a winged girl who has the power to cleanse the air is kidnapped by the criminal known as Buaku, it's up to Leona Ozaki, her mini-tank Bonaparte, and her lovesick companion Al to confront Buaku and his catgirl bodyguards, Annapuma and Unipuma, to bring their crime wave to an end. *Conflict 1—No More Noise* continues the hi-jinks with Anna and Uni joining the police force as Sergeant Ozaki tries to survive a hard day at work, as well as catch the sky pirate Urushi-Maru. The manga was also adapted into an anime series called <u>Dominion: Tank Police</u>.

> *Tank Police.* 3d ed. 2000. 224pp. 1-56971-488-6.
> *Conflict 1—No More Noise.* 1997. 160pp. 1-56971-233-6.

Dr. Radium. Written and illustrated by Scott Saavedra. Slave Labor Graphics/Amaze Ink, 2004–2005. T

In the far future, when the world is considered "perfect," there is no need for science since everything has been decided for people. The last true scientist of the future, Dr. Radium, continues his mad-scientist-like investigations into the heart of the unknown, with reckless abandon. Meanwhile he's out to save the world from the Elvi, an alien race that worship Elvis, encounters time-traveling scientists from the 1950s, battles Phil the King of the Pill Bugs, and many more zany adventures.

> *Vol. 1: Dr. Radium Battles Phill, King of the Pill Bugs!* 2004. 112pp. 0-943151-84-8.
> *Vol. 2: Dr. Radium and the Gizmos of Boola Boola!* 2004. 112pp. 0-943151-92-9.
> *Vol. 3: It's Science with Dr. Radium.* 2005. 128pp. 1-59362-013-6.

Dr. Slump. Written and illustrated by Akira Toriyama. VIZ Media, LLC, 2005– . T ◎ Japanese manga. あ

DR. SLUMP © 1980 by Akira Toriyama/SHUEISHA Inc.

Dr. Slump is known as Dr. Senbei Norimaki (which translates in Japanese to "little rice cracker") of Penguin Village. He's a crazy inventor and has just created his finest work—a robot that appears to be a cute thirteen-year-old girl. He names "her" Arale (which translates to "even littler cracker") , but even though she's super-strong, she's near-sighted and is innocently constantly getting herself into trouble. From problems attending middle school, to the one thing that girls have but Arale doesn't, to X-ray specs, to time travel, to pet bears, Arale and Senbei are constantly getting into calamitous trouble. The series is a reprinting of the eighteen-volume collection originally published in Japan. The manga series was also adapted into several anime series, including several television shows and movies.

> *Vol. 1.* 2005. 192pp. 1-59116-950-X.
> *Vol. 2.* 2005. 192pp. 1-59116-951-8.
> *Vol. 3.* 2005. 200pp. 1-59116-991-7.
> *Vol. 4.* 2005. 200pp. 1-4215-0165-1.

Vol. 5. 2006. 200pp. 1-4215-0173-2.
Vol. 6. 2006. 200pp. 1-4215-0174-0.
Vol. 7. 2006. 200pp. 1-4215-0631-9.
Vol. 8. 2006. 200pp. 1-4215-0632-7.
Vol. 9. 2006. 200pp. 1-4215-0633-5.
Vol. 10. 2006. 200pp. 1-4215-0634-3.
Vol. 11. 2007. 208pp. 1-4215-0635-1.
Vol. 12. 2007. 192pp. 1-4215-1056-1.

Drakuun: Rise of the Dragon. Written and illustrated by Johji Manabe. Dark Horse Comics, 1998–1999. **O Japanese manga.**

Her sister's kingdom besieged by the vicious Romunilian Empire, Princess Karula, the warriorlike Dragon Princess of the kingdom of Ledomiam, is on the run after a failed assassination attempt on the evil the Emperor Gustav of the Romunilian Empire. Surviving on her wits as well as the help of her new-found companions, she must do what she can to end the reign of Emperor Gustav, even if it means forging an alliance with another evil adversary. The concluding volume of the series has yet to be published.

Vol. 1: Rise of the Dragon Princess. 1999. 168pp. 1-56971-302-2.
Vol. 2: The Revenge of Gustav. 1999. 160pp. 1-56971-368-5.
Vol. 3: Shadow of the Warlock. 1999. 160pp. 1-56971-406-1.

***Emily and the Intergalactic Lemonade Stand.* Written by Ian Smith. Illustrated by Tyson Smith.** Amaze Ink/Slave Labor Graphics Publishing, 2004 104pp. 0-943151-96-1. **A**

© 2006 by Ian Smith and Tyson Smith.

All eleven-year-old Emily wants is a pony of her own. His name is Marcus, and he'll one day be hers, but first she has to earn enough money for him. What better way than with her own lemonade stand?! With her robot Juicer and his transdimensional portal, she makes the freshest lemonade on Earth and within four million light years. Even Emily's scheming arch-nemesis Daisy can't come close to beating Emily and Juicer when it comes to making lemonade. When alien invaders come to Earth to terraform the planet into their own amusement park, the U.S. government wants to use Juicer as the ultimate weapon against the aliens. How can one girl help save Earth and make enough money to buy her pony?

FLCL. Written and illustrated by Hajime Ueda. TOKYOPOP, 2003. **T Japanese manga.** あ

8

Naota is a teen living in a world where nothing makes much sense. His father is a pervert, his older brother's ex-girlfriend is hitting on him, and now an alien named Haruko has joined the family after hitting him on the head with a guitar. When Naota spews robots from his head and is instantly turned into a mutant warrior, something mighty peculiar is up. Maybe there's more to Haruko than meets the eye. The series was inspired by the anime series of the same name.

Vol. 1. 2003. 176pp. 1-59182-396-X.
Vol. 2. 2003. 208pp. 1-59182-397-8.

Geobreeders. Written and illustrated by Ahihiro Ito. CPM Manga, 2002–2004. **T Japanese manga.**

The shape-shifting Phantom Cats are taking control of the electronics and phone lines of the world, seeking world domination. Only the six agents of Kagura Security Company are trained to seek out and destroy the ghost-cats in the machine, that is, if the agents don't destroy Earth in the process! Some might say the Kagura Security Company agents are completely mad, and they might be right. Every day for the comedic lunatics of Kagura Security Company is a nonstop calamity of explosions, gunfire, and mass destruction as they chase the elusive cybernetic invading cats around Japan. CPM republished the first three volumes in a smaller digest-sized format, but discontinued the line before the last two volumes could be republished.

Book 1. 2d ed. 2004. 216pp. 1-58664-929-9.
Book 2. 2d ed. 2004. 216pp. 1-58664-946-9.
Book 3. 2d ed. 2004. 208pp. 1-58664-949-3.
Book 4. 2002. 224pp. 1-58664-864-0.
Book 5. 2003. 248pp. 1-58664-877-2.

Girl Genius. Written and illustrated by Phil Foglio and Kaja Foglio. Airship Entertainment, 2002– . **T**

On an Earth where the Industrial Revolution never ended, steam-powered robots called "clanks," flying airships, and alien creatures roam the world. At Transylvania Polygnostic University, Agatha Clay is a lab assistant trying her best to become a mad scientist (or "Spark") , but her experiments fail most of the time. She becomes entangled with the ruthless Spark Baron Klaus Wulfenbach and his impatient son, and Agatha discovers that she's the last of a heroic Heterodyne bloodline.

Book 1: Agatha Heterodyne and the Beetleburg Clank. 2002. 96pp. 1-890856-19-3.
Book 2: Agatha Heterodyne and the Airship City. 2005. 112pp. 1-890856-30-4.
Book 3: Agatha Heterodyne and the Monster Engine. 2005. 128pp. 1-890856-33-9.
Book 4: Agatha Heterodyne and the Circus of Dreams. 2006. 128pp. 1-890856-36-3.

***The Hitchhiker's Guide to the Galaxy: The Authorized Collection.* Based on the novel by Douglas Adams. Adapted by John Carnell. Illustrated by Steve Leialoha.** Paradox Press/DC Comics, 1997. 144pp. 1-56389-271-5. **T** 🎬

The adaptation of the classic science fiction comedy novel by Douglas Adams. Mere seconds before Earth is destroyed by an alien construction crew for a hyperspace motorway, Arthur Dent and his alien friend Ford Prefect are whisked away onto a Vorgon cruiser. Now planetless, they wander the galaxy, getting into one horrible mess after another, encountering strange aliens, including President of the Galaxy Zaphod Beeblebrox, his lovely assistant Trillian, and Marvin the depressed robot. The classic science fiction comedy novel was also adapted as a feature film in 2005.

Hyper Police. **Written and illustrated by MEE.** TOKYOPOP, 2005– . **O Japanese manga.** あ

In the future, humans are an endangered species and the monsters of the world have taken over . . . our jobs!? With crime still rampant, the monster Police Company still tries to maintain order on the streets of Shinjuku. Natsuki, a young cat-girl with magical powers and the annoying tendency to shoot her own partners by accident, is slowly learning the tricks of the bounty hunting trade with her mentor Batanen Fujioka, the werewolf. Natsuki's latest partner is Sakura, a nine-tailed female fox who wants Natsuki for something else: to gobble her up and consume her magic! Will this partnership last, or will the fox consume the cat? The series was also adapted as a twenty-five-episode anime series in Japan.

Vol. 1. 2005. 192pp. 1-59532-294-9.
Vol. 2. 2005. 192pp. 1-59532-295-7.
Vol. 3. 2005. 184pp. 1-59532-296-5.
Vol. 4. 2005. 192pp. 1-59532-297-3.
Vol. 5. 2006. 192pp. 1-59532-298-1.
Vol. 6. 2006. 184pp. 1-59532-299-X.
Vol. 7. 2006. 192pp. 1-59532-300-7.
Vol. 8. 2007. 192pp. 1-59532-301-5.

Hyper Rune. **Written and illustrated by Tamayo Akiyama.** TOKYOPOP, 2004–2005. **T Japanese manga.**

With a mad scientist for a grandfather, eighth-grader Rune Ayanokouji's life is certainly never dull. Her grandfather constantly calls Rune the "Space Queen" and designs costumes for her to wear to find the ideal costume for a Space Queen. A plot to conquer Earth is revealed as two alien races come to the planet, one good, one evil. Rune seeks the aid of her twin friends, who mysteriously are able to transform into robot forms similar to the appearance of the aliens. Now Rune and her two friends have to discover which of the alien races is the evil one and prevent an alien conquest of Earth. Sounds like a job for the Space Queen!

Vol. 1. 2004. 192pp. 1-59532-241-8.
Vol. 2. 2005. 192pp. 1-59532-242-6.
Vol. 3. 2005. 192pp. 1-59532-243-4.
Vol. 4. 2005. 192pp. 1-59532-244-2.

Imperfect Hero. **Written and illustrated by Gureko Nankin.** Dr Master Publications, 2004–2006. **T Japanese manga.**

A spoof of the classic Japanese team hero manga and anime series including Gatchaman, Voltron, and Power Rangers. Yugi Midorikawa is learning the hard way of life as a super-hero. He's a high school student who's also known as "Green," the bumbling member of the Gakusei 5 (G5) team of heroes based at his school. He and his teammates—Blue, Red, Yellow, and Pink—regularly defend Earth from the invading race of aliens called the Gurdark. It turns out that being a villain isn't so great, either. Time and time again Queen Mayura of the Gurdark has been defeated by G5, yet she's never even spent time on Earth, a planet that one day she swears she will conquer. When Yugi finds the

Queen in a park one day, she says she wants to put the Gurdark lifestyle behind her and find a boyfriend; Yugi takes pity on her and brings her in. Now on top of saving Earth and balancing homework, how can Yugi keep it a secret that he has the G5 archenemy staying at his own house?

> *Vol. 1.* 2004. 200pp. 1-58899-235-7.
> *Vol. 2.* 2006. 200pp. 1-58899-317-5.
> *Vol. 3.* 2006. 208pp. 1-59796-094-2.

***The Lab, Vol. 1: Hey ... Test This!* Written and illustrated by Scott Christian Sava.** The Astonish Factory, 2004. 120pp. 0-9721259-3-0. **Y**

The adventures of Esteban the weasel and Livingston the mole, both lab animals at Itchez Labs. Livingston's job is to sniff armpits and Esteban's is to cause as much trouble as possible. When they're asked to test out a mysterious Product X and record the side-effects, the fun really begins as they sing and dance and blow things up, all in the name of science.

***Littlegreyman.* Written and illustrated by C. Scott Morse.** Image Comics, 1997. 96pp. 1-88727955-5. **T**

The absurd adventures of a little grey alien called Littlegreyman and his sidekick robotic turtle. On the run from the "cinematic trio"—what appear to be real-life incarnations of movie characters played by Clint Eastwood, Toshiro Mifune, and Chow Yun Fat—they're out to drive him off the planet, for reasons unknown. Littlegreyman finds himself involved in a plot littered with men in black and their sexy agents. Can one lone alien withstand spoofs from cinema, music, and a plot to destroy Earth's cows with a genetically engineered Pine Martin who can fly a spaceship?

***Lum—Urusei Yatsura: Perfect Collection.* Written and illustrated by Rumiko Takahashi.** VIZ Media, LLC, 1997. 400pp. 1-56931-019-X. **T Japanese manga.** あ

The world has just been invaded by ogre-like aliens and the Earthling chosen to save it is the teen lecher Ataru Morobishi! If Ataru can win in a game of tag and touch the horns of the alien's representative, the green-haired and beautiful Lum, the aliens will retreat. When Ataru's girlfriend Shinobu offers to marry him if he wins, it gives Ataru the courage to do what must be done to win the game. The next day, Ataru finally touches the flying Lum. In his happiness he exclaims that now they can be married, but Lum thinks he means that she's going to marry Ataru and calls herself Ataru's "wife." What's a man to do? A classic science fiction comedy from the creator of *Ranma ½* and *InuYasha*. The title was adapted as an anime series.

Nadesico. **Written and illustrated by Kia Asamiya.** CPM Manga, 2003–2004. **Japanese manga.** あ

A heavily armed and deadly armada from Jupiter has recently begun its conquest of the rest of the universe. The recently colonized Mars has fallen to the might of the Jovian forces, and Earth is next. Against their massive force of warships, the United Earth Government's fleet fights valiantly but fails to protect Earth. There's still hope: the Space Battleship *Nadesico*. Fitted with alien technology and created by the Nergal Corporation, it's the best and last hope for Earth, even though the hapless crew is still a little wet behind the ears. It is commanded by Yurika Misumaru, a cute and headstrong girl who graduated top of her class but has never faced real battle. She and her crew, piloted by the Martian immigrant Akito Tenkawa, may not have the experience, but they'll prove to the planet that they mean business and will fight the Jovian forces or die trying. The series ran for twenty-six episodes as an anime series in Japan.

> *Vol. 1.* 2003. 184pp. 1-56219-901-3.
> *Vol. 2.* 2004. 168pp. 1-58664-907-8.
> *Vol. 3.* 2004. 168pp. 1-58664-940-X.
> *Vol. 4.* 2004. 192pp. 1-58664-941-8.

***Pinky and Stinky.* Written and illustrated by James Kochalka.** Top Shelf Productions, 2002. 208pp. 1-891830-29-5. **Y**

© 2006 by James Kolchalka.

The adventures of two talking pig astronauts who crash land on the moon after being hit by an asteroid. Their journey to Pluto put on hold, they're stranded and have to make the best of it. They locate a nearby space station that is run by some unscrupulous humans who aren't too thrilled to find pigs in space. After falling into a chasm, the two pigs encounter some unhappy residents of the moon living beneath the surface. Will the pigs become friends with the moon aliens, and will they ever get back into outer space? A subtle story of friendship, colonization, and accepting people for who they are . . . with pigs in space!

Psychic Academy. Written and illustrated by Katsu Aki. TOKYOPOP, 2004–2006 **T Japanese manga.**

Everyone wants Ai Shiomi to follow in his big brother's footsteps, but he definitely has big shoes to fill since his brother is known as "The Vanquisher of the Dark Overlord," the only psychic who was able to defeat the most vile evil psychic user and single-handedly saved the world. Now Ai has been accepted to the Psychic Academy, a school made for new children exhibiting psychic abilities, only Ai doesn't think he has what it takes to be at the school; in fact, Ai has no skill at all! Now everyone at school thinks Ai will be just as special as his brother, but boy, are they about to be disappointed! Now Ai is a joke, his best friend is a psychic rabbit who gives him dating advice, and worst all, his brother is one of his teachers at the Academy!

> *Vol. 1.* 2004. 192pp. 1-59182-621-7.
> *Vol. 2.* 2004. 192pp. 1-59182-622-5.
> *Vol. 3.* 2004. 192pp. 1-59182-623-3.
> *Vol. 4.* 2004. 192pp. 1-59182-624-1.
> *Vol. 5.* 2004. 192pp. 1-59182-625-X.
> *Vol. 6.* 2005. 192pp. 1-59532-425-9.
> *Vol. 7.* 2005. 192pp. 1-59532-426-7.
> *Vol. 8.* 2005. 192pp. 1-59532-427-5.
> *Vol. 9.* 2005. 192pp. 1-59532-428-3.
> *Vol. 10.* 2005. 192pp. 1-59532-429-1.
> *Vol. 11.* 2006. 192pp. 1-59532-430-5.

Sardine in Outer Space. **Written by Emmanuel Guibert. Illustrated by Joann Sfar.**
First Second, 2006– . **Y**

© 2006 Emmanuel Guibert
and Joann Sfar.

The adventures of Sardine, a pint-sized swashbuckling heroine with a grand thirst for adventure. She and her cousin Louie, and her pirate uncle Captain Yellow Shoulder, fly across the galaxy in her uncle's ship, the *Huckleberry,* ready to take on any quest and bad guy no matter how big or absurd they are. Whether it's Sardine's dim-witted arch-nemesis Supermuscleman, cosmic squids, talking clouds, a dancing space queen slug, or other oddities, Sardine will be there to save the day. The series was originally published in Europe and is now being reprinted in North America.

> *Vol. 1.* 2006. 126pp. 1-59643-126-1.
> *Vol. 2.* 2006. 126pp. 1-59643-127-X.

Sgt. Frog. **Written and illustrated by Mine Yoshizaki.** TOKYOPOP, 2004–2005. **T Japanese manga.**

When Sgt. Keroro, a small, froglike alien commander from the planet Keron's invasion force, accidentally blows his cover in front of brother and sister Fuyuki and Natsume, his mission to gather information for the invasion of the planet "Pokopen" (Earth) has been compromised, and he and his platoon are stuck millions of miles from home. But even though he wants to take over the planet, maybe this planet's "Pokopenians" aren't so bad after all. Maybe. In exchange for doing chores around the Hinata family household, he has a room of his own, where he can try to locate his lost comrades and think of new ways to take over the world.

> *Vol. 1.* 2004. 188pp. 1-59182-703-5.
> *Vol. 2.* 2004. 188pp. 1-59182-704-3.
> *Vol. 3.* 2004. 196pp. 1-59182-705-1.
> *Vol. 4.* 2004. 188pp. 1-59182-706-X.
> *Vol. 5.* 2004. 188pp. 1-59182-707-8.
> *Vol. 6.* 2005. 192pp. 1-59182-708-6.
> *Vol. 7.* 2005. 192pp. 1-59532-448-8.
> *Vol. 8.* 2005. 192pp. 1-59532-449-6.
> *Vol. 9.* 2005. 192pp. 1-59532-796-7.
> *Vol. 10.* 2005. 192pp. 1-59182-344-7.

Tokyo Mew-Mew. **Written by Ikumi Miya. Illustrated by Yoshida Reiko.**
TOKYOPOP, 2003–2005. **Y Japanese manga.** あ

Eleven-year-old Ichigo Momomiya just wants to date the dreamy Ayoma, but something incredible happens to her one night: her DNA is merged with an almost-extinct mountain wildcat! Now she and four of her friends, who have the DNA of a bird, sea creature, monkey, and wolf, have formed a team called Tokyo Mew Mew to help fight a group of aliens who are using animals of the world to take over the world. Can five girls with animal powers save the planet from aliens and nasty bad guy named Deep Blue and keep their identities safe at school? The manga series was adapted into a fifty-two-episode anime from Japan.

> Tokyo Mew Mew, 1st[t] series. 2003–2004.
> > *Vol. 1.* 2003. 176pp. 1-59182-236-X.
> > *Vol. 2.* 2003. 176pp. 1-59182-237-8.

Vol. 3. 2003. 176pp. 1-59182-238-6.
Vol. 4. 2003. 176pp. 1-59182-239-4.
Vol. 5. 2004. 168pp. 1-59182-548-2.
Vol. 6. 2004. 200pp. 1-59182-549-0.
Vol. 7. 2004. 208pp. 1-59182-550-4.
<u>Tokyo Mew Mew a la Mode.</u> 2005.
Vol. 1. 2005. 208pp. 1-59532-789-4.
Vol. 2. 2005. 216pp. 1-59532-790-8.

<u>The World of Narue.</u> Written and illustrated by Tomohuro Marukawa. CPM Manga, 2004–2005. **T Japanese manga.** あ

High school student Kazuto Izuka has always wanted a girlfriend, so when he meets up with the strangely quiet but captivating girl named Narue, he can hardly believe his luck—she's really half-alien and half-human! She is honest with him from the beginning after saving his life from a cute-but-deadly alien in disguise as a puppy, and they develop a strong friendship from their first date. Though most of the school can hardly believe her story, after she teleports Kazuto with her to see a view of the alien spacefleet, he's not one to argue with her. After all, they've been through everything from fighting androids and aliens, to school pressure and even Narue's half-sister, and Kazuto's and Narue's relationship has never been stronger. The manga was adapted as an anime and was released in Japan in 2003.

Book 1. 2004. 192pp. 1-58664-961-2.
Book 2. 2004. 192pp. 1-58664-962-0.
Book 3. 2004. 192pp. 1-58664-963-9.

Super-Hero Humor

These stories show the humorous side of being a super-hero. Although the story is still mainly about the heroes and fighting crime, often the tales focus on the absurdity of the characters themselves, including their silly costumes, funny occurrences when they are saving the day, and the cynical side of super-heroics. Popular stories include the comedic antics of Plastic Man, the screwball antics of a super-hero team such as the Justice League International, and even the over-the-top black comedy of such anti-heroes as Marshal Law. For more standard super-hero fare, see chapter 1.

<u>Alpha Flight.</u> Written by Scott Lobdell. Illustrated by Clayton Henry. Marvel Comics, 2004–2005. **T**

The comical adventures of the latest Canadian super-hero team, called Alpha Flight. Led by Sasquatch, the all-new team is made up of Centennial, Major Mapleleaf, Nemesis, Puck, and Yukon Jack. Together the misfit team is out to rescue the original Alpha Flight team, captured by an alien race called the Plodex.

Vol. 1: You Gotta Be Kiddin' Me. 2004. 136pp. 0-7851-1430-0.
Vol. 2: Waxing Poetic. 2005. 144pp. 0-7851-1569-2.

🗣 **Bizarro Comics.** **Written and illustrated by various.** DC Comics 2001–2005. **T** ◎

© 2006 DC Comics.

When the best alternative comics writers and artists get their hands on classic DC Comics heroes and villains, the results are bizarro! Includes work by Eddie Campbell, Gilbert Hernandez, Will Pfeifer, Evan Dorkin, Kyle Baker, Jeff Smith, Matt Groening, Tony Millionaire, Brian Ralph, Dylan Horrocks, Bob Fingerman, and others, sharing their own takes on the quirky world of alternative comics blended with tales of the heroic. The highlight of the collection is Kyle Baker's "Letitia Lerner: Superman's Babysitter," which shows the trials and tribulations of a sitter out to watch a toddler Clark Kent with super-human strength. The story won an Eisner Award in 2000 for Best Short Story and a Harvey Award for Best Anthology. *Bizarro World* continues the same off-beat alternative look at super-heroes and includes work by Craig Thompson, Harvey Pekar, Chip Kidd, Tony Millionaire, Kyle Baker, Peter Bagge, and many others.

> *Bizarro Comics.* 2001. 240pp. 1-56389-779-2, hardcover; 2003, 1-56389-958-2, paperback.
> *Bizarro World.* 2005. 200pp. 1-4012-0656-5, hardcover.

Buzzboy. **Written and illustrated by John Gallagher.** Sky Dog Press, 2002–2003. **T**

After the hero of the world, Captain Ultra, declares martial law and becomes its ruler, only the last remaining hero can save the day: Buzzboy, the comic sidekick of Captain Ultra! An oddball hero with a penchant for quoting obscure pop culture references and gorging on fast food, with the power of his mysterious Buzzbelt Buzzboy is able to fight crime one burrito at a time. He is helped in his quest to vanquish "Lord Ultra" by Doc Cyber, a former arch-nemesis who is now his weapons designer and banker; a reality-warping high school student named Becca; Dream Angel Pandora, a guardian of dreams; and Zoomer, a former teen-hero like Buzzboy who has the power of super speed. Together they're able to take on any bad guys who dare to threaten New Paradise and to eat free meals at the local Tastee Diner.

> *Vol. 1: Trouble in Paradise.* 2002. 144pp. 0-9721831-0-8.
> *Vol. 2: Monsters, Dreams, & Milkshakes!* 2003 144pp. 0-9721831-1-6.

Defenders: Indefensible. **Written by Keith Giffen and J. M. DeMatteis. Illustrated by Kevin Maguire.** Marvel Comics, 2006. 120pp. 0-7851-1762-8, softcover; 0-7851-2152-8, hardcover. **T**

The super-hero team called the Defenders, formed in humanity's most desperate hour, was one of the most unlikely and odd super-hero teams. The founding members of the team, the Hulk, Doctor Strange, the Sub-Mariner, and the Silver Surfer, served as core members of the team starting with the team's first appearance in 1971 in the pages of the Marvel Comics series *Marvel Feature* #1, battling a mystical foe. Now years after the team has disbanded, Doctor Strange must bring together the Defenders to battle against the dreaded mystical foes Dormammu and Umar. While the fate of the world hangs in the balance, can the dysfunctional heroes stand working with each other one more time or will they kill each other first before they even fight against Dormammu and Umar? The series was created by the team best known for their now legendary humorous take on DC Comics' <u>Justice League</u> series from the mid-1980s, which is listed below.

Electric Girl. Written and illustrated by Michael Brennan. AiT/Planet Lar, 2001–2005. **Y**

Virginia has never really been a "normal" teenager, but she tries to be. There's something special about her: ever since she was a baby she has had the power to control electricity. She's not using it to fight crime, but it sure does come in handy. She's always tried her best to fit in with her unique power, but it's almost impossible to do that, especially with the company she keeps. She owns a loveable and mischievous pet dog named Blammo, and to top it off, she is the only one who can see the trouble-making gremlin named Oogleeoog. Since no one else can see or hear him, she's always getting into trouble with his "help." *Volume 1* received recognition from YALSA's Popular Paperbacks for Young Adults committee in 2002 on the "Graphic Novels: Superheroes and Beyond" list.

> *Vol. 1.* 2001. 156pp. 0-9703555-0-5.
> *Vol. 2.* 2002. 156pp. 0-9703555-1-3.
> *Vol. 3.* 2005. 160pp. 1-932051-38-4.

Fanboy. **Written by Mark Evanier and Sergio Aragonés. Illustrated by various.** DC Comics, 2001. 144pp. 1-56389-724-5. **Y**

© 2006 DC Comics.

Finster has spent a few too many hours reading comic books, and he dreams about them all day long while working at the local comic book store. He's in love with all the wrong women, and his dating track record shows it. Instead of finding the "right one," who is practically standing right in front of him, he makes up for his lack of dates by daydreaming that he's hanging out with his favorite DC Comics heroes. Illustrated by legendary artists including Jerry Ordway, Frank Miller, Gil Kane, Neal Adams, Dick Sprang, Bill Sienkiewicz, Brent Anderson, Joe Kubert, Brian Bolland, Bruce Timm, Kevin Nowlan, Wendy Pini, Phil Jimenez, Bernie Wrightson, Dave Gibbons, Steve Rude, Dick Giordano, and Mike Grell, this is a tribute to the heroes of yesterday and a comedic look at how one obsessed fan's life can change if he just really opens his eyes.

The Freshmen. **Written by Hugh Sterbakov. Illustrated by Leonard Kirk.** Image Comics. 2006. 176pp. 1-58240-593-X. **T**

When danger calls and Earth is in need of a heroic team to save the day—pray that you don't have the Freshmen team come to your aid. New heroes on the block (and new college students, too), after a science experiment goes wrong and they're given strange powers, the students decide to form a super-hero team. The biggest league of heroic misfits ever seen, the oddball squad is made up of the Puppeteer, Seductress, The Quaker, Wannabe, the Intoxicator, the Drama Twins, Green Thumb, Squirrel and Beaver, and the school mascot, and thy're ready to save the day! The series is co-created by actor Seth Green.

***G.L.A.: Misassembled.* Written by Dan Slott. Illustrated by Paul Pelletier.** Marvel Comics, 2005. 144pp. 0-7851-1621-4. **T**

When the West and East Coast Avengers are too busy to take on the rampaging bad guys in Mid-America, there's only one team for the job: the Great Lakes Avengers! Made up of the farcical team of Mr. Immortal, Dinah-Soar, Big Bertha, Flatman, and the Doorman, they take on the bad guys and try to save the day from the most ruthless villains in the Midwest, even if it costs them their lives or are they sent a cease and desist order to stop using the name "Avengers." A parody of the Marvel Comics <u>Avengers: Disassembled</u> series.

🎖 *Herobear and the Kid: The Inheritance.* **Written and illustrated by Mike Kunkel.** Astonish Comics, 2003. 150pp. 0-9721259-1-4. **A** ◎

© 2006 Mike Kunkel.

After his grandfather passed away and his family moved into his grandfather's mansion, a young boy named Tyler finds that his beloved grandfather has left him an old stuffed toy bear and a pocketwatch as his inheritance. Initially dismissing the gifts, Tyler wishes that his grandfather had never passed away and tosses the toy bear aside. When the toy is tapped on the nose, a magical secret is revealed: it transforms into a magical large white polar bear with a red cape—Herobear is here! After teaming up with Herobear on a slew of adventures as his sidekick, facing the fiendish robot X-5 and even school bullies, Tyler finds out that his grandfather is really much more than he could ever have imagined. As even more secrets are revealed and Tyler inherits his grandfather's legacy, he discovers that you don't need superpowers or a Herobear at your side to truly be a hero. The title won several Eisner Awards, for Best Title for Younger Readers/Best Comics Publication for a Younger Audience (2002–2003), and received recognition from YALSA's Popular Paperbacks for Young Adults committee for the 2004 list.

<u>Hyper Dolls.</u> **Written and illustrated by Shimpei Itoh.** Studio Iron Cat, 2002–2003. **T Japanese manga.**

The comic misadventures of Maika Minazuki and Miyu Fumizuki, two alien female super-heroes sent by the Central Galaxy to battle gigantic monsters that threaten Earth. The giant monsters may not be the biggest threat to the cities, since whenever Maika and Miyu attack, you can be sure there's plenty of destruction! Stuck on Earth until their main target is defeated, girls are disguised as two ordinary high school students. Only one fellow student, a boy named Ikai Hideo, has discovered their secret identities. Will he be able to keep the girls' real identities a secret for long?

> *Vol. 1.* 2002. 230pp. 1-929090-05-6.
> *Vol. 2.* 2003. 230pp. 1-929090-23-4.
> *Vol. 3.* 2003. 230pp. 1-929090-32-3.
> *Vol. 4.* 2003. 218pp. 1-929090-50-1.
> *Vol. 5.* 2003. 208pp. 1-929090-67-6.

Jack Staff. **Written and illustrated by Paul Grist.** Image Comics, 2004. **T**

Twenty years ago Great Britain's favorite super-hero from Castletown disappeared from the public eye, but what really happened to him? Becky Burdock, an investigative reporter for the local tabloid newspaper, is trying to find out. While investigating a series of murders possibly committed by a vampire, she uncovers what really happened to the patriotic hero. When an ancient villain threatens the town after last being seen during the Blitzkreig, Jack Staff has to come out of retirement, face his fears, and fight alongside the heroes of today to defeat an old foe. A light parody of super-hero, science fiction, and horror comic books with an indelible British sense of humor.

> *Vol. 1: Everything Used to Be Black and White.* 2004. 352pp. 1-58240-335-X.
> *Vol. 2: Soldiers.* 2004. 160pp. 1-58240-392-9.

Joker/Mask. **Written by Henry Gilroy and Ronnie del Carmen. Illustrated by Ramon Bachs.** Dark Horse Comics, 2001. 96pp. 1-56971-518-1. **T**

The Joker, chalk-faced Clown Prince of Crime, has just vandalized a museum exhibit in Gotham City and has stolen the infamous 3,000-year-old relic mask that takes away a person's inhibitions and gives the wearer powers beyond belief. Since the Joker is already insane, the mask has given the Joker what he's always wanted: the power and the strength to eliminate Batman! Now with the Dark Knight Detective out of the way, the Joker has the entire city of Gotham to himself. Bored by his easy success defeating Batman, what else can an invincible madman with no inhibitions do after he has accomplished everything he's ever wanted?

♣ Justice League. Written by Keith Giffen and J. M DeMatteis. Illustrated by Kevin Maguire. DC Comics. **Y**

A humorous take on the classic super-team, mixing witty humor with super-heroic action, collecting the earliest stories from the now-classic 1980s tales of the Justice League. Rebuilt with the guidance of financial tycoon Maxwell Lord, the team, composed at first of Batman, Black Canary, Green Lantern Guy Gardner, Blue Beetle, Booster Gold, the Martian Manhunter, Mr. Miracle, Captain Marvel, Dr. Fate, and Dr. Light, became a United Nations-sponsored team. The 2004 and 2005 Justice League spin-offs reunited some of the members of the Justice League. Maxwell Lord has an unscrupulous deal to bring back the old Justice League members Captain Atom, Fire, Elongated Man, Blue Beetle, Booster Gold, and new recruit Mary Marvel in his worst idea yet: as a super-team-for-hire group set up in a local New York strip mall! Old habits die hard as the humorous heroes remember just what made them want to leave their comical former Justice League in the first place. After handling a well-spoken superpowered street gang and being kidnapped by the villain Roulette, can they handle an invasion by the shiny golden cosmic overlord Manga Khan, or will the real Justice League have to save the day? *Formerly Known as the Justice League* won an Eisner Award in 2004 for Best Humor Publication.

8

Justice League, 1991–1992.
> *Justice League: A New Beginning.* 1991. 192pp. 0-930289-40-4.
> *Justice League International: The Secret Gospel of Maxwell Lord.* 1992. 144pp. 1-56389-039-9.

Formerly Known as the Justice League. 2004. 144pp. 1-4012-0305-1.

I Can't Believe It's Not the Justice League. 2005. 144pp. 1-4012-0478-3.

League of Super Groovy Crimefighters. **Written by Jan-Ives Campbell. Illustrated by James Taylor, Mitch Massey, and Michael Kelleher.** Ancient Studios, 2003. 136pp. 0-9744216-0-X. **T**

> Parody of the 1970s heroes. As the downtrodden Sergeant America tries to find a new job after government budget cuts, he's out to prove he's the best hero in New York City. But the hero faces stiff competition from the League of Super-Groovy Crime Fighters, and they won't be second-place heroes. When the Syndicate of Evil Bad Guys breaks out of prison, can the heroes settle their differences and take down the jive-talkin' bad guys?

Lethargic Lad: The Big Book of Lethargic Lad. **Written and illustrated by Greg Hyland.** Destination Entertainment, 1998. 146pp. No ISBN. **T**

> A satirical look at pop culture through the eyes of a crude-looking, pencil-drawn hero called Lethargic Lad. Larry Ladhands has amazing powers of lethargy and was given them after being bombarded by cosmic rays, caught in a gamma bomb explosion, and bitten by a radioactive spider. From his secret Lad-Cave he prepares to fight absurd villains, including Mr. Mimico, Evil Girl, and Mr. Cheese, and pop culture will never be the same. The series is also a Webcomic, viewable at http://www.lethargiclad.com.

Lovebunny and Mr. Hell. **Written by Josh Blaylock, Tim Seeley, and Brendan Hay. Illustrated by Josh Blaylock, Tim Seeley and various.** Devil's Due, 2004. 112pp. 1-932796-10-X. **O**

> The adventures of the world's most dysfunctional super-hero duo. When Lovebunny, a popular former teen sidekick, decides to strike out as a hero, she finds she's constantly rebuked. After visiting the old home of a now-deceased 1960s villain called Conjura, she runs afowl of a tentacled demon, and she finds a crime-fighting partner in Mr. Hell, an honest-to-gosh demon. Though Lovebunny doesn't have any powers, she'd like to get more respect, but when your partner is a demon, that can be a little difficult. Luckily Mr. Hell has a big heart for a demon (and a crush on Lovebunny, too), and he takes her advice on how to be a hero in good part. Can they work together well enough to defeat the villains and one-up Lovebunny's ex-boyfriend, the hero called Electric Bill?

🎯 ***Mad About Super Heroes.*** **Written and illustrated by The Usual Gang of Super-Idiots.** MAD/DC Comics, 2002. 176pp. 1-56389-886-1. **Y** ◉

> See what happens when the Usual Gang of Idiots at *Mad Magazine* get their hands on popular super-heroes such as Batman, Superman, Wonder Woman, Spider-Man, the X-Men, the Hulk, the Teenage Mutant Ninja Turtles, and many more. Includes spoofs

of the comic book, movie translations, and television shows, too. The collection received recognition from YALSA's Quick Picks for Reluctant Readers committee for the 2003 list.

Madman. **Written and illustrated by Mike Allred.** Dark Horse Comics, 1996–2001 and Oni Press, 2002–2003. **T**

When kooky Snap City needs rescuing from the mutant street beatniks, the evil genius Mr. Mondstadt, renegade robots, the Puke, and other oddball enemies, there's only one zany undead masked hero for the job: Madman! Alias Frank Einstein, he was reanimated and now wears a mask and costume to conceal his disfigured face and body. Only Frank's true love, the freckle-faced Joe, loves him for the man he is inside. Joined by a colorful cast of madcap and goofy characters, including Dr. Flem, the Big Guy, G-Men from Hell, and more, Frank and Joe are on the wackiest and hippest adventures possible, taking them back in time, to Hell, on top of the giant brain of Dr. Boiffard, and much more. With Madman here, Snap City is in good hands, but it's one groovy and wild ride.

Text and illustrations of Madman Comics © & ™ 2005 Michael Allred.

Madman Comics: Yearbook '95. 1996. 160pp. 1-56971-091-0.
The Complete Madman Comics Vol. 2. 1996. 152pp. 1-56971-186-0.
The Complete Madman Comics Vol. 3. 2000. 136pp. 1-56971-470-3.
The Complete Madman Comics Vol. 4. 2001. 136pp. 1-56971-581-5.
Madman: The Oddity Odyssey. 2002. 152pp. 1-929998-28-7.
Madman Adventures. 2002. 128pp. 1-929998-29-5.
Madman Super-Groovy King-Size Special. 2003. 56pp. 1-929998-63-5.

Magic Pickle. **Written and illustrated by Scott Morse.** Oni Press, 2002. 128pp. 1-929998-33-3. **A**

Little Jo Jo Wigman has the strangest super-hero of all living under her floorboards—the mysterious and rather short vegetable hero who dills out justice like no other hero before: Weapon Kosher! Revived after fifty years in hibernation, to track down Chili Chili Bang Bang, the Phantom Carrot, and the rest of the Brotherhood, Weapon Kosher is ready to fight with his fists and a little help from Jo Jo, and plenty of bad produce jokes all around.

Major Damage. **Written and illustrated by Chris Bailey.** Sky-Dog Press, 2005. 96pp. 0-9721831-4-0. **T**

Eight-year-old Melvin Grimes was trick or treating on Halloween night dressed as his favorite super-hero, Major Damage, when he was abducted by the Mucus Men from Outer Space. The harmless scientists see his Major Damage costume and mistake him for the "real" Major Damage. They presume he's had some kind of accident and want to help him. They give him "back" his powers and return him to Earth.

Marshal Law. **Written by Pat Mills. Illustrated by Kevin O'Neill.** Titan Books, 2003. **M**
◎

Welcome to San Futuro, a rebuilt San Francisco of the near future that was decimated
in a crippling earthquake and has become a haven for heroes. When the heroes cross
the line, there's only one licensed vigilante to take them down: Joe Gilmore, the
leather-clad and heavily armed warrior called Marshal Law. Joe was once one of many
super-soldiers who fought in "The Zone," a South American war in which the United
States created the ideal super-soldiers who felt no physical pain, but were also unable
to feel empathy. Since returning from the war, the heroes have committed terrible
atrocities without fear or mercy, and now Marshal Law is playing clean-up and doling
out extremely brutal punishments to all the "heroes" who have committed violent
crimes. Originally published in 1987 under Marvel Comics' Epic imprint and later by
Dark Horse Comics, the series was ahead of its time and highly regarded by critics for
its scathingly humorous look at the world of super-heroes as well as religion, hypoc-
risy, war, and the establishment. The series has continued in several prose novels, but
they are not listed in this publication.

> *Fear and Loathing.* 2003. 200pp. 1-84023-452-0.
> *Blood, Sweat and Fears.* 2003. 168pp. 1-84023-526-8.
> *Fear Asylum.* 2003. 176pp. 1-84023-699-X.

The Mask. **Created by John Arcudi. Illustrated by Doug Mahnke.** Dark Horse Comics,
1993-1996. **T** ▰

When neurotic loser Stanley Ipkiss puts on an ancient mask that he purchased for his
girlfriend, it brings out the worst in him, literally. The mask gives the wearer a grin-
ning, green face and the powers of invulnerability and reality-warping, as well as extremely lowered inhibitions. Now with the powers of a walking Tex Avery cartoon,
Stanley takes lethal vengeance against anyone who ever wronged him. As others try on
the Mask, including a police officer and a small-time mobster, they soon find that the
Mask is one of the most deadly and dangerous of creations, able to seduce anyone with
its powers. The story inspired the 1994 movie *The Mask,* starring Jim Carrey. Dark
Horse Comics claims no responsibility for the dreadful 2005 sequel *Son of the Mask.*

> *The Mask.* 1993. 152pp. 1-878574-50-7.
> *The Mask Returns.* 1994. 112pp. 1-56971-021-X.
> *The Mask Strikes Back.* 1996. 128pp. 1-56971-168-2.

🎖 **Plastic Man.** **Written and illustrated by Kyle Baker.** DC Comics, 2004– . **T** ◎

With his alter ego Eel O'Brian framed for the murder of his longtime obese friend
Woozy Winks, the oddball hero called Plastic Man recounts his humorous origin while
trying to figure out who set him up. A criminal who was exposed to chemicals in a
botched robbery of a chemical plant and found himself able to stretch his body into any
shape imaginable, Plastic Man was trained by monks, who taught him the error of his
ways. Now he fights against crime as Plastic Man, the goofiest and lighthearted hero of
all time. The series won an Eisner Award for Best New Series (2004), Best Writer/Art-
ist: Humor (2004–2006), and Best Title for Younger Readers/Best Comics Publication
for a Younger Audience (2005), as well as several Harvey Awards for Best New Series
(2004) and Special Award for Humor (2005).

> *Vol. 1: On the Lam.* 2004. 144pp. 1-4012-0343-4.

Vol. 2: Rubber Bandits. 2006. 144pp. 1-4012-0729-4.

Powerpuff Girls. Written by Sean Carolan and Abby Denson. Illustrated by Mike DeCarlo, Dan Fraga, and Phil Moy. DC Comics, 2003. **A** 🖳

When Professor Utonium was trying to create the perfect little girl, he added a little sugar, spice, everything nice, plus an accidental dosage of Chemical X, and the Powerpuff Girls were born! Now Blossom, Bubbles, and Buttercup use their superpowers to save the city of Townsville from fiends like their simian arch-rival Mojo Jojo, Fuzzy Lumpkins, the Gang Green Gang, giant monsters, and more. Based on the hit cartoon show on the Cartoon Network.

Vol. 1: Titans of Townsville. 2003. 112pp. 1-4012-0171-7.
Vol. 2: Go, Girls, Go. 2003. 112pp. 1-4012-0172-5.

The Pro. **Written by Garth Ennis. Illustrated by Amanda Conner.** Image Comics, 2004. 72pp. 1-58240-383-X. **M**

What happens when a mysterious alien called the Viewer (or is it the "Voyeur?" ') grants super-human powers to one of the most unexpected people on Earth: a New York City street hooker? Even though she's a hooker who curses like a sailor, she is asked to become a member of the League of Honor—a spoof on DC Comics' Justice League of America—if she has what it takes to become a hero. Given an unbearably tight heroine costume, the Pro has the powers to fight evil—and also to earn money as New York City's resident hooker heroine. Filled with Garth Ennis's trademark black humor and a dose of gratuitous sex and violence. The world of super-heroes is turned upside down, and the League of Honor will never be the same once they meet the Pro.

ps238. Written and illustrated by Aaron Williams. Dork Storm Press, 2004–2006. **Y**

Welcome to ps238, the only school designed to help train and prepare the metahumans of tomorrow. Located three miles below the surface of seemingly normal Excelsior Public School for normal students, the special students with super-human powers train in the underground facility to prepare them for a life of crime-fighting adventure and even the occasional life of crime. While their parents fight elsewhere against the forces of evil, the students—including Captain Clarinet, Suzi Fusion, Emerald Gauntlet, evil genius Zodon, Victor VonFogg, Guardian Angel, and Tyler Marlocke, a boy whose parents are heroes but who has no powers at all—must learn to do battle against such fearsome challenges as field trips to other planets, super-hero themed homework assignments, and much more.

Vol. 1: With Liberty and Recess for All. 2004. 160pp. 1-930964-69-2.
Vol. 2: To the Cafeteria . . . For Justice! 2005 160pp. 1-933288-13-2.
Vol. 3: No Child Left Behind. 2006. 160pp. 1-933288-24-8.

Quantum and Woody. Written by Christopher Priest. Illustrated by M. D. Bright. Acclaim Comics, 1997–1999. **T**

Eric and Woody have been best friends since they were kids despite their skin color and personalities. When the mysterious deaths of their fathers bring them back together, they have a new mission in life: to help out the citizens of Long Island and become the super-hero team known as Quantum and Woody. Along with their pet goat Vincent, they're out to save the day. A humorous and sometimes poignant series that boasts the "world's worst super hero team."

The Director's Cut. 1997. 96pp. No ISBN.
Kiss Your Ass Goodbye. 1999. 96pp. No ISBN.
Holy S-Word—We're Canceled. 1999. 96pp. No ISBN.
Magnum Force. 1999. 96pp. No ISBN.

Shades of Blue. **Written by James S. Harris and Rachel Nacion. Illustrated by Greg Grucel and Carl Slayton.** Devil's Due Publishing, 2005. **T**

Heidi Page is a typical Chicago teen who wakes one morning to find that her hair has turned blue and she has gained power over electricity! Maybe now with her powers she'll get up the nerve to talk to the boy she has a crush on in class. Maybe. At the urging of her friends, she dons her very own costume, with striped stockings, and becomes a super-hero of sorts. When other teens and a sexy substitute teacher also gain superpowers, something seems strange at Harrington High, and it's up to Heidi to find out what.

Vol. 1. 2005. 144pp. 1-932796-26-6.
Vol. 2. 2005. 144pp. 1-932796-31-2.

She-Hulk. **Written by Dan Slott. Illustrated by Juan Bobillo.** Marvel Comics, 2004–2005. **T** ◎

The hilarious super-hero side of the law. When Bruce Banner (the Hulk) gave his meek cousin an emergency blood transfusion, she acquired the jade skin color of the Hulk as well as similar powers, but none of the extreme rage. A former Avenger and member of the Fantastic Four, "Shulkie" now works as a lawyer for the Superhuman Law division of the Goodman, Lieber, Kurtzberg, & Holliway law firm, handling some of the most bizarre and humorous cases ever, including her long-time enemy Titania, the Greek god Hercules, and even cases from interdimensional space. For all you trivia geeks out there, the She-Hulk is also one of the only characters in Marvel Comics who fully realizes that she is a comic book character.

Vol. 1: Single Green Female. 2004. 144pp. 0-7851-1443-2.
Vol. 2: Super-Human Law. 2005. 144pp. 0-7851-1570-6.
Vol. 3: Time Trials. 2006. 120pp. 0-7851-1795-4.

The Tick: The Naked City. **Written and illustrated by Ben Edlund.** Marlowe, 1996. 176pp. 1-56924-828-1. **T** ▢

With his battle-cry of "Spoon!," the insane, nigh-invulnerable, blue-costumed avenger known as The Tick is out to save the city—though the city probably needs to be saved from him. Joined by his sidekick The Moth, as well as Paul the Samurai, the ninja warrior Oedipus, and the Caped Wonder, The Tick is out to fight against ninja and "work for hire" super-villains and to prove that he's a hero.

Action and Adventure Humor

These tales include heavy amounts of humor, including black comedy, slapstick, sarcasm, and the like, to serve as a counter to the action and adventure in the plot. Note that the humor helps to alleviate the tension of the action and adventure plot.

Black Heart Billy. **Written and illustrated by Kieron Dwyer, Rick Remender, and Harper Jaten.** AiT/Planet Lar 2001 96pp. 1-932051-02-1. **O**

In an absurd, twisted, and hilariously spoofed world, there's only one person willing to beat all the conformists of the world with his skateboard—Black Heart Billy! A punk skateboarder with a crude attitude and a robot head (he got it after a bad skating accident), Billy has to save the world and stop the second coming of Hitler, whose brain has been transplanted into the body of Grateful Dead singer Jerry Garcia! Yes, Hitler/Garcia has come back from the dead to create a new Third Reich in which everyone is a hippie, and naturally, anarchist Billy won't have anything to do with that. He and his British skater pal Oi Boy are out to take on music store terrorists, coffeehouse employees of the month who won't let Billy use the bathroom, and more.

Blade for Barter. **Written by Jason DeAngelis. Illustrated by Hai.** Seven Seas Entertainment, 2005– . **T ◎ Neo-manga.**

© 2004 Seven Seas Entertainment, LLC and Jason DeAngelis

Ryusuke Washington is a young samurai-for-hire just looking for another meal and another job in New Edo—a busy mega-city where towering skyscrapers and quaint Asian dojos blend together and samurai and ninja walk the streets. Ryusuke's dangerous dealings put him at arm's length from the corrupt Samurai Union, the Mafuza (Mafia/Yakuza), the Ninja Union of clumsy ninja, and even Lord Hoseki, the heavily jeweled ruler of New Edo. Luckily Ryu has friends in the slapstick city, including his loyal dog Hachiko; Mac, the hyperactive female ninja; and Sushi Shop owner Tagosaku, a man whose brute strength and skill with a blade are unmatched.

Vol. 1. 2005. 192pp. 1-933164-01-8.

Vol. 2. 2005. 192pp. 1-933164-05-0.

Chikyu Misaki. **Written and illustrated by Iwahara Yuji. CMX/DC** Comics, 2005–2006. **Y Japanese manga.**

Deep in the depths of Lake Hohoro resides a mythological monster called the Hohopo. The beast is said to be a plesiosaur-like dinosaur, just like the famous Loch Ness Monster—or so the legends say. When schoolgirl Misaki Makishima inherits her maternal grandmother's house near the lake, she and her klutzy widower father move into the house. Misaki soon discovers that the Hohopo isn't a myth; it's real, and the pint-sized plesiosaur can shape-shift into a little boy! Now Misaki has a new prehistoric, shape-shifting friend, but how long can she keep her secret safe?

Vol. 1. 2005. 196pp. 1-4012-0799-5.

> *Vol. 2*. 2006. 196pp. 1-4012-0800-2.
> *Vol. 3*. 2006. 212pp. 1-4012-0801-0.

Cryptozoo Crew. Written by Allan Gross. Illustrated by Jerry Carr. NBM Publishing. 2005–2006. **Y**

Tork and Tara Darwyn are more than just husband and wife;—they're world-renowned cryptozoologists. Out to study hidden and undiscovered animals, there's no place on Earth that the globetrotting duo can't go,—although Tara would rather be shopping than out running into danger and rescuing her pun-spouting husband. From the high mountains of the Himalayas to search for the Yeti; to the jungles of the Congo home of the pygmy dinosaur Mokele-Mbembe; to Puerto Rico, home of the chupacabra, if there's something mysterious and dangerous, you can believe the Darwyns will try to solve it. If only Tork would be able to get the last word in edgewise with Tara: now that's impossible!

> *Vol. 1*. 2005. 96pp. 1-56163-437-9.
> *Vol. 2*. 2006. 96pp. 1-56163-466-2.

GetBackers. Written by Yuya Aoki. Illustrated by Rando Ayamine. TOKYOPOP, 2004– . **O ◎ Japanese manga.** あ

When you've had something stolen and you want it back, there's only one duo you need to call: the superpowered duo known as the GetBackers! With their almost 100 percent success rate, they're practically swimming in . . . poverty? Both blessed with powers, Ginji Amano, the blonde, cool-headed, and kind teen who generates electric currents with his body like an electric eel, and Ban Mido, the brunette teen with the ability to create illusions in the eyes of his victims with his "Evil Eye," they're the best in Japan. Unfortunately, netting a decent-paying client or mooching a free meal off some pretty girls is tough, and some good luck better start heading this bumbling duo's way soon, or they're going to starve to death! The popular series is still being published in Japan, with more than thirty-one volumes, and has also been adapted as an anime series.

> *Vol. 1*. 2004. 216pp. 1-59182-633-0.
> *Vol. 2*. 2004. 200pp. 1-59182-634-9.
> *Vol. 3*. 2004. 200pp. 1-59182-635-7.
> *Vol. 4*. 2004. 192pp. 1-59182-636-5.
> *Vol. 5*. 2004. 208pp. 1-59182-637-3.
> *Vol. 6*. 2004. 192pp. 1-59182-638-1.
> *Vol. 7*. 2005. 200pp. 1-59182-969-0.
> *Vol. 8*. 2005. 200pp. 1-59182-970-4.
> *Vol. 9*. 2005. 200pp. 1-59182-971-2.
> *Vol. 10*. 2005. 192pp. 1-59182-972-0.
> *Vol. 11*. 2005. 192pp. 1-59182-973-9.
> *Vol. 12*. 2005. 192pp. 1-59182-974-7.
> *Vol. 13*. 2006. 192pp. 1-59182-975-5.
> *Vol. 14*. 2006. 192pp. 1-59182-976-3.
> *Vol. 15*. 2006. 192pp. 1-59182-977-1.
> *Vol. 16*. 2006. 192pp. 1-59182-978-X.
> *Vol. 17*. 2007. 192pp. 1-59182-979-8.

Grampa and Julie: Shark Hunters. **Written and illustrated by Jef Czekaj.** Top Shelf Productions, 2004. 128pp. 1-891830-52-X. **A**

Most kids' summer vacations are pretty boring, but not Julie's! She spent the entire summer with her goofy Grampa, a world-famous ichthyologist and all-around jokester, searching for Stephen, the world's biggest shark. As their search for the elusive shark takes them to the wackiest places on the planet and beyond, they meet pirates, rapping squirrels, and more. Julie's story about what she did on her summer vacation will certainly top them all.

GTO: Great Teacher Onizuka. Written and illustrated by Tohru Fujisawa. TOKYOPOP, 2002–2005. **O ◎ ▢ Japanese manga.** あ

Twenty-two-year-old Eikichi Onizuka is a former street motorcyclist with a second-degree black belt in karate and no ambitions but to succeed in life on the easy street to fame, fortune, and plenty of girls. After countless rejection letters, he has a revelation about a career that could snag him plenty of young girls—becoming a high school teacher! Though his intentions are less than honorable, he soon finds out that his unusual methods of persuasion as a student teacher make him formidable, and now even the blackmailing punks in the school won't give him any lip. But even though he has discovered there's more to school than cute girls, Eikichi has his work cut out for him if he really wants to be the "Great Teacher." The hit series was adapted as an anime series as well as a live-action television series in Japan.

Vol. 1. 2002. 192pp. 1-931514-93-3.
Vol. 2. 2002. 184pp. 1-931514-96-8.
Vol. 3. 2002. 200pp. 1-931514-49-6.
Vol. 4. 2002. 200pp. 1-59182-028-6.
Vol. 5. 2002. 200pp. 1-59182-029-4.
Vol. 6. 2002. 200pp. 1-59182-030-8.
Vol. 7. 2002. 200pp. 1-59182-031-6.
Vol. 8. 2002. 200pp. 1-59182-032-4.
Vol. 9. 2003. 200pp. 1-59182-070-7.
Vol. 10. 2003. 200pp. 1-59182-106-1.
Vol. 11. 2003. 208pp. 1-59182-135-5.
Vol. 12. 2003. 208pp. 1-59182-136-3.
Vol. 13. 2003. 216pp. 1-59182-137-1.
Vol. 14. 2003. 200pp. 1-59182-138-X.
Vol. 15. 2003. 200pp. 1-59182-139-8.
Vol. 16. 2004. 200pp. 1-59182-140-1.
Vol. 17. 2004. 200pp. 1-59182-141-X.
Vol. 18. 2004. 200pp. 1-59182-142-8.
Vol. 19. 2004. 192pp. 1-59182-143-6.
Vol. 20. 2004. 192pp. 1-59182-144-4.
Vol. 21. 2004. 216pp. 1-59182-455-9.
Vol. 22. 2005. 192pp. 1-59532-410-0.
Vol. 23. 2005. 192pp. 1-59532-411-9.
Vol. 24. 2005. 200pp. 1-59532-412-7.
Vol. 25. 2005. 192pp. 1-59532-413-5.

8

<u>Gunsmith Cats.</u> Written and illustrated by Kenichi Sonoda. Dark Horse Comics, 1996–2002. **O Japanese manga.** あ

Fun-loving bounty hunters ready to take down Chicago's toughest and most-wanted criminals, Rally Vincent and Minnie-May Hopkins, the Gunsmith Cats, are always on the case and ready to bring the next criminal to justice. From taking on Bonnie & Clyde, hired guns, mad bombers, and the thief known as the Bean Bandit, to the climactic battle of wits between Rally and the bisexual Amazon assassin crime lord Goldie, the Cats have their hands full with plenty of nonstop action and a good dose of humor along for the ride. The series was also adapted as an anime series in Japan.

> *Vol. 1: Bonnie and Clyde.* 1996. 176pp. 1-56971-215-8.
> *Vol. 2: Misfire.* 1997. 184pp. 1-56971-253-0.
> *Vol. 3: The Return of Gray.* 1999. 248pp. 1-56971-299-9.
> *Vol. 4: Goldie versus Misty.* 1999. 192pp. 1-56971-371-5.
> *Vol. 5: Bad Trip.* 2000. 170pp. 1-56971-442-8.
> *Vol. 6: Bean Bandit.* 2000. 224pp. 1-56971-453-3.
> *Vol. 7: Kidnapped.* 2001. 232pp. 1-56971-529-7.
> *Vol. 8: Mister V.* 2001. 224pp. 1-56971-550-5.
> *Vol. 9: Misty's Run.* 2002. 176pp. 1-56971-684-6.

🌱 *Kyle Baker Presents You Are Here.* **Written and illustrated by Kyle Baker.** Vertigo/DC Comics, 1998. 160pp. 1-56389-442-4. **M** ◎

Temporarily reformed criminal Noel Coleman just met the girl of his dreams, a beautiful and sensitive red-head named Helen. Naturally, Noel lies to Helen to hide his phenomenally checkered past. Just as Helen discovers the truth about Noel's background, a serial killer is out to get Noel for seducing his wife. Will love survive the truth, and will anyone survive at all? The story won a Harvey Award in 1999 for Best Graphic Album of Original Work.

The Last Knight: An Introduction to Don Quixote by Miguel de Cervantes. **Adapted from the works by Miguel de Cervantes. Written and illustrated by Will Eisner.** NBM Publishing, 2003. 32pp. 1-56163-251-1. **Y**

A retelling of the classic work by Miguel de Cervantes, in which Pancho Villa, a noble but delusional gentleman, takes it upon himself to become a knight, finding humorous misfortune on his journey across the Spanish countryside attacking windmills, rescuing criminals, and taming sleepy lions. Through his actions, he inspired his "squire," Sancho Panza, and others to never forget the power of imagination and to never stop chasing windmills.

Mister Blank Exhaustive Collection. **Written and illustrated by Christopher J. Hicks.** Amaze Ink/Slave Labor Graphics, 2000. 354pp. 0-943151-25-2. **T** ◎

Bumbling everyman Sam Smith is a nobody at his corporate job. The paperwork is never-ending, and to top it off, he's too shy to ask out a cute coworker. After stumbling upon a sinister plot to destroy his office building, Sam goes from zero to haphazard hero when he finds himself up against robot spies, a superpowered mime, time-traveling twin brothers, an immortal brotherhood who secretly rule the world, a clone of himself, a giant samurai robot, and God's first woman, in a roller coaster of an adventure.

Monkey vs. Robot. Written and illustrated by James Kochalka. Top Shelf Productions, 2000–2003. **T**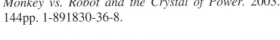

© 2006 James Kochalka.

A factory of self-creating robots is stripping the jungle's natural resources to build moree robots, and when a nearby monkey colony is threatened, war is soon declared between the primates and the robots. The two-part series is an age-old tale of technology versus nature, with a good heaping of simple storytelling and fun mixed in.

> *Monkey vs. Robot.* 2000. 160pp. 1-891830-15-5.
> *Monkey vs. Robot and the Crystal of Power.* 2003. 144pp. 1-891830-36-8.

Mutant, Texas: Tales of Sheriff Ida Red. **Written by Paul Dini. Illustrated by J. Bone.** Oni Press, 2003. 128pp. 1-929998-53-8. **Y**

From the most mystically irradiated town in the Southwest, where everyone's a mutant, comes the spunky and cute teenager Ida Red, the toughest heroine in the state of Texas. Orphaned and raised by Tia Oso, a bear-woman, she's one of many special residents in the sleepy town of Mutant, Texas, with the ability to fly, shoot energy out of her hands, manipulate matter, and more. She and her jaguar companion, Cat, are ready to take down a posse of poachers, led by a corrupt sheriff and a giant snake, who have been stealing the residents from the community to sell them to a traveling freak show.

One Piece. Written and illustrated by Eiichiro Oda. VIZ Media, LLC, 2003– . **T** 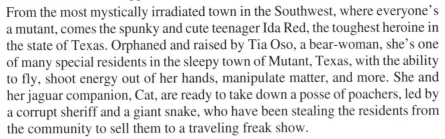 **Japanese manga.** あ

ONE PIECE © 1997 by Eiichiro Oda/SHUEISHA Inc.

Monkey D. Luffy has wanted to be a pirate ever since he was rescued by his pirate friend, "Red Haired" Shanks. Indebted to Shanks for his bravery, Monkey will do whatever it takes to be as noble and tough as his mentor, and he vows to find the hidden treasure left by the "Pirate King" Gold Roger. Luffy also has an odd power: he accidentally ate the "devil's fruit"—the gum-gum fruit—that makes the eater's body stretch like rubber. Now with his unique power and his small crew, made up of the skilled swordsman Roronoa Zoro, the cute and spunky thief Nami, and others, there's nothing to stop Luffy from being the new Pirate King. The series originally debuted in Japan in 1997 and is still being published, with over thirty-eight volumes published to date overseas. The manga series has also been adapted as an anime series, currently airing in North America on the Cartoon Network.

 8

> *Vol. 1: Romance Dawn.* 2003. 216pp. 1-56931-901-4.
> *Vol. 2: Buggy the Clown.* 2003. 200pp. 1-59116-057-X.
> *Vol. 3: Don't Get Fooled Again.* 2004. 208pp. 1-59116-184-3.
> *Vol. 4: The Black Cat Pirates.* 2004. 200pp. 1-59116-337-4.
> *Vol. 5: For Whom the Bells Tolls.* 2004. 200pp. 1-59116-615-2.
> *Vol. 6: The Oath.* 2005. 200pp. 1-59116-723-X.

Vol. 7: The Crap-Geezer. 2005. 200pp. 1-59116-852-X.
Vol. 8: I Won't Die. 2005. 192pp. 1-4215-0075-2.
Vol. 9: Tears. 2006. 208pp. 1-4215-0191-0.
Vol. 10: Okay, Let's Stand Up!. 2006. 208pp. 1-4215-0406-5.
Vol. 11: Meanest Man in the East. 2006. 208pp. 1-4215-0663-7.
Vol. 12. 2006. 208pp. 1-4215-0664-5.
Vol. 13. 2007. 208pp. 1-4215-0665-3.
Vol. 14. 2007. 208pp. 1-4215-1091-x.

Polly and the Pirates. Written and illustrated by Ted Naifeh. 2006. O

© 2006 by Ted Naifeh.

Young Polly-Anne Pringle was the most refined girl at her local boarding school. Dull and proper, she is surprised one day to be kidnapped by the crew of Meg Malloy, the Pirate Queen, to become their new captain. It seems that Polly-Anne's father never told her the truth about her mother. Polly-Anne's mother was not a prim and proper lady, but the rowdy and adventurous Meg Malloy! Now that Meg has gone missing, Polly-Anne is forced to lead the pirates. Can prim and proper Polly-Anne fill her mother's shoes and lead the pirates to high adventure?

Vol. 1. 2006. 168pp. 1-932664-46-7.

Rosemary's Backpack. Written by Anthony Johnson. Illustrated by Drew Gilbert. Cyberosia Publishing, 2002. 112pp. 0-9709474-7-X. Y

After bumping into a complete stranger who exchanged backpacks with her on the way to school, shy technogeek Rosemary Grant has one of the coolest backpacks around. What makes it so special? It's named Pablo, it's fuzzy, it can talk, and it has a really sarcastic sense of humor. Now fourteen-year-old Rosemary and Pablo have the attention of a shadowy organization led by a cyborg general, who want back what was once theirs. But they're going to have to put up a fight to get it, and Rosemary's playing for keeps.

Saint Tail. Written by Naoko Takeuchi. Illustrated by Megumi Tachikawa. TOKYOPOP, 2001–2002. A Japanese manga. あ

A mysterious figure known only as "Saint Tail" is stealing from the rich and giving to the poor like a modern-day Robin Hood. St. Paulia Junior High student Asuka Jr. has made it his mission to discover the thief's identity and apprehend him. Little does he know that Saint Tail is actually his friend Meimi Haneoka. With the assistance of her friend, a nun-in-training who listens to the prayers of the poor and less fortunate and then assists them, Meimi steals from those who don't deserve their wealth. With her magical powers and a little prayer, she's doing God's work. The series was also adapted as an anime series.

Vol. 1. 2001. 192pp. 1-892213-65-6.
Vol. 2. 2001. 192pp. 1-892213-88-5.
Vol. 3. 2001. 176pp. 1-892213-89-3.
Vol. 4. 2002. 176pp. 1-892213-90-7.
Vol. 5. 2002. 192pp. 1-931514-20-8.

Vol. 6. 2002. 176pp. 1-931514-21-6.
Vol. 7. 2002. 176pp. 1-931514-22-4.

***Scurvy Dogs: Rags to Riches.* Written by Andrew Boyd. Illustrated by Ryan Yount.** Ait/Planet Lar, 2005. 160pp. 1-932051-27-9. **O**

Avast ye mateys! The famous Captain Blackbeard and other pirates of legend are amazingly alive and well in the twenty-first century and getting by, with disastrous results. From losing their ship, to escaping from the Hobo Mafia King, to getting real jobs to make money, to getting revenge on Michael Nesmith, to Blackbeard's reunion with his long-lost brother, the high seas have never been more silly.

Humorous Fantasy

These are fantastic tales of dragons, barbarians, elves, wizards, gods and goddesses, and other staples of the fantasy genre, blended with a heavy helping of humor. The formulaic characters, plots, and settings are spoofed in these stories, taking a lighthearted look at the worlds of fantasy. Highlights include the clumsy mendicant barbarian called Groo, the lighthearted romance between Keiichi and the Norse goddess Belldandy in <u>Oh! My Goddess</u>, and the adventures of Santa Claus's rebel daughter, Jingle Belle.

***Amy Unbounded: Belondweg Blossoming.* Written and illustrated by Rachel Hartman.** Pug House Press, 2002. 208pp. 0-9717900-0-0. **Y**

The charming daily life adventures of Amy of Eddybrook, a typical young girl living in the medieval kingdom Goredd. She's preparing for her tenth birthday, avoiding her chores, and spending time with her best friend, Bran Ducanahan. Her mother is a barbarian clockmaker and her father a shepherd/weaver, and all Amy wants to do is have a life half as exciting as that described in the epic poem of Belongweg, the Queen who helped keep Goredd from invaders and united its people. As Amy finds, life may not be quite like fiction, but it has its ups and downs. As the people from Goredd interact with Amy and her family—including friends from town, Amy's uncle who is a banished knight, and even the scholarly dragon called Lalo (who is in disguise as a human)—what transpires is a deeply moving and humorous journey of a young woman living in a subtle fantasy world.

<u>Asterix.</u> **Written by René Goscinny. Illustrated by Albert Uderzo.** Orion, 2002– . **A** ◎

Around the year 50 B.C., in northwest Armorica near ancient Gaul, one last city has escaped the wrath of Julius Caesar and the Roman Empire. The citizens of Gaul have a secret ace up their sleeves to defeat the Romans: Getafix, a druid from the city, has concocted a magical potion that grants the villagers temporary super-strength. And when the trouble gets tough, there's only one Gaul for the job—Asterix! A short blonde-haired man with a mustache and a winged Viking helmet, he's the most cunning of all the Gauls. Joined by his companion, the oafish Obelix, he experiences many misadventures fighting against the Roman Empire. Beloved the world over, Asterix and his friends have been among the most popular comic book characters from France since their first appearance in 1959. The list of titles below is only a small sampling of what is available.

> *Asterix and Son.* 2002. 48pp. 0-7528-4775-9.
> *Asterix the Gaul.* 2004. 48pp. 0-7528-6605-2.
> *Asterix at the Olympic Games.* 2004. 48pp. 0-7528-6626-5.
> *Asterix and the Great Crossing.* 2005. 48pp. 0-7528-6648-6.
> *The Mansions of the Gods.* 2005. 48pp. 0-7528-6639-7.
> *Asterix and the Soothsayer.* 2005. 48pp. 0-7528-6642-7.
> *Obelix and Co.* 2005. 48pp. 0-7528-6652-4.

<u>Dungeon.</u> Written by Lewis Trondheim. Illustrated by Joann Sfar. NBM Publishing, 2004– . **T** ◉

© 2006 Lewis Trondhein and Joann Sfar.

In a fantasy world where heroic barbarian champions regularly battle hordes of monsters, there's only one place to go for your fix of fighting and prizes: the Dungeon! Run by the old bird called the Dungeon Keeper, the keep is a haven for ghouls, beasts, assorted monsters, dark labyrinths, and a large fire-breathing dragon. Like any good business, it needs to attract more customers; it does this by hiring the best monsters as well as having the best treasure trove ever to attract fresh champions. Herbert of Craftiwich, a timorous talking duck and a simple messenger for the Dungeon, is mistakenly chosen to be the new guardian of the Dungeon. With such a klutz as the hero (even with the help of a magical sarcastic sword), the Dungeon Keeper has assigned Herbert a much more capable partner, Marvin, the vegetarian dragon, to keep the Dungeon safe. <u>The Early Years</u> goes back in time and revisits the origins of the Dungeon when the Dungeon Keeper is barely an adult and setting out for the adventure of a lifetime, with plenty of humor along the way. <u>Twilight</u> focuses on an aging Marvin, who realizes that the world is doomed and heads for the legendary dragon cemetery to face the end but finds himself teamed up with a rabbit warrior and a timid bat against the most vile of enemies: a much-changed Herbert.

> <u>Dungeon.</u> 2004–2005.
>> *Vol. 1: Duck Heart.* 2004. 96pp. 1-56163-401-8.
>> *Vol. 2: The Barbarian Princess.* 2005. 96pp. 1-56163-421-2.
> <u>Dungeon: The Early Years.</u> 2005–2006.
>> *Vol. 1: The Night Shirt.* 2005. 96pp. 1-56163-439-5.
> <u>Dungeon: Twilight.</u> 2006.
>> *Vol. 1: Dragon Cemetery.* 2006. 96pp. 1-56163-460-3
>> *Vol. 2.* 2006. 96pp. 1-56163-477-8.

Far West. **Written and illustrated by Richard Moore.** NBM, 2001. 112pp. 1-56163-297-X. **M**

Set in an alternate Wild West of old where elves, ogres, fire-breathing dragons, and shape-shifters roam the land. Meg, a tough-as-nails bounty hunter with a good sense of humor, along with her talking bear sidekick Phil, are hot on the trail of a high-profile bounty: a dangerous train robber named Darien Voss. No ordinary train thief, he robs trains atop a red fire-breathing dragon, and Meg thinks she has what it takes to bring him in. Meanwhile, someone's been making threats against her life, and Meg doesn't take to that kindly.

🏃 <u>Groo.</u> Written by Sergio Aragonés and Mark Evanier. Illustrated by Sergio Aragonés; lettered by Stan Sakai. Dark Horse Comics, 1998–2003. ◉

People run and hide when the name "Groo the Wanderer" is mentioned. Groo is the stupidest barbarian in the world, causing destruction and mayhem wherever he goes. Ships sink when he sets one foot on them, cities burn just for taking him in, and woe be it if anyone should call Groo a "mendicant." He has no idea what the word means, but he can get violently angry when he hears someone call him one! A large-nosed buffoon, Groo is also a master swordsman, capable of defeating entire armies for no reason at all except that it's a chance to participate in a fray. He and his dog companion Rufferto roam the fantasy-land countryside, encountering a large cast of characters, including the Sage, con men Pal and Drumm, the Minstrel, and many more as they search for money, cheese dip, food, and frays. Mostly food. A hilarious parody of Robert E. Howard's *Conan the Barbarian*. Groo first appeared in 1981 and has been one of the most successful creator-owned comic book series ever. It has switched publishers over the years and is now published through Dark Horse Comics. The series is regarded by many fans in the comic book industry as one of the best humorous fantasy titles. The series has won Eisner Awards for Best Humor Publication (1992, 1999) and Best Writer/Artist: Humor (1996) and Harvey Awards for Best Cartoonist (1998) and Special Award for Humor (1991–1993, 1995, 1997–2001).

> *Sergio Aragonés' Groo: The Most Intelligent Man in the World.* 1998. 112pp. 1-56971-294-8.
> *The Groo Houndbook.* 1999. 96pp. 1-56971-385-5.
> *The Groo Inferno.* 1999. 96pp. 1-56971-430-4.
> *Sergio Aragonés' Groo and Rufferto.* 2000. 112pp. 1-56971-447-9.
> *The Groo Jamboree.* 2000. 96pp. 1-56971-462-2.
> *The Groo Kingdom.* 2001. 96pp. 1-56971-478-9.
> *The Groo Library.* 2001. 96pp. 1-56971-571-8.
> *Sergio Aragonés' Groo: Mightier than the Sword.* 2002. 112pp. 1-56971-612-9.
> *The Groo Maiden.* 2002. 96pp. 1-56971-756-7.
> *The Groo Nursery.* 2002. 96pp. 1-56971-794-X.
> *Sergio Aragonés' Groo: Death and Taxes.* 2003. 112pp. 1-56971-797-4.
> *The Groo Odyssey.* 2003. 96pp. 1-56971-858-X.

Gutwallow the Gingerbread Man. Written and illustrated by Dan Berger. Digital Webbing, 1999–2003. **T**

The fun adventures of a walking and talking gingerbread man, created by a Necromancer. Named Gutwallow. He is joined by two female friends, a warrior woman called Leafale and a shaman priestess called J'Sika, as well as other companions. Discovered by the female fighters when they try to recover an ancient artifact stolen by the Necromancer from J'Sika's people,

Gutwallow, as well as the Necromancer's bat, join them on their adventures as they encounter goblins, dwarves, and more on their quests to save the realm from even the most unlikely adversaries of all: outer space!

>*Vol. 1: The Trek to Nara Dim.* 1999. 312pp. 0-9704366-0-2.
>*Vol. 2: Fury of the Furry.* 2003. 112pp. No ISBN.

Jingle Belle. Written by Paul Dini. Illustrated by Stephen DeStefano, Jose Garibaldi, and various. Oni Press, 2000–2003, and Dark Horse Comics, 2005– . **T** ◎

Jingle Belle™ © 2006 Paul Dini.

The crazy and fun misadventures of Santa Claus's mischievous teenage daughter, Jingle Belle. An immortal, she's been stuck in the teenage years for a long time and is sick of receiving a lump of coal every year on her dad's Naughty list. Tired of her dad spending all of his time making other children happy instead of his own daughter, she does what any girl would do: she gets even! Join her as she fills in for a mall Santa, saves Christmas from the Blizzard Wizard, and more, just to spread Christmas cheer and to ensure that someday she'll get a real present for Christmas.

>*Vol. 1: Naughty and Nice.* Oni Press, 2000. 128pp. 1-929998-08-2.
>*Vol. 2: Cool Yule.* Oni Press, 2002. 120pp. 1-929998-36-8.
>*Vol. 3: Dash Away All.* Oni Press, 2003. 136pp. 1-929998-61-9.
>*Jingle Belle.* Dark Horse Comics, 2005. 96pp. 1-59307-382-8.

Negima!: Magister Negi Magi. Written and illustrated by Ken Akamatsu. Del Rey Manga/Random House, 2004– . **O** ◎ **Japanese manga.** あ

Ten-year-old Negi Springfield has just graduated, the youngest in his class of apprentice wizards in England. All graduating students must pass one more trial: each must be assigned a career in the human world until he is old enough to be given the title of wizard. Negi has been assigned to be the youngest-ever English teacher at an all-girls' high school in Japan! Though most of his students think he's adorable, one girl, Asuna Kagurazaka, despises Negi for replacing the teacher she had a crush on. Though Negi is forbidden to use his magic powers, sometimes he just can't resist, and after Asuna discovers Negi's powers, she vows to make his career as short as possible. The hit manga, which is still ongoing in Japan, has also been adapted as an anime series.

>*Vol. 1.* 2004. 208pp. 0-345-47046-X.
>*Vol. 2.* 2004. 208pp. 0-345-47120-2.
>*Vol. 3.* 2004. 224pp. 0-345-47180-6.
>*Vol. 4.* 2004. 208pp. 0-345-47784-7.
>*Vol. 5.* 2005. 208pp. 0-345-47785-5.
>*Vol. 6.* 2005. 208pp. 0-345-47786-3.
>*Vol. 7.* 2005. 208pp. 0-345-47787-1.
>*Vol. 8.* 2005. 208pp. 0-345-46540-7.
>*Vol. 9.* 2006. 208pp. 0-345-48273-5.
>*Vol. 10.* 2006. 208pp. 0-345-48441-X.
>*Vol. 11.* 2006. 208pp. 0-345-49231-5.
>*Vol. 12.* 2006. 208pp. 0-345-49463-6.
>*Vol. 13.* 2007. 208pp. 0-345-49505-5.

Nodwick Chronicles. **Written and illustrated by Aaron Williams.** Dork Storm Press, 2002– . **T**

> The fantasy and other genre-spoofing adventures of Nodwick, a young hench-man with a talent for being crushed, flattened, flayed, and eaten and also for carrying large objects like stolen treasure. Don't worry, every time he is killed he comes right back to life. He has contracted into three adventurers—Piffany, Yeager, and Artax—who are more destructive in their adventuring than any force of evil and have a knack for destroying whole towns rather than saving the day. Together they roam the countryside, stealing treasure as they fight against the evil god Baphuma'al. Features many pop culture references from movies, television, comic books, much-hated operating systems, and gaming.

> > *Vol. I.* 2003. 160pp. 1-930964-80-3.
> > *Vol. II: Of Gods and Henchmen.* 2002. 156pp. 1-930964-81-1.
> > *Vol. III: Songs in the Key of "Aiiieeee!"* 2003. 160pp. 1-930964-82-X.
> > *Vol. IV: Obligatory Dragon on the Cover.* 2004. 160pp. 1-930964-97-8.
> > *Vol. V.* 2005. 160pp. 1-933288-11-6.
> > *Vol. VI.* 2005. 160pp. 1-933288-12-4.
> > *Chronicles I and II.* 2005. 160pp. 1-933288-10-8.

🌱 **Oh My Goddess!** **Written and illustrated by Kosuke Fujishima.** Dark Horse Comics, 1997– . ◎ **Japanese manga.** あ

Oh My Goddess! © 2006 by Kosuke Fujishima. All rights reserved. New and adapted artwork and text copyright 2006. Dark Horse Comics, Inc.

> What would you do if you accidentally dialed the wrong number and instead of ordering pizza, you dialed up your very own goddess? That's what college student Keiichi Morisato has done, and now the beautiful and shy Norse goddess Belldandy has been delivered to his dorm room with one wish to grant him. When Keiichi wishes for a girl just like Belldandy to stay with him forever, his wish is granted, and now the goddess is living at his place and ex-periencing what life is all about. When Belldandy's sisters, the techno-savvy Skuld and the vixenish Urd, decide to move in, too, it's more and more hi-jinks as Heaven and Earth collide. As Keiichi's life gets turned upside down liv-ing with three goddesses, he learns about the pluses and mi-nuses of getting exactly what you wished for. *Wrong Number* received recognition from YALSA's Popular Paperbacks for Young Adults committee in 2002 on the "Graphic Novels: Superheroes and Beyond" list as well as the 2003 Quick Picks for Reluctant Readers list. In late 2005 Dark Horse Comics started reprinting the series in the original right-to-left format from Japan and has also reissued the original volumes in the traditional right-to-left format.

> *Vol. 1: Wrong Number.* 2002. 160pp. 1-56971-669-2; 2d ed., 2005, 192pp., 1-59307-387-9.
> *Vol. 2: Leader of the Pack.* 2002. 152pp. 1-56971-764-8; 2d ed., 2006, 192pp., 1-59307-457-3.
> *Vol. 3: Final Exam.* 2002. 152pp. 1-56971-765-6; 2d ed., 2006, 192pp., 1-59307-539-1.

> *Vol. 4: Love Potion No. 9.* 1997. 192pp. 1-56971-252-2; 2d ed., 2006, 192pp., 1-59307-623-1.
>
> *Vol. 5: Sympathy for the Devil.* 1999. 160pp. 1-56971-329-4; 2007. 184pp. 1-59307-708-4.
>
> *Vol. 6: Terrible Master Urd.* 1999. 176pp. 1-56971-369-3.
>
> *Vol. 7: The Queen of Vengeance.* 1999. 152pp. 1-56971-431-2.
>
> *Vol. 8: Mara Strikes Back.* 2000. 176pp. 1-56971-449-5.
>
> *Vol. 9: Ninja Master.* 2000. 152pp. 1-56971-474-6.
>
> *Vol. 10: Miss Keiichi.* 2001. 232pp. 1-56971-522-X.
>
> *Vol. 11: The Devil in Miss Urd.* 2001. 176pp. 1-56971-540-8.
>
> *Vol. 12: The Fourth Goddess.* 2001. 280pp. 1-56971-551-3.

Oh My Goddess! © 2006 by Kosuke Fujishima. All rights reserved. New and adapted artwork and text copyright 2006. Dark Horse Comics, Inc.

> *Vol. 13: Childhood's End.* 2002. 216pp. 1-56971-685-4.
>
> *Vol. 14: Queen Sayoko.* 2002. 240pp. 1-56971-766-4.
>
> *Vol. 15: Hand in Hand.* 2003. 256pp. 1-56971-921-7.
>
> *Vol. 16: Mystery Child.* 2003. 272pp. 1-56971-950-0.
>
> *Vol. 17: Traveler.* 2003. 256pp. 1-56971-986-1.
>
> *Vol. 18: The Phantom Racer.* 2004. 256pp. 1-59307-217-1.
>
> *Vol. 19/20: Sora Unchained.* 2005. 312pp. 1-59307-316-X.
>
> *Vol. 21.* 2005. 176pp. 1-59307-334-8.
>
> *Vol. 22.* 2005. 176pp. 1-59307-400-X.
>
> *Vol. 23.* 2006. 176pp. 1-59307-463-8.
>
> *Vol. 24.* 2006. 176pp. 1-59307-545-6.006.
>
> *Vol. 25.* 2006. 176pp. 1-59307-644-4.
>
> *Colors.* 2006. 192pp. 1-59307-408-5.
>
> *Adventures of the Mini-Goddesses.* 2000. 88pp. 1-56971-421-5.

Record of Lodoss War: Welcome to Lodoss Island! Written and illustrated by Rei Hyakuyashiki. Based on the creations by Ryo Mizuno. CPM Manga, 2003. **T Japanese manga.** あ

A tongue-in-cheek look at the fantasy Lodoss Island, where stereotypes are mocked with wanton glee. The cast is represented in "chibi" (superdeformed) style to add to the comedy. Join the inept knight Parn and his campaigners as they try to vanquish evil from the island. *Volume 1* tells about the attempt to destroy the evil witch Karla, and Parn seeks the aid of King Kashew to rescue Princess Fiona. In *Volume 2,* Parn and Deedlit try to save King Kashew's kingdom from a neighboring tribe and enlist the aid of a djinn to stop the fight. The story was also released as an anime in Japan.

> *Vol. 1.* 2003. 136pp. 1-58664-879-9.
>
> *Vol. 2.* 2003. 136pp. 1-58664-884-5.

***The Replacement God, Vol. 1.* Written and illustrated by Zander Cannon.** Amaze Ink/Slave Labor Graphics, 1997. 216pp. 0-943151-18-X. **O**

In the land of Mun, a young man called Knute has been a problem prisoner. A slave, he has tried to escape from the king's dungeon more than 346 times. Knute lucks out when he is pardoned as a sign of goodwill following a great victory. Too bad for the king that Knute is foretold to be the replacement god of Death, a title that the king wanted for himself, to live forever. Now Knute and Anne, a simple girl from a nearby village, are on the run from the king and his beatnik Visigoth Death Horde.

The Ruler of the Land. **Written by Jeon Keuk-Jin. Illustrated by Yang Jae-Hyun.** ADV Manga, 2004. **T Korean manhwa.**

Lecherous young buffoon Bi-Kwang Han is a master swordsman, and his skills are desired by the House of a Thousand Horses, but his lust for beautiful women constantly gets him into trouble. He is recruited by Hwa-Rin, a beautiful woman in disguise as a man, to help her search for her grandfather, a legendary master of the White Lightning technique. She carries with her the coveted Sword of Flowers, a mythic weapon that may be a key to locating her grandfather. The Sword of the Flowers is desired by Lord Yoo and his armies of hired swordsmen, bandits, thieves, and cut-throats, and she'll need to work together with Bi-Kwang if they're to survive their experience, unless she kills him first!

> *Vol. 1.* 2004. 200pp. 1-4139-0031-3.
> *Vol. 2.* 2004. 200pp. 1-4139-0037-2.
> *Vol. 3.* 2004. 200pp. 1-4139-0057-7.

Slayers. **Written by Hajime Kanzaka. Illustrated by Shoko Yoshinaka.** CPM Press, 1999–2005. **T Japanese manga.** あ

The adventures of Lina Inverse, one of the most powerful and short-tempered sorceresses to roam the land. Able to destroy a dragon with a simple spell, she's met her match in her own biggest fan and enemy: the busty sorceress Naga the White Serpent. They battle monsters, demons, and thieves in search of money and free food. Later on, as chronicled in *Slayers Super-Explosive Demon Story*, Lina teams up with thick-as-a-brick swordsman Gourry Gabriev, carrier of the powerful Sword of Light. They're joined by their companions, the sorcerer Zelgadis Greywords and the young female cleric Amelia Wil Tesla Seyruun, in their quest to destroy evil and get plenty of free food. The hilarious series was also released as an anime in Japan.

> *Slayers, Book 1: Medieval Mayhem.* 1999. 160pp. 1-56219-913-7.
> Slayers Special. 2002–2003.
>> *Book 1: Touch of Evil.* 2002. 192pp. 1-58664-865-9.
>> *Book 2: Notorious.* 2003. 184pp. 1-58664-902-7.
>> *Book 3: Lesser of Two Evils.* 2003. 176pp. 1-58664-903-5.
>> *Book 4: Spellbound.* 2003. 184pp. 1-58664-904-3.
> Slayers Super-Explosive Demon Story. 2002–2004.
>> *Book 1: Legend of Darkness.* 2002. 192pp. 1-58664-866-7.
>> *Book 2: Legacy of the Dragon God.* 2002. 192pp. 1-58664-867-5.
>> *Book 3: Red Priest.* 2003. 176pp. 1-58664-913-2.
>> *Book 4: Return.* 2003. 136pp. 1-58664-914-0.
>> *Book 5: City of Lost Souls.* 2004. 184pp. 1-58664-915-9.
>> *Book 6: Lina the Teenage Sorceress.* 2004. 176pp. 1-58664-930-2.
>> *Book 7: The Claire Bible.* 2004. 184pp. 1-58664-937-X.
> *Slayers Premium, Vol. 1.* 2005. 184pp. 1-58664-973-6.

8

Tales of the Realm. **Written by Robert Kirkman. Illustrated by Matt Tyree.** Image Comics, 2004. 144pp. 1-58240-394-5. **T**

In a world like modern Earth but where fantasy is an everyday part of life, and dragons, ogres, goblins, and magic are everywhere, Thomas Danbec, James Meyehr, and the elf Amy Nolan are three actors starring in the popular television series *Tales of the Realm.* They've had plenty of fame from the show, but they want a crack at becoming movie stars. When the famous movie director Kyle Stifotel is kidnapped, the three actors, who play warriors on television, set out to rescue him in the hope that they'll be able to launch a movie career adventure-style, as a reward for saving the director. Can three actors who don't have the slightest clue how to rescue anyone, and who carry prop weapons in battle, really save the day? A lighthearted comedy that pokes fun at Hollywood and high fantasy tales.

<u>Vampire Game.</u> **Written and illustrated by Judai.** TOKYOPOP, 2003–2006. **T Japanese manga.**

A battle waged centuries ago between the Phelios, the king of Saint Pheliosta, and the vampire Dusel ended with the vampire being defeated but vowing he would fight his enemy in the next life. Now that time has come, but Dusel has been reincarnated as a cute housecat (albeit with magical powers) and his owner is none other than Ishtar, the great-granddaughter of his ancient enemy. The game begins again, but who is Saint Phelios reincarnated as, and just who's side is Ishtar really on, anyway?

> *Vol. 1.* 2003. 200pp. 1-59182-369-2.
> *Vol. 2.* 2003. 208pp. 1-59182-370-6.
> *Vol. 3.* 2003. 208pp. 1-59182-371-4.
> *Vol. 4.* 2004. 200pp. 1-59182-556-3.
> *Vol. 5.* 2004. 200pp. 1-59182-557-1.
> *Vol. 6.* 2004. 208pp. 1-59182-558-X.
> *Vol. 7.* 2004. 208pp. 1-59182-559-8.
> *Vol. 8.* 2004. 208pp. 1-59182-560-1.
> *Vol. 9.* 2004. 208pp. 1-59182-561-X.
> *Vol. 10.* 2005. 192pp. 1-59532-440-2.
> *Vol. 11.* 2005. 208pp. 1-59532-441-0.
> *Vol. 12.* 2005. 192pp. 1-59532-442-9.
> *Vol. 13.* 2005. 192pp. 1-59532-443-7.
> *Vol. 14.* 2006. 192pp. 1-59532-444-5.
> *Vol. 15.* 2006. 192pp. 1-59816-212-8.

<u>Van Von Hunter.</u> **Written and illustrated by Mike Schwark and Ron Kaulfersch.** TOKYOPOP, 2005–2006. **T Neo-manga.**

In the farcical fantasy land of Dikay, three years have passed since a climactic battle between the powerful Archmage and the warrior Van Von Hunter and his band of heroes, which resulted in most of the local populace having a massive case of amnesia and Van Von Hunter receiving the power to point out the obvious. Van Von Hunter has returned home to his mansion along with his nameless cute sidekick, unsure of what future awaits him since most of the land has been cleansed of evil. Luckily for him, trouble is beginning to appear in the form of the ousted former ruler of Dikay—the Flaming Prince and his legions of evil. Van Von Hunter is joined in his fight against evil by Amanda Beaumont, a mysterious and klutzy guardian of the mystical Ebony Eye, and the newly emerging evil doesn't stand a chance against Van Von Hunter and his amnesiac sidekick. The series is also available online as a Web comic at http://www.vanhunter.com.

    Vol. 1. 2005. 184pp. 1-59532-692-8.
    Vol. 2. 2005. 192pp. 1-59532-693-6.
    Vol. 3. 2006. 192pp. 1-59532-694-4.

Chapter 9

Nonfiction

Though not as common as fictional graphic novels, nonfiction graphic novels are still published today and tackle a variety of topics, including biographies, science, religion, and history. The majority of titles are published by smaller presses or by mainstream book publishers rather than by the larger comic book publishers such as Marvel and DC Comics. For readers interested in graphic novels featuring tales of true crime, see chapter 5 for a selection of titles.

Art—Comics, Comic Books, and Graphic Novels

Several publications have been released that use a graphic novel format to explain the medium of comic books, comic strips, and graphic novels. Below are listed some of the best-known publications focusing on the intricacies that make the medium so appealing for storytelling.

Comics and Sequential Art. **Written and illustrated by Will Eisner.** Poorhouse Press, 1985. 164pp. 0-9614728-1-2. **T**

> Legendary comic art veteran Will Eisner's guide to the basic principles of graphic storytelling. Adapted from his art class taught at the New York School of Visual Arts, the guide examines the basic anatomy of sequential art and practical applications of using the art form of words and pictures to tell a story.

Graphic Storytelling and Visual Narrative. **Written and illustrated by Will Eisner.** Poorhouse Press, 1996. 164pp. 0-9614728-2-0. **T**

> A companion to Will Eisner's publication *Comics and Sequential Art*. Includes storytelling samples by not only Will Eisner, but also Pulitzer Prize winner Art Spiegelman, Robert Crumb, Milton Caniff, and Al Capp.

Making Comics: Storytelling Secrets of Comics, Manga, and Graphic Novels. **Written and illustrated by Scott McCloud.** HarperPerennial, 2006. 272pp. 0-06-078094-0. **T**

> A guide for all of those interested in creating their own manga, graphic novel, or Webcomic. Scott McCloud takes the beginning artist on a tour of tips and secrets found nowhere else. Topics include selecting appropriate moments for comic book panels, how to guide the reader's eye in the comic book layout, understanding body and facial language, an overview of genres, and more.

Reinventing Comics: How Imagination and Technology Are Revolutionizing an Art Form. **Written and illustrated by Scott McCloud.** HarperPerennial, 2000. 252pp. 0-06-095350-0. **T**

> A sequel to Scott McCloud's *Understanding Comics*, this publication shifts the focus to other aspects of the medium, including creator's rights, comics as an art form and literature, and the online potential of Webcomics.

Understanding Comics: The Invisible Art. **Written and illustrated by Scott McCloud.** HarperPerennial, 1994. 216pp. 0-06-097625-X. **T** ◎

© 1993 Scott McCloud.

> In this groundbreaking book, creator Scott McCloud offers professionals of the comics medium, longtime readers of comics, and even novice readers a complete overview of the comics medium, illustrated in a comic book format. Hosted by Scott McCloud, the highly regarded publication dissects many facets of comic, including the origins of comics, basic facts of the medium, the secret language of comics, how a comic book is made, and other informative observations about the medium.

Biography/Autobiography/Memoir

These collections of biographies, autobiographies, and memoirs include tales of heroism and heartache during wartime, life on the street, and everyday angst by renowned comic book artists, and stories about people whose stories have inspired us all.

🎗 *The Amazing "True" Story of a Teenage Single Mom.* **Written and illustrated by Katherine Arnoldi.** Hyperion Press, 1998. 176pp. 0-7868-6420-1. **O**

> As the title indicates, this is the true story of a teenage single mother and the hardships, sacrifice, and small rewards that come into her life after her baby is born. Without the support of her family or her child's father, Kathy drops out of school and works two jobs to get by and to provide for her child. With her dreams of college and traveling the world put on hold, Kathy is helped and encouraged by the kindness of strangers she meets, such as a truck driver and fellow mothers, to continue to seek out her dream of college and to continually exceed in life. The graphic biography has received recognition from YALSA's Best Books for Young Adults and the Quick Picks for Reluctant Readers committee on the 1999 lists.

American Splendor. Written by Harvey Pekar. Illustrated by various. Four Walls Eight Windows and Ballantine Books, 1994– . **M**

> The down and out life of Harvey Pekar. The series has been written since 1976, when Pekar was working as a file clerk at a Veterans Administration hospital in Cleveland, Ohio. The various collections highlight everyday life, including his coworkers, his daily grind, problems unclogging a toilet, relationships, how to have a car survive a Cleveland winter, his short-lived fame on the *Late Night with David Letterman* show, and even his bout with cancer. Since Pekar is not an artist, he has relied on a number of artists to tell his tales, including Robert Crumb, Gary Dumm, Frank Stack, Dean Haspiel, Kevin Brown, and Joe Zabel. The life of Harvey Pekar was also adapted into a 2003 film called *American Splendor,* starring Paul Giamatti as Pekar. Below are listed the various volumes of *American Splendor.*
>
>> *The New American Splendor Anthology.* Four Walls Eight Windows. 1991. 300pp. 0-941423-64-6.
>> *Our Cancer Year.* Four Walls Eight Windows, 1994. 252pp. 1-56858-011-8.
>> *American Splendor Presents: Bob & Harv's Comics.* Four Walls Eight Windows, 1996. 96pp. 1-56858-101-7.
>> *American Splendor: The Life and Times of Harvey Pekar.* Ballantine Books, 2003. 320pp. 0-345-46830-9.
>> *American Splendor: Our Movie Year.* Ballantine Books, 2004. 176pp. 0-345-47937-8.
>> *Best of American Splendor.* Ballantine Books, 2005. 336pp. 0-345-47938-6.

American Splendor: Unsung Hero. **Written by Harvey Pekar. Illustrated by David Collier.** Dark Horse Comics, 2003. 80pp. 1-59307-040-3. **O**

> The Vietnam War recollections of Robert McNeil, a black war vet and coworker at the Cleveland VA Hospital of *American Splendor* creator Harvey Pekar. At the young age of seventeen, Robert enlisted in the Marines with hopes of an early discharge. From training at Camp Pendleton in California to the front lines overseas, McNeil tells, through Pekar's writing, an honest and sometimes humorous portrait of one African American man's experiences as a soldier.

AutobioGraphix. **Written and illustrated by various.** Dark Horse Comics, 2003. 104pp. 1-59307-038-1. **O**

> A collection of short autobiographical and nonfiction stories by some of the comic book industry's best-known writers and artists, including Frank Miller, Will Eisner, Stan Sakai, Paul Chadwick, Sergio Aragones, and Eddie Campbell.

🎖 *Blankets.* **Written and illustrated by Craig Thompson.** Top Shelf Productions, 2002. 592pp. 1-891830-43-0. **O** ◎

> The autobiographical, touching tale of Craig Thompson's youth growing up in his rigid fundamentalist home with his brother Phil, as well as his awkward and touching first experience with love while attending a youth church camp. Raised in a strict Midwest household where his overbearing parents often sent him and his brother to a claustrophobic storage chamber nicknamed "the

cubby hole" for punishment for inappropriate schoolboy behavior, Craig emerged from his youth a shattered, vulnerable teen. At a church camp he meets a kindred spirit in Raina and her friends. As their relationship blossoms, their brightly burning, raw, emotional, physical, and even spiritual love for each other helps to inspire Craig's future endeavors as a creator and to help erase some of the pain of his youth. The story has won many awards, including two Eisner Awards for Best Graphic Novel: New (2004) and Best Writer/Artist (2004); a Harvey Award for Best Artist (2004), Best Cartoonist (2004), and Best Graphic Album of Original Work (2004); and several Ignatz Awards, including Outstanding Artist (2004) and Outstanding Graphic Novel or Collection (2004). The graphic novel has also received recognition from YALSA's Best Books for Young Adults committee in 2004 as well as the Popular Paperbacks for Young Adults committee in 2005.

Carnet de Voyage. **Written and illustrated by Craig Thompson.** Top Shelf Productions, 2005. 224pp. 1-891830-60-0. **O**

© 2006 Craig Thompson.

A personal travel log by Craig Thompson of his three months traveling through Barcelona, the Alps, and France, as well as Morocco, to promote his book *Blankets*. The sketches and commentaries are true reflections of a wandering creator experiencing different cultures and countries. Thompson's solitary journey across many cultures is a quiet and poignant look at a man surrounded by couples, unique friendships, good food, as well as beautiful and exotic locations

Edu-Manga: Anne Frank. **Written by Etsuo Suzuki. Illustrated by Yoko Miyawaki.** Digital Manga Publishing, 2006. 160pp. 1-56970-974-2. **Y Japanese manga.**

An illustrated look at the life of one of the most deeply moving figures from World War II. A German-born Jewish girl, Anne and her family escaped to Amsterdam during the Nazi occupation of Germany. After two years of hiding, she and her family were captured, and Anne died of typhus in the Bergen-Belsen concentration camp at the young age of fifteen. Her diary chronicling the events of her life from 1942 to 1944 was published after her death by the only surviving member of her family, her father. In English, the book is called *The Diary of a Young Girl*, and because of it Anne Frank is one of the best-known Holocaust victims. The manga is hosted by Astro Boy, the popular manga character created by Osamu Tezuka.

Edu-Manga: Helen Adams Keller. **Written by Sozo Yanagawa. Illustrated by Rie Yagi.** Digital Manga Publishing, 2006. 160pp. 1-56970-976-9. **Y Japanese manga.**

An illustrated look at the life of one of the most inspirational people of the twentieth century. Born in 1880, Helen Keller lost both her sight and hearing at the tender age of one and also lost the ability to speak. With the aid of tutor Anne Sullivan, Helen learned Braille, sign language, and eventually how to speak. Helen graduated from Radcliffe College, becoming the first deaf and blind person to earn a bachelor of arts degree, and continued to be an inspiration to many of those born with disabilities through her lectures and appearances across the world, until her death in 1968. The manga is hosted by Astro Boy, the popular manga character created by Osamu Tezuka.

***Epileptic*. Written and illustrated by David B.** Pantheon Press/Random House, 2005. 368pp. 0-375-42318-4. **M**

A poignant memoir of the writer's youth, set in the 1960s. When the author was a five-year-old called Pierre-François Beauchard, his elder brother, Jean-Christophe, was diagnosed with epilepsy. As Pierre-François witnesses his brother's long-term deterioration from the incurable disease, their parents take Jean-Christophe all around Europe to find a miracle cure for his condition, to no avail. As the disease continues to worsen, Pierre-François watches his elder brother descend into madness. Pierre-François also retreats into his own private madness—a fantasy world to protect himself from the ravages of his brother's illness.

***Ethel and Ernest: A True Story*. Written and illustrated by Raymond Briggs.** Knopf/Random House, 2001. 104pp. 0-375-71447-2. **T**

A touching, true-life tale of the author's parents, Ethel and Ernest, from their marriage in 1930 until their deaths, mere months apart, in 1971. Living a working-class life in London, Ernest worked for thirty-seven years as a milkman and Ethel was a housemaid. Together they braved the London bombings, visits from stepmothers, sadness at hearing the career choice of their son, the amazing introduction of modern technologies into the household, and other daily life experiences, proving the universal message that love knows no boundaries or class distinctions.

🖋 *Fax from Sarajevo*. **Written and illustrated by Joe Kubert.** Dark Horse Comics, 1998. 224pp. 1-56971-346-4. **T**

The harrowing and true account of how comic book creator Ervin Rustemagic and his family survived, trapped in their hometown of Sarajevo, during the Serbian bombardment from 1992 to 1994. Only by contacting the outside world via fax were they able to tell their friends and loved ones of their struggles to survive. The story won an Eisner Award in 1997 for Best Graphic Novel: New and a Harvey Award for Best Graphic Album of Original Work (1997), and was also recognized by YALSA's Popular Paperbacks for Young Adults' 2002 "War: Causes and Consequences" selection list.

***Fortune and Glory: A True Hollywood Comic Book Story*. Written and illustrated by Brian Michael Bendis.** Oni Press, 2000 136pp. 1-929998-06-6. **O**

Brian Michael Bendis first hit it big in the comic book industry with his gritty and realistic writing in titles such as *Goldfish, Fire,* and *Torso.* Join him as he relates his true-life adventure of dealing with the most humorous place of all: Hollywood! From shady deals, to actresses vying for attention, to empty promises, Brian's tale makes a great comedy, but unfortunately it's all true!

9

***Godspeed: The Kurt Cobain Graphic.* Written by Barnaby Legg and Jim McCarthy. Illustrated by Flameboy.** Omnibus Press, 2003. 96pp. 0-7119-9763-2. **T**

A first-person account of the life of Kurt Cobain, the troubled lead singer and guitarist of the grunge band Nirvana. Cobain's personal conflicts, bouts of depression, bronchitis, and chronic addiction to heroin resulted in him taking his own life April 5, 1994.

***It's a Bird.* Written by Steven T. Seagle. Illustrated by** Teddy Kristiansen. Vertigo/DC Comics, 2005. 136pp. 1-4012-0311-6 **M**

The semiautobiographical story of writer Steven Seagle's anticipation and dread of writing the adventures of Superman—an icon to millions around the world, but not a hero with whom he can easily relate. Are the heroic qualities of Superman still relevant in this day and age? After dealing with other family setbacks, including the looming family curse of inheriting Huntington's disease, Steve soon finds that even though he is powerless against many things, perhaps he's found a kindred spirit in the Man of Steel after all.

***King: Complete Edition.* Written and illustrated by Ho Che Anderson.** Fantagraphic Books, 2005. 240pp. 1-56097-622-5. **O**

An unflinching biography of the youth, adulthood, and death of the Reverend Martin Luther King Jr. An honest look at the man's life, treating the Reverend not as a saint, but as a normal man who believed in his cause and was willing to die for it so millions could be truly free.

🎋 **Maus: A Survivor's Tale. Written and illustrated by Art Spiegelman.** Pantheon Books/Random House Publishing, 1986–1997. **O** ◎

The tragic, acclaimed series in which a father recounts the horrors of trying to survive through the Jewish Holocaust and an estranged family tries to mend wounds that will never heal. Vladek Spiegelman, a Jewish survivor of Hitler's Holocaust, and his cartoonist son Art have had a troubled relationship. Vladek's first wife, who also survived the camps, committed suicide years ago, and the family has always been broken. Told in flashbacks taking the reader back to Vladek's life in Poland before the war, during the Nazi concentration camps, and in the present, the story features anthropomorphized versions of humans: Jews are mice, Germans are cats, Poles are pigs, French are frogs, Americans are dogs, Swedes are reindeer, and Gypsies are moths. The story has won multiple awards, including a Pulitzer Prize Special Award in 1992 for *Maus I*; an Eisner Award for Best Graphic Novel: Reprint (2002) for *Maus II*; and a Harvey Award for Best Graphic Album of Previously Published Work for *Maus II*. Art Spiegelman also received recognition in the Will Eisner Hall of Fame in 1999 for his contributions to the comic book industry. The series has also received recognition from YALSA: both volumes were selected for the Popular Paperbacks for Young Adults' selection list in 1997.

I: My Father Bleeds History. 1986. 0-394-54155-3.
II: And Here My Troubles Began. 1991. 0-394-54155-3.
The Complete Maus. 1997. 0-679-40641-7, hardcover.

Mom's Cancer. **Written and illustrated by Brian Fies.** Harry N. Abrams, 2006. 115pp. 0-8109-5840-6. **O**

> Originally featured as an online Webcomic, the collected features the poignant as well as uniquely humorous true story of how Fies's mother suffered and battled against advanced-stage lung cancer and the toll it takes on not just those suffering from the disease, but the stress and anguish that family and loved ones suffer as well.

Palestine. **Written and illustrated by Joe Sacco.** Fantagraphics, 2001. 288pp. 1-56097-432-X. **O**

> A true account of the creator's journey to Jerusalem in 1991. The creator spent many weeks in the Gaza Strip and interviewed more than 100 Jews and Palestinians in an effort to better understand the conflict that has plagued the region for decades.

🏮 *Pedro and Me: Friendship, Loss, and What I Learned.* **Written and illustrated by Judd Winick.** Henry Holt & Company, 2000. 192pp. 0-8050-6403-6. **T**

© 2000 by Henry Holt and Company

> In 1994 MTV's *Real World*, cartoonist Judd Winick was a roommate of Pedro Zamora, a young man who was slowly dying from AIDS. For millions of viewers who never knew anyone with the disease, Pedro became a symbol for AIDS awareness, and shortly after the filming of the show he died at the age of twenty-two from complications of the disease. Through the medium of the graphic novel Judd retells the life of Pedro and how this young gay man, dying from a horrible disease, could inspire, educate, and teach us all how to live and what it truly means to be alive. The graphic novel has received recognition from YALSA's Best Books for Young Adults in 2001; Popular Paperbacks for Young Adults committee for the 2002 "Graphic Novels: Superheroes and Beyond" list; and the Quick Picks for Reluctant Readers list in 2001.

Perfect Example. **Written and illustrated by John Porcellino.** Drawn & Quarterly Publications, 2005. 144pp. 1-896597-75-0. **M**

> A collection of the creator's King-Cat minicomics showcasing the author's awkward years of late high school starting in 1987. With college looming on the horizon, John experiences drunken rock concerts, arguments with his parents, make-out sessions, and ultimately a deteriorating relationship with his longtime girlfriend. An honest and true depiction of the life of a high school student unsure of the path that lies ahead and the challenges that await him.

🏮 <u>Persepolis.</u> **Written and illustrated by Marjane Satrapi.** Pantheon Books/ Random House Publishing, 2004. **O**

> Based on the author's own life in Iran and abroad. It is her memoir recounting her youth during the Islamic Revolution in Iran, the downfall of the Shah's regime, the deadly conflict with Iraq, and what life is like under repressive rule. At the age of fourteen she was sent to live in Vienna, and where *Volume II* con-

tinues, she learns about love and growing up, and eventually returns to Iran. But is her homeland where Marjane wants to permanently live and go to college, or have both she and her homeland changed? The series won a Harvey Award for Best American Edition of Foreign Material in 2004. *Volume 2: The Story of a Return* won an Ignatz Award for Outstanding Graphic Novel in 2005. The graphic novel series has also received recognition from several of YALSA's selection list committees, including Best Books for Young Adults for *Volume 1* (2004) and *Volume 2* (2005), respectively, as well as Outstanding Books for the College Bound (2004) and an Alex Award (2004) for *Volume 1*.

> *Vol. 1: The Story of a Childhood.* 2004. 160pp. 0-375-71457-X.
> *Vol. 2: The Story of a Return.* 2004. 192pp. 0-375-42288-9.

🎗 *Pyongyang: A Journey in North Korea*. Written and illustrated by Guy Delisle. Drawn & Quarterly Publications, 2005. 184pp. 1-896597-89-0. **T** 🏵

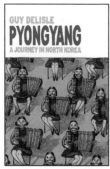

© 2000 Guy Delisle.

The true story of Guy Delisle, a Quebec-born, France-based animator, and his short time living in the bleak country of North Korea. While staying in the city of Pyongyang for two months while overseeing the production of a kids' cartoon, Delisle captures the oddities of the quirky people of North Korea, from their bland customs to the endless line of sites dedicated to North Korea's late founder Kim Il Sung and his son, current leader Kim Jong Il. A stranger in an even stranger land, Delisle's frank look at life in a sheltered country is an awakening appreciation for free countries and the beauty of free expression. The book was awarded recognition on YALSA's Best Books for Young Adults 2006 list.

***The Quitter*. Written by Harvey Pekar. Illustrated by Dean Haspiel.** Vertigo/DC Comics, 2005. 104pp. 1-4012-0399-X. **M**

The childhood and young adult life of Harvey Pekar, author of the ongoing series <u>American Splendor</u>. Pekar focuses on the difficult times growing up in Cleveland, Ohio, as a young Jewish boy in an increasingly African American neighborhood and his attempts to find out where he belongs. Pekar was his own worst enemy, too. He was always too hard on himself when things didn't go his way and quit when push came to shove. Pekar's successes, though small, helped to encourage him on his path toward eventual fame and recognition.

🎗 *Safe Area Gorazde: The War in Eastern Bosnia 1992–95*. Written and illustrated by Joe Sacco. Fantagraphics, 2002. 240pp. 1-56097-470-2. **O**

A harsh and realistic look at the cost of the Bosnian war. Sacco visited the "safe area" of Gorazde four times through 1996. He recounts his interviews with locals as well as historical facts about the city and the conflict that prompted the so-called ethnic cleansing by the Serbs against the Muslim population. The story won an Eisner Award in 2001 for Best Graphic Novel: New and was also recognized by YALSA's Popular Paperbacks for Young Adults' 2002 "War: Causes and Consequences" selection list.

Shenzhen: A Travelogue from China. **Written and illustrated by Guy Delisle.** Drawn & Quarterly Publications, 2006. 152pp. 1-894937-79-1. **T** ◎

© 2000 Guy Delisle.

A follow-up to the highly recognized *Pyongyang: A Journey in North Korea* that continues the true-life tales of Guy Delisle, a Quebec-born animator, and his experiences living in China while overseeing the production of a kids' cartoon. Once again Delisle captures the oddities and humorous side of life in a communist country, where his animation studio outsources work. Delisle showcases the differences between Western and Eastern culture and the small moments when freedom is savored in a country where no one is truly free.

Streetwise: Autobiographical Stories by Comic Book Professionals. **Written and illustrated by various.** TwoMorrows Publishing, 2000. 160pp. 1-893905-04-7. **T**

A collection of autobiographical stories from a wide variety of comic book creators. Contributors include Will Eisner, Jack Kirby, Rick Veitch, Walter Simonson, Barry Windsor-Smith, Sergio Aragonés, Art Spiegelman, Paul Chadwick, and many more.

To the Heart of the Storm. **Reprint ed. Written and illustrated by Will Eisner.** DC Comics, 2000. 208pp. 1-56389-679-6. **O**

An autobiographical look at the life of comic book veteran Will Eisner, from his days as a youth, to his earliest days struggling as an artist, to his family's struggle with being Jewish, and how anti-Semitism affected his life. Onboard a train headed to a boot camp for enlisted men during World War II, Will stares out the window, and we see through his eyes in flashback sequences the life he led and how it made him the man he became.

Total Sell Out. **Written and illustrated by Brian Michael Bendis.** Oni Press, 2003. 184pp. 1-58240-287-6. **O**

A collection of multiple Eisner Award-winning writer Brian Michael Bendis's short stories and comic strips, including crime stories written by Warren Ellis and James Hudnall, as well as true biographical and slice-of-life stories from the comic book industry circuit and about miscellaneous average days that are hysterical and true.

True Story Swear to God. **Written and illustrated by Tom Beland.** AiT/Planet Lar, 2003– . **O**

© 2006 Tom Beland.

I swear to God I'm not making this up. It's all true. Tom never really believed in the power of fate and taking chances, but that's all about to change. When Tom goes on a work-related trip to Walt Disney World, little does he know that he'll meet the love of his life there. While at a concert he meets the fun and carefree Lily, and sparks do fly. There's only one problem: they live 9,000 miles apart. Can a cartoonist from California and a journalist from Puerto Rico find true love? The story of how writer/artist Tom Beland met and fell in love with his wife, Lily—and it's all true. *100 Stories* is a collection of short stories featuring Tom and Lily as they travel the comic book convention circuit and more.

> *Vol. 1: Chances Are . . . .* 2003. 176pp. 1-932051-09-0
> *Vol. 2: This One Goes to Eleven.* 2005. 176pp. 1-932051-34-1
> *100 Stories.* 2004. 136pp. 1-932051-21-X

***We Are on Our Own: A Memoir by Miriam Katin*. Written and illustrated by Miriam Katin.** Drawn & Quarterly, 2006. 132pp. 1-896597-20-3. **T**

The illustrated true story of the escape of Esther Katin and her young daughter, Miriam, from Nazi-controlled Budapest from 1944 to 1946. With her husband enlisted in the army and the Jews in Budapest facing certain death, Esther flees her beloved home along with Miriam in search of freedom from persecution. Abandoning everything they know and love, they travel secretly through battlefields to simple farm houses trying to find some sense of normalcy in a time of great upheaval.

History

These books take look at history both old and new from an entirely new perspective—the graphic form. The books feature current subjects as well as ancient history. Highlights include the history of the United States and of the universe, courtesy of Larry Gonick.

***Cartoon History of the United States*. Written and illustrated by Larry Gonick.** HarperPerennial/HarperCollins, 1991. 400pp. 0-06-273098-3. **T**

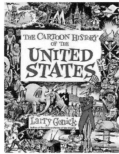

© 1991 HarperPerennial.

From the foundation of the Colonies to the first Gulf War, the book covers the history of the United States in a fun and humorous style. Both factual and irreverent, the collection succinctly highlights the birth of the nation and its history in a way that is both educational and fun.

🎗 **Cartoon History of the Universe. Written and illustrated by Larry Gonick.** 1992–2002. **T**

An ambitious project by Gonick still in the making today that includes the "Big Bang," the formation of Earth, the time of the dinosaurs, the origins of world faiths, the rise of great conquerors and ancient civilizations, and the modern ages of humans. Particular detail is devoted to showcasing perspectives from other cultures. Gonick's work is an impressive and thorough look at civilizations worldwide and is both educational as well as humorously entertaining. At the time of this printing only three volumes have been published, with more to come. *Volume III: From the Rise of Arabia to the Renaissance* received a Harvey Award for Best Graphic Album of Original Work in 2003.

The graphic novel series has also received recognition from YALSA's Popular Paperbacks for Young Adults committee for the 1997 list.

> *Vol. 1.* Doubleday Publishing, 1997. 368pp. 0-385-26520-4.
> *Vol. II: From the Springtime of China to the Fall of Rome.* Main Street Books/Broadway Books, 1992. 320pp. 0-385-42093-5.
> *Vol. III: From the Rise of Arabia to the Renaissance.* W. W. Norton, 2002. 320pp. 0-393-32403-6.

Japanese Drawing Room. **Written and illustrated by Sakura Mizuki.** Boychild/Russell-Cotes Museum. 100pp. 0-905173-80-5. **T Japanese manga.**

A cultural look at nineteenth-century Japan through the eyes of two European travelers to the country during the Victorian Age. Set during the Meiji era (1885). The couples are witnesses to many historical events in the country as well as historical accounts that have shaped Japan to become the country it is today. The manga was published in conjunction with the Russell-Cotes Art Gallery and Museum in Bournemouth, UK.

♠ *Louis Riel.* **Written and illustrated by Chester Brown.** Drawn + Quarterly, 2004. 260pp. 1-896597-63-7. **T**

An ambitious and eloquent look at the life of Louis Riel, a Canadian national who campaigned in several resistance movements for the rights of the Métis people of the Canadian prairies. His beliefs in rights for all ultimately led him to be executed for treason in 1885, but he is considered by many today to be a father of human rights in Canada and the Canadian Confederacy. The story received a Harvey Award for Best Writer (2004), as well as Best Graphic Album of Previously Published Work (2004).

9 of 1: Window to the World. **Written and illustrated by Oliver Chin.** Frog in Well, 2003. 112pp. 1-58394-072-3. **T**

A proactive look at how nine teenagers learned to better understand the world and the current state of events following the 9/11 attacks. As they ask questions and get answers about the history of the world and the cycle of violence, there is hope to pass on the knowledge of peace and understanding.

The 9/11 Report: A Graphic Adaptation. **Adapted by Sid Jacobson and Ernie Colon.** Hill and Wang/Farrar, Straus & Giroux, 2006. 160pp. 0-8090-5739-5. **T**

Originally released in prose form on December 5, 2005, the *9/11 Report*, the findings of an independent council's look into what went wrong and right before and since the terrorist attack on September 11, 2001. The dense manual has been adapted into an accessible source that every American can easily comprehend and shows how our country can benefit from the commission's recommendations and help to best fight the war against terrorism.

Still I Rise: A Cartoon History of African Americans. **Written by Roland Laird. Illustrated by Elihu Bey.** W.W. Norton, 1997. 206pp. 0-393-04538-2. **T**

An in-depth documentary in graphic novel format of the history of African Americans, from their struggle for freedom as slaves to their continuing plights and triumphs. The narrative includes a historical time line of major events as well as famous African Americans and their struggles, hardships, sacrifices, and successes.

***The Story of the Jews: A 4,000-Year Adventure.* Written and illustrated by Stan Mack.** Jewish Lights Publishing, 2001. 288pp. 1-58023-155-1. **T**

A humorous and lighthearted but authoritatively detailed look at the major events in the history of the Jewish people. From Abraham's meeting with God in 2000 B.C., to the birth of Moses, to Jesus Christ, to the Inquisition, to the horrors of the Holocaust and recent events in the Middle East, the experiences of the Jewish people are briefly covered in a focused but fun manner.

Science and Math

The world of science comes alive in the graphic novel format. What could be thought of by some as stodgy and difficult to understand takes on a whole new light. The majority of books in this chapter can be credited to three individuals: Larry Gonick for his guides to such principles as physics and chemistry; Jim Ottaviani for his dedication to a wide range of scientific history, including the life of Niels Bohr, and the history early dinosaur bone hunters; and Jay Hosler and his whimsical looks at science, from the lifecycle of a bee to the theories of Charles Darwin.

***Bone Sharps, Cowboys, and Thunder Lizards: A Tale of Edwin Drinker Cope, Othniel Charles Marsh, and the Gilded Age of Paleontology.* Written by Jim Ottaviani. Illustrated by Zander Cannon and Shad Petrovsky.** GT Labs, 2005. 176pp. 0-9660106-6-3. **T** ◎

© 2006 Jim Ottaviani.

An embellished account of the controversial early years of paleontology in the late nineteenth century, when scientists Edwin Drinker Cope and Othniel Charles Marsh scrambled to one-up each other in their search to discover the bones of "thunder lizards." Both scientists came from wealthy families and were able to fund their very competitive expeditions out West, which became known as the Bone Wars. Competition was so fierce that expeditions in search of Cretaceous fossils were also accompanied by sensationalized accounts of thievery, bribery, and spying that sullied the name of American paleontology for years.

***Cartoon Guide to Chemistry.* Written by Larry Gonick and Craig Criddle. Illustrated by Larry Gonick.** HarperResource/HarperInformation, 2005. 250pp. 0-06-093677-0. **T**

A lighthearted overview of the science of chemistry, the history of the subject, and common principles and practical applications of the theory used today and why it continues to be an important scientific field.

Cartoon Guide to the Environment. **Written by Larry Gonick and Alice Outwater. Illustrated by Larry Gonick.** HarperResource, 1996. 240pp. 0-06-273274-9. **T**

> An entertaining and educational look at the importance of environmental and ecological concerns such as nutrient cycles, producers versus consumers, population biographies, and much more. The book also examines the fate of Easter Island, which we're doomed to repeat unless we learn from yesterday's mistakes.

Cartoon Guide to Physics. **Written by Larry Gonick and Art Huffman. Illustrated by Larry Gonick.** HarperResource/HarperCollins, 1991. 224pp. 0-06-273100-9. **T**

> A simplified yet in-depth look at the fundamentals of the science of understanding and calculating matter, energy, and minute particles. The laws, theories, and fields of physics are included, as well as theoretical physics and famous physicists, in a humorous and informational collection.

Cartoon Guide to Statistics. **Written by Larry Gonick and Woollcott Smith. Illustrated by Larry Gonick.** HarperResource/HarperInformation, 1993. 240pp. 0-06-273102-5. **T**

> A humorous and educational primer of the mathematical computation of data analysis, which is used today to collect and analyze data. Statistics use computations to decide the effect of changes of an independent variable on a dependent variable.

🏵 *Clan Apis.* **Written and illustrated by Jay Hosler.** Active Synapse, 2000. 152pp. 0-9677255-0-X. **Y** ◎

> A unique look at the lifecycle of the honeybee from a humorous, charming, and informative point of view: as a biography. Join honeybee Nyuki from the earliest stages of her life as a larva to her role in the overall relationship with her hive and the flowers and insects that live in her world. From her birth to her death, every aspect of a honeybee's life is treated with added humor and attention to detail. The graphic novel was recognized by YALSA's Popular Paperbacks for Young Adults as a 2002 pick for the "Graphic Novels: Superheroes and Beyond" selection list.

Dignifying Science: Stories About Women Scientists. 2d ed. **Written by Jim Ottaviani. Illustrated by Donna Barr, Lea Hernandez, Carla Speed McNeil, and various.** GT Labs, 2003. 144pp. 0-9660106-4-7. **T**

Science has been stereotyped as a profession for men only, but Ottaviani's collection showcases seven women who have left their indelible mark in the field of science. The profiled women include Marie Sklodovska, Hedy Lamarr, Lise Meitner, Rosalind Franklin, Barbara McClintock, Birute Galdikas, and Marie Curie. The artwork is handled by a handful of talented female artists, including Marie Severin, Carla Speed McNeil, Jen Sorensen, Stephanie Gladden, Donna

Barr, Roberta Gregory, Linda Medley, Lea Hernandez, and Anne Timmons.

***Fallout: J. Robert Oppenheimer, Leo Szilard, and the Political Science of the Atomic Bomb.* Written by Jim Ottaviani. Illustrated by Jeff Parker, Steve Lieber, and various.** GT Labs, 2001. 240pp. 0-9660106-3-9. **O** ◎

A look at the creation of the atomic bomb as seen from the perspectives of Leó Szilárd, a pioneering physicist who first thought of the possibility of creating the atomic weapon, and J. Robert Oppenheimer, the physicist in charge of the famed Manhattan Project, as they worked in an uneasy alliance with the U.S. government. The project was created during the height of World War II and resulted in the design, production, and detonation of the atomic bombs dropped over Hiroshima and Nagasaki in Japan in 1945.

© 2001 Jim Ottaviani.

***Imagination Rocket: Science and Social Studies.* Edited by Brian Clopper. Art by various.** Behemoth Books, 2002. 124pp. 0-9700659-2-2. **Y**

Designed as a classroom guide to help stimulate and inform readers, the collection covers a wide variety of subjects and presents them in an entertaining but informative format. Subjects include how to make a camera, a humorous look at how the dinosaurs really disappeared, and cultural differences between the United States and Japan. Includes works by creators including Mark Crilley, Stuart Immonen, C. Scott Morse, Bill Knapp, and others.

***The Sandwalk Adventures.* Written and illustrated by Jay Hosler.** Active Synapse, 2003. 152pp. 0-9677255-1-8. **T** ◎

Ever wonder what Charles Darwin would say to a follicle mite named Mara who's living in his left eyebrow? In Jay Hosler's humorous and informative style, Charles and Mara strike up an unlikely friendship while strolling though his thinking path, called the Sandwalk. After reassuring Mara that he's no deity, Charles explains to her his theories on natural selection, a subject he knows a great deal about, and how we all fit together in our roles in the universe.

© 2003 Jay Hosler.

***Suspended in Language: Niels Bohr's Life, Discoveries, and the Century He Shaped.* Written by Jim Ottaviani. Illustrated by Jay Hosler, Linda Medley, and various.** GT Labs, 2004. 332pp. 0-9660106-3-9. **O**

An ambitious look at the life of Niels Bohr, a Danish physicist who helped to define the significance of the atomic structure and quantum mechanics. His work as a scientist earned him the Nobel prize in 1922, and after escaping from occupied Denmark during World War II, he eventually made it to America, where he spent time as a consultant in the creation of the Manhattan Project.

Two-Fisted Science: Stories About Scientists. 2d ed. Written by Jim Ottaviani. Illustrated by various. GT Labs, 2001. 128pp. 0-9660106-2-0. **T**

A collection of stories about famous scientists and oddball inventors, from nuclear physicists to amateur locksmiths, who helped change the world in their own creative ways. Includes stories and funny anecdotes about Albert Einstein, Niels Bohr, and Richard Feynman that celebrate their services to science but also showcase their humanity.

Oddities and Miscellany

True tales of the odd and weird have their place on the shelves of libraries. Featured here are the graphic novel collections focusing on this odd bunch, is often people. The graphic books featured include a *Ripley's Believe It or Not* collection as well as the highly recommended <u>Factoid Books Big Book</u> series, including true tales of the biggest freaks, weirdos, thugs, and worse that have ever lived.

♣ <u>**Factoid Books Big Books.**</u> **Written and illustrated by various.** Paradox Press/DC Comics, 1995-2001. **O**

Published from 1995 through 2001, this ambitious series by DC Comics' Paradox Press imprint brought a rotating staff to write and illustrate a wide variety of topics and subjects that ranged from the bizarre, to the off-beat, to the humorous. Each volume features artwork by an impressive list of creators, all working on a separate short story for each respective collection. The majority of the volumes feature short biographical stories, though for some publications, such as *The Big Book of Grimm*, the stories are collections of adapted stories. Several collections have received awards and recognition: *The Big Book of Urban Legends* and *The Big Book of Conspiracies* received Eisner Awards in 1995 and 1996, respectively. *The Big Book of Little Criminals* and *The Big Book of Weirdos* were recognized by YALSA's Popular Paperbacks for Young Adults in 1997. In 2001, *The Big Book of the Unexplained* was selected by the committee's "Paranormal" list. *The Big Book of Weirdos* and the *Big Book of Grimm* were recognized by the Quick Picks for Reluctant Readers book selection committee in 1996 and 2001, respectively.

The Big Book of Bad: The Best of the Worst of Everything. 1998. 192pp. 1-56389-359-2.
The Big Book of Conspiracies. 1995. 224pp. 1-56389-186-7.
The Big Book of Death. 1995. 224pp. 1-56389-166-2.
The Big Book of Freaks: 50 Amazing True Tales of Human Oddities. 1996. 224pp. 1-56389-218-9.
The Big Book of Grimm. 1999. 192pp. 1-56389-501-3.
The Big Book of Hoaxes: True Tales of the Greatest Lies Ever Told! 1996. 192pp. 1-56389-252-9.

The Big Book of Little Criminals: 63 True Tales of the World's Most Incompetent Jail-birds! 1996. 192pp. 1-56389-217-0.

The Big Book of Losers: Pathetic but True Tales of the World's Most Titanic Failures! 1997. 192pp. 1-56389-253-7.

The Big Book of Martyrs: Amazing but True Tales of Faith in the Face of Certain Death! 1997. 192pp. 1-56389-360-6.

The Big Book of Scandal: Trashy but True Tales from the Tawdry Worlds of Celebrity, High Society, Politics, and Big Business! 1998. 192pp. 1-56389-358-4.

The Big Book of the '70s. 2000. 192pp. 1-56389-671-0.

The Big Book of Thugs: Tough As Nails True Tales of the World's Baddest Mobs, Gangs, and Ne'er do Wells! 1996. 192pp. 1-56389-285-5.

© 1999 DC Comics.

The Big Book of the Unexplained. 1997. 192pp. 1-56389-254-5.

The Big Book of Urban Legends: 200 True Stories, Too Good to Be True! 1995. 224pp. 1-56389-165-4.

The Big Book of Vice: True Tales of Humanity's Worst Habits! 1998. 192pp. 1-56389-454-8.

The Big Book of the Weird Wild West: How the West Was Really Won! 1998. 192pp. 1-56389-361-4.

The Big Book of Weirdos: True Tales of the World's Kookiest Crackpots and Visionaries! 1995. 224pp. 1-56389-180-8.

The Big Book of Wild Women. 2001. 192pp. 1-56389-672-9.

***Ripley's Believe It or Not.* Written by Haden Blackman. Illustrated by Cary Nord.** Dark Horse Comics, 2003. 80pp. 1-56971-909-8. **Y**

A collection of highlights of the strange and the bizarre, including a look at unsolved mysteries of Amelia Earhart.

Appendix 1

Recommended Additional Book Sources

Recommended General References on Comic Books and Graphic Novels

Caputo, Tony C. *Visual Storytelling: The Art and Technique.* New York: Watson-Guptill, 2002.

Eisner, Will. *Comics and Sequential Art.* 2d ed. New York: Poorhouse Press, 1994.

———. *Graphic Storytelling.* New York: Poorhouse Press, 2001.

Gravett, Paul. *Graphic Novels: Everything You Need to Know.* New York: Harper Design International, 2005.

McCloud, Scott. *Making Comics: Storytelling Secrets of Comics, Manga, and Graphic Novels.* New York: HarperTrade, 2006.

———. *Reinventing Comics: How Imagination and Technology Are Revolutionizing an Art Form.* New York: HarperTrade, 2000.

———. *Understanding Comics: The Invisible Art.* New York: HarperTrade, 1994.

Weiner, Steve. *Faster Than a Speeding Bullet: The Rise of the Graphic Novel.* New York: NBM Publishing, 2003.

Year's Best Graphic Novels, Comics, and Manga. Edited by Byron Preiss and Howard Zimmerman. New York: St. Martin's Griffin Press, 2005.

Books about Asian Comic Books, Manga, and More

Schodt, Frederick L. *Dreamland Japan: Writings on Modern Manga.* New York: DIANE Publishing, 2001.

———. *Manga! Manga!: The World of Japanese Comics.* New York: Kodansha International, 1998.

Wong, Wendy Siuyi. *Hong Kong Comics: A History of Manhua*. New York: Princeton Architectural Press, 2002.

Graphic Novel Collection Development Titles by Librarians for Libraries

Crawford, Philip Charles. *Graphic Novels 101: Selecting and Using Graphic Novels to Promote Literacy for Children and Young Adults!*. New York: Hi Willow Research & Publishing, 2003.

Goldsmith, Francisca. *Graphic Novels Now: Building, Managing, and Marketing a Dynamic Collection*. Chicago: American Library Association, 2005.

Gorman, Michele. *Getting Graphic!: Using Graphic Novels to Promote Literacy with Teens*. New York: Linworth Publishing, 2003.

Lyga, Allyson A. W., with Barry Lyga. *Graphic Novels in Your Media Center: A Definitive Guide*. Englewood, CO: Libraries Unlimited, 2004.

Miller, Steve. *Developing and Promoting Graphic Novel Collections*. New York: Neal-Schuman, 2005.

Rothschild, D. Aviva. *Graphic Novels: A Bibliographic Guide to Booklength Comics*. Englewood, CO: Libraries Unlimited, 1995.

Weiner, Stephen. *The 101 Best Graphic Novels: A Guide to This Exciting New Medium*. Rev. ed. New York: NBM Publications, 2006.

History of the Comic Book and Specific Characters

Bender, Hy. *The Sandman Companion: A Dreamer's Guide to the Award-Winning Comic Series*. New York: DC Comics, 2000.

Bongco, Mila. *Reading Comics: Language, Culture and the Concept of the Superhero in Comic Books*. New York: Garland, 2000.

Chinn, Mike. *Writing and Illustrating the Graphic Novel*. New York: Barron's Educational Series, 2004.

Conroy, Mike. *500 Comic Book Villains*. New York: Barron's Educational Series, 2004.

———. *500 Great Comic Book Action Heroes*. New York: Barron's Educational Series, 2003.

Daniels, Les. *Batman: The Complete History*. New York: Chronicle Books, 2004.

———. *DC Comics: A Celebration of the World's Favorite Comic Book Heroes*. New York: Watson-Guptill, 2003.

———. *Marvel: Five Fabulous Decades of the World's Greatest Comics*. New York: Harry N. Abrams, 1993.

Duin, Steve, and Mike Richardson. *Comics Between the Panels*. 2d ed. Milwaukee, WI: Dark Horse Comics, 1998.

Gertler, Nat, and Steve Lieber. *Comic Book Culture: An Illustrated History*. New York: Collectors Press, Incorporated, 2004.

———. *Complete Idiot's Guide to Creating a Graphic Novel*. New York: Alpha Books, 2004.

Goulart, Ron. *Comic Book Encyclopedia: The Ultimate Guide to Characters, Graphic Novels, Writers, and Artists in the Comic Book Universe*. New York: Morrow/Avon HarperEntertainment, 2004.

Jones, Gerard. *Men of Tomorrow: Geeks, Gangsters, and the Birth of the Comic Book*. New York: Basic Books, 2004.

Panel Discussions: Design in Sequential Art Storytelling. 2d ed. New York: TwoMorrows Publishing, 2002.

Saavedra, Scott. *Flee, Puny Humans: The Comic Book Heaven Collections*. Portland, OR: Slave Labor Graphics, 2003.

Sabin, Roger. *Comics, Comix & Graphic Novels: A History of Comic Art*. London: Phaidon Press, 2001.

Talon, Durwin. *Comics Above Ground: Sequential Art Affects Mainstream Media*. New York: TwoMorrows Publishing, 2004.

Weist, Jerry. *100 Greatest Comic Books*. New York: Whitman Publishing, 2004.

Recommended Periodical Sources

Brenner, Robin. "Graphic Novels 101: FAQ." *Horn Book Magazine* 82, no. 2 (March/April 2006): 123–125.

Crawford, Philip. "A Novel Approach: Using Graphic Novels to Attract Reluctant Readers and Promote Literacy." *Library Media Connection* 22, no. 5 (February 2004): 26–28.

Foster, Katy. "Graphic Novels in Libraries: An Expert's Opinion." *Library Media Connection* 22, no. 5 (February 2004): 30–32.

Galley, Michelle. "Going 'Graphic': Educators Tiptoe Into Realm of Comics." *Education Week* 23, no. 23 (February 18, 2004): 6.

Gorman, Michele. "Graphic Novels and the Curriculum Connection." *Library Media Connection* 22, no. 3 (November 2003): 20–22.

———. "What Teens Want." *School Library Journal* 48, no. 8 (August 2002): 42–45.

Ireland, Kerry. "Build It and They Will Come: Graphic Novels for Your Collection." *School Libraries in Canada* 23, no. 3 (2004): 18–23.

Kan, Kat. "Core Collection: Great Graphic Novels for Younger Readers." *Booklist* 102, no. 14 (March 15, 2006): 62.

———. "Getting Graphic at the School Library." *Library Media Connection* 21, no. 7 (April/May 2003): 14–19.

Lavin, Michael R. "Comic Books and Graphic Novels for Libraries: What to Buy." *Serials Review* 24, no. 2 (1998): 31–45.

Lyga, Allyson A. W. "Graphic Novels for (Really) Young Readers." *School Library Journal* 52, no. 3 (March 2006): 56–61.

Michaels, Julia. "Pulp Fiction." *Horn Book Magazine* 80, no. 3 (May/June 2004): 299–306.

Mooney, Maureen." Graphic Novels: How They Can Work in Libraries." *Book Report* 21, no. 3 (November/December 2002): 18–19.

Pawuk, Michael. "Creating a Graphic Novel Collection @ Your Library." *Young Adult Library Services* (Fall 2002): 30–35.

Raiteri, Steve. "Graphic Novels." *Library Journal* 127, no. 18 (November 1, 2002): 64–67.

———. "Graphic Novels." *Library Journal* 128, no 1 (January 1, 2003): 80.

———. "Graphic Novels." *Library Journal* 128, no. 8 (May 1, 2003): 94.

———. "Graphic Novels." *Library Journal* 128, no. 18 (November 1, 2003): 58.

———. "Graphic Novels." *Library Journal* 129, no 8 (May 1, 2004): 91.

———. "Graphic Novels." *Library Journal* 130, no. 1 (January 2005): 87.

———. "Graphic Novels." *Library Journal* 130, no. 9 (May 15, 2005): 98–103.

———. "Graphic Novels." *Library Journal* 130, no. 12 (July 1, 2005): 60.

Rudiger, Hollis Margaret. "Graphic Novels 101: Reading Lessons." *Horn Book Magazine* 82, no. 2 (March/April 2006): 126–134.

Sangiacomo, Michael. "Checking Out the Comics: Illustrated Storybooks Get Boost from Enthusiast on the Staff at Library System's Brooklyn Branch." *Cleveland Plain Dealer*, November 23, 2000, sec. B1.

Smith, Jeff. "Graphic Novels—Why in the World Do I Do It?" *Booklist* 102, no. 14 (March 15, 2006): 64–65.

Weiner, Stephen. "Beyond Superheroes: Comics Get Serious." *Library Journal* 127, no. 2 (February 1, 2002): 55–58.

Weiner, Steve. "Building a Strong Collection." *School Library Journal* 49, no. 5 (May2003): 33.

———. "Graphic Novels in Libraries." *School Library Journal* 50, no 5 (May 2004): 28.

Wilson, Rachel. "Multicultural Graphic Novels." *Library Media Connection* 24, no 6 (March 2006): 32–33.

Publishing Companies on the Internet

Mainstream Publishers

The comic book industry has hundreds of publishing companies, from large publishers to small, independent publishing companies. Below are listed some of the most popular large publishers of graphic novels and comic books.

Archie Comics (www.archie.com)

The adventures of Archie Andrews and his Riverdale friends have sold continuously for nearly sixty years, and remain as popular as ever. Archie Comics are the most steadfastly kid-friendly comics on the market, and the publisher works hard to maintain its wholesome reputation. It is believed that Archie Comics is the third largest comics publisher in America. Unlike most comic book publishers, most of Archie's revenues come from sales to "newsstand" distributors rather than comic book stores.

Dark Horse Comics (www.darkhorse.com)

Founded in 1986, Dark Horse Comics has quickly grown to be one of the best-respected publishers in the industry. Dark Horse publishes one of the most consistently diverse lines of comics in America today, including adult humor; detective stories; realistic fiction; fantasy; science fiction; horror; movie/television adaptations, including properties such as <u>Star Wars</u> and <u>Aliens</u>; realistic drama; historical fiction; Japanese manga; and the occasional super-hero title.

DC Comics (www.dccomics.com)

Founded in 1935, DC Comics is the oldest comic book company in America and features the most widely recognized comic book characters, including Superman, Batman, and Wonder Woman. DC Comics publishes the largest variety of comic books today and has branched out with several imprints: Vertigo for fantastic horror, fantasy, and mature-adult stories; Paradox Press for "strange" specialty projects; WB for series featuring characters licensed from the Cartoon Network cable station, and Jim Lee's WildStorm Productions, publisher of Alan Moore's America's Best Comics series of titles, *Planetary*, *Ex Machina*, and *Kurt Busiek's Astro City*.

Image Comics (www.imagecomics.com)

Founded in 1992, Image Comics is divided into three houses: Todd McFarlane Productions (www.spawn.com), Top Cow (www.topcow.com), and Image Central. Each of the creators/owners maintains a separate studio, incorporated independently of Image and employing its own writers, artists, and editors. Image Central promotes creator-owned work under the general banner of Image Comics and includes works such as Colleen Doran's *A Distant Soil*, Erik Larsen's *Savage Dragon*, Eric Shanower' *Age of Bronze*, Michael Avon Oeming's *Hammer of the Gods*, and Robert Kirkman's *Walking Dead* and *Invincible*.

Marvel Comics (www.marvel.com)

Marvel Comics, along with DC Comics, is one of the two powerhouses of the comic book industry. The company was founded in 1939, but it wasn't until 1961 that Marvel Comics came into its own when Stan Lee and Jack "King" Kirby created its own brand of super-heroes, including the Fantastic Four, Spider-Man, the X-Men, the Hulk, Captain America, and many other memorable heroes and villains. Marvel also has a new imprint, called Marvel MAX, which was created to focus on more mature titles and themes, as well as the creator-owned Icon imprint, which is the home for Brian Michael Bendis's <u>Powers</u> series.

Independent Publishers

There are many independent publishers, from those who self-publish only one comic book title to companies that publish a variety of titles in a graphic novel format. Here's a very small sample of some of the best independent publishers; the list includes mainstream North American companies as well as publishers of Asian titles. Mind that this is just a very short list and that there are hundreds of other smaller publishing companies currently publishing comic books and graphic novels.

ADV Manga (www.advmanga.com)

One of the foremost publisher of Japanese anime, the company recently expanded to releasing Japanese manga with such popular titles as *Azumanga Daoh*, *Cromartie High School*, *Full Metal Panic*, and *Chrono Crusade*.

AiT/PlanetLar (www.ait-planetlar.com)

Founded by Larry Young, popular titles include *Astronauts in Trouble: Live from the Moon*, *Channel Zero,* and *Couscous Express*

Alternative Comics (www.indyworld.com/altcomics)

Alternative Comics releases some of the most original and intelligent titles being created today. Popular titles include *Grickle* and the poignant *9-11: Emergency Relief*.

Antarctic Press (www.antarctic-press.com)

One of North America's longest-running publishers of neo-manga titles, including the cult-hit favorites *Gold Digger*, *Neotopia*, *Ninja High School*, *The Courageous Princess*, and many more.

Bongo Comics Group (www.littlegreenman.com)

Matt Groening, creator of *The Simpsons* and *Futurama* TV shows, publishes his own line of comic books. Ongoing titles include the flagship Simpsons comic, *Bart Simpson*, *Futurama*, and the annual *Bart Simpsons' Treehouse of Horror*. The trade paperback collections are published through HarperCollins Publishers.

Cartoon Books (www.boneville.com)

Created by Jeff Smith in 1991, Cartoon Books came into the independent comic book market with Jeff's comic book *Bone,* and became an instant hit with fans all over the world. Bone has won numerous awards, including the Eisner and Harvey Awards, since 1993. Recent other titles include the Rose miniseries, written by Jeff Smith with art by Charles Vess.

Devil's Due (www.devilsdue.net)

The company was started in 1999 and is best known for the licensed revamp of *G.I. Joe* in 2001. The company also has other licensed properties, including *Army of Darkness, Street Fighter*, *Dark Stalkers*, as well as *DragonLance* and *Forgotten Realms*. The studio also publishes its own lines of titles, including *Hack/Slash*, *Black Harvest*, *Kore*, *Misplaced*, and others.

Digital Manga Publishing (www.dmpbooks.com)

Founded as a bridge between Japan and the Western world for anime, manga, and other licenses, the company has recently expanded as a publisher of Japanese manga. Titles are available for all ages, including the Edu-Manga series, g *Berserk*, *Trigun*, *Hellsing*, and even Yaoi homosexual romance titles, for older audiences.

Drawn and Quarterly (www.drawnandquarterly.com)

Based in Canada, this independent publisher was founded in 1992 and is one of the best-known publishers of literary graphic novels. The title of the company comes from the highly regarded anthology of the same name. The publisher is also known for publishing works by such highly regarded creators as Adrian Tomine, Seth, Chester Brown, Joe Matt, Julie Doucet, James Sturm, and Debbie Drechsler

Fantagraphics Books (www.fantagraphics.com)

Founded by the creators of the magazine *The Comics Journal* in 1976, the Seattle-based company produces some of the most striking and compelling alternative comic book titles. From the Los Hernandez Brother's *Love and Rockets,* to Peter Bagge's *Hate*, to Daniel Clowes' *Ghost World*, Fantagraphics Books maintains a high standard of comics for an audience that appreciates comics as a serious means of expression on the same level of film, theater, or literature.

Humanoids Publishing (www.humanoids-publishing.com)

The books, comics, and trade paperbacks from Humanoids Publishing feature groundbreaking comic art from the world's finest creators. Imaginative and sophisticated, Humanoids' science fiction and heroic fantasy stories are designed to be read and enjoyed by an audience older than that of a typical American comic book. Popular titles include *The Metabarons* and *The Incal*.

NBM Publishing (www.nbmpub.com)

Among one of the first publishers to bring the graphic novel to the United States, in 1976, Nantier, Beall, Minoustchine (NBM) specializes in paperback and hardcover graphic novels for a variety of ages. Genres include realistic fiction, mystery, fantasy, science fiction, humor, children's literature, and adaptations of classic literature. Among the outstanding titles in its backlist are Vittorio Giardino's acclaimed *A Jew in Communist Prague*, P. Craig Russell's adaptation of *Fairy Tales of Oscar Wilde*, and Will Eisner's *Last Knight*.

Oni Press (www.onipress.com)

Oni Press has received critical acclaim for its diverse line of quality comics. Highlights include *Blue Monday*, *Whiteout*, *Queen & Country*, *Alison Dare*, *The Adventures of Barry Ween Boy Genius*, *Courtney Crumrin*, *Geisha*, and *Fortune & Glory*.

Seven Seas Entertainment (www.gomanga.com)

A relative newcomer, this is an up-and-coming publisher of neo-manga titles that look and feel nearly identical to Japanese manga title, including printing the books in the traditional right-to-left Japanese manga format. Highlights of its small-but-promising line-up include *Amazing Agent Luna*, *Blade for Barter*, *Last Hope*, *Captain Nemo*, *Unearthly,* and *No Man's Land*. Many more titles are forthcoming.

Slave Labor Graphics (www.slavelabor.com)

Focuses on dark and twisted humor for older readers. Representative titles include *Milk & Cheese*, *Johnny the Homicidal Maniac*, *Lenore*, and *Squee*. A newer, more serious title for older teens is *Gloomcookie*. SLG also publishes humor titles suitable for younger readers, including *Patty Cake* and *Little Gloomy*.

TOKYOPOP (www.tokyopop.com)

One of the leading publishers of Japanese manga and Korean manhwa, TOKYOPOP publish a variety of titles that are popular with teens, including *Sailor Moon*, *Gundam Wing*, *Cardcaptor Sakura*, and *Harlem Beat*. Recently TOKYOPOP has also begun its own line of North American-made neo-manga.

Top Shelf Productions (www.topshelfcomix.com)

Top Shelf graphic novels and comix are crafted with exquisite attention to detail; characterized by a unique, engaging art style; and complemented by a thought-provoking subtext full of social realism, humor, and heart. Highlights include *Good-Bye, Chunky Rice*, *Box Office Poison*, *Monkey vs. Robot*, and *From Hell*.

Viper Comics (www.vipercomics.com)

Started in 2001, this independent publishing company is best known for Josh Howard's cult-hit *Dead@17* and the YALSA-recognized title *Daisy Kutter* by Kazu Kibuishi.

VIZ Media, LLC (www.viz.com)

VIZ Media, LLC is the leading U.S. publisher of Japanese comics (Manga) for English-speaking audiences. Founded in 1987, VIZ serves a growing market of dedicated fans of all ages. Based in San Francisco, it publishes dozens of popular Japanese titles, such as *Ranma ½, Dragon Ball Z, Nausicaá of the Valley of Wind,* and *Battle Angel Alita.* VIZ is a wholly owned subsidary of Shogakukan, one of Japan's three largest publishers of manga. VIZ also distributes both dubbed and subtitled anime for English-speaking countries.

Mainstream Book Publishers

Many mainstream book publishers of prose fiction and nonfiction titles also publish graphic novels. Some publishers, such as Random House, with its Pantheon Press imprint, have been publishing graphic novels for over a decade; Roaring Brook Press, with its First Second: 01 imprint, began publishing graphic novels in 2006. Following is a small sample of such book publishers. Note that they are listed by their specific imprint.

Del Ray Manga (www.randomhouse.com/delrey/manga)

Random House's Del Rey launched its first titles in May 2004, when Random House and the Japanese manga publisher Kodansha entered into a publishing agreement. The first four titles were Ken Akamatsu's *Negima,* CLAMP's *Tsubasa* and *xxxHOLiC,* and Sunrise's *Gundam SEED,* and many new titles are released each year.

First Second: 01 (www.firstsecondbooks.com)

Launched in 2006 by Roaring Brook Press, a division of Holtzbrinck Publishers, the line debuted with six series titles, including several translations of works such as Stassen's *Deogratias: A Tale of Rwanda,* Lewis Trondheim's *A.L.I.E.E.E.N..* Joan Sfar's *Vampire Loves,* and Sfar and Emmanuel Gilbert's *Sardine in Outer Space.* Also launched in 2006 were Eddie Cambell's *The Fate of the Artist* and *The Lost Colony* by Grady Klein. Many more titles will be released in 2007.

Graphix (www.scholastic.com/graphix)

This imprint of Scholastic Books launched its line of titles in 2005 with Jeff Smith's Bone series in full color. Other notable titles equally suitable for tweens and teens include Chyna Clugston's *Queen Bee,* and adaptations of *The Baby-Sitter's Club* and *Goosebumps.* More titles are forthcoming.

Pantheon Press (www.randomhouse.com/pantheon/graphicnovels/home.pperl)

This imprint from Random House is best known for being the publisher of Art Spiegelman's Maus in graphic novel format. Known for serious works, it also publishes works such as Marjane Satrapi's autobiographical graphic novel *Persepolis,* Jessica Abel's *La Perdida,* Chris Ware's *Acme Novelty Library,* Joann Sfar's *The Rabbi's Cat,* and Charles Burns's *Black Hole.*

Web Sites on Comic Books and Graphic Novels

The Internet has greatly changed how we use information, not only as librarians but also for personal searches. Here's just a small sample of the plethora of comic book Web sites.

Comic Book Industry News

Web sites that provide daily or weekly news in the comic book industry, publisher press releases, as well as other news from the industry.

Comic Books Resources (www.comicbookresources.com)

Online since 1995, CBR has received a wide variety of acclaim and recognition for its well put together information on the comic book industry, including previews, reviews, and movie news.

Comics Continuum (www.comicscontinum.com)

An excellent source of daily news from the comic book industry and many comic book-related media projects, including television and movies.

Newsarama (www.newsarama.com)

Newsarama is one of the best sources for daily information on the comic book industry, including headline news, previews of titles, company press releases, and Mike Sangiacomo's "Journey into Comics" articles.

The Pulse (www.comicon.com/pulse)

Hosted at Comicon.com, The Pulse is one of the best sources for daily information on the comic book industry, including headline news, interviews with creators, and a blog by Heidi MacDonald.

Reviews and Recommendations

Web sites by professional reviewers as well as fans that review graphic novels and comic books.

Comics Get Serious: Graphic Novel Reviews (www.rationalmagic.com/Comics/Comics.html)

Created by D. Aviva Rothschild, author of *Graphic Novels: A Bibliographic Guide to Book-Length Comics,* this Web site has reviews of graphic novels published by both large and independent companies. The site is not updated, but is a nice supplement to her 1995 publication.

The Fourth Rail (www.thefourthrail.com)

Features reviews of monthly comic book titles as well as graphic novels from longtime Internet reviewers Don MacPherson and Randy Lander.

Miscellaneous Online Journals and Information Sources

A listing of Web sites that include basic information for beginners on graphic novels and comic books as well as well as links to a variety of miscellaneous sites.

Comic Book Award Almanac (www.enteract.com/~aardy/comics/awards)

A listing of the past winners of awards honored in the comic book and comic strip industry. The list is almost complete and a great source of award-winning comics.

Comicon.com (www.comicon.com)

The "world's largest comic book convention," featuring links to a potpourri of well-known writers and artists.

Comics: The Language of the World. (library.thinkquest.org/3177/main.html)

A wonderful fan site on comics from both the United States and Japan. The site covers a wide range of topics and has a useful FAQ section.

The Comics Journal (www.tcj.com)

Official Web site of the comic book magazine from the Fantagraphics publisher.

Comics Research Bibliography (www.rpi.edu/~bulloj/comxbib.html)

This is an international bibliography of comic books, comic strips, animation, caricature, cartoons, and related topics. The bibliography is divided into four sections, arranged alphabetically by author, for ease of use.

History of Super-Hero Comic Books (www.geocities.com/Athens/8580/)

It's just what it sounds like!

New Comics Releases List (www.comiclist.com)

> A staple on the Web for years, this is a weekly listing of all the comic book and graphic novel titles available for the coming week at your local comic book shop. The site also has links to reviews, publishers, and professionals on the Internet.

Sequential Tart (www.sequentialtart.com)

> An Internet magazine published by an eclectic band of women. Interviews, articles, reviews, and commentaries are included.

Wizard: The Guide to *Comics* (www.wizardworld.com)

> The official Web site to the popular comic book magazine.

Web Sites Created by Librarians

Web sites created by librarians for librarians containing all sorts of comic book and graphic novel information.

Comic Books for Young Adults (ublib.buffalo.edu/libraries/units/lml/comics/pages)

> Created by Lockwood Memorial Librarian Michael R. Lavin, this site is a great introduction for all librarians on the role of comic books in the library. Included are collection development issues, recommendations, Internet links, and publisher highlights.

No Flying, No Tights (www.noflyingnotights.com)

> Created by librarian Robin Brenner, the site is a very useful and user-friendly source to a wide variety of graphic novels. It is broken down into three divisions for kids, teens, and older audiences and features titles from a wide variety of genres. One of the best Web sites for library-appropriate reviews.

Recommended Graphic Novels for Public Libraries (my.voyager.net/~sraiteri/graphicnovels.htm)

> Created by Greene County Public Librarian Steve Raiteri, this site is a great listing of recommendations of graphic novels suitable for public libraries. ISBNs and prices are listed as well.

Intellectual Freedom Issues

Comic Book Legal Defense Fund (www.cbldf.org)

> The official site for one of the most important nonprofit organizations in the comic book industry. The CBLDF's guiding principle is that comics should be accorded the same constitutional rights as literature, film, or any other form of expression.

Comic Book and Graphic Novel Awards and Recognition

As for most media, there are many awards and forms of recognition given to the comic book and graphic novel industry. The awards can come from within the industry, such as the Will Eisner awards, or be recognition from fans and libraries. Below are listed some main Web sites of the most popular awards given out to the comic book industry, as well as some recognition from other sources. For a full list of awards cited in this book, see the introduction.

Comic Book Awards Almanac (users.rcn.com/aardy/comics/awards)

A Web site with links to all the award-winning comic books and graphic novels, from American awards to non-American awards; includes all major awards, such as the Kirbys, Ignatz, Eisners, and Harveys, and many more both from professionals and from fans.

Harvey Kurtzman Awards (www.harveyawards.org)

Awarded at the Baltimore Comic-Con, the Harveys are named in honor of writer and cartoonist Harvey Kurtzman, best remembered for founding *MAD* magazine. The awards recognize the best in the comic book industry in more than twenty categories. The awards were created in 1988.

Ignatz Awards (www.spxpo.com/ignatz.shtml)

Awarded at the Small Press Expo, these recognize outstanding achievement in comics and cartooning.

Will Eisner Awards (www.comic-con.org/cci/cci_eisners_main.shtml)

Awarded each year at the San Diego Comic-Con International, the awards are named in honor of pioneering cartoonist Will Eisner and recognize the best in comic book industry. The Eisners have been awarded each year since 1988.

YALSA Booklists and Book Awards (www.ala.org/ala/yalsa/booklistsawards/booklistsbook.htm)

The Young Adults Library Services Association (YALSA), a division of the American Library Association (ALA), regularly recognizes the works of graphic novels. This site includes lists of all the titles—both prose and graphic novel—that have been recognized in such award categories as Popular Paperbacks for Young Adults, Best Books for Young Adults, and Quick Picks for Reluctant Young Adult Readers. In 2006 a new selection group, Great Graphic Novels, was created by YALSA to recognize the best graphic novels with young adult appeal. All YALSA titles awarded prior to 2007 are listed in this book in the appropriate chapters.

Author Index

Illustrator Index

Subject Index

Characters for which several entries appear in the book are included in this index.

About the Author

Michael Pawuk has worked as a teen services librarian for more than ten years at the Cuyahoga County Public Library system in Northeast Ohio. An avid collector of comic books and graphic novels since he was a boy, he's been recognized as one of the leading librarians in the United States on the subject. In 2002 he chaired the all-day YALSA preconference "Get Graphic @ your library," which included guest speakers Neil Gaiman, Art Spiegelman, Jeff Smith, and Colleen Doran, and he regularly speaks on building graphic novel collections for libraries. He lives in Parma Heights, Ohio, with his wife Laurie, son Nathan, and pet cat Zuzu.